CANADA AND ASIA

*To my wife Margaret,
my children Pamela, Michael and Lesley,
and my grandchildren
Kelley, Kristen and 'Ale*

CANADA AND ASIA

Guide to Archive and Manuscript Sources in Canada

Volume 1

Alberta – Ontario (Toronto: Presbyterian Church in Canada)

G. Raymond Nunn

MANSELL
London and New York

First published in 1999 by

Mansell Publishing Limited, *A Cassell Imprint*

Wellington House, 125 Strand, London WC2R 0BB

370 Lexington Avenue, New York, NY 10017–6550

© Raymond Nunn 1999

All rights reserved. no part of this publication may be reproduced or transmited in any form or by any means, electronic or mechanical, including photocopy recording or any storage or retrieval system without permission in writing from the publishers or their appointed agents.

ISBN Vol. 1 0–7201–2372–0
ISBN Vol. 2 0–7201–2373–0

Printed and bound in Great Britain by Cromwell Press, Ltd, Trowbridge, Wiltshire

PREFACE

Researchers in countries that were once colonial territories must work under the hardship that the primary sources they need to consult are held in the libraries and archives of the colonizing nations. The International Council of Archives (ICA) recognized this problem and encouraged and supported the compilation of a series of inventories that would help to make these sources more accessible (through photocopy and inter-library loan) to researchers who were unable to visit these collections in person.

In my work on *Asia and Oceania: A Guide to Archival and Manuscript Sources in the United States* (Mansell, 1986) I became aware of the rich resources held in Canadian institutions. Canada was not a colonizing country, but its research collections have features similar to those of the colonial powers. These include Asia-related documents of government departments (particularly External Affairs and Immigration), executive offices, military records, and archives with reference to missionary endeavours.

I have defined 'Asia' as the geographical area covered by the academic term 'Asian Studies' – from Afghanistan in the west to Hokkaido and the Kuriles in the east, but excluding the former Soviet Asia. Since the projected ICA coverage of the Middle East included only the Arab countries, I have added Turkey and Iran. The Pacific Islands are included because of their omission in other studies. The significant immigration from the Indian sub-continent to Trinidad, Tobago and British Guiana (Guyana) determined my inclusion of these areas.

Sources of information

I compiled the inventory by transcribing, abstracting, scanning and downloading the finding aids and catalogues provided by institutions. Published sources are listed on pp. ix–x and identified in individual entries. Where none is cited, the entry has been established by personal examination of files, correspondence, or 'in-house' (unpublished) finding aids.

Wherever possible I have given enough specific information so that inter-library requests for microfilm or photocopies can be arranged. Please note, however, that some files are closed or designated as restricted access. Occasionally when non-classified material is included in a classified file it may be possible to locate a copy in another file. Access must be negotiated, of course, with the appropriate officials.

Masters' theses and doctoral dissertations are an invaluable source of information on Asia and Asians in Canada. I used *Canadian Theses*, library files and the computer records of the National Library, Ottawa to locate them. Microfilm copies are available from the Library.

The guide is arranged by province, city, institution, and sub-divisions within the institution. Full information is given for each institution and collection to make it possible for researchers to contact them.

Index

The index has approximately 50,000 entries and is the key to the inventory. It brings together the material in the missionary records, the national, provincial, local and university collections, and the photograph collections. Almost all the entries are in pairs, that is they are entered under both location and subject. For instance information about Dr A. Stewart Allen, a United Church medical missionary to China, will be found under his name and under the names of the cities where he worked. Dates have been added to further sharpen the focus.

It is important to remember that citations are to page number only and both columns must be scanned since there may be two or more citations on the same page. For example, one of the references to Dr Allen is on page 876 – there are two entries on that page. It is also important to look at the preceding and following pages: it has sometimes happened that during the typesetting process the entry has shifted from its position on my computer file from which I compiled the index.

Entries for military groups appear on the first page of the index since they are listed by regimental, division or squadron number: 2 Royal Canadian Regiment; 2 Infantry Division; 435 Squadron R.C.A.F.

Decisions on terminology

'Indian' has been used rather than 'East Indian'.
'Hindu' often includes Sikhs. The substantial Sikh group is not well represented in file titles.
'Oriental' refers to 'East Asians', specifically Chinese and Japanese.

Note

The cut-off date for inclusion of items in each major archive varies:
United Church of Canada Central Archives: 1992
National Archives of Canada, Ottawa: 1992
National Archives of Canada, Vancouver: 1994
Diefenbaker archives: spring 1996.

Acknowledgements

Archivists and librarians throughout Canada have given me unstinting support.
Among them:

Alberta

Calgary

Janet Pieschel
Archivist
Glenbow-Alberta Institute Library

Marlys Chevrefils
University Archives
University of Calgary

Edmonton

Keith Stotyn
Senior Archivist
Provincial Archives of Alberta

Peter Freeman
Director
University Library
University of Alberta

Gertrude B. McLaren
University Archives and Collections
The Rutherford Library
University of Alberta

Lethbridge

Greg Ellis
Archivist
Archives and Records Management
City of Lethbridge

British Columbia

Burnaby

Frances Fournier
Archivist
W.A.C. Bennett Library
Simon Fraser University

Ian Forsyth
University Archivist
Simon Fraser University Archives

Vancouver

Jay Gilbert
Archivist
Vancouver Federal Records Centre

Su M. Baptie
City Archivist
City of Vancouver Archives

Robert Stewart
British Columbia Conference
United Church of Canada

Judy Capes
Deputy Director
Vancouver Public Library

Doreen Stephens
Anglican Archivist
Anglican Provincial Synod of British Columbia

George Brandak
Special Collections
University of British Columbia

Victoria

David Mattison
Archivist
British Columbia Archives and Record Service

Chris Petter
University Archivist
McPherson Library
University of Victoria

Manitoba

Winnipeg

Barry Hyman
Assistant Provincial Archivist
Provincial Archives of Manitoba

Nicole Michaud-Oystryk
Head Reference Services

Elizabeth Dafoe Library
University of Manitoba

New Brunswick

Fredericton

Alan C. Burk
Harriet Irving Library
University of New Brunswick

Saint John

Jane Lodge Smith
New Brunswick Museum

Newfoundland

St. John's

Bert Riggs
Archivist
Centre for Newfoundland Studies

Nova Scotia

Antigonish

Kathleen MacKenzie
University Archivist
St. Francis Xavier University

Halifax

William F. Birdsall
University Librarian
Izaak Walton Killam Memorial Library
Dalhousie University

Allan C. Dunlop
Associate Provincial Archivist
Public Archives of Nova Scotia

Carolyn Earle
Archivist
Maritime Conference Archives

Wolfville

Patricia Townsend
University Archivist
Acadia University

Ontario

Guelph

Nancy Sadek
Archival and Special Collections
University of Guelph Library

Hamilton

Charlotte A. Stewart
Archives and Research Collections
Mills Memorial Library
McMaster University

Judith Colwell
Librarian
Canadian Baptist Archives
McMaster Divinity college

Kingston

D. F. Macdermid
University Archivist
Queen's University

North York

Peter Mitchell and Kent M. Haworth
University Archivists
York University

Ottawa

Cromwell Christie
Directorate of History Library
Department of National Defence

David Holmes
University Librarian
Carleton University

Dorothy F. Thomson
Libraries
University of Ottawa

Ghislain Mallette, at the start of my
research, of the Manuscript Division
Paul Marsden, John Bell, and Paulette J. Dozois
Archivists, National Archives of Canada

Roanne Mokhtar, Jacqueline Nicolls, Dianne
Duguay, and Sarah Montgomery
Reference Services
National Archives of Canada

Ursula Schultz
Computerized Information Service
Rosalie Fox
Reference Services
National Library of Canada

Toronto

Richard W. Ramsay
Portfolio Manager
Archives of Ontario

Marianne Nicholls
General Synod Archives
Anglican Church of Canada

Kim Arnold and Loren Fantin
Presbyterian Church in Canada

David Mitchell
China Inland Mission/Overseas Missionary Fellowship

Ruth Dyck Wilson and Jean E. Dryden
Chief Archivists
United Church of Canada
Central Archives

Gayle Garlock
Director
Development and Public Affairs
University of Toronto Libraries

Windsor

Robin M. Owen
University Archivist
University of Windsor

Québec

Montréal

E. Phoebe Chartrand and Robert Michel
Archivists
McGill University Archives

Mary G. Mason
Reference Department
McGill University Libraries

Eleanor Maclean
Blacker-Wood Library
McGill University

A. Joffre-Nicodeme
Université de Montréal

Québec

Robert Crispo
Bibliothèque
Université Laval

Saskatchewan

Regina

Shelley Sweeney
University Archivist
University of Regina

Saskatoon

Steve Billington, Cheryl Avery and Chris Kitsan
Diefenbaker Centre
University of Saskatchewan

I gratefully acknowledge the assistance of Dr Norman T. London, Academic Relations Officer, Canadian Embassy, who secured two faculty Canadian Studies research grants for my travel to and in Canada; the support and encouragement of Mr Stuart Hughes, Consul of the former Canadian Consulate-General, San Francisco; Miss Pamela Johnson, Canadian Consulate-General, Los Angeles; and Dr Rudolf Schmerl, Research Relations Office, University of Hawai'i, who made possible further travel to Canada.

This book, which has taken over ten years to compile, could not have been completed without the encouragement and support of my wife Margaret and my family.

G. Raymond Nunn

SOURCES

ACADIA	**A Catalogue of the Maritime Baptist Historical Collections in the Library of Acadia University.** Kentville, Kentville Publishing, 1955.	GUENETTE	Canada. National Archives. **Inventory of the Collections of the National Film, Television and Sound Archives.** Ottawa, 1983.
BC	Provincial Archives of British Columbia. Sound and Moving Images Division. **Inventory and Subject Index of Provincial Oral History Collection.** Victoria, 1985 and Supplement.	IVANOW	Ivanow, Wladimir. **Annotated Catalogue of the Casey A. Wood Collections of Persian, Arabic and Hindustani Manuscripts.** Bombay, 1927.
BC ARCH	**British Columbia Archives Union List**(on line)	MCCANDLESS	McCandless, Kate, and others. **The Institute of Pacific Relations, an Inventory of its Records, 1931-1961.** Vancouver, University of British Columbia, 1981
BROWNE	Browne, Colin. **Motion Picture Production in British Columbia, 1898-1940, a Brief Historical Background and Catalogue.** Victoria, Province of British Columbia, Ministry of the Provincial Secretary and Government Service, 1979 (British Columbia Provincial Museum Heritage Record No.6)	MCMASTER	McMaster University. Archives and Research Collections. **A Guide to Archives and Research Collections.** Hamilton, 1951.
		MELNYK	Melnyk, T.W. **Canadian Flying Operations in South East Asia, 1941-1945.** Hull, Canadian Government Publishing Centre, 1976.
CGT	Canada. National Library. **Canadian Graduate Theses in the Humanities and Social Sciences.** Ottawa, 1957.	MITCHELL	Mitchell, Peter M. **Guide to Archival Resources on Canadian Missionaries in East Asia, 1890-1960.** Toronto, Joint Centre on Asia Pacific Studies, University of Toronto and York University, 1987.
COOK	Canada. National Archives. **Federal Archives Division.** Ottawa, 1983.		
CT	Canada. National Library. **Canadian Theses,** 1947-	MG 26/MG 27	Canada. National Archives. Manuscript Division. **General Inventory, Manuscripts. MG 26 MG 27.** Ottawa, 1972.
DUFFY	Duffy, Dennis J. **Camera West, British Columbia on Film, 1941-1965.** Victoria, Province of British Columbia, Provincial Archives, 1979.	MG 30	Canada. National Archives. Manuscript Division. **Preliminary Inventory, Manuscript Group 30, Twentieth Century Manuscripts.** Ottawa, Roger Duhamel, Queen's Printer and Controller of Stationery, 1966.
EPBC	Archivists of the Ecclesiastical Province of British Columbia and Yukon. **Guide to the Archives of the Ecclesiastical Province of British Columbia and Yukon,** Toronto, Anglican Church of Canada, General Synod Archives, 1993.	NABATA1	Nabata, Terry. **An inventory to the papers and records in the Japanese Canadian Research Collection in the Library of the University of British Columbia Special Collections.** 1975.

NABATA2	Nabata, Terry. **Japanese Canadian photograph collections, an inventory of the collection in the Library of the University of British Columbia Special Collections Division.** 1986.
NL	National Library Computer source.
ONTARIO	Ontario Ministry of Citizenship and Culture. **Guide to the Holdings of the Archives of Ontario,** Toronto, 1986.
QUEENS	Queen's University. **A Guide to the Holdings of Queen's University Archives,** Kingston, 1986-1987. 2 volumes.
REP/1959-69	Canada. National Archives. **Report, 1959-1969.** Ottawa, Information Canada, 1971.
REP/1972-73	Canada. National Archives. **Report, 1972-1973.** Ottawa, Information Canada, 1974.
SEIFRIED	Canada. National Archives. **Guide to Canadian Photographic Archives.** Ottawa, 1984.
THORGRIMSSON	Thorgrimsson, Thor. **Canadian Naval Operations in Korean Waters, 1950-1955.** Ottawa, Department of National Defence, 1965.
UBC	**Guide to the Archive Research Collections in the Special Collections and University Archives Division. Vancouver, University of British Columbia Library.** 1994.
UBC1	**Guide to the Holdings of the University of British Columbia Archives. Vancouver, University of British Columbia Archives.** 1994.
UBC2	**Sources for Researching the History of Japanese Canadians in British Columbia in the Special Collections and University Archives Division. Vancouver, University of British Columbia Library.** 1991.
UBC3	**Sources for Researching the History of Chinese Canadians in British Columbia in the Special Collections and University Archives Division. Vancouver, University of British Columbia Library.** 1992.
ULM	Canada. National Archives. **Union List of Manuscripts in Canadian Repositories,** Revised 1975 edition. Ottawa, 1975. 2 v. 26,000 entries. 1968 edition has 11,000 entries.
ULM1	**Supplement, 1976.** Ottawa, 1976. 5,000 entries.
ULM2	**Supplement, 1977-1978.** Ottawa, 1979. 3,000 entries.
ULM3	**Supplement, 1979-1980.** Ottawa, 1982. 3,300 entries.
ULM4	**Supplement. 1981-1982.** Ottawa, 1985. 9,000 entries.
ULM5	Unpublished entries for the fifth supplement.
WILSON	Wilson, Ruth Dyck, **Archives, a Record of Service.** Occasional Paper No. 1. Toronto, United Church of Canada Central Archives. 1992.

CONTENTS
Volume 1
Alberta – Ontario (Toronto: Presbyterian Church in Canada)

ALBERTA

Calgary
Glenbow-Alberta Institute Library.................................. 1
University of Calgary 7

Edmonton
Provincial Archives of Alberta 9
University of Alberta.
    University Archives and Collections 24

Lethbridge
City of Lethbridge. Records and Archives Management 24

BRITISH COLUMBIA

Burnaby
National Archives of Canada. Vancouver Federal
    Records Centre.. 26
Simon Fraser University.
    W.A.C.Bennett Library 29
    University Archives.. 31

Vancouver
Japanese Canadian Archives 32
United Church of Canada.
    British Columbia Conference Archives 32
University of British Columbia.
    Museum of Anthropology Archives 34
    Special Collections and University Archives Division............ 35
Vancouver City Archives 61
Vancouver Public Library 67

Victoria
Anglican Church of Canada. Diocese of British Columbia. Archives .. 76
Provincial Archives of British Columbia 77
University of Victoria.
    McPherson Library. University Archives and Special Collections .. 98
City of Victoria. Archives Division................................ 100

MANITOBA

Winnipeg
Provincial Archives of Manitoba................................... 101

United Church of Canada.
    Conference of Manitoba and North Western Ontario. Archives
    Committee 102
University of Manitoba.
    University Libraries. Archives and Special Collections 102

NEW BRUNSWICK

Fredericton

University of New Brunswick.
    Harriet Irving Library 105

Saint John

New Brunswick Museum. Library and Archives................... 108

NEWFOUNDLAND

St. John's

Memorial University of Newfoundland.
    Centre for Newfoundland Studies. Archives 109

NOVA SCOTIA

Antigonish

Saint Francis Xavier University.
    Angus L. MacDonald Library. Archives........................ 111

Halifax

Dalhousie University... 112
    Killam Memorial Library. Archives 114
Nova Scotia Museum Library 114
Public Archives of Nova Scotia 115
United Church of Canada. Maritime Conference.................... 115

Wolfville

Acadia University.
    Harold Campbell Vaughan Memorial Library................... 116

ONTARIO

Guelph

University of Guelph
    Library. Archival and Special Collections 118
    Documentation and Research Centre 118

Hamilton

McMaster University Library.
    William Ready Division of Archives and
    Research Collections 120
    Divinity College. Canadian Baptist Archives 126

Kingston

Queen's University.
    Archives 128

London
University of Western Ontario.
   D.B.Weldon Library 131

North York
York University.
   Scott Library. Special Collections and Archives 132

Ottawa
Canada Department of National Defence.
   Directorate of History Library 134
Carleton University
   Mac Odrum Library 200
University of Ottawa.
   Morriset Library.
   Special Collection Division..................................... 202

NATIONAL ARCHIVES OF CANADA

Manuscript Division. Manuscript Groups

9. Provincial, Local & Territorial
   Records 205
10. Records of Foreign Governments 205
11. Colonial Office(C.O.) Great Britain............................ 205
17. Religious Archives 207
18. Pre-Conquest Papers... 207
24. Nineteenth Century pre-Confederation papers................... 207
26. Papers of the Prime Ministers 207
   A. MacDonald, John Alexander, 1815-1891 208
   B. MacKenzie, Alexander, 1822-1892........................... 208
   C. Abbott, John Joseph Caldwell, 1821-1893 208
   E. Bowell, MacKenzie, 1823-1917 208
   F. Tupper, Charles, 1821-1915................................ 209
   G. Laurier, Wilfrid, 1841-1919 209
   H. Borden, Robert Laird, 1854-1937 220
   I. Meighen, Arthur, 1874-1960 220
   J. King, William Lyon MacKenzie, 1874-1950 221
   K. Bennett, Richard Bedford, 1870-1947....................... 224
   L. St.Laurent, Louis Stephen, 1882-1973...................... 226
   M. Diefenbaker, John G., 1895-1979 229
   N. Pearson, Lester Bowles, 1897-1972......................... 265
   O. Trudeau, Pierre Elliot, 1919– 280
27. Political figures, 1867-1950
I. Cabinet ministers, 1867-1896 280
   C. Lieutenant-Governors, 1867-1896........................... 280
   D. Cabinet ministers, 1867-1896.............................. 280
   E. Members of the House of Commons and Senate,
   1867-1896... 281
II. Cabinet ministers, 1896-1921
   C. Lieutenant-Governors, 1896-1921........................... 281
   D. Cabinet ministers, 1896-1921.............................. 281

III. Cabinet ministers, 1921-1950
    B. Cabinet ministers, 1921-1948 281
    C. Members of the House of Commons and the
    Senate, 1921-1950 282
    E. Consuls and diplomatic representatives, 1921-1950 282
    G. Related political papers, 1921-1950 283
28. Records of Post-Confederation corporate bodies
I.   Societies and associations 283
III. Business establishments 289
V.   Ethno-cultural organizations 289
29. Nineteenth Century Post-Confederation Manuscripts
    C. Social 292
    D. Cultural 292
30. Manuscripts of the First Half of the Twentieth Century
    A. Business 292
    B. Scientific 292
    C. Social 293
    D. Cultural 295
    E. Professional and public life 298
31. Manuscripts of the Second Half of the Twentieth Century
    B. Economic and Industrial Development 309
    C Exploration and Travel 309
    E. Law, Judiciary and Public Life 310
    F. Churches and Clergy 313
    G. Military Figures and Events 313
    H. Local, Regional and Ethnic History 314
    I. Miscellaneous 315
    K. Social Development 315
32. Political figures, 1950-
    B. Cabinet Ministers 316
    C. Members of the House of Commons and Senate 317
    F. Correspondents of Political Figures 318
    G. Related Political Papers 318
40. Records and Manuscripts from British Repositories 318
42. London. The Dominions Office 319
54. Foreign Documents 319
55. Miscellaneous documents 319
    /24. Nineteenth Century Pre-Confederation Papers 319
    /28. Records of Post-Confederation Corporate Bodies 319
    /29. Nineteenth Century Post-Confederation
         Manuscripts 319
    /30. Manuscripts of the First Half of the
         Twentieth Century 319
    /31. Manuscripts of the Second Half of the
         Twentieth Century 320

Government Archives Division. Record Groups
2. Privy Council Office 320
3. Post Office 332
6. Secretary of State 332

7. Governor General's Office 336
9. Militia and Post-Confederal Records 343
12. Transport 343
13. Justice 343
14. Parliament 351
15. Interior 352
16. National Revenue 352
17. Agriculture 352
18. Royal Canadian Mounted Police 352
19. Finance 354
20. Trade and Commerce 355
21. Energy, Mines and Resources 396
22. Indian Affairs and Northern Development 396
23. Fisheries and Oceans 396
24. National Defence 396
25. External Affairs 422
26. Citizenship and Immigration, 1949-1966 560
27. Labour 561
29. National Heath and Welfare 563
30. Canadian National Railways 563
33. Royal Commissions 563
35. Interdepartmental Committees 564
36. Boards, Offices and Commissions 564
38. Veterans' Affairs 566
42. Marine Branch 566
43. Railways and Canals 566
44. National War Service 566
55. Treasury Board 567
58. Auditor General 567
64. Wartime Prices and Trade Board 567
68. Registrar General 567
74. External Aid Office, 1955-1976 567
76. Immigration, 1865-1977 568
82. Immigration Appeal Board 594
84. Parks Canada 594
85. Northern Affairs Program 594
88. Surveys and mapping 594
117. Office of the Custodian of Enemy Property 595
118. Manpower and Immigration 596
   Documentary Art and Photography Division 596
   National Film, Television and Sound Archives 601
   Historical Sound Recording Section 608

Saint Catharines

Brock University
   Library 609

Toronto

ANGLICAN CHURCH OF CANADA. GENERAL SYNOD ARCHIVES

Missionary Society of the Church in Canada — 609
Council for Social Service — 615
World Mission — 618
Primate's World Relief and Development Fund — 628

Canadian Institute for International Affairs
   The John Holmes Library — 636
China Inland Mission/Overseas Missionary Fellowship — 637
Metropolitan Toronto Reference Library — 639
Archives of Ontario — 639

PRESBYTERIAN CHURCH IN CANADA. ARCHIVES

Presbyterian Church in Taiwan — 640
Korean Christian Church in Japan — 650
Church of North India — 653
Church of Christ in China — 659
Afghanistan. International Mission — 660
Nepal. United Mission — 660
Presbyterian Church of Korea — 660
Inter Church Organizations — 660
Tours — 661
Special Gifts — 662
Overseas Visitors — 662

Administrative Records of the General Board of Missions/Board of World Mission

Correspondence — 662
Women's Missionary Society — 665
   China — 665
   British Guiana — 666
   India — 666
   Formosa — 667
   China — 667
Overseas Missions — 667
   British Guiana — 667
   India — 668
   Japan — 669
   Formosa — 669
   China — 667
Women's Missionary Society — 670
   Publications Department — 670
   Scrapbooks — 671

ALBERTA

Calgary

Glenbow-Alberta Institute Library,
Glenbow Centre, 130 Ninth Avenue,
Calgary, Alberta, T2G 0P3.
Tel: (403)264-8300.

Manuscripts

Aoki, Ted T.
18 leaves, typewritten.
Address "Man with a history, dangers of ahistorical social studies", Calgary, 1979.
Japanese in Alberta.

Baureiss, Gunter A.
1 vol. 192 leaves, photocopy.
The city and the subcommunity, the Chinese of Calgary. M.A. thesis, University of Calgary, 1970.
Chinese in Calgary, Chinese in Canada.

Bescoby, Isabel M.L.
1 reel, microfilm.
Some social aspects of the American mining advance into the Cariboo and Kootenay. Thesis, University of British Columbia, 1935.
Chinese in British Columbia.

Brown, J.C.F., 1856-1833.
39 document boxes, 33 volumes, and 12 items oversize.
Correspondence, legal papers, etc. of lawyer, Calgary and Edmonton, 1865-1946.
Chinese in Alberta.

Bryden, Alexander.
1 cm. photocopy.
Travel diary, 1910.
Chinese in Calgary.

Burtwell, H.D.
1 item, photocopy.
Letter of introduction in Chinese to Ho Lem, Calgary, from Regina, 1951.
Chinese in Canada, Chinese language.

Calgary, City Clerk.
1 document box and 635 items oversize.
Blueprints, specifications, etc., for various Calgary buildings, 1904-1955.
Chinese in Calgary.

Canadian Historical Society.
2.5 inches, photocopy.
Historical papers presented at Conference, Montreal, 1972.
Chinese in British Columbia, Japanese in British Columbia.

Canadian Pacific Railway.
150 ft.
Papers re colonization, land and natural resources Western Canada, 1886-1958.
Chinese in British Columbia.

Cass, Douglas E.
44 leaves, photocopy.
Essay "Aspects of ethnicity in Southern Alberta coal mining camps, 1880-1920."
Chinese in Alberta.

Cassillis, Kennedy F.W.
3 leaves, photocopy.
Articles, "The Japanese in Canada", London, England, 1925.

Chan, Helen.
2 fiche.
Family organization and change among the Chinese in Calgary. M.A. thesis, University of Calgary, 1980.
Chinese in Calgary.

Chapman, Terry.
175 leaves, typewritten.
The drug problem in Western Canada, 1900-1920. M.A. thesis, University of Calgary, 1976.
Chinese in Canada.

Cochrane, William Edward, d. 1929.
1 document box, written, typewritten and printed.
Diaries, ranch papers, correspondence, 1885-1919.
Chinese in Alberta.

Coyote Flats Historical Society, collector.
1 document box, written and typewritten.
Manuscripts relating to history and personalities of Picture Butte, Shaughnessy, Turin, Barrhill and Iron Springs, Alberta, ca. 1975.
Japanese in Alberta.

Dawson, J. Brian.
Collector.
10 cassettes, tape outline.
Interview of Chinese pioneers of Calgary and district, Chinese Canadian Heritage Program, Calgary, 1974.
Chinese in Alberta, Chinese language.

Dawson, J. Brian.
2 fiches.
Chinese urban communities in Southern Alberta, 1885-1925. M.A thesis, University of Calgary, 1976.
Chinese in Alberta.

Foran, Maxwell Laurence.
330 leaves, typewritten.
Draft of book "Urban growth on the Canadian frontier, Calgary, 1875-1960." Calgary, 1978.
Chinese in Calgary.

Fort McLeod History Book Committee.
2 document boxes, written and typewritten.
Family histories prepared for local history:Fort McLeod, our colourful past, 1977.
Chinese in Alberta.

Glenbow-Alberta Institute,.
Collector.
l cm., printed, illustrated, 11 items oversize.
Civic election pamphlets and posters, October 1980.
Chinese in Calgary.

Glenbow-Alberta Institute.
Collector.
.5 inch, printed and illustrated and 2 items oversize.
Civic election pamphlets and posters, October 1974.
Chinese in Alberta.

Ho Lem, George.
1 cassette-tape outline.
Interview conducted by Tom Kirkham, Calgary, 23 February 1982.
Chinese in Calgary.

Hong, Louie.
2 leaves, photocopy.
Biographical information on Chinese settler, Cluny, Alberta, 1969.
Chinese in Alberta

Iwaasa, Katzuo.
1 reel, tape outline.
Interview re recollections of Japanese experiences in Western Canada, 1918-1973.
Japanese Canadian Citizenship Council, Japanese in Alberta, Japanese in British Columbia.

Iwaasa, Mitsuo.
1 reel, tape outline, side 2.
Recollections of Japanese experiences in Western Canada, 1919-1973.
Japanese in Alberta, Japanese in British Columbia.

Jameson, Sheilagh S.
Collector.
13 document boxes, written, typewritten and printed, 13 items oversize.
Documents relating to history re Chatauqua Organization in Western Canada, 1909-1981.
Chinese in Canada.

Longman, O.S.
Collector.
4 boxes and 3 volumes.
Papers relating to beet sugar industry in Western Canada, 1902-1960.
Japanese in Alberta.

Lucas, Edward Alexander.
1.5 in. typewritten.
Manuscripts, autobiography, and articles on Calgary's history, ca. 1952-1959.
Chinese in Alberta.

Macdonald, Elizabeth.
116 leaves, typewritten.
Japanese Canadians in Edmonton, 1969, an exploratory search for patterns of assimilation. M.A. thesis, University of Alberta, 1970.
Japanese in Alberta.

McHugh, John O.
1 volume of 262 leaves, typescript.
Manuscripts. "The reminiscences of H2 Jack." 1960.
Chinese in Alberta.

Morrish, Jack.
1 cassette, tape outline.
Recording of press conference re Fording Coal Mine at Shaughnessy, Lethbridge, 26 May 1981.
Japanese in Alberta.

Nippon Silk and Products Company, est. ca. 1911.
Papers, ca. 1911-1964.
Legal papers, ledgers, etc.
ULM5

Nowlin, C.L.
Collector.
.5 inch, written.
Invoice book of cafe and store run by Long Gum, Retlaw, Alberta, 1930.
Chinese in Alberta.

Orr, Wesley F., 1831-1898.
Volume 3 of 5 volumes.
Letter books of alderman and mayor, Calgary.
Chinese in Alberta.

Palmer, Howard.
464 leaves, photocopy.
Nativism and ethnic tolerance in Alberta, 1920-1972. Ph.D. dissertation, York University, 1973.
Chinese in Alberta, Japanese in Alberta.

Palmer, Howard.
295 leaves, photocopy.
Responses to foreign immigration, nativism and ethnic tolerance in Alberta, 1880-1920. M.A. thesis, University of Alberta, 1971.
Chinese in Alberta.

Ryan, Mrs. Ada T.
42 leaves, typewritten.
Articles re early Alberta pioneers, 1934-1936.
Chinese in Alberta.

Sauder, J.A
1 reel, tape outline.
Interview regarding Penrose M. Sauder, n.p., n.d.
Chinese in Alberta.

Short, Ross, Selwood, Shaw and Mayhood.
12 ft., written and printed.
Estate, property and defense papers of Calgary law firm, 1885-1967.
Chinese in Alberta.

Steinhauser, Gussie, collector.
2 leaves, printed.
Forms related to Japanese farm labour, ca. 1942-1945.
Japanese in Alberta.

Tamagi, James, collector.
1 cm., photocopy.
Information leaflet and menu re Bridge Band Good Services, Ltd., Calgary, 1938, 1980.
Japanese in Alberta.

Tamagi, James.
1 cassette, tape outline.
Interview conducted by Tom Kirkham, Calgary, 29 August 1980.
Japanese in Alberta.

Tamaki, Michigoro.
1 reel, transcript, side 1.
Interview with Mr. and Mrs. M. Tamaki, re Japanese experiences in Western Canada, 1919-1973.
Japanese in British Columbia.

Tamaki, Mr. and Mrs. Michigoro.
3 items, printed.
Identification cards issued to Japanese.
Japanese in Alberta.

Terrill's Flowers Limited.
2 document boxes, 51 volumes.
Business papers of a Calgary florist, 1920-1971.
Chinese in Alberta.

Tighe, John Joseph.
4 cm., written and typewritten.
Correspondence and articles re Patrick Burns, 1937-1956 and n.d.
Chinese in Alberta.

Traill family papers.
4 document boxes, written, photocopy and typescript.
Consists of correspondence, journals, financial records, etc. of William E. Traill and Walter J.S. Traill, 1863-1914.
Chinese in British Columbia.

Turcotte, Judge Louis S. Herman.
1 cassette, tape outline.
Interview conducted by Tom Kirkham, Lethbridge, 4 August 1981.
Japanese in Alberta.

Underwood, Thomas.
3 ft., written and typewritten.
Correspondence, legal documents, etc. re business, church and personal affairs, Calgary, 1904-1948.
Chinese in Alberta.

Wai, Hayne Yip.
1 reel, microfilm.
The Chinese and their voluntary associations in British Columbia, a political machine interpretation. M.A. thesis, Queens University, 1970.
Chinese in British Columbia.

Williams, Tom, collector.
3 leaves, printed and written.
Menu from Pekin Chop Suey cafe, Calgary, ca. 1947-1969.
Chinese in Alberta.

Yamashita, Nobuo.
1 reel, tape outline.
Comments re Japanese experiences in Western Canada, ca. 1925-1973.
Japanese in Alberta, Japanese in British Columbia.

Yamashita, Tatsuzo.
1 reel, tape outline, side 1.
Interview with Mr. Tatsuzo Yamashita and his daughter-in-law, Ruriko Yamashita, re recollections of Japanese experiences in Western Canada, 1908-1973.
Japanese in Alberta, Japanese in British Columbia.

Yuan Lin-shih.
1 volume, written(restricted). 2 volumes, photocopy(for use).
Letterbook of Chinese consul re Chinese immigrants, Vancouver, 1914-1915.
Chinese in British Columbia, Chinese in Canada, Chinese language.

Yuen, Charlie.
1 leaf, typewritten.
Biographical notes re Chinese cook at Alley farm, ca. 1891-1938: 1967.
Chinese in Alberta.

Photographs

NA-103-30
Sam Wing, Innisfail Laundry, 1904.
Chinese in Alberta.

4 • Alberta – Calgary

NA-103-33
Sang Lung, Chinese resident of Innisfail, ca. early 1900's.
Chinese in Alberta.

NA-370-46
Lem's restaurant, High River, extreme right, Lem Foy.
Chinese in Alberta.

NA-387-27
Chinese section men on handcars, Canadian Pacific Railway, ca. 1886.

NA-548-1
Completion of Canadian Pacific Railway through the Rockies. Actual driving of last spike, 1885.
Chinese in Alberta, and British Columbia.

NA-671-(14-16)
Fire in Chinatown, Calgary, 1912.

NA-915-31
Chee You, Chinese cook for Grand Trunk Pacific surveyors, ca. 1910-1911.
Chinese in Alberta.

NA-963-9
Chinese cook at Rawlinson Ranch with large hailstones, ca. 1900-1907.
Chinese in Alberta.

NA-1043-7
Chinese feast at a funeral in Vancouver, British Columbia, early 1900's.

NA-1098-(21-24)
Chinese YMCA annual picnic, Calgary, Alberta.

NA-1215-6
View of CC Ranch, Mosquito Creek, Alberta. ca. 1890's. Son of owner, W.F.Cochrane, and Chinese cook. Latter at CC Ranch for years.
Chinese in Alberta.

NA-1241-1095
Calgary Stampede parade, float sponsored by the Chinese-Canadian club, 1946.

NA-1455-7
Placer mining at Wild Horse Creek, Windermere Valley, British Columbia, 1880's.
Chinese labourers worked this region for gold for over 70 years.

NA-1497-9
Chinese parade, Calgary, 1905.
Chinese in Alberta.

NA-1604-82
Gravestone in Chinese cemetery, Calgary, early 1920's.

NA-1753-25
Work on the Baillie-Grohman canal between Columbia Lake and Kootenay, ca. 1888.
Chinese in British Columbia.

NA-1753-40
Group outside Wild Horse Post Office, Kootenay, British Columbia. Chinese in group, ca. 1886-1889.

NA-1786-16
Chinese cook and cook-house, Walter Fork, Alaska, 1914.
Chinese in Alaska.

NA-1786-45
A.Herbert Eckford and Chinese cook at High River horse ranch, Alberta, ca. 1913.
Chinese in Alberta.

NA-1852-1
Sam Wong, Chinese businessman, New Sedalia, Alberta, 1932. Owner of restaurant and pool room.

NA-1891-1
Delegates to meeting of Chinese Freemasons, Lethbridge, Alberta, 1924.

NA-1900-22
Dr. Tehyi Hsieh, Chinese American, late 1920's. Dr. Hsieh was a lecturer on the Chatauqua circuits.

NA-1945-1
Group at Japanese Settlement, Hardieville, Alberta, 1920.
Settlement of Okinawans, started ca. 1911, originally Canadian Pacific railway workers.

NA-1978-1
Wong Yet store, Olds, Alberta, 1904-1905.
Chinese in Alberta.

NA-2026-6
Chinese band wagon, Vancouver, British Columbia, ca. 1912.

NA-2127-2
Railway Avenue, Olds, Alberta.
Chinese in Alberta.

NA-2131-1
Chinese YMCA group, Calgary, 1914. In front of Chinese mission, 120-2 Avenue, S.W., Calgary.

NA-2186-33
Hop Wo laundry being moved, Calgary, Alberta, 1920's.

NA-2193-8
Boys at Chinese YMCA, Calgary, in front of Chinese mission, 120-2nd Avenue, S.W.

NA-2307-(49 & 50)
Chinese cook working in kitchen, and wielding dinner bell at ranch, in Southern Alberta, 1905-1906.
Chinese in Alberta.

NA-2512-1
Chinese in Alberta, 1901.

NA2574-(59 & 60)
Personalities of Hesketh, Alberta, 1923 and 1926. Show group of residents behind Wong Kai's restaurant, and Wong Kai, Chinese restaurant owner.

NA-2575-4
Pupils and teachers of Chinese mission, Calgary, 1902. Rev. James Camers Herdman, Presbyterian minister at Knox Church in centre of photo.
Chinese in Alberta.

NA-2622-(31, 32 & 38)
Chinese gathering, parade and laundries, Calgary, Alberta, 1905 and 1911.
Chinese in Alberta.

NA-2622-50
Mok-Lien, Chinese cook at Alpine Club camp, Lake O'Hara, British Columbia.

NA-2626-1
View of Vulcan, Alberta business area, ca. 1914.
Chinese in Alberta.

NA-2645-(44-52)
Schools, homes, and business buildings in Chinatown community, Calgary, 1966-1973.

NA-2652-82
Chinese grave, Kamloops, British Columbia.

NA-2685-(69 & 74)
Street scene in Vulcan, Alberta, shows Fung laundry.

NA-2798-6
Asiatic immigrant workers in Southern Alberta outside building, possibly employment office, ca. 1908-1910.
Chinese in Alberta.

NA-2854-(1-3)
Fire in Chinatown, Calgary, 1912.

NA-2961-2
Charles Yuen, Chinese cook, Bow Valley farm, Midnapore, Alberta, ca. 1937 or 1938.

NA-2968-79
Group on board **Empress of Canada,** Vancouver, British Columbia, 1925.
Includes Chinese steward.

NA-2979-(1-10)
Interior of Wing Chong laundry, High River, Alberta, 1974. Chinese-Canadian heritage program.

NA-2991-(1 & 2)
Children at village school, Clover Bar, Alberta, 1934-1937.
Japanese in Alberta.

NA-3020-4
Chinese parade, Rossland, British Columbia, ca. early 1900's.

NA-3047-9
Hewitt Bostock family, Monte Creek, British Columbia, ca. 1895.
Chinese in British Columbia.

NA-3186-(1,2)
J.C. Prokovski, Wing Lee and son, Yee Wing, Jr., Calgary, 1915, 1920.

NA-3212-2
Wing Lang's restaurant, right foreground, 1910.
Chinese in Alberta.

NA-3369-(1 & 2)
Japanese workers in sugar beet field, Southern Alberta, and in armed forces, 1941-1945.
Japanese in Canada.

NA-3489-26
Grand Trunk railway car beside Skeena River, British Columbia, ca. 1910.
Includes Chinese cook standing on observation platform.

NA-3543-71
School children beside school, Viking, Alberta, 1923.
Chinese in Alberta.

NA-3596-2
Construction of Alma Block, Hanna, Alberta, showing Chinese restaurant in centre right. 1912-1913.

NA-3644-6
Hotel Northern, Fernie, British Columbia, owned by Bill Eschwig and wife. Many of their servants were Chinese, ca. early 1900's.

NA-3658-46
Grand Trunk railway construction camp, British Columbia, ca. 1913.
Signs for the B.C. Hotel, and Yee Chong's restaurant.

NA-3740-29
Chinese work gang, Canadian Pacific tracks near Summit, British Columbia, 1889.

NA-3766-(16,17)
Tombstones in Chinese cemetery, Calgary, Alberta, 1912-1913.

NA-3811-21
Steam laundry, Maple Creek, Saskatchewan.
Chinese in Saskatchewan.

NA-3871-3
Grade I class, Victoria School, Moose Jaw, Saskatchewan, 1915.
Chinese in Saskatchewan.

NA-3903-(1 & 62)
Front Street, Bellevue, Alberta, showing Bellevue Chinese cafe.

NA-3910-(5,6, & 18)
Group at Anglican mission, group of men at St. Paul's School, Cardston, Alberta, 1950. Includes Canon Nakayama.

NA-3971-1
Executive and teachers of Chinese Mission, Calgary, Alberta, 1921.

NA-3976-(1-4)
Chinese man, Chinese lady, in living room, Sam Wing, Chinese, Sam Wing's laundry, Bowden, Alberta, 1912-1915.
Chinese in Alberta.

NA-3986-1
Henry Wise Wood, farm leader and Japanese hosts, Japan, 1922.

NA-3992-2
View of 4th Street, S.W. Calgary, Alberta, ca. 1929.
Chinese in Alberta.

NA-4049-4
Group at entrance to Inn, Lac la Biche, Alberta. Chinese cook and waiter, left.
Chinese in Alberta.

NA-4081-4
Survey camp at Cassils, Alberta, 1909.
Chinese in Alberta.

NA-4262-25
Contestants for queen at Potato Conference, Brooks, Alberta. Some Japanese girls in group.

NA-4461-34
Workers removing rock debris from railway tracks after rock slide. Include Chinese labourers.

NA-4571-(27 & 28)
Chinese working at hydraulic mining, Lilloet area, British Columbia.

NA-4571-(29-30)
"Mow", Chinese cook with dinner bell, "Mow", Chinese cook on CC ranch, ca. 1905-1906.
Chinese in Alberta.

NA-4577-8
Chinese servant, Calgary, ca. 1907-1908.
Chinese in Alberta.

NA-4680-3
John, Chinese cook, at No.2 Firehall, Calgary, 1913.

NA-4697-(112 & 134)
Group outside Grand Central Hotel, Field, British Columbia, 1885-1886. Chinese in group.

NA-4786-(12-14)
WK and Jade Palace restaurants, Chinatown, Calgary. n.d.
Chinese in Alberta.

NA-4792-1
John L. Quan from Calgary, on hunting trip near Bowden, Alberta, 1941.

NA-4884-27
Pig "village", 2,000 pigs raised on Grand View farm, Nobleford, Alberta, 1942-1943.
Built by Japanese Canadian workers, to assist in supplying bacon for Britain in the war years.

NA-4893-13
Lady and child in Chinese costume, Calgary, 1956. First ethnic fashion show in Penley's Ballroom, Calgary.

NA-4893-14
Sadako Hironaka, in Japanese costume, Calgary, 1956. In first ethnic fashion show in Penley's Ballroom, Calgary.

NC-6 and ND-3 groups.
McDermid collection, 1921-1930.
Chinese in Alberta.

NC-7-(35,142,362,268,444,457,458 & 538)
Views of Chinese men in Alberta.

NC-7-142
Portraits of Cardston and district residents, 1897-1914. Include Chinese.

NC-7-362
Portraits of Cardston and district residents. Include Chinese.

NC-26-(26-29)
Views of Hing Wah Company, Calgary. Chinese gardeners, views of greenhouses and gardens.

ND-2-(106, 108-112, 133, 321-323)
Views of Chinese restaurants, members of Chinese community, Lacombe, Alberta, 1946.

ND-3-6226
Sing Lee laundry, Edmonton, Alberta, 1932.

ND-27-(28,29)
Chinese family, Cardston, Alberta, ca. 1920's.

**University Archives,
MacKimmie Library,
University of Calgary,
2500 University Drive, N.W.
Calgary, Alberta, T2N 1N4.
Tel:(403)220-7271.**

Theses and dissertations

A microfilm copy is located in the Microforms Department, MacKimmie Library.

Allen, Derek.
Linguistic determinism, bilingualism and Chinese noun classifiers. M.A. thesis 1983.
NL

Allen, Rebecca K.S.
The social organization of migration: an analysis of the uprooting and flight of Vietnamese refugees. M.A. thesis 1983.
NL

Amery, Anwer Mike.
Canadian policies in the Middle East. M.A. thesis 1986.
NL

Assadollahnejad, Majid R.
Iran's foreign policy in the 1970s. M.A. thesis 1976.
CT

Basdeo, Sahadeo.
The development of East Indian immigration to the British West Indies, 1838-1860. M.A. thesis 1972.
CT

Baureiss, Gunter A.
The city and the subcommunity, the Chinese of Calgary. M.A. thesis 1970.

Chan, Elaine Y.
Chinese students from Hong Kong at the University of Calgary: their problems and socio-cultural orientation. M.A. thesis 1987.
NL

Chan, Helen.
Family organization and change among the Chinese in Calgary. M.A. thesis 1980.

Chapman, Terry.
The drug problem in Western Canada, 1900-1920. M.A thesis 1976.
Chinese in Canada.

Chauduri, Esha R.
Participation, learning and change: a study of selected urban and rural programmes of nonformal education for adult women in West Bengal, India. Ph.D. dissertation 1983.
NL

Cho, Sook Whan.
The acquisition of word order in Korean. M.A. thesis 1981.
NL

Chow, Kenneth Y.
An extended care facility for Victoria's Chinatown. M.E.Des. thesis 1986.
NL

Chow, Richard Douglas.
A Chinese cultural centre for Calgary. M.E.Des. thesis 1985.
NL

Chu, Simon Fook Keung.
An analysis of the **Hsin Ch'ing Nien**(New Youth) as a reflection of intellectual trends in China, 1915-1921. M.A. thesis 1975.
CT

Dann, Christopher Francis.
Public opinion on the First Anglo-Chinese War as expressed in some British journals. M.A. thesis 1972.
CT

Dawson, John Brian.
Chinese urban communities in Southern Alberta, 1885-1925. M.A thesis 1976.
CT

Donovan, Mark A.
Guru devotion in Tibetan Buddhism. M.A. thesis 1986.
NL

Enters, Thomas.
Community forestry: a case study in Sri Lanka. M.E.Des thesis 1987.
NL

Ford, Susan Janelle.
Erotic implications in Ukiyo-e prints. M.A. thesis 1975.
CT

Fox, Wendy Cecilia.
An exploratory study of Lao Buddhism: religion in village setting. M.A. thesis 1976.
CT

Gibson, Alistair Fraser.
Problems of inter-island shipping in the Solomon Islands. M.Sc. thesis 1981.
NL

Haley, Rupert David.
The development of Canadian policies toward Communist China. M.A thesis 1968.
CT

Hayakawa, Sei.
Japan's view of the Northern Territories dispute. M.A. thesis 1986.
NL

Hitch, Doug.
Central Asian Brahmi palæography: the relationships among the Tocharian, Khotanese and old Turkic Gupta scripts. M.A. thesis 1981.
NL

Hoffman, Arelene Rochelle.
The role of the school in social reconstruction: a comparative analysis of the half-work, half-study program in China, and the basic education program in India. M.A. thesis 1974.
CT

Hove, Philo H.
Buddhist causality and emptiness: a comparative study of the Nikayas and Nagarjuna. M.A. thesis 1988.
NL

Hu, Shi-chi.
Some aspects of the Sino-American cultural conflicts arising from trading contacts in the nineteenth century. M.A. thesis 1971.
CT

Hui, Kit Chow Albert.
Searching for dignity: the case of Chinese elderly in Calgary. M.A. thesis 1987.
NL

Hume, Lynne.
Making Lengwasa: analysis of a women's pig-killing ritual on Maewo, Vanuatu. M.A. thesis 1982.
NL

Knott, Yvette Yvonne Lucille.
A case study on the Canadian policy and Calgary Community response to the Southeast Asian refugees, 1979-1980. M.A. thesis 1982.
NL

Lin, Sen.
Ideology and the politics of Chinese socialist legality, 1978-1987. M.A. thesis 1988.
NL

Lin, Tsong-yuan.
The nature of dozoku: a comparison of the Japanese dozoku and the Chinese tsungtsu. M.A thesis 1970.
CT

Lin, Zhiqui.
Politics and the autonomy of the Chinese criminal justice system, 1978-1988. M.A. thesis 1989.
NL

Ma, Qing-he.
The design of an ESL test for students in China. M.A. thesis 1988.
NL

Man, Ronald Chi-wing.
Trade and industrialization in the ASEAN region. M.A. thesis 1979.
NL

Moody, Frank.
Equality of conditions and opportunity: China's university admissions policies, 1966-1982.
NL

Nielsen Elizabeth H.
Recognizing power, the underestimation of female power in New Guinea by anthropologists. M.A. thesis 1988.
NL

Osei-Afriyie, Francis.
Import substituting industrialization in India. M.A. thesis 1980.
CT

Paragg, Ralph Ramsarup.
The relation between civilization and politics in Gandhi's thought. M.A. thesis 1971.
CT

Peers, Douglas Mark.
Aspects of the military history of the British in eighteenth century India. M.A. thesis 1984.
NL

Pitman, Kaye.
A strategy for planning curriculum change in a teacher education programme at a church agency teachers' college in Papua, New Guinea. M.A. thesis 1977.
CT

Rooke, Patricia Thelma.
Socio-cultural implications of U.S. educational technical assistance with illustrative reference to Thailand. M.A. thesis 1973.
CT

Rowsell, Lorna V.
An ergative analysis of Kapampangan. M.A. thesis 1983.
NL

Serfaty, Meir.
Jan Sangh: an Indian party in transition. M.A. thesis 1969.
CT

Singh, Pashaura.
Sikh self definition and the Bhagat Bani. M.A. thesis 1987.
NL

Sirisena, Wannanayaka.
Land, policy and social change in Sri Lanka: a study of land tenure and the politics of land reform from the eighteenth to the twentieth century. M.A. thesis 1977.
CT

Sterner, Judith Anne,
High altitude adaptations: physiology and culture in the Andes and the Tibetan Plateau. M.A. thesis 1985.
NL

Sunahara, Muriel Ann.
Federal policy and the Japanese Canadians, 1942-1950. M.A. thesis 1977.
CT

Suzuki, Yoshiko.
The acquisition of Japanese pronouns. M.A. thesis 1985.
NL

Taplin, John Mark.
A study of the educational policy towards immigrants in Alberta, with emphasis upon English as second language instruction and the Indo-Chinese refugee movement. M.A. thesis 1987.
NL

Wang, Zhi Jin.
Cancer mortality of Chinese population in Canada, 1980-1984. M.Sc. thesis 1987.
NL

Watt, Ian.
The marketing of agricultural inputs in Fiji. Ph.D. dissertation 1981.
NL

Webster, Margaret Alexa.
The hawkers and vendors of the urban informal sector of Kota Bharu, Malaysia a case study. M.A. thesis 1982.
NL

Edmonton

Provincial Archives of Alberta,
12845 102nd Avenue,
Edmonton, Alberta, T5N 0M6.
Tel:(403)427-1750.

Alberta. Department of Advanced Education and Manpower.
Manpower Services Division. Records, 1977-1980. 21 cm. 83.131.

Alberta. Department of the Attorney General.
Administrative services records, 1908-1956. 5.8 metres. 83.192.
File 89. Chinese lotteries, 1936-1937.

Alberta. Department of the Attorney General.
Records, 1880-1958. 42.36 metres. 66.166.
File 1236. commissions to administer interrogatories, general file, 1913-1917, Japan.
Records re: Conference on Asian Refugees.

Alberta. Department of Consumer and Corporate Affairs.
Records, 1943. .5 cm., 86.287.
Concerning Kobai Kumiai Association of Raymond, Alberta.

Alberta. Department of Economic Development.
Records, 1973-1979. 84.311.
Files concerning trade missions to Saudi Arabia and Malaysia.

Alberta. Department of Economic Development.
Industrial Development Branch. Records, 1968-1978. 2.85 cm., 83.372.
Files concerning market opportunities in countries throughout Asia.

Alberta. Department of Health and Social Development.
Baker Memorial Sanitarium records, 1922-1965. 1.52 metres. 73.315.
File 24. Japanese evacuees, 1942-1945. Tuberculosis treatment.

Alberta. Legislative Assembly.
Records, 1909-1960. 26 metres. 70.414.
File 721 sessional paper re: shipments to Japan, 24 March 1925.

Alberta. Premier's Office.
Records, 1921-1959. 62.4 metres. 69.289.
Files 519, 1014, 1023 unemployment relief, 1921-1937. Chinese(particularly file 1023 Calgary, Chinese unemployed, 1936-1937)
Files 178, 1206, 1207, 1231, 1496, 1501, 1888, various files containing references to Japanese, primarily re: World War II. 1923, 1936-1953.

Grant, Charles H.
Papers, 1913-1972. 77.22.
Files 165-165. National Parks Highway Association/Jasper Park Development Committee, 1940-1948. Japanese internees doing roadwork.

Sœurs de l'Assomption de la Sainte Vierge.
Records, 1869-1971. 4.8 metres. 73.80.
SASV/40/1-2. Japanese Internment camps, Slocan valley, British Columbia, 1944-1945.

Record Group 76. IMMIGRATION BRANCH.

A. Central Registry Files. First Central Registry Series, 1873-1968.
Volumes 1-692 on microfilm.

Volumes 1-676.
Files on all subjects.

Finding aids. There is a complete file list.

Index to First Central Registry Files, 1892-1024. 21 reels, T5571-T5592.

Index to First Central Registry Files, 1924-ca. 1946. 5 microfilm reels, M-1986-M-1990.

Volume 83.
File 9309, part 1, reel C-4750.
Japanese emigration, 1891-1908.

File 9309, part 2, reel C-4750.
Japanese emigration, 1908.

Volume 84.

File 9309, part 3, reel C-4750.
Clippings Japanese immigration (report of inquiry), 1908-1909.

File 9309, part 4, reel C-4750.
Japanese immigration, 1909-1910.

File 9309, part 6, reel C-4750.
Japanese immigration, 1912-1914.

File 9309, part 7, reel C-4750.
Japanese immigration, 1914-1917.

File 9309, part 8, reel C-4751.
Japanese immigration, 1917-1918.

Volume 85.

File 9309, part 9, reel C-4751.
Japanese immigration, 1918-1919.

File 9309, part 10, reel C-4751.
Japanese immigration, 1919-1920.

File 9309, part 11, reel C-4751.
Japanese immigration, 1921-1923.

File 9309, part 12, reel C-4751.
Japanese immigration, 1923-1925.

File 9309, part 13, reel C-4751.
Japanese immigration(lists), 1925-1930.

Volume 86.

File 9309, part 14, reel C-4751-C-4752.
Japanese immigration, 1930-1936.

File 9309, part 15, reel C-4752.
Japanese immigration, 1936-1938.

File 9309, part 16, reel C-4752.
Japanese immigration, 1938.

File 9309, part 17, reel C-4752.
Japanese immigration(report), 1938-1941.

File 9309, part 18, reel C-4752.
Japanese immigration(report), 1941-1947.

Volume 87.

File 9309, part 19, reel C-4752.
Japanese immigration(report), 1947-1949.

File 9309, part 19, reel C-4753.
Japanese immigration, 1947-1949.

File 9309, part 20, reel C-4753.
Japanese immigration, 1947-1949.

File 9309, reel C-4753.
Reports of board of review on illegal immigration(Japanese), 1938.

File 9309, part 1, reel C-4753.
Japanese immigration, form file(lists), 1908-1909.

File 9309, part 2, reel C-4753-C-4754.
Japanese immigration, form file(lists), 1909-1910.

File 9309, part 3, reel C-4753.
Japanese immigration, newspaper clippings, 1942-1945.

Volume 88.

File 9309, part 3, reel C-4754.
Japanese immigration, form file(lists), 1910-1911.

File 9309, part 4, reel C-4754.
Japanese immigration, form file(lists), 1911.

File 9309, part 5, reel C-4754.
Japanese immigration, form file(lists), 1911.

File 9309, part 6, reel C-4754.
Japanese immigration, form file(lists), 1911-1912.

File 9309, part 7, reel C-4754.
Japanese immigration, form file(lists), 1912.

File 9309, part 8, reel C-4754.
Japanese immigration, form file(lists), 1912.

Volume 89.

File 9309, part 9, reel C-4755.
Japanese immigration, form file(lists), 1912.

File 9309, part 10, reel C-4755.
Japanese immigration, form file(lists), 1912-1913.

File 9309, part 11, reel C-4755.
Japanese immigration, form file(lists), 1913.

File 9309, part 12, reel C-4755.
Japanese immigration, form file(lists), 1913.

File 9309, part 13, reel C-4755.
Japanese immigration, form file(lists), 1913.

Volume 90.

File 9309, part 14, reel C-4755.
Japanese immigration, form file(lists), 1913.

File 9309, part 15, reel C-4755.
Japanese immigration, form file(lists), 1913-1914.

File 9309, part 16, reel C-4756.
Japanese immigration, form file(lists), 1914.

File 9309, part 17, reel C-4756.
Japanese immigration, form file(lists), 1914.

File 9309, part 18, reel C-4756.
Japanese immigration, form file(lists), 1914.

Volume 91.

File 9309, part 19, reel C-4756.
Japanese immigration, form file(lists), 1914.

File 9309, part 20, reel C-4756.
Japanese immigration, form file(lists), 1914-1915.

File 9309, part 21, reel C-4756.
Japanese immigration, form file(lists), 1915-1916.

File 9309, part 22, reel C-4757.
Japanese immigration, form file(lists), 1916.

File 9309, part 23, reel C-4757.
Japanese immigration, form file(lists), 1916.

Volume 92.

File 9309, part 24, reel C-4757.
Japanese immigration, form file(lists), 1916-1917.

File 9309, part 25, reel C-4757.
Japanese immigration, form file(lists), 1917.

File 9309, part 26, reel C-4757.
Japanese immigration, form file(lists), 1917.

File 9309, part 27, reel C-4757.
Japanese immigration, form file(lists), 1917-1918.

File 9309, part 28, reel C-4757 to C-4758.
Japanese immigration, form file(lists), 1918.

File 9309, part 29, reel C-4758.
Japanese immigration, form file(lists), 1918.

Volume 93.

File 9309, part 31, reel C-4758.
Japanese immigration, form file(lists), 1918-1919.

File 9309, part 32, reel C-4758.
Japanese immigration, form file(lists), 1919-1920.

Volume 121.

File 23635, part 1, reel C-4784.
Chinese immigration, 1895-1909.

File 23635, part 2, reel C-4784.
Chinese immigration, report by W.L.MacKenzie King, 1908-1911.

File 23635, part 3, reel C-4784.
Chinese immigration, 1911-1918.

File 23635, part 4, reel C-4784.
Chinese immigration, 1918-1919.

File 23635, part 5, reel C-4784.
Chinese immigration, 1919-1924.

File 23635, part 6, reel C-4785.
Chinese immigration, 1924-1943.

Volume 122.

File 23635, part 7, reel C-4785.
Chinese immigration, 1943-1948.

File 23635, part 8, reel C-4785.
Chinese immigration, 1948-1949.

File 23635, part 9, reel C-4785.
Chinese immigration, 1949-1950.

File 23635, part 10, reel C-4785.
Chinese immigration, 1951-1952.

Volume 125.

File 27114, reel C-4736,
Immigration of Armenians to Western Canada.
D.M.Quin, manager. 1895-1905.

Volume 215.

File 89616, part 1, reel C-7366.
Armenian relief fund. Admissions of orphans to Canada(photographs) 1922-1926.

File 89616, part 2, reel C-7366.
Armenian relief fund. Admission of orphans, 1926-1928.

File 89616, part 3, reel C-7366.
Armenian relief fund. Bringing orphans to Canada, 1928-1934, 1944.

Volume 223.

File 111414, reel C-7372.
Registration of Chinese in Canada under section 18 of the Chinese Immigration Act of 1923, 1942-1943, 1958.

Volume 226.

File 116193, part 1, reel C-7375.
Hong Kong(photographs and plans), 1923-1942.

File 116193, part 2, reel C-7375.
Administration and inspection at Hong Kong, 1945-1949.

Volume 280.

File 536999, part 1, reel C-10279-C-10280.
Emigration of Hindoos, 1904,1906-1907.

File 536999, part 2, reel C-10280.
Emigration of Hindoos(including British Honduras, labour(East Indian) ordinances, 1908), 1907-1908.

File 536999, part 3, reel C-10,280.
Emigration of Hindoos, 1908-1911.

File 536999, part 4, reel C-10,280.
Emigration of Hindoos, 1911-1912.

Volume 300.

File 279907, part 1, reel C-7849,
Immigration from Turkey and Armenia, 1903-1915, 1919-1923.

File 279907, part 2, reels C-7849-C-7850.
Immigration from Turkey and Armenia, 1923-1928.

File 279907, part 3, reel C-7850.
Immigration from Turkey and Armenia, 1929-1934, 1936-1938, 1940, 1946-1949.

Volume 342.

File 361435, reel C-10250.
Fred Yoshi, alias Kiyoshi Suhinto, Vancouver, smuggling Japanese into Canada, 1920-1921, 1928-1932.

Volume 363.

File 462223, reel C-10264.
White Canada Association, Vancouver, British Columbia, information on statistics on Japanese in Canada, 1934-1938.

File 467977, part 1, reel C-10264 to C-10265.
Consul-general for Japan, Ottawa, 1906-1911, 1912-1925.

File 467977, part 2, reel C-10265.
Consul-general for Japan, Ottawa, Ontario, 1928, 1930-1931, 1933-1944, 1948.

Volume 368.

File 488557, reel C-10268.
Privy Council reference from Colonial Office relating to Armenians in Brantford, Ontario, who wish to obtain permission for their families to rejoin them from Armenia, 1906-1907.

Volume 382.

File 532462, reel C-10278.
Investigation by Royal Canadian Mounted Police of illegal entry of Japanese, 1931-1934.

Volume 385.

File 536999, part 5, reel C-10280.
Emigration of Hindoos, 1912-1913.

File 536999, part 6, reel C-10280.
Emigration of Hindoos, 1913.

File 536999, part 7, reel C-10280.
Emigration of Hindoos(appeals against deportation), 1913.

File 536999, part 8, reel C-10280.
Emigration of Hindoos, 1913-1914.

File 536999, part 9, reel C-10280.
Emigration of Hindoos, 1914-1916.

File 536999, part 10, reel C-10280.
Emigration of Hindoos(including **Extracts from Minutes of Proceedings and Papers laid before the Imperial War Conference), 1917,** 1916-1918.

Volume 386.

File 536999, part 11, reel C-10280 to C-10281.
Emigration of Hindoos(including **Extracts from Minutes of Proceedings and Papers laid before the Imperial War Conference**), 1917, 1917-1919.

File 536999, part 12, reel C-10281.
Emigration of Hindoos(including **Summary of proceedings and documents on Conference of Prime Ministers**), 1921, 1919-1921.

File 536999, part 13, reel C-10281.
Emigration of Hindoos(copies of acts), 1921-1923.

File 536999, part 14, reel C-10281.
Emigration of Hindoos(copies of acts)(lists),1922-1935.

File 536999, part 15, reel C-10281.
Emigration of Hindoos, 1934-1939.

Volume 387.

File 536999, part 16, reel C-10281.
Emigration of Hindoos(lists), 1939-1943.

File 536999, part 17, reel C-10281.
Emigration of Hindoos(lists), 1943-1947.

File 536999, part 18, reel C-10281 to C-10282.
Emigration of Hindoos(lists), 1947-1948.

File 536999, part 19, reel C-10282.
Emigration of Hindoos(lists), 1948-1949.

File 536999 R.O., part 1.
Registering certificates of identification to Hindoos leaving on a visit, 1913-1919.

Volume 388.

File 536999 R.O., part 2, reel C-10282.
Registering certificates of identification to Hindoos leaving on a visit(pamphlet), 1919-1922.

File 536999 R.O., part 3, reel C-10282.
Registering certificates of identification to Hindoos leaving on a visit, 1923-1954

File 536999 British, part 1, reel C-10282.
Reports from W.C.Hopkinson on Hindoo matters(copies), 1914-1919.

File 536999 British, part 2, reel C-10282.
Reports from W.C.Hopkinson on Hindoo matters, 1919-1921.

File 536999 clippings, part 1, reel C-10282.
Newspaper clippings on Hindoos, 1913-1914.

File 536999 clippings, part 2, reels C-10282 to C-10283.
Newspaper clippings on Hindoos, 1914-1915, 1918.

File 536999 clippings, part 3, reel C-10283.
Newspaper clippings on Hindoos, 1918, 1920, 1922.

Volume 393.

File 561280, reel C-10286.
Ocean Steamship Company, Liverpool, England. Bonds covering escape of two Japanese, T.Obano and M.Ohishi(in Vancouver, British Columbia), 1906.

Volume 397.

File 565225, reel C-10289.
Chick Sexing Association of America, admission of chick sexing experts from Japan, 1933-1937.

Volume 401.

File 574351, reel C-10292.
G.L.Milne(medical inspector and immigration agent) Vancouver, British Columbia, escape of Japanese from schooner **Swan maru**, 1906.

Volume 470.

File 716275, reel C-10407.
G.L.Milne sends fine of $350.00 for allowing seven Japanese to land at Union Bay, British Columbia, without properly entering customs at that place, German ship S.S. **Wanguard**, 1907.

Volume 474.

File 729921, part 1, reel C-10410.
Asiatics, Orientals(Japanese, Chinese, East Indians), (list), 1907-1922.

File 729921, part 1, reel C-10410.
Asiatics, Orientals(Japanese, Chinese and East Indians), (pamphlets), 1922-1925.

File 729921, part 3, reel C-10410 to C-10411.
Asiatics, Orientals(Japanese, Chinese and East Indians), 1925-1932, 1934-1939.

File 729921 clippings, reel C-10411.

Newspaper clippings on Asiatic immigration(Japanese, Chinese and East Indians) 1907, 1909-1922.

Volume 491.

File 761402, reel C-10425.
A.Lavergne, member of Parliament, Montmagny, Québec. Japanese syndicate acquiring land in Alberta in order to settle colonists there, 1906, 1908, 1913.

Volume 503.

File 781181, reel C-10606.
Richard L.Drury, Victoria, British Columbia, appointed as a special officer of the Immigration branch for immigration work in Japan, 1908-1909.

Volume 512.

File 817172, reel C-10653.
J.B.Harkin wants employment in the fishing industry retained for Canadians(Japanese):1910-1948.

Volume 546.

File 304845, reel C-10632
Inquiries from the Fiji islands, 1908-1911.

Volume 550.

File 805806, reel C-10634.
Khoren Andonian, destitute at Batoum, Russia, makes application for repatriation to Canada(Armenian), 1908-1909.

Volume 551.

File 806018, reel C-10635.
Francis W. Giddens, Department of Labour, Ottawa, Ontario, statement re Chinese, Japanese, and Hindu immigration, 1908-1909.

Volume 556.

File 806652, reel C-10638.
Business manager, **Free Press**, Ottawa, Ontario. Printing pamphlet, **East Indians in British Columbia**(copies), 1909.

Volume 561.

File 808722, part 1, reel C-10641.
W.C.Hopkinson, Vancouver, British Columbia, appointed to the immigration staff at Vancouver, British Columbia(Hindu immigration), 1909-1914.

File 808722, part 2, reel C-10,641.
W.C.Hopkinson, Vancouver, British Columbia, appointed to the immigration staff at Vancouver, British Columbia(Hindu immigration), 1914-1916, 1918.

Volume 563.
File 808904, reel C-10644.
General enquiries from Persia, 1909, 1912-1913.

Volume 566.

File 806977, reel C-10638.
United States Commissioner of Immigration, Montréal, Québec. Report on number of Japanese and Hindoos entering United States, 1907 and 1909.

Volume 568.

File 812274, reel C-10647.
A.B.Barnard, Deputy Director of Intelligence, India, photographs and fingerprints of reports(Hindus), 1909, 1911-1912, 1920-1926.

Volume 576.

File 815661, reel C-10652.
Chinese conditions: 1912, 1921-1932, 1935-1938.

Volume 578.

File 817172, reel C-10653.
J.B.Harkin wants employment in the fishing industry on the Fraser River to be retained for Canadians(Japanese), 1910, 1912-1916, 1918-1919, 1933 and 1948.

Volume 584.

File 820636, reel C-10658.
Honourable Frank Oliver, Minister of the Interior, Ottawa, Canada. prevalence of hookworm among Hindus applying for admission to U.S. and among the negroes(blacks) of the U.S., 1910-1914, 1918, 1922-1923, 1943.

Volume 601.

File 879545, part 1, reel C-10,669.
Hindoo immigration, sailing of 400 Hindoos by chartered vessel S.S. **Komagata maru**, 1914.

File 879545, part 2, reel C-10,669.
Hindoos sailing from Shanghai to Vancouver, British Columbia on S.S. **Komagata maru**, 1914.

File 879545, part 3, reel C-10,669.
Hindoos sailing from Shanghai to Vancouver, British Columbia on **Komagata maru**, S.S.(photograph), 1914.

File 879545, part 4, reel C-10,669.
Hindoos sailing from Shanghai to Vancouver, British Columbia on **Komagata maru**, 1914.

Volume 602.

File 879545, part 5, reel C-10,669 to C-10,670.
Hindoos sailing from Shanghai to Vancouver, British Columbia on **Komagata maru**, S.S. (publication), 1914.

File 879545, part 6, reel C-10,670.
Hindoos sailing from Shanghai to Vancouver, British Columbia on **Komagata maru**, S.S., 1914-1915.

File 879545, part 7, reel C-10,670.
Hindoos sailing from Shanghai to Vancouver, British Columbia on **Komagata maru**, S.S., 1915-1922.

File 879545, part 8, reel C-10,670.
Hindoos sailing from Shanghai to Vancouver, British Columbia on **Komagata maru**, S.S., 1936, 1938, 1942, 1952.

Volume 647.

File A66589, part 1, reel C-10586.
Repatriation of Japanese(lists), 1941-1943, 1945.

File A66589, part 2, reel C-10587.
Repatriation of Japanese(lists), 1946-1947.

Volume 669.

File C57382, reel C-10603.
Transit of German refugees from Shanghai, China through Canada(Jewish), 1949.

Volume 674.

File C92656, reel C-10677.
Admission of Jewish refugees from Shanghai(lists), 1950.

File C92656, reel C-10677.
Admission of Jewish refugees from Shanghai, China(lists), 1950.

Volume 675.

File D46144, reel C-10677.
Greek Embassy, Ottawa, Ontario, admission of 200 Greeks from China(lists) , 1951-1952.

Volume 712.

Reel C-13421.
Control certificates, Chinese immigration(C.1, 5, 28, 30, 36), 1899-1953.

B. Central Registry Files. Second Central Registry series("500" block) 1911-1970 (volumes 676, 677, 689 to 692, and 743 to 930), 7 microfilm reels(C-10678, C-10687 to C-10688, C-13487, and M-1983 to M-1985).

l. Central Registry files, "500" block, 1911-1971. 40.2 metres (volumes 689-692, 718-725, 743-930), and 2 microfilm reels(C-10687 to C-10688).

This series consists of the Immigration Service's core policy and subject files active in the period from World

War II to 1966.

Volumes 743 to 930 are the main run of files in this series. Volumes 689 to 692, reels C-10,687 and C-10,688, document questions and answers in the House of Commons, including individual cases, immigration and employment policy and statistics, U.S. draft dodgers and deserters, and refugees issues from 1957 to 1970.

Volumes 718-725 relate to the Immigration Inspection Service on irregularities in immigration.

Finding aids.
Subject index to "500" block and related files, ca. 1925-1962. 3 microfilm reels M-1983 to M-1985.
Complete list of files in this series available.

The file classification manual indicates some of the files created in this series.

Volume 713.

Reel C-13421.
Register of Chinese Immigration, Central District(Toronto), 1923-1953.

Volume 796.

File 546-1-526, part 1.
Medical examinations of immigrants from China and Hong Kong, 1950-1957.

File 546-1-526, part 2.
Medical examinations of immigrants from China, Hong Kong and Formosa, 1958-1966.

Volume 802.

File 547-5-567.
Security examination of immigrants in India, 1962-1966.

File 547-5-580.
Security examination of persons from Korea, 1963-1966.

File 547-5-611.
Security examination of immigrants in the Philippines, 1961-1966.

Volume 803.

File 547-5-629.
Security examination of immigrants in Thailand, 1966.

File 548-8, part 1.
Processing of Chinese applications (including form 55b procedures), 1951-1956.

File 548-8, part 2.
Processing of Chinese applications (including form 55b procedures), 1956-1961.

Volume 804.

File 548-8, part 3.
Processing of Chinese applications (including form 55b procedures), 1961-1963.

File 548-8, part 4.
Processing of Chinese applications (including form 55b procedures), 1964-1966.

Volume 808.

File 548-12-578.
Processing of applications, Japan, 1965-1966.

Volume 819.

File 552-1-5-522.
Immigration from Burma, 1963-1966.

File 552-1-524.
Immigration from Ceylon, 1960-1065.

File 552-1-526, part 1.
Immigration from China, general files, 1952-1955.

File 552-1-526, part 2.
Immigration from China, policy and instructions, 1955-1958.

File 552-1-526, part 3.
Immigration from China, policy and instructions, 1958-1962.

File 552-1-526, part 4.
Immigration from China, policy and instructions, 1962-1963.

Volume 820.

File 552-1-526, part 5.
Immigration from China, policy and instructions, 1964-1966.

Volume 821.

File 552-1-548.
Immigration from the Fiji Islands, general file , 1953-1966.

Volume 822.

File 522-1-567, part 1.
Immigration from India, 1950-1961.

File 522-1-567, part 2.
Immigration from India, 1961-1966.

Volume 823.

File 552-1-537.
Immigration from Iran, general file, 1951-1956.

File 552-1-569.

Immigration from Indonesia, 1950-1964.

File 552-1-570.
Immigration from Iran, general file, 1951-1966.

Volume 824.

File 552-1-578, part 1.
Immigration from Japan, general file, 1950-1957.

File 552-1-578, part 2.
Immigration from Japan, general file, 1957-1964.

File 552-1-578, part 3.
Immigration from Japan, general file (reading list enclosed), 1964-1966.

File 552-1-580.
Immigration from Korea, general file, 1896-1966.

Volume 826.

File 552-1-606.
Immigration from Pakistan, general file, 1953-1966.

File 552-1-611, part 1.
Immigration from the Philippines, 1929-1963.

File 552-1-611, part 2.
Immigration from the Philippine Islands, 1929-1963.

Volume 829.

File 552-1-632.
Immigration from Turkey, general file, 1951-1966.
Volume 831.

File 5521-10-567, part 1.
Canada-India immigration agreement, policy and instructions, 1951-1952.

File 5521-10-567, part 2.
Canada-India immigration agreement, policy and instructions, 1953-1954.

File 5521-10-567, part 3.
Canada-India immigration agreement, policy and instructions, 1955-1956.

File 5521-10-567, part 4.
Canada-India immigration agreement, policy and instructions, 1957-1959.

Volume 832.

File 5521-10-567, part 5.
Canada-India immigration agreement, policy and instructions, 1959-1962.

File 5521-10-567, part 6.
Canada-India immigration agreement, policy and instructions, 1963-1966.

File 552-10-606, part 1.
Canada-Pakistan immigration agreement, policy and instructions, 1951-1956.

Volume 850.

File 553-148-567.
Admission to Canada of students from India, 1920-1966.

File 553-148-578.
Movement of students from Japan, 1960-1965.

File 533-148-592.
Movement of students from Malaysia (formerly Malaya, Singapore, etc.) policy and instructions, 1960-1964.

File 553-10-606.
Movement of students from Pakistan, 1962-1964.

Volume 854.

File 554-3, part 1.
Immigration to Canada of Armenians, general file, 1950-1961.

File 554-3, part 2.
Immigration to Canada of Armenians, general file, 1961-1966.

File 554-5.
Asiatics, general policy, 1953-1963.

File 554-6.
Asiatic immigration, 1923-1950.

Volume 861.

File 555-54-526, part 1.
Chinese refugees in Hong Kong(and refugees in China) general file, 1946-1961.

File 555-54-526, part 2.
Chinese refugees in Hong Kong(and refugees in China) general file, 1962-1963.

File 555-54-526, part 3.
Special movement of Chinese refugees from Hong Kong, operational control, 1962-1963.

Volume 862.

File 554-54-526-5.
Tibetan refugees, general file, 1959-1966.

Volume 866.

File 555-54-632.
Refugees in Turkey, general file, 1951-1963.

Volume 867.

File 556-1-524.
Immigration laws and regulations, Ceylon, 1942-1961.

Volume 868.

File 556-1-567.
Immigration laws and regulations, India, 1945-1950.

File 556-1-570.
Immigration laws and regulations, Iran, 1960.

File 556-1-606.
Immigration laws and regulations, Pakistan, 1948-1950.

File 556-1-611.
Immigration laws and regulations, Philippines, 1930-1963.

Volume 870.

File 556-3-570.
Alien labor laws and regulations, Iran, 1959.

Volume 871.

File 557-3-578, part 2.
Establishment of Japanese enterprises and entry of personnel, 1961-1966.

Volume 873.

File 557-40-12, part 1.
Canadian church organizations proposals for entry of Chinese immigrants from Hong Kong, 1960-1963.

File 557-40-12, part 2.
Canadian church organizations proposals for entry of Chinese immigrants from Hong Kong, 1964-1966.

Volume 876.

File 560-2-578.
Citizenship regulations, Japan, 1916-1950.

File 560-2-606.
Citizenship regulations, Pakistan, 1951.

File 560-6-526, part 1.
Status adjustment of Chinese illegally in Canada, 1960-1961.

File 560-6-526, part 2.
Status adjustment of Chinese illegally in Canada, policy and procedure, 1961-1962.

File 560-6-526, part 3.
Status adjustment of Chinese illegally in Canada, policy and procedure, 1962-1963.

Volume 877.

File 560-6-526, part 4.
Status adjustment of Chinese illegally in Canada, policy and procedure, 1962-1963.

File 560-6-526, part 5.
Status adjustment of Chinese illegally in Canada, policy and procedure, 1965-1966.

File 560-6-567.
Status adjustments of East Indians who have entered Canada illegally, 1961-1965.

Volume 895.

File 569-2.
Passport and visa regulations for Chinese nationals, 1938-1964.

Volume 896.

File 569-9-510.
Passport regulations, Cambodia, 1954.

File 569-9-524.
Passport regulations, Ceylon, 1950-1965.

Volume 898.

File 569-9-561.
Passport regulations, Maldive Islands, 1966.

File 569-9-567.
Passport regulations, India, 1953-1966.

File 569-9-569.
Passport regulations, Indonesia, 1950-1964.

File 569-9-570.
Passport regulations, Iran, 1954-1966.

Volume 899.

File 5.
Passport regulations, Japan, 1918-1965.

Volume 900.

File 596-9-606.
Passport regulations, Pakistan, 1953-1963.

File 569-9-611.
Passport regulations, Philippines, 1953-1964.

File 569-9-621.
Passport regulations, Singapore, 1960-1965.

Volume 901.

File 555-54-632.
Refugees in Turkey, general file, 1951-1963.

File 569-9-641.
Passport regulations, Vietnam, 1953-1966.

Volume 903.

File 569-30-522.
Issuance of Canadian visas to persons from Burma,

File 569-30-5
Issuance of Canadian visas to persons from India, 1950-1963.

File 569-30-526.
Issuance of Canadian visas to persons from China, 1949-1960.

Volume 904.

File 569-30-567.
Issuance of Canadian visas to persons from India, 1950-1965.

File 569-30-569.
Issuance of Canadian visas to persons from Indonesia, 1960-1961.

File 569-30-570.
Issuance of Canadian passports to persons from Iran, 1958-1966.

File 569-30-578.
Issuance of visas to persons from Laos, 1959.

Volume 905.

File 569-30-578.
Issuance of Canadian visas to persons from Japan, 1959-1966.

File 569-30-592.
Issuance of Canadian visas to persons from Malaysia(formerly Malaya, Singapore, etc.), 1950-1958.

File 569-30-611.
Issuance of Canadian visas to persons from the Philippines, 1953-1963.

File 569-30-621.
Issuance of Canadian visas to nationals from Singapore, 1965.

File 569-30-632.
Issuance of Canadian visas to persons from Turkey, 1953-1966.

File 569-30-580.
Issuance of Canadian visas to persons from Korea, 1960.

File 569-30-589.
Issuance of Canadian visas to persons from North Korea, 1963-1964.

File 569-30-606.
Issuance of Canadian visas to persons from Pakistan, 1955-1962.

Volume 906.

File 569-36-524.
Passport and visas agreements, Ceylon, 1949-1950.

Volume 907.

File 569-36-570.
Passport and visa agreements, Canada-Iran, 1959-1961.

File 569-36-578.
Passport and visas agreements, Canada-Japan, 1954-1965.

File 569-36-632.
Passport and visa agreements, Canada-Turkey, 1949-1963.

Volume 914.

File 581-3-2, part 1.
Japanese agricultural students, general file, 1955-1959.

File 581-3-2, part 2.
Japanese agricultural students, general file, 1960.

Volume 917.

File 584-2-641.
Entry of nationals of Vietnam for medical treatment, 1965-1966.

Volume 920.

File 585-12-578.
Repatriation of Japanese from Canada, 1945-1966.

C. Central Registry Files. Third Central Registry series(5000 block), 1948-1979.
The Third Central Registry series of immigration records contains the core policy and subject files of Immigration headquarters in Ottawa between 1966 and 1977. This was replaced by a fourth series, 8000 block about 1977.

1. Central Registry Files, 5000 block(unclassified files), 1967-1973, 67.5 metres

VI. Chinese immigration records, 1885-1953, .9 metres(volumes 693-703, 712, 713), 5 microfilm reels, C-9510 to C-9513, C-13421.

The Department of Customs was made responsible for the administration of the Chinese Immigration Act of 1885, and a general register was to be maintained for Chinese immigrants who entered Canada. In 1893, the Department of Trade and Commerce was established, and customs officers, as controllers of Chinese immigration were to report to the Deputy Minister of Trade and Commerce. In 1911, the administration of the Act was transferred to the Immigration branch of the Department of the Interior, and the Immigration branch was responsible for the administration of the Act until 1947

A CI.6 certificate was issued to all Chinese who had entered Canada before 1885, and a CI.5 certification to Chinese immigrants who arrived after 1885, and paid the head tax. CI.9 and CI.9A certificates were issued to persons wishing to leave Canada temporarily.

A. General registers of Chinese immigration, 1885-1903, .9 metres(volumes 694-703), 4 microfilm reels, C-9510 to C-9513.
Gives information on Chinese immigrants, some as early as 1860, including village and province of birth in China. General registers numbers 11-to 18, 1903-1949, are found in Record Group 76, accession 84-85/062, with a microfilm version in 84-85/238.

B. New Westminster Agency, register of Chinese immigration, 1887-1808, 1907 and 1908, .075 metres(Volume 693), one microfilm reel(C-9510).

In 1885, the Collectors of Customs at Victoria, Nanaimo, New Westminster, and the sub-Collectors of Customs at Osoyoos and Kootenay and all collectors and acting collectors of customs, as controllers of Chinese immigration, having to register Chinese immigrants, collect head tax, and issue C.I. certificates of identification.

1. Register of Chinese immigrants, Port of New Westminster, 1887--1898, 1907 and 1908, .075 metres(volume 693), one microfilm reel, C-9510.

List of Chinese immigrants who registered and paid the head tax at New Westminster, British Columbia.

C. Central district, registers and certificates of Chinese immigration, 1899-1953, .05 metres,(volumes 712,713), one microfilm reel, C-13421.

Immigration activities for Toronto were controlled by Central District Headquarters. Chinese moving in or out of Canada were required to register their movement with the controllers of Chinese immigration at Toronto.

1. Register of Chinese immigration (Toronto), 1923-1953(Volume 713), one microfilm reel, C-13421.

Chinese register number 2, created in the Office of Immigration's central district(Toronto), and used to control Chinese immigration to and temporary emigration from Canada, particularly outward CI.9 registrations. Register number 1 for registrations before 1923 has apparently not survived.

2. Sample C.I. certificates, C.I.5, CI.28, C.I.30, and C.I.36, 1899-1953(Volume 712), one microfilm reel, C-13421.

The certificate system was used to control the movement of Chinese in and out of Canada, and of seamen sailing out of the Great Lakes system These certificates seem to have never been used.

University Library,
University of Alberta,
Edmonton, Alberta, T6G 2J4
Tel:(403)432-3790.

Theses and dissertations

Ahmed, Mohammed.
Some aspects of urban mapping, Edmonton and Hyderabad. M.Sc. thesis 1976.

Ali, Mehrunnisa.
Federalism in Pakistan, a study of the division of power. M.A. thesis 1970.

Anantrasirichai, Arunsri.
The bureaucratic characteristics of supervisory units at the provincial level in Thailand. Ph.D. dissertation 1988.
NL

Andrews, Mathew Puthupparampil.
Population dynamics of a minority community, Christians of Kerala, India. Ph.D. dissertation 1980.

Baksh, Ishmael Jymshed.
Some factors related to educational expectation among East Indian and Negro students attending public secondary schools in Trinidad. Ph.D. dissertation 1974.

Banta, Gordon Roy.
Asian cropping systems research, microeconomic evaluation procedures. Ph.D. dissertation 1980.

Cassel, Donald F.
Vocational education in Japan a survey from 1868 to 1980. M.Ed. thesis 1984.
NL

Cham, Boon Ngee.
Towards a Malaysian Malaysia, a study of political integration. Ph.D. dissertation 1971.

Chan, Ho Man.
The revival of the Manchu monarchy in early Republican China with special reference to the restoration movement of Chang Hsun. M.A. thesis 1988.
NL

Cheng, Pui-wan.
Visual recognition of Chinese characters by adult Chinese readers. M.Ed. thesis 1986.
NL

Cheng, Wing-chung.
The development of primary teacher education in an urban Chinese community. Ph.D. dissertation 1986.
NL

Cheng, Yeewah.
Schooling and colonialism, a Hong Kong experience. M.Ed. thesis 1985.
NL

Cheng-Jardine, Candy.
Factors associated with the educational participation of Chinese immigrant women. M.Ed. thesis 1988.
NL

Cheung, Sik Lee.
Anaphora production in Cantonese narration. M.Sc. thesis 1986.
NL

Cho, Sook Whan.
Issues in the structure and acquisition of Korean anaphora. Ph.D. dissertation 1985.
NL

Choi, Soo-hyang.
School class differences in mother's speech in Korea. M.Ed. thesis 1985.
NL

Chowdhury, Kowsar P.
Educational development Bangladesh with special emphasis on universalization of primary education. M.Ed thesis 1983.
NL

Chuang, Chen-kuan.
The nature of American diplomacy and commerce on the China coast, 1784-1900. M.A. thesis 1965.

Clark, Harvey.
Chinese grain trade. M.Sc. thesis 1982.
NL

Congear, Damkerng.
The management of industrial arts equipment maintenance program for the comprehensive schools in Thailand. M.Ed. thesis 1974.

Connell, Bruce A.
The interaction of tone and intonation in Mandarin Chinese. M.Sc. thesis 1982.
NL

Cook, David Lawrence.
Subnational interests and the formulation of Chinese foreign policy decisions. Ph.D. dissertation 1980.
NL

Cook, Eung-do.
Embedding transformations in Korean syntax. Ph.D. dissertation 1969.

Cullen, M.D.
The evolution of petroleum concession in Iran and Alberta. LL.M. thesis 1981.
NL

Dhami, Sadu Singh.
Philosophy of John Dewey in the light of Oriental philosophy. M.A. thesis 1934.

Dhir, Rakesh Kumar.
Education and Japanese economic growth, a sociological analysis. M.A. thesis 1983.
NL

Dua, Bhagwan Dass.
Presidential rule in India, 1950-1974, a study of crisis politics. Ph.D. dissertation 1977.

Duvurry, Nata.
Economic analysis of the role of primary credit cooperatives in agricultural development, a case study in Andhra Pradesh, India. M.A. thesis 1976.

Furuyama, Eiji.
An analysis of critical growth factors in the Japanese economy, 1952-1961. M.A. thesis 1964.

Garstin, Marguerite Kathleen.
Revolutionary perspectives on African literature: Mao Tse-tung's **Yenan Talks** and the Writings of Ngugi wa thiong'o and Sembene Ousmane. M.A. thesis 1979.

Ghorayshi, Fatemeh Parvin.
Recent land reform in Iran and Cuba, comparison of a capitalist and a socialist case. M.A. thesis 1976.

Gietz, Ron E.
The potential for Sino-Canadian joint ventures in beef production. M.Sc. thesis 1988.
NL

Given, Brian J.
A study of Tibetan Tantric psycho-religious technology. Ph.D. dissertation 1986.
NL

Hague, Mary Jo Michelle.
Cultural diplomacy, Canada-China a case study: the exhibition of archeological finds of the People's Republic of China held at the Royal Ontario Museum from 8 August-November 16, 1974. M.A. thesis 1987.
NL

Hisatomi, Setsuko.
Social context and reading second/foreign languages, Canada, Japan. M.Ed. thesis 1985.
NL

Hong, Ki hyung.
Prevention of dropout in the air and correspondence high school in Korea. Ph.D. dissertation 1982.

Huq, Mohammad Obaidul.
Public policy in Pakistan, a content analysis. Ph.D. dissertation 1970.

Hur, Sook.
Understanding the meaning of teacher competence, an interpretive study of a teacher education curriculum in Korea. Ph.D. dissertation 1986.
NL

Indrapana, Nat.
Sport and physical education in Thailand, 1932-1965. Ph.D. dissertation 1973.

Islam, S.M.Shafiqul.
A stochastic model of human fertility in Bangladesh. Ph.D. dissertation 1986.
NL

Ji, Changho.
The Juche Idea and economic stagnation in totalitarian North Korea. M.A. thesis 1988.
NL

Juma, Sadrudin.
The social structure, educational disparities and elite schooling in Pakistan. M.Ed. thesis 1987.
NL

Kao, Yu-hsin
Effects of Public Law 480, surpluses, on economic development with special reference to Taiwan. M.A. thesis 1964.

Kawashima, Michiko.
The development of Japanese connectives of sequence and simultaneity. Ph.D. dissertation 1987.
NL

Keawkungwak, Sriruen.
Therapeutic approaches in Theravada Buddhism and existentialism, a comparison. M.Ed. thesis 1971.

Khatun, Hafiza.
Inter-urban residential migration of East Indian people in Edmonton. M.A. thesis 1984.
NL

Kowalski, Kenneth Reginald.
The West China Mission of the Methodist Church of Canada, Szechuan, China, 1891-1911. M.A. thesis 1970.

Kubicek, Robert.
Henry L.Stimson's policy during the first phase of the Manchurian crisis. M.A. thesis 1958.

Kuneliu, Joyce.
A phonological program for Chinese speakers of English. M.Ed. thesis 1971.

Kupfer, Geneva Eileen.
Education and national development, the case of Papua, New Guinea. M.A. thesis 1973.

Lack, Ervin Roy Walter.
Export marketing in the Japanese environment. M.B.A. thesis 1976.

Langub, Jayl.
Rural development in Ba Kelalan, Sarawak, Malaysia interaction between government and community. M.A. thesis 1983.
NL

Lau, Becky Po-Lin.
Word recognition, memory span in Chinese-English bilingual readers. M.Ed. thesis 1988.
NL

Lau, Lawrence Pok Ming.
The significance and extent of Taoist influence on the government of the early man. Ph.D. dissertation 1981.

Lau, Laurence P.C.
The concept of Tao in Lao Tzu and Chuang Tze, ca. 600-200 B.C. M.A. thesis 1972.

Lee, Jena Chi-yung.
Chinese-English bilingual education parental attitudes and bilingual schooling. M.A. thesis 1984.
NL

Lin, Jenn Shann Jack.
Chinese-English bilingual children's acquisition of language, a case study of an advantaged group. Ph.D. dissertation 1979.

Liu, Jiang.
Women's education in the People's Republic of China. M.Ed. thesis 1987.
NL

Ma, Stephen Kwokchuan.
Current reforms in China's public administration, the rise of the bureaucracy and decentralization. M.A. thesis 1985.
NL

McBlane, Rorri.
Developments in Papua, New Guinea and their effects on language policy. M.Ed. thesis 1985.
NL

Macdonald, Elizabeth.
Japanese Canadians in Edmonton, 1969, an exploratory search for patterns of assimilation. M.A. thesis 1970.

McNally, George Frederick.
Odlum, Canada's first ambassador to China. M.A thesis 1977.

Macrury, Katherine Anne.
The occupational adjustment of Vietnamese refugees in Edmonton, Canada. M.Ed thesis 1979.

Mah, Cheng Lian.
Investment incentives in Sri Lanka: legal aspects. LL.M. thesis 1971.

Mah, Hilda.
A history of the education of Chinese Canadians in Alberta, 1885-1947. M.Ed thesis 1987.
NL

Mahadoo, Balwanth.
Romain Rolland, India and Vedanta. Ph.D. dissertation 1982.

Mahamwal, Naveen Kumar.
Regulation of foreign investment in India. LL.M. thesis 1987.
NL

Manouchehri, Shahram.
Inflation in less developed countries, the case of Iran, 1959-1977. Ph.D. dissertation 1982.

Martin, Vincent Joseph.
The development of education in Papua New Guinea and the impact of external aid, 1975-1985. Ph.D. dissertation 1988.
NL

Miles, Michael Sheridan.
Community development in Thailand, a meeting of paradigms. M.A. thesis 1980.

Mishra, Jai Prakash.
Economic analysis of energy use in the modernization of Indian agriculture. Ph.D. dissertation 1977.

Morris, Kimball John.
The socio-economic impact of merchant capital on the mode of production of the Semaq Beri in Peninsular Malaysia. M.A. thesis 1985.
NL

Moten, Abdul Rashid.
Political elites and political instability in Pakistan. Ph.D. dissertation 1977.

Mu, Hai.
A study of the characteristics of Chinese ESL learners in MBA programs at Canadian universities. Ph.D. dissertation 1987.
NL

Mung, Kwok-choi.
Soong Ching-ling, a political profile. M.A. thesis 1973.

Nakagomi, Yasuyo.
A contrastive study of Japanese and English syntax, selected topics from phrase structure and transformation. M.A. thesis 1967.

Nakamura, Mari Louise.
Structure-trade links in Japanese cereal agriculture. M.Sc. thesis 1988.
NL

Oh, Mahn Seug.
The meaning of morality and moral education, an interpretive study of the moral education curriculum of Korea. Ph.D. dissertation 1986.
NL

Padmanabhan, Pallipuram Seshadri.
The influence of Vedanta and Buddhism on the poetry and drama of T.S Elliot. Ph.D. dissertation 1979.

Palakkamannil, Thomas Mathai.
Community development and primary health care in developing countries with particular reference to India. M.A. thesis 1985.
NL

Palmer, Howard.
Responses to foreign immigrants in: nativism and ethnic tolerance in Alberta, 1880-1920. M.A. thesis 1971.
Chinese in Alberta.

Pannu, Rajinder Singh.
A sociological survey of teachers from India teaching in Alberta, 1958-1965. M.Ed. thesis 1966.

Patnaik, Bishnupriya.
Rabindranath Tagore, educator and social reformer. M.Ed thesis 1977.

Pendleton, Brian Blair.
The People's Republic of China and the Olympic movement, a question of recognition. Ph.D. dissertation 1978.

Pettigrew, Judith.
A cognitive analysis of the beliefs and practices surrounding childbirth, Edmonton Chinese community. M.A. thesis 1988.
NL

Phua, Swee liang.
Ability factors and familial psycho-social circumstances, Chinese and Malays of Singapore. Ph.D. dissertation 1976.

Piya-ajariya, Laeka.
The introduction of an individualized reading program in the Thai curriculum for primary grades. M.Ed. thesis 1972.

Plouffe, Gregory L.
The United States, Britain and civil-military relations in Thailand, 1932-1948. M.A. thesis 1983.
NL

Pornsima, Aurapan.
Students' perception of distance learning programs at Stou in Thailand. Ph.D. dissertation 1984.
NL

Pornsima, Direk.
The legal status of teachers in Thailand. Ph.D. dissertation 1984.
NL

Prachongchit, Sanan.
A study of the need for faculty development as perceived by faculty and administrators of a selected university in Thailand. Ph.D. dissertation 1984.
NL

Prasad, Gaya.
A comparison of secondary school social studies programmes of Fiji, Western Samoa and Tonga. M.Ed. thesis 1967.

Pun, Samuel Yin Lun.
A Chinese character software system. M.Sc. thesis 1986.
NL

Qureshi, Regula Burckhardt.
Qawwali, sound, context and meaning in Indo-Muslim Sufi music. Ph.D. dissertation 1981.

Ramaiah, Al.
A study of the perceived need for instructional development at the University of Malaya. Ph.D. dissertation 1984.
NL

Ren, Hai.
A comparative analysis of ancient Greek and Chinese sport. Ph.D. dissertation 1989.
NL

Root, Deborah.
Un lac de sang, French images of the Orient, 1800-1900. M.A. thesis 1983.
NL

Rothrock, Willy.
The development of Dutch-Indonesian primary schooling, a study in colonial education. M.Ed. thesis 1975.

Sabater, Jose Enriquez.
Comparative analysis of the tax treatment of business income in France, the United States, Canada and the Philippines. LL.M. thesis 1971.

Sadighian, Masoud.
A comparative analysis of university goals and governance in North America and Iran. Ph.D. dissertation 1975.

Salopek, Marijan.
A survey of Western Canadian concerns and fears during the Korean War, 1950-1954. M.A. thesis 1984.
NL

Seif, Bishara Theneyan.
Mother tongue usage and attitudes towards preservation within Korean families in Canada. M.Ed. thesis 1984.
NL

Shobany-ghaznivi, Mansoureh.
Iran's foreign trade, an analysis of recent trends and patterns. M.A. thesis 1974.

Shrestha, Binod K.
Perception and behaviour of Nepalese hill farmers towards forest resource use and conservation. M.Sc. thesis 1984.
NL

Singh, Mahendra Prasad.
Schism in a predominant party, the Indian National Congress in 1969. Ph.D. dissertation 1975.

Sirichoti, Chirapan.
Grade XII external examinations in relation to university achievement in Thailand. M.Ed. thesis 1971.

Sirisri, Alisara.
A critical analysis of the junior high school science curriculum in Thailand. Ph.D. dissertation 1986.
NL

Sodhi, Satpa Kaur.
Gandhi's philosophy, in theory and in practice. M.A. thesis 1969.

Srisuthep, Ashara.
English proficiency text and achievement of Thai students. M.Ed. thesis 1972.

Stott, David Charles.
Improvement and reform, a comparative study of the village level change agent in China and India. M.A. thesis 1975.

Stubbs, Richard.
Political leadership, colonial government and the Malayan emergency. Ph.D. dissertation 1975.

Sung, Il Je.
A critical understanding of technology and educational development, a case study of the Korean Education Development Institute. Ph.D. dissertation 1986.
NL

Suwanamalik, Piengchai.
A contrastive study, predicting interference for Thai students in learning English statement sentences. M.Ed. thesis 1967.

Tan, Binky.
Chinese humanism and western sociology. Ph.D. dissertation 1978.

Taza, Ameria Rizuia.
International ideology and interpersonal ideology, the case of Pakistan students. M.A. thesis 1970.

Teal, Greg Leroy.
Urban anthropology and the problems of the formation of social classes with reference to Korean immigrants in Edmonton. M.A. thesis 1979.

Thoburn, John Thomas.
Exports in the economic development of West Malaysia. Ph.D. dissertation 1972.

Thomas, M.M.
Harijan education in India. M.Ed. thesis 1987.
NL

Thompson, Leyland Fitzgerald.
An evaluation of the industrial arts program in the government secondary schools in Guyana. M.Ed. thesis 1978.

Tjatera, I.Wayan.
The impact of high yielding varieties on small-holder rice farming in East Indonesia. M.Sc. thesis 1989.
NL

Tse, John Wing Ling.
The relationship between decoding speed and comprehension skill among skilled and less skilled Chinese primary school readers. M.Ed. thesis 1987.
NL

Tulaha-Martin, Noami.
Community participation in community schools in a study of the North Solomons Province. Ph.D. dissertation 1988.
NL

Upathomp, Vitoon.
The achievement of all Thai industrial arts students in the Thai comprehensive school project. M.Ed. thesis 1973.

Venkateswarlu, Tadebeyina.
Agriculture in Indian economic planning. M.Sc. thesis 1967.

Villaiprom, Kamil.
An evaluation of the industrial arts program in the thirteen comprehensive schools in Thailand. M.Ed. thesis 1971

Wajansoontorn, Dilok.
A study of teachers' attitudes towards working conditions in selected comprehensive secondary schools in Thailand. M.Ed. thesis 1971.

Wiber, Melanie.
Communal, corporate and cooperative, the property relations of the Ibaloi of Northern Luzon, Philippines. Ph.D. dissertation 1986.
NL

Wong, Edy L.
An empirical study of the interplay between the Asian currency market and the ASEAN economies. Ph.D. dissertation 1984.
NL

Wong, Irene Foong-Heng.
Object complements in Malay. Ph.D. dissertation 1970.

Wong, Kayau.
Political ideals, economic demands, and educational reforms of China, 1949 to 1976. M.Ed. thesis 1987.
NL

Wu, Zhou.
Linguistic shaping of thought revisited, do English and Chinese speakers really think differently. M.Ed. thesis 1988.
NL

Yee, Suey.
Adjustment concerns of Hong Kong visa students. M.Ed. thesis 1980.
NL

Zhang, Lihua.
Subjekt im Deutschen und Chinesischen. M.A. thesis 1987.
NL

**University Archives and Collections,
The Rutherford Library,
University of Alberta,
Edmonton, Alberta, T6G 2J4
Tel:(403)432-5146/5834**

Ronning, Chester.
When the National Film Board produced **China Mission,** the story of Chester Ronning's family, 39 interviews were recorded and deposited in the University Archives. They describe the experiences of Norwegian/Lutheran missionaries in China before the Boxer Rebellion. There were no verbatim transcripts of the interviews, but there is a summary of the contents prepared by the National Film Board. Five tapes record Dr. Ronning's description of his return to China in 1975, to revisit the site of the mission.

Lethbridge

**Records and Archives Management,
City of Lethbridge,
910 4th Avenue,South,
Lethbridge, Alberta, TIJ OP6.
Tel:(403)320-3898**

Bailey, Mary E.
Term paper.
Chinese Language Schools in Lethbridge. Paper contains a brief history of Chinese immigration to Southern Alberta, the two main Chinese organizations in Lethbridge and the two Chinese Language schools.

Chinese-English Address/Notebook.
Contains a list of names written in English and Chinese. Book belonged to a Chinese who came to Canada in 1909.

Film in two parts.1. People voting, 2. Japanese dancers at Japanese gardens.

Part 1 is in colour and shows people voting. Part 2 is black and white and shows Japanese dancers at Nikka Yuko Japanese Garden.

Japanese Canadian Centennial Society.
Guest Book.
Japanese Canadian Centennial Society contains signatures of senior citizens guests.

List of Names for Japanese Centennial.
9 pages. 1977.
List of 232 names and addresses. Some names have check marks by them. Names of senior citizens invited to take part in Japanese Canadian Centennial Concert.

Takeyasu, George.
Papers. 13 pieces(2 copies for all except No.1 which has three.)
1.)National Selective Service notice of separation for George Takeyasu.
2. Letter to Japanese Department of Labour requesting a job in Toronto, from George Takeyasu.
3. Letter from Radio College of Canada in Edmonton, giving information on classes and fees.
4. Telegram to George Takeyasu regarding night class and accommodation.
5. Temporary travel permit for George Takeyasu from Picture Butte to Toronto and return by Canadian Pacific Railway.
6. Letter to George Takeyasu from Radio College expressing their regret that he is unable to make it by 15th March, but that another class in June is open.

Takeyasu, George.
Evacuation, 1942.
Manuscript telling story of one family's forced evacuation from British Columbia to Alberta.

Photograph Collection.

Over 80 photographs of Japanese ranging in date from 1896 to 1974, and 11 photographs of Chinese ranging in date from 1903 to 1973.

BRITISH COLUMBIA

Burnaby

National Archives of Canada,
Vancouver Federal Records Centre,
2751 Production Way,
Burnaby, British Columbia, V5A 3G7
Tel: (604)666-8243

Accession V84-85/261.

1.2 metres.
Immigration case files from the Vancouver Immigration Centre; relating to landings, verification of entry, deportations, private visitors, and applications for permanent residence.

Accession V84-85/266.

Immigration branch, Victoria office, lookout and Hindu and Chinese case files, ca. 1920-1970, 8.4 metres, boxes 1-18.
These regional files break down into three areas. The first and fifth boxes of "H" files are case files relating to Hindu immigration from the 1920s to 1960s, including sponsorships, case histories, etc. "Look out files" for undesirables who may have attempted to enter the country, with a brief description of aliases, criminal activity, etc., for the use of immigration agents at points of entry, fill the next three boxes. Boxes 6-18 contain "CH" files which are case files for Chinese immigrants.
Finding aid.

Accession V84-85/319.

28.2 metres.
Immigration case files from the Vancouver office containing sponsorship records, letters of application, departmental investigations, entry permits, deportations, correspondence with American police and other authorities and interviews, 1950-1980.

Accession V85-86/362.

Pacific Regional Office, Planning and Analysis Coordinator, Ugandan expellees program, 1972-1977, 3.3 metres, boxes 1-11.
These records were created by or accumulated in the office of the Planning and Analysis Coordinator, Pacific Region Headquarters, to document the British Columbian phase of the Uganda expellee program(UGX or project 32). This program was announced in September 1972 to deal with the immigration to Canada, mainly of East Indian extraction, expelled from Uganda in that year. Special adjustment assistance was offered to those expellees wishing to come to Canada, including recoverable loans and non-recoverable grants for passage money, accommodation, clothing, other necessities, and medical expenses; these moneys were paid mostly in the period 1973-1974. The project was implemented in the British Columbia Centre's immigration reception center on Howe Street. In 1974, the Federal Auditor General questioned expenditures by the Pacific region UGX program which he deemed to be overpayments; much of the material in this collection relates to investigations arising from his report.
Boxes 1 to 7 contain case files documenting payment of moneys and services rendered to individuals for passage, incidentals, accommodation and medical bills. They contain copies of IMM.1000 forms for each person, documentation on family relationships, bills and invoices, accounting tabulations, and in some cases extended correspondence on repayment of loans. All these files bear the number 5129 and are organized alphabetically by name of immigrant. Box 7 also contains skeleton files on persons who did not seek or receive assistance, and lists of names apparently relating to medical examinations.
General descriptive, administrative and financial records on implementation of the program are found loose in box 7. Boxes 8 and 9 contain hotel and department store bills, the working papers on the 1974-1975 overpayment investigation, including rough notes and edited sheets on each individual immigrant, account ledgers, correspondence, public accounts committee submissions, and indexed books of correspondence on attempts to recover overpayments from individual immigrants are in boxes 9 to 11.
Finding aid.

Accession V85-86/418.

Pacific Regional Office - Registry files(5000 and 8000 block), 1965-1976. .9 metres, boxes 1-3.
These records consist of Immigration Registry subject files dated from 1965 to 1976 at Pacific Regional Headquarters of Employment and Immigration Canada at Vancouver. Topics covered include narrative and statistical reports of immigration activities, inquiries from the public, appointment of formal inquiry officers, federal provincial agreements on medical services to immigrants, changes to the Immigration Appeal Board act, allocation of work permits to individual employers and immigrants in British Columbia, miscellaneous

procedural files, records on immigration cases appealed to the Federal Court of Canada, and immigration of Chilean refugees and East Indian expellees from Uganda. Finding aid is a file list.

Accession V85-86/472

Canada Immigration Centre, Vancouver Metro-immigration case files(p/pd series) and Asian immigration case files, ca. 1960-ca. 1971, 5.7 metres, boxes 1-19.
Two groups of immigration case files created or accumulated in the Vancouver Metro Canada Immigration Centre. The first group consists of one or two files each in three special case file series relating to immigrants of "Hindu" origin(H series), Malaysians/Indonesians(M series) and Thais(T series)(Box 1).
Finding aid.

Accession V85-86/475.

Pacific Regional Office, Chinese case files, ca. 1900-ca. 1980, 5.1 metres, boxes 1-17.
These records are Chinese case files accumulated(and generally speaking also created) in the Vancouver Regional Office of the Immigration Branch.
In content and format they resemble Chinese case files of other Record Group 76 accessions originally held at Immigration headquarters in Ottawa, except that the subjects of the case files are largely residents of British Columbia. Many of the files were used in status adjustment claims procedures.
Finding aid is a file list.

Accession V85-86/476.

Canada Immigration Centre, Vancouver Metro-immigration case files(5153 and P/PD series, "F" sample) and Chinese immigration case files, ca. 1900-ca.1980, 10.5 metres, boxes 1-35.
These records consist of regular immigration case files created or accumulated in the Vancouver Metro Canada Immigration Centre, and containing documents dated from about 1900 to about 1980.
Includes Chinese case files(ca. 1900 - ca. 1980) are numbered in the CH(including PCH and PDCH) series. They are similar in content and format to those in the Accession V85-86/475(boxes 5-35).
Finding aid is a file list by file number only.

Accession V85-86/478.

Immigrant Reception Centre, Vancouver, client case files, 1976-1978, .9 metres, boxes 1-3.
The Vancouver Immigrant Reception Centre is an office responsible for the reception, counselling and assistance of recent immigrants requiring special services: these are notably, but not exclusively refugees, previously stateless persons, and persons arriving under assisted passage arrangements. These records are case files for clients assisted in 1976, 1977 and 1978, arranged alphabetically by client name within each year. Many of the persons assisted were refugees from such areas as Cambodia, Vietnam.
Finding aid is a Federal Records Centre list.

Accession V86-88/218.

Canada Immigration Centre, Vancouver Metro Chinese case files, XY series, 1952-1980, 11.4 metres, boxes 1-38.
These records are Chinese case files accumulated and, in the vast majority of cases, created in the Vancouver Regional Office of the Immigration Branch. While a very few documents on the earlier files date back to the 1950's and 1960's, the great bulk of the material is from the 1969-1980 period. While the files have been renumbered in the XY series on the list provided, the file jackets bear the prefixes PCH or 5133-CH. The individuals concerned are or were residents of British Columbia.
Finding aid is a Federal Records Center list.

Accession V86-87/226.

Canada Immigration Centre, Vancouver Metro Chinese language case files and subject files, 1913-1972, 6.9 metres, boxes 1-23.
This accession consists for the most part of individual Chinese language immigration case files created in the Vancouver Metro Immigration Centre. The files are numbered in the CH, CH-1 and P-CH ranges. The bulk of the material is dated in the decade of the 1960s, but a significant quantity, particularly in the earlier files, was created well before World War II. While the vast majority of these files are for individual immigrants, normally to British Columbia, a few files in the early boxes cover such non-individual subjects as native-born Chinese language.
Finding aid is a Federal Records Centre list.

Accession V86-87/240.

Canada Immigration Centre, Victoria, immigration case files("Hindu" and sponsorship series), 1969-1980, 6.6 metres, boxes 1-21.
This accession contains two distinct types of case files from the Victoria Immigration office, dealing with immigration activities on Vancouver Island. The first, in boxes 497416-497426(11 boxes) consists of immigrant case files similar to others previously accessioned and numbered in the "H" series(Hindu).
The second series, numbered consecutively, are sponsorship files containing all papers and correspondence for the sponsorship of visitors and immigrants. The file titles are the name of the sponsor rather than the visitor/immigrant. Most sponsors are relatives, but others can be educational, religious, charitable or commercial organizations.
Finding aid is a Federal Records Centre list.

Accession V86-87/244.

Canada Immigration Centre, Vancouver Metro, immigration case files, regular and "Hindu" series, 1965-1980, 7.2 metres, boxes 124.-36
The accession consists of two groups of immigration

case files, created or accumulated in the Vancouver Metro Canada Immigration Centre. The first boxes contain case files relating to immigrants of "Hindu" origin(H or PH series). The second consists of regular case files in the series P(or 5133) covering subnumbers 2 through 8, arranged numerically.
Finding aid is a Federal Records Centre list.

Accession V-1987-88/278.

Immigration. Canada Immigration Centre. Vancouver Metro. Vancouver, B.C., Adjudication Department, Case Files1980-1985, I.50 metres, Boxes 1-5.
These records are photocopies of decisions of the Immigration Appeal Board (IAB and Federal Court of Canada (FCC) regarding appeals by immigrants against deportation orders originating in the Vancouver Metro Canada Immigration Centre. These appear to be a reference series of files, not being in official departmental file jackets. The files are not cumulative: appeals to the FCC and do not contain in the file earlier appeals to the IAB or departmental records. The IAB files are photocopies of the Adjudication hearing (which is a summary of proceedings, not verbatim) relevant documents, passport, birth certificate), deportation notice, IAB hearing (verbatim transcript), and decision.
The FCC files contain a notice of appeal, miscellaneous covering correspondence, the FCC verbatim transcript, and decision. The files are chronologically arranged, there is no separation in large logical blocks by box of the IAB versus the FCC files.
There is no finding aid for this material.

Accession V-1987-88/311.

Immigration. Canada Immigration Centre, Lower Mainland and Vancouver Island, Chinese Case Files. 1900-1980, 45.00 metres, Boxes l-150
These records are Chinese Case Files containing applications for admission and supporting documentation. For a fuller description see accession V-1985-86/475.
Finding aid is an Federal Records Centre list.

Accession V- 1987-88/312.

Immigration. Canada.Immigration Centre, Vancouver Metro, Chinese Case Files.1980-1981.21.30 metres. Boxes 1-71.
This accession consists of immigration case files. For a fuller description see Accession V-1986-87/218.
Finding aid is an Federal Reecords Centre list .

Accession V-1987-88/321.

Immigration, Canada Immigration Centre, Vancouver Metro, Chinese Case Files.1980-1982. 7.50 metres. Boxes 1-25.
This accession consists of immigration case files. For a fuller description see Accession V-1986-87/218.
There is no finding aid for this material.

Accession V-1987-88/322.

Immigration, Canada Immigration Centre, Vancouver Metro, Chinese Case Files.1980-1982. 21.30 metres. Boxes 1-71.
This accession consists of Chinese immigration case files. For more information see Accession V-1986—87/218.
The finding aid is an Federal Records Centre list .

Accession V-1987-88/323.

Immigration, Canada Immigration Centre, Vancouver, Chinese Case Files.1980-1982. 8.40 metres. Boxes 1-28.
This accession consists of Chinese immigration case files. For more information see. accession V-1986 87/218.
The finding aid is an Federal Records Centre list .

Accession V-1987-88/324.

Immigration, Canada Immigration Centre, Vancouver Metro, Chinese Case Files.1940-1980. 12.90 metres. Boxes 1-43.
This accession consists of Chinese immigration case files. For more information see Accession V-1986-87/218.
The finding aid is a Federal Records Centre list .

Accession V-1987-88/329.

Immigration, Canada Immigration Centre, Vancouver, Case Files. 1967-1968, 44.10 metres. Boxes 1-147.
This 147-box accession of case files from the Canada Immigration Centre, Vancouver Office, contains files documenting individuals wishing to immigrate to Canada.
Most of the files are regular case files in the 5133-file and "P" file blocks but there are also "Hindu" files (H or PH prefix) There are a few "J-files" relating to Japanese individuals and for employers in box 1; the files are organized by name of employer making applications for immigrant employees (e.g. form IMM-1102, "Employment Authorization" or "Canada Admission Record and Employment Visa"; IMM-1097, "Visitor Record" or "Canada Entry Records"; and IMM-1249", "Application to Vary or Cancel Terms of Admission"). For similar files see accession V-1987-88/334. All of the case files in this accession appear to contain more than routine documentation such as original correspondence; a few have "urgent" stickers on them.
There is no finding aid for this material.

Accession V-1987-88/334.

Immigration, Canada Immigration Centre, Vancouver, Metro Immigration Case files, 1950-1970, 37.50 metres, Boxes 1-125
These records consist of immigration case files created or accumulated in the Vancouver Metro Canada Immigration Centre. They include regular case files with file number prefixes 5133-11 or 5133-12 (see

Accession V-1985-86/474 for similar records) "Hindu" case files with file prefixes H and PH (see similar records in accession V-1985-87/240); and Japanese "J" files similar to those described in Accession V-l987-88/329.
The finding aid is a Federal Records Centre list

Accession V-1992-93/129.

Immigration immigrant Reception Centre. Vancouver G.C., Client Case files. 1982-1983. 3.30 metres, Boxes 1-11.
The Vancouver Immigration section and Office responsible for the reception counseling. and assistance of recent immigrants who require special services These immigrants are notably but not exclusively refugees, previously stateless persons. and those arriving under assisted passage arrangements. This accession consists of individual case files related to several classes of clients assisted by this office in l982 and l983. These clients include Small Boat Refugees (Vietnamese), Polish Ship Jumpers, and EXP Refugees. The files all contain applications, basic data records, contribution arrangements and correspondence related to adjustment assistance programs. An example of these would be the summary ledger card which provides details of each payment, cheque number, amount, cumulative total of assistance, and the purpose of the claim (food shelter, clothing, etc.). In addition to the above documentation the records related to the Polish Ship Jumpers (boxes 3-4) contain copies of Minister's Permits granted to the sailors. All of the above files are grouped by subject and arranged alphabetically by surname therein.
There are no finding aids for this material.

Accession V-1993-94/070.

Immigration, Canada Immigration Centre, Vancouver, Chinese Case Files, XY Series. 1952-l982, 4.50 metres Boxes 1-16.
The Records in this accession consist of Chinese Immigration case files accumulated and, in the majority of cases, created in the Vancouver Regional Office of the Immigration Branch. Although the inclusive dates of these files are 1952-1982, the predominant dates of the records are 1975-1982. While the majority of the files have been classified or reclassified into the XY series, many of the file jackets still bear the prefixes PCH or 5133-CH.
There are no finding aids for this material.

Accession V-1993-94/417.

Immigration, Canada Immigration Centre, Victoria, British Columbia, Immigration Canada. Files 1977-1985, 4.80 metres, Boxes 1-16.
This accession is comprised of a variety of immigration case files created and used by the Canada Immigration Centre in Victoria They include "H" series (Hindu), "XY" and "CH" Series (Chinese), as well as case files from the general immigration series The individual files include such documents as the Immigration Assessment Record (IMM 1104, the Immigration Visa and Record of Landing (IMM 1000), related correspondence, memos, documents submitted by the applicant .
medical reports, telexes, and various support There are no finding aids for this material
HRB Accession Number 121-000417-8
V-1993-94/417

Accession V-1993-94/475.

Immigration, British Columbia Region, Immigration Case Files 1923-1979, 3.00 metres, Boxes 1-10.
This accession consists of a variety of immigration case files created, accumulated, and used by immigration officials within the British Columbia Region The records, which appear to have been selected from a larger accession, consist of "F" sample case files, CH/XY case files, as well as several files related to unusual and/or precedent setting cases. All files in this accession are drawn from the 5133 file block.
There are no finding aids for this material.

Accession V-1993-94/476.

Immigration, British Columbia Region, Immigration Case Files l925-1981, 1.50 metres, Boxes 1-5
This accession consists of a variety of immigration case files created, accumulated, and used by Immigration officials within the British Columbia region. The records, which appear to have been selected from a larger accession, consist of pre-1967 immigration case files, case files from the "CH" Series as well as "F" sample case files.
There are no finding aids for this material.

W.A.C. Bennett Library,
Simon Fraser University,
Burnaby, British Columbia, V5A 1S6.
Tel:(604)291-5946

Theses and dissertations

Amritavalli, Raghavachari.
Negation in Kannada. M.A. thesis 1978.
CT

Aronsen, Lawrence Robert.
Postwar perceptions of the China market, a study of American business attitudes, 1943-1949. M.A. thesis 1974.
CT

Buchigani, N.L.
Immigration, adaptation, and the management of ethnic identity: an examination of Fijian East Indians in British Columbia. Ph.D. dissertation 1977.

Cakiroglu, Saziye.
Phonological acquisition, a construction through case studies of two Turkish children. M.A. thesis 1987.
NL

Chen, Kathleen Shee Yin.

British Columbian fiction attitudes towards Chinese. M.A. thesis 1984.
NL

Chen, Sun-i.
Argumentative discourse structure in Chinese language and English writing: a comparative analysis. M.A. thesis 1986.
NL

Chong, Mick Yoke Loon.
Conflict, law and social control, a descriptive study of the relationship between Chinese and the legal system in British Columbia, 1858-1923. M.A. thesis 1985.
NL

Daur, Phille Phillip.
The Papuan plantation termite, a little known pest of forest trees and structural timber in Papua New Guinea. M.P.M. thesis 1987.
NL

Dhaliwal, Baljeet.
Sikhs in the Vancouver region, a descriptive study of certain Sikhs views of education since 1904. M.A. thesis 1985.
NL

Duguid, Stephen Ralph.
Centralization and localism, aspects of Ottoman policy in Eastern Anatolia, 1878-1908. M.A. thesis 1970.
CT

Guo, Changlin.
The U.S. factor in China's reunification, the Taiwan Relations Act and beyond. M.A. thesis 1987.
NL

Hall, Gerald Herman.
Analysis of the People's Republic of China's behaviour in the United Nations, 1971-1978. M.A. thesis 1979.
CT

Hollebaugh, Ace Leroy.
The geographical, social and political implications of de-urbanisation and de-centralisation in the People's Republic of China. M.A. thesis 1975.
CT

Howard, Patricia M.
Communication, cooperation, and conflict in China's countryside, 1978-1985. Ph.D. dissertation 1986.
NL

Howe, Robert Brian,
Intellectuals and democratic development, the case of modern India. M.A. thesis 1981.
NL

Ibrahim, Ali Wan.
Insect pest management in cocoa in Malaysia. M.P.M. thesis 1979.

Indra, Doreen Marie.
Ethnicity, social stratification, and opinion formation, an analysis of ethnic portrayal in the Vancouver newspaper press, 1905-1976. Ph.D. dissertation 1979.

Iqbal, Mahmood.
An analysis of energy demand in Pakistan, 1960-1981. Ph.D. dissertation 1985.

Ironside, Linda L.
Chinese- and Indo-Canadian elites in Greater Vancouver, their views on education. M.A. thesis 1985.
NL

Jo, Yukiko.
Japan's postwar rearmament and reactions of East Asian States. M.A. thesis 1986.
NL

Kamath, Kiran.
Les emprunts du Français aux langues indiennes de l'Inde(Dix-septième - vingtième siècles)M.A. thèse 1985.
NL

Kamath, Shyam Janardhan.
The political economy of suppressed markets, controls, rent-seeking and interest-group behaviour in the Indian sugar and cement industries. Ph.D. dissertation, 1986.
NL

Leong, Cheng Woh.
Wild pigs in West Malaysia, with special reference to their role as pests in agricultural land development. M.P.M. thesis 1981.
NL

Marie, Gillian.
Attitudes toward Chinese immigrants to British Columbia, 1858-1885. M.A. thesis 1976.
CT

Martin, Randall W.
Some evidence for contrastive analysis, negative questions in Japanese and English. M.A.(Ed.) thesis 1983.
NL

Millen, D. Bruce.
A strategy for personal and community protection against the vectors of malaria in Papua New Guinea with emphasis on the evaluation of bednets impregnated with Permethrin. M.P.M. thesis 1986.
NL

Mohammad, Faiz.
An analysis of the structure and performance of agricultural markets in Pakistan. Ph.D. dissertation 1983.
NL

Nazeman, Hamid.
A macro-econometric model for Iran. M.A. thesis 1979.
CT

Nyaw, Mee Kau.
Export expansion and industrial growth in Singapore. Ph.D. dissertation 1978.

Plant, Christopher M.
Peacesat and development in the Pacific islands. M.A. thesis 1979.
CT

Rahman, A.B.M. Shafiqur.
The matrix of institutional communication in development projects, a case study of the Barisal irrigation project, Bangladesh. Ph.D. dissertation 1986.
NL

Ravindranathan, Tachat Ramavarna.
The Young Turk revolution, July 1908 to April 1909, its immediate effects. M.A. thesis 1970.
CT

Seah, Hong Chee.
Contrastive analysis, error analysis and interlanguage in relation to adult Chinese speakers learning second language. Ph.D. dissertation 1981.

Shanmugan, Vijaysegaran.
Radiofrequency disinfestation application to stored rice in West Malaysia. M.P.M. thesis 1979.
NL

Seehra, Baldev S.
Evaluation of the status of pesticide use and pest management by East Indian berry and cole crops producers in the Fraser Valley, British Columbia. M.P.M. thesis 1988.
NL

Sharma, Shalendra.
Agrarian structure and social change, a case study of Bihar, India. M.A. thesis 1985.
NL

Shiels, Martin.
Across the black water, a study of two Hindu sects in North America. M.A. thesis 1978.
CT

Sproul, Larry Rowland.
A thematic content analysis of Peking and Hong Kong elementary school children, Chinese language texts used in 1974-76. M.A. thesis 1978.
NL

Sze-peng, Tee.
The rice weevil on stored rice in Malaysia. M.P.M. thesis 1979.
NL

Tanaka, Hiroshi.
Pilgrim places, a study of the eighty-eight sacred precints of the Shikoku pilgrimage, Japan. Ph.D. dissertation 1975.

Yeung, David Yuen.
China's politics of modernization. M.A. thesis 1982.
NL

**University Archives,
Simon Fraser University,
Burnaby, British Columbia, V5A 1S6
Tel:(604)291-3261**

Halpern family fonds 1865-1989.
Textual records 2.3 metres.
George Robert Halpern(1902-1989)was born in Poland He received a Ph.D. in chemistry from the University of Vienna in 1927. In 1938 they left for Shanghai, then in 1939 moved to Vancouver where he established Dr.G.Halpern(Vienna) Laboratories. which manufactured pharmaceutical products, and in 1954, opened another business, G.R. Chemicals, Ltd. which operated until 1986. Fanny Gisela Halpern (1899-1953) graduated in medicine from the University of Vienna in 1924, and went to China in 1932 to teach at the Medical College of China in Shanghai. In 1935 she organized the Shanghai Mercy Hospital for Nervous Diseases and became the hospital's medical director. The fonds consists of personal and or professional archives of members of the Halpern family, primarily correspondence and business records.
BCARCH-8300

Pacific Region Science Conference fonds 1976-1977.
Textual records. 19.5 cm.
The Fifth Pacific Region Science Conference was held in 1977 in Vancouver, British Columbia. The conference was sponsored by the Western Regional Science Association and the Japan Section of the Regional Science Association. Simon Fraser University was the host of the conference. The focus of the conference was on the regional impact of the law of the sea changes. Pacific Rim resources and regional development planning; problems and prospects of Pacific island economies, and tourism and Pacific regional development. Mailing lists, announcements, leaflets, financial records, correspondence(1976-1977), committee records and proceedings.
BCARCH-7658.

Sikh Archives.
Photocopies, 3 cm. ca. 1900-1981.
Journal articles, theses, photographs and newspaper clippings pertaining to the Sikh community in British Columbia.

Vancouver

**Anglican Church of Canada,
Provincial Synod of British Columbia,
6000 Iona Drive,
Vancouver, British Columbia, V6T 1L4
Tel:(604)228-9031, ext. 239.**

Record Group 1. Provincial Synod.

Series 4. Provincial Board of Missions to Orientals.
Anglican minutes and reports, 1924-1934, 1942.
Minutes - 1956-1965.

Record Group 3.

Series 2. General Synod Journals, 1893-1986.
Reports re Committees working with Orientals.

**Japanese Canadian Archives,
511 East Broadway Street,
Vancouver, British Columbia V5T 1X4
Tel:(604)874-8187**

Five metres of manuscripts and records covering period 1890 to 1950.
Over 2,000 photographs, and 300 oral history tapes, of which 200 are additional to those held by the University of British Columbia.

Akatsuka, Shokichi.
42 photographs, [ca. 1910-1930].
Photographs of Japanese Canadians and events and activities of the Japanese-Canadian community in and around Vancouver.
BCARCH-37762

Hayashi family.
55 photographs[ca.1900-1946]
Family photographs of the Hayashi family, including scenes of Japanese-Canadian life in Vancouver, New Denver and in Schreiber, Ontario.
BCARCH-37754.

Japanese Canadian Archives Photograph Collection, [ca. 1890]-1994.
ca. 2,000 photographs.
The Japanese Canadian Archives was established in 1993 by the Japanese Canadian History Preservation Committee of the Japanese Canadian Citizens Association. The Archives collects and preserves archival materials which illustrate the heritage and history of Japanese Canadians.
The collection consists of photographs, people, events, organizations, and institutional activities relating to the Japanese-Canadian community, primarily in British Columbia. Many of the photographs depict scenes of the Japanese-Canadian life in the internment and relocation camps and after World War II.
BCARCH-37861

Duggan, John W.
49 photographs, 1942-1946.
John Duggan was an Royal Canadian Mounted Police officer who policed relocation camps in the Kootenay area of British Columbia.
Photographs depict people, events and views relating to the relocation of Japanese Canadians during World War II. Includes photographs depicting relocation camps at Slocan City, Lemon Creek, Tashme and New Denver.
BCARCH-37846

Sanmiya family.
Photogaphs of the Sanmiya family, [ca.1905]-1933.
Koichiro Sanmiya immigrated to Canada in 1905 and first worked as a cattle herder. Sanmiya was one of the founders and early presidents of the Japanese Canadian Association in Vancouver. He had various business interests, and was active in community organizations in Vancouver.
Photographs of the Sanmiya family and of Koichiro Sanmiya, including photographs of Japanese-Canadian groups and activities of the Japanese-Canadian community in Vancouver.
BCARCH-37804

Yoshitake, Masao.
29 photographs, 1937-1946.
Masao Yoshitake was a Japanese Canadian who lived in road camps and internment camps in British Columbia during World War II, including Red Pass Camp, Black Spur Camp, Tete Jaune Camp, East Lillooet Camp, and Tashme.
Yoshitake's photographs primarily depict life in road camps and internment camps in the interior of British Columbia.
BCARCH-37770

**United Church of Canada,
British Columbia Conference Archives,
Vancouver School of Theology Library,
6000 Iona Drive,
Vancouver, British Columbia, V6T 1L4
Tel(604)228-9031**

Bunt, William Percy, b.1888.
Textual records,1928-1965. 70 cm.
Born in Ontario and educated at McGill University. In 1920 he was ordained as a Methodist minister in Vancouver, and was appointed Superintendent of Home Missions for British Columbia in 1939. He served in that position until his retirement in 1958. As Supertintendent, he was especially active on behalf of Japanese Canadians during World War II.
Bunt's general administrative files as Superintendent of Home Missions, and of correspondence and reference material pertaining to Bunt's activities in assisting Japanese Canadians during and after World War II.
Inventory available
BCARCH-37127

Fleming, Everett S., 1895-
Textual records, 1917-1976. 42 cm.
Ordained in 1926 and served various pastoral charges in British Columbia.
Includes letters from Rev.J.Kabayama of Ocean Falls, who had been removed to a Japanese-Canadian internment camp.
Inventory available.
BCARCH-367631

Kelowna, British Columbia. Okanagan Japanese United Church.
Church Records (Diary), 1924-1947.
Membership Roll, 1926-1951.
Subscription List, 1922-1925(Methodist).
Christian Girls Association, Record 1930.
Christian Mothers Association, Record, 1932-1949.
Ledger, 1925-1927, 1928-1964.
Home Mission Record Book, 1946. (includes Lemon Creek Internment Camp)
Kelowna Japanese Language School. Record and Credential, 1932-1941.

Komiyama, Takashi, 1915-1968.
Minister of the United Church of Canada. Original, 6 inches, 1938-1944.
Educated at the University of British Columbia and Union College, and active in the British Columbia Young People's Christian Conference. He was ordained in 1942 and served the Japanese Christian mission of the United Church in the internment camps at Lemon Creek, New Denver, and the Slocan Valley. He also served Japanese United Churches in Vancouver, Montreal and Hamilton.
Reports, lectures, clippings and memorabilia, primarily concerning the treatment of Japanese Canadians during World War II.
BCARCH-36749/ULM

Mission, British Columbia. Fraser Valley Japanese United Church.
Account Book, 1942.
Account Book, 1934-1942(Maple Ridge)
Building Fund Account Book, 1942.
Cash Book, 1935-1942.
Congregational Meeting, Minutes, 1941-1942.
Membership and Attendance Roll, Bible Class, 1942.
Committee Meetings, Minutes, 1942.
Official Board. Minutes, 1940-1942.
Sunday School, Cash Book, 1934-1942.
Sunday School, Minutes, 1938-1942.
Sunday School, Record Book, 1941-1942.
Trustees. Minutes, 1940-1941.
Cash Book, 1936-1942.
Canadian Girls in Training. Cash Book, 1936-1941.
Record Book, 1935-1942.
Young People's Society. Membership Roll, 1938-1939.

Missionary Society.
The papers of James Henry White, Superintendent from 1902 to 1923 are listed in a finding aid.
The White papers include:
Records of the Oriental Committee, 1910-1925, 1 cm.
Minutes of meetings, 1910-1925. The United Church Oriental Committee continued to use the same minute book.

New Westminster, British Columbia. Japanese United Church.
Account books.
Baptismal registers and other records and minutes(7 books).
Minute Book. 1922-1925(Methodist)
Bible Class. Minutes, 1934-1942(In English)
Church Service record Book, 1933-1942.

Oriental Committee and Oriental Missions Society.
The Oriental Committee was concerned with the United Church of Canada's mission among Canadians of Oriental descent. It was a subcommittee of the Conference Home Missions Committee.
Record Book, 1924-1947, 3 cm.
Minutes of meetings of the Oriental Committee, 1925-1935(and minutes of meetings of the Methodist committee, 1915-1925), a copy of the Oriental Committee's act of incorporation, minutes of Society meetings, 1931-1937, copy of a report entitled Indian and Oriental Mission fields in British Columbia by S.S. Osterhout, 1925.

Oriental Home and School.
In 1885, John Endicott Gardiner arrived in Victoria and became involved in Methodist missionary work in the Chinese community. Of particular concern to him was the traffic in Chinese women and girls for prostitution purposes. Gardiner began caring for some of these women in his own home and attracted the support of some members of the Metropolitan United Church including its minister, J.R.Starr. The Woman's Missionary Society(Toronto) was petitioned for help and a "rescue home" for Chinese girls was established in 1888. The home was commonly called the Chinese Girls Home. Classes were offered to the girls and the mission became known as the Oriental Home and School. The United Church continued to operate the Home after church union in 1925, providing care for children and needy women. During the Second World War most of the residents of the home were removed to Saskatchewan. After the war, the Home never achieved its prewar status.
Records of the Home and School 1886-1947, 40 cm.
Includes the original report sent to the Woman's Missionary Society by Rev. J.R.Starr, 1887, 24 p.; registers of residents and accompanying comments, 1886-1942, 8 cm; files on individual residents, 1891-1942, 6 cm.; financial record books, 1888-1947, 21 cm.; quarterly and annual reports of the Home, 1926-1928, and 1933; blueprints and related documents of the proposed new buildings, 1908-1909; scrapbook and photographs.

Superintendent of Home Missions.
In British Columbia, there was an emphasis on work with Native Indians, Japanese Canadians, and on the coastal marine missions and hospital work.
William Percy Bunt was superintendent from 1938-1958. As Superintendent he was especially active on

behalf of Japanese Canadians during the Second World War.
Finding aid: Inventory I-18.
Records relating to Japanese Canadians, 1936-1965, 43 cm.
Most of the files are made up of correspondence, and have been arranged in four series, beginning with the General Administration Series which contains the following: correspondence between Bunt and Japanese Christian ministers, the Board of Home Missions, and the British Columbia Security Commission; files on various committees, and conferences concerned with the Japanese situation, and other miscellaneous files, including newspaper clippings and pamphlets. The second series, Internment Camps and Other Relocation Sites, is made up of correspondence between Bunt and Japanese Canadian ministers and other individuals who lived and worked in the camps. Series three, Files Dealing with Former Japanese Property, contains information on what happened to the property, including church property which had been confiscated from the Japanese. The final series contains general correspondence with other Japanese Canadians.

Vancouver, British Columbia. Chinese United Church.
Annual Reports, 1955-1985.
Baptismal stubs, 1950-1977(6 volumes)
Canadian Girls in Training. Sui Lin Fah Group. Minutes, 19653-1966.
Cash Book. 1906-1939(Methodist and United Mission)
Christian Education Committee. Minutes, 1956-1971.
Congregational meetings. Minutes, 1941-1959, 1976-1988(2 volumes)
History of Chinese United Church, 1888-1981.(l volume)
Marriage Registers. 121-1983(12 volumes)
Official Board. Minutes, 1918-1959; 1976-1988(3 volumes)
Stewards. Minutes. 1961-1966.
Strathcona Community worker. Records, 1973-1980(3 files)
Sunday School. Minutes, 1948-1960.
Chinese Independent Mission. Official Board Minutes. 1914-1922(Presbyterian, in English)

Vancouver, British Columbia. Japanese United Church.
Baptismal Register. 1918-1930(Methodist/United)
Baptismal Register, 1930-1941(also membership roll)
Diary, 1911.
Historical Record.
Junior Church School. Minutes. 1936-1942(English)
Membership Roll. 1918-1930(Methodist/United)
Membership Roll. 1930-1941.
Membership Cards and Family Records.
Japanese Ministerial Association. Minutes, 1931-1941.
Official Board. Minutes. 1921-1942(4 books)(Methodist/United).
Record of Church Services. 1896-?
Session. Minutes. 1933-1942.
The Shepherd's Call:1933-1942.
Social Service Committee. Minutes.
Stewards. Minutes. 1929-1942(5 books).
United Church Weekly. 1928-1932(5 books).
Sunday School Teachers' Meetings. Minutes,1932-1941.
Young People's Society, 1931-1937.

Victoria, British Columbia. Chinese United Church(previously Methodist).
Account Books, 1899-1920.
Children's Groups: Bluebirds. Minutes, 1937-1940.
Christian Girls in Training. Minutes, 1927-1939, Chinese Girls Mission Band, 1897-1928, 1932-1943, 1960.
Explorers. Minutes, 1938-1942.
Friday Group Attendance roll, 1897-1903.
Marriage Registers. 1917-1921, 1923.
Oriental School Attendance records, 1907-1935.
Official Board. Minutes. 1897-1921.
Sunday School Record books, 1909-1927.
Women's Groups. Chinese Mission Circle. Minutes. 1920-1928;1936-1942.
Women's Missionary Society. Minutes. 1940-1955.
Women's Auxiliary. Minutes. 1909-1942.

Victoria, British Columbia. Japanese United Church(previously Methodist).
Canadian Girls in Training. Sunbeam Group. Minutes. 1931-1933.
Girls Mission Band. Minutes. 1913-1933.
Marriage Registers. 1908-1916.
Sunday School. Minutes. 1908-1917.

Woman's Missionary Society(Methodist) British Columbia Conference Branch.
Textual records, 1904-1923. 5 cm.
Organized in Victoria in 1888 to set up a "rescue home" for Chinese women and girls who had been forced into prostitution. Other local auxiliaries soon appeared through the province and, in 1891, were unified through the establishment of the British Columbia Conference Branch. In 1925 merged into the Woman's Missionary Society of the United Church of Canada. Minutes (1908-1923) of the Advisory Committee of the Japanese Mission, later called the Oriental Mission. Minutes of the Victoria District meetings(1904-1911) and Westminster District meetings(1905-1923)
Finding aids available.
BCARCH-36814

Photographs

Oriental Home.
39 photographs.

McGregor,Lily M.
41 photographs relate to her work with Chinese United Church in Vancouver.

**University of British Columbia,
Museum of Anthropology Archives,
6393 NW Marine Drive,
Vancouver,British Columbia, V6T 1Z2.
Tel:(604)822-3825.**

Davidson, James Wheeler, 1872-1933.
131 slides.
James Davidson was a war correspondent in the Sino-Japanese War and then American consul in Shanghai in 1906. He was there at the time of the Japanese takeover of Formosa. He published **The Island of Formosa, Historical View from 1430 to 1900** in 1903.
Lantern slides taken in Formosa and Japan,1894-1902 by James Davidson. He used the slides for his lectures.
Item listing available.
BCARCH-9852

Schofield, Stuart James, 1883-1947.
208 photographs,1923-1924.
In 1920 he was appointed Professor of Structural Geology at the University of British Columbia. He contributed to the understanding of the geology of British Columbia and Hong Kong.
Nitrate negatives of photographs taken in China, 1923-1924, as well as some postcards.
Caption list available.
BCARCH-9829.

**University of British Columbia,
Special Collections and University Archives Division,
University Library,
1956 Main Mall,
Vancouver, British Columbia, V6T 1Z1
Tel:(604)822-2521**

Archives and Manuscripts

ABC Packing Company, Henry Doyle, Chuck On.
Contain information on Asian workers in the canning industry.

Akagawa, Yoshimitsu.
Minister, Manitoba.
Original, 15 cm. ca. 1893-1956.
Diaries, notebooks, correspondence, documents and clippings. Includes diary 1893-1950, daily notes and appointments. Diary 1933-1942, 1944 records of daily acitivities, 1947-1949 records of families in Manitoba, trip expenses and mileage, and 1949-1951 record of visits. Also includes a list of Japanese families in Manitoba and newspaper clippings about the relocation of the Japanese in English, and about the war in Japan, and on the sale of property, repatriation and church articles.
ULM1/NABATA1

Ames, Michael, 1933-
Textual records - 1967-1982. 1.2 metres.
Michael Ames was born in Vancouver and attended the University of British Columbia where he graduated with a B.A. in anthropology in 1956. He continued his education at Harvard University, earning his Ph.D. in social anthropology in 1961. Ames returned to the University of British Columbia as an assistant professor in 1964 rising to full professor in 1970. In addition to his work in the department, Ames also became Director of the Museum of Anthropology in 1974. From 1974 to 1976 Ames served as president of the Shastri Indo-Canadian Institute which was established in 1969 with funding from the Indian Government to promote Indian studies in Canada.
Included are records of the Board of Directors of Shastri Indo-Canadian Institute(1967-1979). The Shastri material includes records generated or collected by Ames and other members of the Institute at the University of British Columbia.
Inventory available.
BCARCH/UBC

Angus, Henry Forbes(1891-1991).
Economist. Head of the Department of Economics from 1930 to 1956.
Interested in plight of Japanese in World War II.
BCARCH/UBC1

Aoki, Aki.
Vancouver.
Photocopies, 1 item, 1942.
A travel permit from the British Columbia Security Commission.
ULM1/NABATA1

Aoki, S.
Vancouver.
Photocopies, 7 pages, undated.
Handwritten notes in Japanese of one aspect of Nobu Suzuki.
ULM1/NABATA1

Beans Collection.
The George H. Beans collection of Japanese maps of the Tokugawa period is one of the finest outside Japan.
Includes manuscript maps. Inventory.
BC

Binning, Bertram Charles, 1909-1976.
Textual records, 1947-1976, 1.3 metres,
Head of the Department of Fine Arts from 1955 to 1968. Binning was concerned in the negotiations for the planning of the Nitobe Memorial Garden.
File list available.
BCARCH/UBC1

Bowen, Roger W., 1947-
Roger Bowen fonds -1926-1984. Roger Bowen teaches at Colby College, Waterville, Maine. He has written two books on E.Herbert Norman: **E.H.Norman: His Life and Scholarship** and **Innocence is Not Enough: The Life and Death of Herbert Norman.**
The fonds consists of material accumulated by Roger Bowen in order to write his biography of E.Herbert Norman. It includes various research materials including copies of records from the Federal Bureau of Investigation.

Inventory available.
BCARCH/UBC

Burridge, Kenelm, 1922-
Textual records. 53 cm. 1950-1987.
Burridge was born in Malta, and obtained a Ph.D. in Anthropology from Australian National University in 1953. He conducted his fieldwork in New Guinea, Malaya, Australia and the Melanesian Islands. Published and unpublished material and reports showing Burridge's anthropological interests, particularly in the areas of religion and mythology.
Inventory available.
BCARCH/UBC1

Canada. Canadian Broadcasting Corporation. Radio Canada International.
Transcripts, 60 pages. 1977-1979.
Thirty sound recordings of radio programs broadcast in Japan by Canadian Broadcasting Corporation on Canadian topics, with transcripts in Japanese summarizing these recordings.
ULM3

Canada. National Archives of Canada.
Prints of Japanese evacuation.
NABATA2

Canadian Japanese Young Men's Christian Association.
Minute book, 1931-1942, 2 cm.
Minutes of the Canadian Japanese Young Men's Christian Association written in Japanese, 1931-1942.
BCARCH/UBC2

China. Consul. Vancouver.
Chinese Consul of Vancouver fonds - 1914-1915.
The fonds consists of a photocopied letterpress copybook used in consul business between 1914 and 1915. The correspondence was generated under the direction of Chinese consul Lin Shih Yuan.
BCARCH/UBC

Chinese Canadian Research Collection, 1870-1979.
Textual records 9.1 metres.
Collection consists of records accumulated by Edgar Wickberg, Graham Johnson and William Wilmot of the University of British Columbia in the course of research projects relating to Chinese Canadians. Contains an index to the **Chinese Times**, research files composed of materials gathered from archival respositories, original records including scrapbooks, the papers, Chinese Benevolent Association Lottery records(1933-1934),and ledgers and other financial records from Vancouver and Victoria Chinatowns, and miscellaneous, newspapers, periodicals, theses, papers and publications broadly relating to the history of Canadian Chinese.
Inventory available.
BCARCH-9068/UBC1

Chock On.
Chock On fonds -1928-1940.
Textual records. 26 cm.
Chock On was a labour agency operating from a house on Pender Street in Vancouver. It contracted Chinese labourers to various canneries along the British Columbia coast.
The fonds consists of correspondence(1929-1940) miscellaneous receipts(1928-1936), address books in Chinese. The fonds includes letters sent to Chock On by overseas Chinese to be distributed to relatives that may have worked in canneries as well as correspondence between Chock On and its Chinese contractors at various canneries including Bones Bay Cannery
BCARCH/UBC

Cowan, Harry, collector.
Harry Cowan collection -1891-1912.
Textual records. 13 cm.
The collection consists of two scrapbooks which record events relating to the Vancouver Trades and Labour Council and the Asiatic Exclusion League, Vancouver.
BCARCH/UBC

Crook, Rudolf and Edith.
150 slides, 100 prints, 16 pages manuscript on a trip to Tibet, summer 1930. Slides and prints also on life in Szechuan, 1920s - ca. 1950, by Baptist medical missionary couple.
MITCHELL

Cumberland Museum Collection.
Print of a Japanese family. 7 people.
NABATA2

Cumyow, Won Alexander, 1861-1955.
Vancouver, civic employee.
Original 14 cm, 1888-1950.
Correspondence, journals, documents, clippings and photographs relating to his business, personal and civic duties, which include the position of interpreter for the Vancouver city police. The papers also include correspondence pertaining to the Chinese Empire Reform Association.
Black and white. 17 photographs, undated.
Portraits and casual photos of Mr. Cumyow and his family; headquarters of the Chinese Empire Reform Association and its first executive.
SEIFRIED/ULM

Department of Commerce.
Textual records, 1940-1950. 6.5 cm.
The Department of Commerce at University of British Columbia was established in 1939. Ellis H.Morrow served as its first head until his retirement in 1950. In 1941 six Japanese-Canadian students were enrolled in the Commerce program. However in 1942, after the bombing of Pearl Harbour, the Government ordered the removal of "enemy aliens" from the coast to the interior of the province. During the turmoil, the Class of '42 graduated, but the future of the six Japanese-Canadians was bleak as they could not seek employment in white-collar jobs. Morrow remained keenly interested in the fate of these students , maintained contact with them at

least until his retirement in 1950.
The fonds consists of student records and correspondence between E.H.Morrow and Fred Sasaki, Oyama Kazuhiko, David Shiozake, Peter Yamada and George Yamashita(1940-1950).The correspondence files provide a very interesting account of the treatment accorded Japanese-Canadians in the 1940s. There is also a copy of an article from **Viewpoints** inspired by the information in the files, as well as some follow -up correspondence with the former students.
BCARCH/UBC1

Discovery (H.M.S.)
Transcripts, 1776-1901, 312 pages.
Typewritten transcript of James Burney's "Journal of the proceedings of his majys. sloop the Discovery, Chas. Clerke, Commander, in company with the Resolution, Capt. James Cook". February 10, 1776 - August 24, 1779. Portion of an incomplete journal by Thomas Edgar, Master of H.M.S. **Discovery**, 1788.
Originals in Mitchell Library, Sydney. Catalogued with call number FC 3821.2433 B8.
ULM

Edamura, Shingejiro.
Prints showing departure for camps. 1940s.
NABATA2

Elrod, J.McRee, 1932-
J.McRee Elrod fonds. - 1968-1976. 13 cm.
J.McRee Elrod moved to Vancouver in 1967 and was head of the University of British Columbia's Library Cataloguing Division until 1978. Also a minister-at-large, Elrod participated in the North Shore Unitarian Church Social Action Committee. In this capacity he placed advertisements in prominent American periodicals offering assistance to any young men and women dislocated as a result of the selective service system during the time of the Vietnam war.
The fonds consists of correspondence with American war objectors between 1968 and 1976 to whom Elrod offered advice to those wishing to emigrate to Canada. The fonds includes records of the North Shore Unitarian Church Social Action Committee.
BCARCH/UBC1

Ennyu, Sanosuke.
Toronto.
Travel diary of trip in Canada, in 1894, in Japanese and including a few drawings of working tools and fish, clippings pertaining to Japanese associations in Toronto, 1946, and notes on the Townsmen's Defence Committee, 1947.
ULM1/NABATA1

Escott, Harold, 1881-1979.
Original, 1.2 metres, 1917-1978.
Handwritten diaries commenting on current events and personal experiences, 1919-1978; two manuscripts: "War as I saw it", and "Stray impressions", 1917-1918; as well as letters, prose, poems and two photograph albums relating to India.
ULM3

Fujiwara, Sakae.
Photographs of Powell Street in 1941, and Roseberry and Fort Williams Camps.
NABATA2

Fukunaga, Sukeo.
Photograph of Red Pass Road Camp, 1942, and Buddhist Churches in Vancouver.NABATA2

Goode, Jim.
A list of material relevant to Japanese Canadians in the Public Archives of Canada, compiled in the summer of 1972.
NABATA1

Gough, Kathleen, 1925-1990.
Kathleen Gough fonds.- 1947-1990.
Textual records 5.7 metres.
Kathleen Gough was born in England in 1925. She was trained as an anthropologist in both Cambridge and Oxford Universities and received her Ph.D. in 1950. Her extensive research fieldwork in India(Kerala-1947-1949 and Tanjore District - 1950-1953) forms the basis for much of her subsequent published work. Her books include **Ten Times More Beautiful: The Rebuilding of Vietnam**(1978), **Rural Society in Southeast India**(1981), **Rural Change in Southeast India, 1950's-1980's**(1989)and **Political Economy in Vietnam**(1990). Her most prominent teaching positions included:Brandeis University(1961-1963), the University of Oregon(1963-1967) and Simon Fraser University(1967-1970). In each instance her deeply held political views helped to precipitate her departure. From 1947 until her death, Gough held the rank of Honorary Research Associate at the University of British Columbia.
The fonds consists primarily of Gough's notes of her Ph.D. field work in Kerala(1947-1949) and her return visit in 1964, as well as her major fieldwork in the Tanjore District(1950-1953) and then again in 1974. The fonds also includes lectures and other notes and typescript copies of articles. It also includes the complete manuscript for her last book, **Political Economy of Vietnam**(1990)
There are access restrictions on this fonds.
Inventory available
BCARCH/UBC

Harnetty, Peter, 1927-
Peter Harnetty fonds. - 1962-1992.
Textual records. 53 cm.
Peter Harnetty was born in Engand in 1927. He completed his B.A. at the University of British Columbia in 1953 and then attended Harvard University where he received his M.A. in 1954 and Ph.D. in 1958. He began teaching at the University of British Columbia in 1958 and was promoted to full professor in 1971. From 1958 to 1992 Harnetty held a joint appointment in the Departments of Asian Studies and History. He served first as acting head of the Department of Asian Studies in 1970/1971 and then as head from 1975 to 1980.
The fonds consists of minutes from the Departments of

Asian Studies(1968-1992) and History(1964-1992) as well as committee material and other records generated by these two units(1962-1992). Harnetty has provided a number of detailed lists which serve as abstracts for much of the material.
Inventory available.
BCARCH/UBC1

Hayashi, Rintaro.
Steveston.
Original, 3 cm., 1941-1945.
Documents, letters and mimeographed material in Japanese and English relating to the evacuation of the Japanese from the coast, the National Japanese Canadian Citizens Association, Japanese associations in Steveston and the Steveston Community Society.
NABATA1 Box 1, folder 6 contains incoming correspondence to Steveston. It includes agenda for meetings in Greenwoord and letters pertaining to its organization, lists of names of repatriated Japanese, documents from the Department of Labour, Royal Canadian Mounted Police, British Columbia Security Commission, etc. There is another group of items from around 1950 dealing with problems in the use of the money of the treasuries of various clubs and associations in British Columbia which dissolved at the end of World War II owing to the return to Japan of some and relocation of other Japanese-Canadians in Eastern Canada. Some memorandum and notes also deal with this, in addition to *habeas corpus* cases and the cancellation of repatriation. There are also items which deal with conditions in Eastern Canada.The quality of the print of some of these documents is very bad.
NABATA1 Box 3, folder 7 contains Department of Labour:General Notice to Persons of Japanese Race Who have Applied for Repatriation to Japan, 1946(translated into Japanese), rough notes and a clean copy of explanations in Japanese of the Orders in Council PC 7355, 7356 and 7357 about repatriation, and several printed sheets in Japanese about the war and the government. Some are translations of official government pronouncements and others seem to be comments by Japanese citizens.
NABATA1 Box 3, folder 8. Mimeographed materials include Constitution of National Japanese Citizens Association, November 7, 1919, amended by 3rd National Conference, Constitution of the National Japanese Canadian Citizens Association, March 26, 1951, amended by 4th National Conference, Japanese Canadian Citizens Association **Bulletins**, March 23, 1951 to September 14, 1953, mostly reports and agenda of meetings. List of Japanese families and addresses, Draft Constitution of Vancouver Japanese Canadian Citizens Association, and Draft Constitution of Steveston Japanese Citizens Association.
NABATA1 Box 3, folder 9A contains materials on the British Columbia Japanese Canadian Citizens Associations for 1953 and1954, and the Steveston Community Society, 1959-1960, and1964. A Report of the Department of Labour on Administration of Japanese Affairs in Canada, 1942-1944, and Japanese in Montreal, An Ecological and Sociological Survey, March1953, by Kuni Uchida.
NABATA1 Box 3, Folder 9B. Guest book by prominent Japanese visitors to the Steveston Japanese Community, 1917-1935.
Photographs of prewar Steveston, Lemon Creek Camp, and a modern kendo tournament.
ULM1/NABATA1/NABATA2

Hazuto, Kiyozo.
Photographs of Tashme Camp.
NABATA2:

Hikida, Kaichi.
Photocopies, 24 pages, 1942-1948.
Incoming letters and personal documents relating to economic loss to the Japanese Canadians owing to their evacuation from the coast(in Japanese and English) and a report of the Strawberry Hill Japanese Farmers' Association, 1946(in Japanese). Includes inventory of chattels belonging to Hikida Kaichi, 1942, notice of sale of land,1944, public auction of chattels, 1944.
ULM1/NABATA1

Homma, Hasue(Mrs).
Photocopies, 8 pages, 1902.
Printed material on court case brought before the House of Lords, Privy Council(Cunningham and Attorney-General for British Columbia for British Columbia -Appellant T. Homma and Attorney-General for Canada - respondent) on the right to vote for Japanese who were British subjects.
ULM1/NABATA1

Imada, Ito(Mrs).
Photocopies, 155 pages, undated.
Reminiscences relating to her early life in Canada(in Japanese).
ULM1/NABATA1

Imamura, Mary.
Photographs of Lemon Creek Camp, 1942.
NABATA2

Inoue, Makato.
l page, 1890's.
Advertisement for Japanese goods by Jin and Amura Company, Vancouver, British Columbia.
ULM4/NABATA1

Institute of Pacific Relations.
Records, 1931-1961, mostly 1950-1960.

l. Boxes 1-58 Boxes includes publication records for 1940-1960, William L. Holland's correspondence files, 1952-1960(1955 lacking), Pacific Council of Institute of Pacific Relations correspondence, 1952-1957, American Institute of Pacific Relations correspondence, 1952-1954, annual reports, conference papers and records, photographs, pamphlets, etc.

Boxes 1-14. Institute of Pacific Relations publications series records, including publications, correspondence with authors and publishers, manuscripts, galley

Boxes 14-16. Institute of Pacific Relations Inquiry series records, with similar material as in boxes 1-14.

Boxes 17-18. Miscellaneous business records.

Boxes 18-21. Reviews of Institute of Pacific Relations publications.

Box 21. **Pacific Affairs** records.

Boxes 22-32. W.L.Holland correspondence, 1952-1964, arranged by correspondent.

Boxes 32-36. W.L.Holland correspondence, 1956-1957, arranged by correspondent.

Boxes 36-40. William L.Holland correspondence, 1958-1959, arranged by correspondent.

Boxes 40-41. William L.Holland reading files, 1954-1955 copies of outgoing correspondence, arranged by date.

Boxes 41-44. William L.Holland correspondence with Institute of Pacific Relations national councils, 1952-1957.

Box 44. Pacific council correspondence, 1952-1957.

Boxes 44-45. American Institute of Pacific Relations correspondence, 1952-1954.

Box 45. Annual reports of American Institute of Pacific Relations and national Institutes of Pacific Relations councils.

Boxes 46-51, 53-55. Institute of Pacific relations financial series include auditor's reports, financial statements, worksheets, inventories, vouchers and deposits, withholding tax records, payroll registers, miscellaneous records, and one folder of correspondence with the Rockefeller Foundation.

Boxes 55-58. Institute of Pacific Relations conference series. Additional conference records and records of short conferences, agendas and lists of delegates. These are apart from the complete set of Institute of Pacific Relations conference papers to be found in the main stacks of the University Library of the University of British Columbia.

Box 58. American Institute of Pacific Relations conferences.

2. Boxes 59-64. Random files, related to the McCarran hearings 1951-1952, the Owen Lattimore trial 1954-1955, and the Institute of Pacific Relations tax case, 1955-1960. Includes documents from the 1930's and 1940's lent to the Federal Bureau of Investigation in Institute of Pacific Relations before the McCarran hearings, and returned in 1952-1953.

Boxes 59-62. McCarran Subcommittee hearings, 1951-1952. Selected documents from 1947-1953 including clippings, magazine articles, correspondence statements, testimonials and miscellaneous documents.

Box 62. Owen Lattimore trial. Documents, 1951-1954, including statements, court transcripts, correspondence subpoenaed as evidence, Lattimore's **Pacific Affairs** correspondence, 1941-1942, notes prepared for Lattimore by Derk Bodde, 1953.

Box 63-64. Institute of Pacific Relations tax case, 1955-1960. Related documents including court documents, correspondence, memoranda, clippings, and miscellaneous documents.

Boxes 65-68. Miscellaneous printed material, including records of the Senate Judiciary Committee on Internal Security.

3. The bulk of the Institute of Pacific Relations files (about 472 boxes), dating from 1925-1955 was given to Columbia University Library in 1961, and are now in the Rare Books and Manuscript Division of the Columbia University Library. A guide and partial inventory is held by Columbia University Library. Another substantial collection of Institute of Pacific Relations papers is held by the University of Hawaii Library.

Ito, Roy
Annotated photograph of a group portrait of staff and students of the Japanese Language School, Royal Canadian Army, Vancouver, August 1945. Photocopies of position taken by Honourable Ian Mackenzie on the evacuation of Japanese-Canadians during World War II; related correspondence.
NABATA1

Japan. Ministry of Foreign Affairs. Diplomatic Record Office.
Photographs depict buildings which sustained damages during the riots at Vancouver in 1907. Names of persons and claims for damages to property are listed on the back of each print. One photograph pertains to Japanese Canadian veterans and three relate to ocean voyages of Japanese immigrants to Canada.
NABATA2

Japanese-Canadian Centennial Project Collection.
Includes list of photographs, donors and descriptions in the exhibition at the Centennial Museum, Vancouver, June 14 to July 7 1976, and on tour thereafter, booklet in Japanese describing the Centennial Project, the donors and containing essays and personal reminiscences of Issei, poster for the display, advertisement for the National Film Board film **Enemy Aliens**, and statement of goals and aims and lists of researchers.
NABATA1

Japanese-Canadian Research Collection.
Textual records. -1900-1970. 2.5 metres.
The Japanese Canadian Research Collection is a set of material assembled by a number of individuals interested in documenting the experiences of Japanese

Canadians, particularly in British Columbia. The records consist of approximately fifty small collections donated by individuals and organizations. The scope of the collection encompasses a wide range of tropics including relocation to internment camps during World Wart II, Farming, fishing, lumbering, religious activities and personal reminiscences, as well as various organizational records.
Individual collections have been arranged and described separately and filed in alphabetical order. Most of the manuscript material is written in Japanese and has been photocopied from original documents. It includes material from the following individuals or organizations: Yoshimitsu Akagawa, Rintaro Hayashi, Japanese Fishermen's Benevolent Association, Kishizo Kimura, Masajiro Miyazaki, Japanese Canadian Citizens Association, Hideichi Nosaka, Yoshio Ono, Yukio Shimoda, Rinkichi Tagashira, Shingeichi Uchibori, Chiyo Umezuki, Tokikazu Tanaka, Yasutaro Yamaga, Tameo Kanabara, Richmond Berry Growers' Association*, Shogo Kobayashi, Skeena Fishermans' Association*, Jisaburo Wakabayashi, Camp and Mill Workers Federal Labour Union*, and Mitsuru Shimpo.
*Not represented in fuller detail in the accompanying entries.
An Inventory to the Papers and Records in the Japanese Canadian Research Collection in the Library of the University of British Columbia Special Collections by Terry Nabata(NABATA1 in this guide)
BCARCH/UBC2/NABATA1

Japanese-Canadian Photograph Collection.
Black and white, 780 photographs, 1907-1950.
Photographs taken by Japanese Canadians reflecting their social and economic activities on the West Coast of British Columbia prior to World War II and throughout Canada after their evacuation from the coast during the war period.
Inventory available.
SEIFRIED

Japanese Fisherman's Benevolent Association, British Columbia.
Photocopies, 11 pages, 1900.
Second annual report of the Association, 1900(in Japanese) and two personal accounts.
ULM1/NABATA1

Japanese Language School Collection, Vancouver.
Original, 7.5 cm., 1914, 1918-1919.
Three diaries bound with notes and tables((holidays, astrological data, the Japanese Imperial family, etc. in Japanese) Diaries donated by the School.
Pictures taken from miniatures hanging in hall of Japanese Language School and includes roll of Honour of Soldiers from World War I.
ULM1/NABATA1/NABATA2

Kadota, Kantaro.
Surrey.
Photocopies, 2.5 cm., 1905-1963.
Documents and reminiscences, 1913-1916, relating to his various activities and movements between Canada and Japan, 1905-1963(in Japanese). Includes list of 61 names of persons repatriated to Japan in 1946.
Photographs of Tashme Camp.
ULM1/NABATA1/NABATA2

Kanbara, Tameo.
Original, 69 pages, ca. 1942-1945.
Manuscript diary pertaining to the evacuation from the Lower Mainland, British Columbia, 28 March-16 June l942(in Japanese), letters and documents relating to the mass evacuations including those circulated in Angler Internment Camp, Ontario and concerning requests for evacuation in family groups(in Japanese and English).
ULM2/NABATA1

Kawase, Chugi.
Daily notes on activities, charts of sales, and other activities of the Richmond Berry Growers Association(in Japanese). Reports on membership, acreage cultivated, with a total of 324 acres, acreage of different crops, quantities of berries sold wholesale and to canneries, and Association financial report for November 1940- December 1941.
ULM1/NABATA1

Kazuta.
Original, 3 cm., undated., 1942-1943.
Notes, clippings, and printed material relating to Japanese immigration and relocation of Japanese from the coast(in Japanese and English). Includes a summary of the 1943 fact-finding Royal Commission, report, reminiscences on World War II experience in Canada, newspaper clippings on evacuation news from the **New Canadian**, a telephone directory of Japanese in British Columbia, and **Canada no Nakutsu**(Canada's Brothels) 1909.
ULM1/NABATA1

Kimura, Kishizo.
Original, 2 cm., 1933-1934, 1942.
Briefs and data relating to salt salmon and salt herring production, 1933-1934, and a memo on the circumstances of the disposal of Japanese owned fishing boats, 77 pages incomplete. Includes records on salt salmon production, 1895-1939, salt herring production, licences issued by racial origin and type of fishing, 1922-1937, tariff papers and invoices,1933, and an Inquiry in Vancouver into Japanese owned Property, December 1942(in Japanese)
Photographs of prewar fishing and impounding Japanese vessels during World War II.
ULM1/NABATA1/NABATA2

Kimura, T.Y.
Photocopies, 8 pages, 1942, 1965-1966.
"Notice to enemy aliens", 1942, and two letters concerning the activities of the Maple Leaf Cultural Association, 1965-1966.
ULM1/NABATA1

Kinoshita, W.
Five pictures of Slocan Camp, 1946?

NABATA2

Knowlton, Willson Edmond, d.1982,
Collector.
Willson Knowlton collection - 1858-1884.
Textual records. 1 cm.
The collection consists of photocopies of legal and financial documents including receipts, promissory notes, orders, agreements which relate to the business transactions of Kwong Lee and Company, Sansum Copper Mining Company and the Grouse Creek Flume Company.
BCARCH/UBC

Kobayashi, Peter.
Photocopies, 139 p. 1942.
Records of the activities of the All Kelowna Society(in Japanese).
ULM1/NABATA1

Kobayashi, Shogo.
Personal documents relating to his education and a diary describing school life at the Lemon Creek Camp, 1945. Photographs of Lemon Creek High School.
ULMl/NABATA1/NABATA2

Kubota, Sanosuke.
World War I Legion picnic, 1914-1932.
NABATA2

Lee Family.
Lee Family fonds,1895-1939. 2m.
After emigrating from China in 1892, Lee Thung secured his first job as kitchen help at Victoria's Empress Hotel. He later moved to Vancouver and became one of the most prominent Chinese businessmen in the community. He founded the Lee Yun Company, acquired considerable real estate holdings and constructed a number of Chinatown buildings. Lee Thung also contracted with the fishing industry to provide Chinese labour to the canneries. His son, Lee Kepment, became principal manager of the business until its demise in the late 1920s. After serving as court interpreter, he became manager of KamYan Jan Sausage Company in the early 1930s. He was prominent in Chinese Liberal politics.
The fonds consist of financial records associated with the various business activities of Lee Thung and Lee Kepment.

Louie, H.Y.(Lei Hsuei-yi).
Vancouver, wholesale grocer.
Four silk rolls containing an eulogy to H.Y.Louie(in Chinese).
ULM1/UBC3/BCARCH

MacKenzie, Norman Archibald MacRae.
President of the University of British Columbia.
Papers.
Include an unpublished biography of MacKenzie. MacKenzie linked to Institute of Pacific Relations.

Maeda, Genzo.
Tete Jaune Road Camp, # 24.
NABATA2

Maple Leaf Cultural Association.
Photographs of Slocan, Lemon Creek and Angler,Ontario Camps.
NABATA2

Miller, Jessie M., 1910-1974.
66 hand-tinted lantern slides, 25 cm.
Show Tokyo street life of 1930s, missionary summer resort at Nojiri-ko, and activities of Miller.
MITCHELL

Miyasaka, Chiyoko.
Papers, 1 cm., 1940s, 1956.
Mimeographed material relating to activities of the Japanese Canadian Citizens Association on behalf of Japanese Canadians after World War II; including the Constitution of the Vancouver Chapter of the Japanese Canadian Citizens' League, submission to theRoyal Commission on Japanese Property entered by the National Japanese Canadian Citizens Association, brief re: Repatriation of Japanese Canadians submitted by the Cooperative Committee on Japanese Canadians, Submission to the Prime Minsiter and Members of the Government in the matter of Japanese Canadian Economic Losses Arising from Evacuation entered by the National Japanese Canadian Citizens Association,1950, and Submision to the Premier of British Columbia and members of the governemt in the matter of certain restrictive enactments and regulations affecting Canadian Citizens of Japanese ancestry by the National Japanese Canadian Citizens Association, 1949, clippings relating to repatriation; photographs and a copy of a drama in Japanese, ca. 1956.
ULM4/NABATA1

Miyazaki, Masajiro.
Lillooet, osteopath.
Original, l0 cm., photocopies, 2.5 cm., 1926-1975.
Draft memoirs and related correspondence, 1974-1974; vital statistics of Japanese in British Columbia and printed surveys, 1926-1940, correspondence, memoranda, notes and lists, relating to the village of Lillooet and East Lillooet settlement, 1945-1973; clippings 1938-1974. photocopies of survey reports, 1935, 1938; an address by Sherwood Lett on legal disabilities of the Japanese in Canada, 1934; and "The Japanese contribution to Canada", 1940, published by the Canadian Japanese Association.
Correspondence, notes and clippings relating to his various experiences in sixty years in Canada, records of the Canadian Japanese Association, 1935-1940, records of the Kaidema club, and agenda of meeting of committee to combat the boycott of Japanese goods, 1934.
Group photographs with names included, of 1924-1939 University of British Columbia student clubs
ULM1/NABATA2

Murakami, J. Shingo.
Print of 9th Vancouver Japanese Canadian Citizens Association picnic with **Nippon Maru** cadets and crew as guests, June 1958 print of Honourable Shigeru Yoshida, Prime Minister of Japan, with Norman MacKenzie, University of British Columbia President

and Honourable Sherwood Lett, University of British Columbia Chancelor in front of Dr.Inazo Nitobe's memorial stone lantern on University of British Columbia campus.
Prints of Prince and Princess Chichibu at the Hotel Vancouver, Japanese Garden,University of British Columbia and Japanese Language School, Vancouver 1937.
Print of Crown Prince Akihito of Japan in front of Old Administration building,University of British Columbia,1953.
NABATA2

Nakano, Ujo.
Photocopies, 60 pages, undated.
Reminiscences relating to his activities(in Japanese) and excerpts from his book, **The Collected Works of Ujo Nakano**, pp. 186-294, describing his experiences during World War II.
Photographs of Pt. Hammond, Steveston Strawberry Fram and Greenwood, 1914-1943.
ULM1/NABATA1/NABATA2

Naser, Richard.
Japanese Canadian Evacuation Questionnaire, 1975. 1 cm.
Richard Naser(B.A. 1974) was a student in the University of British Columbia Department of History who used a questionnaire as part of his History 404 project about Japanese-Canadians and World War II. Materials consist of eighteen completed questionnaires, each posing a series of twelve questions about the World War II treatment of Japanese-Canadians and World War II.
BCARCH/UBC2

National Japanese Canadian Citizens Association Collection.
Photocopies, 15 cm., 1909-1961.
Constitution, by-laws, declaration, 1909, and extraordinary resolution, 1923, of the Canadian Japanese Association; minutes of the Vancouver chapter of the Japanese Canadian Citizen's League, 1936-1949, material concerning the 500 Club, a branch of the J.C.C.S.; papers concerning the Skeena Fisherman's Association, 1929-1932, 1939-1942; constitution, by-laws, correspondence and records of the Camp and Mill Workers Federal Labour Union no. 31, Vancouver and vicinity, undated, 1940-1942; and reminiscences of thirty entrants to the N.J.C.C.A. history contest on various topics. Material in both Japanese and English.
ULM1

Nemoto, M.
Photographs of camp life.
NABATA2:

Nishikihama, Konosuke.
Photocopies. 216 p., undated.
Copies of five notebooks in Japanese of his reminiscences; childhood and youth, manhood memoirs of World War II; youth to old age and the Canada Mio Villagers Association and Mio public hall. Mr. Nishikihama was a fisherman from Steveston and the notebooks refer to his activities.
ULM4/NABATA1

Nishi, Erik.
Photographs of Slocan City and New Denver.
NABATA2

Nishimura, T.
Copies of five letters pertaining to T.Nishimura's search for employment after the evacuation of Japanese Canadians from British Columbia's coast, March 1942-April 1943.
NABATA1

Norman, E. Herbert, 1909-1957.
E.Herbert Norman fonds - 1941-1950.
Textual records. 26 cm. 1 film.
E.Herbert Norman was born in Japan to missionary parents. He was educated by his mother, and then attended the Canadian Academy at Kobe. Ill with tuberculosis in 1926, he returned to Canada where he finished his senior matriculation in Ontario in 1928. He received his B.A. from the University of Toronto in 1933, and then completed a second B.A. in classics in 1935, his M.A. at Harvard in 1937 and his Ph.D. in 1940. Norman joined the External Affairs Department and was posted to Tokyo in 1940. He was interned after the Japanese entry into World War II but returned to Canada in 1942. Following World War II Norman served as Canada's highest ranking diplomat in Japan. In 1953 Norman was made High Commissioner to New Zealand and was then sent to Egypt in 1956. Allegations of Norman's communist sympathies led him to commit suicide in 1957.
The fonds consists of business and personal correspondence, clippings, ephemera, a black and white film of E.Herbert Norman's Award Presentation, manuscripts, legal documents pertaining to his published works, speeches, conference papers by Japanese scholars and miscellaneous Japanese material. Inventory available.
BCARCH/UBC

Norman family.
Norman family fonds - 1922-1986.
Textual records, 13 cm., 31 photographs.
Howard Norman was born in Japan and after graduating from the University of Toronto he studied to become a minister. Ordained in 1931, he returned to Japan where he served until 1941. Norman was minister at St.George's United Church(Vancouver) from 1941 to 1947 during which time he was very active on behalf of Japanese Canadians. After returning to Japan in 1947 where he served in various capacities, Norman retired to Canada in 1972.
The fonds consists of correspondence (including 15 items of general correspondence from Herbert Norman to family members while growing up in Japan, 1922-1927)between E.Herbert Norman and his family(1922-1957), Norman's will and photographs of him and other family members. There are also articles about his career

and other biographical information gathered for tributes after his death. The fonds also includes material generated by Howard Norman.
Inventory available.
BCARCH/UBC

Nosaka, Hideichi, 1894-1973.
Hope. Labourer in forest products industry.
Documents, notebooks, diaries and printed material in Japanese, relating to his activities in Canada. Much of the material relates to his efforts to become a member of the Roman Catholic Church.
ULM/NABATA1

Odlum, Victor Wentworth, 1880-
Soldier.
Original, 61 cm., undated, 1910, 1940's.
Clippings relating to his activities during World War II, an address relating to Asian immigration, 1910.
ULM1

Ogata, Dye.
Group photograph of staff and students of the Japanese Language School of the Royal Canadian Army, August 1945. Most of the persons depicted were identified by Mr.Roy Ito on an annotated photocopy in the Japanese Canadian Manuscript Collection, Box 49, Folder 1. Clippings concerning the school, letters from United States and Canadian officials concerning Mr. Ogata's military service and permission for his wife to join him in Vancouver.
NABATA1/NABATA2

Oikawa, Beatrice.
Japanese tennis club, including Mrs. Oikwaa.
NABATA2

Omachi, Kitazo.
Film, 8 mm film, less than minute, shows a parade related to the Japanese Festival,Vancouver,1937-1938.
NABATA1

Ono, Yoshio.
Cumberland. Minister.
Original, 12 cm., 1942-1943.
Diary of letters pertaining to his work at the Hastings Park Clearing Station in the evacuation of Japanese from the West Coast, lists of residents of Fanny Bay, Cumberland, Royston, Oyster Bay, Union Bay; letters pertaining to the Tashme Camp, British Columbia, including lists of names of people in the camp, participants in camp organizations, and letter with the Spanish vice-consul in Vancouver about conditions in the camp.
ULM1

Osborne, Tom.
Photographs of the Kishi Boatworks in Richmond. Two photographs of the shed and two photographs of the slipway.
NABATA2

Oyagi, Chukichi.
Photocopies, 119 pages, undated, 1942-1946.
Documents and notices relating to the evacuation of the Japanese from the West Coast, problems of repatriation and civil rights, and a plan to go to Switzerland; papers relating to activities at the Lemon Creek Camp High School.
ULM1

Phillips, N.D.Blagdon.
Black and white, 149 photographs, 1907-1932.
Trains, railroads and ships in India, and other places.
SEIFRIED

Pitt Meadows Japanese Farmers' Association.
Pitt Meadows Japanese Farmers' Association fonds - 1937-1942.
Textual records. 39 cm.
The fonds consists of correspondence, financial records, receipts, invoices, printed material, and related items pertaining to the activities of the Pitt Meadows Japanese Farmers' Association(1937-1942) and the Canadian Japanese Association in Vancouver. There are references to the Japanese Language School and the town of Mission, as well as printed material pertaining to the Sino-Japanese War.
BCARCH/UBC

Rafi-zaideh, H.
Author.
Original, .5 cm., 1973.
Typescript, "A letter to your majesty from one of your countrymen relating to Iranian affairs and the Shah's psychological behaviour".
ULM1

Sakai, Shizuo.
Photograph of an association of Japanese Canadian ladies in Vancouver. Originally taken in front of the Japanese Buddhist Church in Vancouver, 1920.
NABATA2

Sasaki, S.
Photographs of 1937 visit of Prince and Princess Chichibu. Detention camp and camp life.
NABATA2

Sato, T.
Vancouver. Principal, Japanese Language School.
Photocopies, 7.5 cm., undated.
Reminiscences about Powell Street, Vancouver, during the evacuation of the Japanese from the West Coast in novelette form and clippings dealing with the Japanese Language School and Mr.Sato(in Japanese).
ULM1/NABATA1

Shimizu, Kosaburo, 1892-1962.
Photocopies, 3.4 metres.
Kosaburo Shimizu was born in Japan and emigrated to British Columbia in 1907. He was ordained a minister of the United Church in 1926. He worked in Vancouver through the 1920s and 1930s to build up and reinforce Japanese Christian fellowship. Shimizu devoted much of his efforts to bridging the growing rifts between the first and second generation Japanese Canadians and between the Anglo-Saxon Canadians and the Japanese

Canadians. During World War II Shimizu was relocated by the Federal Government to the internment camp at Kalso, British Columbia. In 1945 he was transferred to Toronto where he organized the United Church's work in the Church of all Nations.
The fonds consists of diaries(1909-1961), notebooks, copies of sermons and miscellaneous materials related to Shimizu's work in various Japanese churches in British Columbia and Ontario.
BCARCH/UBC/ULM1

Shimizu, Kunio.
Halford Wilson brief on the Oriental situation, 1938. Legal status of Japanese in Canada in 1936, a collection of statutes and law cases which effect Japanese in Canada.

Shimizu, Suzu.
Personal documents including a school certificate from Japan, Nagano prefecture, passport from the Japanese government, and other Meiji documents including a will in Japanese.
NABATA1

Shimoda, Yukio.
Original, 21 pages, 1942-1943.
Manuscript diary relating to his evacuation from the Lower Mainland, British Columbia, 28 March-27 April 1942(in English), and a typescript of an interview between inspector Saul and Major Barbara of the Registrar General of Enemy Aliens, with internees Masaru Sora, Hideo Takahashi, and Shimoda at the Angler Internment Camp, Ontario, 6 October 1943, relating to the mass evacuation of Japanese Canadians frm the West Coast of Canada.
ULM2/NABATA1

Shimpo, Mitsuru.
Textual records. 4.7 metres. 1960-1983. 8 sound tape reels.
Mitsuru Shimpo was born in Manchuria. He graduated from the International Christian University in Japan in 1957 and then received his M.A. in Sociology from the Tokyo Educational College. After his graduation, Shimpo returned to International Christian University as a lecturer(1959-1962). He then emigrated to British Columbia and completed an M.A. in Sociology at the University of British Columbia in 1963. Shimpo then worked as a researcher sociologist at the Center for Community Studies at the University of Saskatchewan. After returning to the University of British Columbia to pursue doctoral studies, Shimpo went to Japan to carry out fieldwork. He subsequently held positions at the Universities of Alberta and Waterloo. Shimpo has authored a number of books which focus on the sociological aspects of native Indians in Canada and Japanese Canadians.
The fonds consist of correspondence(1960-1983), scrapbooks(1970-1977), and diaries(1962-1976). In addition there are eight sound recordings(1971) Includes 3 cm of transcripts of interviews with about 65 Japanese-Canadians on various topics and sound recordings relating to the Powell Street riots, 1907, immigration in the 1920's and 1930's, the Showa Club, and the evacuation of the Japanese Canadians from the West Coast to various areas, including the Lemon Creek Camp and other internment and road camps. The sound recording on the Lemon Creek Camp has been recorded in English.
Photographs of Bon Festival, Steveston, and of 1971 remains of Tashme Camp.
BCARCH/UBC/ULM1/NABATA2

Shiomi, Richard Alan, 1947-
Textual records, 40 cm., 1977-1982.
R.A.Shiomi, writer and amateur musician, was born in Toronto and received his B.A. from the University of Toronto in 1970. He afterwards came to British Columbia to study at Simon Fraser University. From 1972-1974 he travelled the world, returning to Vancouver in 1975 to teach at Langara College until 1976. In 1977, as a member of the Japanese Canadian Citizens' Association, he participated in the Japanese Canadian Centennial. He was also involved in producing audio-visual material about Japanese-Canadian history and the history and goals of the Elizabeth Fry Society. From 1980 to 1981 he lived in San Francisco, but afterwards returned to Vancouver. He was a member of the Powell Street Review and in 1980 he was co-editor of the anthology **Inalienable Rice**.
The fonds consists of correspondence and writings of R.A.Shiomi and material relating to the activities of and Shiomi's participation in the Japanese Canadian Citizens' Association. There is some material on the issue of the internment of Japanese Canadians during World War II.
BCARCH/UBC

Shirakawa, Masanao.
Correspondence and notes on the funeral of Shirakawa, and the Maple Leaf Cultural Association, 1965, which helped transfer his ashes from Canada to Japan.
NABATA1

Smith, Anne M.
Anne Smith funds - 1937-1967.
Textual records, 1.6 metres.
Anne Smith graduated from the University of British Columbia in 1921. She later received a B.L.S. from the University of Washington and M.A. in Library Science from the University of Michigan. Smith joined the University of British Columbia Library as a reference librarian in 1930. She served as acting University Librarian in 1949 and 1951. Interest in international library cooperation led her to accept a term appointment to teach Library Science in Japan.
The fonds consists of office and personal correspondence and subject files that span much of Smith's long career with the University of British Columbia Library
Finding aid available.
BCARCH/UBC1

University of British Columbia – Special Collections • 45

Sugiyama, I.
Comments on the Japanese right to vote and other matters. Newspaper clipping on I.Sugiyama as the only Japanese with the right to vote in Vancouver.
NABATA1

Summerland Japanese Farmers Association Collection.
Financial records and notes 1917-1935, including regulations and lists of members.
NABATA1

Tagashira, Rinkichi.
Vancouver.
Photocopies, 5 cm., 1945-1955.
Correspondence to various benefit associations, insurance companies and the Custodian relating to legal matters and financial settlements owing to the evacuation of the Japanese Canadians from the West Coast.
ULM1

Tahara, Mits.
Photographs of Road Camp.
NABATA2

Takashima, Shizue.
Original, 169 pages, photocopies, 1 cm., 1942-1948.
Typescripts(edited) of "A child in prison camp," 169 pages, relating to a young girl's memories of the evacuation of the Japanese Canadians from the Lower Mainland of British Columbia, 1942-1945; news clippings of articles dealing with relocation and deportation, 55 pages.
ULM2/NABATA1

Takimoto, Shichiro.
Photographs of Tashme Kindergarten, road camp workers in the Rockies, aerial view of Tashme.
NABATA2

Tanaka, Jisaburo.
Photocopies, 1 cm., 1942.
Letters and notes relating to the evacuation, report of Paul D. Murphy about his Ottawa trip on the Japanese evacuation, 1942; notes on the education question during the evacuation; and biography of O.E. Kotaro.
ULM1/NABATA1

Tanaka, Toshikazu.
Photocopies, 12 cm., 1942-1946.
Letters to and from T. Tanaka relating to his position as leader of the Petawawa Internment Camp, Angler, Ontario, 1942-1946. Letters from family members describing their life in the Kaslo and Tashme camps of British Columbia, 1944-1945.
Photographs of Angler Internment Camp, Ontario.
ULM1/NABATA2

Taneda Collection.
History of the Steveston Buddhist Church, 1967(In Japanese).
NABATA1

Tashme camp, Tashme, British Columbia.
Original, 1.2 cm., 1943.
Copies of the **Tashme Camp News,** a camp newspaper in Japanese.
ULM1/NABATA1

Tibetan Refugee Aid Society of Canada.
Original, 3.8 metres., photocopies, 1963-1979.
The Tibetan Refugee Aid Society was founded by Professor and Mrs. George Woodcock and became an official society in British Columbia in 1962. The Woodcocks became concerned about the welfare of the children of the exiled Tibetans in India and developed individual sponsorships and collective projects. It later transformed its program to include broader and longer-term projects. The name of the Society was changed in 1990 to the Trans-Himalayan Aid Society. The fonds consist of records detailing the work of the Society from its foundation, including its projects in North and South India, Nepal and Bhutan. In addition to correspondence, minutes and financial statements, there are journals and other printed materials pertaining to the Tibetan Refuge Aid Society, including reports by the Canadian International Development Association, copies of the **Tibet Society Bulletin**, the **UNHRCV Bulletin, The Tibetan Review** and **UNICEF News**.
Inventory available.
BCARCH/UBC/ULM2

Tomiye, K.
Photographs of Lemon Creek Camp, and Yellowhead Road Camp, ca.1942-1945.
NABATA2

Tsuyuki, U.
Correspondence(two letters with Mori Genichi, a repatriated Japanese in Fukuoka prefecture to U.Tsuyuki in Shinagawa prefecture. Discuss hardships in Canada and post-war Japan.
NABATA1

Turner, George Frederick, 1882-1975.
Diary.
Peking from November 12, 1911 to May 12, l912, when Turner was involved in construction work there.
MITCHELL

Uchibori, Shigeichi.
Photocopies, 5 cm., 1942-1946.
Letters to S. Uchibori at Slocan from the Citizenship Defence Committee in Toronto and persons from Tashme, Greenwood, and Lemon Creek dealing generally with the situation in the camps at that time and specifically with the "voluntary repatriation." Notes from standing committee meetings and records of the Slocan Mass Evacuation Society, undated.
ULM1

Umezuki, Chiyo.
Vancouver, editor and union official.
Photocopies, 17 cm., undated, 1942.
Letters, manuscripts and clippings relating to his

columns in **The New Canadian** including columns on the labour movement and clippings of Retsu Suzuki, founder of the Camp and Mill Workers Federal Labour Union, and personal letters to Umezuki pertaining to the evacuation and relocation of Japanese from the West Coast.
ULM1

Uyeda, Umeo.
Two unpublished essays, on migration from British Columbia to Quebec and Japanese in Canada, evacuation and relocation.
NABATA1

Uyede, Jitsuo
Photographs of Prince Fushimi in Vancouver,1907, the Japanese training ship **Soya**, 1909, and the Japanese training ship **Aso**,1909.
NABATA2

Uyeno, Mrs. Yoshi.
Photographs of a farm at Lillooet, British Columbia,1942. Mr. Toyokichi Uyeno aboard a fishing boat, ca. 1930-1941.
NABATA2

Vancouver Japanese Canadian Citizens Association.
First annual picnic, 1950.
NABATA2

Vancouver Vietnam Action Committee.
Vancouver Vietnam Action Committee fonds - 1966-1972.
Textual records, 60 cm.
The Vancouver Vietnam Day Committee was formed in1966 through a coalition of several organizations that opposed the Vietnam war. A coodinating committee was established in1968 to establish addtional committees and organize demonstrations. A schism in the movement in 1969 led to the formation of the Vancouver Committee to End the War in Vietnam, which turned its assets over to the Vancouver Vietnam Action Committee later that year.
The fonds consists of minutes, correspondence, financial records and printed material from the various organizations opposed to the war inVietnam.
Inventory available
BCARCH/UBC

Wakabayashi, Jisaburo.
Photocopies, 1 cm., 1940s.
Copy of an album(correspondence, documents and photographs)created by J. Wakabayashi that pertains mainly to his activities as spokesman for the Japanese nationals at the Roseberry Camp, British Columbia. Some post-camp correspondence pertains to property settlements.
ULM4/NABATA1

Wakayama Group Vancouver.
Photographs with numbers included.
NABATA2

Whaun, Thomas Moore, 1914-1984.
Thomas Moore Whaun fonds,1914-1984, 26 cm.
Whaun emigrated toCanada in 1907 and became a citizen in 1950. He worked in the newspaper industry as an advertising manager for the **Canada Morning News** and the **New Republic Daily**. He is known for his nation-wide letter writing protest against the Chinese Exclusion Act. Whaun was the first non-white resident of West Vancouver and the first Chinese Canadian graduate of the University of British Columbia.
The fonds consists almost entirely of correspondence with people such as John Diefenbaker, Hugh Keenleyside, and Douglas Jung, as well as family and friends. The correspondence is generally accompanied by newspaper clippings pertaining to the correspondent or the situation. Diaries and a few photographs are also included.
Inventory
BCARCH/UBC3

Women's Missionary Society of the Methodist Church, Japanese Auxiliary.
Textual records, 2 cm., 1911-1925.
Minutes and membership rolls.
BCARCH/UBC

Wong, Soon Sien, d. 1971.
Textual records. 8 metres, 1907-1971.
Foon Sie Wong was a spokesman for the Chinese Canadian community in Vancouver. In 1945 he advocated the granting of the franchise to Chinese Canadians after they bcame subject to the World War II military draft. On many occaisions, he travelled to Ottawa to pursue the rights of Chinese Canadians, particularly urging the lifting of the strictures on Chinese immigration which often separate families from one another. He also served for a time on the Vancouver Consultative Committee on Redevelopment, and throughout his life, fought unflaggingly to end discrimination against, not just Chinese Canadians, but all minority groups.
The fonds consist primarily of clippings and articles relating to international affairs, Chinese customs preserved in Canadian life in Vancouver's China Town and social and political problems confronted by Chinese Canadians. The fonds also includes correspondence as well as printed and published material.
Inventory available
BCARCH

Yamada, Mary.
Photograph of Japanese Laundress' Association of Canada, July 1936.
NABATA2

Yamaga, Yasutaro.
Original, 1.5 metres, 1906-1969.
Photocopies, 10 cm., 1955-1965.
Born in Japan,Yasutaro Yamaga came to British Columbia in 1908. After working as a labourer, he purchased ten acres of land near Haney, British

Columbia. Yamaga led the Japanese Farmer's Union in the Fraser Valley. After World War II he moved to Ontario, where at Beamsville he established the first home for Japanese Canadian senior citizens(Nipponia Home) in Canada.
Typescript, "My footsteps in B.C.," in Japanese, annual reports and church bulletins from the Hamilton United Church; and agenda, addresses, and statistics about the United Church at the Japanese Conference, Winnipeg, 1962.
Records, correspondence, reports, diaries, manuscripts and clippings relating to the Haney Agricultural Association, Fraser Valley Japanese Language School, and the Nipponia Home, Beamsville, Ontario. Most of the papers relating to his various interests and activities as a leader of the Japanese Farmers' Union in Fraser Valley and a founder of the Japanese Senior Citizens' Home(Nipponia Home).
ULM 1/ULM2/NABATA1

Yamakami, Mrs. Onobu.
Photographs of His Imperial Japanese Majesty's **Azuma** and His Imperial Japanese Majesty's **Yakumo** in First Narrows, Vancouver.
NABATA2

Yamamoto, Masaharu,
Photographs of Sandon Camp, Malakwa Road Camp, Bay Farm Camp and Kamloops BuddhistChurch.
NABATA2

Yokota, Junichiro.
Photographs of group activities at Slocan camp.
NABATA2

Yoshioka, Rev.
Photocopies, 1 cm. 1933-1939.
Diary pertaining to ministry and activities(in Japanese).
ULM1

Young, Albert Collection.
1926 article on the redirection of fishing licences among Japanese and related material, on a 1937 brief opposing franchise in province of British Columbia, by Tom Reid, M.P. Collection also includes Telephone Directory of Japanese at Tashme, 1942, a Telephone Directory of Japanese in British Columbia, 1941,
NABATA1

Audio tapes

Mackenzie, N.A.M., Impressions of Japan. 20 March 1957. UBC 126.

Wilson, Tuzo J., A scientist in China. 20 March 1972. UBC 160.

Holland,William L., The founding and early years of the Institute of Pacific Relations. UBC 203-204.

Woodside, Alex, China and Viet Nam, the new era. Vancouver Institute lecture. 1977. UBC 460

Wilson, J.Tuzo, Earthquakes in China and elsewhere. Vancouver Institute. 19 February 1977.UBC 462

Holland, William, Interviewed by John Howes. 21 April 1980. UBC 924.

Dalai Lama of Tibet, The Buddhist view of reality. Vancouver Institute lecture. 23 October 1980

Dalai Lama of Tibet, Tibet in the Modern world; a spiritual contribution. UBC auditorium, 24 October 1980. UBC 945.

Dore, Ronald, The inner mechanism of Japan, Inc. 26 September 1981. UBC 984. No copying.

Franklin, Ursula,The interplay of technology and society, the case of ancient China. Vancouver Institute lecture. UBC 1082. 19 November 1983. No copying.

Franklin, Ursula, The organization of Bronze production in early China. Cecil and Ira Green lecture. 17 November 1982, UBC 1085.

Franklin, Ursula, The Chineseness of Chinese technology. Cecil and Ira Green lecture. 18 November 1983, UBC 1086.

Tanaka, Hideo, The role of law in Japan, comparisons with West. Vancouver Institute lecture, 15 September 1984, UBC 1108

Tanaka, Hideo, Legal equality in Japan. Cecil Green lecture. 17 September 1984, UBC 1124.

Moltke, Wilhelm von, Guyana in the 1960's. 26 September 1979. UBC 1166.

Moltke, Wilhelm von, Istanbul in the 1970's. 3 October 1979. UBC 1167

Akune, Misaye, Japanese community in the Lower Mainland during the first half of the 20th century, Alison Minto interviewing. 1953. UBC 1212.

Mizuguchi, Yutaka, His experiences prior to and following the 2nd World War. Ron Schell interviewing. 1953. UBC 1218.

Barthling, Hedwig, The Japanese internment in Southern Alberta. Kathleen Brennan interviewing. 1984. UBC 1225

Uyeda, Roy, The internment of Japanese in British Columbia with commentary. David Driesum interviewing. 1984, UBC 1233

Theses and dissertations

Adam-Moodley, Kogila.
Resistance and accommodation in a racial polity, responses of Indian South Africans. Ph.D. dissertation 1977.

Alam, Muhammed Mustafa.
Problems of size-tenure structure in Bangladesh agriculture and prospects of a land reform programme in developing the rural economy of the country. Ph.D. dissertation 1980.

Ames, Roger Thomas.
An exegesis on the 'Ta tsung shih' chapter of the Chuang tzu. M.A. thesis 1973.
CT

Anderson, Kay.
East as West, place, state and the institutionalization of myth in Vancouver's Chinatown, 1880-1980. Ph.D. dissertation 1987.
NL

Annamma, Joy.
Accommodation and cultural persistence, the case of the Sikhs and the Portuguese in the Okanagan Valley of British Columbia. Ph.D. dissertation 1982.

Ansley, Clive Malcolm.
Hai Jui dismissed from office, its role in the great proletarian cultural revolution. M.A. thesis 1968.
CT

Apandi, Aca Sughandy.
The impact assessment of tourism development on agricultural land use, a case study of the impact of traditional village land use patterns in Bali. M.Sc. thesis 1980.
NL

Arbour, Kenneth F.
The export of British Columbia lumber products to Japan in the coming decade, cracking a hard nut. M.A. thesis 1980.
NL.

Arnott, Norman Montyque.
Pulmonary tuberculosis among South East Asian refugee immigrants to British Columbia. M.Sc. thesis 1982.
NL

Arntzen, Sonja Elaine.
The poetry of the "Kyounshu" "Crazy Cloud Anthology" of Ikkyu Sojun. Ph.D. dissertation 1979.

Arntzen, Sonja Elaine.
A presentation of the poet Ikkyu with translations from the Kyounshu Mad Cloud Anthology. M.A. thesis 1970.
CT

Arshad, Fatimah B.
The etiology of iron deficiency anemia during pregnancy among rural mothers in Malaysia. Ph.D. dissertation 1984.

Bailey, Paul John
Popular education in China,1904-1919, new ideas and developments. Ph.D. dissertation 1982.

Bajpai, Kanti Prasad.
An inquiry into colonial disengagement, the colonial delegation to India, March to June 1946. M.A. thesis 1979.
NL

Bakony, Edward Gregory Joseph.
Economic factors contributing to the outbreak of war in Asia. M.A. thesis 1948.
CT

Barker, John.
Maisin Christianity, an ethnography of the contemporary religion of a seaboard Melanesian people. Ph.D. dissertation 1985.
NL

Barnett, Ronald Allen.
Comparative studies in Homeric epic and other heroic narrative, especially Sanskrit and Celtic, with special reference to the theory of oral improvisation by means of formulary language. Ph.D. dissertation 1979.

Basham, Ardythe Maude Roberta.
Army service and social mobility, the Mahars of the Bombay Presidency, with comparisons with the Bene Israel and Black Americans. Ph.D. dissertation 1986.
NL

Bent, Colin George.
Input output analysis and the first Malaysia plan, 1969-1970. M.A thesis 1970.
CT

Berger, Mark Theodore.
From commerce to conquest, the dynamics of early British Imperial expansion into Bengal. M.A. thesis 1983.
NL

Bhargava, Jagdish Prasad.
Urbanization, migration and housing, a case study for India. M.A. thesis 1964.
CT

Bishop, Mary Fraser.
From "left" to "right", a perspective of the role of volunteers in family planning in the West and in South Asia. M.A. thesis 1971.
CT

Blackaller, David William.
The significance of "Maya" in Indian philosophy. M.A. thesis 1938.
CGT

Bose, Mandakranta.
Supernatural intervention in Kalidasa's **Abhijnanakuntala** and Shakespeare's **The Tempest**. M.A. thesis 1979.
CT

Braun, Nickolai G.
Community ideology and the ideology of community, the Orokaiva case. M.A. thesis 1982.
NL
Papua New Guinea

Brinkley, Taylor Francis.
Chi tsang. M.A. thesis 1972.
CT

Brosnan, Vivienne.
The International Control Commission for Vietnam, the diplomatic and military context. M.A. thesis 1975.
CT

Brown, Janice Carole Lucas.
The celebration of struggle, a study of the major works of Hayashi Fumiko(Japan). Ph.D. dissertation 1985.

Brown, Janice Carole Lucas.
The static and the dynamic, a study of the hidden world of Ibuse Masuji. M.S. thesis 1980.
CT

Brown, William Nimmo.
Saisei Itchi, the identity of religion and government in the early Meiji years, 1867-1872. M.A. thesis 1984.
NL

Bryant, Daniel Joseph.
The high T'ang poet Meng Hao-jan, studies in biography and textual history. Ph.D dissertation 1978.

Bult, Timothy Paul.
Schema labelling applied to hand-printed Chinese character recognition. M.Sc. thesis 1987.
NL

Calabia, Gerardo S.
The development of a land use data bank for community and regional planning, a case of the Philippines. M.Sc. thesis 1968.
CT

Calder, John Gilchrist.
The political determinants of fertility control policy in South Asia. M.A. thesis 1982.
NL

Calkowski, Marcia Stephanie.
Power, charisma, and ritual curing in a Tibetan community in India. Ph.D. dissertation 1986.
NL

Campbell, Michael Graeme.
The Sikhs of Vancouver, a case study in minority-host relations. M.A. thesis 1978.
CT

Carter, Rosalie Gale.
Takamura Itsue, social activist and feminist theorist, 1921-31. M.A. thesis 1982.
NL

Cassin, Agnes Marguerite.
Class and ethnicity, the social organization of working class East Indian immigrants in Vancouver. M.A. thesis 1978.
CT

Catliff, Christopher Edward.
Japan's government and steel industry policies towards coking coal procurement, the implications of industrial restructuring for the Northeast coal project. Ph.D. dissertation, 1986.
NL

Chan, Marjorie Kit Man.
Zhong Shan phonology, a synchronic and diachronic analysis of a Yue(Cantonese) dialect. M.A. thesis 1980.
NL

Chandra, Rajesh.
Industrialization in Fiji. Ph.D. dissertation 1985.
NL

Charlebois, Carol Ann Ruth.
An application of Rosenau's pre-theory to the Sino-Indian and Sino-Burmese boundary disputes. M.A. thesis 1969.
CT

Chen, Lijuan.
Urban housing policy and housing commercialization in socialist countries, China and Hungary. M.Sc. thesis 1988.
NL

Chen, Robert Shan-mu.
Aspects of cyclic myth in Chinese and Western literature. M.A. thesis 1978.
CT

Cho, George Chin Hust.
Residential patterns of the Chinese in Vancouver, British Columbia. M.A. thesis 1970.
CT

Chung, Frances Po-chu.
Rural urban migration, a case study of the People's Republic of China. M.A. thesis 1977.
CT

Chung, Rosamond C.
Underemployment and the Chinese immigrant of former professional status, a qualitative exploratory study. M.A. thesis 1988.
NL

Clarke, Robert Ebersole.
Land and neighbourhood as features of Malay urbanism. Ph.D. dissertation 1976.

Crone, Donald Kendall.
Dependency, diversification and regionalism, the Association of South East Asian Nations. Ph.D. dissertation 1981.

Curmi, Charles Edward Stuart.
American efforts to raise China to great power status, 1942-1945. M.A thesis 1972.
CT

Darling, Elizabeth Gillian.
Merit feasting among the Kalash Kafirs of North Western Pakistan. M.A. thesis 1979.
CT

Darmono, Juanita Amanda.
A.S.E.A.N.'s diplomatic strategy after the Vietnamese invasion of Kampuchea. M.A. thesis 1987.
NL

Darrough, Masako Naganuma.
Intertemporal allocation of consumption, savings and leisure, an application using Japanese data. Ph.D. dissertation 1975.

Das, Nitya Nanda.
Factors affecting timing and size of Hilsa shad(Hilsa ilisha) in Bangladesh and Pakistan. M.Sc. thesis 1985.
NL

Dehani, Amina Hatim.
Land use for rubber and rice in Malaya, 1947-1960. M.A. thesis 1962.
CT

Dhillon, Pritam Singh.
India and the Far East since 1947. M.A. thesis 1953.
CT

Dinggat, Paul Kadany Arak.
The Sarawak National Party and the interpretations of its nationalism. M.A. thesis 1979.
CT

Dionne, Francis.
The value of British Columbia's natural gas used as a liquified natural gas(LNG) for export to Japan. M.Sc. thesis 1981.
NL

Dizon, Jesus A.N.
Taman Kampung Kuantan, a study of Malay urban participation in West Malaysia. Ph.D. dissertation 1983.

Djwa, Peter Djing Kloe.
An analysis of industrial location factors with particular reference to Indonesia. M.B.A. thesis 1960.
CT

Dumdaeng, Sompong Gunavaro.
Buddhist philosophy, principles and practice. M.A. thesis 1978.
CT

Dunlap, William Devereux.
The Katyayani myth in the **Vamana Purana**(18, 39-21, 52). M.A. thesis 1976.

Duval, Jean-marc.
Japanese joint ventures in British Columbia. M.Sc. thesis 1974.
CT

Erickson, Bonnie Heather.
Prestige, power and the Chinese. M.A. thesis 1966.
CT

Farber, Carole Marie.
Prolegomenon to an understanding of the Jatra of India, the travelling popular theatre of the State of West Bengal. Ph.D. dissertation 1979.

Filteau, Carolyn Helen.
Kali worship and its implications for the study of Bengali women. M.A. thesis 1979.
CT

Fong, Grace Sieugit.
Wu Wenying and the art of Southern Sung 'Ci' poetry. Ph.D. dissertation 1984.

Fowler, Vernon Keith.
Contextual hierarchies in the Shang oracle-bone inscriptions. M.A. thesis 1984.
NL

Friesen, Heather Jean.
Help-giving sources preferred by Chinese international students. M.A. thesis 1983.
NL

Frieson, Kate G.
The rise and fall of the Cambodian revolution, the rationale for Pol Pot's Democratic Kampuchea. M.A. thesis 1986.
NL

Frisch, Matthew Ezra.
The "illumination of the Buddha" in the context of the social/philosophical milieu of the Chin-Liu Sung period. M.A. thesis 1985.
NL

Fulbright, Timothy Calhoun.
The Marching rule, a Christian revolution in the Solomon Islands. M.A. thesis 1986.
NL

Gansner, James Hill.
Agricultural development and fertility patterns in the dry zone of Sri Lanka, 1946-1971. M.A. thesis 1985.
NL

Gardner, Joanne Marie.
Construct validity of the K-ABC for Cantonese, English and Punjabi speaking Canadian children. Ed.D. dissertation 1986.
NL

Gebert, Rita Ingrid.
The Cauvery River dispute, hydrological politics in

Indian federalism. M.A. thesis 1983.
NL

Gibb, Heather R.
Re-examining Japan incorporated, Japanese coal procurement and Western Canadian coal. M.A. thesis 1984.
NL

Gilday, Edmund Theron.
Honen Shonin and the Pure Land movement. M.S. thesis 1980.
CT

Gill, Kuldip.
A Canadian Sikh wedding as a cultural performance. M.A. thesis 1982.
NL

Gill, Kuldip.
Health strategies of Indo-Fijian women in the context of Fiji. Ph.D. dissertation 1988.
NL

Gill, Naranjan Singh.
A study of the development of teacher education in India, its history, philosophy and certain modern trends and needs. M.A. thesis 1954.
CT

Godde, James Thomas.
Adjustment to less-developed country competition in some Japanese industries. Ph.D. dissertation 1983.

Goh, Ethel See Kean.
On the structure of negation in Japanese and its related problems. M.A. thesis 1975.
CT

Goh, Lek-oon.
The operator scheduling for Singapore mass transit system. M.A. thesis 1984.
NL

Golay, Jaqueline.
A study of Setsuwa literature with emphasis on the **Nihon Ryoiki**. M.A thesis 1970.
CT

Golay, Jacqueline.
Le **Shasekishu**, miroir d'une personalité, miroir d'une époque. Ph.D. dissertation 1975.

Goode, James Thomas.
Japan's postwar experience with technology transfer. M.Sc. thesis 1976.
CT

Goode, James Thomas.
Adjustment to less-developed country competition in some Japanese industries. Ph.D. dissertation 1983.
NL

Greenwood, George Blair.
The British administration of Cyprus, 1925-60. M.A. thesis 1962.
CT

Griffin, Helen Wodehouse.
The case of three paintings by Wang Meng. M.A. thesis 1968.
CT

Gruetter, Robert James.
The Kwantung peasant movement, 1922-1928. M.A. thesis 1972.
CT

Hadi, Yusuf Bin.
Planning timber supply from the forests of Peninsular Malaysia. Ph.D. dissertation 1982.

Hagiwara, Takao.
The notion of order in R.W.Emerson and Chuang tzu. M.A. thesis 1979.
CT

Hanson, Nervin Viggo.
The Trikaya, a study of the buddhology of the Early Vijnanavada school of Indian Buddhism. Ph.D. dissertation 1980.

Haq, Ziaush Shams.
Determinants of the spatial dynamics of population movements within Bangladesh. Ph.D. dissertation 1974.

Harmankaya, Nejat Cemil.
Monetary and banking system of Turkey. M.A. thesis 1957.
CT

Hasbullah, Shahul Hameed.
The fertility behaviour of Muslims of Sri Lanka. M.A. thesis 1984.
NL

Hawkey, Thora Elizabeth.
Conflict and compromise in a Japanese village. M.A. thesis 1963.
CT

Hawkins, John Noel.
The theory and practice of education in the People's Republic of China. M.A. thesis 1969.
CT

Hentschel, Klaus Gunther.
The position of the South East Asian communist parties in the Sino-Soviet dispute. M.A. thesis 1967.
CT

Herforth, Derek Dane.
Two philological studies in the Mawangdui Laozi manuscripts. M.A. thesis 1980.
NL

Herschkowitz, Linda.
The porcelain ricebowl, the revival of the urban

individual economy in the People's Republic of China. Ph.D. dissertation 1987.
NL

Hind, Joseph Winton.
Lloyd George and the Turkish question, an examination of Lloyd George's Turkish policy, 1918-1922. M.A. thesis 1979.
CT

Ho, Kwok Keung.
Science education and the medium of instruction, Chinese or English. Ed.D. dissertation 1980.

Horvat, Andrus.
The wall that Kobo built, four short stories by Abe Kobo. M.A. thesis 1971.
CT

Hosoi, Tadatoshi.
The Nagasaki naval training school in the context of Japanese-Dutch relations in the mid-nineteenth century. M.A. thesis 1979.
CT

How, Thomas Richard.
The transfer of technology of Taiwan, a look at the question of technical dependency and several factors affecting the choice of technology. M.B.A. thesis 1980.
NL

Howard, Roger William
"Grasp revolution, promote production," struggles over socialist construction in China, 1973-1978. Ph.D. dissertation 1981.

Howard-Gibbon, John Edward.
Hsu Shu-cheng and the cancellation of self government in Outer Mongolia. M.A. thesis 1971.
CT

Hsu, William Chang Nang.
Chinese education in Malaya, one dimension of the problems of Malayan nationhood. M.A. thesis 1969.
CGT

Huber, Walter Alexander.
From millenia to the millenium, an anthropological history of Bastar State. M.A. thesis 1984.
NL

Hung, Chiu-ling.
An empirical analysis of direct foreign investments in manufacturing in Hong Kong. Ph.D. dissertation 1981.

Hunter, Harriet Jean.
The Japanese Hasso Nirvana tradition of paintings, an iconological study. M.A. thesis 1986.
NL

Huque, Ahmed Shafioul.
The problem of local government reform in Rural Bangladesh, the failure of "Swanirvar Gram Sakkar." Ph.D. dissertation 1984.

Hutchinson, Harold Keith.
Dimensions of ethnic education, the Japanese in British Columbia. M.A thesis 1972.
CT

Imai, Hiroshi.
The role of case law in Japan, a comparative study of Japanese and Canadian company law. LL.M. thesis 1983.
NL

Inglis, Stephen Robert.
Creators and consecrators, a potter community in South India. Ph.D. dissertation 1984.

Ip, David Fu-keung.
The design of rural development, experiences from South China, 1949-1976. Ph.D. dissertation 1979.

Ironside, Linda L.
Chinese- and Indo-Canadian elites in Greater Vancouver, their view of education. M.A. in Education thesis 1985.
NL

Ishikawa, Shoichiro.
Electronic surveillance and the police, a comparative study of the Canadian and Japanese systems. LL.M. thesis 1987.
NL

Ishaklebbe, Mohamed Ussian.
Plantations in the development of the Sri Lanka economy. An evaluation of the dual economy approach. M.A. thesis 1980.
CT

Jacobs, Elisabeth Maria.
The Redhaired in Japan, Dutch influence on Japanese cartography, 1640-1853. M.A. thesis 1983.
NL

Jenks, Robert Darrah.
The politics of opposition in Republican China. Chiang Kai-shek and the Extraordinary Conference of 1931. M.A. thesis 1974.

Jeyaratnam, Kanagaratnam.
Racial factors in the political development of Malaya. M.A. thesis 1958.
CT

Jhappan, Carol R.
Resistance to exploitation, East Indians and the rise of the Canadian Farmworkers Union in B.C. M.A. thesis 1983.
NL

Jiang, Shougang.
Applicability of some organization behaviour theories in the People's Republic of China. M.Sc.(Bus.Admin.)

thesis 1987.
NL

Johal, Sarbjit Singh.
The Emergency and constitutional change in India. M.A. thesis 1978.
CT

Johnson, Carol Evelyn.
A history of the life of Chinese women, the development of Chinese feminism. M.A. thesis 1974.
CT

Johnstone, James Carl.
Planning in the People's Republic of China, the role of the city in creating a modern socialist society. M.A. thesis 1978.
CT

Joy, Annamma.
Accommodation and cultural persistence, the case of the Sikhs and the Portuguese in the Okanagan Valley of British Columbia. Ph.D. dissertation 1982.
NL

Judd, Ellen Ruth.
The revolution in the theatre in the People's Republic of China. M.A. thesis 1973.
CT

Judd, Ellen Ruth.
A study of directed change in Chinese literature and art. Ph.D. dissertation 1981.

Kabir, Muhammed Ghulam.
Minority politics in Bangladesh:1947-1971. M.A. thesis 1978.
CT

Kaganayakam, Chelvanayakam.
The writings of Zulfikar Ghose. Ph.D. dissertation 1985.

Kalimuthu, K. Ramanathan.
Politics of language education, a case study of West Malaysia:1930-1971. M.A. thesis 1979.
CT

Kan, Lisa.
Identification of risk groups, study of infant mortality in Sri Lanka. M.Sc. thesis 1988.
NL

Kanetkar, Raminder B.
The application of passive techniques in housing design in hot and dry climates, with special emphasis on India. M.A.S.A. thesis 1988.
NL

Kavic, Lorne John.
In search for peace and security, a study of Indian foreign policy in the Cold War. M.A. thesis 1960.
CT

Kawano, Madoka.
An analysis of cultural contents of high school English textbooks in Japan. M.A. thesis 1987.
NL

Keerawella, Gamini Bandara.
The growth of superpower naval rivalry in the Indian Ocean and Sri Lankan response. Ph.D. dissertation 1988.
NL

Kelly, Clarence William.
An examination of the T-shaped painting from the Western Han tomb no. 1 at Ma-wang-tui, Ch'ang-sha, Hunan. M.A. thesis 1979.
CT

Kent, Duncan Alexander.
The integration of politics and economics. China's search for a revolutionary model of factory organization. M.A. thesis 1977.
CT

Kim, Hye Soon.
Hedda Gabbler, a Korean translation. M.A. thesis 1987.
NL

King, Richard Oliver
A shattered mirror, the literature of the Cultural Revolution. Ph.D dissertation 1984.

King, Sallie Behn.
Tsung mi, commentary to the Hua-yan dharma-realm meditation, translated with an introduction and notes. M.A. thesis 1976.
CT

Kingscott, Anne Underhill.
A mortuary analysis of the Dawenkou Cemetery site, Shandong, China. M.A. thesis 1983.
NL

Kleeman, Terry Frederick.
A history of Ch'eng-han. M.A. thesis 1979.
CT

Kleemeier, Christine Jeanette.
A study of the modern Chinese novel, Gao Yubao and its author Gao Yubao. M.A. thesis 1981.
NL

Koch, Thomas.
Concepts of space and time in traditional China - notes towards a preective theory of culture. M.A. thesis 1978.
CT

Kreag, John Paul.
The Theravada Buddhist conceptual map of bondage and freedom. M.A. thesis 1978.
CT

Ku, Wei-ying.
The political theories of Ku Yen-wu and the Manchu conquest. Ph.D dissertation 1983.

Kuo, Chang-lu.
A study of regional peace machinery in the Pacific. M.A. thesis 1944.
CGT

Kuprovsky, Stephan George.
The practice of Chinese medicine in the contemporary urban context, herbalism in Vancouver's Chinatown. M.A. thesis 1983.
NL

Kurihara, Tamiko.
Japanese direct foreign investment in the United States and Canada by sogo shosha since 1951. Ph.D. dissertation 1986.
NL

Kwok, Kian-chow.
The tomb of Fu Hao. M.A. thesis 1984.
NL

Lai, Magdalene Claudia.
Living with diabetes, the perspectives of the Chinese elderly. M.S.N. thesis 1988.
NL

Lal, Brij.
East Indians in British Columbia:1904-1914, a historical study in growth and integration. M.A. thesis 1976.

Langrick, Helena.
An anthropological perspective on the role of Chinese trade ceramics in the prehistory of a Philippine culture. M.A. thesis 1985.
NL

Law, Louise Yi-shu.
The San Qu of Ma zhi yuan. M.A. thesis 1978.
CT

Lee, Beverly.
Strangers and sensemaking, an ethnography of Japanese housewives. M.A. thesis 1981.
NL

Lee, Ching Man.
Huang Tsun-hsien's interpretation of Meiji Japan's economic development, an early stage of China's intellectual response to modern Japan. M.A. thesis 1976.
CT

Lee, Christina Chau-ping.
Acculturation and value change, Chinese immigrant women. Ed.D. dissertation 1984.

Lee, Elizabeth Eusee.
Asian immigrants and locus of control. M.A. thesis 1982.
NL

Lee, Robert.
The artisans of Ching-te-chen in late Imperial China. M.A. thesis 1980.
NL

Leicester, Pewter Frederick.
Multiple response free-word association and the syntagmatic-paradigmatic shift in Japanese adults learning English as second language. M.A. thesis 1981.
NL

Leigh, Woh-peng.
The evolution of Overseas Chinese social organization in nineteenth century western Malay states. M.A. thesis 1974.
CT

Leung, Gaylord Kai-loh.
The pottery of Hsu Chih-mo. M.A. thesis 1969.
CT

Leung, Winnie Lai-fong.
Liu Yung and his tz'u. M.A. thesis 1977.
CT

Lim, Bea Fung.
Prestige deprivation and responses, Chinese professionals in Vancouver. M.A. thesis 1981.
NL

Lim, Choi Kwa.
A re-evaluation of the life and works of Wei Ying-wu, ca. 737-? M.A. thesis 1977.
CT

Liu, Bernard Tin Chun.
Chuang tzu's untrammelled wandering in and the Hsiang-kuo commentary. M.A. thesis 1972.

Liu, Francis King-yin.
An analytical study on the trade relations between the People's Republic of China and Hong Kong. M.Sc. thesis 1977.
CT

Louis, Randolph William Craig.
The Chinese People's Liberation Army in the 1960s, ideal and reality. M.A. thesis 1974.
CT

Ludwig, Barbara M.
Planning for the health care of the South East Asian refugees, a review. M.Sc. thesis 1981.
NL

McDonald, James Andrew.
Trying to make a life, the historical political economy of Kitsumkalam. Ph.D. dissertation 1985.

McMullin, Neil Francis.
Oda Nobunaga and the Buddhist institutions. Ph.D. dissertation 1977.

Mahfoz, Napsiah.
The role of key teachers in the implementation of a new history curriculum in Malaysia, a study of perceptions. Ed.D. dissertation 1983.

Malhotra, Deshpal Singh.
The Indian urban slum, myth and reality. M. Arch. thesis 1972.
CT

Malhotra, Lorraine Margaret.
Religion, identity and cultural change, some themes from nineteenth century India. M.A. thesis 1972.
CT

Malik, Mohammed Akram.
Cultural factors which obstruct or facilitate case work in Pakistan. M.S.W. thesis 1963.
CT

Maminta, Rosario Esperanza.
An investigation of the language structures in beginning readers compared with the language structures taught for oral proficiency in the teaching of English as second language in the Philippines. Ed.D. dissertation 1969.

Mamun, Kazi Asadul.
The Farakka Barrage dispute, conflict and cooperation in Bangladesh-India relations. M.A. thesis 1984.
NL

Marican, Y. Mansoor.
The political accommodation of primordial parties, DMK(India) and PAS(Malaysia). Ph.D. dissertation 1977.

Mark, Kenneth Young.
Li Te-yu and the campaign against Chao-I(Tse-lu), 834-844. M.A. thesis 1978.
CT

Martin, Norris.
Three case studies on transportation in Malaya. M.A. thesis 1966.
CT

Matsuda, Hiroshi.
A transformational study of Japanese reflexivization. M.A. thesis 1975.
CT

Maund, Jacqueline K.
The implications for Japanese resource procurement strategy for staple resource regions, an examination of coal mining in South Eastern B.C. M.A. thesis 1984.
NL

Mauzy, Diane Kathleen.
Consocialationism and coalition politics in Malaysia. Ph.D. dissertation 1978.

May, Louise Ann.
Worthy warriors and unruly amazons, Sino-western historical accounts and imaginative images of women in battle. Ph.D. dissertation 1985.

Merken, Kathleen Chisato.
The evolution of Tanizaki Junichiro as a narrative artist. Ph.D. dissertation 1979.

Mia, Essop.
Toponyms and cultural regions, an examination of the place names of the Chota Nagpur. M.A. thesis 1970.
CT

Mian, A.Hafeez.
A micro-analysis of collocation in the case of Pakistani adults learning English as second language. M.A. thesis 1988.
NL

Mian, Abdul Waheed.
The measurement of railway operating performance with an application to Pakistan railways. M.Sc. thesis 1981.
NL

Miyanaga, Kuniko.
Social reproduction and transcendence, an analysis of the Sekai Mahikari Bunmei Kyodan, a heterodox religious movement in contemporary Japan. Ph.D. dissertation 1983.

Mok, Ru-ping.
The use of Chinese geomancy in contemporary architectural design. M.Arch. thesis 1979.
CT

Moody, Janet Louise.
A evaluation of the effects of bilingual instruction in the acquisition of English on young East Indian children. M.A. thesis 1974.
CT

Morley, Carolyn Anne.
Four kyogen plays in haikai. M.A. thesis 1977.
CT

Mozer, Douglas Stephen.
Social structure in village India, with particular emphasis on the Panchayati raj. M.A. thesis 1969.
CT

Mu, Hai.
A study of characteristics of Chinese ESL learners in MBA programs at Canadian universities. Ph.D. dissertation 1987.
NL

Mullatti, Leela Laxman.
A comparison of two devotional sects of South Eastern India, the Nirasaivas of Karnatak and the Varakaries of Maharashtra. M.A. thesis 1972.
CT

Muszynski, Alice Catherine.
Yenan principles in Chinese education. M.A. thesis 1973.
CT

Na, Tsung Shun.
A linguistic study of p'i pa chi rhymes. M.A. thesis 1969.
CT

Nair, Leila Karunakaran.
Sex-related differences in mathematics achievement scores in grade 4 and grade 8 in Kerala, India. M.A. thesis 1984.
NL

Nakagawa, Masako.
The theme of the descent in the **Tale of Genji** and the **The Ramayana**. M.A. thesis 1980.
CT

Nakayama, Kiyoshi.
Transfer pricing taxation, Canadian perspective and Japanese perspective. LL.M. thesis 1987.
NL

Natividad, Pablo Evangelista
A taxonomic phonological analysis of Tagalog and Pampango. M.A. thesis 1967.
CT

Ng, Roxana.
The marriage law and family change in China with special reference to Kwantung province, 1950-1953. M.A. thesis 1976.
CT

Nicholson, Howard Groces.
The new Japan. M.A. thesis 1930.
CGT

Nikitin, Afanasii Nikitich.
The journey beyond three seas of Afanasij Nikitin in A.D. 1466-1472, establishment of text, translation and commentary by Gregory Belkov. M.A. thesis 1950.
CT

Nishi Goldstone, Jane Hiroko.
Eschatalogical backgrounds of devotionalism in Buddhist China. M.A. thesis 1979.
CT

Nyhn, Boon Hang.
A comparative study of the recent use of corporate income taxation in Canada and Singapore as a means to stimulate industrial development. M.B.A. thesis 1968.
CT

Ogawa, Nobuo.
On the Japanese passive form. M.A. thesis 1971.
CT

Ogawa, Toshimitsu Augustine.
A study of Japanese relativization. M.A. thesis 1974.
CT

Ohanjanian, Aram Haig.
A study of the agrarian policy of the T'ai p'ing T'ien-kuo. M.A. thesis 1969.
CT

Okoko, Cornelius Amamebi Biije.
A comparative study of the political and economic consolidation policies pursued by the Soviet Union in Kazakhstan, 1917-1933, and Communist China in Sinkiang, 1948-51, M.A. thesis 1973.
CT

Oleya, Norma Peralta.
A phonological grammar of a dialect of Ilokano. M.A. thesis 1967.
CT

Ong, Roberto Keh.
The interpretation of dreams in ancient China. M.A. thesis 1981.
NL

Oshiro, George Masaaki.
Internationalist in prewar Japan, Nitobe Inazo, 1862-1933. Ph.D. dissertation 1985.

Ota, Midori.
Japanese schools overseas, their development and a case study of a supplementary school in Vancouver, Canada. M.A. thesis 1988.
NL

Otto, Lee Ann.
China and the law of the sea. Ph.D. dissertation 1981.

Owsanecki, Peter Franz.
"Kanni-Mangal", a microcosm of Coorg identity toward an alternative interpretation and analysis of the Coorg marriage ceremony. M.A. thesis 1984.
NL

Oyama, Ikuo.
Japan's behavior in foreign resource investments in the post-Second World War period. M.B.A. thesis l972.
CT

Pan, Yuh-kheng.
The position of women in T'ai-p'ing T'ien-kuo. M.A. thesis 1971.
CT

Pandjaitan, Sarda Vincetius,
Agricultural land use alternatives in regional planning, a case study of West Pasaman area development

planning, West Sumatra-Indonesia. M.Sc. thesis 1982.
NL

Paradis, Johanne Catherine.
The syllable structure of Japanese. M.A. thesis 1988.
NL

Parchela, Joseph Jan.
Recruitment of the Burmese political elite in the second Ne Win regime, 1962-1967. M.A. thesis 1969.
CT

Parker, Michael Stewart.
Men, money and machines, the making of modern society in Highland New Guinea. M.A. thesis 1979.
NL

Parrish, Geoffrey Leal.
The tentative leap forward, reforms and experiments in basic level Chinese industrial management policies, 1977-1979. M.A. thesis 1982.
NL

Patnaik, Vineetha.
Family value portrayals in journal advertising, a comparison of North American and Tamil magazine advertisements. M.A. thesis 1984.
NL

Pechey, Ann.
Britain and Malaya, imperialism as the mystification of self image. M.A thesis 1970.
CT

Peck, Pamela J.
Missionary analogues, the descriptive analysis of a development aid program in Fiji. Ph.D. dissertation 1982.
NL

Peralta-Pineda, P.B.
Tagalog transformational syntax, a preliminary statement. M.A. thesis 1967.
CT

Peterson, Glen.
The Overseas Chinese areas of rural Guangdong and Socialist transformation. M.A. thesis 1986.
NL

Petievich, Carla Rae.
The Two School theory of Urdu literature. Ph.D. dissertation 1986.
NL

Phillips, Susan Patricia.
Miyamoto Yuriko, imagery and thematic development from **Mazushiki hitobito no mura** to **Banshu heiya**. M.A. thesis 1980.
CT

Pi, Clara Ming Lee.
Food habits and nutritional status of East Hindu children in British Columbia. M.Sc. thesis 1978.

Placzek, James Anthony.
Classifiers in standard Thai, a study of semantic relations between headwords and classifiers. M.A. thesis 1979.
CT

Placzek, James Anthony.
Perceptual and cultural salience in noun classification, the puzzling case of the Thai "len." Ph.D. dissertation 1984.

Powles, Cyril Hamilton.
Victorian missionaries in Meiji Japan, the Shiba sect, 1873-1900. Ph.D. dissertation 1968.

Prasad, Kamal Kani.
The Gujaratis of Fiji, 1900-1945, a study of an Indian immigrant trader community. Ph.D. dissertation 1978.

Preston, Jennifer Wei-yen Jay.
The Li hsun faction and the Sweet dew incident in 835, a study of a climactic episode in late T'ang politics. M.A. thesis 1977.
CT

Preston, Laurence Wade.
The socio-economic basis of support for the Buddhist religious institutions of Western India circa 200 B.C. to A.D. 200. M.A. thesis 1976.
CT

Price, Ann Mereryd.
Alienation, trains and the journey of life in four modern Japanese novels. M.A. thesis 1987.
NL

Rajan, Mrunalini.
Housing for Sikh seniors. M.A.S.A. thesis 1988.

Ramsay, William James Hope.
Erosion in the Middle Himalaya, Nepal, with a case study of the Phewa Valley. M.Sc. thesis 1985.
NL

Raphael, Andrew Joel.
Responsive community planning in developing countries, the Kota Bahru, Buluh Kubu case study. M.A. thesis 1981.
NL

Ravindram, Santharam.
Seccesionist guerrillas, a study of violent Tamil insurrection in Sri Lanka. M.A. thesis 1988.
NL

Read, John Mark.
The pre-war Japanese Canadian of Maple Ridge, land ownership and the ken tie. M.A. thesis 1976.
CT

Reynolds, Eric Truman.
On the relationship of Advaita Vedanta and Madhyamika Buddhism. M.A. thesis 1976.
CT

Robinson, Frances Mary Playfair.
Humor in Japanese art, a survey of humor in Japanese art from three selected 200-year periods. M.A. thesis 1969.
CT

Robinson, Geoffrey B.
Islamic resurgence and the stability of Malay non-elite support. M.A. thesis 1982.
NL

Robinson, Peter Christopher.
The illusion of influence. Soviet-Indian strategic relations in the 1970's. M.A. thesis 1980.
CT

Ross, Martin John Elroy.
Japanese lexical phonology and morphology. M.A. thesis 1985.
NL

Ross, Patricia Dorothy.
Analysis of the decision to use the atomic bomb against Japan. M.Sc. thesis 1976.
CT

Roth, Garry Bernard.
Equality of educational opportunity in British Columbia, a study of ethnicity and schooling. Ed.D. dissertation 1984.

Rubin, Kyna Ellen.
Literary problems during the war of resistance as viewed from Yan'an, a study of the literature page of the **Liberation Daily**, May 16, 1941 to August 31, 1942. M.A. thesis 1979.
CT

Russell, Terence Craig.
The poetry of Ts'ao Chih, a critical introduction. M.A. thesis 1980.
CT

Sabet-Esfahani, Afsaneh.
The experience of immigration, the case of Iranian women. M.A. thesis 1988.
NL

Sandhu, Kernial Singh.
Indian migration and population changes in Malaya, ca. 100-1957 A.D., a historical geography. M.A. thesis 1961.
CT

Sara, Harkirpal Singh.
Sikhs and the Rebellion of 1897. M.A. thesis 1970.
CT

Saravanamuttu, Jayaratnam.
A study of the content, sources and development of Malaysian foreign policy, 1857-1975. Ph.D. dissertation 1976.

Sawada, Shikyo.
Aki no yo no monogatari, a lengthy story for a long autumn night. M.A. thesis 1976.
CT

Schmidt, Jerry Dean.
The poetry of Yang Wan-li. Ph.D. dissertation 1975.

Schofield, Stephen.
Entsu-ji and generalife landscape and architectural gardens. M.F.A thesis 1982.
NL

Shah, Pravakar Bickram.
Agricultural land evaluation in the Kailali district in Nepal using resource inventory data as a basis for national land use planning. M.Sc. thesis 1984.
NL

Shand, Eden Arthur.
The development of the Japanese market for Pacific Northwest lumber, a historical survey. M.B.A. thesis 1968.
CT

Sharma, Kavita A.
Ownership and control of foreign direct investment India and Canada, LL.M. thesis 1986.
NL

Shen, Qing. Low-income public housing in Hong Kong and Singapore, 1950-1980, a comparative analysis. M.A. thesis 1986.
NL

Sherlock, Eric Thomas.
Kokoro as ecological insight, the concept of heart in Japanese literature. M.A. thesis 1984.
NL

Shih, Feng-yu.
Li Po, a biographical study. Ph.D. dissertation 1983.

Shimpo, Mitsuru.
Economic development and social change in rural Japan, a case study of Shiwa community, Iwate prefecture. Ph.D. dissertation 1970.

Shimpo, Mitsuru.
The social process of community development in India. M.A. thesis 1963.
CT

Singh, Surjeet Kalsey.
Modern Punjabi poetry, an anthology. M.A. thesis 1978.
CT

Smith, John Malcolm.
Chang Nai-ch'i and his critics, the interpretation of the Hundred Flowers movement. M.A. thesis 1978.
CT

Solomon, Devadason.
Manufacturing industries in Malaya. M.A. thesis 1968.
CT

Solomon, Russell Keith.
The role of Japan in United States strategic policy for Northeast Asia. M.A. thesis 1985.
NL

Sponberg, Alan Wayne.
The Vijnaptimarata Buddhism of the Chinese monk K'uei-Chi(A.D. 632-682). Ph.D. dissertation 1979.

Sproul, Larry Rowland.
A thematic content analysis of Peking and Hong Kong elementary school Chinese language texts used in 1974-76. M.A. thesis 1979.
NL

Stanfield, Norman Allen.
The San koten honkyoku of the Kinko-ryu, a study of the traditional solo music for the Japanese vertical end-blown flute, the shakuhachi. M.A. thesis 1978. CT

Stanley, Timothy John.
Bolshevism and the Chinese Revolution, the conceptual origins of the program of the Chinese Communist Party at the time of its first Congress, 1917-1921. M.A. thesis 1981.
NL

Stark, Mary Verna.
The beginning of bronze technology in East Asia. M.A. thesis 1977.
CT

Steven, Chigusa.
Hachikazuki, a companion story. M.A. thesis 1976.
CT

Steven, Robert Philip Gustav.
Cabinet responsibility, the separation-of-powers and the makers and breakers of cabinets in Japanese politics. Ph.D. dissertation 1974.

Stocking, John Robert.
Tradition and individual talent in the theory of Chinese painting(the paradox of Hsieh Ho's first and sixth principles). M.A. thesis 1968.
CT

Stone, David Leigh.
Perceptions of an Imperial crisis, Canadian reactions to the Sepoy Mutiny, 1857-8. M.A. thesis 1984.
NL

Story, Evelyn Sykes.
India and nationhood. M.A. thesis 1926.
CGT

Straaton, Karin Vivian.
The political system of the Vancouver Chinese community, association and leadership in the early 1960s. M.A. thesis 1974.
CT

Stringer, Anne Marie.
A Canadian trading company, an analysis of the potential benefits of transferring a Japanese-style export promotion and marketing concept to the Canadian economic environment. M.A. thesis 1981.
NL

Stuart, Crampton Michael.
Value orientations in Ceylon, a comparative study and technique. M.A. thesis 1965.
CT

Stubbs, Thomas E.
Tour intermediaries and the regional tourism economy, the case of Japanese tour distribution in British Columbia. M.A. thesis 1984.
NL

Sumida, Rigenda.
The Japanese in British Columbia. M.A. thesis 1935.
CGT

Sunoo, Hard Jung-Cooke.
A spatial plan within a contemporary milieu, the Republic of Korea. M.A. thesis 1972.
CT

Suzuki, Yoshiko.
Directional verbs in English and Japanese. M.A. thesis 1979.
CT

Switucha, Ulana Tamara.
The external debt of South East Asia. M.A. thesis 1982.
NL

Takemoto, Toru.
Japan's security policy during the Ikeda cabinet, 1959-1964. M.A. thesis 1969.
CT

Tan, Evangeline K.
The phonology of Tausug, a descriptive analysis. M.A. thesis 1967.
CT

Tan, Xiaobing.
Rural development and peasant adaptation, a South China case. M.A. thesis 1988.
NL

Tang, Karen Kai-Ying.
Empress Wei, consort Shang-kuan and the political conflicts in the reign of Chung tsung. M.A. thesis 1976.
CT

Thakur, Rishee Shri.
Imperialism and nationalism in the Caribbean, the political economy of dependent underdevelopment in Guyana. M.A. thesis 1978.
CT

Thornbury, Barbara Ellen.
Kabuki in New York, 1900-1969, the developing American interest and response. M.A. thesis 1975.
CT

Thornbury, Barbara Ellen.
Sukeroku's double identity, a study in kabuki dramatic structure. Ph.D. dissertation 1979.

Thwaites, John Beckinton.
The role of French Indo-China in the "New Order" for Asia. M.A. thesis 1940.
CGT

Tiers, Jane Elizabeth.
Impressions of Meiji Japan by five Victorian women. M.A. thesis 1986.
NL

Toriumi, Tetsuro.
Directors' duty of care, diligence and skill, a comparative study of Japanese and Canadian law. LL.M. thesis 1983.
NL

Truscott, Eileen Grace.
Ma Shou-chen, Ming dynasty courtesan/artist. M.A. thesis 1981.
NL

Tsao, Ben-yeh Bonny.
Su-chou t'an-tz'u, an economic sociological study of the structural elements of the Chinese southern singing narrative. M.Mus. thesis 1987.
CT

Tse, Sou-mee.
The acquisition of Cantonese phonology. Ph.D. dissertation 1982.

Uchiyama, Hiroyuki.
Foreign direct investment and economic ethno-centrism in Japan. M.B.A thesis 1972.
CT

Ujimoto, Koji Victor.
Aspects of modernization in Japan, the adaptive and transformation processes of late Tokugawa society. M.A. thesis 1969.
CT

Ujimoto, Koji Victor.
Postwar Japanese immigrants in Canada, job transferability, work and social participation. Ph.D. dissertation 1973.

Upal, Swarn Singh.
Banking in India, development and structure. M.A. thesis 1963.
CT

Urapeepatanapong, Kitipong.
Legal aspects of countertrade under the General Agreement on Tariffs and Trade and the national laws of Canada and Thailand. LL.M. thesis 1987.
NL

Uzawa, Kozue.
Foreigners talk in Japanese, speech adjustments of native speakers with intermediate and advanced non-native speakers. M.A. thesis 1986.
NL

Van der Stoel, William.
Communist China's policy towards the Afro-Asian nations. M.A. thesis 1962.
CT

Van Houten, Richard Lee.
The concept of nature(tzu jan) in Kuo Hsiang and its antecedents. Ph.D. dissertation 1981.

Wake, Charles Julian.
The Sanyasi. M.A. thesis 1973.
CT

Walton, Robert Derwent.
The rising companies and the establishment, 1905-1931, the forerunners of Japanese expansion and their struggle for emergence. Ph.D. dissertation 1977.

Ward, Robert Donald.
The May thirtieth incident in Shanghai, Wu-san shih-chien. M.A. thesis 1971.
CT

Wardenier, Rita.
Are part-time and full-time small farms detrimental to agriculture: evidence from Taiwan, 1972-1980. Ph.D. dissertation 1985.

Whalley, Thomas Randall.
A investigation of the origins of tenant unrest in Japan in the 1920s. M.A. thesis 1978.
CT

White, Gary Richard.
Malthusianism and nationalism in Republican China. M.A. thesis 1978.
CT

Wilson, Harold Edmund.
Educational policies in a changing society, Singapore, 1918-1959. Ph.D. dissertation 1975.

Wong, Saintfield F.
The terra-cotta figures of Qin and human representations from the 5th century to the 3rd century A.D. M.A. thesis 1984.
NL

Wood, Marjorie Rodgers.
Changing patterns of family life in urban Gujarat, a study of twelve high-caste working women. M.A. thesis 1972.
CT

Wood, Marjorie Roberts.
Social service agents and Indo-Canadian immigrants in Vancouver, implications of models of social exchange for intercultural transactions. Ph.D. dissertation 1984.

Woon, Yuen Fong.
Social organization of South China, 1911-1949, the case of the Kwaan lineage of Hoi-p'ing. Ph.D. dissertation 1975.

Wright, Judith Helen.
In their own image, Nuwara Eliya, a British town in the heart of Ceylon. M.A. thesis 1988.
NL

Yamaguchi, Yasuo.
Socialization into physical activity in corporate settings, a comparison of Japan and Canada. Ph.D. dissertation 1984.
NL

Yamakoshi, Atsushi.
A study on Japan's reaction to the 1973 oil crisis. M.A. thesis 1986.
NL

Yamashita, Hideo.
Japanese business organization through mentality perspective. M.B.A. thesis 1969.
CT

Yap, Fe Leadoff.
A synchronic analysis of Tagalog phonemes. M.A. thesis 1967.
CT

Yavorsky, Gregory Paul.
Religion: solitude and nature in the poetry of the Zen monk Ryokan. M.A. thesis 1980.
CT

Yasutake, Yuko.
English and Japanese world associations and syntagmatic-paradigmatic shift of Japanese children learning English as second language. M.A. thesis 1985.
NL

Yee, Ernest.
South East Asia labyrinth, restrictive foreign investment regulatory policies of Malaysia, Thailand and Singapore from 1970 to 1980. M.A. thesis 1987.
NL

Yee, Francis Lok-wing.
The historical geography of book markets in China, a case study of Liulichang. M.A. thesis 1983.
NL

Yee, Paul Richard.
Chinese business in Vancouver, 1886-1914. M.A. thesis 1983.
NL

Young, Blake Morgan.
A tale from the **Harusame monogatari** by Ueda Akinari(1734-1809). M.A. thesis 1969.
CT

Young, Blake Morgan.
Ueda Akinari(1734-1809), scholar, poet, writer of fiction. Ph.D. dissertation 1976.

Yu, Teresa Yee-wah.
The tz'u of Ouyang hsiu. M.A. thesis 1978.
CT

**Vancouver City Archives,
1150 Chestnut Street,
Vancouver, British Columbia, V6J 3J9.
Tel:(604)736-8561.**

Canada. Department of the Secretary of State. Office of Custodian, Japan Evacuation Section.
Originals, 1943-1947. 4 in.
The papers consist of the minutes of the weekly meetings of the Advisory Committee, January 1943-June 1945; there is correspondence addressed to the Committee, 1943-1947, including enquiries re properties for sale, individual correspondence from the Secretary of State and from the Department of the Secretary of State; there are listings of individual properties and the history of their disposal, together with general policies re sales, 1943-1947; there is a copy of the Report of the Advisory Committee on Japanese Properties in Greater Vancouver, submitted in June 1945; printed catalogues of unsold property, 1943-1946, and newspaper clippings, 1944-1945.

Cowan, George Henry, b. 1858.
1.1 metres of textual records, 1877-1957.
George Cowan was a lawyer in Vancouver for many years, and Member of Parliament, 1908-1911. In 1894 he organized the First Conservative Association of Vancouver. He was city solicitor for Vancouver and surrounding municipalities, 1907-1910. He was an author and public speaker. Included among his works are **The Chinese Question In Canada**, and **Better Terms for British Columbia**.
Correspondence, briefs, speeches and related notes, certificates and publications concerning the Liberal-Conservative Union in British Columbia, the 1908 federal election campaign, Cowan's term as Member of Parliament, the 1926 campaign of A.D.McRae, and other political activities. Also included is material relating to Cowan's activities as solicitor for the City of Vancouver.
BCARCH-4929

Johnson, Barney Leitch, 1878-1968.
ca. 135 photographs, 1910-1968. 10 cm . of textual records.
Appointed Advisor to the National Defence Department. He also acted on the Japanese Fishing Vessel Disposal Commission.
BCARCH-4010

Knowlton Papers.
Volume 1: "History of the Caribou Road" by Walter Moberly; McLean letter to City Clerk, 15 November 1900; H.J.Cambie letter to J.M.R.Fairbairn, 4 September 1923; W.S.H. Gallagher , Docket, undated; Annual Report of the Vancouver Board of Trade, 1889; Gambling Investigation, 1928(Typescript 11 volumes); Council Minutes, 1889; "Incoming Correspondence," Volume 17, 1885; License Board Report Book, 1886-1889 and 1903-1909.

Kuo Kong Silk Company
Textual records. 1924-1962. 77 cm.
The Kuo Kong Silk Company first appeared in the **Vancouver City Directory** in 1925. The company's subsidiary operations, International Clothing and a national Dry Goods Manufactory, emerged in 1937. Although the Kuo Kong store was based in Vancouver, its business activities were not limited to the city, and its sale agents sold across the country, up Vancouver Island and the British Columbia interior.
Consists of the firm's correspondence, financial records, financial statements, a catalogue of silk samples and customer catalogues.
File list available.
BCARCH-3095

Lett, Sherwood.
Add. MSS. 3651. 138-186. 1908-1966 originals. 1.3 metres.
Include:
Volume 4.
A.Files1-6. 1947. Mission to Japan re Peace Settlement and Revival of Trade.
B. Files 7-12. 1954-1955. International Commission for Supervision and Control in Viet Nam. Includes material on Vietnam through 1964.
Volume 5.
File 1. Photograph scrapbook re work of International Commission.
Volume 8.
File 4. **South China Morning Post.** Newspaper clippings, 1947.
File 5. **Pacific Stars and Stripes**, 1947.
File 6. **Nippon Times**,1947.
Volume 10.
File 3. re Indo-China 1954-1961.
Additional papers deposited in 1992.
Box 1. File 12. Diaries, reports, memoranda from Canadian Commission(member Sherwood Lett) re Vietnam, 1955.
BCARCH-3012

Sheet Metal Workers' International Association, Local 280(Vancouver,British Columbia).
Textual records, 63 cm. 1905-1987.
The Vancouver Local(No. 280) of the Sheet Metal Workers' International Association received its Charter in 1902 from the Amalgamated Sheet Metal Workers' International Association. In 1906 it affiliated with the Vancouver Trades and Labour Council. It also joined the Local Building Trades Council, and eventually, the Metal Trades Council. It joined the British Columbia Federation of Labour in 1911. In 1913 it joined the North West District Council. Local No. 280 was involved in a number of issues, such as sending a delegate to the Asiatic Exclusion League, opposition to Chinese labour by local fruit growers, opposition to the enfranchisement of Orientals, opposition to foreign-speaking labour in and around Vancouver, opposition to conscription during World War I.
22 minute books dated from 1905-1933, 1937-1964, and 1971-1987.
Box list available.
BCARCH-2345.

Stevens, Henry Herbert, 1878-1973.
11 cm. of textual records. 48 photographs.
Stevens served as an alderman, 1910-1911, and M.P. for Vancouver ridings(1911-1930), and for East Kootenay(1930-1940). In 1921 he served as Minister of Trade and Commerce, and in 1926 as Minister of Customs and Excise. From 1930-1934 he was Minister of Trade and Commerce.
Records include the following subjects: East Indian immigration, 1914, 1916; The **Komagata Maru** incident, with photographs, 1915, 1916; immigration matters other than East Indian, 1912-1925.
BCARCH-1354

Wilson family.
7 metres of textual records, and ca. 500 photographs, 1900-1974.
George Halford Wilson(d.1955) became rector of St. Michael's Anglican church in 1903, after being ordained in Calgary and having worked in Banff as missioner. His son, Halford David Wilson(b. 1905) was educated in Vancouver and initially worked as a bank clerk and then an insurance agent. In 1934, he was elected to the Vancouver City Council. During the pre-war and early-war years, Wilson was an advocate of stringent controls on Japanese in British Columbia. In 1940 he joined the Canadian Army, however he continued on City Council until 1942, when he was sent to Britain. Returning to Vancouver after the war, Wilson was defeated in his bid for Mayor in 1946, but was reelected to council in 1947; he served until 1953. Wilson was reelected in 1955, and remained until 1972. Personal papers and church records(including sermons) of George Halford Wilson, and papers(correspondence, reports, scrapbooks) from Halford Wilson's business and political life.
BCARCH-3020

Yip family.
Textual records, 13 metres. 147 photographs, 1895-1989.
The Yip family in Vancouver began with Yip Sang's arrival in British Columbia in 1881. Yip Sang whose real name was Yip Chun Tien was born in China.
 In1864 he left his home village in Kwangtung province to travel to San Francisco, where he worked as a

dishwasher, cook, cigar maker, and labourer in the goldfields. Eventually he left for British Columbia, and in 1881, after first looking for gold in the North, he settled in Vancouver and found work as a peddler, selling sacks of coal from door to door. In 1882 he was employed by the Canadian Pacific Railroad Supply Company, where he worked as bookkeeper, timekeeper, paymaster and then the Chinese superintendant. In 1885, Yip Sang left the company and returned to China. In 1888, he returned to Vancouver and established the import and export firm of Wing Sang Company. Yip Sang was one of the driving forces in the establishment of the Chinese Benelovent Association, the Chinese School and the Chinese Hospital in Vancouver. He was a lifetime governor of the Vancouver General Hospital, and was a benefactor of the Public Hospital in Kwangtung Province in China. Wing Sang was one of the wealthiest firms in the Chinatown area of Vancouver. It engaged in contracting Chinese workers for the Canadian Pacific Railway Company, as a passenger agency with the Canadian Pacific Steamships Ltd., in the import and export of general merchandise from China and Japan, in money remittances from Vancouver to Hong Kong, and in the dry-salt herring business with China. Wing Sang Company was renamed Yip Sang, Ltd. in 1950. Records of the Yip family, including those of Yip Sang, and of Yip Sang Ltd., and its predecessor the Wing Sang Company. Includes financial records(mainly account books, remittance stubs, receipts and invoices), correspondence, published material, kept by the family and photographs.
Box and file list available.
BCARCH-43414.

Newspaper Clipping Collection

Arranged by subject.

J.S.Matthews, the founding archivist, newspaper clipping file, on microfiche, 1930-1973.
References under Chinese, Chinese Bank, Chinese Freemasons, Chinese New Year, Chinese newspapers, Chinese poll-tax, Chinese pigtails, Chinese riots, Japan and Canada Trust Savings Company, Japanese, 1907, 1928, 1929,1936-1939,
1940-1941, 1941, January-February, March-April, May to August, September to December,1943-1972, Japanese distinguished visits, Japanese internees' confiscated lands, Japanese Consulate, Japanese prehistoric voyages.

Continued by new file 1973-1975, and final file 1977- with references for Chinese Benevolent Association, Church-Chinese, Church-Japanese, Chinese United Church, Indians, Japanese.

Pacific Press clipping files, 1935-1975. The first with clippings on Chinatown, Chinese in Vancouver, East Indians in Vancouver, Japanese in Vancouver, and the second with clippings for **Chinese Times**, Chinese discrimination, Chinese Development Association, Indian traders.

Sam Kee Company.
Originals, 1888-1935. 4.24 metres.
The Sam Kee Company was one of the wealthiest Chinese merchant firms in Vancouver. Its business operations were extensive; the company manufactured charcoal, contracted Chinese labour to shingle mills, canneries, and sugar beet farms, and operated a herring saltery in Nanaimo. It imported and exported food products(rice and fish) to and from China, and served as agent for the Blue Funnel Steamship line. The company also possessed sizable real estate holdings. The unit contains the correspondence and financial records of the Sam Kee Company, and or related firms and operations. Almost all the account books, and a large portion of the correspondence is in Chinese. Photographs have been transferred to the Archives photograph collection. Finding aid for detailed listing.

Vancouver Board of Trade.
Originals, 1887-1964, 19 feet.
Consists of minute books, correspondence, briefs, scrapbooks, pamphlets, and books, tapes and photographs.
Full description in Finding aid 33.

v.148. Special Committee Minutes, January 19, 1932- June 6, 1935. Includes records on China Committee, and trade between Canada and Japan.

v.149. Special Committee. Minutes. Includes records of immigration.

Walker, Elizabeth,.
Collector.
Photocopies, 4 pages, 1921.
Rolls of the Japanese who served in the Canadian Expeditionary Force during World War I.
ULM4

Yamamoto family.
Vancouver, landowners and restaurant operators.
Original 2.5 inches, ca. 1922-1925.
Financial records and school exercise book(in Japanese).
ULM

Photographs

Association of Pacific and Far East Ports, Vancouver.
Black and white photographs:1931.
Group photograph of the 18th Annual Convention of the Association, August 14, 1931.
SEIFRIED

J.S.Matthews Collection.
Some 21,000 entries including:

Chinatown, Vancouver. Ca. 1905. Dist.P.168.

Chinese, 1878. Working men form protective association against great influx of Orientals. Misc.P.54 N.45

Chinese, 1885. Chinese camp huts near North Bend, during Canadian Pacific Railway construction. CAN.P.91.N.66. OUT.P.41.

Chinese, 1903. Canal diggers at work at Capilano Dam, 1903. C.V.P.Ci.Dept.9 N.Ci.Dept.19.

Chinese arch, 1896. Chinese arch erected in honour of Li Hung Chang on Canadian Pacific Railway dock, foot of Howe Street, 15 September 1896. C.V.Arch.P. 25, N17.

Chinese arch. For visit of Duke and Duchess of Cornwall & York, September 1901. Hastings Street looking east from Carrall Street. C.V .P.Arch.15. N49 N.52.

Chinese arch, 1901. Just east of Carrall Street on Hastings, looking west. British Columbia Electric Tram Station decorated in honour of visit of Duke and Duchess of Cornwall and York, September 1901. C.V. P.Duke C&Y.49.

Chinese arch. Dupont Street, erected for the visit of Duke of Connaught, 1912, taken from Carrall Street, looking West on Dupont Street. C.V .P. Arch 9 C.N.332.

Chinese arch and pagoda. Golden Jubilee. C.V.N.Ar.20. P.Arch 65.

Chinese building, 100 block, East Pender Street, 1913. The heart of Chinatown, 1913. Bu,.P. 717 B.609.

Chinese building. Pender and Carrall Street. C.V .P.Bu 253 N.Bu.158.

Chinese church. Joss table,1923. CVh.N.43. P.173.

Chinese coolies, 1885. Cutting, 55 feet deep, at Quoieek, Canadian Pacific Railway, main line, excavated with baskets. CABN.P. 145 N.112.

Chinese gardens. Marine Drive at Ontario. January 25th 1933. The wreck left by storm and flood. Str.N.315 P 474.

Chinese gardens, River Road before 1910(Marine Drive) Looking north up Main Street from river bank. STR.P.120 N.273 P.119. N.272.

Chinese girl dancer. CV.V.P.Port, 561.

Chinese gold miners, 1891. Near North Bend. OUT.P.803 N.362.

Chinese gold miners, 1859-1861. Fraser River, Boston Bar. OUT.P.810 N.369.

Sketch of Chinese gold miners at work at Boston Bar.

From the notebook of Rev. W.B.Crickmer in the possession,1956, of Mr.Cyril Stackhouse, Edmonton. OUT.P.810 N.369.

Chinese, Group of Imperial statesmen. Arrived at Canadian Pacific Railway wharf, 14 September 1896, from liner **Empress of China**, Li Hung Chang. Note the pigtails. ARCH P.63 N .48 S.G.N.1082.

Chinese houseboy, ca. 1900. CV P.Port.705 G.N.878 N.PORT.1064.

Chinese laborers, Yale, 1880-1884, during Canadian Pacific Railway construction. PHO.P.127 N.188.

Construction of Canadian Pacific Railway, 1880-1884. Recollections of W.H.Holmes, supplies storeman at Yale, during construction, Canadian Pacific Railway.

Chinese Labour Battalion. Victoria, British Columbia, 1918. C.V .P.Mil.194. N Mil.185.

Chinese laundry, Granville, 1884. Probably the first laundry in Vancouver, Wah Chong's "Washing & Ironing", facing the beach, now Water Street. Bu.P.403 N.387.

Chinese market garden, Main Street looking North from North Arm river bank, before 1910. C.V. P.Str.120.

Chinese newspaper, Pender and Carrall Street. C.V.N.Bu.157 P.Bu.756.

Chinese orchestra, and Miss Koo-Yu-Ching, dancing, 11 May 1938. CV.P.PORT.824.

Chinese pigtail. Street scene, Hastings at Carrall Street. Chinatown, 1900. Showing Palace Hotel, now Bank of Montreal, Pioneer Square. Good back view of Chinese with queue. STR.P.19 N.28.

Chinese riots, 1887 and 1907. Various accounts by Charlton, A.E.Beck, Albert Foote, as to what happened at the riots of February 1887 and 9 September 1907. PHO.P.307 N.352.

Chinese store, Carrall Street, 1897-1898. Yick Lung Jin, merchant tailors. B Ul.P.3 N.354.

Chinese theatre, 1923. Actors and interior. Port.N.479 P. 1893.

Chinese truck gardens. On Marine Drive at Fraser Avenue, ca. 1924. VLP 58 also Dist.N.64.

Chinese young ladies, 1936. Group of Chinese young ladies, beautiful and exquisitely gowned. Golden Jubilee of Vancouver, 1936. PORT.P.1157N.1071.

"Jap Town", 1912. Powell Street, looking east from Carl Avenue, now Princess. Showing the eastern edge of the Japanese settlement on Powell Street, known as "Jap Town". L.G.N.1213.

Japanese. Building boat. C.V.P.Bo.210. BO N.293.
Japanese arch, West Hastings Street. 1901. Between Hamilton and Homer Streets. Welcome of the Duke and Duchess of Cornwall and York. Arch.P.60.L.G.N.725.

Japanese arch, Hastings Street, 1901. Visit of Their Royal Highnesses The Duke and Duchess of Cornwall and York, September 30, 1901. Arch.P.60. L.G.N.725. N.45.

Japanese arch, Hastings Street, 1901. Between Hamilton and Homer Streets, for visit of Duke and Duchess of Cornwall and York, September, 1901. STR.P.280 N.238.

Japanese arch, 1901. Visit of Their Royal Highnesses The Duke and Duchess of Cornwall and York, 30 September 1901. Arch.P.22. N.16.

Japanese arch, looking west on Hastings Street, from Court House, 1901. C./V.P.C&Y.50.

Japanese arch. Visit of Governor General, September 18, 1912. Hastings and Main Streets. His Royal Highness The Duke of Connaught. Arch P.6. N.44.S.G.NB.334.

Japanese arch, 1901. Visit of Duke and Duchess of Cornwall and York, 30 September 1901. CV.P.Duke C&Y 56. G.N.881.Arch.P.60. L.G.N.725. N.45.

Japanese arch. Hastings Street between Homer and Hamilton Street, erected for visit of Duke and Duchess of Cornwall and York,[30 September 1901] C.V.P.Arch.27. N.53.

Japanese arch, erected in honor of the visit of Duke and Duchess of Cornwall and York, on their visit to Vancouver, 30 September 1901. On Hastings Street between Hamilton and Homer Streets. CV.P.Duke C&Y 63. S.G.N.926.

Japanese arch, 1901. Visit of Duke and Duchess of Cornwall and York, 30 September 1901. CV.P.Duke C&Y 56. G.N.881.Arch.P.60. L.G.N.725. N.45.

Japanese arch, Hastings Street. Royal party with escort approaching the arch, 30 September 1901. CV.P.Duke C&Y .37.

Japanese arch. Hastings Street, between Homer and Hamilton Streets, waiting for the procession of the Royal party the Duke and Duchess of Cornwall and York, 30 September 1901. CV.P.Duke C&Y 38.

Japanese arch, 1901. Visit of Duke and Duchess of Cornwall and York, Hastings Street, 30 September 1901.C.V.G.N.30 P.Arch.26.

Japanese arch, 1901. For visit of Duke and Duchess. Mayor T.O.Townley and wife passing under. CV.P.Duke C&Y 28.

Japanese arch, 1912. Japanese arch of welcome to Duke and Duchess of Connaught, 18 September 1912. Hastings Street east, DUKE CONN P.23. N.4.

Japanese barque **Nippon Maru.** Four prints. Under full sail, English Bay, and entering First Narrows. In English Bay, 17 June 1958. Entered First Narrows, 20 June. Departed Vancouver 25 June. Captain Muneo China. L.P.277.

Japanese church, before 1914. Corner Jackson and Powell Streets. Presented by J.Laurie, 1956. CH.P.131 N.113.See PAN.N .144.

Japanese church, Powell Street. Funeral, 5 March 1927. Southeast corner, Jackson and Powell Streets. Another funeral, same place. PAN.N.143.

Japanese Consulate, the first, 1889. Howe Street, west side, between Dunsmuir and Georgia Streets. STR.P.35.G.N.140.N.252. See also Van, Sc.N.45& 46. P.102 & 103.

Japanese Consulate, the first. This photograph, 1 July 1889, shows the Japanese flag flying, on the extreme left. Van,Sc.N.45& 46. P.102. A larger photograph of the house is S.G.N.140 Str.P. 35.

Japanese Consulate, 1889. Howe and Dunsmuir Streets. BU.P.442 N.429.

Japanese cruiser **Idzumo** in Burrard Inlet, approximately 1920. C.V.P.Bo.97.

Japanese flag, the first, 1889. This photograph, l July 1889, shows the Japanese flag flying over the Japanese consulate - on extreme left of photograph. Van.Sc.N.45 P.102. A larger photograph of the house is S.G.N.140 Str.P.35.

Japanese, first to work at Hastings Sawmill. 1887-1889(about) MI.P.4.N.3.

Japanese funeral ca. 1928. From Buddhist temple,1603 Albert Street, near Woodland Drive. Pan.N.144.

Japanese funeral. (1) 5 March 1927, from Japanese Church, south east corner, Jackson and Powell Streets. (2) Another funeral, same place. PAN.N.143.

Japanese Garden, University of British Columbia. Dr.Nitobe was a distinguished Japanese who visited Vancouver. The gardens are a tribute to his memory. MON.P.126.

Japanese Hall and Japanese School. ca. 1928. PAN.N.145.

Japanese hospital, Steveston, 1900. The front facade. OUT.P.107 N.617. See also OUT.P.689N.296.

Japanese medical doctor, 1897. Early Japanese medical practitioner at Steveston Japanese hospital. OUT.P.689 N.296.

Japanese monument. Stanley Park, 1914-1918.

66 • British Columbia – Vancouver

C.V.P.Mon.9.

Japanese newspaper building. 213 Cordova Street, October 1927. Bu.N.329.

Japanese Prince Chichibu, 29 March 1937. Illuminated address presented by Citizens of Vancouver on occasion of his visit, 29 March 1937. ADD.N.63.

Japanese procession at the Memorial Service, King Edward VII. May 1910. Wearing black mourning sashes. Recreation Park, Home and Smithe Streets, 20 May1910. MIL.P.284.

Japanese roll of honour, 1914-1918. Showing 184 names for Japanese who served with the Canadian Expeditionary Force in the First World War. ADD.P.80 NM.58.

Japanese trade, resumption of, 1951, Arrival at Vancouver, 30 October 1951 of Nippon Yusen Kaisha line. Reopening of trade between British Columbia and Japan. Letter from Mayor of Yokohama, See Geisha doll in glass case, L.P.210.

Japanese training ship **Kaiwo Maru**. First Narrows, outward bound, June 1963. BO.P.559. N.328.

Japanese warships, visit of, 1909. H.I.J.M.S. **Aso** and Sopa entered First Narrows, May 1909. BO.P.440. N.247.

Aso, Sopa.
Japanese warships, three, 1925. Two negative panorama of **Idzumo, Yakumo** and **Asama** at anchor in harbour. 6-12 February 1925. Tragic visit, eleven men drowned. BO.P.513. N.295.

Japanese War Memorial column, 1914-1918. Stanley Park. Unveiled 9 April 1920. MON.P.9. N.46. See ADD.P.80.

Komagata Maru, July 1914. At anchor in Vancouver Harbour with Hindoos on board. L.G.N.1034. BO.P.347

Komagata Maru, 1914. At anchor in Burrard Inlet. East Indians on board. Not permitted to land. BO.P.487 L.G.N.1063.

H.M.C.S. **Rainbow,** Tug **Sea Lion,** Hindu riot, July 1914. CV P.Bo. 238,23. N.Bo. 97,98. L.P.111.

Kompira Maru, Japanese fishing boat.
Boat drifted across Pacific to Queen Charlotte Islands, 1915, from Japan. PHO.P.312 N.56.

2. CVA Collection.
Some 35,000 entries including:

Vancouver - Ethnic groups - Asian. CVA 460-1[1911]
[Group of Asian children with six adults]

Vancouver - Ethnic groups - Chinese.
CVA 287/1-42.
[This collection from the Sam Kee Company of Vancouver contains many images of Chinese people]

Vancouver - Ethnic groups - Chinese.
CVA 178-8, ca. 1891.
[Chinese family group]

Vancouver - Ethnic groups - Chinese.
CVA 352-7 ca. 1895.
[Chinese funeral parade, East Hastings. Urquhart Brothers, Wines and Spirits, 37 East Hastings.]

Vancouver - Ethnic groups - Chinese.
CVA 139/9-20, ca. 1915.
[Chinese Labour Corps: recruited in China travelled via Vancouver to work behind trenches in World War I; boarding train in Vancouver for France.]

Vancouver - Ethnic groups - Chinese.
CVA 689/1-7, 9-15 ca. 1902-1927, [196?]
Photographs of the Yip Sang family and business and the Chinese Students' Athletic League.

Vancouver - Ethnic groups - Chinese.
CVA 99-1395 1921.
Chinese Nationalist League of Canada, 2nd convention, group photograph.

Vancouver - Ethnic groups - Chinese.
CVA 99-3486 ca. 1923
Group of Chinese men - taken for Mr. Chu.

Vancouver - Ethnic groups - Chinese.
CVA 260/452-458, 486-488, 76, 734-737. 1936-1937.
[Sai Woo Chop Suey premises. Chinese parade in Chinatown; Chinese in vegetable fields.]

Vancouver - Ethnic groups - Chinese.
CVA 300-25 ca. 1936-1938
[A group of Chinese men carrying a banner against fascism, war and invasion in a parade.]

Vancouver - Ethnic groups - Chinese.
CVBA 300/194-196, 197-203 ca. 1936-1938
[Views of a Chinese funeral and a Chinese parade featuring a Chinese Dragon Dance.]

Vancouver - Ethnic groups - Chinese.
CVBA 371-1914. ca. 1909
Chinese prayers to their dead, possibly old part of cemetery on North Arm Road.

Vancouver - Ethnic groups - Chinese.
CVA 260-1004, ca. 1939
[Chinese Boy Scout in a parade.]

Vancouver - Ethnic groups - Chinese.

CVA 260/1005-1013, ca. 1939.
Chinese funeral; Chinatown]

Vancouver - Ethnic groups - Chinese.
CVA 260/1264-1268, May15 1939.
[Chinese vegetable gardeners in their fields within Greater Vancouver.]

Vancouver - Ethnic groups - Chinese.
CVA 260-1334, July 1939.
[Chinese shopkeeper inside his small candy and tobacco store.]

Vancouver - Ethnic groups - Chinese.
CVA 180-16520 1950.
[Chinese Girls Drill Team in P.N.E. parade.]

Vancouver - Ethnic groups - Chinese.
CVA 180/65143-6144 1952.
[Taiwanese officials and P.N.E. officer at Horticultural Display.]

Vancouver - Ethnic groups - Chinese.
CVA 180-1953 1955.[Chinese girl dancers at P.N.E.]

Vancouver - Ethnic groups - Chinese.
CVA 180-3818 1958.
[Chinese community float in P.N.E. parade]

Vancouver - Ethnic groups - Chinese.
CVA 180-3409, 3412 1959
Chinese Community Queen and Cathay Queen in P.N.E. parade.]

Vancouver - Ethnic groups - Chinese.
CVA 180-3449, 3458 1959
[Prime Minister John G.Diefenbaker visiting Taiwan exhibit]

Vancouver - Ethnic groups - Chinese.
CVA 468/103-104 ca. 1970
[Halford Wilson and others at Chinese Benevolent Association.]

Vancouver - Ethnic groups - Chinese.
CVA 468/103-104 ca. 1970
[Halford Wilson and others at Chinese Benevolent Association.]

Vancouver - Ethnic groups -East Indians.
CVA 139/5-6, ca. 1910,
[East Indian labour crew clearing the Shaughnessy area]

Vancouver - Ethnic groups -East Indians.
CVA300/23, 24. ca. 1936-1938.
[Views of a woman with three children and Sikh children in a parade.]

Vancouver - Ethnic groups -East Indians.
CVA 260-836.
[Portrait of an elderly Sikh.]

Vancouver - Ethnic groups -East Indians.

CVA 180-6040. 1960.
[Exhibit from India at the P.N.E.]

Vancouver - Ethnic groups -East Indians.
CVA 180-6114. 1965.
[Sikh family at P.N.E. Hobby Show.]

Vancouver - Ethnic groups -Japanese.
CVA 371-1365. ca. 1890.
[Five men from the Japanese Embassy in buggy in front of Hollow Tree, driver Duncan Horne.]

Vancouver - Ethnic groups -Japanese.
CVA 99/924-925, ca. 1920.
[Japanese child dressed in Scottish costume at war memorial.]

Vancouver - Ethnic groups -Japanese.
CVA300/131-141. ca. 1936-1938.
[Views of Japanese floats and women and children in traditional costume in a parade to celebrate the Coronation.]

Vancouver - Ethnic groups -Japanese.
CVA 260/727-732, May 1937.
[Japanese in Coronation Parade.]

Vancouver - Ethnic groups -Japanese.
CVA 99/4207-4208 June 19th, 1932.
B.C.
[Purchases Association Japanese picnic at Hastings; left and right of pan. photo.]

Vancouver - Ethnic groups -Japanese.
CVA 7-204, ca. 1910.
Delegation from Japan with local Japanese community.

Vancouver - Ethnic groups -Japanese.
CVA 180/3506-3545. 1942.
Images showing Japanese-Canadian internment at Hastings Park buildings during World War II.

Vancouver - Ethnic groups -Japanese.
CVA 180/6096-6101. 1959.
Japanese Tea Ceremony at P.N.E.

Vancouver - Ethnic groups -Sikhs.
CVA 312-1. ca. 1905.
Sikhs in Vancouver.

Vancouver - Ethnic groups -Sikhs.
CVA 7-122, July 1914, CVA 141/1-4, see CVA 7.
S.S. Komagata Maru, July 1914.

Vancouver Public Library,
351 West Georgia Street,
Vancouver, British Columbia, V6B 6B1.
Tel:(604)665-35521

Newspaper clipping file.

Business and Economics Division.
Special indexes include Company file index including

company clippings and annual reports.
Clipping files started in late 1950s, and are not purged. Coverage differs, and some files such as those for China and Japan are very substantial. Country files for Asia, 1960-1994, Bangladesh, 1972-1979, Burma, 1960-1990, Myanmar 1990, China, 1960-1993, Hong Kong, 1957-1994, India, 1960-1993, Indonesia 1960-1994, Iran, 1960-1986, Japan, 1960-1994, Korea, 1961-1992, Laos, 1960-1977, Malaysia, 1960-1993, Pakistan, 1960-1993, Philippines, 1960-1994, Thailand, 1961-1992, Turkey, 1973-1991, Vietnam, 1960-1994.

History and Government Division.
Clipping sources vary according to subject. Clippings are purged from time to time, depending on demand. Sources include **Sun, Province, Globe and Mail.**
Arranged by major topics, and subarranged by country. For example: Immigration, subdivided by China, Hong Kong, India, Pakistan, Turkey.; Refugees, subdivided by race, Afghan, Bangladeshi, Burmese, Cambodian Chinese, Cypriot, Indian, Fijian, Filipino, Iranian, Laotian, Pakistani, Sri Lanka, Thai, Tibetan, Turkish, Ugandan, Vietnamese.
Countries divided by topic. For example India, has clippings under antiquities, defence, description and travel, diplomatic and consular service, foreign relations, politics and government, princes, States.

Social Sciences Division
Sun, Province, Globe and Mail, Courier and **New York Times** indexed. Index commenced in 1960.
Has clippings for Chinese in Vancouver, British Columbia, Canada and United States, Chinese New Year, Indians in Vancouver, British Columbia, Canada, Japanese in Vancouver, British Columbia, Canada and United States, Japanese New Year, Koreans in Vancouver, and Sikhs in Vancouver, British Columbia, and Canada.
Also major subject divisions divided by country, such as Crime, divided by Asia, China, India and Japan.
Pacific North West History Collection.
Published materials, journal articles, newspaper articles indexed in 70 drawers of index cards. Some 600 cards for Chinese and Chinatown, 60 for Indians, 300 for Japanese.

Photograph Collection

Chinese Canadian Picture Project.
358 photographs, 1951-1972. Social events in Chinese Canadian communities in Vancouver and Victoria. Many of the early photographs were created by the **Chinatown News** newspaper of Vancouver.
BCARCH-44826:

Chinese Canadians.
Arranged by date.

Undated. Chinatown ceremony. 13636.
Undated. Cookhouse crew, Quatsino. 14006.

Frank, L. Undated.
Chinese man on ship in Vancouver. 10169.

Timms, Philip. Undated.
Group portrait of Oriental men(Railroad workers? Some men sitting on railroad ties) 66958.

Vancouver Public Library. Undated.
Oriental men aboard a Canadian Pacific Railway ship - location unknown. 12866.

Vancouver Public Library. Undated.
Group of Chinese men performing a ceremony near Ross and Howard Iron Works, Ltd. at the foot of Woodland - spectators.13636.

Roozeboom, H.W. donor. 18--
Panorama for Chinese squatters' quarters near North Bend - log cabins with sod roofs. 13389.

Washing for gold. Chinese. 188-. 19977

Bailey, C.S. & Company, photographer, Kilpatrick, T.D., donor. 188-
Chinese men washing for gold near North Bend. 9751, 19977.

Price, A., donor. 1881.
Home of T.H.White, one of the Canadian Pacific Railway Civil Engineers of Spuzzum. T.H.White, 2nd from left - Chinese servant. 402.

Price, A., donor. 1885.
Chinese village opposite Keefers - log cabins - Canadian Pacific Railway personnel - pile of hand hewn ties. 210.

Price, A., donor. 1885.
George A.Keefer's home in Keefers - Canadian Pacific Railway station - men, women and children - Chinese - speeders. 214.

Price, A., donor. 1885.
Group of men at H.B.Smith home, 12 miles above Keefers - Chinese- Indians. 219.

Price, A., donor. 1885.
Home of George A.Keefer's assistant - Chinese. 224.

Bailey Bros. ca.1887.
Panorama from the ground looking east on Pender Street(formerly Dupont) from Carrall - Chinese stores. 13238.

Notman, William. 1887.
Chinese men loading tea from Canadian Pacific Railway's S.S. **Parthia** - see also 1866. 2523.

Christ Church Cathedral, donor. 189-
First rector of Christ Church Cathedral, Reverend Hugh P.Hobson, Baptist with Chinese men - he was also a missionary. 8587.

Christ Church Cathedral, donor. 189-
Portrait of Lee Wah James, first Chinese convert. 8588.

Vancouver Public Library. 1890s.
Group of horse drawn wagons in front of the Hack, Livery, Feed and Sale Stables in New Westminster - Chinese store in background. 12867.

Christ Church Cathedral, donor. 3 May1892.
Portrait of Hin Yu, as Chinese convert. 8583.

Christ Church Cathedral, donor. 3 May1892.
Portrait of Mah Shou Hing and Lee Dye, Chinese converts. 8584.

Christ Church Cathedral, donor. 1892.
Portrait of Lee Wah, a Chinese convert. 8585.

Vancouver Public Library. 1892.
R.A. & I. Exhibition on Columbia Street in New Westminster - Royal Engineers, Chinese men and Indians!

Chinese funeral. ca. 1894. 17064.

Vancouver Public Library. ca. 1895.
Chinese men and small boy in front of Tai Sing Company, Importers and Wholesale Dealers, General Merchandise in New Westminster. 8056, 67636.

Vancouver Public Library. ca. 1895.
Chinese procession(maybe funeral) on Hastings Street, between Carrall and Columbia Streets - Chinese wearing queues(pigtails) -policemen - horses - Urquhart Bros. Saloon. 53.

Vancouver Public Library. 1895.
Chinese joss house in Revelstoke - group of Chinese men in front. 693.

Street arch - Li Hung Chang. 1896. 17063.

Marrion album. 1897.
Chinese street arch erected at the Canadian Pacific Railway station, foot of Granville Street for the visit of Li Hung Chang - bow of the **Empress of Canada** in background - men, women, children. 13525.

Eiglsen, C., donor. 1898.
Chinese at Mission School in Vancouver. 2449.

Price, A., donor. 1899.
Canadian Pacific Railway wooden bridge at M.220,75 - Chinese men on speeder. 326, 355.

Price, A., donor. 1899.
Canadian Pacific Railway wooden bridge at M.204,25 near Ashcroft - Chinese men on speeder - buildings and bridge in distance - Thompson River. 3312.

Sweeney, M.Leo, donor. 19--.
Chinese men working with a barrel machine at Sweeney Cooperage, Ltd., 49 Smithe Street. 3542.

Sailing ship - Moodyville. 190? 22859.

Timms, Philip. 190-
Chinese man unloading of onions from Australia at a Canadian Pacific Railway pier. 2887, 66682.

Timms, Philip. 190-
Chinese men and children boarding the **Baramba** for a picnic - 2977, ship in harbour. 2971.

Timms, Philip. 190-
Group of Chinese and Japanese immigrants aboard a ship docked in Vancouver -Japanese and Sikh military also aboard. 3027.

Timms, Philip. 190-
Carrall and Hastings Streets - Woods Hotel men waiting -Note Chinese with queue. 6531.

Timms, Philip. 190-
Two views, panorama from ground, looking west on Columbia Street from 8th - Canadian Pacific Railway station. Panorama from ground looking west on Front Street from 8th.Chinese vendors -rear of Windsor Hotel. 6910.

Timms, Philip. 190-
Children standing on locie at Britannia mine -engineer- two children are Chinese or Japanese. 6994, 7532.

Timms, Philip. 190-
Ship at Canadian Pacific Railway pier in Vancouver - loading or unloading -Chinese on ship. 7692.

Timms, Philip. 190-
Chinese track gang working on the Canadian Pacific Railway tracks at the foot of Columbia Street. 7742.

Timms, Philip. 190-
Chinese loggers and steam donkey. Location unknown. 78316.

Vancouver Public Library, 190-
Interior of a cannery at Steveston - two men are either Chinese or Japanese.13270.

Vancouver City Hall, Town Planning Department, donor. ca. 1900.
Two views. Panorama from ground of Yick Lung Jin, 426 Carrall Street, tailors. 9498.

Children - Victoria. 190-. 50110-50112

Timms, Philip. 20 September 1901.
Chinese welcome arch erected for the visit of the Duke and Duchess of Cornwall and York in the 200 block Carrall Street - M. Desrosiers, 214 Carrall Street., 7750, 8275.

Timms, Philip. 20 September 1901.
"Welcome" street arch erected at the Canadian Pacific Railway station, foot of Granville Street to welcome the Duke and Duchess of Cornwall and York - Chinese man with a camera. 8280.

70 • British Columbia – Vancouver

Vancouver Public Library. 1901.
"Welcome" street arch erected at the foot of Granville Street to welcome the Duke and Duchess of Cornwall and York - Chinese men. 8280.

Hastings, O.C., Shallcross, Mrs. P.G., donor.1902.
Interior of a Chinese joss house or store in Victoria - Chinese men - abacus on counter. 3114.

Chinese cook/servant. Skagway. 1902. 32250.
Hastings, O.C., Shallcross, Mrs. P.G., donor.1902.
Interior of a Chinese tong, shrine or club in Victoria. 13115.

Timms, Philip. 1903-1905.
Panorama from ground Westminster Avenue at Princess Street(Main at Pender): Chinese funeral. First Baptist choir in procession; City of Vancouver Archives photograph. Major Matthews description. 66980.

Timms, Philip. 1904.
Chinese vendors on Pender Street(formerly Dupont) - horse drawn wagon. 6729, 66659.

Timms, Philip. 1904.
Chinese men taking hogs to market on Front Street in New Westminster - Swanson block - Hotel Fraser on Begbie at Front Streets -donkey engine? 6749.

Timms, Philip. 1904.
Panorama from ground looking west on Pender Street(formerly Dupont) towards Carrall Street from near Abott -Chinese street vendors. 7234, 66646.

Timms, Philip. 1904.
Chinese fish peddlers at waterfront near the foot of Carrall - Canadian Pacific Railway station in background - ship docked.8005, 66677.

Cheverton album. ca.1905.
Three Chinese men sitting on a bench at the wharf at Rivers Inlet "waiting for the steamer"-dog. 8510.

Timms, Philip. ca.1905.
(Two views) Panorama from ground of the entrance to Stanley Park - men, women and children - Chinese men. 5384.

Timms, Philip. ca.1906.
Panorama from ground of the west side of the 500 block Carrall Street - horse drawn wagons - Chinese businesses - 5240, Chinese Empire Reform Association of Canada 529 Carrall Street - horse drawn wagons - Chinese men. 5238, 5240.

Timms, Philip. 1906.
Panorama from ground Canadian Pacific Railway station on Columbia Street corner of 8th in New Westminster - Chinese men -Depot Hotel - Central Hotel. 6951.

Vancouver Public Library. ca.1906.
Chinese band wagon. 6716.

MacKenzie, D.K., donor 1907.
Three women standing in front of buildings at the rear of Chinatown in Kamloops - (album photograph is captioned "back of Chinatown") 12920.

Timms, Philip. ca.1907.
Panorama from ground of southwest Hamilton and Hastings Streets - Inns of Court Building, 423 Hamilton Street - Bank of Hamilton, 2300 West Hastings - Chinese man with a queue. 5245.

Timms, Philip. 1907.
Chinese buildings damaged by race riots in 500 block Carrall, west side. 939.

Timms, Philip. 1907.
Chinese buildings at northwest Carrall and Pender Streets damaged by race riots. 940.

Timms, Philip. 1907.
Chinese building damaged by race riot. 941.

Cartoon on Chinese immigration. 39046-39047.

Timms, Philip. 1907.
Panorama from ground west side of 400 block Carrall Street - Chinese merchants -Methodist Chinese Missions- horse drawn wagons. 6831, 66669

Timms, Philip. 1907.
Chinese cook and two boys in Barnet. 7688.

Bennett, J., donor. ca. 1909.
Great Northern Railway's Chinese track gang - location unknown. 1773.

Broadbridge-Bullen. ca. 1909.
Interior of Steveston salmon cannery - Chinese man preparing equipment for the ovens. 1266.

Price, A. donor. ca. 1909.
Chinese detention shed in Vancouver. 451.

Timms, Philip. 1909.
Three part panorama. New Westminster - Columbia in foreground - Chinese businesses- Hotels - 6962.

Waterfront - sternwheeler on Fraser River- Fraser River Bridge in distance. 6960-6962.

Chinese men sleeping. 191-. 18505.

Timms, Philip. ca. 1910.
Panorama from ground of North Pacific Lumber Company Ltd. shipping yard in Barnet - Canadian Pacific Railway box cars - horse drawn wagon - Chinese man, 7055.

Vancouver Public Library. ca.1911.
Transfer and Feed Stables, maybe Quesnel - men with horses - Chinese man in rear. .295.

Street arch - Pender Street. 30363.
6' wide building - Pender and Carrall Streets. 1912-1976. 17079-17080.

Mills, Olga, donor. 18-21 September 1912.
Chinese street arch at Carrall and Pender Streets - erected for the visit of the Duke of Connaught. 2008.

New Westminster Public Library, donor. 1912.
Group portrait of the Duke of Connaught's Own Rifles as Honour Guard for the visit of the Duke of Connaught on Columbia near Begbie Streets, in front of the Oyster Bay Restaurant - Yee Kee & Company, tailors.9674.

Todd, F.Dundas. 1913.
Two Chinese men at Imperial Cannery in Steveston - one man lighting a pipe - "Just a whiff". 2102.

University Women's Club, Maple Ridge, donor. ca. 1913.
Panorama from ground of the Port Haney Brick Company Ltd. on the banks of the Fraser River - cordwood stacked in foreground was used to fire the kilns - behind cordwood is one of the shacks that housed the Chinese workers. 13069.

Robinson, G. donor. 1915. Oriental men whipsawing timbers for construction at Britannia. 13876.

Chinese Immigration Act 1918-1973. 30625-60326.

Thomson, S. 192-
One man and young Chinese girls at an automobile rally in Vancouver. 13408, 17732.

Chinese men, women and children on ship. 192-. 18282.

Frank, L. ca. 1920.
Log slip at Hasting Sawmill in Vancouver - 3890, two Chinese men. 3890, 3891.

Frank, L. 1920.
Interior of Kitsilano Branch Library - children - Chinese. 10442.

Percy, R. donor. 1920.
Wing Tai & Company one and a half ton Federal truck in front of Federal Motor Company, 2295 Seymour Street. 536.

Schull Lumber Shingle Company, log on conveyor, Chinese worker. ca 1921. 14758.

Chinese convention. 1921. 17726-17727.

Chinese soccer/rugby team. 1921, 17728.

Chinese dragon costume. 1921. 17729-17730.

Chinese soccer/rugby team. 1921. 17731.

Chinese convention - crowds, 1921. 17732.

Chinese convention? 1921. 17855.
Soanes, J.H., donor. 1924.

Chinese man laying Canadian Pacific Railway track near Glenogle. 1746.

Chinese funeral. 1924. 17714-17725.

Thomson, S. 1924.
Chinese School soccer teams. 11207.

Dominion Photo Company, Perry, R., donor. 1925.
C.Yuen Bros. of Ladysmith's Federal-Knight express model truck under the Georgia viaduct. 560.

Frank, L. 1925.
Large timbers being loaded onto flat cars at Hastings Sawmill - Chinese men working. 3653.

Frank, L. 1925.
Lumber on Grand Trunk flatcar at Hastings Mill -men on lumber - Chinese man. 12443.

Percy, R., donor. 1926.
Wong Quoy & Company's Federal truck on Georgia Viaduct -Chinese man. 607.

Portraits from Ward Studio, 1926. 58893- 58922.

Thomson, S. 1926.
Panorama from ground, southeast. Hastings and Main Streets - Royal Bank of Canada. 8944.

Paull, Albert. 7 May 1926.
Group portrait of mill crew at Wood & English, Ltd. , Englewood - Japanese or Chinese men. 1625, 1629, 1630, 1647.

Dominion Photo Company 5 January 1928.
East Pender Street - North side 100 block. 22644., Chinese.

Wing Chong Lee laundry, 1517 West Pender Street. 1928. 39531.

Chinatown stores. 1928. 22642-22644.

Thomson, S. 26 December 1929,
Victoria Chinese Canadian Club Soccer Team at Con Jones Park. 11801.

Thomson, S. 1929-1930.
Vancouver Chinese Students Soccer Team. 11800.

King Studio. 193-
On Lee produce store, Chilliwack, British Columbia. Man and child in doorway, 70242; store front, 70242A. Chinese.

Vancouver Public Library. May 1930's
Group of men gathered at the Cambie Street Grounds(Larwill Park) for a May Day Conference - banners read "145 Chinese Workers Killed by Soup Kitchen - Starved by Anglican Church on

British Columbia – Vancouver

Contract". 8799.

Vancouver Public Library. May 1930's
Chinese men at a May Day Conference. 8838.

Frank, L. 1931.
Panorama looking north from the gasometer, located between Keefer and Georgia Streets, near Main Street - rooftops of Vancouver's Chinatown - B.C.E.R. yards. 4414.
Log buildings. Clinton Chinese store. 1931. 19239.

Frank, L. 1932.
Victoria Produce Company, 1743. Commercial - Chinese market - 7921, interior of market. 7920.

Frank, L. August 1933.
Chinese man in Powell River. Mack Sing. 10038.

Painting: "Oriental with fish". 1934. 23600.

Dominion Photo Company, 1936.
Chinese bamboo arch at Pender and Carrall Streets. 23890.

Sun Toon, interior. 1936. 23789.

Chinese bamboo arch. 1936. 23890, 23897, 23898.

Chinese costume - parade. 1936. 19355.

Chinese carnival queen -parade. 1936. 19356.

Frank, L. 1936.
Chinese arch on Pender Street erected for the Golden Jubilee. 7847.

Vancouver Public Library. 1936.
Panorama - night picture of Chinese contribution to Vancouver's Golden Jubilee - arch and temple, foot of Columbia and Carrall Streets, South side of Pender - gasometer, demolished 196-. 32.

Vancouver Public Library. 1936.
Chinese arch facing Pender near Columbia Streets - imported from China and erected for Vancouver's Golden Jubilee celebrations. 41.

Chinese Benevolent Society float - parade. 1936. 19352.

Vancouver Public Library. 1936.
Panorama from ground of a Chinese street arch erected for Vancouver's Golden Jubilee. 13387.

Frank, L. 1937.
Panorama from ground looking east from Columbia Street on the Northside of the 100 block East Pender Street - Columbia Street block -automobiles. 5306.

Frank, L. 31 May 1937.
Two men and two women being served dinner by Chinese chef in guest house. 10036.

Frank, L. 31 May 1937.
Chinese man in Powell River -Lou Tom. 10037.

Portrait Sun Toon, 50th birthday. Interior of shop. 1938. 24384.

Bestway Merchants, Lillooet, interior and exterior, F.Cheung. 1940's. 34915-34916.

V-J Day parade -Chinatown. 1945. 44922.

Dominion Photo Company 1946-1960.
Interiors and exteriors of various stores in Vancouver. See s-envelope for details. 14 items. 77431.

Soon Town Shop, interior. 1946. 26945.

Old Chinese note - City Museum. 1946. 26960.

Old Chinese robe - City Museum. 1946. 26966-26967.

Chinese barber shop, interior. 1946. 26945.

Chinese Society, Powell Street. 1947. 48886.

Kuo Seun Company, exterior. 1948. 27715.

Soon Town, interior, Chinese New Year. 1951. 28485.

Province Newspaper. 1953.
Chinese funeral procession on Pender Street near Main Street.- automobiles - men walking on road- banners being carried. 13289.

Wong Ham, holdup victim. 1954. 60955.

Chinese women in costume. 1958. 50342.

March for peace in Chinatown. 196-. 45171.

March for peace in Chinatown. 196-. 45171.

Chinese girl and dragon. 196-. 50339.

Chinese children. 196-. 50341.
Armstrong, behind Chinese vegetable grower's home. ca 1960. 345652.

LeBlanc, Don(Croton Studio) 22 May 1960.
Annual Chinese dragon parade in Vancouver's Chinatown; Pender Street. 79795.

Sien Foon. 1961. 60589.

Province Newspaper. 1961.
Panorama from ground looking west on Pender Street from near Columbia Street - Ho Ho Chinese Restaurant - Sun Building - automobiles. 1999, 2001.

Province Newspaper. 1961.
Bamboo Terrace Chinese restaurant, 155 East Pender Street - automobiles. 2000.
Province Newspaper. 1961.

Panorama from the ground west side of 100 block East Pender Street. Chinese business. 2002.

Dominion Photo Company 10 April 1963.
Sun Town and interior of house at 12 East Hastings Street. 77580.

Citizenship Court. 1963. 406536.

Chinese New Year. 1964. 48184.

Chinese kindergarten graduates. 1965-. 50340.

Shing Cheng Pantry Company 1966. 40637-40640, 41103-41105.

Peipei(Chinese guitar player) 1966. 42469.

Chinese dragon - P.N.E. parade. 1966. 43318-43319.

Chinatown Spring Carnival. 1966. 45919.

Chinatown Lions Club Convention. 1969. 48274.

Chinatown - people. 1972. 53954-54007.

Chinese egg vendor and truck. 1972. 54056.

Chinatown. 1972, 54060,54070-54071.

Chinese Canadian Picture Project.
Black and white. 358 photographs. 1951-1972. Donation by Charles Mow of newspaper photographs of social events in Chinese communities in San Francisco, Vancouver and Victoria: British Columbia. Original source of photographs **Chinatown News** and private donations.
SEIFRIED

Indian Canadians

Timms, Philip. 190-
Group portrait of East Indians at North Pacific Lumber Company Ltd. in Barnet. 7641.

Timms, Philip. 190-
Panorama from ground. North Pacific Lumber Company Ltd. yard in Barnet. Horse-drawn wagon loaded with lumber, East Indians. 7642.

Timms, Philip.1904.
Panorama from ground, looking north on Carrall from Hastings Street. Ranier Hotel. East Indian men on street. 6857.

Vancouver Public Library. 1907.
East Indian cremation at Tod Inlet. 13291, 13292.

Timms, Philip.1908.
Panorama from ground of South east Granville and Hastings Streets. Williams Building-Fairfield Building - East Indian men crossing the street, street cars. 5236.

Barrowclough,G.A. 191-

East Indian immigrants at the Canadian Pacific Railway pier loading possessions onto horse-drawn wagons. 9426.

University Women's Club, Maple Ridge, donor. 1911.
A.W.Spilsbury home in Whonnock. Mr. and Mrs Spilsbury ploughing field. East Indians building home.

Todd, F.Douglas. 1913,
East Indians unloading fish from boat at Imperial Cannery in Steveston. 2051,2052.

Todd, F.Douglas. 1913.
Receiving letter at Imperial Cannery in Steveston. East Indian men. 2057, 2058.

Vancouver City Archives, July 1914.
Panorama from ground of the **Komagata maru** in Vancouver harbour. East Indians aboard. 13156-13159.

Vancouver City Archives. July 1914.
Officials standing in tugboat beside the **Komagata Maru**. 13160.

Vancouver City Archives. July 1914.
Five East Indians and an immigration official during the **Komagata maru** incident. Downtown skyline. 13161.

Vancouver City Archives. 21 July 1914.
Panorama from ground of Vancouver harbour during the **Komagata maru** incident. **H.M.C.S. Rainbow** called to aid in deporting Hindus on board **Komagata maru.** 13351.

Nehru's visit to Vancouver, 1949, 462227-462235.

Women in sari. 196- 50335.

Sikhs.

Timms, Philip. 190-
Groups of Chinese and Japanese immigrants aboard a ship docked in Vancouver. Japanese and Sikh military also aboard. 3027

Timms, Philip. 19-
Panorama from ground of City Hall(formerly Market Hall) 411 Main Street(Formerly Westminster) Sikhs crossing the street. Horse-drawn wagons.

Kreb. ca.1910 .
Piles of lumber being air dried - yard crew. Sikh on horseback. East Kootenay.142654.

Canadian Photo Company 23 May -23 July 1914.
Komagata maru incident. Sikhs aboard ship. 119, 121, 127, 132, 133.

Canadian Photo Co, 23 May-23 July 1914.
Komagata maru incident, Officials, newsmen, Sikhs aboard ship, H.H.Stevens on left.122.
Canadian Photo Company 23 May- 23 July 1914

Komagata maru incident. Sikhs aboard **Komagata Maru**. Gurdit Singh wearing light coloured suit, white beard, 136.

Frank, L. 23 May-23 July 1914.
Komagata maru incident. Sikhs aboard ship. 6226, 6230, 6232.

Frank, L. 23 May-23 July 1914.
Komagata maru incident. Sikhs aboard **Komagata Maru**. Gurdit Singh wearing light coloured suit, white beard.6231.
Sikhs. 62202-62203.

Sikh wedding, 1952. 63527-63532.

Moni Gari Singh, 1952. 625466.

Frank, L. 1919.
Sikhs loading lumber at British Columbia Mills. 12452.

Dominion Photo Company 11 October 1936.
Sikh temple, 1860 West 2nd Avenue. 23945, 23046.

Thomson, S. 1936. Portrait of Ranjit Matu, 12653.

Sikh temple congregation,1936. 1866 West 2nd Avenue, Vancouver, 23945-23946.

Japanese Canadians.

Vancouver Public Library.
Japanese bell in Victoria. 66628.

Gunn, Angus, donor, 1900c.
Portrait of three Japanese women, wearing traditional costume. 13467,13468.

Vancouver Public Library, 190-
Interior of a cannery at Steveston - two men are either Chinese or Japanese. 13270.

Timms, Philip. 190-
Group of Japanese and Chinese immigrants aboard a ship docked in Vancouver. Japanese and Sikh military also aboard. 3027.

Timms, Philip. 190-
Children standing on locie at Britannia mine - engineer-two children are Chinese or Japanese. 6994, 7532.

Timms, Philip. 190-
Group of men sitting in snow in Britannia - four men are Japanese. 7006

Vancouver City Hall, Town Planning Department, donor. ca. 1900.
Home of Dr. J.A.Mills at the northwest corner of Dunsmuir and Richards Streets. Japanese man and horse and buggy on boulevard.

Timms,Philip. 20 September 1901.
Japanese street arch erected for the visit of the Duke and Duchess of Cornwall and York on Hastings Street, west of Main Street. 6800, 7749, 8274.

Timms,Philip. 1901.
Japanese street arch at Carrall and Hastings Streets at night -erected for the visit of the Duke and Duchess of Cornwall and York. 7613

Timms,Philip. ca.1907
Japanese Methodist Mission, 502 Powell Street, southeast Jackson and Powell Streets. 6840.

Timms, Philip. June 1907.
Crowds at Canadian Pacific Railway Station to welcome Japanese Prince Fushimi - welcome arch erected at foot of Granville Street. 3010-3012, 6777, 6805-6807, 5224.

Timms, Philip. 1907.
Immigrants aboard the **Kumeric** docked in Vancouver - may be Japanese. 3019, ship docking. 3008, 3009.

Timms, Philip. ca.1908
Japanese men with fish at a cannery in Steveston. 2185.

Timms, Philip. ca.1908 .
Japanese men with dried salmon at a wharf near Steveston. 2142, 2143.

Timms, Philip. ca.1908.
Japanese men repairing a fishing net at a wharf beside the Imperial Cannery in Steveston. 2144.

Timms, Philip. ca.1908.
Panorama from ground of No.1 Road in Steveston - Japanese boys are walking on Moncton. Building on right is the B.C.E.R. Station. Horse and milk wagon. Gas well at end of the street. 2145.

Timms, Philip. ca.1908.
Panorama from the ground of the Japanese Hospital in Steveston. 2173.

Barrowclough, George, Berry John, donor. 26 November 1909.
Great Northern Railway wreck near New Westminster. 23 Japanese were killed. 9909.

Timms, Philip. 1910.
Mount Pleasant Band aboard the **Princess Alexandra**. Japanese men aboard. 3028

Timms, Philip. ca.1910.
Mountain View Cemetery on Fraser between East 31st and East 41st Avenue - 7356, Japanese area of cematary.

Richmond Arts Centre, 1911.
Steveston school children posing for their photograph with their teacher Miss Peck. Two Japanese children. 2426.

Steel, H.A., donor. 1912.

Street arches erected on Granville and Hastings Streets by organizations and ethnic groups to welcome the Duke of Connaught to Vancouver. 742-746.

Mills, Olga, donor. 18-21 September 1912.
Japanese street arch at Hastings Street, near Main Street - erected for the visit of the Duke of Connaught. 2018, 2020.

Broadbridge, R. 1913.
Japanese men "soldering vent hole after exhausting cold air" at the Scottish-Canadian Cannery in Steveston. 8433.

Todd, F.Dundas. 1913.
Japanese men soldering cans a second time after first canning at Imperial Cannery in Steveston. 2088.

Todd, F.Dundas. 1913.
Japanese men testing salmon after first cooking at Imperial Cannery in Steveston. 2087.

Todd, F.Dundas. 1913.
Men and women filling cans with salmon at Imperial Cannery in Steveston - 2067 and 2068, Indian women with children - 2079 and 2071, Japanese women carrying babies on their backs - 2072, White women.

Todd, F.Dundas. 1913.
Soldering machine at Imperial Cannery in Steveston- 2800, Japanese man operating machine - 2081, cans coming from soldering machine.

Todd, F.Dundas. 1913.
Japanese men soldering centre hole of lid at Imperial Cannery in Steveston. 2082.

Todd, F.Dundas. 1913.
Japanese men soldering leaks in cans after water testing at Imperial Cannery in Steveston. 2084.

Todd, F.Dundas. 1913.
Japanese men capping the sanitary cans at Imperial Cannery in Steveston, 2090, 2091.

Todd, F.Dundas. 1913.
Fishing nets being repaired at Imperial Cannery in Steveston. 2108, Japanese men repairing nets. 2107.

Todd, F.Dundas. 1913.
Living quarters for workers at Imperial Cannery in Steveston. 2109. Japanese quarters. 2110. Indian quarters.

Todd, F.Dundas. 1913.
Women and children buying ice cream cones at Imperial Cannery in Steveston. 2111. Two Indian women. 2112. Indian women and children. 2113. Japanese children.

Todd, F.Dundas. 1913.
Two Japanese children playing on wharf at Imperial Cannery in Steveston. 2116.

Print. **Komagata maru** and **H.M.C.S. Rainbow**. 1914. 48569.

Frank, L. 1914.
Japanese men "splitting British Columbia red cedar into quarter blocks from which are made British Columbia edge-grain shingles" Location unknown. 3844, 3849.

Vancouver City Archives. July 1914.
Three Japanese men and one East Indian man aboard a ship -may be the **Komagata maru**. 13162.
Robinson, G. , donor. 1915.
Oriental men whip sawing timbers for construction at Britannia. 13876.

Frank, L. 1918.
Fire in Steveston. Crowds. Japanese people. 9147. Japanese woman and child. 9151A.Fire truck. 9146, 1947, 9150, 9151.

Japanese women. 192- 50386-50387.

Britannia. Chinese or Japanese whip sawing. 1920. 13876.

Frank, L. February 1925.
Japanese visit of state. 11422.
Thomson, S. 13 February 1925.
Japanese Vice-Admiral Hyakutake and Consul Gomyo et al. 11738.

Thomson, S. 13 February 1925.
Mayor L.D.Taylor and high ranking Japanese officers on Court House steps. 11737.

Frank, L. l July 1926.
Japanese float pulled by horses in parade on Georgia Viaduct. 11158.

Paull, Albert. 7 May 1926.
Group portrait of mill crew at Wood & English, Ltd., Englewood. 1629-1630. Japanese or Chinese men. 1625, 1629,1630,1647.

Percy, R., donor. 1926.
K.Shimoyama's Federal-Knight truck. 591.

Dominion Photo Company, Percy, R. donor., 1926.
Y.Yashiki, farm produce of Steveston's Federal-Knight truck in front of the Dominion Canners, British Columbia, 332 Drake Street. 593.

Thomson, S. 1927.
Taishodo Company, Gore and Powell Streets. 11804. Exterior.11805-11806. Interior.

Japan Town. Stores. 1928. 21772-21774

Dominion Photo Company 5 June1928.
East Powell Street at Gore(Japan Town)

Dominion Photo C o.,5 June 1928.
Japanese store on East Powell Street, Bunka Shokai.

Two Japanese children. 21773.

Thomson, S. 1929.
Asahi Baseball Club, Seniors. 11750.

Thomson, S. 1929.
Panorama from ground looking east in the 200 block Powell Street. Japanese business. Automobiles. 13433.

Thomson, S. 1930.
Japanese Rugby Team. Identification on photograph. 11794.

Interned fishing fleet. New Westminster. 194- 26951.
Frank,L. 1942.
Round up of Japanese fishing boats in the Fraser River near New Westminster. 3190,3191.

Province Newspaper.1942.
Japanese evacuation. Royal Canadian Mounted Police posting "To Male Enemy Aliens, Notice" 1343.Japanese men reading notice. 1342. See also 14905-14938.

Province Newspaper.1942.
Japanese evacuation. Japanese fishing boats being seized by **Charlotte T.M.II** from the Fraser River. 1352, 1356, 1357. See also 14905-14938

Province Newspaper.1942.
Japanese evacuation. British Columbia. Packers Ltd. cannery in Steveston. 1354.
See also 124905-14938.

Province Newspaper.1942.
Japanese evacuation. Seized Japanese vehicles held at Hastings Park. Royal Canadian Mounted Police documenting vehicles. 1358-1364, 1366-1376. See also 14905-14938.

Province Newspaper.1942.
Japanese evacuation. Japanese man documenting bicycles in store. 1365. See also 14905-14938.

Province Newspaper.1942.
Japanese evacuation. Japanese men leaving Hastings Park. 1777. Man holding a baby. 1377, 1378, 1400, 1775, 1777. See also 14905-14938.

Province Newspaper.1942.
Japanese evacuation. Japanese men leaving by Canadian National Railways to eastern destinations. 1379-1386. See also 14905-14938.

Province Newspaper.1942.
Japanese evacuation. Japanese women doing exercises. 1387-1389, 1776. See also 14905-14938.

Province Newspaper.1942.
Japanese evacuation. Japanese women in traditional kimonos. 1390, 1391. See also 14905-14938.

Province Newspaper.1942.
Japanese evacuation. Japanese homes in Steveston. Children. 1399. Totem pole. 1392,1395,1397-1399. See also 14905-14938.

Province Newspaper.1942.
Japanese evacuation. Panorama from ground of Japanese stores in Steveston. 1393. Mukai Confectionery. 1394. See also 14905-14938.

Province Newspaper.1942.
Japanese evacuation. Japanese floating homes in Burrard Inlet near grain elevators. 1396. See also 14905-14938.

Vancouver Sun and **Province Newspapers**.1942.
"Notice to All Japanese Persons And Persons of Japanese Racial Origin" signed by Austin C. Taylor, Chairman, British Columbia Security Commission. This notice appeared in **Vancouver Sun** and **Vancouver Province** newspapers.

Hastings Park. Evacuation. 1942. 14905-14938.

Stanley Park War Memorial. 1954. 29096.

LeBlanc, Don(Croton Studio) 20 August 1960.
Japanese "Dance of the Lantern" Jackson Street, Vancouver. 79929.

Walter, Stan (Croton Studio) ll March 1961.
Nippon Exhibition & Bazaar, sponsored by the Japanese Language School, Steveston Community Centre. Joan Taniwa with doll. 79023.

Japanese students. 1966. 44326-44327.

Steveston concert with children. 1966. 44400.

Victoria

**Anglican Church of Canada,
Diocese of British Columbia,
Archives,
912 Vancouver Street,
Victoria, British Columbia, V8V 3V7.
Tel:(604)386-7781.**

Comox Deanery Chapter.
Refugee Action Committee records, 1979-1983. File list available.
Sponsoring of a refugee family from Laos.
5. Good Hope Mission, Victoria.
During the late 1880s and the early 1890s, a Chinese lay catechist was operating a Chinese Mission in the Victoria area. In 1928 the Good Hope Mission(also known as the Victoria Chinese Mission) was established with Diocesan funding. A vestry of nine Chinese communicants was formed that year. The Mission operated until 1955. Some of the documents are written in Chinese.
Originals, undated, 1923-1951. 22 cm.

Include financial statements, register of marriages, and architectural records.

Provincial Board of Missions to Orientals. 1903, 1924-1965. 5 cm.
Set up by provincial canon in 1917, the Provincial Board of Missions to Orientals built on earlier work among Chinese and Japanese in the province. In 1925 four missions were operating under the Superintendent of Anglican Chinese Missions: Good Hope Mission in Victoria, Good Samaritan and Good Shepherd missions in Vernon. Japanese Missions: Holy Trinity Mission in Vancouver, St. Andrew's Mission in Prince Rupert. In 1965 the function of the Provincial Board was transferred to dioceses, resulting in the dissolution of the Board. Scope, minutes, reports and correspondence, financial records and clippings.
Includes report(1903) by Archdeacon S.W.Edwig, Pentreath on the Chinese work in the Diocese of New Westminister.
EPBC

Robin, Peter W.
George Hills, the Anglican Church and the Chinese, 1859-1885. 1983.

Provincial Archives of British Columbia,
655 Belleville Street,
Victoria, British Columbia, V8V 1X4.
Tel:(604)387-5885.

Manuscript and Government Records Division.

Awmack, Winifred J.
Teacher, Papers 1944-1983.
Papers related to the Japanese Relocation Centre at Tashme, British Columbia, accumulated by Mrs. Winifred(McBride) Awmack who taught at the high school operated by the United Church Women's Missionary Society there from 1944 to 1946. The collection includes papers relating to the treatment of Japanese Canadians in general(copies of Orders in Council, notices, etc.) relocation, circular letters from church groups, copies of letters from residents of Tashme cancelling their request for repatriation, and from students 1945 to 1983, from British Columbia, Eastern Canada and Japan, nos 1 and 2 of the **Outlook**, Toronto, 1947, a newssheet circulated among former Tashme students.
Add.MSS.2119/ULM5.

Beall, Gladys W.
History of Oriental Home and Missions in Victoria. 1959. Typescript.
H F B36.

Boulton, Lawrence Beverly Bargemon, 1922-1973.
Assistant District Forester. 5 cm.
Includes an undated gambling book in Chinese.
Add.MSS.1307.

British Columbia. Commercial Fisheries Branch.
Originals. 1911-1972.1.2 metres.
Includes correspondence on Japanese fishermen, 1934-1939.
GR1378

British Columbia. Commission on Charges Contained in Articles in the Vancouver News Herald.
Microfiche (negative). 1942. 2 fiche.
Japanese in British Columbia.
Bf15

British Columbia. Commission on Claims Arising out of Riots in 1913 and 1914 on Vancouver Island, 1916.
Originals, 1916, 72 cm.
Petitions of claimants, commissioners' notes on claims, transcripts of evidence(p.3-323), reports, correspondence and miscellaneous documents relating to court cases arising out of the riots.
Photographs(acc.no.97905-9) in Visual Records Division.
Finding aid: file list and indexes to claims in Box 1 File.
GR518.

British Columbia. Commission on Victoria City Police Commissioners(1910).
Originals, 1910, .01 metres.
Commissioner Peter S. Lampman was appointed March 24, 1910 to inquire into the actions of the Victoria Police commissioners in response to allegations of corruption.
The investigation centred on the actions of the Police commissioners in regard to bawdy houses and gambling establishments in the Chinatown area.
GR0784

British Columbia. County Court(Cumberland)
Originals, 1901-1907, 52 cm.
Probate/estate files.
Finding aid:file list.
Japanese in Vancouver Island.
GR1638.

British Columbia. Department of Education. Elementary Correspondence School.
Includes records of courses provided to Japanese pupils interned during World War II.
GR0470

British Columbia. Department of Health and Welfare. Accounting Division.
Originals. 1945-1969. 60 cm.
Includes materials on Japanese in British Columbia.
Finding list.
GR341

British Columbia. Department of Highways.
Microfilm(negative) 1910-1978. 329 reels.
Includes some files on public buildings, as well as files for the control of Japanese nationals in World War II.
Finding aid.
GR1585

British Columbia. Department of Mines. Gold

Commissioner. Kootenay,
Microfilm (negative), 35 mm., 1872-1886, 1 reel.
Manual of record and conveyances.
Originals, 1865-1872, 4.5 cm. Microfilm
negative), 1865-1872, 35 mm. 243 exp.
Manual of record and record of conveyances for the
Wild Horse Creek district.
GR0232

British Columbia. Department of Mines. Gold Commissioner. Skeena.
Originals, 1897-1934. 3.95metres.
Includes materials on Japanese in British Columbia.
Finding aid.
GR228

British Columbia. Department of Public Lands.
Microfilm(negative) 1910-1970. 247 reels.
Contains files relating to control of Japanese nationals in World War II.
Finding aid.
GR1615

British Columbia. Government Agencies.
Chinese statistics. 1880, 1879.
C C 30.14 C44

British Columbia. Lieutenant Governor (Trutch)
Correspondence re Ah Tuck case and judicial matters in British Columbia.1871.
Chinese in Cariboo.
K J Ahl

British Columbia. Provincial Secretary.
Originals, 1872-1934, 30 cm.
Miscellaneous correspondence inward and outward on diverse topics. Most of these records pertain to the 1920s and early 1930s. Included are files dealing with the exclusion of Orientals (1921)
Japanese in British Columbia.
GR1668

British Columbia. Provincial Secretary.
Originals. 1887-1953, 2.5 cm.
Miscellaneous correspondence and reports, many of which relate to investigations carried out under the Departmental Inquiries Act and the Public Inquiries Act. Other records deal with health and child welfare programmes and juvenile reformatories. Additional records relate to squatters' claims at Granville Townsite (1887), Fraser River Flood Relief work (1894), and proposed sites for the University of British Columbia. Anti-Oriental petitions and the 1924 beer-by-glass plebiscite also included.
Chinese in British Columbia.
GR1665. RESTRICTED

British Columbia. Provincial Secretary.
Originals. 1904-1905, 1948, 4.5 cm.
Record of Japanese and East Indians entering British Columbia.
GR1618

British Columbia. Public Works Department.
Papers. 1910-1970. 247 reels. GR 1615,
Includes files relating to control of Japanese nationals during World War II.
GR0232/ULM5

Canada. Commission on Complaints of Canadian Citizens of Japanese Origin. 1947.
Microfiche(negative) 1950. 1 fiche.
Japanese in British Columbia.
GR1970

Canada. Commission on Unrest and Discrimination among Miners and Mine Workers in British Columbia, 1899.
Microfiche (negatives), 1900, 11 fiche.
Reports(not printed) to the Minister of Justice, including abstracts from evidence(Henderson No. 91).
Chinese in British Columbia.
GR1966

Canada. Department of Agriculture. Willam Head Quarantine Station.
Microfilm(negative)1902-1956, 1 reel, 35 mm.
Annual reports for the William Head Quarantine Station from 1901 to 1932. As well as statistical operational data on the Station, the reports often contain information of occurrences of communicable diseases on connecting shipping routes. Some correspondence is included concerning the isolation and treatment of leprosy in the province.
Chinese in British Columbia.
GR 2005

Canada. Department of Mines and Resources. Yellowhead-Blue River Highway Project.
Textual records. 9 cm.
The Yellowhead-Blue River Project, a project of the Surveys and Engineering Branch of the federal Department of Mines and Resources, ran from 1942 to1944 and employed relocated Japanese-Canadian workers during World War II. The project was based from four camps opening north of Blue River, British Columbia, and involved opening up ten miles of pioneer trail, burning slash, road construction, including the construction of culverts, and the erecting of a truss bridge over the North Thompson River. The records consist of correspondence(1942-1944) and monthly timesheet records(1944) of the Yellowhead-Blue River Project.
BCARCH-465235

Canada. Immigration Branch.
Microfilm(positive), 1873-1968, 583 reels(Provincial Archives reels B-700-B1282), 16 mm., 35 mm.
The following records were presented by the Public Archives of Canada, Diffusion Program, in 1980. The reel numbers given below are the Public Archives of Canada numbers. There is a Provincial Archives of British Columbia conversion file for the Provincial Archives reel numbers.

I. Central Registry File Series.

A. First Central Registry Series, 1873-1968.
Volumes 1-692 on microfilm.

Volumes 1-676.
Files on all subjects.

Finding aids. There is a complete file list.

Index to First Central Registry Files,1892-1924. 21 reels, T5571-T5592.

Index to First Central Registry Files,1924-ca. 1946. 5 microfilm reels, M-1986-M-1990.

Volume 83.

File 9309, part 1, reel C-4750.
Japanese emigration, 1891-1908.

File 9309, part 2, reel C-4750.
Japanese emigration, 1908.

Volume 84.

File 9309, part 3, reel C-4750.
Clippings Japanese immigration (report of inquiry), 1908-1909.

File 9309, part 4, reel C-4750.
Japanese immigration, 1909-1910.

File 9309, part 6, reel C-4750.
Japanese immigration, 1912-1914.

File 9309, part 7, reel C-4750.
Japanese immigration, 1914-1917.

File 9309, part 8, reel C-4751.
Japanese immigration, 1917-1918.

Volume 85.

File 9309, part 9, reel C-4751.
Japanese immigration, 1918-1919.

File 9309, part 10, reel C-4751.
Japanese immigration, 1919-1920.

File 9309, part 11, reel C-4751.
Japanese immigration, 1921-1923.

File 9309, part 12, reel C-4751.
Japanese immigration, 1923-1925.

File 9309, part 13, reel C-4751.
Japanese immigration(lists), 1925-1930.

Volume 86.

File 9309, part 14, reel C-4751-C-4752.
Japanese immigration, 1930-1936.

File 9309, part 15, reel C-4752.
Japanese immigration, 1936-1938.

File 9309, part 16, reel C-4752.
Japanese immigration, 1938.

File 9309, part 17, reel C-4752.
Japanese immigration(report), 1938-1941.

File 9309, part 18, reel C-4752.
Japanese immigration(report), 1941-1947.

Volume 87.

File 9309, part 19, reel C-4752.
Japanese immigration(report), 1947-1949.

File 9309, part 19, reel C-4753.
Japanese immigration, 1947-1949.

File 9309, part 20, reel C-4753.
Japanese immigration, 1947-1949.

File 9309, reel C-4753.
Reports of board of review on illegal immigration(Japanese), 1938.

File 9309, part 1, reel C-4753.
Japanese immigration, form file(lists), 1908-1909.

File 9309, part 2, reel C-4753-C-4754.
Japanese immigration, form file(lists), 1909-1910.

File 9309, part 3, reel C-4753.
Japanese immigration, newspaper clippings, 1942-1945.

Volume 88.

File 9309, part 3, reel C-4754.
Japanese immigration, form file(lists), 1910-1911.

File 9309, part 4, reel C-4754.
Japanese immigration, form file(lists), 1911.

File 9309, part 5, reel C-4754.
Japanese immigration, form file(lists), 1911.

File 9309, part 6, reel C-4754.
Japanese immigration, form file(lists), 1911-1912.

File 9309, part 7, reel C-4754.
Japanese immigration, form file(lists), 1912.

File 9309, part 8, reel C-4754.
Japanese immigration, form file(lists), 1912.

Volume 89.

File 9309, part 9, reel C-4755.
Japanese immigration, form file(lists), 1912.

File 9309, part 10, reel C-4755.
Japanese immigration, form file(lists), 1912-1913.

File 9309, part 11, reel C-4755.
Japanese immigration, form file(lists), 1913.

File 9309, part 12, reel C-4755.
Japanese immigration, form file(lists), 1913.

File 9309, part 13, reel C-4755.
Japanese immigration, form file(lists), 1913.

Volume 90.

File 9309, part 14, reel C-4755.
Japanese immigration, form file(lists), 1913.
File 9309, part 15, reel C-4755.
Japanese immigration, form file(lists), 1913-1914.

File 9309, part 16, reel C-4756.
Japanese immigration, form file(lists), 1914.

File 9309, part 17, reel C-4756.
Japanese immigration, form file(lists), 1914.

File 9309, part 18, reel C-4756.
Japanese immigration, form file(lists), 1914.

Volume 91.

File 9309, part 19, reel C-4756.
Japanese immigration, form file(lists), 1914.

File 9309, part 20, reel C-4756.
Japanese immigration, form file(lists), 1914-1915.

File 9309, part 21, reel C-4756.
Japanese immigration, form file(lists), 1915-1916.

File 9309, part 22, reel C-4757.
Japanese immigration, form file(lists), 1916.

File 9309, part 23, reel C-4757.
Japanese immigration, form file(lists), 1916.
Volume 92.

File 9309, part 24, reel C-4757.
Japanese immigration, form file(lists), 1916-1917.

File 9309, part 25, reel C-4757.
Japanese immigration, form file(lists), 1917.

File 9309, part 26, reel C-4757.
Japanese immigration, form file(lists), 1917.

File 9309, part 27, reel C-4757.
Japanese immigration, form file(lists), 1917-1918.

File 9309, part 28, reel C-4757 to C-4758.
Japanese immigration, form file(lists), 1918.

File 9309, part 29, reel C-4758.
Japanese immigration, form file(lists), 1918.

Volume 93.

File 9309, part 31, reel C-4758.
Japanese immigration, form file(lists), 1918-1919.

File 9309, part 32, reel C-4758.
Japanese immigration, form file(lists), 1919-1920.

Volume 121.

File 23635, part 1, reel C-4784.
Chinese immigration, 1895-1909.

File 23635, part 2, reel C-4784.
Chinese immigration, report by W.L.MacKenzie King, 1908-1911.
File 23635, part 3, reel C-4784.
Chinese immigration, 1911-1918.

File 23635, part 4, reel C-4784.
Chinese immigration, 1918-1919.

File 23635, part 5, reel C-4784.
Chinese immigration, 1919-1924.

File 23635, part 6, reel C-4785.
Chinese immigration, 1924-1943.

Volume 122.

File 23635, part 7, reel C-4785.
Chinese immigration, 1943-1948.

File 23635, part 8, reel C-4785.
Chinese immigration, 1948-1949.

File 23635, part 9, reel C-4785.
Chinese immigration, 1949-1950.

File 23635, part 10, reel C-4785.
Chinese immigration, 1951-1952.

Volume 125.

File 27114, reel C-4736,
Immigration of Armenians to Western Canada.
D.M.Quin, manager, 1895-1905.

Volume 215.

File 89616, part 1, reel C-7366.
Armenian relief fund. Admissions of orphans to Canada(photographs) 1922-1926.

File 89616, part 2, reel C-7366.
Armenian relief fund. Admission of orphans, 1926-1928.

File 89616, part 3, reel C-7366.
Armenian relief fund. Bringing orphans to Canada, 1928-1934, 1944.

Volume 223.

File 111414, reel C-7372.
Registration of Chinese in Canada under section 18 of the Chinese Immigration Act of 1923, 1942-1943, 1958.

Volume 226.

File 116193, part 1, reel C-7375.
Hong Kong(photographs and plans), 1923-1942.

File 116193, part 2, reel C-7375.
Administration and inspection at Hong Kong, 1945-1949.

Volume 280.

File 536999, part 1, reel C-10279-C-10280.
Emigration of Hindoos, 1904,1906-1907.

File 536999, part 2, reel C-10280.
Emigration of Hindoos(including British Honduras, labour(East Indian) ordinances, 1908), 1907-1908.

File 536999, part 3, reel C-10,280.
Emigration of Hindoos, 1908-1911.

File 536999, part 4, reel C-10,280.
Emigration of Hindoos, 1911-1912.

Volume 300.

File 279907, part 1, reel C-7849,
Immigration from Turkey and Armenia, 1903-1915, 1919-1923.

File 279907, part 2, reels C-7849-C-7850.
Immigration from Turkey and Armenia, 1923-1928.

File 279907, part 3, reel C-7850.
Immigration from Turkey and Armenia, 1929-1934, 1936-1938, 1940, 1946-1949.

Volume 342.

File 361435, reel C-10250.
Fred Yoshi, alias Kiyoshi Suhinto, Vancouver, smuggling Japanese into Canada, 1920-1921, 1928-1932.

Volume 363.

File 462223, reel C-10264.
White Canada Association, Vancouver, British Columbia, information on statistics on Japanese in Canada, 1934-1938.

File 467977, part 1, reel C-10264 to C-10265.
Consul-general for Japan, Ottawa, 1906-1911, 1912-1925.

File 467977, part 2, reel C-10265.
Consul-general for Japan, Ottawa, Ontario, 1928, 1930-1931, 1933-1944, 1948.

Volume 368.

File 488557, reel C-10268.
Privy Council reference from Colonial Office relating to Armenians in Brantford, Ontario, who wish to obtain permission for their families to rejoin them from Armenia, 1906-1907.

Volume 382.

File 532462, reel C-10278.
Investigation by Royal Canadian Mounted Police of illegal entry of Japanese, 1931-1934.

Volume 385.

File 536999, part 5, reel C-10280.
Emigration of Hindoos, 1912-1913.

File 536999, part 6, reel C-10280.
Emigration of Hindoos, 1913.

File 536999, part 7, reel C-10280.
Emigration of Hindoos(appeals against deportation), 1913.

File 536999, part 8, reel C-10280.
Emigration of Hindoos, 1913-1914.

File 536999, part 9, reel C-10280.
Emigration of Hindoos, 1914-1916.

File 536999, part 10, reel C-10280.
Emigration of Hindoos(including **Extracts from Minutes of Proceedings and Papers laid before the Imperial War Conference),** 1917, 1916-1918.

Volume 386.

File 536999, part 11, reel C-10280 to C-10281.
Emigration of Hindoos(including **Extracts from Minutes of Proceedings and Papers laid before the Imperial War Conference),** 1917, 1917-1919.

File 536999, part 12, reel C-10281.
Emigration of Hindoos(including **Summary of proceedings and documents on Conference of Prime Ministers**), 1921, 1919-1921.

File 536999, part 13, reel C-10281.
Emigration of Hindoos(copies of acts), 1921-1923.

File 536999, part 14, reel C-10281.
Emigration of Hindoos(copies of acts)(lists),1922-1935.

File 536999, part 15, reel C-10281.
Emigration of Hindoos, 1934-1939.

Volume 387.

File 536999, part 16, reel C-10281.
Emigration of Hindoos(lists), 1939-1943.

File 536999, part 17, reel C-10281.
Emigration of Hindoos(lists), 1943-1947.

File 536999, part 18, reel C-10281 to C-10282.
Emigration of Hindoos(lists), 1947-1948.

File 536999, part 19, reel C-10282.
Emigration of Hindoos(lists), 1948-1949.

File 536999 R.O., part 1.
Registering certificates of identification to Hindoos leaving on a visit, 1913-1919.

Volume 388.

File 536999 R.O., part 2, reel C-10282.
Registering certificates of identification to Hindoos leaving on a visit(pamphlet), 1919-1922.

File 536999 R.O., part 3, reel C-10282.
Registering certificates of identification to Hindoos leaving on a visit, 1923-1954.

File 536999 British, part 1, reel C-10282.
Reports from W.C.Hopkinson on Hindoo matters(copies), 1914-1919.

File 536999 British, part 2, reel C-10282.
Reports from W.C.Hopkinson on Hindoo matters, 1919-1921.

File 536999 clippings, part 1, reel C-10282.
Newspaper clippings on Hindoos, 1913-1914.

File 536999 clippings, part 2, reels C-10282 to C-10283.
Newspaper clippings on Hindoos, 1914-1915, 1918.

File 536999 clippings, part 3, reel C-10283.
Newspaper clippings on Hindoos, 1918, 1920, 1922.

Volume 393.

File 561280, reel C-10286.
Ocean Steamship Company, Liverpool, England. Bonds covering escape of two Japanese, T.Obano and M.Ohishi(in Vancouver, British Columbia), 1906.

Volume 397.

File 565225, reel C-10289.
Chick Sexing Association of America, admission of chick sexing experts from Japan, 1933-1937.

Volume 401.

File 574351, reel C-10292.
G.L.Milne(medical inspector and immigration agent) Vancouver, British Columbia, escape of Japanese from schooner **Swan maru**, 1906.

Volume 470.

File 716275, reel C-10407.
G.L.Milne sends fine of $350.00 for allowing seven Japanese to land at Union Bay, British Columbia, without properly entering customs at that place, German ship S.S. **Wanguard**, 1907.

Volume 474.

File 729921, part 1, reel C-10410.
Asiatics, Orientals(Japanese, Chinese, East Indians), (list), 1907-1922.

File 729921, part 1, reel C-10410.
Asiatics, Orientals(Japanese, Chinese and East Indians), (pamphlets), 1922-1925.

File 729921, part 3, reel C-10410 to C-10411.
Asiatics, Orientals(Japanese, Chinese and East Indians), 1925-1932, 1934-1939.

File 729921 clippings, reel C-10411.
Newspaper clippings on Asiatic immigration(Japanese, Chinese and East Indians) 1907, 1909-1922.

Volume 491.

File 761402, reel C-10425.
A.Lavergne, member of Parliament, Montmagny, Québec. Japanese syndicate acquiring land in Alberta in order to settle colonists there, 1906, 1908, 1913.

Volume 503.

File 781181, reel C-10606.
Richard L.Drury, Victoria, British Columbia, appointed as a special officer of the Immigration branch for immigration work in Japan, 1908-1909.

Volume 512.

File 817172, reel C-10653.
J.B.Harkin wants employment in the fishing industry retained for Canadians(Japanese):1910-1948.

Volume 546.

File 304845, reel C-10632
Inquiries from the Fiji islands, 1908-1911.

Volume 550.

File 805806, reel C-10634.
Khoren Andonian, destitute at Batoum, Russia, makes application for repatriation to Canada(Armenian), 1908-1909.

Volume 551.

File 806018, reel C-10635.
Francis W. Giddens, Department of Labour, Ottawa, Ontario, statement re Chinese, Japanese, and Hindu immigration, 1908-1909.

Volume 556.

File 806652, reel C-10638.
Business manager, **Free Press**, Ottawa, Ontario. Printing pamphlet, **East Indians in British Columbia**(copies), 1909.

Volume 561.

File 808722, part 1, reel C-10641.
W.C.Hopkinson, Vancouver, British Columbia, appointed to the immigration staff at Vancouver, British Columbia(Hindu immigration), 1909-1914.

File 808722, part 2, reel C-10,641.
W.C.Hopkinson, Vancouver, British Columbia, appointed to the immigration staff at Vancouver, British Columbia(Hindu immigration), 1914-1916, 1918.

Volume 563.

File 808904, reel C-10644.
General enquiries from Persia, 1909, 1912-1913.

Volume 566.

File 806977, reel C-10638.
United States Commissioner of Immigration, Montréal, Québec. Report on number of Japanese and Hindoos entering United States, 1907 and 1909.

Volume 568.

File 812274, reel C-10647.
A.B.Barnard, Deputy Director of Intelligence, India, photographs and fingerprints of reports(Hindus), 1909, 1911-1912, 1920-1926.

Volume 576.

File 815661, reel C-10652.
Chinese conditions: 1912, 1921-1932, 1935-1938.

Volume 578.

File 817172, reel C-10653.
J.B.Harkin wants employment in the fishing industry on the Fraser River to be retained for Canadians (Japanese), 1910, 1912-1916, 1918-1919, 1933 and 1948.

Volume 584.

File 820636, reel C-10658.
Honourable Frank Oliver, Minister of the Interior, Ottawa, Canada. Prevalence of hookworm among Hindus applying for admission to U.S. and among the negroes(blacks) of the U.S., 1910-1914, 1918, 1922-1923, 1943.

Volume 601.

File 879545, part 1, reel C-10,669.
Hindoo immigration, sailing of 400 Hindoos by chartered vessel **Komagata maru**, 1914.

File 879545, part 2, reel C-10,669.
Hindoos sailing from Shanghai to Vancouver, British Columbia on S. S. **Komagata maru**, 1914.

File 879545, part 3, reel C-10,669.
Hindoos sailing from Shanghai to Vancouver, British Columbia on **Komagata maru,** S..S. (photograph), 1914.

File 879545, part 4, reel C-10,669.
Hindoos sailing from Shanghai to Vancouver, British Columbia on **Komagata maru**, S.S., 1914.

Volume 602.

File 879545, part 5, reel C-10,669 to C-10,670.
Hindoos sailing from Shanghai to Vancouver, British Columbia on S.S. **Komagata maru** (publication), 1914.

File 879545, part 6, reel C-10,670.
Hindoos sailing from Shanghai to Vancouver, British Columbia on S.S. **Komagata maru**, 1914-1915.

File 879545, part 7, reel C-10,670.
Hindoos sailing from Shanghai to Vancouver, British Columbia on S.S. **Komagata maru**, 1915-1922.

File 879545, part 8, reel C-10,670.
Hindoos sailing from Shanghai to Vancouver, British Columbia on S.S. **Komagata maru**, 1936, 1938, 1942, 1952.

Volume 647.

File A66589, part 1, reel C-10586.
Repatriation of Japanese(lists), 1941-1943, 1945.

File A66589, part 2, reel C-10587.
Repatriation of Japanese(lists), 1946-1947.

Volume 669.

File C57382, reel C-10603.
Transit of German refugees from Shanghai, China through Canada(Jewish), 1949.

Volume 674.

File C92656, reel C-10677.
Admission of Jewish refugees from Shanghai(lists), 1950.

File C92656, reel C-10677.
Admission of Jewish refugees from Shanghai, China(lists), 1950.

Volume 675.

File D46144, reel C-10677.
Greek Embassy, Ottawa, Ontario, admission of 200 Greeks from China(lists) , 1951-1952.

Volume 712.

Reel C-13421.
Control certificates, Chinese immigration(c.1, 5, 28, 30, 36), 1899-1953.

84 • British Columbia – Victoria

B. Central Registry Files. Second Central Registry series("500" block) 1911-1970 (volumes 676, 677, 689 to 692, and 743 to 930), 7 microfilm reels(C-10678, C-10687 to C-10688, C-13487, and M-1983 to M-1985).
l. Central Registry files, "500" block, 1911-1971. 40.2 metres (volumes 689-692, 718-725, 743-930), and 2 microfilm reels(C-10687 to C-10688).

This series consists of the Immigration Service's core policy and subject files active in the period from World War II to l966.

Volumes 743 to 930 are the main run of files in this series. Volumes 689 to 692, reels C-10,687 and C-10,688, document questions and answers in the House of Commons, including individual cases, immigration and employment policy and statistics, U.S. draft dodgers and deserters, and refugees issues from 1957 to 1970.

Volumes 718-725 relate to the Immigration Inspection Service on irregularities in immigration.

Finding aids.

Subject index to "500" block and related files, ca. 1925-1962. 3 microfilm reels M-1983 to M-1985.

Complete list of files in this series available.

The file classification manual indicates some of the files created in this series.

Volume 713.

Reel C-13421.
Register of Chinese Immigration, Central District(Toronto), 1923-1953.

Volume 796.

File 546-1-526, part 1.
Medical examinations of immigrants from China and Hong Kong, 1950-1957.

File 546-1-526, part 2.
Medical examinations of immigrants from China, Hong Kong and Formosa, 1958-1966.

Volume 802.

File 547-5-567.
Security examination of immigrants in India, 1962-1966.

File 547-5-580.
Security examination of persons from Korea, 1963-1966.

File 547-5-611.
Security examination of immigrants in the Philippines, 1961-1966.

Volume 803.

File 547-5-629.
Security examination of immigrants in Thailand, 1966.

File 548-8, part 1.
Processing of Chinese applications (including form 55b procedures), 1951-1956.

File 548-8, part 2.
Processing of Chinese applications (including form 55b procedures), 1956-1961.

Volume 804.

File 548-8, part 3.
Processing of Chinese applications (including form 55b procedures), 1961-1963.

File 548-8, part 4.
Processing of Chinese applications (including form 55b procedures), 1964-1966.

Volume 808.

File 548-12-578.
Processing of applications, Japan, 1965-1966.

Volume 819.

File 552-1-5-522.
Immigration from Burma, 1963-1966.

File 552-1-524.
Immigration from Ceylon, 1960-1065.

File 552-1-526, part 1.
Immigration from China, general files, 1952-1955.

File 552-1-526, part 2.
Immigration from China, policy and instructions, 1955-1958.

File 552-1-526, part 3.
Immigration from China, policy and instructions, 1958-1962.

File 552-1-526, part 4.
Immigration from China, policy and instructions, 1962-1963.

Volume 820.

File 552-1-526, part 5.
Immigration from China, policy and instructions, 1964-1966.

Volume 821.

File 552-1-548.
Immigration from the Fiji Islands, general file , 1953-1966.

Volume 822.

File 522-1-567, part 1.
Immigration from India, 1950-1961.

File 522-1-567, part 2.
Immigration from India, 1961-1966.

Volume 823.

File 552-1-537.
Immigration from Iran, general file, 1951-1956.

File 552-1-569.
Immigration from Indonesia, 1950-1964.

File 552-1-570.
Immigration from Iran, general file, 1951-1966.

Volume 824.

File 552-1-578, part 1.
Immigration from Japan, general file, 1950-1957.

File 552-1-578, part 2.
Immigration from Japan, general file, 1957-1964.

File 552-1-578, part 3.
Immigration from Japan, general file (reading list enclosed), 1964-1966.

File 552-1-580.
Immigration from Korea, general file, 1896-1966.

Volume 826.

File 552-1-606.
Immigration from Pakistan, general file, 1953-1966.

File 552-1-611, part 1.
Immigration from the Philippines, 1929-1963.

File 552-1-611, part 2.
Immigration from the Philippine Islands, 1929-1963.

Volume 829.

File 552-1-632.
Immigration from Turkey, general file, 1951-1966.

Volume 831.

File 5521-10-567, part 1.
Canada-India Immigration agreement, policy and instructions, 1951-1952.

File 5521-10-567, part 2.
Canada-India Immigration agreement, policy and instructions, 1953-1954.

File 5521-10-567, part 3.
Canada-India immigration agreement, policy and instructions, 1955-1956.

File 5521-10-567, part 4.
Canada-India immigration agreement, policy and instructions, 1957-1959.

Volume 832.

File 5521-10-567, part 5.
Canada-India immigration agreement, policy and instructions, 1959-1962.

File 5521-10-567, part 6.
Canada-India immigration agreement, policy and instructions, 1963-1966.

File 552-10-606, part 1.
Canada-Pakistan immigration agreement, policy and instructions, 1951-1956.

Volume 850.

File 553-148-567.
Admission to Canada of students from India, 1920-1966.

File 553-148-578.
Movement of students from Japan, 1960-1965.

File 533-148-592.
Movement of students from Malaysia (formerly Malaya, Singapore, etc.) policy and instructions, 1960-1964.

File 553-10-606.
Movement of students from Pakistan, 1962-1964.

Volume 854.

File 554-3, part 1.
Immigration to Canada of Armenians, general file, 1950-1961.

File 554-3, part 2.
Immigration to Canada of Armenians, general file, 1961-1966.

File 554-5.
Asiatics, general policy, 1953-1963.

File 554-6.
Asiatic immigration, 1923-1950.

Volume 861.

File 555-54-526, part 1.
Chinese refugees in Hong Kong(and refugees in China) general file, 1946-1961.

File 555-54-526, part 2.
Chinese refugees in Hong Kong(and refugees in China) general file, 1962-1963.

File 555-54-526, part 3.
Special movement of Chinese refugees from Hong Kong, operational control, 1962-1963.

Volume 862.

File 554-54-526-5.
Tibetan refugees, general file, 1959-1966.

Volume 866.

File 555-54-632.
Refugees in Turkey, general file, 1951-1963.

Volume 867.
File 556-1-524.
Immigration laws and regulations, Ceylon, 1942-1961.

Volume 868.

File 556-1-567.
Immigration laws and regulations, India, 1945-1950.

File 556-1-570.
Immigration laws and regulations, Iran, 1960.

File 556-1-606.
Immigration laws and regulations, Pakistan, 1948-1950.

File 556-1-611.
Immigration laws and regulations, Philippines, 1930-1963.

Volume 870.

File 556-3-570.
Alien labor laws and regulations, Iran, 1959.

Volume 871.

File 557-3-578, part 2.
Establishment of Japanese enterprises and entry of personnel, 1961-1966.

Volume 873.

File 557-40-12, part 1.
Canadian church organizations proposals for entry of Chinese immigrants from Hong Kong, 1960-1963.

File 557-40-12, part 2.
Canadian church organizations proposals for entry of Chinese immigrants from Hong Kong, 1964-1966.

Volume 876.

File 560-2-578.
Citizenship regulations, Japan, 1916-1950.

File 560-2-606.
Citizenship regulations, Pakistan, 1951.

File 560-6-526, part 1.
Status adjustment of Chinese illegally in Canada, 1960-1961.

File 560-6-526, part 2.
Status adjustment of Chinese illegally in Canada, policy and procedure, 1961-1962.

File 560-6-526, part 3.
Status adjustment of Chinese illegally in Canada, policy and procedure, 1962-1963.

Volume 877.

File 560-6-526, part 4.
Status adjustment of Chinese illegally in Canada, policy and procedure, 1962-1963.

File 560-6-526, part 5.
Status adjustment of Chinese illegally in Canada, policy and procedure, 1965-1966.

File 560-6-567.
Status adjustments of East Indians who have entered Canada illegally, 1961-1965.

Volume 895.

File 569-2.
Passport and visa regulations for Chinese nationals, 1938-1964.

File 569-9-510.
Passport regulations, Cambodia, 1954.

File 569-9-524.
Passport regulations, Ceylon, 1950-1965.

Volume 898.

File 569-9-561.
Passport regulations, Maldive Islands, 1966.

File 569-9-567.
Passport regulations, India, 1953-1966.

File 569-9-569.
Passport regulations, Indonesia, 1950-1964.

File 569-9-570.
Passport regulations, Iran, 1954-1966.

Volume 899.

File 569-9-.
Passport regulations, Japan, 1918-1965.

Volume 900.

File 596-9-606.
Passport regulations, Pakistan, 1953-1963.

File 569-9-611.
Passport regulations, Philippines, 1953-1964.

File 569-9-621.
Passport regulations, Singapore, 1960-1965.

Volume 901.

File 555-54-632.
Refugees in Turkey, general file, 1951-1963.

File 569-9-641.
Passport regulations, Vietnam, 1953-1966.

Volume 903.

File 569-30-522.
Issuance of Canadian visas to persons from Burma, 1953-1966.

File 569-30-524.
Issuance of Canadian visas to persons from India, 1950-1963.

File 569-30-526.
Issuance of Canadian visas to persons from China, 1949-1960.

Volume 904.

File 569-30-567.
Issuance of Canadian visas to persons from India, 1950-1965.

File 569-30-569.
Issuance of Canadian visas to persons from Indonesia, 1960-1961.

File 569-30-570.
Issuance of Canadian passports to persons from Iran, 1958-1966.

File 569-30-578.
Issuance of visas to persons from Laos, 1959.

Volume 905.

File 569-30-578.
Issuance of Canadian visas to persons from Japan, 1959-1966.

File 569-30-592.
Issuance of Canadian visas to persons from Malaysia(formerly Malaya, Singapore, etc.), 1950-1958.

File 569-30-611.
Issuance of Canadian visas to persons from the Philippines, 1953-1963.

File 569-30-621.
Issuance of Canadian visas to nationals from Singapore, 1965.

File 569-30-632.
Issuance of Canadian visas to persons from Turkey, 1953-1966.

Issuance of Canadian visas to persons from Korea, 1960.

File 569-30-589.
Issuance of Canadian visas to persons from North Korea, 1963-1964.

File 569-30-606.
Issuance of Canadian visas to persons from Pakistan, 1955-1962.

Volume 906.

File 569-36-524.
Passport and visas agreements, Ceylon, 1949-1950.

Volume 907.

File 569-36-570.
Passport and visa agreements, Canada-Iran, 1959-1961.

File 569-36-578.
Passport and visas agreements, Canada-Japan, 1954-1965.

File 569-36-632.
Passport and visa agreements, Canada-Turkey, 1949-1963.

Volume 914.

File 581-3-2, part 1.
Japanese agricultural students, general file, 1955-1959.

File 581-3-2, part 2.
Japanese agricultural students, general file, 1960.

Volume 917.

File 584-2-641.
Entry of nationals of Vietnam for medical treatment, 1965-1966.

Volume 920.

File 585-12-578.
Repatriation of Japanese from Canada, 1945-1966.

VI. **Chinese immigration records, 1885-1953**, .9 metres(volumes 693-703, 712, 713), 5 microfilm reels, C-9510 to C-9513, C-13421. The Provincial Archives has only the records up to 1903.

The Department of Customs was made responsible for the administration of the Chinese Immigration Act of 1885, and a general register was to be maintained for Chinese immigrants who entered Canada. In 1893, the Department of Trade and Commerce was established, and customs officers, as controllers of Chinese immigration were to report to the Deputy Minister of Trade and Commerce. In 1911, the administration of the Act was transferred to the Immigration Branch of the Department of the Interior, and the Immigration Branch was responsible for the administration of the Act until 1947.

A.CI.6 certificate was issued to all Chinese who had entered Canada before 1885, and a CI.5 certification to Chinese immigrants who arrived after 1885, and paid the head tax. CI.9 and CI.9A certificates were issued to persons wishing to leave Canada temporarily.

A. General registers of Chinese immigration, 1885-1903, .9 metres(volumes 694-703), 4 microfilm reels, C-9510 to C-9513.
Gives information on Chinese immigrants, some as early as 1860, including village and province of birth in China. General registers numbers 11-to 18, 1903-1949, are found in Record Group 76, accession 84-85/062, with a microfilm version in 84-85/238.

B. New Westminster Agency, register of Chinese immigration, 1887-1808, 1907 and 1908, .075 metres(Volume 693), one microfilm reel(C-9510).
In 1885, the Collectors of Customs at Victoria, Nanaimo, New Westminster, and the sub-Collectors of Customs at Osoyoos and Kootenay and all collectors and acting collectors of customs, as controllers of Chinese immigration, having to register Chinese immigrants, collect head tax, and issue C.I. certificates of identification.

1. Register of Chinese immigrants, Port of New Westminster, 1887--1898, 1907 and 1908, .075 metres(Volume 693), one microfilm reel, C-9510.

List of Chinese immigrants who registered and paid the head tax at New Westminster, British Columbia.

C. Central district, registers and certificates of Chinese immigration, 1899-1953, .05 metres,(volumes 712,713), one microfilm reel, C-13421.

Immigration activities for Toronto were controlled by Central District Headquarters. Chinese moving in or out of Canada were required to register their movement with the controllers of Chinese immigration at Toronto.

1. Register of Chinese immigration (Toronto), 1923-1953(Volume 713), one microfilm reel, C-13421.

Chinese register number 2, created in the Office of Immigration's central district(Toronto), and used to control Chinese immigration to and temporary emigration from Canada, particularly outward CI.9 registrations. Register number 1 for registrations before 1923 has apparently not survived.

2. Sample C.I. certificates, C.I.5, CI.28, C.I.30, and C.I.36, 1899-1953(Volume 712), one microfilm reel, C-13421.

The certificate system was used to control the movement of Chinese in and out of Canada, and of seamen sailing out of the Great Lakes system. These certificates seem to have never been used.

Chen, Kathleen Swee Yin.
Typescript, 1984, 2 cm.
British Columbia fiction: attitudes towards Chinese.
187 leaves. Thesis (M.A.), Simon Fraser University
Add.MSS.2389

Chinese Grocery.
Originals, 25 cm.
Account book written in Chinese.
Add.MSS.1031.

Chinese ledger, Choate, British Columbia
Originals, undated(2 items).
Account ledger; Chinese language book; A story, either personal or copied appears near the back of the language book.
Presented by W.A. Armstrong, Emery Camp, Choate, B.C. on l October 1932.
Add.MSS.135

Chinese letters, account books, etc.
1865, 1870s, 1898. Originals.
Form of contract passage ticket, vessel
Maria, Hong Kong to Victoria, 1865 (87 items).
Free miner's certificate, mining receipt,
Te Ah Che, 1898 (2 items)
Medicine books, account books, written in Chinese(6 items), (Volume 1).Letters to father in British Columbia in the 1870s, containing information relating to crops, family news, information re investment of remittances, written in Chinese (1/2 inch) (Volume 2).
Description of the material in Chinese was provided by Charles Sedgwick, M.A. University of Victoria.
K EA C43

Claxton Family(Cecil Claxton, 1886-1977)
Originals. 88 cm, 1890-1972.
Correspondence between and documents relating to Cecil Claxton, his wife Helen, and their son Peter, and correspondence between them and relatives in England and China. Major series include letters from Captain Claxton to his wife written when he was Staff Captain on the Canadian Pacific's Trans-Pacific route, 1924-1934; letters between Captain and Mrs. Claxton, 1942-1943, written when Claxton was in Vancouver as Superintendent of Pilots for British Columbia; and letters from Mrs. Claxton's mother and sister in China, ca. 1927-1946.
Finding aid. File list.
Add.MSS.2183

Cook, James, 1728-1779.
Navigator.
Transcripts, photocopies, 1776-1780.
Autograph draft of Cook's second voyage, 6-26 January 1774.
Photographed and transcribed by John Steelquist, April 1972.
ULM

Cook, James, 1728-1779.
Transcripts, 80 pages, 1776-1780.
A brief account of Cook's third voyage, containing his instructions and orders from the Admiralty, and letters written by Captains Cook, Gore and King.
ULM

Cook, James, 1728-1779.
Transcript, 5 inches, 1776-1779.
A journal by Captain James Cook preserved in the British Museum and transcribed by hand.
ULM

Cook, James, 1728-1779.
Transcripts, 7 inches. 1776-1779.
Journal of H.M.S. **Resolution**, transcribed by hand.
ULM

Cook, James, 1728-1779.
Transcripts, 4.5 inches, 1776-1778.
Log of H.M.S .**Resolution**, transcribed by hand. original in the Public Record Office.
ULM

Dallas, Alexander Grant, 1818-1882.
Governor-in-Chief of Rupert's Land.
Originals. 6 cm. 1832-1855.
Sketchbook(1832) and miscellaneous prints; journals(1837-1840) providing accounts of voyages to Italy, Calcutta(via the Cape of Good Hope), and logbook of a voyage from China to California and Mexico(1853-1855); miscellaneous notes and newspaper clippings.
Add.MSS.745

Dickie, Francis Joseph, 1890-1976.
Quadra Island; writer.
Originals, 1932-1952, 178 cm., Correspondence, manuscripts, accounts, photographs and newspaper clippings.
Finding aid: file list.
Japanese in British Columbia.
Add.MSS.6

Dickie, Robert Ronald.
Reminiscences (of India). Undated.

Drury, Richard Law.
Correspondence and papers relating to mission to Japan, 1908.
E D D843

Duval, Jean-Marc, 1948-
Microfiche(positive), 1975, 2 fiche.
Japanese joint ventures in British Columbia, 1974. 152 leaves. M.Sc. Business Administration thesis, University of British Columbia, 1974.
Add.MSS.1708.

Ebenezer Dorr(Firm)
Textual records, 1790-1819. 6 cm.
Correspondence regarding news of the fur trade and documents of ships engaged in the triangle trade between Boston, the West Coast and China. Ebenezer Dorr was a ship's merchant in Boston, Massachusetts.
Add.MSS.828/BCARCH-38240

Ellison, Price, 1851-1932.
Vernon, British Columbia; rancher, politician.
Photocopy, 1884-1966. Microfilm(negative, 1884-1966, 1 reel, 35 mm.
Consists of correspondence, accounts, agreements, an indenture and newspaper clippings.
Finding aid.
Orientals in British Columbia.
Add.MSS.0007

Frost, Robert.
Transcripts(typed), 5 cm. ca. 1979.
 Reminiscences of life in China from 1916, first as a ship's officer and later as cargo superintendent with Jardine Matheson; "To Russia with love from the Persian Gulf": an account of his work organizing the unloading of wartime cargo at Abadan in 1943, My Affair with Kuan Yin: the memoirs of Robert Frost(Victoria, British Columbia, Morris Printing Company, Ltd, 1983).
Add.MSS.1079

Great Britain. India Office.
Transcripts, 1 inch, 1786-1787.
Official journal of a voyage to the Northwest coast of America by Captain James Charles Stuart Strange for the Bombay Council of the East India Company.
ULM

Great Britain. India Office.
Transcripts, 2 cm., 1785-1789.
Extracts from Factory Records(China), 1787-1789; Minutes of the Committee of Correspondence, 1785-1788; Court Minutes, 1785-1788, miscellaneous letters received, 1785-1788.
ULM

Harris, Joseph Colebrook, 1871-1951.
New Denver, British Columbia; rancher,
Originals, 1919-1950, 52 cm.
Personal correspondence; letters to editors; essays, articles and lectures; poems and songs, most of which reflect socialist viewpoint.
Finding aid: file list.
Japanese in British Columbia,
Add.MSS.807.

Harris, Richard Colebrook, 1900-
New Denver, British Columbia, rancher.
Originals, 1978, 12 leaves.
Biography of Joseph Colebrook Harris, New Denver area rancher, dairy farmer and essayist, prepared by his son.
Japanese in British Columbia.
Add.MSS.819.

Harrison, Eli, 1852-1930.
Victoria, B.C.; County Court Judge.
Originals, 1886, 1 leaf.
Letter from Caspar Phair, Sheriff of Lillooet, to Mr. Justice Harrison regarding the sitting of County Court and the gold discoveries made by Chinese miners at Cayoosh Creek.
Add.MSS.1304.

Hayes, M., D.H. Perry and J. Gray, defendants.
Judge's summation in trial of Hayes, Perry Hand Gray

for murder of Yee Fook, 8 May 1883, 3 September 1883. Transcript (handwritten). Chinese in British Columbia.
9 leaves
K JA H32

Henry, Arthur, 1876-1946.
Microfilm(negative) 165 mm. 1897-1936. 2 reels.
Diaries, 1896-1900.
Henry was in the Royal Marines Artillery on board H.M.S. *Victorious* on the China Station; he emigrated to British Columbia in 1911.
Add.MSS.1502

Hobson, H.B. Cariboo district(British Columbia)
Microfilm(negative), 1897-1898, 1914, 1 reel.
Diary of weather and events April 1897-March 1898.
Japanese in British Columbia.
Add.MSS.2724.

Imai, Matsuo(Frank) b. ca. 1904.
Original. 4 pages, 1974.
Japanese text of a speech given by Mr. Imai at the dedication of Imai Park, Scotch Creek, 1974. Also transcript of English translation.
Add.MSS.84
ULM1

Japanese fishing vessels disposal committee. Report. 1942.
J G J2

Jones, James Williams, 1869-1954. Kelowna, Victoria; businessman, politician.
Originals, 1908-1934, 2.16 metres.
Private and official correspondence and newspaper clippings. Finding aid: file list.
Japanese in British Columba.
Add.MSS.23.

Kermode, Francis, 1874-1946.
The arrival of the "Kermodes" and the first Japanese in Victoria. Undated. Typescript.
E E N421K

Klassen, Herbert C.
Federal disallowance of British Columbia legislation, 1885-1914, 1954-1955. Typescript.
Chinese in British Columbia.
K K66

Knowlton, William E.
Collector.
Originals 1 cm, 1858-1884.
Materials relating to Chinese businessmen and settlers in British Columbia.
Photocopies in National Archives of Canada.
Add.MSS.1053/ULM4

Kwong Lee and Company,
Originals, 6 cm, 1885.
Statement of account in the matter of Kwong Lee and Company; receipts, account books.
ULM4

Lee, Jack H.
Victoria, British Columbia.
Originals, 1957, 15 items.
Draft transfers, bank money orders, receipts re payments of money sent to his family in China in 1957.
Add.MSS.2107.
BCARCH-34116

Lee, Quong, fl. 1870-1890.
Centreville, British Columbia. Miner.
Originals, 1879-1887. 5 leaves.
Free Miners Certificates, one of which is made out in the name of Dree Quong.
Chinese in British Columbia.
Add.MSS.646.

Lee, Stephen.
The coming of the Chinese people to Canada-Chinese in British Columbia. Undated. Typescript.
H A L51.

Lew, David C.
Letter book. June 7, 1907 - Sept. 22, 1910.
901 [i.e. 133, 49, 13] leaves . 31 cm.
Note: leaves 134-193 consist of a hand written essay by P.X. Belinsky. A memo concerning its origin is inside the front cover of the letter book. leaves 887-900 consist of letters written by Lew on his own behalf and on behalf of the Chinese Benevolent Association.
E D 1910 l58

Lim, Le Bang, 1880-1974.
Victoria. Businessman.
Original. 1 page, 1911.
Letter from Dr. Sun Yat-sen regarding fund raising for Nationalist China, written in Chinese.
Add.MSS.1027/ULM3

Lougheed, Nelson S.
Originals, 1920, 9 cm.
Scrapbook of cuttings kept by Nels Lougheed of the British Columbia Conservation Society relating to agriculture, elections, emigration. education, government, industry, legislation, mining, Orientals, politics, roads, reclamation, taxes, timber and logging, women and politics.
Add.MSS.2594.

Lun Chung and Company
Victoria.
Original, 4 pages, 1890, 1891.
Four customs forms for the importation of goods, including opium from Hong Kong.
ULM

MacKenzie, John Peter.
Military engineer.
1 page, 1946.
Letter from Sam L. Bedson about efforts by Vancouver Chinese merchants to export goods to China, and offering comments about strikes and rumours of strikes in the Vancouver area.

Add.MSS.1039/ULM4

McLeod, Malcolm, 1821-1899.
Originals, 1823-1899. 1.3 metres.
Includes correspondence with Ranald Macdonald, who taught English in Japan: 1848-1849, reminiscences and Japanese glossaries by Macdonald, manuscripts by McLeod entitled: "Japan, story of adventure of Ranald Macdonald". Finding list.
Add.MSS.1249./ULM4

MacMillan Bloedel, Limited, Alberni Pacific Division,.
Alberni, British Columbia.
Microfilm, 1 reel, 1930-1979.
Schedule showing wages paid to apprentices, equipment operators, labourers, tradesmen and others at the Alberni operations of MacMillan Bloedel Limited and its predecessors, 1930-1979. Includes wage scale surveys and nominal list of Chinese, Indians and Japanese employed at Great Central Sawmill, 1934-1941.
Japanese in Vancouver Island. Chinese in Vancouver Island.
Add.MSS. 1641./ULM4

Marlatt, Daphne.
Steveston Recollected. Victoria, Provincial Archives, 1975.

Meares, Cecil Henry, 1877-1937.
Traveller, British military officer.
Originals, 1910-1923, 13 cm., also on microfilm(negative).
Three letters and a postcard, 1910-1913, relating to the British Antarctic Expedition, letters written to his wife from the trenches, fall of 1914, letters and certificates re Service with the British mission in Japan, 1921-1922, manuscript entitled "The Land of the Budorchus", printed articles re travels in Western China ca. 1908-1909. Finding aid.
Add.MSS.455

Minoura, Yasuko, 1939-
Mirofiche(positive), 1977, 2 fiche.
Value orientations found in British Columbia and Japanese schoolbooks; the 1920's- the1970's. 1975.
M.A. thesis, University of Victoria, 1985.
Add.MSS.1748.

Nakayama, Timothy Makoto.
Anglican Japanese missions in Canada.
Typescript. 55 p.
H A N15

Ng Family,
British Columbia.
Originals, 24 cm.
History of the Ng family in 20 volumes(in Chinese)
Add.MSS.2674.

Ng, Chee Chiu Clement.
Microfiche, 1986, 4 fiche.
The Chinese Benevolent Association of Vancouver: 1885-1923, a response to local conditions. 293 p.
M.S.W. thesis, University of Manitoba,1986.
Add.MSS.2674

Oriental Home and School(Victoria, British Columbia) Advisory Committee.
Microfilm(negative), 1896-1915, 35 mm. 103 exposures.
Minute book of the Advisory Committee of the Chinese Rescue Home, 1896-1915(the name of the home was changed to the Oriental Home and School in August 24 1909)
Copies from the original borrowed from the Metropolitan United Church, Victoria, British Columbia, 1987.
Add.MSS.2439./BCARCH-30544

Plant, Charles J.E., 1891-1978.
La Jolla, California; Forest Industry Manager.
Bound photocopy, 1975, 81 p.
A Canadian manufacturing executive discusses the Western red cedar shingle industry [transcript of an interview with Charles Plant conducted by Elwood R.Maunder], 81 p. Santa Cruz, California,Forest History Society, 1975.
Transferred from Audio-Visual Records.
Chinese in British Columbia.
MS 2833

Presbyterian Church in Canada. Synod of British Columbia.
Microfilm(negative), 1902-1925, 1 reel. Printed minutes of the Synod of British Columbia for the years 1902 to 1925 inclusive except for 1904, 1905 and 1906, when the two western provinces combined to form the Synod of British Columbia and Alberta, reverting to individual provincial synods in 1907. The minutes include officers of the Synod, Rolls of Synod, brief committee reports on ecclesiastical and secular isssues, and obituaries, as well as regular business. These minutes are the precursor of the minutes of the British Columbia Conference of the United Church of Canada which commence in 1925.
Add.MSS.2697

Read, John Mark, 1945-
Microfiche(positive), 1976, 2 fiche.
The pre-war Japanese Canadians of Maple Ridge: land ownership and the **ken** tie. 1975. 96 leaves.
M.A. thesis, University of British Columbia, 1975.
Add.MSS.1720

Robinson family.
24 Photographs.1927-1931.
Photographs of Margaret and and family of the Anglican Church, Chinese kindergarten in Victoria, Sunday School Mission at 70 Mile House and Tattla Lake.
9892097-94/BCARCH-29520

Robson, Ebenezer, 1835-1911.
Reminiscences and miscellaneous articles.
Various dates. (In Ebenezer Robson collection)
Originals and typescripts, also newspaper clippings.
Chinese in British Columbia.

H D R57

Rockingham, John M. b. 1911.
Soldier, executive.
Photocopy, typescripts, 1975. 84 pages. "Recollections of Korea" by Major-General John M. Rockingham, First Commander, 25 Canadian Infantry Brigade Group.

Scott, William Alfred, 1898-1979.
China, Victoria, mechanic, Chinese Maritime Customs, ca. 1924-1975, 1.8 cm.
Subject files reflecting his interest in philosophy, civil liberties, local politics, correspondence, reports and diaries re life and work in China, family papers and correspondence. Finding list.
Add.MSS.1075/ULM4

Sedgwick, Charles P.
Typescript, 1973, 224 leaves.
The context of economic change and continuity in an urban overseas Chinese community(1973) M.A. thesis, University of Victoria, 1973.
Add.MSS 58.

Smith, Eustace, 1867-1964.
West Vancouver, British Columbia; timber cruiser, businessman.
Originals, 1930-1970, 8.5 cm.
Business and personal records of Eustace Smith, particularly relating to his mining activities, typewritten reminiscences and correspondence regarding timber business. Maps transferred to Map Division.
Japanese Property Claims Commission.
Add.MSS.960

Smithers, British Columbia; bakery.
Microfilm (negative), 35 mm., 1932, 1944-1954. 2 metres.
Account book, in Chinese, undated, and English, 1932 and 1944-1954.
Original loaned for copying by Bulkley Valley Historical and Museum Society.
Add.MSS.1579

Star Shipyard(Mercers) Limited, 1908-1970.
New Westminster; shipbuilders.
Originals, 1908-1970, 10 metres.
General correspondence, construction, repair and refit files. Photographs, plans and pamphlets transferred to Visual Records, Map Division and Northwest Collection.
Finding aid: file list and list of vessels by construction number, name, type and owner.
Japanese in British Columbia.
Add.MSS.448

Sumida, Rigenda.
Typescript, 1935.
The Japanese in British Columbia. 635 leaves.
M.A. thesis, University of British Columbia, 1935.
Add.MSS.2302

Sunahara, M. Ann.
Microfiche(positive), 1977, 2 fiche.
Federal policy and the Japanese Canadians, 1942-1950. 175 leaves.
M.A. thesis, University of Calgary, 1977.
Add.MSS.1943

Tiarks, John Gerhard.
Notes from the Far West, 1889-1890.
Letters to Weston Super Mare **Mercury**?
Chinese in Victoria.
E C T43

Trousdell, Hilda P.(Buncombe).
Diary of journey to Japan by the Siberian railway, 1908, diary of a journey to England via Honolulu and America, 1914, 1915.
E D T75

Tuttle, Annie(Leake)
Reminiscences. Undated. Xerox copy.
Chinese in British Columbia.
E E T88

Tye Chung Lung & Company
Originals, 1875, 2 cm.
Bankruptcy records(in Chinese)
Chinese in Victoria.
Add.MSS.2562/BCARCH-27680

United Church of Canada. British Columbia Conference.
Microfilm(negative), 1925-1954, 3 reels.
Typed minutes recording the First British Columbia Conference of the United Church of Canada, held in Vancouver in 1925 through to the thirtieth conference in 1954. As well as the regular minutes of conferences, this collection includes appendices which contain special reports to Conference of secular and ecclesiastical items of contemporary interest.
Finding aid:reel list.
Originals held by the Vancouver School of Theology.
Orientals in British Columbia.
Add.MSS.2693

Ward, William Peter, 1943- .
Microfiche (positive), 1975, 4 fiche.
White Canada forever: British Columbia's response to Orientals, 1858-1914. 1972. 292 leaves.
Ph.D. dissertation, Queen's University, 1973.
Add.MSS.1712

Wheeler, Edward Oliver, 1890-1962.
Diaries relating to early life in Ontario and Alberta, service as an engineer in India, trips on leave from India to Canada, U.S.A., England, South Africa, Asia, South Pacific and New Zealand.

Wilson, Halford David, 1905-
Vancouver, British Columbia, Insurance agent, Alderman.
Originals,1938-1942, 30.5cm.(for microfilm see reel A-660)

Correspondence and papers re:Wilson's anti-Oriental stand 1938-1942; papers, briefs, pamphlets re:Orientals in British Columbia and west coast.
Finding aid:detailed file list.
Include material on Japanese Canadians.
Add.MSS.12.

Wing Chong Company.
Victoria, British Columbia.
Original, 7 cm. 1902-1907.
Six account books(in Chinese)
Add.MSS.2537.

Wynne, Robert Edward.
Reaction to the Chinese in the Pacific North-west and British Columbia, 1850 to 1910. 1964. 511 p.
Ph.D. dissertation, University of Washington,1964. UBC NW 325.711 W989

Yee, Paul Richard.
Microfiche (positive), 1983, 2 fiche.
Chinese business ln Vancouver, 1886-1914. 198. 143 leaves.
M.A. thesis, University of British Columbia, 1983.
Add.MSS.24

Yee Lun Ark Kee, Ltd.
Victoria, British Columbia, merchant.
Originals, 1924-1969, 11 cm.
Correspondence and notes on a variety of subjects: bank draft to Chian Kai, 1942; notes in Chinese; letters in English from lawyers re business dealing; list of dental expenses; City of Victoria road and polltax receipt for inhabitants of 534 Fisgard(l folder).Permits to import fireworks and license for magazines. Brokerage firms records re items, mainly food stuffs, imported by Yee Lun Ark Kee, Ltd.
Finding aid: description of collection by G.Keddie(donor)
Add.MSS.2537/BCARCH-26914

Yep Sing and Company. fl. 1890-1910-
McDame, B.C.; Mining company.
Originals 1897-1908, 81.
Receipts for water rights and mining licenses.
Add.MSS.649

Young, Raymond Edgar, 1946-
Microfilm(positive), 1976, 2 fiche.
Street of T'ongs: planning in Vancouver's Chinatown, 1975. 125 leaves.
M.A. thesis, University of British Columbia, 1975.
Add.MSS.1742

Sound and Moving Images Division

Visual Records Division.

Barff, Lionel.
Contributors to the **Illustrated London News**. Boxer Rebellion.
Chinese artists. Works.

Photographs.

Chinese.

Ashcroft - Industries - Farming
Chinese farmer watering horses on Soney's Ranch. 23284.

Barkerville - Chinese and Chinatown.
Family out for an outing. 57847

Barkerville - Chinese and Chinatown.
Group of young children. 578746.

Barkerville - Chinese and Chinatown.
Chinese funeral. Coming with the coffin. 576575.

Barkerville - Chinese and Chinatown.
Funeral rites. 57676.

Barkerville - Chinese and Chinatown.
Two young children. 57845.

Barkerville - Chinese and Chinatown.
Young Chinese man. On right is seen the first Chinese Masonic Building. 57848.

Barkerville - Chinese and Chinatown.
Barkerville Chinatown, August 1933. 57849.

Barkerville - Chinese and Chinatown.
Chinatown., 57852.

Barkerville - Chinese and Chinatown.
Chinatown. Good general view.

Barkerville - Chinese and Chinatown.
Arrival of the mourners at a Chinese funeral, Barkerville, British Columbia. 57955.

Barkerville - Chinese and Chinatown.
Worshipping rites. 57956.

Barkerville - Chinese and Chinatown.
Chinese family at Barkerville, with a friend. 58177.

Barkerville - Chinese and Chinatown.
General view of Chinatown. 58200.

Barkerville - Chinese and Chinatown.
General view of Chinatown, 1 July 1900.

Barkerville - Chinese and Chinatown.
l July 1900. Races held in Chinatown at Barkerville, British Columbia. 58217.

Barkerville - Chinese and Chinatown.
Two small children.

Barkerville - Chinese and Chinatown.
General view of Chinatown, September 1925. 69940.

British Columbia - Industries -Lumbering.
D.L.Mullan Collection. 90210.

94 • British Columbia – Victoria

British Columbia - Industries - Lumbering.
D.L.McMullan Collection. 90212.

British Columbia - Industries - Mining.
Shows Chinese washing gold on the Fraser River Canyon, British Columbia. 32322.

British Columbia - Industries - Mining.
Shows Chinese washing for gold near North Bend, British Columbia. 77719.

British Columbia - Industries -Mining - From Department of Mines Album.
Shows Chinatown at Keithley Creek.

British Columbia - Industries -Mining - From Department of Mines Album.
Ah Sam's claim on Manson Creek, British Columbia.72955. 72951.

British Columbia - Industries - Mining - From Department of Mines Album.
Shows "Toy" - celebrity of Keithley Creek. 73056.

British Columbia - Industries - Mining -From Department of Mines Album.
Shows Chinese buildings at Quesnel Forks. 74106.

British Columbia - Railways - Canadian Pacific Railway(Deville Album)
Chinese camp at Kamloops, British Columbia. 67602.

British Columbia - Railways - Canadian Pacific Railway(Deville Album)
Chinese gamblers at Kamloops, British Columbia. 67603.

British Columbia - Railways - Canadian Pacific Railway(Deville Album)
Chinese camp at Kamloops, British Columbia. 67604.

British Columbia - Railways - Canadian Pacific Railway(Deville Album)
Chinese camp at Kamloops, British Columbia, British Columbia. 67607.

British Columbia - Railways - Canadian Pacific Railway(Deville Album)
Chinese camp at Kamloops, British Columbia. 67608.

British Columbia - Railways - Canadian Pacific Railway(Deville Album)
Chinese camp at Kamloops, British Columbia. 67609.

British Columbia - Railways - Canadian Pacific Railway(Deville Album)
Chinese camp at Kamloops, British Columbia. 67610.

British Columbia - Railways - Canadian Pacific Railway(Deville Album)
Chinese street scene, Victoria, British Columbia. 67634.

British Columbia - Railways - Canadian Pacific Railway(Deville Album)
Street scene, Victoria, British Columbia. 67637.

British Columbia - Railways - Canadian Pacific Railway(Deville Album)
Chinese quarters, Victoria, British Columbia. 67644.

British Columbia - Railways - Canadian Pacific Railway(Deville Album)
Chinese street scene, Victoria, British Columbia. 67645.

British Columbia - Railways - Canadian Pacific Railway(Deville Album)
Interior view of Chinese Joss house, Victoria, British Columbia. 67646.

Kamloops - Organization - Fraternal - Chinese Masons.
Procession in connection with opening of Chinese Free Masons. 33244.

Kamloops - Organization - Fraternal - Chinese Masons.
Procession in connection with opening of Chinese Free Masons Hall, ca. 1910. 33245.

Kamloops - Organization - Fraternal - Chinese Masons.
Procession in connection with opening of Hall ca. 1910. 33247.

Kamloops District.
Possibly Mrs. Louie and family.

Nanaimo - Buildings - Churches
Group of Chinese outside Chinese Mission at Nanaimo, British Columbia. 55493.

Nanaimo - Chinatown
Pine Street, Main Street of Nanaimo's Chinatown, during late 1940's. 65504.

Nanaimo - Chinatown
Nanaimo's Chinatown is built on a hill. The 12-acre townsite is fenced and this photograph taken from the bottom of the hill shows part of the fence and the back of the buildings. 65505.

Nanaimo - Chinatown
Pine Street, Main Street of Nanimo's Chinatown, during late 1940's. 65506.

Onderdonk, Andrew(Canadian Pacific Railway)
(Photographs from Onderdonk Album)
Shows exteriors of some Chinese men's(labourers) houses. 75088

Quesnel Forks
Chinese quarters, 13317.

Vancouver - Orientals - Chinese.
Vegetable Chinatown ca.1898. 30169.

Vancouver - Orientals - Chinese.
Chinese vegetable vendor in Vancouver. 33726.

Vancouver - Orientals - Chinese.
Bedroom where sixteen Chinese sleep. 59639.

Vancouver - Orientals - Chinese.
An improved sitting-room on Pender Street. 59040.

Vancouver - Orientals - Chinese.
Pender Alley, showing sleeping room, kitchen, dining-room, boot shop and laundry. 59641.

Vancouver - Orientals - Chinese.
Illustration showing Chinese, copied from **MacLean's Magazine**, 7 May 1960. 69164

Vancouver - Orientals - Chinese.
"Home from the War" - copied from the **Vancouver Daily Province**, Saturday, 5 January 1946. 69165.

Vancouver - Orientals - Chinese
Chinese Mission School in Vancouver, British Columbia, ca. 1899. 74147.

Victoria - Orientals - Chinese.
Two young Chinese men. 11810.

Victoria - Orientals - Chinese.
Teachers and children. 18577.

Victoria - Orientals - Chinese.
Chinese Joss House, formerly situated on Cormorant Street, south of Government.

Victoria - Orientals - Chinese.
Chinese quarters. 21951.

Victoria - Orientals - Chinese.
Interior view of a Joss House. 23897.

Victoria - Orientals - Chinese.
Ah Suen, Chinese cook at the Menzies Street residence of Richard Wolfenden. Photograph was taken ca. 1911. 29488.

Victoria - Orientals - Chinese.
Ah Suen and his son Ling. Ah Suen is the Chinese cook at the Richard Wolfenden residence. 29489.

Victoria - Orientals - Chinese.
Street scene, Victoria Chinatown. 30170.

Victoria - Orientals - Chinese.
In Chinatown, Victoria, British Columbia. 34781.

Victoria - Orientals - Chinese.
Views in the Chinese quarter, Victoria, British Columbia. 39975.

Victoria - Orientals - Chinese.
Headquarters of the Chinese Reform Association. 39976.

Victoria - Orientals - Chinese.
An idol in the Confucian Temple. 39977.

Victoria - Orientals - Chinese.
"Littler Pete" Fong Ching and his family. 52058.

Victoria - Orientals - Chinese.
Chinatown, Victoria, British Columbia, at Chinese New Year, February 1900. 54020.

Victoria - Orientals - Chinese.
A. Tyee's son in gala attire at Chinese New Year, February 1900. 54021.

Victoria - Orientals - Chinese.
A Chinaman carrying baskets on pole carrier, Victoria, British Columbia. 55972.

Victoria - Orientals - Chinese.
Chinese School. 57214.

Victoria - Orientals - Chinese.
Chinese Flower peddler, ca 1958. 60605.

Victoria - Orientals - Chinese.
Street scene showing Chinese Lion dance, 617899.

Victoria - Orientals - Chinese.
North side of Fisgard Street, about 1892. To the extreme right is the north west corner of Government Street and Fisgard. 68266.

Victoria - Orientals - Chinese.
Second Mandarin. Arrived in Victoria, ca.1890. 68676.

Victoria - Orientals - Chinese.
Interior view of Chinese Joss House. 68812.

Victoria - Orientals - Chinese.
Chinese procession on Government Street. 68813.

Victoria - Orientals - Chinese.
Chinese Joss House(interior view)on Government Street. 68814.

Victoria - Orientals - Chinese.
Two young Chinese men. 68815.

Victoria - Orientals - Chinese.
Little Chinese girl. 68817.

Victoria - Orientals - Chinese.
Group of Chinese in front of the Parliament Buildings, Victoria, British Columbia, May1904. 75161.

Victoria - Orientals - Chinese.
Three Chinese servants. 76066.

Wild Horse Creek.
One of the old Chinese cabins built on Wild Horse Creek. 70427.

Ah, Bau.
Cariboo Chinaman who was a "white" man. Blew his

stake with the boys like an oldtimer. Lake, house, and Creek named after him. 10940.

Ah, Hoo.
A miner of 1871. Mined the Germansen Creek, Manson Creek, and Omineca areas, In this photograph he is 63 years of age. 68806.

Jack, Lee.
Last of the Chinese miners on Wild Horse Creek, ca. 1918, 46259.

Jack, Lee.
Panning on Wild Horse Creek. 46260.

Jack, Lee.
Oldest placer gold miner of the Wild Horse Creek mining region. 46285, 52084.

Jack, Lee.
Lee Jack, the first and the last of the original miners on the Wild Horse, Fort Steele, British Columbia. 52096.

Kim, Lum.
Gardener, was also a miner of Wild Horse Creek area in early days. 79559.

Lim, Bang.
Lim Bang as a young man. He was born in Victoria, British Columbia, in 1880. He later built the Douglas Hotel, and was the owner of the Gim Fook Yuen store in early 1900s. 79079.

Lim, Bang.
Lim Bang's wife. 79080.

Lim, Bang.
Shows Lim Bang family. 79081.

Lim, Bang.
Shows Lim Bang family. This photograph was taken in Vancouver, British Columbia. 79082.

Nan, Sing.
"First Chinese man in Cariboo" 68805.

East Indians.

Burrell, Martin.
Packing fruit on Grand Forks ranch. 38453.
Carrying apples. 38466.
Group of workers. 39467.
Group of workers. 38468.

E & N Railway XI.
Track laying, Alberni, 1911. 93791.

Queen Charlotte Islands-Industries - Lumbering.
Group of East Indian mill workers. 67501.
Queen Charlotte Islands:Queen Charlotte Islands:Timber industry

Saanich.

Hindu town, Tod Inlet, Saanich, British Columbia.

Shipping - Merchant - **Komagata maru**.
Scene in Vancouver Harbour on 21 July 1914. H.M.S. **Rainbow** was called to aid in deporting Hindus on board S.S. **Komagata maru**. 3759.

Shipping - Merchant - **Komagata maru**.
Scene on board the **Komagata maru**. 68631.

Shipping - Merchant - **Komagata maru**.
Sightseers going out to the **Komagata maru**.

Shipping - Merchant - **Komagata maru**.
Komagata maru bringing East Indians to Canada. 70895.

Shipping - Merchant - **Komagata maru**.
Komagata Maru being escorted to Cape Flattery by H.M.C.S. **Rainbow**, 23 July 1914. Trial Island is in background. 72634.

Shipping - Merchant - **Komagata maru**. **Komagata maru** during scene in Vancouver Harbour on 21 July 1914. 75599.

Shipping - Merchant - **Komagata maru**.
Komagata maru incident, Vancouver Harbour, British Columbia, on 21 July 1914. 75600.

Shipping - Merchant - **Komagata maru**.
East Indians on board the **Komagata maru**, Vancouver, British Columbia. 75601

Shipping - Merchant - **Komagata maru**.
East Indians on board the **Komagata maru**, Vancouver, British Columbia. 756502.

Japanese.

British Columbia - Industries -Mining(from Department of Mines Albums)
A Japanese man at Horsefly Mine(copied from Department of Mines Album, 1896) 73059.

British Columbia - Industries -Mining(from Department of Mines Albums)
A Japanese man at Horsefly Mine. 73059.

Hedley.
Group photograph showing Japanese houseboy at the Day Reduction Company Ltd. at Hedley, British Columbia, 14 July 1907. 23653.

Japanese men clearing for new streets, Crofton, British Columbia, January1902. 71713.

Japanese.
Japanese bazaar, Fort Street, Victoria, ca 1890s. 90250.

Lillooet - Buildings- Miscellaneous.
Japanese evacuation cabins at Lillooet, British

Columbia. These were in use until 1950. 58300.

Mission City - Buildings - Churches.
New Japanese Church(United), Mission, British Columbia. 29052.

Mission City - Buildings - Miscellaneous.
Japanese Hall at Mission City, British Columbia. 29052.

Mission City - Miscellaneous.
Group of Japanese Canadian Girls in Training Girls, Mission, British Columbia. 40518.

Queen Charlotte Islands.
Japanese camp at Ikeda Bay. 32566.

Queen Charlotte Islands.
Engine at a Japanese mine at Ikeda Bay. 32567.

Ruskin.
Group of Japanese kindergarten children. 29054.

Shipping - merchant - Japanese fishing vessels.
Vessel that have been confiscated. North Trots near Robson Island. 51808.

Shipping - merchant - Japanese fishing vessels.
Seized fishing vessels at Annieville Dyke, Fraser River, prior to sale in 1942. 54694.

Steveston.
Showing Japanese fisherman drying nets. 30071.

Vancouver - Orientals - Japanese.
Japanese tea room, Vancouver, British Columbia. 72959

Victoria - Orientals - Japanese.
Group. Victoria, British Columbia.55478.

Victoria - Orientals - Japanese.
Japanese Language School, Victoria, British Columbia, 1931. 55479.

Victoria - Orientals - Japanese.
Japanese Language School, Victoria, British Columbia, 1932. 55480.

Victoria - Orientals - Japanese.
A Japanese family, Victoria, British Columbia. 55482.

Victoria - Orientals - Japanese.
Group of Japanese girls. 55503.

Oral History Collection

Collection contains some 7,000 interviews with about 4,500 individuals. 20% of the interviews have been transcribed in some 45,000 pages of transcripts.

Chinese Canadians - Sidney, British Columbia.
Sydney-North Saanich Oral History Collection.
14 interviews. No transcripts.
Chinese in early Sidney-North Saanich region.
BC

Chinese Canadians - Vancouver, British Columbia.
Strathcona Project Collection. 62 interviews, nearly all have been transcribed.
Include Chinese in Strathcona neighbourhood of Vancouver.
BC

Chinese Canadians - Vancouver, British Columbia.
Downtown Eastside Women's Chinese Collection.
12 interviews, no transcripts.
Life histories of women in the Vancouver urban core, include some interviews with Chinese women with separate English translation.
BC

Chinese Canadians -Victoria, British Columbia.
27 interviews, 1 transcript.
Miscellaneous subjects mostly related to people and events in Victoria, British Columbia. Includes Chinese, Japanese and Indians.
BC.

Chinese Women at Work in British Columbia.
9 interviews, no transcripts.
Experiences of Chinese women in British Columbia.
BC

Reynoldston Research and Studies Collection.
227 interviews, half transcribed.
Includes Steveston Japanese, Uganda-Asian immigrants.
BC

Richmond Art Centre Collection.
68 interviews, no transcripts.
History of Richmond, particularly fishing industry. Includes Japanese.
BC

Howie Smith Collection.
52 interviews, no transcripts.
Interviews of workers and unionists about British Columbia labour movement. Includes Japanese.
BC

Provincial Archives of British Columbia. Staff interviews.
207 interviews. Includes Chinese and Japanese.
BC

United Church History.
28 interviews. Nearly all transcribed.
Early United Church of Canada activities in British Columbia, including ministries in numerous communities.
BC

Bob Bassin Collection.
59 interviews, 6 transcribed.

Includes Japanese in early West of Vancouver Island, especially Tofino-Clayoquot area.
BC

Hudson Blake Collection.
4 interviews, no transcripts.
Reminiscences of Victoria, 1920s-1970. Canadian Navy at Esquimalt. Japanese included.
BC

Vera Rosenbluth Collection
5 interviews, no transcripts.
Women in politics. **Komagata Maru** incident. Vancouver in 1930 depression
BC

Moving Images Division

Good Citizens.
Canadian Broadcasting Corporation, 1964. 2 x 27.3 minutes, sound. black and white. 16 mm. ca. 20000 feet/610 metres. Series: Camera West. Documentary: a two-part study of the Chinese in Western Canada.
1. Search for the Past. The history of anti-Chinese prejudice in Canada and the United States, and their response to it, including the 1910 anti-Chinese riot in Vancouver.
2. Search for the Future. How the new generations of Chinese-Canadians deal with the problems that stem from the continued westernization of their community. The subject is revealed from the viewpoint of Bob Lee, a young Chinese Canadian who appears in both programs. Other participants include: University of British Columbia physicist Bill Lee; ex-magistrate Oscar Orr; labour spokesman Grant Mitchell; lawyer Harry Chow; public health nurse Effie Chow.
Location:Vancouver(Chinatown).
DUFFY

Gum Sahn
Canadian Broadcasting Corporation, 1961. 59.5 minutes. Sound. Black and white. 16 mm. 2142 feet/653 metres.
Documentary: The Chinese in British Columbia: history and early immigration; education; commerce; restoration of old customs; immigration. Shows the shops and streets of Vancouver's Chinatown, as well as Nanaimo's Chinatown; an old Chinese graveyard; labourers on the banks of the Fraser; a lion dance and parade; the **Chinese Times** newspaper; etc. "Gum Sahn"(Golden Mountain) was the name given to British Columbia by the early Chinese immigrants.
Locations:Nanaimo, Vancouver(Chinatown), Cumberland.
DUFFY

Japanese Canadians.
Canadian Broadcasting Corporation, 1960. 2 x 28.3 minutes. Sound. Black and white.16 mm. ca. 2040 feet/622 metres.
Series:Explorations.
Alternative title:Exodus.
Documentary" a two-part study of the Japanese-Canadians as a racial group. Traces their immigration from Japan to such communities as Steveston; the prejudice they encountered; their internment and loss of property during World War II; their eventual re-establishment and assimilation after the war. Interviewees include:Professor Ronald P.Dore of the University of British Columbia; fisherman Tatsuro "Buck" Suzuki of Steveston; W.McArthur, major of Greenwood during World War II; Seiji Onozuka of Greenwood. Programs were possibly adapted from a "Special Report" telecast in 1959.
Locations:Greenwood; Steveston; Tashme, Vancouver.
DUFFY

Nippon maru.
Canadian Broadcasting Corporation, 1958. 30 minutes. Sound. Black and white. 16 mm. ca.1100 feet/335 metres.
Series:Here and There.
Documentary: A voyage from Victoria to Vancouver on the four-masted **Nippon maru**, a cadet training vessel of the Japanese merchant marine which visited British Columbia as part of the 1958 centennial celebrations. Includes: routine of crew; judo drill; arrival and welcome in Vancouver harbour.
Locations:Straits of Georgia; Vancouver(harbour)
DUFFY

Summer Afternoon.
Canadian Broadcasting Corporation, 1956. ca. 30 minutes. Sound. Black and White. 16 mm. ca. 1080 feet/329 metres.
Series:Pacific 13.
Documentary:Follows two young Chinese boys at play in and around the shops, streets and waterfront of Vancouver's Chinatown. Presented without commentary.
Locations:Vancouver(Chinatown)
DUFFY

**McPherson Library,
University Archives and Special Collections,
P.O.Box 1800, University of Victoria,
Victoria, British Columbia, V8W 3H5.
Tel:(604)721-8211.**

Manuscripts

Cavenagh Family Papers.
Residence or location: The Straits Settlements, Malaya, Singapore and Penang.Principal occupation: British Army officers and officers of the East India Company.
Inclusive dates of material: 1790-1893.
Description of material.
Sir Orfeur Cavenagh, James Gordon Cavenagh, Gordon Cavenagh: commissions, certificates, orders, proclamations, documents.
Plan of battle of Maharajpore.
Pictures of initiations ceremony, Chinese Secret Society.

Manuscripts: "Translations from the Koran," "Concerning the Poor Laws and Private Charity;" Correspondence between Matthew Cavenagh Kinsey, Canada East and R.Calvert, London(1864-1867) Letter book: Henry William Dent, 1881-1893; Sir Orfeur Cavenagh's private letter books and diaries, 1837-1888; Printed Ephemera, 1847-1862.

Theses and dissertations.

Adam, Robert David.
Myths and realities of Vancouver's Oriental trade, 1886-1942. M.A. thesis 1980.
CT

Andressen, Betty V.
Travel and geographic learning, a study of perception and attitude change in a Japanese tourist segment. Ph.D. dissertation 1988.
NL

Andressen, Curtis A.
Vietnamese refugees in Canada, a case study of integration. M.A. thesis 1986.
NL

Baek, Eung Jin.
A phonological study of Sino-Korean, a comparative study of the initial consonants. M.A. thesis 1975.
CT

Brooks, Jean.
Ours is the dance, a source and demonstration of power on the Island of Yap in the Caroline Islands of Micronesia. M.A. thesis 1989.
NL

Campbell, Mark David.
Social interaction of Chinese visa students, reference groups and morphological age assessments. M.A. thesis 1987.
NL

Crawford, John William.
Japanese studies, a framework for curriculum development. M.A. thesis 1988.
NL

Ellis, Catherine Anna.
Identity formation, a comparison between Sikh and non-Sikh Canadian female adolescents. M.A. thesis 1986.
NL

Fukushima, Masayuki.
Error analysis, a hierarchy of difficulty encountered by Japanese students learning English as a second language. M.A. thesis 1986.
NL

Gallaiford, Neil.
Pitch declination in Japanese, an instrumental study. M.A. thesis 1983.
NL

Gross, Michael Laurence.
Symbol and function in the architecture and mausoleum of Humayun Padshah. M.A. thesis 1980.
CT

Haddon, Rosemary M.
A history and annotation of Taiwan Hsieh-shih(Realist) fiction, 1920-1979. M.A. thesis 1986.
NL

Hall, Gerald Herman.
Analysis of the People's Republic of China's behaviour in the United Nations, 1971-1978. M.A. thesis 1979.
NL

Harwood, Bruce John.
Canada's relations with Japan, 1931-1941. M.A. thesis 1986.
NL

Henderson, Lalitha P.
A phonological contrastive study of Tamil and English. Ph.D. dissertation 1984.
NL

Im, Dong Young.
Factor abundance and Korea's comparative advantage in international trade. M.A. thesis 1986.
NL

Khoury, Nuha Naim Narallah.
Safawid epigraphy in Isfahan, the Masjid-i Shah. M.A. thesis 1983.
NL

Kim, Yong-Bum.
A fragment of Korean phrase structure grammar. Ph.D. dissertation 1988.
NL

Kinugawa, Kazuhide.
American policy toward Japan's military capability during the Occupation, from disarmament to rearmament. M.A. thesis 1985.
NL

Kuluak, Albert John.
The ethnographic history of Kurti people on Manus Island, Papua New Guinea to 1919,
M.A. thesis 1977.
CT

Lovatt, Elizabeth Dickerman.
The Indus Valley seals, a method for their study. M.A. thesis 1978.
CT

Minoura, Yasuko.
Value orientation found in British Columbian and Japanese schoolbooks, the 1920s-the 1970s. M.A. thesis

1976.
CT

Mulligan, Vicki Bridge.
The effect on primary children's classification of occupations by sex of a social studies unit on life in rural China. M.A. thesis 1979.
CT

Nelson, Lloyd George.
The dairy industry in Sri Lanka, problems and prospects. Ph.D. dissertation 1976.

Polume, Samson Mamau.
Papua New Guinea, economic development of a dependent economy. M.A. thesis 1981.
NL

Scott, Linda Beryl.
Baby bystanders, an exploratory study of the determinants of altruism comparing Canada and the People's Republic of China. Ph.D. dissertation 1989.
NL

Sedgwick, Charles Peter.
The context of economic change and continuity in an urban overseas Chinese community. M.A. thesis 1973.
CT

Tatsuki, Masaaki.
The effect of loan words on the phonology of contemporary Japanese. M.A. thesis 1980.
CT

Tatsuki, Masaaki.
Thematic structure of Japanese with reference to two theoretical approaches. Ph.D. dissertation 1982.
NL

Thompson, David George.
An analysis of recent Japanese economic involvement in three South East Asian countries, Malaysia, Singapore and Indonesia. M.A. thesis 1977.
CT

Wedlake, Barbara Fair.
The Mau movements in Western and American Samoa, an ecological approach. M.A. thesis 1983.
NL

Wikkramatileke, Jacqueline Claire.
The Chinese in West Malaysia: the continuing connection to 1979. M.A. thesis 1979.
NL

Wright, Elaine Julia.
The shamsa in Iranian illuminations. M.A. thesis 1989.

Archives Division,
City of Victoria
1 Centennial Square,
Victoria, British Columbia, V8V 1P6.
Tel:(604)361-0375

Lee, George,1880-1960.
Papers, 1880-1960. 2 boxes. Correspondence, legal documents, some in Chinese, immigration papers, certificates. Daybook accounts 1887-1888.

Lim Bang.
Papers. 1915-1934. 27 files. Some materials are in Chinese. Correspondence, some with Hawaii. Newsclippings.

Man Tuck Tong fonds.
Business records of a local herbalist, 1940s-1976. 12 boxes.

Canada-China Friendship Association.
Records, 1936-1989. 3 boxes. Minutes, correspondence, publications and membership lists.

Newspaper clippings index

Contains entries for Chinese cemeteries, Crime, Gambling, Opium, for ethnic groups as Chinese, 1958-1987, Indians, 1925,1979, Japanese 1970-1985, neighbourhoods as Chinatown, 1962-1991.

Photographs

Chinese, Indians and Japanese. Neighbourhoods as Chinatown.

MANITOBA

Winnipeg

Provincial Archives of Manitoba,
200 Vaughan Street,
Winnipeg, Manitoba, R3C 1T5.
Tel:(204)944-3971.

Manuscripts and Records Section.

Manuscript Group 10.
C8-5 Women's Institute of Manitoba. Pembina-District.
Chinese,1963-1974, correspondence.

P599-a Bichitra-Bengali Association of Manitoba.
1978-1986, originals, 6 cm.
Immigrants from Bengal first arrived in Winnipeg in 1957.
Records consist of minutes(1978-1984), correspondence, constitution and by-laws, copies of **Bichitra Samachar**(1985; news-magazine of the Association) and **Agonomi**(1982-1985); **Durga Puja** magazine(in Bengali and English) and miscellaneous documents.

P828-830. Multi-cultural Centre, Thompson.
Established 1975 by the Thompson Citizenship Council, to provide services to immigrants and new Canadians. Records include: minutes, annual reports, statistics, financial statements, brochures, 1973-1980. 6 cm, subject files, 1973-1982, correspondence, 1973-1982, scripts, 1975-1980, and scrap books, 1974-1980.

P827-8 Koo, Paul.
Collection.
1979, 1984, originals, photocopies, 3.5 cm.
Paul Koo came to Canada in 1960, and is active in the Chinese community in Winnipeg.
Anniversary publication of the Manitoba Academy of Chinese Studies, 1974-1984(in Chinese and English, 128p.) and "The History of the Chinese Community of Winnipeg", by G.Baureiss and J.Kwong, unpublished research paper, 1979, 138 p., photocopy.

P827f.4-7 Kato, Taichi, 1903-1985.
n.d., 1942-1976, originals, .5 cm., photocopies, 2.5 cm.
Taichi Kato, a Canadian of Japanese descent, a resident of British Columbia in 1941. In February 1942, evacuation of approximately 21,000 Japanese Canadians from coastal areas was ordered. Half of the evacuees were sent to interior housing centres. These centres were located in old mining towns - Greenwood, Slocan City, New Denver, Roseberry, Sandon, and Kaslo, and two "new towns" - Tashme and Lemon Creek. Documents from most of these centres are included in the Kato papers, reflecting the anxiety experienced by the internees in relation to financial and family matters, relocation and especially repatriation to Japan.
Mr. Kato was interned at Slocan City, actively participated in the camp administration. In 1947, the family relocated to Winnipeg.
Documents and notices related to Japanese internment and repatriation, n.d., 1942-1946, include correspondence, interviews, reports, agreements, petitions, lists of internees, newspaper clippings.
Also included are documents related to the Manitoba Buddhist Church, 1946-1976.

P2759f26 Eliason, M.
Chinese - street name changes, -1985, subject files.

P2765f23-f24 Eliason, M.
Chinese - Chinatown Development Corporation. -1986, reports.

P2767f20 Eliason, M.
Chinese - Chinese Cultural and Community Centre. -1985, subject file.

Record Group 3.
Manitoba. Department of Attorney-General.
C1(40)Miscellaneous files, <1884>-1925.
Chinese, 1918. Curbing of restaurants.

Moving Images and Sound Section

C433 Dafoe, John Wesley, 1866-1944.
n.d. 1936, originals and copies, 4 discs and 2 audio tapes(64.00 min.).
J.W.Dafoe joined the **Free Press** staff in 1886. He attended the Imperial Press Conferences of 1909, 1920, 1925 and 1930, was attached to the Canadian delegation at the Paris Peace Conference, 1919.
Tapes, first in a series of radio broadcasts by WERF New York of highlights of the 6th Biennial Conference of the Institute of Pacific Relations held at Yosemite National Park in 1936. Broadcast on 20 August 1936, features a discussion on the American Recovery Program. Discussants included Dr. <Chin>, Chinese economist and historian.

Bichitra-Bengali Association of Manitoba.
Photographs of Bichitra activities.

Multi-Cultural Centre, Thompson.
Two photograph albums, presented in 1985.

United Church of Canada,
Conference of Manitoba and North Western Ontario,
Archives Committee,
c/o Rare Book Room, Library,
University of Winnipeg,
515 Portage Avenue,
Winnipeg, Manitoba, R3B 2E9.
Tel:(204)786-7811, ext. 559.

Japan Conference of the Methodist Church Records, 1902.

Foreign Missions Board of the Methodist Church Records, 1903.

University Libraries,
Department of Archives and Special Collections,
University of Manitoba,
Elizabeth Dafoe Library,
Winnipeg, Manitoba, R3T 2N2.
Tel:(204)474-9986.

Papers and manuscripts

Allen, Lillian B. 1904-
Papers, 1889-1985. 1.75 metres.
Contains diaries, correspondence and travel logs on her travels to Asia, 1937.

Dafoe, John Wesley, 1866-1944.
Papers, 1892-1943. 3 metres.
Contains correspondence(5 folders) with E.J.Tarr, who along with Dafoe helped found the Canadian Institute of Pacific Relations. The goal of the Institute was to study the conditions of the Pacific peoples with a view for the improvement of their mutual relations(1925-1943).

Tarr, Edgar J.
Papers, 1929-1961. ca. 1.5 metres.
Along with Dafoe, founded the Canadian Institute of Pacific Relations.
Collection not yet processed, May 1987.

University of Manitoba. Office of the President.
Records of the Office of the President, 1887-1977. 27 metres.
Contains some files re University of Manitoba's Faculty of Agriculture student/teacher exchange program in the 1960s.

Winnipeg Tribune.
Collection, 1935-1980. 175 metres.
Contains news clippings, photographs and other reference sources on many of the countries of Asia and Oceania - Japan, Turkey, Iran etc.

Also available on microfilm.

Theses and dissertations

Abbott, S.E.
The socio-economic impact of tourism in the Khumbu region of Nepal. M.N.R.M. thesis 1985.
NL

Amin, Abu Taher Mohammed Nurul.
An analysis of labour force and industrial organization of the informal sector in Dacca. Ph.D. dissertation 1982.
NL

Basnayake, Asoka Kumari.
Soil erosion in the tea lands of Sri Lanka. M.Sc. thesis 1985.
NL

Bramananan, Wasana.
The Campus Centre of Khonkaen University, City of Khonkaen, Thailand. M.Arch. thesis 1969.
CT

Briggs, Rodney J.N.
The use of force in Chinese foreign policy, a case study of the Sino-Vietnamese War. M.A. thesis 1982.
NL

Buduhan, Cleto.
An urban village, the effect of migration on the Filipino garment workers in a Canadian city. M.A. thesis 1972.
CT

Cantelo, Brenda.
The symbolism of the Hindu temple, a study in the Manasara. M.A. thesis 1987.
NL

Chiang, Tung-yeung.
A study of China's agricultural production, inputs, and productivity, 1952-1984. M.Sc. thesis 1987.
NL

Choi, Kwei-hang.
The Chinese Cultural Revolution and the Sino-Soviet border disputes. M.A. thesis 1979.
CT

Chowdury, Abu S.M. Anisuzzaman.
An attempt at integrating macroeconometrics and input-output models, the case of Bangladesh. Ph.D. dissertation 1983.
NL

Chowdhury, Hasanuzzaman.
Underdevelopment, state and mode of production in Bangladesh. M.A. thesis 1984.
NL

Chowdhury, Muhammad Khorshed Alam.

Analysis of the food problem in Bangladesh, an econometric investigation. Ph.D. dissertation 1986.

Copeland, Nancy Cecelia.
Adaptation to resettlement by Southeast Asian adolescents. M.Sc. thesis 1984.
NL

Cowie, Geraldine.
Vidyaranya's Pancadasi, a study of its theory of concsciousness and its Sanskrit terminology. M.A. thesis 1985.

Darsono, Suseno.
Rainfall data generation, Pemali-Comal irrigation area, Java, Indonesia. Ph.D. dissertation 1987.
NL

Dutta, Mirinal Kanti.
A spatial analysis of the ecological patterning of crimes in the metropolis of Calcutta. Ph.D. dissertation 1976.

Enns, Robert.
The potential of agricultural cooperative societies as a means of agricultural development in Bangladesh. M.A. thesis 1980.
NL

Futz, Douglas Neal.
Development of Canadian fresh chilled pork exports to Japan, logistical and economic potential. M.Sc. thesis 1989.
NL

Greenberg, Charles.
The adaptation process of riverbank erosion displacees in an urban environment, a case study of squatters in Serajganj, Bangladesh. M.A. thesis 1986.
NL

Haque, Chowdhury Emdadul.
Patterns, structure and growth of the labour force in Bangladesh, a spatial and temporary analysis. M.A. thesis 1982.
NL

Islam, Muhammad Sadequi.
Structural interdependence, income distribution, and industrial growth, with special reference to Bangladesh and India. Ph.D. dissertation 1983.

Khan, Md. Abu Obaida Ansari.
Statistical analysis of bank erosion of the Brahmaputra River in Bangladesh. M.Sc. thesis 1988.
NL

Kroeker, Randolph H.
The confluence of Zen Buddhism and counselling. M.Ed. thesis 1984.
NL

Lam, Tak M.
Was Singapore a nonaligned country during the period of 1965-1971. M.A. thesis 1985.
NL

Lee, Jae Joung.
A study of Korean church history and Minjung theology. M.A. thesis 1986.
NL

Lee, Po-chu.
A Chinese garden in Winnipeg's Chinatown. M.Land. Arch. thesis 1984.
NL

Mahmood, Amir.
The role of remittance spending in Pakistan. M.A. thesis 1984.
NL

Mak, Magdalen Shunyee.
A cross-cultural study on achievement, causal attribution, and adolescent perception of parent behaviour among Euro-Canadian, Chinese-Canadian and Hong Kong Chinese adolescents. Ph.D. dissertation 1988.
NL

Martyn, Elaine.
The adjustment of North American teachers in China, a case study. M.Ed. thesis 1988.
NL

Mellen, Mary Eleanor Susan.
An interpretation of the anti-Confucius campaign, 1973-1975. M.A. thesis 1977.CT

Mingma, Norbu.
Conservation for survival, a conservation strategy for resource self-sufficiency in the Khumbu region of Nepal. M.N.R.M. thesis 1985.
NL

Nathan, Jivanandam Aloysius.
International tourism and its role in Singapore's economic development. M.A. thesis 1981.
NL

Ng, Chee Chiu Clement.
The Chinese Benevolent Association of Vancouver: 1885-1923, a response to local conditions. M.S.W. thesis 1987.
NL

Ong, Amoy Yuk Mui.
An exploratory study of the life of the single Asian immigrant woman in Winnipeg, implications for social work practice. M.S.W. thesis 1987.
NL

Pereira, Cecil Patrick.
East Indians in Winnipeg, a study of the consequences of immigration for an ethnic group in Canada. M.A. thesis 1971.

Rahi, Khan S.
Social class and social development, the case of Egypt and Turkey. M.A. thesis 1980.
NL

Roberton, Elizabeth.
The Vedanta philosophy. M.A. thesis 1922.
CGT

Sadeq, Abul Hassan Muhammad.
Transport and economic development in rural Bangla Desh. Ph.D. dissertation 1984.

Siddiqui, Baker Ahmed.
Macroeconometric models for developing countries, a case study of Bangladesh. Ph.D. dissertation 1988.
NL

Singh, Harshendra Kumar.
A study of India's international trade with special reference to exports(1951-1964). M.S. thesis 1967.
CT

Sison, Jerome Fronda.
The effects of small farm mechanization on production, income and employment in selected rice growing areas in the Philippines. Ph.D. dissertation 1982.

Soenyoto.
Theoretical plan for increasing the level of utilization of labour force on the agricultural area in Panjatan District, Indonesia. M.N.A.M. thesis 1979.
CT

Steenburg, David John Frederick.
The role of intention in perception according to Vasubhandu's Abhidarmakosabhasya, the background to Buddhist soteriology. M.A. thesis 1987.

Tan, Siow Yue.
Pattern of trade and development in Malaya with special reference to the postwar period. M.A thesis 1963.
CT

Unruh, Kathryn Irma.
The influence of the Noh plays of Japan on the dramatic art of W.B.Yeats. M.A. thesis 1968.
CT

Vanprapa, Som.
The role of the industrial sector in the economic development of Thailand. M.A. thesis 1968.
CT

Wong, Ka-ying Timothy.
Western sociological theory and the Chinese cultural tradition, an assessment. M.A. thesis 1988.
NL

Yoon, Bok-nam.
The adjustment problems and educational needs of Korean immigrant women in the Winnipeg garment industry. M.Ed. thesis 1983.
NL

Zaman, Mohammad Q.
Leadership and mass mobilization at the grass roots, the Ulashi experiment of Bangladesh. M.A. thesis 1981.
NL

Zhong, Fu-ning.
China's grain production and trade. M.Sc. thesis 1986.
NL

NEW BRUNSWICK

Fredericton

Harriet Irving Library,
University of New Brunswick,
P.O. Box 7500,
Fredericton, New Brunswick, E3B 5H5.
Tel:(306)453-2500.

Bennett, Richard Bedford, 1870-1947.
Prime Minister of Canada, 1930-1935.
Originals. Microfilm copy in the National Archives of Canada.

Microfilm, 1878-1947, 435 reels. Finding aid 434.
Papers deposited at the University of New Brunswick.

Political papers, 1878-1947.

Asia- and Pacific-related files in the Political papers, as listed on Reel C4495, are:

Washington Armaments Conference(1 file)

External Affairs, China, 1926(1 file)

Lausanne Treaty(1 file)

Immigration, India, 1922(1 file)

External Affairs, India, 1929(1 file)

Sino-Russian dispute, 1929(1 file)

London Naval Conference, 1930-1935(2 files)

Imperial Conference, 1930-1932(many files)

Pacific Health Conference, 1935(1 file)

External Affairs, China, 1930-1936(6 files)

Conference, International Red Cross, Tokyo, 1934(1 file)

Chinese-Japanese dispute, 1931-1936(9 files)

External Affairs,
Trade with China, 1930-1932(3 files)

External Affairs,
Canadian Minister to China, 1931-1932(2 files)

External Affairs,
India, 1930-1936(8 files)

External Affairs,
India Round Table Conference, 1932-1935(4 files)

External Affairs,
Japan, 1930-1936(10 files)

External Affairs,
Japan, Japanese Minister to Canada, 1930-1935(3 files)

External Affairs,
Japan. Canadian Minister to Japan, 1930(11 files)

External Affairs,
Japan. Canadian Legation, 1930-1934(1 file)

External Affairs,
Japan. Canadian Minister to Japan, 1931-1935(5 files)

External Affairs,
Japan. Trade relations(5 files)

External Affairs,
British Ambassador to Japan, 1934(3 files)

External Affairs,
Japanese Ambassador to London, 1934(1 file)

External Affairs
Persia, 1933(1 file)

External Affairs,
Trade with Persia, 1932-1933(4 files)

External Affairs,
Siam, 1930-1931(4 files)

External Affairs,
Turkey, 1932-1933(4 files)

External Affairs,
Pacific Halibut Treaty, 1931(2 files)

Immigration,
Japanese, 1933(1 file)

Immigration,
Chinese, 1930(1 file)

Immigration,
Japanese and Chinese, 1935(1 file)

Immigration,
Oriental, 1930(1 file)

Immigration,
Indian, 1935(1 file)

London Disarmament Conference:1932(21 files)

Invitation and Clippings Series.

Volume 1061

(Reel 4496) p.672.
Cables, Pacific, 1926.

External Affairs.

Volume 1104

(Reel M4511) p.78-91.
China, 1932-1933.

Volume 1105

(Reel M4511) p.93-104.
China, 1935-1937.

(Reel M4511) p.105-107.
China, Consuls, 1934-1935.

(Reel M4511) p.108-273.
China, Sino-Japanese War, 1931-1933(2 files).

(Reel M4511) p.274-300.
China, Sino-Japanese war, Lytton Report, 1932-1933.

Volume 1109

(Reel M4511) p.360-361.
Consuls, China,1926.

(Reel M4512) p.380-412.
Disarmament, 1931-1932.

(Reel M4512) p.413-461.
Disarmament Conference, 1932-1933.

(Reel M4512) p.462-476.
Disarmament, London Naval Conference, 1930,1931.

(Reel M4512) p.477-478.
Disarmament, London Naval Conference, reports, 1931.

Volume 1119

(Reel M4515) p.1003-1061.
India, Lord Willingdon, 1931-1932.

(Reel M4515) p.1071-1120.
Institute of Pacific Relations, 1931-1933.

Volume 1122

(Reel M4516) p.1103.
Japan, Consuls, 1926.

(Reel M4516) p.1104-1142.
Japan, Economy, 1931-1935.

(Reel M4516) p.1143-1190.
Japan, Legation, 1931-1935.

(Reel M4516) p.1191-1217.
Japan, Legation, Tokugawa, 1930-1935(2 files).

(Reel M4516) p.1218-1219.
Japan, Legation, Kato Sotomatsu, 1935.

(Reel M4516) p.1220-1226.
Japan, Canadian legation:1931-1934.

(Reel M4517) p.113-193.
Japan, Trade relations, 1935.

(Reel M4517) p.194-241.
Japan, Trade relations, Japan-German pact, 1935-1937.

Volume 1123

(Reel M4517) p.320.
Orient, Trade relations, 1926.

(Reel M4517) p.321-327.
Orient, Trade relations, 1930.

(Reel M4517) p.328-359.
Orient, Trade relations, 1931.

(Reel M4517) p.360-370.
Orient, Trade relations, 1932-1933.

(Reel M4517) p.371-384.
Orient, Trade relations, 1934.

(Reel M4517) p.385-387.
Orient, Trade relations, 1935.

(Reel M4517) p.388.
Pacific Foreign Trade Council, 1931.

(Reel M4517) p.401-407.
Pan-Pacific affairs, 1926.

Volume 1148

(Reel M4525) p.353-365.
Fisheries Pacific,1930-1933.

(Reel M4525) p.366-368.
Fisheries, Salmon sea fishing statistics, 1930-1932.

Immigration.

Volume 1170

(Reel M4532) p.264-267.
Oriental, 1930-1933.

Imperial Conferences.

Volume 1173

(Reel M4533) p.384-418.
India, 1930-1931.

Volume 1218

(Reel M4547) p.618-626.
Pacific Science Congress, 1930, 1933.

Tariff
Volume 1277

(Reel M4566) p.711-714.
Silk, 1932-1933.

Weiner, Theodore.
University of New Brunswick Oral History Programme. 97 p.
Dr. Weiner taught in the British University in Shanghai from 1939 to 1942. After the war, he taught at the Shanghai American School until 1947, when he came to Canada. The Shanghai section is less than a quarter of the manuscript.

Theses and Dissertations

Arsenault, Wayne David.
The United States, Great Britain and China in Burma, 1941-1945. M.A. thesis 1984.
NL

Bineypal, Rajinder Singh.
A comparative study of educational provisions in the Canadian and Indian constitutions. M.Ed. thesis 1973.
CT

Breau, Gerald Joseph.
Some insights into Advaita Vedanta of Shankara-Karya. M.A. thesis 1979.
CT

Cassar, George Harris.
The Dardanelles operation from the perspective of the Bonar Law papers. M.A. thesis 1963.
CT

Chaimankong, Chaiyos.
A survey of Thailand's manpower policies. M.A. thesis 1971.
CT

Chan, Kim-man.
China's relations with the United States during the administration of President Yuan Shih-k'ai, 1912-1914. M.A. thesis 1923.
CT

Chen, Chin-yuan.
The changing status of women in modern China, 1880-1927. M.A. thesis 1978.
CT

Chow, Wah Hon.
China's relations with the United States, 1927-1941. M.A. thesis 1970.
CT

Chu, Pao Liang.
A comparative study of the foreign policies of Great Britain and Japan respecting China, 1923-1928. M.A. thesis 1968.
CT

Dhahir, Sanna.
Women in V.S.Naipaul's fiction, their roles and relationships. Ph.D. dissertation 1986.

Faizer, Rizwi Shuhada.
Muslim ethnopolitics in Sri Lanka. M.A. thesis 1984.
NL

Fernando, Laksim Piyadesa.
Political violence in Sri Lanka, the April 1971 Youth Insurrection. M.A. thesis 1977.
CT

Fernando, Thelge Winifred J.
The development of university education in Sri Lanka, 1963-1971. Implications for employment. M.Ed. thesis 1976.
CT

Gangopadhyay, Subhamay.
Forecasting passenger levels for the bus system in Bombay Metropolitan Region. M.Sc. thesis 1987.
NL

Horigan, Damien Patrick.
Buddhist and Christian responses to Marxism. M.A. thesis 1986.
NL

Keith, May Anne.
Canadian foreign policy and the Manchurian crisis. M.A. thesis 1960.
CT

Kulasegaram, Gunaseelan.
The Association of Southeast Asian Nations(ASEAN), the formative phase, 1967-1975, a framework for internation political cooperation. M.A. thesis 1986.
NL

Lau, Ambrose.
The pattern of Hong Kong's industry and foreign trade, 1947-1962. M.A. thesis 1964.
CT

Law, Sophia Woei-jiann.
The adjustment problem of Chinese students in New Brunswick. M.Ed. thesis 1978.
CT

Macmillan, Bonnie.
Developmental implementation of East Asian history in senior high schools. M.Ed. thesis 1976.
CT

McNeil, Paul Roderick.
The China lobby and its effects on the United States government policy, 1945-1950. M.A. thesis 1989.
NL

Mohamed, Alios Bin.
The Pan-Malayan Islamic Party's decision to join the National Front Government of Malaysia. M.A. thesis 1979.

Noble, Bruce Alexander.
Majority-minority relations, the French in Quebec and the Sinhalese in Sri Lanka. M.A. thesis 1980.
CT

Perera, Senath Walter.
Protest in the English fiction of Kenya and India, the novels of Raja Rao, Khushwant Singh, Ngugi wa Thiong'o and Meja Mwangi. M.A. thesis 1987.

Sastry, Kuruganty Ramaswamy.
Social background of the Dravida Munnetra Kazhagam(DMK) legislative elite. M.A. thesis 1978.
CT

Sawarajah, Ambalavanar.
The strategy of an ethnic minority party in government and in opposition, the Tamil Federal Party of Sri Lanka, 1956-1970. M.A. thesis 1978.
CT

Su, Xiaofan.
Reforms of the higher education system in China, 1949-1988. M.Ed. thesis 1988.
NL

Wetmore, Brian Ralph.
Pragmatic quixote, commitment and pragmatism in the development of Jawaharlal Nehru's world view and style. M.A. thesis 1979.

Saint John

**New Brunswick Museum Library and Archives,
277 Douglas Avenue,
Saint John, New Brunswick, E2K 1E5.
Tel:(506)643-2300.**

Fritz, Clara Winnifred, 1890?
Seven letters, January to March, 1904.
Letters to her mother, written from Tourane(Da Nang) and Haiphong. Fritz' father was captain of the S.S. **Troop.** Relate mainly to activities on board ship and the weather.

Hanington, Mabel
Ningteh.
Passport, written in Chinese, 1913.

Y's Men's Club, Osaka.
Letter in Japanese to Saint John Y.M.C.A. re club activities and international friendship. December 1938.

NEWFOUNDLAND

St. John's

Centre for Newfoundland Studies Archives, Queen Elizabeth II Library,
Memorial University of Newfoundland,
Elizabeth Avenue,
St. John's, Newfoundland A1B 3YI.
Tel:(709)737-7475-6.

Manuscripts

Aid to New Newfoundlanders '79
1979-1981. St. John's.
Original, 1979-1983, 6 cm.
Records of a group formed in August 1979 to sponsor a family of Vietnamese refugees. Includes documents, correspondence, newsletters relating to the Sen family in St. John's, and published material concerning the private sponsorship of boat people in Canada.

Andrews, Donald McLachlan, 1907-
Fisheries development consultant.
Papers relating to his career as a fish processor. Include advisor to the government of Papua New Guinea.

Banks, Joseph, 1743-1820.
Botanist.
Photographs, 1768-1771, 30 cm.
Journal of the voyage of the **Endeavour** to the South Seas.
Original in the Mitchell Library, Sydney.

Gushue-Taylor, George, 1883-1954.
Medical missionary, Formosa.
Correspondence concerning pensions, retirement, will and letters probate, news clippings and biographical material, photocopied in 1983 from originals in the United Church of Canada Archives, Toronto, Ontario.

Hoogendoorn, Robert. fl. 1968.
Photocopy, ca. 1968, 1 cm.
Typewritten notes and partial draft of a report on the Chinese in St. John's.

Steele, James Robert.
Lieutenant, 1st Newfoundland Regiment.
21 mounted photographs of Royal Newfoundland Regiment in Eastern Mediterranean include:
  1. Newfoundlanders digging fire recesses at Gallipoli
  2. Newfoundlanders digging fire recesses at Gallipoli.
  3. Newfoundlanders tackling reserve dugouts(their first work) at Suvla.
  4. Newfoundland officers protecting themselves against flies while taking their meals.
  5. Newfoundlanders in their trenches at Gallipoli.
  6. Trenches built by Newfoundlanders near Salt Lake, Gallipoli.
  7. Trenchmaking, Gallipoli.
  8. Men in the trenches.
  9. Officers in dugout.
  10. Burial ground.
  11. Newfoundland Regiment en route to Indros.
  12. Gunners on board troopship.

Welcome to Canada.
Collection, 1989. 1 cm and video cassette.
Feature film about arrival of Southeast Asian (Tamil) refugees in Newfoundland.
Script, publicity package, clippings, poster and video cassette of National Film Board of Canada -John M.Smith feature film 'Welcome to Canada".
Acquired from the National Film Board of Canada, Montreal, Quebec, 1989.
Finding aid.

Theses and Dissertations

Chang, Yuen-loong.
Women's status in post revolutionary China. M.A thesis 1979.
CT

Chiam, Keng Woon.
The development of education in Singapore, 1959-1969. M.Ed. thesis 1976.
CT

Chit Maung, Yi Yi.
The role of economic planning in the development of Southeast Asia(with special reference to Burma). M.A. thesis 1966.
CT

Devani, Manubhai V.
Neglected aspects in agricultural policies of the Indian Five-Year Plan. M.A. thesis 1972.
CT

Herafeen, Helaluddin Khan Shamsul.

The Hindu caste model and the Moslem system of stratification in Bangladesh. M.A. thesis 1976.
CT

Hong, Robert G.
"To take action without delay":Newfoundland's Chinese Immigration Act of 1906. B.A. honours dissertation, 1987.

Kearney, Derrick Joseph.
The United States Army in small wars: theory and practice in South Vietnam, 1965-1972. B.A. honours dissertation 1991.

Kozar, Seana.
Unmasking a "sitting ghost"" a cross-generic exploration of the Chinese heroine in stories told by Chinese in Newfoundland. M.A. thesis 1993.

Liu, Jianxiang.
Continuation and acculturation: a study of foodways of three Chinese immigrant families in St. John's, Newfoundland. M.A. thesis 1991.

Lu, Zhong-Ying.
The preverbal NPs in Chinese. M.A. thesis 1991.
NP=Noun phrase.

MacKinnon, Marian E.M.
Towards meeting the health care needs of the Chinese elderly: meaning and potential health consequences associated with care receiving for the Chinese elderly. M.N. thesis, 1993.

Peters, Gordon Ross.
The problem of the North West Frontier of India, 1800-1880. M.A. thesis 1968

Power, Donald Frances.
Some aspects of the political and commercial relationships between British India and Tibet, from 1890-1914. M.A. thesis 1968.
CT

Ren, Ying.
Hierarchical attributed graph representation and recognition of handwritten Chinese characters. M.Sc thesis 1991.

Rompkey, Ronald George.
A study of Orientalism in English literature, 1707-1824. M.S. thesis 1968.
CT

Sun, Wei Ping.
Mandarin classifiers from a semantic point of view. M.A. thesis 1989.

Ten, Ping-teng.
The making of Britain's new Malayan policy, 1857-1874, the interplay of imperial and colonial interests. M.A. thesis 1972.
CT

Thomson, Margaret Jillian.
"To let the children know": the traditions of the Chinese community of the Avalon Peninsula. M.A. thesis 1991.

Zhu, Niangqiang.
Told by the Newfoundland Chinese: a translation, contextual description and analysis of the jokes collected from two groups in the St. John's Chinese community. M.A. thesis 1991.

NOVA SCOTIA

Antigonish

Saint Francis Xavier University Archives,
Angus L. MacDonald Library,
Saint Francis Xavier University,
Antigonish, Nova Scotia, B2G 1C0.
Tel:(902)867-2201.

The Coady International Institute was founded in 1959, in memory of Rev. Dr. Moses M.Coady, who was the first director of the University's Extension Department established in 1929. He was instrumental in the establishment of adult education, cooperative and credit union movements in Canada and the United States. His ideas and philosophy spread internationally. Asia and Pacific related materials are noted below:

1. Asia- and Coady International Institute, 1960-1970.
Enquiries from Ceylon, China, East Pakistan, Formosa, India, Indonesia, Iran, Japan, Korea, Malaysia, Pakistan, Thailand and Vietnam in files of Monsignor Smyth.
RG50-2/7/1-542

2. Pakistan, East- and Coady International Institute.
Correspondence re assistance of Frank Glasgow; re a seminar on cooperatives, report of Extension Training Center and evaluation report on rural development program in files of Monsignor Smyth.
RG50-2/7/61-78

3. Korea- and Coady International Institute, 1962-1969.
Correspondence from Sister Mary Gabriella Mulherin and Hee Sup Park on the Voluntary Co-operative Center and effects of "Canadian Save the Children Fund:" (1963); history of the Credit Union movement in Korea, in files of Monsignor Smyth.
RG50-2/7/316-499

1. Pacific Islands-and Coady International Institute, 1969-1979.
Correspondence from Caroline Islands, Guam, Mariana Islands and Philippines in files of Monsignor Smyth.
RG50-2/5/1-242

2. Philippines-and Coady International Institute.
Correspondence re Frank Glasgow lecturing at College, "The Bantug Story"; information on "Foundation Little Philippines"; and some correspondence in files of Monsignor Smyth.
RG50-2/5/12-153-201

3. Philippines- and Coady International Institute, 1964-1977.
Correspondence, with report of visits to the Islands by J.F.Glagow in 1964, Monsignor Smyth 1966, Father MacIver 1970 and Charles Enriquez 1985.
RG50-2/5/154-201

4. Asia- and Coady International Institute, 1955-1985.
Files for Bangladesh, Ceylon, China, India, Korea, Malaysia and Pakistan.
RG50-2/7/543-872

6. Ceylon- and Coady International Institute, 1954-1975.
Correspondence of A.H.MacDonald, his draft report of "Fishermen's co-operative program in Ceylon"(1966), and other reports, student's comments on his courses, other correspondence and Asian Development Report(1974) in Colombo.
RG50-2/7/544-666

7. China- and Coady International Institute.
Student's report of his time at St.Francis Xavier(1960) and report of Asian Development Seminar in Hong Kong(1974).
RG50-2/7/676-681

8. India- and Coady International Institute, 1953-1985.
Some students' reports on their courses at St.Francis Xavier, correspondence of Alex Laidlaw re his fisheries assignment to India(1955-1957) with reports; other correspondence, Monsignor Smyth's report on his trip 1966, reports of seminars, 1978 in Calcutta, Mangalore 1980, 1981, 1984, and 1985.
RG50-2/7/682-753 & 900-987

10. Korea- and Coady International Institute.
T.W.Kim's report of study at St. Francis Xavier, Hee Sup Park's report on Coady graduates, first annual report of Catholic Central Credit Union in Seoul, 1961, Wang's report on leadership training program 1973, and Father Topshee's hand written notes of his trip, 1978.
RG50-2/7/755-822 & 988-995

11. Malaysia- and Coady International Institute, 1958-1966.
A student's reaction to courses at Extension, correspondence, and Monsignor Smyth's report of his visit there in 1966.
RG50-2/7/8723-832

12. Pakistan- and Coady International Institute, 1952-

1963.
Dr. Hussain's "Cooperation in Pakistan", "Agricultural co-operation in Pakistan" and other reports with some of Rev. M.J.McKinnon's hand written notes.
RG50-2/7/833-872

13. Asia-and Coady International Institute, 1972-1982.
Correspondence re community projects, etc., from Bangladesh, China, India(including the Calcutta Project), and Korea.
RG50-2/7/873-995

91. Chinese Embassy, Ottawa, 1966-1970.
Correspondence re a visit by Monsignor Smyth to China, and assistance in enrolling students-in Coady International Institute files.
RG50-1/1/4009-15

96. Coady Credit Union. New Aberdeen, Nova Scotia, 1966-1967.
Correspondence from Rev. F.J.Smyth requesting assistance for another Coady Credit Union-in Korea to translate Dr. Coady's book into Korean-in files of Monsignor Smyth, Coady International Institute.
RG50-1/1/4115-17

166. Lemieux, Most Rev. M.J. Ottawa and India.
Correspondence in files of Monsignor Smyth, Coady International Institute.
RG50-1/1/7394-99

236. Rankin, Rev. John A.Glendale, Cape Breton.
Correspondence re working in India-in files of Monsignor Smyth, Coady International Institute.
RG50-1/1/109.098-103

253. SELA Conference, Hong Kong, 1964-1965.
Correspondence, promotion, and list of delegates-in files of Monsignor Smyth, Coady International Institute.
RG50-1/1/10692-648

305. Gillis, Dr. Duncan Hugh.
Reports to Canadian International Development Agency on visit to Pacific Trust Territories and South Asia-in files of Coady International Institute.
RG50-1/1/14624-655

Halifax

**Killam Memorial Library,
Dalhousie University,
Halifax, Nova Scotia, B3H 4H8.
Tel:(902)424-3601.**

Harrington, Charlotte Geddie.
Original, black and white. 25 photographs. ca. 1850.
Rev. John Geddie and his family, Geddie's mission to Aneityum(Anatom), New Hebrides, mission houses of fellow missionaries in New Hebrides, mission ship

Dayspring.
SEIFRIED

Canada-China Friendship Association.
Halifax, 1973-1979.
Original, 45 cm., 1973-1980.
Correspondence, 1973-1980; steering committee minutes, 1973-1979; general membership meeting minutes, 1973-1978; sub-committee minutes, 1973-1978; sub-committee reports, 1973-1978; program materials, 1974-1978; newsletters, 1975-1979; documents, 1975-1979. Other publications, 1974, 1976; membership lists, 1974-1979.
ULM4

Theses and dissertations

Ahmed, Abu Ishaque Mahbub U.
Political elites in Bangladesh. M.A. thesis 1976.
CT

Amirkhalkhali, M.S. Saleh.
Development planning and growth in Iran. M.A. thesis 1981.
NL

Asan, M. Yousuf.
Adult education in Bangladesh, a strategy for development. M.A. thesis 1979.
CT

Bixby, Christopher Diki.
Revolutionary stability and the Chinese Communist Party, 1949-1959, the party's agrarian policies and the organizational capacity to bring them to fruition. M.A thesis 1974.
CT

Chang, Moonchul.
The UNCTAD model marine hull and cargo insurance clauses, recent development in marine insurance laws from the Korean perspective. LL.M. thesis 1985.
NL

Chen, Shenjie.
A theory of the socialist firm in the People's Republic of China. M.A. thesis 1986.
NL

Das Gupta, Malabika.
Big business houses and their impact on the Indian economy. M.A. thesis 1974.
CT

Das Gupta, Malabika.
The distribution of benefits from growth in rural India. Ph.D. dissertation 1976

Dias, Dayakanthi R.
Money and credit supply in Sri Lanka, 1974-1980. M.A. thesis 1984.
NL

Ells, Margaret Elizabeth.
The horns of the Persian dilemma. M.A thesis 1930.
CGT

Evans, Paul M.
Fairbank, intellect and enterprise in American China scholarship, 1936-1961. Ph.D. dissertation 1982.

Fouillard, Anne.
Agroforestry in Indonesia, a case study of the Penghijauan Programme in the Jatipurwo, Central Java. M.E.S. thesis 1985.
NL

Ghosh, Anosuya.
The Phillips curve, a summary and macroeconomic applications in Indian data, 1951-1971. M.A. thesis 1982.
NL

Hasan, M. Yousuf.
Adult education in Bangladesh, a strategy for development. M.A. thesis 1979.
NL

Jarayabhand, Srisuda.
Assessment of coastal zone management and planning in Thailand, a case study of the Eastern Seaboard Region. M.E.S. thesis 1988.
NL

Jha, Lakshmi.
Balanced and unbalanced growth, a case study of India. M.A. thesis 1972.
CT

Lim, Michael Jin Kok.
Problems of political integration in Malaysia. M.A. thesis 1971.
CT

Lin, Jinding.
Mobilization of surplus labor resources in China. M.D.E. thesis 1987.
NL

Lin, Zhengxi.
The Marxian monetary theory and China's monetary policy. M.A. thesis 1987.
NL

Mahbar, Zabidi Bin.
Privatization of public enterprise, a case study of Malaysia. M.D.E. thesis 1988.
NL

Malhotra, Surinder Saroop.
A sociological survey of teachers from India teaching in Nova Scotia, 1962-1972. M.A. thesis 1978.
NL

Martell, Ann Patricia.
The Canadian Presbyterian Mission to Trinidad's East Indian population, 1868-1912. M.A thesis 1975.
CT

Martosubroto, P.
Fishery dynamics of the demersal resources of the Java Sea. Ph.D. dissertation 1982.
NL

Mo, Shijian.
China and its maritime boundaries, a study on boundary making problems in the Yellow Sea, the East China Sea, and the South China Sea. LL.M. thesis 1986.
NL

Moreen, Lori Elyse.
Conflict theory and the iron law of oligarchy reexamined, the case of the People's Republic of China. M.A. thesis 1979.
CT

Moy, Martin M.
An essay of the pre-conditions for rapid expansion in manufacturing exports, Britain 1780-1800, Japan 1953-1973, South Korea 1960-1980. M.A. thesis 1981.
NL

Mukakanya, Patrick J.M.
The portrait of the native in Conrad's African and Malayan fiction. M.A. thesis 1983.
NL

Mullen, Vernon.
Radhakrishnan's idea of the divine in man. M.A. thesis 1965.
CT

Mydin, Mohd Yousoff.
Regional economic integration, the experience of the Association of Southeast Asian Nations. M.D.E. thesis 1987.
NL

Naini, Abbas A.
An econometric study of demand for domestic and imported automobiles in Iran, 1963-1978. Ph.D. dissertation 1980.

Nambiar, Prithi.
Canadian development assistance to India, 1951-1984. M.D.E. thesis 1984.
NL

Pahariya, Nemi Chand.
Factor intensity analysis of India's foreign trade structure. M.A. thesis 1984.
NL

Patayanikorn, Sombot.
A test of the consistency of projected samples of a demand for professional and technical manpower in Thailand, 1971-1980. M.A. thesis 1974.
CT

Philipupillai, Salvathy.
The balance of payments experience of Sri Lanka, 1950-1985. M.D.E. thesis 1988.
NL

Phillips, James Robert.
The development of British authority in Southern India, the Nawab of Arcot, the East India Company, and the British government, 1775-1785. Ph.D. dissertation 1983.

Pilando, Teofilo S.
Transnational corporations, international investment, and related policy with special reference to the Philippine experience. M.D.E. thesis 1988.
NL

Piracha, Zafur Iqbar.
Income distribution and growth in Pakistan. M.A. thesis 1971.
CT

Poudel, Byas Jee.
Canadian development assistance to Nepal. M.D.E. thesis 1987.
NL

Sandhu, Sukhdev Singh.
Adjustment problems of a minority group(East Indian) in the Halifax and Dartmouth area. M.A. thesis 1978.
CT

Singh, Uday Raj.
The Fiji sugar industry, an assessment of linkage and marketing strategies. M.D.E. thesis 1989.
NL

Sirisena, Tilakaratne Arachchige Don.
Monetary expansion as a means of capital formation in underdeveloped countries, illustrated with reference to Ceylon. M.A. thesis 1965.
CT

Tay, Kuang-Yak.
An assessment of the Asian Development Bank and its contribution to Malaysia. M.D.E. thesis 1987.
NL

Teehan, Mark F.
The Russian 'threat' to India and Anglo-Indian defence policy. Ph.D. dissertation 1979.

Tien, Chen-ya.
The functions of the militia system in Chinese nation building after the civil war of 1949. M.A. thesis 1972.
CT

Trood, Russell B.
The origins of Australian-United States involvement in the Vietnam war, 1945-1965. Ph.D. dissertation 1989.
NL

Varchese, Mary Noozhumurry.
The East African Indian National Congress 1914 to 1939, a study of Indian political activity in Kenya. Ph.D. dissertation 1976.

Villareal, Lolita B.
The Philippines in the international shrimp market, 1970-1985. M.D.E. thesis 1988.
NL

Wilson, George Alan.
The growth of Anglo-Japanese understanding, 1894-1902. M.A. thesis 1950.
CT

Wimalasena, R.K.P.
Export and import demand functions for Sri Lanka, an econometric study. M.A. thesis 1988.
NL

Wong, Paul Kwok Wai.
Organization and administration of primary and secondary education in Hong Kong. M.A. thesis 1974.
CT

Yadav, Sanjay Singh.
Interpretations of the Sino-Indian War, a study in sociology of knowledge. Ph.D. dissertation 1987.
NL

Zohir, Sajjad.
Rural credit in Noakhali district, Bangladesh. M.A. thesis 1982.
NL

Zoughi, Iraj.
The decline of British influence and the emergence of American dominance in Iran, 1941-1948. Ph.D. dissertation 1980.

**Archives,
Killam Memorial Library
Dalhousie University,
Halifax, Nova Scotia, B3H 4H8.
Tel:(902)494-6490.**

Murray, Robert and family.
Papers, original, 40 cm.
Letters from Dr. Florence Murray and other family to father, Rev. Robert Murray. Papers of Dr. Florence Murray include letters from family members, manuscript of a published and an unpublished book, notes and articles on her work in Korea, 1912-1973. Also 96 photographs, 478 negatives and 66 postcards from Korea.
MITCHELL

**Nova Scotia Museum Library,
1747 Summer Street,
Halifax, Nova Scotia, B3H 3A6.
Tel:(902)424-7374.**

Geddie, John.
Photographs.

Small collection(less than a dozen) of ambrotypes and stereoscopic slides taken in the New Hebrides in the l860's. Forms part of the artifact collection of the Museum's Historical Section.

**Public Archives of Nova Scotia,
Coburg Road,
Halifax, Nova Scotia, B3H 1Z9.
Tel:(902)423-9115.**

Annand, Joseph, 1844-1932.
Missionary.
Original, 10 cm., 1871-1903.
Journals kept by the Rev. Joseph Annand who left Halifax, 5 November 1872, for the New Hebrides; Nova Scotia, 1 May l871 to 15 November l872, Tririki Fate, New Hebrides, 1 March 1874 to 1 May 1876; Santo, New Hebrides, 1 February 1902 to 31 July 1903.
ULM4

Letters, 1891-1930.
From the Rev. Joseph Annand to his niece, Bertha R. (Lynch) Grant.
ULM5

Foote, William Rufus, 1869-1930.
Letters and diaries, 1898-1930.
Foote accompanied Rev. D.M.MacRae and Dr. Robert Grierson in the early group of Canadian missionaries to Korea. He also served in Manchuria and Siberia.
MITCHELL

Geddie, John, 1815-1872.
Diaries, 1848-1857 of Rev. John Geddie, a Presbyterian missionary in the New Hebrides.
Microfilm copy purchased from the Pacific Manuscripts Bureau, Research School of the Pacific Studies.
ULM5

Grierson, Robert, 1868-1965.
Diaries, 1898-1901.
A graduate of Dalhousie in medicine and Pine Hill in theology, Dr. Robert Grierson was one of the mission's original founding fathers, remaining in Korea from 1898 until 1937.
MITCHELL

Mackenzie, John William.
Papers, 1870-1969.
Papers of the Rev. John William Mackenzie, who was a missionary to Erakor and Epang, Efate, New Hebrides.
ULM5

McNab, James Burrows Davis, ca. 1809-ca. 1871.
Journal, 1827-1830, kept on the whaling ship **Pacific** on a voyage from Halifax to the coast of Japan, 1827-1830.
ULM5

MacRae, Duncan Murdoch, 1867-1949.
Letters, diaries, books and notebooks, 1896-1949.
MacRae, accompanied by his wife Edith, arrived in Korea in 1898 in company with Dr. Robert Grierson and Rev. Foote, agriculturist and builder as well as evangelist, he became well known for his willingness to question the measures of the Japanese occupation authorities.
MITCHELL

Maritime Missionaries to Korea.
Papers, ca. 1890-ca. 1975, 16 metres.
Correspondence, journals, financial accounts, photographs, periodicals and audio tapes related to the Presbyterian mission in North Korea, includes papers of Rev. Duncan MacRae, Dr. Robert Grierson, Rev. W.R.Foote, Rev. Luther Young, the Robb family, and Dr. Florence Murray.
Canadian Presbyterian Missionary Council. Minutes of annual meeting, 1913-1918.
Presbyterian Church in Canada. Council of Korea Mission. Annual meetings, 1919-1920, 1922.
United Church of Canada. Korea Mission. Minutes and reports of annual meetings, 1936-1940. United Church of Canada. Board of Foreign Missions. Rev. A.E.Armstrong, correspondence, 1913-1933.
ULM5

Murray, Florence Jessie, 1894-1975.
Papers.
Daughter of a Presbyterian minister and a school teacher, Dr. Florence Jessie Murray, went to Korea in 1921 after graduating from Dalhousie Medical School. She was part of the 1942 exchange for Japanese POWs, returning to serve once again, 1947-1969.
MITCHELL

Robb, Alexander Francis, -1935.
Letters.
Left for Korea in 1901, and two years later, he and his wife were joined in their work by his sister, Jennie Barclay Robb.
MITCHELL

Young, Luther Lisar, 1875-1950.
Papers.
Left for Korea in 1906, after graduating from Dalhousie and Pine Hill, and except for the war years, served there until his death.
MITCHELL

**United Church of Canada. Maritime Conference.
c/o The Atlantic School of Theology,
Francklyn Street,
Halifax, Nova Scotia, B3H 3B5.
Tel:(902)429-4819.**

F & I. Family and individual.

Box 43.
Envelope 103
Rev. John Geddie. Letters from Geddie to various individuals, 1847-1850.

Envelope 103(a)
Letters from Geddie to various individuals and

institutions(Board of Foreign Missions), 1851-1856.

Envelope 103(b)
Letters from Geddie to various individuals, 1856-1871.

Envelope 103(c)
Letters from Geddie to various individuals and institutions(London Missionary Society), 1857-1867.

Envelope 103(d)
Excerpts from Geddie's journal, 1831-1857 (handwritten).

Envelope 103(e)
Mrs. Geddie's letters to (mostly) family members, 1851-1873.

Envelope 104(b)
Correspondence, minutes, accounts, re Geddie's departure, 1844-1846.

Envelope 104(e)
Correspondence re the centenary of the birth of John Geddie, 1915.

Envelope 105
Miscellaneous material from a scrapbook, some correspondence, mostly unidentified scraps.

Envelope 109(e)
Notebook(in Geddie's handwriting) of guide to translation of native(Samoan) language into English.

Envelope 110
Dr. Geddie's manuscript. Book of Psalms translated into "native" Samoan.

Envelope 111(a)
Pen-and-ink sketches of John Geddie(three copies).

Envelope 111(b)
Photograph of Mrs. Geddie, taken in Halifax(undated).

Envelope 111(c)
Group photograph of missionaries in the New Hebrides(undated), damaged.

Box 44.

Envelope 113
Rev. George Gordon. Typed history of the Rev. and Mrs. George Gordon, author unknown.
Typed history of James Gordon, brother of George, author unknown.

Envelope 113(d)
Collection of letters from various missionaries.
Box 45.

Envelope 116
Dr. A.G.Sinclair. Diary deals exclusively with a trip to the Far East.

Mis. Missions.

Korea.

Box 1.

Envelope 1
Letters from William G.McKay in Korea to Mrs. and Mrs. Lane of Stewiacke, Nova Scotia, 1894, 1 May 1895.

Envelope 2
Letter to Mrs. A.E.McLean, Newcastle, New Brunswick from Anna McLeod in Tokyo, Japan, 25 October 1910.

Envelope 3
Report of Dr. M.McRae from the mission field, Wonsan, Korea, 1904.

Envelope 4
Synopsis of minutes of the seventeenth annual meeting of the Council of the Korea Mission of the Presbyterian Church in Canada, 5 July 1915 (in poor condition).

Photograph Cabinet.

Photograph cabinet contains collections of photographs, etchings, lantern slides pertaining to the missions, include; collection of photographs of churches, schools, catechists' homes on Trinidad, Demarara. All identified.

Collection of lantern slides of scenes, people in the New Hebrides, possibly to accompany the lecture of Rev. Robert Steel(envelope 2, box 2).
Photograph of Rev. J.W.McKenzie.
Photograph of Mr. and Mrs. J.Annand.
Etching of Rev. D.Morton.

Wolfville

Harold Campbell Vaughan Memorial Library,
Acadia University,
Acadia Street, Box D,
Wolfville, Nova Scotia, B0P 1X0.
Tel:(902)542-2201.

Manning, Sarah J.(Bigelow), 1850-1922.
1 vol., manuscript.
(Scrapbook of pictures of the Canadian Baptist Mission in India).
ACADIA

Maritime Provinces' Telugu Baptist Mission Conference.
Minutes of the semi-annual and annual sessions. Semi-annual 1st-3rd, 1889-1891. 5th-11th, 1893-1900, 13th-15th, 1901-1903. Annual: 1st-10th, 1889-1898, 12th, 1900; 14th-17th, 1902-1905.
ACADIA

Tupper, Charles, 1794-1881.
Vindication of the Baptist translators in India, in reply to the Rev. Thomas Trotter's letters, "on the meaning of baptism". Pictou, Nova Scotia, Eastern Chronicle office.
ACADIA

United Baptist Women's Missionary Union of the Maritime Provinces.
Mission band lessons, no.2, work among the Telugus from 1875-1895, no.3, work among the Telugus from 1895-1900, no. 4, work among the Telugus from 1900-1911.
ACADIA

Theses and dissertations

Brown, Gerald Saxon.
The Eastern Question and the Crimean War. M.A. thesis 1937.
CGT

Fox, Bradford Brendon.
Counterinsurgency, Kenya, Malaya and South Vietnam, 1955-1965. M.A. thesis 1978.
CT

Okano, John Kozo.
Prayer and Christian fellowship from the viewpoint of Christian education in Japan. M.Div. thesis 1973.
CT

Perkin, John Conway.
The end of the great game, Anglo-Russian relations concerning Central Asia, 1899-1907. M.A. thesis 1985.
NL

Thomas, Roderick Michael.
Perception and misperception, the American intelligence failure in Iran. M.A. thesis 1983.
NL

Wan, Ming.
Pierre Trudeau and China, the establishment of diplomatic relations with the People's Republic of China. M.A. thesis 1989.
NL

ONTARIO

Guelph

**Archival and Special Collections,
University of Guelph Library,
Guelph, Ontario, N1G 2W1.
Tel:(519)824-4120, ext.3413.**

Abell, Helen C.
East Indonesia regional development studies(E.I.R.D.S.), 8 boxes.
Helen Abell was a consultant on the E.I.R.D.S. Canadian project sponsored by the Canadian International Development Agency and the Provincial Government of Alberta.
Correspondence, reports, surveys, notes and resource materials, 1962-1976.

Abell, Helen C.
Report of preparatory mission to Nepal, India, Sri Lanka, and Pakistan, 6 February- 20 March 1977, by J.P.Goddijn

Abell, Helen C.
Helen Abell worked as consultant for Canadian International Development Agency and Crippen International in Lombok during the summers of 1973 and 1974.
Water feasibility study, Lombok, Indonesia, correspondence, field notes, reports, 1973-1975.

Abell, Helen C.
Helen Abell worked as consultant for Montreal Engineering Company and the World Bank on the West Java project, November-December 1976.
West Java steam power plant social impact study, correspondence, reports, notes and resource materials, 1971-1976.

All about us.
A collection by Dr. Betty Nickerson of 5,000 works of art, and 100,000 pieces of creative writing by children from 6 to 18, mostly by Canadian children, but including some works by children in Fiji, Japan and Malaysia.

McConkey, Oswald Murray, 1891-1970.
Professor of field husbandry(1922-1957), postwar worker with U.N.R.R.A. and F.A.O. in China and Manchuria.
Papers, 15 boxes.

Box 1. General correspondence, including Korean agriculture, 1950.
Box 7. Photographs, including China, illustrating topics as wind and water erosion, soil rehabilitation, irrigation, reforestation, contour farming.
Box 14. Resource materials, including China(1944-1947), Indonesia(1952), West Pakistan(1956).
Box 15. Includes collection on agriculture in China, l map, 13 photographs, 2 bundles of photographic negatives, and 4 plates, manuscripts, documents, studies, collected by Dr. McConkey while he was agricultural rehabilitation officer with United Nations Relief and Rehabilitation Administration and F.A.O., from 1946 to 1948.

**Documentation and Research Centre,
University Library,
University of Guelph,
Guelph, Ontario, N2G 2W1.
Tel:519)824-4280.**

Theses and Dissertations

Bindra, Gusharn Singh.
A study of the nutritional status of a selected sample of East Indian Punjabi immigrants to Canada. Ph.D. dissertation 1986

Cheng, Louis Kam-loi.
Mao Tse-tung's theory of foreign relations. M.A thesis 1969.
CT

Fu, Carly Yee-bing.
A study of the social adjustment of the Chinese family in Toronto. M.A. thesis 1967.
CT

Gardner, J.Douglas.
The influence and efforts of the People's Republic of China in Africa. M.A. thesis 1971.
CT

Gee, Joyce.
Cultural conflicts among Chinese-Canadian adolescents. M.Sc thesis 1981.
NL

Grover, Indu Shobha.
The British policy of westernization of Indian education. M.A. thesis 1971.
CT

Halladay, Judith Lynn.
A study of maternal and child health information sources in South Sulawesi, Indonesia. M.Sc. thesis, 1987.
NL

Heikinkeimo, Pirkko Sisko.
The adaptation of South East Asian and African students at the University of Guelph. M.Sc. thesis 1984.
NL

Huddle, Janet-Marie.
Production and distribution of food, a study of the green and blue revolutions. M.A. thesis 1988
NL

Kado, Koji.
Factors influencing Japan's agricultural import liberalization. M.Sc. thesis 1975.
CT

Legge, Terrence H.
Ideology, tradition and power in China, the Foreign Ministry in the Cultural Revolution. M.A. thesis 1977.
CT

Lofquist, Bruce H.
Chinese Communist Party policy and units of area administration for agricultural production, 1921-1966. M.A. thesis 1975
CT

Loi, Kuong-soon.
General and classification of selected soils intermediate between the red-yellow podzolic and lateritic groups in Sarawak, Malaysia. M.Sc. thesis 1981.
NL

MacPhail, Fiona.
The impact of irrigation on women, a case study of technical change in South Sulawesi, Indonesia. M.A. thesis 1987.
NL

Malik, Allah Ditta.
Achievement motive, higher education and modernization, an exploration of their relationships in the case of Pakistan. M.A. thesis 1972.
CT

Mathison, William Carl.
The reaction of the British press to the Afghan and Sind War(1838-1842). M.A. thesis 1976.
CT

Nitsmer, Semart.
Simulation of agricultural credit policies of the Thai Bank for Agriculture and Agricultural Cooperatives. M.Sc. thesis 1988.
NL

Phillips, Patricia Michelle.
Chinese spatial construction, policy and practice, 1949-1970. M.A. thesis 1975.
CT

Pieri, Renato Gabrielle.
The North American Japanese pork industries, an economic analysis. M.Sc. thesis 1975.U.S.:Japanese:-1975
CT

Pekuril, Anil.
An impact evaluation of the small farmer development program in the Eastern Development Region of Nepal, sub projects Kakarvitta, Dulari, Bokhim and Bhirgaon. M.A. thesis 1987.
NL

Ptak, Roderich.
Macao and its foreign trade to China and Japan,1557-1640. M.A. thesis 1981.
NL

Roleas, Pensa Misiel.
A case study of development administration in Papua New Guinea. M.A. thesis, 1987.
NL

Ross, Jay S.
Subsistence under stress nutritional implications in the Wosera, Papua New Guinea. M.Sc. thesis, 1984.
NL

Smaller, Elizabeth.
Economic transformation and production relations in an Indian farming village, the case of Vashist, Himachal Pradesh. M.A. thesis 1988.
NL

Song, Changqing.
An analysis of farm structural change in Heilungjiong, China, a linear programming approach. M.Sc. thesis 1988.
NL

Strimas, Daniel Thomas.
A rationale for the discrepancies existent in Sino- and Soviet revolutionary theory and practice. M.A. thesis 1972.
CT

Usman, Sunyoto.
Interagency coordination in designing and implementing projects at the sub-district level in Indonesia, a Yogyakarta case study. M.A. thesis, 1986.
NL

Villamayor, Frederico G.
Growth and yield of potatoes(solanium tuberosum l) in the lowlands of the Philippines. Ph.D. dissertation 1984.
NL

Watson, Dwight Jan.
Fish production and community structure in a tropical rainforest river system of Northern Borneo(Sarawak, Malaysia) M.Sc. thesis 1983.
NL

Wilson, Robert Sydney.
The British evangelical reaction to the Indian Mutiny of 1857. M.A. thesis 1967.
CT

Yadava, Ramesh.
Some computer-based international development information systems and their relevance in rural development in the third world. M.A. thesis 1986.
NL
India.

Yasmin, Marziya.
Ethnic identity retention of the Bangladeshi immigrants in the Toronto Census Metropolitan Area. M.A. thesis 1982.
NL

Hamilton

William Ready Division of Archives and Research Collections,
McMaster University Library,
1280 Main Street W,
Hamilton, Ontario, L8S 4L6.
Tel:(416)525-9140, ext.4737.

Brittain, Vera Mary, 1896?-1970.;
Feminist and pacifist.
The Vera Brittain Archive consists of over 100 books and 156 feet of original materials. The original materials consists of manuscripts of all Miss Brittain's published and unpublished books and articles, her correspondence, diaries and journals, and large group of news clippings and articles relating to varied interests as a feminist, journalist, novelist and above all, pacifist. Some correspondence with feminist and pacifist groups in India

Cooperative Committee on Japanese Canadians; Archive.
Committee formed in June 1943 by a group of concerned Toronto citizens to assist relocating Japanese Canadians with housing, jobs, and recreation. The committee became active in lobbying nationally for the rights of Japanese Canadians and against Bill 135 on disenfranchisement and the "voluntary repatriation" plan of l945. By the end of the war, the committee had become an organization representing over forty local and national groups including the Y.W.C.A., the Y.M.C.A., churches, trade unions, youth groups, and the Toronto Council. It had branches in Vancouver, Edmonton, Calgary, Lethbridge, Regina, Saskatoon, Winnipeg, Ottawa, Montreal, Guelph, Brantford, Hamilton and London.

The archive consists of correspondence files, minutes from 1943 to 1951, reports, publications and research files. The collection was donated by Edith Fowke.
MCMASTER

Crosthwaite-Dufferin correspondence.
The collection consists of correspondence between Lord Dufferin, Viceroy of India, and Sir Charles Hawkes Todd Crosthwaite, Commissioner of Burma. The letters are mounted in two volumes, one of correspondence from Lord Dufferin to Sir Charles, dating from 1884 to 1888, and one of letters from Sir Charles to Lord Dufferin, dating from 1887 to 1890. There are over l00 pieces of correspondence in the collection, which gives an excellent view of the British administration in an Indian province during the period of the Third Burmese War(1885-1886) and the settlement afterwards.
MCMASTER

Culhane, Claire Eglin, 1918-
One of Canada's foremost peace activists.
Correspondence, 1966-1977.
In 1968, Culhane resigned her position as administrator of the Canadian Anti-tuberculosis Hospital in Quang Ngai, South Vietnam, in protest over Canada's role in the Indochina War.
Her papers include important exchanges with key government and opposition leaders, spokesmen for the Democratic Republic of (North)Vietnam and the National Liberation Front of South Vietnam, leading peace activists throughout the world, and numerous journalists, editors and publishers. There are manuscripts and typescripts of her speeches and articles, and many difficult-to-obtain documents on the Indochina War, Canadian foreign aid and related topics.
MCMASTER

Harrison, James Graham.
Manuscripts of an unknown provenance entitled: "The visual arts of the South Pacific".
ULM5

Robertson, John Henry, 1909-1965.;
Known under the pen name of John Connell.
Connell was the Chief Military Censor in India during World War II, and also directed British propaganda efforts in the Middle East. The war years had a considerable influence on Connell which shows up in his later novels and biographies, several of which concern military figures.
Includes typescripts of smaller articles and reviews for newspapers, radio and television, and typescripts of many unpublished articles and drafts for longer works. There is much correspondence with literary, political and military figures, amounting to some 14,000 pieces.
Catalog.
MCMASTER

Russell, Bertrand;, 1872-1970.
The Bertrand Russell Archives contain over 250,000 pieces of manuscript and other unpublished material, approximately 335 feet.

Russell's relationship with Asia and the Pacific, include his visit to China and Japan in 1920-1921, his correspondence with Chinese leaders in the 1960's, his condemnation of the Bikini H-bomb test and during the Sino-Indian border conflict and the Cuban missile crisis, he intervened with heads of states and with U Thant on the United Nations. Also during the later l960's Russell attacked U.S. policies in Vietnam, and convened the International War Crimes Tribunal in this connection.
MCMASTER

Classification 220. Articles and speeches.

1924. Memorandum on the Boxer indemnity.

1945. The future in China and Japan. 5 pages.

What the European victory means to China.

The future in India. 4 pages.

1959. Mr. Nehru's foreign policy. 4 pages.

1965. On Indo-Pakistani relations. 6 pages.

Foreword to 1966 edition of the problem of China. 1 page.

The threat of Pakistan 2 to 9 pages.

1966. On the Tashkent agreement, for **Morning News**(Dacca), 6 pages.

Classification 940. Tape recordings.

Tapes no. 1 and 2.

Victims of Hiroshima and Nagasaki and condemnation of U.S.A. and U.S.S.R. tests.

Classification 971. Newsclippings.

Classification 710. Personal correspondence.

Brockway, Fenner, letter from B.R.'s secretary to secretary of British Council for Peace in Vietnam;

British Labour Council for Chinese Freedom, 1926.;

Bridgeman, R.(re 'Les amis du peuple chinois'), 1935.

Chhatapur, Maharaja Bahadur of;.
Under another name this Maharaja appears in Forster's **Passage to India,** 1916-1919.

China and Japan, l920-1921.
Extensive correspondence

Classification 640. World affairs.
Arranged by country.

Ceylon, 1957-1958.

China, 1958-1965
(Sino-Indian dispute), 1962-1964.

Indonesia, 1966.

Iran, 1964-1965.

Japan, 1956-1965

Pakistan, 1963-1965.

Vietnam, 1963-1966.

Classification 650. Heads of state.

Cambodia, 1964-1966, with Prince Sihanouk.

Ceylon, 1963-1964. with Prime Minister Bandaranaike, mostly on the Sino-Indian dispute.

China, People's Republic of, 1962-1964, on Sino-Indian dispute.

India, 1955-1966, mostly with Prime Ministers Nehru, Shastri, and Indira Gandhi.

Indonesia, 1960-1966.

Iran, 1964-1965.

Pakistan, 1964-1966, mostly with Ayub Khan; and Z.A.Bhutto.

Philippines, 1963-1966, with Macapagal and Marcos.

United Nations, 1962-1966, with U Thant.

Vietnam, Democratic Republic of, 1964-1966, with Ho Chi Minh.

World War I Collection.
Includes trench maps for Gallipoli.
MCMASTER

Theses and dissertations

Archival and second copy held in the University Library.

Ahmed, Salehuddin.
Rural-urban interactions in economic development, a two-sector model for Bangladesh. Ph.D. dissertation 1978.

Anderson, Leona May.
Sakra in early Buddhist art. M.A. thesis 1979.
CT

Anderson, Leona May.
A study of Indian Spring festivals from ancient and medieval Sanskrit texts. Ph.D. dissertation 1986.
NL

Barrett, Ralph Victor.
Soka Gakuin, a response to modernization. M.A. thesis 1968.
CT

Bhadra, Bipul Kumar.
The mode of production, social classes and the state in colonial India, 1757-1947, a case study of the process of dependent capitalist development. Ph.D. dissertation 1984.

Bhadra, Bula.
Marx's views on India, a critique of the Asiatic mode of production. M.A. thesis 1980.
NL

Bhadra, Bula.
Marx's views on India, a sociological appraisal of the "Asiatic" mode of production. Ph.D. dissertation 1986.

Blythe, Jennifer Mary.
Following both sides, processes of group formation in Vitu. Ph.D. dissertation 1979.
Papua New Guinea

Bowlby, Paul William Reid.
The lotus and the chariot, a study of the root meaning of "dharma" in the Indian religious tradition. Ph.D. dissertation 1976.

Brown, Ross Owen.
Ko Hung, alchemy, immortality and religious Taoism. M.A. thesis 1977.
CT

Byram, Terence Arthur.
Korea and United States foreign policy during the Truman administration. M.A. thesis 1964.
CT

Cheung, Yet-Wah.
Parental influence on ethnic language retention by children. The case of Chinese in urban Canada. M.A. thesis 1978.
CT

Connoly, Gaiyle Jean.
Visual forms of the Kuan-wu-liang-shou-fu ching; in Far Eastern art as aids to release. M.A. thesis 1979.
CT

Dar, Atul Aditya.
Saving, capital imports and growth, a macroeconomic study of India. Ph.D. dissertation 1981
NL

Dayananda, Muhandiramge Don.
Potential cartelization in a monopsonistic market structure, a model of the world tea market, with special reference to Sri Lanka. Ph.D. dissertation 1977

Dollarhide, Kenneth James.
Nichiren's Doctrine of the Age of the Last Law according to the **Senji sho.** Ph.D. dissertation, 1981.
NL

Dubey, Shri Prakash.
An analysis of Rudolf Ott's interpretation of Hinduism. M.A. thesis 1969.
CT

Due, Evan.
Tourism and development, examining the case of Sri Lanka. M.A. thesis 1980.
NL

Duggan, John Francis.
Hanuman. M.A. thesis 1978.
CT

Faroque, M.A.
Employment maximization in a labour-surplus economy, an application to Bangladesh. Ph.D. dissertation, 1983.
NL

Flower, Theresa J.
Millenarian themes in the White Lotus society. M.A. thesis 1976.
CT

Forde, Janice Carol.
The concept of Saksi in Advaita Vedanta. M.A. thesis 1975.
CT

Foster, Donald James.
The phenomenology of self realization in thephilosophy of Sankaracarya, a study of **Vivekacudamani** and **Aparoksanuphuti.** M.A. thesis 1973.
CT

Freedman, Michael.
Popular elements in some of the Pali sutras. M.A. thesis 1973.
CT

Freedman, Michael.
The characterizaton of Ananda in the "Pali canon" of the Theravada, a hagiographic study. Ph.D. dissertation 1977.

Gadsden, Stephen Lomas.
Causality in Advaita metaphysics. M.A. thesis 1977.
CT

Gidney, Robert Douglas.
Turkey and the powers, from Montreux to the Truman Doctrine. M.A. thesis 1964.
CT

Goswami, Chitto Rajan.
The soul culture in the Upanishads in the light of Sri Aurobindo's thought. M.A. thesis 1969.
CT

Guha, Srghya.
The effects of alternative income distributions on resource allocation in India. Ph.D. dissertation 1976.

Gummoe, Anna Jean.
Contributions of the Osmanli to Muslem dynasties. M.A. thesis 1922.
CGT

Habib, Mohammed Ahsan.
Optimal research, induced innovation, and agricultural development, an application to Bangladesh. Ph.D. dissertation 1980

Hendricks, Norman Cecil.
An explication of the writings on the **Bhagavad Gita** in the published works of Simone Weil. M.A. thesis 1969.
CT

Hendricks, Norman Cecil.
Simone Weil and the Indian religious tradition. Ph.D. dissertation 1972.

Hettiarachchy, Tilak.
Peasants in a changing economy, ecological change among the Sinhalese peasants, 1796-1909. M.A. thesis 1978.
CT

Hill, Peter Graham.
The overseas Chinese in Southeast Asia. M.A. thesis 1967.
CT

Hoda, Mohammad Hashem.
Macroeconometric and input-output model of Iran. Ph.D. dissertation 1984.
NL

Hodgson, Raymond.
Indra and Vrtra, a study of continuity and change in the Indian religious tradition. Ph.D. dissertation 1976.

Horne, John Varnald.
The Japanese immigration problem in Canada. M.A. thesis 1924
CGT

Jillard, Frederick Thomas.
The Canadian Baptist foreign mission enterprise in India and Indian nationalism. B.D. thesis 1956.
CT

Jones, Pauline Mary Milton.
The relationship between the microcosm and the macrocosm as expressed in the principal Upanishads. M.A. thesis 1970.
CT

Kabir, Muhammed.
A disaggregated econometric model of price behaviour in Bangladesh. Ph.D. dissertation 1981.

Karunasena, Aluthgedara.
A macroeconometric model for Sri Lanka. Ph.D. dissertation 1983.
NL

Khandker, Shahipur Rahman.
Farm household decision-making, theory and evidence from a rural economy. Ph.D. dissertation 1983.

Khetan, Chandra Prakash.
A quarterly econometric model of the Indian monetary sector. Ph.D. dissertation 1973.

Khilji, Nasir Mahmood.
Growth prospects of a developing economy, a macroeconometric study of Pakistan. Ph.D. dissertation 1982.

Khosla, Renu Chopra.
A Canadian perspective on the Hindu woman, a study in identity transformation. M.A. thesis 1980.
NL

Kim, Su Il.
The variations of Che Ju Do Korean life styles in Tokyo, Japan. Ph.D. dissertation 1985.
NL

Koppendrayer, K.I.
The interplay of ideas behind the question of untouchability, the interaction of the British, Ambedkar and Gandhi. M.A. thesis 1982.
NL

Lachman, Charles Henry.
The Ch'an master Shen-hsiu(606?-706), three literary portraits of a patriarch manque. M.A. thesis 1974.
CT

Lahiri, Sushil Kumar.
The role of the mother goddess cult in the religious consciousness cult of Bengal. M.A. thesis 1969.
CT

Lanza, Lucille Josephine.
Three metaphors in Wang Yang-ming's discussion of mind. M.A. thesis 1979.
CT

Licorish, Cedric Courtney.
Dependence, class and race in a colonial formation, an analysis of Guyana, 1600-1917. M.A. thesis 1977.
CT

Lovell, Peter Raymond.
Children of blood, children of shame creation and procreation in Longana, East Aoba, New Hebrides. Ph.D. dissertation 1981.
NL

McBride, Stephen Kenneth Maxwell.
The Japanese annexation of Manchuria. M.A. thesis 1970.
CT

McLellan, Dusan.
Reciprocity and exploitation, peasant women in Malaysia's industrialization process. Ph.D. dissertation 1986.
NL

McKnight, John Michael.
The Gupta temple movement, a study of the political aspects of the early Hindu temple. M.A. thesis 1973.
CT

Martin, Judith Grace.
The pedagogy of conciliation in the **Bhagavata purana**, a sporting way of understanding Jnana Yoga. M.A. thesis 1975.
CT

Matthews, Victor Bruce.
The concept of craving in early Buddhism. Ph.D. dissertation 1974.

Morikawa, Tamotsu.
The Japanese in Canada. B.D. thesis 1958
CT

Morris, Paul Martin.
Adhyasa and Nama-Rupa in the Advaita Vedanta of Sankara. M.A. thesis 1979.
CT

Mukerji, Bithika.
Towards an understanding of the ontology of bliss in the conflict of modernity. Ph.D. dissertation 1981.

Mullins, Mark Richardson.
Minority churches among Japanese Canadians, a sociological study. Ph.D. thesis 1985
NL

Oh, Kang-nam.
A study of the Chinese Hua-yen Buddhism with special reference to the "Dharmadhatu"(Fa-chieh) doctrine. Ph.D. dissertation 1976.

Ostroff, Pearl.
The demon-slaying Devi, a study of her Puranic myths. M.A. thesis 1978.
CT

Pandey, Lakshiman.
The Buddha as an omniscient religious teacher. M.A. thesis 1970.
CT

Pandey, Lakshiman.
Buddhist conception of omniscience. Ph.D. dissertation 1972.

Parkhill, Thomas Chittenden.
The forest threshold, princes, sages and demons in the Hindu epics. Ph.D. dissertation 1980.

Parkhill, Thomas Chittenden.
A perception of bubblings in the Indian world view, a journey into the **Narayanjiya**. M.A. thesis 1974.
CT

Pas, Julian Francis.
Shen-tao's commentary on the **Amitayur-buddhanusmrti sutra..** Ph.D. dissertation 1973.

Penner, Peter.
The James Thomason 'school' in Northern India, 1822-1853, a biographical and administrative study. Ph.D. dissertation 1971.

Post, Kenneth Howard.
The knowledge of the absent entity in the Advaita Vedanta. M.A. thesis 1971.
CT

Rathor, Pushpa Devi.
The relationship between ethical experience and political existence in the works of Mahatma Gandhi. Ph.D. dissertation 1981.

Rodman, Margaret.
Customary illusions, land and copra in Longana, Vanuatu. Ph.D. dissertation 1981.
NL

Roth, Harold David.
The Taoist influence on Chinese Buddhism in the fourth century, case study: Chih Tun's understanding of the **Prajnaparamita.** M.A. thesis 1974.
CT

Rupwate, Daniel David.
The Lokamanya Bal Gangadhar Tilak's **"Srimad Bhagavadgitarahasya"** in the light of the saintly tradition of Maharashtra. Ph.D. dissertation 1980.

Sschopen, Gregory Robert.
Three studies in Buddhist non-Tantric cult forms. M.A. thesis 1975.
CT

Scaletta, Naomi M.
Primogeniture and primogenitor firstborn child and mortuary ceremonies among the Kabana(Bariai) of West New Britain, Papua New Guinea. Ph.D. dissertation 1985.
NL

Sen, Anupan.
The social background and social character of Bangla Desh nationalism. M.A. thesis 1975.
CT

Sen, Anupam.
The state, industrialization and class formations in India, a neo-Marxist perspective on colonialism, underdevelopment and development. Ph.D. dissertation 1979.
NL

Shahabuddin, Quazi.
Uncertainty and allocative behaviour in peasant agriculture, a study of small-holding farmers in Bangladesh. Ph.D. dissertation 1983.
NL

Shahidullah, Muhammed.
Modernization versus dependency in the context of colonial Bengal. M.A. thesis 1977.
CT

Shih, Patricia Feng-yu.
Female pollution in Chinese society. M.A. thesis 1978.
CT

Shatsena, Chatsumarn.
A study of an early Buddhist institute of nuns bhikkunis based on the **Patimokkha**. M.A. thesis 1971.
CT

Shiwcharan, Clement Toolsie.
Problems of class formation in Guyana. M.A. thesis 1977.
CT

Simon, Francis Edward.
Sankara as theologian. M.A. thesis 1978.
CT

Sinclair, Donald Keith.
Decision "makers" images in the foreign policy process, the case of the Korean War. M.A. thesis 1969.
CT

Sinha, Braj Mohan.
Problem of time and temporality in Samkhya-yoga; and Abhidarma; Buddhism. Ph.D. dissertation 1976.

Sinha, Manju Kumari.
A comparison of Glock's dimensions of religiousity, the ways of Yoga; and the mechanisms of sacralization. M.A. thesis 1975.
CT

Tan, Bee Heng.
The conception of 'Nien-fo' in the **Ching-t'u-shih-i-lun**(treatise on the Ten Doubts concerning the Pure Land). M.A. thesis 1979.
CT

Thamrongvech, Sucart Thada.
A macro-econometric model of Thailand. Ph.D. dissertation 1983.
NL

Thomas, Muntanattu David.
The relationship of Bhakti and Prapatti in Ramanuja's Moksopaya;. M.A. thesis 1969.
CT

Thomas, Pillachari Mathew.
Swami Vivekananda, his reconstruction of Hinduism as a universal religion. M.A. thesis 1969.
CT

Thomas, Pillachira Mathew.
Twentieth-century Indian interpretations of the "Bhagavadgita;", a selective study of patterns. Ph.D. dissertation 1975.

Thompson, James Ian.
The Japanese in Canada, symbolic politics in action. M.A. thesis 1980.
CT

Thurston, William Roy.
The phonology of Anem, a non-Austronesian language of West New Britain. M.A. thesis 1976.
CT

Van den Brul, Gerard Nicholas.
An examination of the modernization process and ethnic mobilization among the Nagas of Northeastern India. M.A. thesis 1981.
NL

Van Weert, Petronella Maria.
The politics of Canada's foreign aid programme, Indonesia, a case study. M.A. thesis 1979.
NL

Waghmare, Ramesh Ramchandra.
The portfolio behaviour of industrial corporations in India. Ph.D. dissertation 1976.

Watson, Norman Lorne.
Being and manifestation in the Tantric tradition. M.A. thesis 1969.
CT

Welter, Albert Franklin.
Huang-po's notion of mind. M.A. thesis 1978.
CT

Welter, Albert Franklin.
The meaning of myriad good deeds, a study of **Yung-ming yen-shou** and **Wan-shan t'ung-kuei chi**(Treatise on the common end of myriad good deeds). Ph.D. dissertation 1987.
NL

Whillier, Wayne Kenneth.
Reality, speech and speaking in the early Indian religious tradition. Ph.D. dissertation 1973.

Wilkie, Fiona Margory.
Heroism in Vietnam archetypal patterns in selected American prose and drama. Ph.D. dissertation 1985..
NL

Winch, Mary Elizabeth.
The theology of grace in the Saiva Siddhanta, in the light of Umapati Sivacharya's Tiruarupayan. M.A. thesis 1975.
CT

Winokur, Matthew Neidle.
Hui-yuan's doctrine of the spirit, a case study in Chinese Buddhist syncretism. M.A. thesis 1977.
CT

Yao, Ju.
Ethnic heterogeneity, a study of Chinese students. M.A. thesis 1975
CT

Yu, Chai-shin.
A comparative study of the founder's authority, the community, and the discipline in early Buddhism and in early Christianity. Ph.D. dissertation 1973.

Yu, Chai Shin.
A critical examination of Suzuki's understanding of Ch'an(Zen) Buddhism. M.A. thesis 1969.
CT

Zelenietz, Martin Charles.
After the despot, changing patterns of leadership and social control in Kilenge, West New Britain province, Papua New Guinea. Ph.D. dissertation 1980.

**Canadian Baptist Archives,
McMaster Divinity College,
Hamilton, Ontario. L8S 4K1
Tel: (416)525-9140 Ext.23511.**

Contains records of the Canadian Baptist Federation, including the Baptist Convention of Ontario and Quebec, the Baptist Union of Western Canada, the Union des Églises Baptistes Françaises, also records of McMaster University to 1957, John Milton Society for the Blind in Canada.

Under India, a card index notes materials for:

Akidu;

Americans in India

Andhra

Associations of India

Avanigadda

Baptist Convention of Ontario and Quebec Foreign Board, India.

Baptist Union of India

Bengal, Orissa

Blueprints - India

Calcutta

Canadian Baptist Missions to India

Chicacole

Churches

Coconada

Guadavelleru

Hospitals

Institutions-Council of India. Legal files and letters

Medical Schools - India

Missionary Conferences

National Christian Council of India

Newsclippings - India

North IndiaWnokur, Matthew Neidle.

Northern Circars

Photographs and scrapbooks - India

Photographs of specific places

Pithapuram

Primary material from India

Properties. Canadian Baptist Foreign Mission Board India

Publications

Ramachandrapuram

Samalkot, Godavari District

Savaras

Schools

Serampore

Serango

Soras-Oriyas

Telugus- Canadian Baptist Foreign Mission Board

Temperance

Vizagapatam

Vizianagaram

Vuyyuru

Western Ganjam

Women in India. Canadian Baptist Foreign Mission Board

Zenanas

India Miscellaneous

Canadian Baptist Overseas Mission Board. 86-70 India. Andhra Theological College.
Correspondence, 1977-1979.

Canadian Baptist Overseas Mission Board. India. 88-177. Andhra Christian Theological College, Hyderabad
Report by the Principal, 1964-1973. 4 p.

Canadian Baptist Overseas Mission Board. India. 83-28. Andhra Pradesh - files.

Scheme for establishing one united Theological College for Andhra Pradesh at Luthergiri, Rajahmundry, 1961.

Theological education in Andhra Pradesh(The Kretzmann Commission; Report) 1969. Report for Andhra Christian College.

Canadian Baptist Foreign Mission Board. India. Canadian Baptist Telugu Mission.
Annual reports, 1873-1940.
Name changed to **Among the Telugus.**
Loose set not complete.

Bound sets: 1898-1904, 1905-1910, 1911-1916, 1916-1921, 1922-1924, 1881-1891, 1908-1918, 1916-1927.

Baptism Records.
Baptism record books of people who were baptized in the Soras and Oriya Churches, 1907-1944.
4 books, fragile.

Baptist Convention of Ontario and Quebec. Foreign Mission Board Index.
Manuscript record of the general work in the Narsapatnam field from 1892 to about 1910.

Baptist Convention of Ontario and Quebec. Foreign Mission Board.
Newspaper clippings, 1950s and 1960s.

Baptist Convention of Ontario and Quebec. Foreign Mission Board Index.
Correspondence 1872-1890 .
To Shenstone and John McLaurin from Timpany, Bates, Boggs, McLaurin, in India, Burma and Siam.

Baptist Convention of Ontario and Quebec. Foreign Mission Board. India.
Missionary Conference. Minutes.
January 1887-July 1904,
July 1905-July 1911

Baptist Convention of Ontario and Quebec. Foreign Missions. Board. India.
Joint Conferences of missionaries of the Ontario and Quebec Provinces and the Maritime Provinces. Minutes 1890-1912. Manuscript.

Baptist Convention of Ontario and Quebec. Foreign Mission Board. India.
Legal documents re court suit over land site of Srurangaputam; School, 1902.

Baptist Convention of Ontario and Quebec. Foreign Mission Board. India.
Yellmanchili field. Treasurer's records, 1895-1902.

Canadian Baptist Overseas Missions Board. India.
Ganjam, Malia, Oriya Baptist Churches Association, Minutes. 1957-1970(includes Constitution)

Canadian Baptist Overseas Mission Board. India. 87-041 Box 1. 87-218

1975-1982. Utkal Baptist Association.

1980-1984. Utkal Baptist Association.

1980-1982. Utkal Baptist Mandala Sammilani (formerly Utkal Baptist Churches Association, Ganjam, Malia, Oriya Baptist Association).

Canadian Baptist Overseas Missions Board. India. 87-041, 87-218. Box 2.

Sora Baptist Association, 1980-1982.

Canadian Baptist Overseas Mission Board. India. 87-041 87-218.

Box 2.
Files on national workers, 1980-1982.

Canadian Baptist Overseas Missions Board. India. 86-70.

Canadian Baptist Mission in India, 1970-1974.

Missions India.
89-035 microfilm.

Narsapatnam Record, 1892-1910.
Sora Oriya minutes, 1957-1972.
Baptisms, 1907-1944.

Krishna Women's Association, Treasurer 1916-1958.

Women's Work Committee of Conferences and Council, July 1922-July 1946.

Theses and papers

Ban, Joseph.
Canada-India connection: An Historical and Contemporary Study of Canadian Baptist Influence in the State of Orissa. 1991:

Baxter, Samuel John.
The development of a ministry at the Immanuel Baptist Church, Toronto, Canada to integrate multicultural peoples. D.Min. 1982.

Cann, Roger.
Theological reflection on a project in mission in India. 1983.

Carder, Gordon.
Church union in North and South India - a comparison. 1958.

Clutton, Edith.
Canadian Baptist women's evangelism in India. n.d.

Cornutt-O'Brien, C.
Burning Issue, Sati, 1988.

Cosman, Patricia.
Mission and the church in contemporary India. 1988.

Cullen, Tom.
Cross cultural evangelism in India. 1988.

Findlay, Matilda.
Christians in Service, 1988.

Findlay, Samuel H.
Protestant agricultural missions in India, 1945. B.D. 1945.

Fitch, Jessie.
Mission and the church in contemporary India, Development ministries.

Frankland, Doreen.
India

Ghosh, Shonu.
Ministry in the rural church of Bengal, 1988.

Jillard, Fred T.
The Canadian Baptist Foreign Mission Enterprise in India and Indian Nationalism. B.D., 1956.

Johnson, Clara Agnes.
Church union in India from a Baptist viewpoint, B.D. 1962.

Knight, Kenneth.
The Baptists and the ecumenical movement in India, 1959.

Majhi, Satya Ranjan.
Curriculum for Christian Education and Sunday School of Orissa, 1991.

Majhi, Satya Ranjan.
Teaching the Gospel in the Hindu and Christian Village of Rayagoda, Ganjam District, in the State of Orissa, India, M.R.E. 1991

Moore, Dorothy.
Ministries of love and hope, 1988.

Pugh, Elizabeth.
History of single lady missionaries to India, 1986.

Pugh. Elizabeth.
Experiential journey to the Baptist Mission in India, 1988.

Pugh, William H.
Living experience in mission, 1988.

Purchase, Lee Ann.
Mission and the Church in Contemporary India, 1988.

Rao, Sreemnthula.
Smalkot Boys' Boarding School, 1882-1935, Canadian Baptist Mission, with an Evaluation of the School's Contribution. 1973.

Schroeder, J.M.
Nurses in India, 1963.

Stidsen, Catherine.
Analysis of the leadership of the Most. Rev. Leobard D'Souza of the Roman Catholic Archdiocese of Nagpur, India, 1988.

Timbers, Karen.
Reflections of an visit to Edurumondi, 1988.

Kingston

**Queen's University Archives,
Kathleen Ryan Hall,
Queen's University,
Kingston, Ontario, K7L 3N6.
Tel:(613)547-3226.**

Altrincham, Edward William Macleary Grigg, 1879-1955.
Papers, ca. 1916-1944, 15 reels.
British journalist and parliamentarian.
Correspondence, memoranda, notes of diplomatic correspondence, speeches and news clippings. Includes subject files on tour of Prince of Wales in 1920, and Imperial relations 1918-1922. In 1907-1908, toured world, visiting India. 1919-1920 military secretary on the staff of the Prince of Wales and toured Pacific islands in 1920.
Inventory.
QUEEN'S

Bowell, Mackenzie, 1823-1917.
Prime Minister of Canada, 1894-1896, Minister and Controller of Customs, September 1885-January 1892, and Minister of Trade and Industry, May 1893-December 1894.
Customs, then later Trade and Industry, was responsible for Chinese immigration, 1885-1911.
Scrapbooks, 1895-1917. 1 microfilm reel.
QUEEN'S

Cartwright, Richard John.
Minister of Trade and Commerce, July 1896 to May

1911. Trade and Industry responsible for Chinese immigration. Papers

Chandrasekhar, Sripati, 1918-
Population growth in China and India[Address at Queen's University 1 sound cassette, ca. 60 minutes. Former Minister of Health and Family Planning in India.
QUEEN'S

Chek, Sokhom, 1940-
Interview, ca.μ 36 minutes. Sound cassette. Recorded in Kingston, 1985.
Mrs. Chek immigrated from Cambodia in 1975 and now works in New Canadian Service, discusses problems that new immigrants face in Canada.
QUEEN'S

Dunlop, J.G.
Clergyman, Japan.
Letter 1908, Japan to friend.
Describes life in Japan and personal matters
QUEENS

Edgar, Mary Susanne, 1889-1973.
Diaries for 1899, 1920-1921, 1924, 1927, 1934-1935, 1962, 1970 and 1971.
The 1920 and 1920-1921 diaries contain about 100 and 200 manuscript pages respectively, the first on Japan, and the second on Hong Kong and China.

Edgar, Mary Susanne, 1889-1973.
Black and white, 100 photographs, 1925-1970.
Photographs taken during extensive travels abroad, including many views of Japan
SEIFRIED

Flavelle, Joseph Wesley, 1896-1938.
Papers contain 2 boxes of related correspondence. Flavelle was a financier and Methodist layman, and served as chairman of the Board of Directors of the West China Union University from 1922-1926. He was also a long time participant in the Canadian missionary establishment's fundraising and policy decision activities.
MITCHELL

Grier Collection.
Papers, 6 feet.
Letters, diaries, photographs and documents of the Cartwright family and branches, relating to Kingston, India and army in World War II, overseas.
ULM5

Lam, Judie, 1938-
Sound cassette, 25 minutes. Kingston.
Mrs. Lam describes circumstances of her immigration to Canada and first impressions of Canada and Kingston. Issue of discrimination, her occupation and the Chinese community in Kingston.
QUEEN'S

Mahabarata Bhagavad-gita.
Original,1 cm., 1841.
The Bhagavadgita; in Sanskrit, written in the Kannada alphabet.
ULM4

Playfair, A.A.
Letters, 1905-1906. Tokyo. 1 cm.
Include descriptions of life in Japan.
QUEEN'S

Russian-America Company.
Records, 1802-1867. 77 reels.
Correspondence, logs of ships and journals of exploration.
Contains limited information on fur trade with China, and with Manila.
Originals in the National Archives, Washington.
QUEEN'S

Slade, Edmund John Ware, 1859-1928.
Papers, 3 reels.
Correspondence, diaries, general remark book, H.M.S. *Algerine*, China Station, 1899, minute and letter book of Commander in Chief, East Indies, 1909.
QUEEN'S

Woodcock, George Meredith;, 1912-
Writer, Vancouver.
Papers, ca. 1928-1981. 20 metres.
Correspondence, manuscripts, photographs, diaries and subject files.
Woodcock travelled and wrote extensively about India, Tibet and the Pacific Rim.
QUEEN'S

Theses and Dissertations

Copies are held in Queen's University Archives as well as in departmental libraries.

Ahmed, Emajuddin.
The role of bureaucratic elites in segmented economic growth(class and regional terms), a case study of Pakistan and Bangla Desh. Ph.D. dissertation 1977.

Alam, Salauddin Mohd Shamsul.
Modes of production and social formation of colonial Bengal. M.A, thesis 1983.
NL

Ashbury, Frederick Dale.
China in ferment, education and modernization. M.A. thesis 1986.
NL

Baker, Jack Sidney.
A cost benefit analysis of an oil palm estate in Pahang State, West Malaysia. M.A. thesis 1974.
CT

Bhalla, Madhu.
Changing perceptions of the Chinese American journalists and Chinese Communists, 1936-1938. M.A. thesis 1983
NL

Bhuiyan, Abul Hossain Ahmed.
State, economy and class formations in Bangladesh. M.A. thesis 1982.
NL

Borovali, Ali Fuat.
Kemalist tradition, political change and the Turkish military. Ph.D. dissertation 1985.

Camp, Murray Arnold.
Caught in the crossfire, Jacob Gould Schurman and the Philippines, 1898-1902. M.A. thesis 1988.
NL

Caoili, Manuel Albano.
The government of metropolitan Manila. Metropolitan organization in a developing country. Ph.D. dissertation 1982.
NL

Caoili, Olivia R. del Castgello.
Science policy in the Philippines, the education and training of scientists and engineers. Ph.D. dissertation 1980.
NL

Charusiri, Boonsiri.
Ore mineralogy of manganese deposits in Thailand. M.Sc. thesis 1988.
NL

Crisp, Colin Frederick George.
Canada's export trade with Japan, 1957-1966. M.A. thesis 1980.
CT

Earl, E.Louise.
Prophets without honour, State Department officers and the development of a flexible response to China, 1945-1948. M.A. thesis 1986.
NL

Eastman, Julia Antonia.
Race, ethnicity and class, the response to discrimination of East Indians in Toronto. M.A. thesis, 1980.
NL

Galvin, Jeremy Roy.
The Kennedy administration and the Sino-Soviet conflict, American perceptions of a changing world. M.A. thesis 1980.
CT

Garsch, Hans-Jurgen Rudolph.
India and the exotic elements in Heine's poetry and prose. M.A. thesis 1973.
CT
Heinrich Heine and India

Ho, Kwok Keung.
Design and implementation of a multi-layered Chinese text editor. M.Sc. thesis 1987
NL

Kato, Takao.
Training and mobility within the firm, an economic analysis of Japanese and North American internal labour markets. Ph.D. dissertation 1985.
NL

Kim, Ulchol.
Acculturation of Korean immigrants to Canada, psychological, demographic and behavioural profiles of emigrating Koreans, non-emigrating Koreas and Korean-Canadians. Ph.D. dissertation 1988
NL

Li, Jinyan.
Issues in tax treaty policy with particular reference to the People's Republic of China. LL.M. thesis 1987
NL

Lippens, Robert Edward.
Multimaturity texts in international financial markets of efficient market hypothesis, a comparative study of Japan and Canada. Ph.D. dissertation 1985
NL

Liyanagama, Manel C.
Analysis of a multi-purpose multi-reservoir system(Mahaweli Project, Sri Lanka). M.Sc. thesis, 1983.
NL

Moghisi, Haideh.
Women and economic development in Iran. M.A. thesis 1987.
NL

Moore, Dennison.
The origins and development of racial ideology in Trinidad. Ph.D. dissertation 1980.

O'Riordan, Mary Margaret.
Johnson and Vietnam, the decline of a President. M.A. thesis 1983.
NL

Pasugswad, Suwan.
The post-war growth and patterns of the government expenditure in Thailand. M.A. thesis 1968.
CT

Prattas, Zaharias Jack C.
The Aegean Sea continental shelf dispute between Greece and Turkey, historical realities and joint schemes. LL.M. thesis 1986.
NL

Qian, Luqing.
Secured transaction in the People's Republic of China. LL.M. thesis 1988.
NL

Rahneema, Saeed.
Industrialization and revolution in Iran, the political economy of imported-technology-based industrialization. Ph.D. dissertation 1988.
NL

Siddiqui, Muhammed Rafi Ullah.
Determinants of money supply in Pakistan, 1948-1967. M.A. thesis 1970.
CT

Sirisena, Tilakaratne Arachchige don.
Foreign trade policy in less developed countries, a theoretical analysis and an examination of some aspects of the foreign trade policy of Ceylon. Ph.D. dissertation 1968

Thakur, Ramesh Chandra.
Canada, India and the Vietnam War, peacekeeping, foreign policy and international politics. Ph.D. dissertation 1978.

Wai, Hayne Yip.
The Chinese and their voluntary associations in British Columbia, a political machine interpretation. M.A. thesis 1971:
CT

Ward, W. Peter.
White Canada Forever, British Columbia's response to Orientals, 1858-1914. Ph.D. dissertation 1974.

Yap, Connie Sze-cheng.
Internal balance and external threat, Malaysia and the Vietnamese refugees. M.A. thesis 1980.
CT

Yip, Alice Chi-sang.
Kiakhta, a Sino-Russian trading centre. M.A. thesis 1972.
CT

Zheng, Hsiao-Feng.
Chinese securities regulation, regulating market institutions in a non-market economy. LL.M. thesis 1989.
NL

London

**D.B.Weldon Library,
University of Western Ontario,
1151 Richmond Street N,
London, Ontario, N6A 3K7,
Tel:(519)661-3162.**

Newton, Richard H. and Evangeline Marion(Sutherland), 1888-1971.
Missionaries and teachers.
Original, 90 cm., ca. 1906-1919.
Letters between R.H.Newton and his fiancee, and after 1912, his wife Evangeline Marion Sutherland, 1906-1919. The Newtons went to China as missionaries and later returned to London, Ontario, to teach school.
ULM4

Theses and Dissertations

Bancheli, Tozun Shah.
Constitutionalism and bi-communal government in Cyprus. M.A. thesis 1968.
CT

Bentley, Lorne William.
Canada and Vietnam, open mouth diplomacy, 1972-1973. M.A. thesis 1973.
CT

Brown, Cheryl Ann.
An examination of the relationship between sport policy and Canadian foreign policy with specific reference to the People's Republic of China and the 1976 Olympic issue. M.A. thesis 1979.
CT

Cham, Boon Ngee.
The Sino-Indian border dispute, a study of the foreign policy of the People's Republic of China. M.A. thesis 1965.
CT

Chang, Chak-yan.
Political violence in Malaysia and Singapore. M.A. thesis 1971.
CT

Chowdhury, M.A.Tayeeb.
Dimensions of development and change in Bangladesh, 1960-1980. M.A. thesis 1988.
NL

Clark, John Campbell.
The disparity between Truman's Far Eastern and European foreign policies. M.A. thesis 1978.
CT

Delaurentis, Giovanna Ann M.
The interpretation of Indian non-alignment. M.A. thesis 1977.
CT

Halli, Shivalingappa S.
Asian ethnic fertility in Canada, an application of the minority group status hypothesis. Ph.D. dissertation 1984.
NL

Harland, Bonnie Arlene.
The population policy of the People's Republic of

China, the societalist approach to fertility reduction. M.A. thesis 1978
CT

Kosche, Ludwig.
The Turco-German alliance of August 1914(July-November 1914). M.A. thesis 1969.
CT

Krahn, Harvey Jacob.
Pluralism or dependency structural correlates of power concentration in eighty four South Indian villages. M.A. thesis 1978.
CT

Lee, Kwo-Charng.
Sun Yat-sen, an examination of his political life. M.A. thesis 1980.
CT

Muchlas, Makmuri.
An evaluation of a community based mental health course in Indonesia. Ph.D. dissertation 1986.
NL

Noh, Samuel.
Socio-economic status and assimilation of Korean immigrants in Toronto, Canada. M.A. thesis 1979.
CT

Ong, Lu King.
Nonalignment and foreign policy, the case of Singapore. M.A. thesis 1972.
CT

Sadjimin, Tonny.
An evaluation of a village health worker program in Indonesia. Ph.D. dissertation 1986.
NL

Somasundaram, Nahni Priyadarchini.
Communalism as a spatial process in Sri Lanka. M.A. thesis 1976
CT

Tampoe, Tara J.
Geochemical constraints on the future of agriculture in Sri Lanka. Ph.D. dissertation 1989
NL

Tanaka, Hiroshi.
The Japanese department store, spatial patterns as related to cultural change. M.A. thesis 1971
CT

Wai, Lokky.
Social status, value of children and fertility in Mardan, Pakistan. Ph.D. dissertation 1988.
NL

North York.

Special Collections and Archives.
305 Scott Library,
York University,
4700 Keele Street,
North York, Ontario, M3J 1P3.
Tel:(416)736-5601.

Operation Lifeline.
Papers, 1979-1984, 24 feet.
Manuscripts, correspondence, financial records, mailing lists, clippings, photographs, tapes of an organization to assist Vietnamese refugees

Sibbald Family.
Correspondence, diaries, journals, financial and business papers, and family histories, 1771-1914. 12 reels.
Includes diaries and journals of individual members of the family in the British army and navy who visited China, Japan, Philippines, Thailand, etc.

Student Affairs, Assistant Vice President.
Records.
Include International Students' Association, 1968-1973; Committee to End the War in Viet Nam, 1968; Viet Nam Mobilization Committee, 1970; International Peace Club, 1968; Pakistan Crisis, 1971

Toronto Telegram Photographic Collection, 1919-1970.
The **Toronto Telegram** was published from 1876 to 1971.
The Photographic Collection numbers approximately 1,297,115 images covering the period from 1915 to 1971, in 446.61 metres.
Prints 67 boxes, 1225 manuscript cases, 288.61 metres. 1875-1971(bulk 1950-1971).
Negatives 3 boxes, 444 trays, 160 metres. 1937-1971(bulk 1950-1971).
Miscellaneous formats.

The collection is in three distinct groups: photography(consisting of both prints and negatives), clippings, and miscellaneous formats. It represents the period from the 1950's onwards, although some non-print material dates back to 1912, and some print material to 1876. The materials are filed by folders, and there is a complete list of files by title, the title indicating the subject assigned to the file. An exception to this was the photoprint series, where prints were individually filed and identified. Finding aid.

Prints: Series I.

This series consists of approximately 466,500 photographs, ranging in date from 1876 to 1971, arranged in nine subseries.

Series I.1. Prints: Subjects/1923-1955 (bulk 1930s-1940s). .38 metres.
Described in finding aid. Order of files generally alphabetical by subject. File names include topical

subjects, geographic names, and personal names. Among possible Asia and Pacific related files are "Wars and Rebellions", "Ethnic Groups", and "Immigrants and Immigration".

Series I.2. Prints: Subjects/Towns. 1919-1970(bulk dates 1950-1965). 1.83 metres.
3,499 positive prints arranged by town name. Described in finding aid.

Series I.3. Prints: Subjects. 1909-1971(bulk dates 1950-1965). 74.83 metres.

Series I.4. Prints: Editorial Staff /Personalities. 1876-1971(bulk dates 1952-1971). .74 metres.

Series I.5. Prints: Personalities.1935-1971(bulk dates 1950-1971). 200.17 metres.

Series I.6. Prints: Personalities/Politicians. 1944-1971(bulk dates 1950-1971). 5.18 metres.

Series I.7. Prints: Servicemen/individuals. 1939-1966(bulk dates 1939-1945). 8.85 metres.

Series I.8. Prints: Printed material removed from Photo Collection. 1925-1969(bulk dates 1950-1969). .91 metres.

Series I.9. Prints: Servicemen/Groups. 1939-1958. 2.74 metres.

Negatives: Series II.

This series consists of approximately 830,300 images, mainly for the period 1954 to 1971. Some material in subseries 1 and 5 dates back to the 1930's and 1940's. There are five negative subseries as follows:

Series II.1. Negatives: Subjects/1947-1967(bulk dates 1960s). .71 metres.
Described in finding aid.

Series II.2. Negatives:Personalities. 1937-1971(bulk dates 1954-1971). 56.76 metres.
Handlists and box lists.

Series II.3. Negatives:Personalities./Telegram Staff. 1958-1971(bulk dates 1954-1971). 1.37 metres.
Handlists and box lists.

Series II.4. Negatives: Subjects 1950-1971(bulk dates 1960-1971). 100.54 metres.
Handlists and box lists.

Series II.5. Negatives: Miscellaneous 1970-1971. 7.21 metres.
Handlists and box lists.

Theses and Dissertations

Ahmed, Abu Ishaque Mahbub Uddin.
Class and ethnic consciousness among the Bangladeshis in Toronto historical bases and current patterns. Ph.D. dissertation 1985.
NL

Ahmed, Kh. Arif.
Women in transition in social change. Ph.D. dissertation 1987.
NL
Bangladesh.

Bhargava, Guruadhari.
Becoming a doctor, a study in the professional identification of women medical students in India. Ph.D. dissertation 1978.

Brouwer, Ruth Compton.
Canadian women and the foreign missionary movement, a case study of Presbyterian women's involvement at the home base and in Central India, 1876-1914. Ph.D. dissertation 1987.
NL

Chan, Anthony Bernard.
Chinese warlords and the western armaments trade, 1920-1928. Ph.D. dissertation 1980
NL

Cheng, John Yeuk Yee.
Personal networks and help seeking behaviour, an exploratory study of Toronto's Chinese speaking immigrants from China, Hong Kong, and Vietnam. M.S.W. thesis 1986.
NL

Chowdury, Mustafa.
The politics of bureaucracy in Pakistan, 1947-1969. Ph.D. dissertation 1981.
NL

Gordon, Donald Duncan.
An analysis of American literature on Japanese management and its relationship to American society, a study of the appropriation of culture. Ph.D. dissertation 1986
NL

Iolthorpe, Christopher Alan.
Chinese commercial aviation during the Nanking period. M.A. thesis 1975.
CT

Kho, David S.
The transition to Communism in North Korea(1953-1970), a critical analysis. Ph.D. dissertation 1981.
NL

Lai, Vivien Wai-yeng.
The assimilation of Chinese immigrants in Toronto. M.A. thesis 1970.
CT

Lam, Lawrence.
Vietnamese-Chinese refugees in Montreal. Ph.D.

dissertation 1983.
NL

Leighton, Stewart Ian.
Narcotics in Fukien province, 1918-1930. M.A. thesis 1977.
CT

Lum, Janet May.
Private space and public order in contemporary China. Ph.D. dissertation 1983
NL

McLellan, Janet.
The ethnoreligous identity of Tibetans in Lindsay, Ontario. M.A. thesis 1986.
NL

Mallick, Ross.
Hindu-Muslim nationalism in colonial Bengal, 1903-1947. M.A. thesis 1978.
CT

Mathur, Lakshmi Narain.
Freedom of religion under the Indian and American constitutions. LL.M. thesis 1971
CT

Minden, Karen Paula.
Missionaries, medicine and modernization, Canadian medical missionaries in Sichuan, 1925-1952. Ph.D. dissertation 1981.
NL

Moeno, Sylvia Ntlantla.
The "non-white" South Africans in Toronto, a study of the effects of "institutionalized" apartheid in a multicultural society. Ph.D. dissertation 1981.

Mottale, Morris Mehrdad.
The arms build-up in the Persian Gulf. Ph.D. dissertation 1982.
NL

Moy, Frank Kunyin.
The political economy of Chinese labour in Canada, 1858-1923. M.A. thesis 1979.
CT

Palmer, Howard.
464 leaves, photocopy.
Nativism and ethnic tolerance in Alberta, 1920-1972. Ph.D. dissertation, York University, 1973.
Chinese in Alberta, Japanese in Alberta.

Rashid, Modh Razha Bin Ahmad.
One way street to Alor Setar, a case study of migration, adaptation and ethnicity in a Malaysian town. M.A. thesis 1978.
CT

Tharamangalam, Joseph.
Rural class conflict, the political mobilization of agricultural labourers in Kuttanad, South India. Ph.D. dissertation 1977.

Yu, Guanghua.
Joint-venture investment in the People's Republic of China, law and administration. LL.M. thesis 1988.
NL

Ottawa

**Directorate of History Library,
Canada Department of National Defence,
2429 Holly Lane,
Ottawa, Ontario, K1A 0K2.
Tel:(613) 998-7062.**

Canadian Forces Headquarters.

Directorate of History.

Royal Canadian Air Force.

Air 2; Air Ministry Correspondence, 1914-1945.
MELNYK

Air 15; Coastal Command Correspondence, 1938-1945.
MELNYK

Air 20; Unregistered Papers from the Air Ministry.
MELNYK

Air 23; Overseas Commands, Royal Air Force.
MELNYK

Air 25; Group Operations Record Books.
MELNYK

Air 27; Squadron Operations Record Books, Royal Air Force.
Copies of originals held in the Public Records Office.
MELNYK

District Headquarters India and South East Asia daily diary.
MELNYK

Document Collection.
MELNYK

no. 413 Squadron Operations Record Book.
MELNYK

no. 435 Squadron Operations Record Book.
MELNYK

no. 436 Squadron Operations Record Book.
MELNYK

Biographical Files.
MELNYK

Permanent Reference Files.
MELNYK

Kardex File

Records noted below in the Kardex file of the Directorate of History are held in the Directorate or have been transferred to the National Archives.

Armor - enemy - Korea.

1. Intelligence notes on enemy armour and enemy intelligence notes on United Nations tactics in Korea.
410B25.019(D170)

British Army - Korea.

1. War diary - HQ 28th British Commonwealth Brigade. War diary of HQ 28th British Commonwealth Brigade April and May 1951.
112.3H1.008(D4)

2. War diary - Main HQ BCKB War diary of Main HQ of British Commonwealth Korean Base, October-December 1950.
112.3H1.008(D4)

British Commonwealth Forces.

1. Strength states of BCFK October 1954 to November 1955 received from CAHLO, January 1956.
681.065(D6)

2. DSD summary of revisions necessary for integration of 25 Canadian Infantry Brigade into BCFK, 9 August 1951.
112.3M2(D296)

3. Minutes of BCFK meeting re integration of British, Canadian and Australian Movement Control Units, 6 December 1951.
410B25.019(D244)

4. Australian Department of Defence letter re reorganization of Base facilities of BCFK 4 March 1952, BCFK Provost report for April 1952, 10 May 1952.
410B25.019(D244)

5. Periodic reports of Command British Commonwealth Forces in Korea for period 2 May 1951-1 August 1953 received from DMO&P, 16 August 1956.
681.013(D76)

6. Letter from Australian Department of Defence re reorganization of B.C.F.K. Base facilities because of rundown of Occupation Forces Japan, February 1952.
681.046(D1)

7. Australian Department of Defence plan for disposal of surplus of B.C.F.K pool owned stores, 14 November 1953.
681.084(D1)

British Occupation Forces - Japan.

1. Draft instruction to General Robertson, Command BCOF Japan re integrated Commonwealth forces of Korea, 30 November 1950.
112.3M2(D295)

Britcom Sub-Area - Tokyo.

1. Directive for Britcom Sub-Area Tokyo, 28 September 1955
681.009(D15)

2. Directive for Commander Britcom Sub-Area, Tokyo. Copy of HQ Britcom Forces Korea letter KB1250-4 containing directives for Commander Britcom Sub-Area, Tokyo. From DMO&P file 31.4 Volume 2.
112.3M2.1(D4)

British Forces in Korea.

1. Instructions and reports on patrols and raids on and by U.S. and British Forces, January 1952-May 1953.
410B25.019(D145)

2. Correspondence and reports re organization and establishments of British Army, especially force for Korea, July 1950-September 1952.
493.009(D72)

British prisoners of war - Korea.

1. Prisoners of war-Korea. DMO&P file TSG2970-1-Prisoners of war-generally-containing paper "Chinese Communist and North Korean treatment of British prisoners of war in Korea"; 7 May 1954
1123M2.009D213)
British troops in Japan.

1. Directive for Britcom Sub-Area, Tokyo, 28 September 1955.
681.009(D15)

Burma.

1. CALE file TS 9490-4 volumes 1 and 2. War Office Weekly Intelligence Summary. Period 7 December 1953-13 July 1956; Vietnam, Burma, France, Vietcong, Indo-China.
439.009(D10)

Burma Aerial reconnaissance of.

1. U.S. Air Force - Photo Intelligence Report no. 451 - issued 25 February 44 - Tabingaung Landing Field, Burma.
181.003(D2830)

2. U.S. Air Force - Photo Intelligence Report no. 452 - issued 25 February 44 - Alon Landing Field, Lower Chindwin, Burma.
181.003(D2831)

3. U.S. Air Force - Photo Intelligence Report no. 453 - issued 23 February 1944 - Ywataung Landing Fields (North and South Tayetmyo, Burma.
181.003(D2832)

Burma - Air Operations in.

1. "Despatch covering Operations of 3 TAF from 1 June to 4 December 1944, by A/N W.A.Croyton directed to the Air Commander-in-Chief, Air Command, South East Asia.
181.003(D1001)

2. A review of R.A.F. Transport Support Operations in the Burma Campaign, December 1944-August 1945, by Air Vice Marshal J.D.I.
Hardmand, HQ no. 232 Group.
181.003(D1002)

3. Despatch on Operations against the Japanese by Strategic Air Force(EAC) 1 June-26 November 1944. Refer to no. 5 OTU(Canada) 181.003(D 1003)

4. Despatch on Air Operations in EAC(South East Asia) 15 December 1943-31 March 1944, by Major General George M.Stratemeyer, U.S. Army.
181.003(D 1005)

5. Despatch covering operations of no. 224 Group R.A.F. in support of Arakan Campaign, 15 October 1944-15 May 1945, Air Vice Marshal the Earl of Brandon.
181.003(D 1006).

6. Weekly Summary of Burma Operations, March-31 May 1945. 181.003(D 1010)

7. Report by Air Chief Marshal Sir Keith Park, Air Command, South East Asia, Despatch on Air Operations, 1 June 1944-2 May 1945.
181.003(D2944)

Burma - air transport operations.

1. Combat Cargo Task Force Review of Operations Reports no. 2, 4 and 5, covering period 16-31 March and 16 April-15 April-15 May 1945. Task Force was component of Allied Air Command, South East Asia. Reports concern air transport operations in Burma.
181.003(D3078)

Burma - Reports of Strikes and Operations.

1. Collection of reports re strikes and other operations of R.A.F. Coastal Command(for period 23 August 1943-1 December 1943) and India Command and South East Air Command(for period 21 August 1943-2 December 1943). Arranged chronologically.
181.003(D3463)

Burma - Routes in.

1. "Routes in Burma" - Routes "M"Tenasserim - Route book, 1 March 1945, published by Inter-Service Topographical Department (British)- Text and map.
181.009(D829

2 "Routes in Burma" Routes "H" Central Upper Burma - Route book, 15 March 1945, published by Inter-Service Topographical Department (British)- Text and map.
181.009(D830)

Burma - R.C.A.F.

1. Burma - List of Airfields and Seaplane Stations. Most information as 15 October 44. Prepared in Office of Assistant CAS Washington by U.S. & British collaboration with CIO, HQ South East Asia Air Command.
181.005(D 104)

Cambodia.

2. Report of Military Component of Canadian delegation-Cambodia, 8 August 1954-30 March 1955 received from DMO&P, January 1957.
491.013(D1)

3. **Ottawa Journal**. Press clippings. Article in **Ottawa Journal** 13 August 1964. "Canadian troops to serve in 10 world 'Hot spots' Korea, Vietnam, Laos, Cambodia, Egypt, Israel, Yemen, Kashmir, Cyprus, N.A.T.O, U.N.O.
956.009(D44)

4. Copy of text of Geneva Conference - Indo-China. Agreement on the cessation of hostilities in Viet-Nam, 1954. Joint Commission and International Commission for Supervision and Control in Viet-Nam, Agreement on Cessation of Hostilities in Laos; Agreement for the Cessation of Hostilities in Cambodia, 1954. Received from External Affairs, September 1965.
653.009(D9)

5. Historical Report No.4, dated 22 October 1965,prepared by Lt. J.LGranatstein. Early attempts to implement the United Nations Organization. U.N.T.S.O., U.N.M.O.G.I.P,. and U.N.I.P.O.M,. Korea and "United for Peace", Intercommunications, U.N.E.F., U.N.O.G.I.L., U.N.O.C., U.N.T.E.A., and U.N.T.O.M., U.N.F.I.CYP., International Supervisory Commissions No file number stated.

Cambodia Supervisory Commission.

1. International Commission for Supervision and Control Cambodia, Interim Reports no 1-7, International Commission, Supervision and Control, Cambodia. Received from External Affairs, September 1965.
653.009(D11)

2. International Commission for Supervision and Control Cambodia, Interim Reports 8 and 9, special message 2 November 1962. Special Report 15 June 1964, International Commission for Supervision and Control in Cambodia. Received from External Affairs, September 1965.

653.003(D12)

Canadian Medical Detachment - Korea.

1. Establishment-Canadian Component Commonwealth Contingent proposed establishment for Canadian Medical Detachment, Korea. Canadian Component, Commonwealth Contingent, Korea, from BDF 31-4 volume 2.
112.3M2.0-05(D2)

Canadian Army in Korea.

1. Comments by Colonel H.W.Stone, Major General J.M.Rockingham and Major C.J.A.Hamilton on Part IV of Canada's Army in Korea, July-August 1955.
681.013(D70)

2. Comments on Short History of Canada's Army in Korea by Lieutenant Colonel L.R.Crue, Lieutenant Colonel G.R.Gimmell, Wing Comdr. F.W.Hitchins, Brigadier M.P.Dogert, Cr. E.C.Russell.
681.013(D70)

3. Comments by Brigadier J.V.Allard on Part IV of D.Hist. Short History of Korean War, particularly on RCR Battle of 2/3 May 1953, 23 July 1955, in Korean War
681.013(D70)

Canadian assistance in Korean War.

1. Minutes of CSC meeting of 17 July 1950 re the following: Canadian assistance in the Korean situation(DMO&P BDF30 volume 11).
112.3M2(D121)

Canadian Base Provost Detachment (Korea).

1. Interview with Majors J.M.Walsh and H.V.Davies re activities of Canadian Base Provost Detachment in Korea, received from Captain F.R McGuire, January 1953.
41OB25.013(D30)

Canadian Base Units-Far East.

1. Order of battle and location statement of Canadian Base Units, Far East, June 1953.
41OB25.053(D5)

Canadian Base Units-Korea.

1. Report on visit to Korea, Canadian Base Units and Kobe Area 1/15 January 1955, by DMO&P.
681.013(D65)

Canadian Forces-Far East.

1. Detailed memorandum on reorganization of Canadian Forces in Far East as a result of an Armistice, June 1952.
410B25.019(D107)

2. Far East Theatre - Report on administration state. Letter HQTS 2001-122/1 volume 4 over HQTS 1750-1930/29 volume 12 containing report on administrative state-Far East Theater, BD31-4 volume 2.
112/3M2.003(D7)

Canadian Forces-Korea and Japan.

1. Canadian Forces - Korea and Japan. Letters discussing policy on reduction of forces in Korea and Japan. From BDF 31-4 volume 2.
112.3N2.003(D8)

Canadian Liaison Commission- Korea.

1. CGS BDF 15/1/Far East volume 6 for period July 1957-September 1963 contains terms of reference for Canadian representative Military Armistice Commission Korea, Canadian Liaison Mission Korea.
112.009(D102)

Canadian Liaison Commission-Tokyo.

1. Report by Mr. A.R.Menzies of Department of External Affairs on impressions of his visit to 25 Canadian Infantry Brigade in Korea 12/17 October 1951.
681.001(D1)

Canadian Operations in Korea.

1. The Chinese April offensive in the West, 22 April-1 May 1951 27 Britcom Infantry Brigade in Kapyong action from Historical Section narrative "Canadian operations in Korea, 25 June 1950/31 March 1952. Captain Madden, 27 January 1954.
41OB25.013(D63).

Canadian participation in Korean War. Part I

1. Comments on Historical Section report no. 62 "Canadian participation in the Korean War", part 1, 25 June 1950-1 March 1952 by Brigadier J.M.Rockingham, 1 July 1953.
410B25.009(D 5)

Canadian participation in Pacific War.

1. U.S. proposals to War Committee on the Cabinet re Canadian Army participation in Pacific War and in occupation of Germany 23 August 1944.
112.3M2(D 284)

Canadian participation in war against Japan.

1. Group of high level papers on Canadian participation in War against Japan, 1945.
112-3M2(D 307)

Canadian Provost Corps - Korea.

1. Interviews with Majors J.M.Walsh and H.V.Davies re activities.

410B25.013(D30)

Canadian troops for Korea.

1. Cabinet conclusions of 11 April re Canadian Army and Canadians in Korea
112.3M2(D296)

Canadians in Korea.

1. Canadian share in Commonwealth Base and L & C organization in Japan and Korea, prepared by Major H.W.Thomas for Brigadier C.N.Barclay.
HQC 1454-121/1

Casualties-Chinese Communist forces.

1. DMI statistics on strength of United Nations and Communist Forces also casualties of United Nations and Communist forces in Korean War, 6 May 1955.
681.065(D5)

Casualties-Korean War.

1. Canadian Army Operations Research team preliminary report on battle casualties of 25 Canadian Infantry Brigade in Korea for February-November 1951 received from Captain G.D.Corry, 11 February 1952.
41OB25.065(D1)

2. DMI records state on casualties of 25 Canadian Infantry Brigade in Korea for 1952 by category, day and month.
HQS-1454-151/25 Vol.3.

3. DMI statistics on strength of United Nations and Communist Forces also casualties of United Nations and Communist forces in Korean War 6 May 1955.
681.065(D 5)

Censorship - Korea.

1. Correspondence and instructions re censorship and control of Press releases from Korea.
410B25.019(D164)

China.

1. Reports and messages re operations in China and Chinese need for material aid, 19 April-7 August 1944(CAS/1-17-1)314009(D350).

2. Report on observations made during a motor trip in China by Captains H.S.P.Hopkinson and C.R.Boxer, 12 - 23 April 1938.
112.3L009(D69)

3. Intelligence notes & summaries on Chinese Eastern Railway, and Russian, Japanese, Chinese struggle for control, 1922-1928.
112.3M1009(D63)

4. Military report on the Imperial Railways of North China, by Director, Military Intelligence, War Office, 1903.
112.3M1009)(D92)

5. Despatches Nos 83, 28 August and 105, l5 September 1943 by General V.W. Odlum on military conditions in China with comments by CGS & DMI
112.1009(D3)

7. Ops Research Office of Johns Hopkins University Study on China: An Area Manual. Vol. 1. Geographical, Historical & Military Background received from CAORE, 10 March 1955
494.023(D)

8. Submission dated 14 July 1943 from CSC re amendments to earlier submission re items required by Canadian Mutual Aid Board for release to Russia & China
193.00009(D21)

9. Correspondence, extracts from CSC meetings, etc. dated 10-14 July 1943 re certain items of equipment for China, under Canadian Mutual Aid Board to be marked "deferred defense" instead of "no release".
193.009(D21)

10. Reports of Combined Communications Committee telegrams, memos, etc., 21 September 1942-28 August 1943 re disclosure of radar information to Russians and Chinese.
193.009(D22)

11. Correspondence, messages, extracts from CSC meetings, reports by Combined Intelligence Committee etc., 30 November 1943-1 February 1944, re disclosure of military information to the Chinese.
193.009(D27)

12. Report of League of Nations commission of enquiry into appeal by Chinese Government over Sino-Japanese war, dated 1932.
934.009D385A)

13. Microfilm of Japanese monographs: no. 167 Malay Operations received by 29th Army, no. 177 North China Operations, no. 178 Central China Operations and 179 South China Operations.
983.013(D3)

14. Canadian arsenals. File from M.A.Ross, CM and CTO from April 1948-November 1950 on sale of arms, ammunition, clothing, equipment to Greece, Turkey, Belgian Congo, Nicaragua, Siam, China, India, Pakistan, Haiti.
111.21.01(D17)

15. A paper entitled "Japan's Record by Henry H.Douglas. The paper is not dated, it appears to have been written before Japan's entry into the Second World War. Passed to Historical Section by Lieutenant Noble, September 1964.

958.001(D5)

16. Report of Ottawa Air Training Conference held in Ottawa on 18 May 1942.
112.3HH1.006(D5)

17. War Office paper on Japanese position in Manchuria and attitudes of Russia, China, U.S. and U.K, 27 July 1928.
112.3M2(D496)

18. External Affairs Paper 65/22 "International Tensions and the United Nations". Address by Paul Martin at Fifty-Fourth meeting
of Inter-Parliamentary Union, Ottawa - 9 September 1965. League of Nations - United Nations - NATO, Warsaw Pact - China - Peaceful Coexistence - Soviet Union - Czechoslovakia - Disarmament - Peace-keeping India and Kashmir- United Nations Charter. Obtained by Lieutenant J.L.Granatstein.
651.003(D16)

19. Paper by John W.Holmes "Peacekeeping in Asia" prepared for delivery to the Institute of Strategic Studies, Oxford, September 1964. Received from Lieutenant-Colonel R.B.Tackaberry, D.Ops, 11 February 1966.
958.009(D24)

20. Statements and Speeches -- Information Division -- Department of External Affairs no. 47/12-54/25. Passed to Department of History by Lieutenant J.L.Granatstein.
653.003(D29)

21. Statements and Speeches - Information Division - Department of External Affairs, no. 56/1 - no. 65/28. Passed to Department of History by Lieutenant J.L.Granatstein, September 1965.
653.003(D30)

22. Glossaries Burmese, Thai, Japanese, Chinese, Dutch, Malay(in English orthography) Malay(in Dutch orthography), Romanized Khmer, Romanized Thai, (Laos and Tonkin), Romanized Annamese by G.S.G.S. War Office, London.
181.009(D775)

23. Collection of U.S.A.A.F. Photo Intelligence Reports nos. 290-348 incomplete on a variety of geographic locations in Burma, French Indo-China, China, Hong Kong, Thailand, Corsica, Italy and Sicily, June 28 1943-15 December 1943.
181.003(D854)

24. Collection of U.S. Photo Intelligence Reports, 1943-1944, on locations in China, Kiungshan, Hankow, Nanking, Shanghai, Hainan, Kinhwa, Hangchow, Formosa
181.003(D861)

China - Aerial Reconnaissance of.

1. U.S. Air Force - Photo Intelligence Report no. 484 - issued 24 June 1944 - Yuncheng, Shansi, China.
181.003(D2833)

2. U.S. Air Force - Photo Intelligence Report no. 460 - issued 15 April, 1944 - Soochow, China.
181.003(D2833)

3. U.S. Air Force - Photo Intelligence Report no. 466 - issued 22 March 1944 - Kienow, Fukien Province, China.
181.003(D2833)

China Area Aerial Operations.

1. "Japanese Studies in World War II" Monograph 76: China "Incident" Greater East Asia War, China Area Aerial Operations
982.013(D4)

China Goods Transit Board.

1. Telegram, 1 October 1943 from Canadian Joint Staff Washington re proposed China Goods Transit Board to administer China Aid Goods in India.
193.009(D24)

"China Incident".

1. History of the "China Incident" in photographs (4 volumes) by Asahi Shimbun Publishing Company, 1938
982.003(D2)

2. AT & I Section, S.W.P.A. translation of Japanese distributions of awards for China Incident operation, 15 August 1943
982.009(D36)

3. "Japanese Studies in World War II Monograph 76: "China Incident" Greater East Asia War, China Area Aerial Operations
982.013(D4)

China/Japanese Clashes.

1. Declaration on Sino-Japanese clashes issue by the Servants' Society of South Manchurian Railway Company, Dairen, Manchuria, October 31(no year cited)
003(D4)

China - Politics.

1. Report on the situation in the Far East, dealing with War in China, 31 May 1938. India Intelligence Summary on the spread of Bolshevik Russian influence in China, 28 July 1925.
Naval Intelligence Summary on spread of Bolshevism China,, August 1925.
War Office reports on political parties in China, 1927/1928
Notes on Kuo-Min-Tang government of China and relations with Russia
Royal Canadian Mounted Police Report on Kuo-Min-Tang in Canada,

dated 22 February 1927
Brief outline of organization of Kuo-Min-Tang in China and in Canada, July 1925.
112.3M1009(D59)

"China, Western Influence in".

1. For Western influence in China by Lieutenant-Colonel G.T.Pearkes, see GAQ Files(4-32).

China Mail(The).

1. Copy of newspaper "**The China Mail**" issue 16 November 1941, published in Hong Kong. Passed to Department of History by Mr. J.S. Fairnie, Department of Works, August 1964. Description of arrival of Canadian contingent.
958.009(D12)

"Chindits, The".

1. "The Chindits" report by Lieutenant-Colonel B.R.Mullaly, G.S.O. I (Intelligence) Pacific Command, 24 September 1943.
322.023(D1)

Chinese Affairs.

1. Telegram - Secretary of State for External Affairs - re visit of Dr. T.V.Soong to United Kingdom, 19 August 1943(CAS File 2-15-2).
3124.009(D2)

Chinese Armed Forces.

1. Notes on the Chinese Armed Forces by U.S. Command and General Staff School, November 1944.
631.009(D3)

Chinese Army firepower.

1. Department of the Army Intelligence Review no. 198 "Increased firepower in Chinese Communist infantry units" received from Captain F.R.McGuire, 22 December 1952.
681.083(D6)

Chinese Army in Korea.

1. Translation of 19th Chinese Army Group report on operations for penetration of Imjin River in Korea, December 1950 received from Captain F.R.McGuire, 29 August 1952.
410B25.023(D2)

Chinese Artillery - Korea.

1. Extract from **Journal of Royal Artillery**, volume LXXX (80) 1953 on a short history of 1st Commonwealth Divisional Artillery including Chinese Artillery tactics and certain technical aspects by Brigadier Pike, 1st Commonwealth Division(Attached are comments by Captain J.D.Choron, R.C.A.).
956.009(D207)

2. Notes **Journal of Royal Artillery**, volume LXXX (80), 1953 on counter bombardment in Korean by Major E.V.Thomas, Royal Artillery, together with additional notes on Chinese gun emplacements.
956.009(D208)

Chinese Communist Forces.

1. U.S. intelligence study on attack technique of CCF Army, September 1954.
410B25.019(D119)

2. Miscellaneous intelligence notes, summaries and reports on North Korean and Chinese Communist tactics July 1952-November 1953.
410B25.019(D166)

3. Intelligence reports on infantry equipment and clothing of North Korean and Chinese armies 1950-1952.
410B25.019(D181)

Chinese Communist Forces.

1. 25 Canadian Infantry Brigade on new CCF tactics in Korea, 19 August 1952 received from Captain F.R.McGuire, 3 September 1952.
410B2256.023(D3)

2. Psychological warfare leaflets used by United Nations Forces against Chinese Communist Forces in Korea in 1952.
681.009(D2)

3. Miscellaneous 8th Army order of battle maps of CCD in Korea.
681.023(D1)

4. 25 Canadian Infantry Brigade paper on Chinese Communist Forces tactical techniques from Captain J.R.Madden, 27 January 1954.
410B25.013(D64)

5. Translation of enemy combat orders in Korean War supplied from 1 U.S. Corps Periodic Intelligence Report. Captain J.R. Madden, 27 January 1954.
410B25.013(D65)

6. 2nd U.S. Infantry Division report on Chinese tactics and lessons learned from same received from Captain J.R.Madden, 27 January 1954.
410B25.013(D68)

7. 1 U.S. Corps notes on CCF tactics and attack indications received from Captain J.R.Madden, 27 January 1954.
410B25.013(D75)

8. Account of CCF attack on outpost Vegas, Berlin and East Berlin May 1953 received from Captain J.R. Madden, 27 January 1954.
410B25.013D77)

Chinese Labour.

1. Correspondence, instructions, orders, reports, etc., re organization of special railway company to escort Chinese coolies across Canada on their way to the United Kingdom, March 1917-February 1918.(PCC152).
322.009(D808)

Chinese language.

1. Memorandum re system of learning Chinese ideograms by Canada, J.M.A.E.Marbois, R.C.N.R.
3124.009(D154)

Chinese Language School.

1. Correspondence, extracts from C.S.C. meeting, etc., 1 October 1942-12 September 1943 re proposed study of Chinese and Japanese languages at Carleton College, by intelligence personnel of three services as suggested by "Y" Committee.
193.009(D23)

Chinese Mines.

C.R.E. 1st Commonwealth Division, Liaison Letters 1-10, 28 July 1951-31 July 1954. This particular subject is discussed in Liaison Letters No.2-
112.3E1.003(D1)

Chinese nationals.

1. Correspondence, questionnaire, messages, memoranda, extracts from C.S.C. meetings reports of Mr. T.V.Soong visit, 29 October 1943-4 January 1944, re employment of a Chinese national at Research Enterprises, Ltd, to study radar.
193.009(D27)

Chinese offensive - April 1951.

1. Reports of Chinese offensive near Kapyong in Korea, 22-25 April 1951 against 27 British and 29 British Infantry Brigades forwarded by Captain Corry. Letter from Brigadier Burke Command 27 British Brigade to Lieutenant General H.Robertson re operations of 27 British Brigade in Chinese offensive 22-25 April 1951. News report by Roland Batchelor describing "Battle of Kapyong" Chinese offensive 22-25 April 1951(mentions Princess Patricia's Canadian Light Infantry) 29 British Infantry Brigade report on "Battle of the Injim" Chinese offensive 22-25 April 1951 with attached traces.
497.01(D3)

2. The Chinese April offensive in the West(22 April-1 May 1951) 27 British Commonwealth Infantry Brigade in Kapyong action from Historical Section narrative "Canadian operations in Korea, 25 June 1950/31 March 1952". Captain Madden, 27 January 1954.
410B25.01(D63)

Chinese representation in United Nations.

1. Statements and speeches - Information Division, Department of External Affairs, no. 56/1-no. 655/28. Passed to Department of History by Lieutenant J.L.Granatstein, September 1965
653.003(D30)

Chinese soldiers, Canadian.

1. Memorandum re Canadian soldiers of Chinese origin, September 1944(D.C.G.S. File).
112.21009(185)

2. Correspondence, messages, instructions, nominal rolls, reports, etc. re loan of Canadian born Japanese and Chinese personnel to British Security Coordination for service in Australia, 27 September 1944-4 May 1945(DSD/BDF 1-42-1(Volume 1)).
112.3S2009(D191)

3. Correspondence, nominal rolls, attachments, loans, etc. - Chinese soldiers serving in Canadian Army, January-April 1945(K.S. 673).
163.009(D25)

4. C.G.S. appreciation on the suggestion to raise Chinese infantry battalions, 13 April 1942(NP/6-0-6).
322.009(D357)

Chinese soldiers in Canadian Army.

1. Instructions, nominal rolls, etc. re attachment of Canadian born Chinese soldiers to British Army, January-February 1945
340.A20009(D4)

Choksong-Myon area.

1. Account of interview given by Lieutenant Colonel N.G.Wilson Smith(HQ 1 Commonwealth Division) to Captain F.R.McGuire in Chokson-Myon area, 19 June 1952, received in Department of History 15 July 1952.
681.013(D14)

2. Account of interview with Lieutenant Colonel J.R.Cameron re the activities of 1 Princess Patricia's Canadian Light Infantry(May-October 1952) and the handover 1-3 Princess Patricia's Canadian Light Infantry given on 27 October 1952, Choksong-Myon area received from Captain F.R.McGuire, 1 December 1952.
410B25.013(D25)

Chosen Reservoir.

1. Extract from statement of an Army officer in Chosen Reservoir breakout.
432.RCA(D2)

Chronology-Korean War.

1. Chronological summary of activities of 25 Canadian Infantry Brigade Group for period 4 May-28 September 1951 prepared by Captain G.D.Corry, Historical Officer.

410B25.013(D5)

2. Chronological summary of events of 25 Canadian Infantry Brigade Group in Korea 4 May 1951-1 February 1952 by Captain G.D.Corry.
410B25.013(D5)

3. A chronology of the Korean War 25 June 1950-31 July 1953 produced in the Department of History by Major Thomas.
6821.013(D12)

4. Notes on chronology of Korean War 25 June 1950-12 May 1952 by Major Thomas of Department of History.
681.013(D130)

5. Chronology of the Royal Canadian Navy in Korean War June 1950-12 February 1954, prepared by Naval Historian 5 May 1954.
681.013(D57)

6. A chronology of the Korean War, 25 June 1950-12 May 1952. Prepared in Department of History, 23 October 1953.
681.013(D92)

Command Britcom Subarea - Tokyo.

1. Directive for Commander Britcom Sub-Area Tokyo. Copy of HQ Britcom Forces Korea letter KB 1250-4 containing Directives for Commander Britcom Sub-Area Tokyo. From DMO&P BDF file 31-4 volume 2.
112.3M2.1(D4)

Commander in Chief, GHQ Far East Land Forces.

1. Commander in Chief Far East Land Forces - Directive from War Office. Copy of War Office Directive to Commander in Chief, Far East Land Forces on his responsibility for the Commonwealth Contingent Korea. Letter HQS 2001-121/1 volume 4, 11 July 1956. From DMO&P BDF 31-4 volume 2.
112.3M2.1(D7)

Commander in Chief, GHQ Far East Land Forces-Directives.

1. Directives to Commander in Chief, GHQ Far East Land Forces and Commander Commonwealth Contingent, Korea, copy of letter HQS 2001-121/1 TD 6121(DMO&P 1B) undated.
112.2M2.1(D5)

Communist military activities.

1. Brief intelligence reports on Communist military activities in Far East, July 1951-September 1952.
5493.009(D68)

Communist Spring Offensive, April 1951.

1. "The Communist First Phase Spring Offensive April 1951" prepared by 1 U.S. Corps received from Captain

J.R.Madden, 5 August 1953.
681.013(D36)

Communist treatment of prisoners of war.

1. Prisoners of war-Canadian policy. CGS files 1150-1 volumes 1 and 2 on experiences of British prisoners of war, Communist treatment of prisoners of war, instructions regarding interrogation on capture, Soviet interrogation system, report of Advisory Panel on Prisoner of War Conduct after Capture, conduct of Canadian prisoners of war after capture, from December 1954-November 1959(these files are retained in the office of the Chairman Chief of Staffs Committee. Used by Colonel Wood for Korean history May 1963).
112.1.009(D26)

Communist victory in China.

1. Minutes of CSC meeting of 27 June 1949 re the following: Appreciation of strategic advantages to Soviet Union of Communist victory in China(DMO&P BDF 30(volume 10)
112.3M2(D120)

Cyprus.

1. Operation SNOWGOOSE. Copy of Operation Order no.64/1(Operation SNOWGOOSE) Issued by Chief of General Staff, 13 March 1964 on proposed dispatch of Contingent to Cyprus: contains operation order 64/1 Annex A-intelligence annex; annex C-organization of Canadian Contingent Cyprus, annex D-priority of movement; annex E-Adm O 64/1; Annex G- Allotment of WS, Radio diagram; Annex H-Signals instructions.
112.1.006(D1)

2. Operation SNOWGOOSE. DQOP Log sheets on operation SNOWGOOSE covering the period 1755Z-March 1964-2000Z-13 April 1964.
114.3Q1(D13)

3. Paper presenting Canadian view on peace-keeping in Cyprus - 12 February 1964. Objective - impact in the United Nations - Canadian interest.
653.003(D14)

4. Personal narrative(first draft) 25 September 1967, **The War of the Peacekeepingers** and paper **The Military Officer and United Nations peacekeeping Operations,** August 1966 by Major-General Bruce MacDonald, D.S.O.,C.D.
958.001(D10)

5. Canadian Army Liaison Establishment file 2390-34/80 volume 1. Operations-Cyprus 31 January 1964-17 March 1964.
493.009(D188).

6. Three volumes of correspondence from February 1964-November 1964 concerning Canadian participation since formation of Cyprus force received from DSD.

112.3S2.00

7. List of files received from Canadian Contingent Cyprus for period September 1961-September 1969. Files noted with letter "R" in Department of History under above number, remainder have been destroyed.
419CYP.009(D1)

Defence-Korea.

1. Notes for guidance of study of the defence "Defence of Korea" Canadian Army Training Instructions no. 45, received from DMI.
112.3M303(D2)

Demilitarized Zone-Korea.

1. 25 Canadian Infantry Brigade Operation Instruction no. 65. Amendments re Demilitarized Zone, July-August 1953.
410B25.019(D52)

2. 25 Canadian Infantry Brigade Operation instruction no. 68, 2 September 1953 re recovery of bodies from Demilitarized Zone.
410B25.019(D57)

3. 25 Canadian Infantry Brigade Operation order December 1952-May 1954 including orders and instructions re recovery of bodies from Demilitarized Zone.
410B25.019(D64)

4. Reports and courts of enquiry into unauthorized crossing into Demilitarized Zone by Private J.R.Lamothe, 6 December 1953.
410B25.019(D109)

5. Correspondence, reports, messages, instructions, standing orders, etc. for patrols of Demilitarized Zone, Demarcation Line and No Pass Line, August 1953-November 1954.
410B25.019(D110)

Demin official correspondence - Brigadier Rockingham.

1. Files of demin official and personal correspondence of Brigadier J.M.Rockingham, 22 October 1951-27 April 1952.410B25.019(D18)

Developments in Far East - Post hostilities.

1. Post hostilities in Far East (retained in safe file no. 1).
S9072-9

Efficiency of Army in Korea.

1. Study on employment efficiency of artillery with 8th(U.S.) Army in Korea, October 1951-July 1953, HQS3640-34/78(338)volume 8.

Enemy tactics in Korea.

1. Intelligence reports and notes on enemy infantry tactics in Korea.
410B25.019(D171)

2. Intelligence notes and sketches on enemy anti-tank artillery tactics in Korea.
410B25.019(D172)

3. Translation of enemy offensive tactics in Korea 1953.
410B25.019(D173)

4. Intelligence reports and studies on enemy defensive tactics in Korea, 1952-1953
410B25.019(D174).

GHQ Far East Land Forces-Directives to C-in-C

1. Directives to C-in-C, GHQ Far East Land Forces and Commander Commonwealth Contingent, Korea. Copy of letter HQS 2002-121/1 TD 6121 (DMO&P 3B)undated.

Far East .

1. "Far East Military Intelligence Notes" a roundup of Far Eastern affairs, by DMI February 1952.
112.3M1029(D3)

2. Note no. 57 of Office of High Commissioner for U.K. in Canada, 7 December 1940 attaching notes of Britain, U.S. and Netherlands discussions in London on Far Eastern situation, October-November 1940.
112.3M2009(D82)

3. Post Hostilities in Far East (retained in safe file no. 1).
S9072-9

4. Far East Land Forces Military Intelligence Reviews, June 1950-June 1955, from British sources.
952.023(D37)

5. Brief Intelligence reports on Communist military activities in Far East, July 1951-September 1952.
493.009(D68)

6. Papers stripped from DMO&P BDF 8-4 volume 5, "Canadian Army Korea", May 1955-August 1957.
112.3M2(D6 & &)

7. Far East Theatre - Report on Administrative States Letters HQTS 2001-122/1 Volume 4 over HQTS 1750-1930/29 Volume 12 containing report on Administrative State - Far East Theatre.
HDF 31-4 volume 2.

8. Directives to C-in-C GHQ Far East Land Forces and Commander Commonwealth Contingent Korea. Copy of letter HQS 2001-121/1 TD 6121 (DMO&P 1B) undated.
112.32.1(D5)

9. Commander Commonwealth Contingent Korea -

Duties. Copy of War Office directive on duties of Commander Commonwealth Contingent Korea. Letter HQS 2001-121/1 volume 4, 12 July 1955. From DMO&P BDF 31-4 volume 2.
112.2M2.1(D6)

10. C-in-C Far East Land Forces - Directive from War Office. Copy of War Office Directive to C-in-C Far East Land Forces on his responsibilities for the Commonwealth Contingent, Korea.
112.3M2.1(D7)

11. Reduction of forces in Far East. Copies of messages dealing with proposed reduction of forces in the Far East, from DMO&P BDF 31-4 volume 2.
112.3M2.01(D6)

12. Chronology - United Nations operations in Korea, from 25 June 1950-1 April 1956. Prepared by Department of History, 4 April 1956.
112.3H1.003(D7)

13. Canadian Army Special Forces. DQOP BDF 15-27 volume 1 - 4 August 1950-23 November 1954 DQOP BDF 15-27-1 volume 1 from 4 August 1950-23 November 1954, on organization Canadian Army Special Force 25 Canadian Infantry Brigade, equipment and stores, ACANTHUS Maintenance Project Accommodation, 25 Infantry Brigade Replacement Group, Reinforcements. Reduction of forces Far East.
114.3Q1.009(D2)

14. CGS Office. CGS BDF 15-1/Far East volume 4 - period January 1954-26 March 1955. Policy re Korean awards, terms of reference and CMMFE, reduction of forces Korea, U.N. airlift operations, Chinese intervention in Indo-China, Press clipping from **The Times** on Indo-China, status of U.N. Forces Korea, report to Minister in visit to Korea and Japan by JAG, biography of Major General Bierwith, CMCBCFK, report on visit Korea, Canadian Base Units and Kobe area.
112.009(D94)

15. CGS Office. CGS BDF 15-1-25 Canadian Infantry Brigade volume 6, period April 1952-March 1953, Canadian Army Special Force statistics as of 31 March 1953, AG Administration Order no. 134, return of units from Far Eastern Theatre, Director to Command 25 Canadian Infantry Brigade on operational research, report on VD incidence in 25 Canadian Infantry Brigade, rotation 25 Canadian Infantry Brigade, general notes on Army buildup - pre-Korea and after.
112.009(D95)

16. CGS Office. CGS BDF 15-1-25 TD 3 August 1950-March 1952. Commonwealth Division and Commonwealth Administrative HQ, Canadian contribution to Commonwealth Division, U.S. awards - Korea, Formation of Commonwealth Division, Biography of Major General Cassels, Divisional Patch Commonwealth Division, SD 1 letter no. l 4293, Organization HQ First Commonwealth Division United Nations Command.
112.009(D96)

17. CGS Office. CGS BDF 15-1/Far East volume 5 from 29 March 1955-5 June 1957, withdrawal 2 Battalion QBR from Korea, article in **Nippon Times** by William Courtney, terms of reference, Command CMMFE, 4 June 1956, record of Cabinet decisions on withdrawal of Canadian Forces Far East.
112.009(D97)

18. CGS Office BDF 15-1/25 TD 2 on Canadian Army Special Force - reduced Contingent period October 1950-February 1951. Reinforcements 2 Princess Patricia's Canadian Light Infantry - 25 Canadian PR Unit, Command instructions - CO 2nd Battalion, Princess Patricia's Canadian Light Infantry, Message - possible request for officers to serve in Military Government - North Korea, PC 5578 - Powers for Commander 25 Canadian Infantry Brigade, Royal Canadian Air Force Transport.
112.009(D99)

19. CGS Office BDF 15-1/25 period 24 February 1951-19 April 1951, on despatch of 25 Canadian Infantry Brigade to Korea, Organization 25 Canadian Infantry Brigade and Adm. Sp., terms of reference to CMMFE, Administrative Plan - 25 Canadian Infantry Brigade 16 March 1951, SD 1 letter no. 4196 on move overseas.
112.009(D100)

20. CGS BDF 15-1/Far East volume 1 from 11 September 1950-28 April 1952 Security Council resolution of 27 June 1950, Joint Intelligence Committee report on Korea, 29 June 1950, terms of reference CMMFE, despatch of Canadian Forces-Korea, paper on provision of occupation forces in Korea, memorandum to Cabinet Defence Committee, 11 January 1952.
112.009(D101)

21. Organization of Special Force. CGS BDF 15-1/25 Canadian Infantry Brigade TD 3 August 1950-November 1956. Papers on organization of Canadian Army Special Force, passed to History 1 by DD History - December 1963, memorandum to CGS from JAG 17 November 1956 on basic documents relating to the organization of the Canadian Army Special Force, together with following appendices.
112.3H10.09(D59)

22. War diary-HQ 28th British Commonwealth Brigade, April-May 1951.
112.3H1.008(D4)

23. War diary Main HQ BCKB. War diary of Main HQ British Commonwealth Korean Base. October-December 1950.
112.3H1.008(D4)

24. MacArthur interview, copy of Department of External Affairs message of reports of 1954 Lucas

interview with General MacArthur who criticized senior American generals and British government, published by Scripps-Howard newspapers.
951.009(D 47)

25. Canadian Army Liaison Establishment-file TS9490-33/29 volume 2. Intelligence Far East, Japan, China, Indo-China, Korea, March 1956-31 December 1961.
493.009(D180)

Far East Land Forces.

1. Far East Land Forces Intelligence Reviews(monthly) February-October 1948.
6809.0232(D1)

Far East military intelligence notes.

1. "Far East Military Intelligence Notes" a roundup of Far Eastern affairs by DMI, February 1952.
112.3M1029(D3)

Far Eastern Advisory Commission.

1. Correspondence, messages, decisions, minutes of meetings Far Eastern Advisory Commission re control of Japan October 1945-October 1947
112.3M2(D317)

H.M.C.S. Ontario(1941-1962)

Papers re disposal of Ontario's drum major's mace and samurai sword, 1958, including acquisition of the sword, 1945.
H.M.C.S. Ontario(1941-1958) 8000

History of H.M.C.S. Ontario(1941-1958), prepared 10 March 1958.
H.M.C.S. Ontario(1941-1958) 8000

History of H.M.C.S. Ontario(1941-1960), prepared 21 March 1962.
H.M.C.S. Ontario(1941-1958) 8000

H.M.C.S. Prince David;

Narratives on three Prince Ships Second World War; History 1930-1939; Acquisition; Fitting out, 1940; Conversion to Armed Merchant Cruisers 1940; Alterations and additions 1940-1943; Conversion 1943.

H.M.C.S. Prince David 8000.

Impact of Pearl Harbor on R.C.N.; Service of Prince ships; West Coast corvettes and minesweepers; internment of Japanese fishing vessels, December 1941.

H.M.C.S. Prince David 8000.

Correspondence and interviews re the three Prince ships acquired by the R.C.N. 1939-1940.
H.M.C.S. Prince David 8000.

H.M.C.S. Prince Henry

Notes re R.C.N. operations in Aleutians, 1942 and 1943.
Ops Aleutians, 1650-239/255

H.M.C.S. Prince Robert.

Notes on R.C.N. participation in Aleutian operations August-October 1942 and the Kiska landings August 1943(Ships involved) 1942.
Ops Pacific 1650-239/5

Draft narrative(62 pages) re the acquisition and conversion of the Prince ships to 1943, reference H.M.C.S. Prince Robert.
Armed Cruisers General 8000.

Claim that Prince Robert sighted the Japanese fleet prior to the attack on Pearl Harbour. Pictures of Prince Robert and Weser(Press)
H.M.C.S. Prince Robert 8000.

Hill 355, Korea.

1. Korea-Hill 355-November 1951. Extracts from United States Command Reports on operations at Hill 355, in Korea, during November 1951. Prepared by Captain F.R.McGuire, March 1963.
112.3HI.003(D3)

History - Korea.

2. War Diary-HQ 28th British Commonwealth Brigade. War Diary-HQ 28th British Commonwealth Brigade, April-May 1951,
112.3H1.008(D4)

3. War diary - Main HQ BCKB War diary of Main HQ British Commonwealth Korean Brigade's. Months of October-December 1950.
112.3H1.008(D4)

Hong Kong.

1. High level messages and reports re defence plans for Hong Kong received from CAHLO, October 1940-October 1941(24/Liaison/2/Hist/5 January 1951).
593.012(D1)

2. Copies of papers re "C" Force Hong Kong received by Department of History from C.G.Power in 1953.
111.1009(D2)

3. Extracts from Hong Kong situation reports (1941/1942) Appendix 1.
593.013(D22)

4. Report of Royal Commission(Duff Commission) into Hong Kong June 1942(DMO&P BDF 13).
112.3M2(D83)

5. Minutes of DMO&P meetings 9 and 14 October 1941 re preparation for despatch of "C" Force to Hong

Kong(2) Order of detail to Brigadier J.K.Lawson for control of "C" Force to Hong Kong October 1941.
112.3M2(D251)

6. Chronology of GS action re despatch of Canadian troops to Hong Kong, 23 September-22 October 1941(2) Report by Brigadier W.H.S.Macklin on action by DSD re despatch of "C" Force to Hong Kong, October 1941.
112.3M2(D251)

7. Report by Brigadier R.B.Gibson on action by DMO&P re despatch of Canadian troops to Hong Kong(2). Notes on press conferences with Mr. B.A.Proulx re operations of "C" Force at Hong Kong, 17 July 1942.
112.3M2(D251)

8. Memorandum re statement in **Montreal Gazette** of 13 April 1945 by Mr. D.G.E.Middelburg re Canadian troops sent to Hong Kong(2). Correspondence re activities of C.S.M. Tughy M.C. while a prisoner of war of the Japanese, October 1945.
112.3M2(D251)

9. Correspondence and reports on Canadian operations at Hong Kong also on employment of Coast Artillery in defence of Hong Kong, November 1941-August 1949.
112.3M2(D252)

10. Historical Section report on Intelligence re Japanese intentions previous to the attack of 7 December 1941.
593.0232(D2)

11. Loose assorted papers of DSD re move, selection and employment of Hong Kong Force, 1941-1942.
112.3S20(D4)

Hong Kong, Canadian operations at.

1. Correspondence and reports on Canadian operations at Hong Kong also on employment of Coast Artillery in defence of Hong Kong November 1941-August 1949.
1121.3M2(D252)

Impact on United Nations-Cyprus.

1. Paper representing Canadian view on peace-keeping in Cyprus, 12 February 1964. Objectives - Impact in the United Nations-Canadian interest.
653.003(D14)

India-Secret.

1. BGS(Plans) memorandum re exchange of service officers with India and Pakistan to attend Staff College, 24 October 1949(DMO&P BDF 30(volume 10)).
112.3M2(D120)

2. Minutes of CSC meeting at 25 October 1949 re the following: Attendance at Canadian Staff College of Indian and Pakistan officers(DMO&P BDF(volume 10)).
112.3M2(D192)

3. Brief on British defence negotiations with India and Pakistan, September 1947. (2) Correspondence, instructions, reports, messages, etc. re liaison with India and Pakistan.
112.3M2(D192)

4. Memorandum on debriefing of Kashmir(U.N.M.O.G.I.P.) observers-interview with Lieutenant Colonel Wygand, 23 March 1950, Major McClelland, 17 May 1955. Received from External Affairs by Lieutenant J.L.Granatstein. Duties of observers-incidents-attitudes of Army officers-political attitudes in Kashmir-Naikowal incident-British officers in Pakistan and Indian Armies.
653.003(D24)

5. Canadian position on United Nations peacekeeping 1961-United Nations peacekeeping machinery - India, Pakistan, Balkans, U.N.T.S.O., U.N.M.O.G.I.P., Greece, Lebanon, Spinelli Mission, Middle East, Beck Friis Mission, Secretary-General United Nations Dag Hammarskjold, U.N.E.F., United Nations, External Affairs paper obtained by Lieutenant J.L.Granatstein.
653.003(D28)

6. Statement of Mr. G.S.Murray, Head of United Nations Division, Department of External Affairs to Orientation Course of Directorate of Military Intelligence, 18 March 1963, entitled "Peace-keeping activities of the United Nations". Received from External Affairs.
653.009(D6)

7. Message Cairo/Department of External Affairs, 5 June 1967 re United Arab Republic request for withdrawal of U.N.E.F. (Yugoslav/Indian indication of positions).
951.009(D66)

8. CDLS(London) file S531-8-3-Ferrying six Dakota aircraft Trenton to India, 6 November 1952-30 November 1962.
493.009(D197)

India.

1. Supplement to **London Gazette,** 20 April 1948(no.38266). Despatch submitted by Field Marshal Viscount Wavell, C-in-C India, on operations in the India Command, 1 January-20 June 1943:
002.011(D43)

2. Operations in the Indo-Burma Theatre based on India, 21 June-15 November 1943, by Field Marshal Claude J.E.Auchinleck, C-in-C India. Supplement to **London Gazette**(38274).
002.011(D50)

3. Operations in Eastern Theatre based on India from

March 1942-31 December 1943. Despatch by Field Marshal Wavell.
002.011(D9)

4. Notes on operational research India, 1943-1944
770.013(D1)

5. Notes from operational research, India, 1943-1944, by Brigadier J.Welsh, BGS, India, November 1944(DCGS file).
112.21009(D209)

6. Director of Special Weapons and Vehicles report on tour to India/S.E.A.C.-Australia/S.W.P.A. and U.S.A/Canada, 13 June 1945.
171.009(D15)

7. Report by Major J.S.Mulholland, attached 1st British Army, India and Burma, July 1944(including Scotcol).
171.009(D55)

8. Draft narrative of the Hong Kong campaign(8-25 December 1941) by Combined Inter Services Historical Section(India and Pakistan)(HQC/1450-34/148).
593.013(D3)

9. Canadian comments on draft narrative of Hong Kong campaign(8-25 December 1941) by Combined Inter Services Historical Section(India and Pakistan), 27 October 1950.
 HQC/1450-34/148.

10. Report on tour of Director of Special Weapons and Vehicles to India, S.E.A.C., Australia, S.W.P.A. and U.S., March-June 1945(RMC/C1 3-4).
171.009(D131)

11. Supplement no. 39171 to **London Gazette** - Despatches on operations in Burma and North East India,16 November 1943-22 June 1944, by General Sir George G.Gifford, 13 March 1951(HQS/1450-3).
002.011(D76)

12. Correspondence, nominal rolls, memoranda, and instructions re loan of VG or C personnel to British Army for mule transport to India, September-November 1944(DSD/BDF 1-33 four volumes)
112.3S2009(D185)

13. Study of arrangements re loan and interchange of Canadian officers and those of U.K., India and other Dominions, 24 April 1944(DSD/BDF 1-33-1 three volumes).
112.3S2009(D186)

14. "The Pacific Story". Radio dramatization of the Story of India at War by National Broadcasting Company, 27 February 1944.
658.011(D1)

15. Statistics received from War Service Records showing total Canadian Army personnel proceeded to Asiatic Zone 1939-1945, 13 June 1947.

HQC 1915-75/58).

16. Correspondence reports on personnel orders and instructions re personnel of VG of C for mule convoy to India, February 1944-November 1946, two volumes.
113.3V1009(D1032)

17. Notes on operational research in India, 1943-1944(PCS 504-1-43).
322.009(D542)

18. Telegraph 1 October 1943 from CJS Washington re proposed China Goods Transit Board to administer China Aid Goods in India.
193.009(D24)

19. British participation in War against Japan by Office of Information British Supply Council, 25 May 1945, including special contributions of Australia, New Zealand and India.
193.009(D45)

20. British Information Services Weekly War Notes, 8 May 1943 re Dr. Khare, a new member of the Government of India.
314.009(D46)

21. Correspondence, messages, reports, nominal rolls, instructions etc., 19 March 1941-19 March 1945 re loan of Canadian personnel to British Army as muleteers for shipment of mules to U.K. and India.
314.009(D242)

22. Lecture on India and Pakistan by Commander J.S.Dallison, June 1948.
179.009(D3)

23. Report on the Quetta Earthquake of 1935 published by the Government of India.
934.009(D225)

24. DMI translation of Russian documents re visit of Marshal Zhukov to India and Burma in 1957.
112.3M1023(D80)

25. McN file correspondence L.S. Amery Secretary of State for India and Burma.
PA6-9-A-3.

26. A critical analysis of the principal medical lessons of Second World War, based on official medical histories of Australia, Canada, India, New Zealand and U.K. by Dr. W.R.Feasby
147.013(D11)

27. Canadian arsenals. File from Mr. A.Ross, CM & CTO from April 1948-November 1950, on sale of arms, ammunition, clothing equipment to U.S., Greece, Turkey, Belgian Congo, Nicaragua, Siam, China, India, Pakistan and Haiti.
111.21.01(D17)

28. Breakdown of C.E.F. personnel by Provinces, British possessions and foreign born. Prepared by

Department of Records, 6 December 1927.
112.3HI.005(D1)

29. Report no. 3. Historical Section, CFHQ-material in the Department of External Affairs relating to Canada and Peace-keeping operations prepared by Lieutenant J.L.Granatstein, 9 September 1965. Subjects: Armed Forces, Canadian Army, Canadian delegation International Truce Commission, Collective security, Congo, Cyprus, Egypt, Emergency Force, Guard Force, India, Indo-China, Indonesia, Kashmir, Lebanon, New Guinea, Pakistan, Palestine, Royal Canadian Air Force, Royal Canadian Navy, San Francisco Conference, United Nations, Yemen.

30. Newspaper clippings of the **Gagetown Gazette,** edition 9 February 1967 containing photographs of Canadian military advisers, and truce missions in India and Pakistan.
956.009(D121)

India-Air Command-HQ-routine orders-Royal Canadian Air Force.

1. R.C.A.F. file. Air Commands India and South East Asia. Air Marshal Sir Richard Peirse, Air Officer Commanding in Chief-Routine orders. Volume 1. India- 28-4 -11-11-43. Volume 2. South East Asia- 20-11-43 -9 -6- 44.
181.009(D47 69)

India-Air Headquarters-personnel-Royal Canadian Air Force.

1. R.C.A.F. file-Air Force HQ, India and South East Asia. Daily postings and attachments list aircrew and grounded aircrews, 27 volumes, April 1943-June 1945.
181.009(D5 128)

India-air operations in.

1. "Despatch covering operations of 3 TAF from 1 June-4 December 1944 by Air Marshal A.W.Coryton", directed- Air Commander in Chief Air Command South East Asia.
181.003(D1001)

2. Despatch on operations against the Japanese by Strategic Air Force(EAC), 1 June-26 November 1944. Ref to no. 5 OTU(Canadian).
181.003(D1003)

3. Despatch on air operations in Bengal Command, 21 June-15 November 1943, by Air Vice-Marshal T.M.Williams.
181.003(D1004)

4. Despatch on air operations in EAC(South East Asia), 15 December 1943-31 March 1944, by Major General George M.Stratemeyer, U.S.A.
181.003(D1005)

5. "The Siege of Imphal" report prepared by Air Staff HQ Air Command South East Asia, 3 February 1944.

181.003(D1007)

India and South East Asia-District HQ(Royal Canadian Air Force).

1. R.C.A.F. file 14-3 District HQ, India and South East Asia. R.C.A.F. Personnel repatriation and unscrambling-embarkation list. Volumes 1-3, 12 July 1945-19 December 1945.
181.005(D1499)

2. R.C.A.F. file 14-41 District HQ, India and South East Asia. Personnel-tour of duty, 15 August 1944-3 July 1945.
181.009(D3968)

India-Canadian Air Liaison Mission.

1. District HQ(R.C.A.F.), India file 12/1/1 volume 1- "Canadian Air Liaison Mission." Covers August 1944- January 1945.
181.009(D900)

India Command.

1. **Illustrations of the Modern Japanese Army,** December 1943 by GHQ India Command
982.009(D92)

2. "Duty G/C resume of air operations" no. 1143, 1 February 1943 to 1344, 21 August 1943. Brief report of R.A.F. operations all commands.
181.009(D480)

India-District HQ-Royal Canadian Air Force.

1. R.C.A.F. file P-9-1-District HQ(R.C.A.F.), India and South East Asia. Visits of Air Marshal L.S.Breadner and Air Marshal G.O.Johnson, 19 December 1944-21 September 1945.
181.009(D4466)

2. R.C.A.F. file BPO-23-1-District HQ(R.C.A.F.), India - Personnel movements general, 5 March 1943-1 February 1945
181.009(D4823)

3. R.C.A.F. file 413 CS-S-131-Air no. Group(R.A.F.)- Ceylon-Administrative instructions, 7 October 1943-14 April 1944
181.009(D5103)

4. R.C.A.F. file 41-3-District HQ(R.C.A.F.), India. Postal services, October 1943-May 1945.
181.009(D5121)

5. R.C.A.F. file 9-4-District HQ(R.C.A.F.), India. Staff officers - also officers appointed-represent R.C.A.F. staff officer in R.A.F. units with Canadian personnel - Reports and other correspondence, 10 July 1944-8 August 1945.
181.009(D5654)

6. R.C.A.F. file 9-5-District HQ(R.C.A.F.), India.

Communications-telephone, 10 June-7 December 1945.
181.009(D5655)

7. R.C.A.F. file 6-2--District HQ(R.C.A.F.), India. Press relations-correspondence, 27 May 1944-19 November 1945.
181.009(D5656)

8 R.C.A.F. file 3-1-District HQ(R.C.A.F.), India . Establishments and amendments to, March 1944-November 1945.
181.005(D2078)

9. R.C.A.F. file 41-4-District HQ(R.C.A.F.), India. Weekly minutes of Commanding officers' conferences, February-September 1945
181.003(D5165)

10. R.C.A.F. file 13-2-2-District HQ(R.C.A.F.), India Auxiliary services-Supervisor's station reports and minutes, 10 December 1943-30 August 1945
181.003(D5202)

11. R.C.A.F. file 21-33-District HQ(R.C.A.F.), India Airmail bulletins received from Wartime Information Board, Ottawa, Canada-referring to Canadian political, economic, etc. topics, 16 May 1944-16 July 1945.
181-003(D5278)

India-District HQ-Royal Canadian Air Force-Air Regulations.

1. R.C.A.F. files 28-5-District HQ(R.C.A.F.), India. Regulations and orders. Air Ministry orders, October 1943-April 1945.
181.009(D6067)

India-District HQ-Royal Canadian Air Force-auxiliary services.

1. R.C.A.F. file 13-3-1-District HQ(R.C.A.F.), India Auxiliary Services-organization and administration-auxiliary helpers, 31 January-17 September 1945.
181.009(D4328)

2. R.C.A.F. file 13-3-0-District HQ(R.C.A.F.), India . Auxiliary Services-organization and administration, January 1944-27 September 1945.
181.009(D4329)

3. R.C.A.F. file 13-2-4-District HQ(R.C.A.F.), India. Auxiliary Services Entertainment Committee. Reports and minutes, 25 February 1944-2 July 1945.
181.003(D4810)

4. R.C.A.F. file 13-4-0-District HQ(R.C.A.F.), India. Auxiliary Services-Areas general, December 1944-4 July 1945.
181.009(D4351)

5. R.C.A.F. file 13-2-3-District HQ(R.C.A.F.), India Auxiliary Services. Marine Drive Camp reports and minutes, 18 September 1944-9 March 1945.
181.003(D5242)

6. R.C.A.F. file 13-2-0-District HQ(R.C.A.F.), India. Auxiliary Services reports and minutes, August 1944-26 May 1945.
181.003(D5241)

7. R.C.A.F. file 13-2-2-District HQ(R.C.A.F.), India. Auxiliary Services. Supervisor's station reports and minutes, 10 December 1943-30 August 1945.
181.009(D4504)

8. R.C.A.F. file 13-2-1-District HQ(R.C.A.F.), India. Auxiliary Services. Special Services Officer reports and minutes, December 1944-14 April 1945.
181.009(D4347)

9. R.C.A.F. file 13-2-3-District HQ(R.C.A.F.), India. Auxiliary Services. Special Services Officer reports and minutes, December 1944-14 April 1945.
181.003(D4813).

India-District HQ-Royal Canadian Air Force-communications.

1. R.C.A.F. file 9-2-District HQ(R.C.A.F.), Bombay. India communications. Signals, 18 September 1944-1 October 1945.
181.009(D4764)

2. R.C.A.F. file 9-1-District HQ(R.C.A.F.), Bombay. India . Communications generally, 11 June 1943-22 August 1945.
181.009(D4765)

3. R.C.A.F. file 9-3-District HQ Bombay. India(R.C.S.A.F.). Communications. Conduct of correspondence. Command airgram instructions, 22 August 1943-16 October 1945.
181.009(D4763)

India-District HQ-Royal Canadian Air Force-demobilization.

1. R.C.A.F. file 8-1-District HQ(R.C.A.F.), Bombay. India. Demobilization, 29 May-28 August 1945.
181.009(D4768)

India-District HQ-Royal Canadian Air Force-dental services.

1. R.C.A.F. file 8-1-District HQ(R.C.A.F.), Bombay. India. Canadian Dental Corps, 19 March 1943-29 January 1945.
181.009(D4767)

India-District HQ-Royal Canadian Air Force-discipline.

1. R.C.A.F. file 18-1-District HQ(R.C.A.F.), India. Discipline generally, 29 June 1944-11 October 1945.
181.009(D4370)

2. R.C.A.F. file 18-3-District HQ(R.C.A.F.), India.

Discipline-airmen, 9 September 1943-3 November 1945.
181.009(D4371)

3. R.C.A.F. file 18-2. District HQ(R.C.A.F.), India Discipline. Officers, 2 February-16 November 1945.
181.009(D4372)

India-District HQ-Royal Canadian Air Force-honours and awards.

1. District HQ(R.C.A.F.), India Honours and awards, May 1943-October 1945.
181.009(D6817).

India-District HQ-Royal Canadian Air Force-keeping operational records

1. R.C.A.F. pamphlets-District HQ(R.C.A.F.), India. Operational records. Instructions on preparing, July 1943.
181.009(D6512)

India-Royal Canadian Air Force.

1. Handwritten daily diary-R.C.A.F. District HQ. India and South East Asia.
181.008(D3)

2. R.C.A.F. OS HQ file S 2-9-4 volume 1, March 1943-November 1945, "Organization-R.C.A.F." Records detachment - India re location Bombay.
181.003(D1165).

3. File 23-1 R.C.A.F. District HQ, India and South East Asia records, document policy, April-September 1945.
181.009(D1148)

4. R.C.A.F. file 21-34-District Headquarters, India-nos. 435 and 436 Squadrons(R.C.A.F.)-progress reports, 1 January 1945-18 August 1945.
181.009(D2967)

5. R.C.A.F. Overseas HQW file 22-5-2 "Records-Nominal rolls-R.C.A.F. personnel-India Command" volumes 1-3. Listing R.C.A.F. personnel with their units, 26 August 1943-12 March 1945.
181.005(D1300)

6. R.C.A.F. file 28-7-District HQ(R.C.A.F.), India-Regulations and orders -minutes of conferences-Liaison conference with Overseas HQ, April 1943-June 1944.
181.005(D125?)

India-Royal Canadian Air Force - District HQ.

1. R.C.A.F. Overseas HQ file 2-15-3 "Organization - R.C.A.F. District HQ-India" correspondence December 1942-February 1945 re organization and staffing of District HQ and problems peculiar-area.
181.002(D267)

2. R.C.A.F. District HQ India -File 15-21-" Appointments to Commissions-Policy" covers period December 1942-October 1943.
181.009(D1319)

3. R.C.A.F. HQ file S.50-60-6-Intelligence-Organization of Forces in the Middle East and South East Asia Command,14 October 1943-18 May 1944.
181.009(D16522)

4. R.A.F. file ME-21-2-4-R.C.A.F. District HQ, India-Returns-Nominal Rolls Personnel-Ceylon and India, 23 February 1943-16 June 1944.
181.005(D12276)

5. R.C.A.F. HQ file S-2-15-District Headquarters Generally - re organization and other matters concerning units and formations overseas in U.K., India, South-East Asia and Italy, 6 March 1943-15 March 1946.
181.009(D2251)

6. R.C.A.F. HQ file S-22-5-2-- District HQ(R.C.A.F.), India-R.C.A.F. Personnel-Nominal Rolls.
Volume 4 -1, 1 June 1945-1 July 1945,
Volume 5 - 1, 1 August 1945-18 September 1945.
181.005(D125)

7. File-21-36-District HQ(R.C.A.F.), India-returns, strengths and establishments, 21 April 1944-31 December 1945.
181.005(D1223)

8. R.A.F. file-District Headquarters(R.C.A.F.), India-Returns-Medical Liaison Officer Reports, 28 February-5 July 1945.
181.003(D3063)

9. File 221-30-District HQ India-Returns Base Records Officer's Progress Reports, 10 February 1944-19 October 1945.
181.003(D3064)

10. R.C.A.F. file 21-31-District HQ(R.C.A.F.), India-Canadian Forces Postal Services-Returns-Reports-volume 1, 7 October 1944-5 May 1945, volume 2, 12 May 1945-10 October 1945.
181.003(D3065)

11. File 21-23-District HQ. India-Returns District HQ Liaison Reports, 23 January 1944-30 May 1945.
181.003(D3068)

12. Base Personnel Office R.C.A.F.-Air Command India-Casualty lists-2 volumes covering period from 12 May 1943-1 June 1945.
181.003(D4015)

13. R.C.A.F. file S-21-50-4-District HQ(R.C.A.F.), India-Monthly Strength returns-nominal rolls, establishments, 31 January 1944-5 March 1945.
181.005(D1216)

14. File 6-2-2-District HQ(R.C.A.F.), India-Daily Routine Orders. Volume 1, 18 May 1943-21 September

Canada Department of Defence – Directorate of History Library • 151

1943, volume 2, 5 November 1943-6 July 1944, volume 3, 7 July 1944-30 January 1945.
181.009(D1851)

15. R.C.A.F. District HQ, India -Establishment correspondence, 13 May 1943-21 September 1945.
181.009(D1852)

16. R.C.A.F. District HQ-India-Dental services-policy, correspondence 26 July 1943-19 October 1944.
181.009(D1853)

17. R.C.A.F. District HQ, India -Organization-Field Liaison -monthly letter. Correspondence, 4 April 1944-7 September 1945.
181.009(D1854)

18. R.C.A.F. District HQ India-Press-Policy, 22 December 1944-20 August 1945.
181.009(D1855)

19. R.C.A.F. District HQ India-Organization-Canadian Forces Post-Tobacco Depot-Correspondence, 8 August 1944.
181.009(D1856)

20. R.C.A.F. District HQ file, India-Organization-Field Liaison-Correspondence, 30 March-23 July 1945.
181.009(D1857)

21. File 2-2-R.C.A.F. District HQ, India-Organization District HQ-Change of designation is noted in this file-"District HQ India" S.E.Asia" effective 16 March 1945-Correspondence, 16 March 1943-16 January 1946.
181.009(D1858)

22. File 2-1-R.C.A.F. District HQ, India-Organization policy-correspondence, 20 May 1944-22 November 1945.
181.009(D1859)

23. R.C.A.F. District HQ, India-Organization-nos. 435 and 436 Squadrons, formation of. Correspondence, 12 July 1944-11 January 1945.
181.003(D4079)

24. R.C.A.F. District HQ-India-Organization nos. 435 and 436 Squadrons withdrawal. Correspondence, 28 August-9 October 1945.
181.003(D4079)

25. R.C.A.F. District Headquarters, India-Dental Services-Correspondence, 25 September 1943-16 July 1945.
181.003(D4080)

26. R.C.A.F. District HQ, India-Organization Canadian Forces Postal Services. Correspondence, 19 October 1943-20 October 1945.
181.003(D4081)

27. R.C.A.F. District HQ-India-Organization Formation-R.A.F. detachment, Delhi, India-Correspondence, 16 June-28 August 1943(includes materials relating to medical services).
181.003(D4093)

28. R.C.A.F. HQ file 43-4-R.C.A.F. overseas - Educational Services - Monthly reports of Education Officers-visits to R.A.F. stations where R.C.A.F. personnel based, in United Kingdom, Middle East, India and North-West Liberated Europe. Volumes 1-4, 2 December 1943-1 March 1946.
181.003(D4443)

29. R.C.A.F. file- District HQ, India and South East Asia-Daily Casualty Reports, 11 July-12 November 1945
181.003(D4125)

30. R.C.A.F. HQ file-R.C.A.F. District HQ, New Delhi, India-Summary-Operations Record Book, July 1943.
181.003(D4221)

31. R.C.A.F. file 53-1-District HQ, R.C.A.F., India-Estates-Disposal, 30 December 1943-30 January 1945.
181.009(D3016)

32. R.C.A.F. file 56-1-District HQ, Base Air Force South East Asia-Personnel counselling policy and procedure, 2 volumes, covering period 14 January 1944-15 September 1945.
181.009(D3018)

33. R.C.A.F. file 63-2-District HQ, India-R.C.A.F.-Canadian prisoners of war-Hong Kong, 15 August-3 October 1945.
181.009(D3100)

34. R.C.A.F. files 65-1 and 65-2-District HQ, R.C.A.F. India. Survey of continued services-"Second phase"-policy-correspondence-policy-65-1, 30 May-22 October 1945, correspondence-65-2, 5 June-9 October 1945.
181.009(D3105)

35. R.C.A.F. file 63-1-District HQ India(R.C.A.F.)-Canadian prisoners of war-correspondence, 8 May-14 November 1945.
181.009(D3137)

36. R.C.A.F. file 80-1-District HQ-R.C.A.F.-India-Canadian Army policy - deals with loan and interchange with of Chinese and Japanese-born personnel or others graduated from Far Eastern Language schools, 24 March 1945-25 July 1945.
181.009(D3104)

37. R.C.A.F. file 46-1-District HQ India and South East Asia-Dominion of Canada election-account of experiences gained carrying ballots to front lines in Burma-lists of Asiatic polling stations-and other correspondence, July 1944-28 September 1945.
181.009(D3513)

38. R.C.A.F. file 14-24-District HQ, R.C.A.F.,India-repatriation of personnel-nominal rolls-number of volumes-2, 17 August 1944-29 November 1945.

181.009(D3962)

39. R.C.A.F. file-District HQ(R.C.A.F.), India-Photos of R.C.A.F. personnel in India and Burma.
181.009

40. R.C.A.F. file S-21-6/1 DHQ-District HQ(R.C.A.F.),India and South East Asia - progress report for July 1945
181.003(D3450)

India-Royal Canadian Air Force District HQ.

1. R.C.A.F. file S-21-6-413-R.C.A.F. District HQ. India-Personnel in no. 413 Squadron(R.C.A.F.), 9 December 1943-March 1945.
181.005(D861)

2. R.A.F. file 21-24-District Headquarters, R.C.A.F., India-returns detachments -Liaison reports-Visits to stations, 21 November 1944-16 March 1945
1821.003(D2953)

3. R.A.F. file 21-21-District Headquarters, India(R.C.A.F.)-returns-progress reports, 14 July 1943-1 November 1945.
181.003(D2954)

4. District HQ, (R.C.A.F.), India - booklet on "Monsoon flying" distributed by no. 229 Group(R.A.F.), 12 June 1945.
181.009(D1695)

5. R.A.F. file 21-37-District HQ(R.C.A.F.), India. Fortnightly accommodation and strength returns refers to personnel, 29 December 1944-31 October 1945.
181.005(D1202)

6. R.C.A.F. HQ file S-22-5-2-District HQ, (R.C.A.F.), India-R.C.A.F. personnel-nominal rolls. Volume 4, 1 June 1945-1 July 1945, volume 5, 1 August 1945-18 September 1945.
181.005(D125?)

India-Royal Canadian Air Force - District HQ - Education

1. R.C.A.F. 13-39-District HQ, (R.C.A.F.), India correspondence re education, 31 October 1944-27 September 1945.
181.009(D3232)

2. R.C.A.F. 13-38-District HQ, (R.C.A.F.), India. R.C.A.F. detachment, Calcutta, Education. 6 October 1944-8 February 1945.
181.009(D3233)

3. R.C.A.F. 13-33-District HQ, (R.C.A.F.), India, Education-Liaison reports, 21 December 1943-17 April 1945.
181.009(D3234)

India-Royal Canadian Air Force-operations.

1. File of no. 413(R.C.A.F.) Squadron 413CS/S,14/AIR-"Operational flying"-covers period April 1941-August 1942, instruction information, squadron reports.
181.009(D16514)

2. R.C.A.F. file -13-38-R.C.A.F. District HQ, India, R.C.A.F. detachment, Calcutta, Education, 6 October 1944-8 February 1945.
181.009(D3232)

India-District HQ-Royal Canadian Air Force-medical services.

1. R.C.A.F. file -R.C.A.F.(I) 10-1-District HQ, (R.C.A.F.), India and South East Asia-Medical-policy, 20 August 1943-27 September 1945.
181.009(D4762)

India-District HQ-Royal Canadian Air Force-movements personnel.

1. R.C.A.F. file 17-22-District HQ(R.C.A.F.),India. Movement of personnel-Temporary duty-detachments and HQ, 28 November 1944-25 October 1945.
181.009(D4345)

India-District HQ-Royal Canadian Air Force-nominal rolls.

1. R.C.A.F. file 21-6-District HQ(R.C.A.F.),India. Returns-nominal rolls personnel in India, 27 June 1943-18 September 1945.
181.005(D1533)

2. R.C.A.F. file BPO-21-4-15-District HQ(R.C.A.F.), India. Personnel returns-nominal rolls, April 1943-December 1944.
181.005(D1817)

India-District HQ-Royal Canadian Air Force-personnel.

1. R.C.A.F. file District HQ(R.C.A.F.), India. and South East Asia. Postings-notifications of personnel embarking ex-India-experience of operations tours-leave-repatriation volumes 1, 2, 4, 25 August 1943-1 July 1945.
181.009(D4189)

2. R.C.A.F. file 14-3-District HQ(R.C.A.F.), India posting of personnel-airmen volumes 1-4, 19 April 1943-22 September 1945.
181.009(D4302)

3. R.C.A.F. file 14-21-1-District HQ(R.C.A.F.), India. Postings of personnel generally. Daily postings and attachments list. Volume 1-8-10-43-30-4-45, volume 2 2-20-6-21-7-45, volume 3 9-8--25-8-45, volume 54, 18-8-26-10-45, volume 5 3-10-6-11-45.
181.009(D4199)

4. R.C.A.F. file 15-1-District HQ(R.C.A.F.), India. Promotions and appointments-policy, 17 December

1942-8 September 1945
181.009(D4357)

5. R.C.A.F. file 15-1--District HQ(R.C.A.F.), India. Promotions and Appointments General, 10 June 1944-19 May 1945.
181.009(D4358)

6. R.C.A.F. file 21-T--District HQ(R.C.A.F.), India. no. 222 Group(R.A.F.) Ceylon-returns-weekly return of officers and aircrew newly arrived in Ceylon, 26 May 1943-23 March 1945
181-009(D4368)

7. R.C.A.F. file 21-4-District HQ(R.C.A.F.), India. Returns-weekly return of officers and aircrew newly arrived in India, 4 May 1943-February 1945.
181.009(D4369)

8. R.C.A.F. file 14-2-District HQ(R.C.A.F.),India. Postings of personnel officers, volume 1, 2 June 1943-25 June 1945, volume 2, 2 July 1945-26 October 1945.
181.009(D4665)

9. R.C.A.F. file S-21-6-5- (R.C.A.F.), Strength in Middle East, particularly in India. Nominal rolls personnel in India and Ceylon, 11 September 1942-15 September 1945.
181.005(D1566)

10. R.A.F. file P--15-District HQ(R.C.A.F.), India and South East Asia. Personnel promotions and reclassifications - policy, 25 March 1944-8 September, 1945 181.009(D5853)

11. R.A.F. file P--15--1-District HQ(R.C.A.F.), India and South East Asia. Officers-promotion-temporary and acting rank, 4 September 1944-14 September 1945.
181.009(D5854)

12. R.C.A.F. file 28-6-District HQ(R.C.A.F.), India. Regulations and orders-personnel - field liaison bulletins, May 1943-May 1945.
181-009(D5953)

13. R.C.A.F. file 28-8-District HQ(R.C.A.F.), India. Regulations and orders-overseas bulletins-cover subjects connected with R.C.A.F. Ground Tradesmen, July 1943-March 1945.
181.009(D5954)

14. R.C.A.F. file 15-3-District HQ(R.C.A.F.), India. Promotions and appointments-issue of airmen. 2 volumes covering period 22 April 1943-December 1945.
181.009(D4450)

15. R.C.A.F. file 15-3-1-District HQ(R.C.A.F.), India-promotions and appointments-eligible list - airmen, aircrew, 11 July-19 September 1945.
181.009(D4451)

16. R.C.A.F. file BPO-23-3-District HQ(R.C.A.F.), India-movements -airmen, 12 June 1943-8 January 1945.
181.009(D4788)

17. R.C.A.F. file BPO-23-2-1-District HQ(R.C.A.F.), India-Personnel-remustering and reclassification-general. 3 volumes covering period 26 April 1943-5 February 1945.
181.009(D4829)

18. R.C.A.F. file 24-1-District HQ(R.C.A.F.), India-Personnel, remustering and reclassification-general. 3 volumes covering period 26 April 1943-5 February 1945.
181.009(D4856)

19. R.C.A.F. file 45--1-District HQ(R.C.A.F.), India Leave and passes policy, December 1944-October 1945.
181.009(D5155)

20. R.C.A.F. file 17--22-District HQ(R.C.A.F.), India. Movement of personnel-temporary duty-detachment and HQ, 28 November 1944-25 October 1945.
181.003(D4812)

India-District HQ-Royal Canadian Air Force-personnel occurrence reports.

1. R.C.A.F. file 21-2-District HQ(R.C.A.F.), India-returns-personnel occurrence reports-general, 31 December 1942-19 October 1943.
181.009(D4445)

2. R.C.A.F. file -District HQ(R.C.A.F.), India - no. 436 Squadron(R.C.A.F.)-returns-personnel occurrence - reports - general, 27 September-28 December 1945.
181.009(D4481)

India-District HQ-Royal Canadian Air Force-personnel-records.

1. R.C.A.F. file 31-1-District HQ(R.C.A.F.), India India-Records-Office-Personnel records-General: Volume 1-4, June 1943-26 April 1944, volume 2, 2 May 1944-26 April 1945.
181.009(D4344)

2. R.C.A.F. file 23-2-District HQ, India(R.C.A.F.),Personnel orders-repatriation-R.C.A.F. personnel in R.A.F. units, 6 July-26 November. 1945.
181.009(D4790)

India-District HQ-Royal Canadian Air Force-personnel-transportation.

1. R.C.A.F. file 17.5-District HQ(R.C.A.F.), India-transportation of personnel - general - orders and instructions, 1 February-1 August 1945.
181.009(D4319)

2. R.C.A.F. file 17-7-District HQ(R.C.A.F.), India-transportation by rail of baggage and personnel, 16 March-29 October 1945.
181.009(D4320)

India-District HQ-Royal Canadian Air Force-Personnel-visits.

1. R.C.A.F. file S-21-85-R.C.A.F. Overseas-Reports by Squadron Leader W.C.Sanderson on visits to Italy, India and Middle East re personnel matters, 30 March-1 September 1944.
181.009(D5187)

India-District HQ-Royal Canadian Air Force Postings.

1. R.C.A.F. Records-District HQ(R.C.A.F.), India-Records of aircrew returned to United Kingdom and Canada for disposal, and of aircrew posted to Middle East for non-operational duties and to United Kingdom for medical reasons- Nominal rolls, 1944-1945.
181.009(D6274).

India-District HQ-Royal Canadian Air Force Repatriation.

1. R.C.A.F. file 14-23-1-District HQ(R.C.A.F.), India-India-repatriation-radar personnel-volume 1, October 1944-24 December 1944, volume 2, 3 January 1943-4 May 1945.
181.009(D3966)

2. R.C.A.F. file 14-24-District HQ(R.C.A.F.), India-repatriation of personnel-nos. 435 and 436 Squadrons(R.C.A.F.),16 January-17 May 1945.
181.009(D39677)

3. R.C.A.F. file-P-2-3-District HQ(R.C.A.F.), India and South East Asia-organization-Unscrambling R.C.A.F. from R.A.F. policy, 20 March-27 August 1945.
181.009(D4462)

4. R.C.A.F. file P2-3-1-District HQ(R.C.A.F.), India and South-East Asia-Unscrambling R.C.A.F. from R.A.F.-repatriation-correspondence and report, 2 July-6 October 1945.
181.009(D4430)

5. R.C.A.F. file 14-4-District HQ(R.C.A.F.), India and South East Asia-postings-repatriation. Volumes 1-5 from 19 January-30 June 1945.
181.009(D4430)

India-District HQ-Royal Canadian Air Force Routine orders.

1. R.C..A.F. file 28-2-District HQ(R.C.A.F.)-India-Regulations and orders-Unit Routine Orders, September 1943-October 1945.
181.009(D5098)

2. R.C.A.F. file 6-2-1-District HQ, (R.C.A.F.), India-Routine Orders-Unit correspondence, 11 June 1943-11 May 1944.
181.009(D4766)

India-District HQ-Royal Canadian Air Force Second Phase.

1. R.C.A.F. file P-2-5-District HQ(R.C.A.F.), India and South East Asia - reorganization of the R.C.A.F. for Second Phase-policy, 31 May-3 August 1945.
181.009(D4471)

India-District HQ-Royal Canadian Air Force Shipments.

1. R.C.A.F. file 17-1-District HQ(R.C.A.F.), India freight shipments to India-policy,12 January-23 March 1945.
181.009

India-District HQ-Royal Canadian Air Force Standing orders.

1. R.C.A.F. file 28-3-District HQ(R.C.A.F.), India-Regulations and Orders-Station Standing Orders, July-August 1945.
181.009(D5099)

India-District HQ-Royal Canadian Air Force-Transportation.

1. R.C.A.F. file 17-6-District HQ(R.C.A.F.), South East Asia - transportation of personnel by air, 19 February 1945-15 January 1946.
181.009(D4322)

India-District HQ-Royal Canadian Air Force Visits.

1. R.C.A.F. file 17-21-District HQ(R.C.A.F.), India-visits and inspections-Correspondence on visiting-personnel, 27 December 1943-5 October 1945.
181.009(D4346)

"India, Iran: The Key to".

1. "Iran: the Key to India"-from **Montreal Gazette**, 18 April 1946.(DCGS(AB)34).
112.21009(D157)

India-Operations-R.A.F./R.C.A.F.

1. R.C.A.F. file - no. 222 Group, R.A.F., Indian Ocean-Weekly Intelligence Summaries, Part 1. Volume 1, 15 April 1945-30 June 1945, Part 2. volume 2, 1 July 1945-11 August 1945, volume 3, 15 August 1945-September 1945.
181.003(D3486)

India/Pakistan.

1. Correspondence pertaining to possible emergency evacuation of Canadians from India/Pakistan during 1965.
112.3M2.003.

India/Pakistan U.N.E.F.

1. Canadian participation -United Nations peacekeeping operations. Return on cost of Canadian participation in peacekeeping operations, 1948-1964.
112.3H1.009(D109)

Canada Department of Defence – Directorate of History Library • 155

India-personnel-records.

1. R.C.A.F. file 22-7-District HQ(R.C.A.F.), India Records personnel-Forwarding documents. Part 1, May 1943-January 1945, Part 2, January-June 1945.

India-R.A.F. in Ceylon-R.C.A.F.

1. R.C.A.F.-India-R.A.F. in Ceylon-no. 413 Squadron (R.C.A.F.) sortie reports, July-August 1945.
181.003(D3523)

2. R.C.A.F. file-India-R.A.F. in Ceylon-no. 413 Squadron(R.C.A.F.), Sortie reports, October-November 1944.
181.003(D3524)

India-R.A.F. organization.

1. R.A.F. file R.A.F. establishments India, 1 April 1931.
181.005(D532)

India-training.

1. Excerpts from Army in India Training Memorandum no. 22 August 1943 re Jungle Warfare.
171.009(D79)

Indian Air Force.

1. Report on "Operation Longhaul"(the flying of "Liberator" HE 773 which was a gift to Canada from the Indian Air Force) by Colonel A.J.Pudsey, Royal Canadian Air Force. See Annual Report for Aircraft Maintenance Development Unit on S1326-2488.

Indian and Dominion forces, British, Italy.

1. List of "Operations of British, Indian and Dominion Forces in Italy" reports (2 September 1943/2 May 1945) by British Historical Section, Central Mediterranean.
952.013(D45)

Indian Army.

1. British official war photographs of France. Second World War(0.92-0.1900)(O & F 2001-O & F 4822) Two volumes.
112.3P1(D1331)

2. War Office detailed statement of British, Indian and African formations in existence as of December 1944.
602.065(D2)

Indian Army, Transfer of officers to.

1. Correspondence re request from Mr. L.S.Amery, Secretary of State, India, for transfer of Lieutenant E.H.Hale, RCA to Indian Army, 28 January-5 February 1942. File 1 Canadian Corps GOC 6-6-3 Indian formations under command Canadian formations.
222C1(D295)

Indian Formations under Command Canadian Formations.

1. List of British and U.S. formations and their commanders under Command 1st Canadian Army NWE June 1944/May 1945 and British, Indian South Africa and New Zealand formations under command 1 Canadian Army in Italy, 1944. (by DHS(GS) May 1949).
959.015(D3)

Indian History Section.

1. The Indian History Section "Experentia docet" as contained in the **United Services Institution Journal**, April 1948.
658.043(D1)

2. Draft narrative of the Hong Kong campaign(8-25 December 1941) by Combined Inter Services Historical Section(India and Pakistan) (HQC/1450-34/148).
593.013(D3)

3. Canadian comments on draft narrative of Hong Kong campaign(8-25 December 1941) by Combined Inter Services Historical Section(India and Pakistan), 27 October 1950.
HQC/1450-34/148

Indian Ocean general reconnaissance operations review.

1. "TOGROPS REVIEW" volume 1, nos. 1-3(August 1944-January 1945) re Indian Ocean General Reconnaissance Operations including operations, aerial reconnaissance and Japanese U boats.
181.003(D4686)

Indian operations.

1. Notes from "Operations of British, Indian and Dominion Forces in Italy, 21 December 1946 by Major-General G.W.L.Nicholson.(Italy/43/AFHQ/B/F DOC III).
204A5.013(D1)

Indian operations research.

1. Report by 10 Indian Operations Research Group on long range patrols behind Japanese lines in Burma, 24 August 1944(Research BDF 17-130-6).
770.009(D4)

Indian political leaders.

1. Copy of statement of Viceroy of India to conference of Indian political leaders, 14 July 1945.
193.009(D45)

Indo-Burma theatre.

1. Operations in the Indo-Burma theatre based on India, 21 June 1943 by Field Marshal Sir Claude J.E.Auchinleck, C-in-C India, supplement to the

London Gazette.(38274)
002.011(D50)

Indo-China.

1. Disease and public health in Indo-China by Dr. C.Wilcocks, Bureau of Hygiene and Tropical Diseases. File "1 Canadian Army/156/Geog Rep/2(Med)".
212C1.7009(D11)

2. Indo-China notes 1954 by DMI. Part I. General situation, topography, military background. Part II. Notes on history of war and forces involved and military situation at time of cease fire. Part III Comparative notes on armistice supervision in Korea, Kashmir and Palestine.
112.3M1012(D22)

3. Report on liaison visits to Indo-China by Lieutenant-Colonel D.H.Rochester of AG(Plans), 25 October 1954.
113.003(D2)

4. Liaison report on visit to Indo-China by Lieutenant-Colonel V.D.Mooney, 6-17 October 1954.
114.003(D1)

5. Letter from Major H.W.Thomas on conditions in Indo-China late April 1954.
Hist 10-1-15 May 1956

6. Report of Military Component of Canadian delegation to Cambodia for period 8 August 1954-30 March 1955, received from DMO&P January 1957.
491.013(D1)

8. Correspondence reports re operations of Truce Team in Indo-China, January 1954-March 1955.
112.3M2(D598)

9. Historical information on background of Canadian overseas commitments including U.N.E.F., Palestine(U.N.T.S.O.), NATO, Indochina and Kashmir, 25 March 1960.
400.019(D2)

10. Standing orders for Canadian Military Component in Viet Nam and Indo-China agreement on cessation of hostilities there, July 1954.
685.016(D1)

12. Progress reports on implementation of Geneva Agreement and Interim Reports of International Commission on Indo-China, August 1954-May 1958.
685.013(D2)

13. Monthly reports of Command, Military Components, Canadian delegation to Indo-China for November 1954-December 1959(3 folders).
685.013(D1)

14. DPR press release 10 September 1962-retirement of Colonel A.R.Campbell.
Biography Drawer "C"

15. DPR press release of 10 September 1962-Colonel Peck to be promoted Brigadier and appointed SMA-Indo-China.
Biography drawer "P"

16. Personnel strength of military component -- Canadian delegation, Indo-China. Research on comparative strength of Canadian, Polish and India personnel in Indo-China. Material was intended for publication in **Army Journal**, 1958.
685.005(D1)

17. International Commission for Supervision and Control. Viet Nam Reports 1 to 11, International Commission Supervision and Control-Viet Nam; Special Reports June 1952 and February 1965. Received from External Affairs, September 1965.
653.003(D10)

18. Report no 3. Historical Section, CFHQ - Material in the Department of External Affairs relating to Canada and Peace-Keeping Operations. Prepared by Lieutenant J.L.Granatstein, 9 September 1965. Subjects: Armed Forces; Canadian Army; Canadian delegation International Truce Commission; Collective Security; Congo, Cyprus, Egypt; Emergency Force; Guard Force; India;, Indo-China; Indonesia; Kashmir; Lebanon; New Guinea; Pakistan; Palestine; Royal Canadian Air Force; Royal Canadian Navy; San Francisco Conference; United Nations; Yemen.
(no file cited)

19. History Report no 4, 22 October 1965, prepared by Lieutenant J.L.Granatstein: Canada and Peace-Keeping Operations, Copies, no. 2, 3 and 4. Subjects covered: Introduction; Canada and the League of Nations; The Second World War; Creation of the United Nations Organization; Early Attempts to Implement the Charter; the United Nations Guard Force; U.N.T.S.O., U.N.M.O.G.I.P. and U.N.I.P.O.M.; Korea and "United for Peace"; Intercommunication; U.N.E.F., U.N.O.G.I.L., U.N.O.C.; U.N.T.E.A.; and U.N.T.O.M.; U.N.F.K.CYP; International Supervisory Commission.
(no file cited)

20. Paper by John W.Holmes "Peacekeeping in Asia", prepared for delivery to the Institute of Strategic Studies, Oxford, September 1964. Received from Lieutenant-Colonel R.B.Tackaberry, D Ops, 11 February 1966.
958.009(D24)

21. Collection of U.S.A.A.F. Photo Intelligence Reports no. 290 incomplete on a variety of geographic locations in Burma, French Indo-China, China, Hong Kong, Thailand, Corsica, Italy and Sicily, June 28-15 December 1943.
181.003(D854)

22. Collection of U.S. Photo Intelligence Reports, February 1944, on locations in French Indo-China: Tonkin, Hai Duong, Phu Tho, Touraine, Hue.
181.003)(D860)

23. Interservice Topographical Department report June 1945. Geology, topography and climate of Indo-China.
181.009(D461)

24. Glossaries Burmese, Thai, Japanese, Chinese, Dutch, Malay(in English Orthography) Malay(in Dutch orthography), Romanized Khmer, Romanized Thai(Laos and Tonkin), Romanized Assamese by G.S.G.S. War Office, London.
181.009(D775)

25. Notes on the International Commission, Viet Nam, 1954-1955. These notes were prepared by Major-General W.J.Megill, D.S.O., C.D., on request by Directorate History(see file HQC 1450-2, 12 May 1960).
958.001(D9)

26. 89 general correspondence files received from MCCD Viet Nam Indo-China, 19 February 1970(Files cover period October 1960-July 1968). File list included.
685.003(D2)

Indo-China(Secret).

1. DGPO file of papers re Canadian personnel for Indo-China, July 1954-September 1956(DGPO BDF 8).
410.019(D1)

2. Correspondence, orders, plans, nominal rolls, etc. re setup, organization and administration of Indo-China Truce teams, June 1954-September 1955(3 volumes).
112.3M2(D568)

3. External reports, instructions, messages, etc. re setting up and activities of Indo-China Truce Commission, July-December 1954(2 volumes).
112.3M2(D569)

4. Correspondence, instructions, terms of references, monthly reports, etc. re operations of Truce Teams in Indo-China, October 1955-July 1957(2 volumes).
112.3N2(D567)

5. Correspondence, and reports re availability of air transport for Supervising Staff in Indo-China, August-October 1954.
112.3M2(D664)

6. Correspondence, terms of reference and weekly reports on operations of Canadian Truce delegations in Indo-China, August 1957-May 1958.
112.3M2(D671)

7. Impressions of the work of the Canadian delegation, Indo-China. Account by Brigadier R.M.Bishop given to a narrator, Historical Section(G.S.) AHQ, 12 January 1959.
685.003(D1)

8. Terms of Service - Military Component Canadian delegation Indo-China - letters and despatches received from Department of External Affairs.

685.002(D1)

Indo-China Agreements-1954.

1.Geneva Conference - Compilation of Documents on the Indo-China Armistice Agreements - July 1954.
113.046(D4)

Indo-China-Canadian delegation.

1.Canadian Forces Medical Services Training Centre CFMSTC file 2001-1 Org and Adm, 16 April 1959-15 December 1961 - AHQ Org chart; RCAF Stn Camp Borden - Organization - Function; AGI 61/5 Canadian delegation Indo-China.
325.009(D753)

Indonesia.

1. Joint Planning Staff memo on strategic importance of Indonesia.
112.3M2(D124)

Indonesia-aerial reconnaissance of.

1. U.S. Air Force Photo Intelligence Report no. 454 issued 24 February 1944, Boela, Ceram Island, Netherlands East Indies.
181.003(D2845)

Indonesian Army.

1. 57 Canadian Signal Unit file 1730-1-Regulations and Orders-Dress, 24 September 1960-2 June 1961. Specimen of rank badges, tunics, Indonesian Army.
144.009(D51)

Indonesian Problem.

1. Joint Planning Staff summing up of Indonesian problem 1946. 2. Text of Council(Security) resolution on Indonesian problem, 31 October 1947.
112.3M2(D124)

2. Suggestions of Joint Planning Staff on help to be given to by Canadian member of Security Council in Indonesian problem 1946.
112.3M2(D124)

Integrated Commonwealth Forces - Korea.

1. Draft instructions to General Robertson Comd B.C.O.F. Japan re integrated Commonwealth Forces for Korea, 30 November 1950.
112.3M2(D295)

Intelligence-China.

1. Joint U.S. Army Navy Intelligence study of China South Coast, March 1945, Chapter I. Brief, Chapter II. Military geography, Chapter III. Oceanography, Chapter IV. Coast and landing beaches, Chapter V. Climate and weather, Chapter VI. Port facilities, Chapter VII. Transport and telecommunications,

Chapter VIII. Cities and towns, Chapter IX. Resources and trade, Chapter XI. Health, Chapter XII. Defences, Chapter XIII Navy, Chapter XIV. Air facilities, Chapter XV. Gazetteer.
112.3M10(D23)
Intelligence-Cyprus.

1. Operation SNOWGOOSE. Copy of Operation Order no. 64/1(Operation SNOWGOOSE) issued by Chief of General Staff, 13 March 1964 on proposed dispatch of Contingent to Cyprus, contains operation order 64/1., Annex A -Intelligence annex - Priority of movement; Annex E. Adm O 64/1.Annex G, Allotment of WS, radio diagram; Annex H - Signals instructions.
112.1.006(D1)

Intelligence, Enemy(Korea).

1. Intelligence notes on enemy armour and enemy intelligence notes on U.N. tactics in Korea.
410B25.019(D170)

2. Intelligence studies and collection of enemy codes used in Korea, 1952.
410B25.019(D176)

3. Intelligence reports on enemy morale in Korea, 1951-1953.
410B25.019(D178)

4. Reports and examples of enemy intelligence and counter intelligence activities in Korea, September 1951-May 1952.
410B25.019(D179)

Intelligence-Japan.

1. Historical Section report on intelligence re Japanese intentions previous to the attack of 7 December 1941
593.023(D2)

Intelligence-Korea.

1. Air photographs of Kapyong area in Korea taken from Captain J.R.Madden also two rolls of file used for photos and well as Photo Recce report.
681.014(D2)

2. Letter from Lieutenant Colonel Frank White including points of value for 25 Canadian Infantry Brigade in preparation for Korea.
112.3M2(D293)

3. Joint Intelligence Committee Situation reports on Korea from 1950 as received from DQOP, 18 August 1958.
681.023(D24)

Intelligence notes-Far East military.

1. Far East Military Intelligence Notes, a roundup of Far Eastern Affairs, by DMI, February 1952.
112.3MI029(D3)

Intelligence notes - Korea.

1. Canadian Army Intelligence Notes on Korea Supplement, no. 4.
4354.RCA(D4)

Intelligence reports - Cyprus.

1. List of files received from Canadian Contingent Cyprus for period September 1965-September 1969. Files noted with letter "R" are retained in Directorate History, under above number, remainder have been destroyed.
4190

Intelligence reports 8th U.S. Army.

1. Periodic Intelligence Reports of HQ 8th U.S. Army(Korea) no. 297, 5 May 1951 to current.
681.013(D9)

Intelligence reports-Far East.

1. Reports and routine reports of Commander Canadian Military Mission Far East, 4 October 1950 to current, received from DMO&P, 17 February 1955.
683.023(D1)

2. Far East Land Forces Military Intelligence Reviews, June 1950-June 1955 from British sources.
952.023(D37)

Intelligence reports - Korea.

1. Intelligence report on new enemy 60 mm new mortar bomb used by Red forces in Korea, received 2 July 1952 from Captain F.R.McGuire.
681.083(D1)

2. 25th Canadian Infantry Brigade Intelligence Report on enemy weapons and techniques in Korea, as received from Captain F.R.McGuire, 9 July 1952.
410B25.023(D1)

3. Periodic Intelligence Reports by X U.S. Corps in Korea for December 1950 and January 1951.
681.023(D2)

4. 25 Canadian Infantry Brigade Intelligence Reports, November 1952 received from Captain F.R.McGuire, 17 January 1953.
410B25.023(D7)

5. Document from Military Intelligence Section, Far East Command entitled History of the North Korea Army.
681.023(D26)

Intelligence- Korean War.

1. Intelligence extract re enemy tactics in Korean War, 1 January 1953, received from Captain F.R.McGuire, 13 January 1953.
681.023(D4)

2. Joint Intelligence Committee Situation reports on Korea, nos. 1-71, 29 January-5 October 1950 received in Directorate History from DMO&P, 31 March 1953.
681.023(D5)

3. Joint teletype situation report on Korea War from Washington no. 379 1 November 1951-no. 529, 29 August 1952, received from DMI, April 1953.
681.023(D7)

Interrogation of prisoners of war-Korea.

1. Intelligence interrogation reports on Privates J.W.Cranston, K.H.Dawe, E.J.R.Fields, G.E.Griffiths, B.Jewer, E.J.McInnes, R.B.Watson, and Lance Corporal D.F.Orson of Royal Canadian Regiment after their repatriation as prisoners of war received from Captain J.H.R.Madden, 5 October 1953.
410B25.O23(D17)

2. 25 Canadian Infantry Brigade interrogation reports on enemy tactics, armour, methods, 4 August 1952, received from Captain F.R.McGuire, 18 August 1952.
681.023(D3)

3. Interrogation reports on 2/Lieutenant C.G.Owen of 1 Royal Canadian Regiment, repatriated prisoner of war from Korea, received from Captain J.R.Madden, 2 October 1953.
410B25.023(D19)

4. Interrogation reports on enemy prisoners of war in Korea, October 1953-July 1954.
410B254.019(D185)

Iwo Jima.

1. Comparative studies of Iwo Jima and Korea, 5 September 1950.
112.3M2(D196)

Japan(Secret).

1. Canadian share in Commonwealth Base and Line of Communication organization in Japan and Korea prepared by Major H.W.Thomas for Brigadier C.N Barclay, 1954.
HQC 1454-121/1

2. Post War Planning - Canadian Army Japan.
S9072-2-5

3. Directive for Britcom Sub Area Tokyo, 28 September 1955.
681.009(D15)

4. JPC summary of military aspects of peace settlement with Japan, 29 July 1947(DMO&P BDF 30(volume 8)).
112.3M2(D118)

5. Report on visit to Korea and Japan by Lieutenant Colonel Bult-Francis, 22 March-6 June 1952.
410B25.019(D244)

Japan.

1. Defence in the Far East 1921-1939. The Far East during war in Europe and the Middle East, September 1939-December 1941. Plans and policy, Japan as the Eastern partner of the Axis. Hong Kong, Singapore and Malaya.(Compiled by Captain W.Miles, Historical Section, Cabinet Office).(Kept in Vault -Drawer 7a).
840.013(D2)

2. Memoranda and notes re Japan and Japanese Army by Intelligence Section, (GS), 25 August 1941(MD 12 RS 4-7-11).
168.009(D8)

3. U.S. Manhattan Engineering District report on atomic bombings in Japan, 23 July 1946 by U.S. Information Service, London, England.
168.009(D8)

4. U.S. Strategic Bombing Survey report on atomic bombings in Japan, 23 July 1946 by U.S. Information Service, London, England.
956.013(D4)

5. Summary report of U.S. Strategic Bombing Survey in the Pacific.
956.013(D5)

6. The war against Japan - directive(Vault-drawer 11C)
955.0165(D1)

7. Inter-Service Intelligence Summary no. 3, 31 May 1946, by U.K. Liaison Mission in Japan(Received from DMI - 13 July 1949)(HQS 143-22-16-1 MI-Int)(DHS 2-9-0)(Filed in vault).
112.3M1023(D4)

8. Intelligence bulletins re Japan, May-July 1945, by Camp Borden, including events leading up to war with Japan, 1931-1945.
171.009(D19)

9. Letter from A.G., 18 January 1946, laying down instructions for provision of Canadian Army guards for repatriation of Japanese internees from Canada to Japan(MD 11 S602-1-27-6 volume 2).
322.009(D23)

10. Notes on Japanese system of reckoning time, August 1943(PCS/540-3-3-1).
322.009(D23)

11. Nominal roll of prisoners of war at camps in Japan by drafts and nominal rolls of deaths in Hong Kong, 19 June 1943-29 April 1944.
593.065(D4)

12. Intelligence notes and summaries on Chinese Eastern Railway and Russian, Japanese and Chinese struggle for control, 1922-1928.
112.3M1009(D63)

13. Statistics received from war service records total Canadian Army personnel proceeded to Asiatic Zone, 1939-1945, 13 June 1947.
HQC 1915-75/58.

14. Correspondence, messages, studies, appreciations, plans, etc. re participation by Canadian Armed Forces in the war against Japan, 26 May 1944-6 June 1946.
112.3M2009(D79)

15. Privy Council instruction and Canadian proclamation of state of war with Japan, 7 December 1941.
951.016(D2)

16. "The War Against Japan" volume 1, parts 1 and 3, Part of War Office **Official History of the Second World War** by Major General S.W.Kirby(first draft).
952.013(D101)

17. List of Canadian Army units in Japan showing designations, period served there by commanding officers.
410.065(D1)

19. British **Official History of the Second World War** "The War Against Japan" volume 1, part 3, appendices, including map: re Hong Kong battle, received in History 4, from Colonel C.P.Stacey, 17 February 1955(refers to 952.013(D101).
982.013(D6)

20. Memorandum 30 September 1941 by CSC recommending approval of Joint Canadian/U.S. Basic Defence Plan no. 2(ABC 22) against Japan, also to include Germany and Italy, 17 December 1941.
193.009(D3)

21. Memorandum 18 October 1941 from CSC recommending approval of report of Special Interdepartmental Committee on measures to be taken in event of war with Japan, 28 July 1941. Memorandum to CGS,27 October 1941.
193.009(D3)

22. Abstract of a CAORE report on significance of atomic casualties in Japan by Dorothy K.Clark, 4 February 1953.
770.0132(D6)

23. Letter, 13 January 1944, from Secretary CSC re plan from defeat of Japan.
193.009(D27)

24. Extract from minutes of CSC meeting, 4 April 1944, re policy for development of equipment likely to be used against Japan.
193.009(D30)

25. Correspondence, extracts from CSC meetings, comments, etc., 25 April to 12 May 1944, re Canadian Joint Intelligence Committee's reports "Estimates of Japan's present position and its potentialities", 3 April 1944.
193.009(D31).

26. Message 10 December 1945 from CJS Washington and extract from CSC meeting, 13 December 1945 re visit of Colonel Solandt to Ottawa following visit to Japan to inspect and assess scientifically the effects of atomic bombs
193.009(D50)

27. Memorandum re Japan, 25 August 1941, by Intelli
3143.009(D156)

28. Paper "German inducements to keep Japan loyal to Tripartite Pact, 18 September 1941"(2) Supplement to RCMP memorandum - information re vulnerable points in Japan.
3134.009(D156)

29. **Gazetteer of Japanese place names**, received 8 January 1956 from DMI.
982.009(D134)

30. "War on all Continents" - Canadian declaration of war against Hungary, Rumania, Finland, Japan, statements by Hon.W.M.King, December 1941.
509.011(D9)

31. Guest books(2) of Canadian Maple Leaf Club in Tokyo, Japan, September 1952-April 1955.
410B25.009(D104)

32. A paper entitled "Japan's Record" by Henry H.Douglas. The paper is not dated, it appears to have been written before Japan's entry into the Second World war. Passed to Historical Section by Lieutenant Noble, September 1964.
958.001(D4)

33. General Crerar's personal file - visit to Japan, 1947, as head of Canadian Mission to Japan, Itinerary; report on visits.
958C.009(D286)

34. Envelope containing booklets: The Constitution of Japan; travel literature on Hawaii; Occupation of Japan; travel literature -Philippines; Map of Japan; Travel literature-Philippines; Map of Japan.
958C.009(D331)

35. General Crerar's personal papers - address on "Canada and Japan", October 1947.
958C.009(D377)

36. Extract from **Canada Gazette** no 28 - Volume LXXXV. Proclamation from declaring an end to the state of war with Japan, 28 April 1952
006,013(D2)

37. Glossaries Burmese, Thai, Japanese, Chinese, Dutch, Malay(in English orthography), Malay(in Dutch orthography), romanized Khmer, romanized Thai(Laos and Tonkin), romanized Assamese by G.S.G.S. War Office, London.
181.009(D775)

38. Directive for British Commonwealth Sub Area, Tokyo, 28 September 1955.
681.009(D15)

39. Report on visit to Korea and Japan by Lieutenant Colonel D.S.Bult-Francis, 22 March-6 June 1952.
410B25.019(D244)

Japan-aerial reconnaissance of.

1. U.S. Air Force: Special Photo Intelligence Report no. 2. Photographed 18 July 1943. Paramushiro/Shimushu Islands(Kurile Group)Japan.
181.003(D2846)

2. U.S. Air Force - Special Photo Intelligence Report no. 13 - report 31 December 1943. Sasebo and vicinity, Japan.
181.003(D2847)

3. U.S. Air Force - Special Photo Intelligence Report no. 14 - report 31 December 1943. Target Nagasaki and vicinity, Japan.
181.003(D28248)

Japan-air operations against.

1. Report by Air Chief Marshal Sir Keith Park - "Air Command, South East Asia, Despatch on Air Operations, 1 June 1944-2 May 1945".
181.003(D2994)

Japan-armed forces.

1. R.C.A.F. HQ file 50-5-31 "Intelligence Transport Command Notes on Japan" including notes for aircrew going to India, Japanese Empire, Japanese psychology and tactics, interrogation methods used by enemy, transport operations to Burma, nature of India Burma Theatre, May 1944-February 1945.
181.003(D2712)

Japan-Canadian units in.

1. Interview with Lieutenant W.P.Stoker, Tokyo Provost Detachment received from Captain F.R.McGuire, 23 April 1953.
410B25.053(D3)

Japan - guided missiles.

1. **Handbook on Guided missiles of Germany and Japan** prepared by Military Intelligence Division, War Department, Washington, D.C., 1 November 1945. Received from Air His April 1966.
180.009(D29)

Japan intelligence.

1. Excerpts from R.C.A.F. Overseas HQ file 50-1(b) "Intelligence" contains report 28 February 1944 on Operational Air Photography, report 15 April 1944 on the Turkish Air Force, report 15 March 1945 on known information re Japan, information re interrogation of Swedish ship crews by RCMP, information re Russian Army operations in 1944 and Russian Air Force, particularly operations in the Ukraine in 1944, results of economic warfare on Germany.
181.002(D257)

Japan-intelligence bulletins.

1. Intelligence bulletins on Japan produced by GS(Intelligence)Borden Comd HQ, volume 1, nos. 1-4, May-June 1945.
982.023(D6)

2. Personal letters on jungle warfare, 20 May 1945(Intelligence Bulletin May 1945, volume 2, nos. 1-2), produced by GS(Intelligence)Borden Command HQ).
749.2021(D1)

3. Japanese weapons and equipment -Australian Technical Intelligence Summary no. l, April 1943. Allied LMQ.
982.023(D5)

4. Correspondence, reports, appreciation's statements, etc. re intelligence on Japan generally, August 1943-10 November 1944(PCS/540-3-3-1).
322.009(D157)

5. Notes on Japanese capabilities - Joint Intelligence Committee, Pacific Command August 1943. Descriptions and drawings of Japanese optical instruments - Australian Intelligence Service, 30 July 1943.
Notes by Mr. S.H.Dawes on topography, weather, facilities, etc. re parts of Japan.
Reports on changes in Japanese strategy from confidential agent of U.S. Navy intelligence, 10 March 1943.
Pamphlet **Morale and Social Conditions in Japan and Occupied Countries**, OSS, 23 March 1941(PCS/540-3-3-1).
322.009(D157)

6. Notes on racial and regional characteristics, Japanese press editorial, Japanese personalities, glossary of military terms, etc. re Japanese people dated 1941, 10 November 1944. Pamphlet "Regional characteristics of the Japanese People"-DMI(undated) List of Japanese personalities of current interest - Department of External Affairs, 17 August 1943(PCS/540-3-1-1 Volume 1).
322.009(D158)

7. Notes on background, qualities, etc. of Japanese soldier, possibilities of escape from prisoner of war camps, Japanese uniforms(with diagrams), August 1942-30 June 1945(PCS/540-3-3-1-7).
322.009(D159)

8. Orders of battle, organization charts, locations, states, etc. re Japanese Army, May 1944-6 August 1945.(PCS/540-3-3-1-8(volume 3).
322.009(D160)

9. Correspondence, descriptions, silhouettes, captured orders, etc., re Japanese Navy, 26 September 1942-21 November 1944.
Notes, organization charts, instructions, etc., re Japanese naval landing forces and pioneer units, 26 September 1942.
Identification Bulletin on Japanese and U.S. naval vessels.
Notes on aircraft carriers(Japanese), 8 February and 3 and 25 September 1942,(PCS/540-3-3-1-14).
322.009(D161)

10. Correspondence, reports, studies, charts, etc., re Japanese methods of training and warfare, 9 June 1942-24 November 1944.
Notes on Japanese warfare - Bulletins 6-10 - War Department Intelligence Division, U.S. Army, 9 January 1942-23 April 1942.
Japanese impressions of Allied combat methods -HQ Allied Land Forces, S.W.P.A., December 1943.
Japanese combat training plans- AI&T Section, S.W.P.A., 28 December 1943.(PCS/540-3-3-1-20(volume 1)).
322.009(DF162)

11. Correspondence and directive of intelligence methods of Japanese, 15 November 1944-19 February 1945. Japanese document "Notes on Intelligence Work from Experience in the Greater East Asia War", 17 August 1943(PCS/540-3-3-1-22 volume 1).
322.009(D163)

12. Intelligence notes and pictures of Japanese AA and Anti-tank guns, gunnery manuals, orders, instructions, etc. re Japanese AA and anti-tank guns, December 1941-9 March 1945.
Orders of No.2 Battery, 47 Field AA Gun Battalion-Japanese, November 1941-June 1942, AT&I Section S.W.P.A. Translation no.11, 12 May 1943.
Index to Flakintel Bulletins 1-40(including HQ Allied Land Forces S.W.P.A., 10 January 1945).
Flakintel Bulletin no.41 - New developments in Japanese AA artillery. HQ Allied Air Forces - S.W.P.A., 31 January 1945.
Flakintel Bulletin no. 44 -Japanese AA defences at Luzon - HQ Allied Air Forces, S.W.P.A. 21 February 1943(PCS/540 3-3-4-10).
322.009(D166)

13. Intelligence correspondence, drawings, descriptions and bulletins on Japanese mines and booby traps, 1 July 1942-9 May 1945.
Intelligence Information Bulletin no. 19 - Axis Booby Traps - War Department, Washington, 1 July 1942(PCS/540-3-3-4-12).
322.009(D1667)

14. Intelligence notes and drawings on Japanese AFVs, wireless equipment, AFV weapons, etc., 30 January 1943-9 January 1945 (PCS/540-3-3-4-13).
322.009(D168)

15. Intelligence drawings and notes on Japanese bombs and mortars, 29 July 1942-29 January 1945.
Flakintel Bulletin no. 41 - Japanese defence tactics at Clark Field, 18 January 1945(PCS/540-3-34-15).
322.009 D(179)

16. Intelligence notes and data on Japanese operations South Pacific, 24 November 1942-15 February 1945.
War Office Bulletin-"Notes from a Theater of War, no. 17", Far East, April-November 1943,May 1944.
Engineer Technical Information Bulletin no. 10 -CE GHQ S.W.P.A., 30 January 1944(PCS/540-3-3-6-2).
322.009(D170)

17. Intelligence notes on Japan and the mandated islands, 1921-1946. Received in the Directorate of History from DMI.
112.3M1023(D17)

Japan-navy vessels-Royal Canadian Air Force.

1. R.C.A.F. file -District HQ Middle East - no. 413 Squadron(R.C.A.F.), Intelligence from no. 222 Group(R.A.F.) Ceylon - re Japanese war vessels, 28 July 1943-April 1944.
81.009(D5033)

"Japan News".

1. Clippings from "Japan News" re Canadian troops on Koje Island and visit of Lord Alexander-Korea, received from Captain F.R.McGuire, 2 July 1952.
497.009(D2)

Japan-Post surrender policy.

1. Reports by working committees FEAC - Post-surrender policies for Japan.
680.013(D4)

Japan-rearmament.

1. Ref CGS; Rearmament -Japan. Background information on U.S. proposal to allow Japanese rearmament and the Canadian position concerning this June 1953.
112.002(D2)

Japan-Royal Canadian Air Force prisoners of war.

1. R.C.A.F. HQ file - R.C.A.F. personnel reported prisoners of war in Japanese hands- policy - instructions on communicating with - attempts to trace same, 2 June-1 October 1943.
181.009(D2966)

Japan-Russia War 1904.

1. Paper prepared by Dr. J.M.Hitsman, Directorate of History "Canada's First Military Attache"(1904) when Captain H.C.Thacker was attached to the 2nd Imperial Japanese Army(prepared May 1967).
112.3H1.009

2. Article on "Canadian Military Attache - 1904" prepared in Directorate of History by Staff Sergeant

P.R.Marshall for publication in **The Sentinel** series of articles "Over Our Shoulders?"(Negative of photos and maps included.)
112.3H1(D2005)

Japan-social conditions.

1. Pamphlet "Morale and Social Conditions in Japan and Occupied Countries" OSS, 23 March 1941(PCS/540-3-3-1).
322.009(D157)

Japan-the Royal Canadian Navy war against.

1. Historical Report no. 53, October 1965, prepared by Mr. F.E.MacLeod: "The Prince Ships, 1939-1945" Copies no. 2 and 3. Subjects covered: H.M.C.S. **Prince Robert** H.M.C.S. **Prince David**; H.M.C.S. **Prince Henry**; Evaluation of Prince ships; Many merchantmen taken in prize by ships of the Royal Canadian Navy; German disguised raider KOMET; Canadian soldiers in Hong Kong; U.K., North Africa convoys; The R.C.N. at war against Japan; Combined Operations, Royal Canadian Navy; Royal Canadian Navy Assaults groups J-1 and J-2 in the invasion of Normandy; Troops transported by H.M.C.S. ships **Prince David** and **Prince Henry**; "SITKA" Assault for operation "Dragoon"; Role of Free French 1st Groupe de Commmandos; the Greek Civil War; landing craft ferried by H.M.C.S. **Prince Henry**, Commissions and Commanding Officers of the Prince ships in the Second World War.

Japan-trade with Germany.

1. "Patent contracts with Japan" U.S.A.F.E. documents from translated German sources re trade with Japan in war materials, 21 September 1945.
181.009(D519)

"Japan, The War against".

1. "The War against Japan" - an appreciation of strategical, tactical and equipment problems involved(undated and unsigned).
171.009(D87)

2. Report - 220 Military Mission, copy no. 36, 25 March 1944. Characteristics of War against Japan received from DED, June 1965.
113.3E2.001(E1)

Japan-United Nations airlift-post-war.

1. AFHQ - Director of Flight Safety - Statistics Flying Times - Miles Flown - Ground Speeds - U.N. Airlift to and from Japan 1950 - special flights, etc., 1947-1954.
181.005(D2067)

Japan, war with.

1. Defence Scheme no. 2, a plan for maintenance of Canadian neutrality in event of war between U.S. and Japan, including notes on neutrality with respect to land, naval and air warfare, 11 April 1938.
114.1(D2)

2. War against Japan - British plans, August 1944, Prime Minister to Prime Minister cable(from External Affairs).
951.023(D9)

3. War against Japan - correspondence with General Odlum, Canadian ambassador in China, 1945(from External Affairs).
951.023(D10)

4. Brief summary of measures affecting Pacific Command that have been taken either before or after outbreak of war with Japan, 13 December 1941.(DCGS file).
112.21009(D204)

5. Intelligence Bulletins re Japan, May to July 1945, by Camp Borden, including events leading up to war with Japan, 1931-1945.
171.009(D19)

6. General Staff Policy Statement no. 14, 1 September 1944, re organization for the war in Far East and including organization table of the Light Division, showing war establishment, etc.
171.009(D75)

7. Defence Scheme no. 2 - plan for the maintenance of Canadian neutrality in the event of a war between U.S. and Japan, by General Staff, 11 April 1938.
322.016(D12)

8. Memoranda, work sheets and statement of estimate of Canadian Government expenditure in war against Japan prepared by DSD, 4 April-10 May 1946(DSD/BDF 3-8-10-1).
112.3S2009(D71)

9. War Office manuscripts on Far Eastern Theatres of Operations (1) War with Japan (2) The Fall of Hong Kong (3) The Loss of Malaya and the Fall of Singapore. Prepared by the Historical Section Cabinet Office.
952.013(D94)

Japanese.

1. Removal of Japanese from Protected Areas. Report by British Columbia Security Commission, 4 March-31 October 1942.
951.073(D1)

2. For movement of Japanese, correspondence, prisoner of war records etc. MD 13, 1942, see Military District 13(C/S 12-9-volume 1).
169.009(D5)

3. "Position of Japanese in British Columbia" by T.W.S.Parsons, Commissioner of British Columbia Police, 24 September 1940, and report of meeting by Attorney-General of British Columbia, 1 October 1940

to discuss civil security of British Columbia, Japanese concentrations and activities along British Columbia coast, 24 June 1940. File MD 11/VS-38-1-1-1 volume 5.
1698.012(D2)

4. Complaints, correspondence, movement orders, hospitalization instructions, instructions, messages, etc. re Japanese internees in Canada, 20 October 1942-9 April 1946.
Letter from Attorney-General, 18 January 1946, laying down instructions for provision of Canadian Army guards for repatriation of Japanese internees from Canada to Japan(MD 11 S602-1-27-6(volume 6).
322.009(D23)

5. Memorandum re riot by Japanese internees at Immigration Building, Vancouver, British Columbia, 1942.(NP/6-0-7).
322.009(D358)

6. Report on enlistments of Nisei and Canadians of Japanese ancestry as well as requests for their services in Second World War, prepared by DMI, 1 October 1945.
133.065(D612)

7. RCMP reports on background and operations of Japanese at Sidney Inlet Mining Company, 20 September 1942.(PCS/508-1-1-1(Volume 2)).
322.009(D595)

8. Instructions for enlistment and discharge of Canadian Nisei in Canadian Army, June 1944-November 1945(PC 71-2).
322.009(D845)

9. Minutes of 10th meeting of JSC, Pacific Command, 19 December 1941 showing discussion of the following (a)Enlistment of Canadian born Japanese in Armed Forces (b) Liaison with U.S. Services (c) Dissemination of air raid warnings (d) Ground defence against air attack (e) Censorship and control of radio broadcasts (f) Camouflage of industrial premises (g) Strategic map - common grid - Canada-U.S.A. (h) Measures for security of industrial plants (i) definition of areas susceptible to blackout.
193.008(D3)

10. Minutes of 11th meeting of JSC Pacific Command, 9 January 1942, re the following (a) Liaison with U.S. Services (b) Japanese subscribers on telephone circuits (c) Security of industrial plants on Sea Island (d) Censorship and control of radio broadcasts (e) Strategic map - common grid Canada/U.S.A dealing with Japanese in coastal waters in case of emergency (f) Appreciation of the situation (g) Fire hazard(forest fires by incendiary bombing) (h) Bella Coola as a vulnerable point (i) location of Operations HQ.
193.009(D3)

11. Minutes of 13th meeting of JSC Pacific Coast, 20 January 1942, re the following (a) Major Gladstone Murray discussion use to be made of CBC in ARP arrangements (b) Dealing with Japanese in coastal waters in event of an emergency (c) Protection of the railway to Prince Rupert.
193.009(D4)

12. Minutes of 14th meeting of JSC Pacific Coast, 30 January 1942, re (a) Coordination of intercommunications system of navy, army and Air Force - U.S. (b) Patrolling arrangements in sea approaches to fortresses and defended ports (c) Dealing with Japanese in coastal areas in event of an emergency (d) Ground defence against air attacks (e) Measures to be taken for security of industrial plants.
193.009(D4)

13. (f) Camouflage of industrial premises (g) Protection of railway to Prince Rupert (h) Large scale operations map (j) Blackout headlights (difference between military and civilian vehicles) (k) Installation of boom defence at Bella Coola (l) Protection of air bases (m) Protection of Sea Island dyking system against sabotage (n) Remarks by DMO&I CSC re above matters, 14 & 18 February 1942.
193.009(D45)

14. Extracts from minutes of 14th meeting of JSC Pacific Coast, 13 February 1942, dealing with Japanese in coastal area in case of emergency.
193.009(D4)

15. Minutes of 15th meeting of JSC Pacific Coast, 19 February 1942, (a) Dealing with Japanese in cases of emergency (b) Possibility of enemy landing on beaches of Vancouver and Queen Charlotte Island (c) Anticipated scales of attack.
193.009(D4)

16. Minutes of 12th meeting of JSC Pacific Coast, 16 January 1942, re (a) Strategical maps of Pacific Coast for common use of three services and for liaison with U.S. (b) Measures to be taken for security of industrial plants, etc. (e) Control of private R/T stations (f) W/T interception (g) Duties of Communications Sub Committee (h) Fire hazard(incendiary bombing).
193.009(D4)

17. Notes on Joint Services Security Intelligence Bureau and minutes of meeting, 3 August and 1 September 1943, re Japanese.
193.009(D24)

18. Correspondence, orders, instructions, regulations, restrictions, extracts from meetings, messages, maps, etc., 31 March 1942-19 March 1943, re travel of Japanese in Canada.
193.009(D27)

19. Report on removal of Japanese from Protected Area of British Columbia during Second World War by British Columbia Security Commission.
934.009(D431)

20. Glass slide showing Japanese troop locations, World War II.

Canada Department of Defence – Directorate of History Library • 165

643.02(D1)

Japanese action.

1. Appreciation of possible Japanese action on Pacific Coast by Intelligence Pacific Command, 16 February 1942.(PCS 508-1-1-1 (volume 1)).
322.009(D594)

Japanese activities.

1. Patrol report of H.M.C.S. **Cougar** re Japanese activities on British Columbia coast, 27 December 1941(NP/6-0-7).
322.009(D358)

Japanese air bases.

1. Summary of Japanese Army air bases giving location, length of runways, protection, capacity and installations, 1 August 1945.
982.009(D95)

Japanese Air Force.

1. Japanese air record - from Japanese periodical **Chuo Koron** 1934(1 volume) (HQRC/1450-2).
982.003(D3)

2. Order of battle of Japanese Army Air Force as of 28 October 1944 issued by Intelligence Division of U.S. War Department.
934.009(D2)

3. R.C.A.F. Intelligence Digest, May 1944-February 1945.
181.003(D3)

4. Narrative of personal experiences of Flight/Lieutenant R.D.Millar, with 84 Squadron RSAF, Malaya, Dutch East Indies, prisoner of war of Japanese.
181.001(D4)

5. Intelligence Summary HQ R.A.F. West Africa, nos. 26-68, 1 August 1943-21 May 1945.
181.003(D143)

6. Air Command South East Asia Weekly Intelligence Summaries nos. 65-76(11 February-29 April 1945) Operations in Burma, Malaya, Indochina, Thailand, Japanese aircraft and operations.
181.003(D909)

7. Intelligence- Disposition of Japanese Air Force(Air Ministry reports, March 1943-15 July 1945).
181.009(D5120)

8. Material from R.C.A.F. District HQ Air Command South East Asia. Air Command South East Asia HQ statistical tables giving synopsis of bomb effort against Japanese, December 1941-August 1945. Similar statistical synopsis of R.A.F.-U.S.A.A.F. bombing against Japanese by types of targets. Also intelligence papers on Japanese Air Force, including radar equipment and anti-aircraft defences.
181.009(D759)

9. Report of London Conference on Japanese Air Force October 1943, includes details of strength, organization of Japanese Army and Navy Air Services.
181.009(D77)

10. R.C.A.F. Command Intelligence Summary nos. 7-10, 17 March-7 April 1945(19 May-15 August 1945) re Japanese aircraft, air operations in SW Pacific flak, Japanese Air Force, miscellaneous intelligence.
181.003(D1428)

11. R.C.A.F. Western Air Command- File 14 - General correspondence from 3 May-17 July 1945, with papers on various types of R.C.A.F. equipment, Staff conferences, accident supplement, and notes on Japanese Navy, Army Air Force, aircraft carriers, aircraft weapons and defence and piloted rocket bomb.
181.003(D2415)

12. Lecture notes for R.C.A.F. Staff College. Japanese Air Force, 15 December 1943.
181.009(D1214)

13. Undated report circa February 1945 "Organization Japanese Army Air Force".
181.009(D1461)

14. Air Ministry Handbook issued February 1945 "Organization of the Japanese Army and Navy Air Forces" including notes on aircraft, supporting services, etc.
181.009(D1462)

15. R.C.A.F. file - Allied Technical and Intelligence Unit, South East Asia - U.S. Navy performance and characteristics data on Japanese aircraft, September and October 1944
181.009(D5588)

Japanese aircraft.

1. Recognition and data manual on Japanese aircraft by U.S. Office of Naval Intelligence, 5 December 1942
1212.3M1009(D119)

2. Intelligence Summary HQ West Africa nos. 26-68, 1 August 1943-31 May 1945.

3. Air Command South East Asia Weekly Intelligence Summaries no. 65-76(11 February-29 April 1945) Operations in Burma, Malaya, Indo-China, Thailand. Japanese aircraft and operations.
181.003(D909)

4. Air HQ R.A.F. East Africa Intelligence Summary 45-79, 15 November 1944-1 May 1945.
181.003(D915)

5. R.A.A.F. Command Intelligence Summary nos. 7-10,

17 March-7 April 1945, 16-29, 19 May-15 August 1945, re Japanese aircraft, air operations in SW Pacific flak, Japanese air force, miscellaneous intelligence.
181.003(D1428)

6. U.S. Navy Intelligence Supplements nos. 1 and 2, issued 19 March and 27 April 1945 to Supplement TAIC Manual 1 "Japanese aircraft - Performance and characteristics".
181.009(D1057)

Japanese aircraft carriers.

1. "Japanese aircraft carriers" extract from Air Ministry Weekly Intelligence Summaries, 25 September 1942(ACC/3-10-9-0 volumes 1-4).
321.009(D59)

Japanese aircraft operations.

1. Situation reports on Japanese and aircraft activities in North America area, September 1942-September 1944(PRD 3-2-0).
341.PR009(D7)

Japanese aircraft-R.C.A.F.

1. R.C.A.F. file - R.C.A.F. HQ - Air Staff Division Directorate of Intelligence - Information gathered from crashed Japanese aircraft, February 1942.
181.009(D5360)

2. R.C.A.F. file S0-50-7-1-Air Ministry-Intelligence-A.I.2(g) reports -Japanese and German aircraft and engines - Flying bombs, January-August 1945.
181.009(D6430)

3. R.C.A.F. file S-50-7-1-Air Ministry-Intelligence - A.I.2(g) reports - Japanese and German aircraft and engines - Flying bombs, November 1943-November 1944.i.6Japanese
181.009(D6431)

Japanese Air Force-aircraft-weapons.

1. R.C.A.F. HQ(Ottawa)(file S.50-7-1(DAS/INT) volume 1 - "Intelligence - A.I2(g) Reports" covers period November 1943-February 1945. Reports on German and Japanese aircraft, air weapons, aircraft equipment.
181.003(D3006)

Japanese Air Force-airfields.

1. List of airfields and seaplane stations in Enemy-occupied Malaya, prepared in Office of Assistant Chief of Air Staff, Intelligence, Washington, D.C,. by combined personnel of U.S. and British Services. 31 May 1945.
181.009(D776)

2. Provisional airfield list - Netherlands East Indies(and New Guinea) Prepared in Office of Assistant Chief of Air Staff, Intelligence, Washington, D.C. by combined personnel of U.S. and British Services. Enemy Airfield Information Report no. 5, 15 September 1944.
181.009(D779)

3. Provisional Airfield List - Philippine Islands. Prepared in Office of Assistant Chief of Air Staff, Intelligence, Washington, D.C. by combined personnel of U.S. and British Services. Enemy Airfield Information Report no. 4, 10 August 1944.
181.009(D812)

4. Provisional Airfield List - South East Asia(Burma, French Indo-China, Malaya, Thailand). Prepared in Office of Assistant Chief of Air Staff, Intelligence, Washington, D.C. by combined personnel of U.S. and British Services. Enemy Airfield Information Report no. 3, 25 July 1944.
181.009(D813)

Japanese Air Force intelligence.

1. Intelligence - Japanese Forces file S 322, 9 January 1942-February 1944.
181.003(D266)

2. Information Intelligence Summary issued by Assistant Chief of Air Staff, Intelligence(U.S.A.A.F.) nos. 43-52 to 43-44 and 44-1 to 44-10(10 December 1943-30 March 1944) and 44-12 to 44-31(10 April-15 October 1944) and 44-33 to 44-37(30 October-30 December 1944) Miscellaneous Intelligence re U.S.A.A.F. operation, enemy opposition and tactical developments.i.6Japanese
181.009(D1058)

Japanese Air Force-Kamikaze.

1. Intelligence reports issued by HQ Air Command South East Asia, nos. 6 & 8 February 1946 re Japanese kamikaze training and Japanese anticipation of Allied plans.
181.009(D521)

Japanese Air Force-messages.

1. Letter 20 March 1943 from Colonel W.W.Murray Chairman "Y:" Committee recommending that R.C.A.F. set up an Air Force Discrimination Unit to intercept Japanese Air Force messages.
193.009(D17)

Japanese Air Force-tactics.

1. Selected papers issued January 1942-August 1944 covering Japanese air tactics in landing operations(January 1942), defences(February 1944), air tactics up to May 1944(July-August 1944). Issued by Air Ministry
181.003(D2671)

2. R.A.F. Papers on Japanese air tactics - TC-30, TC-40, TC-41, and TC-45. Tactics in landing operations; air

tactics and types of aircraft in Pacific; bomber and fighter tactics, aircraft defences, etc.; and aircraft and defences 9 November 1942, September and October 1943 and February 1944.
181.009(D2729)

3. R.A.F. Paper TC-43 - and addendum to - Japanese Air Tactics, up to May 1944. Deals with bomber fighter tactics, use of radio and radar.
181.009(D2730)

4. R.A.F. Paper TC-43 - Japanese Air Tactics against naval and merchant shipping, February 1944.
181.009(D2594)

5. R.C.A.F. file S-322-16 - U.S. Intelligence Summaries- Battle of Midway - Review of Japanese Air Force.
181.009(6225)

Japanese ammunition.

1. Table of Japanese small arms ammunition, 12 December 1942, by War Office(ACS/3-10-9-5 volumes 1 and 2).
321.009(D84)

Japanese Armed Forces.

1. Booklet of uniforms and insignia of German, Turkish and Japanese armed forces received in Directorate History from DMI.
112.3M1089(D1)

2. **Handbook for Japanese Language Officers in R.A.F.,** 23 July 1944.
181.009(D518)

Japanese-Armed Forces-intelligence.

1. Intelligence - Japanese Forces file S-322, 8 January 1942-February 1944.
181.003(D266)

Japanese Army.

1. Intelligence tables and notes on the Japanese Army, August 1943-April 1945(C.I.8-2).
982.023(D3)

2. **Handbook on Japanese Military Forces** by War Department, Washington, 1 June 1945(2 copies).
982.023(D4)

3. Japanese Army defence against naval attack(a Japanese report) extracts from WOWIRS.
982.023(D14)

4. Draft charge sheet against Major General Ryosaburo Tanaka, CO, 229th Regiment, 38 Division, Imperial Japanese Army for atrocities committed at Hong Kong, 17-27 December 1941, by War Crimes Committee(Hung, Major General Chan Ying, War Crimes Investigation Unit, Hong Kong).
982.023(D122)

5. Charge sheet on Major General Shoji Toshishige of Japanese Army for war crimes committed at Hong Kong between 17 and 27 December 1941.
982.023(D13)

6. Memoranda and notes re Japan and Japanese Army by Intelligence Section(GS), 15 August 1941(MD 12 RS 4-7-11).
168.009(D8)

7. Comparison tables on Japanese-U.S.-Australian infantry divisions, 2 September 1943(organization charts)(DCGS file).
112.21009(D192)

8. Order of battle of Japanese ground forces, 28 September 1945 by DMI.
171.009(D11)

9. Extracts from WOWIRS and War Office(Restricted)Intelligence Summaries, October 1944- June 1945, re German and Japanese organization, tactics, equipment, training, etc.
171.009(D66)

10. Comparison tables re Japanese, U.S. and Australian infantry divisions by Allied Land Forces, S.W.P.A., 21 July 1944(ACS/3-10-9-10-0 volumes 1-3).
321.009(D91)

11. Japanese Army record - from Japanese periodical **Chuo Koron** 1934(1 volume) (HQC/1450-2).
982.003(D4)

12. War Office Intreps on Japanese Army by officers who have been attached to it, 1928-1932.
952.023(D29)

13. Correspondence. DMI reports, instructions, organization re Japanese Army organization and tactics, April-August 1945(KGS 3).
163.009(D29)

14. Illustrations of the modern Japanese Army, December 1943 by GHQ India Command.
982.009(D92)

15. **Soldiers guide booklet to Japanese Army, its arms, uniform and equipment,** issued by the U.S. War Department, 15 November 1944.
934.009(D11)

16. War Office pictorial pamphlet of Japanese soldier and his armament, 23 February 1942.
934.009(D12)

17. War Office illustrated pamphlet on weapons of Japanese Army, September 1944.
934.009(D13)

18. War Office periodical notes on the Japanese Army nos. 1 to 8, 1942-1945.
934.009(D16)

19. AT&I Section, S.W.P.A. translation of Japanese regulations re employment of prisoners of war and supervision of troops returning to Japan 4 December 1944.
982.009(D94)

20. AT&I Section, S.W.P.A. translation of alphabetical list of Japanese Army officers, publication no. 2, May 1943.
982.065(D2)

21. Intelligence cables from DMI Far East Singapore on Japanese Army dispositions, 17 December 1941-8 January 1943.
114.1009(D5)

22. Order of battle of Japanese Army, July 1943.
230C6.009(D27)

23. U.S. Intelligence Bulletins re Japanese Army, its arms, and tactics, February 1942-July 1945(MD 13 C/S 78-13-1).
169.009(D182)

24. Intelligence notes on organization of Japanese Army, May 1943(CS 504-1-10-2 FD 15).
322.009(D506)

25. Notes on Japanese Army August 1941 by DMO&I.
112.100(D25)

26. Report on the study of military history by Russian and Japanese armies prepared by DMI September 1956.
112.1009(S25)

Japanese Army - Air Force.

1. Report of London Conference on the Japanese Air Force October 1943, includes details of strength and organization of Japanese Army, Navy and Air Forces.
181.009(D779)

"Japanese Army in Pictures-The".

1. **The Japanese Army in Pictures,** pamphlet published by the War Office, 23 February 1942.
982.009(D133)

Japanese art.

1. Painting of Hong Kong operations,1941, by Japanese artists, published in **Life** magazine, 27 February 1950.
593.009(D3)

Japanese artillery.

1. Handbook on education and training of Japanese Field Artillery, prepared by War Office 1909.
952.009(D40)

Japanese atrocities.

1. Memorandum of interview with Major G.B.Puddicombe at Historical Section AHQ 11 July 1947 re prosecution of Japanese officers accused of war crimes committed at Hong Kong, 1941(Including Major-General Tanaka and Major-General Shoki).
593.(D35)

3. Correspondence, messages, etc. re the maltreatment of prisoners of war in Japanese hands, British publicity campaign against Japanese atrocities, 6 December 1943-27 February 1945(National War Services File FD 550-14).
951.059(D12)

4. Reports on Japanese atrocities against Canadian personnel January 1944.
113.3R2009(D21)

Japanese attitudes.

1. Cipher messages Circular M310, 20 September 1941; 317, 4 October 1941, 330, 18 October 1941 and 343, 31 October 1941 - Secretary of State for Dominion Affairs to External for Prime Minister describing situation re Japanese attitude in Far East.
352.009(D1)

Japanese balloon bombs.

1. Clipping of article by T./Sgt. Cornelius W.Conley "Japanese bomb U.S. and Canada", a short history on use of balloon bombs by Japanese during Second World War.
956.009(D1238)

Japanese balloons.

1. "Japanese balloon-Launching site" by Captain S.Ambrose Freedman, U.S. Army, in **Pacific Stars and Stripes,** 11 May 1947, and forwarded to Historical Section by Lieutenant -Colonel O.Orr, Officer in charge Canadian War Crimes Liaison Detachment, Japanese Theatre, Tokyo.
(TOK-1-2-11)028.001(D1)

2. Account of "Japanese Balloons" in Progress Report no.189, Canadian Army, 14 June 1945(HQS 8538-6 volume 15)(Memorandum from Colonel C.P.Stacey, 10 July 1947).
Progress Report no.189, Canadian Army.

4. Balloon attacks on Canada, story of Japanese device(See **The Times,** London, 7 September 1945).

5. Reports, instructions, messages, correspondence, etc. re Japanese balloons landing in Canada, 13 January-30 May 1945(MD 12, RS 4-7-45).
168.009(D11)

6. Incidents, summaries, technical data, photographs, re Japanese balloons landed in U.S. and Canada, 16 December 1944-16 April 1945(MD 12 RS 4-7-45A).
168.009(D12)

7. Correspondence, recommendations, minutes of

meetings, etc., Joint Services Committee Pacific Coast, 2 April 1945-8 April 1946(including information re Japanese balloons)(Pac Comd 6-1).
169.009(D23)

8. Correspondence, directives, charts, maps, incident summaries, etc. re Japanese balloons and defences against them, by Pac. Comd, 6 April-1 June 1945(including information on enemy mines)(Pac Comd File 1-13).
169.009(D25)

9. Memoranda, correspondence, etc. re organization of Bomb Disposal Company, RCE, disbandment of Civil Defence in Canada and retention of ARP organizations in Pac. Comd due to increase in number of Japanese balloons, February 1945(DCGS(AB) 40).
112.21009(D162)

10. Letter re Japanese balloon incidents from W/C Hitchins, Air Historian, R.C.A.F., 28 September 1949.
182.013(D4)

11. " Those Japanese Balloons" - article in **Readers' Digest,** August 1950, by Brigadier-General W.N.Wilbur, U.S. Army.
000.5(D8)

12. Reports of balloon incidents in MD 11, December 1944 and 4 April 1945(MD 11 - S602027-1 volume 3).
322.009(D24)

13. Correspondence, directives, instructions, data, etc. re Japanese balloons - PCMR, 22 January-17 May 1945. Pac Comd directive no. 19. reporting routine on Japanese balloons, 22 March 1945. Pac Comd circular letters no.99/45 - Technical data re 4.6 kg. incendiary and 15 kg bombs carried by Japanese balloons, 2 May 1945(MD11/S619-27-1-3 volume 1).
322.009(D10988)

14. Reports of Japanese balloon incidents and 23 Company PCMR MD 11, 19 March and 1 April 1945(MD 11-2-27-2-23 volume 1).
169.009(D890)

15. Routine correspondence and reports re activities of no. 70 Company, PCMR - Terrace, British Columbia (including report of balloon incident 23 July 1945) 14 April 1942-31 July 1945(MD 11-2-27-2-70).
169.009(D84

16. Correspondence, reported incidents, descriptions, directives, minutes of meetings of JSC Pac. Comd, etc. re Japanese balloons, 16 December 1944-13 August 1945. Detailed descriptions of Japanese balloons which have landed in U.S., 16 December 1944(PCS/508-1-14)(FD 156 JSC).
322.019(D47)

17. Summary of policy re Japanese balloon incidents, 5 January 1945. List of balloons reported over North America, 25 January 1945(PCS/508-1-1-4(FD 156 JSC).

322.019(D47)

18. U.S. Joint Army/Navy news release 8 February 1946 re Japanese balloons, giving descriptions, number sent, method and purpose of sending, etc.
959.0132(D17)

19. AHQ Intelligence reports re Japanese balloon incidents in Canada, 15 March-6 August 1945(TS-21-9-3).
325.009(D303)

20. Correspondence, instructions, description of balloons, reports of incidents, etc. re Japanese balloon operations against West Coast of North America, January-December 1945(PCS 508-2-1-23(volumes 1-7)).
322.009(D660)

21. Studies, meetings, findings and reports of Joint Services Committee on Japanese balloons, January-February 1945(PCS 508-2-1-23(FD1)).
322.009(D661)

22. Photographs and technical reports and studies of Japanese balloons, January-December 1945(PCS 508-2-1-232-1).
322.009(D662)

23. Sighting and finding reports on Japanese balloons in North America, February-October 1945(PCS 508-2-1-23-2 (volumes 1-3).
322.009(D663)

24. Correspondence, instructions, orders, reports, etc. re Ex "Ram": to test anti-fire methods of West Coast defences in case of enemy action, e.g. balloons, April-May 1945(PCS 508-2-1-23-4).
322.009(D664)

25. Notices and reports of Pac Comd conferences re Japanese balloons, March-August 1945(PCS 508-2-1-23-5).
322.009(D665)

26. Correspondence, instructions, reports, etc. re operations of British Columbia Provincial Committee on Japanese balloons, June-July 1945(PCS 508-2-1-23-6).
322.009(D666)

27. U.S. periodic and incident reports on Japanese balloons and mines on Pacific Coast, January 1945-February 1946(PCS 508-2-1-23-7).
322.009(D667)

28. Correspondence, instructions, reports, orders, re danger of biological warfare through Japanese balloons, March-September 1945(PCS 508-2-1-24).
322.009(D668)

29. Correspondence, instructions and reports re Japanese balloon incidents in MD 12, May 1945-September 1947(RS 54-7-45).

168.009(D98)

30. Instructions and directives re action to be taken re suspected and actual Japanese balloon incidents, January-July 1945(RS 4-7-45ED).
168.009(D99)

31. Letter 23 January 1945 from JSC Pac Coast re situation arising out of reports of sightings and finds of balloons of suspected enemy origin on the Pacific Coast. (2) letter,27 January 1945, from Air Marshal J.A.Sully, Chief of Air Staff re Japanese balloons.
193.009(D40)

32. Letter, 27 January 1945, from DMO&P re balloon occurrences. (2) Message, 27 January 1945, to Pac. Comd re instructions on coordination and responsibilities in dealing with balloon incidents.
193.009(D40)

33. Joint directive re action to be taken by R.C.N., Army and R.C.A.F. in coordination of measures to deal with balloons of suspected enemy origins on Canadian Pacific Coast, 7 February 1945, JSC Pac Coast.
193.009(D40)

34. Message, 12 February 1945, from Pac. Comd; letter, 15 February 1945, from DMO&P from CSC meeting, 16 February 1945, re proposal to retain civil defence and ARP organizations in British Columbia in view of increased number of balloon incidents.
193.009(D40)

35. Memoranda from JSC Pac. Coast, CGS and extract from CSC meeting, 16-20 April 1945, re measures for dealing with forest fires resulting from Japanese balloon incidents.
193.009(D42)

36. The Japanese balloon enterprise against North America(F.R. McGuire, 15 October 1949).
AHQ Report (D28)

37. CAORG memoranda, incidents, reports, meetings, circuit charges, maps, messages, coordination. procedure, press releases, etc., 21 February-8 September 1945, re Japanese balloons.
314009(D15)

38. Canadian Army Progress Report for PJDB, 7 April 1945, re Japanese balloons.
314.009(D17)

39. Canadian Army Progress Report of 1 November 1945 re Japanese balloons(RCMP to destroy old ones).
314.009(D17)

40. The Japanese balloon enterprise as extracted from six years of war.
934.009(D258)

41. Intelligence Summary HQ R.A.F. West Africa, nos.26-68, 1 August 1943-31 May 1945
181.003(D143)

42. R.C.A.F. Northwest Air Command HQ file 104-9 "Operations - Japanese Balloons" dealing with reporting and recovering of Japanese balloons.
181.002(D268)

43. R.C.A.F. Northwest Air Command File 204-9 "Operations - Japanese Balloons". Correspondence re plans for combatting, tactics to be employed, and possible use of balloons by enemy or transporting agents and biological weapons. Covers period from January-June 1945
181.002(D269)

44. R.C.A.F. File S-604-14- Japanese balloons - Descriptions of, methods of handling, Western Air Command -correspondence from 15 February-25 June 1945
181.003(D2362)

45. R.C.A.F. file S-4-5-No.2 Filter detachment, Victoria, British Columbia, Operations W.A.C. Operations. Orders include paper on defence against Japanese balloons. Correspondence from 20 October 1943-7 August 1945
181.003(D2368)

46. R.C.A.F. File S-4-10 No.2 Filter Detachment, Victoria. Operations/Reports on Japanese balloon incidents, with photographs of balloons, diagram and instructions on how to handle. Correspondence from 16 February-10 August 1945.
181.003(D2374)

47. File S-8- R.C.A.F. Station, Mountain View, Ontario, no. 2 1 Air Command - Defence of Canada and Station Defence - includes miscellaneous intelligence material, instructions in respect to defence against Japanese balloons and possible air raids on area in Command. From 19 March 1943-19 November 1945
181.009(D1252)

48. Western Air Command HQ file 241-2-1-2 "Staff Conferences - WACHQ" Minutes(incomplete) of Staff conferences, 11 July 1944-26 July 1945.
181.006(D408).i.6Japanese

49. R.C.A.F. file S-50-1-Intelligence-General-R.C.A.F., 21 March 1943-30 November 1945.
181.009(D3021)

50. R.C.A.F. file -Air Historian questions - War Services of Air gunners - Anti-submarine warfare - raids on German cities - Japanese balloons -Transatlantic glider crossings - R.C.A.F. in D-Day invasion-Histories of growth of air power and of R.C.A.F., 1948-1951.
181.009(D5054)

51. R.C.A.F. file S-204-14-1-Western Air Command Enemy operations- Unknown and enemy ships - movements of aircraft and suspected submarines sightings - daily intelligence summaries -reports of Japanese balloons - inquiry into reported shelling near Nootka Sound, 18 December 1941-7 July 1945.

181.003(D36535)

52. R.C.A.F. file S-39-8-Western Air Command - R.D.F. Instructions General, February 1944-July 1945.
181.009(D5889)

53. R.C.A.F. Secret file S-4-1-North West Air Command - HQ Edmonton, Alberta. Alaska Highway and R.C.A.F. Army cooperation- Japanese balloon incidents, January 1945-January 1946.
181.009(D6416)

54. R.C.A.F. file - D-33-R.C.A.F. Station, Trenton, Ontario. Operations - Japanese balloons, November 1944-July 1945.
181.009(D6448)

Japanese balloons - No.2. Air Command(R.C.A.F.).

1. R.C.A.F. file - No.2 Air Command, HQ, Winnipeg, Manitoba. Description of, Instructions for handling and other information relating to Japanese balloons, January-March 1945
181.009(D5992)

Japanese balloons-No.2 Air Command(R.C.A.F.).

1. R.C.A.F. file - War Office(R.A.F.) Intelligence Summaries nos. 74, 77-79, 81-82, 3 January-3 July 1945. Includes summaries on Political Notes, Operations, German and Japanese Army organizations.
181.003(D3245)

Japanese-battle experience against.

1. "Battle experience against Japanese" by HQ U.S. Forces, European Theatre, 17 July 1945. File 1 CIN INF DIV/1 CD/1/G.
230C1(D80)

2. "Battle experience against the Japanese" by S.H.A.E.F.,18-23 July 1945.File 1 CDN ARMY/CSO/2-13/1.
212C1.4009(D34)

3. Intelligence notes by 96 U.S. Infantry Division, 8 July 1945, and XXIV U.S. Corps, 11 July 1945, on Japanese weapons and battle tactics(PCS 504-1-40 Volume 1).
322.009(D32)

Japanese campaign pay.

1. Memoranda re special rates of pay for CAPF, January-July 1946(DCGS(AB)16-1-20 Temp 6).
112.21009(D29)

2. Memorandum, 14 January 1946, re special rates of pay CAPF by DCGS(A)(DCGS(A) 16-1-20 Temp 6).
112.21009(D29)

3. Privy Council Instruction, 17 March 1949, authorizing Japanese Campaign pay for "C" Force personnel who fought at Hong Kong.
951.056(D3)

Japanese capabilities.

1. Notes on Japanese capabilities-Joint Intelligence Committee, Pacific Command, August 1943(PCS/540-3-3-1).
322.009(D157)

Japanese casualties.

1. German, Italian and Japanese U-boat casualties during the war - statistical statement and particulars of destruction by 1st Lord of the Admiralty to Parliament, June 1946.
981.013(D10)

Japanese characteristics.

1. Notes on racial and regional characteristics, Japanese press editorials, Japanese personalities, glossary of military terms, re Japanese people dated 1941, 10 November 1944.
Pamphlet "Regional characteristics of the Japanese people" DMI(undated)(PCS/540-3-3-1-1 volume 1).
322.009(D158)

Japanese/China clashes.

1. Declaration on Sino-Japanese clashes issue by the Servants' Society of South Manchurian Railway Company, Dairen, Manchuria, October 1931.
003(D4)

Japanese census.

1. AT&T Section, S.W.P.A. translation of census of Japan, October 1940.
982.009(D43)

Japanese commerce.

1. The **Japan Advertiser** - Annual Review of Japanese Finance, Industry and Commerce, 1939-1940.
982.029(D1)

Japanese communications.

1. AT&T Section, S.W.P.A. translation of communication instructions for 21st Japanese Independent Mixed Brigade, 6 June 1943.i.6Japanese
982.009(D31)

Japanese counter measures.

1. DMT notes on tactics and counter measures used by Japanese Army, 1942.
934.009(D14)

Japanese customs.

1. Notes on Japanese system of reckoning time, August 1943(PCS/540-3-3-1).

322.009(D157)

Japanese defence forces.

1. Intelligence reports on Japanese Defence Forces as collected and prepared by Brigadier R.E.A. Morton, July 1953-September 1954(2 volumes).
410B25.019(D304)

Japanese defences.

1. Flakintel Bulletin no. 44 - Japanese defences at Luzon. HQ Allied Air Forces, S.W.P.A., 21 February 1945(PCS/540-3-4-10).
322.009(D166)

Japanese Department of Information.

1. AT & I Section, S.W.P.A. translation of "The Weekly", an information pamphlet of Japanese Department of Information, 8 January 1944.
982.009(D98)

Japanese developments.

1. Flakintel Bulletin no. 42. New developments in Japanese AA artillery - HQ Allied Air Forces, S.W.P.A., 31 January 1945(PCS/540-3-3-4-10).
322.009(D166)

Japanese discrimination units.

1. Extracts from CSC meetings, correspondence, recommendations, etc., 30 March-6 July 1943, re establishment of housing of Japanese discrimination units.
193.009(D20)

2. Minutes of 31st meeting of "Y" committee, 11 June 1953, re the following: Reports of subcommittee on proposed housing of the service Japanese discrimination unit.
193.009(D20)

Japanese documents.

1. Translation of captured Japanese documents, September 1942.
982.023(D2)

2. Translation of an account of the attack on Hong Kong December 1941 as given by Major General Tanaka Ryusaburo, OC 229 Regiment of 38 Division, Imperial Japanese Army.
982.011(D1)

3. Translation of a personal account of the fall of Hong Kong by Lieutenant General Ito Takeo, on 23 July 1947.
982.011(D2)

4. Operation record of Japanese operations in China theatre, volume II, by First Demobilization Bureau received Washington(including Hong Kong, Changsha, Chekiang, Kiangsi, Ssu-chuan, Leichow Peninsula and Kwanchow Bay, Changte, Yangtse River, etc.).
982.013(D4)

5. Material concerning Hong Kong and Aleutians operations from Japanese sources compiled by J.J.McArdle and forwarded by Mr. E.H.Norman, Canadian Liaison Mission in Japan, to Historical Section, 26 October 1949(HQC 1453-10(DHS1-5-1).
982.013(D4)

6. Global situation report for February 1944. Captured Japanese intelligence documents by Allied Translation and Interpreter Section, S.W.P.A. =272,8 January 1945(HQC 1450-2).
982.023(D15)

7. Correspondence, descriptions, silhouettes, captured orders, etc. re Japanese navy, 26 September 1942-21 November 1944. Notes, organization charts, instructions, etc. re Japanese naval landing forces and pioneer units, 26 September 1942.
Japanese manual on landing operations AT & I Section, S.W.P.A. Bulletin no. 12, 24 May 1943(PCS/540-3-3-1-14).
322.009(D161)

8. Japanese document -"Notes on Intelligence work from experiences in the Greater East Asia War, 17 August 1943"(PCS/540-3-3-1-22 volume 1).
322.009(D1653)

9. Intelligence notes and pictures of Japanese AA and Anti tank guns, gunnery manuals, orders, instructions, etc. re Japanese AA and Anti-tank guns, November 1941-9 March 1945.
Orders of No.2 Battery - 47 Field Gun AA Gun Battalion - Japanese, November 1941-June 1942 - AT&I Section, S.W.P.A. Translation no. 11, 12 May 1943.
Japanese reference manual for AA gunners AT&I Section, S.W.P.A. Translation no. 18, 6 June 1943.
Japanese AA and Anti-submarine Training instructions AT&I Section, S.W.P.A. Translation no. 19, 16 June 1943(PCS/540-3-3-40-10).
322.008(D166)

10. Japanese Bulletin "Notes for Japanese gunners" Allied Land Forces S.W.P.A., 2 November 1943(PCS/540-3-3-4-3).
982.003(D1)

11. List of Japanese language documents received from Joint Intelligence Bureau, Defence Research Board, 27 January 1951.
982.003(D1)

12. List of translations of Japanese documents received in Directorate of History from DMI produced by the Allied Translator and Interpreter Section, S.W.P.A.
982.009(D1)

13. AT&I Section S.W.P.A. translation of alphabetical list of Japanese Army Officers, publication no. 2, May

1943.
982.065(D2)

14. Microfilm of Japanese document -notebook of ensign Nakamura received from U.S. Department of the Navy and CAS Washington, 31 January 1953. Prints of portion of Nakamura notebook microfilm dealing with Japanese evacuation of Kiska.
982.018(D1)

15. History of Army Section Imperial GHQ 1941-1945 Japanese narrative received from Cabinet Office, London.
952.001(D1)

16. ATIS pamphlet of Japanese military conventional signs and abbreviations, March 1943.
982.055(D1)

17. War Office general report on Japanese system of military education and training, 1906.
952.023(D38)

18. Pamphlet on Japanese uniforms, including army and navy ranks and insignia, March 1943.
982.085(D1)

19. Microfilm of Japanese monographs; no. 167 Malay Operations received by 29th Army; no. 177, North China Operations; no. 178 Central China Operations and no. 179 South China Operations.
983.013(D3)

20. Guide to Japanese Monographs and Japanese studies on Manchuria, 1945-1960, by Office of Chief of Military History, U.S. Army.
980.005(D1)

Japanese economy

1. Japanese Economic Record - from Japanese periodical **Chuo Koron,** 1934 (1 volume)HQC /1450-2).
982.003(D9)

Japanese embassies

1. Guide no. 15 - Records of former German and Japanese Embassies, 1890-1945, 1960, 63 pages.
981.005(D35)

Japanese evacuation from British Columbia

1. Correspondence and PC Orders 1942 re Japanese evacuation from British Columbia protected area(CGS office file).
112.1(D37)

2. Memorandum to Joint Service Committee from Commodore R.C.N., Pacific Coast, 2 May 1941, re rounding up of Japanese nationals and Japanese boats(PCS 638-1-5-Volume 1).
322.009(D53)

3. Correspondence, reports, proclamations, newspaper articles, orders, plans, etc. re evacuation of Japanese from protected areas in British Columbia, 17 February 1942-23 February 1944.
322.009(D358)

4 . Proclamation re removal of male enemy aliens from protected areas in British Columbia, February 1942. Memorandum re riot by Japanese internees at Immigration Building, Vancouver, British Columbia 1942(NP/6-0-7).
322.009(D358)

5. Report by British Columbia Security Commission on removal of Japanese from protected area, 4 March-31 October 1942.
322.009(D400)

Japanese field logs.

1. AT&I Section S.W.P.A. translation of Japanese field log of Sakigawa Tai, July-August 1942, 16 July 1943.
982.009(D51)

Japanese forces.

1. Extracts from War Office(Restricted) Intelligence Summaries(re Japanese distribution and organization), March-September 1944(DCGS file).
112.21009(D192)

2. Disposition and movement of Japanese ground forces, 1941-1945 a special study - Military Intelligence Division, U.S. War Department, 10 December 1945(including orders of battle and maps).
171.009(D88)

3. Japanese air record - from Japanese periodical **Chuo Koron,** 1934(l volume) HQC/1450-2).
982.003(D3)

4. Japanese Army record - from Japanese periodical **Chuo Koron,** 1934(1 volume) (HQC/1450-2)
982.003(D4)

5. Japanese Navy record - from Japanese periodical **Chuo Koron,** 1934(1 volume)(GQC/1450-2).
982.003(D5)

6. War Office Intreps on Japanese Army by officers who have been attached to it, 1929-1932.i.6Japanese
952.0232(D29)

7. War Office Intelligence Summary on strength and distribution of Japanese forces by area,1 April 1944(DSD/BDF 1-5-7(volumes I & II).
112.3S2009(D17)

8. Charts showing organization of a standard Japanese division - Organization chart, U.S. Infantry Division 1945(K.G.S 8-X-l).
163.009(D31)

9. Correspondence, descriptions, silhouettes, captured orders, etc. re Japanese Navy, 16 September-21

November 1944. Notes, organization charts, instructions, etc. re Japanese naval landing forces and pioneer units, 16 September 1942.
Identification Bulletin on Japanese and U.S. naval vessels.
Notes on aircraft carriers(Japanese), 8 February and 3 and 25 September 1942(PCS/540-3-3-1-14).
332.009(D161)

10. Correspondence, reports, studies, charts, etc. re Japanese methods of training and warfare, 9 June 1942-24 November 1944.
Notes on Japanese warfare - Bulletins 6-10 - War Department Intelligence Division, U.S. Army, 9 January-23 April 1942.
Japanese impressions of Allied combat methods - HQ Allied Land Forces, S.W.P.A., 4 December 1943.
Japanese combat training films AT&I Section -S.W.P.A., 28 December 1943(PCS/540-3-3-1-20(volume 1).
322.009(D162)

11. Correspondence, and directive on intelligence methods of Japanese, 15 November 1944-19 February 1945.
Japanese document "Notes on intelligence work from experiences in the Greater East Asia War",17 August 1943(PCS/540-3-3-1-22(volume 1)).
322.009(D163)

12. Intelligence notes and pictures of Japanese AA and anti-tank guns, gunnery manuals, orders, instructions, etc. re Japanese AA and anti-tank guns, November 1941-9 March 1945.
Orders of no. 2 Battery- 47 Field Gun Battalion - Japanese November 1941-June 1942. AT&I Section S.W.P.A. Translation no. 11, 12 May 1943.
Index to Flakintel Bulletins 1-40(inclusive) HQ Allied Air Forces S.W.P.A., 10 January 1945.
Flakintel Bulletin no. 42-New developments in Japanese AA artillery HQ Allied Air Forces - S.W.P.A., 31 January 1945.
Flakintel Bulletin no. 44 - S.W.P.A. -Japanese AA defences in Luzon -HQ Allied Air Forces, S.W.P.A., 21 February 1945(PCS/540-3-3-4-10).
322.009(D166)

13. Intelligence correspondence, drawings, descriptions and bulletins on Japanese mines and booby traps, 1 July 1942-9 May 1945.
Intelligence Information Bulletin no. 19 - Axis Booby traps -War Department, Washington, 1 July 1942.(PCS/540-3-3-4-13).
322.009(D167)

14. Intelligence notes and drawings on Japanese AFVs, wireless equipment, AFV weapons, etc., 30 January 1943-2 January 1945(PCS/540-3-3-4-13).
322.009(D168)

15. Intelligence drawings and notes on Japanese bombs and mortars, 29 July 1942-29 January 1945. Flakintel Bulletin no. 41 - Japanese defence tactics at Clark Field, 18 January 1945(PCS/540-3-3-4-15).

322.009(D169)

16. Intelligence notes and data on Japanese operations, South Pacific, 24 November 1942-15 February 1945, Theatre of War no. 17.- Far East, April-November 1943, May 1944.
Engineer Technical Information Bulletin no. 10 -CE GHQ S.W.P.A., 29-30 January 1945 (PCS/540-3-3-4-15).
322.009(D170)

17. Intelligence Notes on Japan and the Mandated Islands, 1921 and 1936, received in the Directorate of History from DMI
113.3M1023(D17)

Japanese forces intelligence reports on.

1. Army Intelligence, File S 22-3 Volume 5, April-August 1942.
181.003(D269)

Japanese foreign relations.

1. Japanese foreign relations record from Japanese periodical **Chuo Koron,** 1934(1 volume) (HQC/1450-2)
982.003(D6)

Japanese Government - orders from Allied Powers.

1. Orders from Supreme Commander for Allied Powers to Japanese Government, November 1945-February 1946.
982.046(D1)

Japanese Imperial Headquarters.

1. British Joint Staff Mission in Washington document entitled "Japanese Surrender", 25 September 1945(contains orders issued by General MacArthur to Japanese Imperial Headquarters).
193.009(D48)

Japanese impressions.

1. Japanese impressions of Allied Combat methods - HQ Allied Land Forces, S.W.P.A., December 1943(PCS/540-3-3-1-20 (volume 1)).
322.009(D1652)

Japanese in Aleutian Islands. Royal Canadian Air Force.

1. R.C.A.F. file - Army Intelligence Reports - War against the Japanese in the Kurile and Aleutian Islands, 22 May-14 July 1943.
181.003(D3226)

Japanese in Canada.

1. Correspondence, regulations, recommendations of JSC Pac Comd etc., re areas inhabited by Japanese in Pac Comd, 23 May 1942-13 February 1945(PCS/508-

1-1-4(FD 79 JSC)).
322.019(D15)

2. Report on conference in Victoria re Civil Security as it applies to Japanese in Canada 1 October 1940. British Columbia Police Report to British Columbia Security Committee re Japanese problem, 1 October 1940(NP/6/-0-7).
322.009(D358)

3. Newspaper reports, reports and recommendations of committees etc. re public opinion against Japanese in British Columbia, 5 July 1939-4 June 1942(NP/6-0-8).
32009(D361)2

4. Correspondence, reports and instructions re handling of Japanese in British Columbia, June 1942-February 1945.
322.009(D601)

5. Statistics on Japanese population in Canada - 1946.
327.009(D214)
Japanese in Canada, 1939-1945. Royal Canadian Air Force.

1. R.C.A.F. file S-657-3-Western Air Command-Situation of the Japanese in Canada, 13 December 1939-21 March 1942.
181.009(D5546)

Japanese industry.

1. Japanese industrial record from Japanese periodical **Chuo Koron,** 1934(1 volume)(HQC/1450-2).
982.003(D8)

2. AT&I Section, S.W.P.A. translation of Japanese weekly into bulletin with editorial on wartime industrial organization, 19 January 1945.
982.009(D47)

3. **The Japan Advertiser Annual Review of Japanese, Finance, Industry and Commerce 1939-1940.**
982.029(D1)

Japanese information extracts

1. Japanese Information Extracts prepared by the DMO, March 1943-December 1944.
983.023(D1)

Japanese inquiry

1. Report of Judge J.C.A. Cameron re Japanese Inquiry at Vancouver, 1942.(NP-6-0-7-1).
322.0099-359)

Japanese intentions.

1. Japanese intentions, February 1941. Telegrams from Dominion Office.
951.023(D2)
Japanese internees.

1. Complaints, correspondence, movement orders, hospitalization instructions, repatriation instructions, messages, etc. re Japanese internees in Canada, 20 October 1942-9 April 1946.
Letter from Attorney-General, 18 January 1946, laying down instructions for provision of Canadian Army guards re repatriation of Japanese internees from Canada to Japan(MD 11 S602-1-27-6 volume 2).
322.009(F23)

Japanese internal situation.

1. AT&I Section, S.W.P.A. translation of Japanese publication "The Weekly" covering the internal situation, 9 October 1943.
942.009(D42)

Japanese internment camps.

1. Statement and reports re repatriates on conditions in Japanese internment camps, 1941-1945, various sources passed by DMI, 12 February 1950.
982.061(D1)

2. Radio talk by Mr. Joseph Grew ex-U.S. Ambassador to Japan describing events before Pearl Harbour, Japanese treatment of prisoners of war, Japanese tactics, etc., December 1942(PCS/540-3-3-1).
322.009(D157)

Japanese press.

1. Notes on racial and regional characteristics, Japanese press editorials, Japanese personalities, glossary of military terms, etc. re Japanese people, 1941-10 November 1944(PCS/540-3-3-1-1 Volume 1).
322.009(D158)

Japanese prison camps.

1. Notes on atrocities in Japanese prison camps by Lieutenant-Colonel O.Orr, W.C.I.S., 8 January 1946.
593.(D8)

2. See also "Hong Kong".

3. Nominal rolls of prisoners of war at camps in Japan and of deaths at Hong Kong(passed by Colonel Crawford, D.G.M.S.(AMD 8))
593.065(D2)

4. Notes on background, qualities, etc. of Japanese soldier, possibilities of escape from prisoner of war camps, Japanese uniforms(with diagrams), August 1942-30 January 1945(PCS/540-3-3-1-7).
322.009(D159)

5. Reports, instructions, signed statements, nominal rolls, correspondence, re liberated prisoners of war from Far East, 11 November 1945-12 April 1946(L.S. 343-11-3).
161.009(D6)
6. "Groups" of Japanese camps. Many of the camps are divided into "Groups" for administrative purposes.

Example: the name of the place from which it is governed, though individual camps may be some distance, each generally bears an individual name. Also map showing location of prisoner of war camps in the Far East; China, Japan, Chosen(Korea), Manchoukuo, Philippines, Taiwan(Formosa), Indo-China, Thailand(Siam), and Malaya.
113.3R2.009(D21)

Japanese - prisoners of war.

1. Correspondence, instructions, proceedings on trial of Japanese prisoners of war at Petawawa, 4 July-22 September 1942(K-36-216 B).
325.009(D471)

Japanese Promotions and Appointments.

1. AT & I Section. S.W.P.A. translation of Japanese naval promotion and appointment bulletins, January 1944, 28 December 1944.
982.009(D61)

Japanese - Radar.

1. R.A.F. Intelligence Report on Japanese radar locations, 5 May 1944.
181.009(D517)

Japanese raids.

1. Story of Japanese raids on West coast of North America from Second World War from **Ottawa Citizen**, 7 April 1950.
934.011(D2)

Japanese records.

1. AT & I Section. S.W.P.A. translation of Japanese miscellaneous personnel records Horii Butai, 8 September 1943.i.6Japanese
982.009(D87)

Japanese regulations.

1. AT & I Section. S.W.P.A. translation of Japanese Western New Britain garrison regulations, 13 May 1944.
982.009(D75)
2. AT & I Section. S.W.P.A. translation of Japanese interim duty and discipline regulations, 27 March 1944.
982.009(D76)

3. AT & I Section. S.W.P.A. translation of Japanese troopship regulations, 23 July 1944.i.6Japanese
982.009(D78)4

1. AT & I Section. S.W.P.A. translation of Japanese communication regulations of Moto Group Signal Tai, 5 June 1943.i.6Japanese
982.009(D86)
Japanese reports.

1. AT & I Section. S.W.P.A. translation of Japanese report on guerrilla activities in the Philippines, 28 April 1945.
982.009(D13)

2. AT & I Section. S.W.P.A. translation of Japanese reports on Allied air raids on Tsurubu, 24 April 1944.
982.009(D90)

Japanese resistance.

1 .Joint Intelligence Committee study on possible post war resistance by Japanese Army after surrender, 24 March 1944(JIC, 29 March 44).
112.3M1(D5)

Japanese rule.

1. Paper on Philippines under Japan, 12 April 1943(based mainly on U.S. press reports)
314.009(D46).

Japanese security.

1. Handbook of standard translations of Japanese security gradings by AT & I Section, S.W.P.A.
982.009(D2)

Japanese shelling -Canada.

1. Messages, reports, etc., re enemy attacks on U.S. and Canada(including Brookings, Oregon and Estevan Point), June-September 1942(NA1-0-2).
312.009(D182)

Japanese shipping.

1. EAC file 322-6 "Intelligence - Merchant shipping", 4 May 1943-3 October 1945, with notes re miscellaneous ships and list of Japanese vessels believed converted to wartime uses
181.009(D241)

Japanese signs.

1. AT & I Section. Pamphlet of Japanese military conventional signs and abbreviations, March 1943.
982.055(D1)

Japanese-Sino clashes.

12. Declaration on Sino-Japanese clashes issue by the Servants' Society of South Manchurian Railway Company, Dairen, Manchuria, October 1931.
003(D4)

Japanese ski-troop training.

1. Japanese ski-troops training - extracts from WOWIR's, 4 July 1945(2 copies).
982.023(D7)

Japanese small boat operations.

1. AT & I Section. S.W.P.A. translation of Japanese notes on small boat operations, 20 July 1944.
982.009(D32)
2. AT & I Section. S.W.P.A. translation of Japanese boat unit regulations between Bogo and Surigao, 11 September 1944.
982.009(D68)

Japanese studies - Second World War.

1. Microfilm of Japanese Studies nos. 51 and 57 in Second World War "The Aleutians Islands Campaign" and "Naval Operations in the Northern Area" received from CAS(W), 4 September 1952(see reel no. 3171, Item nos. 3766-56).
In possession of Mr. Steiger see also 983.013(D2).

2. "Japanese Studies in World War II" Monograph 76: "China Incident", Greater East Asia War, China Area Aerial Operations.
982.013(D4)

Japanese submarine operations.

1. Situation reports on Japanese submarine and activity in North America Area, September 1942-September 1944(PRD 3-2-0).
341.PR009(D7)

Japanese submarines.

1. Royal Canadian Navy and lightkeepers' reports on shelling of Estevan by Japanese submarine, 20 June 1942(PCS 508-1-1-1(Volume 2).
322.009(D595)

2. Intelligence Summary H.Q. R.A.F. West Africa, nos. 26 -68, 1 August 1943-31 May 1945.
181.003(D143)

3. "IOGROPS REVIEW" Volume 1, nos. 1-3(August 1944-January 1945).
181.003(D4686)

Japanese surrender.

1. Miscellaneous personal messages November 1944 - May 1945 from various Commands and including message from His Majesty the King re surrender of Japan.i.6Japanese
012. (D1)

2. Letter, 11 August 1945 from Cabinet to MND outlining action to be taken following the surrender of Japan(DCGDS(A) 16-1-15 Volumes 1 and 2).
112.2009(D14)

3. Correspondence, messages, directives, orders, instructions, instruments of surrender, etc. re Japanese surrender, 10 August-18 October 1945. Surrender document between Admiral Mountbatten and Siamese Commanders, 8 September 1945(CAS/1-4-21).
314.009(D346)

4. Instrument of surrender of Japanese forces in Southern Region, signed at Singapore, 12 August 1945. General Order No.1 by General MacArthur issued on surrender of Japanese forces, 5 September 1945(CAS/1-4-21).
314.009(D346)

5. AT & I Section. S.W.P.A. translation of Japanese documents submitted to Supreme Command of Allied Forces by Japanese mission to negotiate surrender at Manila, 19 August 1945.
List of Japanese mission to the surrender negotiations.
982.009(D95)

6. Imperial rescript appointing Lieutenant-General Kawabe Japanese emissary to Supreme Command Allied Forces for Surrender. Japanese statistics of air raid damages done to major cities of Japan as of 15 August 1945.
Statistics re strength of Japanese Army, Air Force in planes as of 15 August 1945Summary of Japanese Army Air Bases giving location, length of runways, protection, capacity and installations, 1 August 1945.
List of Commanders of Japanese Naval Forces, as of 15 August 1945.
Strength of Japanese Navy Air Force in planes as of 1 August 1945 with dispositions of air fleets.
Names, locations and operational states of ships of Japanese Navy, 15 August 1945.
982.009(D95)

7. Strength and location of Japanese Navy personnel as of 1 August 1945.
Deployment of surface and underwater special attack weapons of Japanese Navy, 10 August 1945.
List of Allied naval prisoners of war in Japanese hands as of 15 August 1945.
Statistical tables giving number of Allied prisoners of war in Japan and occupied areas as of 15 August 1945.
982.009(D95)

8. DPR photographs of signing of Japanese armistice on board U.S.S. **Missouri**, September 1945.
112.3P1(D1406)

9. Joint Intelligence Committee study on possible postwar resistance by Japanese Army after surrender, 29 March 1944(JIC 181 29 March 1944).
112.3M1(D5)

10. British Joint Staff Mission in Washington document entitled "Japanese Surrender", 25 September 1945(contains orders issued by General MacArthur to Japanese Imperial Headquarters)
193.009(D48)

Japanese Surrender documents.

1. AT & I Section. S.W.P.A. translation of Japanese documents submitted to Supreme Command of Allied Forces by Japanese Mission to negotiate surrender at Manila, 19 August 1945.

List of Japanese mission to the surrender negotiations Imperial rescript appointing Lieutenant-General Kawabe Japanese emissary to Supreme Command Allied Forces for Surrender. Japanese statistics of air raid damages done to major cities of Japan as of 15 August 1945.
Statistics re strength of Japanese Army Air Force in planes as of 15 August 1945.
Summary of Japanese Army Air Bases giving location, length of runways, protection, capacity and installations, 1 August 1945.
List of Commanders of Japanese Naval Forces, as of 15 August 1945.
Strength of Japanese Navy Air Force in planes as of 1 August 1945 with dispositions of air fleets.
Names, locations and operational states of ships of Japanese Navy, 15 August 1945.
Strength and location of Japanese Navy personnel as of 1 August 1945.
Deployment of surface and underwater special attack weapons of Japanese Navy, 10 August 1945.
List of Allied naval prisoners of war in Japanese hands as of 15 August 1945.
Statistical tables giving number of Allied prisoners of war in Japan and occupied areas as of 15 August 1945.i.6Japanese
982.009(D95)

3. "The End of the War in the Pacific", Japanese Surrender Documents in facsimile, published by the National Archives of the United States, 1945.
670.006(D2)

Japanese Surrender Mission.

1. List of Japanese mission to the surrender negotiations. Imperial rescript appointing Lieutenant-General Kawabe, Japanese Emissary to Supreme Command Allied Forces for Surrender.
982.009(D95)

Japanese tactics.

1. Extracts from WOWIR's on German tactics, training, equipment, etc., February-May 1944, and Japanese tactics in Arakan, May 1944(ACC/3-10-9-0-6 volumes 1-3).
321.009(D64)

2. Radio talk by Mr. Joseph C.Grew, ex U.S. Ambassador to Japan describing events before Pearl Harbour, Japanese treatment of prisoners of war, Japanese tactics, etc., December 1942(PCS/540-3-3-1).
322.009(D157)

Report on changes in Japanese strategy from confidential agent of U.S. Navy, 10 March 1943(PCS/540-3-3-1).
322.009(D157).i.6Japanese

3. Appreciation of possible Japanese action on Pacific coast -Pacific Command Intelligence, 16 February 1942(PCS/540/3-3-1).
322.009(D157)

4. Notes, organization charts, instructions, etc., re Japanese naval landing forces and pioneer units, 26 September 1942(PCS/540-3-3-1-14).
322.009(DF161)

5. Correspondence, reports, studies, charts, etc., re Japanese methods of training and warfare, 9 June-24 November 1944, Notes on Japanese warfare - Bulletins 6-10, War Department Intelligence Division, U.S. Army, 9 January 42-23 April 1942(PCSD/540-3-3-1-20 Volume 1).
322.0009(D162)

6. Flakintel Bulletin no. 41 - Japanese Anti-aircraft defence tactics at Clark Field, 18 January 1945(PCS/540-3-3-4-15).
322.009(D169

7. U.S . Joint Army/Navy release, 8 February 1946 re Japanese balloons, giving descriptions, numbers sent, method and purpose of sending, etc.
959.013(D17)

8. AT & I Section. S.W.P.A. translation of Japanese notes on automatic weapons and infantry gun, including tactics, 5 July 1943.
982.009(D15)

9. Manual on Japanese tank and methods of fighting published by Military Intelligence Division, U.S. War U.S. War U.S. War
Department, 25 June 1945.
934.009(D6)

10. Manual describing Japanese tanks and tank tactics, issued by U.S. War Department, 15 November 1944.
934.009(D8)

11. Booklet summarizing battle tactics of Japanese Army, issued by U.S. War Department Intelligence Services, 1942.i.6Japanese
934.009(D10)

12. DMT notes on tactics and counter measures used by Japanese Army, 1942.i.6Japanese
934.009(D14)

13. Notes on strategy, organization and tactics of Japanese troops employed against Hong Kong, December 1941, by Captain P.A.MacMillan, Royal Artillery.
352.009(D1)

14. U.S. Intelligence Bulletins re Japanese Army, arms and tactics, February 1942-July 1945(MD 13/C/S 78-13-1).
169.009(D182)

Japanese tank and anti-tank warfare.

1. Japanese tank and anti-tank warfare, 25 June 1945, by Military Intelligence Division, War Department, Washington(2 copies).

982.(D1)

2. Manual on Japanese tank and anti-tank methods of fighting, published by Military Intelligence Division, U.S. War Department, 25 June 1945.i.6Japanese
934.009(D6)

3. Manual describing Japanese tanks and tank tactics, issued by US. War Department, 15 November 1944.
934.009(D8)

Japanese-Training.

1. Extracts from WOWIR's and War Office(Restricted) Intelligence Summaries, October 1944-June 1945, re German and Japanese organization, tactics, equipment, training, etc.i.6Japanese
171.009(D66)

2. Japanese combat training plans - brief enemy publications no. 69, December 1943 by Allied Translator and Interpreter Section, S.W.P.A.
171.009(DF79)

3. Correspondence, reports, studies, charts, etc., re Japanese methods of training and warfare, 9 June 1942-24 November 1944. Japanese Combat Training plans, A.T. & I. Section. S.W.P.A., 28 December 1943(PCS/540-3-3-1-20 Volume 1)
322.099(D1652)

4 Technical pictures and descriptions of Japanese mortars and artillery precis, 1943-24 July 1945. Japanese Bulletin "Notes for Japanese gunners" - Allied Land Forces, S.W.P.A., 2 November 1943.(PSC/540-3-3-4-3).
322.009(D164)

5. Intelligence notes and pictures of Japanese anti-aircraft and anti-tank guns, gunnery manuals, orders, instructions, etc., re Japanese anti-aircraft and anti-tank guns, November 1941-9 March 1945. Japanese reference manual for anti-aircraft gunners, A.T. & I. Section. S.W.P.A. Translation no. 18, 6 June 1943.
322.008(D166)

Japanese anti-aircraft and anti-submarine training Instructions, A.T. & I. Section. S.W.P.A. translation no. 19, 16 June 1943(PCS/540-3-3-450-10).
322.009(D166)

6. AT & I Section. S.W.P.A. translation of Japanese manual of engineer training methods, 31 July 1943.i.6Japanese
982.009(D21)

7. AT & I Section. S.W.P.A. Translation of Japanese pamphlet on anti-aircraft and anti-submarine shipboard training Instructions, 16 June 1943.
322.009(D111)

8. Handbook on education and training of Japanese field artillery, prepared by War Office, 1909.i.6Japanese
952.009(D40)

Japanese Treatment - liberated prisoners of war.

1. Reports, instructions, signed statements, nominal rolls, correspondence, re liberated prisoners of war from Far East, 11 November 1945-12 April 1946(-11-3).
162.009(D6)

Japanese treatment of prisoners of war.

1. Radio talk by Mr. Joseph C.Grew, ex U.S. Ambassador to Japan describing events before Pearl Harbour, Japanese treatment of prisoners of war, Japanese tactics, etc., December 1942 (PCS/540-3-3-1).
322.009(D157)

2. "Regulations for prisoners" - orders given to U.S. prisoners of war who were being transported by sea, 1943(PCS/540-3-3-1).
322.009(D157)

Japanese uniforms.

1. Notes on background, qualities, etc. of Japanese soldier, possibilities of escape from prisoner of war camps, Japanese uniforms(with diagrams), August 1942-30 January 1945(PCS/540-3-3-1-7).i.6Japanese
322.009(D159)

2. Coloured charts of uniforms and insignia of armed forces of Germany, Japan, and Turkey by U.S. Intelligence Services.i.6Japanese
112.3M1009(D111)

Japanese war.

1. Tiger Force -strategic background and the Air plan, July 1945.
181.003(D253)

2. Copy of signal MND for Air Power to A.O.C.-in-C, R.C.A.F. O.S. Breadner, 17 June 1944 re policy on deployment and uses of R.C.A.F. squadrons after end of German war. Also formation of new R.C.A.F. squadrons, for current employment with R.A.F.
181.009(D1044)

Japanese warfare.

1. See Equipment, Japanese.

2. Notes on Japanese warfare, Information Bulletins no. 6 (9 January 1942)-no. 10 (21 March 1942) by Military Intelligence Division, War Department, Washington.
982.023(D1)

3. See Organization and Tactics, German and Japanese.

4. Japanese Army defence against naval attack, a Japanese report. Extracts from WOWIR's, 7 May 1945.
982.023(D14)

5. Japanese weapons and equipment - Australian Technical Intelligence Summary, No.2, April 1943, Allied Headquarters.
982.023(D5)

6. Balloon attacks on Canada, story of Japanese device, see **The Times**(London) 7 September 1945.

7. A summary of Japanese warfare by Military Intelligence Service(Organization, Equipment, etc.).
982.043(D1)

8. History of the "China Incident" in photographs (4 volumes) by Asahi Shimbun Publishing Company, 1938.
982.003(D2)

Japanese wartime punishments.
AT & I Section. S.W.P.A. translation of Japanese bulletin of wartime punishments, 3 June 1943.
982.009(D84)

Japanese - West Coast.

1. Minutes of 15th meeting of JSC Pacific Coast, 15 February 1942, re the following: Dealing with Japanese in Coastal Areas in case of emergency.
193.009(D5)

2. Minutes of 19th meeting of JSC Pacific Coast, 12 March 1942, re the following: Dealing with Japanese in Coastal Areas in event of emergency.
193.009(D5)

Koje Island.

2. Clippings from "Japan News" re Canadian troops on Koje Island and visit of Lord Alexander to Korea, received from Capt. McGuire, 2 July 1952.
497.009(D2)

3. CGS office file re move of Royal Canadian Regiment to Koje Island, June-July 1952(CGS 15-l/25CIB TD 6).
112.009(D88)

4. Correspondence(High level) and reports re tour of duty of Royal Canadian Regiment on Koje Island, June 1952, received from CGS Office.
112.0909(D92)

5. Excerpt from British Parliamentary Debates- 5 series, 19 -30 May 1952.
612.0032(D1)

Korea.

1. Korea Handbook prepared by DMI, 8 September 1950.
See Confidential Index.
112.3MI.023(D12)

2. Memorandum from Colonel C.P.Stancey to Adjutant General commenting on wording of recommendations for award to Canadian personnel in Korea, 28 June 1951(PN - 171-51).
713.009(D1)

3. List of Korean place names suffixes as received from Lieutenant H.D.Martin, Directorate of History, 16 October 1951.
680.005(D1)

4. "Korean Journey" Broadcast speech by Hon. Brooke Claxton, MDN, on his visit to Korea and 25 Infantry Brigade, 20 January 1952.
111.2(D1)

5. "A Brief History of the Korean People" U.S. Operations Research Office Technical Memorandum ORO-T-7(FEC), 10 March 1951 held in DWD(see HQS 2382-34/338(DWD 3), 21 January 1952.

6. Clippings from "Japan News" re Canadian troops on Koje Island and visit of Lord Alexander to Korea, received from Capt. McGuire, 2 July 1952.
497.009(D2)

7. Newspaper clipping depicting new type winter clothing used by troops in Korea, December 1952.
1956(068)

8. List of Command and Staff appointments in 25 Canadian Infantry Brigade to November 1953.
681.065(D3)

9. CAORE Internal memorandum no. 7 - Manpower flow in 25 Canadian Infantry Brigade, April 1951- September 1952, by A.C.Lauriston, May 1953.
112.3W1013(D12)

10. CAORE notes on operations research in Korea by Mr. G.D.Kaye, 18 April 1952.
112.3W1013(D13)

11. Captions and colour films of rolls 8,9, 10 to 16 pictures taken in Korea by Captain J.R.Madden, received 21 December 1953.
681.009(D12)

12. List of Canadian Army units in Korea showing designations, period of service and commanding officers prepared in Directorate of History, March 1954.
410B25.063(D6)

13. Miscellaneous DPR photographs of 25th Canadian Infantry Brigade in Korea, 1953-1954.
112.3P1A(D3)

14. Statistical report on casualties(all types) of 25 Canadian Infantry Brigade in Korea up to 15 April 1954 supplied by Directorate of Records, 6 May 1954.
133.065(D651)

15. Photographs of 25 Canadian Infantry Brigade in Korea taken by Captain J.R.Madden, 1953(rolls 1-6).
43310B25.019(D25)

16. DPR photographs of visits of Rt. Hon. L.S.St.Laurent to 1st and 25th Canadian Infantry Brigades in Germany and Korea, 1954. 112.31A(D8)

17. Photographs of operations area of 25 Canadian Infantry Brigade in Korea taken for Captain J.R. Madden, 29 September 1953.
410B25.019(D26)

18. Photographs of 25 Canadian Infantry Brigade operations area in Korea, taken for Captain J.R.Madden, 29 September 1953.
410B25.019(D27)

19. Photograph of 25 Canadian Infantry Brigade operations area in Korea taken for Captain J.R. Madden, 29 September 1953(Pack 6).
410B25.019(D28)

20. Photograph of Lee-Enfield rifle presented to Queen's Own Regiment by Queen Victoria in 1864 being taken ashore in Korea by 2nd Battalion Queen's Own Regiment April 1954.
1452Q2.009(D2)

21. Photographs of 25 Canadian Infantry Brigade area in Korea received by Captain Madden from Major P.A.Mayer in 1954.
410B 25.012(D1)

22. Photographs taken by Captain J.R.Madden of 25 Canadian Infantry Brigade on Exercise "Shakeup", November 1953.
410B 25.019(D29)

23. Photographs of visit of Rt. Hon. L.St.Laurent to 25 Canadian Infantry Brigade taken by Captain J.R.Madden, 9 March 1954.
410B 25.019(D30)

24. Photographs of 25 Canadian Infantry Brigade taken by Captain J.R.Madden(colour negatives). Rolls 17 and 18.
410B 25.019(D31)

25. Photographs of operations area of 25 Canadian Infantry Brigade in Korea taken for Captain J.R.Madden, October 1953.
410B 25,019(D32)

26. Actual count of decorations of 25 Canadian Infantry Brigade in Korea, 1950-1953.
410B 25.065(D6)

27. Captions and colour plates of photographs of Korean war zone taken by Captain J.R.Madden, 30 July 1953(Roll 10).
681.029(D1)

28. Reference paper by Information Division of Department of External Affairs re Canada and the Korean Problem, December 1953-March 1954.
681.013(D60)

29. DPR tape recording of an interview with two cooks of 1 Royal Canadian Regiment in Korea(Tape No.1)
41B35.011(D2)

30. DPR tape recording(No.2) of interview by Bill Ross of Private A.S.Baker on Operation "Little Switch" in Korea.
410B25.011(D3)

31. DPR tape recording (no. 11) of Prime Minister's address to 25 Canadian Infantry Brigade at Maple Leaf Theatre, March 1954.
410B 25.011(D11)

32. List of Canadian Army units which have served in Korea, 1951-1954, prepared in Directorate of History, August 1954.
410B25.045(D1)

33. List of honours and awards of personnel of 25 Canadian Infantry Brigade in Korea, August 1954.
410B 25.0655(D8)

44. List of (a) Canadian Army units served in Korea (b) List of Canadian decorations in Korea (c) List of fatal Canadian casualties in Korea, prepared for Mr. Hugh Pond, August 1954.
HQC1453-6-2.

45. Photographs of 25 Canadian Infantry Brigade in Korea, Roll 20 taken by Captain J.R.Madden, 27 March 1954.
410B25.019(D33)

46. Photographs of 25 Canadian Infantry Brigade in Korea, Roll 21, taken by Captain J.R.Madden, 27-30 April 1954.
410B25.019(D324.

47. Indo-China notes 1954 by DMI: Part I. General situation, topography, military background: Part II. Notes on history of war and forces involved and military situation at time of cease fire: Part III. Comparative notes on armistice supervision in Korea, Kashmir and Palestine.
112.3M1012(D22)

48. "The Communist War in Prisoner of War Camps", a report on background of incidents among Communist prisoners of war in Korea by Headquarters, U.N. Command, 28 January 1953.
681.013(D62)

49. DPR photographs used in **Canadian Army Journal** article "Canada's Army in Korea, Part I".
112.3P1(D1404)

50. DPR(Army) press release(PN 72-55) 25 Canadian Infantry Brigade in Korea.
681.013(D69)

51. Roll of colour photographs with negatives of 25 Canadian Infantry Brigade area and activities in Korea.
410B25.009(D35)

52. Miscellaneous DPR photographs of 25 Canadian Infantry Brigade in Korea, 1950-1953.
681.009(D14)

53. Comments on Part IV of "Canada's Army in Korea" by Lieutenant- Colonel E.A.C.Amy, 23 January 1956.
681.013(D74).

54. Report on a visit to Korea to check performance of equipment in the field, May-June 1952 by Lieutenant-Colonel D.A.G. Waldock of Directorate of Armament Development.
115.32A1(D2)

55. Photographs of "The Hook" position in Korea, May 1953.
681.014(D4)

56. An annotated bibliography of publications in Western languages re Korea, August 1950.
681.005(D1)

57. Regimental history of the Norwegian Mobile Surgical Hospital in Korea, 1951-1954.
681.013(D75)

58. London **Times** book review on **Gallipoli** by Alan Moorehead and **From Pearl Harbour to Korea** by General C.A.Willoughby and John Chamberlain.
934.009(D156)

59. See also Confidential Index.

60. Photographs of 25 Canadian Field Historical Detachment taken on 21 August 1952.
410B25.009(D409)

61. Magazine article re President Rhee's visit to East coast troops - Korea - **Korean Survey**, page 13, Volume 6, January 1957.
956.009(D18)

62. Complete list of Canadian Army units which have served in Korea, giving dates of arrival and departure.
4120B 25.065(D11)

63. Statement of financial recoveries from Canadian Government(Korea) with supporting claims, March-June 1957.
410K.009(D3)

64. Armistice agreement Volume II Maps(Korea) received in Directorate of History, September 1958.
681.004(D1)

65. Booklet on Korea prepared for Canadian troops by Bureau of Current Affairs.
934.009(D373)

66. Extract from **The Nation**, 25 June 1960 - "The Case of Korea" "Our Falling Ramparts" by Alfred Crolts.
68P1.001(D2)

67. Reports on activities of 3 Transport Company, Royal Canadian Army Service Corps, in Korea, April-November 1954.
146.65T3(D1)

68. Extract from **The Legionnary** June 1962. A summary of events for the three services. World War II and Korea.

69. End of Second World War. Termination of war with Germany, 10 July 1951(in **Canada Gazette** 14 July 1951). Termination of war with Japan, 28 June 1952. Conclusion of war for army 30 September 1947(CAO 216-1, Issue 27 of 1947). Cease fire in Korea, 27 July 1953.

70. Copy of CAORE DOC 1-15-8 "Notes on Operational Experience in Korea" gathered by a member of DRB from time to time during the period December 1950-June 1952.
494.013(DB9)

71. Operation - Korea. Copies of transcripts of interviews with Colonel Stone and Brigadier Rockingham, and Brigadier Brodie.
6812.011(D3)

72. A paper received from DVA entitled "The Korean Operation of 1950-1953."
681.009(D27)

73. Booklet entitled "The Dedication of the Korea Book of Remembrance by the Governor-General of Canada".
100.009(D4)

74. Excerpt from British Parliamentary Debates - 5 series, 19 May-30 May 1953.
612.003(D1)

75. 1st Canadian Infantry Division file I450-1 Volume 1. "Historical Matters Generally" December 1954-September 1956, contains a history of Korea Operations, 1st Canadian Infantry Division, 1915-1955, 1st Brigade 1914-1954.
41001.009(D5)

76. Associate Deputy Minister National Defence, file 23-4."Canadian Forces, Korea General" containing correspondence on equipping and financial arrangements with U.S. and U.K. for 25 Canadian Infantry Brigade, October 1950 -June 1951.
509.05(D1)

77. List of files received from 1 Ground Liaison Group in December 1962.
142.99(D16)

78. 1 Ground Liaison Group file S 3-3-1 "65 CBGLS H.M.S. **Ocean**" Operations in Korea", 1 May-30 September 1952.

142.99(D17)

79. 1 Ground Liaison Group file 2390-1 "Operations - Naval aviation in Korea", 1 March 1950-22 October 1951.
142.99(D20)

80. 1 Ground Liaison Group file 3-3-1 "63 CBGIS H.M.S. **Theseus** - Operations in Korea", 14 August 1950-31 March 1951.
142.99(D21).

81. 1 Ground Liaison Group file 3-3-1 "67 18 March-30 September 1951.
142.99(D22).

82. 1 Ground Liaison Group file 3-3-1 "65 CBGLS H.M.S. **Triumph** - Operations in Korea", 1 June-30 September 1950.
142.99(D23).

83. 1 Ground Liaison Group file 3-3-1 "67 CBGIS, H.M.S. **Glory** -Operations in Korea", 1 June-30 April 1952.
142.99(D24).

84. 1 Ground Liaison Group file S3-3-1 "63 CBGLS H.M.S. **Glory** - Operations in Korea", 6 November 1952- 6 July 1953.
142.99(D25).

85. 1 Ground Liaison Group file ACLS/1-4-2 Army/Air operations - CBGLS Bulletins, April 1946-December 1954.
142.99(D28)

86. Korea - Prisoners of war. Press releases on Squadron Leader Andy Mackenzie captured by Communists during mission over Korea.
189.009(D1)

87. Korea - Prisoners of war. Copy of narrative by Major J.H.B. George, General Staff Officer II, HQ Saskatchewan Area, relating capture of a Chinese soldier in Korea.
410B 25,001(D1)

88 Power - Commander of 25 Canadian Infantry Brigade, Copy E.C. 4973, 17 October 1950 defining power of Commander, 25 Canadian Infantry Brigade, and/or his representative. From DM's file 23-3(Ross paper).
111.21.01(D7)

89. Korean airlift - Canadian Pacific Airlines. Copies of correspondence from DM's files on cost of Korean airlift.
111.21.01(D10)

90. Defence Appropriation Act - 1950. From D.M.(Mr. A.Ross) file from 15 September-17 November 1950 containing copy of Defence Appropriation Act, 15 September 1950.
111.21.01(D20)

91. Capitation Rates Korea - Canadian Army file from DM(Mr. Ross) on capitation rates for Canadian Army in Korea from December 1950-3 July 1951.
111.21.01(D21)

92. Capitation Rates U.S.A./Canadian Army. File from DM(Mr. A.Ross)on capitation rates U.S.A. for Canadian Army in Fort Lewis; maintenance costs from 3 October 1950-13 July 1951.
111.21.01(D25)

93. Canadian Army units who served in Korea. List of Canadian Army units who served in Korea. Letter HWTS 200l-122/1 Vol. 7(DMO&P 3B), 6 August 1957(BDF 31-4 Vol. 2).
112.3M2.005(D1)

94. Expression of appreciation to Australian Military Authorities MSG Ops 139, 29 June 1956, sent by CGS in appreciation of work done by Australian Military Authorities in non-operational control and administrative support of Commonwealth contingent - Korea.
112.3M2.005(D105)

95. Liaison Officer - Canadian Section Headquarters 1 Commonwealth Division -replacement. Copy of brief HQWTS 2001-122/1 Vol.(DMO&P 1B), 23 September 1955, commenting on replacement of Liaison Officer.

96. Commander-in-Chief, British Commonwealth Forces, Korea -Position. Copy of letter HQWWTS 2001-122/1 Vol. 6, 29 June 1956, discussing position of Commander-in-Chief, British Commonwealth Forces, Korea. From DMO&P BDF 31-4 Vol. 2.
1122.3M2.1(D3)

97. 27th British Commonwealth Division. Copies of War Diary of 27th British Commonwealth Division for months of February, March and April 1951. Received from War Office.
952.008(D1)

98. Photographs. 35 mm photographs and negatives-photographs of Korea and AAGOR(during Second World War?).
112.3PI.009(D19)

99. Photographs. Miscellaneous photographs of Canadian Army Special Force Korean visit of Field Marshal Alexander of Tunis, Lieutenant-General Guy Simonds, Hon. Brooke Claxton. Photographs from DPR as above.
112.3P1.009(D21)

100. Liaison letters - CRE 1 Commonwealth Division. 10 volumes of CRE 1 Commonwealth Division Liaison letters for period 28 July 1951-31 July 1954. Passed to Directorate of History by CE office, July 1963. Index of contents(18 volumes).
112.3E1.003(D1)

101. The inevitable step - Editorial. Photocopy of editorial published in the Ottawa **Evening Journal**, 28

July 1950, on Canada's obligations to the U.N. following Korean Communist occupation of South Korea
956.009(D41)

102. Photographs. DPR photographs of Senior officers serving with Canadian Army in Korea, Prime Minister L. St. Laurent and American officers.
12.3P1.009(D30)

103. Honours and awards. List of personnel who received awards and/or foreign decorations during Korean Campaign. Prepared in Hist 1 - September 1963.
112.3P1.009(D35)

104. CGS Office, CGS BDF 15-1/Far East Vol. 3 from 8 January-30 December 1953. Organization of Headquarters, CBU Far East, SDD letter no. 53/15; Canadian Commonwealth Z Detachments British Commonwealth Forces Korea - SDF 1 Letter no. 53/15; Exchange of prisoners of war; Trials of prisoners of war; Korea, Defence Committee meeting-92nd, Security of Troop Movements - Korea, Post-Armistice Plans; Military Implications U.N./R.O.K. as result of Armistice negotiationss.
112.09(D98)

105. Interview with Major-General J.V.Allard. Paper on interview with Major-General J.V.Allard by Lieutenant-Colonel H.F.Wood on 17 December 1963. General Allard was commenting on the draft chapters of the Korean War History covering his period as Commander of 25th Canadian Infantry Brigade.
112.3H1.001(D78)

106. Flashbacks. Photograph used with Flashback no. 42, Cease fire in Korea, July 1953 and Volume XVII no. 4 - 1963, showing 3rd Battalion Royal Canadian Regiment clearing out, July 1953.
112.3P1(D1445)

107. Copy of message from Secretary of State for External Affairs to Canadian High Commissioner for External Affairs, Ottawa, 28 August 1950, on proposal for a Commonwealth Division to fight in Korea. Passed to Hist 1 by DD Hist, 3 March 1964.

109. Photographs - Korea. Coloured and Black and White transparencies of the Korean War. Passed to Hist.1 by DD Hist, March 1964.
112.3H1.009(D67)

110. Statistics - Korean War. Miscellaneous statistical papers on Korean War, passed to Hist. 1 by DD Hist, March 1964; Rejection statistics; Capitation rates, Department of National Defence Appropriations, 1945-1955, United Kingdom Brigade Group for dispatch to Korea, Special Force recruiting, 8-9 August 1950.
112.3H1.0009(D68)

111. Photograph of visitors at 25th Canadian Infantry Brigade Headquarters in Korea, 1951. Photograph used in **Canadian Army Journal**, Flashback no. 43, **Canadian Army Journal** Issue no. 3, 1963.
112.3P1.009(D39)

112. Honours and awards - Korea. Draft copy of list of personnel who received awards during the Korean Campaign. Prepared in Directorate of History, September 1963. Compiled from CAO. To be used as Appendix to Official history of Korean War.
112.3H1.009(D7)

113. History of Royal Canadian Air Force. Paper "Milestones in the Development of Canada's Air Power" - a chronological account of the development of the Royal Canadian Air Force. Received from Air Historian, 21 April 1964.
189.009(D2)

114. History of the Royal Canadian Air Force. A short history of the Royal Canadian Air Force prepared for 40th Anniversary of the Royal Canadian Air Force (1924-1964). Received from Air Historian, 21 April 1964.
189.001(D1)

115. History of the Royal Canadian Navy. Brief digest of the History of the Royal Canadian Navy, prepared by Naval Historian, April 1964.
120.003(D4)

116. History of the Canadian Army, Paper "A Brief History of the Canadian Army" covering period from early French regime to present day. Paper prepared in Department of History by Mrs. A.S. Sorby M.B.E., April 1964.
112.3H.009(D72)

117. Patches. Sample cloth patches of British Commonwealth Division in Korea and S.H.A.P.E. in Paris.
112.3H1.009(DF73)

118. Notes prepared by Lieutenant-Colonel H.F.Wood, after interview with Major-General J.M.Rockingham in Montreal - March 1960, regarding events of 1950, Organization of Special Force, Korean War.
112.3H1.009(D73)

119. **Ottawa Journal**. Press clipping - Article in **Ottawa Journal** 13 August 1964 "Canadian Troops service in 10 World 'Hot Spots'" - Korea - Vietnam - Laos - Cambodia - Egypt - Israel - Yemen - Kashmir - Cyprus - N.A.T.O. - U.N.O.
956.009(D44)

120. Papers on Administration in Korea; Logistic Support 25th Canadian Infantry Brigade; Letter from Canadian Joint Staff Washington to Directorate of History, 25 July 1955, on Administration in Korea; Movement 25th Canadian Infantry Brigade to Far East; Administrative Instructions and Command 25th Canadian Infantry Brigade and Command CMMFE; Paper on Canadian Defence Policy. Passed to Hist. 1 by Acting Director, September 1964.

112.3H1.009(D113)

121. A paper entitled "Japan's Record" by Henry H.Douglas. The paper is not dated, it appears to have been written before Japan's entry into the Second World War. Passed to Historical Section by Lieutenant Noble, September 1964.
958.001(D4)

122. A chronology of the United Nations Operation - Korea, 25 June 1950 - April 1956. Prepared in Directorate of History, 4 April 1956. Passed to Hist. 1 by DD Hist. November 1964.
681.013(D91)

123. Statistics on battle casualties, Royal 22e Regiment, Second World War and Korea. Information supplied by Miss Dignard of War Service Records on 9 December 1964.
112.3H1.009(D125)

124. Paper prepared in Hist 1 by Mrs. A.Sorby, January 1965, on French-Canadian participation in War.
112.3H1.003(D22)

125. Developments in North East Korea - July 1935. Paper prepared by K.P.Kirkwood, Canadian Legation, Tokyo, Japan, 6 August 1935. Received from IP 3-2, June 1965.
112.3M12.003(D13)

126. 1st Manuscript Draft, Official History of the Canadian Army in the Korean War. Colonel Stacey's comments. Received from DD Hist, 3 May 1965.
112.3H1.009(D146)

127. Draft copy - Official History of the Canadian Army in the Korean War, Chapters IX to XVII(2 volumes). Received from DD Hist, 3 May 1965.
112.3H1.009(D147)

128. U.S .detailed comments - incorporated in revised draft - Official History of Canadian Army in the Korean War - Chapters I to IV. Received from DD Hist, 3 May 1965.
112.3H1.009(D148)

129. Colonel Stacey's comments - Official History of the Canadian Army in the Korean War - Chapters I to IV. Received from DD Hist, 3 May 1965.
112.3H1 009(D149)

130. Colonel Stacey's comments - References to Official History of the Canadian Army in the Korean War. Received from DD Hist, 3 May 1965.
112.3H1.009(D150)

131. Chronology of formation, redesignations, locations and moves of 1st, 2nd and 3rd Battalions of the Royal Canadian Regiment. Prepared by Sergeant Azar, War Diary Section, June 1965.
112.3H1.009(D157)

133. Historical Report no. 4, 22 October 1965, prepared by Lieutenant J.L.Granatstein: Canada and Peacekeeping operations, Copies no. 2, 3, and 4. Subjects covered: Introduction; Canada and the League of Nations; The Second World War; Creation of the United Nations Organization; Early Attempts to Implement the Charter; The United Nations Guard Force; UNTSO; U.N.M.O.G.I.P. and U.N.I.P.O.M.; Korea and"Uniting for Peace"; Intercommunications, U.N.E.F.; U.N.O.G.I.L.; U.N.O.C. ; U.N.T.E.A.; and U.N.Y.T.O.M.; U.N.F.I.CYP.; International Supervisory Commissions. (no file cited)

134. Narrative entitled "History and Role of Dietitians in the Canadian Army" Cowritten by Major J.Clarke of Department of Food Services and Captain Dorothy M.Dobson(retired). Received February 1966. Paper covers period from First World War to Integration of Canadian Armed Forces in 1964.
959.001(D1)

135. Photocopy of article published in Survival VI(July-August 1964) by Rt. Hon. Lester B.Pearson "Keeping the Peace". Passed to D Hist by Lieutenant J.L.Granatstein, September 1965.
958.009(D37)

136. Photocopy of article published in **International Affairs**, Vol. 40, no. 2, April 1964. "Peace-keeping and the United Nations, the Broader View", by The Hon. Paul Martin. Passed to D. Hist by Lieutenant J.L.Granatstein.
958.009(D28)

137. Envelope containing Korean War photographs not used for the Official History.
112.3Hi.009(D228)

138. DMO&P BDF 8-4 for period 18 April 1955-19 December 1961, containing intelligence correspondence relating to the Canadian Army, Korea.
112.3M2.005(D3)

139. Report by Lieutenant-Colonel D.S.F. Bult-Francis on liaison visit to Far Eastern Theatre, 22 March -6 June 1952.
410B25.093(D1)

140. Account of interview with Major J.M.R.Gendron and Major W.G.Harris re administration of 25 Canadian Reinforcement Group in Korea by Captain F.R.McGuire, 3 September 1952.
410B25.056(D1)

141. Programme for visit of Lieutenant-General G.G.Simmonds, Chief of Staff, Canadian Army to Korea, 22-25 January 1952.
410B25.019(DF13)

142. Programme of visit of Hon. Brooke Claxton, MND to Korea, 31 December 1951-3 January 1952.
410B 25.019(D14)

143. Training syllabus of 25th Canadian Infantry Brigade Junior N.C.O.'s School in Korea, April 1952.
410B25.019(D17)

144. Memorandum of interview given by AG on his return from Korea, 26 April 1953.
113.003(D1)

145. Summary of activities of 25th Canadian Infantry Brigade August 1950-June 1952, prepared by History Officer, 25th Canadian Infantry Brigade at request of Republic of Korea Ministry of National Defence(Part I).
410B25.013(D58)

146. Map and information re roads in 1 Commonwealth Division in Korea supplied on 20 December 1952 by Captain D.G.Raschen, IORE Commonwealth Division(Hist 9-24-4-2, 21 December 1952).
681.074(D1)

147. Photograph of operations area of 25th Canadian Infantry Brigade in Korea, 26 June 1952, received from Captain F.R.McGuire, 19 August 1952.
410B25.014(D1)

148. Photographs of operations area of 25th Canadian Infantry Brigade 26 June 1952, received from Captain F.R.McGuire, 18 August 1952.
410B25.014(D2)

149. Photographs of Operations area of 25th Canadian Infantry Brigade August-October 1952, received from Captain F.R.McGuire, January 1953.
410.B25.014(D3)

150. Panoramic photographs and traces of Kapyong area in Korea taken for Captain J.R.Madden, 29 September 1953.
681.019(D2)

151. 1 Commonwealth Division History of Korean War received from Captain J.R.Madden, 27 September 1954.
410B25.013(D79)

152. Interim report on activities of U.N. Command Military Armistice Commission in Korea, 23 June-27 July 1953, received from Captain J.R.Madden, 16 March 1954.
61.013(D51)

153. U.N. Command, Military Armistice Commission report on activities in September and October 1953, received from Captain J.R.Madden, 25 March 1954.
681.013(D52)

154. U.N. Command Military Armistice Commission report for November 1953, received from Captain J.R.Madden, 30 March 1954.
681.013(D53)

155. Statistics on issues and wastages of clothing in 25th Canadian Infantry Brigade in Korea, June 1951-March 1954, received from Captain J.R.Madden, 7 June 1954.
410B25.085(D1)

156. Marked map of area 6528 II NW in Korea, showing positions of 25th Canadian Infantry Brigade(undated).
410B25.009(D9)

157. Summary of experiences of 3rd Battalion Royal Canadian Regiment in Korea, 1953-1954, by Lieutenant-Colonel K.L.Campbell.
145.2R13019(D1)

158. "25th Canadian Infantry Brigade in Korea", 27 July 1953-23 May 1954, prepared by Captain J.R.Madden, September 1954.
410B25.013(D86)

159. Summary of activities of 25th Canadian Infantry Brigade, July 1952-May 1953, prepared by History Section, Army Headquarters, at request of Republic of Korea Ministry of National Defence(Part 2).
410B25.013(D59)

160. Publication "Enemy Frontline Positions in Korea" prepared by Headquarters 8th U.S. Army and received from Captain J.R.Madden, 25 September 1953.
681.023(D18)

161. Climatological study of Korea for the autumn season, September-November 1953, received from Captain J.R.Madden, 5 October 1953.
681.023(D19)

162. Notes prepared by 1 Commonwealth Division on ways to defeat the Korean winter, received from Brigadier J.V.Allard, Commander, 25th Canadian Infantry Brigade, 28 October 1953.
681.023(D21)

163. Air photographs of Kapyong area in Korea taken for Captain J.R.Madden, also two rolls of film used in takes for photographs as well as Photographic Reconnaissance report.
681.014(D2)

164. Account of 2nd Battalion, Princess Patricia's Canadian Light Infantry action in Kapyong area in Korea, 23 -26 April 1951, by Captain A.P.McKenzie, 26 November 1954.
145.2P7013(D5)

165. Address by Major-General H.Murray and Army Headquarters officers on 16 December 1954, re operations and morale of 1 Commonwealth Division in Korea, with comments by Captain F.R.McGuire and Major F.W.Thomas.
681.011(D2)

166. Report on operations in Korea, April 1953-April 1954, by 4th Battalion, Royal Canadian Horse Artillery.

410B25.0123(D87)

167. Report on postal operations for fiscal year 1953/1954 by Captain F.T.Burgess of Canadian Postal Unit, 10 May 1954.
410B25.013(D88)

168. Personal recollections of the field works of Wyoming, Jamestown and Kansas lines in Korea, prepared by Captain J.R.Madden, September 1954.
681.011(D1)

169. Statistics on breakdown of sorties flown by 1903 Air OP Flight in Korea in January and May 1953.
681.015(D2)

170. Extracts from War Diaries of 27th Commonwealth Brigade and 1st Battalion Kings Own Scottish Borderers for April 1953 re action at Kapyong River received from CAHLO.
681.015(D2)

171. Marked map of troop dispositions on demarcation line in Korea, 1954.
681.024(D2)

172. Statistics on number of artillery and mortar rounds received in 9 U.S. Corps area in Korea, January-July 1953.
681.085(D1)

173. Report on visit to Korea and Japan by Lieutenant-Colonel D.S.Bult-Francis, 22 March-6 June 1952.
410B25.019(D244)

174. Terms of reference of Major J.P.Beer, Canadian representative on United Nations Military Armistice Commission Korea, 13 January 1954.
681.0165(D12)

175. Report on visit to Korea, Canadian Base Units and Kobe Area, 1-15 January 1955 by DMO&P.
681.013(D65)

176. Correspondence and report by Brigadier J.V.Allard on 25th Canadian Infantry Brigade requirements for extra wireless sets in Korea, July 1953-October 1954.
410B 25,082(D1)

177. 1 CAORT Memorandum no. 5 "Effects of three flood producing rains on military operations in Korea" by Major J.R.Stafford, 11 May 1954.
681.013(D66)

178. Summary of flame actions experienced by 8 U.S. Army in Korea, including addenda on the Hush Flare, Napalm Satchel Charge, Bunker Bomb, Napalm Mine, July 1952-February 1953.
681.013(D67)

179. Miscellaneous papers concerning reduction and withdrawal of Canadian troops from Korea.
112.1.009(D40)

180. Correspondence reference behaviour of Canadian troops in Korea.
112.1(D157)

181. Intelligence Review. Canadian Forces participation in International organizations prepared by DMI.
020.023(D1)

182. British Commonwealth missing in action and prisoner of war lists, Korea, 1 July 1953.
112.3M2.003(D28)

Korea - 1st Commonwealth Divisional Artillery.

1. Extract from **Journal of Royal Artillery**, Vol. LXXX(80) on a short history of 1st Commonwealth Divisional Artillery, including Chinese artillery tactics and certain technical aspects by Brigadier Pike, CRA, 1st Commonwealth Division(Attached are comments by Captain J.D.Choron, Royal Canadian Artillery)
956.009(D207)

Korea - Battle honours.

1. Battle honours and memorials. CALE file 1075-1 on Battle Honours and Memorials. Period 7 November 1952-17 January 1958.
493.009(D159)

Korea - Casualties.

1. Resume of Canadian casualties in Korea, 1951.
112.3H1.009(D309)

Korea - Cease-fire.

1. Korean War. Statistics on commencement of hostilities, cease-fire, dates of qualifying service for pensions Navy - Army - Air Force. Information obtained from Superannuation Branch, Department of Finance- by Mrs. Sorby(Hist 1).
112.3H1.009(D40)

Korea - Command and Staff Appointments.

1. Command and Staff Appointments. List of Command and Staff appointments, Korea, period May 1951-1955. Prepared in Directorate of History, by Sergeant Azar, June 1964.
112.3H1.009(D60)

Korea - Commencement of Hostilities.

1. Korean War. Statistics on commencement of hostilities, cease-fire, dates of qualifying service for pensions Navy - Army - Air Force. Information obtained from Superannuation Branch, Department of Finance- by Mrs. Sorby(Hist 1).
112.3H1.009(D40)

Korea - Counter Bombardment and Chinese Artillery.

2. Notes **Journal of Royal Artillery**, volume 80, 1953 on counter bombardment in Korea by Major E.V.Thomas, Royal Artillery, together with additional notes on Chinese gun emplacements.
956.009(D208)

"Korea in War, July 1951-June 1952".

1. Translation of the section on Canada in the South Korean publication "Korea in War July 1951-June 1952", received from Captain J.R.Madden, 16 July 1953.
410B25.013(D54)

Korea - Military Operations.

1. Photocopy of extract from CAMT 1-36, Canadian Army Manual of Staff Procedures - 1958 - Volume 1. Military writing, designation of World Wars and Military Operations.
112.3H1.009(D235)

Korea - Position of Commander-in-Chief, British Commonwealth Forces, Korea.

1. Commander-in-Chief - Position. Copy of letter HQTS 2001-122/1 Volume 6., 29 June 1956, discussing position of Commander-in- Chief, British Commonwealth Forces, Korea. From DMO&P BDF 31-4 Vol. 2.
112.3M2.1(D3)

Korea - Royal Canadian Air Force Pilots.

1. List of Royal Canadian Air Force pilots who served with U.S. formations in Korea.
112.3H1.009(D273)

Korea - Royal Canadian Air Force Sabre Pilots with United States Air Force.

1. Photographs, correspondence etc. concerning Royal Canadian Air Force pilots who served in Korea with United States Air Force.
181.003(D5423)

Korea - United Nations Expeditionary Force.

1. Canadian Participation- U.N. Peacekeeping operations. Return on cost of Canadian Participation in Peacekeeping operation, 1948-1964.
112.3H1.009(D109)

Korea - U.S. Air Reconnaissance - Royal Canadian Air Force.

1. Royal Canadian Air Force file - Report on visit to inspect United States Air Force Photographic Reconnaissance Organizations in Japan and Korea to compare with Royal Canadian Air Force requirements, May 1952.
181.009(D4264)

Korean Armistice.

2. Temporary agreement supplementary to Korean Armistice Agreement.
Korean Armistice Agreement Volume 1.
Text of Agreement.
92nd Supplement to summary of events Military Armistice Conference at Panmunjon, Korea, 14-20 June 1953.
25 Canadian Infantry Brigade instructions re control of movement of military stores to and after armistice from Korea.

3. Armistice Agreement Volume II(Korea) received in Directorate of History, September 1958.
681.004(D1)

Korean Armistice.

1. Marked map of troop dispositions on demarcation line in Korea, 1954.
681.024(D2)

2. 1 Commonwealth Division instructions and plans for Operation "Iceland"(reorganization on armistice, March-September 1952).
410B24,019(D86)

3. Correspondence, orders, instructions, reports, etc. re reorganization and administration of 25 Canadian Infantry Brigade after Armistice in Korea, June-August 1953 (2) Detailed memorandum on reorganization of Canadian Forces in Far East as result of an Armistice, June 1953. (3) Korean Armistice - Text of Agreement.
410B25.019(D107)41

Korean Army.

1. Questionnaire re use of KATUSA's(Korean Augmentation Troops)

KATCOM(Korean Augmentation Troops).

1. Central Registry file S2715-42/1787. Personnel employment - general - Korean Army - KATCOM, July 1952-June 1953
111.41(14)

2. Correspondence, reports, instructions, etc. re integration and administration of Korean Augmentation Troops(KATCOM) into 1 Commonwealth Division, February 1953-August 1954.
410B25.019(D245)

3. Orders, instructions and reports on organization and administration of KATCOM in 25 Canadian Infantry Brigade, February 1953-August 1954.
410B25.019(D267)

Korean Campaign.

1. Final Report of Battles Nomenclature Committee re Names of battles during Australian Campaign in South West Pacific and New Zealand Campaign in South

West Pacific, 1942-1944, and Korean Campaign, 1950-1953.
952.013(D133)

2. Canadian Army Orders, D Hist Suggestions, etc., re Korean Campaign Battle Honours for Canadian Army, 1958.
410.B25.019(D315)

Korean Citations.

1. Citations for honours and awards-members of 25 Canadian Infantry Brigade in Korea War received from Honours and Awards Section, 5 March 1954.
410B25.063(D3)

2. Nominal Roll of officers' citations for honours and awards from 25 Canadian Infantry Brigade up to December 1953.
410B25.063(D4)

3. Nominal Roll of men's citations for honours and awards from 25 Canadian Infantry Brigade up to December 1953.
410B25.063(D5)

Korean Climate

1. Notes prepared by 1 Commonwealth Division on ways-defeat the Korean winter, received from Brigadier J.V.Allard, Commander, 25th Canadian Infantry Brigade, 28 October 1953.
681.023(D21)

2. Studies and reports on Korean weather and climate, 1952-1954.
419.3F Sqn(D12)

Korean Farming Zones.

1. Instructions and traces re limits of Korean farming areas in forward zone of 25 Canadian Infantry Brigade, July 1954.
410B25.019(D163)

2. Correspondence and instructions, orders, reports etc. re Civil Affairs status of Korean farming areas inside demilitarized zone, March-September 1954.
410B25.019(D268)

"Korean Journey".

1. "Korean Journey" Broadcast speech by Hon. Brooke Claxton, MND on his visit to Korea and 25 Canadian Infantry Brigade, 20 January 1952.
111.2(D1)

2. "Korean Journey" Broadcast of Hon. Brooke Claxton on his first visit to Korea, 20 January 1953.
410B25.019(D244)

Korean Labour.

1. Correspondence, instructions and returns re Korean indigenous labour used by 25 Canadian Infantry Brigade, February-November 1954.
410B 25.019(D270)

Korean Medal.

1. Photograph of U.N. medal for Korea.
681.009(D22)

2. Photographs of Korean Medal.
6891.009(D23)

Korean Operations.

1. Enemy documents - Korean Operations Copy nos. 80,164, 86, 136, and Interrogation Report Copy no. 78.
681.023(D25)

Korean Operations - Royal Canadian Air Force.

1. Booklet - Directorate of Air Intelligence, Air Force Headquarters. Royal Canadian Air Force Intelligence Summary for June 1951 - deals particularly with Korean War.
181.003(D32235)

Korean Personnel.

1. Central Registry file S2715-42/1787. Personnel employment - general - Korean Army - KATCOM, July 1952-June 1953.
111.41(14)

Korean Statistics.

1. Korean statistics. Total number of Canadians who served in Far East up to 27 July 1953: 21,940. Peak Canadian strength in Far East: 8123. Number of Canadians serving on 27 July 1953: 7134. Statement of Special Force enlistments, showing those with Far East Service and Canadian Army active force personnel with Far East service by Province of enlistment. Statistical report on Battle Casualties(Far East) as of 4 February 1955.
133.(D4)

Korean War-Diaries.

1. List of War Diaries passed to PARC, April 1968. Units of United Nations Expeditionary Force and The Congo, United Nations in Korea, and N.A.T.O.
1122.3H1.008(D60)

Korean Weather.
1. Studies and reports on Korean weather and climate, 1952-1954.
419.3FSqn(D12)

Lines of Communication - Korea.

Canadian share in Commonwealth Base and Line of Communication organization in Japan and Korea. Prepared by Major H,W.Thomas for Brigadier

C.N.Barclay, 1954.
HQC 1454-121/1

Laos.

2. **Ottawa Journal**. Press clipping -article in **Ottawa Journal**, 13 August 1964. "Canadian troops serve in 10 World 'Hot Spots" - Korea-Vietnam - Laos - Cambodia - Egypt - Israel - Yemen - Kashmir - Cyprus - NATO - UNO.
956.009(D44)

3. Copy of text of Geneva Conference - Indo-China, Agreement on the cessation of hostilities in Viet-Nam, 1954. Joint Commission and International Commission for Supervision and Control in Viet-Nam; Agreement on Cessation of Hostilities in Laos; Agreement for the Cessation of Hostilities in Cambodia, 1954, Received from External Affairs, September 1965.
653.003(D9)

6. Paper by John W.Holmes, "Peacekeeping in Asia", prepared for delivery to the Institute of Strategic Studies, Oxford, September 1964. Received from Lieutenant Colonel R.B.Tackaberry, D Ops, 11 February 1966.
958.009(D24)

7. Newspaper clipping - **The Gagetown Gazette** edition 2 February 1967 and photographs on Canadians serving in Laos and Vietnam.
956.009(D101)

8. Intelligence Review. Canadian Forces Participation in International Organizations, prepared by DMI
020.023(D1)

Laos(Secret)

1. Establishments of Canadian Military Truce Teams for Viet Nam, Cambodia and Laos, with effect from 26 August 1954, prepared by AHQ, 30 September 1954.
410.045(D2)

2. DMO&P file SG1750-1930/181 volume 9. Military Reports and Returns Canadian delegations Laos, 1 June 1963 - 4 August 1964.
112.3M2.009(D272)

3. DMO&P S2001-1980/181 volume 6 - Organization and Administration Military Components - Canadian delegations- Laos, 2 May 1963 -10 July 1964. Messages from External Affairs on situation in Laos.
112.3M2.009(D277)
Liaison letters - Korea.

1. ADMS 1 Commonwealth Division Liaison Letter, March 1953, received from Captain J.R.Madden, 24 December 1953.
681.013(D46)

Malaya.

1. See Singapore

840.013(D2)

2. Operations and Malaya Command 8 December 1941-15 February 1942 by Lieutenant General A.E.Percival former GOC Malaya, supplement to **London Gazette**, 20 February 1948(38215).
002.011(D36)

3. Report on air operations during campaigns in Malaya and Netherlands East Indies, 8 December 1941-12 March 1942, by Air Vice Marshal Sir Paul Maltby, Assistant Air Officer Command Far East Command, R.A.F. Supplement to **London Gazette,** 20 February 1948.
002.0111(D38)

4. #19 Singapore.
952-013(D94)

5. #8 Singapore.

6. AT & I Section S.W.P.A. Translation of Japanese reports of naval operations in area of Hawaii-Malaya, 27 March 1943.
982.009(D114)

7. AT & I Section S.W.P.A. Translation of miscellaneous records of Japanese Southern Expeditionary Force in Malaya and the Philippines, 10 April 1943.
982.009(D117)

9. British policy, situation reports and bulletins from Far East (Malaya Command, etc), 2 January-12 February 1942.
314.009(D283)

11. Photos of Malayan roads prepared by Inter Service Topographical Section, United Kingdom(1945).
181-003(O65)

12. Interservice Topographical Department, Maps and plans of Malaya.
181.009(D450)

13. Photos illustrating Malayan resources prepared by Interservice Topographical Department, 1945.
181.009(D462)

14. Interservice Topographical Department report June 1945. Coast, ports, resources and inland towns, Malaya(5 volumes).
181.009(D465)

15. Interservice Topographical Department report, May 1945. Road communications in Malaya, July 1945, Signals, history, geography and medical facilities(3 volumes).
181.009(D464)

16. Interservice Topographical Department. Volume of photos on Malaya.
181.009(D466)

17. Air Command South East Asia Weekly Intelligence Summaries no. 65-74(11 February-29 April 1945) Operations in Burma, Malaya, Indochina and Thailand. Japanese aircraft and operations.
181.003(D909)

18. Interservice Topographical Department. Report on Malaya, April-August 1944.
181.009(D467)

20. Provisional airfield list. South East Asia(Burma, French Indo-China, Malaya, Thailand), prepared in Office of Assistant Chief of Staff, Intelligence, Washington, D.C. by combined personnel of U.S. and British services. Enemy airfield information report no. 3, 25 July 1944.
181.009(D813)

Malaya-air operations in.

1. Despatch on operations against the Japanese by the Strategic Air Force(EAC) from January-26 June 1944.
181.003(D1003)

Malaya-enemy aircraft.

1. List of airfields and seaplane stations in enemy occupied Malaya, prepared in offices of Assistant Chief of Staff Intelligence, Washington D.C. by combined personnel of U.S. and British services, 31 May 1945.
181.009(D776)

Malaya-general.

1. Report on Malaya prepared by U.K., Interservice Topographical Department. August 1945, dealing with language, history, geology, topography, resources, medical problems, railways, roads, waterways, signal communication, ports and towns.
181.009(D35)

Military Component Canadian delegation - Cambodia.

1. DMO&P file SG-1750-1930/57 volume 6. Military Reports and Returns Canadian delegations - Cambodia, 20 June 1957 - 16 March 1964.
112.3M2.009(D270)

Military Component Canadian delegation - Indo-China.

1. Impressions of the work of the Canadian delegation, Indo-China. Account by Brigadier R.M.Bishop, O.B.E. E.D., given to a narrator, Historical Section(G.S.)AHQ, 12 January 1959.
685.003(D1)

2. Terms of service - Military Component Canadian delegation Indo-China - Letters and despatches received from the Department of External Affairs.
685.002(D1)

3. DMO&P file SDG1750-1930/114 volume 13. Reports and Returns Military Components Canadian delegations Indo-China, 27 April 1963-12 November 1964.
112.3M2.009(D271)

4. DMO&P file S2001-1930/114 volume 3. Organization and Administration - Military Components - Canadian delegation - Indo-China Messages and External Affairs.
112.3M2.009(D275)

5. Situation Reports, Policy Decisions, Conference minutes, Team Close Out orders. Alleged North attack on Police Post, 2 March 1966, Operations Committee decisions, copy of 11th interim report on Cambodia, 1 January -31 December 1964.
685.003(D3)

Military Component Canadian delegation - Laos.

1. DMO&P file SDG1750-1930/181 volume 9 - Military Reports and Returns Canadian delegations Laos, 1 June 1963-5 August 1964.
112.3M2.009(D272)

2. DMO&P file SG1750-1930/181 volume 9. Military Reports and Returns Canadian delegations Laos, 1 June 1963 - 4 August 1964.
112.3M2.009(D272)

3. DMO&P S2001-1980/181 volume 6 - Organization and Administration Military Components - Canadian delegations, Laos, 2 May 1963 -10 July 1964. Messages from External Affairs on situation in Laos.
112.3M2.009(D277)

Mission - Indo-China.

1. DMO&P file S2001-1930/114 volume 3. Organization and Administration - Military Components - Canadian delegation - Indo-China Messages - External Affairs.
112.3M2.009(D275)

Morale - Enemy(Korea)

1. Intelligence reports on enemy morale in Korea, 1951-1953.
410B25.019(D178)

Navy, China.

1. Joint U.S. Army/Navy Intelligence study of China South Coast, March 1945. Chapter 1. Brief, Chapter II. Military Geography, Chapter III Oceanography, Chapter IV. Coast and Landing Beaches, Chapter V. Climate and Weather, Chapter VI. Port facilities, Chapter VII Transport and Telecommunication, Chapter VIII. Cities and Towns, Chapter IX . Resources and Trade, Chapter XI. Navy, Chapter XIV. Air facilities, Chapter XV. Gazetteer.
112.3M1012(D23)
Notes on Korean fighting.

1. Notes on fighting in Korea - Bulletins 2-(current), 19 September 1950- (current) by DMI.
112.3M1023(D13)

2. Notes on fighting in Korea, no. 2, August 1950- no. 6, 22 January 1951.
112.3M2(D437)

Occupation of Japan.

1. Order of Battle of Commonwealth Occupation Forces in Japan as of 19 July 1947.
112.3M2(D184)

2. Letter from Australian Department of Defence re reorganization of British Commonwealth Forces Korea base facilities because of rundown of Occupation Forces Japan, February 1952
681.046(D1)

Official History - Korea.

7. War Diary - HQ 28th British Commonwealth Brigade War Diary, HQ 28th British Commonwealth Brigade, April and May 1951(Kept in safe).
112.3HI.008(D4)

8. War Diary -Main HQ British Commonwealth Korean Base. War Diary of Main HQ British Commonwealth Korean Base. Months of October-December 1950.
112.3HI.008(D4)

Operation Institutions - 8th U.S. Army(Korea)

1. Operation Orders, instructions and reports of 8th U.S. Army in Korea, 1951(25 CIB 1-1-1).
410B25019(D9)

Operation Reports - Korean War.

1. G3 Operations Reports U.N. Command, no. 133, 4 November 1950-no. 615, 22 February 1952, received from DMI, 29 April 1952.
681.013(D7)

2. G2 Operations Reports U.N. Command no. 3035, 31 December-current, received from DMI, 15 May 1952.
681.013(D8)

Operation Reports - U.S. Formations - Korea.

1. Operational Reports of 3 U.S. Infantry Division, 7 U.S. Cavalry Regiment, 65 and 24 U.S. Infantry regiments in Korean War for June-August 1951, received from Captain Corry, October 1951.
681.0123(D1)

2. Operational reports of 25 U.S. Infantry Division in Korean War, 25 May-27 July 1951, received from Captain Corry, 5 November 1951. (History 2-22-9, 5 November 1951).
681.013(D2)

3. Operational reports of 1 U.S. Cavalry Division in Korea, 19 June- 5 August 1951, as received from Captain Corry, 5 November 1951.(Hist 2-22-9, 5 November 1951).
681.013(D3)

4. Periodic operation reports by 1 U.S. Corps in Korea, 18 July-27 September 1951, as received from Captain Corry, 5 November 1951.(Hist 2.22-9, 5 November 1951)
681.013(D4)

Operational Reports - Korea.

1. Operational reports on Korean War from Britcom, Japan, no. GO 202, March 1953 - GO June 1953, received from DMO&P, 16 July 1953.
681.013(D32)

2. Britcom Japan Operational reports on Korean War from 5 June 1952-16 January 1953 and 18 April -31 July 1953 from DMI, May 1957.
681.013(D80)

Operations - Chinese.

1. Special intelligence aspects of Chinese Communist Forces attacks on The Hook, 24-26 July 1953, received from Captain Madden, 27 January 1954.
410B 25.013(D70)

2 Summary of enemy action on 1 U.S. Corps front in Korea, 30 April-31 May 1953, received from Captain Madden, 27 January 1954.
410B 25.013(D72)

3. Report on enemy offensive action on 9 U.S. Corps sector in Korea, 19-20 June 1953 received from Captain Madden, 27 January 1954.
410B 25.013(D73)

Operations- Korea.

1. Korea - Hill 355 - November 1951. Extracts from U.S. Command Reports on operations at Hill 355, in Korea, during November 1951. Prepared by Captain McGuire, March 1963.
112.3HI.003(D3)

2. Chronology - United Nations Operations in Korea from 25 June 1950 to 1 April 1956. Prepared by Directorate of History, 4 April 1956.
112.3HI.003(D7)

3. Paper - Canadian Operations in Korea - 25 June 1950 - 31 March 1952. Prepared by Major H.W.Thomas, Directorate of History, 25 September 1953.
6581.013(D93)

Operations - Korean War.

1. Report on enemy activity in Korea for July 1952 received from Captain F.R.McGuire, 3 September 1952.

681.013(D21)

2. Joint Situation Reports on Korean War, nos. 617 to 624, 3 to 27 July 1953, prepared by the Combined Joint Staffs Washington and received from DMO&P 18 November 1953.
681.013(D43)

3. 1 CAORT memorandum no. 6 "Effects of three flood-producing rains on military operations in Korea" by Major J.R.Stafford, 11 May 1954.
681.013(D66)

4. DMO&P Top Secret TD 1750-1930/29 TD 7050 High Level Correspondence and cables - Korea, October 1950 - June 1953.
112.3M2(D695)

5. DMO&P Top Secret file 1750-151/25 TD 7049 Weekly Cables, on Korean situation, October 1950-March 1951. High Level.

Order of battle - Commonwealth Forces in Japan.

1. Order of Battle of Commonwealth Occupation Forces in Japan, as of 19 July 1947
112.3M2(D184)

Organization and Administration - Cyprus.

1. List of files received from Canadian Contingent Cyprus for period September 1961-September 1969. Files noted with Letter "R" are retained in Directorate of History, under above number, remainder have been destroyed.
419CYP.009(D1)

Organization - North Korean Engineers.

1. 8th U.S. Army Engineer Intelligence Team reports on organization of North Korean Engineers and route map with symbols, November 1952 received from DMI May 1953.

Organization and Administration - Canadian delegation - Laos.

1. DMO&P file Secret G2001-1930/181 Volume 1-4. Organization and Administration Canadian delegation - Laos, 22 March 1961-28 March 1963.

Pacific War Council.

1. Memorandum by Right Honourable William Lyon Mackenzie King re meeting of Pacific War Council, 15 April 1942 at Washington, D.C.
951.001(D1)

2. Minutes of meetings of Pacific War Council, February 1942-January 1943.
112.3M2(D513)

Pacific Strategy.

1. Memorandum by Mr. G.G.Geer to Prime Minister on Pacific strategy with comments of senior officers, April 1942 - July 1946.
112.3M2(D482)

Peace Settlement with Japan.

1. JPC summary of military aspects of peace settlement with Japan,29 July 1947(DMO&P BDF 30(volume 8)).
112.3M2(D118)

Philippines.

1. Provisional airfield list Philippine Islands, prepared in office of Assistant Chief of Staff, Intelligence, Washington, D.C. by combined personnel of U.S. and British Services. Enemy airfield report, no. 4, 10 August 1944.
181.009(D12)

2. Operation Instruction no. l26, 21 February 1945 re Zamboanga, etc. by 13 Air Force Transport doctrine, Amphibious Forces, U.S. Pacific Fleet support aircraft in amphibious operations(undated).
171.009(D46)

3. Field Order no 20, 17 February 1945 re Zamboanga and Palawan operations by 8th U.S. Army. Field Order no. 10, 28 February 1945, re "V.4" Zamboanga area, by 41 U.S. Infantry Division Administrative Order no. 6, 17 February 1945 re Zamboanga and Palawan operations by 8th U.S. Army "V/4" operations report 12 March 1945 by 543rd U.S. Engineer Boat and Shore regiment(Zamboanga Area map of Central and South Philippine Islands, overprinted to show enemy situation, 5 May 1945 by 8th U.S. Army
171.009(D46)

4. Report by Captain J.E.Streater RCCS on operations of U.S. Signal Corps during invasion of Zamboanga Peninsula, Philippine Islands) - including Guerrilla Command, including maps)
171.009(D50)

6. AT & I Section, S.W.P.A. Translation of a report on guerrilla activities in the Philippines, 28 April 1945.
981.009(D13)

7. AT & I Section, S.W.P.A. Translation of Japanese 65th Brigade Combat Team report on Philippine Operation, January 1942. 19 March 1945.
982.009(D39)

8. AT & I Section, S.W.P.A. Translation of Japanese attacks on airfields on Philippines, Borneo, Malaya and Burma, 25 April 1944.
982.009(D91)

9. Note on Operation "Mike One" landing at Lingayen Gulf, Philippine Islands, 9 June 1945, compiled from report of Australian officer attached to U.S. formation.
112-3M1009(D67)

10. AT & I Section, S.W.P.A. Translation of Japanese Intelligence Reports from operations in the Philippines, December 1941-March 1942, 20 February 1943.
982.009(D112)

11. AT& I Section, S.W.P.A. Translation of miscellaneous records of Japanese Southern Expeditionary Force in Malaya and the Philippines, 10 April 1943.
982-009(D117)

15. Combined Operations HQ Bulletins Y/4, 6 April 1945 "Combined Operations against Leyte, October 1944".
181.0031516)

Prisoner of War Camps - Korea.

1. 1 Commonwealth Division orders and directive re tour of duty of "B" Company 1 Royal Canadian Regiment at Koje Island Prisoner of War Camp, received from Captain F.R.McGuire, 12 September 1952.
681.016(D9)

Prisoners of War - Far East.

1. Correspondence re activities of Company Sergeant-Major Tughy M.C . while a prisoner of war of Japanese, October 1945.
112.3M2(D251)

Prisoners of War - Korea.

1. Prisoners of War - Korea. DMO&P file TS G.2970-1 - Prisoners of War - Generally - containing paper "Chinese Communist and North Korean Treatment of British Prisoners of war in Korea", 7 May 1954. Use of Australian troops to guard prisoners of war in Korea.
112.3M2.009(D213)

2. Prisoners of war. DMO&P file TS2970-1 volume 2. Personnel service - prisoners of war generally. Prisoners of war policy, Chief of Staff Committee Paper -Working Group on Prisoners of war, Inquiry re Captain Harry D.Moreland, Jr., prisoner of war in Korea.
112.3M2.009(D240)

Prisoners of war - Korean War.

1. Reports and returns on return of prisoners of war from enemy hands,August-September 1953.
410B25.019(D112)

2. Correspondence, reports, instructions, orders, etc. re handling of enemy prisoners of war in Korea, October 1951-September 1954.
410B25.019(D165)

3. Interrogation, reports on enemy prisoners of war in Korea, October 1953-July 1954.
410B25.019(D185)

4. Heavily stripped file re reports and returns of l Commonwealth Division including report on conditions on Koje Island, April 1952-August 1956.
6891.013(D77)

Public Relations - Cyprus.

1. List of files received from Canadian Contingent Cyprus for period September 1961-September 1969. Files noted with Letter "R" are retained in Directorate of History, under above number, remainder have been destroyed.
419CYP.009(D1)

Repatriated Prisoners of war - Korea.

1. Intelligence Interrogation reports on J.W.Cranston, K.H.Dawe, E.J.R.Fields, G.E.Griffiths, B.Jewer, E.J.McInnes, R.B.Watson and Lance Corporal D.F.Orson of Royal Canadian Regiment after their repatriation as prisoners of war in Korea, received from Captain J.R.Madden, 5 October 1953.
410B25.023(D17)

2. Interrogation report on Private J.P.Dufour, repatriate prisoner of war from Korea, received from Captain J.R.Madden, 6 October 1953.
410.B25.023(D18)

3. Interrogation report on Second Lieutenant C.G.Owen of 1 Royal Canadian Regiment, repatriated prisoner of war from Korea, received from Captain J.R.Madden, 2 October 1953.
410B 25.023(D19)

7. Interrogation report on Private G. St. Germain, Royal 22e Regiment, repatriated prisoner of war from Korea, received from Captain J.R. Madden, 19 October 1953.
410B 25.023(D23)

8. Interrogation report on Private J.Binette of Royal 22e Regiment repatriated prisoner of war from Korea, received from Captain J.R.Madden, 19 October 1953.
4120B25.023(D24)

Report - Administrative State - Far East.

1. Far East Theatre - Report on Administrative State. Letter HQTS 2001-122/1 volume 4 over HQTS 1750-1930/29 volume 12, containing report on Administrative State, Far East Theatre, BDF-4 volume 2.
112.3M2.003(D7)

Report - 1 U.S. Corps - Korea.

1. Korea - Hill 355 - November 1951. Extracts from U.S. Command Reports on operations at Hill 355, in Korea, during November 1951. Prepared by Captain McGuire, March 1963.
112.3HI.003(D3)

Reports and Returns - Cyprus.

1. List of files received from Canadian Contingent Cyprus for period September 1961-September 1969. Files noted with Letter "R" are retained in Directorate of History, under above number, remainder have been destroyed.
419CYP.009(D1)

Reports - Canadian delegations - Cambodia.

1. DMO&P file SG-1750-1930/57 volume 6, Military Reports and returns - Canadian delegations -Cambodia, 20 June 1957-16 March 1964.
112.3M2.009(D270)

Reports - Canadian delegations - Laos.

1. DMO&P file SG1750-1930/181 volume 9. Military Reports and Returns Canadian delegations Laos - 1 June 1963 - 4 August 1964.
112.3M2.009(D272)

Republic of Korea.

1. G199 extract from DIB no. 620,26 June 1953. Republic of Korea, received from DMO&P, 16 July 1953.
681.009(D3)

Republic of Korea Army.

1. Description of Republic of Korea defence of outpost '128' 5-6 June 1953, received from Captain Madden, 27 January 1954.
410B25.0123(D76)

2. Report on Republic of Korea Army by Brigadier R.E.A.Morton, 7 July 1954.
410B25.019(D119)

3. Report on Republic of Korea Army by Brigadier R.E.A.Morton,15 June 1955.
410B25.019(D217)

Responsibilities of Commander in Chief Far East Land Forces.

1. Commander in Chief Far East Land Forces - Directive from War Office. Copy of War Office Directive to Commander in Chief Far East Land Forces on his responsibilities for the Commonwealth Contingent Korea. Letter HQS 2001-121/1 volume 4, 11 July 1956. From DMO&P BDF 31-4 volume 2.
112.3M2.1(D7)

Return of prisoners of war from Korea.

1. Reports and returns on return of prisoners of war from enemy hands, August-September 1953.
410B25.019((D112).

Royal Thai Navy.

1. Correspondence, messages, instructions etc. re visit from Royal Thai Navy to Canada, July 1950-July 1952.
112.009(D72)

Rundown of Canadians in Korea.

1. DGPO papers re return and rundown of Canadian troops in Korea, December 1954-May 1955(DGPO BDF7).
410.019((D2)

South East Asia Command.

1. Organization on charts of S.E.A.C.(South East Asia Command)
112.3M2(D195)

Singapore.

1. Defense in the Far East, 1921-1939. The Far East during war in Europe and the Middle East, September 1939 - October 1941, Plans and policy, Japan as the Eastern partner of the Axis. Hong Kong, Singapore and Malaya(Compiled by Captain W, Miles , Historical Section, Cabinet Office(Kept in Vault drawer 7a))
840.013(D2)

2. For Defense of Far East, 1921-1939 by Captain W.Miles, see Far East, Defense.
840.013(D1)

3. Memorandum on "The Singapore Base" by Overseas Defence Sub-Committee of the Committee of Imperial Defence -Imperial Conference, 1930(Copy no. 2).
951.003(D6)

4. Establishment of Naval Base at Singapore and its effect upon the foreign and naval policy of the Empire - 1923(Copy no. 8).
951.003(D7)

5. Provision of Air Forces for cooperation in the Defence of Singapore - Committee of Imperial Defence, 30 March 1933(Copy no. 50).
951.003(D8)

6. Report on Singapore Base - air units for cooperation with the new Armament Committee of Imperial Defence, 1933(Copy no. 51).
951.003(D9)

7. Report on Singapore Defences - Committee on Imperial Defence, 5 April 1933(Copy no. 51)
952.003(D9)

8. Note on Military Work contemplated for the Singapore base, Committee of Imperial Defense, 1935(Copy no. 52).
951.003(D11).

9. Air requirements for defence of Singapore, Report by Chiefs of Staff, Chiefs of Sub-Committee, Committee of Imperial Defence, dated 20 April 1934(Copy no. 5).
951.003(D12)

10. Singapore Local Defences. Memo by Overseas Defence Sub-Committee of Committee of Imperial Defence dated 16 March 1934(Copy no. 51).
951.003(D13)

11. Singapore. Defences. Defense of Calder Harbour. Memo by Joint Overseas and Home Defence Sub-Committee of Committee of Imperial Defense, dated July 1936.
951.003(D14)

12. Singapore Defences by Committee of Imperial Defence, 1935.(Copy 53).
951.003(D15)

13. Memorandum by Chiefs of Staff Sub-Committee on Singapore, acceleration of provision of defences. Committee of Imperial Defence, dated 9 July 1935(Copy no. 55)
951.003(D16)

14. Singapore defences. Report of Sub-Committee of Defence, policy and requirements. Committee of Imperial Defence, dated 19 July 1935(Copy no. 55).
951.003(D17)

15. Report on Singapore to Imperial Conference, 1930- Committee of Imperial Defence(Copy No. 56).
951.003(D128)

16. Singapore. Anti-Motor Torpedo boats defences(Booms, guns, lights) Committee of Imperial Defence, dated 4 December 1936(Copy no. 59).
951.003(D21)

17. Singapore. A.A. Defences- Committee of Imperial Defence, dated 2 December 1936(Copy no. 62).
951.003(D20)

18. Singapore. Anti-Motor torpedo boat defences.(Booms, guns, lights)Committee of Imperial Defence dated 4 December 1936(Copy no. 70).
952.003(D21)

19. War Office manuscripts on Far Eastern Theater of Operations.
(1.) War with Japan. (2.) Fall of Hong Kong.
(3.) The Loss of Malaya and the Fall of Singapore. Prepared by the Historical Section of Cabinet Office.
952.013(D94)

20. Instrument of surrender of Japanese forces in Southern Region. signed at Singapore, 12 August 1945. (CAS/1-4/21).
314.009(D346)

21. Intelligence cables from DMI Far East, Singapore on Japanese Army dispositions dated 17 December 1941/8 January 1942.
114.1009(D5)

22. British official news photographs of the Far East(FE 1-FE 492).
112.3PI(D1332)

23. "Problems of the Pacific" from Military Intelligence Summary of 14 August 1926.
934.009(D203)

Situation Reports - Korean War.

1. Joint situation reports on Korean War received from CAS Washington and DMO&P no. 370,19 December 1950 to no. 572,26 January 1953(incomplete) received in Directorate of History, 7 March 1953. (HQC 1450-2 4 March 1953).
681.013(D25)

2. Korean War weekly review, 3 December 1950 - 31 January 1953 from Britcom, Japan, received in Directorate of History from DMO&P 5 March 1953.(HQC 1450-2, 4 March 1953).
681.013(D26)

3. Joint situation reports on Korean War received from CAS Washington and DMO&P nos. 582 to 589, received in Directorate of History, 31 March 1953.
681.0123(D27)

7. Joint teletype situation report on Korean War from Washington - no. 379 1 November 1951 - no. 529 29 August 1952, received from DMI, April 1953.
681.023(D7)

8. U.S. War Department daily situation reports on Korean War no. 418 29 December 1951-589 25 March 1953, received from DMI April 1953(3 volumes).
681.023(D8)

9. Joint situation reports on Korean War from Canadian Joint Staff, Washington, no. 500 April 1953-no. 616, June 1953, received from DMO&P, 16 July 1953.
6891.023(D15)

Situation in Korea.

1. D.M.I. Briefs on Situation in Korea, 28 June - 11 September 1950, received in Directorate of History from DMO&P, 31 March 1953.
681.023(D6)

2. 13 Chinese Communist Forces Army Group appreciation of the situation for an attack on United Nations, made at Kakson, October 1953.
410B25.019(D289)

South East Asia Command.

1. Organization on charts of S.E.A.C.(South East Asia Command).
112.3M2(D195)

South West Pacific Area(S.W.P.A.)

1. Extract from reports of Captain J.R.Lind, Canadian Army Observer attached-U.S. Forces, S.W.P.A., February-May 1950.
112.3M2(D196)

Canada Department of Defence – Directorate of History Library • 197

Status U.N. Forces - Korea.

1. CGS Office. CGS BDF 15-1/Far East volume 4 - period January 1954-26 March 1955. Policy re Korean Awards; Terms of Reference and CMMFE; Reduction of Forces, Korea; U.N.Airlift Operations; Chinese Intervention in Indo-China; Press Clippings from **The Times** on Indo-China; Status of U.N. Forces Korea; Report to Minister in visit to Korean and Japan by JAG; Biography of Major-General Bierwith, CMC British Commonwealth Forces, Korea; Report on visit Korea, Canadian Base Units and Kobe Area by Command CMMFE, 20 January 1955; Rotation of Units from Far East.
112./009(D94)

Strength States - U.N. Forces in Korea.

1. CMMFE report no. 11 22 November 1950 on operational conditions in Korea including strength state of U.N. forces.
112.3M2(D318)

Tughy, C.S.M.

1. Correspondence re activities of Company Sergeant-Major Tughy M.C., while a prisoner of Japanese, October 1945.
112.2M2(D251)

Turkey.

1. Combined JPC and JIC study on association of Greece and Turkey with N.A.T.O.,19 June 1951.
112.3M2(D349)

2. Combined Chiefs of Staff paper CCS59/2, 28 May 1942 on German capabilities in Turkey.
112.3M2(D483)

3. Paper presenting Canadian View on Peace-Keeping in Cyprus, 12 February 1964. Objectives - Impact in the United Nations - Canadian Interest.
 653.003(D14)

4. Canadian Joint Staff(London) - file 1038-CJ-3(SO Sup) volume 1 - Sabre - Supply to Greece, Turkey and Italy, 1 April 1954-16 May 1958.
493.009(D178)
Turkish Army.

1. Report of U.S. Quartermaster General Branch on clothing for Turkish Army, March 1951.
112.3M2(D197)

Turkish Cypriots.

1. Order of Battle - Greek Cypriot - Turkish Cypriot, compiled 20 July 1965 by Operations Branch HQ Nicosia Zone. Contained in August 1965 Original Diary of HQ Nicosia Zone.

United Kingdom - Cyprus.

1. Paper presenting Canadian View on Peace-Keeping in Cyprus, 12 February 1964. Objectives - Impact in the United Nations - Canadian Interest.
653.003(D14)

United Nations.

9. Army Council Secretariat folder containing Periodic Memoranda on operation Rapid Step, 9 November - 19 November 1956.
112.3M2.003(D14)

10. Memorandum on debriefing of Kashmir(U.N.M.O.G.I.P.) observers - Interview with Lieutenant-Colonel Wygand, 23 March 1950; Major McClelland 17 May 1955. Received from External Affairs by Lieutenant J.L.Granatstein. Duties of observers - Incidents - Attitudes of Army officers - Political attitudes in Kashmir - Naikowal incident - British Officers in Pakistani and Indian Armies.
653.003(D24)

U.N.I.P.O.M.(United Nations India Pakistan Observer Mission)

1. Personal narrative(first draft), 25 September 1967, **The War of the Peacekeepers** and paper **The Military Officer and United Nations Peace-keeping Operations,** August 1966 by Major-General Bruce E.MacDonald, D.S.O., C.D.
958.001(D10)

U.N. Command

1. G3 Ops Reports U.N. Command no. 133, 4 November 1950-(to current) received from D.M.I. 29 April 1952.
681.013(D7)

2. G2 Ops Reports U.N. Command no. 3035 31 December 1950 to current received from D.M.I. 15 May 1952.
681.013(D8)

3. Interim report on activities of U.N. Command Military Armistice Commission in Korea, 20 June -27 July 1953, received from Captain J.R.Madden, 16 March 1954.
681.013(D51)

4. U.N. Command Military Armistice Commission report on activities September and October 1953 received from Captain J.R.Madden, 25 March 1954.
681.0132(D52)

U.N. Command.

Operation SNOWGOOSE. Copy of Operation Order no. 64/1(Op SNOWGOOSE) issued by Chief of General Staff, 13 March 1964 on proposed dispatch of Contingent to Cyprus; contains Operation Order 64/1, Annex "A" - Intelligence annex; Annex "C"

Organization of Canadian Contingent Cyprus; Annex "D" - Priority of Movement; Annex "E" Administration

Order 64/1. Annex "G" Allotment of WS, radio diagram; Annex H - Signals instructions.
112.1.006(D1)

United Nations - Cyprus.

Paper presenting Canadian View on Peace-Keeping in Cyprus, 12 February 1964. Objectives - Impact in the United Nations - Canadian Interest.
653.003(D14)

Canadian Army Liaison Establishment file 2390-34/80 volume 1 Operations - Cyprus, 31 January-17 March 1964.
493.009(D188)

U.N.E.F. - Canadian Component, Korea.

1. Establishment - Canadian Component, Commonwealth Contingent. Proposed establishment for Canadian Medical Detachment, Korea, Canadian Component, Commonwealth Contingent, Korea - from BDF 31-4 volume 2.
112.3M2.005(D2)

U.N.E.F. - Canadian Forces Korea.

1. Canadian Forces - Korea and Japan. Letters discussing policy on reduction of forces in Korea and Japan, from BDF 31-4 volume 2.
112.3M2.003(D8)

United Nations Forces Contingent - Korea.

1. Commander Commonwealth Contingent Korea - Duties. Copy of War Office directive on duties of Commander Commonwealth Contingent Korea. Letter HQS 2001-121/1 Volume 4, 12 July 1956. From DMO&P BDF 31-4 volume 2.
112.3M2.0(D6)

2. Commander in Chief Far East Land Forces - Directive from War Office. Copy of War Office Directive to Commander in Chief Far East Land Forces on his responsibilities for the Commonwealth Contingent Korea. Letter HQS 2001-121/1 volume 4, 11 July 1956. From DMO&P BDF 31-4 volume 2.
112.3M2.1(D7)

United Nations Forces in Korea.

1. Directive for Commander Britcom Sub-Area, Tokyo, Copy of HQ British Commonwealth Forces Korea letter KB 1250-4 containing directives for Commander Britcom Sub-Area, Tokyo, from DMO&P BDF file 31-4 volume 2.
112.3M2.1(D4)

2. Reduction of Forces in Far East. Copies of messages dealing with proposed reductions of forces in the Far East from DMO&P BDF 31-4 volume 2.
112.3M2.01(D6)

U.N.M.O.G.I.P.(U.N. Military Observation Group in Pakistan).

1. Paper presenting Canadian View on Peace-Keeping in Cyprus, 12 February 1964. Objectives - Impact in the United Nations - Canadian Interest.
653.003(D14)

2. Canadian Position on U.N. Peace-keeping, 1961 - United Nations Peace-Keeping Machinery - India; Pakistan; Balkans; U.N.T.S.O., U.N.M.O.G.I.P.; Greece, Lebanon, Spinelli Mission; Middle East; Beck Friis Mission; Secretary-General United Nations, Dag Hammarskjold; U.N.E.F.; United Nations; External Affairs paper obtained by Lieutenant J.L.Granatstein.
653.003(D28)

3. Statement of Mr. G.S.Murray, Head of U.N. Division, Department of External Affairs to Orientation Course of Directorate of Military Intelligence, 18 March 1963, entitled "Peace-keeping Activities of the United Nations", received from External Affairs.
653.009(D6)

U.N.M.O.G.I.P. -Kashmir.

1. Memorandum on debriefing of Kashmir(U.N.M.O.G.I.P.) observers - Interview with Lieutenant-Colonel Wygand, 23 March 1950; Major McClelland 17 May 1955. Received from External Affairs by Lieutenant J.L.Granatstein. Duties of observers - Incidents - Attitudes of Army officers - Political attitudes in Kashmir - Naikowal incident - British Officers in Pakistani and Indian Armies.
653.003(D24)

United Nations - Military Operations.

1. Joint Staff papers CSC 2195-5(JBDMSD), 1 March 1961. The Role of the United Nations Sponsored Military Forces - received from External Affairs, September 1965.
653.006(D1)

2. AHQ File SD6001-151/25 volumes 1-10 inclusive, Equipment and Stores - Overall - 25th Canadian Infantry Brigade Group, 11 August 1950-30 August 1951.
111.41(D19)

3. A chronology of the Korean War - 25 June 1950-12 May 1952. Prepared in Directorate of History, 23 October 1953.
681.013(D92)

4. Paper - Canadian Operations in Korea - 25 June 1950-31 March 1952. Prepared by Major H.W.Thomas, Directorate of History, 25 September 1953.
681.013(D93)

United Nations Operations -Korea - 1950-1953.

1. This is the official title of Korean Operations

1950/1953. For information see the following headings also: Korean War, Korea, 25 Canadian Infantry Brigade, etc.

2. Chronology - United Nations Operations in Korea from 25 June 1950-1 April 1956. Prepared in Directorate of History, 4 April 1956.
112.3HI.003(D7)

3. Organization of Special Force. CGS BDF 15-1/25CIB TD 3 August 1950-November 1956. Paper on Organization of Canadian Army Special Force, passed to History 1 by DD Hist - December 1963; Memorandum to CGS from JAG, 17 November 1956 on basic documents relating to the organization of the Canadian Army Special Force, together with following appendices.
112.3HI.009(D59)

U.S. Army Field Force(Korea).

1. October 1950 report of British/Canadian Liaison Officer with U.S. Army Field Force(Korea).
112.3M2(D407)

Vietnam.

2. Standing orders for Canadian Military component in Vietnam and Indo-China agreement on cessation of hostilities there, July 1954.
685.016(D1)

3. Canadians in Vietnam. Press release and work accomplished by Canadian Officers with U.N. Control Commission in Vietnam.
113.3Pl-009(D7)

4. Personnel Strength of Military Component - Canadian delegation, Indo-China. Research on comparative strength of Canadian, Polish and Indian personnel in Indo-China. Material was intended for publication in **Army Journal**, 1958.
685.005(D1)

5. **Ottawa Journal**. Press clipping - Article in **Ottawa Journal** 13 August 1964 "Canadian Troops service in 10 World 'Hot Spots'" - Korea - Vietnam - Laos - Cambodia - Egypt - Israel - Yemen - Kashmir - Cyprus - N.A.T.O. - U.N.O.
956.009(D44)

6. Report entitled "Vietnam - as seen by a Team Officer, 1962-1963" by Captain R.H.Mahar, Royal Canadian Regiment.
960.001(D1)

7. Copy of text of Geneva Conference - Indo-China, Agreement on the cessation of hostilities in Vietnam, 1954. Joint Commission and International Commission for Supervision and Control in Vietnam; Agreement on Cessation of Hostilities in Laos; Agreement for the Cessation of Hostilities in Cambodia, 1954, Received from External Affairs, September 1965.
653.003(D9)

11. Address by Air Chief Marshal F.R.Miller, delivered at Warriors' Day Luncheon, C.N.E. Toronto, 21 August 1965. Passed to Director by R.L.Raymon, Executive Staff Officer to C.D.S. The topics covered in the address are: the changing world and military scene; the advances in technology; the creation of peacekeeping forces; the integration of the Canadian Armed Forces and the levels at which integration will be carried out.
101.009(D3)

12. Paper by John W. Holmes "Peacekeeping in Asia" prepared for delivery to the Institute of Strategic Studies, Oxford, September 1964. Received from Lieutenant-Colonel R.B. Tackaberry, D.Ops, 11 February 1966.
958.009(D24)

13. Statements and Speeches - Information Division - Department of External Affairs, no. 56/1-no. 65/28. Passed to Directorate of History by Lieutenant J.L.Granatstein, September 1965.
653.003(D30)

14. Notes on the International Commission, Viet Nam, 1954-1955. These notes were prepared by Major-General W.J.Megill, D.S.O., C.D., on request by Directorate of History(see file HQC 1450-2, 12 May 1960.
958.001(D9)

15. Newspaper clipping - **The Gagetown Gazette** edition 2 February 1967 and photographs on Canadians serving in Laos and Vietnam.

16. 89 general correspondence files received from Military Component Canadian delegation Vietnam, Indo-China, 19 February 1970(Files cover period October 1960-July 1968) File list included.
685.003(D2)

17. Intelligence review. Canadian Forces Participation in International Organizations, prepared by D.M.I.
020.023(D1)

18. Recount of interview with Lieutenant-Colonel R.J.Kerfoot, Princess Patricia's Canadian Light Infantry, on his return from duty with Military Component Canadian delegation, Vietnam, by Commander W.A.B.Douglas, Senior Historian.
956.0012(D5)

19. C-1759-1930114 - Military Component, Canadian delegation in Vietnam, Monthly reports, November-December 1964.
113.023(D2()

20. Geneva Conference - Compilation of Documents on the Indo-China Armistice Agreements, July 1954.
113046(D4)

MacOdrum Library,
Carleton University,
1125 Colonel By Drive,
Ottawa, Ontario, K1S 5B6.
Tel:(613)788-2735

Theses and Dissertations.

Bajpai, Ishwari Prasad.
Declining American interest in India. M.A. thesis 1976.
CT

Banerjee, Nipa.
India's policy of positive neutralism and nonalignment. M.A. thesis 1969
CT

Bellows, Eric.
Effective rural credit delivery in Sri Lanka. M.A. thesis 1987
NL

Booker, D.W.
Organizing for people's power under martial law, the case of the Church and State in the Philippines. M.A. thesis 1986.
NL

Campbell, Colin Alexander Graham.
Power and conflict: the tertius gaudens in the Sino-Soviet-American triad.
M.A. thesis 1984

Chan, Hing Kai.
The decisive years in Sino-Soviet relations, 1962-1963. M.A. thesis 1978.

Chetelat, Lois J.
The role of the traditional birth attendant in the delivery of primary health care in Central Java, Indonesia. M.A. thesis 1986.
NL

Choudhury, Ahmed Fazli Hasan.
The pattern and the process of urbanization in developing countries, a case study of Bangladesh. M.A. thesis 1977.
CT

Creese, Gillian Laura.
Working class politics, racism and sexism: the making of a politically divided working class in Vancouver, 1900-1939. Ph.D. dissertation 1986.

Curtis, Terrance James.
Status inconsistency and international aggression: a case study of Japan: 1890-1940.M.A. thesis 1977.

Diehl, MacLean Roswitha J.
The effects of the green revolution on rural women in three selected states of India. M.A. thesis 1986
NL

Durrant, Edward W.
Hong Kong squatter community, a question of multiple meanings and interpretations. M.A thesis 1977.
CT

Duvadi, Ashok Kumar.
Geology of the Himalayas and Southern Tibet. M.Sc. thesis 1985.

Fisher, Stephen Frederick.
Changing patterns of social organization among the Chinese in Ottawa: a study of internal and external determinants. Ph.D. dissertation 1979.

Galway, Michael Anthony.
Role of the Japanese in the development of the copper-mining industry in British Columbia. M.A. thesis 1974.
CT

Garson, Ronald.
Chinese foreign policy towards Thailand, 1958-1984: from revolution to cooperation. M.A. thesis 1984

Gill, Christopher R.
Japan and the prospects of Siberian investment, a case study of influencing factors. M.A. thesis 1976.
CT

Gunapala, Nanayakkara Jagodage.
Technological change and underdevelopment of the rubber industry of Sri Lanka: a study of public policy and organization behaviour. Ph.D. dissertation 1980

Hakim, Md. Abdul.
Lending policy of the World Bank with special reference to its contribution to the economic development of Bangladesh from 1972 to 1978. M.A. thesis 1980.

Hakim, Md. Abdul.
The colonial legacy in the administrative system of a post-colonial state, the case of Bangladesh, 1971-1985. Ph.D. dissertation 1987.
NL

Halladay, Judith Lynn.
A study of maternal and child health information sources in South Sulawesi, Indonesia. M.Sc. thesis 1987.
NL

Ho, Christopher Tak-chew.
Development administration in West Malaysia. M.A. thesis 1971.
CT

Hoque, Kazi Sadrul.
Land tenure and socio-structural impediments to agricultural modernization in Bangladesh. M.A. thesis 1980.
NL

Huq, Mohdudul.
Low rice productivity in Bangladesh. M.A. thesis 1977.

Islam, Anwarul.
Class structure and social change in an agrarian society, the case of Bangladesh. M.A. thesis 1976.
CT

Islam, Shamsul.
Public corporations in Canada and Pakistan, a comparative study. M.A. thesis 1971.

Ito, Takako.
International regime theory and security cooperation in East Asia. M.A. thesis 1988.
NL

Jain, Prakash Chand.
Colonialism, class and race relations: the case of overseas Indians. Ph.D. dissertation 1985.

Jashanmal, Bhagwan.
The origin of the Nestorian church at Trichur. M.A. thesis 1966.
CT

Joeck, Neil H.
Nixon foreign policy and Chinese-Japanese diplomatic relations, November 1969-September 1972. M.A. thesis 1976.
CT

Johnson, David Curtis.
Island dispute, a case study of Soviet-Japanese relations. M.A. thesis 1976.
CT

Joseph, Thomas Wilfred.
Canada's China policy, 1949-1966. M.A. thesis 1969.
CT

Kapoor, Ilan.
Gandhi's alternative and India. M.A. thesis 1986.
NL

Kapur, Ashok.
India's arms control and nuclear development: A quest of an altered world order. Ph.D. dissertation 1974

Kariyawasam, Manthrie.
The language problem and national unity in Ceylon M.A. thesis 1966.

Khan, Mohammed Mohiuddin.
The Bangla Desh crisis, the role of the major powers. M.A. thesis 1979.
CT

Khonker, Habibul Haque.
Social change, class structure and changing elites in Bangladesh and Kenya, a comparative study of peripheral societies. M.A. thesis 1978.
CT

Kore Shettar, Shivanagappa F.
Disparities in economic development, learning from the growth centre experiences of India's five year plans, 1951-1985
NL

Kozliner, Marsha.
Commercial considerations in Canadian aid, Canada's aid to India's power and transportation sector. M.A. thesis 1974.
CT

Kuruvilla, P.K.
Problems of public administration in developing countries with special reference to India. M.A. thesis 1964

Kuruvilla, P.K.
A comparative study of recruitment and training of higher federal civil servants in Canada and India. Ph.D. dissertation 1972

Lodh, Francoise Suzanne.
Social modernization and Indian caste system. M.A. thesis 1976.
CT

Ma, Joseph.
China's oil industry, self reliance and self sufficiency. M.A. thesis 1978.
CT

Madarshahi, Mehri.
The impact of manpower planning on Iranian economic development. M.A. thesis 1981.

Mars, Pairadeau A.A.
Peasant nationalism and revolutionary political change, the China experience, 1927-1957. M.A. thesis 1970.
CT

Maswood, Syed Javed.
Japan and the liberal economic order, hegemony and system support. Ph.D. dissertation 1987.
NL

Mihara, Asahiko.
Economic relationship between Indonesia and Japan. M.A. thesis 1976.
CT

Morgan, Hywel Rhys.
Krushchev's military aid programmes to noncommunist states in Asia(1955-1964). M.A. thesis 1966.

Ogawa, Shinichi.
Japan's defense policy, options and constraints. M.A. thesis 1977.
CT

O'Malley, Jeffrey.
Thai tourism development policy and socio-economic change. M.A. thesis 1987.
NL

Ono, Hiroko.
China's foreign policy, multifaceted self image and its behaviour. M.A. thesis 1976
CT

Padilla, Perfecto.
Organization and methods practices in the governments of Canada and the Philippines: a comparative study. M.A. thesis 1965.

Pant, Raghab D.
A theoretical and empirical analysis of the sources of inflation: the Asian experiences. Ph.D. dissertation 1980.

Pathirama, Sumith.
Spatial aspects of the development problems of primary agricultural commodities: a study of smallholder tea production in Sri Lanka. M.A. thesis 1983

Philips, Wilkinson Summesh Kumar.
The pulse of the caste system in a village of Marwar. M.A. thesis 1968.
CT

Pond, Patricia Bonita.
Ideology and economic development in Communist China. M.A. thesis 1970.
CT

Postgate, Wilfred Pale.
Linguistic states and the Indian federation, the cases of Bombay and the Punjab. M.A. thesis 1964.
CT

Raghuram, Neelawar Vasudevarao.
Higher personnel recruitment in India and Canada. M.A. thesis 1961.
CT

Rahman, Syed Sajjadur.
The demand for money in a developing economy: evidence for six Asian countries. Ph.D. dissertation 1985.
NL

Sani, Pramila Manik.
The Indian polity, parties and bureaucracy in theory and practice. M.A. thesis 1971.
CT

Saul, Fay Rebecca.
The petroleum industries of the People's Republic of China and Indonesia: an analysis of the bargaining relationship with Japan. M.A. thesis 1978.

Saunders, Eileen Mary.
Women, the economy and the socialist state: the case of China. Ph.D. dissertation 1983

Sekar, Radhika.
The process of pilgrimage, the Ayyappa cultus and Sabarimlal Yatra. M.A. thesis 1988.
NL

Shamin, Choudury M.
Small-state foreign policy, Bangladesh, a case study. M.A. thesis 1977.
CT

Sharma, Girdhar Behari.
Implementation of ombudsman plans in India. M.A. thesis 1978.

Siu, Bobby Chi Yiu.
The women's movements in China, 1900-1949. Ph.D. dissertation 1981.

Tan, Christopher.
Communalism and national integration: a case study of Sarawak, Malaysia. M.A. thesis 1977.

Weatherston, Susan Mary.
Development and equity in Chinese strategies of education. M.A. thesis 1982.

Wong, Warren.
The Philippine land reform program under the new society: the logical framework approach to evaluation. M.A. thesis 1981.
NL

Wood, John Christopher.
Canadian foreign policy and its determination during the Korean war. M.A. thesis 1961.
CT

Yu, Hyung Kyung.
Korean reunification and four major powers in North East Asia. M.A. thesis 1977.
CT

Photographs

Heath, David, 1931-
Photographer and photography instructor.
Black and white 82 photographs, 1952-1961.
Portraits of men, women and children, some taken in Korea.
SEIFRIED

**University of Ottawa Libraries,
Special Collection Division,
Morriset Library
65 Hastey Avenue,
Ottawa, Ontario, K1N 9A5
Tel: (613)564-6813.**

Theses and dissertations

Microfilm and microfiche copies also in Morriset Library Microform Department.

Antoninus, P.A.J.B.
Social and economic aspects of the fishing industry in Ceylon. M.A. thesis 1959.
CT

Bard, Robert F.
The originality of European civilization in the chronicles of travellers to India, mid-seventeenth to mid-eighteenth century. M.A. thesis 1976.
CT

Chan, Kim-khomg.
The Catholic Church in the People's Republic of China, 1979-1983, its life and theological implications. Ph.D. dissertation 1986
NL

Chang, Pin.
The development of party politics in Japan. M.A. thesis 1956
CT

Chau, Peter Hoang-Nhu.
Economic development of Viet Nam. M.A. thesis 1963.
CT

Chen, Stella.
Hong Kong's economy, 1949-1959. M.A. thesis 1961.
CT

Chiang, Haven.
Diplomatic relations between China and Canada. M.A. thesis 1958.
CT

D'Mello, James.
The dual religious marriage celebration in India. Ph.D. dissertation 1985.
NL

D'Costa, Herman.
Intuition and the spirit of man in the philosophy of Sarvepalli Radhakrishnan. M.A. thesis 1969.
CT

Dion, Raymond.
La politique exterieure Chinoise et le cas Angolais. M.A. thèse 1982.
NL

Gagne, Evelyn.
Strategies de developpement en éducation proposées par l'UNESCO pour le Bangladesh, recherche des implications pour l'éducation de la femme bengale. Ph.D. thèse 1978.
NL

Gunaratne, Leslie L.
Human capital and distribution of personal income, a theoretical analysis and an examination of some aspects of income distribution in Sri Lanka. Ph.D. dissertation 1982
NL

Hsieh, David J.T.
Some aspects of the problem of economic development in Taiwan(Formosa). M.A. thesis 1958.
CT

Jacot, Joyce AS.M.
Some linguistic remarks on language reforms, policies and practices throughout the People's Republic of China today M.A. thesis 1982.
NL

Jayasuriya, Joseph.
The problem of juvenile delinquency in Ceylon. M.A. thesis 1955.
CT

Khataie, Mahmood.
The agricultural sector in the economic development of Iran. Ph.D. dissertation 1978
NL

Ki-man, Chan.
The people's communes of Communist China. M.A. thesis 1961.
CT

Kim, Chung-Wha.
Korea's problems of foreign trade and industrialization. M.A. thesis 1961.
CT

Lacombe, Honorius.
Mission Lemieux au Japan(1907-1908). M.A. thèse 1951.
CT

Lee, Samuel Yin Sun.
Some aspects of financing economic development in underdeveloped countries with special reference to Indonesia. M.A. thesis 1963.
CT

Levasseur, Danielle.
Le grand tournant de la politique étrangere chinoise , le rapprochement de la Chine avec les États-Unis 1971-1972. M.A. thèse 1981:
NL

Mao, Yun An.
International technical collaboration with China since 1931. M.A. thesis 1943
CGT

Martin, Elizabeth.
La femme japonaise selon les coutumes et la tradition religieuse. M.A. thèse 1968.
CT

Moore, Michael D.
The foreign aid programmes and policies of the People's Republic of China, 1953-1974. M.A. thesis 1976.
CT

Musa, Mohammad Abu.
Sound changes in modern Bengali. M.A. thesis 1983.
NL

Ng, Yung-tsai.
China as an export market. M.A. thesis 1945
CGT

Painchaud, Marcel.
La Chine et l'appui moral aux mouvements de lutte armée dans les pays du tiers monde. M.A. thesis 1977.
CT

Rainville, Luc.
Spécialisation internationale et branches de la production, le cas de Singapour. M.A. thèse1984.
NL

Robichaud, Emilien.
La révolution dans les pays du tiers monde, origine, nature et évolution des divergences sino-sovietiques. M.A.thèse 1976.
CT

Sahib, Mohammed Ali.
Development of national accounts for Fiji Islands. M.A. thesis 1962.
CT

Siddaramaiah, Chandrashekar.
Lexical morphology and phonology of Kannada. M.A. thesis 1986.
NL

Szeto, Yee-kies
Passive construction in Chinese. M.A. thesis.
NL

Tsui, Man-Shing.
An analytical study on the formation of the rural communes in China. M.S. thesis 1963
CT

Wen, Saul Shu.
Land reform in Taiwan. M.S. thesis 1968.
CT

Zhou, Qi-ying.
A comparison of pre-school learning structures related to cooperation and creativity in China and Canada. M.Sc. thesis 1986
NL

National Archives of Canada,
395 Wellington Street,
Ottawa, Ontario, K1A 0N3.
Tel:(613)995-5138

Manuscript Division.

Manuscript Group 9. Provincial, Local & Territorial Records;

Victoria, British Columbia. Census Returns, 1891.
Originals, 1891. 251 pages. Reel H1408. F3.
Ethnic origins is indicated only for Chinese and Indians.

Manuscript Group 10. Records of Foreign Governments;

MG 10 C .China.

MG 10 C1. China Consular Records.

Xerox copies, 1914-1915, 528 pages. MG 10 C1
Letterbook of Lin Shih Yuan for the period 8 November 1914-29 May 1915. He was the Chinese Consul at Vancouver, B.C., 1914-1915.
Copied from the originals in the Glenbow-Alberta Institute, Calgary. Permission to copy must be obtained from the Institute.

Subjects include head tax payments on Chinese immigrants, deportation of immigrants, estates of dead Chinese, arms shipments to China, and protests against British Columbian laws restricting Chinese employment Two-thirds of the letters are in Chinese, one-third in English. Most of the English letters are addressed to Canadian Government officials.
A nominal index is included at the beginning of the volume.

MG 10 C2. China. Nationalist Consular Records.

Originals, n.d., 1919-1923, 1931-1948, 1960, 1966,1967. 1.3 metres.
Finding aid 1285. MG 10 C2.
The first Chinese consulate in Canada was opened in 1909. Between 1909 and 1970 there were Chinese consulates (for varying periods of time) in Ottawa, Vancouver, Toronto, and Winnipeg. In 1970 the Republic of China (Taiwan) withdrew its diplomatic and consular officials from Canada.
The importance of the Chinese consulate as an integral part of the Chinese Canadian community is illustrated in this collection. Before the establishment of full diplomatic ties with China in 1942 the consul fulfilled many diplomatic functions. The most important subjects dealt with in this collection are registration certificates(Chinese Immigration Act 1923), war relief to China, and Sino-Canadian relationsThere are registration certificates for more than a thousand individuals and families in the collection. A large number of these certificates are for Chinese Canadians residing in the Prairie provinces On the other hand most of the correspondence concerning wartime relief to China is from British Columbia, Ontario, Quebec and the Maritimes. The collection is in both English and Chinese.

Presented in 1981 by Norman Rehder, Ottawa, Ontario.

Registration Forms, n.d., 1931-1948. 61 cm. (volumes 1-3, 7).

Application forms, registration certificates and oath of citizenship forms.

Correspondence, n.d., 1939-1944. 27 cm. (volumes 3-5).
Correspondence concerning registration certificates, wartime aid to China, and correspondence with the Canadian government.

Membership lists, n.d., 1944-1945. 2 cm. (volume 5).
Membership lists for the Kuomintang and the Montreal Chinese Laundry Association. This series also contains two files listing members of the Chinese foreign service

Greeting cards, n.d., 1967. 16 cm. (volume 5-6).
Greeting cards from politicians, Canadian public servants as well as members of the diplomatic corps stationed in Ottawa and Washington.

Published material, n.d., 1919, 1935-1947, 1960, 1966. 20 cm (volume 6).
Manuscripts, periodicals and published reports relating to China and Canada.

NOTE: One poster concerning the Chinese Immigration Act of 1923 has been placed in horizontal shelving

Manuscript Group 11. Colonial Office(C.O.) Great Britain;

Great Britain. Colonial Office.
CO323. MG 11 CO323.

Reel B1720 volume 202, 1825, East India Company.

Reel B1734 volume 242, 1854, East India Company.

Reel B1839 volume 279, 1865, India.

Reel B1843 volume 290, 1868, India.

Reel B1844 volume 290, 1868, India.

Reel B1847 volume 299, 1870, India.

Reel B1849 volume 305, 1871, India.

Reel B1851 volume 308, 1872, India.

Reel B1942 volume 314, 1873, India.

Reel B1943 volume 319, 1874, India.

Reel B1944 volume 322, 1875, India.

Reel B1946 volume 327, 1876, India.

Reel B1947 volume 332, 1877, India.

Reel B1949 volume 336, 1878, India.

Reel B1950 volume 339, 1879, India.

Reel B1953 volume 348, 1881, India.

Reel B1957 volume 355, 1883, India.

Reel B1958 volume 358, 1884, India.

Reel B1960 volume 361, 1885, India.

Reel B1962 volume 365, 1886, India.

Reel B1965 volume 368, 1887, India.

Reel B1966 volume 372, 1888, India.

Reel B1967 volume 376, 1889, India.

Reel B1971 volume 380, 1890, India.

Reel B1973 volume 384, 1890, India.

Reel B1974 volume 384, 1891, India.

Reel B1976 volume 389, 1892, India.

Reel B1981 volume 401, 1895, India.

Reel B1982 volume 401, 1895, India.

Reel B2051 volume 407, 1896, India.

Reel B2055 volume 417, 1897, India.

Reel B2060 volume 430, 1898, Trade and India.

Reel B2073 volume 443, 1899, India and Law Offices.

Reel B2073 volume 443, October and December 1899, India and Law Offices.

Reel B2074 volume 443, 1899, India and Law Offices.

Reel B2081 volume 454, 1900, India, Law and Treasury.

Reel B2086 volume 464, 1901, India and Law Offices.

Reel B2114 volume 475, January to June 1902, India.

Reel B2092 volume 484, 1903, India, Law and Treasury.

Reel B2097 volume 496, 1904, India.

Reel B2101 volume 508, 1907, India.

Reel B2108 volume 528, 1907, India.

Reel B2109 volume 528, 1907, India.

Reel B2306 volume 540, 1908, India.

Reel B2320 volume 554, 1909, India.

Reel B2923 volume 565, 1910, India.

Reel B2928 volume 581, 1911, India.

Reel B2933 volume 597, 1912, India.

Reel B2960 volume 614, 1913, India.

Reel B3108 volume 638, 1914. India.

Reel B3109 volume 638, 1914, India.

Reel B3385 volume 681, 1915, India.

Reel B3511 volume 717, 1916, India.

Reel B3512 volume 717, 1916, India.

Reel B3704 volume 834, 1920, India.

Reel B3783 volume 869, 1921, India.

Reel B3754 volume 896, 1922, India.

Reel B3920 volume 937, 1925, India

Great Britain. Colonial Office.
CO 532. General Correspondence, 1907-1926, on microfilm MG 11 CO532.

Reel B4056 volume 2, 1907, India.

Reel B4059 volume 7, 1908, India.

Reel B4075 volume 31, 1911, India.

Reel B4084 volume 45, 1912, India.

Reel B4103 volume 73, 1914, India.

Reel B4108 volume 80, 1915, India.

Reel B4113 volume 87, 1916, India.

Reel B4123 volume 10l, 1917, India.

Reel B4123 volume 101, 1917, India.

Reel B4141 volume 122, 1918, India.

Reel B4201 volume 188, 1921, India Office.

Reel B4202 volume 188, 1921, India.

Reel B4232 volume 221, 1922, India.

Reel B4233 volume 221, 1922, India.

Reel B4299 volume 293, 1924, India Office.

Reel B4299 volume 294, 1924, India Office.

Reel B4300 volume 294, 1924, India Office.

File continued by Dominions Office, DO35.

Manuscript Group 17. Religious Archives;

MG 17 G. Society of Friends.

Religious Society of Friends.
Originals on deposit at the University of Western Ontario. 58 reels. Finding aid .20. MG 17 G1.

Series B. Records of Canada yearly meeting(Orthodox), 1810-1955, and its subordinate meetings, 1798-1970(115 volumes, 8 cubic feet).

Proceedings and Minutes of Canada yearly meetings, 1810-1955.

Yearly meetings Women's Foreign Mission Society, June 1885-June 1903. Reels M3180.
Executive Committee. May 1899-June 1903.
Executive Committee. December 1887-April 1899.
Includes material on Quaker Foreign Missions to Japan, B-1-11.

Manuscript Group 18. Pre-Conquest Papers;

Cook, James, 1728-1779.
Naval officer.
Originals, 1759. 2 pages.
Account of midshipman William Brann, with H.M.S. **Pembroke** signed by Cook as master, 29 March 1759. Autographed portrait of Cook.
ULM

Cook, James, 1728-1779.
Photocopies, 1777. 2 pages.
Sailing instructions issued to masters of ships under Cook's command, while searching for a passage from the Pacific to the Atlantic. Report on the condition of provisions on H.M.S. **Resolution,** 24 October 1777. Originals in British Columbia Archives.
ULM

Manuscript Group 23. Late Eighteenth Century Papers.

MG 23 G Quebec and Lower Canada Government.

Sewell, Jonathan and family, 1766-1839.
Originals, 1650-1950. Finding aid 149. MG 23 G11 10. Two letters of Rev. Henry D.Sewell, from Constantinople in 1849.

Hale, John, 1764-1868, and family.
Originals, 1739-1954, 41 cm. photocopies 1654, 1826, 6 pages, microfilm, 1817-1826. Reel A-1085. Finding aid 1292. MG 23 G11 18.

Volume 1, pages 28-31, 23, and 29 February 1828.
Address of Lord Amherst to the Council of Calcutta, declining an invitation and the reply.

Volume 3, pages 113-116. 15 June 1826.
Letters of John Hale and his daughter Fanny to Edward Hale, written while Military Secretary to Lord Amherst, Governor-general of India. Photocopy.

Manuscript Group 24. Nineteenth Century pre-Confederation papers.

Baring Brothers & Company, London, England.
Originals, 1781-1878. 37 feet.
Selected papers from the records of Baring Brothers and Company, including Colombo, 1861-1862.
Material also available on microfilm.
ULM

Lay, Horatio Nelson, 1832-1898.
England, public servant and financier.
Original, 12 cm. transcripts, 1 cm, 1842-1966.
Includes correspondence and printed material relating to the career of H.N.Lay, as Inspector of Customs in China, 1859-1864; the Treaty of Tientsin, 1858-1859; biographical and genealogical notes on H.N.Lay and his family.
ULM

Maitland, Peregrine, 1777-1854.
Lieutenant Governor of Upper Canada and Nova Scotia.
Typescript, 1821-1858. 1/2 inch.
Correspondence with the Colonial Office and the East India Company, 1847-1858; addresses to and by Maitland during his governorship of Nova Scotia, Cape of Good Hope, and Madras, 1821-1847. Newspaper articles regarding his incumbencies, 1846-1847.Original Dr. Gwendolyn Carter, Smith College, Massachusetts.
ULM

Manuscript Group 26. Papers of the Prime Ministers.

The papers of the Prime Ministers are rich in materials on Canada's relations with Asia and the Pacific and on Asian Canadians. Reliance has been placed on existing finding aids as a guide to these materials, although the aids are an imperfect cover. All that can be done is to give indications which can be followed. Asia- and Pacific-related material even during World War II were only a very small fraction of the total volume of records.

Records for the Prime Ministers extend beyond the actual period of their ministry, and often contain relevant materials for these periods also. For a fuller but general description of the Prime Ministers' papers from MacDonald through MacKenzie King see: Canada. Public Archives. Manuscript Division. **General Inventory, Manuscripts, MG 26-MG 27**, Ottawa, 1972.

A, MacDonald, John Alexander, 1815-1891

Prime Minister, 1867-1873, 1878-1891.
Originals, 1809-1919, 103 feet, 3 inches. 570 volumes.
Finding aid 104.
Political papers.
Arranged by subject, 1851-1891(volumes 1-185).
Arranged by correspondents, 1843-1891(volumes 186-296).
Miscellaneous, 1836-1891(volumes 297-335).

Among the topics noted in Finding aid 104, Part I are:

Cable, Asiatic, 1880, volume 308, pages 59-70.

Cable, Asiatic, 1883, volume 317, pages 109-125.

Cable, Asiatic, 1884-1885, volume 323, pages 85-94.

Pacific Cable, 1890-1891, volume 332, pages 349-386.

Pacific. Islands, 1887, volume 330, pages 51-109.

Pacific mail service, 1890-1891, volume 332, pages 315-348.

Trade with China, 1888, volume 327, pages 230-255.

B, MacKenzie, Alexander, 1822-1892.

Prime Minister, 1873-1878.
Originals, 1872-1883 13 volumes, 1 foot 5 inches, microfilm 1776-1892, 4 reels, Finding aid 108(Reel C2054).
No Asia or Pacific references in subject index.

C., Abbott, John Joseph Caldwell, 1821-1893.

Prime Minister 1891-1892.
Originals 1884-1892 13 inches 5 volumes. Finding aid 183.

Volume 5. arranged by subject files.
Australia. Cable and steamship connection and trade, 1884-1891.

D, Thompson, John Sparrow David, 1844-1894.

Prime Minister 1892-1894.
Originals, 1867-1895, 50 feet, 297 volumes. Finding aid 156(authors only) Reel C11061.

E, Bowell, MacKenzie, 1823-1917.

Minister and Controller of Customs, September 1885-January 1892.
Minister of Trade and Commerce, March 1893-December 1894.
Customs part of Trade and Commerce and responsibility passed to Trade and Commerce in 1893.
Prime Minister, 1894-1896.
Originals, 1860-1914, 20 feet 8 inches, 135 volumes.
Finding aid 14.
Correspondence 1865-1912, volumes 1-97.

Letters received, 1868-1912, 2 foot 10 inches, volumes 1-15.

Arranged in chronological order with nominal and subject indexes.

Asia and Pacific related topics were:

Volume 3, pages V-1315. April 1883-August 1884.
Shipping, Japan.

Volume 3, pages 1635-1638.
China, Chinese.

Volume 7, pages 3344-3361. May 1888-April 1890.
Shipping, Pacific.

Volume 10, October 1891-December 1892.
Submarine cable to Japan.

Volume 10, pages 4945-5008.
China, Chinese.

Volume 12, pages 5597-5600, October 1893-February 1894.
Shipping, Fiji.

Volume 14, pages 6144-6102, January-December 1895.
Shipping, Pacific.

Departmental letter books, 1877-1912, 8 feet, volumes 16-77.

Letterpress copies of letters by Bowell or his secretaries concerning the departments of which Bowell was Minister. A portion of the first letterbook was written by Isaac Burpee, Bowell's predecessor as Minister of Trade and Commerce.

Private letterbooks, 1879-1894, 2 feet 4 inches, volumes 78-97.
Letterpress copies of a more or less private and political nature written by Bowell.

Memoranda and notes, 1879-1905, 9 inches, volumes 98-101.
Arranged by subject. A list of subjects is available, includes Customs Department and Pacific cable.

Clippings and scrapbooks, 1860-1907, 6 feet 6 inches.

Loose clippings, 1860-1907, 3 feet 1 inch, volumes 102-114.

Scrapbooks, 1860-1907, 3 feet 5 inches, volumes 1155-133.

F, Tupper, Charles, 1821-1915

Prime Minister, 1896.
Originals 1821-1919,1958, 8 feet 5 inches, 28 volumes.
Finding aid 153(Reel C4500).

Two principal Asia- and Pacific-related concerns are the Pacific cable(24 items) from 1886-1912, correspondents including John A. MacDonald and MacKenzie Bowell, and the Transpacific steamship service(12 items) from 1885-1889, correspondents including John A.MacDonald.

G, Laurier, Wilfrid, 1841-1919.

Prime Minister, 1896-1911.

Papers. 1037 volumes, of which 804 are on microfilm. Political papers, 1871-1919. Originals, 185 feet((volumes 1-757). Finding aid 91).

Correspondence.

Author index gives author, subject, date and page numbers of each letter. There is also a subject index. The two indexes are available in original and on microfilm(Reels C-1158(subject index) and C-1606 to C-1608(author index)).

Subject index.

Asia- and Pacific-related topics were:

Armenian question, 1 reference.
British Columbia, Chinese in, 1 reference.
British Columbia, Japanese in, 10 references.
British Columbia, Japanese riot in Vancouver, 8 references.
Cable, Pacific, 171 references.
China, trade with, 2 references.
Drug traffic, 28 references.
Exhibition, Japanese, 1 reference.
Franchise, Japanese, 1 reference.
Immigration ,Oriental, 416 references.
Imperial Conferences , 46 references.
India famine fund, 14 references.
Japan, 12 references.
Japan, trade with, 21 references.
Japan steamship service, 2 items.

Japanese, 7 items.
Opium Conference, 1 reference.
Treaties and conventions, Anglo-Japanese, 6 references.
Turkey, relations with, 1 item.

Author index.

Aberdeen, Lord.
23 January 1897, India famine fund 11362-8.
9 January 1897, India famine fund 11536-41.
8 May 1897, Japanese visitor.
15 November 1900, Pacific cable 215263-4.

Alexander, Skinner, Pender(delegates).
27 October 1911, New Zealand. Imperial trade and steamship services 1901,17.

Alley, R.A.
13 October 1903, Canada-Australia steamship service 77781-4.
26 October 1903, Australia steamship service 78368.
14 March 1904, Canada-New Zealand steamship service 83319-21.
18 March 1904, New Zealand steamship service 83506-8.
5 May 1904, Australia-Canada steamship service 85273-4.
18 August 1904, Vancouver-New Zealand steamship line 89111-3.
13 July 1905, Canada-New Zealand steamship line 99682-4.
27 July 1905, Australia steamship line 100069-70.

Anderson, George.
31 January 1901, Japanese immigration 53063.

Angus, F.
1903, Chinese immigration exclusion 68819-22.

Annable, W.G.
4 August 1906, Chinese immigration 112666-7.

Ansen, J.
1907, Asiatic immigration 117578.

Asiatic Exclusion League.
9 September 1907, resolution - Asiatic exclusion 128836-40.
17 September 1907, Japanese immigration 129651-4.
27 September 1907, Japanese immigration 129771.
6 November 1907, Oriental immigration 131564-
17 January 1909, Oriental immigration 1352768, 136407-8.
4 March 1908, Oriental immigration 137454-5.
14 March 1908, Oriental immigration 137560-1.
1 April 1908, Oriental immigration 138523.
21 April 1908, Asiatic immigration 139366-74.

Auditor general(McDougal, J.L.).
23 December 1903, Grant for Pacific Cable 80221-2.
24 December 1903, Audit Act. Pacific cable 80261-4.
30 December 1903, appropriation for Pacific cable.

80415-6.

Australasian Press Association.
4 December 1909, Pacific cable 163176-80.

Australia, Premier of(Reid, G.H.).
 2 March 1899, Pacific cable 30915-8.
19 January 1905, Pacific cable 52644-7.

Aylesworth, A.B.
November 1905, Pacific cable 102625-6.

Baker, James.
15 September 1896, Chinese immigration 7077-8.

Barton, Edmund(Prime Minister, Australia).
 8 February 1903, Pacific steamship service 215589.
 8 February 1903 Pacific cable 70015-7.
12 February 1903, Pacific steamship service 215580.
 4 March 1903, Pacific cable 70751-5.
 4 March 1903, Pacific cable 275599-602.
 6 March 1903, Pacific cable 70851-55.
18 March 1903, Pacific cable 71199-204.
18 March 1903, Pacific cable 215612.
24 March 1903, Pacific cable 215615.
13 May 1903, Pacific steamship service 215625.
30 July 1903, Pacific cable 215639.
17 August 1903, Pacific cable 75550-2.

Begg, A.
14 June 1900, Royal Commission on Oriental Immigration 46530-7

Belcourt, M.A.
3 March 1904, Agent to Japan 83046-7.

Bickerdike, Robert.
29 March 1897, India 13498-500.

Bostock, Hewitt
17 June 1899, Oriental immigration 46256.
20 June 1900, Oriental immigration 46677-9.
28 June 1900, Oriental immigration 46941.
24 July 1900, Oriental immigration 46956.
24 July 1900, Oriental immigration 47747-8.
 2 August 1900, Oriental immigration 48021.

Brierley, James S.
19 September 1907, Canada-Japan treaty 129517-9

British Columbia(residents).
1907, protest against Japanese immigration 117308-572.

British Columbia government.
20 April 1902, Asiatic labour, Oriental immigration 64479-83.

British Columbia Herring Packers Association.
 7 April 1910, Asiatic labour, Oriental Immigration 169595-6.

British Columbia Lumber and Shingles Manufacturing Company.

31 July 1906, Anglo-Japanese treaty 112493-6.
27 November 1906, Oriental exclusion 116081-3.

Brooke, L.A.W.
29 May 1911, King of Thailand. Coronation 186636-7.

Bryce, P.H.
18 October 1907 Oriental immigration 176693-4.

Burke, James T.
 8 May 1900, Oriental immigration 45359-60.

Burnett, Frank.
19 June 1900, Lieutenant Governor MacInnes. League Oriental poll tax 46643-5.

Burns, Rev.
10 March 1900, famine in India 43216-8.

Caldwell ,A.C.
 6 May 1908 India(R) 14018-14019.

Calgary Trades and Labour Council .
14 October 1907, Asiatic exclusion 130500-
14 October 1907, Oriental immigration 130502.
27 September 1909, Asiatic exclusion 160316-7.

Calgary, Alberta.
19 December 1907, Oriental immigration 134008-11.

Capetown, Anti-Asiatic League.
15 December 1903, Asiatic immigration 215690.

Carey, C.
13 August 1906, tax on Chinese immigrants 112869-76.

Carman, Rev. A.
April 1899, Japanese immigration 31994-5.

Carmichael, Carrie.
12 September 1908, Oriental immigration 144607-15.

Carter-Cotton, F.
7 February 1900, Japanese immigration 42150-2.
4 January 1908, anti-Japanese riots in British Columbia 134721-3.

Cartwright, Richard John.
11 March 1902, Chinese polltax 63607.
11 March 1902, Oriental immigration 95430-3.
15 April 1907, Japanese prince 123908.
 2 September 1907, Japanese immigration 128537-40.
 5 May 1908, Chinese immigration 140087-96.
 8 March 1909, wages for Japanese in British Columbia 153070-71.

Casgrain, J.P.B.
 6 April 1903, Quebec Oriental bill 71850-3.

China, Consul General (K.M.Thoms).
19 October 1910, Chinese consul - interview 175923-4.

Christie, J.A.
21 March 1900, Asiatic immigration 45833-5.

Clark, R.William.
15 August 1911, Hindu immigration 188953-6.

Clute, P.C.
26 November 1900, Chinese immigration 51074-6.
28 January 1901, Chinese commission 52963-4.

Coote, A.
18 May 1898, Pacific cable 23424-8.

Cory, W.W.
28 October 1910, Hindu immigration 176246-52.

Cote, Thomas.
10 April 1908, Japanese immigration 138893-4.

Crafter, A.G.
8 January 1908, Social Reform Party's Oriental immigration 134871-99.

Crawford, John.
15 March 1911, Chinese immigration 183171-2.

Deane, F.J.
6 September 1907, British Columbia politics, Japanese trade and immigration 128721-9.
8 December 1907, Asiatic immigration 133486-90.
16 October 1908, Oriental immigration 245958-9.

Dewdney, E.
6 May 1897, Oriental immigration 14483-509.

Doherty, Keville.
31 May 1905, Japanese matters 98043.

Drinkwater, C.
14 June 1900, Chinese immigration 46538.
28 March 1903, Chinese immigration 71533-42.

Drury, R.L.
9 March 1908, Japanese immigration 137334-60.
13 March 1909, mission to Japan 150367-9.
16 June 1910, exclusion of Asiatics 172164-7.
2 August 1911, Japanese immigration 188444-5.

Duncan, Howard J.
31 July 1907, British Columbia politics and economy - Oriental immigration 127177-96.
9 October 1907, British Columbia. Japanese immigration 130255-60.
28 October 1907, Japanese immigration 131071-5.
31 October 1907, Oriental immigration 131244.
15 January 1908, Asiatic immigration, British Columbia 135234-7.
22 February 1908, Japanese immigration 136743-4.

Duncan, W.S.
31 January 1908, Anglo-Japanese Alliance 135787-9.

Dunsmuir, James.
28 July 1900, Oriental immigration 47877-8.
2 February 1901, Oriental immigration 53138-72.

Edmonton Trades and Labour Council.
10 September 1907, Asiatic exclusion 129053-4.
21 September 1909, Asiatic exclusion 160073-74.

Elgin, Lord.
10 September 1907, Oriental immigration 215894.
17 October 1907, Japanese immigration 21.
13 November 1908, Indian immigration 215903-6.
12 December 1907, Chinese immigration 215915.
20 February 1908, Japanese immigration 215958-62.
29 February 1908, Japanese immigration 215972-86.

Embree, William B.
6 September 1907, Asiatic immigration.

Etsell, J.E.
15 July 1911, Chinese immigration tax 187578-82.

Falconer, R.A. President, University of Toronto.
26 February 1909, scholarships to Chinese students 152490-2.
17 September 1910, Immigration of Chinese students 174870-5.

Federated Trades Council.
1900, Chinese immigration head tax increase 40642.

Fielding, W.S.
1907 Japanese Convention 117574a.

Fisher, Sydney A.
15 March 1903, Japan-Canada treaty 71057-65.
1 April 1903, Japan-Canada trade 71685-93.
25 September 1905, Japan-British trade treaty 101491-7.
4 October 1907, Japanese negotiations 130102.
16 October 1907, Japanese treaty 130526-54.
18 October 1907, Japan 130712.

Ford, G.
18 January 1908, Asiatic immigration 135336-8.

Foster, G.E.
20 May 1911, Japanese business 186332a.

Fraser, George L.B.
31 July 1908, British Columbia: Fishing industry, Japanese employment 142992-3.

French, F.P.
3 October 1907, Asiatic immigration 130047-54.

Galliher, W.A.
30 December 1907, views(Laurier's on Oriental immigration 134378-85).

Garneau, F.G.
June 1900, Japanese immigration 46119.

Gavin, F.J.
5 June 1903, Chinese immigration 73872-6.

Gibson, J.M.
21 March 1911, charity - China relief 183601-3.

Gifford, A.
13 February 1906, Canadians in China 107096-8.

Governor-General's Office.
19 October 1907, relations with Japan 130722-4.

Grant, Gordon M.
9 September 1907, Oriental immigration 128852-3
8 October 1907, Oriental immigration 130251-4.
10 October 1907, Oriental immigration 130317-9
31 December 1907, Asiatic immigration 134417-19

Greely, A.W.
7 October 1904. Asia-America submarine cable 905302.

Greenwood, B.C.
17 October 1907, Asiatic exclusion, Oriental immigration 121038-43.

Greenwood, British Columbia, Miners' Union.
2 December 1907, Oriental immigration 133161-2.

Gregson, J.W.
1900, Oriental immigration 40538-41.

Grey, Lord.
2 January 1906, Japanese trade 203428-9.
12 July 1906, Anglo-Japanese Treaty 215829-32.
13 July 1906, Japan trade 203775-91.
8 January 1907, Japanese immigration 204070-84.
9 May 1907, Japanese mission 125185-6.
15 May 1907, visit of Prince Fushimi 125391-6.
29 May 1907, visit of Japanese prince 125603-7.
13 September 1907, Oriental immigration 204489.
17 September 1907, Oriental immigration 204489-98.
20 September 1907, Oriental immigration 204499-532.
23 September 1907, Oriental immigration 204533-6.
6 October 1907, Oriental immigration 204563-9.
16 November 1907, Oriental immigration 204709-22.
19 November. 1907, Oriental immigration 204738-54.
27 November 1907, Oriental immigration 204775-82.
27 November 1907, Oriental immigration 215907.
5 December 1907, Japanese immigration 204803-9.
20 December 1907, Oriental immigration 204821-31.
21 December 1907, Japanese immigration 204832-7.
27 December 1907, Japanese immigration 204841-54.
13 January 1908, Japanese immigration 204890-5.
16 January 1908, Japanese immigration 204896-9.
8 February 1908, Japanese immigration Honorable William Lyon MacKenzie King, 205000-5.
8 February 1908, Japanese immigration 2115955.
10 February 1908, Japanese immigration 205006-17.
11 February 1908, Japanese immigration 206018-9.
17 February 1908, Japanese immigration 215956-7.
21 February 1908, Japanese immigration 215956-7.
22 February 1908, Oriental immigration 205037-42.
3 March 1908, Japanese immigration 205098-108.
3 March 1908, Japanese immigration 215994-5.
5 March 1908, Japanese immigration 205123.
11 March 1908, Japanese immigration 208150-3.
16 March 1908, Japan 208176-181.
29 March 1908, Japanese immigration 216064.
4 April 1908, Japanese immigration 205232-8.
2 May 1908, Oriental immigration 205304-7.
15 July 1908, opium legislation 205435-40.
12 September 1908, Japanese immigration 205537.
16 November 1908, Oriental immigration 205610-7.
3 December 1908, Hindu immigration 205610-7.
7 December 1908, Oriental immigration 205641-64.
14 December 1908, Hindu immigration 205676-95.
16 April 1909, Japanese ships - visit 206023-40.
5 December 1910, Japan trade 207137-40.
15 February 1911, Japan trade 207244-7.
16 February 1911, Japan trade 207248-9.

Griffith, W.L.
1 September 1898, Pacific cable 26150.

Gundy, J.H.
22 March 1911, Chinese famine relief 183685-7.

Halford, H.J.
7 November 1906, Chinese immigration 115371-2.

Harcourt, Rt. Hon. Lewis.
20 May 1911, Anglo-Japanese treaty 186387-93.

Harling, Thomas.
19 April 1910, Canada-Japan trade 170133-6.
10 May 1910, Japanese trade. Trade and Commerce Department. 170922-8.

Harris, William.
2 July 1908, Oriental immigration 142880-2.

Hartman, C.W.
24 December 1907, Asiatic immigration 134214-5.

Hays, Charles M.
10 November 1909, Oriental immigration 161982-3.
6 April 1911, Steamship service, Canada to Japan 184459-61.

Helmcken, H.D.
21 June 1900, Oriental immigration, Lieutenant Governor, British Columbia 46732.

Herbert, John E.
12 February 1900, Pacific cable 42282-83.

Hope, Charles E.
16 May 1903, Chinese immigration 73387-93.

Hopkinson, William C.
4 September 1908, Oriental immigration 144226-33.

Howard, Sir Esme.
20 August 1908, Opium Conference 216205.

Huxtable, J.J.
18 November 1907, suppression of liquor and opium traffic 132312-314.
14 September 1908, suppression of liquor and opium traffic 144678-9.

Interior Department.
8 October 1910, Hindus in British Columbia, Oriental immigration 175518-23.
18 March 1911, Asiatic immigration 183432-5.
1 May 1911, Hindu immigration 186611-5

Japan. Consul-general.
5 March 1897, routine business 12797-9.
28 February 1899, British Columbia legislation 215026-7.
6 June 1899, Anti-Japanese legislation, British Columbia 34233-38.
25 August 1899, routine business 36822-4.
30 November 1900, Asiatic immigration 51282-4.
21 January 1901, British Columbia Immigration Act 52708-9.
7 March 1901, British Columbia Immigration Act 53980-4.
18 March 1901, farewell 54443.
22 September 1901, British Columbia Immigration Act 59050-51.
30 April 1902, routine business 64751-3.
28 May 1902, routine business 65417-8.
3 June 1902, Canada-Japanese relations 65638-45.
1903,? Japanese immigration 68699-702
24 January 1903, Japanese immigration 69468-71.
3 February 1903, Japanese immigration 69840-55.
5 February 1903, Japanese exhibition 69926-28.
30 March 1903, Japanese immigration 71592-5.
1 April 1903, Japanese trade 71703-6.
20 July 1903, Japanese immigration 75285-92.
13 August 1903, Japanese immigration 76142-7.
17 September 1903, Japanese immigration 77050-3.
20 November 1903, Routine business 79017-8.
4 December 1903, Japanese immigration 79548-9.
4 February 1904, Japanese immigration 81897-901.
17 March 1904, routine business 83439-40.
19 March 1904, Japanese immigration 83547-8.
20 April 1904, Japan and Russia 84675-717.
10 June 1904, routine business 86616-7.
22 August 1904, Routine business 89166-7.
1 September 1904,, routine business 89307.
30 September 1904 routine business 90223-4.
16 March 1906, Japanese famine 95793-4.
8 May 1906, Japanese immigration 97258-9.
4 September 1906, condolences 113346.
18 January 1907, Japanese immigration 118353-75.
18 January 1907, Japanese trade 118425-30.
9 September 1907, Japanese riots, Vancouver 128806-13.
6 February 1908, Japanese-British Columbia 136044-52.
24 April 1908, Japanese consulate 139581-584.
5 May 1908, Japanese consulate 140120-2.
3 June 1908, Grand Exhibition of Japan 141200-36.
18 December 1908, Japanese immigration 149102.
9 January 1909, Japanese immigration 150135-6.
8 February 1909, Japanese immigration 151504.
16 February 1909, Japanese consulate 151862-3.
24 February 1909, Japanese immigration 162383-5.
4 March 1909, Japanese immigration 152985-6.
10 March 1909, Japanese immigration 153144-8.
25 March 1909, Japanese navy 154021-5.
7 April 1909, Japanese immigration 154470-3.
23 April 1909, Japanese consulate 155189-91.
12 May 1909, Japanese immigration 155924-8.
18 May 1909, Japanese consul 156075-6.
9 June 1909, Japanese immigration 156777-83.
24 June 1909, stay in Canada 157307-9.
9 July 1909, Japanese immigration 157773-8.
14 August 1909, Japanese immigration 158919-25.
September 1909, Japanese immigration 159655-71.
20 September 1909, Japanese visit 160064-8.
22 September 1909, invitation 160127-8.
16 October 1909, Japanese immigration 161006-12.
9 November 1909, Japanese immigration 161912-8.
1 December 1909, Japanese immigration 163041-7.
14 January 1910, Japanese immigration 165140-6.
19 February 1910, Japanese immigration 167276-82.
12 March 1910, Japanese in British Columbia 169188.
17 March 1910, Japanese immigration 168387-93.
13 April 1910, Japanese immigration 169872-7.
18 May 1910, Japanese immigration 171246-51.
26 May 1910, visit of Prince Fushimi 171502-6.
14 June 1910, Japanese immigration 172085-90.
5 July 1910, Japanese trade 172867-9.
12 July 1910, Japanese immigration 173038-44.
11 August 1910, Japanese immigration 173826-53.
10 September 1910, Japanese immigration 174605-10.
3 December 1910, removal to Philippines 177738-40.
13 December 1910, Japanese immigration 178076-95.
12 January 1911, Japanese immigration 179949-55.
17 January 1911, Japanese trade 180148-56.
25 January 1911, Canada-Japanese relations 180527-30.
8 February 1911, Japanese immigration 181154-7.
28 February 1911, Japanese trade 182203-48.
8 March 1911, Japanese immigration 182846-8.
3 April 1911, Anglo-Japanese treaty 184328.
8 April 1911, Anglo-Japanese treaty 184545-6.
13 April 1911, Japanese immigration 184767-9.
24 April 1911, Japanese trade 185142-7.
3 May 1911, Japanese immigration 185731-3.
5 June 1911, Japanese immigration 186812-4.
7 July 1911, Japanese immigration 187405-7.
15 July 1911, Anglo-Japanese treaty 187604-31.
5 August 1911, Japanese immigration 188585-7.

Jardine, John.
23 January 1908, Asiatic immigration 135519-21.

Jones, A.G.
16 October 1896, Pacific cable 8074.
20 October 1896, Pacific cable 8166-8.
2 October 1896, Pacific cable 8203-4.
26 December 1896, Pacific cable 10075-9.
7 January 1897, Pacific cable 10775-87.
5 May 1899, Cable, Pacific 225276-82.

Kerr, John(Vancouver).
15 March 1897, Chinese immigration 13070.

Kimura, Baron(Japanese ambassador).
11 May 1907, Japanese visit to Canada 125282-.

King, Hon. William Lyon MacKenzie.
22 October 1907, Oriental immigration 130808-92.
21 March 1908, Oriental immigration 138074-87.

15 July 1908, Oriental immigration 142591-601.
31 October 1908, Opium Commission 146859-74.
19 November 1908, Anti-Opium Commission, Shanghai, Oriental immigration 147988-9.
29 December 1908, Anti-Opium Commission 149482.
31 January 1909, Oriental immigration 151210-6.
17 February 1909, Anti-Opium Commission, Oriental immigration 151924-33.
17 March 1909, Oriental immigration 153673-6.
22 March 1909, Oriental immigration 153843-95.
23 March 1909, Oriental immigration 153946-51.
1 May 1909, arrival from Orient 155499.
20 September 1909, Asiatic exclusion 159970-160043.
6 June 1910, Oriental immigration 171791-5.
23 January 1914 Immigration from India 190590-1.

Kirby, E.B.
13 January 1901, Asiatic immigration 53084-90.

Langley W.H.
25 July 1900, Oriental immigration 47770-1.

Larney, T.C.
17 April 1910, Chinese immigration 170034-40.
15 November 1910, Chinese immigration 176833-4.

Laschinger, E.H.
4 March 1909, routes to Australia 152970-1.

Latta, J.
31 May 1903, Chinese immigration 73750-2.

Lemieux, Rodolphe, 1907.
7 November 1907, Japanese immigration 117307d-e.
27 September 1907, Japan 129769-70.
12 November 1907, trip to Japan 131842-6.
15 November 1907, Japanese immigration. Mission to Japan 132056-183.
16 November 1907, Japanese immigration 132301-11.
22 November 1907, Japanese earthquake 136611-2.
22 November 1907, Japanese immigration 132616-8.
25 November 1907, Japanese immigration 232708-17.
27 November 1907, negotiations with Japan. Japanese immigration 132858-60.
27 November 1907, Japanese immigration 132861-66.
3 December 1907, Japanese immigration 132233-6.
3 December 1907, Japanese immigration 133237-8.
4 December 1907, Japanese immigration 133296-9.
5 December 1907, Japanese immigration 133346-52.
6 December 1907, Japanese negotiations 133409-20.
10 December 1907, Japanese immigration 133709-14.
16 December 1907, Japanese immigration and negotiations 133810-2.
19 December 1907, Japanese immigration 134002-7.
20 December 1907, Japanese immigration 134043-50.
21 December 1907, Japanese immigration 134105-12.
21 December 1907, Japanese immigration 134115-6.
23 December 1907, Japanese immigration 134140-60.
25 December 1907, return from Japan 134229.
4 May 1908, Japanese immigration 140047.
14 July 1908, Oriental immigration 14253956.
8 July 1918 Russia and Japan, interview with Fielding 200914-15.

Lewis, John.
23 February 1900, relief for India 42729-31.

Lytteltown.
16 November 1905, Anglo-Japanese treaty 215789-93.

McBride, Hon. Richard.
9 September 1903, Chinese immigration. Chinese capitation tax 76878-80.
12 June 1908, Chinese immigration 141608-12.

Macdonald, Sir C.M.
23 October 1907, Japan 130855-8.

Macdonald, Sir Claude.
20 September 1907, Japanese riots in British Columbia 129521.
11 October 1907, Asiatic immigration 130359.
11 October 1907, British Columbia riots, Oriental immigration 215895-7.
20 October 1907, Japanese negotiations 130728-32.
23 October 1907, Japanese immigration 130835-42.
23 October 1907, Hon. R. Lemieux mission to Japan 130865.
12 December 1907, Japanese immigration 215913-4.
20 June 1908, Japanese immigration 215926-9.
26 February 1908, Japanese immigration 215967-8.
5 March 1908, Japanese immigration 216000-1.
9 March 1908, Japanese immigration 137332-3.
14 March 1908, Japanese immigration 216035-6.
2 July 1908, Japanese immigration 216201.

MacInnes, T.R.E.
11 September 1907, Asiatic immigration in British Columbia 129162-4.
7 November 1907, Asiatic immigration 131593-600.
12 December 1907, Oriental immigration 134026-30.
28 December 1907, Oriental immigration 134371-2.
3 January 1908, Japanese in British Columbia 134691-4.
10 January 1908, Japanese immigration 134942-44.
13 January 1908, Japanese immigration 135078-9.
26 January 1908, Japanese immigration 135595-603.
29 January 1908, Asiatic immigration 135709-11.
31 January 1908, Oriental immigration 135595-603.
2 February 1908, Oriental immigration 135870-2.
7 February 1908, Asiatic immigration 136107-13.
12 February 1908, Oriental immigration 136303-14.
22 February 1908, Asiatic immigration 136740-42.
8 February 1908, Asiatic immigration 136969-70.
15 March 1908, Oriental immigration 137761-2.
19 March 1908, Hindu immigration 137920-5.
22 March 1908, Oriental immigration 138145-6.
1 July 1908, opium traffic 142187-8.
2 July 1908, opium import 142197-200.
1 February 1910, Japanese in British Columbia 166014-37.
12 September 1910, opium smuggling 174653-5.
22 September 1910, Chinese opium import 175014-9.
5 October 1910, opium in British Columbia 175392-3.
15 October 1910, Chinese opium smuggling 175835-8.
21 October 1910, Chinese opium smuggling 175983-4.
28 October 1910, Chinese Immigration Commission 176811-3.

MacInnes, W.W.B.
13 August 1899, Chinese immigration 36466-70.
28 March 1902, Chinese head tax 63923a.
11 October 1907, Oriental immigration 130357-8.
24 March 1908, Hindu immigration 138181-2.

McKenney, R.R.
28 September 1907, Japanese immigration 129805-6.

Maclean, A.
1902, trip to Japan 68695-6.
30 July 1905, Japanese immigration, Japanese labour and trade 100192-207.

Maclean, A(Australian).
16 March 1900, Pacific cable 43394-6.

MacLeod, Rev. J.R.
19 May 1903, Chinese immigration 73471-4.

MacPherson, R.G.
4 September 1906, Hindu immigration 113371-4.
24 July 1907, Japanese immigration 127059-64.
10 August 1907, Japanese immigration 127623-5.
10 August 1907, Japanese immigration 127979-82.
14 October 1907, Japanese immigration 130484-7.
4 February 1908, Japanese immigration 135955-8.

MacRae, A.B.
17 September 1909, Oriental labour 159908-11.

Magee, H.S.
27 June 1908, Anti-Opium League 142002-4.

Marine and Fisheries Department.
19 March 1901, Pacific cable 54488-90.

Martin, Joseph.
17 January 1899, Oriental immigration 29731-5.

Matheson, A.W.
16 February 1908, Chinese immigration 136400-3.

Methodist Church Conference.
16 February 1908, Chinese immigration tax 74175-7.

Milne, G.L.
14 September 1907, Hindu immigration 129350.
21 April 1899, Pacific cable 32849-52.
27 April 1899, Pacific cable 33012-3.
10 May 1899, Pacific cable 215049.
18 May 1899, Pacific cable 215060.
13 June 1899, Pacific cable 215081.
30 November 1899, Chinese immigration 30754.
2 March 1900, Pacific cable 42909-11.
31 May 1900, Pacific cable 215251.
15 February 1901, Pacific cable 215289.
26 February 1901, Pacific cable 53684-5.
1 November 1901, Pacific cable 215402-5.
6 June 1902, Pacific cable 215526-8.
21 December 1906, situation in India 134079-97.
1 March 1909, William Lyon MacKenzie King. Oriental immigration 152772-3.
17 February 1910, conditions in India 167175-88.

Monroe, A.S. (Immigration Department, Vancouver).
7 September 1907, Japanese immigrants 128794-7.
30 September 1907, Japanese immigration 129827-30.
2 March 1908, Hindu immigrants 137054.

Morinville, Alberta.
17 September 1907, Asiatic Exclusion 129447-50.

Morrison, Aulay.
17 February 1900, Chinese immigration 42483-7.
11 September 1900, Oriental immigration 49007.
8 November 1900, Oriental immigration 50384.

Mulock, William.
10 November 1898, Pacific cable 27970-8.
29 November 1898, Pacific cable 28436-7.
2 January 1900, Pacific cable 40688.
8 January 1900, Pacific cable 40891-2.
5 February 1900, Pacific cable 41990.
3 April 1900, Pacific cable 44281-4.
30 May 1900, Pacific cable 46068.
22 December 1900, Chinese commission 51790.
3 January 1901, Chinese immigration 52177-86.
5 March 1901, Pacific cable 53914-5.
5 March 1901, nationalization of Japanese 53924-8.
11 October 1901, Canada-Australia steamship service. 59288-92.
17 August 1903, Pacific cable 76238-9.

Munn, D.J.
14 August 1900, Oriental Commission 48297.
28 August 1900, Oriental Commission 48635.
22 November 1900, Oriental immigration 50983-4.
24 January 1901, Oriental immigration 52959-62.
4 April 1901, Oriental immigration 55110-2.
6 May 1901, Oriental immigration 55943.
27 July 1901, Oriental immigration 57211-3.
20 February 1902, Oriental immigration 62948-9.
14 March 1902, Oriental immigration 63680-2.
14 March 1902, Oriental immigration 63683-4.
27 May 1902, Oriental immigration 65383-6.

Munnings, Rev. E.
23 July 1911, Hindu immigration 187864-66.

Munro, A.S.
14 September 1907, Hindu immigration 12957.
1 October 1907, Oriental immigration 129896-901.
7 October 1907, Oriental immigration 130155-6.

National Council of Women.
20 August 1898, slavery, immigration of Chinese women 25897-8.

New South Wales Premier.
25 January 1900, Pacific cable 41447.

New Westminster Liberal Association.
20 June 1900, Oriental immigration 46684-6

New Zealand Premier.
27 February 1900, Pacific cable 42816.
6 March 1900, Pacific cable 43083.
18 October 1900, Pacific cable 50029-31.

North West Mounted Police.
23 December 1900, loyalty of Indians during South African War 41328-31.

O'Halloran, G.F.
14 March 1903, British Japanese Treaty 71036.
18 March 1903, Canada-Japan trade 71249-50.
2 April 1903, British-Japanese trade negotiations 71709.

O'Hara, F.C.T.
14 December 1903, discharge of Chinese interpreter 79869.
2 January 1904, Canadian Australia steamship service 80558-9.
13 Augusta 1907, Australia trade 127759.
19 Augusta 1907, Australia trade 127962-3.
21 August 1907, Australia trade 128062-4.
27 August 1907, Australia trade 128217.
5 September 1907, Japanese immigration 128653.
5 September 1907, Australia trade 128657.
6 September 1907, Japanese immigration 128710-11.
13 January 1908, Canada-Australia steamship service 135122.
29 January 1908, Japanese immigrants 135694.
29 February 1908, Japanese immigrants 137005-7.
13 May 1908, Australia trade 140440-5.
10 June 1908, Australia trade 141366-86.
6 July 1908, Australia trade 142330-3.
2 February 1909, Australia steamship service 151319-22.
25 June 1909, timber trade with New Zealand 164114-5.
10 January 1910, Australia steamship service 164918-22.
11 January 1910, Australia steamship service 165017-21.
19 January 1910, Australia steamship service 165476-8.
20 January 1910, Australia steamship service 155542-4.
23 January 1910, Australia steamship service 168675-7.
10 May 1910, Canada Australia steamship service 170901-3.
10 May 1910, Canada Australia steamship service 170904-6.
31 May 1910, Canada Australia steamship service 171639-54.
6 July 1910, Canada Australia steamship service 172904.
23 September 1910, Chinese immigration 175035.
23 September 1910, Australia steamship service 175040-4.
29 September 1910, Chinese smuggling case 175234-6.
24 October 1910, Australia trade 176070-80.
11 November 1910, Chinese immigration 176737.
15 November 1910, Australia steamship service 176835.
20 December 1910, Canada-Australia-New Zealand steamship service 178432-33.
30 December 1910, Canada-Australia-New Zealand steamship service 178974-8.
5 January 1911, Canada Australia steamship service 179265-6.
10 January 1910, Canada-Australia-New Zealand steamship service 179873.
12 January 1911, Australia steamship services 179971-5.
30 January 1911, China and Japan steamship services 180681-96.
9 February 1911, Pacific steamship service 181287-90.
24 March 1911, Chinese immigration 183807-8.
10 May 1911, reciprocal trade, Canada and Australia 186041-57.
24 July 1911, Chinese immigration 187940-50.

Oliver, Frank.
4 July 1900, Chinese immigration 47101-2.
1906, Hindu immigration 104886-7.
16 September 1907, Japanese riots 129383.
16 September 1907, Japanese riots 129397-8.
15 October 1907, Japanese immigration 130518-9.
1 November 1907, Vancouver riots 131254-5.
27 December 1907, Japanese immigration 134317.
16 February 1908, Japanese immigration 136397-9.
22 February 1908, Japanese immigration 136730-1.
25 June 1910, Hindu immigration 170283-9.
3 March 1911, Hindu immigration 185718-.

Page, Z.D.
3 June 1903, Oriental labour migration 73826-7.

Paquette, D.
2 September 1907, Asiatic exclusion 129854-5.

Paris(Ontario) Board of Trade.
1 June 1905, trade with Australia 98089-93.

Parmelee, W.G.
4 August 1898, Canadian Australian steamship service 25556.
28 April 1898, Australian steamship service 33030-2.
13 June 1900, Chinese capitation tax 46425-6.
25 June 1900, Chinese immigration bill 46840-8.
26 March 1903, Chinese bread tax, British Columbia 71488.
8 July 1903, Japanese immigration 74857-8.
9 September 1903, Chinese bread tax 76881-2.
15 September 1903, Chinese immigration 16997.
29 October 1906, Australia-Canada trade 115082-4.
10 December 1906, Australia trade 116488-9.
9 August 1907, Australia trade 127600-2.

Peake, R.E.
1 April 1901, Pacific cable 54967-8.

Philp, Robert.
1 February 1910, Pacific cable 215169.

Pillay, K.S.
Addresses of British Indians in South Africa 59258-9.

Pine, A.J.
11 July 1907, prohibition of opium 126282.

Pope, Sir Joseph.

15 November 1907, Japanese negotiations 132184-5.
9 December 1907, negotiations in Japan re Japanese immigration 133521-7.
9 December 1907, Japanese immigration 133547-53.
25 December 1907, gift from Prince Fushimi 134242-3.
24 August 1910, Japan treaties 174041-5.
10 March 1911, Japanese immigration 182985-7.

Preston, W.J.R.
22 February 1907, Indian immigration 129560-1.
22 October 1907, Japanese immigration 130800-4.
7 October 1909, Japanese delegation 160731.
19 October 1909, Japanese delegation 161109.

Pringle, William R.
17 October 1906, Hindu immigration 114749-52.

Pringle and Guthrie.
24 February 1907, Pacific steamship line. Eastern Canada to Australia and New Zealand 120719-29.

Prior, E.G
27 March 1903, Chinese immigration 71518-20.

Pollen, H.F.
14 December 1906, Oriental immigration 116801-03.

Reed, D.
10 September 1907, Asian immigration 129029-30.

Rigg, O.D.
27 June 1911, Appointment for the Gaekwad of Baroda 187211-3.

Robillard, Jeremie.
14 May 1900, Chinese immigration 56188-91.

Roosevelt, Theodore(President of the United States).
1 February 1908, Oriental immigration 135842-9.

Ross, Sir Charles.
20 June 1906, Canadian commercial agent - China 111419-20.

Ross, D.H.
4 September 1901, export of fish eggs to Australia 58642-3.
6 March 1907, Australian trade 121103.
7 March 1907, Australian trade 121929-39.
11 March 1907, Australian trade 122199-206.
12 March 1907, Australian trade 122275-8.
13 March 1907, Australian trade 122343-7.
20 March 1907, Australian trade 122677-89.
3 April 1907, Australian trade 123483-9.
5 September 1907, Australian tariff 128704-7.
25 November 1907, Pacific cable 132782-97.
17 January 1908, Pacific cable 135296-7.
15 February 1908, Pacific cable 136386--91.
14 March 1908, Pacific cable 137533-6.
11 April 1908, Pacific cable 138937-41.
9 May 1908, Pacific cable 140290-2.
11 May 1908, Pacific cable 140352-4.
20 May 1908, Pacific cable 140688-94.

8 August 1908, Canada -Australia steamship line 143326.
22 November 1909, Trade - Canada-Australia 162574.
10 February 1910, Trade - Canada-Australia 166755-6.
24 August 1910, Australian trade 174197-200.
December 1910, Australian trade 177621-40.
26 August 1911, Canada-Australia steamship service 185372-4.

Roy, Julien.
3 January 1908, Japanese in British Columbia 134687-90.
20 January 1908, Japanese immigration 135393-4
22 January 1908, Japanese immigration 135512-3.
17 February 1908, Japanese immigration 136432-4.
18 February 1908, Japanese immigration 136497-8.
24 February 1908, Japanese immigration 136828-33.

Rutherford, J.G.
26 March 1900, famine in India 43936-44.

Scott, R.W.
22 November 1901, Pacific cable 60124.
8 August 1905, Baron Kimura's visit 100469-70.
5 August 1906, visit of Baron Kimura 122671-2.
29 January 1907, Australia-Canada trade 118877-8.
29 April 1907, Japanese immigration 124678.

Scott, W.D.
30 June 1910, Hindu immigration 172714-6.

Scully, John.
25 June 1900, Chinese immigration 46787-91.

Seddon, Hon. R.J
10 October 1898, New Zealand Canada trade 27097-8.
23 January 1900, Pacific cable 215160.
13 February 1900, Pacific cable 215192.
20 February 1900, Pacific cable 42627-9.
25 February 1900, Pacific cable 215198-9.
2 November 1900, Pacific cable 50261.
31 October 1902, Pacific cable 67806-17.
9 March 1903, Pacific steamship service 215606-8.
26 September 1903, Pacific steamship service 215659-62.

Semlin, C.A.
3 June 1899, British Columbia Japanese legislation 34144-5.

Senkler, J.N.
3 October 1910, Chinese smuggling frauds 175515-7.
10 October 1910, opium 175587.
18 October 1910, opium 175884-6.

Shaughnessy, Sir Thomas G.
15 April 1899, trade with China and Japan 32587-8.
26 January 1900, Chinese immigration 41460-2.
2 June 1902, Australia-Canada steamship service 65528.
27 August 1907, Steamship service, Hong Kong-Liverpool 128285-6.

7 September 1907, Pacific cable 128758.
9 September 1907, Pacific cable 128841-3.
26 December 1907, Pacific cable 134262.
24 February 1908, Trans-Pacific services 136827.
28 February 1908, Pacific steamship service 136980.
2 February 1910, Pacific cable 166060.
24 December 1910, Canadian Pacific Railway Pacific mail subsidy 178732-5.

Shaw, Joseph.
10 September 1907, Asiatic exclusion 129055-6.

Shaw, L.C.
28 October 1907, Japanese trade treaty 131100-3.

Sherwood, A.P.
7 September 1907, Japanese riots Vancouver 128781.
29 January 1908, Japanese troubles, British Columbia 135712-5.

Shibusawa, Baron.
1 November 1909, Japanese Commercial Commission 161571-2.

Shields, R.
2 April 1906, China-Canada trade 109066-72.

Singh, A
21 September 1910, Indian subjects in United States 174949.

Singh, Hira.
19 October 1908, Sikhs in British Columbia 146051-2.
2 July 1910, Hindu immigration, admission in Canada 172809-.
27 July 1911, Admission to Canada of wife and child 188187-95.

Singh, S
24 July 1911, Hindu immigration 187951-73.

Smith, Ralph.
10 May 1901, Japanese immigration 56100-4.
2 August 1907, Japanese immigration 127322-4.
January 1908, Japanese immigration 134619-20.
18 January 1908, Japanese immigration 135313-21.
25 May 1909, Canada-New Zealand steamship service 156237-8.
20 September 1910, Grand Trunk Pacific Oriental labour 174916-9.

Staples, John J.
19 May 1908, Asiatic immigration 140630-47.

Stephens, George V.
4 June 1903, Oriental immigration 73852-5.

Stephens, Roy.
12 August 1907, Asiatic immigration 127701.

Strathcona, Lord (Smith, Sir Donald).
22 August 1896, China, visit of diplomat 224379-80.
19 December 1896, Pacific cable 9862-8.
22 December 1899, Pacific cable 215130.

1900, Pacific cable 215254.
12 February 1900, Pacific cable 215191.
17 February 1900, Pacific cable 215195-7.
26 February 1900, Pacific cable 215211-6.
6 March 1900, Pacific cable 43084.
4 April 1900, Pacific cable 215229-30.
19 June 1900, Pacific cable 46661.
21 June 1900, Pacific steamship services 215255-6.
13 December 1900, Pacific cable 51659.
24 January 1901, Pacific cable 217279.
25 January 1901, Pacific cable 215319.
16 February 1901, Pacific cable 215281.
16 February 1901, Pacific cable 215329.
16 February 1901, Pacific cable 215333.
19 February 1901, Pacific cable 215285.
23 February 1901, Pacific cable 215338-9.
12 April 1901, Pacific cable 215287-91.
22 April 1901, Pacific cable 215295-6.
19 August 1901, Pacific cable 54229.
11 June 1901, Pacific cable 65787-800.
16 March 1903, Pacific cable 71118-9.
12 March 1904, Pacific cable 215709.
7 May 1904, Pacific cable 85801-3.
10 September 1907, Anti-Japanese riots 129058-9.
6 December 1907, Pacific cable 133434-6.
19 February 1908, Pacific cable 151999-2033.
17 June 1909, Chinese consul 157075.
5 August 1909, Pacific cable 158686-95.
17 September 1909, Pacific cable 159907.
18 November 1909, Pacific cable 162302.

Sully, Robert.
10 September 1907, Asiatic immigration 129025-8.

Swan, Howard.
24 June 1905, Manchurian question 98948-50.

Takahashi, K.T.
1897, Japan immigration 10271-85.

Templeman, William.
23 March 1900, Chinese immigration 40486a-6.
26 June 1900, Oriental immigration 46891-3.
24 July 1900, Oriental immigration 47428-33.
18 May 1903, Chinese immigration 73410-2.
9 July 1903, Japanese immigration 74900-1.
1 September 1906, Hindu immigration 113247-6405.
30 July 1907, Japanese immigration 127113-5.
9 August 1907, Japanese immigration 127574-6.
27 September 1907, Oriental immigration William Lyon MacKenzie King 129789-80.
12 February 1908, Oriental immigration 136244-8.
10 July 1908, Japanese immigration 142451-5.

Thorn, J.O.
20 October 1909, Australia steamship 161135-40.

Toronto Board of Trade.
25 May 1899, Pacific cable 33859.

Toronto Trades and Labour Council.
4 April 1909, Asiatic exclusion law 161062-3.

Trade and Commerce, Departments.

1 March 1900, Chinese immigration 42869-71.
4 July 1900, Japanese immigration 57168-9.
23 July 1903, Japanese immigration 75370-2.
1 August 1903, Japanese immigration 75691-734.
February 1906, Canada Australia steamship service 106686-731.
6 August 1906, Australia trade, New Zealand trade 112683-726.
January 1907, New Zealand trade 117698-709.
16 April 1907, Pacific cable 123984-9.
5 September 1907, Pacific cable 128693-8.
23 August 1909, Australia trade 159125-30.
27 August 1909, Australia trade 159250.
6 October 1909, Australia trade 160681.
21 November 1910, Pacific cable 177093.

Trail Liberal Association.
28 December 1908, Chinese immigration 149437-8.

Turriff, J.G.
15 October 1909, Canada Australia steamship service 160964.

Vail, W.B.
13 December 1896, Pacific cable 9737-40.

Vancouver Board of Trade.
27 December 1907, Canada-Australia steamship line 134344.
6 July 1908, Australia steamship service 142302-3.

Vancouver City Council.
27 November 1906, Indian immigration 116102-4.
2 November 1907, Japanese immigration 131345-7.

Vancouver Hindu Association.
5 October 1909, release of Hindu student 160653.

Vancouver Liberal Association.
14 June 1900, Oriental immigration 46496.
26 July 1907, Japanese immigration 126840-1.
1 August 1907, Oriental immigration 127244-7.
2 October 1907, Oriental immigration 129963-6.
11 November 1907, Asiatic immigration 131718.
29 August 1909, Canada Australia steamship services 155426.

Vancouver, Mayor of.
11 September 1907, Japanese riots 129117-21.
11 September 1907, Hindu immigration 129135-47.

Vancouver Trades and Labour Council.
7 February 1903, Oriental immigration 69995-6.

Vancouver Young Men's Liberal Club.
24 February 1898, Chinese immigration 20942.

Van Horne, Sir William C.
17 July 1896, Immigration Chinese 5746-50.
26 July 1898 Canadian-Australian steamship services 25356-61.

Victoria(British Columbia) Board of Trade.
8 April 1904, British Columbia fisheries, Oriental immigration 84326-9.
Victoria Trades and Labour Council.
25 August 1906, Hindu immigration 113129-134.
29 July 1907, Oriental immigration 127065-7.
18 August 1910, Oriental immigration 174000-2.

Von Olegar, David.
16 June 1897, Pacific cable 15530-2.

Ward, Sir Joseph G.
8 June 1904, Pacific steamship service 215733.
9 January 1905, Pacific steamship service 93494.
14 January 1908, Canada Australia steamship service 135137-9.
18 November 1909, Pacific cable 162296-301.
1 January 1910, Canada Australia steamship service 164721-2.
2 September 1910, Canada Australia, New Zealand steamship service 174376.
19 June 1911, Canada New Zealand steamship service 180265-7.

Warren, Fulk.
2 January 1907, Oriental immigration 117771-5.

Watson, J.H.
March 1908, Oriental immigration 137046-9.

Weston, W.W.
30 March 1908, Asiatic immigration 138435-8.

White, Fred.
29 September 1899, Visit of Kang Yu-wei, North West Mounted Police escort 37665.

Wood, Benjamin(Society of Friends).
2 October 1907, Oriental immigration 129955-7.

Wood, T.W.(Vancouver **Daily Province**).
23 November 1908, Hindu immigration 148107-15.

Woodbury, Dr. H.
10 November 1908, Chinese immigration 147448-56.

Woods, A.
14 August 1896, Canada-Australia trade 6262-8.
11 December 1901, Trade with Australia 60707-1

Woods, Garson.
2 November 1896, Trade with Australia 8472-5.
9 December 1896, Australia trade 9627-8.

Woods, E.H.M.
4 March 1908, Hindu immigration 140074-80.
26 October 1909, Asiatic exclusion 161337-40.
27 August 1910, Oriental immigration 174166-9.

Zimmerman, W.
21 September 1906, Hindu immigration 113962-4.

Correspondence on the Colonial Conferences, 1907, 1911.

Volumes 750-756.

Despatches concerning external relations, chiefly copies of the Governor General's secret or confidential correspondence sent to Laurier for information.

Scrap-books, 1897-1921. 2 feet, 4 inches,(volumes 804-805, 815-826).
Contain clippings on the Colonial Conference of 1897, and the Imperial Conferences of 1907 and 1911.

H. Borden, Robert Laird, 1854-1937.

Prime minister, 1911-1920.
Originals, 1836-1938, 150 feet, 440 volumes. Finding Aid 833(a computer sorted index(reels C4819-C4829) divided into chronological index, subject index and correspondent index).
Reels C4823 and C4824 only consulted. Asia- and Pacific-related topics were:

China, 1914-1926(42 items).

China-Canada relations, 1914-1922(69 items).

Chinese Canadians, 1914-1920(31 items).

Dutch East India, 1916(1 item).

Immigration, Asiatic, 1917(2 items).

Immigration, Chinese, 1913- (85 items).

Immigration, Hindu, 1907-1921(332 items, with heavy emphasis on 1914, the date of the **Komagata maru** incident).

Immigration, Japanese, 1908-1914(34 items).

Immigration, Japanese, 1908-1921(41 items).

Immigration, Oriental, 1906-1935(81 items).

India, 1913-1934(93 items).

Japan, 1912-1933(42 items).

Japanese-American relations, 1913-1916(22 items).

Japanese-Canadian relations, 1907-1935(109 items).

Japanese Canadians, 1913-1917(17 items).

Trade with China, 1915-1919(7 items).

Trade with India, 1917(3 items).

Trade with Japan, 1906-1917(23 items).

In addition there was correspondence on the Imperial Conferences of 1907, 1911, 1921, 1923, 1926, and 1930, which peripherally related to India.

Borden headed the Canadian delegation to the Paris Peace Conference of 1919, where Canada had a special role in relation to the Dominions and India. Memoranda by Borden on the work of the Canadian delegation at the Paris Conference, 6 January-10 May 1919, in volume 296, 2 inches, and also the papers of the Canadian delegation, 6 feet, volume 427-444.
Borden participated in the Washington Disarmament Conference, 5 November 1921-7 February 1922, 1 inch, in volume 297.

The index by correspondents indicates 35 items from 1912-1926 to the Japanese Consul General and one on the Japanese treaty of 1911.

I. Meighen, Arthur, 1874-1960.

Prime minister, 1920-1921, 1926.
Originals, 1917-1960, 90 feet 8 inches, 272 volumes. Finding aid 883(a computer sorted index in three parts: chronological, subject and by correspondent, reels C4831-C4833). The aid was consulted for its subject index, and Asia- and Pacific-related topics were:

Chanak incident, 1922, 1922-1924(186 items).

Great Britain was close to war with Turkey, and Canada would not participate.

China, 1921-1926(16 items).

Chinese Canadian relations, 1938(1 item).

Immigration, Armenian, 1924-1926(4 items).

Immigration, Chinese, 1921-1927(10 items).

Immigration, Indian, 1921-1922(16 items).
Immigration, Japanese, 1921(32 items)

Immigration, Oriental, 1922-1925, 1942(14 items)

Imperial Conferences, 1917, 1921, 1923, 1926, 1930, 1932, and 1937(355 items) India would be represented.

Imperial Economic Conferences, 1923,1926, and 1932(211 items).

India, 1920-1953(41 items).

Japan, 1920-1938(15 items).

Japanese representative in Canada, 1923(1 item).

Japanese American relations, 1935(3 items).

Japanese Canadian relations, 1920-1940(9 items).

Japanese Canadians, 1921-1940(3 items).

Trade with India, 1926-1932(6 items).

Trade with Japan, 1924(2 items).

Trade with Malaya, 1932(1 item).

Turkey, 1922-1924(94 items).

Turkish Canadian relations, 1922-1924(4 items).

The index by correspondent indicates 6 items to the Japanese government, 4 for 1933 and 2 for 1926.

J. King, William Lyon MacKenzie;, 1874-1950.

Prime Minister 1921-1925, 1926-1930, and 1935-1948. Originals, 1641, 1703, 1840, 1884-1950, 825 feet 4 inches. Finding aid 502 indexes the Primary Series, correspondence 1889-1950, originals 148 feet 8 inches, volumes 1-446. The Primary Series Correspondence is on microfilm to 1945.

The Asia- and Pacific-related topics included:

China, 1922-1940**(299 items).**

    Arms, 1925(1 item).

    Arms embargo, 1926-1929(8 items).

    Arms shipment, 1926(1 item).

    Boxer Rebellion, 1930(1 item).

    Cabinet Minister, 1935(2 items).

    Civil War, 1935(1 item).

    Communism, 1935(1 item).

    Cost of living, 1942(1 item).

    Defense policy, 1928(1 item).

    Economic conditions, 1935-1941(10 items).

    Extraterritoriality, 1929-1942(49 items).

    Food prices, 1942(1 item).

    Foreign missions, 1928, 1929(2 items).

    Foreign policy, 1928-1942(4 items).

    Government, 1929(4 items).

    International Settlements, 1929(1 item).

    Legal system, 1929-1930(10 items).

    Liberalism, 1929(1 item).

    Malnutrition, 1940(1 item).

    Military situation, 1929, 1937(3 items).

    Missionaries, 1924-1939(34 items).

    Missionary shootings, 1939(1 item).

    Monetary policy, 1936(1 item).

    Monetary reform, 1936(1 item).

    Shanghai riots, 1925(1 item).

    Shipping Yangtse, 1939(2 items).

    Silver smuggling, 1935(1 item).

    Sun Yat-sen memorial, 1930(1 item).

    Tientsin, International Bridge, 1939(1 item).

China, North, autonomy, 1935(1 item).

Chinese Canadians, 1924-1940(8 items).

Chinese Immigration, 1939(1 item).

Chinese-American relations, 1939-1941(3 items).

Chinese-American relations. Medical relief, 1937(2 items).

Chinese-Canadian relations, 1927-1942(28 items).

Chinese-Soviet relations, 1929(1 item).

Diplomats in Japan, 1936(2 items).

Disarmament Japan, 1929(1 item).

High Commissioner to India, 1940(1 item).

Immigration

    Immigration, Chinese, 1923-1942(12 items).

    Immigration, Hindu, 1923(1 item).

    Immigration, India, 1922-1939(8 items).

    Immigration, Japanese, 1924-1941(39 items).

    Immigration, Oriental, 1922-1940(52 items).

Japan, 1922-1942(171 items).

    Anti-Semitism, 1939(1 item).

    Armed forces, 1935(2 items).

    Armed forces, Manchuria, 1935(1 item).

    British Commonwealth relations, 1936(1 item).

    Budget, 1939(1 item).

    Cabinet appointments, 1941(2 items).

Cabinet resignations, 1941(3 items).
> Civil liberties, 1941(1 item).
> Commercial policy, 1941(3 items).
> Communism, 1941(1 item).
> Currency, 1937(1 item).
> Customs, 1936(1 item).
> Defence, Navy, 1938(5 items).
> Earthquake, 1923-1924(6 items).
> Economic conditions, 1929-1942(32 items).
> Economic situation, 1936(1 item).
> Education minister, 1938(1 item).
> Emigration, 1942(1 item).
> Emperor, 1940(1 item).
> Emperor's palace, New Year's celebration, 1937 (1 item).
> Espionage, 1936-1941(2 items).
> Exports, 1934(1 item).
> Extra territoriality, 1929-1936(3 items).
> Family allowances, 1941(1 item).
> Financial policy, 1936-1937(2 items).
> Food control, 1941(2 items).
> Food requirements, 1941(1 item).
> Foreign Affairs ministers, 1928(1 item).
> Foreign policy, 1936-1941(190 items).
>> Amur incident, 1937(1 item).
>> Germany, 1939(1 item).
>> Italy, 1939(1 item).
> Foreign relations, 1935-1936(5 items).
> Foreign relations, Manchuria, 1935-1936(2 items)
> Foreign trade, 1935(1 item).
> Franciscan missionaries, 1936(2 items).
> Immigration, 1937(2 items).

Industrial Control Law, 1935(1 item).
Interests in British Columbia, 1939(1 item).
Japan Trade Council, 1935(1 item).
Justice, 1936(1 item).
Law enforcement, 1936(2 items).
Legislation, 1941(2 items).
Military situation, 1936(16 items).
Missionaries, 1941(2 items).
> Roman Catholic, 1935(2 items).
National Defense Security Act, 1941(1 item).
National policy, 1936(1 item).
Naval forces, 1935(1 item).
Naval policy, 1935-1937(39 items).
Parliament, 1940(1 item).
> Dissolution, 1936(1 item).
> Proceedings, 1941(1 item).
Political crisis, 1936(8 items).
Political situation, 1935-1941(76 items).
> February uprising, 1937(1 item).
> Hayashi cabinet, 1937(1 item).
> Hirota cabinet, 1937(1 item).
> Keelung, 1937(2 items).
> Premier Hayashi, 1937(1 item).
Population growth, 1941(2 items).
Relief, 1923(5 items).
Religion, 1936(14 items).
Religious discrimination, 1936-1941(5 items).
Religious order, 1941(1 item).
Representatives in Canada, 1928-1941(35 items).
> Departure, 1940(1 item).
> Diplomatic status, 1941(3 items).

Representation in Germany, 1941(1 item).

Representation in the United States, 1929,1941(2 items).

Representation in China, 1938(1 item).

Riots, Oshima Island, 1935(1 item).

Royal family, 1937(3 items).

Shipping, 1938-1941(6 items).

Tariff policy, 1936(3 items).

Tourists, 1936(1 item).

Trade, 1937(2 items).

Trade policy, 1936-1938(10 items).

Trade situation, 1936(1 item).

Trade with Australia, 1936(8 items).

    China, 1936(2 items).

    Dutch East Indies, 1935(1 item).

    Germany, 1936(1 item).

    United States, 1936(i item).

    U.S.S.R. 1936(1 item).

Japan-Canada Society, 1935(3 items).

Japanese-Canadians, 1927-1941(30 items).

    British Columbia, 1929,1940(2 items).

    Discrimination, 1939(1 item).

    Franchise, 1936(1 item).

    Pacific Coast, 1938(1 item).

    Racial discrimination, 1937(1 item).

Japanese Christian Brotherhood, 1941(1 item).

Japanese American relations, 1922-1941(110 items).

    China, 1938(1 item).

    Far East, 1939(7 items).

    Liquor, 1929(1 item).

    Shipping, 1939(1 item).

Japanese-Australian relations, 1936(2 items).

Japanese-Canadian relations, 1922-1942(140 items).

Espionage, 1936(2 items).

Fisheries, 1939(1 item).

Immigration, 1938(1 item).

Japanese-Dutch relations, 1940-1941(7 items).

Japanese Fishing Associations, 1939(1 item).

Japanese-German relations, 1936-1941(15 items).

Japanese-Italian relations, 1936(1 item).

Japanese-Korean relations, 1941(1 item).

Japanese-Philippine relations, 1936(1 item).

Japanese-Siam relations, 1940-1941(19 items).

Japanese-Soviet relations, 1936-1937(21 items).

Japanese-Spanish relations, 1936(1 item).

Japanese-Thailand relations, 1941(1 item).

Japanese-Vatican relations, 1942(1 item).

Pacific Cable, 1923-1929(210 items).

Pacific relations, 1925-1940(14 items).

    Conference, 1928(15 items).

Persia, 1924-1942.

    Oil, 1929(1 item).

    Political situation, 1942(6 items).

    Shah, 1941, 1942(2 items).

    Trade embargoes, Japan, 1935-1941(33 items).

    War materials, 1939(1 item).

Trade with China, 1922-1942(25 items).

Trade with Fiji, 1924(1 item).

Trade with Japan, 1922-1942(180 items).

    Aluminum, 1940(1 item).

    British Columbia, 1935-1939(3 items).

    Copper, 1934(1 item).

    Dumping, 1935(1 item).

    Lead, 1940(1 item).

    Metals, 1936-1940(4 items).

Molybdenum, 1940(1 item).

Nickel, 1941(2 items).

Salmon, 1939(1 item).

Scrap iron, 1940(1 item).

Textiles, 1932(1 item).

Trade summary, 1935(1 item).

War materials, 1938(1 item).

Trade with Persia, 1927-1929(3 items).

Trade with Turkey, 1922(2 items).

Treaties, Lausanne, 1923, 1923-1924(100 items).

Turkey, 1922-1942(120 items).

Damage assessment, 1925(6 items).

Foreign policy, 1936-1939(5 items).

Political situation, 1934, 1942(7 items).

K. Bennett, Richard Bedford, 1870-1947.

Prime Minister, 1930-1935.
Microfilm, 1878-1947, 435 reels. Finding aid 434.
Papers deposited at the University of New Brunswick.

Political papers, 1878-1947.

Asia- and Pacific-related files in the Political papers, listed on Reel C4495, are:

Washington Armaments Conference(1 file).

External Affairs, China, 1926(1 file).

Lausanne Treaty(1 file).

Immigration, India, 1922(1 file).

External Affairs, India, 1929(1 file)
Sino-Russian dispute, 1929(1 file).

London Naval Conference, 1930-1935(2 files).

Imperial Conference, 1930-1932(many files).

International Red Cross, Tokyo, Conference, Conference, Conference, 1934(1 file).

Pacific Health Conference, 1935(1 file).

External Affairs, China, 1930-1936(6 files).

Chinese-Japanese dispute, 1931-1936(9 files)

External Affairs,
Trade with China, 1930-1932(3 files).

External Affairs,
Canadian Minister to China, 1931-1932(2 files).

External Affairs,
India, 1930-1936(8 files).

External Affairs,
India Round Table Conference:1932-1935(4 files).

External Affairs,
Japan. 1930-1936(10 files).

External Affairs,
Japan. Japanese Minister to Canada, 1930-1935(3 files).

External Affairs,
Japan. Canadian Minister to Japan, 1930(11 files).

External Affairs,
Japan. Canadian Legation, 1930-1934(1 file).

External Affairs,
Japan. Canadian Minister to Japan, 1931-1935(5 files).

External Affairs,
Japan. Trade relations(5 files).

External Affairs,
British Ambassador to Japan, 1934(3 files).

External Affairs,
Japanese Ambassador to London:1934(1 file).

External Affairs
Persia, 1933(1 file).

External Affairs,
Trade with Persia, 1932-1933(4 files).

External Affairs,
Siam, 1930-1931(4 files).

External Affairs,
Turkey, 1932-1933(4 files).

External Affairs,
Pacific Halibut Treaty, 1931(2 files).

Immigration,
Japanese, 1933(1 file).

Immigration,
Chinese, 1930(1 file).

Immigration,
Japanese and Chinese, 1935(1 file).

Immigration,

Oriental, 1930(1 file).

Immigration,
Indian, 1935(1 file).

London Disarmament Conference, 1932(21 files).

Invitation and Clippings Series.

Volume 1061(Reel 4496) page 672.
Cables, Pacific, 1926.

External Affairs.

Volume 1104(Reel M4511) pages 78-91.
China, 1932-1933.

Volume 1105(Reel M4511) pages 93-104.
China, 1935-1937.

Volume 1105(Reel M4511) pages 105-107.
China, Consuls, 1934-1935.

Volume 1105(Reel M4511) pages 108-273.
China, Sino-Japanese War, 1931-1933 2 files.

Volume 1105(Reel M4511) pages 274-300.
China, Sino-Japanese War, Lytton Report, 1932-1933.

Volume 1109(Reel M4511) pages 360-361.
Consuls, China, 1926.

Volume 1109(Reel M4512) pages 380-412.
Disarmament, 1931-1932.

Volume 1109(Reel M4512) pages 413-461.
Disarmament Conference, 1932-1933.

Volume 1109(Reel M4512) pages 462-476.
Disarmament, London Naval Conference, 1930,1931.

Volume 1109(Reel M4512) pages 477-478.
Disarmament, London Naval Conference, reports, 1931.

Volume 1119(Reel M4515) pages 1003-1061.
India, Lord Willingdon, 1931-1932.

Volume 1119(Reel M4515) pages 1071-1120.
Institute of Pacific Relations:1931-1933.

Volume 1122(Reel M4516) pages 1103.
Japan, Consuls, 1926.

Volume 1122(Reel M4516) pages 1104-1142.
Japan, Economy, 1931-1935.

Volume 1122(Reel M4516) pages 1143-1190.
Japan, Legation, 1931-1935.

Volume 1122(Reel M4516) pages 1191-1217.
Japan, Legation, Tokugawa, 1930-1935, 2 files.

Volume 1122(Reel M4516) pages 1218-1219.
Japan, Legation, Kato Sotomatsu, 1935.

Volume 1122(Reel M4516) pages 1220-1226.
Japan. Canadian legation, 1931-1934.

Volume 1122(Reel M4516) pages 1227-1258.
Japan. Canadian Legation, Marler, Herbert, 1930-1934.

Volume 1122(Reel M4516) pages 1259-1324.
Japan. Canadian Legation. Marler, Herbert, speeches, 1930-1936.

Volume 1122(Reel M4517) pages 0-111.
Japan. Trade relations, 1930-1935.

Volume 1122(Reel M4517) pages 113-193.
Japan. Trade relations, 1935

Volume 1122(Reel M4517) pages 194-241.
Japan. Trade relations, Japan-German pact 1935-1937.

Volume 1123(Reel M4517) pages 320.
Orient. Trade relations, 1926.

Volume 1123(Reel M4517) pages 321-327.
Orient. Trade relations, 1930.

Volume 1123(Reel M4517) pages 328-359.
Orient. Trade relations, 1931.

Volume 1123(Reel M4517) pages 360-370.
Orient. Trade relations, 1932-1933.

Volume 1123(Reel M4517) pages 371-384.
Orient. Trade relations, 1934.

Volume 1123(Reel M4517) pages 385-387.
Orient. Trade relations, 1935.

Volume 1123(Reel M4517) page 388.
Pacific Foreign Trade Council, 1931.

Volume 1123(Reel M4517) pages 401-407.
Pan-Pacific affairs, 1926.

Volume 1148(Reel M4525) pages 353-365.
Fisheries, Pacific, 1930-1933.

Volume 1148(Reel M4525) pages 366-368.
Fisheries. Salmon sea fishing statistics, 1930-1932.

Immigration.

Volume 1170(Reel M4532) pages 264-267.
Oriental, 1930-1933.

Imperial Conferences.

Volume 1173(Reel M4533) pages 384-418.
India, 1930-1931.

Volume 1218(Reel M4547) pages 618-626.
Pacific Science Congress, 1930, 1933.

Tariff.

Volume 1277(Reel M4566) pages 711-714.
Silk, 1932-1933.

L. St.Laurent, Louis Stephen, 1882-1973.

Prime Minister, 1948-1957.
Originals, 1935-1958, 258 feet 8 inches, 183 volumes.
Finding aid 530.

Correspondence and memoranda, pre 1948.

Department of External Affairs, 1947-1948.

Volume 13.

File 70-d.
Immigration - cases - Chinese.

Volume 18,

File 100-1-7, 1947-1948.
China.

Volume 18.

File 100-1-9, 1947-1948.
Turkey.

Volume 19.

File 100-14, 1947-1948.
Japan;

File 100-15, 1947-1948.
India;

Prime Minister's Office, 1948-1949. Indexed files volumes 38-241.

Volume 39.

File C-14, 1949.

China, volume 2.

China, volume 3(a)
Advances to China, official and confidential.

China, volume 3(b).
Advances to China, unofficial.

Volume 39.

File C-14-1, 1948-1949.
Trade relations, volume 3.
Shipment of war materials to China.

File C-14-2, 14 September 1948-1949.
Canadian Ambassador to China, volume 1, official and confidential.

Canadian Ambassador to China, volume 2.
Unofficial.

Volume 55.

File I-17, 1949.
Indonesian Republic, volume 2, unofficial.

Volume 56.

File I-20-14, 1948-1949.
Immigration. Asiatic, general.

File I-20-14 & I-20-15-g.
Immigration. Asiatic, general.

Volume 57.

File I-45, 1949.
India, volume 2, unofficial.

File I-45-1, 1949.
India, High Commissioner for Canada in India, volume 1, official and confidential.

Volume 64.

File P-14-1, 1949.
Pakistan, High Commissioner for Canada in Pakistan, volume 1, official and confidential.

Volume 76.

File T-11, 1949.
Turkey, volume 3, Mr. St.Laurent's signature.

Prime Minister's Office, 1949-1953, volumes 79-169.

Volume 85.

File C-18, 1950.
China, volume 1, personal and confidential.
China, volume 2, unofficial.

File C-18-3, 1950.
China, Mr. St.Laurent's signature.

File C-18-3, 1949-1952.
China. Ambassador of China to Canada, volume 3, Mr. St.Laurent's signature.

Volume 86.

File C-18-4, 1950-1952.
China. Chinese Communist regime, volume 3, confidential.

File C-18-4, 1950.
China. Chinese Communist regime, volume 4, arrest of missionary sisters by Chinese Communists.

File C-18-4, 1952.

China. Chinese Communist regime, volume 5, arrest of missionary sisters by Chinese Communists.

File C-18-4, 1951-1952.
China. Chinese Communist regime, volume 5, arrest of missionary sisters by Chinese Communists(3 files).

File C-18-4, 1952.
China. Chinese Communist regime, volume 6, treatment of Canadian nationals in China.

File C-18-4, 1952.
China. Chinese Communist regime, volume 3. Mr. St.Laurent's signature. Rev. Joseph Leon Arcand.

Volume 87.

File C-46, 1951-1953.
Colombo plan, Mr. St.Laurent's signature(2 files).

Volume 88.

File C-67, 1952-1953.
Ceylon, volume 1, personal and confidential.
Ceylon, volume 3, Mr. St.Laurent's signature.

Volume 114.

File I-18, 1950.
Indonesia, volume 1, official and confidential.
Indonesia, volume 2, unofficial.

Volume 115.

File I-20-17, 1952.
Immigration, Asiatic, Mr. St.Laurent's signature.

File I-20-17, 1951.
Immigration, Asiatic, general, Mr. St.Laurent's signature.

File I-20-17, 1949.
Immigration, Asiatic, personal and confidential.

File I-20-09, 1950.
Immigration, China, Mr. St.Laurent's signature.

File I-20-30-m, 1950.
Immigration, China, personal and confidential, Ma Hong, Esq.

Volume 116.

File I-45, 1951-1953.
India, volume 1, personal and confidential.

File I-45, 28 June 1949, 1950-1953.
India, volume 3, Mr. St.Laurent's signature.

File I-45, 1951-1952.
India, volume 5, provision of food for India.

File I-45, 1952.
India, volume 6, secret.

File I-45-1, 28 June 1948, 1950-1951.
India, High Commissioner for Canada in India.

File I-45-2, 28 June 1948, 1950-1951.
India, High Commissioner from India in Canada.

File I-45-2, 1953.
India, High Commissioner from India in Canada.

File I-45-3, 1953.
India, trade relations, volume 3, Mr. St.Laurent's signature.

Volume 117.

File I-52, 1951.
Iran, volume 1, personal and confidential.

Volume 118.

File J-11, 1951-1953.
Japan, volume 3, Mr. St.Laurent's signature.

File J-11-1, 1950,1952,1953.
Japan, trade relations volume 2, unofficial.

File J-11-1, June 28, 1949.
Japan, trade relations, volume 3, Mr. St.Laurent's signature.

File J-11-2, 1951-1952.
Japan, Canadian Liaison Mission, Tokyo, Japan, volume 3, Mr. St.Laurent's signature.

File J-11-2, 1953.
Japan, Canadian Liaison Mission, Tokyo, Japan, volume 4, top secret.

File J-11-3, 1952.
Japan, Japanese Ambassador to Canada, volume 1, personal and confidential.

File J-11-3, 1952-1953.
Japan, Japanese Ambassador to Canada, volume 3, Mr. St.Laurent's signature.

File J-11-4, 1952-1953.
Japan, Canadian Ambassador to Japan, volume 1, personal and confidential.

File K-20-1, 1950.
Korea, Korean situation, volume 3, correspondence with Tim Buck.

File K-20-1, 1953.
Korea, Korean situation, volume 1, personal and confidential.

File K-20-1, 1950.
Korea, Korean situation, volume 2, unofficial.

File K-20-1, 1951-1953.
Korea, Korean situation, volume 2, unofficial.

File K-20-1, 1950-1952.
Korea, Korean situation, volume 4, confidential.

File K-20-1, 1950-1953.
Korea, Korean situation, volume 5, Mr. St.Laurent's signature.

File K-20-1, 1951.
Korea, Korean situation, volume 6, return of war dead for burial in Canada.

File K-20-1, 1952.
Korea, Korean situation, volume 7,
Honours and awards, Mr. St.Laurent to sign.

File K-20-1, 1952-1953.
Korea, Korean situation, volume 7, honours and awards.

File K-20-1, 1953.
Korea, Korean situation, volume 8.
Formosa.

File K-20-1, 1953.
Korea, Korean situation, volume 9, top secret.

File K-20-1, 1953.
Korea, Korean situation, volume 10, armistice.

File K-20-1, 1953.
Korea, Korean situation, volume 10, armistice conference.

File K-20-1-g, 1952.
Korea, Korean situation, volume 2, unofficial.

File K-20-1-I, 1951-1952.
Korea, Korean situation, volume 5, Mr. St.Laurent's signature.

File K-20-1-v, 1952-1953.
Korea, Korean situation, volume 2, unofficial.

Volume 130.

File P-14, 1952.
Pakistan, volume 6, biography of the Quaid-i-Millat. Mr. St.Laurent to sign.

File P-14, 1951.
Pakistan, volume 5, the late Liaquat Ali Khan, Mr. St.Laurent to sign.

File P-14, 1950-1953.
Pakistan, volume 4, Mr. St.Laurent 's' signature

File P-14, 28 June 1949.
Pakistan, volume 3, secret.

File P-14, 1950-1953.
Pakistan, volume 1, personal and confidential.

File P-14, 28 June 1951.
Pakistan, High Commissioner for Pakistan to Canada, volume 1, personal and confidential.

Volume 163.

File T-21, 1952.
Turkey, volume 1, personal and confidential.

File T-21, 1952.
Turkey, volume 3, Mr. St.Laurent to sign.

File T-21-1, 1951-1952.
Turkey. Canadian Ambassador to Turkey, volume 1, personal and confidential.

File T-21-1, 1953.
Turkey. Canadian Ambassador to Turkey, volume 2, unofficial.

File T-21-2, 1952.
Turkey. Turkish Ambassador to Canada.

File U-25-14, 1951.
U.N.,U.N.K.R.A., personal and confidential.

Volume 167.

File U-25-15, 1951.
U.N. Director General of Technical Assistance, admission of the U.N.

File U-25-16, 1952.
U.N. Genocide.

File U-25-17, 1953.
U.N. Admission of Red China to.

Volume 168.

File U-10-4, 1952.
Veterans organization. Hong Kong Veterans, organization of, personal and confidential.

Volume 173.

File C-46, 11 August 1953-1954.
Colombo Plan, personal and confidential.

File C-46-4, 1955.
Colombo Plan, meeting in Singapore. Mr. St.Laurent's signature.

Volume 174.

File D-16-12-N, 1956.
Department of External Affairs.
Important visitors, Jawaharlal Nehru

File D-16-12-N, 1954.
Department of External Affairs.
Important visitors, Dr. S.Radhakrishnan

File D-16-12-S, 1956.

Department of External Affairs.
Important visitors, President Sukarno.

Volume 175.

File D-16-22, 1956.
Department of External Affairs.
Important visitors, Mr. Shigeru Yoshida.

Volume 185.

File I-17, 11 August 1953-1956.
India, volume 1, personal and confidential.

Volume 185.

File I-17, 1954-1955.
India, volume 4, secret.

File I-17-2, 11 August 1953-1956.
India, High Commissioner in India, volume 1, personal and confidential.

File I-17-2, 1954-1957.
India, High Commissioner in India, volume 3, Mr. St.Laurent's signature.

Volume 186.

File C-15, 12 August 1953-1954.
Immigration, Pakistan. Mr. St.Laurent's signature.

Volume 186.

File I-20-25, 1954-1955.
Immigration, Japan.

File I-20-32C, 1955.
Immigration, Chinese. Mr. St.Laurent's signature, Frank Chin.

File I-20-38J,1956.
Immigration, India. Edward Joseph.

File I-26, 1954-1955.
Indo-China, volume 4, secret.

File I-26-R ,1955.
Indo-China, volume 3, Mr. St.Laurent's signature.

File I-26-1, 1954-1955.
Indo-China. Indo-China Commission, Mr. St.Laurent's signature.
International Commission for Supervision and Control in Indo-China:1954-1955;

File J-10, 1954-1957.
Japan, volume 3, Mr. St.Laurent's signature.

File J-10-1, 11 August 1953-1956.
Japan, Canadian Ambassador to Japan, volume 1, personal and confidential.

File J-10-2, 1954-1957.

Japan. Japanese Minister to Canada, volume 3, Mr. St.Laurent's signature.

File J-10-3, 1954.
Japan. Trade with, volume 5. Correspondence with cabinet ministers.

Volume 199.

File P-18, 11 August 1953-1956.
Pakistan, volume 1, personal and confidential.Volume 200.

File P-18, 11 August 1953-1954.
Pakistan, volume 4, military aid to Pakistan from U.S.

File P-18, 11 August 1953-1954.
Pakistan. High Commissioner for Pakistan in Canada, volume 1, personal and confidential.

File P-23, 11 August 1953-1957.
Philippines, volume 1, personal and confidential.

Volume 218.

File T-26, 1956.
Turkey.

File T-6-1-U, 1956-1957.
Turkey, Turkish Ambassador to Canada, Mr. St.Laurent's signature.

Non-indexed papers, 1948-1957.

Volume 232, 1949-1955.
China, Personal communications from British Prime Minister.

Volume 232, 1949-1950.
China, Recognition of Communist China.

Volume 234, 1953-1956.
Far East statements.

Volume 234, 1950.
External Affairs, India and Pakistan.

Volume 234, 1949-1951.
External Affairs, India and Pakistan. Kashmir.

Volume 234, 1950.
Korea, Attlee, Messages to the Prime Minister(2 files).

Volume 234, 1951.
Korea, Attlee, Messages to the Prime Minister.

Volume 236, 1951.
Japanese Peace Treaty.

M. Diefenbaker, John G. 1895-1979.

Prime Minister, 1957-1963.
Originals to be located at the University of

Saskatchewan Diefenbaker Centre. Finding aid 1218. Microfilm, 1888-1979, 343 reels, M-5549 to 5562, M-5900 to M-5901, M-6803 to M-6825, M-7414 to M-7454, M-7547 to M-7582, M-7788 to M-7961, M-8451 to M-8503...These reel numbers refer to National Archives of Canada holdings.

A statement of the Asia-related material in the Diefenbaker papers will also be found under the entry for the Rt. Hon. John G. Diefenbaker Centre, University of Saskatchewan, Saskatoon, and this source has been used in this inventory.

Materials on Asia in the Diefenbaker Center were accessed on world wide web
http:www/usask.ca/archives/dief.html
Repetitious, minor and non-Asia data have been deleted.
* = Available on microfilm in the National Archives of Canada and the Diefenbaker Centre. On interlibrary loan from the Diefenbaker Centre only.

(RSN: 00001478)
Call No.: MG 01/XIV/D/25 Diefenbaker Centre, Row 9, Memoirs Volume 10 Title: Memoirs - Photocopies - World Tour 1958 [before 1974] [textual records]
Physical description: one folder
Summary:This file records the substance of all the important confidential political, economic and military discussions which Prime Minister Diefenbaker held with the Heads of State and Government and other senior functionaries on his 1958 World Tour covering Western Europe and the Commonwealth countries of Asia as well as Australia and New Zealand. In most cases, the reports were prepared by H.B. Robinson, the Prime Minister's principal foreign policy advisor, and were approved by Mr. Diefenbaker. The documents within this file that are restricted relate to views expressed on issues which are still the subject of international negotiation such as arms shipments to the Middle East, agricultural trade, and the Law of the Sea. The following documents are open: (a) PM's conversation with the Secretary General of the United Nations, U Thant, 29 October 1958; (b) Conversation between PM and British Prime Minister Macmillan, London, 3 November 1958, (except pages 8 and 10); (c) Talks with General de Gaulle of France, 5 November 1958; (d) Conversations with Paul-Henri Spaak, Secretary-General of NATO, and with General Norstad, Paris, France, November 1958; (e) Conversations with Adenauer, Chancellor of Germany, and Prof. Hallstein, Chairman of the European Economic Commission (EEC), 7 November 1958; (f) Talks with Fanfani, Prime Minister of Italy and with Gronchi, President of Italy, November 1958; (g) Conversation with Nehru, Prime Minister of India, 19 November 1958; (h) Meeting with the Indian Planning Commission, New Dehli, 22 November 1958; (i) Conversation with Bandaranaike, Prime Minister of Sri Lanka, 26 November 1958; (j) Conversation with Tunku Abdul Rahman, Prime Minister of Malaya, 28 November 1958; (k) Conversation with Dato Abdul Razak, Deputy Prime Minister of Malaya, 28 November 1958; (l) Meeting with the Malayan Cabinet, 29 November 1958; (m)

Discussion with Dr. Djuanda, Prime Minister of Indonesia, 2 December 1958.Restricted:Partially closed. File contains both restricted and open documents. The archivist will have to remove sensitive items and create an interim file that can be consulted by the researcher. Restricted pages: 8, 10, 48-50, 63-65, 108-113,114-119, 124-134. Subject:World Tour - 1958; Commonwealth countries - 1958; U Thant - Secretary-General of the United Nations - 1958; Communist China - 1958; Soviet Union - 1958; Macmillan, Harold - Prime Minister of Great Britain - 1958; deGaulle, General Charles - President of France - 1958; North Atlantic Treaty Organization - NATO - talks regarding, 1958; Spaak, Paul-Henri - Secretary-General of NATO - 1958; Norstad, General - NATO - 1958; Adenauer, Konrad - Chancellor of Germany - 1958; Hallstein, Professor - Chairman of the European Economic Commission - EEC - 1958; Fanfani - Prime Minister of Italy - 1958; Gronchi - President of Italy - 1958; Ayub Khan - President of Pakistan - 1958; Nehru - Prime Minister of India - 1958; India - Indian Planning Commission - Canadian Colombo Plan - funding from Canada - 1958; Wheat - Exports from Canada to members of the Canadian Colombo Plan - 1958; Bandaranaike - Prime Minister of Sri Lanka (Ceylon) - 1958; Ceylon - Rubber and rice deal with Communist China - 1958; Tunku Abdul Rahman - Prime Minister of Malaya - 1958; Communism in Malaya - 1958; Malaya - Defence - 1958; Djuanda, Dr. - Prime Minister of Indonesia - 1958; Sukarno - President of Indonesia - 1958; Menzies - Prime Minister of Australia - 1958. Series Description: RSN 00001476

(RSN: 00013974)
Call No.: MG 01/XI/C.1-C.29 Diefenbaker Centre, Rows 6-8
Title: General Correspondence - S 1967-1979 [textual records] Physical description: 29 folders
Summary:This file contains general correspondence with the public created and accumulated by John Diefenbaker's office from the tme he ceased being Leader of the Opposition until his death. Restricted: Closed until arrangement completed.

(RSN: 00100342)
Call No.: MG 01/VI/(025.1) Diefenbaker Centre, Rows 2-4, Volume 26 Title: Religion - Religious Movements - Moral Re-Armament 1962-1963 Summary:This file contains correspondence, memoranda, press clippings and MRA Bulletins. Microfilm No.: M-7800
*Subject:Buchanan, Frank Communism World Headquarters in Caux, Switzerland Christianity and free enterprise Prime Minister of Burma Ikeda, Hayato - Prime Minister of Japan Imperial Majesty Shahenshah of Iran Chiang Kai-Shek - ChinaNgo Dinh Diem - Prime Minister of Vietnam Hearst, William Randolph Jr. Holyoake, Keith - Prime Minister of New Zealand Garcia, Carlos - President of the Philippines King Michael and Queen Anne of Roumania Lindley, General Nicolas - Peru President San Martin - Uraguay Gandhi, Rajmohan - India Adenauer, Konrad - Chancellor of Germany. American propaganda against Russia MRA Bulletins

Series Description: RSN00002248

(RSN: 00111308) Afghanistan
Call No.: MG 01/VI/(840/A257) Diefenbaker Centre, Row 4 - 6, Volume 550 Title: Canada and Foreign Countries - General - Afghanistan 1962 Microfilm No.: M-8031
* Series Description: RSN00002248

(RSN: 00106579) Burma
Call No.: MG 01/VI/(380/B962.21) Diefenbaker Centre, Row 4 - 6, Volume 336 Title: Governments of Other Countries - General - Burma - Cabinet - Prime Minister 1960 Microfilm No.: M-7939
* Series Description: RSN00002248

(RSN: 00108025) Burma
Call No.: MG 01/VI/(548/B962) Diefenbaker Centre, Row 4 - 6, Volume 398 Title: Minerals and Fuels - Petroleum - Burma 1961
Microfilm No.: M-7962
* Series Description: RSN00002248

(RSN: 00111003) Burma
Call No.: MG 01/VI/(811/B962) Diefenbaker Centre, Row 4 - 6, Volume 537 Title: Canada and the Commonwealth - Commonwealth Members - Burma 1960 Microfilm No.: M-8023
* Series Description: RSN00002248

(RSN: 00111324) Burma
Call No.: MG 01/VI/(840/B962) Diefenbaker Centre, Row 4 - 6, Volume 551 Title: Canada and Foreign Countries - General - Burma 1958-1961,1963 Microfilm No.: M-8031
* Series Description: RSN00002248

(RSN: 00111869) Burma
Call No.: MG 01/VI/(864/B962) Diefenbaker Centre, Row 4 - 6, Volume 560 Title: Diplomatic Representation - Representation of Other Countries in Canada - Burma 1958,1960 Microfilm No.: M-8042
* Series Description: RSN00002248

(RSN: 00009248) Cambodia
Call No.: MG 01/XI/B Diefenbaker Centre, Rows 6-8
Title: Cambodia 1970-1973 [textual records]
Summary:This file contains the reference material created and accumulated by John Diefenbaker's office from after he ceased being Leader of the Opposition to his death. Restricted:Closed until arrangement completed.
Series Description: RSN00003078

(RSN: 00102143) Cambodia
Call No.: MG 01/VI/(307.1.01 - 1957) Diefenbaker Centre, Rows 2-4, Volume 105 Title: Government - Parliament - Opening of Parliament - Speech* Throne - 1957 Summary:This file contains transcripts, memoranda, and reports. Microfilm No.: M-7835
*Subject:Opening of Parliament - agendas Hees, George - Minister of Transport - suggestions for Throne Speech External Affairs - Commonwealth Conference Colombo Plan United Nations Emergency Force Middle East International Supervisory Commissions in Vietnam, Laos and Cambodia North Atlantic Treaty Organization (NATO) Author:Bryce, R.B.
Series Description: RSN00002248

(RSN: 00111543) Cambodia
Call No.: MG 01/VI/(845/I41C176) Diefenbaker Centre, Row 4 - 6, Volume 559 Title: Canada and Foreign Countries - International Situation - Indo-China - Cambodia 1961 Microfilm No.: M-8037
*Series Description: RSN00002248

(RSN: 00111624) Cambodia
Call No.: MG 01/VI/(846/I41C176.1) Diefenbaker Centre, Row 4 - 6, Volume 563 Title: Canada and Foreign Countries - Visits - Indo-China - Cambodia - Heads of State 1962 Microfilm No.: M-8038
*Series Description: RSN00002248

(RSN: 00003926) Ceylon
Call No.: MG 01/VII/A/420 Diefenbaker Centre Row 4, Volume 53 Collection:Prime Minister's Office/ Leader of the Opposition Office Title: Ceylon Buddhist Congress 1961 [textual records]
Physical description: 1 folder
Subject:Sri Lanka
Pages:pp. 30084-30096
Series Description: RSN 00000254

(RSN: 00004395) Ceylon
Call No.: MG 01/XXII/74 Diefenbaker Centre, Row Volume 2
Title: Message to Prime Minister of Ceylon Expressing Sympathy Re Floods 14 January 1958 [textual records]
Physical description: 1 folder
Summary:French included
Series Description: 3081

(RSN: 00007530) Ceylon
Call No.: MG 01/IX/C/402 Diefenbaker Centre, Row 6, Second Leader of the Opposition, Volume 161
Collection:Leader of the Opposition Office
Title: International Affairs - Ceylon 1965 [textual records] Physical description: 1 folder
Series Description: RSN 00003079

(RSN: 00009281) Ceylon
Call No.: MG 01/XI/B Diefenbaker Centre, Rows 6-8
Title: Ceylon 1970-1971 [textual records]
Summary:This file contains the reference material created and accumulated by John Diefenbaker's office from after he ceased being Leader of the Opposition to his death. Restricted:Closed until arrangement completed.
Series Description: RSN00003078

(RSN: 00010464) Ceylon
Call No.: MG 01/XII/A/397 Diefenbaker Centre, row 9, Personal and Confidential, Volume 12
Collection:Prime Minister's Office
Title: Diefenbaker, John G. - Trips and Engagements - World Tour - Ceylon 1958 [textual records] Physical

description: 1 folder
Series Description: RSN 9157

(RSN: 00012508) Ceylon
Call No.: MG 01/XII/F/213 Diefenbaker Centre, row 9, Personal and Confidential, Volume 112
Collection:Prime Minister's and Leader of the Opposition's Offices/Diefenbaker Parliamentary Office
Title: Foreign Affairs - Ceylon n.d.,1960 [textual records] Physical description: 1 folder
Series Description: RSN 9162

(RSN: 00100641) Ceylon
Call No.: MG 01/VI/(046/C425) Diefenbaker Centre, Row 4 - 6, Volume 38 Title: Language and Ethnic Groups - Racial Discrimination - Ceylon 1961 Microfilm No.: M-7805
*Series Description: RSN00002248

(RSN: 00102557) Ceylon
Call No.: MG 01/VI/(313.2.02 R) Diefenbaker Centre, Rows 2-4, Volume 127 Title: Federal Government Executive - The Prime Minister of Canada - Personal - Personal Letters - R 1957-1962 Summary:This file contains correspondence and press clippings. Microfilm No.: M-7845
*Subject:Rajapakse, Sir Lalita - Ceylon 1959 Commonwealth Tour Series Description: RSN00002248

(RSN: 00105460) Ceylon
Call No.: MG 01/VI/(335 Lambton West) Diefenbaker Centre, Row 4 - 6, Volume 292 Title: The House of Commons - Members of the House - Lambton West Constituency 1957-1962 Summary:This file includes correspondence, press clippings, and a photograph, as well as: a memo for Diefenbaker from Joseph Warner Murphy (MP) re Murphy's trip to India, Pakistan and Ceylon; a copy of a speech on Canada given by L.D. Smithers, President of Dow Chemicals of Canada Limited, to the Synthetic Organic Chemical Manufacturers' Association in New York. Microfilm No.: M-7923
* Subject:Polymer Corporation Canadian unions - payment of dues to American head offices Series Description: RSN00002248

(RSN: 00106580) Ceylon
Call No.: MG 01/VI/(380/C425) Diefenbaker Centre, Row 4 - 6, Volume 336 Title: Governments of Other Countries - General - Ceylon 1961 Microfilm No.: M-7939
*Series Description: RSN00002248

(RSN: 00106581) Ceylon
Call No.: MG 01/VI/(380/C425.1) Diefenbaker Centre, Row 4 - 6, Volume 336 Title: Governments of Other Countries - General - Ceylon - Head of State 1960 Microfilm No.: M-7939
*Series Description: RSN00002248

(RSN: 00106582) Ceylon
Call No.: MG 01/VI/(380/C425.21) Diefenbaker Centre, Row 4 - 6, Volume 336 Title: Governments of Other Countries - General - Ceylon - Cabinet - Prime Minister 1957-1960 Microfilm No.: M-7939
*Series Description: RSN00002248

(RSN: 00108095) Ceylon
Call No.: MG 01/VI/(554/C425) Diefenbaker Centre, Row 4 - 6, Volume 402 Title: Power Resources - Private Central Electric Stations - Ceylon 1961 Microfilm No.: M-7963
*Series Description: RSN00002248

(RSN: 00109545) Ceylon
Call No.: MG 01/VI/(722/C425) Diefenbaker Centre, Row 4 - 6, Volume 476 Title: Foreign Trade - Trade By Countries - Ceylon 1961
Microfilm No.: M-7996
* Series Description: RSN00002248

(RSN: 00110918) Ceylon
Call No.: MG 01/VI/(802.1/C425) Diefenbaker Centre, Row 4 - 6, Volume 533 Title: World Relations - Economic Assistance Abroad - Flood Relief Assistance - Ceylon 1957-1958 Microfilm No.: M-8021
* Series Description: RSN00002248

(RSN: 00110926) Ceylon
Call No.: MG 01/VI/(805/C425) Diefenbaker Centre, Row 4 - 6, Volume 534 Title: World Relations - The Colombo Plan - Ceylon 1960
Microfilm No.: M-8022
*Series Description: RSN00002248

(RSN: 00110927) Ceylon
Call No.: MG 01/VI/(805/C425 Conf.) Diefenbaker Centre, Row 4 - 6, Volume 534 Title: World Relations - The Colombo Plan - Ceylon - Confidential 1960
Microfilm No.: M-8022
*Series Description: RSN00002248

(RSN: 00111004) Ceylon
Call No.: MG 01/VI/(811/C425) Diefenbaker Centre, Row 4 - 6, Volume 537 Title: Canada and the Commonwealth - Commonwealth Members - Ceylon 1959,1961 Microfilm No.: M-8023
*Series Description: RSN00002248 .

(RSN: 00111140) Ceylon
Call No.: MG 01/VI/(818.21 PM 1958 Ceylon) Diefenbaker Centre, Row 4 - 6, Volume 542 Title: Canada and the Commonwealth - Visits - Visits to Commonwealth Countries by Canadian Ministers - World Tour - Prime Minister - 1958 - Ceylon 1958-1959
Microfilm No.: M-8026
*Series Description: RSN00002248

(RSN: 00111328) Ceylon
Call No.: MG 01/VI/(840/C425) Diefenbaker Centre, Row 4 - 6, Volume 551 Title: Canada and Foreign Countries - General - Ceylon 1958-1963
Microfilm No.: M-8031
*Series Description: RSN00002248

(RSN: 00111593) Ceylon
Call No.: MG 01/VI/(846/C425) Diefenbaker

Centre, Row 4 - 6, Volume 562 Title: Canada and Foreign Countries - Visits - Ceylon 1958 Microfilm No.: M-8038
*Series Description: RSN00002248

(RSN: 00111757) Ceylon
Call No.: MG 01/VI/(861/C425) Diefenbaker Centre, Row 4 - 6, Volume 568 Title: Diplomatic Representation - Canadian Representation Abroad - Ceylon 1958-1961 Microfilm No.: M-8041
*Series Description: RSN00002248

(RSN: 00111758) Ceylon
Call No.: MG 01/VI/(861/C425 Conf.) Diefenbaker Centre, Row 4 - 6, Volume 568 Title: Diplomatic Representation - Canadian Representation Abroad - Ceylon - Confidential 1958-1959 Summary:This file consists essentially of a "personal and confidential" letter (written at Prime Minister Diefenbaker's request) from Nik Cavell, Canada's High Commissioner in Ceylon (and first Director of Canada's Colombo Plan administration) on how the West in general, and Canada in particular, could combat Communism in Asia. Not available on Microfilm. (This file was classified "Restricted" at the time PMO Numbered series was microfilmed.) Subject:Ceylon - Communist propaganda - 1958-1959; Cavell, Nik - High Commissioner for Canada in Ceylon; Series Description: RSN00002248

(RSN: 00111822) Ceylon
Call No.: MG 01/VI/(862 Ceylon) Diefenbaker Centre, Row 4 - 6, Volume 569 Title: Diplomatic Representation - Canadian Missions Abroad - Ceylon 1958 Microfilm No.: M-8042
*Series Description: RSN00002248

(RSN: 00111870) Ceylon
Call No.: MG 01/VI/(864/C425) Diefenbaker Centre, Row 4 - 6, Volume 560 Title: Diplomatic Representation - Representation of Other Countries in Canada - Ceylon 1958-1961 Microfilm No.: M-8042
*Series Description: RSN00002248

(RSN: 00000256) China
Call No.: MG 01/VII/A/249 Diefenbaker Centre Row 4, Volume 32 Collection:Prime Minister's Office/ Leader of the Opposition Office Title: Canada-China Relations n.d., 1964 [textual records] Physical description: 1 folder Pages:pp. 17362-17375
Series Description: RSN 00000254

(RSN: 00001473) China
Call No.: MG 01/XIV/C/5 Diefenbaker Centre, Row 9, Memoirs Volume 4 Title: CBC Encounter 20 June 1970 [textual records]
Physical description: one folder
Summary:This file contains a transcript of an interview with Diefenbaker conducted by John Robinson, Charles Lynch, and Ron Collister for broadcast on the CBC programme Encounter (20 June 1970). Topics discussed included: Canada's recognition of Communist China. Subject:Trudeau, Pierre Elliott Parliament Greene, Joe (Minister of Energy) Socialism Conservatism
Series Description: RSN 00001461

(RSN: 00001507) China
Call No.: MG 01/IX/B/3 Diefenbaker Centre Rows 5-6, Second Leader of the Opposition, Volume36 Collection:Leader of the Opposition Office
Title: Agriculture - Sale of Wheat to China n.d., [1961], 1965 [textual records] Physical description: 1 folder
Summary:This file contains photocopied press clippings and Hansard re Pearson's statements on grain sales. There are also two letters from Jack McDowell to Diefenbaker about international wheat sales and Wheat Board payments to farmers.
Series Description: RSN 00001512

(RSN: 00001669) China
Call No.: MG 01/XIV/E/51 Diefenbaker Centre, Row 9, Memoirs Volume 12 Title: World Relations - Conferences - Bermuda [197-] [textual records]
Physical description: one folder
Summary:This file contains a photocopied memo (1964) from Wallace B. Nesbitt M.P. re Bermuda Conference.
Subject:NATO Great Britain - nuclear policy Disarmament United States Communist China - recognition of Foreign aid
Series Description: RSN 00001527

(RSN: 00001690) China
Call No.: MG 01/XIV/E/57 Diefenbaker Centre, Row 9, Memoirs Volume 12 Title: World Relations - Republic of China [196-] [textual records] Physical description: one folder
Summary:This file contains printed pamphlets from Communist China and Taiwan.
Series Description: RSN 00001527

(RSN: 00001957) China
Call No.: MG 01/IX/B/195 Diefenbaker Centre, Rows 5-6, Second Leader of the Opposition, Volume42 Collection:Leader of the Opposition Office
Title: Diplomatic Correspondence - China - Hsu, Shuhsi 1964-1967 [textual records] Physical description: 1 folder
Series Description: RSN 00001512

(RSN: 00001959) China
Call No.: MG 01/IX/B/196 Diefenbaker Centre, Rows 5-6, Second Leader of the Opposition, Volume42 Collection:Leader of the Opposition Office
Title: Diplomatic Correspondence - China - Peng, Professor Ming-Min 1965 [textual records] Physical description: 1 folder
Series Description: RSN 00001512

(RSN: 00002168) China
Call No.: MG 01/IX/B/332 Diefenbaker Centre, Rows 5-6, Second Leader of the Opposition, Volume49 Collection:Leader of the Opposition Office
Title: International Affairs - China 1964 [textual records] Physical description: 1 folder
Series Description: RSN 00001512

(RSN: 00002279) China
Call No.: MG 01/VII/B/10 Diefenbaker Centre, Row 5, Volume 267 Collection:Prime Minister's Office/ Leader of the Opposition Office Title: China 1958 [textual records]
Physical description: 1 folder
Pages:pp. 166885-166889
Series Description: RSN 00000255

(RSN: 00003503) China
Call No.: MG 01/VII/F/201 Diefenbaker Centre, Row 5, Volume 300 Collection:Prime Minister's Office/ Leader of the Opposition Office Title: United States-China Relations 1959 [textual records] Physical description: 1 folder
Pages:p. 192624
Series Description: RSN 00002245

(RSN: 00003900) China
Call No.: MG 01/VII/A/445 Diefenbaker Centre Row 4, Volume 55 Collection:Prime Minister's Office/ Leader of the Opposition Office Title: "China Reconstructs" 1966 [textual records]
Physical description: 1 folder
Pages:pp. 31026-31033
Series Description: RSN 00000254

(RSN: 00003901) China
Call No.: MG 01/VII/A/444 Diefenbaker Centre Row 4, Volume 54 Collection:Prime Minister's Office/ Leader of the Opposition Office Title: China - Nationalist n.d.,1961-1967 [textual records] Physical description: 1 folder
Pages:pp. 30886-31025
Series Description: RSN 00000254

(RSN: 00003902) China
Call No.: MG 01/VII/A/443 Diefenbaker Centre Row 4, Volume 54 Collection:Prime Minister's Office/ Leader of the Opposition Office Title: China - Communist n.d.,1957-1967 [textual records] Physical description: 1 folder
Pages:pp. 30687-30885
Series Description: RSN 00000254

(RSN: 00006287) China
Call No.: MG 01/IX/A/1136/*821/C539.1 Diefenbaker Centre, Row 5, Volume33
Collection:Leader of the Opposition Office
Title: Canada and the United Nations - United Nations Membership - China - Communist China n.d., 1964-1966 [textual records] Physical description: 1 folder
Series Description: RSN 00003079

(RSN: 00006288) China
Call No.: MG 01/IX/A/1137/*821/C539.11 Diefenbaker Centre, Row 5, Volume 33
Collection:Leader of the Opposition Office
Title: Canada and the United Nations - United Nations Membership - China - Communist China - Recognition of 1966 [textual records] Physical description: 1 folder
Series Description: RSN 00003079

(RSN: 00006297) China
Call No.: MG 01/IX/A/1146/*840/C539 Diefenbaker Centre, Row 5, Volume 33 Collection:Leader of the Opposition Office
Title: Canada and Foreign Countries - China 1964 [textual records] Physical description: 1 folder
Series Description: RSN 00003079

(RSN: 00006328) China
Call No.: MG 01/IX/A/1174/*864/C539 Diefenbaker Centre, Row 5, Volume 35 Collection:Leader of the Opposition Office
Title: Diplomatic Representations - Representations of Other Countries in Canada - China 1964 [textual records] Physical description: 1 folder
Series Description: RSN 00003079

(RSN: 00007529) China
Call No.: MG 01/IX/C/403 Diefenbaker Centre, Row 6, Second Leader of the Opposition, Volume 161 Collection:Leader of the Opposition Office
Title: International Affairs - China 1963-1967 [textual records] Physical description: 1 folder
Series Description: RSN 00003079

(RSN: 00008015) China
Call No.: MG 01/XI/A Diefenbaker Centre, Row 6, Member of Parliament, Volume 24
Collection:Diefenbaker Parliamentary Office
Title: Lin, Professor Paul n.d.,1969 [textual records]
Physical description: 1 folder
Historical:Canadian born, Chinese name: Lin Ta-kaung; English language secretary to Prime Minister Chou En-Lai 1949-1964; professor of Asian Studies at McGill University. Summary:This file contains press clippings, Hansard, a letter, and a memorandum for the House. Restricted:Closed until arrangement completed
Subject:Company of Young Canadians Canada - foreign relations Lynch, Charles United Church of Canada - promotion of Maoist philosophy Communist China - diplomatic relations Author:Lord, W. (Montreal)
Series Description: RSN00003078

(RSN: 00008118) China
Call No.: MG 01/III/86 Diefenbaker Centre, Row 1, 1940-1956 Series, Volume 9 Collection:Diefenbaker Parliamentary Office
Title: China and Formosa n.d., 1955 [textual records]
Physical description: 1 folder
Microfilm No.: M-7417
* Pages:pp. 6000-6007
Series Description: RSN00002238

(RSN: 00008119) China
Call No.: MG 01/III/87 Diefenbaker Centre, Row 1, 1940-1956 Series, Volume 9 Collection:Diefenbaker Parliamentary Office
Title: China - Admission to the United Nations n.d., 1954-1956 [textual records] Physical description: 1 folder
Microfilm No.: M-7417

* Pages:pp. 6008-6021
Series Description: RSN00002238

(RSN: 00008120) China
Call No.: MG 01/III/88 Diefenbaker Centre, Row 1, 1940-1956 Series, Volume 9 Collection:Diefenbaker Parliamentary Office
Title: China - Recognition of n.d., 1949-1956 [textual records] Physical description: 1 folder
Microfilm No.: M-7417
* Pages:pp. 6022-6141
Series Description: RSN00002238

(RSN: 00008744) China
Call No.: MG 01/XVIII/OH/69 Diefenbaker Centre Collection:Right Honourable John G. Diefenbaker Centre
Title: McIlraith, George 12 July 1989 [sound recording] Physical description: 2 audio cassettes
Historical:Member of Parliament; Senator
Summary:This tape contains Senator George McIlraith's reminiscences of his political career as a Liberal Member of Parliament and his associations with Diefenbaker, as well as an evaluation of Diefenbaker's administrations. . Restricted: Cassette can be consulted at the Centre but may not be reproduced without the interviewee's permission. *Hard copy summary available.
*No working copy available.
Cite as:Diefenbaker Centre MG01, XVIII, Oral History Subseries, tape 69 Subject:Diefenbaker, Edna
Includes Subject:China - sale of Canadian wheat to
Series Description: RSN00008534

(RSN: 00009284) China
Call No.: MG 01/XI/B Diefenbaker Centre, Rows 6-8
Title: China 1973, 1979 [textual records]
Summary:This file contains the reference material created and accumulated by John Diefenbaker's office from after he ceased being Leader of the Opposition to his death. Restricted:Closed until arrangement completed.
Series Description: RSN00003078

(RSN: 00009965) China
Call No.: MG 01/III/1073 Diefenbaker Centre, Row 1, 1940-1956 Series, Volume 85 Collection:Diefenbaker Confectionary Industry
Title: Trade with China n.d., 1956 [textual records]
Physical description: 1 folder
Microfilm No.: M 7452
* Pages:pp. 68273-68277
Series Description: RSN00002238

(RSN: 00011403) China
Call No.: MG 01/XII/B/355 Diefenbaker Centre, row 9, Personal and Confidential, Volume 41
Collection:Prime Minister's Office
Title: Trade - China 1963 [textual records]
Physical description: 1 folder
Series Description: RSN 9157

(RSN: 00011442) China

Call No.: MG 01/XII/B/393 Diefenbaker Centre, row 9, Personal and Confidential, Volume 43
Collection:Prime Minister's and Leader of the Opposition's Offices Title: Wheat Transaction with China n.d.,1961,1963 [textual records] Physical description: 1 folder
Series Description: RSN 9158

(RSN: 00011543) China
Call No.: MG 01/XII/C/95 Diefenbaker Centre, row 9, Personal and Confidential, Volume 52 Collection:Prime Minister's and Leader of the Opposition's Offices Title: China - Wheat Deal 1961-1963 [textual records]
Physical description: 1 folder
Series Description: RSN 9159

(RSN: 00011682) China
Call No.: MG 01/XII/C/233 Diefenbaker Centre, row 9, Personal and Confidential, Volume 63
Collection:Prime Minister's and Leader of the Opposition's Offices Title: Indo-China 1962 [textual records]
Physical description: 1 folder
Series Description: RSN 9159

(RSN: 00012772) China
Call No.: MG 01/XII/F/463 Diefenbaker Centre, row 9, Personal and Confidential, Volume 124
Collection:Prime Minister's and Leader of the Opposition's Offices/Diefenbaker Parliamentary Office
Title: Trade - China n.d.,1961-1962 [textual records]
Physical description: 1 folder
Series Description: RSN 9162

(RSN: 00013298) China
Call No.: MG 01/XI/C Diefenbaker Centre, Rows 6-8
Title: Trips and Engagements - China - China [textual records] Physical description: 1 folder
Summary:This file contains general correspondence with the public created and accumulated by John Diefenbaker's office from the time he ceased being Leader of the Opposition until his death.
Restricted:Closed until arrangement completed.
Series Description: RSN00003078

(RSN: 00014426) China
Call No.: MG 01/XI/C Diefenbaker Centre, Rows 6-8
Title: Trips and Engagements - China - China - Recognition of Red China [textual records] Physical description: 1 folder
Summary:This file contains general correspondence with the public created and accumulated by John Diefenbaker's office from the time he ceased being Leader of the Opposition until his death.
Restricted:Closed until arrangement completed.
Series Description: RSN00003078

(RSN: 00014427) China
Call No.: MG 01/XI/C Diefenbaker Centre, Rows 6-8

Title: Trips and Engagements - China - China - Republic of China - Taiwan [textual records] Physical description: 1 folder
Summary:This file contains general correspondence with the public created and accumulated by John Diefenbaker's office* time he ceased being Leader of the Opposition until his death. Restricted:Closed until arrangement completed.
Series Description: RSN00003078

(RSN: 00014428) China
Call No.: MG 01/XI/C Diefenbaker Centre, Rows 6-8
Title: Trips and Engagements - China Trip [textual records] Physical description: 1 folder
Summary:This file contains general correspondence with the public created and accumulated by John Diefenbaker's office from the time he ceased being Leader of the Opposition until his death. Restricted:Closed until arrangement completed.
Series Description: RSN00003078

(RSN: 00014429) China
Call No.: MG 01/XI/C Diefenbaker Centre, Rows 6-8
Title: Trips and Engagements - China Trip File [textual records] Physical description: 1 folder
Summary:This file contains general correspondence with the public created and accumulated by John Diefenbaker's officetime he ceased being Leader of the Opposition until his death. Restricted:Closed until arrangement completed.
Series Description: RSN00003078

(RSN: 00014432) China
Call No.: MG 01/XI/C Diefenbaker Centre, Rows 6-8
Title: Trips and Engagements - Memo Re: China 1979 [textual records] Physical description: 1 folder
Summary:This file contains general correspondence with the public created and accumulated by John Diefenbaker's office from the time he ceased being Leader of the Opposition until his death. Restricted:Closed until arrangement completed.
Series Description: RSN00003078

(RSN: 00015425) China
Call No.: MG 01/XI/B Diefenbaker Centre, Rows 6-8
Title: Speeches - Reference: China Trip file 1979 1979 [textual records] Physical description: 1 folder
Summary:This file contains general correspondence with the public created and accumulated by John Diefenbaker's Office from the time he ceased being Leader of the Opposition until his death. Restricted:Closed until arrangement completed.
Series Description: RSN00003078

(RSN: 00016082) China
Call No.: MG01/XVII/JGD 6299 Diefenbaker Centre, Photographs and Slides, Volume Title: Election - 1963 1963 [contact sheet]
Physical description: 20 photographs black & white
Historical:Olive Evangeline (Freeman, Palmer) Diefenbaker; b. 14 Apr, 1902; d. 23 Dec, 1976; second wife of JGD Summary:Inscription on reverse indicates that shots of John and Olive Diefenbaker campaigning were taken in Vancouver China Town, circa 1963.
*See Reference File: Election - 1963
Cite as:Diefenbaker Centre, Photographs and Slides, JGD 6299

(RSN: 00016158) China
Call No.: MG01/XVII/JGD 6300 Diefenbaker Centre, Photographs and Slides, Volume Title: Election - 1963 1963 [contact sheet]
Physical description: 20 photographs black & white
Summary:John Diefenbaker meeting people in Vancouver's Chinatown, at Vancouver rally, and at airport, Vancouver, British Columbia, circa 1963.
*See Reference File: Election - 1963
Cite as:Diefenbaker Centre, Photographs and Slides, JGD 6300

(RSN: 00100386) China
Call No.: MG 01/VI/(031) Diefenbaker Centre, Rows 2-4, Volume 29 Title: Education - Provincial Schools 1957-1963
Summary:This file includes: request* University of Arizona re Canada's position on nuclear testing and the admittance of Communist China to the United Nations.
Microfilm No.: M-7801
*Series Description: RSN00002248

(RSN: 00102564) China
Call No.: MG 01/VI/(313.2.02 Stevens) Diefenbaker Centre, Rows 2-4, Volume 127 Title: Federal Government Executive - The Prime Minister of Canada - Personal - Personal Letters - Hon. H.H. Stevens 1957-1962 Summary:This file contains correspondence and ephemera.
Microfilm No.: M-7845
*Subject includes China War Measures Act
Series Description: RSN00002248

(RSN: 00104259) China
Call No.: MG 01/VI/(313.3I2 D - Duncan) Diefenbaker Centre, Rows 2-4, Volume 229 Title: Federal Government Executive - The Prime Minister of Canada - Requests and Appeals - Interviews - James S. Duncan 1957, 1959-1960 Historical:Chairman, Hydro-Electric Power Commission of Ontario Summary:This file includes letters to Diefenbaker from Duncan re Duncan's visit to China. Microfilm No.: M-7893
* Series Description: RSN00002248

(RSN: 00104510) China
Call No.: MG 01/VI/(313.3I2 N - Newell) Diefenbaker Centre, Rows 2-4, Volume 236 Title: Federal Government Executive - The Prime Minister of Canada - Requests and Appeals - Interviews - Mr. J.C. Newell 1961 Summary:This file includes a letter to Diefenbaker from Newell re international policy and the need for rapprochement with China in order to distance it from the Soviet Union. Microfilm No.: M-7896
*Series Description: RSN00002248

(RSN: 00105350) China
Call No.: MG 01/VI/(333) Diefenbaker Centre, Rows 2-4, Volume 287 Title: The House of Commons - The Leader of the Official Opposition 1957-1963
Summary:This file includes: a copy of Lester B. Pearson's speech to the Young Ontario Liberals Association; a copy of Pearson's 1961 New Year's message; a copy of the 1959 convocation address at Bishop's College; a press release re Diefenbaker's broadcast of September 30, 1959; a press statement re civil service salaries. Microfilm No.: M-7920
* Subject:Canadian trade - American control - export of cars to China
Series Description: RSN00002248

(RSN: 00106584) China
Call No.: MG 01/VI/(380/C539.21) Diefenbaker Centre, Row 4 - 6, Volume 336 Title: Governments of Other Countries - General - China - Cabinet - Prime Minister 1961 Microfilm No.: M-7939
*Series Description: RSN00002248

(RSN: 00109460) China
Call No.: MG 01/VI/(711/C539) Diefenbaker Centre, Row 4 - 6, Volume 469 Title: Domestic Trade - Grain Trade - China 1962
Microfilm No.: M-7992
*Series Description: RSN00002248

(RSN: 00109461) China
Call No.: MG 01/VI/(711/C539.1) Diefenbaker Centre, Row 4 - 6, Volume 469 Title: Domestic Trade - Grain Trade - Communist China 1961 Microfilm No.: M-7992
*Series Description: RSN00002248

(RSN: 00109480) China
Call No.: MG 01/VI/(711.3/C539.1) Diefenbaker Centre, Row 4 - 6, Volume 472 Title: Domestic Trade - Grain Trade - Grain Marketing - Communist China 1961-1963 Microfilm No.: M-7994
*Series Description: RSN00002248

(RSN: 00109481) China
Call No.: MG 01/VI/(711.3/C539.1 Conf.) Diefenbaker Centre, Row 4 - 6, Volume 472 Title: Domestic Trade - Grain Trade - Grain Marketing - Communist China - Confidential 1958-1963 Microfilm No.: M-7994
*Series Description: RSN00002248

(RSN: 00109532) China
Call No.: MG 01/VI/(721.1/C539.1 Conf.) Diefenbaker Centre, Row 4 - 6, Volume 475 Title: Foreign Trade - Foreign Trade Policy and Structure - Conferences - Communist China - Confidential 1962 Microfilm No.: M-7996
*Series Description: RSN00002248

(RSN: 00109546) China
Call No.: MG 01/VI/(722/C539) Diefenbaker Centre, Row 4 - 6, Volume 476 Title: Foreign Trade - Trade By Countries - China 1957-1961 Microfilm No.: M-7996

*Series Description: RSN00002248

(RSN: 00109548) China
Call No.: MG 01/VI/(722/C539.1) Diefenbaker Centre, Row 4 - 6, Volume 476 Title: Foreign Trade - Trade By Countries - Communist China 1957-1963 Microfilm No.: M-7996
*Series Description: RSN00002248

(RSN: 00109549) China
Call No.: MG 01/VI/(722/C539.1 Conf.) Diefenbaker Centre, Row 4 - 6, Volume 476 Title: Foreign Trade - Trade By Countries - Communist China - Confidential 1961-1962 Microfilm No.: M-7996
*Series Description: RSN00002248

(RSN: 00109550) China
Call No.: MG 01/VI/(722/C539.1 Secret) Diefenbaker Centre, Row 4 - 6, Volume 476 Title: Foreign Trade - Trade By Countries - Communist China - Secret 1962-1963 Microfilm No.: M-7996
*Series Description: RSN00002248

(RSN: 00109551) China
Call No.: MG 01/VI/(722/C539.11) Diefenbaker Centre, Row 4 - 6, Volume 476 Title: Foreign Trade - Trade By Countries - Communist China - Recognition Of 1958-1961 Microfilm No.: M-7996
*Series Description: RSN00002248

(RSN: 00109679) China
Call No.: MG 01/VI/(725/C539.1) Diefenbaker Centre, Row 4 - 6, Volume 482 Title: Foreign Trade - Exports - Communist China 1958
Microfilm No.: M-7999
*Series Description: RSN00002248

(RSN: 00110568) China
Call No.: MG 01/VI/(740/C539.11) Diefenbaker Centre, Row 4 - 6, Volume 517 Title: Manufactures - General - Communist China - Recognition Of 1961 Microfilm No.: M-8014
*Series Description: RSN00002248

(RSN: 00110894) China
Call No.: MG 01/VI/(802 China) Diefenbaker Centre, Row 4 - 6, Volume 532 Title: World Relations - Economic Assistance Abroad - China 1957 Microfilm No.: M-8021
*Series Description: RSN00002248

(RSN: 00110895) China
Call No.: MG 01/VI/(802/C539.1) Diefenbaker Centre, Row 4 - 6, Volume 532 Title: World Relations - Economic Assistance Abroad - Communist China 1961 Microfilm No.: M-8021
*Series Description: RSN00002248

(RSN: 00110980) China
Call No.: MG 01/VI/(808/C539.1) Diefenbaker Centre, Row 4 - 6, Volume 536 Title: World Relations - Foreign Policy - Communist China 1958 Microfilm No.: M-8023

*Series Description: RSN00002248

(RSN: 00111141) China
Call No.: MG 01/VI/(818.21 PM 1958 China) Diefenbaker Centre, Row 4 - 6, Volume 542 Title: Canada and the Commonwealth - Visits - Visits to Commonwealth Countries by Canadian Ministers - World Tour - Prime Minister - 1958 - China 1958 Microfilm No.: M-8026
*Series Description: RSN00002248

(RSN: 00111177) China
Call No.: MG 01/VI/(820/C539.1) Diefenbaker Centre, Row 4 - 6, Volume 544 Title: Canada and the United Nations - General - Communist China 1961 Microfilm No.: M-8028
*Series Description: RSN00002248

(RSN: 00111181) China
Call No.: MG 01/VI/(821/C539) Diefenbaker Centre, Row 4 - 6, Volume 545 Title: Canada and the United Nations - United Nations Membership - China 1961 Microfilm No.: M-8028
*Series Description: RSN00002248

(RSN: 00111182) China
Call No.: MG 01/VI/(821/C539.1) Diefenbaker Centre, Row 4 - 6, Volume 545 Title: Canada and the United Nations - United Nations Membership - China - Communist China 1961-1962 Microfilm No.: M-8028
*Series Description: RSN00002248

(RSN: 00111183) China
Call No.: MG 01/VI/(821/C539.11) Diefenbaker Centre, Row 4 - 6, Volume 545 Title: Canada and the United Nations - United Nations Membership - Communist China - Recognition Of 1957-1962 Microfilm No.: M-8028
*Series Description: RSN00002248

(RSN: 00111194) China
Call No.: MG 01/VI/(822/C539.1) Diefenbaker Centre, Row 4 - 6, Volume 545 Title: Canada and the United Nations - The General Assembly - Communist China 1961-1962 Microfilm No.: M-8028
*Series Description: RSN00002248

(RSN: 00111331) China
Call No.: MG 01/VI/(840/C539) Diefenbaker Centre, Row 4 - 6, Volume 551 Title: Canada and Foreign Countries - General - China (Formosa) 1958-1963 Microfilm No.: M-8031
*Series Description: RSN00002248

(RSN: 00111332) China
Call No.: MG 01/VI/(840/C539 Liao) Diefenbaker Centre, Row 4 - 6, Volume 551 Title: Canada and Foreign Countries - General - China (Formosa) - Dr. Thomas Liao 1961-1962 Microfilm No.: M-8031
*Series Description: RSN00002248

(RSN: 00111333) China
Call No.: MG 01/VI/(840/539.1) Diefenbaker Centre, Row 4 - 6, Volume 551 Title: Canada and Foreign Countries - General - China - Communist China 1959-1961 Microfilm No.: M-8031
*Series Description: RSN00002248

(RSN: 00111334) China
Call No.: MG 01/VI/(840/C539.1 Conf.) Diefenbaker Centre, Row 4 - 6, Volume 551 Title: Canada and Foreign Countries - General - China - Communist China - Confidential 1959 Microfilm No.: M-8031
*Series Description: RSN00002248

(RSN: 00111335) China
Call No.: MG 01/VI/(840/C539.11) Diefenbaker Centre, Row 4 - 6, Volume 551 Title: Canada and Foreign Countries - General - China - Communist China - Recognition Of 1957-April 1959 Microfilm No.: M-8031
*Series Description: RSN00002248

(RSN: 00111336) China
Call No.: MG 01/VI/(840/C539.11) Diefenbaker Centre, Row 4 - 6, Volume 551 Title: Canada and Foreign Countries - General - China - Communist China - Recognition Of May 1959-1962 Microfilm No.: M-8031
*Series Description: RSN00002248

(RSN: 00111337) China
Call No.: MG 01/VI/(840/C539.11 Conf.) Diefenbaker Centre, Row 4 - 6, Volume 551 Title: Canada and Foreign Countries - General - China - Communist China - Recognition Of - Confidential 1958-1961 Summary:The principal component of this file is a June 1958 memorandum setting out, in classic External Affairs' terms, the pros and cons of recognizing Communist China. The file also contains a report* Canadian High Commission in Wellington on the New Zealand government's attitude on this same question. *Not available on Microfilm. (This file was classified "Restricted" at the time PMO Numbered series was microfilmed.) Subject:Communist China - recognition of Smith, Hon. Sidney E. - Secretary of State for External Affairs - recognition of Communist China New Zealand - attitude toward recognition of Communist China
Series Description: RSN00002248

(RSN: 00111378) China
Call No.: MG 01/VI/(840/I41V666S) Diefenbaker Centre, Row 4 - 6, Volume 552 Title: Canada and Foreign Countries - General - Indo-China - South Vietnam 1959,1962 Microfilm No.: M-8032
*Series Description: RSN00002248

(RSN: 00111541) China
Call No.: MG 01/VI/(845 India-China) Diefenbaker Centre, Row 4 - 6, Volume 559 Title: Canada and Foreign Countries - International Situation - India - China 1962-1963 Microfilm No.: M-8037
*Series Description: RSN00002248

(RSN: 00111542) China
Call No.: MG 01/VI/(845 India-China Conf.)

Diefenbaker Centre, Row 4 - 6, Volume 559 Title: Canada and Foreign Countries - International Situation - India - China - Confidential 1962 Microfilm No.: M-8037
*Series Description: RSN00002248

(RSN: 00111594) China
Call No.: MG 01/VI/(846/C539) Diefenbaker Centre, Row 4 - 6, Volume 562 Title: Canada and Foreign Countries - Visits - China 1957-1961 Microfilm No.: M-8038
*Series Description: RSN00002248

(RSN: 00111595) China
Call No.: MG 01/VI/(846/C539.1) Diefenbaker Centre, Row 4 - 6, Volume 562 Title: Canada and Foreign Countries - Visits - Communist China 1958-1961 Microfilm No.: M-8038
*Series Description: RSN00002248

(RSN: 00111596) China
Call No.: MG 01/VI/(846/C539.1J) Diefenbaker Centre, Row 4 - 6, Volume 562 Title: Canada and Foreign Countries - Visits - Communist China - J 1957 Microfilm No.: M-8038
*Series Description: RSN00002248

(RSN: 00111625) China
Call No.: MG 01/VI/(846/I41L298) Diefenbaker Centre, Row 4 - 6, Volume 563 Title: Canada and Foreign Countries - Visits - Indo-China - Laos 1958-1962 Microfilm No.: M-8038
*Series Description: RSN00002248

(RSN: 00111687) China
Call No.: MG 01/VI/(848/C539.1) Diefenbaker Centre, Row 4 - 6, Volume 565 Title: Canada and Foreign Countries - Passports, Visas, Etc. - China - Communist China 1958 Microfilm No.: M-8039
*Series Description: RSN00002248

(RSN: 00111872) China
Call No.: MG 01/VI/(864/C539) Diefenbaker Centre, Row 4 - 6, Volume 560 Title: Diplomatic Representation - Representation of Other Countries in Canada - China 1958-1961 Microfilm No.: M-8042
*Series Description: RSN00002248

(RSN: 00001260) Chinese
Call No.: MG 01/VII/A/1569 Diefenbaker Centre Row 4, Volume 168 Collection:Prime Minister's Office/ Leader of the Opposition Office Title: Nationalist Chinese 1963-1964 [textual records]
Physical description:1 folder
Pages:pp. 103714-103735
Series Description: RSN 00000254

(RSN: 00003130) Chinese
Call No.: MG 01/VII/A/667 Diefenbaker Centre Row 4, Volume 79 Collection:Prime Minister's Office/ Leader of the Opposition Office Title: Delegations - Chinese Benevolent Association 1959 [textual records] Physical description: 1 folder
Pages:pp. 46753-46757

Series Description: RSN 00000254

(RSN: 00003898) Chinese
Call No.: MG 01/VII/A/447 Diefenbaker Centre Row 4, Volume 55 Collection:Prime Minister's Office/ Leader of the Opposition Office Title: Chinese-Soviet Relations 1963 [textual records]
Physical description: 1 folder
Pages:p. 31036
Series Description: RSN 00000254

(RSN: 00003899) Chinese
Call No.: MG 01/VII/A/446 Diefenbaker Centre Row 4, Volume 55 Collection:Prime Minister's Office/ Leader of the Opposition Office Title: Chinese Investigations 1962 [textual records]
Physical description: 1 folder
Pages:pp. 31034-31035
Series Description: RSN 00000254

(RSN: 00004003) Chinese
Call No.: MG 01/IX/A/72/*045 Chinese Diefenbaker Centre, Row 5, Volume 3 Collection:Leader of the Opposition Office
Title: Language and Ethnic Groups - Ethnic Groups - Chinese 1966 [textual records] Physical description: 1 folder
Series Description: RSN 3079

(RSN: 00004470) Chinese
Call No.: MG 01/XXII/136 Diefenbaker Centre, Row Volume 2
Title:Re: President Eisenhower's Speech (11 Sept. 1958) Concerning Talks Between U.S. and Chinese Communist Representatives 12 September 1958 [textual records] Physical description:1 folder
Series Description: 3081

(RSN: 00005997) Chinese
Call No.: MG 01/IX/A/908/*572.1 Chinese Diefenbaker Centre, Row 7, Volume 26 Collection:Leader of the Opposition Office
Title: Immigration and Citizenship - Immigration Operations - Immigration Cases - Chinese 1964 [textual records] Physical description: 1 folder
Series Description: RSN 00003079

(RSN: 00008825) Chinese
Call No.: MG 01/III/675 Diefenbaker Centre, Row 1, 1940-1956 Series, Volume 57 Collection:Diefenbaker Parliamentary Office
Title: Immigration - Chinese 1953-1955 [textual records] Physical description: 1 folder
Microfilm No.: M-7439
*Pages:pp. 45647-45667
Series Description: RSN00002238

(RSN: 00011544) Chinese
Call No.: MG 01/XII/C/96.1-96.2 Diefenbaker Centre, row 9, Personal and Confidential, Volume 52 Collection:Prime Minister's and Leader of the Opposition's Offices Title: Chinese Immigration n.d., 1960-1963 [textual records] Physical description: 2 folders

Arranged: C/96.1: n.d., 1960-1961; C/96.2: 1962-1963.
Series Description: RSN 9159

(RSN: 00100587) Chinese
Call No.: MG 01/VI/(045 Chinese) Diefenbaker Centre, Row 4 - 6, Volume 35 Title: Language and Ethnic Groups - Ethnic Groups - Chinese 1957-1963
Microfilm No.: M-7804
*Series Description: RSN00002248

(RSN: 00102279) Chinese
Call No.: MG 01/VI/(312 C&I R.A. Bell) Diefenbaker Centre, Rows 2-4, Volume 113 Title: Federal Government Executive - The Cabinet - Minister of Citizenship and Immigration - Hon. R.A. Bell 1962 Summary:This file contains memoranda and correspondence.
Microfilm No.: M-7838
*Subject:Hyndman, Louis B. Jr. - apointment as Bell's executive assistant illegal entries - Chinese Series Description: RSN00002248

(RSN: 00103040) Chinese
Call No.: MG 01/VI/(313.25 ONT - C) Diefenbaker Centre, Row 4 - 6, Volume 160 Title: Federal Government Executive - The Prime Minister of Canada - Personal - Invitations - Ontario - Chinese Community Center's Testimonial Dinner 1962-1963 Microfilm No.: M-7860
*Series Description: RSN00002248

(RSN: 00104212) Chinese
Call No.: MG 01/VI/(313.3I2 B - Beaumont) Diefenbaker Centre, Row 2-4, Volume 227 Title: Federal Government Executive - The Prime Minister of Canada - Requests and Appeals - Interviews - Henry M. Beaumont 1960 Summary:This file includes: a letter from Beaumont advising Diefenbaker on the brief being sent to the Minister of Citizenship and Immigration on behalf of Calgary's Chinese community re existing immigration regulations; a copy of "Representations of the Joint Committee of Oriental Associations of Calgary". Microfilm No.: M-7892
*Subject:Young Progressive Conservatives of Western Canada
Series Description: RSN00002248

(RSN: 00104313) Chinese
Call No.: MG 01/VI/(313.3I2 D - C - Chinese Community Centre) Diefenbaker Centre, Row 4 - 6, Volume 231
Title: Federal Government Executive - The Prime Minister of Canada - Requests and Appeals - Interviews - Delegations - Chinese Community Centre 1959-1960
Microfilm No.: M-7894
*Series Description: RSN00002248

(RSN: 00104433) Chinese
Call No.: MG 01/VI/(313.3I2 H - Hoffman) Diefenbaker Centre, Rows 2-4, Volume 235 Title: Federal Government Executive - The Prime Minister of Canada - Requests and Appeals - Interviews - Paul S. Hoffman 1960 Summary:This file contains a letter from James Duncan of the Electic Power Commission of Ontario re the Chinese Opera Company's tour of Canada and a rally at Tien An Men. Microfilm No.: M-7895
*United Nations Macdonnell, J.M. - Minister Without Portfolio
Series Description: RSN00002248

(RSN: 00108187) Chinese
Call No.: MG 01/VI/(571 Chinese) Diefenbaker Centre, Row 4 - 6, Volume 407 Title: Immigration and Citizenship - Immigration Policy and Administration - Chinese 1958-1963 Microfilm No.: M-7964
*Series Description: RSN00002248

(RSN: 00108188) Chinese
Call No.: MG 01/VI/(571 Chinese Conf.) Diefenbaker Centre, Row 4 - 6, Volume 407 Title: Immigration and Citizenship - Immigration Policy and Administration - Chinese - Confidential 1960-1962 Microfilm No.: M-7964
*Series Description: RSN00002248

(RSN: 00108219) Chinese
Call No.: MG 01/VI/(572.1 Chinese) Diefenbaker Centre, Row 4 - 6, Volume 408 Title: Immigration and Citizenship - Immigration Operations - Immigration Cases - Chinese 1957-1959 Microfilm No.: M-7965
*Series Description: RSN00002248

(RSN: 00108220) Chinese
Call No.: MG 01/VI/(572.1 Chinese) Diefenbaker Centre, Row 4 - 6, Volume 408 Title: Immigration and Citizenship - Immigration Operations - Immigration Cases - Chinese 1959-1963 Microfilm No.: M-7965
*Series Description: RSN00002248

(RSN: 00108221) Chinese
Call No.: MG 01/VI/(572.1 Chinese Conf.) Diefenbaker Centre, Row 4 - 6, Volume 408 Title: Immigration and Citizenship - Immigration Operations - Immigration Cases - Chinese - Confidential 1960-1963 Microfilm No.: M-7965
*Series Description: RSN00002248

(RSN: 00108222) Chinese
Call No.: MG 01/VI/(572.1 Chinese Wong Ging Ken) Diefenbaker Centre, Row 4 - 6, Volume 408 Title: Immigration and Citizenship - Immigration Operations - Immigration Cases - Chinese - Wong Ging Ken 1959-1961 Microfilm No.: M-7965
*Series Description: RSN00002248

(RSN: 00108223) Chinese
Call No.: MG 01/VI/(572.1 Chinese Kwan Siu Lau Conf.) Diefenbaker Centre, Row 4 - 6, Volume 408 Title: Immigration and Citizenship - Immigration Operations - Immigration Cases - Chinese - Kwan Siu Lau - Confidential 1961 Microfilm No.: M-7965
*Series Description: RSN00002248

(RSN: 00108224) Chinese
Call No.: MG 01/VI/(572.1 Chinese Lee) Diefenbaker Centre, Row 4 - 6, Volume 408 Title:

Immigration and Citizenship - Immigration Operations - Immigration Cases - Chinese - Dr. J.C. Lee 1958-1960 Microfilm No.: M-7965
*Series Description: RSN00002248

(RSN: 00108225) Chinese
Call No.: MG 01/VI/(572.1 Chinese PA Conf.) Diefenbaker Centre, Row 4 - 6, Volume 408 Title: Immigration and Citizenship - Immigration Operations - Immigration Cases - Chinese - Prince Albert - Confidential 1962-1963 Microfilm No.: M-7965
*Series Description: RSN00002248

(RSN: 00108226) Chinese
Call No.: MG 01/VI/(572.1 Chinese PA Tom Hum) Diefenbaker Centre, Row 4 - 6, Volume 408 Title: Immigration and Citizenship - Immigration Operations - Immigration Cases - Chinese - Prince Albert - Tom Hum 1962 Microfilm No.: M-7965
*Series Description: RSN00002248

(RSN: 00108227) Chinese
Call No.: MG 01/VI/(572.1 Chinese PA Der Joy King Conf.) Diefenbaker Centre, Row 4 - 6, Volume 408 Title: Immigration and Citizenship - Immigration Operations - Immigration Cases - Chinese - Prince Albert - Der Joy King - Confidential 1958-1962 Microfilm No.: M-7965
*Series Description: RSN00002248

(RSN: 00108228) Chinese
Call No.: MG 01/VI/(572.1 Chinese PA Quong Chum Wah Conf.) Diefenbaker Centre , Row 4 - 6, Volume 408 Title: Immigration and Citizenship - Immigration Operations - Immigration Cases - Chinese - Prince Albert - Quong Chum Wah - Confidential 1953-1963 Microfilm No.: M-7965
*Series Description: RSN00002248

(RSN: 00111570) Chinese
Call No.: MG 01/VI/(845.4 Chinese) Diefenbaker Centre, Row 4 - 6, Volume 560 Title: Canada and Foreign Countries - International Situation - Refugees - Chinese 1960-1963 Microfilm No.: M-8037
*Series Description: RSN00002248

(RSN: 00111571) Chinese
Call No.: MG 01/VI/(845.4 Chinese - George Soo) Diefenbaker Centre, Row 4 - 6, Volume 560 Title: Canada and Foreign Countries - International Situation - Refugees - Chinese - Mr. George Soo 1962-1963 Microfilm No.: M-8037
*Series Description: RSN00002248

(RSN: 00003224) Cyprus
Call No.: MG 01/VII/A/594.1-594.2 Diefenbaker Centre Row 4, Volume 72 Collection:Prime Minister's Office/ Leader of the Opposition Office Title: Cyprus n.d.,1957-1965 [textual records]
Physical description: 2 folders
A/594.1: n.d.; A/594.2: 1957-1965.
Pages:pp. 42106-42503
Series Description: RSN 00000254

(RSN: 00003515) Cyprus
Call No.: MG 01/VII/G/6 Diefenbaker Centre, Row 5, Volume 301 Collection:Prime Minister's Office/ Leader of the Opposition Office Title: Cyprus 1964 [textual records]
Physical description: 1 folder
Pages:pp. 192892-192900
Series Description: RSN 00002246

(RSN: 00003628) Cyprus
Call No.: MG 01/VII/H/89 Diefenbaker Centre, Row 5, Volume 309 Collection:Prime Minister's Office/ Leader of the Opposition Office Title: Cyprus n.d., 1964 [textual records]
Physical description: 1 folder
Pages:pp. 197314-197390
Series Description: RSN 00002246

(RSN: 00005391) Cyprus
Call No.: MG 01/XIII/83 Diefenbaker Centre, Row 9, Volume 10
Collection:Diefenbaker Parliamentary Office/Leader of the Opposition Office Title: Cyprus 1956 [textual records]
Physical description: 1 folder
Series Description: RSN00002240

(RSN: 00006309) Cyprus
Call No.: MG 01/IX/A/1158/*845 Cyprus
Diefenbaker Centre, Row 5, Volume 34
Collection:Leader of the Opposition Office
Title: Canada and Foreign Countries - International Situation - Cyprus 1964-1965 [textual records] Physical description: 1 folder
Series Description: RSN 00003079

(RSN: 00006310) Cyprus
Call No.: MG 01/IX/A/1159/*845 Cyprus Conf.
Diefenbaker Centre, Row 5, Volume 34
Collection:Leader of the Opposition Office
Title: Canada and Foreign Countries - International Situation - Cyprus - Confidential 1964 [textual records]
Physical description: 1 folder
Series Description: RSN 00003079

(RSN: 00007526) Cyprus
Call No.: MG 01/IX/C/406 Diefenbaker Centre, Row 6, Second Leader of the Opposition, Volume 161
Collection:Leader of the Opposition Office
Title: International Affairs - Cyprus 1964-1965 [textual records] Physical description: 1 folder
Series Description: RSN 00003079

(RSN: 00008303) Cyprus
Call No.: MG 01/III/267 Diefenbaker Centre, Row 1, 1940-1956 Series, Volume 22 Collection:Diefenbaker Parliamentary Office
Title: Cyprus n.d., 1956 [textual records]
Physical description: 1 folder
Microfilm No.: M-7422
Pages:pp. 15620-15634
*Series Description: RSN00002238

(RSN: 00009322) Cyprus
Call No.: MG 01/XI/B Diefenbaker Centre, Rows 6-8
Title: Cyprus 1978 [textual records]
Summary:This file contains the reference material created and accumulated by John Diefenbaker's office from after he ceased being Leader of the Opposition to his death. Restricted:Closed until arrangement completed.
Series Description: RSN00003078

(RSN: 00012145) Cyprus
Call No.: MG 01/XII/E/22 Diefenbaker Centre, row 9, Personal and Confidential, Volume 89 Collection:Prime Minister's and Leader of the Opposition's Offices/Diefenbaker Parliamentary Office Title: Cyprus 1964 [textual records]
Physical description: 1 folder
Series Description: RSN 9161

(RSN: 00104391) Cyprus
Call No.: MG 01/VI/(313.3I2 E - Elieff) Diefenbaker Centre, Rows 2-4, Volume 234 Title: Federal Government Executive - The Prime Minister of Canada - Requests and Appeals - Interviews - Very Reverend H. Elieff 1957 Summary:This file includes a copy of "The Cyprus Problem and Macedonia: An Expose of Greece's Oppression of Her Ethnic Minorities".
Microfilm No.: M-7895
*Series Description: RSN00002248

(RSN: 00105740) Cyprus
Call No.: MG 01/VI/(346/C996 Conf.) Diefenbaker Centre, Row 4 - 6, Volume 305 Title: The Judiciary - Judgeships - Cyprus - Confidential 1961-1962 Microfilm No.:
*Series Description: RSN00002248

(RSN: 00108274) Cyprus
Call No.: MG 01/VI/(572.2/C996) Diefenbaker Centre, Row 4 - 6, Volume 411 Title: Immigration and Citizenship - Immigration Operations - Agricultural Workers - Cyprus 1958 Microfilm No.: M-7966
*Series Description: RSN00002248

(RSN: 00110898) Cyprus
Call No.: MG 01/VI/(802/C996) Diefenbaker Centre, Row 4 - 6, Volume 533 Title: World Relations - Economic Assistance Abroad - Cyprus 1961 Microfilm No.: M-8021
*Series Description: RSN00002248

(RSN: 00111005) Cyprus
Call No.: MG 01/VI/(811/C996) Diefenbaker Centre, Row 4 - 6, Volume 537 Title: Canada and the Commonwealth - Commonwealth Members - Cyprus 1959-1960 Microfilm No.: M-8023
*Series Description: RSN00002248

(RSN: 00111006) Cyprus
Call No.: MG 01/VI/(811/C996 Conf.) Diefenbaker Centre, Row 4 - 6, Volume 537 Title: Canada and the Commonwealth - Commonwealth Members - Cyprus - Confidential 1959-1961 Microfilm No.: M-8023

*Series Description: RSN00002248

(RSN: 00111007) Cyprus
Call No.: MG 01/VI/(811/C996 Secret) Diefenbaker Centre, Row 4 - 6, Volume 537 Title: Canada and the Commonwealth - Commonwealth Members - Cyprus - Secret 1959 Microfilm No.: M-8023
*Series Description: RSN00002248

(RSN: 00111346) Cyprus
Call No.: MG 01/VI/(840/C996) Diefenbaker Centre, Row 4 - 6, Volume 552 Title: Canada and Foreign Countries - General - Cyprus 1957-1962 Microfilm No.: M-8032
*Series Description: RSN00002248

(RSN: 00111347) Cyprus
Call No.: MG 01/VI/(840/C996.1) Diefenbaker Centre, Row 4 - 6, Volume 552 Title: Canada and Foreign Countries - General - Cyprus - Heads of State 1961 Microfilm No.: M-8032
*Series Description: RSN00002248

(RSN: 00008826) East Indian
Call No.: MG 01/III/676 Diefenbaker Centre, Row 1, 1940-1956 Series, Volume 57 Collection:Diefenbaker Parliamentary Office
Title: Immigration - East Indians 1956 [textual records]
Physical description: 1 folder
Microfilm No.: M-7439
*Pages:pp. 45668-45675
Series Description: RSN00002238
RSN: 00108233) East Indian
Call No.: MG 01/VI/(572.1 East Indian) Diefenbaker Centre, Row 4 - 6, Volume 409 Title: Immigration and Citizenship - Immigration Operations - Immigration Cases - East Indian 1958 Microfilm No.: M-7965
*Series Description: RSN00002248

RSN: 00111144) Fiji
Call No.: MG 01/VI/(818.21 PM 1958 Fiji) Diefenbaker Centre, Row 4 - 6, Volume 542 Title: Canada and the Commonwealth - Visits - Visits to Commonwealth Countries by Canadian Ministers - World Tour - Prime Minister - 1958 - Fiji 1958 Microfilm No.: M-8026
*Series Description: RSN00002248

(RSN: 00002527) Hong Kong
Call No.: MG 01/VII/A/1134 Diefenbaker Centre Row 4, Volume 130 Collection:Prime Minister's Office/Leader of the Opposition Office Title: Hong Kong n.d. [textual records]
Physical description: 1 folder
Pages:pp. 78031-78032
Series Description: RSN 00000254

(RSN: 00006075) Hong Kong
Call No.: MG 01/IX/A/976/*659.3 Diefenbaker Centre, Row 7, Volume 30 Collection:Leader of the Opposition Office
Title: Veterans Health and Welfare - Other - Hong Kong

Veterans 1964 [textual records] Physical description: 1 folder
Series Description: RSN 00003079

(RSN: 00008815) Hong Kong
Call No.: MG 01/III/665 Diefenbaker Centre, Row 1, 1940-1956 Series, Volume 55 Collection:Diefenbaker Parliamentary Office
Title: Hong Kong Inquiry 1942-1948 [textual records]
Physical description: 1 folder
Microfilm No.: M-7439
*Pages:pp. 44984-45036
Series Description: RSN00002238

(RSN: 00010547) Hong Kong
Call No.: MG 01/XII/A/479 Diefenbaker Centre, row 9, Personal and Confidential, Volume 17 Collection:Prime Minister's Office
Title: Immigration - Hong Kong 1959 [textual records]
Physical description: 1 folder
Series Description: RSN 9157

(RSN: 00109317) Hong Kong
Call No.: MG 01/VI/(659.3) Diefenbaker Centre, Row 4 - 6, Volume 463 Title: Veterans Health and Welfare - Other - Hong Kong Veterans 1958-1960 Microfilm No.: M-7989
*Series Description: RSN00002248

(RSN: 00111372) Hong Kong
Call No.: MG 01/VI/(840/H772) Diefenbaker Centre, Row 4 - 6, Volume 552 Title: Canada and Foreign Countries - General - Hong Kong 1959,1961 Microfilm No.: M-8032
*Series Description: RSN00002248

(RSN: 00001783) India
Call No.: MG 01/XIV/E/126 Diefenbaker Centre, Row 9, Memoirs Volume 14 Title: External Affairs 1959-1966 [textual records]
Physical description: one folder
Restricted:Closed until screening completed.
Subject:India European Economic Duty
Series Description: RSN 00001527

(RSN: 00002391) India
Call No.: MG 01/VII/A/1204.1-1204.3 Diefenbaker Centre Row 4, Volume 138 Collection:Prime Minister's Office/ Leader of the Opposition Office Title: India n.d.,1957-1967 [textual records]
Physical description: 3 folders
A/1204.1: n.d.,1957; A/1204.2: 1963-1964; A/1204.3: 1965-1967. Pages:pp. 83006-83071
Series Description: RSN 00000254

(RSN: 00002468) India
Call No.: MG 01/VII/C/22 Diefenbaker Centre, Row 5, Volume 272 Collection:Prime Minister's Office/ Leader of the Opposition Office Title: India-Pakistan 1965 [textual records]
Physical description: 1 folder
Pages:pp. 169705-169706
Series Description: RSN 00002242

(RSN: 00003523) India
Call No.: MG 01/VII/G/14 Diefenbaker Centre, Row 5, Volume 301 Collection:Prime Minister's Office/ Leader of the Opposition Office Title: India-Pakistan 1965 [textual records]
Physical description: 1 folder
Pages:pp. 193228-193230
Series Description: RSN 00002246

(RSN: 00003580) India
Call No.: MG 01/VII/H/41 Diefenbaker Centre, Row 5, Volume 306 Collection:Prime Minister's Office/ Leader of the Opposition Office Title: Canada-India 1963 [textual records]
Physical description: 1 folder
Pages:p. 195605-195606
Series Description: RSN 00002247

(RSN: 00003745) India
Call No.: MG 01/VII/H/206 Diefenbaker Centre, Row 5, Volume 315 Collection:Prime Minister's Office/ Leader of the Opposition Office Title: India - Defence 1963 [textual records]
Physical description: 1 folder
Pages:pp. 201310-201311
Series Description: RSN 00002246

(RSN: 00004384) India
Call No.: MG 01/XXII/65 Diefenbaker Centre, Row Volume 1
Title: $7 Million Wheat to India as Part of Colombo Plan Programme 2 November 1957 [textual records]
Physical description: 1 folder
Summary:Draft and French included
Series Description: 3081

(RSN: 00004421) India
Call No.: MG 01/XXII/93 Diefenbaker Centre, Row Volume 2
Title: Wheat Grants to India and Pakistan 28 March 1958 [textual records] Physical description: 1 folder
Series Description: 3081

(RSN: 00005142) India
Call No.: MG 01/XXII/535 Diefenbaker Centre, Row Volume 8
Title: Re: Prime Minister's Offer to Act as Mediator Between India and Pakistan 3 September 1965 [textual records] Physical description: 1 folder
Summary:Draft Only
Series Description: 3081

(RSN: 00005454) India
Call No.: MG 01/XIII/146 Diefenbaker Centre, Row 9, Volume 17 Collection:Diefenbaker Parliamentary Office/Leader of the Opposition Office Title: India nd, 1950-1956 (inclusive) [textual records] Physical description: 1 folder
Series Description: RSN00002240

(RSN: 00005455) India
Call No.: MG 01/XIII/147 Diefenbaker Centre, Row 9, Volume 17 Collection:Diefenbaker Parliamentary Office/Leader of the Opposition Office Title: India --

Nehru, Pandit Jawaharlal 1949-1956 (inclusive) [textual records] Physical description: 1 folder
Series Description: RSN00002240
(RSN: 00005540) India
Call No.: MG 01/XIII/232 Diefenbaker Centre, Row 9, Volume 26 Collection:Diefenbaker Parliamentary Office/Leader of the Opposition Office Title: Pakistan 1951-1957 (inclusive) [textual records] Physical description: 1 folder
Summary:This file contains: an issue of "Pakistan News and Views"; a booklet entitled The Republic of Pakistan and the Commonwealth; and a booklet commemorating the Indian Mutiny of 1857 entitled Struggle For Freedom, 1857.
Series Description: RSN00002240

(RSN: 00006280) India
Call No.: MG 01/IX/A/1129/*802 India Diefenbaker Centre, Row 5, Volume 33 Collection:Leader of the Opposition Office
Title: World Relations - Economic Assistance Abroad - India 1967 [textual records] Physical description: 1 folder
Series Description: RSN 00003079

(RSN: 00006281) India
Call No.: MG 01/IX/A/1130/*802/I39 Diefenbaker Centre, Row 5, Volume 33 Collection:Leader of the Opposition Office
Title: World Relations - Economic Assistance Abroad - India 1966 [textual records] Physical description: 1 folder
Series Description: RSN 00003079

(RSN: 00006329) India
Call No.: MG 01/IX/A/1175/*864/139 Diefenbaker Centre, Row 5, Volume 35 Collection:Leader of the Opposition Office
Title: Diplomatic Representations - Representations of Other Countries in Canada - India 1966 [textual records] Physical description: 1 folder
Series Description: RSN 00003079

(RSN: 00007519) India
Call No.: MG 01/IX/C/412 Diefenbaker Centre, Row 6, Second Leader of the Opposition, Volume 161 Collection:Leader of the Opposition Office
Title: International Affairs - India 1964-1966 [textual records] Physical description: 1 folder
Series Description: RSN 00003079

(RSN: 00008826) India
Call No.: MG 01/III/676 Diefenbaker Centre, Row 1, 1940-1956 Series, Volume 57 Collection:Diefenbaker Parliamentary Office
Title: Immigration - East Indians 1956 [textual records] Physical description: 1 folder
Microfilm No.: M-7439
* only Pages:pp. 45668-45675
Series Description: RSN00002238

(RSN: 00010062) India
Call No.: MG 01/XII/A/1 Diefenbaker Centre, row 9, Personal and Confidential, Volume 1
Collection:Prime Minister's Office
Title: Agriculture [510] 1957-1958 [textual records) Physical description: 1 folder
Summary:This file contains memoranda concerning wheat policy, surplus and sales. Subject:United Kingdom - stockpiling India Netherlands - Hoogstraten surplus disposal scheme Spain - Swartz proposal agricultural stabilization bill Author:Menzies, M.W. Reid, Escott McNamara, W.C. (Commissioner Canadian Wheat Board)
Series Description: RSN 9157

(RSN: 00010460) India
Call No.: MG 01/XII/A/393 Diefenbaker Centre, row 9, Personal and Confidential, Volume 11
Collection:Prime Minister's Office
Title: Diefenbaker, John G. - Trips and Engagements - Canada - India [818.01 PM - 1958 India] 1958 [textual records] Physical description: 1 folder
Series Description: RSN 9157

(RSN: 00010468) India
Call No.: MG 01/XII/A/401 Diefenbaker Centre, row 9, Personal and Confidential, Volume 12
Collection:Prime Minister's Office
Title: Diefenbaker, John G. - Trips and Engagements - World Tour - India 1958 [textual records] Physical description: 1 folder
Series Description: RSN 9157

(RSN: 00011040) India
Call No.: MG 01/XII/B/188 Diefenbaker Centre, row 9, Personal and Confidential, Volume 36
Collection:Prime Minister's and Leader of the Opposition's Offices Title: India - Long Term Export Financing 1963 [textual records] Physical description: 1 folder
Series Description: RSN 9158

(RSN: 00011680) India
Call No.: MG 01/XII/C/231 Diefenbaker Centre, row 9, Personal and Confidential, Volume 63
Collection:Prime Minister's and Leader of the Opposition's Offices Title: India 1962 [textual records]
Physical description: 1 folder
Series Description: RSN 9159

(RSN: 00012335) India
Call No.: MG 01/XII/F/51 Diefenbaker Centre, row 9, Personal and Confidential, Volume 97
Collection:Prime Minister's and Leader of the Opposition's Offices/Diefenbaker Parliamentary Office Title: Civil Liberties - India 1958 [textual records]
Physical description: 1 folder
Series Description: RSN 9162

(RSN: 00012833) India
Call No.: MG 01/XI/C Diefenbaker Centre, Rows 6 -8
Title: India 1968-1975 (inclusive) [textual records]
Summary:This file contains general correspondence with the public, as well as newspaper clippings,

created and accumulated by John Diefenbaker's office* time he ceased being Leader of the Opposition until his death. Restricted:Closed until arrangement completed.
Subject:Diefenbaker, John G. - Gifts - Tea
Series Description: RSN00003078

(RSN: 00100983) India
Call No.: MG 01/VI/(154.2 India) Diefenbaker Centre, Row 4 - 6, Volume 52 Title: Defence Research - Atomic Research - Atomic Research Plants (Reactors) - India 1958 Microfilm No.: M-7812
*Series Description: RSN00002248

(RSN: 00101048) India
Call No.: MG 01/VI/(166/I39) Diefenbaker Centre, Row 4 - 6, Volume 55 Title: Defence Production - Arms for Export - India 1962-1963 Microfilm No.: M-7813
*Series Description: RSN00002248

(RSN: 00101049) India
Call No.: MG 01/VI/R/108/(166/I39 Conf.) Diefenbaker Centre, Row 4, Volume 3 Collection:Prime Minster's Office
Title: Defence Production - Arms for Export - India - Confidential 1962 [textual records] Physical description: 1 folder
Summary.
Cite as:Diefenbaker Centre, MG 01, VI, Restricted Subseries, Volume 3, file 108
Series Description: RSN00002248

(RSN: 00101509) India
Call No.: MG 01/VI/(230.2/I39) Diefenbaker Centre, Row 4 - 6, Volume 75 Title: Currency and Banking - General - International Monetary Funds - Banks - India 1961
Series Description: RSN00002248

(RSN: 00101510) India
Call No.: MG 01/VI/(230.2/I39 Conf.) Diefenbaker Centre, Row 4 - 6, Volume 75 Title: Currency and Banking - General - International Monetary Funds - Banks - India - Confidential 1957,1961 Microfilm No.:
*Series Description: RSN00002248

(RSN: 00102285) India
Call No.: MG 01/VI/(312 DPW) Diefenbaker Centre, Rows 2-4, Volume 114 Title: Federal Government Executive - The Cabinet - Minister of Public Works 1957-1963 Summary:This file contains correspondence and memoranda.
Microfilm No.: M-7838
*Subject include: Campbell, Arthur - acting High Commissioner in New Delhi
Series Description: RSN00002248

(RSN: 00102290) India
Call No.: MG 01/VI/(312 Finance Hon. George Nowlan) Diefenbaker Centre, Rows 2-4, Volume 114 Title: Federal Government Executive - The Cabinet - Minister of Finance - Hon. George Nowlan 1957-1962 Summary:This file, in fact, contains memoranda, correspondence, photocopies, reports and ephemera concerning Donald Fleming, Minister of Finance.

Microfilm No.: M-7838
*Subjects include: Indus Waters Dispute between India and Pakistan Japan - trade negotiations Japan - Prime Minister's visit to Ottawa RSN00002248

(RSN: 00102317) India
Call No.: MG 01/VI/(312 T&C) Diefenbaker Centre, Rows
2-4, Volume 115
Title: Federal Government Executive - The Cabinet - Minister of Trade and Commerce 1957-1963
Summary:This file contains correspondence, memoranda, reports and press releases. Microfilm No.: M-7839
*Subjects include:Atomic Energy of Canada Ltd. - Canada-India Reactor Project Author:Churchill, Gordon Menzies, M.W. Fleming, Donald Hees, George Series Description: RSN00002248

(RSN: 00105460) India
Call No.: MG 01/VI/(335 Lambton West) Diefenbaker Centre, Row 4 - 6, Volume 292 Title: The House of Commons - Members of the House - Lambton West Constituency 1957-1962 Summary:This file includes a memo for Diefenbaker from Joseph Warner Murphy (MP) re Murphy's trip to India, Pakistan and Ceylon. Microfilm No.: M-7923
*Subject:Polymer Corporation Canadian unions - payment of dues to American head offices Series Description: RSN00002248

(RSN: 00106600) India
Call No.: MG 01/VI/(380/I39.1) Diefenbaker Centre, Row 4 - 6, Volume 336 Title: Governments of Other Countries - General - India - Heads of State 1960-1962 Microfilm No.: M-7939
*Series Description: RSN00002248

(RSN: 00106601) India
Call No.: MG 01/VI/(380/I39.21) Diefenbaker Centre, Row 4 - 6, Volume 336 Title: Governments of Other Countries - General - India - Cabinet - Prime Minister 1959-1962 Microfilm No.: M-7939
*Series Description: RSN00002248

(RSN: 00108233) India
Call No.: MG 01/VI/(572.1 East Indian) Diefenbaker Centre, Row 4 - 6, Volume 409 Title: Immigration and Citizenship - Immigration Operations - Immigration Cases - East Indian 1958 Microfilm No.: M-7965
*Series Description: RSN00002248

((RSN: 00109462) India
Call No.: MG 01/VI/(711/I39) Diefenbaker Centre,Row 4 - 6, Volume 469 Title: Domestic Trade - Grain Trade - India 1957-1960
Microfilm No.: M-7992
*Series Description: RSN00002248

(RSN: 00109563) India
Call No.: MG 01/VI/(722/I39) Diefenbaker Centre, Row 4 - 6, Volume 477 Title: Foreign Trade - Trade By Countries - India 1957-1958,1961 Microfilm No.: M-

7997
*Series Description: RSN00002248

(RSN: 00109767) India
Call No.: MG 01/VI/(732/I39) Diefenbaker Centre, Row 4 - 6, Volume 486 Title: Transportation and Communication - Railway Transportation - India 1961 Microfilm No.: M-8001
*Series Description: RSN00002248

(RSN: 00110460) India
Call No.: MG 01/VI/(738.5/I39) Diefenbaker Centre, Row 4 - 6, Volume 513 Title: Transportation and Communication - The Press - Newspapers - India 1959 Microfilm No.: M-8012
*Series Description: RSN00002248

(RSN: 00110903) India
Call No.: MG 01/VI/(802/I39) Diefenbaker Centre, Row 4 - 6, Volume 533 Title: World Relations - Economic Assistance Abroad - India 1957-1963 Microfilm No.: M-8021
*Series Description: RSN00002248

(RSN: 00110904) India
Call No.: MG 01/VI/(802/I39 Conf.) Diefenbaker Centre, Row 4 - 6, Volume 533 Title: World Relations - Economic Assistance Abroad - India - Confidential 1958-1961 Microfilm No.: M-8021
*Series Description: RSN00002248

(RSN: 00110919) India
Call No.: MG 01/VI/(802.1/I39) Diefenbaker Centre, Row 4 - 6, Volume 533 Title: World Relations - Economic Assistance Abroad - Flood Relief Assistance - India 1958 Microfilm No.: M-8021
*Series Description: RSN00002248

(RSN: 00110928) India
Call No.: MG 01/VI/(805/I39) Diefenbaker Centre, Row 4 - 6, Volume 534 Title: World Relations - The Colombo Plan - India 1957-1961 Microfilm No.: M-8022
*Series Description: RSN00002248

(RSN: 00110929) India
Call No.: MG 01/VI/(805/I39 Conf.) Diefenbaker Centre, Row 4 - 6, Volume 534 Title: World Relations - The Colombo Plan - India - Confidential 1959,1961 Microfilm No.: M-8022
*Series Description: RSN00002248

(RSN: 00110942) India
Call No.: MG 01/VI/(805.2/I39) Diefenbaker Centre, Row 4 - 6, Volume 534 Title: World Relations - The Colombo Plan - Technical Assistance - India 1957,1959 Microfilm No.: M-8022
*Series Description: RSN00002248

(RSN: 00110990) India
Call No.: MG 01/VI/(810/I39) Diefenbaker Centre, Row 4 - 6, Volume 536 Title: Canada and the Commonwealth - General - India 1961 Microfilm No.: M-8023

*Series Description: RSN00002248

(RSN: 00111009) India
Call No.: MG 01/VI/(811/I39) Diefenbaker Centre, Row 4 - 6, Volume 537 Title: Canada and the Commonwealth - Commonwealth Members - India 1957-1962 Microfilm No.: M-8023
*Series Description: RSN00002248

(RSN: 00111121) India
Call No.: MG 01/VI/(818.1/I39) Diefenbaker Centre, Row 4 - 6, Volume 541 Title: Canada and the Commonwealth - Visits - Visits to Canada of Commonwealth Ministers - India 1958-1960 Microfilm No.: M-8026
*Series Description: RSN00002248

(RSN: 00111154) India
Call No.: MG 01/VI/(818.21 PM 1958 India) Diefenbaker Centre, Row 4 - 6, Volume 543 Title: Canada and the Commonwealth - Visits - Visits to Commonwealth Countries by Canadian Ministers - World Tour - Prime Minister - 1958 - India 1958-1959 Microfilm No.: M-8027
*Series Description: RSN00002248

(RSN: 00111221) India
Call No.: MG 01/VI/(822.613) Diefenbaker Centre, Row 4 - 6, Volume 547 Title: Canada and the United Nations - The General Assembly - Agenda - Resolutions - International Co-operation Year (India) 1961-1963 Microfilm No.: M-8029
*Series Description: RSN00002248

(RSN: 00111375) India
Call No.: MG 01/VI/(840/I39) Diefenbaker Centre, Row 4 - 6, Volume 552 Title: Canada and Foreign Countries - General - India 1957-1963 Microfilm No.: M-8032
*Series Description: RSN00002248

(RSN: 00111376) India
Call No.: MG 01/VI/(840/I39 Secret) Diefenbaker Centre, Row 4 - 6, Volume 552 Title: Canada and Foreign Countries - General - India - Secret 1961 Microfilm No.: M-8032
*Series Description: RSN00002248

(RSN: 00111429) India
Call No.: MG 01/VI/(840/P853-9) Diefenbaker Centre, Row 4 - 6, Volume 554 Title: Canada and Foreign Countries - General - Portuguese India 1961-1962 Microfilm No.: M-8032
*Series Description: RSN00002248

(RSN: 00111496) India
Call No.: MG 01/VI/(843 India) Diefenbaker Centre, Row 4 - 6, Volume 556 Title: Canada and Foreign Countries - Summit Conferences - India 1958 Microfilm No.: M-8034
*Series Description: RSN00002248

(RSN: 00111540) India
Call No.: MG 01/VI/(845/I39) Diefenbaker Centre,

Row 4 - 6, Volume 559 Title: Canada and Foreign Countries - International Situation - India 1962 Microfilm No.: M-8037
*Series Description: RSN00002248

(RSN: 00111541) India
Call No.: MG 01/VI/(845 India-China) Diefenbaker Centre, Row 4 - 6, Volume 559 Title: Canada and Foreign Countries - International Situation - India - China 1962-1963 Microfilm No.: M-8037
*Series Description: RSN00002248

(RSN: 00111542) India
Call No.: MG 01/VI/(845 India-China Conf.) Diefenbaker Centre, Row 4 - 6, Volume 559 Title: Canada and Foreign Countries - International Situation - India - China - Confidential 1962 Microfilm No.: M-8037
*Series Description: RSN00002248

(RSN: 00111620) India
Call No.: MG 01/VI/(846/I39) Diefenbaker Centre, Row 4 - 6, Volume 563 Title: Canada and Foreign Countries - Visits - India 1959-1961 Microfilm No.: M-8038
*Series Description: RSN00002248

(RSN: 00111621) India
Call No.: MG 01/VI/(846/I39 Kotah) Diefenbaker Centre, Row 4 - 6, Volume 563 Title: Canada and Foreign Countries - Visits - India - Maharao of Kotah 1960-1961 Microfilm No.: M-8038
*Series Description: RSN00002248

(RSN: 00111622) India
Call No.: MG 01/VI/(846/I39.1 Secret) Diefenbaker Centre, Row 4 - 6, Volume 563 Title: Canada and Foreign Countries - Visits - India - Heads of State - Secret 1961 Microfilm No.: M-8038
*Series Description: RSN00002248

(RSN: 00111623) India
Call No.: MG 01/VI/(846/I39.21 Secret) Diefenbaker Centre, Row 4 - 6, Volume 563 Title: Canada and Foreign Countries - Visits - India - Cabinet - Prime Minister - Secret 1961 Microfilm No.: M-8038
*Series Description: RSN00002248

(RSN: 00111772) India
Call No.: MG 01/VI/(861/I39) Diefenbaker Centre, Row 4 - 6, Volume 568 Title: Diplomatic Representation - Canadian Representation Abroad - India 1958-1959 Microfilm No.: M-8041
*Series Description: RSN00002248

(RSN: 00111773) India
Call No.: MG 01/VI/(861/I39 Kotah) Diefenbaker Centre, Row 4 - 6, Volume 568 Title: Diplomatic Representation - Canadian Representation Abroad - India - Kotah 1961 Microfilm No.: M-8041
*Series Description: RSN00002248

(RSN: 00111886) India
Call No.: MG 01/VI/(864/I39) Diefenbaker Centre, Row 4 - 6, Volume 571 Title: Diplomatic Representation - Representation of Other Countries in Canada - India 1957-1963 Microfilm No.: M-8042
*Series Description: RSN00002248

(RSN: 00111887) India
Call No.: MG 01/VI/(864/I39 Pillai) Diefenbaker Centre, Row 4 - 6, Volume 571 Title: Diplomatic Representation - Representation of Other Countries in Canada - India - Mr. K. Sankara Pillai 1961 Microfilm No.: M-8042
*Series Description: RSN00002248

(RSN: 00107641) Indo-China
Call No.: MG 01/VI/(437/I41) Diefenbaker Centre, Row 4 - 6, Volume 376 Title: Crime and Deliquency - Narcotics - Indo-China 1962 Microfilm No.: M-7954
*Series Description: RSN00002248

(RSN: 00006330) Indonesia
Call No.: MG 01/IX/A/1176/*864/142 Diefenbaker Centre, Row 5, Volume 35 Collection:Leader of the Opposition Office
Title: Diplomatic Representations - Representations of Other Countries in Canada - Republic of Indonesia 1966 [textual records] Physical description: 1 folder
Series Description: RSN 0000307920:

(RSN: 00010469) Indonesia
Call No.: MG 01/XII/A/402 Diefenbaker Centre, row 9, Personal and Confidential, Volume 12 Collection:Prime Minister's Office
Title: Diefenbaker, John G. - Trips and Engagements - World Tour - Indonesia 1958 [textual records] Physical description: 1 folder
Series Description: RSN 9157

(RSN: 00012516) Indonesia
Call No.: MG 01/XII/F/218 Diefenbaker Centre, row 9, Personal and Confidential, Volume 112 Collection:Prime Minister's and Leader of the Opposition's Offices/Diefenbaker Parliamentary Office
Title: Foreign Affairs - Indonesia 1958 [textual records] Physical description: 1 folder
Series Description: RSN 9162

(RSN: 00017412) Indonesia
Call No.: MG01/XVII/JGD 312 Diefenbaker Centre, Photographs and Slides, Volume Title: Empire Parliamentary Association 1950 [photograph] Physical description: 1 photograph black and white
Summary:Photograph of discussion panel on "Parliamentary Government" which John Diefenbaker opened at the EPA conference, New Zealand. Ceylon's Speaker of the House Sir Francis Molamure is standing and speaking. JGD inscription on back reads: "L to R -- 1/Official of Internal Affairs -- 2/Opener of Discussion on Parlty Govt. -- 3/Sir Frances Molamura (Ceylon) Chairman -- 4/Sir Howard D'Egville -- 5/Dr. Malik Ambassador from Ceylon to Indonesia -- Nov. 29th 1950."
See Reference File: Empire Parliamentary Association-1950 Cite as:Diefenbaker Centre, Photographs and

Slides, JGD 312

(RSN: 00106603) Indonesia
Call No.: MG 01/VI/(380/I42.1) Diefenbaker Centre, Row 4 - 6, Volume 336 Title: Governments of Other Countries - General - Republic of Indonesia - Heads of State 1960-1962 Microfilm No.: M-7939
*Series Description: RSN00002248

(RSN: 00106604) Indonesia
Call No.: MG 01/VI/(380/I42.2) Diefenbaker Centre, Row 4 - 6, Volume 336 Title: Governments of Other Countries - General - Republic of Indonesia - Cabinet 1960 Microfilm No.: M-7939
*Series Description: RSN00002248
Government:Indonesia:1960;

(RSN: 00110905) Indonesia
Call No.: MG 01/VI/(802/I42) Diefenbaker Centre, Row 4 - 6, Volume 533 Title: World Relations - Economic Assistance Abroad - Republic of Indonesia 1961 Microfilm No.: M-8021
*Series Description: RSN00002248

(RSN: 00111155) Indonesia
Call No.: MG 01/VI/(818.21 PM 1958 Indonesia) Diefenbaker Centre, Row 4 - 6, Volume 543 Title: Canada and the Commonwealth - Visits - Visits to Commonwealth Countries by Canadian Ministers - World Tour - Prime Minister - 1958 - Indonesia 1958-1959 Microfilm No.: M-8027
*Series Description: RSN00002248

(RSN: 00111379) Indonesia
Call No.: MG 01/VI/(840/I42) Diefenbaker Centre, Row 4 - 6, Volume 552 Title: Canada and Foreign Countries - General - Indonesia 1957-1962 Microfilm No.: M-8032
*Series Description: RSN00002248

(RSN: 00111380) Indonesia
Call No.: MG 01/VI/(840/I42 Conf.) Diefenbaker Centre, Row 4 - 6, Volume 552 Title: Canada and Foreign Countries - General - Indonesia - Confidential 1962 Microfilm No.: M-8032
*Series Description: RSN00002248

(RSN: 00111381) Indonesia
Call No.: MG 01/VI/(840/I42.1) Diefenbaker Centre, Row 4 - 6, Volume 552 Title: Canada and Foreign Countries - General - Indonesia - Heads of State 1961 Microfilm No.: M-8032
*Series Description: RSN00002248

(RSN: 00111548) Indonesia
Call No.: MG 01/VI/(845/I42) Diefenbaker Centre, Row 4 - 6, Volume 560 Title: Canada and Foreign Countries - International Situation - Indonesia 1962 Microfilm No.: M-8037
*Series Description: RSN00002248

(RSN: 00111774) Indonesia
Call No.: MG 01/VI/(861/I42) Diefenbaker Centre, Row 4 - 6, Volume 568 Title: Diplomatic Representation - Canadian Representation Abroad - Republic of Indonesia 1958 Microfilm No.: M-8041
*Series Description: RSN00002248

(RSN: 00111888) Indonesia
Call No.: MG 01/VI/(864/I42B736) Diefenbaker Centre, Row 4 - 6, Volume 571 Title: Diplomatic Representation - Representation of Other Countries in Canada - Republic of Indonesia - South Borneo 1959-1962 Microfilm No.: M-8042
*Series Description: RSN00002248

(RSN: 00000449) Iran
Call No.: MG 01/VII/A/2383 Diefenbaker Centre Row 5, Volume 260 Collection:Prime Minister's Office/Leader of the Opposition Office Title: Visits - Foreign Heads of State - Shah of Iran 1965 [textual records] Physical description: 1 folder
Pages:pp. 161709-161710
Series Description: RSN 00000254

(RSN: 00005324) Iran
Call No.: MG 01/XIII/20 Diefenbaker Centre, Row 9, Volume 3
Collection:Diefenbaker Parliamentary Office/Leader of the Opposition Office Title: Anglo Iranian Oil Company 1951 (inclusive) [textual records] Physical description: 1 folder
Series Description: RSN00002240

(RSN: 00009523) Iran
Call No.: MG 01/XI/B Diefenbaker Centre, Rows 6-8 Title: Iran 1971, 1979 [textual records]
Summary:This file contains the reference material created and accumulated by John Diefenbaker's office from after he ceased being Leader of the Opposition to his death. Restricted:Closed until arrangement completed.
Series Description: RSN00003078

(RSN: 00106605) Iran
Call No.: MG 01/VI/(380/I65.1) Diefenbaker Centre, Row 4 - 6, Volume 336 Title: Governments of Other Countries - General - Iran - Heads of State 1960 Microfilm No.: M-7939
*Series Description: RSN00002248

(RSN: 00108885) Iran
Call No.: MG 01/VI/(639.2/I65) Diefenbaker Centre, Row 4 - 6, Volume 445 Title: Federal-Provincial Welfare Services - Other - Earthquakes - Iran 1962 Microfilm No.: M-7982
*Series Description: RSN00002248

(RSN: 00111156) Iran
Call No.: MG 01/VI/(818.21 PM 1958 Iran) Diefenbaker Centre, Row 4 - 6, Volume 543 Title: Canada and the Commonwealth - Visits - Visits to Commonwealth Countries by Canadian Ministers - World Tour - Prime Minister - 1958 - Iran 1958 Microfilm No.: M-8027
*Series Description: RSN00002248

(RSN: 00111382) Iran
Call No.: MG 01/VI/(840/I65) Diefenbaker Centre, Row 4 - 6, Volume 552 Title: Canada and Foreign Countries - General - Iran (Persia) 1957-1959 Microfilm No.: M-8032
*Series Description: RSN00002248

(RSN: 00111627) Iran
Call No.: MG 01/VI/(846/I65 Secret) Diefenbaker Centre, Row 4 - 6, Volume 563 Title: Canada and Foreign Countries - Visits - Iran - Secret 1961 Microfilm No.: M-8038
*Series Description: RSN00002248

(RSN: 00111775) Iran
Call No.: MG 01/VI/(861/I65) Diefenbaker Centre, Row 4 - 6, Volume 568 Title: Diplomatic Representation - Canadian Representation Abroad - Iran 1958,1961 Microfilm No.: M-8041
*Series Description: RSN00002248

(RSN: 00111828) Iran
Call No.: MG 01/VI/(862 Iran) Diefenbaker Centre, Row 4 - 6, Volume 569 Title: Diplomatic Representation - Canadian Missions Abroad - Iran 1958 Microfilm No.: M-8042
*Series Description: RSN00002248

(RSN: 00111889) Iran
Call No.: MG 01/VI/(864/I65) Diefenbaker Centre, Row 4 - 6, Volume 571 Title: Diplomatic Representation - Representation of Other Countries in Canada - Iran (Persia) 1957-1962 Microfilm No.: M-8042
*Series Description: RSN00002248

(RSN: 00112036) Iran
Call No.: MG 01/VI/(930/I65) Diefenbaker Centre, Row 4 - 6, Volume 579 Title: History of Other Countries - General - Iran 1958
Microfilm No.: M-8048
*Series Description: RSN00002248

(RSN: 00112067) Iran
Call No.: MG 01/VI/(970/I65) Diefenbaker Centre, Row 4 - 6, Volume 581 Title: Geography of Other Countries - Iran (Persia) 1958 Microfilm No.: M-8048
*Series Description: RSN00002248

(RSN: 00000447) Japan
Call No.: MG 01/VII/A/2385 Diefenbaker Centre Row 5, Volume 260 Collection:Prime Minister's Office/ Leader of the Opposition Office Title: Visits - Prime Minister - Japan 1961 [textual records] Physical description: 1 folder
Pages:pp. 161750-161752
Series Description: RSN 00000254

(RSN: 00000592) Japan
Call No.: MG 01/VII/A/2241.1-2241.2 Diefenbaker Centre Row 5, Volume 242 Collection:Prime Minister's Office/ Leader of the Opposition Office Title: Trade - Japan n.d., 1961-1967 [textual records]
Physical description: 2 folders

*A/2241.1: n.d., 1961-1965; A/2241.2: 1966-1967.
Pages:pp. 154333-154804
Series Description: RSN 00000254

(RSN: 00001281) Japan
Call No.: MG 01/VII/A/1548 Diefenbaker Centre Row 4, Volume 166 Collection:Prime Minister's Office/ Leader of the Opposition Office Title: National Japanese Canadian Citizens Association 1960 [textual records]
Physical description: 1 folder
Pages:pp. 102886-102905
Series Description: RSN 00000254

(RSN: 00001664) Japan
Call No.: MG 01/XIV/E/48 Diefenbaker Centre, Row 9, Memoirs Volume 12 Title: World Relations 1960-1976 [textual records]
Physical description: one folder
Summary:This file has three principal components: 1) private and confidential thoughts and/or advice regarding the appointment of a new Canadian Ambassador to the United States; 2) the draft (but approved) record of a June 1961 discussion between Ikeda, the Prime Minister of Japan, and Diefenbaker; and 3) some extracts from Hansard and/or speech notes on foreign policy themes (dated 1975-1976). Of these three items, only the third is open to researchers. Restricted:Partially closed. File contains both restricted and open documents. The archivist will have to remove sensitive items and create an interim file that can be consulted by the researcher. Subjects include: Japan;
Series Description: RSN 00001527

(RSN: 00001754) Japan
Call No.: MG 01/XIV/E/104 Diefenbaker Centre, Row 9, Memoirs Volume 13 Title: Diefenbaker, J.G. - Trips - Japan 1961 [textual records] Physical description: one folder
Summary:This file contains the programme of Diefenbaker's visit to Japan (26-31 October 1961). Series Description: RSN 00001527

(RSN: 00002333) Japan
Call No.: MG 01/VII/A/1247 Diefenbaker Centre Row 4, Volume 142 Collection:Prime Minister's Office/ Leader of the Opposition Office Title: Japan 1960-1965 [textual records]
Physical description: 1 folder
Pages:pp. 84908-85098
Series Description: RSN 00000254

(RSN: 00004293) Japan
Call No.: MG 01/XXII/12 Diefenbaker Centre, Row 10, Volume 1
Title: Re Rate of Subvention for the Export of Coal 26 July 1957 [textual records] Physical description: 1 folder
Subject:foreign trade - Alberta and Japan British Columbia shipping - Vancouver Series Description: RSN 3081

(RSN: 00004295) Japan
Call No.: MG 01/XXII/14 Diefenbaker Centre, Row

10, Volume 1
Title: Messages from Hon. J.G. Diefenbaker to Adolfo Ruiz Cortines and P.M. Nobusuke Kishi 30 July 1957 [textual records] Physical description: 1 folder
Subject:natural disasters - Mexico and Japan
Series Description: RSN 3081

(RSN: 00004661) Japan
Call No.: MG 01/XXII/207 Diefenbaker Centre, Row 10, Volume 3
Title: Re: Second Grant of $10,000 to the Japanese Red Cross Society Re Typhoon Vera 6 October 1959 [textual records] Physical description: 1 folder
Summary:Drafts, Memorandum and French included
Series Description: 3081

(RSN: 00004667) Japan
Call No.: MG 01/XXII/213 Diefenbaker Centre, Row 10. Volume 3
Title: Donation of 100,000 Lbs. of Canned Pork to Japan - Relief Assistance 26 October 1959 [textual records] Physical description: 1 folder
Summary:Draft included
Series Description: 3081

(RSN: 00004695) Japan
Call No.: MG 01/XXII/241 Diefenbaker Centre, Row 10,Volume 3
Title: Prime Minister of Japan, Hon. Nobusuke Kishe, to Visit Canada Jan. 21, 1960 29 December 1959 [textual records] Physical description: 1 folder
Summary:French included
Series Description: 3081

(RSN: 00004704) Japan
Call No.: MG 01/XXII/250 Diefenbaker Centre, Row 10, Volume 4
Title: Text of Prime Minister's Letter to Mr. W.J. Parker, President of Manitoba Pool Elevators, Concerning Canadian Trade With Japan 12 January 1960 [textual records] Physical description: 1 folder
Series Description: 3081

(RSN: 00004705) Japan
Call No.: MG 01/XXII/251 Diefenbaker Centre, Row 10, Volume 4
Title: Programme for the Visit to Ottawa of Prime Minister of Japan, Jan. 21, 1960 13 January 1960 [textual records] Physical description: 1 folder
Summary:Drafts and French included
Series Description: 3081

(RSN: 00004879) Japan
Call No.: MG 01/XXII/362 Diefenbaker Centre, Row 10, Volume 5
Title: Prime Minister Hayato Ikeda of Japan to Visit Canada, June 25 and 26 29 May 1961 [textual records] Physical description: 1 folder
Summary:French included
Series Description: 3081

(RSN: 00004882) Japan
Call No.: MG 01/XXII/365 Diefenbaker Centre, Row 10, Volume 5

Title: Details of the Programme for the Visit to Canada of the Prime Minister and the Foreign Minister of Japan 15 June 1961 [textual records] Physical description: 1 folder
Summary:French included
Series Description: 3081

(RSN: 00004889) Japan
Call No.: MG 01/XXII/372 Diefenbaker Centre, Row 10, Volume 5
Title: Joint Communique Issued at Conclusion of Visit to Canada of the Prime Minister of Japan 26 June 1961 [textual records] Physical description: 1 folder
Summary:French included
Series Description: 3081

(RSN: 00004912) Japan
Call No.: MG 01/XXII/395 Diefenbaker Centre, Row 10, Volume 6
Title: Further Details - Prime Minister's Visit to Japan 13 October 1961 [textual records] Physical description: 1 folder
Summary:French included
Series Description: 3081

(RSN: 00004919) Japan
Call No.: MG 01/XXII/402 Diefenbaker Centre, Row 10, Volume 6
Title: Joint Statement Issued by Prime Minister Diefenbaker and Prime Minister Ikeda at Conclusion of Visit of Prime Minister Diefenbaker to Japan 31 October 1961 [textual records] Physical description: 1 folder
Summary:French included
Series Description: 3081

(RSN: 00005074) Japan
Call No.: MG 01/XXII/491 Diefenbaker Centre, Row 10, Volume 7
Title: Re: First Meeting of the Canada-Japan Ministerial Committee, Tokyo, Jan.11 and 12, 1963 8 January 1963 [textual records] Physical description: 1 folder
Summary:French included
Series Description: 3081

(RSN: 00005188) Japan
Call No.: MG 01/IX/A/999/*722/J35 Diefenbaker Centre, Row 7, Volume 30 Collection:Prime Minister's Office/ Leader of the Opposition Office Title: Foreign Trade - Trade by Countries - Japan 1965 [textual records] Physical description: 1 folder
Series Description: RSN 00003079

(RSN: 00005471) Japan
Call No.: MG 01/XIII/163 Diefenbaker Centre, Row 9, Volume 20 Collection:Diefenbaker Parliamentary Office/Leader of the Opposition Office Title: Japanese Canadians 1945-1948[textual records]
Physical description: 1 folder
Series Description: RSN00002240

(RSN: 00006219) Japan
Call No.: MG 01/II/200 Diefenbaker Centre, Row 1,

Volume 14
Title: Japan - Keio University 1934 [textual records]
Physical description: 1 folder
Summary:This file contains a telegram from D.L. Burgess to Saskatchewan Minister of Highways A.C. Stewart regarding the character of Llewellyn Fletcher, teacher in English conversation at Keio University.
Microfilm No.: M-6821

(RSN: 00006301) Japan
Call No.: MG 01/IX/A/1150/*840/J35 Diefenbaker Centre, Row 5, Volume 34 Collection:Leader of the Opposition Office
Title: Canada and Foreign Countries - Japan 1965 [textual records] Physical description: 1 folder
Series Description: RSN 00003079

(RSN: 00008868) Japan
Call No.: MG 01/III/718 Diefenbaker Centre, Row 1, 1940-1956 Series, Volume 58 Collection:Diefenbaker Parliamentary Office
Title: Japan n.d., 1955 [textual records]
Physical description: 1 folder
Microfilm No.: M-7440
* Pages:pp. 47037-47062
Series Description: RSN00002238

(RSN: 00008869) Japan
Call No.: MG 01/III/719 Diefenbaker Centre, Row 1, 1940-1956 Series, Volume 59 Collection:Diefenbaker Parliamentary Office
Title: Japanese - Canadians n.d., 1941-1947 [textual records] Physical description: 1 folder
Microfilm No.: M-7440
* Pages:pp. 47063-47099
Series Description: RSN00002238

(RSN: 00008870) Japan
Call No.: MG 01/III/720 Diefenbaker Centre, Row 1, 1940-1956 Series, Volume 59 Collection:Diefenbaker Parliamentary Office
Title: Japanese - Canadians - 1934 Franchise Act 1936 [textual records] Physical description: 1 folder
Microfilm No.: M-7440
* Pages:pp. 47100-47162
Series Description: RSN00002238

(RSN: 00008871) Japan
Call No.: MG 01/III/721 Diefenbaker Centre, Row 1, 1940-1956 Series, Volume 59 Collection:Diefenbaker Parliamentary Office
Title: Japanese - Canadian Evaluation Compensation Committee - 1954 [textual records] Physical description: 1 folder
Microfilm No.: M-7440
* Pages:pp. 47163-47184
Series Description: RSN00002238

(RSN: 00009528) Japan
Call No.: MG 01/XI/B.1-B.2 Diefenbaker Centre, Rows 6-8
Title: Japan 1967-1978 (inclusive) [textual records]
Physical description: 2 folders
Summary:This file contains the reference material created and accumulated by John Diefenbaker's office from after he ceased being Leader of the Opposition to his death. Restricted:Closed until arrangement completed.
Series Description: RSN00003078

(RSN: 00009798) Japan
Call No.: MG 01/XI/B Diefenbaker Centre, Rows 6-8
Title: Trudeau, Pierre Elliott - Visit to Japan 1976 [textual records] Summary:This file contains the reference material created and accumulated by John Diefenbaker's office from after he ceased being Leader of the Opposition to his death. Restricted:Closed until arrangement completed.
Series Description: RSN00003078

(RSN: 00009966) Japan
Call No.: MG 01/III/1074 Diefenbaker Centre, Row 1, 1940-1956 Series, Volume 85 Collection:Diefenbaker Confectionary Industry
Title: Trade with Japan n.d., 1954-1956 [textual records]
Physical description:
1 folder
Microfilm No.: M 7452
* Pages:pp. 68278-68320
Series Description: RSN00002238

(RSN: 00011323) Japan
Call No.: MG 01/XIX/47 Diefenbaker Centre, Library section
Title: Scrapbook #47 Oct. 1959 - May 1960 (inclusive) [textual records] Physical description: 232 pages; 37 x 30 cm.
Language: French
Language: Spanish
Summary:This scrapbook contains press clippings, political cartoons, and ephemera highlighting various Diefenbaker speeches and political policies, as well as clippings regarding Diefenbaker's visit to Mexico in 1960. Cite as:Diefenbaker Centre, MG01/XIX/47.
Subjects include:Kishi, Nobusuke - Prime Minister of Japan
Series Description: RSN00002251

(RSN: 00011410) Japan
Call No.: MG 01/XII/B/362.1-362.2 Diefenbaker Centre, row 9, Personal and Confidential, Volume 41 Collection:Prime Minister's Office
Title: Trips and Engagements - Japan n.d.,23 Oct.-Nov. 1961 [textual records] Physical description: 2 folders
Arranged: B/362.1: n.d.,23 Oct. 1961; B/362.2: 24 Oct.-Nov. 1961. Series Description: RSN 9157

(RSN: 00011685) Japan
Call No.: MG 01/XII/C/236 Diefenbaker Centre, row 9, Personal and Confidential, Volume 63 Collection:Prime Minister's and Leader of the Opposition's Offices Title: Japan 1961 [textual records]
Physical description: 1 folder
Series Description: RSN 9159

(RSN: 00012782) Japan

Call No.: MG 01/XII/F/473 Diefenbaker Centre, row 9, Personal and Confidential, Volume 124
Collection:Prime Minister's and Leader of the Opposition's Offices/Diefenbaker Parliamentary Office
Title: Trips and Engagements - Japan 1961 [textual records] Physical description: 1 folder
Series Description: RSN 9162

(RSN: 00012783) Japan
Call No.: MG 01/XII/F/474 Diefenbaker Centre, row 9, Personal and Confidential, Volume 124
Collection:Prime Minister's and Leader of the Opposition's Offices/Diefenbaker Parliamentary Office
Title: Trips and Engagements - Japan - Confidential n.d.,1959, 1961 [textual records] Physical description: 1 folder
Series Description: RSN 9162

(RSN: 00012856) Japan
Call No.: MG 01/XI/C Diefenbaker Centre, Rows 6-8
Title: Japan 1977 [textual records]
Summary:This file contains general correspondence with the public created and accumulated by John Diefenbaker's office from the time he ceased being Leader of the Opposition until his death.
Restricted:Closed until arrangement completed.
Subject:Yamashita, Tsutomu
Series Description: RSN00003078

(RSN: 00013303) Japan
Call No.: MG 01/XI/C Diefenbaker Centre, Rows 6-8
Title: Trips and Engagements - Expo Japan June 1970 1970 [textual records] Physical description: 2 folders
Summary:This file contains general correspondence with the public created and accumulated by John Diefenbaker's office from the time he ceased being Leader of the Opposition until his death.
Restricted:Closed until arrangement completed.
Series Description: RSN00003078

(RSN: 00014431) Japan
Call No.: MG 01/XI/C Diefenbaker Centre, Rows 6-8
Title: Trips and Engagements - Mementos - Japan 1970 [textual records] Physical description: 1 folder
Summary:This file contains general correspondence with the public created and accumulated by John Diefenbaker's office from the time he ceased being Leader of the Opposition until his death.
Restricted:Closed until arrangement completed.
Series Description: RSN00003078

(RSN: 00014587) Japan
Call No.: MG01/XVII/JGD 1106 Diefenbaker Centre, Photographs and Slides, Volume Title: World Tour - Australia 1958 [photograph]
Physical description: 1 photograph black and white
Summary:John Diefenbaker and Canadian High Commissioner to Australia, Terence W. L. MacDermot, at National War Memorial, inspecting a Japanese midget submarine destroyed in Sydney harbour in World War II , Canberra, 4 Dec, 1958. See Reference File: World Tour - Australia
Cite as:Diefenbaker Centre, Photographs and Slides, JGD 1106

(RSN: 00015059) Japan
Call No.: MG 01/XI/B Diefenbaker Centre, Rows 6-8
Title: Speeches - Reference: June 11, 1969. Canada-Japan Trade Council, Kingston,Ont. 1969 [textual records]
Physical description: 1 folder
Summary:This file contains general correspondence with the public created and accumulated by John Diefenbaker's Office from the time he ceased being Leader of the Opposition until his death.
Restricted:Closed until arrangement completed.
Series Description: RSN00003078

(RSN: 00018981) Japan
Call No.: MG 01/IV/660/722 JAPAN Diefenbaker Centre, Row 1, First Leader of the Opposition Series, Volume 27 Collection:Leader of the Opposition Office
Title: Trade by Countries - Japan Jan. 1957 [textual records] Physical description: 1 folder
Microfilm No.: Microfilm No.:M-5559
*Pages:pp. 19377-19378
Series Description: RSN 00003079

(RSN: 00100343) Japan
Call No.: MG 01/VI/(026) Diefenbaker Centre, Rows 2-4, Volume 26 Title: Religion - Religious Rights 1958, 1960-1962
Summary:This file includes a MRA Bulletin re the opening of the MRA Asian Assembly Centre in Odawa, Japan, and a copy of Peter Howard's "Frank Buchanan's Secret" re race for moral conquest. Microfilm No.: M-7800
*Series Description: RSN00002248

(RSN: 00100600) Japan
Call No.: MG 01/VI/(045 Japanese) Diefenbaker Centre, Row 4 - 6, Volume 36 Title: Language and Ethnic Groups - Ethnic Groups - Japanese 1957-1960
Microfilm No.: M-7804
*Series Description: RSN00002248

(RSN: 00101007) Japan
Call No.: MG 01/VI/(154.5) Diefenbaker Centre, Rows 2-4, Volume 54 Title: Defence Research - Atomic Research - Radioactive Fallout 1957-1961 Summary:This file contains correspondence, memoranda, and ephemera. Microfilm No.: M-7812
*Subject:Women's International League for Peace and Freedom Japanese resolution in the United Nations cessation of nuclear tests radioactive fallout Agricultural Institute of Canada - "Nuclear Energy and its Agricultural Implications" Department of National Health and Welfare Monteith, J. Waldo Visscher, Maurice B. - Governor's Committee on Atomic Energy Development Problems National Committee for the Control of Radiation Hazards National Health Federation - Strontium 90 - cesium 137 Series Description: RSN00002248

(RSN: 00101119) Japan

Call No.: MG 01/VI/(182.1/J35) Diefenbaker Centre, Row 4 - 6, Volume 57 Title: War - World War II - Claims Against Enemy Governments - Japan 1958 Microfilm No.: M-7813
* Series Description: RSN00002248

(RSN: 00101289) Japan
Call No.: MG 01/VI/(216) Diefenbaker Centre, Rows 2-4, Volume 66 Title: Labour - Organized Labour 1961-1963
Summary:This file contains correspondence, memoranda, reports and ephemera. Microfilm No.: M-7819
*Subjects include: situation in LaosJapanese Nationals
Series Description: RSN00002248

(RSN: 00101612) Japan
Call No.: MG 01/VI/(246/J35) Diefenbaker Centre, Row 4 - 6, Volume 80 Title: National Accounts - Canadian Assets Abroad - Japan 1960 Microfilm No.: M-7825
*Series Description: RSN00002248

(RSN: 00102276) Japan
Call No.: MG 01/VI/(312 Agriculture) Diefenbaker Centre, Rows 2-4, Volume 113 Title: Federal Government Executive - The Cabinet - Minister of Agriculture 1957-1963 Summary:This file contains correspondence and reports.
Microfilm No.: M-7838
*Subjects include:Japanese wheat sales
Series Description: RSN00002248

(RSN: 00102290) Japan
Call No.: MG 01/VI/(312 Finance Hon. George Nowlan) Diefenbaker Centre, Rows 2-4, Volume 114 Title: Federal Government Executive - The Cabinet - Minister of Finance - Hon. George Nowlan 1957-1962 Summary:This file, in fact, contains memoranda, correspondence, photocopies, reports and ephemera concerning Donald Fleming, Minister of Finance.
Microfilm No.: M-7838
*Subjects include: trade negotiations Japan
Series Description: RSN00002248

(RSN: 00102428) Japan
Call No.: MG 01/VI/(313.12 Ikeda) Diefenbaker Centre, Row 4 - 6, Volume 120 Title: Federal Government Executive - The Prime Minister of Canada - Permanent Residence - Social Functions - Prime Minister of Japan and Mrs. Ikeda 1961 Microfilm No.: M-7841
*Series Description: RSN00002248

(RSN: 00102799) Japan
Call No.: MG 01/VI/(313.23) Diefenbaker Centre, Rows 2-4, Volume 143 Title: Federal Government Executive - The Prime Minister of Canada - Personal - Gifts To and From Feb. 1959-Feb. 1960 Summary:This file contains correspondence, press clippings, memorabilia and photographs. Microfilm No.: M-7852
*Subjects include:Japanese Embassy - stamps commemorating marriage of Crown Prince Akihito of Japan and Michiko Shoda

Series Description: RSN00002248

(RSN: 00102801) Japan
Call No.: MG 01/VI/(313.23) Diefenbaker Centre, Rows 2-4, Volume 144 Title: Federal Government Executive - The Prime Minister of Canada - Personal - Gifts To and From Aug. 1961-Dec. 1962 Summary:This file contains correspondence, memoranda, and press clippings.

(RSN: 00104933) Japan
Call No.: MG 01/VI/(313.45/J35) Diefenbaker Centre, Row 4 - 6, Volume 258 Title: Federal Government Executive - The Prime Minister of Canada - Travel, Trips, Visits, Etc. - Official Visits - Japan 1961-1962 Microfilm No.: M-7906
*Series Description: RSN00002248

(RSN: 00104934) Japan
Call No.: MG 01/VI/(313.45/J35 Conf.) Diefenbaker Centre, Row 4 - 6, Volume 258 Title: Federal Government Executive - The Prime Minister of Canada - Travel, Trips, Visits, Etc. - Official Visits - Japan - Confidential 1961-1962 Microfilm No.:
*Series Description: RSN00002248

(RSN: 00105124) Japan
Call No.: MG 01/VI/(324 Brunt) Diefenbaker Centre, Rows 2-4, Volume 276 Title: The Senate - Members of the Senate - Hon. W.R. Brunt 1957-1962 Summary:This file contains correspondence, memoranda, press clippings, and reports. Microfilm No.: M-7915,M-7916
*Subjects include:Wheat - sales to Japan
Series Description: RSN00002248

(RSN: 00105145) Japan
Call No.: MG 01/VI/(324 Gladstone) Diefenbaker Centre, Rows 2-4, Volume 277 Title: The Senate - Members of the Senate - Senator [James] Gladstone 1958-1962 Summary:This file contains: a memo from Diefenbaker for Allister Grosart re Gladstone touring Indian reserves in the western provinces to swing the Indian vote from the C.C.F.; a memo from Neil Crawford to Diefenbaker re Gladstone's views on the need to reform the Indian Act and his views on current Indian sentiment. Microfilm No.: M-7916
*Subjects include:Kishi, the Hon. Nobusuke
Series Description: RSN00002248

(RSN: 00001281) Japan
Call No.: MG 01/VII/A/1548 Diefenbaker Centre Row 4, Volume 166 Collection:Prime Minister's Office/Leader of the Opposition Office Title: National Japanese Canadian Citizens Association 1960 [textual records]
Physical description: 1 folder
Pages:pp. 102886-102905
Series Description: RSN 00000254

(RSN: 00105605) Japan
Call No.: MG 01/VI/(335 Sherbrooke) Diefenbaker Centre, Rows 2-4, Volume 300 Title: The House of Commons - Members of the House - Sherbrooke Constituency 1958-1962 Language: French

Summary:This file includes: a report on the textile industry around Sherbrooke; correspondence between the Department of Trade and Commerce and the Trade Commissioner in Hong Kong re Maurice Allard's unofficial visit to Japan and his statements in the Japanese press; Allard's notes re his trip to Japan, Formosa and Hong Kong, his meeting with General Chiang Kai-shek,and his views on international affairs and agricultural reform. Microfilm No.: M-7926
*Subject:pensions federal-provincial financial relations
Author:Allard, Maurice (MP)
Series Description: RSN00002248

(RSN: 00106616) Japan
Call No.: MG 01/VI/(380/J35) Diefenbaker Centre, Row 4 - 6, Volume 336 Title: Governments of Other Countries - General - Japan 1960 Microfilm No.: M-7939
*Series Description: RSN00002248

(RSN: 00106617) Japan
Call No.: MG 01/VI/(380/J35.1) Diefenbaker Centre, Row 4 - 6, Volume 336 Title: Governments of Other Countries - General - Japan - Heads of State 1959-1960 Microfilm No.: M-7939
*Series Description: RSN00002248

(RSN: 00106618) Japan
Call No.: MG 01/VI/(380/J35.2) Diefenbaker Centre, Row 4 - 6, Volume 336 Title: Governments of Other Countries - General - Japan - Cabinet 1959-1960 Microfilm No.: M-7939
*Series Description: RSN00002248

(RSN: 00106619) Japan
Call No.: MG 01/VI/(380/J35.21) Diefenbaker Centre, Row 4 - 6, Volume 336 Title: Governments of Other Countries - General - Japan - Cabinet - Prime Minister 1961 Microfilm No.: M-7939
*Series Description: RSN00002248

(RSN: 00108198) Japan
Call No.: MG 01/VI/(571/J35) Diefenbaker Centre, Row 4 - 6, Volume 407 Title: Immigration and Citizenship - Immigration Policy and Administration - Japanese 1958-1961 Microfilm No.: M-7965
*Series Description: RSN00002248

(RSN: 00108199) Japan
Call No.: MG 01/VI/(571/J35 Conf.) Diefenbaker Centre, Row 4 - 6, Volume 407 Title: Immigration and Citizenship - Immigration Policy and Administration - Japanese - Confidential 1961 Microfilm No.: M-7965
*Series Description: RSN00002248

(RSN: 00109463) Japan
Call No.: MG 01/VI/(711/J35) Diefenbaker Centre, Row 4 - 6, Volume 469 Title: Domestic Trade - Grain Trade - Japan 1960
Microfilm No.: M-7992
*Series Description: RSN00002248

(RSN: 00109483) Japan
Call No.: MG 01/VI/(711.3/J35) Diefenbaker Centre, Row 4 - 6, Volume 472 Title: Domestic Trade - Grain Trade - Grain Marketing - Japan 1960 Microfilm No.: M-7994
*Series Description: RSN00002248

(RSN: 00109566) Japan
Call No.: MG 01/VI/(722/J35) Diefenbaker Centre, Row 4 - 6, Volume 477 Title: Foreign Trade - Trade By Countries - Japan 1957-1962 Microfilm No.: M-7997
*Series Description: RSN00002248

(RSN: 00109567) Japan
Call No.: MG 01/VI/(722/J35 Conf.) Diefenbaker Centre, Row 4 - 6, Volume 477 Title: Foreign Trade - Trade By Countries - Japan - Confidential 1961-1962 Microfilm No.: M-7997
*Series Description: RSN00002248

(RSN: 00109568) Japan
Call No.: MG 01/VI/(722/J35 Ministerial Committee Conf.) Diefenbaker Centre, Row 4 - 6, Volume 477 Title: Foreign Trade - Trade By Countries - Japan - Ministerial Committee - Confidential 1961 Microfilm No.: M-7997
*Series Description: RSN00002248

(RSN: 00109639) Japan
Call No.: MG 01/VI/(724 Iron) Diefenbaker Centre, Row 4 - 6, Volume 481 Title: Foreign Trade - Imports - Iron 1960
Microfilm No.: M-7999
*Series Description: RSN00002248

(RSN: 00109660) Japan
Call No.: MG 01/VI/(724.1/J35) Diefenbaker Centre, Row 4 - 6, Volume 482 Title: Foreign Trade - Imports - Restrictions - Japan 1957-1961 Microfilm No.: M-7999
*Series Description: RSN00002248

(RSN: 00109683) Japan
Call No.: MG 01/VI/(725/J35) Diefenbaker Centre, Row 4 - 6, Volume 482 Title: Foreign Trade - Exports - Japan 1958-1959
Microfilm No.: M-7999
*Series Description: RSN00002248

(RSN: 00109736) Japan
Call No.: MG 01/VI/(728.1/J35) Diefenbaker Centre, Row 4 - 6, Volume 485 Title: Foreign Trade - Tariff and Trade Agreements - Tariff Policy - Japan 1960 Microfilm No.: M-8000
*Series Description: RSN00002248

(RSN: 00109749) Japan
Call No.: MG 01/VI/(728.2 Japan - 1959) Diefenbaker Centre, Row 4 - 6, Volume 486 Title: Foreign Trade - Tariff and Trade Agreements - General Agreement on Tariff and Trade Conference (GATT) - Japan - 1959 1959 Microfilm No.: M-8000
*Series Description: RSN00002248

(RSN: 00110254) Japan
Call No.: MG 01/VI/(736.5/J35) Diefenbaker Centre, Row 4 - 6, Volume 506 Title: Transportation and Communication - Wire and Wireless Communication - Television - Japan 1962 Microfilm No.: M-8009
*Series Description: RSN00002248

(RSN: 00110908) Japan
Call No.: MG 01/VI/(802/J35) Diefenbaker Centre, Row 4 - 6, Volume 533 Title: World Relations - Economic Assistance Abroad - Japan 1958-1959
Microfilm No.: M-8021
*Series Description: RSN00002248

(RSN: 00111392) Japan
Call No.: MG 01/VI/(840/J35) Diefenbaker Centre, Row 4 - 6, Volume 553 Title: Canada and Foreign Countries - General - Japan 1957-1962 Microfilm No.: M-8032
*Series Description: RSN00002248

(RSN: 00111634) Japan
Call No.: MG 01/VI/(846/J35) Diefenbaker Centre, Row 4 - 6, Volume 563 Title: Canada and Foreign Countries - Visits - Japan 1958-1962 Summary:This file contains correspondence and memoranda related to visits to Canada by Japanese VIPs, and vice versa. Of particular interest is a memorandum to Prime Minister Diefenbaker dated 5 September 1958 to which is attached a comprehensive brief concerning the Japanese Foreign Minister Fujiyama's 1958 visit to Canada. This provided Diefenbaker with an excellent summary of the state of Canadian-Japanese relations at that time, and of the Canadian viewpoints on a number of world problems of common concern. Not available on Microfilm. (This file was classifed "Restricted" at the time PMO Numbered series was microfilmed.)
Subject:Japan - Prime Minister Diefenbaker's visit to - 1961; Kishi, Hon. Nobusuke - Prime Minister of Japan - Visit to Canada - 1960; Japan - Economic cooperation with Canada; Immigration - Admission of Japanese managers and technicians to Canada - 1960; Hutchison, Bruce - Editor of The Times - Visit to Japan - 1959; Sato, Hon. Eisako - Minister of Finance of Japan - Visit to Canada - 1959; Fujiyama, Hon. Aiichiro - Minister of Foreign Affairs of Japan - Visit to Canada - 1958; Canadian-Japanese relations - Summary - 1958; Fleming, Donald - Minister of Finance - Trip to the Far East - 1958.
Series Description: RSN00002248

(RSN: 00111635) Japan
Call No.: MG 01/VI/(846/J35.1) Diefenbaker Centre, Row 4 - 6, Volume 563 Title: Canada and Foreign Countries - Visits - Japan - Heads of State 1959-1960
Microfilm No.: M-8038
*Series Description: RSN00002248

(RSN: 00111636) Japan
Call No.: MG 01/VI/(846/J35.21) Diefenbaker Centre, Row 4 - 6, Volume 563 Title: Canada and Foreign Countries - Visits - Japan - Cabinet - Prime Minister 1961 Microfilm No.: M-8038
*Series Description: RSN00002248

(RSN: 00111637) Japan
Call No.: MG 01/VI/(846/J35.21 Conf.) Diefenbaker Centre, Row 4 - 6, Volume 563 Title: Canada and Foreign Countries - Visits - Japan - Cabinet - Prime Minister - Confidential 1961 Microfilm No.: M-8038
*Series Description: RSN00002248

(RSN: 00111780) Japan
Call No.: MG 01/VI/(861/J35) Diefenbaker Centre, Row 4 - 6, Volume 568 Title: Diplomatic Representation - Canadian Representation Abroad - Japan 1958,1960-1961 Microfilm No.: M-8041
*Series Description: RSN00002248

(RSN: 00111894) Japan
Call No.: MG 01/VI/(864/J35) Diefenbaker Centre, Row 4 - 6, Volume 571 Title: Diplomatic Representation - Representation of Other Countries in Canada - Japan 1958-1962 Microfilm No.: M-8042
*Series Description: RSN00002248

(RSN: 00005471) Japanese
Call No.: MG 01/XIII/163 Diefenbaker Centre, Row 9, Volume 20 Collection:Diefenbaker Parliamentary Office/Leader of the Opposition Office Title: Japanese Canadians 1945-1948[textual records]
Physical description: 1 folder
Series Description: RSN00002240

(RSN: 00008869) Japanese
Call No.: MG 01/III/719 Diefenbaker Centre, Row 1, 1940-1956 Series, Volume 59 Collection:Diefenbaker Parliamentary Office
Title: Japanese - Canadians n.d., 1941-1947 [textual records] Physical description: 1 folder
Microfilm No.: M-7440
* Pages:pp. 47063-47099
Series Description: RSN00002238

(RSN: 00008880) Korea
Call No.: MG 01/III/730 Diefenbaker Centre, Row 1, 1940-1956 Series, Volume 59 Collection:Diefenbaker Parliamentary Office
Title: Korea 1950-1953 [textual records]
Physical description: 1 folder
Microfilm No.: M-7440
* Pages:pp. 47422-47438
Series Description: RSN00002238

(RSN: 00009543) Korea
Call No.: MG 01/XI/B Diefenbaker Centre, Rows 6-8
Title: Korean War 1978 [textual records]
Summary:This file contains the reference material created and accumulated by John Diefenbaker's office from after he ceased being Leader of the Opposition to his death. Restricted:Closed until arrangement completed.
Subject:Stone, Jim
Series Description: RSN00003078

(RSN: 00012517) Korea
Call No.: MG 01/XII/F/219 Diefenbaker Centre, row 9, Personal and Confidential, Volume 113
Collection:Prime Minister's and Leader of the Opposition's Offices/Diefenbaker Parliamentary Office Title: Foreign Affairs - Korea 1960 [textual records]
Physical description: 1 folder
Series Description: RSN 9162

(RSN: 00012874) Korea
Call No.: MG 01/XI/C Diefenbaker Centre, Rows 6-8
Title: Korea 1974-1975 [textual records]
Summary:This file contains general correspondence with the public created and accumulated by John Diefenbaker's office from the time he ceased being Leader of the Opposition until his death.
Restricted:Closed until arrangement completed.
Series Description: RSN00003078

(RSN: 00018059) Korea
Call No.: MG01/XVII/JGD 5733 Diefenbaker Centre, Photographs and Slides, Volume Title: Korea 1953 (photograph)
Physical description: 1 photograph black & white
Summary:Full length photo of the back of comedian John Pratt (Stinky) looking out over the crowd of servicemen in Korea for whom he is performing, circa 1953. The photo is autographed and reads: "To The Prime Minister and Mrs. Diefenbaker with my very best wishes John Pratt, Korea, 1953." Cite as:Diefenbaker Centre, Photographs and Slides, JGD 5733

(RSN: 00101127) Korea
Call No.: MG 01/VI/(183) Diefenbaker Centre, Row 4 - 6, Volume 57 Title: War - Korean War 1962-1963
Microfilm No.: M-7814
*Series Description: RSN00002248

(RSN: 00101128) Korea
Call No.: MG 01/VI/(183.1) Diefenbaker Centre, Row 4 - 6, Volume 57 Title: War - Korean War - Prisoners 1958-1961
Microfilm No.: M-7814
*Series Description: RSN00002248

(RSN: 00101129) Korea
Call No.: MG 01/VI/(183.1/W255) Diefenbaker Centre, Rows 2-4, Volume 57 Title: War - Korean War - War Claims Commission 1958
Summary:is file contains correspondence and press clippings. Microfilm No.: M-7814
*Subject:Hyndman, Justice J.D.
Series Description: RSN00002248

(RSN: 00111394) Korea
Call No.: MG 01/VI/(840/K84 S) Diefenbaker Centre, Row 4 - 6, Volume 553 Title: Canada and Foreign Countries - General - South Korea 1957,1959-1962
Microfilm No.: M-8032

*Series Description: RSN00002248
(RSN: 00111639) Korea
Call No.: MG 01/VI/(846/K84.2) Diefenbaker Centre, Row 4 - 6, Volume 563 Title: Canada and Foreign Countries - Visits - South Korea 1961 Microfilm No.: M-8038
*Series Description: RSN00002248

(RSN: 00002143) Laos
Call No.: MG 01/VII/A/1338 Diefenbaker Centre Row 4, Volume 151 Collection:Prime Minister's Office/ Leader of the Opposition Office Title: Laos 1964-1965 [textual records]
Physical description: 1 folder
Pages:pp. 91934-91945
Series Description: RSN 00000254

(RSN: 00004396) Laos
Call No.: MG 01/XXII/75 Diefenbaker Centre, Row Volume 2
Title: Visit of Prime Minister of Laos - Jan.16-19, 1958 14 January 1958 [textual records] Physical description: 1 folder
Summary:French included
Series Description: 3081

(RSN: 00004626) Laos
Call No.: MG 01/XXII/196 Diefenbaker Centre, Row Volume 3
Title: Statement Re Laos 14 August 1959 [textual records] Physical description: 1 folder
Summary:Draft included
Series Description: 3081

(RSN: 00009548) Laos
Call No.: MG 01/XI/B Diefenbaker Centre, Rows 6-8
Title: Laos 1970-1971 [textual records]
Summary:This file contains the reference material created and accumulated by John Diefenbaker's office from after he ceased being Leader of the Opposition to his death. Restricted:Closed until arrangement completed.
Series Description: RSN00003078

(RSN: 00011703) Laos
Call No.: MG 01/XII/C/250 Diefenbaker Centre, row 9, Personal and Confidential, Volume 64
Collection:Prime Minister's and Leader of the Opposition's Offices Title: Laos 1961 [textual records]
Physical description: 1 folder
Series Description: RSN 9159

(RSN: 00012518) Laos
Call No.: MG 01/XII/F/220 Diefenbaker Centre, row 9, Personal and Confidential, Volume 113
Collection:Prime Minister's and Leader of the Opposition's Offices/Diefenbaker Parliamentary Office Title: Foreign Affairs - Laos 1958,1961 [textual records]
Physical description: 1 folder
Series Description: RSN 9162

(RSN: 00101289) Laos
Call No.: MG 01/VI/(216) Diefenbaker Centre, Rows 2-4, Volume 66 Title: Labour - Organized Labour 1961-1963
Summary:This file contains correspondence, memoranda, reports and ephemera. Microfilm No.: M-7819
*Subjects include: situation in Laos
Series Description: RSN00002248

(RSN: 00102143) Laos
Call No.: MG 01/VI/(307.1.01 - 1957) Diefenbaker Centre, Rows 2-4, Volume 105 Title: Government - Parliament - Opening of Parliament - Speech from the Throne - 1957 Summary:This file contains transcripts, memoranda, and reports. Microfilm No.: M-7835
*Subjects include: Colombo PlanInternational Supervisory Commissions in Vietnam, Laos and Cambodia
Series Description: RSN00002248

(RSN: 00106602) Laos
Call No.: MG 01/VI/(380/I41L298) Diefenbaker Centre, Row 4 - 6, Volume 336 Title: Governments of Other Countries - General - Indo-China - Laos 1960 Microfilm No.: M-7939
*Series Description: RSN00002248

(RSN: 00111377) Laos
Call No.: MG 01/VI/(840/I41L298) Diefenbaker Centre, Row 4 - 6, Volume 552 Title: Canada and Foreign Countries - General - Indo-China - Laos 1959-1961 Summary:File consists of letters re: MEDICO, Dr. Thomas Dooley's foundation's work in Laos, persons volunteering to serve on the International Commission (ICSC) on Laos. etc. An External Affairs telegram (8 July 1961) to Delhi is a key policy statement (in the form of a "personal" message from Prime Minister Diefenbaker to Indian Prime Minister Nehru) setting out basic objectives which Canada would wish to achieve in participating in the Laos commission. Not available on Microfilm. (This file was classified "Restricted" at the time PMO Numbered series was microfilmed.) Subject:Laos - International Commission - 1959 Dooley, Dr. Thomas A. - founder of MEDICO MEDICO - Medical International Co-operation - Laos
Series Description: RSN00002248

(RSN: 00111544) Laos
Call No.: MG 01/VI/(845/I41L298) Diefenbaker Centre, Row 4 - 6, Volume 559 Title: Canada and Foreign Countries - International Situation - Indo-China - Laos 1959-1962. Not available on Microfilm. (This file was classified "Restricted" at the time PMO Numbered series was microfilmed.)
Series Description: RSN00002248

(RSN: 00111545) Laos
Call No.: MG 01/VI/(845/I41L298 Conf.)
Diefenbaker Centre, Row 4 - 6, Volume 559 Title: Canada and Foreign Countries - International Situation - Indo-China - Laos - Confidential 1962 Summary:This file consists of a confidential, but rather "pro forma", exchange between the United Kingdom and Canadian Prime Ministers upon the conclusion of the 1962 Laos Conference and the resumption of duty by Canada on the International Control Commission in Laos. Not available on Microfilm. (This file was classified "Restricted" at the time PMO Numbered series was microfilmed.) Subject:Laos - 1962 Conference; Laos - International Control Commission.
Series Description: RSN00002248

(RSN: 00111546) Laos
Call No.: MG 01/VI/(845/I41L298 Secret) Diefenbaker Centre, Row 4 - 6, Volume 560 Title: Canada and Foreign Countries - International Situation - Indo-China - Laos - Secret 1961 Microfilm No.: M-8037
*Series Description: RSN00002248

(RSN: 00111625) Laos
Call No.: MG 01/VI/(846/I41L298) Diefenbaker Centre, Row 4 - 6, Volume 563 Title: Canada and Foreign Countries - Visits - Indo-China - Laos 1958-1962 Microfilm No.: M-8038
*Series Description: RSN00002248

(RSN: 00111626) Laos
Call No.: MG 01/VI/(846/I41L298 Conf.)
Diefenbaker Centre, Row 4 - 6, Volume 563 Title: Canada and Foreign Countries - Visits - Indo-China - Laos - Confidential 1962 Summary:This file consists of three memoranda to Prime Minister Diefenbaker on a possible visit by the King of Laos to the thirteen signatories of the Laos Accord of 1962 (including Canada). The Prime Minister was not enthusiastic about receiving this distinguished visitor, and these memoranda reveal what arguments were used to persuade the Prime Minister to receive the Laotian monarch in February 1963. Not available on Microfilm. (This file was classified "Restricted" at the time PMO Numbered series was microfilmed.) Subject:Laos - Geneva Accord - 1962; King of Laos - Proposed visit to Canada - 1962 Series Description: RSN00002248

(RSN: 00000920) Malaysia
Call No.: MG 01/VII/A/1910 Diefenbaker Centre Row 4, Volume 205 Collection:Prime Minister's Office/ Leader of the Opposition Office Title: Rahman, Tunku Abdul - Prime Minister of Malaysia n.d., 1964 [textual records] Physical description: 1 folder
Pages:pp. 132944-132986
Series Description: RSN 00000254

(RSN: 00001395) Malaysia
Call No.: MG 01/VII/A/1434 Diefenbaker Centre Row 4, Volume 157 Collection:Prime Minister's Office/ Leader of the Opposition Office Title: Malaysia n.d., 1965 [textual records]
Physical description: 1 folder
Pages:pp. 96141-96143
Series Description: RSN 00000254

(RSN: 00006302) Malaysia
Call No.: MG 01/IX/A/1151/*840 Malaysia
Diefenbaker Centre, Row 5, Volume 34

Collection:Leader of the Opposition Office
Title: Canada and Foreign Countries - Malaysia 1964
[textual records] Physical description: 1 folder
Series Description: RSN 00003079

(RSN: 00004721) Nepal
Call No.: MG 01/XXII/267 Diefenbaker Centre, Row Volume 4
Title: Visit to Canada by His Majesty Mahendra Bir Bikran Shah Deva, King of Nepal, May 27,28, 1960 12 April 1960 Physical description: 1 folder
Summary:French included
Series Description: 3081

(RSN: 00111411) Nepal
Call No.: MG 01/VI/(840/N439) Diefenbaker Centre, Row 4 - 6, Volume 553 Title: Canada and Foreign Countries - General - Nepal 1960 Microfilm No.: M-8032
*Series Description: RSN00002248

(RSN: 00111648) Nepal
Call No.: MG 01/VI/(846/N439.1) Diefenbaker Centre, Row 4 - 6, Volume 563 Title: Canada and Foreign Countries - Visits - Nepal - Heads of State 1959 Microfilm No.: M-8039
*Series Description: RSN00002248

(RSN: 00001130) Pakistan
Call No.: MG 01/VII/A/1699 Diefenbaker Centre Row 4, Volume 181 Collection:Prime Minister's Office/ Leader of the Opposition Office Title: Pakistan n.d., 1957-1964 [textual records]
Physical description: 1 folder
Pages:pp. 111888-111901
Series Description: RSN 00000254

(RSN: 00001580) Pakistan
Call No.: MG 01/XIV/E/26 Diefenbaker Centre, Row 9, Memoirs Volume 11 Title: [Government - Executive - Prime Minister] - Diefenbaker, J.G. - Trips/Travel 1958 [textual records] Physical description: one folder
Summary:This file contains itineraries, printed ephemera and press releases from Diefenbaker's world tour, and a letter from General Mohammed Ayub Khan, President of Pakistan.
Series Description: RSN 00001527

(RSN: 00001787) Pakistan
Call No.: MG 01/XIV/E/130 Diefenbaker Centre, Row 9, Memoirs Volume 14 Title: External Relations - India [and Pakistan] 1958 [textual records] Physical description: one folder
Summary:This file contains Diefenbaker's summary of discussions with General Mohammed Ayub Khan, President of Pakistan.
Series Description: RSN 00001527

(RSN: 00002468) Pakistan
Call No.: MG 01/VII/C/22 Diefenbaker Centre, Row 5, Volume 272 Collection:Prime Minister's Office/ Leader of the Opposition Office Title: India-Pakistan 1965 [textual records]
Physical description: 1 folder
Pages:pp. 169705-169706
Series Description: RSN 00002242

(RSN: 00003523) Pakistan
Call No.: MG 01/VII/G/14 Diefenbaker Centre, Row 5, Volume 301 Collection:Prime Minister's Office/ Leader of the Opposition Office Title: India-Pakistan 1965 [textual records]
Physical description: 1 folder
Pages:pp. 193228-193230
Series Description: RSN 00002246

(RSN: 00004185) Pakistan
Call No.: MG 01/XXII/9 Diefenbaker Centre, Row 10, Volume 1
Title: Visit of the Prime Minister of Pakistan 17 July 1957 [textual records] Physical description: 1 folder
Language: French
Subject:Suhrawardy, H.S.
Series Description: RSN 3081

(RSN: 00004292) Pakistan
Call No.: MG 01/XXII/11 Diefenbaker Centre, Row 10, Volume 1
Title: Cancellation of Visit of Prime Minister Suhrawardy to Canada 24 July 1957 [textual records] Physical description: 1 folder
Summary:This file a draft press release.
Subject:Pakistan
Series Description: RSN 3081

(RSN: 00004421) Pakistan
Call No.: MG 01/XXII/93 Diefenbaker Centre, Row Volume 2
Title: Wheat Grants to India and Pakistan 28 March 1958 [textual records] Physical description: 1 folder
Series Description: 3081

(RSN: 00004754) Pakistan
Call No.: MG 01/XXII/300 Diefenbaker Centre, Row Volume 4
Title: International Financial Agreement - Australia, Germany, New Zealand, Pakistan, U.K., U.S. and International Bank for Recons. & Development 19 September 1960 [textual records] Physical description: 1 folder
Summary:Draft and French included
Series Description: 3081

(RSN: 00005043) Pakistan
Call No.: MG 01/XXII/469 Diefenbaker Centre, Row Volume 7
Title: President Fr. Ayoub of Pakistan will Pay a State Visit to Canada in Sept. 1962 20 August 1962 [textual records] Physical description: 1 folder
Summary:French included
Series Description: 3081

(RSN: 00005052) Pakistan
Call No.: MG 01/XXII/478 Diefenbaker Centre, Row Volume 7
Title: Further Details Concerning the Visit to Canada of the President of the Republic of Pakistan 14 September

1962 [textual records] Physical description: 1 folder
Summary:French included
Series Description: 3081

(RSN: 00005142) Pakistan
Call No.: MG 01/XXII/535 Diefenbaker Centre, Row Volume 8
Title: Re: Prime Minister's Offer to Act as Mediator Between India and Pakistan 3 September 1965 [textual records] Physical description: 1 folder
Summary:Draft Only
Series Description: 3081

(RSN: 00005540) Pakistan
Call No.: MG 01/XIII/232 Diefenbaker Centre, Row 9, Volume 26 Collection:Diefenbaker Parliamentary Office/Leader of the Opposition Office Title: Pakistan 1951-1957 (inclusive) [textual records] Physical description: 1 folder
Summary:This file contains: an issue of "Pakistan News and Views"; a booklet entitled The Republic of Pakistan and the Commonwealth; and a booklet commemorating the Indian Mutiny. of 1857 entitled Struggle For Freedom, 1857 Series Description: RSN00002240

(RSN: 00006312) Pakistan
Call No.: MG 01/IX/A/1161/*845 Indo-Pakistan Diefenbaker Centre, Row 5, Volume 34
Collection:Leader of the Opposition Office
Title: Canada and Foreign Countries - International Situation - Indo-Pakistan Relations 1964 [textual records] Physical description: 1 folder
Series Description: RSN 00003079

(RSN: 00007514) Pakistan
Call No.: MG 01/IX/C/415 Diefenbaker Centre, Row 6, Second Leader of the Opposition, Volume 162
Collection:Leader of the Opposition Office
Title: International Affairs - Pakistan 1967 [textual records] Physical description: 1 folder
Series Description: RSN 00003079

(RSN: 00010472) Pakistan
Call No.: MG 01/XII/A/405 Diefenbaker Centre, row 9, Personal and Confidential, Volume 12
Collection:Prime Minister's Office
Title: Diefenbaker, John G. - Trips and Engagements - World Tour - Pakistan 1958 [textual records] Physical description: 1 folder
Series Description: RSN 9157

(RSN: 00011778) Pakistan
Call No.: MG 01/XII/C/324 Diefenbaker Centre, row 9, Personal and Confidential, Volume 69
Collection:Prime Minister's and Leader of the Opposition's Offices Title: Pakistan 1961 [textual records]
Physical description: 1 folder
Series Description: RSN 9159

(RSN: 00012068) Pakistan
Call No.: MG 01/XII/D/158 Diefenbaker Centre, row 9, Personal and Confidential, Volume 87
Collection:Prime Minister's and Leader of the Opposition's Offices/Diefenbaker Parliamentary Office
Title: Pakistan - Letter from President and Reply 1960-1961 [textual records] Physical description: 1 folder
Series Description: RSN 9160

(RSN: 00012525) Pakistan
Call No.: MG 01/XII/F/227 Diefenbaker Centre, row 9, Personal and Confidential, Volume 113
Collection:Prime Minister's and Leader of the Opposition's Offices/Diefenbaker Parliamentary Office
Title: Foreign Affairs - Pakistan 1962-1963 [textual records] Physical description: 1 folder
Series Description: RSN 9162

(RSN: 00012972) Pakistan
Call No.: MG 01/XI/C Diefenbaker Centre, Rows 6-8
Title: Pakistan [textual records]
Summary:This file contains general correspondence with the public created and accumulated by John Diefenbaker's office from the time he ceased being Leader of the Opposition until his death.
Restricted:Closed until arrangement completed.
Series Description: RSN00003078

(RSN: 00015378) Pakistan
Call No.: MG01/XVII/JGD 3810 Diefenbaker Centre, Photographs and Slides, Volume Title: World Tour - Pakistan 1958 [photograph]
Physical description: 1 photograph black and white
Summary:Aerial view of the Warsak project (hydropower and irrigation development project) from over the plane's left wing, 17 Nov, 1958.
See Reference File: World Tour - Pakistan
Cite as:Diefenbaker Centre, Photographs and Slides, JGD 3810

(RSN: 00015387) Pakistan
Call No.: MG01/XVII/JGD 1030 Diefenbaker Centre, Photographs and Slides, Volume Title: World Tour - Pakistan 1958 [photograph]
Physical description: 1 photograph black and white
Summary:Elmer, Olive, and John Diefenbaker posing outside the Pakistani hospital on the Warsak Project site with members of hospital's staff, Nov 1958.
See Reference File: World Tour - Pakistan
Cite as:Diefenbaker Centre, Photographs and Slides, JGD 1030

(RSN: 00015388) Pakistan
Call No.: MG01/XVII/JGD 1029 Diefenbaker Centre, Photographs and Slides, Volume Title: Diefenbaker, Olive 1958 [photograph]
Physical description: 1 photograph black and white
Summary:As nurse looks on, Olive Diefenbaker talks to a patient in a Pakistani hospital on the Warsak Project site during the World Tour, Nov 1958.
See Reference File: Diefenbaker, Olive
Cite as:Diefenbaker Centre, Photographs and Slides, JGD 1029

(RSN: 00015389) Pakistan

Call No.: MG01/XVII/JGD 1028 Diefenbaker Centre, Photographs and Slides, Volume Title: World Tour - Pakistan 1958 [photograph]
Physical description: 1 photograph black and white
Summary:John Diefenbaker talking to four female members of the nursing staff at a Pakistani hospital on the Warsak Project site, Nov 1958.
See Reference File: World Tour - Pakistan
Cite as:Diefenbaker Centre, Photographs and Slides, JGD 1028

(RSN: 00015391) Pakistan
Call No.: MG01/XVII/JGD 1014 Diefenbaker Centre, Photographs and Slides, Volume Title: Diefenbaker, Olive 1958 [photograph]
Physical description: 1 photograph black and white
Summary:As others look on, Olive Diefenbaker talks to a young patient in a Pakistani hospital on the Warsak Project site during the World Tour, Nov 1958.
See Reference File: Diefenbaker, Olive
Cite as:Diefenbaker Centre, Photographs and Slides, JGD 1014

(RSN: 00015400) Pakistan
Call No.: MG01/XVII/JGD 966 Diefenbaker Centre, Photographs and Slides, Volume Title: Diefenbaker, Olive 1958 [photograph]
Physical description: 1 photograph black and white
Historical:Olive Diefenbaker; b. 14 Apr, 1902; d. 23 Dec, 1976; second wife of J.G.D. Summary:Olive Diefenbaker greeting group of boys and young men on the Warsak Project site during World Tour, Pakistan, Nov 1958.
See Reference File: Diefenbaker, Olive
Cite as:Diefenbaker Centre, Photographs and Slides, JGD 966

(RSN: 00015411) Pakistan
Call No.: MG01/XVII/JGD 951 Diefenbaker Centre, Photographs and Slides, Volume Title: World Tour - Pakistan 1958 [photograph]
Physical description: 1 photograph black and white
Summary:Road building at Warsak Project construction site, 17 Nov 1958.
See Reference File: World Tour - Pakistan
Cite as:Diefenbaker Centre, Photographs and Slides, JGD 951

(RSN: 00015412) Pakistan
Call No.: MG01/XVII/JGD 950 Diefenbaker Centre, Photographs and Slides, Volume Title: World Tour - Pakistan 1958 [photograph]
Physical description: 1 photograph black and white
Summary:John Diefenbaker in hat at Warsak Project construction site, Canadian workers in background and Pakistani soldiers in foreground, 17 Nov 1958.
See Reference File: World Tour - Pakistan
Cite as:Diefenbaker Centre, Photographs and Slides, JGD 950

(RSN: 00015413) Pakistan
Call No.: MG01/XVII/JGD 946 Diefenbaker Centre, Photographs and Slides, Volume Title: World Tour - Pakistan 1958 [photograph]
Physical description: 1 photograph black and white
Historical:Olive Diefenbaker; b. 14 Apr, 1902; d. 23 Dec, 1976; second wife of J.G.D. Summary:John and Olive Diefenbaker at Warsak Project construction site with crowd of workmen in the background, 17 Nov 1958.
See Reference File: World Tour - Pakistan
Cite as:Diefenbaker Centre, Photographs and Slides, JGD 946

(RSN: 00015414) Pakistan
Call No.: MG01/XVII/JGD 945 Diefenbaker Centre, Photographs and Slides, Volume Title: World Tour - Pakistan 1958 [photograph]
Physical description: 1 photograph black and white
Historical:Olive Diefenbaker; b. 14 Apr, 1902; d. 23 Dec, 1976; second wife of J.G.D. Summary:John and Olive Diefenbaker and official party, walking around Warsak Project construction site, 17 Nov 1958.
See Reference File: World Tour - Pakistan
Cite as:Diefenbaker Centre, Photographs and Slides, JGD 945

(RSN: 00015415) Pakistan
Call No.: MG01/XVII/JGD 944 Diefenbaker Centre, Photographs and Slides, Volume Title: World Tour - Pakistan 1958 [photograph]
Physical description: 1 photograph black and white
Summary:View from above of the Warsak Project construction site, 17 Nov 1958.
See Reference File: World Tour - Pakistan
Cite as:Diefenbaker Centre, Photographs and Slides, JGD 944

(RSN: 00015416) Pakistan
Call No.: MG01/XVII/JGD 943 Diefenbaker Centre, Photographs and Slides, Volume Title: World Tour - Pakistan 1958 [photograph]
Physical description: 1 photograph black and white
Summary:John and Olive Diefenbaker and official party entering tunnel at the Warsak Project construction site, 17 Nov 1958.
 See Reference File: World Tour - Pakistan
Cite as:Diefenbaker Centre, Photographs and Slides, JGD 943

(RSN: 00015417) Pakistan
Call No.: MG01/XVII/JGD 942 Diefenbaker Centre, Photographs and Slides, Volume Title: World Tour - Pakistan 1958 [photograph]
Physical description: 1 photograph black and white
Summary:John Diefenbaker speaking with a Canadian manager at the Warsak Project construction site, 17 Nov 1958.
See Reference File: World Tour - Pakistan
Cite as:Diefenbaker Centre, Photographs and Slides, JGD 942

(RSN: 00015418) Pakistan
Call No.: MG01/XVII/JGD 940 Diefenbaker Centre, Photographs and Slides, Volume Title: World Tour - Pakistan 1958 [photograph]
Physical description: 1 photograph black and white
Summary:View of the Warsak Project showing

workmen at bottom of dam construction site, 17 Nov, 1958.
See Reference File: World Tour - Pakistan
Cite as:Diefenbaker Centre, Photographs and Slides, JGD 940

(RSN: 00015505) Pakistan
Call No.: MG01/XVII/JGD 3973 Diefenbaker Centre, Photographs and Slides, Volume Title: World Tour - Pakistan 1958 [negative]
Physical description: 1 photograph black and white
Summary:View of Warsak Project with three native men in foreground, Nov 1958.
See Reference File: World Tour - Pakistan
Cite as:Diefenbaker Centre, Photographs and Slides, JGD 3973

(RSN: 00102290) Pakistan
Call No.: MG 01/VI/(312 Finance Hon. George Nowlan) Diefenbaker Centre, Rows 2-4, Volume 114 Title: Federal Government Executive - The Cabinet - Minister of Finance - Hon. George Nowlan 1957-1962
Summary:This file, in fact, contains memoranda, correspondence, photocopies, reports and ephemera concerning Donald Fleming, Minister of Finance.
Microfilm No.: M-7838
*Subjects include: Indus Waters Dispute between India and Pakistan Japan - trade negotiations Japan - Prime Minister's visit to Ottawa
Series Description: RSN00002248

(RSN: 00106628) Pakistan
Call No.: MG 01/VI/(380/P152.1) Diefenbaker Centre, Row 4 - 6, Volume 337 Title: Governments of Other Countries - General - Pakistan - Heads of State 1959-1961 Microfilm No.: M-7939
*Series Description: RSN00002248

(RSN: 00106629) Pakistan
Call No.: MG 01/VI/(380/P152.1 Secret) Diefenbaker Centre, Row 4 - 6, Volume 337 Title: Governments of Other Countries - General - Pakistan - Heads of State - Secret 1961 Microfilm No.:
*Series Description: RSN00002248

(RSN: 00106630) Pakistan
Call No.: MG 01/VI/(380/P152.2) Diefenbaker Centre, Row 4 - 6, Volume 337 Title: Governments of Other Countries - General - Pakistan - Cabinet 1960 Microfilm No.: M-7939
*Series Description: RSN00002248

(RSN: 00110094) Pakistan
Call No.: MG 01/VI/(735.5/P152 Conf.) Diefenbaker Centre, Row 4 - 6, Volume 502 Title: Transportation and Communication - Civil Air Transportation - Private Airlines - Pakistan - Confidential 1962-1963 Microfilm No.: M-8007
*Series Description: RSN00002248

(RSN: 00110911) Pakistan
Call No.: MG 01/VI/(802/P152) Diefenbaker Centre, Row 4 - 6, Volume 533 Title: World Relations - Economic Assistance Abroad - Pakistan 1957

Microfilm No.: M-8021
*Series Description: RSN00002248

(RSN: 00110912) Pakistan
Call No.: MG 01/VI/(802/P152 Official) Diefenbaker Centre, Row 4 - 6, Volume 533 Title: World Relations - Economic Assistance Abroad - Pakistan - Official 1961
Microfilm No.: M-8021
*Series Description: RSN00002248

(RSN: 00110933) Pakistan
Call No.: MG 01/VI/(805/P152) Diefenbaker Centre, Row 4 - 6, Volume 534 Title: World Relations - The Colombo Plan - Pakistan 1957-1958 Microfilm No.: M-8022
*Series Description: RSN00002248

(RSN: 00110934) Pakistan
Call No.: MG 01/VI/(805/P152 Conf.) Diefenbaker Centre, Row 4 - 6, Volume 534 Title: World Relations - The Colombo Plan - Pakistan - Confidential 1960
Microfilm No.: M-8022
*Series Description: RSN00002248

(RSN: 00111020) Pakistan
Call No.: MG 01/VI/(811/P152) Diefenbaker Centre, Row 4 - 6, Volume 537 Title: Canada and the Commonwealth - Commonwealth Members - Pakistan 1957,1959-1960 Microfilm No.: M-8024
*Series Description: RSN00002248

(RSN: 00111126) Pakistan
Call No.: MG 01/VI/(818.1/P152) Diefenbaker Centre, Row 4 - 6, Volume 541 Title: Canada and the Commonwealth - Visits - Visits to Canada of Commonwealth Ministers - Pakistan 1959 Microfilm No.: M-8026
*Series Description: RSN00002248

(RSN: 00111127) Pakistan
Call No.: MG 01/VI/(818.1/P152.1) Diefenbaker Centre, Row 4 - 6, Volume 541 Title: Canada and the Commonwealth - Visits - Visits to Canada of Commonwealth Ministers - Pakistan - Heads of State 1960-1961 Microfilm No.: M-8026
*Series Description: RSN00002248

(RSN: 00111128) Pakistan
Call No.: MG 01/VI/(818.1/P152.2) Diefenbaker Centre, Row 4 - 6, Volume 541 Title: Canada and the Commonwealth - Visits - Visits to Canada of Commonwealth Ministers - Pakistan - Cabinet 1961
Microfilm No.: M-8026
*Series Description: RSN00002248

(RSN: 00111162) Pakistan
Call No.: MG 01/VI/(818.21 PM 1958 Pakistan) Diefenbaker Centre, Row 4 - 6, Volume 543 Title: Canada and the Commonwealth - Visits - Visits to Commonwealth Countries by Canadian Ministers - World Tour - Prime Minister - 1958 - Pakistan 1958-1960 Microfilm No.: M-8027
*Series Description: RSN00002248

(RSN: 00111423) Pakistan
Call No.: MG 01/VI/(840/P152) Diefenbaker Centre, Row 4 - 6, Volume 553 Title: Canada and Foreign Countries - General - Pakistan 1957-1963 Microfilm No.: M-8032
*Series Description: RSN00002248

(RSN: 00111656) Pakistan
Call No.: MG 01/VI/(846/P152) Diefenbaker Centre, Row 4 - 6, Volume 564 Title: Canada and Foreign Countries - Visits - Pakistan 1957-1960 Microfilm No.: M-8039
*Series Description: RSN00002248

(RSN: 00111657) Pakistan
Call No.: MG 01/VI/(846/P152 Ayub) Diefenbaker Centre, Row 4 - 6, Volume 564 Title: Canada and Foreign Countries - Visits - Pakistan - President Ayub 1961-1962 Microfilm No.: M-8039
*Series Description: RSN00002248

(RSN: 00111787) Pakistan
Call No.: MG 01/VI/(861/P152) Diefenbaker Centre, Row 4 - 6, Volume 568 Title: Diplomatic Representation - Canadian Representation Abroad - Pakistan 1957-1960 Microfilm No.: M-8041
*Series Description: RSN00002248

(RSN: 00111837) Pakistan
Call No.: MG 01/VI/(862 Pakistan) Diefenbaker Centre, Row 4 - 6, Volume 569 Title: Diplomatic Representation - Canadian Missions Abroad - Pakistan 1958 Microfilm No.: M-8042
*Series Description: RSN00002248

(RSN: 00111901) Pakistan
Call No.: MG 01/VI/(864/P152) Diefenbaker Centre, Row 4 - 6, Volume 571 Title: Diplomatic Representation - Representation of Other Countries in Canada - Pakistan 1958-1963 Microfilm No.: M-8042
*Series Description: RSN00002248

(RSN: 00106631) Philippines
Call No.: MG 01/VI/(380/P551.1) Diefenbaker Centre, Row 4 - 6, Volume 337 Title: Governments of Other Countries - General - Philippines - Heads of State 1959-1961 Microfilm No.: M-7939
*Series Description: RSN00002248

(RSN: 00111433) Sarawak
Call No.: MG 01/VI/(840/S243) Diefenbaker Centre, Row 4 - 6, Volume 554 Title: Canada and Foreign Countries - General - Sarawak 1962 Microfilm No.: M-8032
*Series Description: RSN00002248

(RSN: 00010474) Singapore
Call No.: MG 01/XII/A/407 Diefenbaker Centre, row 9, Personal and Confidential, Volume 12 Collection:Prime Minister's Office
Title: Diefenbaker, John G. - Trips and Engagements - World Tour - Singapore 1958 [textual records] Physical description: 1 folder
Series Description: RSN 9157

(RSN: 00111023) Singapore
Call No.: MG 01/VI/(811/S617) Diefenbaker Centre, Row 4 - 6, Volume 537 Title: Canada and the Commonwealth - Commonwealth Members - Singapore 1959 Microfilm No.: M-8024
*Series Description: RSN00002248

(RSN: 00111167) Singapore
Call No.: MG 01/VI/(818.21 PM 1958 Singapore) Diefenbaker Centre, Row 4 - 6, Volume 544 Title: Canada and the Commonwealth - Visits - Visits to Commonwealth Countries by Canadian Ministers - World Tour - Prime Minister - 1958 - Singapore 1958-1959 Microfilm No.: M-8027
*Series Description: RSN00002248

(RSN: 00111436) Singapore
Call No.: MG 01/VI/(840/S617) Diefenbaker Centre, Row 4 - 6, Volume 554 Title: Canada and Foreign Countries - General - Singapore 1958-1959 Microfilm No.: M-8032
*Series Description: RSN00002248

(RSN: 00001690) Taiwan
Call No.: MG 01/XIV/E/57 Diefenbaker Centre, Row 9, Memoirs Volume 12 Title: World Relations - Republic of China [196-] [textual records] Physical description: one folder
Summary:This file contains printed pamphlets from Communist China and Taiwan. Series Description: RSN 00001527

(RSN: 00013316) Taiwan
Call No.: MG 01/XI/C Diefenbaker Centre, Rows 6-8 Title: Trips and Engagements - Taiwan - June [textual records] Summary:This file contains general correspondence with the public created and accumulated by John Diefenbaker's office from the time he ceased being Leader of the Opposition until his death. Restricted:Closed until arrangement completed. Series Description: RSN00003078

(RSN: 00014427) Taiwan
Call No.: MG 01/XI/C Diefenbaker Centre, Rows 6-8 Title: Trips and Engagements - China - China - Republic of China - Taiwan [textual records] Physical description: 1 folder
Summary:This file contains general correspondence with the public created and accumulated by John Diefenbaker's office from the time he ceased being Leader of the Opposition until his death. Restricted:Closed until arrangement completed. Series Description: RSN00003078

(RSN: 00000281) Thailand
Call No.: MG 01/VII/A/273 Diefenbaker Centre Row 4, Volume 35 Collection:Prime Minister's Office/ Leader of the Opposition Office Title: Canadian Alumni Group of Thailand 1961 [textual records] Physical description: 1 folder
Pages:pp. 19383-19414
Series Description: RSN 00000254

(RSN: 00000620) Thailand
Call No.: MG 01/VII/A/2211 Diefenbaker Centre Row 4, Volume 239 Collection:Prime Minister's Office/ Leader of the Opposition Office Title: Thailand 1962-1966 [textual records]
Physical description: 1 folder
Pages:pp. 152970-152989
Series Description: RSN 00000254

(RSN: 00004925) Thailand
Call No.: MG 01/XXII/408 Diefenbaker Centre, Row Volume 6
Title: Governments of Canada and Thailand Have Agreed to Enter Into Diplomatic Relations and to Exchange Representatives at the Rank of Ambassador 8 November 1961 [textual records] Physical description: 1 folder
Summary:French included
Series Description: 3081

(RSN: 00006331) Thailand
Call No.: MG 01/IX/A/1177/*864/T364 Diefenbaker Centre, Row 5, Volume 35 Collection:Leader of the Opposition Office
Title: Diplomatic Representations - Representations of Other Countries in Canada - Thailand (Siam) 1965 [textual records] Physical description: 1 folder
Series Description: RSN 00003079

(RSN: 00111446) Thailand
Call No.: MG 01/VI/(840/T364) Diefenbaker Centre, Row 4 - 6, Volume 554 Title: Canada and Foreign Countries - General - Thailand (Siam) 1960-1963 Microfilm No.: M-8032
*Series Description: RSN00002248

(RSN: 00111662) Thailand
Call No.: MG 01/VI/(846/T364) Diefenbaker Centre, Row 4 - 6, Volume 564 Title: Canada and Foreign Countries - Visits - Thailand 1960 Microfilm No.: M-8039
*Series Description: RSN00002248

(RSN: 00111909) Thailand
Call No.: MG 01/VI/(864/T364) Diefenbaker Centre, Row 4 - 6, Volume 571 Title: Diplomatic Representation - Representation of Other Countries in Canada - Thailand (Siam) 1962 Microfilm No.: M-8042
*Series Description: RSN00002248

(RSN: 00111447) Tibet
Call No.: MG 01/VI/(840/T553) Diefenbaker Centre, Row 4 - 6, Volume 554 Title: Canada and Foreign Countries - General - Tibet 1960 Microfilm No.: M-8032
*Series Description: RSN00002248

(RSN: 00111554) Tibet
Call No.: MG 01/VI/(845/T553) Diefenbaker Centre, Row 4 - 6, Volume 560 Title: Canada and Foreign Countries - International Situation - Tibet 1958-1963 Microfilm No.: M-8037
*Series Description: RSN00002248

(RSN: 00111572) Tibet
Call No.: MG 01/VI/(845.4/T553) Diefenbaker Centre, Row 4 - 6, Volume 560 Title: Canada and Foreign Countries - International Situation - Refugees - Tibet 1962 Microfilm No.: M-8037
*Series Description: RSN00002248

(RSN: 00104907) Turkey
Call No.: MG 01/VI/(313.4/T939) Diefenbaker Centre, Row 4 - 6, Volume 257 Title: Federal Government Executive - The Prime Minister of Canada - Travel, Trips, Visits, Etc. - Turkey 1960 Microfilm No.: M-7905
*Series Description: RSN00002248

(RSN: 00105370) Turkey
Call No.: MG 01/VI/(335 Bran-Sour) Diefenbaker Centre, Rows 2-4, Volume 288 Title: The House of Commons - Members of the House - Brandon-Souris Constituency 1957-1960 Summary:This file includes: a copy of a letter from Derek Bedson to Walter Dinsdale (MP) re Dinsdale's need to apologize to Diefenbaker; a letter from Dinsdale re NATO installations in Turkey, and the NATO Parliamentarians Conference. Microfilm No.: M-7921
*Series Description: RSN00002248

(RSN: 00106642) Turkey
Call No.: MG 01/VI/(380/T939.1) Diefenbaker Centre, Row 4 - 6, Volume 337 Title: Governments of Other Countries - General - Turkey - Heads of State 1958 Microfilm No.: M-7939
*Series Description: RSN00002248

(RSN: 00110427) Turkey
Call No.: MG 01/VI/(738/T939) Diefenbaker Centre, Row 4 - 6, Volume 512 Title: Transportation and Communication - The Press - Turkey 1958 Microfilm No.: M-8011
*Series Description: RSN00002248

(RSN: 00111269) Turkey
Call No.: MG 01/VI/(832/T939) Diefenbaker Centre, Row 4 - 6, Volume 549 Title: Canada and the North Atlantic Treaty - The Treaty Organization (NATO) - Turkey 1958 Microfilm No.: M-8030
*Series Description: RSN00002248

(RSN: 00111451) Turkey
Call No.: MG 01/VI/(840/T939) Diefenbaker Centre, Row 4 - 6, Volume 554 Title: Canada and Foreign Countries - General - Turkey 1958,1960 Microfilm No.: M-8033
*Series Description: RSN00002248

(RSN: 00111452) Turkey
Call No.: MG 01/VI/(840/T939.21) Diefenbaker Centre, Row 4 - 6, Volume 554 Title: Canada and Foreign Countries - General - Turkey - Cabinet - Prime Minister 1958-1959 Microfilm No.: M-8033
*Series Description: RSN00002248

(RSN: 00111664) Turkey
Call No.: MG 01/VI/(846/T939) Diefenbaker

Centre, Row 4 - 6, Volume 564 Title: Canada and Foreign Countries - Visits - Turkey 1958-1960 Microfilm No.: M-8039
*Series Description: RSN00002248

(RSN: 00111816) Turkey
Call No.: MG 01/VI/(861.1/T939 Conf.) Diefenbaker Centre, Row 4 - 6, Volume 569 Title: Diplomatic Representation - Canadian Representation Abroad - Accommodation - Turkey - Confidential 1961-1962 Microfilm No.: M-8042
*Series Description: RSN00002248

(RSN: 00111841) Turkey
Call No.: MG 01/VI/(862 Turkey) Diefenbaker Centre, Row 4 - 6, Volume 569 Title: Diplomatic Representation - Canadian Missions Abroad - Turkey 1958 Microfilm No.: M-8042
*Series Description: RSN00002248

(RSN: 00111911) Turkey
Call No.: MG 01/VI/(864/T939) Diefenbaker Centre, Row 4 - 6, Volume 571 Title: Diplomatic Representation - Representation of Other Countries in Canada - Turkey 1957-1961 Microfilm No.: M-8042
*Series Description: RSN00002248

(RSN: 00000461) Vietnam
Call No.: MG 01/VII/A/2371.1-2371.7 Diefenbaker Centre Row 4, vols. 258,259 Collection:Prime Minister's Office/ Leader of the Opposition Office Title: Vietnam n.d., 1963-1967 [textual records]
Physical description: 7 folders
A/2371.1: n.d., Volume 258; A/2371.2: 1963-1965, Volume 258; A/2371.3: Jan. 1966, Volume 259; A/2371.4: Feb.-May 1966, Volume 259; A/2371.5: July-Dec. 1966, Volume 259; A/2371.6: Jan.-March 1967, Volume 259; A/2371.7: April-May 1967, Volume 259. Pages:pp. 160286-161222
Series Description: RSN 00000254

(RSN: 00001508) Vietnam
Call No.: MG 01/IX/B/4 Diefenbaker Centre, Rows 5-6, Second Leader of the Opposition, Volume36 Collection:Leader of the Opposition Office
Title: Aiken, George D. 1967 [textual records]
Physical description: 1 folder
Historical:United States Senator
Summary:This file contains correspondence between Aiken and Diefenbaker about the Liberal Government's foreign policy. Subject:United States - Canada Parliamentary Association Vietnam Gordon, Walter
Series Description: RSN 00001512

(RSN: 00002171) Vietnam
Call No.: MG 01/IX/B/335 Diefenbaker Centre, Rows 5-6, Second Leader of the Opposition, Volume 49 Collection:Leader of the Opposition Office
Title: International Affairs - Vietnam 1967 [textual records] Physical description: 1 folder
Series Description: RSN 00001512

(RSN: 00005788) Vietnam
Call No.: MG 01/XI/A Diefenbaker Centre, Row 6,
Member of Parliament, Volume 38
Collection:Diefenbaker Parliamentary Office
Title: Whitestone, Bruce 1967-1972,1974 [textual records] Physical description: 1 folder
Historical:one of Diefenbaker's special assistants during the 1965 election Summary:This file contains correspondence and clippings on a variety of political issues. Restricted:Closed until arrangement completed Subjects include: Vietnam war
Series Description: RSN00003078

(RSN: 00005845) Vietnam
Call No.: MG 01/XI/A Diefenbaker Centre, Row 6, Member of Parliament, Volume 36
Collection:Diefenbaker Parliamentary Office
Title: Turner, John H.F. 1971,1973 [textual records]
Physical description: 1 folder
Historical:former general manager for Europe, Bank of Montreal Summary:This file contains personal correspondence.
Restricted:Closed until arrangement completed
Subject:Sharp, Mitchell Vietnam war
Series Description: RSN00003078

(RSN: 00006316) Vietnam
Call No.: MG 01/IX/A/1164.1/*845 Vietnam - 1164.2/*845 Vietnam Diefenbaker Centre, Row 5, Volume 34 Collection:Leader of the Opposition Office Title: Canada and Foreign Countries - International Situation - Vietnam 1964-1967 [textual records]
Physical description: 2 folders
Arranged: A/1164.1: n.d., 1964-1965; A/1164.2: 1966-1967.
Series Description: RSN 00003079

(RSN: 00007506) Vietnam
Call No.: MG 01/IX/C/423 Diefenbaker Centre, Row 6, Second Leader of the Opposition, Volume 164 Collection:Leader of the Opposition Office
Title: International Affairs - Vietnam - P.A. 1966 [textual records] Physical description: 1 folder
Series Description: RSN 00003079

(RSN: 00007507) Vietnam
Call No.: MG 01/IX/C/422.1 - 422.6 Diefenbaker Centre, Row 6, Second Leader of the Opposition, Vols. 163-164 Collection:Leader of the Opposition Office
Title: International Affairs - Vietnam n.d., 1963-Sept. 1967 [textual records] Physical description: 6 folders
Arranged: C/422.1: Volume 163, n.d., 1963-Oct. 1965; C/422.2: Volume 163, Nov. 1965-16 Feb. 1966; C/422.3: Volume 163, 18 Feb.-11 July 1966; C/422.4: Volume 163, 18 July 1966-Mar. 1967; C/422.5: Volume 164, Apr.-May 1967; C/422.6: Volume 164, June-Sept. 1967.
Series Description: RSN 00003079

(RSN: 00009834) Vietnam
Call No.: MG 01/XI/B Diefenbaker Centre, Rows 6-8 Title: Vietnam n.d., 1956-1974 (inclusive) [textual records] Summary:This file contains the reference material created and accumulated by John Diefenbaker's office from after he ceased being Leader

of the Opposition to his death. Restricted:Closed until arrangement completed.
Series Description: RSN00003078

(RSN: 00013319) Vietnam
Call No.: MG 01/XI/C Diefenbaker Centre, Rows 6-8 Title: Trips and Engagements - Vietnam - June 1970 1970 [textual records] Summary:This file contains general correspondence with the public created and accumulated by John Diefenbaker's office from the time he ceased being Leader of the Opposition until his death. Restricted:Closed until arrangement completed.
Series Description: RSN00003078

(RSN: 00102143) Vietnam
Call No.: MG 01/VI/(307.1.01 - 1957) Diefenbaker Centre, Rows 2-4, Volume 105 Title: Government - Parliament - Opening of Parliament - Speech from the Throne - 1957 Summary:This file contains transcripts, memoranda, and reports. Microfilm No.: M-7835 *Subjects include:Colombo Plan Middle East International Supervisory Commissions in Vietnam, Laos and Cambodia North Atlantic Treaty Organization (NATO) Author:Bryce, R.B.
Series Description: RSN00002248

(RSN: 00111378) Vietnam
Call No.: MG 01/VI/(840/I41V666S) Diefenbaker Centre, Row 4 - 6, Volume 552 Title: Canada and Foreign Countries - General - Indo-China - South Vietnam 1959,1962 Microfilm No.: M-8032
*Series Description: RSN00002248

(RSN: 00111547) Vietnam
Call No.: MG 01/VI/(845/I41V666S) Diefenbaker Centre, Row 4 - 6, Volume 560 Title: Canada and Foreign Countries - International Situation - Indo-China - South Vietnam 1962 Microfilm No.: M-8037
*Series Description: RSN00002248

(RSN: 00111842) Vietnam
Call No.: MG 01/VI/(862 Vietnam) Diefenbaker Centre, Row 4 - 6, Volume 569 Title: Diplomatic Representation - Canadian Missions Abroad - Vietnam 1958 Microfilm No.: M-8042
*Series Description: RSN00002248

N. Pearson, Lester Bowles, 1897-1972.

Prime Minister, 1963-1968.
Secretary of State for External Affairs, 1948-

Led Canadian delegates in Commonwealth Foreign Affairs Conference in Ceylon 1950.
Japanese Peace Treaty Conference, San Francisco, 1951.
Served on three-man United Nations Commission to draw up truce plans for Korea, 1950-1951.
Permission needed to see materials and to view indexes.

Originals, 1911-1973. 348 metres. Finding aid 877.

Pre-1958 correspondence, N1 series, 1931-1957, originals 8.4 metres(volumes 1-82).

Nominal files, 1935-1957. 1.8 metres(volumes 1-17)

Files arranged alphabetically by correspondent chiefly relating to Pearson's career in the Department of External Affairs.
Bajpai, Girja. India External Affairs, 1949-1954.

Kaur, Rajkumari. Indian politician, 1950-1954.

Nehru, Jawaharlal. Indian statesman, 1949.

Saksena, R.R. India. External Affairs, 1952.

Sarper, S. Turkey. External Affairs, 1949.

Small, Walter. Missionary to China, 1952.

Subject files, 1931-1957. 5.6 metres (volumes 18-72)
These files are arranged alphabetically by subject.

China, recognition, 1949-1956.

Formosa and offshore islands, 1955.

India-Canada relations, 1947-1957.

Indo-China, 1954-1957.

Korea, Canadian membership of U.N.C.U.R.K.(United Nations Commision for the Unification and Rehabilitation of Korea), 1947-1948.

Korea, cease-fire, 1950-1957.

Korea, Canadian policy, 1950-1957.

Korea, discussion at Seventh U.N. Assembly, 1952-1953.

Pacific Relations, Institute of, 1942-1943.

Tarawa(Gilberts), 1943.

Leader of the Opposition correspondence, N2 series 1958-1963, originals 18.4 metres (volumes 1-174).

Numbered subject files, 1958-1963. 6.1 metres (volumes 1-59) file list and card index.

1. Chinese, 1958-1959.

2. Japanese, 1961-1962.

46. Trade with Communist China, 1958-1962.

46. Trade with Japan, 1959-1962.

49. Recognition of Communist China, 1959

85. Colombo Plan, part 1, 1950-1960.

85. Colombo Plan, part 2, 1957-1960.

87. Indo-China crisis, 1962.

88. Recognition of Red China, 1952-1960.

Prime Minister's Office correspondence, N3 series, 1963-1965, originals, 68.7 metres (volumes 1-337).

Numbered subject files, 1963-1965. 64.6 metres (volumes 1-317)

File list and nominal and subject card indexes.

Volume 25.

File 045, Armenians
Language and ethnic groups - Armenians, July 1964-September 1965.

Volume 25.

File 045, China.
Language and ethnic groups - Chinese, October 1964-October 1965.

Volume 25.

File 045. Japan.
Language and ethnic groups - Japanese, November 1963-July 1964.

Volume 30.

File 100.5.
Defense troops. Cyprus, June 1964.

File 183.
War. Korea, March 1964-June 1965

Volume 92.

File 312.25, India.
Prime Minister of Canada. Personal invitations. India, June 1963.

Volume 92.

File 312.25, 234.
Prime Minister of Canada. Personal Invitations, Malaya, June 1964.

Volume 106.

File 313.253J.
Patronage. Japanese Art Exhibition 19 October 1965-10 November 1965.

File 313.253J.
Patronage. Japanese Art Exhibition, May 1965.

Volume 183.

File 380/B425.21.
Governments of other countries, Ceylon, Cabinet, Prime Minister, February 1964-April 1965.

File 383/I 39, Conf.
Governments of other countries, India, confidential, June 1965.

File 383/I39.2.
Governments of other countries, India, Cabinet, July 1964.

File 383/I39.21.
Governments of other countries, India, Cabinet, Prime Minister, June 1964.

Volume 184.

File 383/I39.21.
Governments of other countries, India, Cabinet, Prime Minister, June 1963-July 1965.

File 383/I39.21, Conf.
Governments of other countries, India, Cabinet, Prime Minister Conference, June 1963-August 1964.

File 383/I39.21, death of.
Governments of other countries, India, Cabinet, Prime Minister, death of, May-August 1964.

File 380/J35.21.
Governments of other countries, Japan, Cabinet, Prime Minister, August 1963-April 1965.

File 380/M241, Conf.
Governments of other countries, Malaysia, confidential, June 1965.

File 380/P152.1.
Governments of other countries, Pakistan, Heads of State, August 1963-July 1965.

Volume 208.

File 572.1, Kung.
Immigration and citizenship. Immigration operations, Ching Kung, September 1963-February 1964.

File 572.1, Park.
Immigration and citizenship. Immigration, Dr. Jai Park, April-November 1963.

Volume 209.

File 577.2/H772.
Immigration and citizenship. Immigration, agricultural workers, Hong Kong, July 1964-January 1965.

Volume 239.

File 711/C539.1.
Domestic trade, Grain trade, Communist China, August 1963.

File 711.3/C539.1.
Domestic trade, Grain trade, Grain marketing, Communist China, June 1963-March 1965.

File 711.3/I39.
Domestic trade, Grain trade, Grain marketing, India, March 1965.

Volume 240.

File 722/C539.
Foreign trade, trade by countries, Communist China, February-May 1965.

File 722/C539.11.
Foreign trade, trade by countries, Communist China, Recognition of, October 1965.

File 722/I35.
Foreign trade, trade by countries, India, December 1963.

File 722/J35.
Foreign trade, trade by countries, Japan, June 1965-August 1965.

File 722/J35, Conf.
Foreign trade, trade by countries, Japan, Conf., October 1963.

File 722/K4S, Conf.
Foreign trade, trade by countries, Korea, South, Conf. September 1965.

Volume 264.

File 802/C425.
World relations, economic assistance abroad, Ceylon, November 1963-September 1965.

File 802/I39.
World relations, economic assistance abroad, India, September 1964-September 1965.

File 802/I39, Conf.
World relations, economic assistance abroad, India, Conf., May 1963.

File 802/I39, Military Assistance, Conf.
World relations, economic assistance abroad, India, military assistance, Conf., July-August 1965.

File 802/I42.
World relations, economic assistance abroad, Indonesia, September 1964.

File 802/P152.
World relations, economic assistance abroad, Pakistan, July 1965.

Volume 271.

File 821/C539.1.
Canada and the U.N., U.N. membership China, Communist China, August 1963-June 1965.

File 821/C539.11.
Canada and the U.N., U.N. membership Communist China, Recognition of September 1963-November 1965

File 821/C539.11, Conf.
Canada and the U.N., Communist China, Recognition of, Conf., November 1965.

File 821/I42.
Canada and the U.N., Indonesia, Republic of, January-February 1965.

File 821/S617.
Canada and the U.N., Singapore, August 1965.

Volume 272.

File 828/F.A.O. Canada-Mysore project.
Canada and the U.N., specialized U.N. agencies, Food and Agriculture Organization, Canada- Mysore project, November 1963-September 1965.

828 Canada-Mysore project gift, January-October 1965.
Canada and the U.N. Canada- Mysore project gift.

File 828, WHO Easter Island.
Canada and the U.N., World Health Organization, Easter Island, January 1962-October 1965.

Volume 274.

File 840/B962.
Canada and foreign countries, Burma, December 1963-July 1965.

File 840/C425.
Canada and foreign countries, Ceylon, January 1964-September 1965.

File 840/C539.
Canada and foreign countries, China, May 1964-May 1965.

File 840/C539.1.
Canada and foreign countries, Communist China, August 1963-October 1965.

File 840/C539.11.
Canada and foreign countries, Communist China, Recognition of, July 1963-July 1965.

File 840/C996.
Canada and foreign countries, Cyprus, February 1964-January 1965.

Volume 275.

File 840/H772.
Canada and foreign countries, Hong Kong, May 1963-April 1964.

File 840/I39.
Canada and foreign countries, India, July 1963-November 1965.

File 840/I39, Conf.
Canada and foreign countries, India, confidential, May 1964-March 1965.

File 840/I39, Rann of Kutch.
Canada and foreign countries, India, Rann of Kutch, April-June 1965.

File 840/I41, C176.
Canada and foreign countries, Cambodia, May-June 1963.

File 840/I41, L298.
Canada and foreign countries, Laos, May 1963.

File 840/I41, V666.
Canada and foreign countries, Vietnam, April 1964-July 1965.

File 840/I41, V666S.
Canada and foreign countries, South Vietnam, November-December 1964.

File 840/I42.
Canada and foreign countries, Indonesia, Republic of, August 1964-February 1965.

File 840/I65.
Canada and foreign countries, Iran, June 1964-May 1965.

File 840/J35.
Canada and foreign countries, Japan, May 1963-September 1965.

File 840/J35, Pers. and Conf.
Canada and foreign countries, Japan, personal and confidential, December 1964.

File 840/J35, Ministerial committee.
Canada and foreign countries, Japan, Ministerial committee, September 1963-September 1965.

File 840/K48S
Canada and foreign countries, Korea, South, July 1964-March 1965.

File 840/M239.
Malaysia, August 1963.

File 840/M241.
Malaysia, August 1963-September 1965.

File 840/M241 ,Conf.
Malaysia, confidential, March-September 1965.

File 840/M241, Military assistance.
Canada and foreign countries, Malaysia, military assistance, August 1964-March 1965.

File 840/M241, Military assistance, Conf.
Canada and foreign countries, Minister, Malaysia, military assistance, April 1964-March 1965.

File 840/M241, Military assistance, Conf.
Canada and foreign countries, Malaysia, military assistance, confidential, March 1965.

File 840/M241, Comments.
Canada and foreign countries, Malaysia, military assistance.

File 840/M743, Conf.
Canada and foreign countries, Mongolia, confidential, December 1963.

File 840/P152.
Canada and foreign countries, Pakistan, May 1963-October 1965.

File 840/P152, Conf.
Canada and foreign countries, Pakistan, confidential, February 1965.

Volume 276.

File 840/P551.
Canada and foreign countries, Philippines, April 1963-April l965.

File 840/S191.
Canada and foreign countries, Samoa, Western, March 1965.

File 840/S617.
Canada and foreign countries, Singapore, October 1965.

File 840/S617, Conf.
Canada and foreign countries, Singapore, confidential, August 1965.

File 840/S617, Policy.
Canada and foreign countries, Singapore, policy.

Volume 277.

File 840/T553.
Canada and foreign countries, Tibet, December 1964.

File 840/T939.
Canada and foreign countries, Turkey, October-May 1963.

File 845/C996.
Canada and foreign countries, international situations, Cyprus, February 1964-April 1965.

Volume 278.

File 845/C996.
Canada and foreign countries, international situations, Cyprus, January-February 1964.

Volume 279.

File 845/I39.
Canada and foreign counties, international situations, India, September 1963-July 1964.

File 845/I39, Goa freedom movement.
Canada and foreign countries, international situations, India, Goa freedom.

File 845/I41 V666, Cdn entente.
Canada and foreign countries, international situations, Vietnam, Canadian entente, August 1965.

File 845/I41 V666, Commission.
Canada and foreign countries, international situations, Vietnam Commission.

File 845/I41 V666, Crisis 1964.
Canada and foreign countries, international situations, Vietnam, crisis 1964, November 1963-December 1964.

File 845/I41 V666, Crisis 1964 Conf.
Canada and foreign countries, international situations, Vietnam, crisis, confidential, July-September 1964.

File 845/I41 V666-845 V666, Crisis, 1965.
Canada and foreign countries, international situations, crisis 1965.

File 845/I41 V666, Crisis, 1965.
Canada and foreign countries, international situations, crisis 1965, June 1965.

File 845/I41 V666, Crisis 1965.
Canada and foreign countries, international situation, Vietnam, June-July 1965.

File 845/I41 V666, Crisis 1965.
Canada and foreign countries, international situations, Vietnam, crisis, August 1965.

File 845/I41 V666, Crisis 1965.
Canada and foreign countries, international situations, Vietnam, crisis, August-September 1965.

File 845/I41 V666, Commission, Conf.
Canada and foreign countries, international situations, Vietnam, Commission, March 1965.

File 845/I41 V666, Crisis 1965.
Canada and foreign countries, international situations, Vietnam, crisis, 1965, December 1964-February 1965.

File 845/I41 V666, Crisis 1965.
Canada and foreign countries, international situations, Vietnam, crisis, 1965. February 1965.

File 845/I41 V666, Crisis,1965.
Canada and foreign countries, international situations, Vietnam, crisis, February-March 1965.

File 845/I41 V666, Crisis 1965.
Canada and foreign countries, international situations, Vietnam, crisis, 1965, February-March 1965.

File 845/I41 V666, Crisis 1965.
Canada and foreign countries, international situations, Vietnam, crisis 1965, March 1965.

File 845/I41 V666, Crisis 1965.
Canada and foreign countries, international situations, Vietnam, crisis 1965, April 1965.

Volume 280.

File 845/I41 V666, Crisis 1965.
Canada and foreign countries. international situations, Vietnam, crisis, April 1965.

File 845/I41 V666, Crisis 1965.
Canada and foreign countries, international situations, Vietnam, crisis, April-May 1965.

File 845/I41 V666, Crisis 1965.
Canada and foreign countries, international situations, Vietnam, crisis, May 1965.

File 845/I41 V666, Crisis Vietnam 1965.
Canada and foreign countries, international situations, Vietnam, crisis, May 1965.

File 845/I41 V666, Crisis 1965.
Canada and foreign countries, international situations, Vietnam, crisis, May 1965.

File 845/I41 V666, Crisis 1965.
Canada and foreign countries, international situations, Vietnam, crisis, May-June 1965.

File 845/I41 V666, Crisis 1965.
Canada and foreign countries, international situations, Vietnam, crisis, June 1965.

File 845/I41 V666, Crisis Vietnam, 1965.
Canada and foreign countries, international situations, Vietnam, crisis, June-July 1965.

File 845/I41 V666, Crisis 1965.
Canada and foreign countries, international situations, Vietnam, crisis, August 1965.

File 845/I41 V666, Crisis 1965.
Canada and foreign countries, international situations, Vietnam, crisis, August-September 1965.

File 845/I41 V666, Crisis 1965.
Canada and foreign countries, international situations, Vietnam, crisis, October-November 1965.

Volume 281.

File 845/I41 V666, Crisis 1965 Conf.
Canada and foreign countries, international situations, Vietnam, crisis, 1965 confidential, February-July 1965.

File 845/I41 V666, Pers. and Conf.
Canada and foreign countries, international situations, Vietnam, crisis 1965, personal and confidential, April-September 1965.

File 845/I41 V666, Crisis 1965, Policy.
Canada and foreign countries, Vietnam, crisis, policy, April-June 1965.

File 845/I41 V666, Crisis 1966, Canadian troops.
Canada and foreign countries, international situations, Vietnam, crisis, Canadian troops, October-November 1965.

File 845/I41 V666, Crisis 1965, Pauling.
Canada and foreign countries, international situations, Vietnam, crisis, Dr. Linus Pauling, 8 March-August 1965.

File 845/I41 V666, Crisis 1965, P.M.'s statements.
Canada and foreign countries, international situations, Vietnam, crisis, Prime Minister's statements, February-March 1965.

File 845/I41 V666, Crisis 1965, Use of gas.
Canada and foreign countries, international situations, Vietnam, crisis, use of gas, March-May 1963.

File 845/I41 V666, Crisis 1965, Use of gas. Conf.
Canada and foreign countries, international situation, use of gas confidential, May 1965.

File 845/I41 V666S.
Canada and foreign countries, international situations, Indo-China and S.Vietnam, June 1963-January 1965.

File 845/I42.
Canada and foreign countries, international situations, Indonesia, January-March 1965.

Volume 282.

File 846/J35, Conf.
Canada and foreign countries, Japan, confidential, March-April 1964.

File 846/J35, Pers. and Conf.
Canada and foreign countries, Japan, personal and confidential, December 1964-January 1965.

File 846/M241.
Canada and foreign countries, Malaysia, June-July 1964.

File 846/M241 Conf.
Canada and foreign countries, Malaysia, confidential, June-July 1964.

Volume 283.

File 846/P152.
Canada and foreign countries, Pakistan, September 1963.

Volume 284.

File 855.1 Choy.
Canada and the United States immigration regulations. U.S. immigration cases, Wayson S.Choy, May-November 1963.

Volume 286.

File 861/C425.
Diplomatic representation, Canadian diplomatic representation abroad, Ceylon, February 1964.

File 861/I39, Michener.
Diplomatic representation, Canadian representation abroad, India, July 1964.

File 861/I39.
Diplomatic representation, Canadian representation abroad, India, May 1964-July 1965.

File 861/I39.
Diplomatic representation, Canadian representation abroad, India, personal, October 1964-February 1965.

File 861/I65.
Diplomatic representation, Canadian representation abroad, Iran, June 1963-February 1965.

File 861/J35.
Diplomatic representation, Canadian representation abroad, Japan, February-March 1965.

File 861/M241.
Diplomatic representation, Canadian representation abroad, Malaysia, September 1963.

File 861/P152.
Diplomatic representation, Canadian representation abroad, Pakistan, August 1963.

Volume 287.

File 862, Pakistan Conf.
Diplomatic representation, Canadian representation abroad, Pakistan confidential, June 1964.

File 863/I39.
Diplomatic representation, Canadian consulates abroad, India, September 1, 1965

Volume 288.

File 864/B962.

Diplomatic representation. representation of other countries in Canada, Burma, June 1964-December 1965.

File 864/C425.
Diplomatic representation, representation of other countries in Canada, Ceylon, June 1963-September 1965.

File 864/C539.
Diplomatic representation, representation of other countries in Canada, China, December 1963-June 1965.

File 864/I39.
Diplomatic representation, representation of other countries in Canada, India, May 1964-September 1965.

File 864/I42.
Diplomatic representation, representation of other countries in Canada, Indonesia, May 1964-August 1965.

File 864/I65.
Diplomatic representation, representation of other countries in Canada, Iran, October 1964-September 1965.

File 864/J35.
Diplomatic representation, representation of other countries in Canada, Japan, March 1963-April 1965.

File 864/K84S.
Diplomatic representation, representation of other countries in Canada, South Korea, June l964-August 1965.

Volume 289.

File 864/P152.
Diplomatic representation, representation of other countries in Canada, Pakistan, June 1963-September 1965.

File 864/T364.
Diplomatic representation, representation of other countries in Canada, Thailand, September 1963-October 1964.

File 864/T939.
Diplomatic representation, representation of other countries in Canada, Turkey, January 1964-September 1965.

File 264/T939, Conf.
Diplomatic representation, representation of other countries in Canada, Turkey, confidential, October-November 1965.

Secret Subject files, 1963-1965. 1 metre (volumes 318-322).

Volume 318.

File 139/I39, Secret.
Air forces operations, India, secret.

Volume 321.

File 820.21, Secret.
Canada and the United Nations, peace-keeping operations, Cyprus crises, secret.

File 840/I30, Rann of Kutch.
Canada and foreign countries, India, Rann of Kutch, secret.

File 840/M241, Secret.
Canada and foreign countries, Malaya, secret.

File 8450/S716, Secret.
Canada and foreign countries, Singapore, secret.

Volume 322.

File 845/C996, Secret.
Canada and foreign countries, international situations, Cyprus, secret.

Volume 322.

File 845/I41V666, Crisis,1964, Secret.
Black binder, Vietnam background, 22 September 1964.

File 845/I41V666.
Canada and foreign countries, international situations, Vietnam crisis, 1965, secret.

File 845/I41V666, Commission, Secret.
Canada and foreign countries, international situations, Vietnam crisis, Commission, secret.

File 845/I41V666, Crisis,1965.
Canada and foreign countries, international situations, Vietnam crisis, 1965, President Johnson policy.

File 845/P152, Cease-fire proposal, Secret.
Canada and foreign countries, international situations, Pakistan, Cease-fire proposal, secret.

File 846/I65, Secret.
Canada and foreign countries, visits, Iran, secret.

File 846/M241, Secret.
Canada and foreign countries, visits, Malaysia, secret.

File 864/B962, Secret.
Diplomatic representation, representations of other countries in Canada, Burma, secret.

File 864/I39, Secret.
Diplomatic representation, representation of other countries in Canada, India, secret.

Prime Minister's Office correspondence, N4 series, 1965-1968, originals, 61 metres (volumes 1-301).

Volume 12.

File 008.
Visits of heads of state and governments, Burma, May 1967.

File 008.
Visits of heads of state and governments, India, June-July 1967.

Volume 13.

File 008.
Visits of heads of state and governments, Iran, June 1967.

File 008.
Visits of heads of state and governments, Japan, July 1967.

File 008.
Visits of heads of state and governments, Korea, June 1967.

File 008.
Visits of heads of state and governments, Republic of China, October 1967.

File 008.
Visits of heads of state and governments, Thailand, June 1967.

Volume 32.

File 045.
Language and ethnic groups, Armenian, July 1966-July 1967.

Volume 32.

File 045.
Language and ethnic groups, Chinese, November 1965-August 1967.

File 045.
Language and ethnic groups, Japanese, September 1966.

Volume 39.

File 154.2/I39, Conf.
Defense research, atomic research, atomic research plant, India, confidential, December 1966.

Volume 40.

File 183.
War, Korea, January 1967.

Volume 94.

File 313.25/I939.
Turkey, September-October 1966.

Volume 120.

File 313.45/I39, Conf.
Prime Minister of Canada, travel, trips, visits, etc., official visits, India, confidential, July 1966.

Volume 157.

File 380/I39.21.
Governments of other countries, India, Prime Minister, January-November 1966.

Volume 158.

File 380/I67, Conf.
Governments of other countries, India, Prime Minister, death of, January 1966.

File 380/J35, Conf.
Governments of other countries, Japan, cabinet, Prime Minister, February 1967.

File 380/J35.21.
Governments of other countries, Japan, cabinet, Prime Minister, February 1967.

File 380/M241.21.
Governments of other countries, Malaysia, Prime Minister, November 1965.

File 380/P152.1.
Governments of other countries, Pakistan, heads of state, December 1965-May 19867.

File 380/P551.1.
Governments of other countries, Philippines, heads of state, December 1965.

Volume 158.

File 380/T939.l.
Governments of other countries, Turkey, heads of state, August 1966.

Volume 191.

File 571/J35, Conf.
Immigration and citizenship, immigration policy and administration, Japan, confidential, January-February 1966.

Volume 220.

File 722/C539.1.
Foreign trade, trade by countries, Communist China, December 1965-March 1968.

File 722/J35.
Foreign trade, trade by countries, Japan, April 1966-

October 1967.

File 722/K84S.
Foreign trade, trade by countries, Korea, South, April 1966.

Volume 237.

File 802/C425.
World relations, economic assistance abroad, Ceylon, May 1966-March 1968.

File 802/I39.
World relations, economic assistance abroad, India, December 1965-April 1968.

Volume 238.

File 802/I41 V666-S, Pers. and Conf.
World relations, economic assistance abroad, Indo-China, Vietnam South, personal and confidential, February 1968.

File 802/K845.
World relations, economic assistance abroad, Korea, South, February 1966-November 1967.

File 802/M241.
World relations, economic assistance abroad, Malaysia, May 1967.

File 802/P152.
World relations, economic assistance abroad, Pakistan, June 1966-January 1967.

File 802/P551.
World relations, economic assistance abroad, Philippines, March-May 1966.

File 805.
World relations, the Colombo Plan, February 1966-February 1967.

File 805.4.
World relations, the Colombo Plan, information, January 1966-May 1967.

Volume 239.

File 811/I39.
Canada and the Commonwealth, Commonwealth members, India, January 1967.

Volume 242.

File 821/C539.1, Conf.
Canada and the United Nations, United Nations membership, China, Communist China, September 1966-October 1967.

File 821/C539.11.
Canada and the United Nations, United Nations membership, Communist China, recognition, November 1965-June 1967.

File 821/C539.11, Conf.
Canada and the United Nations. United Nations membership, Communist China, Recognition, confidential, November 1966.

Volume 245.

File 840/B962.
Canada and foreign countries, Burma, January 1966-December 1967.

File 840/C425.
Canada and foreign countries, Ceylon, May 1967-March 1968.
1967.

File 840/C425, Conf.
Canada and foreign countries, Ceylon, confidential, April-June 1967
File 840/C539.
Canada and foreign countries, China, June 1967.

File 840/C539, Conf.
Canada and foreign countries, China, confidential, March 1966.

File 840/C539.1.
Canada and foreign countries, Communist China, December 1966-June 1967.

File 840/C539.1, Conf.
Canada and foreign countries, Communist China, confidential, July-August 1967.

File 840/C539.11.
Canada and foreign countries, Communist China, Recognition of, December 1966.

File 840/C539.11, Conf.
Canada and foreign countries, Communist China, Recognition of, confidential, May-December 1966.

Volume 246.

File 840/H772.
Canada and foreign countries, Hong Kong, May 1967.

File 840/I39.
Canada and foreign countries, India, November 1965-July 1967.

File 840/I39, Conf.
Canada and foreign countries, India, confidential, June-August 1966.

File 840/I41C176.
Canada and foreign countries, Cambodia, January 1966.

File 840/I41l290, Conf.

Canada and foreign countries, Laos, confidential, May-June 1966.

File 840/I42, Conf.
Canada and foreign countries, Indonesia, confidential, June 1966-May 1967.

File 840/I42.
Canada and foreign countries, Iran, May 1966-November 1967.

File 840/I42, Conf.
Canada and foreign countries, Iran, confidential, January 1966-August 1967.

Volume 247.

File 840/J35.
Canada and foreign countries, Japan, December 1963-September 1967.

File 840/M241.
Canada and foreign countries, Malaysia, March 1960-August 1967.

File 840/N287.
Canada and foreign countries, Nauru, January 1968.

File 840/N532.7.
Canada and foreign countries, Territory of New Guinea, January 1968.

File 849/P152.
Canada and foreign countries, Pakistan, September 1967-January 1968.

File 840/P152 Conf.
Canada and foreign countries, Pakistan, confidential, April 1966-April 1967.

File 840/P551.
Canada and foreign countries, Philippines, November 1966-January 1967.

File 840/S617, Conf.
Canada and foreign countries, Singapore, June 1966.

Volume 248.

File 840/T364.
Canada and foreign countries, Thailand, June 1966-June 1967.

File 840/T665.
Canada and foreign countries, Tonga, December 1965.

File 840/T939, Conf.
Canada and foreign countries, Turkey, confidential, June 1966.

File 840/T939, GK Orthodox residents.
Canada and foreign countries, Turkey, Greek Orthodox residents, July 1964-May 1966.

Volume 249.

File 845/I41 V666.
Canada and foreign countries, international situations, Vietnam, January 1966-October 1967.

File 845/I41V666, Conf.
Canada and foreign countries, international situations, Vietnam, confidential, December 1965-August 1966.

File 845/I41V666, Canadian troops.
Canada and foreign countries, international situations, Vietnam, Canadian troops, June 1966-June 1967.

File 845/I41V666, Cdn Volunteer Corps.
Canada and foreign countries, international situations, Vietnam, Canadian Volunteer Corps, February-June 1966.

Volume 250.

File 845/I41V666, Canadian Volunteer Corps, Conf.
Canada and foreign countries, international situations, Vietnam, Canadian Volunteer Corps, confidential, February 1966.

File 845/I41V666, Commission.
Canada and foreign countries, international situations, Vietnam, Commission, February 1966-February 1968.

File 845/I41V666, Commission, Conf.
Canada and foreign countries, international situations, Vietnam, Commission, confidential.

File 845/I41V666, Crisis, S.U.P.A. 1965.
Canada and foreign countries, international situations, Vietnam, crisis 1965, Student Union for Peace Action, November 1965-December 1965.

File 845/I41V666, Crisis, 1965.
Canada and foreign countries, international situations, Vietnam, crisis 1965, November-December 1965.

File 845/I41V666, Crisis,1965, part 1.
Canada and foreign countries, international situations, Vietnam, crisis 1965, part 1, June 1966.

File 845/I41V666, Crisis,1965, part 2.
Canada and foreign countries, international situations, Vietnam, crisis, 1965, part 2, February 1966.

File 845/I41V666, Crisis,1965, part 3.
Canada and foreign countries, international situations, Vietnam, crisis, 1965, part 3.

File 845/I41V666, Crisis,1965, part 4.
Canada and foreign countries, international situations, Vietnam, crisis, 1965, part 4.

File 845/I41V666, Crisis,1965, part 5.
Canada and foreign countries, international situations, Vietnam, crisis, 1965, part 5.

File 845/I41V666, Crisis,1965, part 6.
Canada and foreign countries, international situations, Vietnam, crisis, 1965, part 6.

File 845/I41V666, Crisis,1965, part 7.
Canada and foreign countries, international situations, Vietnam, crisis, 1965, part 7.

File 845/I41V666, Crisis,1965, part 8.
Canada and foreign countries, international situations, Vietnam, crisis, 1965, part 8.

Volume 251.

File 845/I41V666, Crisis, 1965, part 9.
Canada and foreign countries, international situations, Vietnam, crisis, 1965, part 9.

File 845/I41V666, Crisis, 1965, part 10.
Canada and foreign countries, international situations, Vietnam, crisis, 1965, part 10.

File 845/I41V666, Crisis, 1965, part 11.
Canada and foreign countries, international situations, Vietnam, crisis, 1965, part 11.

File 845/I41V666, Crisis,1965, part 12.
Canada and foreign countries, international situations, Vietnam, crisis, 1965, part 12.

File 845/I41V666, Crisis,1965, part 13.
Canada and foreign countries, international situations, Vietnam, crisis, 1965, part 13.

File 845/I41V666, Crisis,1965, part 14.
Canada and foreign countries, international situations, Vietnam, crisis, 1965, part 14.

File 845/I41V666, Crisis,1966, Conf.
Canada and foreign countries, international situations, Vietnam, crisis, 1966, confidential, January-December 1966.

File 845/I41V666, Honolulu Mtg.
Canada and foreign countries, international s ituations, crisis, 1966, Honolulu meeting, February 1966.

File 845/I41V666,1966 Pearson.
Canada and foreign countries, international situations, crisis, 1966, Mr. Anthony Pearson, July-August 1966.

File 845/I41V666,1966, Use of gas.
Canada and foreign countries, international situations, crisis, 1966, use of gas, January 1966-June 1967.

File 845/I41V666,1966.
Canada and foreign countries, international situations, Vietnam, crisis, 1966, U.S.A. prisoners, July-August 1966.

File 845/I41V666,1966, War crimes.
Canada and foreign countries, international situations, Vietnam, crisis, 1966, war crimes, August-September 1966.

File 845/I41V666,1967, part 1.
Canada and foreign countries, international situations, Vietnam, crisis, 1967, part 1, January 1966-January 1967.

Volume 252.

File 845/I41V666,1967, part 2.
Canada and foreign countries, international situations, Vietnam, crisis, 1967, part 2, February 1967.

File 845/I41V666,1967, part 3.
Canada and foreign countries, international situations, Vietnam, crisis, 1967, part 3, March 1967.

File 845/I41V666,1967, part 4.
Canada and foreign countries, international situations, Vietnam, crisis, 1967, part 4, April-15 May 1967.

File 845/I41V666,1967, part 5.
Canada and foreign countries, international situations, Vietnam, crisis, 1967, part 5, 16-19 May 1967.

File 845/I41V666,1967, part 6.
Canada and foreign countries, international situations, Vietnam, crisis, 1967, part 6, 30 May 1967.

File 845/I41V666,1967, part 7(a).
Canada and foreign countries, international situations, Vietnam, crisis, 1967, part 7(a), 31 May 1967.

File 845/I41V666,1967, part 7(b).
Canada and foreign countries, international situations, Vietnam, crisis, 1967, part 7(b), 31 May 1967.

File 845/I41V666,1967, part 8.
Canada and foreign countries, international situations, Vietnam, crisis, 1967, part 8, 1 June 1967 only.

Volume 253.

File 845/I41V666,1967, part 9.
Canada and foreign countries, international situations, Vietnam, crisis, 1967, part 9, 2-14 June 1967.

File 845/I41V666,1967, part 10.
Canada and foreign countries, international situations, Vietnam, crisis, 1967, part 10, 15-30 June 1967.

File 845/I41V666
Canada and foreign countries, international situations, Vietnam, crisis, 1967, part 11, July-September 1967.

File 845/I41V666, Crisis, 1967.
Canada and foreign countries, international situations, Vietnam, crisis, 1967, part 12, October-December 1967.

File 845/I41V666, Crisis, 1967.
Canada and foreign countries, international situations, Vietnam, crisis, 1967, April-June 1967.

File 845/I41V666, Crisis, 1967.
Canada and foreign countries, international situations, Vietnam, crisis, 1967, September 1967.

File 845/I41V666, Crisis, 1967.
Canada and foreign countries, international situations, Vietnam, crisis, 1967, September 1967.

File 845/I41V666, Crisis, 1967 Conf.
Canada and foreign countries, international situations, Vietnam, crisis, 1967, confidential, January-September 1967.

File 845/I41V666, Crisis, 1967 policy.
Canada and foreign countries, international situations, Vietnam, crisis, 1967, policy, June-August 1967.

File 845/I41V666, Crisis, Pers. and Conf.
Canada and foreign countries, international situations, Vietnam, crisis, 1967, personal and confidential, April 1967.

File 845/I41V666, Crisis, 1967, Use of gas.
Canada and foreign countries, international situations, Vietnam, crisis, 1967, use of gas.

Volume 254.

845/I41V666, Crisis,1968 part 1.
Canada and foreign countries, international situations, Vietnam, crisis, 1968 part 1, 1 January 1968-29 February 1968.

File 845/I41V666, Crisis,1968, part 2.
Canada and foreign countries, international situations, Vietnam, crisis, 1968, part 2, 1 March-April 1968.

File 845/I41V666, Crisis,1968.
Canada and foreign countries, international situations, Vietnam, crisis, 1968, March 1968.

File 845/I41V666, Crisis,1968, Conf.
Canada and foreign countries, international situations, Vietnam, crisis, 1968, confidential, March-April 1968.

File 845/I41V666, Crisi,1968, Pers. and Conf.
Canada and foreign countries, international situations, Vietnam, crisis, 1968, personal and confidential, January-March 1968.

File 845/I41V666, Crisis,1968, Pers. and Conf.
Canada and foreign countries, international situations, Vietnam, crisis, 1968, personal and confidential, September 1967.

File 845/I41V666, Crisis,1968, Use of gas.
Canada and foreign countries, international situations, Vietnam, crisis, 1968, use of gas, January 1968.

File 845/I41V666, Five Power Mtg., Conf.
Canada and foreign countries, international situations, Vietnam, Five Power meeting, confidential, September 1967-March 1968.

File 845/I41V666, March on Ottawa.
Canada and foreign countries, international situations, Indo-China Vietnam, March on Ottawa, February-March 1966.

File 845/I41V666, March on Ottawa, Conf.
Canada and foreign countries, international situations, Indo-China, Vietnam, March on Ottawa, confidential, March 1966.

File 845/I41V666, Ottawa Committee to End the War in Vietnam.
Canada and foreign countries, international situations, Vietnam, Ottawa Committee to End the War in Vietnam, February 1966-November 1967.

File 845/K84N.
Canada and foreign countries, international situations, Korea, North, January-April 1968.

File 845/K84S.
Canada and foreign countries, international situations, Korea, South, March 1968.

Volume 257.

File 845.4 Tibetan.
Canada and foreign countries, international situations, refugees, Tibetan, March 1966-November 1967.

File 846/I39.
Canada and foreign countries, visits, India, April 1966-October 1967.

File 846/I39, Conf.
Canada and foreign countries, visits, India, confidential, June 1967-January 1968.

File 846/I41V666, Conf.
Canada and foreign countries, visits, Vietnam, confidential, May 1966-October 1967.

File 846/I65.

Canada and foreign countries, visits, Iran, December 1966.

File 846/I65, Conf.
Canada and foreign countries, visits, Iran, confidential, September 1967.

File 846/J35.
Canada and foreign countries, visits, Japan, April-December 1967.

File 846/J35, Conf.
Canada and foreign countries, visits, Japan, confidential, May-December 1967.

Volume 262.

File 846/K84S.
Canada and foreign countries, visits, Korea, South, December 1966-June 1967.

File 846/M241.
Canada and foreign countries, visits, Malaysia, May-September 1967.

File 846/M241, Pers. and Conf.
Canada and foreign countries, visits, Malaysia, personal and confidential, January 1968.

File 846/S627, Pers. and Conf.
Canada and foreign countries, visits, Singapore, personal and confidential, December 1967-April 1968.

File 846/T364.
Canada and foreign countries, visits, Thailand, June l964-March 1968.

File 846/T939.
Canada and foreign countries, visits, Turkey, confidential, August-September 1967.

Volume 265.

File 861/C425.
Diplomatic representation, Canadian representation abroad, Ceylon, May 1967-February 1968.

File 861/C539.
Diplomatic representation, Canadian representation abroad, China, September 1966-February 1967.

File 861/H772.
Diplomatic representation, Canadian representation abroad, Hong Kong, May 1967.

File 861/I39.
Diplomatic representation, Canadian representation abroad, India, November 1965-March 1968.

File 861/I39, Conf.
Diplomatic representation, Canadian representation abroad, India, confidential, August 1966.

File 861/I39, Pers. and Conf.
Diplomatic representation, Canadian representation abroad, India, personal and confidential, October 1965-April 1967.

File 861/I41V666, Conf.
Diplomatic representation, Canadian representation abroad, Vietnam, confidential, January 1967.

Volume 266.

File 861/J35.
Diplomatic representation, Canadian representation abroad, Japan, May-December 1967.

File 861/M241.
Diplomatic representation, Canadian representation abroad, Malaysia, August-November 1967.

File 861/S617.
Diplomatic representation, Canadian representation abroad, Singapore, August 1967-February 1968.

File 861/T364.
Diplomatic representation, Canadian representation abroad, Thailand, February-March 1967.

File 861/T939.
Diplomatic representation, Canadian representation abroad, Turkey, July 1966.

Volume 267.

File 864/C539.
Diplomatic representation, representation of other countries in Canada, China, November 1965-December 1967.

File 864/C539, Conf.
Diplomatic representation, representation of other countries in Canada, China, confidential, February-August 1967.

File 864/I39.
Diplomatic representation, representation of other countries in Canada, India, January 1966-June 1968.

File 864/I39,Conf.
Diplomatic representation, representation of other countries in Canada, India, confidential, July 1966.

File 864/I42.
Diplomatic representation, Diplomatic representation of other countries in Canada, Indonesia, December 1965-March 1968.

File 864/I65.
Diplomatic representation, Diplomatic representation of other countries in Canada, Iran, January 1966-May 1967.

Volume 268.

File 864/I65, Conf.
Diplomatic representation, Diplomatic representation

of other countries in Canada, Iran, Confidential, May 1967.

File 864/J35.
Diplomatic representation, Diplomatic representation of other countries in Canada, Japan, May 1966-February 1968.

File 864/K84S.
Diplomatic representation, Diplomatic representation of other countries in Canada, Korea, South, December 1965-March 1968.

File 864/M241.
Diplomatic representation, Diplomatic representation of other countries in Canada, Malaysia, February-September 1967.

File 864/N439, Conf.
Diplomatic representation, Diplomatic representation of other countries in Canada, Nepal, Confidential, May 1966.

File 864/P152.
Diplomatic representation, Diplomatic representation of other countries in Canada, Pakistan, March 1966-January 1967.

File 864/P152, Conf.
Diplomatic representation, Diplomatic representation of other countries in Canada, Pakistan Confidential, February-March 1966.

File 864/T364.
Diplomatic representation, Diplomatic representation of other countries in Canada, Thailand, May 1967.

File 864/T939.
Diplomatic representation, Diplomatic representation of other countries in Canada, Turkey, December 1965-December 1967.

File 864/T939, Conf.
Diplomatic representation, Diplomatic representation of other countries in Canada, Turkey, Confidential, January 1966.

Prime Minister's Office Correspondence, 1965-1968. Secretariat Series.

Volume 277.

File 313-312 D-F.
Prime Minister of Canada, Requests and Appeals, interview Delegations Faculty Committee on Vietnam, Secret, 5 January-16 March 1967.

File 313.45/I39, Secret.
Prime Minister of Canada, Travel Trips, Visits, etc. Official Visits, India, Secret, 8 June-10 August 1966.

File 380/I39.21.
Governments of other countries, India, Cabinet, Prime Minister, Secret, 12 July-10 August 1966.

Volume 279.

File 821-C539.1, Secret.
Canada and the United Nations. United Nations Membership, China, Communist China, 27 November 1966 only.

File 821-C539.1, Secret.
Canada and the United Nations. United Nations. Communist China, Recognition of, Secret, 12 July-17 November 1966.

File 821-C539.1, Secret.
Canada and the United Nations. United Nations. Communist China, Recognition of, Secret, 12 December 1966-9 February 1967.

Volume 280.

File 845/I41V666, Crisis,1965 Secret.
Canada and foreign countries, International Situations, Vietnam Crisis, 1965, Secret, 28 December 1965 only.

Volume 281.

File 845/I41V666, Crisis,1966 Honolulu Meeting, Secret.
Canada and foreign countries, International Situations, Vietnam Crisis, 1966, Honolulu Meeting, Secret, 10 March 1966.

File 845/I41V666, Crisis,1967
Canada and foreign countries, International Situations, Vietnam Crisis, 1967, Secret, February-June 1967.

File 845/I41V666, Crisis,1968.
Canada and foreign countries, International Situations, Vietnam Crisis, 1968, 9 January-14 February 1968.

File 845/I41V666, Commission, Secret.
Canada and foreign countries, International Situations, Vietnam Commission, Secret, 30-31 July 1967.

File 845/I41V666. Vietnam Truce, 1966, Secret.
Canada and foreign countries, International Situations, Vietnam Truce 1966, Secret, 29 December 1965-19 January 1966.

Post-April 1968 Papers, N5 series, 1968-1972, Originals, 13.2 metres(volumes 1-65)

Commission on International Development, chaired by LBP in August 1968, to study consequences of previous twenty years of development assistance and to propose policies for the future. Findings of the Commission was "Partners in Development"(1969). Series consists of administrative files of LBP and his assistant Albert F.Hearst, research papers, drafts of the report and press coverage.

Commission on International Development.

L.B.Pearson Files.

Volume 1.

Proposals and suggestions, August 1968-October 1969.

Volume 2.

Correspondence, November 1968-October 1969. Seminars and conferences, include Bangkok, 7-16 March 1969, and trips, Africa-Asia, November 1969-October 1969(include India, Japan, Pakistan and Singapore).

Volume 3.

A.F.Hearst files.

Volume 4.

Trips and conferences include:
Ankara, August 1968-June 1969.
India and Pakistan, September 1968-June 1969.

Volume 5.

Japan, September 1967-July 1969.
Singapore, January-April 1969.

Volume 6.

SP/M5a
R.Gauhati, Debt Problems, February 1969.
B.Jalan, Debt Servicing Capacity, January-February 1969.
D.P.Ghat, Issues in Trade Policy, February 1969.

Staff Papers and Commissioned Studies(unnumbered series)

Bhattachajee, A . The Effects of Different Growth Rates, April 1969.

Dapice, David. Costs and Benefits of PL 480 Programs, May 1969.

Employment in Agriculture and Migration to the Cities(India) n.d.

Japan. Economic Research Center. Aid Philosophy and Mechanisms in Japan. March 1969.

Volume 7.

Lateef, K.S. Foreign Investments in India, April 1969.

Lateef, K.S. Technical Assistance-India, April 1969.

Narain, D. Agricultural Programmes and Prospects(India) April 1969.

Srinivasan, T.R. Impact of Variations in the Supply of Foreign Resources on the Growth of the Indian Economy, (1969-1970-1980-1984) March 1969.

Stern, J.J. and Falcon, W.P. Pakistan's Growth and Development Policies, May 1969.

Thailand: Political and Historical Background. n.d.

Yanal, O. A Brief Survey of Turkish Economic Development. May 1969.

Volume 8.

Malaysia. Memorandum on Malaysia's Development Experience. April 1969.

Chenoy, R.R. Notes on Indian Union Budget for 1969-1970, 1969.

Singh, K. Comments on High Commissioner's Speech in Jammu, India, February 1969.

Turkey. Basic Aspects of Turkey's Development Planning and Policies, June 1969.

General Subject Files, 1958-1968.

Volume 6.

China. Recognition of Communist China.

Pearson Statements, 1958-1969.

Paul Martin to NATO.

Ministerial Council, 1959-1964.

Hansard Statements, 1959-19643.

Memorandum, 19 February 1959.

China. Representation at U.N.

November 1966. Early Memoranda for Prime Minister, May-July 1966.

Memoranda for Prime Minister on Canadian Strategy and Proceedings, 4-28 November 1966.

Volume 7.

China. Representation at U.N.

Proposed Canadian Resolution and Amendments, November 1966.

Memorandum to Prime Minister on Cabinet Discussion, 15 November 1966.

U.S. reaction, Memoranda and Correspondence, November 1966.

Japanese reaction. Memoranda, July-November 1966.

Japanese reaction.
Canadian Press Story, Memoranda, 9 November 1966.

Japanese reaction.
Speech to U.N. by Paul Martin, 23 November 1966.

Statements and Replies to Anticipated Questions, by the Prime Minister, November 1966-1967.
Communism.

Statements by Pearson, 1960-1962.

Pearson and Communism.

Correspondence, 1958-1961.

Press Clippings, 1958-1962.

Cyprus Riots.

August 1964. Pearson Diary and Notes.

August 1964. U Thant Statement.

Hansard Clippings, 10 August 1964.

Far East Situation, 1958 and Background Material.

India. Reports of Conversations with the High Commissioner, subject: Tashkent, China, Wheat, Vietnam, Kuala Lumpur, Conference on Tensions in Development, February 1964, Conference on Development and Cooperation in the South Asia Pacific Region. Report on Conference by Nick Gavett.

Volume 9.

Tashkent Meeting. Canadian Note to Soviet Union, on Participation in Tashkent Meeting, 25 January 1966.

Trade, Wheat sales to China, 1963.

Volume 10.

Vietnam.

Memoranda for Prime Minister on developments, 1966-

Correspondence and memoranda with U.S., 1965-1966.

Correspondence with Ho Chi Minh, 24 January 1966.

Statement in the House of Commons, 1965-1968.

Pearson Statements, April 1965. Persian Gulf.

Miscellaneous Statements on the War. Newspaper articles.

Correspondence, Faculty Committee on Vietnam, Victoria College, January-February 1967.

Volume 20.

Canadian Memorial Service, Japan, 1967.

China, Speech by Shushi Hsu re recognition of Communist China, 25 November 1965.

Pearson N8 Series.

Diaries and Personal Papers.

Volume 1.

Diary of the activities of the Cease Fire Committee of the United Nations, 1950-1951.

Closed:

Black binder containing diary entries concerning:

Korean Discussion, November 1952.

Day-to-Day Entries, January-March 1952.

Nine-Power Conference, London, September 1954.

Commonwealth Prime Ministers' Conference, London, January-February 1955.

Visit to the Soviet Union, South and Southeast Asia and the Middle East, September-November 1955.

O. Trudeau, Pierre Elliot, 1919-

Prime Minister, 1967-1984.

Original, 1965-1984, 684.92 metres Microfilm, 1975-1978, 31 reels, H-1834-H-1864. Finding aid 1900.

Recieved on security deposit from Mr.Trudeau from 1974-1980. Transferred to the National Archives of Canada 1986-1992. Closed for thirty years. Restrictions to be determined after thirty years.

Includes 15 file-card indexes and 156 computer-printout indexes(combined total of 1,043,136 pages) relating to the various Prime Minister's Office Correspondence Series.

Manuscript Group 27. Political figures 1867-1950.

I. Cabinet ministers, 1867-1896.

MG 27 IC. Lieutenant-Governors, 1867-1896.

Chapleau, Joseph Adolphe.
Minister and Controller of Customs, January-November 1892. MG 27 IC3.
Customs was responsible for Chinese immigration from 1885-1911.

MG 27 ID. Cabinet Ministers, 1867-1896.

Costigan, John.
Acting Minister of Trade and Industry, January 1896.
MG 27 ID5. Trade and Industry responsible for Chinese.

MG 27 IE. Members of the House of Commons and Senate, 1867-1896

Wallace, Nathaniel Clarke.
Minister and Controller of Customs, December 1892-March 1893. MG 27 IE36.
Customs was responsible for Chinese immigration from 1885-1911

MG 27 II. Cabinet Ministers, 1896-1921.

MG 27 IIC. Lieutenant-Governors, 1896-1921.

Brodeur, Louis Philipe, 1862-1924.
Ottawa. Minister.
Original, 52 cm. transcripts, 1.5 cm, photocopies, 33 pages, microfilm, 22 reels, 1838, 1891, 1904-1943. MG 27 IIC4.

Correspondence, memoranda, newspaper clippings, articles, drafts of speeches, and of the Naval bill, conference proceedings and background pages including the l907, l908 and l911 Imperial Conferences. ULM 4

MG 27 IID. Cabinet Ministers, 1896-1921

Cartwright, Richard John.
Minister of Trade and Industry from July 1896-May 1911. MG 27 IID4
Trade and Industry was responsible for Chinese immigration from 1893-1911

Foster, George Eulas, 1847-1921.
Teacher and Cabinet Minister.
Originals, 1867-1931, 32 feet, 2 inches. Finding aid 64. MG 27 IID7.

Political papers:
Notes, n.d., and 1909-1921. Originals, 1 foot, 8 inches(volumes 11, 76b-77 and 110-112)
Includes an autobiographical sketch, and an account of a trip to Australia, New Zealand and the Far East, 1913(volume 1)

Lemieux, Rodolph, 1866-1937.
Minister of Labour and Postmaster General.
Papers. MG 27 IID10
Signed "gentlemen's agreement" with Count Hayashi, Japanese Minister of Foreign Affairs.

Mission au Japon, 1907-1908.
Originaux, 13 pouces(volumes 3-9)
Arrangée en ordre chronologique(volumes 3-7) et compte rendu de la mission (volumes 8-9), consistent en un rapport imprimé, en mémoires et en dépêches officielles.

King, William Lyon MacKenzie.
MacKenzie King, memo. on his mission to England, 2 May 1908, securing cooperation on Indian immigration problem.

Sifton, Arthur Lewis, 1859-1921.
Politician.
Originals, 1883-1921, 1.3 metres Finding aid 816. MG 27 II D19.

Attended the Paris Peace Conference of 1918-1919. Subject files include Paris Peace Conference, 1918-1919, 10cm.(volume 5-6)

MG 27 III.. Cabinet ministers, 1921-1950.

MG 27 IIIB.. Cabinet Ministers, 1921-1948.

Gouin, Lomer, 1861-
Papers, 1888-1929, 23 feet, microfilm C2335-C2371. Finding aid 167. MG 27 IIIB4.

Correspondence, 1922-1929, volume 25-29, 5 feet.

Volume 25.

File 6.
Asiatic Exclusion League(Mrs. M.Barber) 1923 Treaty with Japan.

Volume 30.

File 52.
Dr. Joseph Gavreau. Against participation in a European war(Turkey 1922)

Volume 35.

File 96.
A.W.Neill. 1922-1924 Asian migration

Volume 61.

File 91.
Politique internationale en général. Turquie.

MacKenzie, Ian Alistair.
Member of Parliament from British Columbia and Cabinet Minister under MacKenzie King.
Papers. MG 27 IIIB5.

Volume 19.

J.H.McVety, General Superintendent, British Columbia Office, Employment Service of Canada to Gordon Sloan, April 15, 1935. Re relief to Chinese and Japanese.

Volumes. 24, 25 and 32.

MacKenzie's belief that his anti-Asian stand inhibited the Canadian Commonwealth Federation in British Columbia.

Volume 32, X-81.

Conference on the Japanese problem in British Columbia, report, and Ian MacKenzie to W.L.MacKenzie King.

Stevens, H.H.
Member of Parliament from British Columbia and Cabinet Minister under R.B.Bennett.
Papers. MG 27 IIIB9.

Volumes 1, 3,12, 22 on Oriental immigration and correspondence with H.H.Marler, 1911-1934

Dupre, Maurice, 1888-1941.
Solicitor general.
Originals, 1919-34, 3 feet. MG 27 IIIB16.

Papers relating to the Imperial Conference, 1930; correspondence, memoranda, confidential prints, and clippings. Geneva Disarmament Conference, 1932: Correspondence, memoranda, confidential prints and clippings. Materials on political affairs, 1929-1934, mostly clippings, also correspondence and memoranda.
ULM

Ralston, James Layton.
Minister of National Defense, 1940-1941.
Papers, Finding aid 533. MG 27 IIIB17.

Public papers, 1935-1948.

House of Commons.

General, 1940-1944.

Volume 69.

Hong Kong enquiry, 1942.

Volume 73.

Canadian American coastal defence talks, 1943. Attu, Aleutians.

Military, 1939-1948.

Volume 40.

Casablanca, Japanese shipping situation, 1943.

Volume 46.

Far Eastern situation, conference re London, 1940.

Volume 49.

Indian situation, 1946.

Canadian army participation in the war against Japan, 1944

Volume 61.

Employment of Canadian army, Far East, 1944.

Hanson, Richard Burpee.
Conservative party leader, and wartime leader of the opposition.
Papers. MG 27 IIIB22.
Volume 92.

FIle on the Japanese consisting of a mimeographed report issued by the British Columbia Security Commission on the "Removal of Japanese from protected areas", 4 March-31 October 1942.

MG 27 IIIC. Members of the House of Commons and the Senate, 1921-1950.

Nielsen, Dorise Winnifred(Webber), 1902-1980.
Canada and People's Republic of China, politician.
MG 27 IIIC30.

Memoirs, n.d. detailing Nielsen's early life in Britain and Canada, prior to her political career; correspondence, memoranda, notes and ephemera, 1938-1976, relating to her Canadian political career and associates and to her life in China; political notebooks and travel journals, n.d., 1964-1977, dealing with Chinese topics.
ULM 4

MG 27 IIIE. Consuls and diplomatic representatives.

Kirkwood, Kenneth P., 1899-1968.
Diplomat.
Originals, 1901-1978, 1.66 metres. Photocopies, 1929-1939, 12 cm. Finding aid 398. MG 27 IIIE3.

On the staff of the International College, Smyrna, 2nd secretary to the Canadian Legation, Tokyo, 1929-1939, High Commissioner to Pakistan, 1952-1954

Volume 1.

"Turkish journal - Smyrna blue", 2 cm.
Turkish travels and impressions while on staff of International College at Smyrna, 1922-1925. Comments on Dr. Alexander MacLachlan, 234 pages, typescript.

"Fair house, a bachelor's musings" - 1.7 cm. Tokyo, 1931, 169 pages typescript.

A journal of travel through Soviet Russia, Siberia and Manchuria(Russian journal) 2 cm. May 1932, 209 pages typescript.

Journal of a tour through Formosa. 1.3 cm. October 1932, 134 pages typescript.

Journal of a tour of China. 1.8cm. September 1933, 194 pages typescript and photographs

Journal of a tour through Korea, 2.3 cm. July 1935, 215

pages typescript and photographs.

Journal of a tour through Hokkaido, Japan. 2 cm. July 1930, typescript.

Volume 2.

Journal of travels in Japan, summer of 1934, 2.5 cm. typescript.

Diplomatic diary, Canadian Legation, Tokyo, part I.1929-1931. 2.5 cm. typescript. The diary and journal contain descriptions of places Kirkwood visited. He comments on the people he meets and the political, social and cultural life. His interests extended beyond Japan to world affairs in general.

Scrapbook, Canadian Legation, part II, 1930, 1 cm.

Manchurian journal, 1931, 2 cm. typescript.

1932 journal, 1.8 cm. typescript. Includes the Japanese attitude towards Manchuria and fellow diplomats as Hugh Keenleyside and U.S. ambassador, Joseph Clark Grew

Volume 3.

1933-1935 journals. 3.7 cm. typescript. Comments on world affairs, observations of life in Japan, descriptions of events at the legation and comments on colleagues

Volume 4.

The Buddhist pantheon in Japanese arts. 3 cm. typescript, 1934

Volume 5.

Essays while in Tokyo.

The Tokyo revolt, a diary, 26-29 February 1936.

Tokyo's four days - a dramatic narrative and synopsis, 26-29 February 1936.

Gulliver in Japan.

The Imperial cherry blossom garden party, 27 April 1930.

An Imperial duck-netting party, 17 March 1930.

Kamakura, 1 December 1929.

English poetry in relation to Japan.

Volume 6. Press clippings.

Turkey, 1922-1925.

Japan, 1929-1938.

Pakistan, 1951-1954.

Dr. Herbert Norman, 1957-1977.

MG 27 IIIG. Related political papers.

Reid, Escott Meredith, 1905-
Diplomat.
Photocopies, 1918-1969, 1 foot. transcripts, 1930-1932, 2 inches. Finding aid 54. MG 27 IIIG5

High Commissioner in India from 1952-1957, and from 1962-1966, Director of Operations in South Asia and the Middle East for the World Bank

Manuscript Group 28. Records of Post-Confederation corporate bodies.

MG 28 I.. Societies and associations.

Theatre Canada. Finding aid 438. MG 28 I50.

Volume 143. Chinese Musical Society of Vancouver, 1974.

National Council of Young Men's Christian Associations of Canada. est.. 1912.
Originals n.d., 1856-1978, 62.5 metres MG 28 I95.

Volume 169.

2. Y.M.C.A. Ceylon. Correspondence, 1955-1972.

3. Y.M.C.A. China. Reports(1), 1920-1931.

4. Y.M.C.A. China. Reports(2), 1920-1931.

5. Y.M.C.A. China. Scrapbook of newspaper clippings, 1928-1930.

6. Y.M.C.A. China. Miscellaneous, 1930-1934.

7. Y.M.C.A. China. Miscellaneous(1),1931-1933.

8. Y.M.C.A. China. Miscellaneous(2), 1931-1933.

Volume 172.

7. Y.M.C.A. India. Miscellaneous 1923-1933.

8. Y.M.C.A. India. Correspondence, 1931-1936.

9. Y.M.C.A. India. Burma and Ceylon, Miscellaneous, 1938-1947.

10. Y.M.C.A. India. Correspondence, 1935-1938.

11. Y.M.C.A. India. Burma and Ceylon, miscellaneous, 1938-1947.

12. Y.M.C.A. India. Miscellaneous(1), 1938-1958.

13. Y.M.C.A. India. Miscellaneous(2), 1938-1958.

14. Y.M.C.A. India. Miscellaneous, 1939-1946.

Volume 173.

1. Y.M.C.A. India. Correspondence, 1952-1958.

2. Y.M.C.A. India. Hamilton-Mangalore project, 1970.
Volume 174.

12. Y.M.C.A. Japan. Miscellaneous(1), 1962-1968.

13. Y.M.C.A. Japan. Miscellaneous(2), 1962-1968.

14. Y.M.C.A. Korea. Miscellaneous, 1930-1934.

15. Y.M.C.A. Transfer of funds from Canadian aid to China fund, 1951-1952.

Volume 175.

3. Y.M.C.A. Malaya. Correspondence, 1952-1956.

4. Y.M.C.A. Malaya. Correspondence, 1955-1956.

7. Y.M.C.A. New Guinea. Vancouver-New Guinea project, 1969.

8. Y.M.C.A. New Guinea. Vancouver-New Guinea project(1), 1970-1971.

9. Y.M.C.A. New Guinea. Vancouver-New Guinea project(2), 1970-1971.

10. Y.M.C.A. New Guinea. Vancouver-New Guinea project(3), 1970-1971.

11. Y.M.C.A. New Guinea. Vancouver-New Guinea project, 1970-1973.

12. Y.M.C.A. New Guinea. Vancouver-New Guinea project, 1972-1973.

13. Y.M.C.A. New Guinea. National Council project, 1973.

Volume 176.

1. Pakistan. Correspondence, 1955-1956.

3. Y.M.C.A. Philippine Islands. Miscellaneous, 1933-1934.

4. Y.M.C.A. Philippine Islands. Miscellaneous, 1935-1951.

12. Y.M.C.A. Siam. Correspondence, 1933.

13. Y.M.C.A. Siam. Miscellaneous, 1935-1956

18. Y.M.C.A. Thailand. Miscellaneous, 1953-1970.

19. Y.M.C.A. Thailand. Chiang Mai-Sarnia, Windsor and Chatham project 1970.

20. Y.M.C.A. Thailand. Chiang Mai-Sarnia, Windsor and Chatham project 1970.

21. Y.M.C.A. Thailand. Chiang Mai-Sarnia, Windsor.

and Chatham project(1) 1971.

22. Y.M.C.A. Thailand. Chiang Mai-Sarnia, Windsor and Chatham project(2) 1971.

23. Y.M.C.A. Thailand. Chiang Mai-Sarnia, Windsor and Chatham project(1) 1972.

24. Y.M.C.A. Thailand. Chiang Mai-Sarnia, Windsor and Chatham project(2) 1972.

Volume 177.

1. Y.M.C.A. Thailand. Chiang Mai-Sarnia, Windsor and Chatham project. includes photographs,1972-1974.

2. Y.M.C.A. Thailand. Contract Thailand project, 1973-1974.

10. Y.M.C.A. Turkey. Miscellaneous, 1933-1949.

11. Y.M.C.A. Turkey. Camp leadership program, 1970-1971.

Volume 185.

15. Aid to refugees and migrants. Vietnam projects. Correspondence, 1967-1969.

Canadian Commission for UNESCO.
Finding aid 725. MG 28 I97.

UNESCO Fellows, 1957-1963.
From, including Pakistan, India, Turkey, Japan, Malaya, Indonesia and Burma.

Files 64-79.
Regional Cultures study grants.

Volume 6.

Files 80-83.
Japan, Taiwan, Hong Kong.

Volume 13.

File 170.
Ceylon Association of Teachers of Western Music, Speech, and Dramatic Art, 1963. Correspondence.

File 173.
Japanese Regional Seminar on the Museum.

File 175.
Japanese folk tales.

Volume 14.

File 186.
East-West major project, 1963-1964. International Conference of Orientalists in Delhi.

Volume 15.

File 211.
Indian National Commissions, 1963.
Survey on research in social sciences and humanities in and concerning Asia, Correspondence.

File 214.
International Conference of Orientalists, New Delhi, 1962-1963, Correspondence.

File 217.
International Symposium in Fine Art in the East and West, Tokyo, 1966.

Young Women's Christian Association of Canada.
Finding aid 926.MG 28 I198.

Volume 35. World Service.

Caroline MacDonald, National Secretary to Japan. Correspondence, 1904-1931.

Study kit. Vietnam, 1964-1967.

Volume 36.

Work in Japan, 1959-1965.
Work in Pakistan and Ghana, 1965.

Japanese Women's tour of Canada and U.S., 1966.

United Nations Association in Canada. est. 1946.
Original 8 metres n.d. 1953-1977. MG 28 I202.

Correspondence and memoranda on administration, educational services, membership projects, and the Habitat Conference in Vancouver, British Columbia, 1976, included are projects, like the Canada/Mysore project, 1965-1967, International cooperation year, 1963-1965, the Peace Rose project, 1966-1970. and Civil Liberties, 1967-1971.
ULM 4

Voice of Women, est. 1960.
Women's peace organization.
Ontario Voice of Women knitting project for Vietnamese children, 1966-1977. Originals 1.8 metres(Volume 24-32) MG 28 I218.

Correspondence and printed material related to the knitting project.

Canadian Institute of International Affairs/Institut Canadien des Affaires internationales.
Originals, 1911, 1925-1967. 4.4 metres. Microfilm, 5 reels, M-4618 to M-4622. Finding aid 1081.
Papers presented to the National Archives of Canada in 1976 and 1978. Microfilmed by the National Archives on five reels, M-4618 to M-4622.

Minute Books, 1928-1961.
Minute books of the Institute.
1932-1961. 66 cm.(volumes 1-4)
Papers relating to various conferences, miscellaneous correspondence relating to World Affairs and general information on both the Canadian Institute of International Affairs and the Institute of Pacific Relations. There is also included some personal material concerning Edgar J.Tarr.

Volume 1.

Correspondence, 1932-1950.

Volume 2.

Conferences.
Atlantic Conference, 1941-1942.
British Commonwealth Conference: Agenda Committee, 1937.
British Commonwealth Relations Conference - London, 1945. 1943-1945.
Commonwealth Nations Conference 1948-1949.
International Studies Conference 1937, 1940.
Montebello Conference 1943.
Sydney Conference, 1937-1938.

General
Reid, Escott - special memorandum - "The Future of the Institute" 1938.

Rockefeller Foundation, 1936-1944.

World Affairs.
Correspondence, 1936-1943.

Volume 3.

World Affairs.

Conferences
Atlantic City Conference, 1943-1946
Hot Springs Conference 1944-1945
Mont Tremblant Conference 1942.
Mont Tremblant Conference: Canadian Group
Ottawa Conference Sir Frederick Whyte 1943.
Yosemite Conference 1935.

General
India 1935-49
International Research -D .P.E.Corbett 1932-1947

Volume 4.

Personal
Correspondence, China, 1937-1950.

Norman A.M.MacKenzie, 1911, 1927-1966. 66 cm.(volumes 4-7)

The majority of the MacKenzie papers deals with the Canadian Institute of International Affairs, while a small portion consists of general information and material relating to the Institute of Pacific Relations. Canadian Institute of International Affairs, 1927-1928.

Volume 4.
Canadian Institute of International Affairs 1927-1928.

Volume 5.

Canadian Institute of International Affairs 1929-1930.

Volume 6.

Canadian Institute of International Affairs 1931-1933.

Volume 7.

Canadian Institute of International Affairs, January-July 1934.

Volume 8

15th Annual Study Conference - "Canada in a Two Power World", "Canada's Economic Future", "Canada and the Far East" 1948.

Volume 9

32nd Annual Study Conference - "Canada and the Asian World", 1963-1965.

Volume 11.

Institute of Pacific Relations - 4th General Session - Held in China 1931.

Institute of Pacific Relations - Documentation , 1952.

Institute of Pacific Relations, 1953. 1951-1954.

Institute of Pacific Relations - General 1951-1960.

Volume 12.

Conferences

Institute of Pacific Relations - Proposal and Admission of Councils 1932- 34.

Institute of Pacific Relations - Review 1933-34.

Institute of Pacific Relations - Finances 1933-34.

Institute of Pacific Relations - Canadian Data Paper- Manuscript 1954.

Institute of Pacific Relations -1957, 1956-57.,

Institute of Pacific Relations - 1958, 1954-58.

Institute of Pacific Relations - 1960. 1959-61...

West Point Conference 1955, 1956. 1955-57.

West Point Conference 1957. 1956-58.

West Point Conference 1958. 1958-59.

West Point Conference 1960. 1960.

West Point Conference 1961. 1961-62.

West Point Conference 1962. 1961-63.

West Point Conference 1963. 1963-64.

West Point Conference 1964. 1964-65.

West Point Conference 1965. 1965-66.

West Point Conference 1966. 1966-67.

Volume 14.

General Conferences.

British Commonwealth- U.S. Relations - Round Table 1945-46.

Volume 18.

University of Guelph, 1968. "Conference on China" 1966-68.

Volume 20.

General.

Pacific Affairs - University of British Columbia 1960-62.

Volume 21.

Institute of Current World Affairs, 1961-1974. 30 cm. (volumes 21-22).
There are ten file folders of newsletters concerning topical news items and information from countries around the world.

File #3 and File # 4, Newsletters.

Hong Kong, 1962-66.
Japan 1966-68.

File #5, File #6 and File #7, Newsletters.

Papua and New Guinea 1967- 71.

File #8 File #9 and File #10, Newletters.

Japan 1973.

Thailand 1973-74.

University Service Overseas(CUSA).
Originals 1960-1986. 41.21 metres. Finding aid 1379. MG 28 I323.

Meetings including 1961-1982, 6 metres (Volumes 10-11, 28-30, 33-34, 88-92, 96-105, 109-110, boxes 81-28, 81-34, and 81-7, Volumes 111-115.).
Administrative, training and recruitment. 10.2 metres, 1961-1983.(Volumes 21-23, 26-27, 32, 35-37, 78-88, 106).

Project reports and plans. 1960-1983. 13.2 metres(Volumes 11-21, 24-25, 67-71, 93-95, 106-108).
Projects funded by other agencies, unapproved and discretionary projects, 1073-1977, 2.45 metres(Volumes 30-31).

Funding and finances, 1969-1983. 8.6 metres(Volume 1-10, 24, 72-75, 108).

Volume 12.

South Pacific, 1968-1977.

Papua New Guinea, 1969-1976.

Volume 13. Fiji-Tonga, 1972-1975.

Volume 16.

Western Samoa, 1972-1977..

Cook Islands, 1976.

Papua New Guinea, 1971-1979.

Volume 17. New Hebrides, 1968-1971.

Volume 80-21.

1. CUSA-Asia/Financial management manual, volume 1, 2, 3, 1974.

3. CUSA-Thailand Report. Technical volunteer program, 1974.

Volume 81-25. Project Department.

5. Drought in Gujarat, India.

16. Japan agricultural machinery.

17. T.E.F.L. Course, Malaysia.

Projects Various States.

20. Bangladesh-Jute.

31. Malaysia- Mobile Library for Sabah.

32. Manila-Regional Centre for Graduate Study and Research in Agriculture.

37. Philippines-Philippine National Volunteer Service Coordinating Office(P.N.V.S.C.O.)

38. Sabah-Primary readers project.

40. South Vietnam, Support to released prisoners.

Volume 81-26 Country Files. General and Discretionary.

Asia.

Malaysia-General.

PNG.

Papua New Guinea-General.

Volume 81-27.

31. PNG-Forestry Seminar.

32. PNG-Yarapo High School.

39. Thailand-Science Campage.

40. Western Samoa- Prawn and Catfish farming.

Volume 81-31.

The Volunteer and the Bureaucrat. Case studies from India.

1111-2-1-India(John Wood and Steve Wood) January 1963-January 1964.

Sarawak(Michael Dillon, Coordinator).

518 Asia - Regional Field Secretary(Director).

Volume 81-33.

8. Fiji-Tonga-discretionary, 1973-1974.

9. Fiji-Tonga-General, 1973-1974.

10. India-General, 1973-1974.

11. Indonesia-Discretionary and general, 1973-1974.

12. Laos-Discretionary, 1973-1975.

13. Laos-General, 1973-1975.

18. Papua New Guinea-Discretionary, 1973-1975.

22. Thailand-Discretionary file(1), 1973-1975.

23. Thailand-Discretionary file(2), 1971-1972.

24. Thailand-General, 1973-1975.

Volume 81-35. Project.

Asia RFD General 1977.

Laos Discretionary.

Bangladesh Discretionary.

Thailand Discretionary.

Volume 81-44.

223-10.1 Japan. General.

223-11.1 Korea, General.

228-5.1 Indonesia survey.

210-14-1 Guyana Country Plans.

Volume 81-54 University of British Columbia linkage with Asian Institutions.

223-15.1 Philippines - General.

223-14.1 Vietnam.

Volume 81-55 Project.

PNG discretionary.

PNG general.

Volume 76.

CUSA Bangladesh- Handbook 1973.

Bangladesh - CUSA 1972-1973.

Volume 77.

CUSO India handbook, 1968.

CUSO India handbook, 1969.

CUSO Papua New Guinea information.

CUSO Papua New Guinea, 1978.

CUSO Papua New Guinea orientation, 1980.

Tonga, South Pacific.

CUSO Tonga handbook.

CUSO Malaysia, 1973.

CUSO Thailand information.

CUSA Thailand handbook, 1973.

Papua New Guinea. PNG.

Volume 92. Asia-Pacific.

Papua New Guinea. PNG Education project evaluation 1980.
Education project, financial statement, 1980.

Papua New Guinea. PNG Education project. Selection orientation, 1980.
Education project, financial statement, 1980.

CUSO Bhutan, Burma, Ceylon, 1961-1963.
Education project, financial statement, 1980.

CUSO India, 1961-1963.

Volume 110 Asia-Pacific(APO).

Bangladesh draft: "Joint proposal for collaboration with U.N. Organization in Bangladesh".

Volume 111. "Bangladesh" booklet by CUSO "CUSO Bangladesh" Now what? Bangkok.

Thailand. Report of the Bangladesh Task Force, September 1974.

Bangladesh trip(pre-Study and correspondence), 1973-1974.

Papua New Guinea Country Plan and Budget, 1975-197, Volume 1.

Papua New Guinea. Report, 1971-1981.

Papua New Guinea. Meeting, 1977-1981.

Canadian Council for International Cooperation, est. 1968. MG 28 I367.
Originals, 1961-1982. 13.4 metres Finding aid 1541.

Council worked in the field of international development overseas, largely in third-world countries. Records document most of the private initiative activities of Canada in developing countries. Video cassettes, slides, recordings on magnetic tape and 16 mm files(191 items in all) have been transferred to the National Film, Television and Sound Archives.

a) Administrative files, 1969-1982. 55 cm. (volumes 1-3).

b) Correspondence, 1963-1982. 70cm.(volumes 3-7).

c) Policies and programmes, 1971-1982. 65 cm. (volumes 7-10).

d) Relations with government bodies and other aid institutions, 1963-1982. 2.9 metres(volumes 10-24). Including the Canadian International Development Agency, and the United Nations.

e) Project clearing house, 1970-1981. 5.55 metres(volumes 25-32).
Case files of aid projects, including Asia and Oceania, country programme profile on non-government organization aid to India.

f) Special projects, 1969-1979. 1.50m (volumes 52-60).

g) Press material and subject reference files, 1961-1981. 1.55 metres(volumes 60-67).

MG 28 III. Business establishments.

Canadian-Australia Steamship Company.
Photocopies, 1893. 14 pages. MG 28 III51.
Temporary agreement between James Huddart representing the owners of the steamers Miowera and Warrimo, and the Canadian Pacific Railway establishing a monthly trans-Pacific steamship service, May 1893.
ULM

Toronto Board of Trade.
Papers. MG 28 III56. Finding aid 1237.

Volume332. Foreign trade missions.

6. Japanese Iron and Steel Mission, 1957.

7. Japanese delegates - conference with, 1958.

8. Visit of K.V.Lall, Director General of Foreign Trade for India. Indian Coir Board delegation, 1958, 1959.

9. Engineering trade delegation from India, 1960.

10. Japanese trade mission, 1962.

16. Trade mission from China, 1964.

18. Japanese industrial mission, 1964.

Chamber of Commerce, est. 1935.
Originals, 1923-1975, 16 metres Finding aid 1269. MG 28 III62.

Committees.

Volume 47. 422. Business and industry advisory committee.

Greek-Turkish cooperation project, 1966-1967.

Volume 48. 428.

Private investment. Thailand, 1966-1968.

Volume 48.429.

Private investment. Turkey, 1962-1967.

MG 28 V. Ethno-cultural organizations.

Cooperative Committee on Japanese Canadians.
Originals, 1942-1956. 29 cm. photocopies, 1943-1946. 1 cm. Finding aid 341. MG 28 V1.

The Cooperative Committee on Japanese was set up in Toronto in 1942 to aid in the resettlement of Japanese Canadians who were arriving from relocation centres in British Columbia. Besides providing assistance in problems of housing, employment, etc., the committee compiled briefs concerning deportation and repatriation and on the repeal of these measures took an active part in the question of compensation for losses resulting from repatriation.
Originals presented in l958 by the former secretary Miss M.K.Boos, copies of minutes, 1943-1946, presented in 1977 from McMaster University Library(Edith Fowkes papers).
Finding aid 341 is file list.

Minutes and correspondence, 1943-1953. 2.5 cm. (Volume 1)

Statements, 1947-1952, 1956. 5 cm.(Volume1)
Claims fund statements, property claims returns, lists of claimants.

Briefs and submission, 1944-1950. 2.5 cm. (Volume1)

Subject files, 1942-1951. 10 cm.(Volume2).
Correspondence, bulletins, depositions, copies of judgments, etc. arranged by subject list.

Printed materials, 1943-1953. 10 cm.(Volume3)

News bulletins and clippings list.

Japanese Canadian Citizens Association,1947-
Community Association.
Originals, 1922-1968. 3.5 metres Finding aid 1281. MG 28 V7.

The Japanese Canadian Citizens Association(J.C.C.A.) was formed in 1947 to act as a national organization for Japanese Canadians. Its first major function was to assist claimants before the Royal Commission on Japanese Property Losses(Bird Commission). The J.C.C.A. was also in the forefront of the successful post-war struggle against discriminatory legislation. Because of a change in the organization's structure in 1953, most of the records in this collection are from the early period of its activity. The records in this collection are essential for the study of Japanese Canadians during World War II and its aftermath. The evacuation of Japanese Canadians from the "protected area" of British Columbia in 1942 led to the destruction of most archival material pre-dating 1941. Although much of the material in the collection relates to the issue of property losses which provided the impetus for a national organization in 1947, there are many other subjects covered by these files. The rebuilding of an ethno-cultural community, the struggle for basic civil rights and the activities of a national ethnic organization are all well documented.

Precursors of the J.C.C.A., 1936-1947. 33 cm.(volumes 1-2)
Minutes of the Japanese Canadian Citizens League, Vancouver chapter, 1936-1940. Japanese Canadian Citizens League, Vancouver chapter, 1936-1940; Canadian Citizens Council, 1942 and the British Columbia:Japanese Canadian Citizens Association,

1946-1948 minutes, Canadian Citizens Association:British Columbia, 1946-1948 correspondence, financial records and subject files of the J.C.A.A., 1943-1947. Reels C-12818, C-12819 and C-12836.
Japanese Canadian Citizens Association, 1947-1968. 3.07 m (volumes 2-17).
Executive committee, 1947-1968. 16 cm. (volumes 2-3).
Executive committee minutes, bulletins and information sheets. Reels C-12819, C-12820.
Financial, 1948-1953, 1963. 10 cm. (volume 3)
Budgets, balance sheets, auditors reports correspondence and lists of donors. Reel C-12820.
National office general, 1947-1953. 28 cm.(volumes 3-4)
General housekeeping records, including address listings, executive officers correspondence, publicity and news releases and membership material. Reels C-12820, C-12821.

Evacuation claims, 1922,-1932, 1942, 1947-1954. 52 cm. (volumes 4-7)
Memoranda, bulletins, newsletters, reports, and correspondence relating to the Japanese Canadian property loss claims, and the activities of the Cooperative Committee on Japanese Canadians. Material relating to the claims can also be found in other sources such as minutes, bulletins, J.C.C.A. records as well as other series. Also included in this series are three files relating to fishing licenses 1922-1932, 1942-1950 and the Fishing Vessel Disposal Committee. Reels C-12821, C-12822, C-12823.

Provincial, local and general correspondence, 1947-1966. 44 cm. (volumes 7-9)
Correspondence arranged by Province from east to west and general correspondence arranged chronologically which related primarily to the property claims issue. Other subject and activities are also included particularly for the 1950's and 1960's material. Reels C-12823, C-12824, C-12825.

Government - submissions, reports, correspondence, 1948-1953. 14 cm. (volume 9).
Various briefs submitted to the Federal and British Columbia government on regulations and discrimination against Japanese Canadians and general routine correspondence with government departments. Reels C-12825, C-12826.

Immigration and strandee correspondence, 1947-1958. 44 cm. (volumes 9-11).
Correspondence and case files of individuals who returned to Japan and sought re-entry into Canada as well as correspondence.

Conferences, 1947-1962. 23 cm. (volume 12-13).
Correspondence, memoranda, reports and briefs relating to annual national conferences and some provincial and local conferences. Reels C-12829, C-12830.

American Citizens League, 1947-1950, 1960. 8 cm. (volume 13).

Correspondence between the J.C.C.A. and the J.A.C.L., which outlines the Japanese-American fight for civil rights and a speech by Mike Masaoka, President of the J.A.C.L., at the first J.C.C.A. Conference, Toronto, 1947. Reel C-12830.

Organizations, 1947-1955, 1962. 23 cm. (volumes 13-14).
Out of the struggle for civil rights and the desire to be a contributing part of society, the executive of the J.C.C.A. established contact with many organizations with common goals. The files in this series contain mostly printed material relating to the various organizations. Reels C-12830, C-12831.

Civil rights, 1947-1951. 4 cm. (volume 14).
Correspondence, briefs to the Senate Committee on Human Rights and Fundamental Freedoms, newsletters of civil rights groups, newspaper clippings and a speech by G.Tanaka to the British Columbia United Fishermen and Allied Workers Convention, 1969. Reel C-12831.

Subject files, n.d., 1950-1953. 5 cm. (volume 24).
Correspondence, reports, printed material, a poem "Call my people home" by Dorothy Livesay and the script for a play "Minority groups vs. Canadian public - a mock trial" by Pattie Turner. Reel C-12831.

J.C.C.A. projects, 1947-1958. 13 cm. (volume 14).

Correspondence and reports on various national projects including immigration restrictions, fishing licenses, property claims, fund drives, Nipponia home and the Japanese Canadian Cultural Centre. Reels C-12832, C-12833

Memoirs and history contest entries, n.d., 1936, 1958. 8 cm. (volume 16).

Account of a pilgrimage in 1936 of Issei veterans to the unveiling of the Vimy Memorial, by Saburo Shinobu and submissions to the J.C.C.A. historical context in 1958. The winning submissions appeared in the "New Canadian". Reel C-12833.

Bulletins and minutes, 1948-1965. 29 cm. (volumes 16-17).
Incomplete runs of bulletins, minutes and reports of various local and provincial chapters of the J.C.C.A. Reels C-12834, C-12835.

Miscellaneous, n.d., 1936, 1945-1949. 3 cm. (volume 17).

A complete run of **Nisei Affairs,** a 1949 issue of the **Québec Directory**, and a paper by Judge Helen G.McGill, 1936, "The Oriental delinquent in the Vancouver juvenile court", Reel C-12835.

Four photographs were transferred to the National Photography Collection and one reel of film, "Japanese Canadians at Play", to the National Film Archives.

United Council of Filipino Associations in Canada, est. 1971.
Originals, 1964-1975. 8 inches. MG 28 V30.

Although an earlier organization of the same name was established in 1964, in Vancouver, British Columbia, the present council dates from 1971. Its purpose is to serve as a national voice for Filipinos in Canada, as a link between local constituent groups and the Filipino and Canadian governments, and to emphasize the role of Filipinos in a developing multicultural society.

Presented in 1975 by Dr. Manuel Garcia. A number of recordings were transferred to the Historical Sound Records Section of the National Film Archives.

Correspondence, memoranda, bulletins, resolutions and related material concerning the United Council of Filipino Associations in Canada, and its links with constituent organizations.

Japanese Canadian Collection.
Originals, 1918-1973. 2.5 cm. photocopies, n.d., [1914], 1972. 2.5 cm. MG 28 V73.

The Japanese Canadian Collection is a unit that has been created from a variety of smaller units that have come from a variety of donors.

Presented in 1976 by various individuals.

Exit permit and registration cards, 1918, 1944. originals, 3 pages.

Official Canadian government permit and cards of Mr. Tokutaro Sakamoto.

Newspaper clippings, [1940's]. originals, 2.5 cm.

Material relating to significant events in Japanese-Canadian history, particularly to the internment.

Report, memoirs, n.d. photocopies, 2.5 cm.

Report to the Minister of Fisheries regarding the sale of impounded fishing boats and the memoirs of Mr. Matsumoto, a Japanese ship builder in British Columbia, who relates his experiences in the Slocan Internment camp and various events in his life. Both items are in Japanese. Copies of newspaper clippings relating to Japanese labour leader Joe Miyazawa.

Chinese Freemasons Society, Cumberland, British Columbia.
A political organization.
Originals, n.d., 1929-1955. 16 cm. MG 28 V94.

Transferred in 1978 from Dr. B.S.Hoe, CCFCS, National Museum of Man.

Nomination forms for choosing the Association's executive, financial records, lottery books, membership records and books. All material is in Chinese.

(oversize items are in horizontal storage cabinets).

Raymond(Alberta) Young Peoples Society, 1942-1947.
Social organization.
Originals, 1942-1947. 1 cm. MG 28 V101.
Presented in 1978 by Miss Betty Bartling of Vancouver.

Minute book of the Raymond Young Peoples Society which was organized as a social and educational group. Its membership was primarily Japanese Canadian. Photographs of the first Japanese Canadian child born to evacuee parents in Lethbridge was transferred to the National Photograph Collection.

Chinese Canadian Association, f. 1951
Community organization.
Originals, 1951-1972. 15 cm. MG 28 V145.

The Chinese Canadian Association was founded in 1951, in Toronto, with the following objectives: to gain for Chinese Canadians fair play and justice; to promote good citizenship; and to promote better relations amongst Chinese Canadians and Canadians of all other ethnic origins. It continues, to this day to pursue its goals actively.
Presented in 1984 by Margaret Ko, Toronto, Ontario.

Constitution(1951), minutes(1951-1972), financial statements(1966-1969), immigration briefs and statements(n.d., 1957), topical files on redevelopment of Toronto Chinatown(1969-1971), correspondence(19864-1971), CCA newsletter(1963-1971), announcements and address lists. Most of the material is in English.

Immigrant Aid Services(Toronto). Est. 1972
Aid organization.
Originals, 1972-1984. 3 cm. MG 28 V146
The Indian Immigrant Aid Services, founded in 1972, is an organization dedicated to helping East Indian immigrants in Canada; it gives counsel and advice in the areas of job search, housing problems, and family difficulties.
Presented in 1985 by the Indian Immigrant Aid Services, Scarborough, Ontario.
Constitution and by-laws of the I.I.A.S., various brochures, pamphlets, and newsletter, a needs assessment study entitled **South Asians in Transition** and annual reports(1981, 1982, 1983, 1983-1984)

National Association of Canadians with Origins in India(NACOI).
Originals 1985. 190 pages MG 28 V150.
N.A.C.O.I., with its head office in Ottawa, was founded in 1976 to organize the East Indian community in Canada, with the purpose of preserving the Indian cultural heritage. N.A.C.O.I .also represents the East Indian community before the government, making known to the government the concerns, desires and aims of the Indian community in Canada.

Annual reports of the national, provincial and town chapter executive bodies of N.A.C.O.I; annual reports of various N.A.C.O.I. standing committees, reports on employment discrimination, submissions on multiculturism and media, agenda and notes on annual general meeting(1985), and notes on the crash of Air India flight 182.

Manuscript Group 29. Nineteenth-Century Post-Confederation Manuscripts.

MG 29 C. Social.

Bilbrough, Ellen Agnes, 1841-1900.
Organizer of child immigration from Great Britain. Photocopies, 1896-1900, 3 metres MG 29 C106.

Includes a daily diary across the Pacific to China and Japan, describes sights visited, missionaries encountered, spread of Christianity and living conditions.

Wallace, Robert, 1855-1932.
Clergyman and husband of Ellen Agnes Bilbrough. Treasurer of China Inland Mission, 1915-1929. Photocopies 1862-1929. 15 pages MG 29 C107.

Includes information on missionary voyage to China and Japan with his wife.

Caddick, Helen. fl. 1891-1892.
Transcripts 1891. 1 cm. MG 29 C125.

Excerpt from a travel diary including Canada and China in 1891-1892. She describes the Chinese in British Columbia.

MG29 D. Cultural.

Grant, George Munro.
Clergyman, educationalist, principal of Queen's University, 1877-1902. MG 29 D38.

Volume 1. pages 769-7984 6 December 1878.
Presbyterian Church, India Mission to Rev. John Campbell.

Volume 3. pages 1882g-I, 5 October 1884.
Re Chinese to Lord Lansdowne.

Volume 5. pages 3389-3405, 12 July 1895.
Chinese immigration to D.J.O'Donoghue

Volume 5. pages 3432-3434, 24 September 1895.
Chinese immigration to Robert Campbell

Volume 5. pages 3458-3477, 23 December 1897.
Pacific cable to Sir Sandford Fleming.

Volume 5. pages 3511-3514, 19 March
Presbyterian Church. Turkish Missions to Alexander MacLachan.

Volume 5. pages 3858-3862, 31 January 1899.

Pacific cable to Mrs. G.M.Grant.

Volume 5. pages 3895 a-g., 10 June 1899.
Pacific cable to Lord Aberdeen.
Volume 6. pages 3933-3938, 18 January 1900.
American Collegiate Institute, Turkey to James P.MacNaughton.

Manuscript Group 30. Manuscripts of the First Half of the Twentieth Century.

MG 30 A. Business.

Flavelle, Joseph Wesley, 1896-1938.
Financier and industrialist.
Correspondence and papers, 31 ft., 8 inches. Finding aid 66. MG 30 A16.

Miscellaneous papers(volumes 75-76) include missions and Korean College supported by the Methodist Church of Canada.

Ross, Charles, 1862-1972.
Papers. Finding aid 1027. MG 30 A95.

iii. Chinese business ventures, 1895-1903.

a) Memoranda, reports, clippings, legal documents, 1897-1900.

1. Railways, 1897-1898.

2. Mines, 1899-1900.

3. Tramways.

4. Miscellaneous, 1897-1898.

5. Accounts, 1897-1899.

Correspondence, 1855-1903.

Aikawa, Frank S., 186?-1955.
Businessman.
Photocopies, n.d., 1892-1913, 16 pages. MG 30 A97.
Frank S.Aikawa emigrated from Japan to San Francisco in 1855. In 1889 he established a fish cannery at Port Simpson, near Port Rupert, British Columbia. He spent about thirty years in Canada involved in various fishing and farming activities, in which he employed Japanese immigrants, before returning to his native village, Isezaki City, Gumma prefecture, Japan.

Copies in 1977, from originals in the possession of Aikawa Family Museum, Isezaki City, Japan.
Personal and business documents including land titles, naturalization certificate, fishing licenses and copies of photographs.

MG 30 B. Scientific.

Bethune, Norman, 1890-1939.
Surgeon.

Original, 4 pages, photocopies, 11 cm. 1926-1982. MG 30 B55. Finding aid 1391.
Son of a clergyman, educated at the University of Toronto Faculty of Medicine. Helped to organize the Montréal Group for the Security of the People's Health, an organization devoted to establishing socialized medicine. During the Spanish Civil War he set up a blood transfusion service, and in 1938 went to China to attend to the wounded during the Sino-Japanese War. He died there in 1939.

Additional material may be found in Bethune, Endicott and West China Union University collection, MG 30 C230.
Exchange of documents with China, led to the acquisition of 18 documents relating to Bethune in China, and also available on microfilm(reel K-169).

Matsuda, R.D. 1986.
Entomologist.
Originals, approximately 7 metres MG 30 B164.

Correspondence, research notes and original manuscripts of Dr. Matsuda, dealing with both morphology and entomology of insects, and also dealing with evolution.

MG30 C. Social.

Foster, Margaret.
Missionary.
Originals, 1942-1950, 4 cm. MG 30 C69.
In the 1940's Margaret Foster was a missionary among immigrant groups in Slocan City, British Columbia. Petitions, resolutions, circular letters, newsletters, reports, articles, pamphlets and official forms and instructions, relating to the evacuation and deportation of Japanese Canadians, scrap-book relating to the Etsuyi Morii affair, 1942, newspaper clippings, 1942-1950, concerning the evacuation and resettlement of Japanese Canadians.

Makishi, Anno Abraham, 1875-1960.
Fireman, farmer.
Originals, 1907-1960. 8 pages, MG 30 C115.
Considered to be the first Okinawan to settle in Canada, came to Canada in 1900. A number of photographs transferred to the National Photographic Collection.

Canadian naturalization certificate(1907), Japanese passports issued to Anno and Kiyo Makishi(1911), Canadian citizenship certificate(1954), obituaries(1960) and hymns from Anno Makishi's funeral(1960).

Miyagawa, George Suteichi, 1899-
Storekeeper.
Originals, n.d., 1922-1941, 1975. 16 pages photocopies, n.d. ,1907-1942, 7 pages. MG 30 C117.
Arrived in Canada in 1906, and evacuated to Vernon, British Columbia in 1942. Returned to Vancouver after the war.
Correspondence 1923-1925, concerning G.S. Miyagawa's unsuccessful efforts to obtain a 4th class engineer's certificate; correspondence, 1975, concerning his life in Canada, letters of reference. n.d., 1922, certificates, n.d. ,1907-1942, including a school certificate from Kyoritsu Nippon Kokumin Gakko, a certificate of discharge as a seaman, Japanese and Canadian registration documents, and newspaper clippings. A number of photographs were transferred to the National Photography Collection.

Endicott, James Gareth, Dr., 1898-
Missionary and peace activist.
Originals, n.d., 1891-1984, 16.77 metres photocopies, 1983-1984. 8 pages. Finding aid 1474. MG 30 C130.
James Gareth Endicott was born in Szechuan province, in 1898, the son of missionary parents. Attended Victoria College, University of Toronto, graduating in 1925 as an ordained minister. He moved to Chungking as a missionary with the West China Mission of the United Church. Fluent in Szechwan dialect, and eventually loaned to the New Life Movement of Madame Chiang Kai Shek. In 1941, he returned to Canada and lectured on behalf of China, although uneasy at the reactionary nature of the Chinese Nationalist government. He returned to China in 1944, but was increasingly at odds with the missionary movement, and in 1947, he returned to Canada to speak for the Chinese Revolution. This led to the organization of the Canadian Peace Congress in 1948, of which he was chairman to 1981. Transfers of material were made to the National Photography Collection. Also see Bethune, Endicott and West China Union University papers, MG 30 C230.

Peace movement, n.d., 1948-1975. 7.07 metres(volumes 1-35).

Endicott family papers, n.d. 1892-1978, 4.12 metres (volumes 36-56).

Manuscripts and notes, - J.G.Endicott, n.d., 1926-1975. 46 cm. (36/667-38/817).

Sermons, speeches, statements, press releases, notes, tour itineraries, pamphlets.

The **Far Eastern Newsletter** n.d., 1948-1976. 21 cm. (38/818-39/817) Volumes 1(1948)-28(1976), guide lines for office procedure, notices to subscribers, correspondence, orders, and background material. Subject files - J.G. Endicott, n.d., 1915-1973. 25 cm. (39/854-40/883a) biographical sketches, diaries, school records, notes, correspondence and broadcasts for the New Life Movement, reports to the United States Office of Strategic Services, the **Shanghai Newsletter,** correspondence, statements, and clippings on J.G.Endicott's resignation, 1946, correspondence, documentation and clippings on germ warfare charges, 1952, statements and clippings on the Stalin Peace Prize, 1952, correspondence and clippings on his resignation from the Canadian Peace Congress.

Language teaching - J.G. Endicott, n.d., 1932-1948. 12

cm. (40/884-41/902).
Correspondence, background material, teaching manual, and teaching aids for direct method English, criticisms of "Basic English", the **Gin I Middle School English Weekly**

Clippings on J.G. Endicott, n.d., 1932-1975. 41 cm. (41/903-43/921).

Reports of speeches and rallies, editorial and other attacks.

Mary Endicott - manuscripts and subject files, n.d., 1907-1967. 41 cm.(43/922-45/976).
Diary, essays, articles, notes, reviews of and correspondence re: **My Journey for Peace,** material on **Five Stars over China**- reviews, correspondence, promotion and distribution, foreign editions, poetry, obituaries.

Austin family correspondence, n.d., 1893-1975, 38 cm. (45/977-47/1013).
Childhood correspondence of Mary Endicott and family, later correspondence of Mary Endicott, and her father, sister and nephew.

James Endicott, sr., Norman Endicott, Steven Endicott, n.d., 1892-1967. 38 cm.(47/1015-48/1026).
Speeches, correspondence, notes, pamphlets, clippings, school records, articles.

Endicott family correspondence, n.d., 1907-1978. 1.69 metres (48/1027-56/1175).
Subject files, specific, n.d., 1915-1980. 3.14 metres (volumes 56-72).

Personalities, n.d., 1915-1980. 56 cm. (56/1175-58/1243).
Correspondence, pamphlets, notes and clippings.

China, n.d., 1927-1979. 78 cm. (58/1244-63/1315).
Manuscripts, clippings, speeches, visitors' and journalists' reports.

American foreign policy, n.d., 1943-1964, 48 cm. (65/1357-68/1389).
Clippings, speeches, articles.

Canadian foreign policy, n.d., 1933-1976. 12 cm. (68/1390-1402).
Documents, clippings and statements
The arms race and arms control, n.d., 1945-1970. 39 cm. (68/1403-70/1439).
Clippings, reports, statements and articles.

The church and peace/Christianity and Communism, n.d., 1940-1972. 29 cm. (70/1440-72/1490).
Clippings, correspondence, statements, publications and sermons.

Microfilms, 1927-1976. reels H-1747 to H-1754.
Eight reels of microfilm, duplicates of films sent to the First Historical Archives in the People's Republic of China, under the auspices of the cultural exchange agreement between China and Canada. The particular subject files were selected by Chinese archival officials.

On the microfilms, the following information is captured: Endicott's personal records (schooling, marriage, ordination, etc.) direct method English, a system of teaching English to Chinese-speakers, devised by Endicott, commentary on China under the war lords and Chiang Kai-shek; information of the Japanese occupation of China, Endicott's growing disenchantment with Chiang and his conversion to supporter of the revolutionary Communist movement; the mechanics of Communist victory; Communist China and the West, especially U.S. opposition to the acceptance of China into the world community, information on the cold war and the Korean War, the Christian Church in China; and the world peace movement.

Thompson, Grace, fl. 1930-1940's.
Photocopies, n.d., 1945-1948. 1.5 cm. MG 30 C160.

Presented in 1978 by Mrs. G. Thompson, Winnipeg.

Letters, petitions and news clippings concerning the plight of Canadians of Japanese descent, part of the campaign of the Cooperative Committee on Japanese Canadians to ensure the restoration of civil rights in the postwar period. Much of the correspondence is of Thelma Scrambler

Sato, Stephen S. 1899-
Originals, (1930-1960) 6 cm. MG 30 C161.

Presented in 1978 by Mr. and Mrs. K.A.Ellis, Winnipeg.
Material relating to Sato's property, the Japanese Property Claims Commission and the Office of the Custodian of Enemy Property.

Lists of Japanese families in Steveston slated for relocation, places of designation and correspondence on relocation.

Various correspondence, certificates and insurance policy receipts.

Book in Japanese, printed in 1961, titled **History of the Japanese Congregations of the United Church of Canada, 1892-1959.**

Sakamoto, Mas, fl.1930-1940's.
Originals, 1934, 1942, 1945. 2 cm. MG 30 C162.
Presented in 1978 by Mr. Mas Sakamoto, Lethbridge, Alberta.

Book concerning the Japanese navy on a visit to North America (in Japanese), a letter from the British Columbia Security Commission, 1942, and a notice, 1945, concerning the "repatriation" of Canadians of Japanese origin to Japan

Uyede, Mr. fl.1910-1920's.

Photocopies, 1907- [1910], 5 cm. MG 30 C163.

Presented in 1978 by Mrs. Lilly Uyede, Toronto via Toyo Takata.

Diaries of Mr. Uyede noting his day by day activities, written largely for the purpose of practicing his English.
Davies, John W.(Jack) 1899-1978.
Montréal sports executive. MG 30 C164.

Correspondence, and subject files of Colonel J.W.Davies pertaining to sport and various sports organizations, both Canadian and international including the Commonwealth Games Association of Canada, Commonwealth Games Federation, and individual Commonwealth Games, 1930-1978, International Amateur Athletic Federation.
ULM 4.

Bethune, Endicott, and West China Union University.
Microfilm, 1926-1983. Reel K-180. MG 30 C230.

This collection consists of documents by and concerning, Dr. N.Bethune and Dr. J.G.Endicott. For biographical information on these figures, see the following inventory entries: Dr. N. Bethune, MG30 B55; Dr. J.G. Endicott, MG 30 C130.

Presented in 1986 by the First Historical Archives of China, Beijing, People's Republic of China.

The Bethune File consists of a number of testimonials to Dr. Bethune following his death, and several articles written by him on medicine and the Chinese revolution. All files are in the Chinese language. Six photographs have been transferred to the National Photography Collection.

The Endicott Files consists of copies of articles taken from the Chinese(most are out of **Heavenly Wind**). They deal with Endicott's support of the Chinese revolutionaries and his international peace activity.

The West China Union University Files are copies of correspondence between the Board of Foreign Overseas Missions of the United Church of Canada and the administration of the West China Union, University in Chengtu, Szechwan, funded and administrated by the Board. Most of the correspondence is between A.W.Lindsay, Vice-Chancellor of the University, and J.H.Arnup, who headed the Board of Foreign Missions. L.G.Kilborn (Director of the University), S.H.Fong (University President), and J.D.Robertson (also Vice-Chancellor) are also prominent among the correspondents. There are only several letters by Endicott in the files, but much of the correspondence concerns him and his activities. The correspondence also reflects the following concerns: administrative, pedagogical and financial difficulties of the university during China's difficult era of civil war, foreign occupation and revolution; political situation in China in all its complexity and J.Endicott's growing disenchantment with the Nationalist movement. The final several letters of recent date (1983) address the matter of a film to be made in China depicting Endicott's contribution to the victory of the Chinese Communist movement. The correspondence is all in English.Also available in photocopies.

Sharman, Henry Burton, 1865-1953.
Biblical scholar and professor.
Originals, n.d. 1869-1976. 7.45 metres. Finding aid 1697. MG 30 C224.

Volume 17 - 18 , Mandarin Bibles, English-language missionary publications and hymnbooks, circular letters from missionaries, correspondence and printed materials relating to Peking University, Chinese student work and the 1922 World Student Christian Federation Conference in Peking.

MG 30 D. Cultural.

Dafoe, John Wesley, 1886-1944.
Winnipeg. Journalist. One of the founders of the Canadian Institute of Pacific Relations.
Microfilm, 11 reels, n.d.<1808>, 1857, 1896-1948.
Finding aid 51. Originals in the University of Manitoba Library. MG 30 D45.

General correspondence including letters from Wilfrid Laurier, Clifford Sifton, Charles Tupper, W.L.MacKenzie King, R.L.Borden, Vincent Massey, Henri Bourassa, Lord Beaverbrook, and Grant Dexter. Subject files include the Paris Peace Conference and the Boy Scouts movement; family papers including speeches and notes relating to the imperial relationship. Also available is a complete set of photocopies made from the microfilm, and some transcripts.
Anglo-Japanese treaty, 30 June 1921.
Armenia and Canadian foreign policy, 3 April 1922
Chanak crisis, 18,26, 28 September, 4 October 1922.
Institute of Pacific Relations, 19 November 1928.
Canadian Institute of International Affairs, 28 November 1928, 17 July 1929, 6 January 1930, 7 February 1930, 7 March 1930, 8 August 1930, 19 August 1930.
Institute of Pacific Relations, 19 June 1931.
Canadian Institute of International Relations, 27 November 1931.
Institute of Pacific Relations, 7 August 1931.
Institute of Pacific Relations Conference, 7 July 1931, 19 June 1931, 19 September 1931, 13 October 1931, 23 November 1931, 14 September 1931.
Institute of Pacific Relations, 7 January 1931. 16 January 1931.
Canadian Institute of International Affairs, 9 March 1932, 23 March 1932, 9 January 1932, 18 January 1932,8 March 1932.
Institute of Pacific Relations, Canadian Institute of International Affairs, 14 March 1932.

Institute of Pacific Relations meeting, 21 April 1932.
Canadian Institute of International Affairs, 17 May

1932, 23 January 1932, 31 August 1932, 23 January 1932.

Jenkins, Frank M.S.,1859-1930, and Annie. 1866-1952.
Ottawa. Musicians.
Papers, 6 volumes. Finding aid, 1131. MG 30 D183
Includes correspondence from their daughter, Ruth Jenkins, while engaged in missionary work in China, 1920-1927, with the Anglican Mission.

Volumes 3-5. Correspondence from Ruth Jenkins, 1920-1938. 37 cm.
Letters written to her family in Canada by Ruth Jenkins while she was with the Anglican Mission in China, 1920-1927, describing her daily life in China, excursions, acquaintanceships with other missionaries, involvement in missionary work, observation on Chinese customs and politics, and other aspects of her Chinese experiences, also letters 1927-1938 written by Ruth Jenkins while living in Japan with her husband, H.G.Watts.

Nakayama, Gordon Goichi, 1900- Clergyman.
Correspondence, 1936-1978. 1.3 m (volumes 3-9).MG 30 D197.
Varied correspondence of the Reverend Nakayama. There is some early correspondence on Vancouver property and its disposition, and on evacuation and relocation. Most of the correspondence is of later date (1960's and 1970's): much of it is with persons in Japan, Brazil, Paraguay, Okinawa and Taiwan, dealing with missionary and church related matters, and the lifestyle of Japanese communities in those lands. Scattered throughout is some of the correspondence of other Nakayama family members.

Church of the Ascension - Records, n.d., 1930-1952. 16 cm. (volume 10).
Various registers of church activity in Vancouver, Slocan and Coaldale, Alberta.

Church of the Ascension - Bulletins, Reports and Announcements, 1927-1978. 54 cm. (volumes 10-13). Various mimeographed information sheets put out by the Japanese Anglican Church of the Ascension in its various locations (Vancouver, B.C., Slocan, B.C. and Coaldale, Alta.). There are newsletters, flyers and other material detailing the activity of the church parish and its parishioners. Included are "The Church News" of 1928-1930, and the "Vancouver Japanese Anglican Churches Weekly Bulletin", ca.1920-1930's, which deal with Japanese-Canadian Anglicans in British Columbia.

Various Publications - Press, n.d., 1934-1977. 13 cm. (volumes 13-14).
A number of religious serials, largely printed abroad. There are no complete runs.

Various Publications - Books and Pamphlets, n.d., 1946-1975. 17 cm. (volume 14).
Various pamphlets, some of which are as follows; a mimeographed History of Slocan (1946), fact sheets on Japanese-Canadians, Rev. Nakayama's sermons published under the title **The Divine Love,** and Rev. Nakayama's publication entitled **My Missionary Trip Around the World.**

Various, n.d., 1941-1946. 20 cm. (volume 15).
Diverse material, consisting of newspapers and clippings, some posters, calligraphed material, etc.

Tucker, M. Grace, 1902-
Missionary.
Originals, 1942-1951, 1968. 10 cm. MG 30 D200

Grace Tucker was born in London, England, and came to Canada as a child in 1905. She was educated in Peterborough, Ontario, and after several years in secretarial work she entered the Anglican Women's Training College in Toronto. Following her graduation Miss Tucker was assigned to Vancouver, British Columbia for work among Japanese Canadians. From 1942-1946 she was a welfare worker at Slocan Relocation Centre in the interior of British Columbia. In 1946, the Anglican Church assigned her to Toronto where she helped with the resettlement of Japanese Canadians in various parts of Ontario, until 1952. She later moved to Prince Albert, Saskatchewan, where she worked with the Anglican Church until her retirement in 1967.

Presented in 1975 by Miss M.Grace Tucker.

Correspondence, 1945-1947, 1968; agendas, minutes, treasurers reports and financial statements, news bulletins, lists. and memoranda, 1946-1951, of the Cooperative Committee on Japanese-Canadians; Anglican Japanese Mission reports, 1942-1943; articles on Japanese evacuation and repatriation. 1942-1945, B.C., Security Commission works sheets, Slocan; memoranda forms, permits, and printed material.

Mark, Ernest C., 1896-1973.
Newspaper publisher.
Originals, 1928-31, 1942, 1957, 1972, 1973. 21 cm. MG 30 D219.

Ernest C. Mark came to Canada from China in 1916 to study medicine at the University of Toronto. Active in social and political organizations, he was unofficial mayor of Toronto's Chinatown for several years and was an active elder of the Chinese Presbyterian church. He was publisher of the **Shing Wah Daily News**, the largest Chinese newspaper in North America and one of the oldest surviving ethnic newspapers in Canada. In 1951, Mr. Mark was predeceased by his first wife Yuk Fong Mark. He later married Nancy Lau Mark.

Presented in 1976 by Mrs Nancy Lau Mark via **Shing Wah Daily News.**

Scrapbooks, 1925-39, 1942, 1957. Originals, 19.5 cm. Newspaper clippings and photographs relating to the career and activities of E.C. Mark publisher of the **Shing Wah Daily News**. This material also

documents the relief efforts of the Chinese-Canadian community after the Japanese invasion of Manchuria, the activities of the Chinese Nationalist League of Canada (Kuomintang), Eastern Division and the Chinese Patriotic Federation of Ontario. There are photographs of executive members and of 2 airplanes bought for the distribution of leaflets. Most of this material is in Chinese.
Booklets, 1972, 1973. Originals, 1.5 cm.
Two 50th anniversary booklets of the **Shing Wah Daily News** published in Chinese and one booklet, **A Tribute to Ernest C.Mark** in English and Chinese.

Sato, Tsutae, 1891-1983, and **Hanako.**
Teacher, educator.
Originals, 1923-1981, 2.90 cm. Finding aid 1418. MG 30 D221.

Born in the village of Tanikura, Tsukushima prefecture, Japan. Trained at the Teachers' Training College in Tokyo in 1908. In 1917, the Japanese consul in Vancouver transmitted a request from the Japanese community in Vancouver for an additional Japanese-language teacher. The Ministry of Education recommended Tsutae Sato, and he arrived in 1917 in Vancouver to take up his duties with the Nippon Kokumin Gakko(Japanese National School). In 1922, he became its principal. He married Hanako Awaka in 1921, and she too had graduated from the Teachers' Training College in Tokyo, and had also received an invitation to teach from the Vancouver Japanese Joint Language Schools.
The Satos played important roles in the educational and cultural life of the Japanese community in Canada. They dedicated much time to the founding of the Japanese Library and to the building of a Japanese hall in Vancouver. They were also instrumental in organizing the Japanese Language Schools Society, meant to embrace all Japanese language schools in Canada. In this venture they were very successful. At the first conference only seven schools were represented, by 1942, 54 schools were involved.
In 1941, anti-Oriental hysteria, against the background of World War II, was reaching alarming proportions. It led directly to the closure of the Japanese Language School in Vancouver in 1941. The Satos, evicted from the evacuation zone with most of their fellow Japanese, subsequently spent the next ten years of their lives on a farm near Lacombe, Alberta.
In 1951, they returned to Vancouver, and once again took up teaching in the newly reopened Japanese Language School. They retired from teaching in 1966, and continued to reside in Vancouver until their deaths in 1983.

Photographs(55) were transferred to the National Photographs Collection. Three tape recordings and two records were transferred to the National Film, Television and Sound Archives.

Correspondence, 1938-1974. 1 cm.(volume 1).
Several letters from Japanese notables.

Diaries, 1941-1980. 55 cm.

Bound diaries maintained by the Satos.

Publications and writings of Tsutae and Hanako Sato, 1923-1980. 30 cm. (volumes 4-5,17).

Published manuscripts writings of the Satos on Japanese language education, their various experiences in Canada and generally on Japanese in Canada.
Records and texts of the Japanese Language School, 1923-1976. 74 cm. (volumes 5-8).
Minutes of general meetings of the Japanese Language Schools in Canada Association, records of the Japanese Language School after World War II, several guides of moral instruction, Japanese language texts and other publications related to the Japanese Language School in Vancouver.
Scrapbooks, 1923-1970(volume 9).
Scrapbooks of press clippings related to Japanese Language Schools in Canada, the Satos' trip to Japan in 1938, and the visit of Prince and Princess Chichibu in 1937
Printed materials, 1959-1973. 36 cm.(volumes 10-11).
Printed texts on Japanese in North America from the Satos' library, some of which are annotated.
Newsletters, 1958-1971, 54 cm. (volumes 11-14).
Runs of Japanese newspapers: **Kaiho**(Japanese Immigrants' Association newsletter) for 1978-1982 and **Geppo**(Japanese Canadian Citizens Association) for 1958-1981.
Oversize items, 1929-1977. 20 cm. (volumes 15-16).
Several pictorials of Japan, scrapbooks of World War II events and Mr. Sato's diplomas and commendations and calligraphed poems by Japanese literati.

Wong, Leung Doo Collection.
Originals, 1908-1962. 21 cm. photocopies, 1894-1931. 7 pages. MG30 D250.

Personal and business correspondence relating to activities in the Province of Québec and material concerning the Teatro Chung Wa in Havana,Cuba; relating to members of the Wong family, several booklets in Chinese, personal photographs; photocopies of immigration documents. Most of the documents are in Chinese.

Story, Norah, 1902-1978.
Toronto. Archivist and historian.
Originals. 20 cm. n.d., 1968-1975. MG 30 D256.

Includes typescript of Norah Story's biography of Paul Martin, **The member for Essex East, the career of Paul Martin**, and related correspondence, 1975, from the Canadian Institute of International Affairs, correspondence between Norah Story and Paul Martin regarding the biography, 1968-1973.
ULM 4

Gordon, Margaret Elizabeth, 1905-1962.
Originals, 1937. 20 cm. MG 30 D299.

While teaching at the MacLean High School in Maple

Ridge, British Columbia, she began to study the Japanese language to better deal with some of her students, of whom one-third were of Japanese origin. In this connection she was the only Canadian high school teacher who accompanied a group of American high school teachers on a tour of Japan at the request of the Japanese government in 1937.

One scrapbook, two photo albums, one studio photograph and two pictorials of Japan, relating to M.E.Gordon's tour of Japan at the request of the Japanese Board of Tourist Industry(volumes 1 and 2).

MG 30 E. Professional and public life.

McHaffie, George Addison, l887-
Army officer.
Originals, 1919. 31 pages. MG 30 E22

Correspondence, relating chiefly to supplies for the Canadian Expeditionary Force, Siberia.
ULM

Christie, Loring Cheyney, 1885-1941.
Diplomat.
Originals, 1904-1917. 4 inches. Finding aid 189. MG 30 E44.

Papers, consisting of memoranda and reports, arranged under subject headings. Subjects concerned are imperial and dominion affairs, Paris Peace Conference, 1919, the Washington Disarmament Conference and military and legal matters.

Anglo-Japanese alliance 003, 041, 042.

Immigration, Oriental. 013-040, 068

India. 014-105.

Peace Conference, 1919. 1920-1921, 062.

Turkey. 024-025.

Washington Conference, 1921-1922. 026.

Beaudry, Laurent.
Senior official, Department of External Affairs.
Papers. MG 30 E50.

Folder 13. Japanese passports taken by the Royal Canadian Mounted Police from Japanese sailing on the **Gripsholm**, 1943.

Volume 5. Folder 105. Memorandum on position of Japanese in British Columbia, 1943.

O'Hara, Francis Charles Trench, 1870-1954.
Journalist and public servant.
Papers. 1896-1954. MG 30 E104
Photographs and clippings include albums relating to the Pan-Pacific Commercial Conference held in Honolulu, 1922.

Robertson, Norman, 1904-1968.
Ottawa. Public servant.
Originals, 3.21 metres transcripts, 5 cm. 1915-1968, 1981.
MG 30 E163

Correspondence, memoranda, and printed material relating to Robertson's career in the Department of External Affairs, with the Canadian delegation to the League of Nations, as delegate to various international conferences, and as advisor to imperial conferences, 1920-1941.
ULM 4

McNaughton, Andrew George Leslie, 1897-1965.
Military officer, scientist, public servant, cabinet minister.
Original, 1764-1966. 48.99 metres Finding aid 417. MG 30 E133.

Permanent Joint Board of Defence and United Nations.
Original, 1946-1953. 1 metres Volume 296-301.
Subject files include the work of the Atomic Energy Commision and the Kashmir Dispute which are the personal working files and verbatim records of the United Nations Security Council.

Corlett, Charles H.
U.S. military officer. MG 30 E197.

Copy of a portion of General Corlett's unpublished autobiography in which he describes the Joint Canadian-American landing on Kiska, Aleutian Islands, 15 August 1943. 28 pages.
REP/1972-1973.

Sparling, Albert Walter.
Letter with three memoranda, 1941-1942. MG 30 E240.

A letter from Colonel J.F.Preston, Canadian Army General Staff, Pacific Command, enclosing three memoranda written during September 1941 by Colonel B.R.Mullaly. The memoranda deal with the Far East situation during the early period of World War II with emphasis on conditions in Japan, Japanese imperialism and the Tripartite Alliance. In addition there is a file of newspaper clippings dealing with the Japanese problem in British Columbia during January 1941-January 1942.

Cherniack, Saul M., 1917-
Lawyer and politician.
Originals, 1946-51. 75 cm., photocopies, 1942-1951, 1976. 5 cm. Finding aid 583. MG 30 E266.
Born and educated in Winnipeg, receiving an LLB in 1939. In 1947 he acted as counsel in Manitoba for the Cooperative Committee on Japanese Canadians, representing many Japanese claimants before the Royal Commission on Japanese Property Losses, 1947-1950(frequently called the Bird Commission). Correspondence, 1942-1951, 1976. photocopies 5 cm. (volume 1). Originals in the possession of the Manitoba Provincial Archives.

Material relating to Cherniack's activities as legal representative in Manitoba and North-Western Ontario for the Cooperative Committee on Japanese Canadians before the Royal Commission on Japanese Property Losses including correspondence with claimants, other lawyers, the office of the Custodian of Enemy Property and the executive of the Cooperative Committee on Japanese Canadians. Financial statements, miscellaneous forms, completed economic loss survey forms and the constitution and correspondence of the Steveston Japanese Women's Society.
Case files, 1946-1951, originals, 75 cm.(volumes 1-4). Correspondence, property evaluation forms and court transcripts relating to Japanese claims represented by Cherniack. Files are listed alphabetically.

Angus, Henry Forbes, 1891-
Lawyer and professor.
Originals, 1914-1966. 18 cm. transcripts, 1914-1919. 3 cm. MG 30 E274.
Born in Victoria, British Columbia. In World War I served in India, 1914-1916, and in Mesopotamia, 1916-1919. Has written on domestic and international topics, and has been a member of the Institute of Pacific Relations, the Royal Commission on Dominion-Provincial Relations, and others, and has served as Special Secretary to the Under-Secretary of State for External Affairs.

Transcripts are from originals in the possession of Henry Forbes Angus.

Speeches, n.d., 1953-1961. Originals, 2 cm.
Unpublished speeches on a variety of topics delivered in the 1950's and 1960's.
Articles, book reviews, reports, originals, 4 cm.
Offprints of various articles and reviews by Angus on such topics as immigration, civil rights, international relations, copies of reports and his activities on government commissions in British Columbia and studies.
Autobiography, 1966. Originals, 7 cm.
Mastercopy of the autobiography of H.F.Angus which describes many political and economic events in the 20th century.
Books, n.d., 1951, originals, 3 cm.,transcripts, 1914-1919. 3 cm.
Letters from her son transcribed by Mrs. M.E.Angus into five books which represent H.F.Angus' war diaries(1914-1919). Mrs. Angus wrote and privately published two books, **Diary of M.E.Angus, 1914-18**, which complements the transcribed war correspondence from her son.

Singh, Kartar, fl.1910-1935.
Publisher and editor.
Originals, 1911-1936. 5 cm. MG 30 E281
Kartar Singh emigrated from India to Canada in 1912, and became active in the Sikh community, publishing the newspaper **Samsar**. A graduate of the Faculty of Arts, Khalsa College, Amritsar, in 1909, he became involved in the struggle for equality and justice through his newspapers and the Khalsa Diwan societies of the first Sikh temples. In the late 1920's, Mr. Singh started another publication, **India and Canada**, an English language periodical, to promote better cultural understanding. The economic problems of the depression led to the suspension of this project

Various newspapers collected or edited by Kartar Singh, including **The Indian Immigrant**, 1914-1918, **The Aryan**, 1911-1912, and the **India and Canada**, 1929-1936, in English and Punjabi, and one issue of **The Hindustanee**, 1914. 1916-1919.

Odlum, Victor Wentworth, 1880-1971.
Soldier, journalist and diplomat.
Originals, 1890-1978, 10.9 metres Finding aid 1149. MG 30 E300.
First Canadian ambassador to China, 1941-1942, Canadian ambassador to Turkey, 1947-1952.

Volume 1.

Ahmad Bashir M. Pakistan ambassador to Turkey. Private correspondence and press releases on anti-British sentiment in Pakistan, 1949-1951.

Allen, Dr. Stewart, Chairman, Canadian Aid Fund to China. Relate to Allen's internment by Chinese Communists, 1945-1952.

Ankara Golf Club, 1952-1954.

Bayer, Celai, President of Turkey, Odlum to Bayer, 1951.

Bell, Dr. Gerald, 11 letters from Bell on Canadian missionary property rights in China, 1943-1945.

Volume 2.

Brown, Margaret, missionary activity in China, November 1942-February 1946.

Canadian aid to China organization. Fund raising in Vancouver, 1947-1949.

Red Cross China Committee,1945;

Canadian legation to Tokyo, 1930-1931.

Casey, Richard, Governor of Bengal. Discussion of Indian politics, 1945-1946.

Chang, Caron, see also: diplomatic series, China, correspondence through, 1944.

Chang, Chia-Chu("C.C.") includes article "China's urge for industrialization", 1945-1946.

Chang, General Chun, Secretary-general to the President, Republic of China, and Governor of Szechwan province, 1946-1951.

Chang, S.L., Chinese merchant, 1945-1948

Charles, Noel, British ambassador to Turkey, includes official correspondence, 1949-1953.

Che, Lin-shou, 1959-1960.

Chen, Li-tu, Dr. Includes copies of letters from Odlum. Some of Chen's letters are in Chinese, 1943-1951.

Chen, R.C. Manager, Bank of China, 1944.

Chen, Shih-tsau, 1943-1944.

Cheng, Tien-fong, Vice-chancellor, Central Political Institute, 1943-1946.

Chen, T.K., Curator, West China Union University Museum, 1943.

Chiang, Kai-shek, Madame. Includes 12 autographed letters from Madame Chiang, with references to Chinese politics, 1943-1959

Ch'ien, Ch'eng, Vice-chief of General Staff, 1944.

Childers, Colonel James S. Personal, 1943-1944.

China-American Council, 1944-1945.

Chinese War Relief fund, 1943.

Volume 3.

Davis, T.C. Canadian arms to China, 1946-1951, copies of dispatches and official correspondence on China, December 1946-January 1955.

Derin, Hadlun. Chef du cabinet, Turkey, 1948-1949.

re volume Missionary activity in China, 1944-1946

Dorr, Russell T. U.S. minister. Special mission to Turkey, 1950-1962.

Volume 4.

Dye, Dr. Daniel. China Union University, 1944.

Endicott, Dr. James. Includes some despatches and clippings on Endicott's problems in China, missionary and political, and his personal observations and confrontations in Chinese politics, 1945-1952.

Fan, Chong-shi. Chinese businessman. Includes original Chinese script and translation.

Volume 5.

Gauss, C.E. U.S. ambassador to China, 1943-1948.

Ghani, Ghassame. Iranian ambassador to Turkey, 1949-1952.

Goker, Muzaffer. Turkish ambassador to Canada, semi-official, 1948-1949.

Graham, Rev. David. West China Border Research Society, 1944.

Gulek, Kasim. Turkish Minister of Public Works, 1948-1952.

Volume 6.
Hurley, Patrick. Private correspondence, 1945-1951.

Kilborn, Leslie Gifford, Rev, West China Union University, 1943-1960;

Volume 9.

Menon, K.P.S. Agent-general for India. Correspondence and diplomatic relations concerning Indian politics.

Moran, H.O. Ambassador to Turkey, semi-official, includes Turkish immigration to Canada, 1952-1956.

Munro, D.W. Department of External Affairs. Semi-official and personal correspondence re Turkish embassy matters, 1949-1953.

Volume 10.

Pearson, Lester Bowles. Drafts and copies of Odlum's letters and telegrams. 27 items are from Pearson in a semi-official and official capacity on Turkey, U.N. and liberal leadership, 1943-1968.

Ralston, James Layton, Minister of National Defence. Telegrams, personal correspondence, despatch on Ralston's resignation, Chinese press interpretation of conscription, Turkish-Canadian textile transaction, 1940-1949.

Reid, Escott Meredith, Under Secretary of State. Official correspondence re China, Dr. James Endicott, 1944-1949.

Volumes 33-42.

China(1940-1967).
Correspondence(1940-1947) volumes 39-40.
Files include official, semi-official and private correspondence, both outgoing and incoming letters, alphabetically arranged. In some instances an attempt was made to cite significant correspondence or list significant correspondents. All correspondents in all files are not listed.

Volume 33.

Correspondence, regarding Odlum's posting to China(43 items) - includes congratulatory letters, as well as advice re legation, Sino-Canadian trade, November 1940-December 1942.

Correspondence en route to China(67 items- includes reports of meetings with influential Chinese and Americans, and a series of letters of introduction.)

Among the correspondents are J.Bassett, Harry Hussey, Hugh B.Keenleyside, W.L.MacKenzie King, and Agnes Smedley, January-March 1943.

Correspondence on India(36 items) - includes reports on the Indian political situation and India's view of Canada and Britain, April 1943.

Correspondence in China as first minister(55 items) - correspondents include Hugh Keenleyside, Leslie Kilborn, and M.E.Nichols, May-June 1943

Correspondence in China as first minister(50 items) - included are letters from Odlum(copies) to MacKenzie King, relating to Dr. Wilder Penfield, and to Hugh Keenleyside, August 1943.

Correspondence in China as first minister(85 items) - correspondents include Pearl S.Buck, J.H.King, and Lieutenant-General J.W.Stilwell, September 1943.

Correspondence in China as first minister(57 items), October 1943.

Correspondence in China as first minister(50 items) - included is correspondence re the status of the Canadian Legation. Correspondents include the Women's Missionary Society of the United Church of Canada, M.E.Nichols, T.V.Soong, November 1943.

Correspondence as Canadian ambassador to China(62 items), December l943.

Correspondence as Canadian Ambassador to China(43 items) - includes correspondence from C.E.Gauss, Orville Kay, Hugh Keenleyside, N.S.Robertson, January 1944.

Correspondence as Canadian ambassador to China(55 items) - includes copies of documents creating Odlum ambassador. Among the correspondents are Brigadier Sherwood Lett, M.E.Nichols, N.A.Robertson and Freda Utley, February 1944.

Correspondence as Canadian ambassador to China(51 items) - correspondents include Ralph E.Collins, Harry Letson, R.M.Macdonnell, March 1944.

Correspondence as Canadian ambassador in China(49 items) - included are letters from J.H.King, C.J.MacKenzie, M.E.Nichols, N.A.Robertson, April 1944.

Correspondence as Canadian ambassador to China(43 items) - correspondence includes discussion of press tour controversy, correspondents include Madame Sun Yat-sen, May 1944

Correspondence as Canadian ambassador to China,(29 items) - correspondents include Norman MacKenzie, Brigadier General Thomas B.Wilson, and Madame Chiang Kai-shek, June 1944.

Correspondence as Canadian ambassador to China(49 items) - correspondents include Hugh Keenleyside, Sherwood Lett, Gerald G.McGeer, and M.E.Nichols, July 1944.

Correspondence as Canadian ambassador to China(61 items), August l944.

Correspondence as Canadian ambassador to China(84 items) - includes correspondence re Madame Sun Yat-sen, and correspondents such as Harry Hussey and Madame Chiang Kai-shek, September-December 1944.

Correspondence as Canadian ambassador to China(67 items) - correspondents include Tao Hsi-sheng, Arthur Lowndes, and W.L.MacKenzie King, January-April 1945.

Correspondence as Canadian ambassador to China(89 items) - includes correspondence re Sino-Canadian trade, Irvine Keenleyside, R.M.Macdonell, Gerald G.McGeer, C.J.MacKenzie, M.E.Nichols, W.L.MacKenzie King, Madame Sun Yat-sen, and Georges P.Vanier(from Odlum), May-June 1945.

Correspondence in China as Canadian ambassador - includes a message from W.L.MacKenzie King to Chiang Kai-shek, July 1945.

Correspondence in China as Canadian ambassador(56 items) - correspondents include H.D.Robertson, A.C.Wedemeyer, and W.L.MacKenzie King to Chiang Kai-shek, August 1945.

Correspondence in China as Canadian ambassador(84 items) - includes correspondence re Canadian loan to China. Among correspondents are Edwin A.Locke, W.L.MacKenzie King, Tao Hsi-sheng, and K.W.Taylor, September-October 1945.

Correspondence in China as Canadian ambassador(49 items)- correspondents include Tao Hsi-sheng and Freda Utley, November 1945

Correspondence in China as Canadian first minister(86 items) - correspondents include Senator J.H.King, V.J.MacKenzie, Norman MacKenzie, James A.Mackinnon, and Tao Hsi-sheng, December 1945.

Volume 34.

Correspondence as Canadian ambassador to China(91 items)- correspondents include Arthur Lowndes, N.A.MacKenzie, M.E.Nichols, G.S.Patterson, Harold R.Robertson and Freda Utley, January 1946

Correspondence as Canadian ambassador to China(87 items) - includes correspondence relating to Yalta, and from Leslie Kilborn, M.E.Nichols, and Tao Hsi-sheng, February l946

Correspondence as Canadian ambassador to China(86 items) - correspondents include Sherwood Lett and Chester Ronning, April- May 1946

Correspondence in China as Canadian ambassador(24

items) - include correspondence regarding loss and damage to mission property in Suchow, June-July 1946.

Correspondence in China as Canadian ambassador(27 items) - includes correspondence from H.D.Robertson re Odlum's next possible appointment, August 1946.

Correspondence in China as Canadian ambassador(57 items) - includes correspondence regarding Chinese Communist Party, correspondents include G.S.Patterson, H.D.Robertson and T.P.O'Kelly, September-December 1946.

Correspondence in China relating to China(21 items) - correspondents include Madame Chiang Kai-shek(original) and Chien Li-fu, February-December 1947

Correspondence in China(11 items)n.d.

Memorabilia(n.d., 1941-1946)

Volume 40.

Business receipts re China, 1942-1946.

Cartoon, "A tale of two cities", 1945.

Collins, Ralph E. - Wedding announcement, 1945.

Funeral notice in Chinese, with eulogies, n.d.

Greeting cards, Chinese, 1943-1946.

Greeting cards from Chou En-lai(2 items), 1945-1946.

Greeting cards, 1943-1946.

Invitations, Canadian and American, re China, 1941-1946.

Invitations in China from Chinese, 1943-1946.

Invitations, Chinese, to Odlum, with translations, n.d.

Invitations, Chinese with translations, 1943-1946.

Invitations, from Generalissimo and Madame Chiang Kai-shek, 1945-1946.

Invitations from various embassies, 1943-1946.

Public appearances by Odlum, 1943-1946.

Despatches and memoranda(1943-1950) volumes 34-36.

China, despatches and memoranda, May-August 1943.

China, despatches and memoranda, September-October 1943.

China, despatches and memoranda, November-December 1943.

China, despatches and memoranda, January 1944.

China, despatches and memoranda, February 1944.

China, despatches and memoranda, March-April 1944.

Volume 35.

China, despatches and memoranda, May 1944.

China, despatches and memoranda, June 1944.

China, despatches and memoranda, July 1944.

China, despatches and memoranda, August 1944.

China, despatches and memoranda, September 1944.

China, despatches and memoranda, October 1944.

China, despatches and memoranda, November 1944.

China, despatches and memoranda, December 1944.

China, despatches and memoranda, January-March 1945.

China, despatches and memoranda, April-May 1945.

China, despatches and memoranda, June 1945.

China, despatches and memoranda, July-August 1945.

China, despatches and memoranda, September-October 1945.

China, despatches and memoranda, November 1945.

China, despatches and memoranda, December 1945.

Volume 36.

China, despatches and memoranda, January 1946.

China, despatches and memoranda(1 of 2), February-March 1946.

China, despatches and memoranda(2 or 2), March 1946.

China, despatches and memoranda, April-May 1946.

China, despatches and memoranda, June 1946.

China, despatches and memoranda, July 1946.

China, despatches and memoranda, August 1946.

China, despatches and memoranda, September-October 1946.

External affairs circular despatches, 1947.

External affairs circular despatches, 1949.

External affairs circular despatches, 1950.

China subject files(1941-1951) volumes 36-58 - includes some despatches, memoranda and related correspondence.

Armed forces of China, 1943-1945.

British despatches, 1942-1945.

Burma campaign, 1941-1944.

Canadian embassy move to Nanking, September 1945-February 1946.

Canadian embassy move to Nanking, March-July 1946.

Volume 37.

Canadian mission property rights in China, October 1943-July 1946.

"C.C. Clique"(the Chang brothers), 1946-1948.

Censorship in China, 1943-1946.

Chiang Kai-shek, 1943-1946.

Civil war in China, 1944-1946.

Civil war in China, military operations, March 1945-September 1946.

Civil war, negotiations with Communists, June 1944-July 1946.

Communist held territory in China, 1944-1946

Communist-Kuomintang ideological factionalism, 1945-1946.

Communist position in China, 1943-1946.

Diplomatic lists of dignitaries, 1942-1946.

Economics in China, statistical information, 1943-1946.

Economic letters, Bank of China, 1943-1946.

Economic situation in China, 1943-1946.

Endicott, Dr. James Gareth. - correspondence and despatches regarding his activities in China, October 1944-May 1945.

Foreign policy, Chinese, 1944-1946
General reports, impressions of China, 1944.

Health problems in China, 1943-1946.

Industrialization of China, 1945.

Japanese military operations in China and the Far East, 1943-1945.

Volume 38.

Korean situation, 1944-1946.

Kuomintang-Communist negotiations, 1944-1945.

Kuomintang reports and statements, 1944-1945.

Lin-sen, death of, 1943.

Military operations in the Chinese theatre, 1943-1945.

National Resources Commission of China, technical committee visit to Canada, 1944.

Official Chinese government move to Nanking, 1945-1946.

Pearson, Lester Bowles. Statement to the U.N. re China, 1951.

Press, Chinese and foreign, 1944-1946.

Prisoners of war in China and Far East, 1943-1946.

Recovered Chinese cities, 1944-1946.

Shanghai internees, 1945.

Sino-American relations, 1943-1946.

Sino-British relations, 1943-1946.

Sino-Canadian immigration draft treaty, 1944.

Sino-Canadian loan proposals, 1945-1946.

Sino-Canadian relations - purpose and work of the Canadian legation, 1943.

Sino-Canadian relations, general.

Sino-Canadian trade relations, 1945-1946.

Sino-Canadian relations, the Kuling talks, 1946.

Sino-Japanese relations, 1943-1945.

Sino-Soviet relations, 1943-1948.

Szechwan province, 1944-1946.

"Who's who" in China(c-k), n.d.

"Who's who" in China(l-z), n.d.

"Who's who" lists, 1942-1946.

United Nations, planning of, 1945.

World War II, China and Indo-China, 1943-1945.

Reference material relating to China(1943-1967)

volumes 38-43 - includes Odlum's personal notes and a variety of printed material.

Volume 38.

Addresses of Chinese and international dignitaries, n.d.

Canadian embassy guest lists, 1944.

Central Planning Board organization, [1946].

Chinese Democratic Party - notes, n.d.

Chinese language lessons, n.d.

Chinese officials, 1944-1946.

Chinese political situation - notes, n.d.

Chinese stamps and postmarks, examples, 1943-1946.

Chinese traffic signals - posters, 1945.

Diaries of events in China, November 1942-December 1945.

Volume 39.

Diary of appointments in China, 1944-1946.

Diplomatic officials in China, 1945-1946.

Odlum's personal notebook relating to dignitaries and language lessons, 1943.

American Digest - Bulletin, 1945.

Australia's Neighbours - bulletin, 1954, 1964, 1967.

British bulletins, 1942-1962.

Canadian bulletins, including one published by the Canadian Legation, 1943-1955.

China News Service; - bulletin. 1947-1963.

Constitution of the Republic of China, 1937, 1947.

Constitutional government and national reconstruction of China" prepared by Canadian Embassy in China. n.d.

Far Eastern Survey - bulletin, 1949-1952

Fitzgerald, C.P., "A series of two articles and a lecture", 1951.

Free China Weekly - bulletin, 1967.

Manifestos of the Central Committee of the Chinese Communist Party - leaflet, 1945-1946.

New Republic - journal, 1945.

Articles re China, 1939-1949.

Articles re China, 1950-1966.

Newspapers within China - including **Chungking Reporter, National Herald,** and a Chinese language paper, 1944-1946.

Press releases re China, 1943-1944.

Press releases in China, 1945.

Press releases in China, 1946-1951.

Press releases re China and the United Nations, 1955-1952.

Newspaper clippings re China, n.d.

Newspaper clippings re China, 1941-1946.

Volume 40.

Newspaper clippings re China, 1947-1949.

Newspaper clippings re China, 1950-1967.

Publications re China and the Far East.

American publications(16), 1943-1949

American publications(9), 1950-1966.

American - foreign policy bulletin(9) 1945-1946.

American - Harry Hussey(1), n.d.

British publications(5), 1938-1942.

Canadian government publications re Japan(1), 1942-1944.

Canadian pamphlets re China(6), n.d.

Madame Chiang Kai-shek - speeches and pamphlets(9), 1942-1966.

China - documents re constitution and government(4) - includes **National Congress and draft of the constitutional law"**(in Chinese), n.d., 1925.

China, general(7), 1932-1941.

China, general(5), 1943-1944.

Volume 41.

China, official publications of the Kuomintang(3) - includes essays by Sun Yat-sen.

Chinese language publications(3), n.d.

Chinese authors(4), 1942-1945.

Chinese patriotic songbook(1), n.d.

Chinese publications - Communist Chinese(9), 1942-1949.

Diplomatic lists and directory of Chungking(4), 1942-1946.
Financial agreement between Canada and China(2), 1946.

India(3), 1942-1948.

International publications(7), 1927-1961.

Japan-China conflict(3), n.d.

Japanese-Canadians(3), 1927-1945.

Japan-general(14), 1925-1958.

Volume 42.

Japan-Manchurian problem(2), 1931, 1933.

Manchuria-**Contemporary Manchuria**(1), 1937.

Republic of China-**Free China Review**(3), 1951-1959.

Republic of China(4), 1959-1964.
Republic of China, specific issues(4), 1949-1957.

United Nations and China, 1948-1958.

Photographs reflecting Odlum's ambassadorship in China. The majority of the photos were transferred to the National Photography Collection.

C. Turkey(1941-1955), volumes 43-46.

Correspondence and memorabilia(1941-1952), volume 50.

Volume 43.

Correspondence(6 items) - includes original letters from Lester B.Pearson, and correspondence relating to Odlum's proposed appointment to South Africa, 1941-1946.

Correspondence(30 items)-includes details of the move to Turkey, arrangement of staff, Odlum's appointment, 1947.

Correspondence(15 items) - personal letters to Odlum, 1948-1950.

Correspondence (17 items) - largely regarding arrangements from Odlum's move to Canada, 1951.

Correspondence(36 items), 1952.

Accounts at Ankara, 1948-1952.

Addresses and telephone directory, 1952

Archeology, Turkey - correspondence and information, including the Harran discovery, 1951-1952.

Credentials of the Canadian ambassador and laissez-passer(copies), [1947].

Dominion day - receptions, 1949-1951.

Embassy House staff, Ankara - correspondence, memos and letters of recommendation, 1947-1951.

Invitations, n.d.

Invitations and programmes, 1947-1952.

Kelly, David sr.- farewell dinner, 1949.

Menus, 1949-1951.

Officials, lists of, 1947-1952.

Social notes by Odlum, 1950-1951.

Turkish lessons - notes, 1947-1949.

Turkey, despatches and memoranda(1947-1952), volumes 43-45.

Odlum's despatches and memoranda were bound together in folders and arranged chronologically, despatches are also numbered. Not all topics discussed are highlighted; only a rough guide is provided.

Turkey, despatch - regarding Canadian Legation to Turkey(from Louis St. Laurent), 5 December 1947.

Turkey, despatches and memoranda - includes information regarding the Arab-Israeli situation, Czechoslovakia and Greece, 2 December 1947-5 March 1948.

Turkey, despatches and memoranda - correspondence is included to T.C.Davis; despatches include information regarding aid plan to Turkey, Czechoslovakia, Russia and the Eastern bloc, March-May 1948.

Turkey, despatches and memoranda - includes information regarding tension between Russia and Turkey, possibility of World War III, May-July 1948.

Turkey, despatches and memoranda - includes correspondence to J.F.Bingham, T.C.Davis, and Colonel Kenyon, and discussion of Democratic Party of Turkey, Turkish by-elections, and Dutch-Turkish relations, July-November 1948.

Turkey, despatches and memoranda - includes information regarding Turkish economic plans for

1949, Russian-Turkish tension, Turkish-Netherlands hostility, Russian diplomatic tactics re Turkey, November-December 1948.

Turkey, despatches and memoranda - correspondence include Colonel L.E.Kenyon and the Netherlands ambassador, topics include situation in Indonesia, Turkish political parties and cabinet, Turkey-U.K. finances, and Economic Congress in Istanbul, January-February 1949.

Turkey, despatches and memoranda - topics include Canadian Embassy operations, cold war, military-strategic position of Turkey, proposed Atlantic Pact, Turkish resources, American estimates of Turkey's position, and an immigration application from the Don Cossacks, February-March 1949.

Turkey, despatches and memoranda, topics include Canadians in Lebanon, Turkish defence systems, and issue of invitation to Sadat to visit Canada, March-May 1949.

Turkey, despatches and memoranda - topics include embassy administration, Arab-Israeli clash, China, Soviet threat to Turkey, and Turkish army training, May-June 1949.

Volume 44.

Turkey, despatches and memoranda, includes reports re Chaman Lall, India and Pakistan conflict, Turkish defence, and political parties in Turkey, June-July 1949.

Turkey, despatches and memoranda - includes appeal re former Hungarian ambassador to Turkey, appointment of Turkish ambassador to Canada, bilateralism and barter re Turkey, Canada-Turkey trade, organization of Ministry of National Defense and Turkish General Staff, July-August 1949.

Turkey, despatches and memoranda - includes information re coup d'état in Syria, Turkish economics and political parties, August-October 1949.

Turkey, despatches and memoranda - includes an article from **Time** magazine, talks with Prime Minister Gunalty, Turkish defence strategy, and the Kurds of Syria, October-November 1949.

Turkey, despatches and memoranda - includes correspondence from Dr. Li Tsi-au, also includes information regarding Cyprus and World Bank mission to Turkey, December 1949-February 1950.

Turkey, despatches and memoranda - includes information regarding the Cypriot situation, and Massey-Harris survey team in Turkey, March-April 1950.

Turkey, despatches and memoranda - includes information regarding British position re Turkey, Turko-Israeli relations and the Turkish election, 10 April-31 May 1950.

Turkey, despatches and memoranda - includes correspondence from Chen Li-fu and A.D.P.Heeney; also includes platform of new Turkish government, discussion of Middle Eastern situation, and map of "Principal holy places" of Jerusalem, 1 June-11 July 1950.

Turkey, despatches and memoranda - includes discussion of Cyprus, fear of war in Turkey, a study of Nationalist China, 11 July-3 August 1950.

Turkey, despatches and memoranda - includes discussion of Turkish defences near Erzerum, Turkish contingent for Korea and the Atlantic Pact, 4-25 August 1950.

Turkey, despatches and memoranda - includes discussion of Turkish Tobacco Congress, cotton exports, NATO, Turko-Bulgarian relations, 25 August-1 December 1950

Turkey, despatches and memoranda - correspondence from the Canadian Secretary of State, Jerusalem, Turko-Bulgarian hostilities, Atlantic Pact, the Turkish army, 22 September-23 October 1950

Turkey, despatches and memoranda - memoranda re the writing of despatches and routine embassy business, Turkish Parliament, 23 October-28 November 1950.

Turkey, despatches and memoranda - includes annual report, 1950; Turkish party politics, Turko-Korean contingent, 28 November 1950-16 January 1951

Turkey, despatches and memoranda - includes information regarding budget for Turkey, Turkish courts, Korea, Russian threat and U.S. interference in Turkey, 18 January-2 March 1951.

Turkey, despatches and memoranda - includes material relating to implication of Turkish budget, Middle East command, Massey-Harris and cotton, immigration selection, 2 March-14 April 1951.

Turkey, despatches and memoranda - includes information regarding strategic material in Turkey, position of Turkish armed forces, 16 April-29 May 1951.

Turkey, despatches and memoranda - includes information regarding the Middle East Command, article on "Zionist espionage ring in Baghdad", 3 May-19 June 1951.

Turkey, despatches and memoranda - includes information relating to anti-British sentiment, anti-Ataturk campaign, and consular work in Istanbul, 19 June-24 August 1951.

Turkey, despatches and memoranda, includes information regarding Turkish by-election, Turkey and NATO, transport of Turkish troops to Korea, 4 September-15 October 1951.

Turkey, despatches and memoranda -includes report on Cyprus, Middle East defence, and top secret re Turkey in NATO, 20 October-26 November 1951.

Volume 45.
Turkey, despatches and memoranda - includes information regarding preparation for emergency or war, Turkish budget, 28 November 1951-26 January 1952.

Turkey, despatches and memoranda - includes information regarding Indian-Pakistani relations in Turkey, NATO, Turkish politics and military, 29 January-1 April 1952

Turkey, despatches and memoranda - includes information regarding foreign trade to Turkey, war prospects, Bulgarian protest to Turkey, 4 April-31 May 1952.

Turkey, despatches and memoranda, 2 June-16 July 1952.

Turkey, despatches, indices - detailed and in chronological order, 1947-1952.

Turkey, memoranda, 1948-1952.

Turkey, reference material(1938-1950) volume 45-46.

Bulletins relating to Turkey, 1946, 1953.

Information relating to Turkey, n.d.

La turquie kemaliste(2 files) - incomplete, multilingual journal, April 1938-March 1948.

Volume 46.

Publications, miscellaneous, 1947-1950.

"Turkey, a past and a future"(article), 1927.

Press releases(in Turkish), n.d.

Press releases relating to Turkey, 1947-1948.

Press releases relating to Turkey, 1950.

Press releases relating to Turkey, 1951-1952.

Press clippings, articles, 1948-1955.

Press clippings, 1938-1955.

Press clippings in Turkish, n.d.

V.W.Odlum's diaries of events, January-December 1949.

Photographs reflcting Odlum's ambassadorship in Turkey. The majority of the photographs were transferred to the National Photograph Collection.

Tam, Yee Yee, 1880-1977.
Community organizer.
Originals, 1913-1960. 8 pages. MG 30 E314.
Transferred in 1978 from Canadian Centre for Folk Culture Studies (Dr. Ban Hoe).

Immigration certificate, issued to Tam Yee Yee by the Department of the Interior on 22 December 1913. Mr. Tam arrived at Victoria on 8 August 1899.
Canada:Chinese:1899-

Certificate of appointment issued to Mr. Tam Yee Yee as an "authorized agent" of the Chinese Freemasons, by the Chee Kung Tong, in Victoria on 15 August 1924 (20 Years' restriction as requested by Mr. Tam Yee Yee).

Certificate of appointment which empowered Mr. Tam Yee Yee to "investigate and standardize" the Freemasons; work in a building known as "The Temple of Peace"(20 years' restriction as requested by Mr. Tam Yee Yee).

Certificate of appointment issued to Mr. Tam Yee Yee by the Chee Kung Tong in San Francisco in 1921.

Certificate of appointment issued to Mr. Tam Yee Yee by the Chee Kung Tong in Victoria in 1921.

Receipt of a donation of $50 given by Mr. Tam Yee Yee (issued by the Freemason Lodge in Toronto in 1960).

War bond (issued by the National Republican Government in China) for the purposes of organizing an air force and buying planes.

Ebdon, Frank Williams, 1901-
Soldier.
Original 12.5 cm. photocopies .5 cm. n.d., 1928-1980.
MG 30 E328.

Personal diary, regulations, work sheets, standing orders, nominal rolls, notebook and other papers concerning Ebdon's imprisonment in the Japanese prisoner of war camp at Shamshuipo on the Kowloon peninsula, China and Omine, near Kawasaki, Kyushu, Japan, 1942-1945. Included also are military papers, personal correspondence, newspaper clippings, sketch, publications and photographs concerning the service of the Royal Rifles of Canada in Newfoundland, 1940 and Hong Kong, 1941, and the wartime and postwar experiences of Canadian Hong Kong prisoners of war.
ULM 4

Green, John Joseph.
Ottawa, aeronautical engineer and public servant.
Originals, 1926-1984. 3.9 metres Finding aid 1032. MG 30 E343.

Correspondence and working papers of various national and international aeronautical and technical organizations, including the Asian Institute of Technology.

Institution, association and foundation series.

Volume 10.
Asian Institute of Technology.
Memoranda, correspondence, 1977, 1979-1980.

Asian Institute of Technology.
Correspondence re search for a new president, 1981-1982.

Asian Institute of Technology.
Memoranda, reports, re educational policy committee, 1977-1979.

Asian Institute of Technology.
Memoranda, reports re educational policy committee, 1980-1981.

Asian Institute of Technology.
Reports, minutes of meetings re student relations committee, 1980-1982.

Asian Institute of Technology.
Yearbook, 1979.

tute of Technology, 1959-1979, commemorative printed book of photographs.

Anniversary symposia -AIT and Asia, the next two decades, 1979.

Asian Institute of Technology, creation and development. Report to the U.S. Agency for International Development, 1975.

Volume 13.

Asian Institute of Technology.
Minutes of a regular meeting of the executive committee and the board of trustees, 12-16 February 1973.

Asian Institute of Technology.
Minutes, 1973-1976.

Volume 14.

Asian Institute of Technology.
Minutes, 1976-1978.

Volume 15.

Asian Institute of Technology.
Minutes, 1979-1981.

Volume 16.

Asian Institute of Technology.

Minutes, 1981-1983.

Asian Institute of Technology.
Board of trustees minutes and reports, parts 1-3, 1982.

Asian Institute of Technology.
Correspondence, 1982-1984.

Volume 17.
Asian Institute of Technology.
Minutes, 1983-1984.

Asian Institute of Technology.
Education policy committee minutes, 1978-1981.

Volume 18.

Asian Institute of Technology directory and tracer study, 1979, 1982.

Asian Institute of Technology. Annual reports, 1977-1980, 1983.

Astech - AIT students' magazine, 1974-1981.

Asian Institute of Technology, n.d.

Balasubramanian, A.S. Curriculum vita.

Asian Institute of Technology.
Correspondence, 1982-1984.

Asian Institute of Technology.
Board of trustees handbook, 1982.

Asian Institute of Technology.
Board of trustees handbook, 1982-1983.

Asian Institute of Technology.
Catalogue of courses, 1973-1980.

Asian Institute of Technology.
Donors meeting, agenda and reports, 1982.

Asian Institute of Technology. Human settlements division.
Proposal and plan of operation, 1975, 1980-1981.

Asian Institute of Technology.
Institution plan, 1981-1984, 1981.

Asian Institute of Technology.
Master plan for 1973-1980, 1973.

Asian Institute of Technology.

Miscellaneous brochures, n.d., 1977-1978.

Asian Institute of Technology.
Miscellaneous pamphlets, various dates.

Asian Institute of Technology.
Newsletter, 1973-1978.

Asian Institute of Technology.
Newsletter, 1979-1983.

Asian Institute of Technology.
Promotional photographs, n.d.

Asian Institute of Technology.
Reports and newsletters, 1968-1972.
Asian Institute of Technology.
Research summary, 1973.

Asian Institute of Technology.
Research summary, geotechnical and transportation engineering, 1975-1977.

Asian Institute of Technology.
Research summary, 1975-1977.

Asian Institute of Technology.
Research summary, industrial engineering and management, 1977-1978.

Asian Institute of Technology.
Research summary, Professor A.S. Balasubramanian, n.d.

Asian Institute of Technology.
Research summary, n.d.

Asian Institute of Technology.
Student handwork, 1979.

Asian Institute of Technology.
Technical reports and newsletter, n.d., 1979-1980.

Asian Institute of Technology.
Yearbooks, 1975, 1976,1978,1980.

Swait, Charles Edwards, 1859-1937.
Originals, 1880, 1884, 8 metres MG 30 E467.
Memoirs of Charles Swait, of the 4th battalion, Rifle Brigade, a British military unit sent to India. Describes years 1874-1875. Written in Canada, based on notes taken in India. Describes in detailed manner customs, flora, and fauna of India

Manuscript Group 31. Manuscripts of the Second Half of the Twentieth Century.

MG 31 B. Economic and Industrial Development.

Kagetsu, Eikichi, 1883-1967.
Businessman and community leader.

Originals, 1943-S4. 15 cm. MG 31 B22.

Eikichi Kagetsu was born 5th September 1883, in Wakayama-ken, Hidaka-gun, Yakawa-mura, Takara, after completing his schooling at the Yukawa Elementary school he served with the Japanese Army in Manchuria during the Russo-Japanese War. He emigrated to Canada in 1906 and worked at various jobs prior to 1907 when he worked in a lumber camp That year he bought a tract of forest land and began an independent logging operation north-west of Vancouver. In 1912, a year after his marriage to Toyo Makamoto his business failed during an economic recession. He returned to laboring in lumber camps.

In 1923, with capitalization of $120,000, Mr. Kagetsu bought 300 acres of forest at Fanny Bay, Vancouver Island. His logging operation was continually expanded until his assets were seized in 1942 and held by the Custodian of Enemy Property. By this time he employed about 100 Japanese and Canadian workers.

Until the evacuation, Mr. Kagetsu was a central figure in the Vancouver Japanese community. His contributions as a businessman, philanthropist and civic leader were many. At the end of the Second World War he resettled in Toronto and started a long and fruitless legal battle to seek equitable payment for his holding which were sold at devalued prices by the Custodian of Enemy Property.

Presented in 1978 by Toyo Kagetsu (wife) Hajime Kagetsu and Kimio Takahashi (son & daughter).

Correspondence with lawyers, politicians and the Custodian's Office relating to the Kagetsu-Deep Bay Logging claim and a transcript of the claim hearing before the Royal Commission of Mr. Justice Bird into the claims for compensation. Films of the logging operations, family and community events have been transferred to the National Film Archives.

Laidlaw, Alexander F., 1908-1980.
Educator, Coop leader. Finding aid 1341. MG 31 B32.

Volume 3. File 3.
Laidlaw correspondence with India, 1956-1957.
Consultant to the Government of India and Reserve Bank of India in training of personnel for agricultural credit unions and cooperatives.

Volume 8. File 8-11, 13.
India.

MG 31 C. Exploration and Travel.

Luxford, Nancy C.
Urban planning consultant.
Photocopy 1978. 153 pages. MG 31 C7.
Travel in People's Republic of China in June 1978, under the auspices of the University of Lethbridge.
Copy of "Reflections China 1978" on experience traveling in the People's Republic of China.

MG 31 D. Educational and Cultural Development.

Chauhan, Jay, 1941-
Barrister & Solicitor.
Originals, 1967-1983. 6 cm. MG 31 D6.

Jay Chauhan was born in Dar-Es-Salaam, Tanzania, in 1941. His family was of Indian origin, then living in

East Africa. Between 1958 and 1967, Chauhan studied in England and Germany. He migrated to Canada in 1967, completed his legal studies at Osgoode Hall and York University and was called to the bar in 1972. He resides in Richmond Hill, Ontario and is active in community and local ethnic affairs.

Presented in 1983 by J. Chauhan, Richmond Hill, Ontario.

Record of incorporation of East African Cultural Society, several newsletters, articles authored by Chauhan on immigrants and race relations, correspondence with family in India and one legal case file.

Stursberg, Peter, 1913-
Journalist.
Originals 1922-1981, 7.4 metres Finding aid 467. MG 31 D78.

Alphabetical Files.

Volume 4.

Trilingual education(India), 1966-1967.

Volume 18.

Day diaries, India trip, 1959-1961.

Correspondence and notes, India trip, 1966-1967.

Clippings and printed material, India trip, 1966.

Clippings, Indian High Commissioner, 1966.

Miscellaneous notes, correspondence, India trip, 1966.

Notes, etc., for TV talk on India, 1966.

Notes and articles, China trip 1971.

Notebook, China trip, 1971.

Publications and miscellaneous, China trip, 1971.

Scripts and notes for Canadian Broadcasting System, re China trip, 1971.

Scripts, correspondence and notes, **Newsweek** and **Toronto Star,** China trip 1971.

Canadians in China, correspondence notes,

manuscripts and scripts, 1971-1971

Clippings, interview notes, China trip, 1971.

Volume 21.

Despatches to **Daily Herald,** India, June 1946.
Notes and clippings, India, 1946.

Penlington, Norman, 1908-
Professor.
Original, 34 cm. Transcripts, 1 cm. Photocopies, 1 cm.
1893-1895, 1923, 1935. MG 31 D82.

Includes letters of J.N.Penlington on the Japanese earthquake of 1923.
ULM 4
MG 31 E. Law, Judiciary and Public Life.

Holtom, Edith Ellen, 1893-1978.
Peace activist.
Originals, 1929-1979, 80 cm. MG 31 E1

Includes files of miscellaneous Canadian and American publications published by anti-war organizations and letters to editors in protest against the Vietnam War, 1953-1976.

Shumiatcher, Morris C., 1917- .
Barrister.
Originals, 1946-49. 5 cm. MG 31 E19

Dr. Morris Cyril Shumiatcher was born in Calgary, Alberta, the son of a pioneer Jewish lawyer. He received his B.A. (1940) and LL.B. (1941) from the University of Alberta and his LL.B. (1942) and J.D. (1945) from the University of Toronto. He was admitted to the Bars of British Columbia and Alberta (1943), to the Bar of Saskatchewan (1945) and appointed a K.C. in 1948. He was assistant to the former Premier of Saskatchewan T.C.Douglas and a former Legal Counsel of the Government and Labour Relations Board of Saskatchewan. He has specialized in the areas of constructional law, company law and civil rights. Both he and his wife (Jacquelline Clay) are active in various cultural organizations as well as many Jewish community activities.

Presented in 1976 by Morris C. Shumiatcher.

Correspondence, transcripts of hearings before the Bird Commission, 1946-1949. Originals, 5 cm.
Material relating to nine claims represented by the firm of Shumiatcher & Shumiatcher before the Royal Commission on Japanese Property Losses on behalf of the Japanese Canadian Citizens Association and one file of correspondence with Premier T.C.Douglas of Saskatchewan, Ian A.MacKenzie, Minister of Veterans Affairs, H.Francis G.Bridges, Minister of Fisheries, N.J.Caldwell, M.P., and Sgt. T.Buck Iguzuki who served with the Canadian Army in South-East Asia. This file relates to Mr. Suzuki's attempts to
receive fair compensation for his property, sold by the Custodian of Enemy Property, and to Mr. Suzuki's attempts to receive a commercial fishing license, which under P.C. 25I (1942) could not be granted to persons of Japanese origin.

Bloomfield, Louis M., 1906-
Papers, MG 31 E25.

E. International Law and Legal Affairs.

Volume 5.

Correspondence, reports.

Government of India re Committee on Uses of Waters of International Rivers, International Law Association, 8 parts, 1966-1967
Correspondence, reports, Government of India re Committee on International Water Resources, International Law Association, 3 parts, 1968-1978.

Volume 13.

Correspondence. People's Republic of China, 1971-1974.

Correspondence. People's Republic of China 1975-1977.

Bethune Memorial Hospital. Lecture at Reddy Memorial Hospital, 1976.

Kitagawa, Muriel, 1912-1974.
Writer and community leader.
Originals, n.d., 1931, 1935-1959. 16.5 cm. Photocopies, 1941-1942. 2 cm. MG 31 E26

Muriel Kitagawa(see Fujiwara) was born in Vancouver in 1912. She attended Connaught High School in New Westminster and the University of British Columbia for one year, after which she withdrew to work with her father, a dentist by profession. Evacuated from the "protected zone" of British Columbia, she relocated to Toronto, where she resided until her death in 1974. She was an active campaigner on behalf of the Japanese Canadians' civil rights, working on many various committees of the Canadian Citizens' Association. Presented in 1978 by Ed Kitagawa, Toronto, Ontario.

Personal correspondence with friends and brother, W.Fujiwara, 1938-1942. 1.5 cm. (volume 1).

British Columbia Security Commission Travel Documents and Repatriation of Mrs. T.Fujiwara from Japan to Canada, 1942-1948. 1.5 cm.

Various articles by T.M.Kitagawa, Sue Sada and Margaret Inouye, on Japanese evacuation and relocation, n.d., 1947-1948. 6 cm.

Japanese Canadian Citizens Association, various committees, minutes, submissions and reports, 1946-1959. 4 cm.

National Citizenship Seminar, Minaki (Ontario), correspondence, notes and background papers, 1958. 3 cm.

Miscellaneous notes and pamphlets, 1931-1958. 5 cm.

Belle, Frank, 1924-
Finding aid 1829. MG 31 E29.
Frank Belle, was born in 1924 in Kirkland Lake, Ontario. A graduate of McGill University, he worked in the Citizenship Branch of the Department of the Secretary of State and eventually became head of the Ethnic Press Analysis Service in the Multiculturalism Directorate. He retired in 1987.

The Frank Belle papers consist largely of articles and essays produced by various ethnocultural groups and institutions in Canada between 1953 and 1986. The collection contains translations of newspapers and other articles that were written originally in languages other than English and French. There are also studies and reports on the status of the ethnic press in Canada by Belle and other analysts. This material was accumulated by Frank Belle while he served with the Ethnic Press Analysis Service and other units of the Multiculturalism Directorate. This collection is of particular use to researchers interested in the ethnic press and in the history of ethnocultural groups in Canada.

Volume 1.

1. "The Role of the Ethnic Press, Radio and T.V. in Canadian life, 1967"(unpublished article).

4. Department of Citizenship and Immigration, Canadian Citizenship Branch, Press Review (Review of the Press in Canada other than French or English), May 1954.

5. Canadian Citizenship Branch, Foreign Language Press Review Service: Handbook of editorial policies of various ethnocultural newspapers, 1958.

6. Ethnic Press Analysis Service, Department of the Secretary of State: notes for Minister's address and miscellaneous documents 1972-1973, 1980.

8. Chinese - Ethnic Press Analysis Service, draft translations of various ethnocultural articles. n.d., 1970-1971.

9. Chinese - Ethnic Press Analysis Service, draft translations of various ethnocultural articles, 1971-1974.

24. East Indian and Pakistani - Solomon Nigosian, "The East Indian and Community in Metropolitan Toronto," (unpublished paper prepared for the Department of the Secretary of State),1971.

Volume 2.

2.Canadian Gallop Poll Ltd., 'Problems and Attitudes of Immigrants in Metro Toronto From Six Ethnic Communities' (report produced for the Department of State.) 1978.

13. Japanese - Japanese Canadian Cultural Centre of Montreal Inc. "Montreal Japanese - Canadian Community Survey(Secretary of State Student Community Service Project) 16 p.1978.

14. Japanese - Japanse Canadian Citizen;'s Association Reparations Committeee: reports and news releases.1978.

15. Japanese - Japanese Canadian Citizens Association Greater Vancouver JCCA Bulletin, April 1979

16. Japanese - Ethnic Press Analysis Service, draft translations of various ethnocultural articles, 1970-1975.

21. Chinese - Chinese in Canada: articles and papers, n.d. 1953-1978

22. Chinese - Anonymous unpublished history of Chinese immigration to Canada, 95 pages, ca.1977.

32. Japanese - Japanese Immigration to Canada, chronology, 59 pages, ca. 1962

33. Japanese - **The New Canadian**(Japanese Canadian newspaper), cippings and excerpts on redress questions.

Cadieux, Marcel, 1915-1981.
Diplomat, ambassador to the United States. Originaux, 1934-1983, 8.26 mètres. Instrument de recherche 1241. MG 31 E31.

Journaux personnels.

Volume 9.

Journal personnel. Reports to the Under-Secretary of State for External Affairs and correspondence including Vietnam, 1970.

Journal personnel. General correspondence, included are numerous conversations with American officials and correspondence relating to the International Commission for Control and Supervision in Indo-China, 2 files, April-July 1972.

Volume 10.

Journal personnel. General correspondence, included is correspondence relating to the Vietnam peace talks and the International Commission for Control and Supervision in Indo-China, August-December 1972.

Journal personnel. General correspondence with American personnel and correspondence and memoranda with the Under-Secretary of State for External Affairs, concerning draft evaders, the Middle East and the International Commission for Control and Supervision, January-February 1973.

Journal personnel. General correspondence, included is correspondence related to Canada's participation in the International Commission for Control and Supervision, March 1973.

Volume 18.

Dossiers par pays, includes: Association de l'Asie du Sud-est, 1976-1977.

Bangla Desh - accord de coopération commerçiale, 1977.

Chine - l'ouverture de négociation d'un accord commerçiale, 1975-1977.

Inde - exportations de l'Inde vers la CEE, 1975-1977.

Iran - un accord commerçiale, 1976-1977.

Japon - le dumping japonais, 1975-1977.

Pakistan - un accord commerçiale et pour une assistance technique et économique, 1976.

Sri Lanka - la coopération commerçiale

Vietnam - un accord commerçiale avec la CÉE, 1977.

Reid, Escott Meredith, 1905-
High Commissioner to India, 1952-1957, Director of Operations in South Asia and the Middle East for the World Bank. Wrote **Envoy to Nehru.**
Correspondence and memoranda, papers, 1939-1962, 1.60 m, volumes 5-12. Finding aid 54, MG 31 E46. Created in the Department of External Affairs.

Volume 5.

File 2. Foreign affairs, United States, Washington, February-December 1939.
Includes Far Eastern policy.

File 3. Foreign affairs. United States, Washington. January 1940-March 1941.
Includes U.S. policy in the Far East.

Volume 6.

File 10. Policy papers, Volume 1(201.2), 1946-1960, 1969.
Includes the Korean War.

Volume 7.

File 15. Conferences, December 1949-July 1950.
Includes comments on some Asian problems, diary "after Colombo Conference", impressions of conference.

File 17. Foreign affairs, India, selection of correspondence with Ottawa, volume 1, notes, correspondence, reports. discussion with Sir Archibald Ney on India. reports on conversations with Indian officials.

File 18. Foreign affairs, India, selection of correspondence with Ottawa, volume 11, January-April 1953
Memoranda, despatches, correspondence, etc., (notes on conversations with Indian officials and diplomaticin India, India's Five Year Plan, Korean War

developments, Kashmir and Pakistan development, Indian domestic problems, Canadian aid under Colombo Plan, Indo-U.S. relations).

File 19. Foreign affairs, India. Selection of correspondence with Ottawa, volume 8, September-December 1953.
Despatches, notes, etc., Indo-Pakistan relations, Canadian aid to India under the Colombo Plan, Korean negotiations, U.S.-Pakistan military security arrangements, Nixon's visit to India. India, annual review.

Volume 8.

File 20. Foreign affairs, India. Selection of correspondence with Ottawa, Volume 4, January-June 1954.

Fujiwara, W.N.
Originals, 1925-1973, 7 cm. MG 31 E64.

6/290
Originals, 1940-1952, 4 cm.
Letters between Muriel Kitagawa and her, brother, Wes Fujiwara, largely concerning the Japanese community in British Columbia prior to evacuation. Also, a portion of Muriel's autobiography, entitled "The Crucible". Presented in 1986 by Dr. W.N. Fujiwara, 19 Teddington Park. Ave., Toronto.

86/473
Microfilm, 1925-1973. Reel H-1765.
Correspondence, scrapbook of clippings, Connaught High School file with writings, school reports and certificates and sketches. Manuscript of "Go East", and other documents as described in the above two accessions.
Microfilmed in 1986 from originals in the Public Archives of Canada.

MG 31 F. Churches and Clergy.

Takada, Minoru, 1921- .
Community leader.
Originals, 1845-SO. 10 cm. MG 31 F8.

Minoru Takada was born in Vancouver in 1921. After attending Granview High School of Commerce he spent one year as an accountant before being evacuated to Lethbridge, Alberta. There he worked in lumber camps during the winter and on sugar beets or in canneries in the summer. He became interested in civil liberties and was involved in Nisei activities in Southern Alberta. When the Southern Alberta Youth Councilwas formed his commercial training made him an obvious choice as secretary. The SAYC worked in conjunction with the Cooperative Committee on Japanese Canadians and the Canadian Citizens Association, to assist Japanese Canadians with their property claims and other grievances.
After upgrading his high school credits, Mr. Takada attended the University of Alberta and went on to study for the ministry at St. Stevens College where he graduated as gold medalist in 1956. His first charge was at Bashaw, Alberta. In 1961 he moved to Toronto to become minister of the Japanese United Church Nisei Congregation. He is presently ministering to the Glen Ayre Congregation in Scarborough.

Presented in 1977 by Reverend Min Takada, Toronto. Minutes, correspondence, reports and newsletters relating to the activities of the Southern Alberta Youth Council and its affiliation with various local Nisei groups and national organizations including the Citizens Defense Committee, the Cooperative Committee on Japanese Canadians, the Japanese Canadian Committee for Democracy, the Japanese Canadian Citizens' Association, civil liberties associations, **The New Canadian**, and the Japanese American Citizens League.

MG 31 G. Military Figures and Events.

Roberts, Richard,1915-
Naval officer, medical doctor.
Original, 1958-1986. 0.40metres MG 31 G26.

Volume 1.

Correspondence series, 1962-1984.

1. Planning of Medical Expedition to Easter Island- correspondence, reports, 1963-1964.

2. Medical Team - lists, agreements. 1964-1965.

3. General Correspondence, 1965.

4. General Correspondence, 1966.

5. General Correspondence, 1967-1968.

6. General Correspondence. 1969-1984.

7. Correspondence - Dr. Maureen Roberts. 1962-1965.

8. W.M.C.S. **Cape Scott** - reports, operations, 1964-1965.

9. Reports to Military by R. Roberts, 1965.

Medical Expedition to Easter Island . METEI.

Medical data series, 1964-1971.

10. Census of Easter Island Natives, 1964-1965.

11. Code Sheets for medical examinations. 1964.

12. Tabulations of Medical Data - computer printouts, 1965.

13. Electrocardiograms - sample of tapes, test results, 1965.

14. Electrocardiograms - correspondence, 1966-1971.

15. Genealogies of Easter Island Natives, 1965.

16. Genealogies of Easter Island Natives - cards, 1965.

17. Leprosy - correspondence, 1966-1968.

18. Medical Histories of Individuals - notebook, correspondence, 1966-1969.

19. METEI: tabulations of "Haptoglobulin types and milk precipitin reactions"(1965).

20. METEI: Measurements of Easter Island Natives(1965).

21. METEI: Soil Analysis. n.d., 1967.

22. METEI: Analysis of Urine Tests, 1966.

MISCELLANEOUS SERIES, 1964-1978.

23. General Information on Easter Island, 1965, 1970.

24. METEI: Layout of Camp and Photo of Expedition members, 1964-1965.

25. Rapa-Nui Science Club - newsletters, 1965-1967.

26. Easter Island Symbol Collection, 1965, 1978.

Volume 2.

Scientific studies series, 1922-1986.

1. Franco-Belgium Archeological Expedition of 1934-1935 - articles, 1935, 1983.

2. Language (Rapa-Nui) of Easter Island Natives, 1928, 1964-1966.

3. Polynesian Migration - articles. n.d., 1922-1969.

4. Blood Groups of Polynesians and Easter Island. Natives - articles. n.d., 1967.

5. Preliminary Report of Medical Expedition to Easter Island, (Part 1) 1965.

6. Preliminary Report of Medical Expedition to Easter Island,(Part II) 1965.

11. Canadian Society of Chemotherapy. Symposium on the Medical Expedition to Easter Island(M.E.T.E.I.)1969.

12. METEI: Symposium on Microbiology Project. Montréal - abstracts, agenda, list of contributors, 1971.

13. METEI: Symposium on Microbiology Project, 1971. Montréal - paper by Dr. R.Roberts.

14. Microbiology of Easter Island, Volume 1 G.L. Nogrady, ed., 1974.

15. METEI: Microbiology Project - correspondence and paper relating to volume 2., 1981.

16. METEI: Dental Conditions - papers by A.G.Taylor, [1965].

17. METEI "A Canadian Medical Expedition to Easter Island", correspondence and paper- by J.A.Boutilier, 1985-1986.

18. METEI: Radiological Survey - correspondence and report. n.d., 1966.

19. Scientific Papers relating to Easter Island Natives,(Part I)1966-1969.

20. Scientific Papers Relating to Easter Island Natives,(Part II)1966-1969.

21. Magazine Articles on Easter Island, 1965-1969.

22. Newspaper Clippings, 1964-1984.

23. Canadian Forces Medical Services Clinical Conference - speech notes of Dr. R.Roberts, 1984.

MG 31 H. Local, Regional and Ethnic History.

Miyazaki, Masajiro, 1899-
Osteopath.
Originals. 1926-1974. 8 cm. Photocopies, 1975. 2 cm. MG 31 H63.

Dr. Masajiro Miyazaki was born near Hikone City in Japan and came to Japan with his father at the age of thirteen. He worked his way through school and graduated from the University of British Columbia. Following his graduation from Kirksville College of Osteopathy and Surgery in Missouri in 1929, Dr. Miyazaki received his license to practice from the College of Physicians and Surgeons of British Columbia, and after further training in Los Angeles he opened an office in Vancouver. From 1930 until 1942 he practiced his profession and took an active role in local Japanese affairs, serving as treasurer of the Japanese Association from 1933-1941. Dr. Miyazaki and his family were evacuated in 1942 to the East Lillooet relocation centre. In 1945, he moved to Lillooet and resumed private practice until his retirement in 1970. He published his autobiography **My Sixty Years in Canada** in 1973.

Draft memoirs and related correspondence (1973-1974); vital statistics of Japanese in British Columbia and printed surveys (1926-1940); correspondence, memoranda, notes and lists, relating to the Village of Lillooet and East Lillooet Settlement (1945-1973); clippings (1936-1974). Presented in 1975 by Dr. Miyazaki: A copy of his book has been transferred to the Public Archives Library, and several photographs have been transferred to Picture Division.

Population surveys reports (1935, 1938), an address by Sherwood Lett on legal disabilities of the Japanese in Canada (1934), and "The Japanese contribution to Canada" (1940) published by the Canadian Japanese Association. Copied in 1975 from originals in the possession of Dr. M.Miyazaki.

Tanaka, June K.,1913-
Originals, 1975. 3 pages. Photocopies, 1946, 1970-1971. 11 pages. MG 31 H70.

Mrs. June K.Tanaka, her husband, two young children, and her mother were evacuated in 1942 from Vancouver to Slocan. The family later moved to Kaslo, and in 1946 they joined Mr. Tanaka, who had preceded them to Montréal.

Presented in 1975 by Mrs. June K. Tanaka.

Correspondence with the Office of the Custodian concerning money held in trust for Mr. Tanaka's father, 1946-1975; extracts from a diary kept during the early phases of the Japanese evacuation from the "Protected area" of British Columbia; an essay entitled "Discrimination and Prejudice" written for a sociology course at Loyola College, 1971.

Matsubara, Keitaro, d. 1976.
Clergyman.
Originals, 1942-1969. 30 cm. MG 31 H96.

K. Matsubara was born in Higo, Japan, and emigrated to Canada c.1907. He settled in Eburne, B.C., where he earned a living as a merchant. Subsequently, he became a clergyman . In 1942, he was relocated with his family to a farm near Holmwood, Manitoba, where the family worked on a sugar beet farm. He died in 1976.

Presented in 1979 by Rev. Nobuo Matsubara, Winnipeg, Manitoba.

Diaries of Keitaro Matsubara (1942-1946, 1949-1952, 1955-1960, 1965-1966, 1969) and photographs of the life of the Matsubara family as workers on a sugar beet farm near Holmwood, Manitoba. Diaries are in Japanese. Photographs transferred to National Photography Collection.
Certificate of Naturalization, 1914, and several other documents of the late K.Matsubara. The certificate was registered each year between 1914 and 1941.

Toronto Malayalee Samajan, est. ca.1975.
East Indian Ethnic Organization.
Originals, 1983-1984. 1 cm. MG 31 H132.

The TMS is a social organization serving the community of immigrants from South India living in Toronto.

Presented in 1984 by Mr. J.P.George, Toronto, Ont.

Various flyers and announcements of the Toronto Malayalee Samjam, describing events of notes in the South Indian community of Toronto.

MG 31 I. Miscellaneous.

Josephy, Goldie, 1928-
Pacifist writer. MG 31 I4.

Correspondence and memoranda relating to pacifist organizations. The papers contain extensive correspondence with U.S. draft evaders planning to migrate to Canada.
ULM4

Vo, Thanh Minh, 1906-
Educator, pacifist and poet.
Originals, n.d., 1950-1965. 7.5 cm. MG 31 I6

Dr. Vo, a Buddhist, was a former professor of Ethics at the Universities of Vinh, Hue and Saigon in Vietnam. He left Vietnam in 1949, unable to live under French rule. He went to Geneva, Switzerland where he met with Secretary Generals of the United Nations Trygve Lie and Dag Hammerskjold. He made representations at the 1954 Geneva Conference on Indo-China. While in Europe he spoke about the Vietnam situation before numerous audiences in France and Switzerland. In 1963, he came to U.N. Headquarters where he fasted for 47 days to protest the Bay of Tonkin Incident. In 1965, he came to Canada to attend the Canadian Friends Service Committee National Conference on Vietnam. He then returned to Vietnam

Donated by Murray Thompson of Project Plowshares in 1984.

Poems, Songs, n.d., 1950-1965. 5 cm.
Poems in Vietnamese script and in Chinese characters and in French. Some of the French poems are translations of the Vietnamese poems. The poems largely appear to concern his exile in Switzerland, the war in Vietnam and his political views.

Memoranda, n.d., 1962-1965, 1 cm.
Biographical memoranda on Dr. Vo and leaflets on his Peace Mission to Vietnam issued in Canada.

Clippings, 1965, 1.5 cm.
Clippings concerning the war in Vietnam and Dr. Vo.

MG 31 K. Social Development.

Callwood, June, 1924-
Writer.
Papers, journalism and reference, subject files, n.d. 1958-1984. 83 cm. MG 31 K24.

Include materials on draft evasion and protest against the war in Vietnam

Manuscript Group 32. Political figures, 1950-

MG 32 B. Cabinet Ministers.

Martin, Paul, 1903-
Cabinet minister.
Originals 1905-1968, 63.05 metres. Finding aid 986. MG 32 B12.

Confidential file volumes 6-11, 58 feet.
Volume 8.

90-3 Colombo Plan, 1936-1957.

Unnumbered files.

Volume 10.

Colombo Plan ministerial meeting, 1956.

Subject files, 1943-1958. 9 feet 7 inches, volumes 22-36.

Volume 23.

Asia:Visit:1956, 1956, 1957.

Burma, 1956.

Cambodia, 1956.

Ceylon, 1956-1958.

India, 1956-1959.

Indonesia, 1956.

Laos, 1956-1957.

Pakistan, 1957.

Singapore and Malaysia, 1956-1957.

Thailand, 1956.

Vietnam, 1956.

Volume 34.

Cyprus, 1955-1957.

Volume 35.

Formosa, 1955.

Korea, 1950-1957.

Opposition years.

Subject files 1946-1963, 20 feet, volume 188-217.

Volume 195.

External affairs, China, 1959-1962.

Volume 200.

Immigration. Chinese, miscellaneous, 1958-1960.

External affairs.

Ministerial files 1959-1968, 9 feet 4 inches, volumes 225-238.

Volume 225.
3. China, 1964-1967.

5. Cyprus, 1964-1967.

9. Far East(other than Vietnam and China), 1964-1967.

Volume 227.

25. Vietnam 1964-1968.

Subject files 1954-1968, 43 feet 4 inches(volumes 239-303).

Volume 243.

Citizenship and immigration, Chinese, 3 files, 1965-1967.

Volume 251.

External affairs, China 1964.

External affairs, Cyprus 1964.

Volume 253.

External affairs. Trip to Japan, 1964.

Biographical resume, volume 351-365.

Volume 357.

General conference on Far East, 1954, and 1962.

Indonesia-Canada relations, 1971.

Korea Commission. Cabinet crisis, December 1947-June 1948.

Volume 358.

Korean trip Inauguration of Park Chung-hee.

Korean war 1950-1953.

Dinsdale, Walter Gilbert, 1916-1982.
Politician, Minister of Northern Affairs and Natural Resources.
Originals 1914-1983, 46.5 metres. Finding aid 1465. MG 32 B35.

Volume 32. Citizenship and immigration. Employment.

File 2-8-cheu. Cheu, Kam jin, 1962-1963.

File 2-8-lee. Lee, Tong Owen and Dick, 1962-1963.

File 2-8-yuet. Yuet, Nguyen, 1958-1959.

Volume 34.

File 3-12-2 Sale of wheat to China and Japan, 1961-1963.

Volume 89. Immigration cases. Chinese, 1977-1980.

Volume 92. External affairs.

File 2. Afghanistan, 1973.

File 9. China, 1964-1976.

File 12. Draft dodgers, 1969-1970.

Volume 93.

File 2. Japan - briefing materials n.d.

File 12. Pakistan, 1971.

Volume 94.

File 3. Vietnam, 1965-1975.

Volume 108. Industry, trade and commerce.

File 2. Japan. Trade, 1980-1981.

File 3. Japan auto imports, 1963

MG 32 C. Members of the House of Commons and Senate.

Drew, George Alexander, 1894-1973.
Papers. MG 32 C3.

Include official inquiry on the Canadian contingent caught in Hong Kong, 1941-1943, the Korean War, 1951-1955, and early discussions with Japan over peaceful nuclear energy in the mid-1960s.
MITCHELL

Macrae, John Chester 1912-
Papers 2.94 metres. Finding aid 917. MG 32 C6

Files relate to his career in the House of Commons, 1957-1972.

Volume 5. Hong Kong Veterans Association 1965-1967, and 1972.

Stanfield, Robert Lorne, 1914-
Politician.
Finding aid 1310. MG 32 C21.

Entries in subject index:

China 1971-1972, 4 entries.

Japan 1971-1972, 5 entries.

Japan economy 1971, 1 entry.

Vietnam 1968-1974, 5 entries.

Brewin, Francis Andrew, 1907-
Lawyer, politician.
Originals, 1944-1954. 40 cm. MG 32 C26.
Born in England, and established a law practice in Toronto in 1930.

Correspondence, legal briefs, financial statements, statistics and minutes relating to the activities of Andrew Brewin as general counsel for the Cooperative Committee on Japanese Canadians before the Japanese Property Claims Commission(Bird Commission). The C.C.J.C. organized in Toronto to coordinate efforts with regional branches and with the National Japanese Canadian Citizens Association, sought more equitable payment for property and assets disposed of by the Custodian of Enemy Property under the Defense of Canada Regulations. Mr. Brewin worked in conjunction with the C.C.J.C. and supervised the legal activities of the lawyers in other provinces.
The material is arranged chronologically in two volumes. volume 1, 1944-1948, and volume 2, 1949-1954.

Douglas, Thomas Clement, 1904-1986.
Minister and politician. Premier of Saskatchewan.
Leader of New Democratic Party.
Papers. Finding aid 1412. MG 32 C28.

Leader's Office, 1961-1969.

Volume 3. External affairs.

China 1967-1968.

Vietnam.

1 1965.

2 1965.

3 1966.

4 1967.

5 1967.

6 1967.

7 1968-1969.

Leader's Office, 1968-1971.

Volume 19. External affairs.

Files 9-3 China, 1969-1970.

Volume 20. External affairs.

Files 9-9. Vietnam .

1 1965-1969.

2 1970.

3 1970-1971.

Nesbitt, Wallace Bickford, 1918-1974.
Politician.
Originals 1953-1974. 5.7 metres. Finding aid 1468. MG 32 C56.

Files relating to parliamentary career as MP, 1963-1974. Volume 1-19.

Box 3.

File 5,6. China, U.N. debate, 1966.

Box 9.

File 3. India, famine, 1966-1967.

Box 10.

File 1. Japan, 1955.

Box 12.

File 5. Pakistan, 1971.

File 6. Pakistan High Commissioner, visit to Woodstock, 1953-1954.

Box 14.

File 15. Taiwan and U.S., 1971.

Box 18

File 9. Vietnam, 1965-1966.

File 10. Vietnam, 1967-1973.

MG 32 F. Correspondents of Political Figures.

Vockeroth, Heidi, 1898-
Saskatchewan and Ontario. Teacher.
Original, 58 pages, n.d., 1943-1980. MG 32 F7

Correspondence from Dorise Nielsen, 1902-1980. "Unity" Party, member of parliament(1940-1945) and active Canadian communist, 1932-1957, from Toronto and China, where she became a citizen of China in 1962. Subjects included as Nielsen family, life and politics in China; figures from the Canadian left and international events.
ULM 4

Gratton, Stan, fl. 1970's.
Originals, 1977-1979. 8 pages. MG 32 F8.

Correspondent of Dorise Nielson after she emigrated to China. Two letters describe her travels in South West China, 1979.

MG 32 G. Related Political Papers.

Carter, Thelma Nielsen, 1931-
Original, 10 cm. 1940-1980. MG 32 G10.

Correspondence from T.N.Carter's mother Dorise Winnifred Nielsen, a former member of parliament, describing life in China, 1966-1980, postcards and album from China
ULM 4

Nielsen, Christine Patricia, 1929-
Originals, 20 cm. 1941-1981. MG 32 G11.

Pamphlets written by Dorise Nielsen, 1941-1949; union cards, Chinese citizenship records, passports, and other miscellaneous items belonging to Dorise Nielsen; letters received by Christine Wong from friends of her mother, 1980-1981; letters received from Nielsen documenting her life in China, 1955-1980
ULM 4

McLaren, Ray, 1956-.
Grandson of Dorise Nielsen.
Originals, 2 pages 1979. MG 32 G17.

Letter from Dorise Nielsen on China.

Houston, Robert Laird, 1911-
Consultant.
Originals, c. 1930, 1955-1986. 1 metre. Finding aid 1691. MG 32 G19.

Was Deputy Military Advisor to the ICC in Vietnam. After retiring from the Army joined the Canada-Japan Trade Council as Executive Secretary and became its President in 1967.

Canada-Japan Trade Council, 1964-1981.
Originals 30 cm. Volumes 3-4, files 9-16, especially files 3, 6, 7, 13 and 16

Correspondence and reports concerning Canada-Japan trade politics and activities.

General files, c. 1930, 1955-1986. Originals 20 cm.
Volume 5, files 1-2.
Series contains correspondence and reports on the Asian Centre at the University of British Columbia, 1975-1981.

Manuscript Group 40. Records and Manuscripts from British Repositories.

Great Britain. National Army Museum.
Finding aid 90. MG 40 M3.

1466. National Army Museum.

pages 121-231. British Army units in India.

Manuscript Group 42. London. The Dominions Office.

Formerly contained in MG 11 is now a separate manuscript group.

Manuscript Group 54. Foreign Documents.
and family.
Originals, 1812, 1877, 1879, n.d., 24 pages. MG 54 no. 90.

The letter of Adoniram Judson to Joseph Emerson, with a note from Nancy Judson to her sister(Mrs. J.Emerson), 1812(4 pages) discusses their conversion from Congregationalists to Baptists; with a translation of the letter from Koh-Yih-Djun to the missionary W.D.Rudland, 1879(2 pages), are two documents in Chinese, possibly dated 1877(4 pages), the second of which is missing the lower quarter of the pages; the letter of W.D.Rudland to his friend Mr. Claxton, 1879(8 pages) provides more detail about his missionary activity in China; two documents in Chinese, n.d.(3 pages); one document and a fragment of a document, apparently in Burmese, n.d.(2 pages); printed wrapper advertising quinine wine, n.d.(1 page).

Manuscript Group 55. Miscellaneous documents.

MG 55/24. Nineteenth Century Pre-Confederation Papers

Broadfoot, George, 1807-1845.
Army officer.
Originals 1843-1844. 9 pages. Transcripts 1910. 3 pages. MG 55/24 no. 172.

Two letters concern the British Army in India from H.Havelock to George Broadfoot in 1843, and from George Broadfoot to John Loch, 1844 and a statement of the services of Major General George Broadfoot.

MG 55/28. Records of Post-Confederation Corporate Bodies.

Hong Kong Engineers Institute.
Originals, 1882-1883, 1890-1891. 1 inch. MG 55/28 No. 1.

Minute book of the Hong Kong Engineers Institute 1882-1883 including financial statement with notes on cement companies, 1890-1891.

Civil Liberties Union. est. 1937.
Originals, 1947. 21 pages. MG 55/28 no. 12.

Circular letter, with enclosed copies of letters addressed to Prime Minister; MacKenzie King, concerning the continuing civil disabilities of Canadians of Japanese origin. The letter was issued by the C.C.L.U. Vancouver branch

United Churches.
Originals, 1944-1962. 21 cm. MG 55/28 no. 17.

A partial run of **The shepherd's call** a newspaper for Japanese United churches in Canada, edited by Reverend K.Shimizu of Toronto, and various reports of Japanese United Church congregations, such as minutes of the Nisei congregation of the Toronto Japanese United Church. Part of the material is in Japanese.

Guru Tegh Bahadur Tercentenary Matyrdom Foundation Canada, est. 1975.
Originals, 1975. 127 pages. MG 55/28 no. 23.

The Guru Tegh Bahadur Tercentenary Matrydom Foundation was established to mark the threehundredth anniversary of the martyrdom of Siri Tegh Bahadur Ji, ninth guru of the Sikhs.

MG 55/29. Nineteenth Century Post-Confederation Manuscripts.

Knowlton, Wilson E.
Collector.
Photocopies, 1858-1884. 1 cm. MG 55/29 no. 149.

Photocopies of papers collected by W.E.Knowlton, chiefly pertaining to business in Victoria, Yale, Vancouver and other parts of British Columbia, 1858-1884. Some of the material is written in Chinese; Kwong Lee and Co. are often mentioned in the materials. Originals in the Provincial Archives of British Columbia.

MG 55/30. Manuscripts of the First Half of the Twentieth Century.

Mark, Kwok Chee, ca. 1903-
Original, 1918. 1 page. MG 55/30 no. 116.

Kwok Chee Mark was born in Sun Chan, China, ca. 1903, and landed in Victoria, British Columbia, as an immigrant in 1918. Certificate of payment of head tax of $500.00 on entry into Canada, 25 March 1918.

Komagata maru.
Voyage of the **Komagata Maru** or India's slavery abroad.
Microfilm, n.d. reel K-79. MG 55/30 no. 159.

English translation of Baba Gurdit Singh's account of the **Komagata maru** incident.

Komagata maru.
Microfilm, n.d. reel K-78. MG 55/30 no. 160.

An account of the **Komagata maru** incident and the activities of Baba Gurdit Singh, written in Punjabi by Professor Jaswant Singh Jas.

Sam family, 1881-
Originals, 1922-1943. 9 pages. MG 55/30 no. 166

J.P.Sam, a member of the mandarin class in Kwangtung, China emigrated to Canada in 1899. He worked as a court interpreter and established himself as an influential member in Toronto's Chinatown and the Chinese freemasons. Internal political disagreements where Mr. Sam had established a restaurant business. He continued to act in legal matters concerning Chinese Canadians until his death in 1947.
Membership certificate for the Chinese freemasons, Chinese head tax certificate, and war-time registration certificates.

Sunada, M.
Originals, 1908. 3 pages. MG 55/30 no. 169.

Imperial Japanese government passport 1908, and an Imperial Japanese government "laissez passer".

Ray, Satyendra, fl .1930.
Physicist.
Original, ca. 1930. 2.5 cm. MG 55/30 no. 189.
Satyendra Ray was engaged in physics research at the University of Lucknow during the late 1920's. Collection consists of two pamphlets, two typescripts and three photographs presented by the author to the Royal Society of Canada. The papers deal with the author's views on quantum physics, Compton effect, Raman effect, Barh effect and the philosophy and methodology of science.

MG 55/31. Manuscripts of the Second Half of the Twentieth Century.

Hoe, Ban seng, 1939-
Sociologist.
Originals, 1962, 1977-1979. 1 cm. photocopies n.d. 1974-1980. 1 cm. MG 55/31 no. 58.

Dr. Ban Seng Hoe was born in Malaysia. He received his training in sociology and anthropology at the University of Alberta and Vanderbilt University and did considerable research on the Chinese and other Asian communities in Canada for his personal research and as senior coordinator, Oriental Asiatic Program, Wong Clan Association, Toronto, 1962, giving reasons for amalgamation of the Wong Chia Sia Tang and the Wong Yun Shan Kung So, as well as three conference papers on the Chinese community in Québec and North America.
Photocopies of three published essays concerning the Chinese community in Québec and North America and copies of review of Dr. Hoe's book: **Structural Changes of two Chinese Communities in Alberta.** Also included is an interview in Chinese given by Dr. Hoe to the Ottawa Chinese community newspaper.

Government Archives Division

Record Group 2. Privy Council Office.

a. Office of the Clerk to the Privy Council and Secretary to the Cabinet.

1. Orders-in-Council, 1867-1983.

1a. Minutes and Orders in Council, 1862-1981.

P.C. 1376, 13 September 1871.
Capital case - Chung Say, Cariboo, British Columbia.

P.C. 147, 29 January 1885.
Expenses - Chinese Labour Commission.

P.C. 686, 27 March 1885.
Chinese bill - British Columbia.

P.C. 687, 28 March 1885.
Chinese bill - British Columbia.

P.C. 1622, 1 September 1885.
Department of Customs made responsible for the administration of Chinese immigration acts of 1885.

P.C. 1627, 1 September 1885.
Chinese immigration act - regulations.

P.C. 2136, 1 December 1885.
Petition Anti-Chinese Union, British Columbia, for appointment of a Controller under Chinese immigration act.

P.C. 482, 16 March 1886.
Act of British Columbia to prevent immigration of Chinese.

P.C. 483, 16 March 1886.
Act of British Columbia to prevent immigration of Chinese.

P.C. 38, 12 January 1889.
Admission of Chan Sing Quoi and family - Chinese missionary in British Columbia.

P.C. 56, 8 January 1901.
Appointment of Christopher Foley of Rossland, as Chinese and Japanese immigration commissioner.

P.C. 136, 21 January 1901.
$500 placed for purposes of Chinese and Japanese immigration commission.

P.C. 401, 25 February 1901.
$5000 placed for purposes of Chinese and Japanese immigration commission.

P.C. 363, 5 March 1901.
Landing Japanese by United States revenue cutter **Grant** without reporting to customs.

P.C. 2002, 7 November 1901.
Dismissal of E.H.Blunton, customs officer, Montréal, for irregularities in manifesting of Chinese.

P.C. 2017, 7 November 1901.

Chinese and Japanese commission, payment $300 to Alexander Crawford, disbursement by for.

P.C. 34, 10 January 1902.
Capital case, Ah Quong, Chinese committed(lunacy).

P.C. 40, 17 January 1902.
Acts of British Columbia, 1901, prohibiting employment of aliens, Chinese and Japanese labour.

P.C. 876, 20 May 1902.
Re Chinese and Japanese mission.

P.C. 1052, 12 June 1902.
Statutes of British Columbia 1901- report on employment Chinese and Japanese.

P.C. 1053, 12 June 1902.
Statutes of British Columbia, cap. 46, tax on persons report.

P.C. 1070, 19 June 1902.
Statutes of British Columbia, re employment of Chinese and Japanese.

P.C. 1731-1734, 5 December 1902.
Statutes of British Columbia, cap. 38, 34, and 48 of 1902, re Japanese immigration, disallowance of.

P.C. 158, 3 February 1903.
Appointment of Hon. Sydney Fisher as Commissioner, Japanese exhibition.

P.C. 1591, 18 September 1903.
Chinese capitation tax, payment 50% of said tax to Province of British Columbia.

P.C. 1986, 28 November 1903.
Capital case Kangu Maida, Japanese at Nanaimo, British Columbia law to take its course.

P.C. 265, 12 February 1904.
Acting Chief Controller of Chinese immigration to sign certificates for Chinese visiting United States.

P.C. 670, 19 April 1904.
Chinese Chou Tim Tsun permitted to reenter Canada.

P.C. 1609, 17 August 1904.
Regulation transport of Chinese through Canada.

P.C. 1687, 19 September 1904.
Resignation Yip Yen, Chinese interpreter, Vancouver.

P.C. 1688, 19 September 1904.
Appointment of Yip On, Chinese interpreter, Vancouver.

P.C. 1814-1816, 1836-1837, 30 September 1905.
Disallowance statutes of British Columbia, numbers 67-81 and 82, re immigration(Chinese, etc.) they being chaptered differently as 28, 30 and 36.

P.C. 19, 3 November 1905.

Amending section 1 of the regulations in re Chinese in transit through Canada.

P.C. 569 and 900, 1905.
Refund of Chinese capitation tax, individual cases.
P.C. 360, 20 February 1907.
Regulations re Chinese amended re port of exit.

P.C. 904, 27 April 1907.
Huntingdon, British Columbia, added to list of ports at which Chinese may be manifested on exit from Canada.

P.C. 2170, 12 October 1907.
Anti-Japanese riots in Vancouver, appointment Chief Justice of British Columbia as Commissioner to enquire into losses of Japanese.

P.C. 2256, 12 October 1907.
Mission of Hon. R.Lemieux to Japan to arrange means to prevent recurrence of anti-Japanese disturbances in British Columbia.

P.C. 2435, 5 November 1907.
Appointment of W.L.Mackenzie King, Commissioner to enquire re immigration of Oriental labourers.

P.C. 2471, 12 November 1907.
Japanese losses, Vancouver, British Columbia.

P.C. 458, 2 March 1908.
Immigration of British Indians and from the Orient generally.

P.C. 880, 19 April 1908.
Refunds of Chinese capitation tax.

P.C. 1255, 3 June 1908.
Asiatic immigrants from countries other than those with which arrangements exist required to face at least $200.

P.C. 1396, 13 June 1908.
Chinese losses, Vancouver riots, Ministry of Labour received payment of $27, 990 in settlement, etc.

P.C. 2014, September 1908.
Losses, Chinese and Japanese, Vancouver riots, reports, W.L.Mackenzie King.

P.C. 2470, 16 November 1908.
Regulations, Chinese in transit through Canada.

P.C. 2708, 13 December 1908.
Chinese immigrations, re restriction of, to Canada(W.L.MacKenzie King)

P.C. 625, 7 April 1910.
Case of Han Chu, Chinese British subject who was prevented from reentering Canada from United States.

P.C. 934, 23 April 1908.
Refunds of Chinese capitation tax.

P.C. 1453, 23 June 1908.

Refunds of Chinese capitation tax.

P.C. 1482, 29 June 1908.
Refunds of Chinese capitation tax.

P.C. 1788, 11 August 1908.
Refunds of Chinese capitation tax.

P.C. 2813, 31 December 1908.
Refunds of Chinese capitation tax.

P.C. 977, 4 May 1909.
Re refunding Chinese capitation tax.

P.C. 1155, 26 May 1909.
Re refunding Chinese capitation tax.

P.C. 314, 19 February 1910.
Refund Chinese capitation tax.

P.C. 296, 19 February 1910.
Re note of Count Hayashi not to be communicated to United States.

P.C. 720, 18 April 1910.
Refund Chinese capitation tax.

P.C. 751, 19 April 1910.
Refund Chinese capitation tax.

P.C. 805, 27 April 1910.
Regulations re Chinese in transit.

P.C. 843, 28 April 1910.
Re illegal entrance of Chinese into United States.

P.C. 882, 4 May 1910.
Refund Chinese capitation tax.

P.C. 1272, 22 June 1910.
Chinese smuggling along Canadian frontier.

P.C. 926, 1 August 1910.
Asian immigrants must be in possession of $200.

P.C. 2050, 14 October 1910.
Appointment of T.C.Thom, Chinese Methodist missionary Nanaimo, British Columbia be appointed Chinese interpreter at Nanaimo.

P.C. 2117, 12 November 1910.
Irregularities, Chinese immigration at Vancouver, British Columbia, re report.

P.C. 2281, 12 November 1910.
Commission of enquiry into Chinese immigration frauds at British Columbia, etc.

P.C. 2282, 12 November 1910.
Nip On, Chinese interpreter at Vancouver dismissed.

P.C. 2317, 19 November 1910.
Refund Chinese capitation tax.

P.C. 2423, 30 November 1910.
Refund Chinese capitation tax.

P.C. 2462, 6 December 1910.
Refund Chinese capitation tax.

P.C. 2520, 12 December 1910.
Refund Chinese capitation tax.

P.C. 285, 13 February 1911.
Refund Chinese capitation tax.

P.C. 432, 3 March 1911.
Opium act, bill Canadian parliament to be transmitted to Colonial Secretary.

P.C. 584, 21 March 1911.
Refund Chinese capitation tax.

P.C. 794, 12 April 1911.
Refund Chinese capitation tax, and appointment of Rev. Tom Chue Thom as Chinese interpreter at Nanaimo, British Columbia.

P.C. 1272, 31 May 1911.
Chinese immigration act to be administered by Minister of Interior.

P.C. 1483, 12 July 1911.
Refund Chinese capitation tax.

P.C. 1705, 28 July 1911.
Resignation of Herbert Lee, assistant Chinese interpreter at Victoria, British Columbia, and refund Chinese capitation tax.

P.C. 1810, 7 August 1911.
Refund Chinese capitation tax.

P.C. 2285, 6 October 1911.
Refund Chinese capitation tax.

P.C. 2286, 6 October 1911.
Refund Chinese capitation tax.

P.C. 2409, 6 October 1911.
Refund Chinese capitation tax.

P.C. 2411, 6 October 1911.
Refund Chinese capitation tax.

P.C. 2782, 6 December 1911.
Refund Chinese capitation tax.

P.C. 1354, 6 June 1912.
Regulations under Chinese Immigration Act.

P.C. 1959, 19 July 1912.
Opium and Drugs Act of Canadian Parliament.

P.C. 391, 10 February 1913.
Chinese passing through Canada in bond may not pay head tax and remain in country.

P.C. 2448, 27 September 1913.
Wives and children of East Indians in Canada, regulations re continuous journey cannot be relaxed.

P.C. 24, 7 January 1914.
Immigrants of Asiatic race must have at least $200 upon landing in Canada.

P.C. 304, 23 February 1914.
Re immigration wives and children of East Indians into Canada, S.S. communication Calcutta and Vancouver.

P.C. 493, 23 February 1914.
Immigration regulations re East Indians.

P.C. 3187, 24 December 1914.
Chinese immigration, appointment of A.L.Joliffe as Controller of Vancouver.

P.C. 233, 30 January 1915.
Refund Chinese capitation tax.

P.C. 315, 18 February 1915.
Chinese minister protests against legislation of Ontario and Saskatchewan re employment of white females by Chinese.

P.C. 397, 23 February 1915.
Refund Chinese capitation tax.

P.C. 445, 2 March 1915.
Chinese who have registered out under Chinese Immigration Act may prolong return to Canada without affecting right to free reentry.

P.C. 535, 9 March 1915.
Refund Chinese capitation tax.

P.C. 600, 20 March 1915.
Refund Chinese capitation tax.

P.C. 963, 4 May 1915.
Refund Chinese capitation tax.

P.C. 1158, 20 May 1915.
Refund Chinese capitation tax.

P.C. 1197, 26 May 1915.
Refund Chinese capitation tax.

P.C. 1248, 1 June 1915.
Refund Chinese capitation tax.

P.C. 1340, 10 June 1915.
Refund Chinese capitation tax.

P.C. 1398, 19 June 1915.
Refund Chinese capitation tax.

P.C. 1470, 24 June 1915.
Refund Chinese capitation tax.

P.C. 1523, 28 June 1915.
Refund Chinese capitation tax.

P.C. 1649, 14 July 1915.
Refund Chinese capitation tax.

P.C. 1709, 21 July 1915.
Refund Chinese capitation tax.

P.C. 1861, 7 August 1915.
Refund Chinese capitation tax.

P.C. 1915, 18 August 1915.
Chinese may return to China and prolong return to Canada for six months after termination of the War.

P.C. 1996, 25 August 1915.
Refund Chinese capitation tax.

P.C. 2151, 17 September 1915.
Refund Chinese capitation tax.

P.C. 2220, 24 September 1915.
Refund Chinese capitation tax.

P.C. 2287, 30 September 1915.
Refund Chinese capitation tax.

P.C. 2344, 6 October 1915.
Refund Chinese capitation tax.

P.C. 2422, 15 October 1915.
Refund Chinese capitation tax.

P.C. 2466, 27 October 1915.
Refund Chinese capitation tax.

P.C. 2621, 10 November 1915.
Refund Chinese capitation tax.

P.C. 2680, 16 November 1915.
Refund Chinese capitation tax.

P.C. 2889, 8 December 1915.
Chinese who register out between 1 January and 30 June 1916, permitted to prolong return to Canada.

P.C. 2947, 17 December 1915.
Cases of refund Chinese capitation tax.

P.C. 3095, 6 January 1916.
Cases of refund Chinese capitation tax.

P.C. 7, 4 January 1915.
Cases of refund Chinese capitation tax.

P.C. 70, 12 January 1915.
Cases of refund Chinese capitation tax.

P.C. 163, 23 January 1915.
Cases of refund Chinese capitation tax.

P.C. 17, 8 January 1916.
Refund Chinese head tax.

P.C. 133, 25 January 1916.

Refund Chinese head tax.

P.C. 355, 18 February 1916.
Refund Chinese head tax.

P.C. 572, 11 March 1916.
Refund Chinese head tax.

P.C. 711, 28 March 1916.
Refund Chinese head tax.

P.C. 777, 4 April 1916.
Refund Chinese head tax.

P.C. 834, 11 April 1916.
Refund Chinese head tax.

P.C. 989, 27 April 1916.
Refund Chinese head tax.

P.C. 1069, 8 May 1916.
Refund Chinese head tax.

P.C. 1250, 26 May 1916.
Refund Chinese head tax.

P.C. 1592, 6 July 1916.
Chinese in Canada granted extension of time within which they may return to Canada from visit to China.

P.C. 1645, 13 July 1916.
Refund Chinese head tax.

P.C. 2046, 31 August 1916.
Refund Chinese head tax.

P.C. 2323, 5 October 1916.
Refund Chinese head tax.

P.C. 3189, 13 November 1917.
Return Chinese to Canada 1 January to 15 November permitted until six months after conclusion of the war.

P.C. 111, 17 January 1918.
Military Service Act, exemption from service of persons disqualified from voting and of Indians.

P.C. 1459, 12 June 1918.
Exemption of East Indians from military service under Military Service Act.

P.C. 43, 14 January 1919.
Chinese who have registered out of Canada permitted to prolong return to Canada until six months after proclamation of peace.

P.C. 552, 14 March 1919.
Immigration, prohibiting Germans, Austrians, Bulgarians, Turks, except under permission.

P.C. 697, 2 April 1919.
Chinese who register out of Canada before 31 March 1919, permitted to prolong their return to Canada until one year after proclamation of peace.

P.C. 1506, 22 July 1919.
Chinese taxes, regulations for ascertaining net proceeds whereof one half goes to province where collected.

P.C. 1929, 17 September 1919.
Chinese coolies, expenses of repatriation to China, conveyance through Canada to be charged to demobilization vote.

P.C. 2245, 6 November 1919.
Chinese immigration, amendment regulations re distribution proceeds to taxes paid by Chinese immigrants.

P.C. 1498, 24 December 1919.
Immigration of East Indians, report re reciprocity treaty.

P.C. 4041, 9 November 1921.
Refund Chinese head tax.

P.C. 333, 9 February 1922.
Refund Chinese head tax.

P.C. 472, 2 March 1922.
Refund Chinese head tax.

P.C. 715, 12 April 1922.
Immigration regulations, Asiatics must have $250.

P.C. 846, 12 April 1922.
Refund Chinese head tax.

P.C. 1976, 20 September 1922.
Refund Chinese head tax.

P.C. 2045, 6 October 1922.
Refund Chinese head tax.

P.C. 76, 10 January 1923.
Refund Chinese head tax.

P.C. 182, 31 January 1923.
Immigration regulation re landing in Canada of Asiatics, must have in possession $250.

P.C. 501, 21 March 1923.
Education of Chinese students at Canadian universities, proposed scheme for, submitted to British government.

P.C. 1271-1276, 10 Commission July 1923.
Chinese immigration appointments and regulations.

P.C. 271, 7 March 1924.
Refund head tax.

P.C. 681, 28 April 1924.
Refund head tax.

P.C. 98, 22 January 1925.
Refund head tax.
P.C. 230, 16 February 1925.
Refund head tax.

P.C. 291, 24 February 1925.
Refund head tax.

P.C. 230, 16 February 1926.
Refund head tax.

P.C. 671, 1 May 1926.
Refund head tax.

P.C. 1229, 13 July 1928.
Refund head tax.

P.C. 2115, 16 September 1930.
Immigration regulations amended re admission of Asiatics.

P.C. 2051, 18 October 1930.
Refund head tax.

P.C. 1118, 11 August 1931.
Refund head tax.

P.C. 1760, 13 August 1934.
Naturalization certificates, procedure of issue of to Japanese.

P.C. 308, 6 February 1936.
Extending period Chinese registering out of Canada may remain away for three years.

P.C. 257, 18 February 1933.
Immigration regulations, waived to permit the entry to Canada of an Asiatic person.

P.C. 489, 16 March 1933.
Immigration regulations, waived to permit the entry to Canada of an Asiatic person.

P.C. 812, 29 April 1933.
Immigration regulations, waived to permit the entry to Canada of an Asiatic person.

P.C. 1005, 27 May 1933.
Immigration regulations, waived to permit the entry to Canada of an Asiatic person.

P.C. 1226, 24 June 1933.
Immigration regulations, waived to permit the entry to Canada of an Asiatic person.

P.C. 1769, 29 August 1933.
Immigration regulations, waived to permit the entry to Canada of an Asiatic person.

P.C. 1932, 19 September 1933.
Immigration regulations, waived to permit the entry to Canada of an Asiatic person.

P.C. 2170, 14 October 1933.
Immigration regulations, waived to permit the entry to Canada of an Asiatic person.

P.C. 2296, 6 November 1933.
Immigration regulations, waived to permit the entry to Canada of an Asiatic person.

P.C. 2367, 22 November 1933.
Immigration regulations, waived to permit the entry to Canada of an Asiatic person.

P.C. 2561, 12 December 1933.
Immigration regulations, waived to permit the entry to Canada of an Asiatic person.

P.C. 524, 15 March 1934.
Immigration regulations, waived to permit the entry to Canada of an Asiatic person.

P.C. 2811, 9 September 1935.
Immigration regulations, waived to permit the entry to Canada of an Asiatic person.

P.C. 308, 6 February 1936.
Extending period Chinese registering out of Canada may remain away for three years.

P.C. 9591, 7 December 1941.
Amending Defence of Canada Regulations re registration of Japanese in Canada.

P.C. 9760, 16 December 1941.
Re-registration of all persons of the Japanese race by the Royal Canadian Mounted Police made compulsory.

P.C. 9761, 16 December 1941.
Provision for the control of vessels used or operated by persons of the Japanese race.

P.C. 251, 13 January 1942.
Prohibiting the issuance of fishing licenses to persons of Japanese racial origin; also prohibiting such persons from serving on fishing vessels.

P.C. 288, 13 January 1942.
Constituting committee on the disposal of Japanese fishing vessels - members: Hon. S.A.Smith, Puisne Judge of the Supreme Court of British Columbia, Commander R.L.Johnson, Royal Canadian Naval Reserve; and Kischizi Kimura of Vancouver, British Columbia.

P.C. 365, 16 January 1942.
Amending Defence of Canada Regulations re "protected areas".

P.C. 987, 9 February 1942.
Committee on disposal of Japanese fishing vessels authorized to impose and collect a charge of 1% on all monies involved in transactions for the disposal of such vessels.

P.C. 1074, 13 February 1942.
Amending Defence of Canada Regulations re P.C. 9591 above.

P.C. 1271, 17 February 1942.
Establishing a "Canadian-Japanese Construction

Corps".

P.C. 1348, 19 February 1942.
Authorizing the establishment of work camps for male enemy aliens, including Japanese nationals, on projects located outside of protected areas.

P.C. 1365, 19 February 1942.
Prohibiting the possession of firearms or explosives by persons of the Japanese race.

P.C. 25/1450, 24 February 1942.
$100, 000 to department of mines and resources for construction of Japanese internment camps.

P.C. 1457, 24 February 1942.
Regulating the acquisition of land or any interest therein or the growing of crops in Canada by persons of the Japanese race and by Japanese controlled companies.

P.C. 1486, 24 February 1942.
Amending Defence of Canada Regulations re authority for removal of any or all persons from protected areas.

P.C. 1542, 26 February 1942.
Amending Defence of Canada Regulations re prohibiting or restricting of possession of specific articles.

P.C. 1665, 4 March 1942.
Sets up the British Columbia Security Commission with wide powers to supervise and direct the evacuation of Japanese from protected areas; requisition services of other government departments, etc.

P.C. 2439, 27 March 1942.
Immigration regulations, waived to permit the entry to Canada of an Asiatic person.

P.C. 2542, 31 March 1942.
Defers formation of construction corps.

P.C. 3213, 31 April 1942.
Empowers British Columbia Security Commission to enter into agreements with government of any province relative to placement in each province of persons of Japanese race evacuated from British Columbia protected areas.

P.C. 4615, 2 June 1942.
Approval agreement between British Columbia Security Commission province of Alberta re placement in that province of Japanese.

P.C. 5513, 29 June 1942.
Establishes regulations re agricultural land owned by Japanese and confers on Director of Soldier Settlement wide powers of control and disposition.

P.C. 5965, 10 July 1942.
Housing accommodation for evacuated Japanese in British Columbia; additional funds provided for British Columbia Security Commission.

P.C. 6247, 20 July 1942.
Authorises that boats and equipment owned by persons of Japanese race be vested in and subject to control of custodian.

P.C. 6885, 4 August 1942.
Gives power to officer named by minister to act in absence of Director of Soldier Settlement.

P.C. 7656, 28 August 1942.
Chinese seamen, amendment of P.C. 2041, November 8, 1928, re leave for Chinese seamen.

P.C. 8173, 11 September 1942.
Amends P.C. 1348, so as to make its terms applicable to persons other than those named therein.

P.C. 8225, 14 September 1942.
Immigration regulations, waived to permit the entry into Canada of an Asiatic person.

P.C. 10773, 26 September 1942.
Takes from persons repatriated to enemy territory in time of war their status as British subjects or as Canadian nationals.

P.C. 11037, 3 December 1942.
Appoints George Collins, General Supervisor of Japanese evacuation and maintenance.

P.C. 11561, 22 December 1942.
Amends Defence of Canada Regulations with regard to exempting certain persons of Italian, Austrian, Rumanian, Hungarian or Finnish nationality, resident in Canada, from operation of regulations 24, 25 and 26.

P.C. 469, 19 January 1943.
Empowers the Custodian to "liquidate, sell or otherwise dispose of" property in the protected area belonging to persons of Japanese race.

P.C. 946, 9 February 1943.
Establishes regulations relative to further placement, control and maintenance of persons of Japanese race in Canada.

P.C. 1373, 19 February 1943.
Agreement with Ontario re placement of Japanese in agricultural work.

P.C. 1883, 9 March 1943.
Provisions of P.C. 4759, 27 June 1941, waived for 1943-1944 re Japanese war camps.

P.C. 3831, 10 May 1943.
Immigration regulations, waived to permit the entry to Canada of an Asiatic person.

P.C. 4002, 17 May l943.
Agreement between British Columbia Security Commission and the Alberta government re education of Japanese children.

P.C. 4365, 28 May 1943.

Authorises the utilisation of Japanese labour in wood fuel cutting and timber operations.

P.C. 9702, 20 December 1943.
Amends Defence of Canada Regulation with regard to leasing of buildings by persons of Japanese race.

P.C. 9743, 24 December 1943.
Amends P.C. 946 of 5 February 1943, to make more specific provision government placement, control and maintenance of Japanese.

P.C. 800, 11 February 1944.
Acquisition of various properties in connection with the evacuation of Japanese from protected areas in British Columbia.

P.C. 3378, 5 May 1944.
Chinese Immigration Act, modified re persons passing through Canada.

P.C. 3797, 19 May 1944.
Re holding of property.

P.C. 7811, 6 October 1944.
Amendment P.C. 1274, 10 July 1923, so as to provide free issue of Chinese immigration certificate to replace those worn out or lost.

P.C. 8284, 27 October 1944.
Immigration regulations, waived to permit the entry to Canada of an Asiatic person.

P.C. 8797, 20 November 1944.
Immigration regulations, waived to permit the entry of one immigrant(Asiatic)

P.C. 884, 9 February 1944.
Immigration regulations, waived to permit entry of Asiatics

P.C. 468, 23 January 1945.
Commissioner of Japanese Placement - appointment J.B.Pickersgill.

P.C. 2125, 28 March 1945.
Waiving provision of P.C. 4759, 27 June 1941, re Japanese work camps for another year.

P.C. 5637, 16 August 1945.
Amends certain of Defence of Canada Regulations and revokes others which impose restriction on liberties normally enjoyed by individuals in peace time.

P.C. 5804, 30 August 1945.
Immigration regulations, waived to permit entry of Asiatics.

P.C. 5972, 14 September 1945.
Revoking and amending certain of the Defence of Canada Regulations.

P.C. 5973, 14 September 1945.
Amends P.C.946, 5 February 1943, with respect to the holding or leasing of land, etc.(14-9-45).

P.C. 6738, 30 October 1945.
Immigration regulations, waived to permit entry of Asiatics.

P.C. 7355, 15 December 1945.
Making provision for deportation of Japanese.

P.C. 7356, 15 December 1945.
Revokes naturalisation of persons deported in pursuant of Order in Council P.C. 7355, 15 December 1945.

P.C. 7357, 15 December 1945.
Authorizes appointment of commission to inquire into conduct during the war of persons of Japanese race, etc.

P.C. 7477, 28 December 1945.
Immigration regulations, waived to permit entry of Asiatics.

P.C. 45, 8 January 1946.
Reference to the Supreme Court of Canada of question as to validity of Orders in Council of 15 December 1945, P.C. 7355-6-7 re Japanese.

P.C. 83, 11 January 1946.
Immigration regulations, waived to permit entry of Asiatics.

P.C. 268, 23 January 1946.
Amending P.C. 7355 re deportation of Japanese.

P.C. 269, 23 January 1946.
Revoking six Orders in Council.

P.C. 270, 23 January 1946.
Amending P.C. 946 re: placement, control and maintenance of.

P.C. 238, 31 January 1946.
Immigration regulations, waived to permit entry of Asiatics.

P.C. 1396, 11 April 1946.
Immigration regulations, waived to permit entry of Asiatics.

P.C. 2047, 21 May 1946.
Immigration regulations, waived to permit entry of Asiatics.

P.C. 113, 9 January 1947.
Immigration regulations, waived to permit entry of Asiatics.

P.C. 567, 13 February 1947.
Revoking P.C. 1378, 17 June 1931, which made restrictions on naturalization of Chinese.

P.C. 644, 20 February 1947.
Immigration regulations, waived to permit entry of Asiatics.

P.C. 1584, 22 April 1947.
Immigration regulations, waived to permit entry of Asiatics.

P.C. 2853, 18 July 1947.
Immigration regulations, waived to permit entry of Asiatics.

P.C. 4139, 14 October 1947.
Immigration regulations, waived to permit entry of Asiatics.

P.C. 4688, 14 November 1947.
Immigration regulations, waived to permit entry of Asiatics.

P.C. 5131, 16 December 1947.
Immigration regulations, waived to permit entry of Asiatics.

P.C. 242, 22 January 1948.
Inquiry into claims of persons of Japanese race resident in Canada and evacuated from British Columbia coast as a war measure(P.C. 1810, 18 July 1947) amended: inquiry into claims of corporations of which majority of shares were formerly owned by such persons.

P.C. 299, 30 January 1948.
Immigration regulations, waived to permit entry of Asiatics.

P.C. 632, 20 January 1948.
Immigration regulations, waived to permit entry of Asiatics.

P.C. 1305, 31 March 1948.
Immigration regulations, waived to permit entry of Asiatics.

P.C. 2034, 6 May 1948.
Immigration regulations, waived to permit entry of Asiatics.

P.C. 2314, 26 May 1948.
Immigration regulations, waived to permit entry of Asiatics.

P.C. 299, 30 January 1948.
Immigration regulations, waived to permit entry of Asiatics.

P.C. 632, 20 January 1948.
Immigration regulations, waived to permit entry of Asiatics.

P.C. 242, 22 January 1948.
Inquiry into claims of persons of Japanese race resident in Canada and evacuated from British Columbia coast as a war measure(P.C. 1810, 18-7-47) amended: inquiry into claims of corporations of which majority of shares were formerly owned by such persons.

P.C. 589. 17 February 1948.
Japanese-agreement with Alberta Province re maintenance, educational costs and establishment of residence rights.

P.C. 637, 20 February 1948.
Continuation of Transitional Measures Act - revoking P.C. 7355, 15 December 1945, re repatriation of Japanese in part.

P.C. 804, 2 March 1948.
Continuation of Transitional Measures Act - revoking portions of the Japanese Order P.C. 946, 5 February 1943, on 26 February 1948 and other orders re Japanese.

P.C. 958, 6 March 1948.
Agreement with British Columbia covering provision of maintenance and welfare of indigent Japanese.

P.C. 1305, 31 March 1948.
Immigration regulations, waived to permit entry of Asiatics.

P.C. 2034, 6 May 1948.
Immigration regulations, waived to permit entry of Asiatics.

P.C. 2314, 26 May 1948.
Immigration regulations, waived to permit entry of Asiatics.

P.C. 2613, 10 June 1948.
Immigration regulations, waived to permit entry of Asiatics.

P.C. 3481, 9 August 1948.
Commission of Inquiry into claims of persons of Japanese race.

P.C. 3555, 9 August 1948.
Immigration regulations, waived to permit entry of Asiatics.

P.C. 5243, 19 November 1948.
Immigration regulations, waived to permit entry of Asiatics.

P.C. 3555, 9 August 1948.
Immigration regulations, waived to permit entry of Asiatics.

P.C. 5243, 19 November 1948.
Immigration regulations, waived to permit entry of Asiatics.

P.C. 5632, 16 December 1948.
Revoking P.C. 7355, 15 December 1945, re financial assistance of voluntary repatriation to Japan.

P.C. 126, 18 January 1949.
Immigration regulations, waived to permit entry of Asiatics.

P.C. 897, 24 February 1949.

Immigration regulations, waived to permit entry of Asiatics.

P.C. 1291, 22 March 1949.
Immigration regulations, waived to permit entry of Asiatics.

P.C. 3328, 6 July 1949.
Immigration regulations, waived to permit entry of Asiatics.

P.C. 3831, 3 August 1949.
Immigration regulations, waived to permit entry of Asiatics.

P.C. 3955, 10 August 1949.
Immigration regulations, waived to permit entry of Asiatics.

P.C. 7113, 17 August 1949.
Immigration regulations, waived to permit entry of Asiatics.

P.C. 4392, 31 August 1949.
Immigration regulations, waived to permit entry of Asiatics.

P.C. 4683, 13 September 1949.
Immigration regulations, waived to permit entry of Asiatics.

P.C. 4962, 12 September 1949.
Immigration regulations, waived to permit entry of Asiatics.

P.C. 1291, 22 March 1949.
Immigration regulations, waived to permit entry of Asiatics.

P.C. 3328, 6 July 1949.
Immigration regulations, waived to permit entry of Asiatics.

P.C. 3831, 3 August 1949.
Immigration regulations, waived to permit entry of Asiatics.

P.C. 3955, 10 August 1949.
Immigration regulations, waived to permit entry of Asiatics.

P.C. 7113, 17 August 1949.
Immigration regulations, waived to permit entry of Asiatics.

P.C. 4392, 31 August 1949.
Immigration regulations, waived to permit entry of Asiatics.

P.C. 4962, 12 September 1949.
Immigration regulations, waived to permit entry of Asiatics.

P.C. 4683, 13 September 1949.

Immigration regulations, waived to permit entry of Asiatics.

P.C. 5456, 27 October 1949.
Immigration regulations, waived to permit entry of Asiatics.

P.C. 5767, 15 November 1949.
Immigration regulations, waived to permit entry of Asiatics.

P.C. 6174, December 1949.
Immigration regulations, waived to permit entry of Asiatics.

P.C. 6285, 13 December 1949.
Immigration regulations, waived to permit entry of Asiatics.

P.C. 6378, 21 December 1949.
Immigration regulations, waived to permit entry of Asiatics.

P.C. 6229, 28 December 1949.
Immigration regulations amended to provide for admission of children and husbands of Asiatics.

P.C. 783, 17 February 1950.
Waiving provisions of P.C. 2744, 2 June 1944(re possession of passports) in case of Chinese wives or unmarried children of Canadian citizens legally resident in Canada.

1c. Dormant Orders in Council, 1862-1983.

P.C. 372, 24 February 1885.
Report of commission on Chinese immigration.

P.C. 1146, 10 June 1885.
Chinese Consolidated Benevolent Association, re British Columbia Act.

P.C. 1176, 13 June 1885.
Chinese Consolidated Benevolent Association, re British Columbia Act.

P.C. 3194(5), 12 December 1892.
Apportionment of Chinese tax on immigrants.

P.C. 1505, 12 May 1894.
Chinese labour in Esquimalt fortifications, protest against referred to Minister of Militia and Defence, 12 May 1894, on file with documents.

P.C. 879, April 1898.
Application Chinese immigration act to Japanese.

P.C. 1276, 23 May or 15 June 1898.
Discrimination against Japanese in British Columbia.

P.C. 1303, 26 May or 28 May 1898.
Discrimination against Japanese in British Columbia.

P.C. 1416, 7 June or 8 June 1898.
Discrimination against Japanese in British Columbia.

P.C. 1494, 3 July 1899.
Disallowance anti-Japanese legislation, British Columbia.

P.C. 1903 and 1904, 4 July 1900.
Petition British Columbia inhabitants against immigration of Chinese and Japanese.

P.C. 2457, 19 October and 10 December 1900.
Restricting Japanese immigration.

P.C. 600, 15 March 1901.
Japanese subjects in British Columbia, objection of Japanese government to certain statutes of 1900.

P.C. 665, 27 March 1901.
Chinese immigration, appreciation of appointment of a commission to enquire into.

P.C. 369, 9 March 1902.
Petition Presbyterian Church on behalf of Foreign Mission Board, against more stringent laws against immigration Chinese.

P.C. 448, 1 April 1902.
Chinese Immigration Tax, proportion of tax to be paid to British Columbia increased to one half, etc.

P.C. 1408, 9 September 1902.
Cariboo Gold Fields Company, require redress for grievance suffered through clause in act preventing employment of Chinese and Japanese labour.

P.C. 1663, 6 November 1902.
British Columbia legislation directed against Japanese. Protest of the Japanese Consul-general.

P.C. 131, 30 January 1903.
Memorandum re Mongolian immigration and share of Chinese capitation tax paid to British Columbia.

P.C. 1263, 22 July 1903.
Japanese immigration into British Columbia, Japanese Consul-general, Montréal, with report from Consul, Vancouver.

P.C. 1264, 25 July 1903.
Japanese immigration into British Columbia, Japanese Consul-general Montréal, with report from Consul, Vancouver.

P.C. 2829, 1903.
Report Hon. R.Lemieux of his mission to Japan on subject of immigration Oriental labourers into British Columbia.

P.C. 638, 6 April 1904.
Japanese Consul, expresses thanks of his government for disallowance of acts of immigration.

P.C. 1847, 30 September 1904.
Vancouver City Council protest against immigration of East Indians.

P.C. 2862, 25 January 1907.
Chinese Immigration Act, re repeal of section exempting students from tax.

P.C. 253, 5 February 1907.
Petition Montréal Board of Trade for temporary removal of head tax imposed on Chinese immigrants.

P.C. 24, 6 January 1908.
Oriental immigration, petitions against.

P.C. 137, 21 January 1908.
Japanese matters, correspondence between Mr. Nosse and Sir Wilfrid Laurier.

P.C. 1111, 9 May 1908.
Japanese immigration report, on numbers of immigrants and re passports issued before negotiations.

P.C. 1075, 15 May 1908.
Petition Chinese residents of British Columbia for amendment to criminal law to prevent gambling among Chinese residents.

P.C. 1479, 26 June 1908.
Japanese Consul General 22 June protesting against fishing laws of British Columbia prohibiting employment of Japanese boat pullers.

P.C. 1515, 15 July 1908.
Opium bill, protest 12 July of Chinese opium merchants with suggested amendment.

P.C. 746, 6 August 1908.
Opium trade, Montréal Chinese mission thanks for Act.

P.C. 2715, 11 December 1908.
Visit of Colonel Swayne, Governor of Honduras to Canada re transfer of Hindoos.

P.C. 2716, 11 December 1908.
Transfer British East Indians from British Columbia to Honduras.

P.C. 2640, 15/18 December 1908.
Transfer Hindoos to British Honduras.

P.C. 256, 12 February 1910.
Amendment Criminal Code to punish those who live in open concubinage, petition of British Columbia hierarchy of Canada.

P.C. 704, 6 April 1911.
Complaint British Indians residing in United States of treatment received from Canadian immigrant officials.

P.C. 2538, 9 November 1911.
British Columbia claims, Asiatic legislation, etc.

P.C. 2650, 24 November 1911.
Complaints restrictions imposed upon East Indian

immigrants resident in Canada.

P.C. 475, 29 February 1912.
Asiatic immigration, resolution of British Columbia Legislative Assembly.

P.C. 1151, 6 May 1912.
Asiatic immigration, confidential memo, Honorable MacKenzie King.

P.C. 2420, 30 August 1912.
Canadian-Japanese Association, petition against cap.18, statute Saskatchewan 1912, employment of female help.

P.C. 2448, 27 September 1913.
Wives and children of East Indians in Canada, regulations re continuous travelling.

P.C. 1404, 16 June 1914.
Timber and fishing regulations of British Columbia which operate disadvantageously against Japanese.

P.C. 216, 27 January 1915.
Chinese consul for refund of head tax in cases of Chinese immigrants who cannot get employment.

P.C. 433, 25 February 1915.
Chinese students, universities for admission.

7c. Cabinet War Committee minutes.

Volume 8, Reel C-4274.
Meeting no. 147, 26 February 1942, agenda items 4-5. re Japanese Canadians.

Volume 10, Reel C-4874.
Meeting no. 176, 8 July 1942, agenda items 1-2,
Meeting no. 177, 15 July 1942, agenda item 2,
Meeting no. 189, 9 September 1942, agenda items 7-8;
Meeting no. 195, 23 September 1942, agenda item 4 re Japanese Canadians.

Volume 11, Reels C-4874 to C-4875.
Meeting no. 201, 28 October 1942, agenda item 2;
Meeting no. 224, 11 March 1943, agenda item 6-7;
Meeting no. 260, 22 September 1943, agenda item 8. re Japanese Canadians.

Volume 14, Reel C-4875.
Meeting no. 263, 6 October 1943, agenda items 1-2, re Japanese Canadians.

Volume 15, Reel C-4876.
Meeting no. 277, 12 January 1944, agenda item 4,
Meeting no. 293, 19 April 1944, agenda items 6-7, re Japanese Canadians.

Volume 16, Reel C-4276.
Meeting no. 304, 5 July 1944, agenda item 2;
Meeting no. 315, 23 September 1944, agenda item 3;
Meeting no. 318, 11 October 1944, agenda item 6 re Japanese Canadians.

Volume 17, Reels C-4276-C-4877.
Meeting no. 329, 17 January 1945, agenda item 5;
Meeting no. 339, 11 April 1945, agenda item 9.

A. Cabinet Records, 1867-1956.

A5a. Cabinet, 1867-1955.

A5a. Cabinet Conclusions, 1944-1956, 3.0 metres(volumes 2636-2659, 5775, Reels T-2364 to T-2369).

All items dealing with Canada's relations with Asia and the Pacific, internal matters such as security and defence, along with commercial and trade relations can be found in the records of decisions made by the Cabinet. Although these conclusions do not provide verbatim accounts, they do constitute the only official record of cabinet meetings. The records fall under the provisions of the access to information and privacy legislation, though the overwhelming majority have been cleared. The records are on microfilm and can be ordered on inter-library loan. The records are arranged by the date of the Cabinet meeting.

A5b. Cabinet Committees, 1939-1965.

A5b. Cabinet War Committee, 1938-1945, 1.95 metres(volume 5667-5684, reels C-4654, C-4873 to C-4877, C-11789).

The records in this series consist of the minutes of the defence committee of cabinet 1938-1939 and the minutes and supporting documents of the Cabinet War Committee from December 1939 to May 1945. All items discussed by the Cabinet War Committee dealing with the war with Japan, security, trade and relations with various countries in Asia and the Pacific can be found in this series. The records are all open for researchers under the provisions of the access to information and privacy legislation. The finding aid is the alphabetically arranged subject file list.

B. Administrative records.

B2. Central Registry files, 1938-1955, 50.7 metres(volumes 1-253).

The Central Registry records consist of correspondence, minutes of cabinet committees, sub-committees and inter-departmental committees and supporting documents dealing with a wide variety of subjects concerning Asia and the Pacific. Of particular note are the records on Japanese immigration, trade and commercial records, the formation of the United Nations and Canada's role in providing economic assistance on the Far East along with a variety of files concerning Canada's relations with specific countries. The records are open under the provisions of the access to information and privacy legislation. The finding aids to the material are file lists arranged alphabetically by

subject.
These files fill out the background of the cabinet conclusions.

Volume 1, file C-10-3, December 1940.
War Committee of the Cabinet. Most secret. Orientals in British Columbia, November-December 1940. Report and recommendation of the Special Committee on Orientals in British Columbia.

Volume 25, file M-5-5, 1941-1945.
Military service.

Volume 25 and 26, 1940-1945.
Japanese in Canada, British Columbia Security Commission.

Volume 36, file E-11-1, 1942.
Dominion Elections Act, petition from Khalsa Diwan Society.

Volume 45, file D-15-26, 1940-1942
Treatment of enemy aliens.

Volume 167, 1940-1945.
Japanese in Canada, British Columbia Security Commission, 1950-1951.

Volume 182, file R-20-J, 1950.
Royal Commission enquiries - Japanese claims.

Record Group 3. Post Office..

Volume 655, file 112515.
Question of authorizing postmasters to register persons of Chinese origin or descent.

Record Group 6. Secretary of State.

A. Secretary of State correspondence.

A1. General correspondence, 1867-1952, 18.3 metres(volumes l-210).

Volume 36.

File 237.
Chinese poll tax passed by the Legislature of British Columbia, 1879.

Volume 38.

File 1628.
Francis I.Brown, steamer communication between Japan and Canada, 1879.

Volume 41.

File 1790.
Speaker, Legislative Assembly, British Columbia, for act to empower British Columbia to impose special taxes on Chinese, 1880.

Volume 55.

File 1740 and 1741.
Lieutenant-governor of British Columbia, re immigration.1883.

Volume 59.

File 7718 and 7719.
Resolutions of British Columbia re Chinese immigration.

Volume 60.

File 2235.
Destitutes among Chinese discharged from Canadian Pacific Railway, 1886.

Volume 61.

File 6628.
Pillage by Chinese of chapels of Canadian Presbyterian Mission, 1886.

Volume 65.

File 17127.
Re action of Chinese government, i.e. social relations of Chinese in British Columbia, n.d.

Volume 66.

File 23759.
Treatment of Chinese in British Columbia, 1886.

File 1352.
Re section 20 of 1 Immigration Act, 1887.

Volume 69.

File 8684.
Re treatment of Chinese subjects in British Columbia, 1887.

Volume 70.

File 698.
Re position of Chinese subjects in British Columbia, 1888.

Volume 77.

File 698.
Re proposed changes in Chinese Immigration Act, 1891.

Volume 78.

File 2963-2964.
Re T&LC, to prevent importation of Chinese, 1891.

Volume 79.

File 1313.
Re leprosy among Chinese and establishment of

lazaretto, 1892.

Volume 81.

File 5020.
Re Order in Council proposal by S.Ewata of Yokohama, Japan, for emigration of Japanese labourers to Manitoba, 1892.
Volume 82.

File 1527.
British Columbia government advises inspection of Japanese and Chinese immigrants(see file 1846), 1893.

File 1846.
Re British Columbia report on smallpox epidemic in British Columbia, 1893.

Volume 86.

File 1629.
Chinese residents of Victoria, British Columbia, petition for amendment of certain act, 1894.

Volume 87.

File 6897.
Legislative Assembly of British Columbia, resolution to exclude persons without means from British Columbia from foreign countries, 1894.

Volume 89.

File 4228.
Re Tard L.C. received letter from Rev. Principal Grant re repeal of legislation discriminating against Chinese, 1895.

Volume 91.

File 880.
Re quarantine of vessels stopping at Shanghai due to smallpox, 1896.
File 1344.
Order in Council asking government to aid escape of Mesrob Baghdasarian and family from Turkish atrocity in Armenia, 1896.

Volume 94.

File 340.
Executive Council of British Columbia resolution re amendment of Naturalization Act to prevent Asians from becoming British subjects in Canada, 1900.

Volume 97.

File 1210.
Colonial Secretary re Japanese emigration to Canada, 1900.

File 1600.
Re despatches from Japanese Consul relating to certain provincial acts of British Columbia, 1900.

Volume 100.

File 642.
Re right of petitioning theme of Chinese Reform Association of Canada, 1901.
Volume 101.

File 667.
Re Wong Soon King, resolution of Chinese Board of trade, re Chinese community.

File 668.
Legislative Assembly resolution re amendment of Chinese Immigration Act, 1900-1901.

File 689.
Executive Council of Manitoba, re notice to Japanese government re stipulation of convention at Tokyo to be made applicable to Canada re protection of estates of deceased persons, 1901.

File 728.
Re Legislative Assembly of British Columbia prevents franchise being exercised by naturalized subjects of Japan and China, n.d.

Volume 104.

File 552.
Rev. William H.Grant re resolution of Foreign Mission Branch of Canada re anti-Chinese agitation, 1902.

Volume 106.

File 1269.
Resolution of British Columbia Legislative Assembly re Chinese and Japanese immigration to Canada, 1902.

File 1557.
Legislative Assembly of British Columbia, proposal to check immigration of Chinese and Japanese, 1902.

Volume 108.

File 12.
Newspaper clippings re Japanese labour in British Columbia, 1903.

Volume 109.

File 1003.
Governor of Hong Kong wishes to be supplied with copies of laws, re immigration of Chinese in Canada, 1903.

Volume 119.

File 1724.
Alberta Conference of Methodist Church, resolution against opium traffic with China, 1905.

File 2130.
Methodist Church Conference in Nova Scotia, resolution re opium traffic with China and India, n.d.

File 2209.
Diocese of Niagara re opium traffic, 1905.

Volume 120.

File 838.
Order in Council granting $25,000 relief to famine sufferers in Japan, 1906.

File 947.
Secretary of State for Colonies application for assistance on behalf of certain Armenians, 1896.

Volume 122.

File 1309.
Re Japanese famine fund, 1906.

Volume 124.

File 2886.
Petitioning of Anglican Missionary Society for suppression of opium in all British possessions, 1906.

Volume 129.

File 1382.
Re British Columbia T & L.C. letter re Japanese immigration, 1907.

Volume 130.

File 2822.
Re claim by Chinese subjects for losses incurred in recent rioting in Vancouver, 1907.

File 2878.
Re deportation of Japanese immigrants for insufficient reasons of health, Vancouver, 1907.

Volume 131.

File 91.
Message to be cabled to British consuls at Honolulu, Hong Kong and India, re entrance of immigrants into Canada, n.d.

Volume 132.

File 669K
W.L.Mackenzie King appointed Commissioner to settle Chinese claims for compensation from losses in Vancouver riots, 1908.

File 637.
Re copies of Vancouver **Daily Province** containing details of agreement between Canada and Japan re immigration, n.d.

Volume 133.

File 1053.
Seizaburo Shimizu appointed Consul-general of Japan for Canada, 1908.

Volume 134.

File 1039.
Re sailing of Tung Ching-ling for Canada and inquiries concerning Chinese, 1908.

File 1475.
Fining of Chinese subjects at Sydney, Nova Scotia, 1908.

File 1480.
Re desire of Chinese government to appoint Chinese consular representative to Canada, 1908.

Volume 135.

File 2493.
Resolution passed by Toronto Chinese mission re Opium Bill.

Volume 136.

File 382.
Rev. H.F.Perry, on the Shanghai Opium Conference, 1909.

Volume 138.

File 1186.
T.Sugimuro, proposed visit to Japanese training on coast of British Columbia, 1909.

Volume 139.

File 1585.
Re resolution passed by Toronto Chinese Mission re tax Chinese students, 1909.

Volume 145.

File 946.
Re copy of law re admission of Chinese students to study at Canadian universities, 1910.

Volume 147.

File 2350.
Re proposed issue of Order in Council to enable Turkish consular officers in His Majesty's dominions to administer the estates of Ottoman subjects dying therein, 1910.

Volume 149.

File 786.
Rev. Shearer, resolution re opium traffic, 1911.

File 823.
T.A.Moore, resolution re opium traffic, 1911.

Volume 150.
File 1211.
Petition from Sunder Singh, president, Hindustani Association, re Hindu immigration to Canada, 1911.

Volume 160.

Files 2458-2459.
Order in Council, act to prevent immigration of Chinese, 1885.

Volume 161.

File 5139.
Secretary of State, expenses re Li Hung chang, 1896.

Volume 163.

File 3190.
Re Prince Fushimi's visit to Canada, 1906.

Volume 164.

File 2434.
Hostility towards Japanese in British Columbia, 1907.

Volume 172.

File 1668.
Policy re employment of Japanese, 1913.

Volume 174.

File 2096.
L.Shikyuan re Chinese order, Rev. W.C.White, n.d.

Volume 209.

File 101
Application of Chinese family to enter United States, 1896.

File 190.
Passports for Japanese immigrants in British Columbia, 1892.

File 1876.
J.O.Peeland - passports for Armenians, 1896.

File 3086.
United States Consul-general, Chinese entering United States on Canadian passports.

File 4511.
Re passports to Chinese, 1896.

A3. Unnumbered and subject files, 1862-1965.

Volume 215.
Reports to Privy Council(pages 123, 180) re appointment of Chinese consul in Canada, 1908-1909.
Files 128, 140, 144, 150, 156, 158.
Reports to Privy Council re transportation of Hindus from British Columbia to British Honduras, 1908.

Volume 216.
Telegram re release of Jack Chun or Chung from Westminster Penitentiary, contains other telegrams re individual cases of Chinese, etc., re deportation, naturalization, imprisonment, etc., 1916.

Volume 791.

File 2246.
Re return of Japanese in British Columbia to Japan before Military Reserve Act, 1917.

File 3102.
Offer of detachment of 25, 000 Japanese from the United States, 1917.

C. Secretary of State for the Provinces.

C1. General correspondence, 1867-1973. 3.2 metres(Volume 307-339).

Volume 332.

File 1143.
Lieutenant Governor, Victoria, re poll tax, California, 1872.

E. Chief Press Censor, 1915-1920. 16.5 metres(Volumes 490-656; and microfilm reels T-12 to T-111, and T-745 to T-758).

Censorship Directorate Records, 1939-1945.

E1. Chief Press Censor for Canada.

Volume 590.

File 268-A-1. Reel No. 1-81.
Hairenik, Boston.

Volume 512.

File 141(volume 1).
Indian Nationalist Committee, etc., 1915-1919. Reel T-26-T-27.

Volume 513.

File 141-13.
Censorship of mail, Commander-in-Chief, China Station, 1916. Reel T-27.

Volume 526.

File 168.
Censorship telegraph messages, to and from Chinese consul, Vancouver, 1915-1919. Reel T-36-T-37.

Volume 527.

File 168-A.

Volume 620.

File 331.
Passage of Chinese coolies through Canada, 1917-1918. Reel T-101.

File 332.
Statement in United States papers re Japanese troops crossing Canada, 1917. Reel T-101.

F. Citizenship sector.

F1. Citizenship Registration Branch, 1887-1978, 3 metres(volumes 657-665 and 8121-818).

Since 1881 the Secretary of State has been involved with the issuing of naturalization certificates. Initially this responsibility only covered government employees. Provincial courts were responsible for all other registrations eventually submitting information on members and nationalities to the Secretary of State. This information is available in the **Annual reports** of the department. Since 1914 the department has had full responsibility for issuing naturalization certification. The records received prior to the access to information and privacy legislation are open. Those received since that date must be reviewed. These records have not been microfilmed. Finding aids are available.

F2. Multicultural Directorate, 1971-1979.(volumes 820-823, accession 86-87/342).

This directorate is responsible for the promotion of multicultural programmes aimed at enriching Canada's cultural heritage. This is presently achieved by the administration of a grants system and support. Finding aids are available, although not on microfilm. These records are subject to access to information and privacy legislation.

H. War time records.

H4. Second World War, 1939-1942.

Volume 811.

File 796.
Evacuation of Japanese, 1942.

File 2420.
Repatriation of Japanese from Canada, 1942.

File 2426.
Repatriation of Japanese from Canada, 1942.

Volume 818.
Register of Japanese evacuees, ca. 1946.

Record Group 7. Governor-General's Office.

G1. Register of despatches from the Colonial Office re Japanese in Canada. G1, G2, and G3(secret and confidential)
Records arranged by date.

File 280.
Chinese impostor name Wang-Tsing-Tah, 31 December 1874.

File 341.
Chinese poll tax, British Columbia, 29 November 1877.

File 14.
Act relating to Chinese, British Columbia, 17 January 1879.

File 355.
Chinese poll tax, 29 October 1879.

Volume 308(2)-310(1).

File 76.
Proposal re establishment of an Armenian colony in Canada, 3 March 1886.

File 219.
Chinese Commission, report on social relations of Chinese subjects in British Colonies, 6 October 1886.

File A/3a.
Chinese emigrants telegram, 27 April 1887.

File A/3a.
Chinese emigrants telegram, 30 April 1887.

Circular.
Chinese subjects in Her Majesty's colonies, 23 January 1888.

File 221.
Chinese labourers, entry from Canada or Mexico into the United States, 13 November 1890.

File 246.
Chinese labourers, 27 December 1890.

File 34.
Chinese subjects entering United States through Canada, 25 February 1891.

File 59.
Chinese, entry into United States from Mexico and Canada, 26 March 1891.

File 94.
Chinese, entry into the United States from Canada, 19 May 1891.

File 265.
Chinese entry into United States from Canada, 22 September 1892.

File 327.
Chinese Immigration Act, 1886, copy of note from Chinese Minister in London protesting amendment, 28 November 1892.

File 64.

Chinese Immigration Act, 22 March 1893.

File 226.
Chinese labourers, emigrating to British Guiana via Canada, 14 August 1893.

File 283.
Restriction of Chinese immigration, 10 October 1893.

Volume 308(2)-310(1).

Files 91, 101, 109, 113.
Resolutions re Armenian massacres, 3 March 1896.

Volume 310(2)-312(1).

File 352.
Li Hung chang, Chinese Grand Secretary visit to Canada, 23 November 1896.

Volume 308(2)-310(1).

File 97.
Emigration to Canada of father of an Armenian student at McMaster University, 19 March 1897.

File 111.
Proposed increase of Chinese poll tax, 7/8 May 1897.

File 458.
Chinese poll tax, 18 November 1897.

File 171.
Poll tax on Chinese immigrants into Canada, 4 June 1898.

File 214.
Japanese legislation in British Columbia, 20 July 1898.

File 235.
Chinese naturalized British subjects divesting themselves of their allegiance to China, 2 August 1898.

File 249.
Japanese legislation in British Columbia, 11 August 1898.

File 343.
Anti-Japanese legislation in British Columbia, 24 December 1898.

File 41.
Anti-Japanese legislation in British Columbia, 8 March 1899.

File 58.
Anti-Japanese legislation in British Columbia, 23 March 1899.

Secret.
Chinese reformer, Kang Yu-wei, 11 April 1899.

File 83.
Anti-Japanese legislation in British Columbia, 19 April 1899.

File 89.
Chinese immigration, capitation tax, 29 April 1899.

File 92.
Anti-Japanese legislation in British Columbia, 2 May 1899.

File 102.
Anti-Japanese legislation in British Columbia, 9 May 1899.

File 105.
Chinese capitation tax, 10 May 1899.

File 172.
Chinese poll tax, 29 July 1899.

File 286.
Chinese capitation tax, 30 November 1899.

File 67.
Chinese entering Canada, capitation tax, 8 March 1900.

File 167.
Chinese capitation tax, 23 June 1900.

File 186.
Japanese emigration to Canada, July 1900.

File 193.
Letter, Victoria, British Columbia, for establishing a government employment bureau to keep Asiatics out of British Columbia, 14 July 1900.

File 234.
Chinese Empire Reform Association of Canada, petition, 24 August 1900.

File 272.
Japanese legislation in British Columbia, October 1900.

Confidential.
British Columbia Immigration Act of 1900, Japanese, January 1901.

File 67 and 68.
Chinese Empire Reform Association, memorial, March 1901.

File 114.
Japanese landed in British Columbia by captain of United States revenue cutter **Grant**, April 1901.

File 144.
Act restricting Chinese immigration will not be disallowed, 18 May 1901.

File 50.
Chinese Empire Reform Association, memorial, 12 February 1902

File 292.
Recent anti-Japanese legislation in British Columbia, 2 August 1902.

File 185.
Chinese capitation tax, from 100 to 500 dollars, 21 May 1903.

Confidential.
Legislation affecting Chinese immigrants, 22 October 1903.

File 87.
Chinese emigration to the United States. n.d.

Volume 369(1)-370(2).

File 371.
Armenian tobacco planters, 21 December 1904.

Volume 375(2)-376(2).

File 87.
Application for assistance on behalf of certain Armenians, 21 February 1906.

File 364.
Emigration from Turks in Asia to Canada, 24 August 1906.

File 454.
East Indians immigration into British Columbia, 24 October 1906.

Files 394 and 424.
Lemieux's visit to Japan, October 1907.

File 422 and telegrams.
Indians(British) immigration to Canada, 29 October 1907.

File 507.
(Hindus) Indians, immigration to British Columbia, 27 November 1906.

Library.
Parliamentary papers, statistics, coolie labour, 30 November 1906.

File 535.
Indians(British) immigration to British Columbia, December 1906.

File 387.
Oriental disturbances, Chinese subjects, 7 October 1907.

File 439.
Claims for losses in Vancouver rioting, compensation to Chinese, November 1907.

File 447.
Claims for losses in Vancouver rioting, compensation to Chinese, November 1907.

File 44.
Japanese immigration to Canada, 29 January 1908.

File 52.
Japanese immigration to Canada, 5 February 1908.

File 68.
Indians(British) immigration to Canada, 12 February 1908.

File 241.
Chinese attaché visit to Canada, 6 May 1908.

File 250.
Congress of Orientalists, 15 May 1908.

File 350.
Chinese subjects at Sydney, Nova Scotia, fine and imprisonment, 18 June 1908.

File 395.
Vancouver riots, compensation of Chinese, 4 July 1908.

File 287.
Penalty imposed on steamer **Oceana** for desertion of three Chinese crew members, 11 July 1908.

File 457.
Chinese immigration bill, effect of, 1 August 1908.

File 548.
Asiatic immigration, Indians at Vancouver, 5 September 1908.

File 557.
Chinese in Nova Scotia, treatment of certain, 11 September 1908.

File 660.
Removal of Hindoos from British Columbia to British Honduras, 31 October 1908.

File 749.
Tung Ching ling to visit Canada, 8 December 1908.

G6. Despatches from the British Minister at Washington.

Records arranged by date.

Volume 26.

File 24.
Copy of act of United States Congress prohibiting importation of immigrants into United States, Chinese, Japanese, and Orientals, 1875.

File 26.
Japanese landed in British Columbia by captain, United States revenue cutter **Grant**, 20 March 1901.

File 39.
Japanese landed in British Columbia by captain, United States revenue cutter **Grant**, 31 March 1901.

Volume 37.

File 114.
Re refusal of authorities of British Columbia to receive back Chinese labourers who have crossed into United States, 1885.

Volume 38(1).

File 42.
Re Lum Way, British subject forcibly expelled from town of Tacoma, Washington Territory, United States, 1886.

Volume 20.
Chinese subjects detained at Seattle, Washington, 10 September 1889.

Volume 50.
Case of Chong Sam returned to Canada by order of United States court, 10 October 1891.

Volume 64.
United States government complaint against Canadian Pacific Railway for transporting Chinese to United States, 10 August 1892.

Volume 87.
United States government complaint against Canadian Pacific Railway for transporting Chinese to United States, 3 October 1892.

Volume 88.
Chinese immigration into United States, 5 October 1892.

Volume 33.
Passage through Canada of the Chinese missionary Yung King yen facilitated, 10 May 1895.

Volume 90.
Case of Chinaman Lee Chong who claims to be merchant of Montréal who applied for admission to the United States, 14 November 1896.

Volume 97.
Case of Chinaman Lee Chong who claims to be merchant of Montréal who applied for admission to the United States, 8 December 1896.

Volume 100.
Case of Chinaman Lee Chong who claims to be merchant of Montréal who applied for admission to the United States, 17 December 1896.

Volume 108.
F.Brown of Montréal alleged extorting money from Chinese under threat of arrest for entering the United States, 30 September 1898.

File 124.
J.Dwyer, an Armenian anarchist stated to have escaped after an attempt to kill the Ottoman Consul at San Francisco, 7 December 1898.

Volume 74.
16 Chinese persons, one afflicted with smallpox brought to frontier by Canadian Pacific Railway for purpose of unlawfully entering the United States, 3 July 1899.

Volume 77.
Violation of Chinese exclusion laws at Plattsburg, New York, 13 August 1899.

Volume 8.
Complaint of action of Saunders, Customs official trying to intimidate Chinese witness, re violation of Chinese exclusion laws, 19 January 1900.

Volume 10.
Violation of United States Chinese exclusion laws by Canadian Customs officers, 5 February 1900.

Volume 70 and telegrams.
Oriental situation in Vancouver and Pacific states of the United States, 6 and 20 September 1907.

Volume 21.
Hindu named Taraknath Dass, 3 February 1909.

G10. Drafts of secret or confidential messages to the Colonial Office, 6 feet, (Volumes 1-44).

Records arranged by date.

Volume 37-44.
Re covering letters sent to Colonial Secretary enclosing copies of reports about activities of Hindus, Mohammedans and Sikhs in British Columbia, 1906-1913.

Volume 38.
Immigration regulations(restriction of labour emigration), 9 December 1907.

Volume 38.
Immigration regulations(restriction of labour emigration), 20 December 1907

Volume 38.
Immigration regulations(restriction of labour emigration), 26 December 1907.

Volume 40.
Immigration regulations(restriction of labour emigration), 20 January 1908.

Volume 40(1).
Immigration regulations(restriction of labour emigration), 23 March 1908.

Volume 40(1).
Immigration regulations(restriction of labour emigration), 14 April 1908.

Volume 40(1)
Re immigration, restriction, 22 June 1908.

Volume 40(3)
Re immigration, restriction, 4 May 1909.

Volume 40(3).
Immigration regulations(restriction of labour emigration), 4 May 1909.

G11. Drafts of despatches to Washington.

Volume 3.

File 96.
Reply to despatch, copies of "act to restrict and regulate Chinese immigration into Canada" sent to Minister at Washington, 11 September 1885.

Volume 4(2).

File 30.
Detention of Chinese subjects at Seattle, Washington, "at which place they arrived two years ago from Victoria, British Columbia, " 14 September 1889.

Volume 7(2).

File 71.
Case of Chinaman Lee Chong alleged to have tried to gain admission to United States using papers fraudulently obtained from Canadian officials, 2 December 1896.

Volume 9(1).

File 27.
Alleged violations of United States Chinese exclusion

laws by Canadian Customs official and Canadian Pacific Railway, 22 March 1900.

Volume 11(1).

File 12.
Dominion government authorized Controller of Chinese immigration, F.C.O'Hara to issue necessary certificate to Chinese visiting United States, as required by United States law, 12 February 1904.

Volume 15(1).

File 51.
Proposal to discourage illegal entry of Chinese from Canada to United States, 4 May 1910.

Volume 17(2).

File 21.
Information and proposed action re Har Dyal(Har Dayal), violent anglophobe of frankly anarchist views. Travelled through Oregon and California inciting Hindu workers. Suggested United States authorities arrest him as a dangerous anarchist, 6 February 1914.

Volume 17(2).

File 39.
Letter of appreciation re thanking United States government for help given to Mr. Hopkinson, special agent of Department of Interior, mission in San Francisco to investigate certain phases of Hindu question, 10 March 1914.

G12. Letterbooks of despatches to Colonial Office.

Volume 30.

File 245, page 158.
Privy Council Order disallowing act passed by British Columbia Legislature affecting Chinese, 4 September 1879.

Volume 80.

File 20, page 31.
Correspondence re British Columbia's legislation(poll tax) affecting Chinese residents, whether power of disallowance should be used, 23 December 1878.

Volume 83.

File 69, pages 38-40.
Report of Privy Council on British Columbia's legislation dealing with Chinese immigrants, examines rationale for these bills, 15 April 1884.

File 257, page 330.
Chinese immigration to British Columbia, present act far less stringent than legislation disallowed in 1884-1885, 7 August 1884.

Volume 84.

File 226, page 120.
Chinese government sending a commission to report on "social relations" of Chinese subjects in British Columbia, 15 July 1887.

Volume 87.

File 68, page 80.
United States proposal to prevent clandestine entry of Chinese labourers from Canada. Minister of Customs governed by Chinese Immigration Act, Chinamen cannot reenter Canada legally without paying capitation tax, 7 March 1892.

Volume 88.

File 112, page 143.
Protest by Chinese Minister at Court of St. James against amendment of Dominion Chinese Immigration Act of 1886, Minister of Trade and Industry, 14 April 1893.

File 208, page 246.
Privy Council minute forwarded re petition from Dominion Trades and Labour Congress desiring restriction of Chinese immigration, 14 September 1893.

Volume 90.

File 234, page 391.
Privy Council discouraging establishment of Armenian colony. Climate and conditions too difficult. No funds other than usual in case of ordinary settlers, 21 August 1896.

Volume 93.

File 40, page 321.
Chinese and Japanese labour prohibition legislation of British Columbia, objections of his Imperial Japanese Majesty's consul at Vancouver, 27 February 1899.

File 136, page 127.
British Columbia legislation amending Public Works Loan Act 1897, prohibiting Chinese and Japanese persons to be employed in construction or operation of undertakings subsidized by the Public Works Loan Act, 25 May 1898.

File 145, page 130.
Transmitting communications from the Imperial Japanese Majesty's consul on British Columbia legislation, 30 May 1898.

File 146.
Transmit letter from Japanese consul for Canada and list of British Columbia acts containing anti-Japanese clauses, 8 June 1898.

File 185, page 168.
Answer to Chinese Minister at Court of St. James re no proposed increase of poll tax on Chinese immigrants, 7 July 1898.

Volume 94.

File 205, page 336.
Discussion re action taken to disallow British Columbia's legislation barring Japanese labourers from working on public works projects, 19 July 1901.

G14. Miscellaneous Records, 6 metres, originals, 1774-1913. Finding aid 722.

Volume 110.
Includes correspondence between Lord Grey and Sir C.MacDonald in Tokyo re Japanese immigration to Canada, 1908-1909.

G17a. Letterbooks, Canada, 1839-1910. 13 feet, (79 volumes).

A. Government internal letterbooks, 1830-1909(Volumes 1-17).

G18. Miscellaneous records, 1791-1917. 21 feet, (Volumes 1-117).

Volume 100.
United States-China exclusion laws, complaint of Canadian customs and Canadian Pacific Railway officials violating laws, 1900.

Volume 101.
Canadian Armenian relief fund, 1920-1926.

G20. Civil Secretary's correspondence, 1841-1909. 63 feet, (Volumes 1-416).

Records arranged by date.

File 3835.
Department of Justice, re act passed by Legislature of British Columbia imposing certain taxes on Chinese residents.

File 8154.
Government of Hong Kong, Chinese emigration from Hong Kong, 22 December 1881.

File 230.
Copy of report of Chinese Commission, Secretary of State, 28 March 1885.

File 858.
Her Majesty's consul, San Francisco, Chinese act, 1885, 4 September 1885.

File 1482.
Secretary of State, Chinese Commission to visit Canada, 22 June 1886.

File 1518.
Claim for damages by C.F.Moore for customs taxing his Chinese wife, 5 July 1886.

File 1568.
Claim for damages by C.F.Moore for customs taxing his Chinese wife, 21 July 1886.

File 1595.
Secretary of State, arrest at Port Huron of two Chinese residents of Canada, 18 July 1891.

File 1758.
Consul of Japan, protest against British Columbia anti-Japanese legislation, 1 June 1897.

File 1524.
Governor of Hong Kong, re immigration of Chinese, 18 February 1902.

File 1745.
Governor of Hong Kong, laws re Chinese immigration, 12 May 1893.

File 1872.
C.F.Moore, teaching of Chinese, 17 August 1903.

File 1536.

Chinese immigration, 14 April 1903.

File 1719.
Her Majesty's consul, New York, re intent to land mutinous Chinese at Cape Breton, 1903?

File 1048 and 1069.
Regina Patrons of Industry, resolution re Armenian troubles, 5 and 28 February 1895.

File 1066.
First Presbyterian Church, London, Armenian massacres, 14 February 1895.

File 1758.
Consul of Japan, protest against British Columbia anti-Japanese legislation, 1 June 1897.

File 2570.
Japanese consul, disallowance of British Columbia legislation, 22 September 1901.

G21. Central Registry Series, 1818-1941.
(Volumes 1-734, reels T-184 to T-202, T-820 to T-884, T-1145 to T-1195, T-1371 to T-1401, T-1478 to T-1490, T-2294 to T-2363, T-2503 to T-2535, T-7327).

Before the Department of External affairs was begun in 1909, the Governor General was responsible for the conduct of Canada's foreign relations. The office also had many domestic responsibilities and all of these are covered in the central registry files. The bulk of these records cover the years 1867 to 1941. The records and the finding aid are on microfilm and may be borrowed on interlibrary loan. The series is open for research.

Volume 126.

File 232, reel T-843.
Japanese immigration to Canada, 1898-1904.

Volume 179.

File 304.
Treaty of commerce between Great Britain and Japan, 1894-1912.

File 304, part 2, reel T-1165.
Immigration of Japanese labourers to British colonies, 1895-1896, 1913-1937.

Volume 190.

File 314, part v.
Indians(Hindu) domiciled in Canada, re position under Dominion Franchise Law, 1925, 1925.

Volume 199-211.

File 332, reels T-1172 to T-1176.
Oriental immigration(including Japanese and East Indians), 1907-1930.

Volume 199.

File 332, reel T-1172.
Anti-Oriental disturbances in Vancouver, 1907-

Volume 200-211.

File 332, reel T-1176.
Asiatic immigration(including Chinese) , 1908-1930.

Volume 202-212.

File 332.
Various Hindu immigration into Canada(manifests of ships' passengers), nationalization of aliens, 1913-1930.

Volume 211, 212.

File 332b.
Hindu immigration, **Komagata maru** question, 1914-1916.

Volume 224-235.

File 343, parts 1-14, reels T-1180 to T-1184.
Turco-Greek operations in Anatolia, 1907-1938.

Volume 226.

File 226, reels T-842-T-1172.
Chinese immigration into Canada, 1884-1887.

Volume 402.

File 7683, reel T-2294.
Laws forbidding employment of white girls by Japanese, 1912-1921.

Volume 408.

File 9394, reel T-2296.
Chinese desiring to enter United States require certificates, 1905-1927.

Volume 590.

File 24896, reels T-2350-T-2351.
California anti-alien land bill, inclusive of Japanese, 1913-1927.

Volume 618-628.

File 34386, parts 1-10. Reel T-263, T-2503 to T-2506.
Treaties arising out of the Great War, 1920-1937.

Volume 635.

File 3467, part 1. reel T-2510.
Armenians in Turkey, 1913.

Volume 635-637.

File 34671, part 2. Reel T-2511.

Admission of Turkish nationals in the British Empire, 1924-1925.

File 34671, part 3. Reel T-2511.
Admission of Turkish nationals in the British Empire, 1926-1937.

Volume 637.

Part 3, reel T-2511.
Admission etc., of Turkish nationals in the British Empire, 1926-1937.

Volumes 639-640.

File 34804, parts 1a and 1b, reel T-2513.
Asiatic immigration, land-owning rights of Chinese, Japanese, etc., 1921-1924.

Volume 639-641.

File 34804, reel T-2513-T-2514.
Asiatic immigration, land-owning rights, 1921-1924.

Volume 654.

File 38351.
International law, Asiatic immigration into Canada, land-owning rights, 1921-1924

G26. Central Registry Files, 1859-1966, (volumes 1-119).

This series is a continuation of series G21, mostly covering the years 1941 to 1966.

Because of the lessening role of the Governor General throughout Canadian history, these records are not as concerned with such issues as foreign affairs, trade and immigration. The records are not on microfilms. Access to these records is given by the Governor General's office, though the overwhelming majority of them are open to research.

Record Group 9. Militia and Post-Confederal Records.

IIA2. Reports and Memoranda, 1867-1920.

Volume 33, page 60.
Decision of Militia Council not to proceed with formation of Japanese battalion for service overseas, 1916.
IIA6. Reference papers, 1859-1903.

Volume 6, page 2387.
Copy telegram re offer from Japanese British subjects resident in British Columbia to Her Majesty's government.

Record Group 12. Transport.

Volume 1998-1999.

File 3556-33(six parts).
Andrew Ordendonk, contractor, built section of Canadian Pacific Railway(British Columbia) with Oriental labourers, 1879-1891.

Volume 2079.
File 3606-12.
Oriental labourers on Canadian Pacific Railway in British Columbia, 1880-1884.

A1. Central Registry Files, 1841-1976. 415.5 metres(volumes 1-408, 461-545)

Volume 1483.

File 8038-7.
Merchant navy, manning pools, welfare services, Chinese, 1941-1945.

Volume 1484.

File 8038-29.
Merchant navy, manning pools, welfare service, Chinese shore leave in Canada, 1942.

A2. Classified Registry Files. 1936-1974. 30.6 metres.

Records with a security classification of confidential or higher.

Volume 632.

File 11-16-41.
Defense measures and regulations, radio telegraph and cable prohibiting Japanese nationals the use of short wave radio receiving sets and radio transmitters, 1942-1943.

Record Group 13. Justice..

A2. Central Registry Files, 1845-1959. 154.9 metres(volumes 1-413, 416, 418, 1856-2029, 2113-2130)
Finding aids available.
Entries arranged in order by date.

Volume 53.

File 916.
Re Chinaman keeping Indian women prostitutes, 1882.

Volume 60.

File 544.
Re inquiry as to whether Hong Kong emigrants may land in Victoria, British Columbia, 1884.

Volume 61.

File 1265.
Re suggestion legislate so as to prevent Chinese from acquiring Crown lands, n.d.

Volume 63.

File 1151(63).
Re naturalized Chinaman absent at passing of Restriction Act, therefore head tax, 1885.

Volume 65.

File 1064.
Re acts of British Columbia, entitled act to regulate the Chinese population in British Columbia, 1886.

Volume 68.

File 961.
Re if protector of the Chinese is likely to be appointed, 1887.

Volume 71.

File 797.
Re Imperial despatch relating to Chinese immigration into Australasian colonies, 1888.

Volume 75.

File 1124.
Re certain Chinese subjects being detained at Seattle, 1889.

Volume 78.

File 875.
Re Bowell re Chinese passenger on **Pekin,** 1890.

Volume 81.

File 745.
Re Chinese residents of dominion while travelling in United States, 1891.

Volume 83.

File 1411.
Re land in railway belt, British Columbia to Kwan Lung in trust for Chinese of Kamloops for cemetery purposes, 1891.

Volume 86.

File 475.
Re forged certificates of Chinese immigrants of Canadian Pacific Railways S.S. **Empress of India**, 1892.

Volume 87.

File 751.
Chinaman Wong Chee ping and Hien Wah ling require certificates of identity from Canada to enter United States territories, 1892.

Volume 102.

File 816.
Expenses of Customs collector re arrest of three Chinamen at St. Hyacinthe, 1896.

Volume 104.

File 140.
If Chinamen may come from British Guiana to Canada to study medicine without paying tax, 1897.

Volume 106.

File 967.
Liability of A.N.Patterson, Collector of Customs at Sheep Cree, British Columbia, for cost of prosecution brought against him by a Chinaman, 1899.

Volume 116.

File 697.
Application of Suig Duck, alias Chang Jung for refund of Chinese immigration tax, 1900.

File 801.
If Chinese leaving Canada will now be entitled to return within six or twelve months, 1900.

File 580.
Claim of M.Edaljee of Yokohama, Japan against T.B.Hall of Victoria, 1900.

Volume 117.

File 55.
If Chinese entitled to refund of capitation tax under old act and still entitled to it under the present act, 1901.

Volume 118.

File 306.
Capitation tax on Chinese in transit through Canada to United States, 1901.

File 323.
Despatch from Lord Pauncefote transmitting copy of an Act of Congress, re procedure to be followed in case of arrests for violation of the Chinese exclusion, 1901.

Volume 122.

File 206.
Case of Fred Beowne, American citizen of Montréal, accused of extorting money from Chinamen, 1902.

Volume 123.

File 335.
Despatch from Lieutenant Governor of British

Columbia, re regulation to prevent immigration of Chinese and Japanese, 1902.

Volume 128.

File 499.
Asking date on which Chinese tax comes into force, 1903.

Volume 130.

File 103.
Chinaman detained at Montréal by Canadian Pacific Railway on account of a disagreement, 1904.

Volume 136.

File 197.
For information as to status of Chinese entering Canada, 1905.

Volume 139.

File 1157.
F.D.Shaw, coroner, Coldston, returning account for investigation into death of Yep Goon Han, 1905.

Volume 142.

File 744.
Legality for conviction of certain Chinese for gambling, 1906.

File 836.
Case of Lam Kin convicted at Hamilton of breach of the Chinese act, 1906.

Volume 149.

File 118.
Arrival of Chinamen in Woodstock, New Brunswick, without paying capitation tax, 1908.

Volume 150.

File 228.
Claim of Mai Sing of Blairmore for compensation for unjust imprisonment, 1908.

File 257.
Fines imposed on Chinamen at Sydney, claims for refunds, 1908.

Volume 152.

File 1140.
Errors in act amending the Chinese immigration act, 1908.

Volume 153.

File 1352.
Regulations re education of Chinese, 1908.

Volume 156.

File 866.
Draft bond to be given under Chinese immigration act by the Bank Line of steamers, 1909.

Volume 157.

File 1111.
Money qualifications of Asiatic immigrants, 1909.

Volume 166.

File 522.
Percentage of crimes committed by Chinese, Japanese and Hindu immigrants, 1911.

Volume 167.

File 824.
Draft Chinese Immigration Act, 1911.

File 923.
Hindu immigrants should be allowed to bring in families, 1911.

Volume 168.

File 1227.
Order in Council re apprehension of deserters from Japanese ships, 1911.

Volume 169.

File 1416.
Rejection by Department of Interior of Chinese youths claiming to be minors, 1911.

Volume 173.

File 990.
Registration of the Chinese Board of Montréal, 1912.

Volume 174.

File 1113.
Alleged outrage by mounted police on Chinamen at Unity, Saskatchewan, 1912.

File 1203.
Immigration bond covering Chinese crew of S.S. **Blackheath**, 1912.

Volume 176.
File 1680.
Japanese immigration, questions, 1913.

Volume 181.

File 1319.
Regulations for re-admission to Canada of Hindus who have previously resided here, 1913.

File 1434.

Laws governing Chinese immigration, 1913.

Volume 182.

File 1499.
Petition for indemnity to Chinese sufferers from rioters in British Columbia, 1913.

File 1599.
Status of Chinese women or Canadian women marrying Chinese, 1913.

File 1611.
If naturalization of Chinese improves their status under Chinese Immigration Act, 1913.

File 1673.
Employment of white women by Chinese, 1913.

Volume 179.

File 649.
Immigration regulations re importation of Japanese farm labour, 1914.

Volume 186.

File 831.
Application of Hindoos on a religious mission to enter Canada, 1914.

Volume 187.

File 1173.
Refund of head tax to estate of Jew Haw hop, 1914.

File 1092.
Claim of the Hindu Manooka to deposit of $100.00 as entered in his passbook.

Volume 189.

File 1764.
Protection to an informer re illegal entry of Chinese, 1914.

Volume 192.

File 409.
Naturalization of Armenians, 1915.

Volume 193.

File 817.
Naturalization of Armenians, 1915.

File 857.
Kidnapping of Chinese woman, 1916.

Volume 198.

File 1713.
Rights of Armenians in Canadian courts, 1915.

File 1760.
Chinese and Siam black lists, 1915.

Volume 202.

File 732.
Offering information re smuggling of Chinamen across border, 1916.

Volume 205.

File 1388.
Re Chinese immigrant, 1916.

Volume 206.

File 1624.
Suggested prosecution of Fong Quing and Fong Toy for smuggling opium, 1916.

Volume 216.

File 1902.
Inadequate sentence imposed on Chinaman who seduced girl of 14, 1917.

Volume 217.

File 3110.
Expenses incurred re East Indian prisoners whose evidence was requested by Imperial government, 1917.

Volume 220.

File 347.
Disposal of estate of deceased intestate Chinaman, 1918.

File 350.
Reciprocity with India re immigration, 1918.

File 483.
Labour Education Association of Ontario re Asiatic labour, 1918.

Volume 222.

File 974.
Request for cancellation of charter of Canadian Japanese Social and Athletic Club, Limited, 1918.

Volume 223.

File 1034.
Elimination of clause in mining leases prohibiting employment of Chinese and Japanese, 1918.

Volume 224.

File 1449.
Japanese trading with enemy, 1918.

Volume 225.

File 1586.
Rex versus Wong Han charged with serving beer in prohibited hours, 1918.

Volume 227.

File 2023.
Liability of Chinese to military service, 1918.

File 2033.
Information re Chinese Nationalist League, 1918

Volume 228.

File 2408.
Circulation of Chinese publications, 1918.
Volume 229.

File 2454.
Mail, etc., of Chou Eei ping, Toronto, should be watched, 1918.

Volume 231.

File 13
Reward for apprehension of accessories to murder of Chinese Minister of Vancouver, 1919.

Volume 236.

File 1241.
To prevent Japanese purchasing land in British Columbia, 1919.

File 1293.
British Columbia acts forbidding Orientals to employ white women, 1919.

Volume 239.

File 1840.
Return of money held by Press Censor addressed to Chinese Nationalist League, 1919.

Volume 241.

File 2210.
For permission to use internment camp at Vernon for detention of coolies en route to China, 1919.

File 2382.
Franchise to Orientals, 1919.

File 2407.
Bill re votes of Orientals, 1919.

Volume 249.

File 1042.
Disfranchisement of Chinese in British Columbia and Saskatchewan, 1920.

Volume 256.

File 343.
Power to grant immunity to Chinese willing to give evidence regarding illegal entry, 1921.

File 370.
Mounted Police re literature, 1921.

Volume 257.

File 665.
For government assistance to the Chinese, 1921.

Volume 259.

File 1156.
For permit for Quong Wing to use opium, 1921.

File 1268.
Power of rejecting Chinese immigration, 1921.

Volume 261.

File 1830.
Information re immigration legislation and land-owning rights of Japanese for Washington Conferences, 1921.

Volume 262.

File 1923.
Payment of half of fine on Lee Shing, 1921.

File 2005.
Case of Jang Yin, deduction of taxed costs from deposit, 1921.

File 2080.
Rex versus Wong Mah, re appeal, 1921.

Volume 263.

File 2431.
Immigration re Chinese woman and boy, 1921.
Volume 266.

File 370.
Legality of employment of white girls in Chinese cafes, 1922.

File 549.
Deportation of Wong on release from jail, 1922.

File 567.
Application of woman claiming to be wife of Luin Lun, 1922.

Volume 269.

File 1028.
Detention of two persons, 1922.

File 1149.
Deputy Minister of Justice asking for Chinese interpreter, 1922.

Volume 270.

File 1377.
Cases of two persons(Chinese), 1922.

File 1405.
Bond covering Chinese crew of S.S. **Bethlehem**, 1922.

Volume 272.

File 2041.
Decision of United States Supreme Court that Japanese are not eligible for naturalization in United States, 1922.

File 2220.
Deportation of Samuel Lee, 1922.

Volume 273.

File 2017.
Objection to deportation of Oan Yee jing, 1922.

File 2039.
Cancellation of deportation of three persons(Chinese), 1922.

Volume 274.

File 2279.
Deportability of Chong Kin, 1922.

Volume 275.

File 132.
Form of bond to be used by Chinese teachers, 1923.

File 292.
May wife of Ing Yan yee be deported, 1923?

Volume 276.

File 352.
Deportability of Hum Sin, 1923.

File 526.
Decision of British Columbia court re two Oriental persons, 1923.

File 547.
Deportability of Lung Chong, 1923.

Volume 277.
File 691.
Admission of Ho Guey, 1923.

File 694.
Authority of Dominion to restrict Orientals to certain districts, 1923.

File 743.
Right of province to prohibit sale lease of land to Orientals, 1923.

Volume 278.

File 995.
Suspended sentence of Yee Oan yee alias Yeen Young, 1923.

Volume 280.

File 1277.
Case of Oriental person released, 1923.

Volume 282.

File 1691.
Case of Chou Tung, application for habeas corpus, 1923.

File 1702.
Quon Sing will not perform manual labour, 1923.

File 1805.
Court order, case of Chew Nem, 1923.

File 1835.
Appeals in cases of three Oriental persons, 1923.

File 1842.
Alien land laws of Pacific coast upheld by Supreme Court, United States, 1923.

Volume 283.

File 2056.
Deportation of Oriental persons on ground of vagrancy, 1923.

Volume 286.

File 472.
Deportation of Jun Daw wong, 1924.

Volume 288.

File 802.
Case of Chow Tung, if costs may be deducted from deposit, 1924.

File 819.
Procedure in indicting Chinese on selling opium charges, 1924.

File 877.
Deportation of Jung Fook, 1924.
Volume 289.

File 1014.
Case of Wong Quon Due, if head tax must be returned, 1924.

File 1020.
Case of Low Quong, 1924.

File 1021.
Case of Fong Thick guoy, 1924.

Volume 290.

File 2209.
Technicalities on which convicted Chinese are allowed liberty, 1924.

File 1317.
Fraudulent certifications of registration of Chinese births, 1924.

Volume 291.

File 1455.
If immigration investigating officer may order deportations, 1924.

Volume 292.

File 1821.
Appeals in three cases, 1924.

Volume 295.

File 262.
Japanese Consul-general re relinquishment of Japanese nationality, 1925.

Volume 298.

File 1054.
Status under Civil Service Act of appointments under Chinese Immigration Act, 1925.

Volume 300.

File 1231.
Inquiry from Japanese Consul as to treatment of aliens in Canada, 1925.

Volume 301.

File 1971.
Advisability of appeal in case of Low Hong Hing, 1925.

File 2121.
Inquiry re alleged rule that Orientals shall not be employed on government contracts, 1925.

Volume 303.

File 196.
Case of persons held pending deportation proceedings, 1926.

File 258.
Wang Shun chew, claim to Canadian citizenship, 1926.

File 421.
For investigation into death of Lee Lung when deprived of drugs, 1926.

Volume 304.

File 579.
Fine imposed on man with gun, 1926.

Volume 305.

File 738.
Claims of Chinamen for damages from raids in Montréal, 1926.

Volume 307.

File 1470.
Case of Yip Boc, drug peddler who cannot be deported under provisions of Narcotic Drug Act, 1926.

Volume 308.

File 2790.
Deportability of Charlie Wong, 1926.

Volume 311.

File 437.
Bills in British Columbia legislature restricting Asiatic migration, 1927.

File 357.
Bills in British Columbia legislature restricting Asiatic Mongolians.

Volume 316.

File 1877.
Collection of fine from Hum Lam, alias Hum Lo, 1927.

Volume 320.

File 496.
Deportation order against Loo Dook Foo to be cancelled, 1928.

Volume 321.

File 890.
Re Jackson[?](Chinese) and W.V.Curtis, 1928.

File 1028.
Claim for expenses for two Orientals, 1928.

Volume 323.

File 1487.
Case of Wang Wa, appeal dismissed, 1928.

Volume 325.

File 1985.
Disposal of money found in house of Love Yip during raid, 1928.

Volume 327.

350 • Ontario – Ottawa

File 529.
May stop people from playing cards on Sunday in a Chinese restaurant, 1929.

File 548.
Disposition of $100 paid by Chinaman to policeman, 1929.

Volume 329.

File 978.
Proceedings in rex versus Wong Sack Joe, 1929.

Volume 330.

File 1245.
Authority of Chinese Consul-general to receive assets of deceased intestate Chinamen, 1929.

Volume 331.

File 1351.
Failure of prosecution of Leung Ding for possession of opium, 1929.

File 1395.
Information re Chinese gambling houses, 1929.

File 1589.
Soo Hai Joi, habeas corpus proceedings, 1929.

Volume 332.

File 1809.
To recover certificate from person convicted under Opium and Narcotic Drug Act, 1929.

Volume 333.

File 143.
Authority of Chinese Consul-general to receive assets of deceased intestate Chinamen, 1930.

Volume 339.

File 744.
King versus Lim Looie Foo, should appeal be taken against habeas corpus decision, 1930.

File 796.
Man desires advice re visiting China to study Chinese and smuggling of narcotics, 1930.

File 859.
Case of Gun Ying to go to Supreme Court, 1930.

Volume 344.

File 1478.
Ku Klux Klan asks questions re Orientals, 1930.

Volume 352.

File 394.
Habeas corpus application of Lee Moon koo, alias Dang Hong, 1931.

Volume 354.

File 708.
Rex versus Fong Lee, agent John Murray for instructions, 1931.

File 747.
Request for stated cases, Lee Wah and Lee Chang, 1931.

Volume 357.

File 1097.
Rex versus Ho Fook and Ho Shew, 1931.

File 1175.
Cases against three persons, 1931.

Volume 372.

File 1272.
Wang Quong yuen, payment of head tax, if to be repaid as merchant under Chinese Immigration Act, 1932.

Volume 376.

File 1754.
King versus Wong Fong, 1932.

Volume 379.

File 203.
Excise seizure from two persons of Oriental origin, 1932.

Volume 381.

File 468.
Rex versus Chen Sam, opium prosecution, 1933.

Volume 382.

File 484.
Franchise for Indian settlers in Canada, 1933.

Volume 384.

File 690.
Narcotics charges against two persons of Oriental origin, 1933.

Volume 390.
File 1397.
Payment of fine to enable release of convict Lee Kin, 1933.

Volume 397.

File 236.
Ah Tong, deportation proceedings, illegal entry, 1934.

Volume 400.

File 475.
Administration of oath to Chinamen, 1934.

Volume 403.

File 847.
Rex versus Ng Gin, 1934.

C. Remission Branch.

C1. Remission Branch, 1888-1962. 17.5 metres, 120 microfilm reels(Volumes 1128-1367, reels M-1776 to M-1895).

Volume 1138.

File 3157.
Chin Dow alias Wang Nan, keeper of opium joint, 1911.

Volume 1138.

File 3038.
Lee Ma, opium in possession, 1911.

Volume 1154.

File 7213.
Leong Tin, How Sung, Wong Kow, desertion, 1914.

Volume 1156.

File 8965.
Sing Jalip, unlawful possession of explosives, 1915.

Volume 1157.

File 9133.
Singh, Gundit, unlawful possession of explosives, 1915.

Volume 1167.

File 14076.
Slyman, Mohammed Hessine, possession of beaver skids, arms, ammunition, not reporting as alien enemy(Turkish).

Volume 1181.

File 15623.
Ho Min ling, et al, member of unlawful association, 1919.
Volume 1234.

File 27248.
Eshaya Aziz or Ayis Isohaia(Turkish), manslaughter, 1922.

Volume 1280.

File 53437.
Joe Woe attempted murder, 1933-1947.

Volume 1309.

File 103878.
Kirkorian, R.F., desertion, 1945.

Volume 2116.

File 147715.
Labour report on administration of Japanese affairs in Canada, 1944.

Volume 2123.

File 152189.
Justice, Japanese Claims Commission's expenses, 1948.

File 152189-5.
Justice, Japanese Claims Commission, crop claims, details of settlements recommended.

D1. Capital case files, 1867-1976. 89.4 metres(Volumes 1393-1854).

Volume 1467.

File 525a.
Murder of W.C.Hopkinson(Inspector, Immigration Branch) by Mewa Singh, 1914-1915.

Record Group 14. Parliament..

1st session, 13th Parliament, document 155.
Copy of all petitions, etc., re the importation of coolie labour from 1 September 1917 to date, Sir Wilfrid Laurier, March to May 1918.

2nd session, 16th Parliament, document 127.
Order, return showing Japanese immigration in 1927, January-June 1928.

2nd session, 16th Parliament, document 128.
Order, return showing Chinese immigration in 1927, January-June 1928.

4th session, 16th Parliament, document 126a.
Return showing treaty with Japan limiting Japanese immigration to Canada, February-May 1930.

4th session, 18th Parliament, document 111.
Report of board of review appointed to investigate charges that aliens, in particular, Oriental aliens, had been entering Canada illegally and surreptitiously in large numbers, January-June 1939.

Report of recommendations of special committee on Orientals in British Columbia, 1940-1942.

3rd session, 19th Parliament, document 210b.
Reference No. 108, what was the total number of fishing boats collected from Japanese, giving the number in each respective class of boat? M.Reid, 1942-1943.

3rd session, 19th Parliament, document 210c.
Reference number 207, how many Japanese entered Canada during each year from 1930-1941 inclusive,

1942-1943.

5th session, 19th Parliament, document 182b.
Right of Royal Commission, Order in Council 9489 to investigate welfare of Japanese in Ontario settlements, 1944-1945.

1st session, 20th Parliament, document 152c.
Deportation of Japanese back to Japan, September-December 1945.

D. House of Commons.

D1. Appendices to the journals, House of Commons, 1919-1965, 16.8 metres(Volumes 651, 653-674, 676, 678-680, 685-690, 696-697, 700-703, 705-707, 710-712, 715, 717-718, 727, 729-730, 733, 738-741, 745-746, 750-754, 757-758, 767, 770-771, 787-789, 1022-1033).

Volume 653, appendix No. 8.
Japanese property in British Columbia, sale of reported by Public Accounts Committee, 1947.

D2. Sessional papers. House of Commons, 1916-1983.
304 metres, (Volumes 4-650, 652, 681-682, 684, 691-695, 698-699, 6720-7623, 728, 734, 736-737, 742-744, 747-749, 7565, 759-766, 768-769, 772-786, 790, 801-1021, 1034-1150, 1750-1834, 29044-2182, 2198-2248, 2251-2480; Reels C-6919 to C-6969, C-7516 to C7634, C-7870-C-7906, T-3490 to T-3848, T-460 to T-4686, T-4878 to T-4910).

Volume 434.
Reels C-14473 to C-14474, file 210, parts A-D.
Questions re Japanese Canadians, 1942-1943.

Volume 469.
Reel C-14480, file 182 A, B, E, F, G.
Questions re Japanese back to Japan, 1945.

Volume 533.
Reel C-14496, file 180.
Appointment of Hon. Mr. Justice H.I.Bird to be Commissioner to inquire into certain property claims of persons of the Japanese race who were evacuated from the coast of British Columbia as a war measure, 1947-1948.

Volume 559.
Reel C-14403. File 185a.
Report re Royal Commission on Reparation, 13 June 1950.

Record Group 15. Interior.

Immigration Branch transferred from Department of Agriculture, 1893.

Record Group 16. National Revenue.

Volumes 486-490.
Port records, letterbooks of Port of Vancouver contain correspondence re head and poll tax charged on Chinese immigrants, 1887-1901.

Volumes 599-602.
Letterbooks of Port of Coutts, Alberta, contain correspondence on transport of Chinese in bond to United States, re head tax, etc. Other letterbooks of Port records may also contain references(Chinese), 1890-1910.

Volumes 1138-1139.
Gretna sub collectors letterbook, contains correspondence re head tax collected on Chinese, transport of bonded Chinese to United States. Re some Chinese staying at Gretna, etc., 1883-1892.

Record Group 17. Agriculture.

From 1852-1931, Immigration and Quarantine were the responsibility of the Department of Immigration. Immigration was transferred in 1893 to the Department of the Interior.

Contains records on Chinese and "Asian" immigrants.

Series AI. General letterbooks, 1852-1860, 1865-1896, 12 feet, (Volumes 1490-16526, microfilm reels T-112 to T-131).
Includes immigration.

Series AIII. Immigration letterbooks, 1862-1864.

Record Group 18. Royal Canadian Mounted Poice.

A. Office of the Controller, 1874-1920.

A1. Official correspondence, 1874-1920.

Volume 69.

File 615-92.
Disturbances at Calgary re a Chinese, 1892.

Volume 124.

File 495-96.
Police escort for Li Hung chang while in North West Territories, 1896.
Volume 170.

File 399-99.
Protection for Chinese reformer Kang-tu-wai(sic), 1899.

Volume 241.

File 846-02.
Escort of Chinese lunatic, Moose Jaw to Vancouver, 1902.

Volume 242.

File 12-03.
Cuthbert, superintendent, A.E.K., a Japanese taken to Dawson by, 1903.

Volume 265.

File 81-04.
Allen, Thomas, theft of gold watch from Chinaman Lai Men, 1904.

Volume 492.

File 492.
Maharaja Kapurthala of India, police protection of, while in the West, 1915.

Volume 509.

File 203.
Information re drilling of Chinese in Western Canada, 1916.

Volume 525.

File 48.
Kozue Matsumoto, application for naturalization, 1917.

Volume 536.

File 353.
Yoshioka, a Japanese, murders committed by, at Dawson, 1917.

Volume 577.

File 296.
Doctor Young, Chinese Consul-General for Canada, police assistance to, in British Columbia, 1919.

Volume 585.

File 685.
Investigation into murder of Chinese government Minister at Victoria, police assistance in, 1919.

Volume 590.

File 1012.
Chinese Immigration Act, breaches of, 1919.
Volume 593.

File 1111.
Chinese in Toronto, restaurants, etc., conditions, 1919.

Volume 596.

File 1152.
Naturalization of Japanese, suspected irregularities in, 1919.

B. Office of the Commissioner, 1868-1954.

B1. Royal Canadian Mounted Police: Office of the Commissioner, Official Correspondence, 1876-1920.

Volume 1284.

File 346.
Party of Chinese being driven across the line, 1893.

Volume 1422.

File 169, parts 1 and 2.
(7) Chinamen Ghing Howe fined for illegal liquor selling at Lethbridge, 1893.

File 144, part 1.
Visit of Kang Yu wei to Canada, etc., 1899.

File 174, part 2.
North West Mounted Police acting as guard for Kang Yu wei, 1899.

Volume 1605.

File 133a.
Visit of Prince Fushimi of Japan.

Volumes 1768-1793 include case files, etc. on interned and paroled aliens, etc.

Volume 1779.

File 170, part 455.
Suspect alien(Turk) Sam Kotney, 1914.

Volume 1783.

File 170, part 575.
Interned Turk, Aman Ngen, 1916.

Volume 1788.

File 170, part 766.
Interned Turk, Choschosus Tama, 1916.

B5. Crime reports, 1880-1938.

Volumes 2464-2490.
Individual case files of crime reports, includes references to Chinese, see file list.

Records of the Royal Canadian Mounted Police.

F3. Headquarters security, 1919-1934.

Registry files, 1940-1946, 1.5 metres(volumes 3563-3569)

Volume 3563.

File E-11-19-2-9, parts 1-3.
Removal of enemy aliens from protected areas of British Columbia, 1942.

Volume 3564.

File E-11-19-2-13, parts 1-3.
Release of Japanese from internment, 1942-1946.

File-E-11-19-2-24.
Action taken re Japanese schools, press and fishing fleet, 1941-1944.

File E-11-19-3.
Internment camps for enemy aliens - War Measures Act, 1939-1945.

File E-11-9-3-2.
Regulations governing internment camps and internees, 1951-1953.

File E-11-9-4, part 1.
Apprehension and internment of enemy aliens and others - War Measures Act, 1939-1940.

Volume 3565.

File E-11-19-2-9, part 4.
Removal of enemy aliens from protected areas of British Columbia, 1942-1947.

File E-11-9-4, parts 2, 4.
Apprehension and internment, 1940-1961.

Volume 3566.

File E-315-36-3, parts 3-7.
Repatriation, 1945-1954.

Volume 3567.

File E-315-36-3, supplement A.
List of applicants for repatriation.

File E-3129-1-4, parts 1-3.
British Columbia Security Commission and advisory committee on the Japanese situation; reports, 1942-1957.

Volume 3568.

File E-3129-1-5
Detention of Japanese under P.C. 1665, 1942-1943.

File E-3129-1-6.
Orders and regulations governing the conduct of workers in highway camps, 1942-1944.

File E-3129-1-7.
Strikes by Japanese in labour camps.

File E-3129-1-8, parts 1-2.
Enforcement of British Columbia Security Commission orders by Royal Canadian Mounted Police, 1942-1943.

File E-3129-1-10.
Interdepartmental meetings re reallocation, segregation and repatriation of Japanese, 1943-1946.

File E-3129-1-15, parts 1-2.
Japanese relocation hostels, 1946-1948.

Folders - classification sheets indicating name, address, date of birth - dates of internment.

Volume 3569.

Folders, E-F - classification sheets.

Volume 3569.

Folders G-H- Department of Justice record of internment hearings, 1939-1945.

Volume 3569.
Report on Japanese activities in British Columbia, 1942.

Volume 3569.
Lists of internees by camp.

Record Group 19. FINANCE.

D. Accounting.

D6. Returns.

Volume 2586.
Pages 25-26.
Re appropriation of $10, 775.00 for expenses in connection with settlement of Japanese claims as a result of Vancouver riots.

E. Departmental correspondence.

E2. Deputy Minister's Office correspondence.

Central registry files, volume 1-895, 4630-4634. Key word subject index available.

Volume 506.

File 121-6-0-1.
Japanese labour includes submissions by the National Japanese Canadian Citizens Association, Toronto, on "Japanese Canadian economic losses arising from evacuation", 1943.

File 121-6-0-2.
Claims by Japanese Canadians for property losses, 1950.

File 121-6-0-3.
Japanese Canadian economic losses arising from evacuation, 1948-1950.

Volume 544.

File 135-8.
Interdepartmental committee on the treatment of enemy aliens and enemy alien property, 1940-1941.

E2(b). Outgoing correspondence, 1840-1931.

Volume 3160.

File 10357.
Department of Trade and Commerce re payment due Tom Kee, a Chinese, 1899.

Volume 3214.

File 12854.
Re Chinese immigration in British Columbia, 1903.

Volume 3229.

File 13739.
Re remission of capitation tax on a Chinese named Wong Quong Yick, 1905.

Volume 3249.

File 14958.
Re issue of special warrant for $25, 000, entertainment of Prince Fushimi of Japan, 1907.

Volume 3259.

File 15417.
Re prosecution of certain Chinamen at Sydney, British Columbia, 1908.

Volume 3263.

File 15554.
Re proposed issue of Governor General's warrant in connection with Japanese claims, riot Vancouver, 1907.

File 15588.
Re payment of Messrs. Verret and Baker in connection with Japanese mission, 1903.

Volume 3267.

File 15761.
Papers in connection with "An act to amend the Chinese Immigration Act", 1908.

Volume 3269.

File 15817.
Re vote(financial) for Customs officials for their work with Chinese immigration, 1908.

Volume 3287.

File 16404.
Re Chinese smuggling, 1910.

Volume 3313.

File 17021.
Chief Controller of Chinese Immigration, re $500 head tax deposited by N.P.Freeman on behalf of Thomas Jackson, and re other cheques for Chinese capitation tax, 1912-1913.

Volume 3350.

File 17532.
Provincial Treasurer of British Columbia re payments under Chinese Immigration Act, 1913.

E2c. Deputy Minister's memoranda book, 1903- .

Volume 532.

File 1344.
Royal Canadian Mounted Police, correspondence re Hindoos withdrawing money from government savings banks, 1919-1921.

Volume 544.

File 138-8-3.
Alien enemy bank accounts, property, etc.(re claims of Japanese, etc.), 1932-1952.

E2f. Finance Departmental Files, miscellaneous, 1917-1964.

Volume 544.

File 135-8-3.
Alien enemy bank accounts, property, etc.(re Japanese, Armenian repatriation claims, etc.) 1932-1952.

Volume 3424.
Refugees - general, commission, loans, reports(inclusive report on establishment of Armenian refugees in the Republic of Erivan, etc.) 1922-1929.

F. Department of Finance(new filing system) 1957- .
F2. Central Registry and Departmental Registry.

a. International Trade and Finance Branch.

i. International Economic Relations Division, 1918-1979. 43.9 metres Finding aid 19-16.

ii. International Finance Division, 1941-1975. 20 metres

iii. Tariff Division, 1935-1975. 34.6 metres

vi. International Finance Division, 1952-1976. 20 metres

Record Group 20. TRADE AND COMMERCE.

A. Headquarters. Records of the Department of Trade and Commerce, 1880-1970.

A1. Old Registry Series, 1893-1901, 14.5 metres (volumes 1080-1224)

This early registry series consists of subject files arranged by correspondence numbers. It is the predecessor of the more modern system and contains general correspondence dealing with a wide variety of subjects including steamship subsidies, departmental appointments, tariffs, and foreign trade. A file list facilitates access to this series.

Volume 1081.

File 319.
Resolutions of Trades and Labour Congress on Canada and Chinese immigration, 1893.
Report containing resolution of the Legislative Assembly of British Columbia re Chinese immigration, 1893.

Volume 1082.

File 529.
Expenditure in Chinese accounts, 1893.

Volume 1090.

File 1208.
Passing through Canada of Chinese emigrants to British Guyana, 1894.

Volume 1101.

File 1728.
Action of General Assembly of Presbyterian Church re restriction of Chinese immigration, 1894.

Volume 1104.

File 1928.
Resolutions of Trades and Labour Congress of Canada and Chinese immigration, 1893.
File 328.
Report containing resolution of the Legislative Assembly of British Columbia re Chinese immigration, 1893.
Volume 1111.

File 2202.
British Columbia Executive Council recommendation that Dominion government increase per capita tax on Chinese immigration, 1895.
Volume 1122.

File 2955.
Memorandum from Trades and Labour Council protesting change in existing law re Chinese immigration, 1895.

Volume 1144.

File 4261.
Tax on Chinese entering British Columbia.

Volume 1145.

File 4268.
Order of House calling for all petitions on subject of Chinese immigration, 1896.

Volume 1151.

File 4890.
British Columbia Legislative Assembly re increasing tax on Chinese, 1897.

Volume 1156.

File 5198.
Re naturalization of Chinese and Japanese, 1897.

Volume 1157.

File 5344.
Bill passed by British Columbia Legislature prohibiting employment of Japanese subjects, 1897.

Volume 1174.

File 5922.
Poll tax on Chinese immigrants, 1898.

Volume 1181.

File 6149.
Issue of certificates to Chinese who wish to enter United States, 1898.

Volume 1184.

File 6228.
British Columbia Legislature requests information re Chinese and Japanese landed at various ports, taxes collected, etc., 1899.

Volume 1186.

File 6300.
Legislative Assembly of British Columbia resolution in increasing tax to $500 on Chinese immigrants, 1899.

Volume 1193.

File 6476.
Action of Canadian Pacific Railway in irregularly transporting Chinese into United States, 1899.

Volume 1199.

File 6627.
Pamphlet from United States entitled **Digest on Chinese exclusion laws**, 1899.

File 6633.
Chinese government appointees to report on conditions of Chinese in British Columbia, 1899.

Volume 1205.

File 6813.
Japanese, Collector of customs, S.S. **Milos**, 1900.

Volume 1207.

File 6875.
Asking information re amount of Chinese immigration tax, trade with China, revenue from opium, trade with Japan, 1900.

Volume 1210.

File 6967.
British Columbia Legislature re effective mode of dealing with question of restricting Mongolian immigration, 1900.

Volume 1217.

File 7147.
Correspondence regarding Mongolian immigration, 1901.

Volume 1222.

File 7233.
Immigration laws of Canada, asking for report of Royal Commission on Chinese Immigration, 1901.

A2. 1906 Central Registry System, 1880-1961. 58.1 metres(volumes 1-281, 1360, 1364, 1369-1370, 1529-1536, 1539, 1626-1627).

In 1906 the Department of Trade and Commerce established a new numerical registry system whereby the files were numbered according to the order in which they were created. In some instances correspondence from the earlier registry and from predecessor agencies such the Department of Finance was brought forward and incorporated into the system. Some items of correspondence date from the early 1880s.
In 1911, the Department of Trade and Commerce underwent a reorganization and purged its records, destroying the 1902-1910 correspondence. A computerized finding aid and a file list of files received after a completion of the computerized finding aid are available in the Federal Archives Division.
Most of the items cited below in this series were found in the finding aid **KWOC Index for** (Key Word in Context)**RG20, A2, A3, A5**. In this index volume numbers are cited as box numbers.

Volume 4.

File 10977.
Trade Commissioner's office, Shanghai, 1912

Volume 15.

File 12994.
Anglo-Japanese treaty, volumes 1-7, boxes 15-16, 1911-1947.

Volume 18.

File 14100.
United Development Company, Hong Kong, Proulx B.A. 1942-1948.

Volume 19.

File 14764.
McKee, R. of Vancouver, Special Representative of Trade and Commerce to China, 1944-1945.

Volume 24.

File 25 3.
Canadian incoming trade mission, engineering equipment from New Zealand and the Far East, 1963.

Volume 29.

File 16377.
Supplies for British forces in China, 1931-1941.

Volume 37.

File 17162.
Prohibited imports into India and prohibited exports, volumes 1-2, 1917-1947.

Volume 38

File 7620.
Loan of service of Canadian government officials to other countries, India, etc., 1933-1943.

Volume 39.

File 17704A.
Tariff of Japan, volumes 1-2, 1915-1937.

Volume 41.

File 17973.
China equipment for construction of small arms munitions plant, 1946-1947.

File 18074.
Bounty on bonus paid by Japanese Government, 1917-1939.

File 18104A.
Tariff of India, volumes 1-2, 1921-1931.

Volume 57

File 19664A.
Treaty and tariff negotiations, Empire trade India, volume 1-3, 1930-1940.

Volume 57.

File 19664D.
India treaty and negotiations, 1933-1934.

Volume 72.

File 20481.
Exchange situation in Japan, 1932-1938

Volume 75.

File 20783.
Japanese competition in foreign markets for Canadian fish and other products, volumes 1-2, 1933-1939.

Volume 83.

File 22012.
Economic conditions in Japan, volumes 1-4, 1919-1939.

Volume 87.

File 22185.
Exhibition in Japan, Nagoya, Tokyo, 1918-1946.

Volume 97.

File 22825.
Prohibited imports into Japan, volumes 1-4, boxes 97-98, 1919-1938.

Volume 99.

File 22961.
Market for grain and flour for India, 1941-1945.

File 22961B.
Wheat and flour for India, accounts only, volumes 1-2, 1944-1948.

File 22961C.
Flour for Indian contracts, 1947-1948.

Volume 111.

File 22439.
Economic conditions in China, volumes 1-5, boxes 111-112, 1923-1945.

Volume 112.

File 24460.
Report by Trade Commissioner, Palmer, F. on his mission to China, 1944-1945.

Volume 113.

File 24537.
Visits of Canadian businessmen to Japan, general procedures, 1947-1949.

Volume 135.

File 25793.
Exhibition in Fiji Islands, 1933-1935.

Volume 137.

File 25836.
Import and export, China, 1919-1936.

Volume 152.

File 26587.
Trade with China, civilian trade mission to Japan and China and Manchukuo, volumes 1-2, 1925-1945.

Volume 162.

File 26725.
Placing of Canadian firms on lists of the India or Crown Offices in London, volumes 1-3, boxes 162-163, 1921-1937.

Volume 166.

File 26901.
Turkey, import and export restrictions, n.d.

File 26910.
Turkey, import and export exchange regulations, volumes 1 and 3.

Volume 167.

File 26940.
British trade mission to Manchukuo, volumes 1-2, 1921-1940.

Volume 177.

File 27460A.
Tariff of Siam, 1921-1939.

File 27494.
China merchandise marks, trade marks and labelling, volumes 1-2, 1920-1935.

Volume 179.

File 27569.
Trade with China, volumes 1-4, 1913-1945.

Volume 179.

File 27570.
Market for wood pulp in Japan, 1926-1949.

Volume 180.

File 27633B.
Flour and grain for China, accounts only, 1946-1948.

File 27633C.
Contracts for flour and grain for shipment to China, 1945-1947.

Volume 181.

File 27664.
Visit of Japanese Commercial Mission to the United States, 1921-1950.

Volume 187.

File 27853A.
Tariffs and treaty negotiations, Fiji, 1921-1936.

Volume 195.

File 28137A.
Hong Kong tariff official, 1920-1935.

Volume 199.

File 28522.
Sample and showroom, Shanghai, China, 1922-1932.

Volume 200.

File 28665.
Publicity in China and Japan, 1935-1941.

Volume 201.

File 28717.
Unfederated Malay States, customs duties and tariffs, volumes 1-2, 1922-1936.

File 28717DA.
Unfederated Malay States, documentation, official, 1927-1937.

Volume 201.

File 28717DB.
Unfederated Malay States, customs documentation, 1933-1937.

Volume 204.

File 28835.
Visit of Canadian commercial delegations to Japan and China Conference. Specific relations at Kyoto, 1923-1931.

Volume 205.

File 28880.
Admission of Chinese students in Canada, volumes 1-2, 1914-1945.

Volume 222.

File 29356.
Supplies for China under Mutual Aid Plan, volumes 1-2, 1943-1946.

Volume 225.

File 30160.
Complaint against Brupbacher, E.W. by Caudron K and Co. of Hong Kong re shipment of rayon velvet, 1948.

Volume 229.

File 30736.
United Kingdom goodwill mission to China, 1947-1948.

Volume 232.

File 30983.
Complaint against Ace Manufacturing Co., of Montréal by Howan and Co Ltd., of Hong Kong re shipment of plastic film, 1948.

Volume 232.

File 31124.
Inquiry by Imperial Shipping Committee into position of British shipping in Middle East and Far East waters, 1937-1939.

Volume 238.

File 32046.
Proposed office in Winnipeg of Japanese importers and exporters Central Bureau of Trade Association, 1938-1939.

Volume 247.

File 32712A.
India import and exchange regulations, volumes 1-3, 1931-1945.

Volume 250.

File 7250.
Trade with Japan, 1948-1950.

Volume 252.

File 32837.
Creation of Department of Supply, India, 1944-1947.

Volume 253.

File 32887A.
Straits Settlements of Malaya, import, export and exchange regulations, 1919-1940.

Volume 262.

File T11.
Tariff of Turkey, 1931-1945.

Volume 271.

File A250.
Publicity and advertising, United Arab Republic, Egypt, Sudan, Palestine, Cyprus, Iraq, Syria and Iran,

1964-1965.

Volume 279.

File 36068.
National Resources Commission of China, 1944-1948.

Volume 281.

File 36530.
Indian industrial mission to Australia and Canada, 1946.

Volume 281.

File 36673.
Special mission to Japan by External Affairs and Colonel Cosgrove, Trade and Commerce, re Foreign Advisory Council, 1946.

A3. 1961 Central Registry System, 1940-1972. 152 metres (volumes 562-607, 610-691, 694-1079, 1225-1250, 1356-1359, 1375, 1381-1383, 1431, 1435-1505. 1508-1514, 1526-1528, 1625-1627, 1635-1677, 1918-1986, 1991-2000, 2101).

This registry system was established in 1961 and was operative until 1966. In this system a block number is allotted to a specific branch or program. As an example, all registry files starting with number 8 were created by the Exhibitions branch.
In many instances correspondence from the previous sequentially numbered file system was brought forward and incorporated into this system, resulting in correspondence contained therein dating back to the early 1940's. Also some files will contain correspondence beyond 1966.
A computerized subject finding aid and a list of files received after the completion of the computerized finding aid are available in the Federal Archives Division.
Most of the items cited below in this series were found in the finding aid **KWOC *Index for RG20, A2, A3, A5**. In this index volume numbers are cited as box numbers.
*KWOC an acronym for keyword in context.

Volume 568.

File A187.
Publicity and advertising, Hong Kong and the Philippines, 1947-1965

Volume 571.

File A247.
Publicity and advertising, China and Japan, 1957-1961.

Volume 572.

File A252.
Publicity and advertising, Greece and Turkey, 1932-1965.

File A254.
Publicity and advertising, Burma, India and Ceylon, Volumes 4-5, 1958-1964.

Volume 573.

File A259.
Publicity and advertising, New Zealand, West Indies, Fiji, and Western Samoa, 1947-1966.

File A260.
Publicity and advertising, India and Pakistan, 1947-1965.

Volume 589.

File 3 2 1915.
Foreign petroleum industry, Iran, 1950-1963.

Volume 593.

File 3 10.
Foreign aid and relief, Korea, volumes 1, 4, 1950-1955.

Volume 599.

File 3 51 1.
Canadian nuclear power reactor for India, 1960-1963.

Volume 636.

File 7 442.
Conference of Commonwealth foreign ministers, Colombo:1949-1964.

Volume 636.

File 7 511.
U.K. industrial mission to Pakistan, 1950.

Volume 641.

File 71380.
Japanese trade missions to South America, 1953.

Volume 658.

File 10 138 12.
Wheat Utilization Committee, Joint Mission to Japan, India and Indonesia, 1959-1960.

File 10 143.
Canadian Grain Mission to the Far East, volumes 1-3, boxes 658-659, 1953-1954.

Volume 662.

File 17 58 2.
Canadian Wheat Board Mission, Japan, volumes 1-2, 1954-1957.

Volume 664.

File 17 58 18A.

Canadian Wheat Board Mission to India, 1950-1960.

Volume 674.

File 25 17 1.
India State engineers mission to Canada, 1963.

Volume 676.

File 25 J2 3.
Sulphur mission from Japan, 1964-1965.

File 25 J2 4.
Trade missions, Japan trade and economic mission, 1964-1965.

Volume 681.

File 25 M 70.
Canadian trade missions abroad, Canadian seeds missions to Japan, 1962-1964.

Volume 683.

File 25 M 99 2.
Canadian trade missions abroad, Canadian trade mission, telecommunication and electronics, to Malaysia, volume 1-3, 1963.

Volume 684.

File 25 M 104.
Canadian trade missions abroad, manufactured goods to the Far East, 1963-1964.

Volume 685.

File 25 M 111 1.
Canadian trade missions abroad, consulting engineering mission, Singapore, 1963-1964.

Volume 686.

File 25 M 113.
Canadian trade missions abroad, reconnaissance fisheries mission to Japan, 1964.

File 25 M 117.
Canadian trade missions abroad, Canadian travel missions, trade promotion to Japan, 1964-1965.

Volume 687.

File 25 M 119.
Canadian trade missions abroad, Canadian outgoing trade missions, poultry products to Japan, 1964-1965.

Volume 687.

File 25 M 122.
Canadian trade missions abroad, outgoing fisheries products to Australia, New Zealand, Malaysia and Ceylon, 1965-1966.

Volume 689.

File 25 M 134.
Canadian trade missions abroad, Canadian outgoing trade missions proposed meat mission to Japan, 1964-1965.

Volume 700.

File 4 C1-3.
Ceylon trade treaty negotiations, 1948.

Volume 703.

File 4 P1 3A.
Pakistan trade treaty negotiations, official, 1947-1950.

Volume 704.

File 4 13 3A.
Turkey trade treaty negotiations, official, 1946-1950.

Volume 716.

File 7 C3-1.
Trade with China, 1947-1950.

File 816-1.
Trade and economic conditions in Burma, 1939-1950.

Volume 717.

File 7 C3.
Economic conditions in China, volumes 9-10, 1948-1950.

Volume 720.

File 19434.
Trade with Hong Kong, 1948-1950.

Volume 722.

File 7 792.
Trade and economic conditions in Iran, 1944-1951.

Volume 723.

File M12 1.
Trade with Malaysia, 1946-1950.

File 7 389.
Trade with India, 1946-1950.

File 7 398.
Political and economic conditions in India.

Volume 724

File 7 93 T.
Trade and economic conditions in Korea, 1946-1950.

File 7 512.
Economic conditions in Japan, 1949-1950.

File 7 977.
Business and economic conditions in the Malayan Union, 1946-1950.

File 13250.
Trade between China and Japan, 1948-1949.

Volume 725.

File 7 215.
Pakistan trade, 1947-1950.

Volume 725.

File 7 454.
Economic and financial conditions in the Philippines, 1949-1951.

Volume 727.

File 23921.
Trade with Siam(Thailand) Export Licenses, 1940-1949.

Volume 781.

File 24 11.
Barter trade with Turkey, 1948-1959.

File 24 37.
Barter trade with India, 1949-1962.

Volume 783

File 25 38.
Visitors to and from Communist China, 1964-1965.

File 25 32.
Visit to Europe, Africa and the Far East by Trottier, A., 1961.

File 25 37.
Visitors to and from Japan, 1963-1965.

File 25 37 3.
Japanese business men's committee meetings, 1961-1963.

Volume 818.

File 10 33.
Market for flour and grain in China, volumes 1-4, boxes 818-820, 1932-1965.

Volume 823.

File 10 47.
Market for flour and grain, Pakistan, volumes 3-4, 1958-1965.

File 10 47.
Market for flour and grain, Pakistan, volumes 32-34, 1958-1965.

Volume 825.

File 10 57.
Market for flour and grain, Japan, volumes 20, 23, 26-31, 1959-1965.

Volume 826.

File 10 61.
Market for flour and grain, India, volumes 10-13, 1959-1965.

Volume 827.

File 10 77.
Market for grain and flour, Philippines, 1961-1965.

Volume 829.

File l0 83.
Market for grain and flour, Iran and Iraq, 1960-1964.

Volume 869 .

File 6 24.
Shipping services to and from Japan, 1959-1965.

Volume 886.

File 6 225.
Japanese merchant marine and shipbuilding industry, 1937-1955.

Volume 907.

File 7 36.
Colombo plan documents, still in force, 1958.

Volume 924.

File 7 204.
Extension of credit to India, 1948-1949.

File 7 206.
Suggested long term credit to Pakistan, 1947-1952.

File 7 250 1.
Canada-Japan ministerial meetings, correspondence, 1963-1965.

Volume 932.

File 7 416.
Outstanding mess accounts of National Defence Department incurred in Hong Kong in 1941, 1949-1950.

Volume 942.

File 7 618.
Philippine trade with Japan and China, 1950-1951.

Volume 944

File 7 637.
United States Treasury. Foreign assets control. Regulations, restrictions on trade with China, volumes

1-5, boxes 946-965, 1951-1965.

Volume 945.

File 7 637.
United States Treasury. Foreign Assets Control, trade with China, restrictions grain unloading equipment, volumes 1-2, 1961-1962.

File 7 637 2
United States Treasury. Foreign Assets Control, trade with China restrictions, volumes 1-2, 1959-1963.

Volume 946.

File 7 648
Guarantee loans by Canadian banks to Ming Sung Industrial Co. Ltd., re construction of ships for government of China, volumes 1-3, 1946-1961.

Volume 953.

File 7 799
Reparation claims against Japan, volumes 6-7, 1948-1961.

File 7 859
Export credit guarantee scheme, India, 1956-1964.

Volume 954.

File 7 888 1.
Visit of Prime Minister Diefenbaker to Japan, October 1961, 1954-19651.

Volume 956.

File 7 946.
Industrialization in India, foreign investments, 1953-1961.

File 7 967.
Liquidation of prewar accounts held in Japan on behalf of Canadian firms, 1946-1950.

Volume 959.

File 7 1032.
Trade and economic conditions in the Far East, 1938-1958.

File 7 1036.
Trade between Australia, Japan and China, 1939-1957

Volume 974.

File 71466.
Colombo Plan Consultative Committee Meeting, Ottawa. Country material, Borneo to Vietnam, volumes 1-2, 1954.

File 71466 2.
Colombo Plan Consultative Committee Meeting, Ottawa, Country materials, Borneo to Vietnam, volumes 1-2, 1954.

Volume 980.

File 71560 11.
Malaysia Common Market, 1964-1965.

Volume 983.

File 71590 2.
Canada Foreign Aid Program, India, volumes 1-3.

Volume 1005.

File 18-11.
Trade Commissioner Service post, report of Bombay Trade Commissioner, 1941-1956.

Volume 1015.

File 15 35.
Long term credits(loans) to Greece under section 21a of Export Credits Insurance Act, 1962. 1962-1967.(Turkey)

File 18 70.
Post report, Hong Kong, volumes 1-2, boxes 1015-1016, 1941-1965.

File 18 86.
Post report, Singapore, 1941-1953.

Volume 1017.

File 18 85.
Post report, Shanghai, 1945.

Volume 1018.

File 18 88.
Post report, Tokyo, 1955-1964.

Volume 1026.

File 18 168.
Post report, New Delhi, 1948-1965.

Volume 1030.

File 18 196.
Post report, Colombo, 1950-1962.

Volume 1033.

File 18 213.
Post report, Ankara, 1950-1965.

Volume 1034.

File 18 244.
Trade Commission, Service post, reports, Manila, 1951-1962.

Volume 1035.

File 18-255.
Post report, Rangoon.

Volume 1036.

File 18 283.
Establishment of a Trade Commissioner's Office in Dairen, China, 1931-1933.

Volume 1038.

File 18 345.
Post reports, Djakarta, Indonesia, 1952-1965.

File 8 354.
Post report, Kobe, Osaka, 1953-1954.

Volume 1042.

File 18 440.
Post report, Saigon, 1958-1965.

File 18 477.
Post report, Kuala Lumpur, 1959-1964.

Volume 1043.

File 18 553.
Inspection of Trade Commission Office, Far East, 1961.

Volume 1045.

File 18-1-4.
Trade Commissioner Service, Bombay, annual report, 1964-1965.

Volume 1046.

File 18 2 14.
Miscellaneous reports, Trade Commissioner, Hong Kong, 1955-1965.

Volume 1047.

File 18 2 36.
Miscellaneous reports, Trade Commissioner, Singapore, 1959-1965

Volume 1049.

File 18 2 55.
Miscellaneous reports, Trade Commissioner, Manila, 1959-1965.

Volume 1049.

File 18 2-60.
Miscellaneous reports, Trade Commissioner, Colombo, 1959-1965.

Volume 1051.

File 18 3 60.
Agriculture reports, Trade Commissioner, Ceylon, 1963-1965.

Volume 1052.

File 18 6 14.
Trade Commissioner, economic reports, Hong Kong, 1962-1965.

Volume 1053.

File 18 6 55.
Trade Commissioner, economic reports, Manila, 1956-1965.

Volume 1053

File18-9-54.
Trade Commissioner, Bombay, 1958-1965.

Volume 1056/18 9 55.
Trade Commissioner, Manila, travelling, general, 1963-1965.

Volume 1063/19 55.
United States foreign aid programs, Korea, 1958-1962.

Volume 1064/19 57.
United States foreign aid program, China, 1959-1960.

Volume 1064/19 58.
United States foreign aid programs, Greece and Turkey, 1958-1961.

Volume 1064/19 60.
United States foreign aid programs, India, 1954-1962.

Volume 1365.

File PAC4.
Articles of agreement, British Columbia and China and Australia, 1932-1938.

A4. 1966 Central Registry System, 1950-1972.(Volumes 70, 1430, 1538-1539, 1562-1578-).

When Department of Trade and Commerce records were transferred from an active to a dormant records area, their registry number was cancelled and they were allotted a new sequential number prefixed by the letter "T". This practice was created to facilitate file retrieval. All files sent to dormant storage from the sequentially numbered and first block registry systems were so designated, until the practice was discontinued in 1966.

A computerized subject finding aid and a list of files received after completion of the computerized finding aid are available in the Federal Archives Division.

Volume 1680.

Aid. Ceylon, 1965-1970, India 1969-1970, Pakistan, 1968-1970.

Volume 1686.
Agriculture, meat and meat products. Trade relations, Japan.

Volume 1689.
Electrical and Electronic equipment. Pakistan, 1969-1970.

Volume 1693.
Electrical and Electronic equipment, India, 1968-1969.

Volume 1697.
Agriculture, livestock, Japan, 1968-1969.

Volume 1699.
Trade policy, service. Low cost imports. Market description, Japan, 1967.

Volume 1701.
Trade Policy Service. Canadian diplomatic representatives. Trade relations, Turkey, 1947-1968.

Volume 1712.
Aid. Canadian Aid program. Trade relations, India, 1966-1967.

Volume 1713.
Aid. Canadian Aid program. Trade relations, India, 1967-1969.

Volume 1713.
Aid. Canadian Aid program. Trade relations, Pakistan, 1963-1969.

Volume 2001.
Commodities and industry. Agriculture, dairy products, Japan, 1968-1971.

Volume 2005.
Electrical and Electronic Branch. Foreign markets. Electrical equipment. Ceylon, general, 1968-1972, China(Peking), 1970-1971.

Volume 2006.
Electrical and Electronic Branch. Foreign markets. Electrical equipment, Cyprus, 1968-1972, Cambodia, 1968-1970, Cambodia, Prek Thoat project, 1968-1969.

Volume 2008.
Electrical and Electronic Branch. Foreign markets. Electrical equipment, Hong Kong, 1968-1972, Indonesia, 1969-1972, India, 1969-1972.

Volume 2009.
Electrical and Electronic Branch. Foreign markets. Electrical equipment, Iran, 1968-1970.

Volume 2010.
Electrical and Electronic Branch. Foreign markets. Electrical equipment, Japan, 1968-1970.

Volume 2011.
Electrical and Electronic Branch. Foreign markets. Electrical equipment, Korea, 1968-1972, Laos, 1971-1972.

Volume 2012.
Electrical and Electronic Branch. Foreign markets. Electrical equipment, Malaysia, 1969, Pakistan, 1968-1972.

Volume 2013.
Electrical and Electronic Branch. Foreign markets. Electrical equipment, Philippines, 1969-1972.

Volume 2014.
Electrical and Electronic Branch. Foreign markets. Electrical equipment, Singapore, 1968-1972, Thailand, 1969-1972.

Volume 2015.
Electrical and Electronic Branch. Foreign markets. Electrical equipment, China(Taiwan), 1965-1972.

Volume 2016.
Electrical and Electronic Branch. Foreign markets. Electrical equipment, Vietnam, 1969.

Volume 2017.
Electrical and Electronic Branch. Foreign markets. Electrical equipment, Ceylon, 1972, China, 1971-1972.

Volume 2019.
Electrical and Electronic Branch. Foreign markets. Electrical equipment, Iran, 1970-1972, Japan, 1972-

Volume 2020.
Electrical and Electronic Branch. Foreign markets. Electrical equipment, Malaysia, 1968-1972, Pakistan, 1971-1972, Philippines 1968-1972, Thailand, 1969-1972.

Volume 2023.
Mechanical Transport Branch. Agricultural equipment, Asia, 1966-1971.

Volume 2025.
Mechanical Transport Branch. Agricultural equipment, Ceylon, 1970-1972, China, 1970-1972.

Volume 2026.
Mechanical Transport Branch. Agricultural equipment, Guyana, 1970-1972, Indonesia, 1970-1972, India, 1970-1972.

Volume 2027.
Mechanical Transport Branch. Agricultural equipment, Iran, 1970-1972, Japan 1970-1972, Malaya, 1970-1972.

Volume 2028.
Mechanical transport Branch. Agricultural equipment, Singapore, 1970-1972, Turkey, 1970-1972.

Volume 2031.

Aerospace, Marine and Rail Branch. Railway equipment, Ceylon 1968-1971.

Volume 2030.
Aerospace, Marine and Rail Branch. Railway equipment, China, 1971, Far East, 1968-1971.

Volume 2032.
Aerospace, Marine and Rail Branch. Railway equipment, Hong Kong, India, 1970-1972, Iran, 1969-1971, Japan, 1970-1971, Malaya, 1969-1972.

Volume 2033.
Aerospace, Marine and Rail Branch. Railway, Pakistan, 1971, Thailand, 1970-1972, Turkey, 1968-1972.

C. Records of the Department of Industry, Trade and Commerce.

C2. Branch Records, 1880-1969.

C2d. International Trade Relations Branch, 1915-1969.

Foreign Tariffs Division, 1912-1968. 7.8 metres (volumes 368-377, 382, 384-396, 423-435, 439-442, 449-451).
This material was created or received by the International Trade Relations Branch and related to Canada's foreign trade relations. It contains information on the economic status of foreign countries, as well as tariffs in force, trade negotiations, market, important regulations, duties, preference conditions, safes, banking, currencies, pest and disease control, customs regulation, transportation, packaging, etc., in those countries. A file list is available in the Federal Archives Division.

General Agreement on Tariffs and Trade(GATT), ca.1930-1969, 3.6 metres (volumes 1544-1561), microfilm, 139 reels(reel numbers M-2376 - M-2514).

These records include proceedings of meetings of member states, copies of trade agreements, working papers on domestic and foreign economic matters, published reports, and general administrative files. A file list and a microfilm shelf list serves as indexes to this material.

C2e. Fairs and Missions Branch, 1919-1966.

Correspondence files, 1919-1966, 26.8 metres (volumes 1225-1358).

These records include administrative correspondence relating to incoming and outgoing trade missions. Also included is publicity and advertising material deal with a wide variety of programs, from livestock fairs to fashion shows held in various foreign countries. A file list facilitates access to this series.

C2f. Trade Commissioner Service, 1923-1960.

Reports, 1926-1966, 16.2 metres (volumes 144-1514, 1529-1539).

These files comprise, for the most part, a series of annual reports prepared by trade commissioners posted throughout the world. Included in these reports are detailed economic reports on the post country trade commissioner on industrial centres in his territory, and examples of correspondence with Canadian producers. In countries where there was no Canadian diplomatic mission, the trade commission also reported on his consular duties and involvement with immigration matters. The remainder of the records in the collection are files on the general administration of the trade commissioner service: feature articles for **Foreign Trade**, the departmental magazine, and series of reports from the Inspector of the Trade Commissioner Service. A file of these records is available.
Most of the items cited below in this series were found in the finding aid **KWOC Index for RG20, A2, A3, A5**. In this index volume numbers are cited as box numbers.

Volume 283.

File T 22.
Trade with China, 1946.

Volume 287.

File T214
Tariff on Turkey, 1914-1933.

File T247.
Japanese shipping subsidies, 1914-1937.

Volume 292.

File T10078
Postwar conditions in Japan, Far Eastern control of imports and exports, Allied side, 1945-1946.

File T10104.
Greece and Turkey, relief general, 1947.

Volume 293.

File T10110.
Reparation claims against Japan, 1946-1947.

Volume 295.

File T10182.
Reparations claims against Japan, 1946.

File T10183.
Postwar conditions in Japan, Far Eastern Commission control of imports and exports, Allied trade representation, 1946.

Volume 296.

File T10231.
Regulations re exchange and imports and exports to China, 1937-1946.

Volume 298.

File T10288.
All Japanese treaties. Anglo-Japanese treaties, freezing Japanese assets, 1941-1948.

Volume 300.

File T10361.
Hong Kong tariff, 1935-1940.

Volume 302.

File T10428.
Training Indian students and technicians in Canada, 1945-1947.

Volume 304.

File T10490.
Market for grain and flour in India, 1945-1948.

Volume 304.

File T10532.
Trade with China, 1946.

Volume 305.

File T10565.
Tariff of Korea, 1915-1919.

Volume 306.

File T10591.
Supplies for China, Mutual Aid plan and credits, general, 1946.

Volume 309.

File T10768.
Trade with Hong Kong, 1929-1946.

Volume 310.

File T10815
Reparations claims against Japan, 1947.

File T10825.
Postwar conditions in Japan, Far East, control of imports and exports, Allied trade, 1945-1947.
Volume 316.

File T11103.
Trade with the Malay states, 1939-1947.

Volume 317.

File T11246.
Trade between Canada and Japan, 1937-1947.

File T11348
Economic conditions, China, 1945-1946.

Volume 318.

File T11369.
Industrialization in India, 1943-1947.

Volume 319.

File T11431.
Trade between Canada and Japan, 1947.

Volume 320.

File T11455.
Trade treaty between Canada and Siam, 1932-1938.

File T11465.
Flour for India contracts, 1946-1947.

Volume 322.

File T11490.
Supplies for China under Mutual Aid plans and credits, general, 1946.

Volume 325.

File T11564.
Reparation claims against Japan, 1947.

File T11573.
Supplies for China under Mutual Aid plan and credits, 1947-1948.

Volume 326.

File T11578.
Exchange situation in Japan, 1938-1941.

File T11608.
Emergency laws and regulations of India. Licencing, 1945-1947.

Volume 327.

File T11631.
British Chamber of Commerce in Shanghai, China, 1947.

Volume 328.

File T11653.
Greece and Turkey relief, 1947-1948.

Volume 329.

File T11668.
Singapore and Malayan Union, British Malaya, import control and exchange, regulations, official, 1940-1947.

File T11675.

Trade between Canada and Japan, 1947-1948.

File T11677.
Reparation claims against Japan, 1947-1948.

Volume 330.

File T11707.
Trade with China, 1946-1947.

Volume 331.

File T11731-1.
Supplies for China under Mutual Aid plans and credits, general, 1947-1948.

Volume 333.

File T11806.
Hong Kong imports and exports, restrictions and exchange, 1930-1947.

Volume 334.

File T11822.
Economic conditions in China, 1946-1947.

Volume 335.

File T11880.
Trade between Canada and Japan, 1948.

Volume 337.

File T11927.
Trade with Hong Kong, 1946-1948.

Volume 338.

File T11780.
Opening of new Trade Commissioner's Office in Tientsin, China, 1931-1938.

Volume 339.

File T11968.
U.N.R.R.A. in China, 1945-1948.

Volume 340.

File T11981.
Market for grains and flour in India, 1944-1948.

Volume 347.

File T12008.
Exhibitions in Hong Kong, 1946-1948.

File T12067.
Economic conditions in China, 1946-1947.

Volume 348.

File T12082.

Trade of Japan. Economic conditions, 1939-1949.

C3. Office of the Minister, 1963-1972.

1. Hon. R.H.Winters, 1964-1968, 1.8 metres (volumes 1515-1523).

These office files deal exclusively with Expo '67. A file list is available for this series.

2. Hon. W.Mitchell Sharp, 1963-1965, 40 metres(volumes 1524-1525).

These miscellaneous office files deal with such subjects as foreign trade, international conferences, interprovincial trade, and development of Canadian energy resources. A file list facilitates access to these records.

3. Hon. Jean-Luc Pépin, 1968-1972, 8.4 metres (volumes 1579-1624).

These office files deal with a wide variety of subjects, such as foreign trade, the Canadian Wheat Board, and relations with other government agencies. A file list serves as an index to this material.

Accession 83-84/133.

Canadian Government participation in Expo' 70, Osaka, Japan, 1966-1971, 24.6 metres, PARC Boxes 1-76 and 2 wooden boxes.
This accession contains administrative and operational central registry files of the Department of Industry, Trade and Commerce pertaining to the Canadian Government participation in World Expo '70, held in Osaka, Japan. The records include subject files, press clippings, reports, contractors, personnel files, architectural files and minutes of meetings.
The finding aid is a file list Finding aid 38.

Accession 85-86/063

Box 11.

File 4770-INDI Part 1.
Markets - India 1976-1978.

File 4700-JAPA Part 1.
Markets - Japan 1978

Box 12.

File 4850-CHIN. Part 1.
Marine and Rail Industries - Markets - Marine - China, 1976-1978

Box 13.

File 4850-INDl. Part 1.
Marine and Rail Industries - Markets - Marine - India, 1974 -1976.

File 4850-INDI. Part 2.
Marine and Rail Industries - Markets - Marine - India, 1977-1978.

Box 14.

File 4850 INDO. Part 1.
Marine and Rail Industries - Markets - Marine - Indonesia, 1974-1975.

File 4850-lNDO. Part 2.
Marine and Rail Industries - Markets - Marine - Indonesia, 1976.

File 4850-1NDO. Part 3.
Marine and Rail Industries - Indonesia, 1976-1977.

File 4850-JAPA. Part 1.
Marine and Rail Industries - Markets - Marine - Japan, 1974-1976.

File4850-JAPA. Part 2.
Marine and Rail Industries - Markets - Marine - Japan, 1976.

File 4850-JAPA. Part 3.
Marine and Rail Industries - Markets - Marine - Japan, 1976- 1977.

File 4850-JAPA. Part 4.
Marine and Rail Industries - Markets - Marine - Japan, 1976- 1977.

File 4850-JAPA Part 5.
Marine and Rail Industries -Market - Marine - Japan, 1977-1978.

File 4850-KOR(S). Part 1.
Marine and Rail Industries - Markets - Marine - Korea, South, 1974-1977.

File 4850-MALAY. Part 1.
Marine and Rail Industries - Markets - Marine - Malaysia, 1974-1977.

File 4850-THA. Part .1.
Marine and Rail Industries - Markets - Marine - Thailand, 1974-1976.

File4850-THA.Part 2.
Marine and Rail Industries - Markets - Marine - Thailand, 1976-1977

Box 17.

File 4850-TRIN. Part 1.
Marine and Rail Industries - Markets - Marine - Trinidad, 1974-1975

File 4850-TRIN. Part 2.
Marine and Rail Industries - Markets - Marine - Trinidad, 1976.

File 4850-TUR. Part1.
Marine and Rail Industries - Markets - Marine - Turkey, 1973-1976.

File 4850-TUR. Part 2.
Marine and Rail Industries - Markets - Marine - Turkey, 1976- 1977.

File 4850-TUR. Part 3.
Marine and Rail Industries - Markets - Marine - Turkey, 1977-1978.

File 4942-3-HONG. Part 1.
Vehicle Systems Industry - Markets - Urban Transportation - Hong Kong, 1976-1977

File 4942-HONG . Part 2.
Vehicle Systems Industry - Markets - Urban Transportation - Hong Kong, 1977-1978.

Box 27.

File 4942-SIN. Part 1.
Vehicle Systems Industry - Markets - Urban Transportation Singapore, 1975-1978.

Box 34.

File 5614-J1 Part 1.
Asian Development Bank Increases in Financial Resources, 1977-1978.

File 5614-J1 Part 2.
Asian Development Bank- News Releases and Publications. 1977-1979.

Box 42.

File 7775-2-TOK-78 Part 1. Communications, Mediums and Services - Monthly Reports - Publicity - Tokyo, 1978. General, 1978.

File 7775-2-TOK-78 Part 2. Communications, Mediums and Services - Monthly Reports - Publicity - Tokyo, 1978. General 1978

File 7775-2-TOK-78 Part 3.
Communications, Mediums and Services - Monthly Reports - Publicity - Tokyo, 1978. General 1978

File 7775-2-TOK-78 Part 4. Communications, Mediums and Services-Monthly Reports- Publicity -Tokyo, 1978. General 1978.

Accession 85-86/222.

Finding aid 20-54.

PARC 73.

7-614. Volume 1.
Economic relations between India and Pakistan. December 1949-November 1968.

7-637-2. Volume 3.
United States Foreign Assets Control Trade with China Restrictions. Oriental Commerce, Ltd. Windsor, January 1964-January 1968.

7-1037. Volume 1.
Asia - Economic development general, June 1957-February 1970.

20-82A. Volume 5.
Trade Commissioner Service. Asia, Africa and Middle East, January 1969-May 1970.

20-265-C3. Volumes 1-3.
Canadian China policy, February 1963-September 1969.

20-265-C3. Volume 4.
Canadian China policy, September-October 1969.

25-M-164. Volume 1.
Vocational School Equipment Mission to Malaysia, Thailand, Singapore and the Philippines, January 1967-July 1968.

690-3. volumes 16-19.
Market for grain and flour - China, July 1961-July 1971.

810-B20-1. Volume 1.
Trade Policy Service - Trade relations-Borneo-Trade and economic conditions, September 1946-March 1964.

810-C1-2-1. Volume 1.
Trade policy services - Trade relations - Ceylon - Budget, July 1949-August 1965.

810-C3-3. Volume 1.
Trade Policy Service - Trade relations Barter, China(Communist), December 1949-March 1960.

810-C7-1. Volume 1.
Trade Policy Service-Trade relations-Cyprus-Trade and economic conditions, December 1939-August 1965.

810-F8-1. Volume 1.
Trade Policy Service-Trade relations-Fiji Islands-Trade and economic conditions. November 1945-October 1963.

810-I2-3. Volume 1.
Trade Policy Service-Trade relations-Barter-Indonesia, December 1949-September 1960.

810-I3-2-1. Volume 1.
Trade Policy Service-Trade relations. India-Budget, March 1949-August 1968.

810-J2-3. Volume 1.
Trade Policy Service-Trade relations-Barter-Japan, March 1948-November 1961.

810-N2-1. Volume 1.
Trade Policy Service-Trade relations-New Caledonia-Trade and economic conditions, May 1930-November 1967.

810-P1-3. Volume 1.
Trade Policy Service-Trade relations- Barter-Pakistan, November 1949-October 1963.

810-S19-1. Volume 1.
Trade Policy-Trade relations-Samoa-Trade and economic conditions, January 1915-December 1966.

810-T8-1. Volume 3.
Trade Policy Service-Trade relations. Taiwan(Formosa) Trade and economic conditions.

810-T11-1. Volume 1.
Trade Policy Service-Trade relations-Tahiti-Trade and economic conditions, December 1928-June 1962.

822-B16-1. Volume 1.
Trade Policy Service-Trade relations-Trade treaty negotiations-Burma-Official and general, April 1936-November 1963.

822-C3-1A. Volume 1.
Trade Policy Service- Trade relations-Trade treaty negotiations-China(Communist)-Official, July 1962-August 1969.

822-C14-1. Volume 1.
Trade Policy Service-Trade relations-Trade treaty negotiations-Cambodia-Official and general, December 1957-February 1960.

822-I2-1. Volume 1.
Trade Policy Service-Trade relations-Trade treaty negotiations-Indonesia-Official and general, September 1960-May 1965.

822-I3-1A. Volume 1.
Traded Policy Services-Trade relations-Trade treaty negotiations-India-Official, January 1955-September 1965.

822-J2-2. Volume 1.
Trade Policy Service-Trade relations-Trade treaty negotiations-with Canada-Japan-Official and general, August 1959-December 1960.

822-P1-1A. Volume 1.
Trade Policy Service-Trade relations-Trade treaty negotiations-Pakistan-official, December 1959-July 1964.

822-P5-1. Volume 1.
Trade Policy Service-Trade relations-Trade Treaty negotiations-Philippines-Official and general, October 1947-July 1965.

822-T3-1A. Volume 8.
Trade Policy Service-Trade relations-Trade treaty negotiations-Turkey-official, August 1967.

822-V4-1. Volume 1.

Trade Policy Service-Trade relations-Trade treaty negotiations-Vietnam-Official and general, June 1956-November 1963.

880-11. Volume 9.
Trade Policy Service-International Organizations - United Nations-Eco-Soc-Economic Commission for Asia and the Far East-General Correspondence, January-April 1969.

880-11. Volume 10.
Trade Policy Service-International Organizations - United Nations-Eco-Soc-Economic Commission for Asia and the Far East-General Correspondence, March-April 1969.

880-11. Volume 11.
Trade Policy Service-International Organizations - United Nations-Eco-Soc-Economic Commission for Asia and the Far East-General Correspondence, May-August 1969.

885-5. Volume 6.
Trade Policy Service-International organizations-O.E.C.D. Greek and Turkish consortia, January 1967-December 1969.

8001-317/E2. Volume 1.
Economic Commission for Asia, January-August 1966.

Accession 85-86/223.

Finding aid 20-55.

File 20-I3-C3 1 S.
Foreign diplomatic and trade representatives in Canada. Communist China, November 1964-November 1970.

File 20-I3-C3 2 S.
Foreign diplomatic and trade representatives in Canada. Communist China, January 1971.

File 20-39-1 5 S.
Canada-Japan, trade and economic ministerial. October 1966-February 1969.

File 20-39-1 6 S.
Canada-Japan, trade and economic ministerial, March 1969-August 1971.

File 20-44-6 1 S.
Japan Universal and International Exhibition-Osaka 1970, August 1966-September 1967.

File 20-44-6 2 S.
Japan Universal and International Exhibition-Osaka 1970, January 1968-June 1970.

File 20-82A 6 S.
Trade Commissioner Service, Asia, Africa and Middle East, June 1970-April 1971.

File 20-141-C1 1 S.
Grain and flour. Ceylon, April 1963-November 1971.

File 20-141-C3 6 S.
Grain and flour. China, December 1968-May 1971.

File 20-141-C1 5 S.
Grain and flour. China, January 1968-May 1969.

File 20-141-C7 1 S.
Grain and flour. Cyprus, April 1967-June 1970.

File 20-141-M12 1 S.
Grain and flour. Malaysia, February 1966-May 1970.

File 20-141-P1 2 S.
Grain and flour. Pakistan, October 1964-May 1971.

File 20-141-P5 1 S.
Grain and flour. Philippines, October 1963-September 1970.

File 20-141-R1 1 S.
Grain and flour. Ryukyus, June 1965-April 1969.

File 20-141-T2 1 S.
Grain and flour. Thailand, April 1968-March 1971.

File 20-141-T3 1 S.
Grain and flour. Turkey, September 1963-August 1969.

File 20-141-T3 2 S.
Grain and flour. Turkey, August 1969-October 1970.

File 20-141-T8 1 S.
Grain and flour. Taiwan, December 1964-June 1971.

File 20 125-6 1 2.
Japan-West Canada Freight Conference, July 1967-May 1968.

File 20 321-G38 1 S.
Nationalization of industries in foreign countries. Claims for compensation by citizens. Guyana, September 1964-March 1971.

File 20 321- I3 1 S.
Nationalization of industries in foreign countries. Claims for compensation by citizens. India, July 1969-May 1971.

File 20-374-C3 1 S.
Trade missions from Canada to China, April 1964-July 1971.

File 20E-2-C1 1 S.
Trade and economic conditions, Trade agreements and Trade relations. Ceylon, October 1963-June 1970.

File 20E-2-C3 1 S.
Trade and economic conditions, Trade agreements and Trade relations. China, January 1957-June 1971.

File 20E-2-C7 1 S.

Trade and economic conditions, Trade agreements and Trade relations. Cyprus, October 1964-June 1966.

File 20E-2-C9-5 2 S.
Trade and economic conditions, Trade agreements and Trade relations. Canada-Turkey, March 1960-October 1968.

File 20E-2-C9-5 3 S.
Trade and economic conditions, Trade agreements and Trade relations. Canada-Turkey, March 1969-June 1970.

File 20E-2-E7-5 1 S.
Trade and economic conditions, Trade agreements and Trade relations. European Economic Community. Japan., February 1969-July 1970.

File 20E-2-G8 1 S.
Trade and economic conditions, Trade agreements and Trade relations. Guyana, July 1968-May 1971.

File 20E-2-H5 1 S.
Trade and economic conditions, Trade agreements and Trade relations. Hong Kong, April 1964-August 1967.

File 20E-2-I3 1-2 S.
Trade and economic conditions, Trade agreements and Trade relations. India, April 1963.

File 20E-2-I5 1 S.
Trade and economic conditions, Trade agreements and Trade relations. Iran, July 1969-May 1970.

File 20E-2-I5-1 1 S.
Trade and economic conditions, Trade agreements and Trade relations. Iran-Canada Trade Agreements, December 1959-May 1970.

File 20E-2-J2-2 1 S.
Trade and economic conditions, Trade agreements and Trade relations. Japan, merchandise marks, trade marks and labelling, April 1948-September 1964.

File 20E-2-K1 1-10 S.
Trade and economic conditions, Trade agreements and Trade relations. Republic of Korea(South), September 1962.

File 20E-2-K2 1 S.
Trade and economic conditions, Trade agreements and Trade relations. North Korea, May 1964-September 1965.

File 20E-2-K2-1 1 S.
Trade and economic conditions, Trade agreements and Trade relations. Canada-North Korea, April 1964-May 1969.

File 20E-2-M12 1-2 S.
Trade and economic conditions, Trade agreements and Trade relations. Malaysia, April 1959-February 1971.

File 20E-2-P1 1 S.
Trade and economic conditions, Trade agreements and Trade relations. Pakistan, June 1956-March 1970.

File 20E-2-P5 1 S.
Trade and economic conditions, Trade agreements and Trade relations. Philippines, September 1969-June 1971.

File 20E-2-R1 1 S.
Trade and economic conditions, Trade agreements and Trade relations. Ryukyus, September 1965-February 1971.

File 20E-2-S1 1 S.
Trade and economic conditions, Trade agreements and Trade relations. Singapore, May 1967-July 1968.

File 20E-2-T2 1 S.
Trade and economic conditions, Trade agreements and Trade relations. Thailand, April 1964-May 1969.

File 20E-2-T3 1 S.
Trade and economic conditions, Trade agreements and Trade relations. Turkey, April 1964-February 1971.

File 20E-2-T8 1 S.
Trade and economic conditions, Trade agreements and Trade relations. Taiwan, February 1967-December 1970.

File 20E-2-V4 1 S.
Trade and economic conditions, Trade agreements and Trade relations. Vietnam, January 1965-October 1967.

File 25-J2-6 1.
Canadian(Incoming) Trade Missions 1969/1970. Meat mission from Japan, October 1969-December 1969.

File 25-J2-6 2.
Fairs and Missions Branch. Meat industry mission from Japan, January-October 1969.

File 25-J2-7 1.
Trade Fairs and Trade Missions. Canadian(Incoming) Trade Missions 1969-1970. Rapeseed mission from Japan, September 1968-July 1969.

File 25-J2-7 2.
Rapeseed mission from Japan, July-September 1969.

File 25-M-163 1-3.
Trade Fairs and Trade Missions. Canadian(Incoming) Trade Missions 1968-1969. Fur Mission to Japan and Hong Kong, March 1966-October 1969.

File FM-25-M-201 1.
Fairs and Missions Branch. Hotel Equipment Mission to Pacific Rim countries, March 1968-December 1969.

File FM-25-M-201 2.
Hotel Equipment Mission to South East Asia, December 1969-February 1970.

File FM-25-M-201 3.

Hotel Equipment Mission to Pacific Rim countries, February-April 1970.

File FM 25-M-203 1.
Tobacco Trade Development Mission to Britain, Germany and Japan, December 1969-June 1970.

File 25-N-159 1.
Canadian(Outgoing) Trade Missions 1967-1968. Food Products Mission to Far East, January 1966-August 1968.

File 490-C1 5.
Agriculture - Market for grain and flour. Ceylon, June 1958-July 1970.

File 490-I2 2.
Agriculture - Market for grain and flour. Indonesia, December 1959-July 1970.

File 490-I5 1.
Agriculture - Market for grain and flour. Iran, March 1960-December 1970.

File 490-K1 2.
Agriculture - Market for grain and flour. South Korea, March 1958-December 1969.

File TIP 691-J2-1 1.
Trade Policy Service Japan-USA textile negotiations, June 1970-June 1971.

File 801-C3 2.
Trade Policy Service. Low cost imports - Market disruption - Long Term Textile agreements. China, July-August 1968.

File 801-H5 3.
Trade Policy Service. Low cost imports - Market disruption - Long Term Textile agreements. Hong Kong, January 1965-October 1969.

File 801-I3 2.
Trade Policy Service. Low cost imports - Market disruption - Long Term Textile agreements. India, May 1963-February 1967.

File 810-A6-1 2.
Trade Policy Service. Trade Relations. Afghanistan - Trade and economic conditions, August 1965-June 1970.

File 810-B16-1 2.
Trade Policy Service. Trade Relations. Burma - Trade and economic conditions, September 1958-November 1970.

File 810-B17-1 1.
Trade Policy Service. Trade Relations. Brunei - Trade and economic conditions, October 1959-April 1970.

File 810-C1-1 7-8.
Trade Policy Service. Trade Relations. Ceylon - Trade with, August 1968-March 1971.

File 810-C3-1 23-25.
Trade Policy Service. Trade Relations. Communist China - Trade with, October 1968-March 1971.

File 810-C3-3 2.
Trade Policy Service. Trade Relations. Barter. Communist China, October 1965-July 1968.

File 810-C3-4 1.
Trade Policy Service. Trade Relations. Canadian recognition of Communist China, October 1970-February 1971.

File 810-F5-1 4.
Trade Policy Service. Trade Relations. Far East-Trade and economic conditions, March 1967-March 1969.

File 810-G8-1 3.
Trade Policy Service. Trade Relations. Guyana - Trade and economic conditions, March 1967-March 1969.

File 810-I2-1 3.
Trade Policy Service. Trade Relations. Indonesia -Trade with. January 1968-June 1971.

File 810-I2-1 10.
Trade Policy Service. Trade Relations. Indonesia - Economic conditions, September 1968-April 1971.

File 810-I3-1 6-8
Trade Policy Service. Trade Relations. India -Trade with, July 1965-June 1971.

File 810-I3-2-1 2.
Trade Policy Service. Trade Relations. India - Budget, March 1969-April 1970.

File 810-I3-3 2
Trade Policy Service. Trade Relations. Barter - India, October 1962-December 1965.

File 810-J2-1 18-19
Trade Policy Service. Trade Relations. Japan -Trade with, November 1968-July 1970.

File 810-J2-4 4
Trade Policy Service. Trade Relations. Japan -Trade Canada-Japan Trade Council, August 1968-June 1971.

File 810-L6-1 1-2.
Trade Policy Service. Trade Relations. Laos -Trade and economic conditions, July 1961-June 1964, January-July 1970.

File 810-N9-1 1.
Trade Policy Service. Trade Relations. Nepal -Trade and economic conditions, August 1956-February 1970.

File 810-N10-1 1.
Trade Policy Service. Trade Relations. Nauru -Trade and economic conditions, February 1968-

File 810-P1-3 2.
Trade Policy Service. Trade Relations. Barter -

Pakistan, June 1966-January 1970.

File 810-P5-1 1.
Trade Policy Service. Trade Relations. Philippines - Trade and economic conditions, April 1966-June 1970.

File 810-T1-1 4-5.
Trade Policy Service. Trade Relations. Trinidad -Trade and economic conditions, March 1968-November 1970.

File 810-T1-1-1 2.
Trade Policy Service. Trade Relations. Trinidad - Budget, December 1968-January 1971.

File 810-T2-1 3-4.
Trade Policy Service. Trade Relations. Thailand(Siam) - Trade and economic conditions, January 1959- November 1970.

File 810-T3-1 1.
Trade Policy Service. Trade Relations. Turkey -Trade with, February 1964-February 1970.

File 810-T3-3 2.
Trade Policy Service. Trade Relations. Barter - Turkey, June 1963.

File 822-C1-1 2.
Trade Policy Service. Trade Relations. Ceylon - Official and general, February 1968-March 1969.

File 822-I3-1B 1.
Trade Policy Service. Trade Relations. India - general, June 1967-May 1968.

File 822-I5-1A 2.
Trade Policy Service. Trade Relations. Iran - official, January 1967-September 1970.

File 822-J2-1A 2.
Trade Policy Service. Trade Relations. Japan - official, December 1965-December 1970.

File 822-K1-1 2.
Trade Policy Service. Trade Relations. Korea - official, May 1966-April 1967.

File 822-P1-1A 2.
Trade Policy Service. Trade Relations. Pakistan - official, February 1967-January 1970.

File G.2167-305/J4 1 C.
Duties and tariffs - Imports India, March 1964 -July 1969.

File G.2168-305/C14 2 S.
Duties and tariffs - Low cost imports. China(Mainland), February 1967-October 1969.

File G.2168-305/F5 2 S.
Duties and tariffs - Low cost imports. Formosa(Taiwan), March 1969-

File G.2168-305/H5 7 C.
Duties and tariffs - Low cost imports. Hong Kong, August 1969-April 1970.

File G.2168-305/J15 13 C.
Duties and tariffs - Low cost imports. Japan, March 1969-May 1970.

File G.2168-305/K6 2 C.
Duties and tariffs - Low cost imports. Korea-South, January 1968-December 1969.

File G.2168-305/M4 1-2 C.
Duties and tariffs - Low cost imports. Malaysia, March 1968-March 1970.

File G.2168-305/S35 2 C.
Duties and tariffs - Low cost imports. Singapore, January 1969-May 1970.

File B.8835-305/J15 1 S.
Sale of Equipment - Japan, September 1967-June 1969.

File OST.9010-305/J15 1 S.
Science and technology missions to, and agreement with Japan, March-August 1971.

Accession 85-86/225

Finding aid 20-5t6.

File 18-1-14. Volume 1.
Annual report-1968-Trade Commissioner Office. Hong Kong, February 1968-December 1968.

File 18-1-36. Volume 1.
Annual report-1968-Trade Commissioner Office. Singapore, January 1967-December 1968.

File 18-1-39. Volume 1.
Annual report-1968-Trade Commissioner Office. Tokyo, January-December 1968.

File 18-1-45. Volume 1.
Annual report-1968-Trade Commissioner Office. New Delhi, January-June 1968.

File 18-1-55. Volume 1.
Annual report-1968-Trade Commissioner Office. Manila, December 1967-November 1968.

File 18-1-60. Volume 1.
Annual report-1968-Trade Commissioner Office. Colombo, June-December 1968.

File 18-1-72. Volume 1.
Annual report-1968-Trade Commissioner Office. Tehran, September-November 1968.

File 18-1-88. Volume 1.
Annual report-1968-Trade Commissioner Office. Rawalpindi, February-June 1968.

File 18-1-96. Volume 1.

Annual report-1968-Trade Commissioner Office. Islamabad, September-December 1968.

File 18-40. Volume 1.
Post report. Nicosia, Cyprus, June 1967-May 1969.

File 18-72. Volume 1.
Post report. Trade Commissioners. Karachi, May 1949-June 1969.

File 18-393. Volume 1.
Post report. Tehran, December 1952-January 1969.

File 211-4-39. Volume 1-2.
Administration-Organization. Canadian Government Travel Bureau, Tokyo, April 1954-August 1968.

File 211-11-4. Volume 1.
Administration-Organization. Trade Commissioner Services, Bombay. October 1946-July 1966.

File 211-11-14. Volume 1.
Administration-Organization. Trade Commissioner Services, Hong Kong. October 1928-December 1966.

File 211-11-19. Volume 1-2.
Administration-Organization. Trade Commissioner Services, Karachi. August 1947-October 1967.

File 211-11-35. Volume 1.
Administration-Organization. Trade Commissioner Services, Shanghai. February 1929-January 1952.

File 211-11-36. Volume 1-2.
Administration-Organization. Trade Commissioner Services, Singapore. June 1921-October 1967.

File 211-11-39. Volume 1.
Administration - Organization. Trade Commissioner Services, Tokyo. May 1918-January 1960.

File 211-11-45. Volume 1.
Administration-Organization. Trade Commissioner Services, New Delhi. February 1948-November 1967.

File 211-11-51. Volume 1.
Administration-Organization. Trade Commissioner Services, Calcutta. October 1911-March 1962.

File 211-11-55. Volume 1.
Administration-Organization. Trade Commissioner Services, Manila. February 1947-November 1967.

File 211-11-65. Volume 1.
Administration-Organization. Trade Commissioner Services, Djakarta, July 1925-April 1967.

File 211-11-66. Volume 1.
Administration-Organization. Trade Commissioner Services, Kobe. March 1953-February 1957.

File 211-11-72. Volume 1.
Administration-Organization. Trade Commissioner Services, Tehran. May 1955-September 1960.

File 211-11-88. Volume 1.
Administration-Organization. Trade Commissioner Services, Rawalpindi. October 1959-April 1968.

File 810-C10-1 Volume 1.
Trade Policy Service. Trade relations, Cook Islands-Trade and economic conditions. August 1946-February 1955.

File 810-M11-1 Volume 1.
Trade Policy Service. Trade relations, Manchuria-Trade and economic conditions. October 1932-December 1949.

File 810-S2-1 Volume 1.
Trade Policy Service. Trade relations, Sarawak-Trade and economic conditions, May 1947-June 1952.

File 810-T6-1 Volume 1.
Trade Policy Service. Trade relations, Tonga-Trade and economic conditions, October 1954-May 1955.

File 810-T13-1 Volume 1.
Trade Policy Service. Trade relations, Tibet-Trade and economic conditions, August 1948-July 1954.

File 813-C3-1 Volume 1.
Trade Policy Service. Trade relations, Investments-China(Communist), October 1927-August 1954.

File 955-1 Volume 1-2.
External Trade Promotion. Exhibitions. World Exhibition-Osaka 1970. general April 1965-May 1969.

File 955-2 Volume 1.
External Trade Promotion. Exhibitions. World Exhibition-Osaka 1970. Invitation-Canadian. September-October 1966.

File 955-3 Volume 1.
External Trade Promotion. Exhibitions. World Exhibition-Osaka 1970. Commissioners General. Appointment of General. October 1966-August 1968.

File 955-3-1 Volume 1.
External Trade Promotion. Exhibitions. World Exhibition-Osaka 1970. Commissioners- General. Appointment of Canadian, July 1967-May 1969.

File 955-5 Volume 1.
External Trade Promotion. Exhibitions. World Exhibition-Osaka 1970. Committees, October 1966-March 1969.

File 955-6 Volume 1.
External Trade Promotion. Exhibitions. World Exhibition-Osaka 1970. Services, offer of, April 1966-July 1967

File 955-11 Volume 1.
External Trade Promotion. Exhibitions. World Exhibition-Osaka 1970. Administration, finance, February 1967-March 1969.

File 955-12 Volume 1.
External Trade Promotion. Exhibitions. World Exhibition-Osaka 1970. Commissioners-Administration- personnel general. Appointment of Canadian, July 1967-May 1969.

File 955-13-1 Volume 1.
External Trade Promotion. Exhibitions. World Exhibition-Osaka 1970. Administration Accommodation general, January-May 1969.

File 955-13-2 Volume 1.
External Trade Promotion. Exhibitions. World Exhibition-Osaka 1970. Administration Accommodation Office, April 1969.

File 955-20 Volume 1.
External Trade Promotion. Exhibitions. World Exhibition-Osaka 1970. Buildings and Construction-general. April 1967-November 1968.

File 955-21 Volume 1.
External Trade Promotion. Exhibitions. World Exhibition-Osaka 1970. Buildings and Construction-Site, March 1967-July 1968.

File 955-22 Volume 1.
External Trade Promotion. Exhibitions. World Expo-Osaka 1970. Buildings and Construction-Architecture, June 1967-October 1968.

File 955-22-1 Volume 1.
External Trade Promotion. Exhibitions. World Exhibition-Osaka 1970. Buildings and Construction-Competition, Design of, November 1966-January 1968.

File 955-30 Volume 1.
External Trade Promotion. Exhibitions. World Exhibition-Osaka 1970. Publicity- general, May 1966-March 1968.

File 955-31 Volume 1.
External Trade Promotion. Exhibitions. World Exhibition-Osaka 1970. Publicity-Canadian, December 1966-April 1969.

File 955-33 Volume 1.
External Trade Promotion. Exhibitions. World Exhibition-Osaka 1970. Publicity Publications-general, October 1966-March 1969.

File 955-33-1 Volume 1.
External Trade Promotion. Exhibitions. World Exhibition-Osaka 1970. Publicity-Publications-Exposition News, June 1967-September 1970.

File 955-41 Volume 1.
External Trade Promotion. Exhibitions. World

Exhibition-Osaka 1970. Exhibit- Canadian, March 1967-April 1969.

File 955-45 Volume 1.
External Trade Promotion. Exhibitions. World Exhibition-Osaka 1970. Participation- general, January 1966-May 1968.

File 955-45-1 Volume 1-2.
External Trade Promotion. Exhibitions. World Exhibition-Osaka 1970. Participation-Canadian, September 1966-April 1969.

File 955-45-1-1 Volume 1.
External Trade Promotion. Exhibitions. World Exhibition-Osaka 1970. Participation-Canadian. Cultural Participation, November 1967-April 1969.

File 955-51 Volume 1.
External Trade Promotion. Exhibitions. World Exhibition-Osaka 1970. Visitors-Canadian, October 1967-April 1969.

Accession 85-86/226.

Finding aid 57.

Record Group 20 - Industry, Trade and Commerce. Series A4, B1, C1.
Headquarters Central Registry Files from the Trade and Commerce 1966 system(Series A4); Industry system(Series B1); Industry, Trade and Commerce system(Series C1), 1946-1976, 33.6 metres, boxes 1-112.
The subjects included are missions-China(file block 19)

Accession 85-86/238.

Finding aid 20-58.

Record Group 20. Industry, Trade and Commerce. Series A4, B1, C1.
Headquarters Central Registry files of the Department of Trade and Commerce(1966 system) - Series A4; Department of Industry - Series B1; Department of Industry, Trade and Commerce - Series C1, 1913-1974, 56.1 metres, Boxes 1-187.
The records include service files concerning Expo '70 in Osaka, Japan. Finding aid 20-58.

File TIP7-250-1. 1.
CDA-Japan/Ministerial/Committee. General and unclassified correspondence, September 1966 to May 1971.

File TIP7-637. 2.
United States Treasury - Foreign Assets Control Regulations-Restrictions on trade with China, January 1968-May 1971.

File TIP 7-1036.
Trade Policy Service - Trade between Australia, Japan and China. Pacific Basin Economic Cooperation Committee, July 1970-April 1971.

File GR10-300-C3-1. 1-3.
People's Republic of China-Peking Solo Trade Fair, December 1971-July 1972.

File GR10-300-K1--1. 1.
Korea-Grain terminals, June-November 1971.

File GRl0-300-K1-3. 1.
Oilseed Crushing project-Korea(X Canada), November 1971-January 1972.

File GRl0-300-K1-4. 1.
Korea- Flour mill in Pusan, November 1971.

File TCS18-1-14. 1.
Annual report - Trade Commissioner Service- Hong Kong-1969, January-December 1969.

File TCS18-1-14(70). 2.
Annual report - Trade Commissioner Service- Hong Kong-1970, February-December 1970;

File TCS18-1-16(70). 1.
Annual report - Kuala Lumpur - 1970, March 1970-.

File TCS18-1-39. 1.
Annual report -1969- Trade Commissioner Service- Tokyo, February-December 1969.

File TCS18-1-45. 1.
Annual report - 1969-Trade Commissioner Service-New Delhi, January-November 1969.

File TCS18-1-55. 1.
Annual report - 1969-Trade Commissioner Service- Manila, March-September 1969.

File TCS18-1-65. 1.
Annual report -1970- Trade Commissioner Service- Djakarta, January-March 1970.

File TCS18-1-95. 1.
Annual report - 1969-Trade Commissioner Service- Bangkok, May 1969-.

File TCS18-1-96. 1.
Annual report -1969- Trade Commissioner Service- Islamabad, February 1969-.

File TCS18-3-14. 1.
Agricultural reports -Trade Commissioner - Hong Kong, June 1965-May 1968.

File TCS18-3-19. 1.
Agricultural reports -Trade Commissioner - Karachi-Pakistan agricultural industry, December 1962-November 1968.

File TCS18-3-36. 1.
Agricultural reports -Trade Commissioner - Singapore, June 1956-September 1968.

File TCS18-3-39. 2.
Agricultural reports -Trade Commissioner - Tokyo-Japanese agricultural industry, March 1968-.

File TCS18-3-45. 2.
Agricultural reports -Trade Commissioner - New Delhi-Indian agricultural industry, November 1968-May 1969.

File TCS18-3-60. 2.
Agricultural reports -Trade Commissioner - Agricultural industry in Ceylon, August 1968.

File TCS18-6-14. 3.
Trade Commissioner - Hong Kong-Economic reports, May-August 1968.

File 1TCS8-6-16. 1.
Reports for foreign trade-Economic reports-Trade Commissioner -Kuala Lumpur, January 1966-May 1968.

File TCS18-6-36. 3.
Trade Commissioner -Singapore-Economic reports, May-June 1968.

File 1TCS8-6-39. 2.
Trade Commissioner - Tokyo-Economic reports, May-September 1968.

File 1TCS8-6-40. 2.
Trade Commissioner - Trinidad-Economic reports, October 1965-March 1968.

File 1TCS8-6-55. 3.
Trade Commissioner - Manila-Economic reports, May-June 1968.

File TCS18-10-14(69) l.
Post Program forecast 1969-Five year forecast-Trade Commissioner Office-Hong Kong, February 1969-

File TCS18-10-16(69) l.
Post Program forecast 1969-Five year forecast-Trade Commissioner Office-Kuala Lumpur, Year 1970-1971.

File TCS18-10-36(69) l.
Post Program forecast 1969-Five year forecast-Trade Commissioner Office- Singapore, March 1969-.

File TCS18-10-39(69) l.
Post Program forecast 1969-Five year forecast-Trade Commissioner Office-Tokyo, March-May 1969.

File TCS18-10-45(69) l.
Post Program forecast 1969-Five year forecast-Trade Commissioner Office-New Delhi, Year 1970-1971.

File TCS18-10-55(69) l.
Post Program forecast 1969-Five year forecast-Trade Commissioner Office-Manila, April 1969-.

File TCS18-10-60(69) l.
Post Program forecast 1969-Five year forecast-Trade Commissioner Office-Colombo, Year 1970-1971.

File TCS18-10-65(69) l.
Post Program forecast 1969-Five year forecast-Trade Commissioner Office. Djakarta, March 1969-.

Ontario – Ottawa

File TCS18-10-72(69) l.
Post Program forecast 1969-Five year forecast-Trade Commissioner Office-Teheran, March 1969-.

File TCS18-10-95(69) l.
Post Program forecast 1969-Five year forecast-Trade Commissioner Office-Bangkok, Year 1970-1971.

File TCS18-10-96(69) l.
Post Program forecast 1969-Five year forecast-Trade Commissioner Office-Islamabad, February-March 1969.

File TCS18-10-98(69) l.
Post Program forecast 1969-Five year forecast-Trade Commissioner Office-Ankara, February 1969-.

File TCS18-11-72(70-71) 1.
Post annual plan - 1970/71-Trade Commissioner Office Tehran, December 1970-.

File TCS18-11-96(70-71) 1.
Post annual plan - 1970-1971-Trade Commissioner Office Islamabad, January 1971-.

File TCS18-70. 4.
Post report -Trade Commissioner. Hong Kong, November 1968-March 1971.

File TCS18-86. 2.
Post report-Trade Commissioner -Singapore, August 1955-November 1970.

File TCS18-88. 2.
Post report-Trade Commissioner -Tokyo, August 1969-April 1970.

File TCS18-150. 1.
Post report-Trade Commissioner -Vientiane, Laos, May 1965-June 1968.

File TCS18-168. 3.
Post report-Trade Commissioner -New Delhi, February 1968-July 1970.

File TCS18-196. 3.
Post report-Trade Commissioner - Colombo, Ceylon, February 1968-May 1970.

File TCS18-213. 3.
Post report-Trade Commissioner -Ankara, October 1968-October 1969.

File TCS18-244. 2.
Post report-Trade Commissioner -Manila. September 1968-May 1970.

File TCS18-257. 2.
Trade Commissioner Conference- Asia, January 1968-June 1970.

File TCS18-265. 1.
Post report-Trade Commissioner -Georgetown, British Guyana, July 1965-August 1968

File TCS18-271. 1.
Trade Commissioner Services-Operational audit-Africa, Asia, Australia, January 1970-January 1971.

File TCS18-289. 1.
Post report-Trade Commissioner -Hanoi, Vietnam, October 1969-.

File TCS18-345. 2.
Post report-Trade Commissioner -Djakarta, Indonesia, July 1968-March 1970.

File TCS18-418. 2.
Post report-Trade Commissioner -Saigon, Vietnam, October 1968-February 1971.

File TCS18-477. 2.
Post report-Trade Commissioner - Kuala Lumpur, March 1969-December 1970.

File TCS18-485. 1.
Post report-Trade Commissioner - Phnom Penh, September 1959-December 1968.

File TCS18-578. 1.
Post report-Trade Commissioner-Bangkok, March 1969-

File TCS18-580. 1.
Post report-Trade Commissioner -Islamabad, July 1969-

File FM25/A15-1. 1.
Trade delegations - Delegates Asia and Middle East, 1970-1971, March 1970-February 1972.

File FM25-G1-12. 1.
Logging and sawmill equipment and services mission to South East Asia, June 1969-February 1971.

File FM 25-J2-8. 1.
Technical tobacco mission from Japan =70/84, March 1970-January 1971.

File FM 25M-209. 1.
Rapeseed mission to Japan and Australia, or Japan and South East Asia, April 1970-April 1971.

File TCS211-11-36. 3.
Administration - Organization. Trade Commissioner Service -Singapore, May 1968-April 1970.

File TCS211-11-39. 2.
Administration - Organization. Trade Commissioner Service -Tokyo, November 1960-July 1970.

File TCS211-11-45. 2.
Administration - Organization. Trade Commissioner Service -New Delhi, September 1968-April 1970.

File TCS211-11-55. 2.
Administration - Organization. Trade Commissioner Service -Manila, February 1968-April 1970.

File TCS211-11-60. 2.

Administration - Organization. Trade Commissioner Service -Colombo, June 1950-January 1969.

File TCS 211-11-65. 2.
Administration-Organization-Trade Commissioner Service-Djakarta, April 1967-March 1969.

File TCS 211-11-72. 2.
Administration-Organization-Trade Commissioner Service-Tehran, January 1962-April 1969.

File TCS211-11-95. 1.
Adminstration-Organization-Trade Commissioner Service-Bangkok, July 1965-February 1970.

File TCS211-11-96. 2.
Administration-Organization-Trade Commissioner Service-Islamabad, January 1969-.

File TCS 211-11-98. 1.
Administration-Organization-Trade Commissioner Service-Ankara, July 1969-December 1970.

File TCS 211-11-106. 1.
Trade Commissioner Service-Post establishment-Trade Commissioner Peking, October-November 1970.

File GR490-A6. 1.
Agriculture market for Grain and Flour. Afghanistan. October 1947-October 1971.

File GR490-C3. 20-21.
Agriculture market for Grain and Flour. China, August 1971-October 1972.

File GHR490-C7. 2.
Agriculture market for Grain and Flour. Cyprus, February 1962-September 1971.

File GR490-J2. 37.
Market for Grain and Flour. Japan, December 1971-August 1972.

File GR490-Kl. 3.
Market for Grain and Flour. Korea, January 1970-August 1972.

File GR490-P1. 8.
Market for Grain and Flour. Pakistan, November 1970-December 1971.

File GR490-P5. 13.
Market for Grain and Flour. Philippines, January-August 1971.

File GR490-T3. 3.
Market for Grain and Flour. Turkey, August 1970-March 1971.

File TIP810-C7-1. 2.
Trade Policy Service-Trade Relations-Cyprus-Trade and economic conditions, March 1967-April 1971.

File TIP810-F8-1. 2.
Trade Policy Service-Trade Relations-Fiji Islands-Trade and economic conditions, July 1966-June 1971.

File TIP810-G8-1. 4.
Trade Policy Service-Trade Relations-Guyana-Trade and economic conditions, June 1969-June 1971.

File TIP810-H5-1. 13.
Trade Policy Service-Trade Relations-Hong Kong-Trade and economic conditions, June 1967-March 1971.

File TIP810-J2-1. 20.
Trade Policy Service-Trade Relations-Japan-Trade and economic conditions, August 1970-June 1971.

File TIP810-K1-1. 4.
Trade Policy Service-Trade Relations-Korea-Trade and economic conditions, July 1968-June 1971.

File TIP810-M12-1. 3.
Trade Policy Service-Trade Relations-Malaysia-Trade and economic conditions, October 1968-June 1971.

File TIP810-M12-2. 6.
Trade Policy Service-Trade Relations-Malaysia-Trade and economic conditions, July 1970-February 1971.

File TIP810-P1-1. 4.
Trade Policy Service-Trade Relations-Pakistan-Trade with, July 1968-June 1971.

File TIP810-P5-1. 5.
Trade Policy Service-Trade Relations-Philippines-Trade and economic conditions, August 1970-May 1971.

File TIP810-R1-1. 1.
Trade Policy Service-Trade Relations-Ryukyus-Trade and economic conditions, April 1966-November 1967.

File TIP810-S6-1. 5.
Trade Policy Service-Trade Relations-Singapore-Trade and economic conditions, November 1968-May 1971.

File TIP810-T3-1, volume 2.
Trade and economic conditions, Turkey, June 1970-June 1971.

File TIP810-T8-1, volume 1.
Trade and economic conditions, Taiwan(Formosa), July 1969-May 1971.

File TIP810-V4-1, volume 2.
Trade with Iron Curtain countries-East West Trade, Vietnam, August 1970-June 1971.

File TIP822-C3-1A, volume 2.
Trade Policy Service - Trade Relations -Trade Treaty Negotiations - China(Communist) official, October 1970-April 1971.

File TIP822-I3-1A, volume 2.
Trade Policy Service - Trade Relations -Trade Treaty

Negotiations - India official, January 1966-May 1971.

File TIP822-J3-2, volume 2.
Trade Policy Service - Trade Relations -Trade Treaty Negotiations - With Canada-Japan- official and general, July 1967- March 1971.

File TIP822-P5-1, volume 2.
Trade Policy Service - Trade Relations -Trade Treaty Negotiations - With Canada- Philippines- official and general, May 1966-May 1971.

File TIP822-T3-1A, volume 9.
Trade Policy Service - Trade Relations -Trade Treaty Negotiations - With Canada-Turkey- official, May 1968-May 1971.

File TIP875-T3, volume 2.
Trade Policy Service -International Organizations GATT. Turkey, May-June 1969.

File FM 950-A15-1, volume 1.
External Trade promotion-Exhibition-Asia-general, January 1969-October 1970.

File FM 950-J2-1, volume 3.
External Trade promotion- Japan general, February 1969-September 1970.

File FM 950-J2-2, volume 3.
External Trade promotion- Japan Mobile Trade Displays and Exhibitions, February 1968-November 1970.

File FM950-J2-6, volume 1.
Food Promotion in Japan, March 1968-June 1970.

File FM 950-J2-6, volume 5.
External Trade Promotion Exhibition - In Store Promotion Japan, January 1969-February 1970.

File FM 950-J2-6-1, volume 1.
1970-Keio In Store Promotion, Tokyo, December 1969-March 1970.

File FM 950-J2-6-1, volume 2.
1970-Keio In Store Promotion, Tokyo, January-July 1970.

File FM 950-J2-6-1, volume 3.
1970-Keio In Store Promotion, Tokyo, July 1970-June 1972.

File FM 950-J2-6-1, volume 4.
1970-Keio In Store Promotion, Tokyo, 3-25 April 1970, November 1970-June 1971.

File FM 960-J2-8, volume 1.
Solo Food Fair Seibu and Sapporo, Japan, December 1970-February 1971.

File FM 960-J2-8, -1 volume 2.
Solo Food Fair Seibu and Sapporo, Department Store, Sapporo, Japan, March-July 1971.

File FM 950-J2-9, volume 1.
External Trade Promotion Exhibition - Solo Food Show, Japan. July 1970-May 1971.

File FM 950-M12-2, volume 1.
Festival of Penang - Malaysia, 3-31 December 1970 (Pesta '70), September 1970-April 1971.

Box 186.

OSAKA 70 Files from Mr. L.J.Rodger, General Director of Promotional Services.

1. Advisory Committee Meetings.

2. Administration. Volume 1. May 1967-April 1970, volume 2, May 1970-May 1971.

3. Architectural award.

4. Attendance.

5. Auditor General

6. Disposal of Assets.

7. Entertainment.

8. Gift-Emperor.

9. Miscellaneous correspondence. Volume 1, December 1966-June 1969. Volume 2, July 1969-December 1969. Volume 3, January-June 1970. Volume 4, July-December 1970.

Box 187.

1. Official visitors to Osaka, Accommodation for VIPs, Prime Minister's Visit, Mr. Pépin's Visit.

2. Steering Committee - Commissioner General of Section.

3. Report on Canadian Government Participation, Expo '70, Osaka.

4. Miscellaneous Publications.

Accession 85-86/239

Finding aid 20-59.

Industry, Trade and Commerce - Transportation Branch-Ocean Freight- Shipping Conference Tariff Records.

I. Inbound Services Freight tariffs arranged alphabetically by continent, by country or region of a country and therein numerically by tariff numbers.

Box 1-3. ASIA.

1. Japan-Atlantic Canada, 1969-1973.

2. Japan-Pacific Canada, 1969-1979.

Box 4.

3. Japan-United States Pacific, 1965-1976.

II. Outbound Services Freight Tariffs arranged alphabetically by continent, by country or region of a continent, and therein numerically by tariff number.

ASIA

1. Box 20-21. Canada Atlantic India 1961-1978.

2. Box 22-28 Canada Atlantic Japan, 1964-1978.

3. Box 29-35. Canada Pacific Japan, 1966-1974.

4. Box 36-37. United States Atlantic/Gulf Indonesia, 1960-1978.

5. United States Atlantic/Gulf Singapore, 1960-1978.

ITC- Transportation Services Branch. Ocean Freight-Shipping Conference Tariffs. Storage Reference List.

Box 30.
Atlantic & Gulf/Indonesia Freight Conference Tariff 13, 1960-1965.
Atlantic & Gulf/Singapore Freight Conference Tariff 14, 1900-1966.

Box 30-33.
Atlantic & Gulf/Singapore/Malaya/Thailand Freight Conference, Tariff 14, 1966-1971, Tariff 15, 1971-1978.

Box 34-38.

Tariff 223-226, 1966-1976.

Box 51-52.
Atlantic & Gulf/Indonesia Freight Conference, Tariff 14, 1976-1978.

Box 53-54.
Far East Freight Conference, Tariff 27, 1977-1978.

Box 59A-60.
India/Pakistan/Ceylon Freight Conference Tariff 10-13, 1961-1976.

Box 71-72.
Japan West Canada Freight Conference Tariff 1, 1969-1970.

Box 71-73.
Japan East Canada Freight Conference Tariff 1-2, 1969-1973.

Accession 85-86/657.

Finding aid 20-64

Volume 103.

File 2930-THA. Part 13.
Industry, Trade and Commerce. Marketing-Products-Electrical-Tenders-Thailand, September 1979.

File 2930-THA. Part 14.
Industry, Trade and Commerce. Marketing-Products-Electrical-Tenders-Thailand, September-November 1979.

File 2930-THA. Part 15.
Industry, Trade and Commerce. Marketing-Products-Electrical-Tenders-Thailand, November 1979.

File 2930-TUR. Part 1.
Industry, Trade and Commerce. Marketing-Products-Electrical-Tenders-Turkey, March 1976-April 1978.

Volume 104.

File 2935-INDI. Part 1.
Industry, Trade and Commerce. Marketing-Products-Electrical-Tenders-India, July 1976-May 1978.

File 2935-INDI. Part 2.
Industry, Trade and Commerce. Marketing-Products-Electrical-Tenders-India, May 1978-March 1979.

File 2935-INDI. Part 3.
Industry, Trade and Commerce. Marketing-Products-Electrical-Tenders-India, April-December 1979.

Volume 105.

File 2935-INDO. Part 1.
Industry, Trade and Commerce. Marketing-Products-Electrical-Tenders-Indonesia. Commerce. Marketing-Products-Electronics-Instrumentation. Korea. November 1976-August 1978.

File 2935-KOR. Part 2.
Industry, Trade and Commerce. Marketing-Products-Electronics-Instrumentation. Korea, August 1978-April 1979.
File 2935-TUR. Part 1.
Industry, Trade and Commerce. Marketing-Products-Electronics-Instrumentation. Turkey, January 1977-May 1979.

Volume 107.

File 2937-CHIN. Part 1.
Industry, Trade and Commerce. Marketing-Products-Electronics-Telecommunications. China, June 1971-February 1979.

File 2937-CHIN. Part 2.
Industry, Trade and Commerce. Marketing-Products-Electronics-Telecommunications. China, March-November 1979.

File 2937-CHIN/1. Part 1.
Industry, Trade and Commerce. Marketing-Products-

Electronics-Telecommunications. China, Franco-Chinese Telecommunications Agreement. October 1979.

Volume 109.

File 2937-INDI. Part 1.
Industry, Trade and Commerce. Marketing-Products-Electronics-Telecommunications. India, January 1977-June 1978.

File 2937-INDI. Part 2.
Industry, Trade and Commerce. Marketing-Products-Electronics-Telecommunications. India, June 1978-January 1979.

File 2937-INDI. Part 3.
Industry, Trade and Commerce. Marketing-Products-Electronics-Telecommunications. India, December 1978-July 1979.

File 2937-INDI. Part 4.
Industry, Trade and Commerce. Marketing-Products-Electronics-Telecommunications. India, July-December 1979.

File 2937-INDI/1.
Industry, Trade and Commerce. Marketing-Products-Electronics-Telecommunications. India. Raytheon Q77 transistor, July 1979.

File 2937-INDI/1.
Industry, Trade and Commerce. Marketing-Products-Electronics-Telecommunications. India. Polapa II, May 1979.

File 2937-JAPA. Part 1.
Industry, Trade and Commerce. Marketing-Products-Electronics-Telecommunications. Japan, September 1975-March 1978.

File 2937-JAPA. Part 2.
Industry, Trade and Commerce. Marketing-Products-Electronics-Telecommunications. Japan, July 1977-January 1979.

Volume 110.

File 2937-KOR. Part 1.
Industry, Trade and Commerce. Marketing-Products-Electronics-Telecommunications. Korea, October 1975-May 1979.

File 2937-MALAY. Part 1.
Industry, Trade and Commerce. Marketing-Products-Electronics-Telecommunications. Malaysia, October 1976-February 1979.

Volume 111.

File 2937-SIN. Part 3.
Industry, Trade and Commerce. Marketing-Products-Electronics-Telecommunications. Singapore, August-September 1979.

File 2937-SIN. Part 4.
Industry, Trade and Commerce. Marketing-Products-Electronics-Telecommunications. Singapore, October-December 1979.

File 2937-SRI. Part 1.
Industry, Trade and Commerce. Marketing-Products-Electronics-Telecommunications. Sri Lanka, July 1975-February 1978.

File 2937-THA. Part 1.
Industry, Trade and Commerce. Marketing-Products-Electronics-Telecommunications. Thailand, January 1976-March 1978.

File 2937-THA. Part 2.
Industry, Trade and Commerce. Marketing-Products-Electronics-Telecommunications. Thailand, April 1978-February 1979.

Volume 112.

File 2939-IRAN.
Industry, Trade and Commerce. Marketing-Products-Electronics-Airport and Ground Navigation Equipment. Iran, January 1976-March 1978.

File 2939-KOR.
Industry, Trade and Commerce. Marketing-Products-Electronics-Airport and Ground Navigation Equipment. Korea, January 1976-March 1978.

File 2939-SIN. Part 1.
Industry, Trade and Commerce. Marketing-Products-Electronics-Airport Ground Equipment. Singapore, January 1973-March 1977.

File 2945-IRAN.
Industry, Trade and Commerce. Marketing-Consumer Products and Components. Iran, June 1975-April 1979.

Volume 114.

File 2950-JAPA. Part 1.
Industry, Trade and Commerce. Marketing-Industrial cooperation-Japan, April 1976-December 1977.

Accession 85-86/663.

Finding aid 20-60.

Industry, Trade and Commerce records including.

I. Administration and Operational Files 1934-1975 arranged by type therein alphanumerically.

Box 13.
G.A.T.T. File 22/600 volume 19. Japan, December 1971-August 1974.

C.) International Bureau

Box 43.

File 22/600-CPR Volume 19.
Trade Relations(Canadian Trade with) Resource Industries and Construction. China People's Republic of China, October 1974-August 1975.

File 22/600-CPR-1-3. Volume 3.
Trade Relations(Canadian Trade with) Resource Industries and Construction. China People's Republic of China. February 1973-October 1975.

File 22/600-CPR -1-5. Volume 3.
Trade Relations(Canadian Trade with) Resource Industries and Construction. China People's Republic of China, January 1974-October 1975.

File 22/600-CPR-1-8. Volume 4.
Agriculture, Fisheries and Food. China People's Republic, June 1974-June 1975.

File 22/600-CPR-3. Volume 1.
Agriculture Canada - China - Treatment of United States subsidiaries, June 1971-July 1975.

File 22/600-CPR-5. Volume 1.
Agriculture China's relations with Taiwan i Agriculture annual consultations China, People's Republic. December 1973-February 1975.

File 22/600-CPR-6. Volume 5.
Agriculture annual consultations China People's Republic, February-December 1975.

Box 44.

File 22/600-CPR-8. Volume 1.
Trade relations(Canadian trade with) China - Wheat, June 1971-April 1975.

Box 50.

File 22/600-HOK. Volume 3.
Trade relations(Canadian trade with) Hong Kong, March 1974-June 1975.

File 22/600-INA. Volume 13.
Trade relations(Canadian trade with) India, December 1974-March 1975.

File 22/600-INA. Volume 14.
Trade relations(Canadian trade with) India, March-August 1975.

File 22/600-IND. Volume 6.
Trade relations(Canadian trade with) Indonesia, March 1974-April 1975.

Box 51.

File 22/600-IRA. Volume 5.
Trade relations(Canadian trade with) Iran, November 1974-March 1975.

File 22/600-IRA. Volume 6.
Trade relations(Canadian trade with) Iran, April-June 1975.

File 22/600-IRA. Volume 7.
Trade relations(Canadian trade with) Iran, June-July 1975.

File 22/600-IRA. Volume 8.
Trade relations(Canadian trade with) Iran, August-October 1975.

Box 53.

File 22/600-JAP. Volume 17.
Trade relations(Canadian trade with) Japan, August 1974-February 1975.

File 22/600-JAP. Volume 18.
Trade relations(Canadian trade with) Japan, January-March 1975.

File 22/600-JAP. Volume 19.
Trade relations(Canadian trade with) Japan, April-June 1975.

File 22/600-KON. Volume 2. Trade relations(Canadian trade with) Korea-North, February 1973-August 1975.

File 22/600-KOS. Volume 7.
Trade relations(Canadian trade with) Korea-South, February 1974-July 1975.

File 22/600-KOS-1. Volume 1.
Trade relations(Canadian trade with) Korea-South, November 1973-October 1975.

Box 56.

File 22/600-PAK. Volume 5.
Trade relations(Canadian trade with) Pakistan, October 1973-January 1975.

Box 58.

File 22/600-SIK. Volume 1.
Trade relations(Canadian trade with) Sikkim, April 1973-August 1974.

File 22/600-SIN. Volume 2.
Trade relations(Canadian trade with) Singapore, February 1973-August 1975.

Volume 4.
Trade relations(Canadian trade with) Sri Lanka, November 1973-January 1975.

File 22/600-TAI. Volume 5.
Trade relations(Canadian trade with) Taiwan, March 1974-August 1975.

Box 59.

File 22/600-THA. Volume 5.
Trade relations(Canadian trade with) Thailand,

January 1974-May 1975.

File 22/600-TUR. Volume 5.
Trade relations(Canadian trade with) Turkey, November 1973-July 1975.

File 22/600-TUR. Volume 6.
Trade relations(Canadian trade with) Turkey, July-November 1975.

Box 62.

File 22/600-VNN. Volume 1.
Trade relations(Canadian trade with)(Electrical off-set) North Vietnam, January 1973-April 1975.

Box 67.

File 22/611-JAP. Volume 2.
Trade Agreement Negotiations Treaties Japan, July 1974-July 1975.

File 22/611-TAI. Volume 1.
Trade Agreement Negotiations Treaties, Taiwan, August 1971-November 1974.

Box 68.

File 22/611-USA-8. Volume 1.
USA Trade Agreements with Sino-Soviet Bloc general, May 1973.

File 22/611-USA-8-1. Volume 1.
USA Trade Agreements with Sino-Soviet Bloc general. China People's Republic of, February-March 1973.

Box 71.

File 22/635-1-ASI. Volume 1.
Export and Import controls Asia, July 1971-August 1975.

File 22/635-1-HOK. Volume 1.
Export and Import controls Hong Kong, August 1971-October 1975.

File 22/635-1-KOS. Volume 1.
Export and Import controls Korea, South, May 1971-July 1975.

D.) Industrial Policy

Box 84.

File 23/720-1-11. Volume 2.
Instrument Questionnaire. Japanese Industrial Policy, June 1970-November 1972.

Box 89.

File 23/974-JAPA. Volume 8.
Foreign Countries. Japan, November 1974-May 1975.

File 23/974-JAPA. Volume 9.
Foreign Countries. Japan, June 1975.

File 23/974-JAPA-1. Volume 7.
Foreign Countries. Japan, December 1974-March 1975.

File 23/974-JAPA-1. Volume 8.
Foreign Countries. Japan, November 1974.

E.) Grain Marketing

Box 96.

File 40A/720-BAN. Volume 5.
Markets and Programs Grains. Flour Report Issued by Wheat Board. Bangladesh, November 1974-June 1975.

File 40A/720-CHIN. Volume 5.
Markets and Programs Grains. Flour Report Issued by Wheat Board. China, October 1974-March 1975.

Box 97.

File 40A/720-INDI .Volume 5.
Markets and Programs Grains. India, January-June 1975.

File 40A/720-INDI. Volume 6.
Markets and Programs Grains. India, June-September 1975.

File 40A/720-INDI. Volume 7.
Markets and Programs Grains. India, September-October 1975.

File 40A/720-IRAN. Volume 1.
Markets and Programs Grains. Iran, January 1973-May 1975.

Box 98.

File 40A/720-JAP. Volume 5.
Markets and Programs Grains. Japan, October 1974-May 1975.

File 40A/720-JAP. Volume 6.
Markets and Programs Grains. Japan. April-November 1975.

File 40A/720-KOR(N). Volume 1.
Markets and Programs Grains. Korea North, January 1973-January 1975.

File 40A/720-KOR(S). Volume 2.
Markets and Programs Grains. Korea South, July 1973-November 1975.

File 40A/720-PAK. Volume 3.
Markets and Programs Grains. Pakistan, March 1974-May 1975.

File 40A/720-PAK. Volume 4.
Markets and Programs Grains. Pakistan, June-December 1975.

Box 99.

File 40A/720-TUR. Volume 1.
Markets and Programs Grains. Turkey, January 1973-September 1975.

Box 100.

File 40A/721-BAN volume 1.
Markets for Oilseeds. Bangladesh, January 1973-March 1975.

G.) Aerospace, Marine and Rail

Box 151.

File 42/968-19. Volume 1.
Ocean Expo '75 - Okinawa Japan, February 1972-March 1974.

N.) Agriculture, Fisheries and Food Products

Box 168.

File 49/610-10. Volume 1.
Canada-Japan Trade Matters, March 1972-March 1974.

File 49/610-10. Volume 2.
Canada-Japan Trade Matters, June 1974-November 1975.

Box 169.

File 49/721-90-11. Volume 1.
Livestock-Korea, January 1974-December 1975.

S.) Regional Bureau

Box 183.

File 60/110-2. Volume 1.
Japan Industrial Location Centre Mission to Canada -9-26 June 1975(JILC), April-October 1975.

T.) Science and Technology

Box 188.

File 61/610-16. Volume 5.
Science and Technology International Sphere - countries Japan- general, October 1974 to January 1975.

File 61/610-16. Volume 6.
Science and Technology International Sphere - countries Japan- general, January-April 1975.

File 61/610-16. Volume 7.
Science and Technology International Sphere - countries Japan- general, April-June 1975.

File 61/610-16. Volume 8.
Science and Technology International Sphere - countries Japan- general, July-August 1975.

File 61/610-16. Volume 9.
Science and Technology International Sphere - countries Japan- general, August-September 1975.

File 61/610-16. Volume 10.
Science and Technology International Sphere - countries Japan- general, September-October 1975.

Box 189.

File 67/115-73-CAN-295 1.
Incoming Mission from Indonesia "Airports for Export" October-November 1973. May 1973-January 1975.

V.) Fairs and Missions

Box 226.

File 67/116-2-4(75/76).Volume 1.
Buyer from Hong Kong - Food, November 1975. October-December 1975.

File 67/116-2-5(74/75). Volume 1.
Buyers from Oil and Natural Gas Commission(ONGE) India, May 1974, September 1973-February 1975.

File 67/116-2-9(74/75). Volume 1.
Incoming Buyers from Philippines. Forestry Processing Equipment, October 1974, February 1974-February 1975.

File 67/116-2-10(74/75). Volume 1.
Incoming Buyers from Philippines. Mining Products, pre-November 1974, February 1974-February 1975.

File 67/116-2-12(74/75). Volume 1.
Buyers from Indonesia. Indonesian Power Corporation, May-June 1974.

File 67/116-2-14(74/75). Volume 1.
Buyers from Indonesia. Forestry Equipment, June-July 1974. March 1974-February 1975.

File 67/116-3-1(75/76). Volume 1.
Delegate from University and Polytechnic Grants Committee of Hong Kong, July 1975, June 1974-February 1975.

File 67/116-3-2(75/76). Volume 1.
Delegation from Chin - and Paper, April-May 1974, March 1974-February 1975.

File 67/116-3-3(72/74). Volume 1.
Delegate - Miss Thanya Ruatong of Department of Teacher Training Bangkok, Thailand, August 1973-February 1974.

File 67/116-3-4(75/76). Volume 1.
Delegates from Ministry of the Environment- Hong Kong & China Light Power Co. Ltd, May 1975-July 1975.

File 67/116-3-6(73/74). Volume 1.

Delegate - Mr. Au Man-ho, Civil Aviation Department, Hong Kong, October 1973-March 1974.

File 67/116-3-6(75/76). Volume 1.
Delegates from Indonesian State Electricity Corporation, 6-7 May 1975. April-May 1975.

File 67/116-3-9(75/76). Volume 1.
Delegate from Japan-STOL Promotion, June 1975.

File 67/116-3-11(74/75). Volume 1.
Delegation from Iranian Coast Guard, 1974, June 1974-November 1975.

File 67/116-3-13(75/76). Volume 1.
Delegation from China Geophysical Equipment, 1975, September-October 1975.

File 67/116-3-15(75/76). Volume 1.
Delegation from Hong Kong- Secretary from Ministry of the Environment, August 1975, July -October 1975.

File 67/116-3-18(74/75). Volume 1.
Delegation from Iran Admiral Ardalan Aide 1974, July 1974-January 1975.

Box 227.

File 67/116-3-30(74/75). Volume 1.
Delegation from Ministry of Agriculture, Korea, November 1974, October 1974-January 1975.

File 67/116-3-33(74/75). Volume 1.
Delegates from Japan -STOL, February 1975, January-July 1975.

File 67/116-4-1(73/74). Volume 1.
EOTP. Engineers from Japan, Australia and Israel to Instronics, June-August 1973.

File 67/116-4-1(74/75). Volume 1.
EOTP. Outboard Marine Corporation, Training and Japanese Tech., June 1974, August 1973-January 1975.

File 67/116-4-9(74/75). Volume 1.
EOTP. H.A.Brown, Don Mills - Trainee from Japan, January-February 1975, October 1974-January 1975.

File 67/116-4-1(75/76). Volume 1.
EOTP. Stacpoole Machinery, Scarborough, Training from Japan, September 1975. September 1975.

File 67/116-6-74-649. Volume 4.
Electronics and Scientific Instruments Exhibition, Shanghai, 16-26 April 1974. Volume 3, December 1973, February 1974, March-July 1974.

File 67/116-6-74-666. Volume 1.
Supermarket promotion, Japan, 1974-1975, April 1973-October 1975.

File 67/116-6-74-750. Volume 1.
International Restaurant Fair: Tokyo, 5-8 August 197, November 1973-August 1974.

File 67/116-6-74-792. Volume 1.
Catalogue Show of Forestry Products, Philippines, pre August 1974, March 1974-February 1975.

Box 228.

File 67/116-6-74-793. Volume 1.
Catalogue Show of Mining Products, Philippines, pre December 1974, February 1974-October 1975.

File 67/116-6-74-907. Volume 1.
Turkish Geophysical Society(Information Booth) Ankara, Turkey, January 1975, May 1974-February 1975.

File 67/116-6-75-046. Volume 1.
International Restaurant Equipment Fair, Tokyo, 1975, November 1973-March 1975.

File 67/116-6-75-046. Volume 2.
International Restaurant Equipment Fair, Tokyo, 1975. September 1975,

File 67/116-6-75-083. Volume 1.
Tehran International Trade Fair, Iran, September 1975, December 1973-February 1975.

File 67/116-7-74-714. Volume 1.
Canadian STOL Mission from Japan, September 1974, November 1973-October 1975.

Box 229.

File 67/116-7-74-730. Volume 3.
Outgoing Consulting Engineering Mission to China-June 1974, May 1974-April 1975.

File 67/116-7-74-913. Volume 1.
Incoming Mission from Japan-Auto Services Equipment, March 1975, July-November 1974 .

File 67/116-7-74-931. Volume 1.
Mission from China. Canada-China Joint Trade Committee(JTC), February 1975, February-April 1975.

File 67/116-7-75-236. Volume 1.
Ministerial Mission to South East Asia, February-March 1976, September-December 1975.

File 67/116-7-75-359. Volume 1.
Canada - Iran Joint Economic Commission - Mission from Iran, July 1975, April-July 1975.

File 67/116-7-75-359. Volume 2.
Canada/Iran Joint Economic Commission - Mission from Iran, July 1975, July-November 1975.

X.) Trade Commissioner Services.

Box 241.

File 72/700-6-1-4. Volume 1.
ICER Selection Criteria, Asia and the Pacific, March 1971-July 1975.

Z.) Tourism

Box 248.

File 79/101-66. Volume 1.
Individual fairs and Exhibitions, Okinawa, Japan. International Ocean Exposition, 1975-1976, September 1974-October 1975.

Box 249.

File 79/216-10. Volume 1.
Promotions General, 10th Anniversary, Tokyo, April-December 1974.

Box 263.

File 79/968-13(74). Volume 1.
Conference Pacific Area Travel Association-Indonesia, April 1974-January 1975.

Accession 85-86/665.

Finding aid 20-62.

Box 6.

File 20-28-I2. Volume 1.
GATT tariff negotiations with Indonesia, May 1965-November 1970.

File 20-28-I3. Volume 1.
GATT tariff negotiations with India, April 1962-April 1970.

File 20-28-J2. Volume 4.
GATT tariff negotiations with Japan, January 1967-August 1970.

Box 70.

File 20-28-J2. Volume 5.
GATT tariff negotiations by Japan, January-April 1971.

File 10-28-K1. Volume 1.
General Agreement on Tariffs and Trade Korea, May 1966-May 1971.

File 20-28-P1. Volume 1.
GATT tariff negotiations by Pakistan, June-November 1969.

File 20-28-T3. Volume 2.
GATT tariff negotiations by Turkey, May 1965-July 1969.

Box 8.

File 20-141-A6. Volume 1.
Grain and Flour -Afghanistan, November 1965-October 1972.

Box 9.

File 20-141-B16. Volume 1.
Grain and Flour -Burma, July 1970-June 1972.

File 20-141-B17. Volume 1.
Grain and Flour Bangladesh(East Pakistan). January-December 1972.

File 20-141-C1. Volume 2.
Grain and Flour- Ceylon, January-December 1972.

File 20-141-C3. Volume 7.
Grain and Flour- China, June 1971-May 1972.

File 20-141-C3. Volume 8.
Grain and Flour -China, June-December 1972.

File 20-141-C14. Volume 1.
Grain and Flour Cambodia, December 1971-June 1972.

Box 10.

File 20-141-G8. Volume 1.
Grain and Flour Guyana, June 1968- December 1972.

Box 11.

File 20-141-H5. Volume 1.
Grain and Flour Hong Kong, June 1963- October 1972.

File 20-141-I2. Volume 1.
Grain and Flour Indonesia, May 1964- October 1972.

File 20-141-I3. Volume 2.
Grain and Flour India, April 1966- January 1972.

File 20-141-I3. Volume 3.
Grain and Flour- India, February- December 1972.

File 20-141-I5. Volume 1.
Grain and Flour -Iran, August 1960-December 1972.

File 20-141-J2. volume 3.
Grain and Flour -Japan, July 1969-November 1972.

Box 12.

File 20-141-K1. Volume 1.
Grain and Flour -Korea South, October 1963-May 1972.

File 20-141-K2. Volume 1.
Grain and Flour -Korea North, December 1970-December 1972.

File 20-141-N 9. Volume 1.
Grain and Flour-Nepal, June 1966-August 1972.

File 20-141-P1. Volume 3.
Grain and Flour-Pakistan, June 1971-November 1972.

File 20-141-P5. Volume 2.
Grain and Flour -Philippines, October 1970-September

1972.

Box 13.

File 20-141-S1. Volume 1.
Grain and Flour -Singapore, June 1966-October 1972.

File 20-141-T1. Volume 1.
Grain and Flour -Trinidad and Tobago, October 1965-October 1972.

Box 14.

File 20-141-V4. Volume 1.
Grain and Flour -Vietnam, November 1963-July 1972.

File 20-265-3. Volume 1.
Canadian foreign policy review - Pacific and Asia, July 1969-May 1970.

File 20-265-3. Volume 2
Canadian foreign policy review - Pacific and Asia, March-May 1971.

File 20-265-C3. Volume 5.
Canadian China policy, November 1969-October 1970.

File 20-265-C3. Volume 6.
Canadian China policy, October-November 1970.

Box 47.

Visit by Hon. R.H.Winters-London, The Hague, Rome, Tehran and New Delhi, 1968.

Report by the Canadian Delegation to the Second Session of the United Nations Conference of Trade and Development, 1 February-29 March 1968, New Delhi.

Box 50.

Briefs and References Department, Industry, Trade and Commerce, 1966-1972.

Meeting of the India Consortium, 22 and 23 May 1969.

Asian Development Bank, Second Annual Board of Governors Meeting, Sydney, Australia, 10-12 April 1969.

Meeting of the Pakistan Consortium, 19 and 20 May 1969.

Canada-Japan Ministerial Committee Meeting, Tokyo, 17 and 18 April 1969.

Canada-Japan Ministerial Committee Meeting, 17-18 April 1969, Counterpart discussions -Talking points.

Accession 85-86/667.

Finding aid 20-65.

Volume 103.

File 2930-THA Part 13.
Industry, Trade and Commerce, Marketing-Products-Electrical-Tenders-Thailand, September1979.

File 2930-THA Part 14.
Industry, Trade and Commerce, Marketing-Products-Electrical-Tenders-Thailand, September-November 1979.

File 2930-THA Part 15.
Industry, Trade and Commerce, Marketing-Products-Electrical-Tenders-Thailand, November 1979.

File 2930-TUR Part 1.
Industry, Trade and Commerce, Marketing-Products-Electrical-Tenders-Turkey, March 1976-April 1978.

Volume 104.

File 2935-INDI Part 1.
Industry, Trade and Commerce, Marketing-Products-Electronics-Instrumentation-India, July 1976-May 1978.

File 2935-INDI Part 2.
Industry, Trade and Commerce, Marketing-Products-Electronics-Instrumentation-India, May 1978-March 1979.

File 2935-INDI Part 3.
Industry, Trade and Commerce, Marketing-Products-Electronics-Instrumentation-India, April-December 1979.

Box 105.

File 2935-IND0 Part 1.
Industry, Trade and Commerce, Marketing-Products-Electronics-Instrumentation-Indonesia, December1975-November 1979.

File 2935-KOR Part 1.
Industry, Trade and Commerce, Marketing-Products-Electronics-Instrumentation-Korea, November 1976-August 1978.

File 2935-KOR Part 2.
Industry, Trade and Commerce, Marketing-Products-Electronics-Instrumentation-Korea, August 1978-April 1979.

File 2935-TUR Part 1.
Industry, Trade and Commerce, Marketing-Products-Electronics-Instrumentation-Turkey, January 1977-May 1979.

Box 107.

File 2937-CHIN Part 1.
Industry, Trade and Commerce, Marketing-Products-Electronics-Telecommunications-China, June 1971-February 1979.

File 2937-CHIN Part 2.
Industry, Trade and Commerce, Marketing-Products-Electronics-Telecommunications-China, March-November 1979.

File 2937-CHIN Part 1.
Industry, Trade and Commerce, Marketing-Products-Electronics-Telecommunications-China. Franco-Chinese Telecommunications Agreement, October 1979.

Box 109.

File 2937-INDI Part 1.
Industry, Trade and Commerce, Marketing-Products-Electronics-Telecommunications-India, January 1977-June1978.

File 2937-INDI Part 2.
Industry, Trade and Commerce, Marketing-Products-Electronics-Telecommunications-India, June 1978-January 1979.

File 2937-INDI Part 3.
Industry, Trade and Commerce, Marketing-Products-Electronics-Telecommunications-India, December 1978-July1979.

File 2937-INDI Part 4.
Industry, Trade and Commerce, Marketing-Products-Electronics-Telecommunications-India, July-December 1979.

File 2937-INDI/1.
Industry, Trade and Commerce, Marketing-Products-Electronics-Telecommunications-India, Raytheon Q77 transistor. July1979.

File 2937-INDO/1.
Industry, Trade and Commerce, Marketing-Products-Electronics-Telecommunications-Indonesia, Polapa II. May 1979.

File 2937-JAPA Part 1.
Industry, Trade and Commerce, Marketing-Products-Electronics-Telecommunications-Japan, September 1935-March 1978.

Box 110.

File 2937-KOR Part 1.
Industry, Trade and Commerce, Marketing-Products-Electronics-Telecommunications-Korea, July 1975-May 1979.

File 2937-MALAY Part 1.
Industry, Trade and Commerce, Marketing-Products-Electronics-Telecommunications-Malaysia, October 1975-October 1979.

Box 111.

File 2937-SIN Part 3.
Industry, Trade and Commerce, Marketing-Products-Electronics-Telecommunications-Singapore, August-September 1979.

File 2937-SIN Part 1.
Industry, Trade and Commerce, Marketing-Products-Electronics-Telecommunications-Singapore, October-December 1979.

File 2937-SRI Part 1.
Industry, Trade and Commerce, Marketing-Products-Electronics-Telecommunications-Singapore, July1975-February 1978.

File 2937-THA Part 1.
Industry, Trade and Commerce, Marketing-Products-Electronics-Telecommunications-Thailand, January 1976-March 1978.

File 2937-THA Part 2.
Industry, Trade and Commerce, Marketing-Products-Electronics-Telecommunications-Thailand, April 1978-February 1979.

Box 112.

File 2939-KOR.
Industry, Trade and Commerce, Marketing-Products-Electronics-airport and ground navigation equipment-Korea, March-May1973.

Accession 87-88/061.

Finding aid 20-75.

Box 1.

File 58/800-20-2-1 Part 1.
Financing -Area Projects-South Pacific Islands, 1977.

File 58/800-AFG Part 1.
Financing-Afghanistan -general, 1976-1977.

File 58/800-AFG-1 Part 1.
Financing-Afghanistan -Bilateral Projects, 1975-1978.

File 58/800-AFG-2 Part 1.
Financing-Afghanistan -Multilateral Projects, 1975-1978.

Box 2.

File 58/800-BAN Part 1.
Financing-Bangladesh -general, 1977-1978.

File 58/800-BAN-1 Part 1.
Financing-Bangladesh -Bilateral Projects, 1976-1978.

File 58/800-BAN-2 Part 1.
Financing-Bangladesh -Multilateral Projects, 1976-1978.

Box 3.

File 58/800-BURM Part 1.

Financing-Burma -general, 1976-1978.

File 58/800-BURM Part 2.
Financing-Burma -general, 1978.

File 58/800-BURM -1 Part 1.
Financing-Burma -Bilateral Projects, 1976-1978.

File 58/800-BURM -2 Part 1.
Financing-Burma -Multilateral Projects, 1976-1978.

File 58/800-BSOL-2 Part 1.
Financing-British Solomon Islands -Multilateral Projects, 1976-1977.

Box 4.

File 58/800-CHIN Part 1.
Financing-China(People's Republic of) -general, 1976-1978.

File 58/800-CHIN-1 Part 1.
Financing-China(People's Republic of) -Bilateral Projects, 1977-1978.

File 58/800-CHIN-2 Part 1.
Financing-China(People's Republic of) -Multilateral Projects, 1977-1978.

File 58/800-CYP Part 1.
Financing-Cyprus -general, 1977-1978.

File 58/800-CYP-1 Part 1.
Financing-Cyprus -Bilateral Projects, 1977.

File 58/800-CYP-2 Part 1.
Financing-Cyprus -Multilateral Projects, 1976-1977.

File 58/800-FIJ Part 1.
Financing-Fiji -general, 1977-1978.

Box 5.

File 58/800-FIJ-1 Part 1.
Financing-Fiji -Bilateral Projects, 1977-1978.

File 58/800-FIJ-2 Part 1.
Financing-Fiji -Multilateral Projects, 1977.

Box 6.

File 58/800-GIL Part 1.
Financing-Gilbert and Ellice Islands -general, 1976.

File 58/800-GIL Part 2.
Financing-Gilbert and Ellice Islands -Multilateral Projects, 1976.

File 58/800-GUY. Part 1.
Financing-Guyana -general, 1976-1977.

File 58/800-GUY.-1 Part 1.
Financing-Guyana -Bilateral Projects, 1977-1978

File 58/800-GUY.-2 Part 1.
Financing-Guyana -Multilateral Projects, 1976-1978

Box 7.

File 58/800-HONG. Part 1.
Financing-Hong Kong -general, 1977-1978.

File 58/800-HONG.-1 Part 1.
Financing-Hong Kong -Bilateral Projects, 1976-1978.

File 58/800-HONG.-2 Part 1.
Financing-Hong Kong -Multilateral Projects, 1976-1977.

File 58/800-INDI Part 1.
Financing-India -general, 1976-1978.

File 58/800-INDI-1 Part 1.
Financing-India -Bilateral Projects, 1977.

File 58/800-INDI-1 Part 2.
Financing-India -Bilateral Projects, 1977-1978.

File 58/800-INDI-2 Part 1.
Financing-India -Multilateral Projects, 1976-1977.

File 58/800-INDI-2 Part 2.
Financing-India -Multilateral Projects, 1977-1978.

File 58/800-INDO Part 1.
Financing-Indonesia -general, 1976-1978.

File 58/800-INDO-1 Part 4.
Financing-Indonesia -Bilateral Projects, 1977-1978.

File 58/800-INDO-1 Part 5.
Financing-Indonesia -Bilateral Projects, 1977-1978.

Box 8.

File 58/800-INDO-2 Part 1.
Financing-Indonesia -Multilateral Projects, 1976-1978.

File 58/800-IRAN Part 1.
Financing-Iran -general, 1976-1978.

File 58/800-IRAN-1 Part 1.
Financing-Iran -Bilateral Projects, 1976-1977.

File 58/800-IRAN-2 Part 1.
Financing-Iran -Multilateral Projects, 1977.

Box 10.

File 58/800-NEP Part 1.
Financing-Nepal -general, 1976-1978.

File 58/800-NEP-1 Part 1.
Financing-Nepal -Bilateral Projects, 1976-1977.

Box 11.

File 58/800-NEP-2 Part 1.
Financing-Nepal -Multilateral Projects, 1976-1978.

File 58/800-NEP-2 Part 2.
Financing-Nepal -Multilateral Projects, 1978.

File 58/800-PAK Part 1.
Financing-Pakistan -general, 1975-1978.

File 58/800-PAK-1 Part 2.
Financing-Pakistan -Bilateral Projects, 1977-1978.

File 58/800-PAK-1 Part 3.
Financing-Pakistan -Bilateral Projects, 1978.

File 58/800-PAK-2 Part 1.
Financing-Pakistan -Multilateral Projects, 1975-1978.

File 58/800-PAK-2 Part 2.
Financing-Pakistan -Multilateral Projects, 1978.

File 58/800-PAK-2-1 Part 3.
Financing-Pakistan -Multilateral Projects-Tarbela Project, 1976-1978.

File 58/800-PAK-2-1 Part 4.
Financing-Pakistan-Multilateral Projects-Tarbela Project, 1976-1978.

File 58/800-PAK-2 Part 2.
Financing-Pakistan -Multilateral Projects 500kv Transmission Line, 1976-1978.

Box 12.

File 58/800-PHI Part 1.
Financing-Philippines-general, 1976-1978.

File 58/800-PHI-1 Part 1.
Financing-Philippines -Bilateral Projects, 1976-1978.

File 58/800-PHI-1 Part 2.
Financing-Philippines -Bilateral Projects, 1978.

File 58/800-PHI-2 Part 1.
Financing-Philippines -Multilateral Projects, 1976-1978.

File 58/800-PNG Part 1.
Financing-Papua New Guinea -general, 1976-1978.

File 58/800-PNG-1 Part 1.
Financing-Papua New Guinea -Bilateral Projects, 1976-1978.

File 58/800-PNG-2 Part 1.
Financing-Papua New Guinea -Multilateral Projects, 1976-1978.

Box 13.

File 71/101-10 Part 1.
Tehran International Trade Fair, Iran. 18-31 October 1976, 1976-1977.

File 71/101-16 Part 1.
Tehran International Trade Fair -1978, 1978.

File 71/101-IRAN Part 1.
Fairs and Exhibitions -Iran, 1978.

Box 14.

File 71/112-THA Part 1.
Missions and Visits -Outgoing from Canada -Thailand, 1978.

File 71/400-2-JAPA Part 1.
Transportation Systems Japan, 1978.

File 71/400-3-AFG Part 1.
Transportation Systems -Rail -Afghanistan, 1978.

File 71/400-3-INDI Part 1.
Transportation Systems -Rail -India, 1978.

File 71/400-3-PAK Part 1.
Transportation Systems -Rail -Pakistan, 1977-1978.

File 71/400-4-FIJI Part 1.
Transportation Systems -Road-Fiji, 1978.

File 71/400-4-PAK Part 1.
Transportation Systems -Road-Pakistan, 1978.

Box 15.

File 71/700-BSOL Part 1.
General Information -British Solomon Islands, 1978.

File 71/700-4-NEP Part 1.
General Information -Nepal, 1978.

File 71/700-4-NGUI Part 1.
General Information -New Guinea, 1976.

Box 16.

File 71/704-2-5 Part 1.
Mining Program -Area-Asia and Far East, 1971-1977.

File 71/704-AFG Part 1.
Mining Program -Afghanistan, 1978.
File 71/704-BAN Part 1.
Mining Program -Bangladesh, 1978.

File 71/704-NGUI Part 1.
Mining Program -New Guinea(Australian Mandate), 1977.

File 71/704-PAK Part 1.
Mining Program -Pakistan, 1976-1978.

File 71/704-SRI Part 1.
Mining Program -Sri Lanka, 1978.

File 71/704-VIE Part 1.
Mining Program -Vietnam, 1978.

File 71/705-BURM Part 1.
Forest Industry -Area -Burma, 1976-1978.

Box 17

File 71/705-NEP Part 1.
Forest Industry -Area -Nepal, 1977.

File 71/705-PAK Part 1.
Forest Industry -Area -Pakistan, 1977-1978.

File 71/705-PAP Part 1.
Forest Industry -Area -Papua(New Guinea), 1976-1978.

File 71/705-PHI Part 1.
Forest Industry -Area -Philippines, 1976-1978.

File 71/705-SRI Part 1.
Forest Industry -Area -Sri Lanka, 1977.

File 71/706-HONG Part 1.
Oil and Gas Industry -Area -Hong Kong, 1978.

File 71/706-JAPA Part 1.
Oil and Gas Industry -Area -Japan, 1976.

File 71/709-SIN Part 1.
Port Development -Singapore, 1974-1977.

File 71/710-AFG Part 1.
Industrial Programs and Projects -General Information -Afghanistan, 1977-1978.

File 71/710-BAN Part 1.
Industrial Programs and Projects -General Information -Bangladesh, 1978.

File 71/710-JAPA Part 1.
Industrial Programs and Projects -General Information -Japan, 1978.

File 71/710-MALAY Part 1.
Industrial Programs and Projects -General Information -Malaysia, 1976-1978.

File 71/710-NEP Part 1.
Industrial Programs and Projects -General Information -Nepal, 1976-1977.

File 71/710-TAI Part 1.
Industrial Programs and Projects -General Information -Taiwan, Formosa, 1978.

File 71/712-IRAN Part 1.
Chemical Industry-Iran, 1977-1978.

File 71/712-MALAY Part 1.
Chemical Industry-Malaysia. 1976.

File 71/712-PHI Part 1.
Chemical Industry-Philippines, n.d.

File 71/714-AFG Part 1.
Water and Sewerage. Afghanistan, 1978.

File 71/714-BURM Part 1.
Water and Sewerage. Burma, 1978.

Box 18.

File 71/715-2-7 Part 1.
Agro Industry-Area -Asia and Far East, 1974-1978.

File 71/715-BSOL Part 1.
Agro Industry-Area -British Solomon Islands, 1977.

File 71/715-BUR Part 1.
Agro Industry-Area -Burma, 1977.

File 71/715-JAPA Part 1.
Agro Industry-Area -Japan, 1976-1977.

File 71/715-Part 1.
Agro Industry-Area -New Guinea(Australian Administration), 1976.

File 71/730-IRAN Part 1.
Airborne -Ground Surveys and Service-Iran, 1976-1977.

File 71/730-PAK Part 1.
Airborne -Ground Surveys and Service -Pakistan, 1976.

File 71/733-SRI Part 1.
Housing -Sri Lanka, 1978.

Box 19.

File 71/734-TUR Part 1.
Tire Industry -Turkey, 1977-1978.
File 71/735-AFG Part 1.
Power Industry -Afghanistan, 1978.

File 71/735-BAN Part 1.
Power Industry -Bangladesh, 1977-1978.

File 71/735-NGUI Part 1.
Power Industry -New Guinea(Australian Administration), 1977.
File 71/735-TRI Part 1.
Power Industry -Trinidad and Tobago, 1978.

File 71/736-INDI Part 1.
Telecommunications Systems -India, 1978.

File 71/736-NEP Part 1.
Telecommunications Systems -Nepal, 1978.

File 71/736-PAK Part 1.
Telecommunications Systems -Pakistan, 1978.

File 71/766-2-8 Part 14.
Social -Commodities -Area -Asia and Far East, 1977-1978.

File 71/767-AFG Part 1.
Social -Projects -General Information Afghanistan, 1978.

File 71/767-BAN Part 1.
Social -Projects -General Information -Bangladesh, 1978.

File 71/767-TUR Part 1.
Social -Projects -General Information -Turkey, 1978.

File 71/767-GUY -2 Part 1.
Second World Bank Education Project -Guyana, 1975-1976.

File 71/767-INDO-4 Part 1.
Social -Surabaya Institute of Technology(Asia Development Bank Education Project) -Indonesia, 1974-1976.

File 71/767-INDO-5 Part 1.
Social -Fourth World Bank Education Project -Indonesia, 1975-1978.

Box 20.

File 71/767-KOR(S)-4 Part 1.
Social -Third World Bank Education Project -Korea, South, 1975-1978.

File 71/767-SIN-1 Part 1.
Social -$9.5M IBRD Loan for Higher Technical Education -Singapore, 1976-1978.

File 71/767-THA-2 Part 1.
Social -Third World Bank Education Project: Thailand, 1972-1978.

File 71/777-2-2 Part 4.
Commercial -Market Date -Area -Asia and Far East, 1975-1976.

Box 21

File 71/779-NEP Part 1.
Commercial -Projects -General Information-Nepal, 1978.

File 71/779-PAP Part 1.
Commercial -Projects -General Information-Papua New Guinea, 1976.

Box 22.

File 71/779-INDI-2 Part 1.
Commercial -Projects -Joint Venture -Stadium Complex -India, 1976-1977.

File 71/779-IRAN-2 Part 1.
Commercial -Projects -C.P Hotel -500-600 Rooms- Tehran -Iran, 1975-1976.

File 71/779-IRAN-6 Part 1.
Commercial -Projects -Pahlavi Hotel Project-Iran, 1975-1976.

File 71/779-IRAN-7 Part 1.
Commercial -Projects -Olympic Village Motel Complex -Iran, 1975-1976.

File 71/779-IRAN-8 Part 1.
Commercial -Projects -Stock Exchange -Tehran -Iran, 1975.

File 71/779-IRAN-9 Part 1.
Commercial -Projects -400 Room Hotel and Casino -Abadan -Iran, 1976.

File 71/779-IRAN-10 Part 1.
Commercial -Projects -Bushire Hotel -240 Rooms -Bushire -Iran, 1976.

File 71/779-IRAN-11 Part 1.
Commercial -Projects -1000 Room Luxury Hotel -The Tehran Oberoi Hotel -Iran, 81978.

File 71/779-IRAN-12 Part 1.
Commercial -Projects -Proposed Establishment of Coast Guard in Iran -Iran, 1974-1978.

File 71/779-IRAN-12 Part 1A.
Commercial -Projects -Proposed Establishment of Coast Guard in Iran -Iranian Coast Guard File -Iran, 1975.

File 71/779-PAK-2 Part 1.
Commercial -Projects -Hotel Zainab -Karachi City -Pakistan, 1975-1976.

File 71/779-PHI-3 Part 1.
Commercial -Projects -Beach Resort Hotel Philippines, 1977.

Box 23.
File 71/779-THA-1 Part 1.
Commercial -Projects -World Bank Tourism Study -Phuket -Thailand, 1976-1977.

File 71/779-TRI-6 Part 1.
Commercial -Projects -North Oropouche Water Project -Trinidad and Tobago, 1976-1977.

File 71/779-TUIR-2 Part 1.
Commercial -Projects -Hotel Management Contracts -Turkey, 1976.

Box 24.

File 71/780-BAN Part 1.
Airports for export Program -Bangladesh, 1974-1978.

Box 25.

File 71/780-HONG Part 3.
Airports for Export Program -Hong Kong, 1978.

File 71/780-INDI Part 1.
Airports for Export Program -India, 1971-1977.

File 71/780-IRAN Part 2.
Airports for Export Program -Iran, 1975-1978.

File 71/780-JAPA Part 2.

Airports for Export Program -Philippines, 1975-1978.

Box 26.

File 71/780-HONG.
Airports for Export Program -Hong Kong, 1978.

Accession 87-88/062

Finding aid 20-69.

First part of finding aid lists a group of confidential files on trade negotiations, mostly ranging from 1971-1977, and recommended for destruction in December 1985. The second part of the finding aid records the following files in microform and relating to Asia:

Box 27.

File 24/970.
Companies -C.Itoh and Co.(Canada) Ltd., 1977.

Box 29.

File 24/971 HONG Part 1.
Economic Reports -Hong Kong, 1969-1973.

File 24/971 HONG Part 2.
Economic Reports -Hong Kong, 1973-1974.

File 24/971 HONG Part 3.
Economic Reports -Hong Kong, 1974-1975.

File 24/971-JPN Part 1.
Economic Reports -Japan, 1967-1971.

File 24/971-JPN Part 2.
Economic Reports -Japan, 1971.

File 24/971-JPN Part 3.
Economic Reports -Japan, 1971-1972.

File 24/971-JPN Part 4.
Economic Reports -Japan, 1972.

File 24/971-JPN Part 5.
Economic Reports -Japan, 1972.

File 24/971-JPN Part 6.
Economic Reports -Japan, 1972-1973.

File 24/971-JPN Part 7.

Economic Reports -Japan, 1973.

File 24/971-JPN Part 8.
Economic Reports -Japan, 1973.

File 24/971-JPN Part 9.
Economic Reports -Japan, 1973.

File 24/971-JPN Part 10.
Economic Reports -Japan, 1974.

File 24/971-JPN Part 11.
Economic Reports -Japan, 1974-1975.

File 24/971-JPN Part 12.
Economic Reports -Japan, 1975-1976.

File 24/971-1 Part 1.
Economic Reports -Canada-Japan Ministerial Meeting, 1971-1972.

File 24/971-KOR(S) Part 1.
Economic Reports -Korea -Republic of, 1970-1972.

File 24/971-KOR(S) Part 1.
Economic Reports -Korea -Republic of, 1973-1976.

Accession 87-88/063.

Finding aid 20-76.

Box 11.

File 4770-INDI Part 1.
Markets -India 1976-1978e.

File 4770-JAPA Part 1.
Markets -Japan 1978.

Box 12.

File 4850-CHIN. Part 1.
Marine and Rail Industries -Markets -Marine -China, 1976-1978.
Box 13.

File 4850-INDI. Part 1.
Marine and Rail Industries -Markets -Marine -India, 1974-1976.

File 4850-INDI. Part 2.
Marine and Rail Industries -Markets -Marine -India, 1977-1978.

Box 14.

File 4850-IND0. Part 1.
Marine and Rail Industries -Markets -Marine -Indonesia, 1974-1975.

File 4850-IND0. Part 2.
Marine and Rail Industries -Markets -Marine -Indonesia, 1976.

File 4850-IND0. Part 3.
Marine and Rail Industries -Markets -Marine -Indonesia, 1976-1977.

File 4850-JAPA. Part 1.
Marine and Rail Industries -Markets -Marine -Japan, 1974-1976.

File 4850-JAPA. Part 2.
Marine and Rail Industries -Markets -Marine -Japan,

1976.

File 4850-JAPA. Part 3.
Marine and Rail Industries -Markets -Marine -Japan, 1976-1977.

File 4850-JAPA. Part 4.
Marine and Rail Industries -Markets -Marine -Japan, 1976-1977.

File 4850-JAPA. Part 5.
Marine and Rail Industries -Markets -Marine -Japan, 1977-1978

File 4850-KOR(S). Part 1.
Marine and Rail Industries -Markets -Marine -Korea, South, 1974-1977.

File 4850-MALAY Part 1.
Marine and Rail Industries -Markets -Marine -Malaysia, 1974-1977.

File 4850-THA. Part 1.
Marine and Rail Industries -Markets -Marine -Thailand, 1974-1976.

File 4850-THA. Part 2.
Marine and Rail Industries -Markets -Marine -Thailand, 1976-1977.

Box 17.

File 4850-TRIN. Part 1.
Marine and Rail Industries -Markets -Marine -Trinidad, 1974-1975.

File 4850-TRIN. Part 2.
Marine and Rail Industries -Markets -Marine -Trinidad, 1976.

File 4850-TUR. Part 1.
Marine and Rail Industries -Markets -Marine -Turkey, 1973-1976.

File 4850-TUR. Part 2.
Marine and Rail Industries -Markets -Marine -Turkey, 1976-1977.

File 4850-TUR. Part 3.
Marine and Rail Industries - Markets - Marine - Turkey, 1977-1978.

Box 18.

File 4852-3- CHIN Part 1.
Marine and Rail Industries - Markets - Ocean Industries- China, 1975-1977.

File 4852-3- CHIN Part 2.
Marine and Rail Industries - Markets - Ocean Industries-China, 1978.

File 4852-3-INDI Part 1.
Marine and Rail Industries -Markets -Ocean Industries-India, 1974-1977.

File 4852-3-JAPA Part 1.
Marine and Rail Industries -Markets -Ocean Industries-Japan, 1974-1978.

File 4852-4 Part 1.
Marine and Rail Industries -Markets -Ocean Industries-South East Asian Countries, 1974-1978.

Box 19.

File 4854-CHIN Part 1.
Marine and Rail Industries -Markets -Railway-China, 1975-1977.

File 4854-CHIN Part 2.
Marine and Rail Industries -Markets -Railway-China, 1977-1978.

File 4854-INDO Part 1.
Marine and Rail Industries -Markets -Railway-Indonesia, 1975-1976.

Box 20.

File 5854-PAK Part 1.
Marine and Rail Industries -Markets -Railway-Pakistan, 1975-1977.

File 5854-SRI Part 1.
Marine and Rail Industries -Markets -Railway-Sri Lanka, 1975-1977.

File 5854-THA Part 1.
Marine and Rail Industries -Markets -Railway-Thailand, 1973-1978.

Box 25.

File 4938-TUR. Part 2.
Vehicle Systems Industry -Markets -Automotive -Turkey, 1975-1978.

Box 26.

File 4942-HONG Part 1.
Vehicle Systems Industry -Markets-Urban Transportation-Hong Kong, 1976-1977.

File 4942-HONG Part 2.
Vehicle Systems Industry -Markets-Urban Transportation-Hong Kong, 1977-1978.

Box 27.

File 4942-SIN Part 1.
Vehicle Systems Industry -Markets -Urban Transportation, Singapore, 1975-1978.

Box 34.

File 5614-J1 Part 1.
Asian Development Bank -Increase in Financial

Resources, 1977-1978.

File 5614-N1 Part 1.
Asian Development Bank -News Releases and Publications, 1977-1978.

Box 42.

File 7775-2-TOK-78 Part 1.
Communications, Mediums and Services -Monthly Reports -Publicity -Tokyo, 1978, general, 1978.

File 7775-2-TOK-78 Part 2.
Communications, Mediums and Services -Monthly Reports -Publicity -Tokyo, 1978, general, 1978.

File 7775-2-TOK-78 Part 3.
Communications, Mediums and Services -Monthly Reports -Publicity -Tokyo, 1978, general, 1978.

File 7775-2-TOK-78 Part 4.
Communications, Mediums and Services -Monthly Reports -Publicity -Tokyo, 1978, general, 1978.

Box 27.

File 4942-SIN Part 1.
Vehicle Systems Industry -Markets-Urban Transportation-Singapore, 1975-1978.

Record Group 21. Energy, Mines and Resources.

A. Deputy Minister's Office, 1931-1969.

1. Registry files, 1927-1969, 7.6 metres(volumes 2, 4-47, 151)

Records include the Colombo Plan. Finding aid 1, 3.

Record Group 22. Indian Affairs and Northern Development.

Engineering and Construction Services, Central Registry files, 1913-1955. 5.4 metres(volumes 566-592). These records relate to relief camps operated during the Depression or to wartime labour by Japanese Canadians. Finding aid 5.

Record Group 23. Fisheries and Oceans

Central Registry files, 1894-1970. Volumes 19-77, 431-549, 556-1827).
Volumes 945-947. File 721-4-6 Parts 129-47.
Legislation -British Columbia fishery regulations(restricting licences to Japanese in British Columbia), 1939-1949.

Volumes 1643-44. File 792-17-7 Parts 1-4.
Claims for loss and damage to Japanese fishing vessels, 1942-1954.

Record Group 24. National Defence.

Major series below where one can reasonably expect to find Asia-and Oceania-related materials through consulting available file lists and indexes.

C. Army records.

C1. Army Headquarters records registry systems, 1903-1965.

Volumes 10-142, 147-152, 171-184, 187-189, 224-1146, 1150-1200, 1202-1226, 1229-1588, 1634-1731, 1766-1809, 1947-2939, 2948-2952, 5289-5344, 5697-5823, 5846-5953, 6199-6575, 6596-6651, 9344-9347, 9498-9700, 12873-12910, 13122-13124, 18851-19835(microfilm reels C-4622, C-4857-C-4859, C-4889-C-5035, C-5046-C-5504, C-5547-C-5781, C-5870-C-5874, C-8242-C-8438, C-11628-C-11677, C-14438, T-1665, C-6772-C-6774).
KWOC(Key Word of Context)index available on reels C-6772-C-6774.

Volume 96.

File HQ 1857-2.
Chinese activity in Canada, 1916-1919.

Volume 369.

File HQ 54-3-5.
Circular regarding contributions to a fund for Japanese soldiers' and sailors' widows and families, 1904.

Volume 370.

File HQ 54 3 7 1.
Reports of the British officers attached to the Russian and Japanese forces in Manchuria, 1908-1910.

Volume 1256.

File HQ 593-1-94-1.
Enlistment of Japanese, Canadian Expeditionary Force, 1916-1919.

Volume 2288.

File HQS 23-1.
Internal security intelligence -soldiers of enemy origin -policy, 1943-1947.

Volume 2401.

File HQS 225 1.
Reports of Captain Thacker, Royal Canadian Artillery, re Japanese-Russian War, 1904.

Volume 2437.

File HQS 590 31 1.
Japanese reservists, 1918.

Volume 2640-2642.

File HQS 3488-3-.
Authorized enlistment, 17 January 1945, S.E. Asia.

Volume 2692.

File HQS 5199 a1.
Minutes of Joint Staff Committee re maintenance of Canadian neutrality, re war between Japan and the United States, boxes 2692-2693.

Volume 2730.

File HQS 5199.
Joint Staff Committee -emergency plan for the defence of the West coast, 1940-1941.

Volume 2763.

File HQS 6615-1.
Interdepartmental committee on recruiting of aliens in Canada, 1939-1946.

Volume 4642.

File MD 11-99-4-57.
Mobilization of a Japanese battalion, 1916-1917.

Volume 6584.

File 10-12-33-1A.
Japanese internees, general accounting, 1942.
Reel C-5055.

File HQC.
Japanese activity in Canada and United States, 1908-1940.

Reel C-5069.

File HQC 4498-4499.
Reports on prisoner of war camps in Japan, 1940-1947.

Reel 5079.

File HQC 5533.
Simon Commission Report on India.

Reel C-5392.

File 7236-50.
Disposal of internee's property.

Reel C-8242.

File HQS 21.
Japanese intercepts, general, A-Z(7 files) 1944-1945.

Reels C-8250 to C-8252.

Files 42-A-1 to 42-Y-20.
Intelligence investigation, Japanese aliens, n.d.(includes files on individuals).

Reel C-8317.

File HQS 6265-127.
Internal security, intelligence, Japanese Canadians in the employ of Japan, 1945-1946.

Reel C-8240.

File HQS 7368.
Interdepartmental committee on Orientals in British Columbia, 1939-1942.

Reel C-8340.

File HQS 7368-1. Removal of Japanese and establishment of protected areas, West Coast, 1942-1944.

Job 31. Intelligence.

Reel C-11628.

File TS 9131-33-1.
Far Eastern Advisory Commission re Control of Japan, 1945-1949.

Reel C-11629.

File TS 712-106.
Reports from Canadian embassies and legations, China, 1946-1949.

Reel C-11630.

File S 712-106-1.
Monthly reports from Canadian Embassy, China, 1947-1949.

File TS 112-114.
Reports from Canadian embassies and legations, India, 1946-1949.

File TS 712-116.
Reports from Canadian embassies and legations, Japan, 1949.

File S 712-124.
Reports from Canadian embassies and legations, Netherlands East Indies, 1946-1949.

Reel C-11632.

File S 701-124.
Appreciations, foreign countries, Netherlands East Indies, 1947

File TS 703-106.
Reports from the Canadian military attaché, China, 1946-1949.

File TS 703-106-16-1.
Weekly briefing telegram, Canadian military attaché, China.

Reel C-11634.

File TS 703-267.
Reports from the Canadian military attaché, Turkey, 1948-1949.

Reel C-11635.

File TS 706 100.
War Office reports on the Far East and Pacific Area, 1946-1948.

File S 706-100-16-1.
War Office Chief of the Imperial General Staff summary, Far East, 1947.

File TS 706-101.
War Office reports, Afghanistan, 1948.

File TS 706-106.
War Office reports, China, 1947-1949.

File TS 706-111.
War Office reports, French Indo-China 1949.

File TS 706-114.
War Office reports, India, 1946-1949.

File TS 706-116.
War Office reports, Japan, 1947.

File S 706-117.
War Office reports, Korea, 1948.

File TS 706-120.
War Office reports, Manchuria, 1946-1947.

File TS 706-124.
War Office reports, Netherlands East Indies, 1948.

File TS 706-130.
War Office reports, Siam, 1948.

File S 706-250.
War Office reports, Iran, 1947-1949.

File TS 706-267.
War Office reports, Turkey, 1947-1948.

Reel C-11636.

File TS 707-100-16-1.
United States War Department reports, Far East and Pacific, political intelligence, 1948.

File TS 707-100-16-3.
United States War Department reports, Far East and Pacific, topographical intelligence, 1948.

File TS 707-106-16-5.
United States War Department reports, China, technical intelligence, 1946.

File TS 707-106-16-5.
United States War Department reports, China, military intelligence, 1948-1949.

File TS 707-106-16-7.
United States War Department reports, China, who's who intelligence, 1947-1948.

File TS 707-106-16-9.
United States War Department reports, China, intelligence reviews, 1948.

File TS 707-114-16-6.
United States War Department reports, India, military intelligence, 1948.

File TS 707-116.
United States War Department reports, Japan, 1946-1947.

File TS 707-116-2.
United States War Department reports, Japan, economic intelligence, 1948.

File TS 707-116-6.
United States War Department reports, Japan, military intelligence, 1947.

File TS 707-117.
United States War Department reports, Korea, 1947.

File TS 707-117-16-6.
United States War Department reports, Korea, military intelligence, 1947-1948.

File TS 707-117-16-7.
United States War Department reports, Korea, who's who intelligence, 1948.

File TS 707-117-16-9.
United States War Department reports, Korea, intelligence reviews, 1948.

File TS 707-120.
United States War Department reports, Manchuria.

File TS 707-120.
United States War Department reports, Netherlands East Indies, political intelligence, 1947.

File TS 707-124-16-6.
United States War Department reports, Netherlands East Indies, military intelligence, 1947-1948.

File TS 707-128-16-6.
United States War Department reports, Outer Mongolia military intelligence, 1948.

File TS 707-129.
United States War Department reports, Philippines, 1947.

Reel C-11637.

File TS 707-267.

United States War Department reports, Turkey, 1947.

File TS 707-267-16-6.
United States War Department reports, Turkey, military intelligence, 1949.

TS File 708-100.
Dominions Office reports on Far East and Pacific area, general, 1947.

File S 708-104.
Dominions Office reports, Burma, 1947-1949.

File TS 708-106.
Dominions Office reports, China, 1947-1949.

File TS 708-107.
Dominions Office reports, Ceylon, 1947.

File TS 708-111.
Commonwealth Relations Office reports, French Indo-China, 1947-1949.

File TS 708-114.
Commonwealth Relations Office reports, India, 1947-1949.

File TS 708-116.
Commonwealth Relations Office reports, Japan, 1947-1949.

File S 708-117.
Commonwealth Relations Office reports, Korea, 1949.

File TS 708-119.
Commonwealth Relations Office reports, Malaya, 1948.

File TS 708-124.
Commonwealth Relations Office reports, Netherlands East Indies, 1947-1949.

File TS 708-130.
Commonwealth Relations Office reports, Siam, 1947-1949.

File S 708-250.
Commonwealth Relations Office reports, Iran-Persia, 1948-1949.

File TS 708-267.
Commonwealth Relations Office reports, Turkey, 1947.

File S 709-106.
Reports from sources other than Canadian military attachés, embassies and legations, China, 1948.

File S 709-116.
Reports from sources other than Canadian military attachés, embassies and legations, Japan, 1947.

File S 709-116-16-1.
Reports from sources other than Canadian military attachés, embassies and legations, Japan, Capt.

L.H.Nerlick, Irish Regiment of Canada, 1949.

Reel C-11639.

File S 710-100.
Reports, general, Far East and Pacific Area, 1947.

File S 710-104.
Reports, general, Burma, 1947.

File TS 710-106.
Reports, general, China, 1944-1949.

File TS 710-107.
Reports, general, Ceylon, 1947-1948.

File S 710-109.
Reports, general, Formosa, 1947.

File S 710-111.
Reports, general, French Indo-China, 1948.

File S 710-113.
Reports, general, Hong Kong.

File S 710-114.
Reports, general, India, 1949.

File S 710-115.
Reports, general, Inner Mongolia, 1946.

File TS 710-116.
Reports, general, Japan, 1946-1949.

File S 710-117.
Reports, general, Korea, 1947-1948.

File S 710-124.
Reports, general, Netherlands East Indies, 1947-1948.

File S 710-128.
Reports, general, Outer Mongolia.

File S 710-130.
Reports, general, Siam, 1949.

File S 710-267.
Reports, general, Turkey, 1948.

File S 710-267-16-1.
Reports, general, Turkey, German maps and publications, 1947.

Reel C-11640.

File TS 712-267.
Reports from Canadian embassy and legation, Turkey, 1947-1949.

File TS 720-116-3.
Science and technology, Japanese reports, 1947.

Reel C-11641.

File S 731-101.
Foreign Office reports, Afghanistan, 1948.

File S 731-104.
Foreign Office reports, Burma, 1948.

File S 731-106.
Foreign Office reports, China, 1948.

File S 731-129.
Foreign Office reports, Philippines, 1948.

File S 731-130.
Foreign Office reports, Siam, 1947.

File S 731-267.
Foreign Office reports, Turkey, 1949.

File S 753-104.
Reports to and from Canadian permanent delegate to United Nations re Burma, 1948.

File S 753-106.
Reports to and from Canadian permanent delegate to United Nations re China, 1949.

File S 753-114.
Reports to and from Canadian permanent delegate to United Nations re India, 1949.

File S 753-117.
Reports to and from Canadian permanent delegate to United Nations re Korea, 1948-1949.

File S 753-124.
Reports to and from Canadian permanent delegate to United Nations re Netherlands East Indies, 1948-1949.

Reel C-11642.

File S 754-114.
Reports to Canadian member on Security Council on India, general, 1948-1949.

File TS 756-101.
Liaison with commands re Afghanistan, 1948.

File TS 756-104.
Liaison with commands re Burma, 1949.

File TS 756-114.
Liaison with commands re Pakistan and India, 1949.

File TS 756-116.
Liaison with commands re Japan, 1948-1949.

File TS 756-129.
Liaison with commands re Philippines, 1948.

File TS 756-130.
Liaison with commands re Siam, 1948.

File TS 762-101.
Canadian Joint Intelligence Bureau, information on Afghanistan, 1948.

File TS 762-114.
Canadian Joint Intelligence Bureau, information on India and Pakistan, 1949.

File TS 762-267.
Canadian Joint Intelligence Bureau, information on Turkey, 1948.

Reel C-11647.

File TS 3507.
Intelligence re China, 1946.

File S 6074.
Quarterly liaison letters, India, 1938-1945.

File TS 6532.
Situation in Turkey, 1935-1946.

File TS 6616.
Attitude of United Kingdom government re defence of Netherlands and Netherlands East Indies, 1936-1946.

Reel C-11648.

File S 9074-1.
Reports from military attaché, China, 1941-1946.

Reel C-11649.

File S 9074-3.
Special reports from Canadian Minister in China, 1943-1946.

Reel C-11650.

File S 9015-34/114.
Reports from Canadian Air attachés in French Indo-China, 1952.

File S 9015-34/154.
Reports from Canadian Air attachés in Iran(Persia), 1951.

File S 9017-34/70.
Reports from Royal Canadian Air Force on China, 1949-1951.

File S 9017-34/176.
Reports from Royal Canadian Air Force on Korea, 1950-1951.

File TS 9034-34/70.
Appreciation by Director of Military Intelligence on China, 1949-1952.

File TS 9034-34/178.
Appreciation by Director of Military Intelligence on Korea, 1950-52

File S 9041-33/29.
Appreciation by Joint Intelligence Board(Canadian) on Far East, 1952.

Reel C-11651.

File C 9041-34/6(336).
Appreciation by Joint Intelligence Board(United Kingdom) on Afghanistan, 1951.

File S 9041-34/66(336).
Reports on appreciation by Joint Intelligence Board in Ceylon re United Kingdom.

File S 9041-34/70.
Appreciation by Canadian Joint Intelligence Board on China, 1949-1953.

File S 9041-34/70(336).
Appreciation by United Kingdom Joint Intelligence Board on China, 1954.

File S 9041-34/140.
Appreciation by Canadian Joint Intelligence Board on Hong Kong, 1949.

File S 9041-34/154.
Appreciation by Canadian Joint Intelligence Board on Iran(Persia), 1951.

File TS 9041-34/154(336).
Appreciation by United Kingdom Joint Intelligence Board on Iran(Persia), 1950-1953.

File S 9236-34/84(154).
Canadian embassy and legation, Denmark re Iran, 1952.

File S 9236-34/128(154).
Canadian embassy and legation, Greece re Iran, 1952.

File S 9236-34/330(41).
Canadian embassy and legation, Turkey re Middle East, 1949-1952.

File TS 9236-34/330(154).
Canadian embassy and legation, Turkey re Iran, 1949.

Reel C-11652.

File S 9236-34/342(6).
Canadian embassy and legation, USSR re Afghanistan, 1952.

File S 9236-34/342(150).
Canadian embassy and legation, USSR re Indonesia, 1949.

File S 9236-34/342(170).
Canadian embassy and legation, USSR re Japan, 1952.

Reel C-11655.

File TS 9130-34/140.
Colonial Office reports, Hong Kong, 1949.

File S 9138-34/246.
Commonwealth Relations Office reports, Pakistan, 1952.

File S 9238-34/24(88).
Canadian embassy and legation in Australia. Reports re New Guinea, 1951.

Reel C-11656.

File TS 9336-34/330.
Reports from Canadian military attaché, Turkey, 1949-1950.

Reel C-11657.

File S 9138-34/314.
Commonwealth Relations Office reports, Tibet, 1950.

File S 9236-34/246(314).
Reports from Canadian embassy and legation in Pakistan re Tibet, 1950.

File TS 9236-34/330.
Reports from Canadian embassy and legation in Turkey, 1949-1954.

Reel C-11658.
File S 9335-34/154.
Reports from the British military attachés, Iran, 1951-1953.

File S 9490-34/70.
War Office reports on China, 1949-1952.

Reel C-11659.

File TS 9202-34/178.
Reports from Canadian delegate to United Nations re Korea, 1950-1954.

File TS 9236-34/148.
Reports from Canadian embassy and legation in India, 1949-1954.

Reel C-11665.

File TS 9015-34/170.
Reports from Canadian Air attaché in Japan, 1952-1953.

Reel C-11665.

File S 9042-34/170.
Reports on Japan by Canadian Joint Intelligence Bureau, 1953.

File S 9041-34/256.
Reports on Philippines by Joint Intelligence Board, 1954.

File TS 9042-34/178-3.
Appreciations by Canadian Joint Intelligence center, Korea. Daily situation report, 1950.

File TS 9100-1930/0-1.
Reports from Canadian military mission Far East. Daily intelligence summaries, 1950-1954.

File S 9236-34/300(178).
Reports from Canadian embassies and legation in Sweden re Korea, 1951-1954.

File S 9236-34/302(178).
Reports from Canadian embassies and legation in Switzerland re Korea, 1953-1954.

Reel C-11666.

File TS 9336-34/330.
Reports from Canadian military attaché in Turkey, 1951-1952.

Reel C-11667.

File TS 9471-34/178.
United States War Department reports on Korea, 1949-1953.

File S 9430-34/150.
War Office reports on Indonesia, 1950-1954.

Reel C-11668.

File S 9260-34/70.
War Office reports on China, 1949-1953.

File S 9260-34/114.
War Office reports on French Indo-China, 1950-1954.

File S 9260-34/170.
War Office reports on Japan, 1951-1954.

File S 9336-34/300(29)
Reports from Canadian military attaché in Sweden re Far East, 1951.

File S 9350-34/178.
Reports from other sources on Korea, 1954.

File C 9395-34/178.
Reports from United Nations Secretary General on Korea, 1950.

Reel C-11669.

File TS 1766-1930/29.
Reports and returns, Canadian Military Mission, Far East, 1954-1956.

Reel C-11670.

File TS 9336-36/330.
Reports from Canadian military attachés in Turkey, 1951-1953.

Reel C-11672.

File TS 9138-34/178.
Commonwealth Relations Office reports on Korea, 1951.

File S 9235-34/170.
Reports from British embassy re Japan, 1952.

File TS 9236-34/170.
Reports from Canadian embassy and legation in Japan, 1949-1951.

File S 9236-34/170(70).
Reports from Canadian embassy and legation in Japan, re China, 1949-1954.

File S 9236-34/170(106).
Reports from Canadian embassy and legation in Japan, re Formosa, 1953.

File S 9236-34/170(338).

File TS 9336-34/330.
Reports from Canadian military attachés in Turkey, 1953-1955.

Reel C-11673.

File TS 9042-34/70.
Appreciations by Canadian Joint Intelligence Committee China, 1948-1955.

Reel C-11674.

File S 9165-(170)Y1.
Counter intelligence personalities, Japan, Hugo Yamamoto, 1951.

File TS 9336-34/330.
Military attaché reports, Turkey, 1955-1956.

Reel C-11675.

File TS 9380-34/181-1.
Political intelligence, International Supervisory Commission, Laos, 1954.

C2. Adjutant-general branch, 1870-1966.

C2f. Office of the Special Assistant to the Adjutant general(Canadian prisoners of war in enemy hands) 1941-1946, 4.8 metres (volumes 8018-8029).

Contains numbered files of the Canadian War Crimes Liaison Detachment in the Far East; copies of International Red Cross inspection reports on prisoner of war camps operated by the Axis powers, as well as communications received by the Department of External Affairs relating to these camps, 1941-1945. File list available.

Canadian War Crimes Liaison Detachment, Japanese Theatre.

Volume 8018-8020.
Covers East Asia and South East Asia.

Special Assistant to the Attorney general, 1945.

Volume 8027.
A few files.

Volumes 8028-8029.
Camps in East Asia and South East Asia.

C3. War diaries, 1939-1967. 1007 metres (volumes 6623, 6916, 13200-17509, 17515, 182178, 13176-13182(microfilm reels T-1847 to T-1882, T-6668-T-6698, T-7071-T-7114, T-7599-T-7620.) Finding aid 60.

War diaries of units and formations of the Canadian army, both at home and overseas, during World War II, including Korea.

Korean war.

Volume 12, 178.
25 Canadian Field Punishment Camp(restricted), March-July 1951.

Volume 12, 178.
27 Field Detention Barracks(restricted), July 1951-October 1953.

Volume 18, 220.
Branch of the General Staff, 25 June 1950-31 December 1953.

Volume 18, 220.
Vice Chief of the General Staff, AHQ, 25 August-31 October 1950.

Volume 18, 220.
Notes on Korean situation, Chief of General Staff, 28 June-3 August 1950.

Volume 18, 221.
Notes on Korean situation, Chief of General Staff, 11 July-18 November 1950.

Volume 18, 221.
Branch of the Adjutant General, 1 August-September 1950.

Volume 18, 222.
Branch of the Adjutant General, October 1950-June 1951.

Volume 18, 223.
Branch of the Adjutant General, July 1951-July 1952.

Volume 18, 224.
Branch of the Adjutant General, August 1952-December 1953.

Volume 18, 225.
Branch of the Adjutant General, 1 January-31 December 1954.

Volume 18, 225.
Branch of the Quartermaster General, 1 August-October 1950.

Volume 18, 226.
Branch of the Quartermaster General, January 1952-June 1953.

Volume 18, 227.
Branch of the Quartermaster General, July 1953-31 December 1954.

Volume 18, 227.
Headquarters, Eastern Command, August 1950-31 December 1951.

Volume 18, 227.
Headquarters, Québec command, 1 August 1950-31 December 1951.

Volume 18, 228.
Headquarters, Central Command, 1 August-November 1950.

Volume 18, 229.
Headquarters, Central Command, January-31 December 1951.

Volume 18, 229.
Headquarters, Prairie Command, 1 August 1950-31 December 1951.

Volume 18, 229.
Headquarters, Western Command, 5 August-31 December 1950.

Volume 18, 229.
Headquarters, Eastern Québec Area, 1-30 November 1950.

Volume 18, 230.
Headquarters, Eastern Ontario Area, 1 August-30 November 1950.

Volume 18, 230.
Headquarters, Eastern Ontario Area, 1 May-31 July 1951.

Volume 18, 230.
Headquarters, Western Ontario Area, 1 August-30 September 1950.

Volume 18, 230.
Headquarters, British Columbia Area, 1 August-October 1950.

Volume 18, 231.
Headquarters, British Columbia Area, November 1950-30 April 1951.

Volume 18, 231.
Canadian Section, Headquarters 1(Commonwealth) Division, U.N. Command, 10 June 1951-30 April 1953.

Volume 18, 231.
Headquarters, 1 Canadian Infantry Brigade, 1 November 1953-January 1954.

Volume 18, 232.
Headquarters, 1 Canadian Infantry Brigade, February-July 1954.

Volume 18, 233.
Headquarters, 1 Canadian Infantry Brigade, August-December 1954.

Volume 18, 234.
Headquarters, 1 Canadian Infantry Brigade, June-27 July 1958.

Volume 18, 234.
Headquarters, 2 Canadian Infantry Brigade. 2 Canadian Infantry Brigade (was Headquarters 25 Canadian Infantry Brigade Replacement Group) 5 April 1951-January 1952.

Volume 18, 235.
Headquarters, 2 Canadian Infantry Brigade, February 1952-April 1953.

Volume 18, 236.
Headquarters, 2 Canadian Infantry Brigade, May 1953-31 December 1954.

Volume 18, 237.
Headquarters, 25 Canadian Infantry Brigade. 25 Canadian Infantry Brigade(now Headquarters 4 Canadian Infantry Brigade), 5 September 1950-June 1951.

Volume 18, 238.
Headquarters, 25 Canadian Infantry Brigade, February-June 1951.

Volume 18, 239.
Headquarters, 25 Canadian Infantry Brigade, July-September 1951.

Volume 18, 240.
Headquarters, 25 Canadian Infantry Brigade, October-December 1951.

Volume 18, 241.
Headquarters, 25 Canadian Infantry Brigade, January-March 1952.

Volume 18, 242.
Headquarters, 25 Canadian Infantry Brigade, April-May 1952.

Volume 18, 243.
Headquarters, 25 Canadian Infantry Brigade, May-July 1952.

Volume 18, 244.
Headquarters, 25 Canadian Infantry Brigade, July-September 1952.

Volume 18, 245.
Headquarters, 25 Canadian Infantry Brigade, September-December 1952.

Volume 18, 246.
Headquarters, 25 Canadian Infantry Brigade, December 1952-January 1953.

Volume 18, 247.
Headquarters, 25 Canadian Infantry Brigade, January-February 1953.

Volume 18, 248.
Headquarters, 25 Canadian Infantry Brigade, February-March 1953.

Volume 18, 249.
Headquarters, 25 Canadian Infantry Brigade, March-April 1953.

Volume 18, 250.
Headquarters, 25 Canadian Infantry Brigade, April-May 1953.

Volume 18, 251.
Headquarters, 25 Canadian Infantry Brigade, May-June 1953.

Volume 18, 252.
Headquarters, 25 Canadian Infantry Brigade, June-July 1953.

Volume 18, 253.
Headquarters, 25 Canadian Infantry Brigade, August-November 1953.

Volume 18, 254.
Headquarters, 25 Canadian Infantry Brigade, December 1953-April 1954.

Volume 18, 255.
Headquarters, 25 Canadian Infantry Brigade, May-2 December 1954.

Volume 18, 256.
Headquarters, 27 Canadian Infantry Brigade, 5 June 1951-January 1952.

Volume 18, 257.
Headquarters, 27 Canadian Infantry Brigade, January-July 1952.

Volume 18, 258.
Headquarters, 27 Canadian Infantry Brigade, August-November 1952.

Volume 18, 259.
Headquarters, 27 Canadian Infantry Brigade, December 1952-May 1953.

Volume 18, 260.
Headquarters, 17 Canadian Infantry Brigade 27 Canadian Brigade, June-30 November 1953.

Volume 18, 261.
Headquarters, Canadian Base Units, Europe, 3 July 1952-31 December 1954.

Volume 18, 262.
"C" Squadron, Royal Canadian Dragoons, 1 July 1951-31 October 1953.

Volume 18, 263.
"D" Squadron, Royal Canadian Dragoons, 24 May-31 October 1954.

Volume 18, 263.
"A" Squadron, Lord Strathcona's Horse, 1 March 1953-6 June 1954.

Volume 18, 264.
"B" Squadron, Lord Strathcona's Horse, 1 February 1952-30 April 1953.

Volume 18, 264.
"C" Squadron, Lord Strathcona's Horse, 28 August 1950-May 1951.

Volume 18, 265.
"C" Squadron, Lord Strathcona's Horse, June 1951-31 May 1952.

Volume 18, 265.
"D" Squadron, Lord Strathcona's Horse, 7 November 1953-July 1954.

Volume 18, 266.
"D" Squadron, Lord Strathcona's Horse, August-31 December 1954.

Volume 18, 266.
2 Canadian Armoured Squadron, 3 December 1951-24 February 1952.

Volume 18, 266.
1 Regiment, Royal Canadian Horse Artillery, 1 February-May 1952.

Volume 18, 267.
1 Regiment, Royal Canadian Horse Artillery, June-August 1952.

Volume 18, 268.
1 Regiment, Royal Canadian Horse Artillery, September-October 1952.

Volume 18, 269.
1 Regiment, Royal Canadian Horse Artillery, November 1952-January 1953.

Volume 18, 270.
1 Regiment, Royal Canadian Horse Artillery, February-30 April 1953.

Volume 18, 271.
2 Regiment, Royal Canadian Horse Artillery, 8 August 1950-November 1950.

Volume 18, 272.
2 Regiment, Royal Canadian Horse Artillery, December 1950-July 1951.

Volume 18, 273.
2 Regiment, Royal Canadian Horse Artillery, August 1951-March 1952.

Volume 18, 274.
2 Regiment, Royal Canadian Horse Artillery, April 1952-April 1954.

Volume 18, 275.
2 Regiment, Royal Canadian Horse Artillery, May-December 1954.

Volume 18, 276.
3 Regiment, Royal Canadian Horse Artillery(was 79 Field Regiment, Royal Canadian Artillery), 8 May 1951-January 1952.

Volume 18, 277.
3 Regiment, Royal Canadian Horse Artillery, February-March 1952.

Volume 18, 278.
3 Regiment, Royal Canadian Horse Artillery, April-August 1952.

Volume 18, 279.
3 Regiment, Royal Canadian Horse Artillery, August-September 1952.

Volume 18, 280.
3 Regiment, Royal Canadian Horse Artillery, September 1952-February 1953.

Volume 18, 281.
3 Regiment, Royal Canadian Horse Artillery, March-July 1953.

Volume 18, 282.
3 Regiment, Royal Canadian Horse Artillery, August 1953-February 1954.

Volume 18, 283.
3 Regiment, Royal Canadian Horse Artillery, March-31 August 1954.

Volume 18, 283.
4 Regiment, Royal Canadian Horse Artillery(was 81 Field Regiment, Royal Canadian Artillery), 22 March-June 1953.

Volume 18, 284.
4 Regiment, Royal Canadian Horse Artillery, July 1953-30 April 1954.

Volume 18, 285.
"G" Battery, Royal Canadian Horse Artillery, 9 January-31 March 1951.

Volume 18, 285.
205 Field Battery, Royal Canadian Artillery, 3 May

1951-30 April 1952.

Volume 18, 285.
213 Field Battery, Royal Canadian Artillery, 5 May 1951-31 May 1952.

Volume 18, 285.
1 Field Squadron, Royal Canadian Engineers(was 23 Field Squadron), 1 April 1952-28 February 1953.

Volume 18, 286.
2 Field Squadron, Royal Canadian Engineers(was 57 Canadian Independent Field Squadron), 14 August 1950-May 1952.

Volume 18, 287.
2 Field Squadron, Royal Canadian Engineers, June 1952-31 December 1954.

Volume 18, 288.
3 Field Squadron, Royal Canadian Engineers(was 58 Canadian Independent Field Squadron), 4 May 1951-January 1952.

Volume 18, 289.
3 Field Squadron, Royal Canadian Engineers, February-July 1952.

Volume 18, 290.
3 Field Squadron, Royal Canadian Engineers, July-October 1952.

Volume 18, 291.
3 Field Squadron, Royal Canadian Engineers, November 1952-August 1953.

Volume 18, 292.
3 Field Squadron, Royal Canadian Engineers, September 1953-12 December 1954.

Volume 18, 293.
4th Field Squadron, Royal Canadian Engineers, 1 March 1953-28 February 1954.

Volume 18, 294.
31 Canadian Works Section, Royal Canadian Engineers, 26 February 1952-31 December 1954.

Volume 18, 295.
"J" Troop, 1 Canadian Infantry Divisional Signal Regiment, 1 January 1953-31 December 1954.

Volume 18, 296.
25 Canadian Infantry Brigade Signal Troop, 14 August 1950-30 September 1954.

Volume 18, 297.
2 Regiment, Royal Canadian Horse Artillery Signal Troop, 14 August-31 December 1950.

Volume 18, 297.
2 Regiment, Royal Canadian Horse Artillery Signal Troop, 1 December 1953-31 December 1954.

Volume 18, 297.
3 Regiment, Royal Canadian Horse Artillery Signal Troop, 5 May 1951-31 October 1953.

Volume 18, 298.
No.1 Canadian Base Signal Troop, 10 March 1951-15 October 1952.

Volume 18, 298.
No.2 Canadian Base Signal Troop, 2 January 1952-April 1953.

Volume 18, 299.
No.2 Canadian Base Signal Troop, May 1953-31 December 1954.

Volume 18, 299.
1 Battalion, the Black Watch of Canada(was 1 Canadian Highland Battalion), 30 May 1951-February 1952.

Volume 18, 300.
1 Battalion, The Black Watch, March-September 1952.

Volume 18, 301.
1 Battalion, the Black Watch, September 1952-June 1953.

Volume 18, 302.
1 Battalion, the Black Watch, July-30 November 1953.

Volume 18, 302.
2 Battalion, the Black Watch of Canada(was 2 Canadian Highland Battalion), 8 October 1953-February 1954.

Volume 18, 303.
2 Battalion, the Black Watch, March-31 October 1954.

Volume 18, 304.
1 Battalion, the Canadian Guards, 31 March-31 October 1954.

Volume 18, 304.
2 Battalion, the Canadian Guards, 8 January-October 1954.

Volume 18, 305.
2 Battalion, the Canadian Guards, August-31 December 1954.

Volume 18, 305.
3 Battalion, the Canadian Guards(was 1st Canadian Infantry Battalion), 3 May-November 1951.

Volume 18, 306.
3 Battalion, the Canadian Guards, December 1951-May 1952.

Volume 18, 307.
3 Battalion, the Canadian Guards, June-September 1952.

Volume 18, 308.

3 Battalion, the Canadian Guards, October 1952-April 1953.

Volume 18, 309.
3 Battalion, the Canadian Guards, May-September 1953.

Volume 18, 310.
3 Battalion, the Canadian Guards, October 1953-30 September 1954.

Volume 18, 310.
4 Battalion, the Canadian Guards(was 2 Canadian Infantry Battalion), 5 May 1952-January 1953.

Volume 18, 311.
4 Battalion, the Canadian Guards, February 1953-April 1954.

Volume 18, 312.
4 Battalion, the Canadian Guards, May-31 October 1954.

Volume 18, 312.
1 Battalion, Princess Patricia's Canadian Light Infantry, 17 August-November 1951.

Volume 18, 313.
1 Battalion, Princess Patricia's Canadian Light Infantry, December 1951-March 1952.

Volume 18, 314.
1 Battalion, Princess Patricia's Canadian Light Infantry, March-May 1952.

Volume 18, 315.
1 Battalion, Princess Patricia's Canadian Light Infantry, June-August 1952.

Volume 18, 316.
1 Battalion, Princess Patricia's Canadian Light Infantry, September-31 October 1952.

Volume 18, 317.
2 Battalion, Princess Patricia's Canadian Light Infantry, 7 August 1950-February 1951.

Volume 18, 318.
2 Battalion, Princess Patricia's Canadian Light Infantry, March-July 1951.

Volume 18, 319.
2 Battalion, Princess Patricia's Canadian Light Infantry, August 1951-June 1952.

Volume 18, 320.
2 Battalion, Princess Patricia's Canadian Light Infantry, October 1953-April 1954.

Volume 18, 321.
2 Battalion, Princess Patricia's Canadian Light Infantry, May-September 1954.

Volume 18, 322.

2 Battalion, Princess Patricia's Canadian Light Infantry, October-31 December 1954.

Volume 18, 322.
3 Battalion, Princess Patricia's Canadian Light Infantry, 1 December 1950-June 1951.

Volume 18, 323.
3 Battalion, Princess Patricia's Canadian Light Infantry, July 1951-April 1952.

Volume 18, 324.
3 Battalion, Princess Patricia's Canadian Light Infantry, May 1952-January 1953.

Volume 18, 325.
3 Battalion, Princess Patricia's Canadian Light Infantry, February-May 1953.

Volume 18, 326.
3 Battalion, Princess Patricia's Canadian Light Infantry, June-July 1953.

Volume 18, 327.
3 Battalion, Princess Patricia's Canadian Light Infantry, August-31 December 1953.

Volume 18, 328.
1 Battalion, the Queen's Own Rifles of Canada(was 1 Canadian Rifle Battalion), 2 May 1951-March 1952.

Volume 18, 329.
1 Battalion, the Queen's Own Rifles of Canada, April-June 1952.

Volume 18, 330.
1 Battalion, the Queen's Own Rifles of Canada, July-September 1952.

Volume 18, 331.
1 Battalion, the Queen's Own Rifles of Canada, October 1952-May 1953.

Volume 18, 332.
1 Battalion, the Queen's Own Rifles of Canada, June-October 1953.

Volume 18, 332.
2 Battalion, the Queen's Own Rifles of Canada(was 2 Canadian Rifle Battalion), 1 May-October 1952.

Volume 18, 333.
2 Battalion, the Queen's Own Rifles of Canada, January 1952-January 1954.

Volume 18, 334.
2 Battalion, the Queen's Own Rifles of Canada, February-July 1954.

Volume 18, 335.
2 Battalion, the Queen's Own Rifles of Canada, August-31 December 1954.

Volume 18, 336.

1 Battalion, the Royal Canadian Regiment, 2 January-May 1952.

Volume 18, 337.
1 Battalion, the Royal Canadian Regiment, June-July 1952.

Volume 18, 338.
1 Battalion, the Royal Canadian Regiment, August-October 1952.

Volume 18, 339.
1 Battalion, the Royal Canadian Regiment, November 1952-January 1953.

Volume 18, 340.
1 Battalion, the Royal Canadian Regiment, February-27 April 1953.

Volume 18, 340.
2 Battalion, the Royal Canadian Regiment, 7 August-November 1950.

Volume 18, 341.
2 Battalion, the Royal Canadian Regiment, December 1950-June 1951.

Volume 18, 342.
2 Battalion, the Royal Canadian Regiment, July-September 1951.

Volume 18, 343.
2 Battalion, the Royal Canadian Regiment, October-November 1951.

Volume 18, 344.
2 Battalion, the Royal Canadian Regiment, December 1951-January 1952.

Volume 18, 345.
2 Battalion, the Royal Canadian Regiment, February-March 1952.

Volume 18, 346.
2 Battalion, the Royal Canadian Regiment, October 1953-April 1954.

Volume 18, 347.
2 Battalion, the Royal Canadian Regiment, May-September 1954.

Volume 18, 348.
2 Battalion, the Royal Canadian Regiment, October-31 December 1954.

Volume 18, 348.
3 Battalion, the Royal Canadian Regiment, 10 January-September 1951.

Volume 18, 349.
3 Battalion, the Royal Canadian Regiment, October 1951-September 1952.

Volume 18, 350.

3 Battalion, the Royal Canadian Regiment, October 1952-June 1953.

Volume 18, 351.
3 Battalion, the Royal Canadian Regiment, June-October 1953.

Volume 18, 352.
3 Battalion, the Royal Canadian Regiment, November 1953-12 April 1954.

Volume 18, 353.
1 Battalion, 22e Régiment, 1 February-July 1952.

Volume 18, 354.
1 Battalion, Royal 22e Régiment, August-December 1952.

Volume 18, 355.
1 Battalion, Royal 22e Régiment, January-2 May 1953.

Volume 18, 356.
2 Battalion, Royal 22e Régiment, 10 August 1950-May 1951.

Volume 18, 357.
2 Battalion, Royal 22e Régiment, June-December 1951.
Volume 18, 358.
2 Battalion, Royal 22e Régiment, January-April 1952.

Volume 18, 359.
2 Battalion, Royal 22e Régiment, November 1953-March 1954.

Volume 18, 360.
2 Battalion, Royal 22e Régiment, April-August 1954.

Volume 18, 361.
2 Battalion, Royal 22e Régiment, September-31 December 1954.

Volume 18, 362
3 Battalion, Royal 22e Régiment, 7 January 1951-March 1952.

Volume 18, 363.
3 Battalion, Royal 22e Régiment, April-October 1952.

Volume 18, 364.
3 Battalion, Royal 22e Régiment, April-June 1953.

Volume 18, 365.
3 Battalion, Royal 22e Régiment, June-July 1953.

Volume 18, 366.
3 Battalion, Royal 22e Régiment, August-September 1953.

Volume 18, 367.
3 Battalion, Royal 22e Régiment, October-November 1953.

Volume 18, 368.
3 Battalion, Royal 22e Régiment, January-31 July 1954.

Volume 18, 369.
"F" Company, the Scottish Regiment Princess Mary's), 24 July 1951-31 January 1952.

Volume 18, 369.
"F" Company, the North Nova Scotia Highlanders, 1 December 1951-30 April 1952.

Volume 18, 369.
"E" Company, the Regina Rifle Regiment, 30 April-9 July 1951.

Volume 18, 369.
"F" Company, the Regina Rifle Regiment, 10 July 1951-30 April 1952.

Volume 18, 369.
"F" Company, the Royal Winnipeg Rifles, 12 June 1951-31 March 1952.

Volume 18, 369.
"F" Company, Seaforth Highlanders of Canada, 10 July 1951-30 April 1952.

Volume 18, 370.
No.1 Transport Company, Royal Canadian Army Service Corps(was No. 23 Transport Company), 14 March 1952-28 February 1953.

Volume 18, 370.
No.2 Transport Company, Royal Canadian Army Service Corps(was No. 54 Canadian Transport Company) 5 August 1950-January 1951.

Volume 18, 371
No.2 Transport Company, Royal Canadian Army Service Corps, February 1951-February 1954.

Volume 18, 372.
No.2 Transport Company, Royal Canadian Army Service Corps, March-31 December 1954.

Volume 18, 373.
No. 3 Transport Company, Royal Canadian Army Service Corps (was No. 55 Transport Company), 14 June 1951-August 1952.

Volume 18, 374.
No. 3 Transport Company, Royal Canadian Army Service Corps, September 1952-July 1953.

Volume 18, 375.
No. 3 Transport Company, Royal Canadian Army Service Corps, August 1953-3 October 1954.

Volume 18, 376.
No. 5 Transport Company, Royal Canadian Army Service Corps (was No. 56 Transport Company), 26 February 1953-15 April 1954.

Volume 18, 376.
No. 38 Canadian Motor Ambulance Company, Royal Canadian Army Service Corps, 1 March 1951-28 February 1954.

Volume 18, 376.
No. 38 Canadian Motor Ambulance Company, Royal Canadian Army Service Corps, 1 April-31 May 1954.

Volume 18, 377.
No. 58 General Transport Company, Royal Canadian Army Service Corps(was No. 57 Company), 24 September 1952-May 1954.

Volume 18, 378.
No. 58 General Transport Company, Royal Canadian Army Service Corps, June-31 December 1954.

Volume 18, 378.
No.1 Canadian Movement Control Group, Royal Canadian Army Service Corps, 1 October 1950-March 1953.

Volume 18, 379.
No.1 Canadian Movement Control Group, Royal Canadian Army Service Corps, April 1953-31 December 1954.

Volume 18, 379.
No.2 Canadian Transport, Royal Canadian Army Service Corps, 11 October 1950-March 1952.

Volume 18, 380.
No.2 Canadian Movement Control Group, Royal Canadian Army Service Corps, April 1952-31 December 1954.

Volume 18, 381.
No. 3 Canadian Movement Control Group, Royal Canadian Army Service Corps, 13 August 1951-31 December 1954.

Volume 18, 381.
No. 4 Canadian Movement Control Group, Royal Canadian Army Service Corps, 5 May 1951-September 1952.

Volume 18, 382.
No. 4 Canadian Movement Control Group, Royal Canadian Army Service Corps, October 1952-May 1954.

Volume 18, 383.
No. 4 Canadian Movement Control Group, Royal Canadian Army Service Corps, June-31 December 1954.

Volume 18, 383.
Canadian Section, British Commonwealth Hospital, 1 July 1951-December 1952.

Volume 18, 389.
No. 2 Field Ambulance, Royal Canadian Army Medical Corps, July-31 December 1954.

Volume 18, 389.
No. 3 Field Ambulance, Royal Canadian Army Medical Corps(was No. 79 Field Ambulance) 5 May-December 1951.

Volume 18, 390.
No. 3 Field Ambulance, Royal Canadian Army Medical Corps, January-August 1952.

Volume 18, 391.
No. 3 Field Ambulance, Royal Canadian Army Medical Corps, September 1952-May 1953.

Volume 18, 392.
No. 3 Field Ambulance, Royal Canadian Army Medical Corps, April-31 December 1954.

Volume 18, 393.
No. 4 Field Ambulance, Royal Canadian Army Medical Corps(was No. 38 Field Ambulance), 28 July 1952-July 1953.

Volume 18, 394.
No. 4 Field Ambulance, Royal Canadian Army Medical Corps, August 1953-31 March 1954.

Volume 18, 395.
No. 25 Canadian Field Dressing Station, 14 December 1950-June 1952.

Volume 18, 396.
No. 25 Canadian Field Dressing Station, July 1952-October 1953.

Volume 18, 397.
No. 25 Canadian Field Dressing Station, November 1953-6 November 1954.

Volume 18, 398.
No. 25 Canadian Field Surgical Team, 1 November 1951-31 March 1952.

Volume 18, 398.
No. 25 Canadian Field Surgical Team, 1 June 1952-6 November 1954.

Volume 18, 398.
No. 25 Canadian Field Transfusion Team, 1 November 1951-6 November 1954.

Volume 18, 398.
No.1 Canadian Base Medical Unit, 29 June-31 December 1954.

Volume 18, 398.
No. 1 Canadian Medical Liaison Detachment, 1 April 1952-31 December 1954.

Volume 18, 399.
No.2 Canadian Medical Liaison Detachment, 4 May 1951-31 December 1954.

Volume 18, 400.
No.1 Infantry Divisional Ordnance Field Park, 1 December 1953-31 December 1954.

Volume 18, 401.
No.25 Canadian Infantry Brigade Ordnance Company, 23 September 1950-2 January 1952.

Volume 18, 401.
Canadian Army Ordnance Elements, First(Commonwealth) Division, 1 January-December 1952.

Volume 18, 402.
Canadian Army Ordnance Elements, First(Commonwealth) Division, January 1953-31 December 1954.

Volume 18, 403.
No. 27 Canadian Infantry Brigade Ordnance Company, 5 June 1951-April 1953.

Volume 18, 404.
No. 27 Canadian Infantry Brigade Ordnance Company, May-30 November 1953.

Volume 18, 404.
No.1 Canadian Base Ordnance Unit, 1 October 1951-May 1952.

Volume 18, 405.
No.1 Canadian Base Ordnance Unit, June 1952-September 1953.

Volume 18, 406.
No.1 Canadian Ordnance Liaison Establishment, 1 April-25 October 1951.

Volume 18, 406.
No.2 Canadian Ordnance Liaison Establishment, 2 April-3 November 1951.

Volume 18, 407.
No. 25 Canadian Support Workshop, 1 November 1950-30 November 1951.

Volume 18, 407.
No. 40 Infantry Workshop(was No. 23 Infantry Workshop), 22 March 1953-14 April 1954.

Volume 18, 408.
No. 41 Infantry Workshop(was No. 191 Canadian Infantry Workshop), 5 August 1950-30 April 1953.

Volume 18, 409.
No. 42 Infantry Workshop(was No. 194 Infantry Workshop), 4 May 1951-October 1952.

Volume 18, 410.
No. 42 Infantry Workshop, November 1952-October 1953, April-31 December 1954.

Volume 18, 411.
No. 43 Infantry Workshop(was No. 195 Infantry Workshop), 15 February-31 May 1952.

Volume 18, 411.
No. 43 Infantry Workshop, 7 November 1953-31 December 1954.

Volume 18, 411.

No.1 Canadian Base Repair Section, 20 September 1951-December 1952.

Volume 18, 412.
No. 1 Canadian Base Repair Section, January 1953-31 December 1954.

Volume 18, 412.
1 Canadian Infantry Brigade Light Aid Detachment(was No. 191 Light Aid Detachment), 5 May 1951-April 1953.

Volume 18, 413.
1 Canadian Infantry Brigade Light Aid Detachment, May 1953-31 December 1954.

Volume 18, 414.
4th Canadian Infantry Brigade Light Aid Detachment(was No. 193 Canadian Light Aid Detachment), 1 November 1950-31 October 1954.

Volume 18, 414.
1 Regiment, Royal Canadian Horse Artillery Light Aid Detachment(was No. 170 Light Aid Detachment), 1 August 1952-18 April 1953.

Volume 18, 414.
2 Regiment, Royal Canadian Horse Artillery Light Aid Detachment (was No. 192 Canadian Light Aid Detachment), 1 December 1953-31 December 1954.

Volume 18, 415.
3 Regiment, Royal Canadian Horse Artillery Light Aid Detachment (was No. 197 Light Aid Detachment), 5 May 1951-February 1953.

Volume 18, 416.
3 Regiment, Royal Canadian Horse Artillery Light Aid Detachment, March 1953-31 October 1954.

Volume 18, 416.
4 Regiment, Royal Canadian Horse Artillery Light Aid Detachment (was No. 198 Light Aid Detachment), 18 April 1953-30 April 1954.

Volume 18, 417.
No.1 Field Dental Unit, 24 November 1953-31 December 1954.

Volume 18, 417F.
No. 25 Canadian Field Dental Unit, 17 November 1953-30 November 1954.

Volume 18, 418.
No. 27 Field Dental Unit, 4 May 1951-23 November 1953.

Volume 18, 418.
No. 35 Field Dental Unit, 29 April 1953-31 December 1954.

Volume 18, 418.
No.1 Base Post Office, 11 October 1950-August 1952.

Volume 18, 419.
No.1 Base Post Office, September 1952-31 December 1954.

Volume 18, 419.
No.2 Base Post Office, 1 September 1951-April 1953.

Volume 18, 420.
No.2 Base Post Office, May 1953-31 December 1954.

Volume 18, 420.
No.1 Canadian Overseas Postal Depot, 7 October 1952-31 January 1955.

Volume 18, 421.
No.1 Canadian Communications Zone Postal Unit, 17 November 1950-April 1954.

Volume 18, 422.
No.1 Canadian Communications Zone Postal Unit, May-31 December 1954.

Volume 18, 422.
No.2 Canadian Communications Zone Postal Unit, 9 August 1951-February 1953.

Volume 18, 423.
No.2 Canadian Communications Zone Postal Unit, March 1953-31 December 1954.

Volume 18, 423.
No.1 Canadian Air Division Postal Unit, 1 October 1952-October 1953.

Volume 18, 424.
No.1 Canadian Air Division Postal Unit, November 1953-31 December 1954.

Volume 18, 424.
No.1 Canadian Field Security Section, 1 September 1950-December 1951.

Volume 18, 425.
No.1 Canadian Field Security Section, February-31 December 1954.

Volume 18, 425.
No.2 Field Security Section(restricted), 7 May 1951-February 1954.

Volume 18, 426.
No.1 Canadian Provost Company, 1 February-31 December 1954.

Volume 18, 426.
No. 25 Canadian Provost Detachment(restricted), 28 August 1950-August 1952.

Volume 18, 427.
No. 25 Canadian Provost Detachment, September 1952-31 December 1954.

Volume 18, 428.
No. 27 Provost Detachment, 4 May 1951-December

1952.

Volume 18, 429.
No. 27 Provost Detachment, January 1953-1 February 1954.

Volume 18, 429.
No.1 Field Detention Barracks, 31 July 1951-October 1952.

Volume 18, 430.
No.1 Field Detention Barracks, November 1952-31 December 1954.

Volume 18, 430.
No. 25 Field Detention Barracks, 20 March 1951-December 1952.

Volume 18, 431.
No. 25 Field Detention Barracks, January 1953-16 November 1954.

Volume 18, 431.
No. 25 Canadian Reinforcement Group, 1 October 1950-March 1951.

Volume 18, 432.
No. 25 Canadian Reinforcement Group, April 1961-June 1952.

Volume 18, 433.
No. 25 Canadian Reinforcement Group, August 1953-August 1954.

Volume 18, 434.
No. 25 Canadian Reinforcement Group, September-31 December 1954.

Volume 18, 434.
No. 25 Canadian Field Historical Detachment, 27 April 1951-30 April 1954.

Volume 18, 434.
No.2 Canadian Administrative unit, 1 September 1950-December 1951.

Volume 18, 435.
No.2 Canadian Administrative Unit, January 1953-February 1954.

Volume 18, 436.
No.2 Canadian Administrative Unit, March-31 December 1954.

Volume 18, 436.
No. 3 Canadian Administrative Unit, 4 May 1951-February 1952.

Volume 18, 437.
No. 3 Canadian Administrative Unit, March-December 1952.

Volume 18, 438.
No. 3 Canadian Administrative Unit, January-October 1953.

Volume 18, 439.
No. 3 Canadian Administrative Unit, November 1953-31 December 1954.

Volume 18, 439.
Administrative increment-2 Battalion Princess Patricia's Canadian Light Infantry, 19 December 1950-30 November 1951.

Volume 18, 440.
Headquarters, Canadian Communications Zone Detachments, 1 November 1951-October 1953.

Volume 18, 441.
Headquarters, Canadian Communications Zone Detachments, November 1953-8 November 1954.

Volume 18, 441.
Canadian Military Mission Far East, 20 September 1950-31 December 1954.

Volume 18, 441.
Royal Canadian Horse Artillery Band, 19 June- 31 December 1953.

Volume 18, 442.
Royal Canadian Engineers, 2 August-31 December 1954.

Volume 18, 442.
Royal 22e Band, 1 April-30 June 1953.

Volume 18, 442.
No.1 Canadian Public Relations Unit, 6 May 1951-September 1952.

Volume 18, 442.
Royal Canadian Rifles Band, 28 January-17 August 1954.

Volume 18, 443.
No.1 Canadian Public Relations Unit, October 1952-December 1954.

Volume 18, 443.
No. 25 Canadian Public Relations Unit, October 1950-December 1952.

Volume 18, 444.
No. 25 Canadian Public Relations Unit, January 1953-December 1954.

Volume 18, 444.
79 Field Regiment Signal Troop, May 1951-March 1952.

Volume 18, 445.
79 Field Regiment Signal Troop, April 1952-November 1954.

C5. Director of Internment Operations, 1939-1945, 10.2 metres (volumes 1589-1595, 6576-6595, 11244-11273, 10398, reels T-7020-T-7057).

Most files relate to German and Italian prisoners of war.

Volume 11249. File 9-4-7 and volume 1126. File 12-33-IA deal with Japanese internees.

C6. Army Historical Section, 1919-1964, 23.3 metres(volumes 1732-1765, 1810-1909, 69078-6929, 698-7000).

HQ 683-1-IL, volume 13. File 196.
Japanese enlistment in the Canadian Expeditionary Forces.

Volume 1833. File GAQ 8-36.
Chinese coolies, n.d.

Convert file numbers by Scanlon's indexes.

C8. Military District Records, 1907-1938, 1.5 metres (volumes 1201, 4254-4758, 2331-2339).

Pacific Command records

Volume 4324. File 34-1-171.
Repatriation of Chinese coolies, 1919-1920.

Volume 4642 MD 11 99-4-57, 1916-1917.
Mobilization of a Japanese battalion.

Volume 4740, MD 13448-14-262-1, 1915.
Japanese battalion, not authorized and recruiting.

C9. Adjutant-general Branch, 1870-1964.

C9f. Special assistant to the Attorney-general, 1941-1946.
4.8 metres(volumes 8018-8025).

Volume 8018-8020.
Covers East Asia and South East Asia.

Volume 8027.
A few files.

Volumes 8028-8029.
Camps in East Asia and South East Asia.

D. Royal Canadian Navy, 1903-1970.

D1. Naval Headquarters registry files, 1903-1965.

Volume 3767-9.

File 1043-45-2(volumes 1-15).
Special cases of transportation. Chinese coolies overseas, 1917-1920.

Volume 3771-2.

File 1043-45-1(volumes 1-5).
Return of Chinese coolies from overseas, 1919-1922.

Volume 3864.

File 1023-18-2.
Naval intelligence - Japanese activities in Canada and United States, 1930-1946.

Volume 3884.

File 1029-6-32.
Press censorship re transport of coolies through Canada.

Volume 5598.

File 28-1-10.
Committee - Orientals in British Columbia, 1941.

Volume 8177.

File 1812-12.
Repatriation of Japanese personnel, 1946.

Reel C-5848.

File NSS 1023-1-8.
Naval intelligence from C. in C. China Station, 1916-1939.

NSC 1023-4-16.
Naval intelligence. Organisation and administration. Reports on activities of Far Eastern Intelligence Section, NS Headquarters, 1942.

Reel-5852-3.

NSS 1023-18-1.
Naval intelligence, Japan. 1927-1944.

NSS 1023-18-2.
Naval intelligence. Japanese activities in Canada and the United States, 1932-1941.

NSS 1023-18-5.
Naval intelligence, Japanese naval and mercantile shipbuilding, 1942-1944.

Reel C-5853.

NSS 1023-18-6.
Naval intelligence, Japanese submarines, 1941-1944.

NSS 1023-18-7.
Naval intelligence, notes on Japanese warfare, 1942.

NSS 1023-18-8.
Naval intelligence, Japanese bacteriological warfare, 1942.

Reel C-5855.

File NSS 1023-18-2
Naval intelligence, Japanese activities in Canada and United States, 1932-1941.

Reel C-5857-C-5858.

NSS 1023-42-2.
Naval intelligence received from and transmitted to sources in China area. Monthly intelligence reports from Shanghai, 1931-1941.

Reel C-5858.

NSS 1023-42-3.
Monthly intelligence reports from Shanghai area, relative to China squadron movements, 1925-1935.

NSS 1023-42-4.
Naval intelligence reports from Shanghai area. China intelligence orders, 1935-1940.

Reel C-5858-C-5859.

NSS 1023-42-5.
Naval intelligence reports from Shanghai area. Monthly intelligence reports received from Hong Kong, 1932-1941.

Reel C-5859.

NSS 1023-42-6.
Naval intelligence reports from the Shanghai area, China Station memoranda, 1940-1941.

Reel C-5859-62.

NSC 1023-43-2.
Naval intelligence. Monthly intelligence summaries from Singapore, Straits Settlements, Malaya Command, Intelligence summaries, Fort Canning, 1926-1944.

Reel C-5863.

NSC 1029-6-32.
Transportation of coolies through Canada, 1917.

D2. Ships' logs, 1917-1983. 297.6 metres

World War II.

Ontario(cruiser). Files 8872-8885, 1945-1958.

Prince David(armed merchant cruiser). Files 7749-7750.

Prince Henry(armed merchant cruiser). File 7751, 1940-1945.

Prince Robert(armed merchant cruiser). Files 7752-7754, 1940-1945.

Uganda(cruiser), unnumbered files. Files 7963-7964, 1942-1945.

Korean War.

Athabascan. Files 8556-8571, 1930-1963.

Cayuga. Files 8372-8375, 1931-1964.

Crusader. Files 8416-8425, 1945-1959.

Sioux. Files 9074-9087, 1931-1963.

Haida. Files 8205-8222, 1947-1963.

Huron. Files 8617-8631, 1931-1963.

Iroquois. Files 8637-8653, 1918-1962.

Nootka. Files 8849-8871, 1946-1964.

D4. Naval Intelligence records. Route files.

Volume 3783.

File 47.
Vancouver, routes to China, 1916-1918.

File 50.
Vancouver, routes to Philippine Islands, 1916-1918.

File 56.
Victoria, routes to Japan, 1917.
File 57.
Victoria, routes to Philippine Islands, 1916.

File 86.
Vancouver, routes to Japan, 1918.

Volume 3787.

File 101.
Trade routes, San Francisco to Orient.

File 102.
Trade routes, San Francisco to Manila.

Volume 3788.

File 104.
Trade routes, San Pedro to Orient.

File 105.
Trade routes, San Pedro to Manila.

File 106.
Trade routes, via Panama Canal to Orient.

D5. Korean Operations, 1950-1953, .9 metres, volumes 6984-6987.

Records relating to naval operations in Korean waters, consisting of operation orders, notes and situation reports.

D11. Pacific Command records, 1903-1966. 37.8 metres

Volume 11, 845.
H.M.C.S. **Naden** Gunnery Training Centre. Japanese suicide attacks, 1945.

Volume 11, 846.

File 034.
H.M.C.S. **Naden**, board of inquiry - protective custody, Japanese fishing vessels, 1942.

Volume 11, 847.

File 12-12.
H.M.C.S. **Naden**, confiscation of Japanese equipment, 1942.

Volume 11, 771.

File COPCS 115-146/21.
Air operations, Japan, 1941-1945.

Volume 11, 840.

File 8001-821/4.
General information, Japanese fishing vessels, 1941-1942.

File 8021-821/4.
Acquisition, purchase and officers of ships. Japanese fishing vessels, 1941-1948.

Volume 11, 842.

File 8341-821/4.
Damage to and loss of Japanese fishing vessels, 1942.

Volume 11, 867.

File DE 10-2.
Japanese, 1941-1942.

File DE 10-7-1.
Scheme of rounding up Japanese fishing vessels, 1941-1942.

File DE 10-7-2.
Vessels seized, 1942-1944.

File DE 10-7-3.
Vessels to be requisitioned, 1942-1943.

File DE 10-7-4;
Vessels to be requisitioned by Admiralty, 1941-1942.

Volume 11, 868.

File DE 10-7-7.
Japanese fishing vessels, survey reports, 1942.

File DE10-7-15.
Japanese fishing vessels, work reports, 1942.

File DE10-7-16.
Japanese fishing vessels, theft of equipment, 1942.

File DE 10-7-17.
Japanese fishing vessels, dismantling, 1942.

H.M.C.S. Chatham and NOIC Prince Rupert..

Volume 11, 893.

File 04-14.
Naval intelligence notes, Japanese, 1944-1945.

Volume 11, 894.

File S-75.
Japanese balloons, 1945.

Volume 11, 902.

File AE 6-10-1.
Relations with Imperial Japanese Navy, 1917.

File AE 6-10-2.
Visit of Japanese training squadron.

File AE 6-10-3.
HIJS **Idzumo**, 1914-1915.

File AE 6-10-4.
Visit of H.I.J.S. **Assama**, 1915.

File AE 6-10-9.
Visit of H.I.J.S. **Idzumo**, **Iwate** and **Nisshin**, 1917.

File AE 6-10-10.
Visit of H.I.J.S .**Towika** and **Yukumo**, 1917.

Engineer Officer, West Coast.

Volume 11, 888.

File 15-37.
Disposal of Japanese vessels, 1943-1944.

File 15-37-4.
Japanese fishing vessels. Disposal Committee, 1942.

Volume 11, 880.

File ES 10-4-l.
Japanese boats seized, 1944-1944.

File ES 10-4-2.
Japanese boats purchased by the Admiralty, 1942-1943.

File ES 10-4-3.
Requisition of Japanese fishing boats laid up, 1942.

Staff Officer(Intelligence) West Coast..

Volume 11, 917.

File 5-1-128.
Japanese activities in British Columbia, companies, societies, etc., controlled by Japanese, n.d.

File 5-1-128.
Japanese activities in British Columbia. Details of Japanese fishing vessels, 1935-1942.

File 5-1-128.
Japanese activities in British Columbia. Roundup of Japanese craft in British Columbia, 1941-1942.

Volume 11, 918.

File E59-65-8
Consul-general, Shanghai, 1919.

File E57-65-10.
Ambassador, Tokyo, 1919-1923.

File 9-1-72.
Japanese balloons found in North American continent, 1945.

Volume 11, 919.

File S13-1-49.
Merchant shippers. Neutral ships to Far East, 1940-1941.

Volume 11, 922.
File 19-7-20.
Submarines, particulars of Japanese, 1942-1945.

File 19-7-21.
Submarines, movements of Japanese, 1942-1944.

File 20-1-10.
Trade, cargo shipments to Japan, 1940-1946.

Volume 11, 923.

File 09-6.
Interrogation of Canadian repatriates abroad **Gripsholm**, 1942.

D13. Department of National Defence: Canadian Naval Liaison Records.

Volume 11, 751.

File CS46-1-1.
Far Eastern War, general, 1945.

File CS 46-2-1.
Far Eastern War, base equipment, 1944-1945.

File CS46-4-1.
Fleet train, 1944-1945.

File CS 46-5-1.
Prince ships, 1944-1945.

File CS 46-6-1.
Escort vessels, 1944-1945.

File CS 46-7-1.
Miscellaneous, 1944-1945.

File CS 46-8-1.
Personnel, 1944-1945.

File CS 46-8-1.
Canadian repair facilities, 1945.

E. Royal Canadian Air Force, 1919-1965.

E1. Air Force Headquarters registry files, 1920-1972.
247.2 metres.

Volume 17, 582.

File 004-85/140, 1943-1959.
Cooperation and liaison, Chinese Air Force.

Volume 17, 586.

File 004-85/335, 1947-1965.
Cooperation and liaison, India.

Volume 17, 588.

File 004-85-380, 1954-1964.
Cooperation and liaison, Japan.

Volume 17, 591.

File 004-85/530, 1948-1965.
Cooperation and liaison, Pakistan.

Volume 17, 593.

File 004-85/690, 1946-1965.
Cooperation and liaison, Turkey.

Volume 17, 604.

File S004-100-85/136, 1955-1956.
Cooperation and liaison, Ceylon.

Volume 17, 604-17, 605.

File S004-100-85/250, 1954-1962.
Cooperation and liaison Indo-China.
International Supervisory Truce Commission.

Volume 17, 605.

File S064-100-85/335, 1953-1965.
International Supervisory Truce Commission, India.

Volume 17, 606.

File S064-100-85/340, 1953-1965.
International Supervisory Truce Commission, Indonesia.

File S064-100-85/380, 1954-1963.
International Supervisory Truce Commission, Japan.

File S064-100-85/395, 1952-1961.
International Supervisory Truce Commission, Korea.

File S064-100-85/435, 1959-1964.
International Supervisory Truce Commission,

Malaysia.
Volume 17, 607.

File S064-100-85/530, 1967-
International Supervisory Truce Commission, Pakistan.

File S064-100-85/690, 1955-1964.
International Supervisory Truce Commission, Turkey.

Volume 17, 985.

File D940-100-85/130, 1957.
Intelligence, Ceylon.

Volume 17, 985.

File S940-100-85/140, 1949-1964.
Intelligence, China.

File S940-100-85/250, 1952-1956.
Intelligence, French Indo-China.

E2. Air Board, 1920-1922. .062 metres(volume 3192)

Volume 3192.
Air Board Meeting =143.
Application of Chinese pilot turned down, 1921.

Volume 3192.
Air Board Meeting =160.
Aviation School in Saskatoon for Chinamen.

E7. Royal Canadian Air Force record books and diaries(by squadron, unit or station).

Originals held by Directorate of History, Department of National Defence.

Canadian Armed Forces, 1964.

G3. Directorate of History, 1913-1970. 167.3 metres (volumes 6632, 10399-11006, 11761, 18499-18850, 19836-19838, 20270-20684)(microfilm reels T-2405-T-2468, and T-3972-T-3980).

Records of the Canadian Army participation in the Second World War. Some deal with Canadian participation in the Korean war. Records of the Canadian Air Force, 1932-1966, including South East Asia. Mostly administrative files.

Accessioned/unprocessed records.

Include unprocessed accessions of records from the Second World War through integration of the armed forces in the mid-1960's.

Accession No. 8.

Army Headquarters files. 1903-1947-1950.

Volume 2203-2204.

File 70-14.
Information re Hong Kong, 1941-1947.

Volume 2207.

File 84-9.
Visit of Madame Chiang Kai Shek.

Volume 2249.

File 94-55.
Prisoners of War, Far East.

Volume 2554-2571A.
Siberian Expeditionary Force, 1918-1921.

Volume 2865.
Defence of Hong Kong, 1941-1945.

Volume 2892-2905.
U.N.W.C.C. Japan, 1945-1954(U.N.W.C.C. United Nations War Crimes Commission).

Volume 2916-1917.
Operational research Japanese balloons.

Volume 2924.
Surrender and Occupation of Japan. Force for Pacific area, 1945-1946.

Volume 2951.
Hong Kong Inquiry(Volumes 2, 3, 5 only).

Volume 6518.
Vancouver, Hindu riot, 1914.

Accession 83-84/165.

Finding aid 107. Boxes 36-38, 40, 47-49, 58-60.

Box 37.

2001-1930/29.
Organization and administration, a Canadian military mission for the Far East, 1950-1954.

Box 38.

2001-1930/11.

1. Organization and administration. Military components, Canadian delegation, Indo-China, 1961-1962.

2. Organization and administration, Military components, Canadian delegation, Indo-China, 1962-1963.

2001-1930/18.

5. Organization and administration, military components, Canadian delegation in Laos, 1962-1963.

2001-1930/29.

2. Organization and administration, Canadian military mission Far East, 1954-1955. Organization and administration, Canadian military mission Far East, 1955-1958.

Box 58.

9072-2-5.
Post War Planning Canada Army, Japan, 1944.

9072-9.
Post-hostilities development in Far East, 1945.

Accession 83-84/167.

Finding aid 112, part 2.

Boxes 4879-4914. File blocks 3060 to 3128.

Box 4901.

File 3125-9/80.
1. Welfare. General. Canadian contingent, U.N. forces Cyprus, 1964.

File 3125-9/80.
2. Welfare. General. Canadian contingent, U.N. forces Cyprus, 1964.

File 3125-9/80.
3. Welfare. General. Canadian contingent, U.N. forces Cyprus, 1964-1965.

File 3125-9/80.
4. Welfare. General. Canadian contingent, U.N. forces Cyprus, 1965.

File 3125-9/80-1.
1. Welfare. General. Payment of accounts. Canadian contingent. U.N. Cyprus, 1964.

File 3125-9/80-1.
2. Welfare. General. Payment of accounts. Canadian contingent. U.N. Cyprus, 1964-1965.

Box 4903.

File 3125-33/24.
1. Welfare. General. Troops in Far East, 1950-1951.

File 3125-33/24.
2. Welfare. General. Troops in Far East, 1951-1952.

File 3125-33/24.
3. Welfare. General. Troops in Far East, 1951-1952.

Box 4904.

File 3125-33/29.
4. Welfare. General. Troops in Far East, 1952-1953.

File 3125-33/29.
4. Welfare. General. Troops in Far East, 1952-1953.

File 3125-33/29.
5. Welfare. General. Troops in Far East, 1952-1956.

File 3125-33/29.
6. Welfare. General. Troops in Far East, 1953-1954.

File 3125-33/29.
7. Welfare. General. Troops in Far East, 1954-1955.

File 3125-33/29.
8. Welfare. General. Troops in Far East, 1955-1957.

Box 4907.

File 3125-1930/11.
1. Personnel services. Welfare. Military components Canadian delegation- Indo-China, 1954-1955.

Box 4908.

File 3125-1930/11.
2. Personnel services. Welfare. Military components Canadian delegation- Indo-China, 1955.

File 3125-1930/11.
3. Personnel services. Welfare. Military components Canadian delegation- Indo-China, 1955-1956.

File 3125-1930/11.
4. Personnel services. Welfare. Military components Canadian delegation- Indo-China, 1956-1958.

File 3125-1930/11.
5. Personnel services. Welfare. Military components Canadian delegation- Indo-China, 1957.

File 3125-1930/11.
6. Personnel services. Welfare. Military components Canadian delegation- Indo-China, 1957-1959.

File 3125-1930/11.
7. Personnel services. Welfare. Military components Canadian delegation- Indo-China, 1958-1960.

File 3125-1930/11.
8. Personnel services. Welfare. Military components Canadian delegation- Indo-China, 1961-1962.

File 3125-1930/11.
9. Personnel services. Welfare. Military components Canadian delegation- Indo-China, 1962-1963.

Box 4909.

File 3125-1930/11.
10. Personnel services. Welfare. Military components Canadian delegation- Indo-China, 1963.

File 3125-1930/11.
15. Personnel services. Welfare. Military components Canadian delegation- Indo-China, 1965-1966.

File 3125-1930/11.
16. Personnel services. Welfare. Military components Canadian delegation- Indo-China, 1965.

Box 4910.

File 3126-33/29.
1. Welfare, books, magazines and newspapers for troops in the Far East, 1950-1951.

File 3126-33/29.
2. Welfare, books, magazines and newspapers for troops in the Far East, 1952-1953.

File 3126-33/29.
3. Welfare, books, magazines and newspapers for troops in the Far East, 1953-1955.

File 3126-33/29.
4. Welfare, books, magazines and newspapers for troops in the Far East, 1964.

Box 4910.

File 3126-9/80.
Personnel, welfare, books, magazines and newspapers, for troops in the Canadian contingent, U.N. Cyprus, 1964-1965.

Box 4911.

File 3126-1930/11.
Personnel, welfare, books, magazines and newspapers, for military component Canadian delegation, Indo-China, 1963-1964.

File 3126-33/29.
5. Welfare, books, magazines and newspapers for troops in the Far East, 1955-1957.

File 3126-33/29-1.
Forces editions of newspapers produced in the Far East, 1953.

File 3127-9/80.
Welfare, cigarettes and tobacco, Canadian contingent U.N. Cyprus, 1964.

Box 4912.

File 3227-33/29.
1. Welfare, cigarettes and tobacco, troops in the Far East, 1950-1951.

File 3227-33/29.
2. Welfare, cigarettes and tobacco, troops in the Far East, 1951-1953.

File 3227-33/29.
3. Welfare, cigarettes and tobacco, troops in the Far East, 1953.

File 3227-33/29.
4. Welfare, cigarettes and tobacco, troops in the Far East, 1953-1954.

File 3227-33/29.
5. Welfare, cigarettes and tobacco, troops in the Far East, 1954-1959.

Accession 83-84/167.

Finding aid 112 Part 19. Boxes 6057-6100. File blocks 8905-9440.

Box 6095.

File 9010-35/148.
Intelligence administration, India, 1967.
File 9010-35/170.
Intelligence administration, Japan, 1967.

File 9010-35/178.
Intelligence administration, Korea, 1967.

File 9010-35/226.
Intelligence administration, Nepal, 1967.

File 9010-35/246.
Intelligence administration, Pakistan, 1967.

File 9010-35/338.
Intelligence administration, Turkey, 1964-1967.

Accession 83-84/215.

Finding aid 119 Part 5. Boxes 277-410. File blocks 2001-9145.

Box 385.

File 9010-35/70.
Administration, Canadian military attaché in China, 1947-1950.

Box 389.

File 9010-35/140.
1. Intelligence administration in India, 1961-1963.

File 9010-35/140.
2. Intelligence administration in India, 1962-1963.

File 9010-35/140.
3. Intelligence administration in India, 1963-1964.

Box 390.

File 9010-35/170.
1. Intelligence administration in Japan, 1951.

File 9010-35/170.
2. Intelligence administration in Japan, 1957-1958.

File 9010-35/170.
3. Intelligence administration in Japan, 1958-1959.

File 9010-35/170.
4. Intelligence administration in Japan, 1959-1960.

File 9010-35/170.
5. Intelligence administration in Japan, 1960-1962.

File 9010-35/170.
6. Intelligence administration in Japan, 1962-1964.

Box 392.

File 9010-35/246.
1. Intelligence administration in Pakistan, 1961-1962.

File 9010-35/246.
2. Intelligence administration in Pakistan, 1962-1963.

File 9010-35/246.
3. Intelligence administration in Pakistan, 1963-1964.

Box 395.

File 9010-35/330.
1. Intelligence administration in Turkey, 1948-1951.

File 9010-35/330.
2. Intelligence administration in Turkey, 1951-1954.

File 9010-35/330.
3. Intelligence administration in Turkey, 1954-1955.

File 9010-35/330.
4. Intelligence administration in Turkey, 1956-1957.

File 9010-35/330.
5. Intelligence administration in Turkey, 1957-1962.

File 9010-35/330.
6. Intelligence administration in Turkey, 1962-1963.

File 9010-35/330.
7. Intelligence administration in Turkey, 1963-1964.

Box 399.

File 9055-34/6.
1. Intelligence - Military reports, general Afghanistan, 1961-1962.

File 9055-34/6.
2. Intelligence - Military reports, general Afghanistan, 1962-1963.

File 9055-34/6.
3. Intelligence - Military reports, general Afghanistan, 1963.

File 9075-34/114.
2. Intelligence briefing, Indo-China, 1960-1962.

Box 405.

File 9145-44/6.
Intelligence cooperation and liaison with Ceylon, 1956-1960.

File 9145-44/70.
Intelligence cooperation and liaison with China, 1947-1964.

Box 408.

File 9145-44/115.
Intelligence cooperation and liaison with Indo-China, liaison representatives in Ottawa, 1964.

Box 410.

File 9145-44/148.
1. Intelligence cooperation and liaison with India, 1955-1957.

File 9145-44/148.
2. Intelligence cooperation and liaison with India, 1957-1958.

File 9145-44/148.
3. Intelligence cooperation and liaison with India, 1958-1960.

Accession 83-84/215.

Finding aid 119 Part 6.

Boxes 411-1249. File blocks 9145 to 9480 and 1200.

Box 411.

File 9145-44/148.
4. Intelligence cooperation and liaison with India, 1960-1961.

File 9145-44/148.
5. Intelligence cooperation and liaison with India, 1961-1963.

File 9145-44/148.
6. Intelligence cooperation and liaison with India, 1963.

File 9145-44/148.
7. Intelligence cooperation and liaison with India, 1963-1964.

File 9145-44/148.
8. Intelligence cooperation and liaison with India, 1962-1965.

File 9145-44/148.
9. Intelligence cooperation and liaison with India, 1963-1965.

Box 412.

File 9145-44/154.
Liaison representatives in Iran, 1951-1963.

Box 413.

File 9145-44/170.
Intelligence cooperation and liaison with Japan, 1957-1964.

Box 418.

File 9145-44/330.
1. Intelligence cooperation and liaison with Turkey, 1963.

File 9145-44/330.
2. Intelligence cooperation and liaison with Turkey, 1946-1953.

File 9145-44/330.
3. Intelligence cooperation and liaison with Turkey, 1954-1956.

File 9145-44/330.
4. Intelligence cooperation and liaison with Turkey, 1956.

File 9145-44/330.
5. Intelligence cooperation and liaison with Turkey, 1956-1958.

File 9145-44/330.
6. Intelligence cooperation and liaison with Turkey, 1958-1959.

File 9145-44/330.
7. Intelligence cooperation and liaison with Turkey, 1959-1963.

Box 439.

File 9465-98/8.
1. Treaties, pacts and agreements. U.N. operations Korea, 1950-1953.

File 9465-98/8.
2. Treaties, pacts and agreements. U.N. operations Korea, 1953.

File 9465-98/8.
3. Treaties, pacts and agreements. U.N. operations Korea, 1953-1954.

File 9465-98/8.
4. Treaties, pacts and agreements. U.N. operations Korea, 1954.

File 9465-98/8.
5. Treaties, pacts and agreements. U.N. operations Korea, 1954.

File 9465-98/8.
6. Treaties, pacts and agreements. U.N. operations Korea, 1953-1954.

File 9465-98/8.
7. Treaties, pacts and agreements. U.N. operations Korea, 1954.

File 9465-98/8.
8. Treaties, pacts and agreements. U.N. operations Korea, 1954.

File 9465-98/8.
9. Treaties, pacts and agreements. U.N. operations Korea, 1954.

File 9465-98/8.
10. Treaties, pacts and agreements. U.N. operations Korea, 1954-1955.

File 9465-98/8.
11. Treaties, pacts and agreements. U.N. operations Korea, 1955.

File 9465-98/8.
12. Treaties, pacts and agreements. U.N. operations Korea, 1955.

File 9465-98/8.
13. Treaties, pacts and agreements. U.N. operations Korea, 1955.

File 9465-98/8.
14. Treaties, pacts and agreements. U.N. operations Korea, 1955.

File 9465-98/8.
15. Treaties, pacts and agreements. U.N. operations Korea, 1955.

File 9465-98/8.
16. Treaties, pacts and agreements. U.N. operations Korea, 1955-1956.

File 9465-98/8.
17. Treaties, pacts and agreements. U.N. operations Korea, 1956.

File 9465-98/8.
18. Treaties, pacts and agreements. U.N. operations Korea, 1956.

File 9465-98/8.
19. Treaties, pacts and agreements. U.N. operations Korea, 1956.

File 9465-98/8.
20. Treaties, pacts and agreements. U.N. operations Korea, 1956.

File 9465-98/8.
21. Treaties, pacts and agreements. U.N. operations Korea, 1957.

File 9465-98/8.
22. Treaties, pacts and agreements. U.N. operations Korea, 1957.

File 9465-98/8.
23. Treaties, pacts and agreements. U.N. operations Korea, 1957.

File 9465-98/8.
24. Treaties, pacts and agreements. U.N. operations Korea, 1957.

File 9465-98/8.
25. Treaties, pacts and agreements. U.N. operations Korea, 1957.

File 9465-98/8.
26. Treaties, pacts and agreements. U.N. operations Korea, 1957-1958.

File 9465-98/8.
27. Treaties, pacts and agreements. U.N. operations Korea, 1957-1958.

File 9465-98/8.
28. Treaties, pacts and agreements. U.N. operations Korea, 1958.

File 9465-98/8.
29. Treaties, pacts and agreements. U.N. operations Korea, 1958.

File 9465-98/8.
30. Treaties, pacts and agreements. U.N. operations Korea, 1958.

File 9465-98/8.
31. Treaties, pacts and agreements. U.N. operations Korea, 1958.

File 9465-98/8.
32. Treaties, pacts and agreements. U.N. operations Korea, 1958.

File 9465-98/8.
33. Treaties, pacts and agreements. U.N. operations Korea, 1958-1959.

File 9465-98/8.
34. Treaties, pacts and agreements. U.N. operations:Korea, 1959.

File 9465-98/8.
35. Treaties, pacts and agreements. U.N. operations Korea, 1959.

File 9465-98/8.
36. Treaties, pacts and agreements. U.N. operations Korea, 1959.

Box 445.

File 9470-33/29.
U.S. State Department reports on Far East, 1948-1949.

File 9470-33/29.
U.S. State Department reports on China, 1949.

File 9470-33/106.
U.S. State Department reports on Formosa, 1949.

File 9470-33/154.
U.S. State Department reports on Iran, 1948-1950.

File 9470-33/170.
U.S. State Department reports on Japan, 1948-1950.

File 9470-33/178.
U.S. State Department reports on Korea, 1952-1953.

Accession 83-84/227.

Finding aid 122 and B.

Volume 9263.

File 85/380.
War criminals, Japan, volumes 1-7, 1951-1960.

File 85/395.
War criminals, Korea, 1952-1953.

Volume 9292.

File 85/380.
Reports and returns. Military Component, Canadian Delegation, Indo-China, 1966-1972.

File 5-16530-1513.
Reports and returns. Military Component, Canadian Delegation, Laos, 1964-1967.

Boxes 41-65. 19.6 metres.

United Nations Emergency Force(Middle East) boxes 62-65.

International Commission of Supervision and Control in Indo-China: Vietnam, 1972-1973.

Accession 84-85/167.

Finding aid 127.

Canadian contingency, United Nations Forces in Cyprus, 1973-1974.

Record Group 25. External Affairs.

A. High Commissioner's Office, London.

A1. Correspondence with Canadian and British Government Departments, 1880-1903(volumes 1-38), 7.2 metres(see also Record Group 6, A5). File list available.

Volume 52.
Acknowledgment of a letter on Chinese immigration, 6 October 1891.

Volume 82.

File 727.
Control of Communist agitation in Sikhs community in British Columbia, 1926-1927.

Volume 94.
Chinese immigrants, Peninsular and Oriental Navigation Company, 13 June 1892.

Volume 94.
Chinese immigration to Canada, Peninsular and Oriental Steam Navigation Company, 25 June 1892.

A2. Correspondence with Canadian and British Government Departments, 1904-1945., 20.7 metres.(volumes 139-344, 2166),

Volume 141.

File C 1/96.
Immigration to Canada of Armenian tobacco planters, 1904-1905.

Volume 148.

File C 7/58.
Emigration of certain Armenian villages, 1912- .

Volume 181.

File C 16/68.
British Columbia legislation prohibiting the employment of white girls by Chinese, 1920.

Volume 198.

File I 6/79.
Proposed immigration to Canada of the families of certain naturalized Turks, 1906.

Volume 199.

File I 11/62.
Alleged landings of Sikhs in British Columbia, 1906.

File I 14/29.
Armenians who have been naturalized in Canada, but desire to return to their own country to dispose of property, 1907.

File I 15/40.
Proposed immigration of Turkish family, 1907.

File I 16/18.
Intended emigration of the wife and child of man from Turkey to Canada, 1907.

Volume 200.

File I 19
Proposed emigration of Sahapian family from Turkey, 1908.

File I 20/11.
Proposed Hindu immigration from British Columbia to British Honduras, 1908.

File I 21/24.
Proposed Hindu immigration from British Columbia to British Honduras, 1909.

Volume 229.

File M-60-26.
Chinese coolies across Canada, 1916-1919.

Volume 251.

File N-12-4.
Chinese coolies, transportation, 1921.

Volume 252.

File P-1-27.
Japanese troubles in Vancouver, 1907.

File P-1-36.
Oriental immigration, 1908.

Volume 258.

File P-3-6.
Emigration from India, 1915.

Volume 296.

File P-10-13.
Appeal to settle Armenian question, 1920.

File P-10-18.
Armenian appeals, 1921.

Volume 305.

File S-10-72.
Okanogan valley, sale of land to Japanese in, 1919-1920.

Volume 306.

File T-2-92.
Chinese servant, exemption from Canadian immigration laws, 1906.

A12. Canada House - Secret and Confidential Files, 1936-1955, 1976-1982. 10.5 metres (volumes 2077-2123).

This series of records cover many aspects of Canada's relationship with Asia and the Pacific, for the years 1936 to 1955 with a heavy emphasis on the immediate post war period. Relations with countries such as China, Japan, U.S.S.R., Australia, New Zealand, India and Pakistan are covered along with defence and security questions and the work of the United Nations. Access to these records is subject to the provisions of the privacy legislation. The records are in hard copy form only and the finding aid is a list of subject files.

Volume 2089.

File AR23/15.
Japan - disposal of properties and assets in Canada, 1947.

File AR23/16.
Japan - treatment of Japanese in Canada, 1942-1947.

B3. Washington Embassy, 1927-1970, 11.8 metres (volumes 2124-2165, 2453-2459, 2480-2481, 3175-3176).

The emphasis of the records in this series is the Second World War and in the years immediately following. The records cover such topics as the Mutual Aid Plan, Colombo Plan, and other files on economic assistance. Also included is the Far Eastern Commission along with Canada's relations with Japan, China, Indo-China and the Soviet Union. Access to the records is subject to the provisions of the access to information and privacy legislation. The records are in hard copy only and the finding aid is a list of subject files.

Volume 2163.

File 92, part 1.
Japan - Japanese in Canada, 1950.

B5. Canadian Legation, Tokyo. 10 metres.(volumes 2482, 2611),

Volume 2482.
Visitors' book, 1929-1972.

Volume 2611.
Proposal, Canadian Legation, Japan. Recommendations by Herbert Marler.

B8. International Commission of Supervision and Control in Vietnam, Cambodia and Laos, 1953-1974. 1.2 metres(volumes 3068-3073), Finding aid 51.

C4. Japanese surrender, 1945(Volume 697).

C7. Foreign and Canadian bound Prints, 1803-1949. 5.8 metres(volumes 701-710, 2979-3003).

Volume 704.
Asiatic immigration, 1884-1908.

D1. Office of the Under-Secretary of State for External Affairs, 1908-1962. 1.23 metres (volumes 715-829, 2959-2961, reels T-1445 to T-1771, T-1790 to T-1813, T-2201 to T-2209).

Volume 722.

File 62.
Chinese immigration to Canada, n.d.

Volume 727.

File 83.
Oriental activities in British Columbia, 1939.

File 84, part 1.
Japanese immigration to Canada re Lemieux mission to Japan, 1907-1912.

File 84, part 2.
Questions and speeches in House of Commons re Japanese problem in British Columbia, 1922.

File 84, part 3.
Various problems of Japanese immigration, 1924-1925.

Volume 728.

File 84, part 4.
Press clippings, 1924-1925.

File 84, part 5.
Re Oriental ownership of land, 1925-1926.

File 84, part 6.
Two folders marked "Japanese immigration" and "Japanese immigration, duplicate", correspondence, 1908-1926.

File 84, part 7.
Two folders marked "Japanese immigration" and "Japanese immigration, duplicate", correspondence, 1925-1926.

File 84, part 8.
Same as above, working folder of Dr. Skelton, 1926-1927.

Volume 729.

File 84, part 10.
Memoranda, correspondence, etc., re Japanese immigration, 1938.

File 84, part 11.
Continuation of part 10, 1938-1941.

File 85, part 11.
Japanese fishing licences, 1926-1939.

Volume 803-804.

File 561.
Enfranchising of East Indians in British Columbia. n.d.

Volume 805.

File 573.
Military training of Orientals in British Columbia, 1940.

The records in this series reflect the pivotal role of the Office of the Under Secretary of State and therefore cover all aspects of the department's operations with an emphasis on the inter-war period and the early years of the Second World War. Topics covered include China-Japan relations, Japanese immigration, League of Nations, trade and commercial topics along with defence question in the later 1930's and during the war. The records are on microfilm and can be borrowed on inter-library loan. The finding aid is a list of subject files.

E1. Clippings, 1881-1973(volumes 858-890, 2549-2577, 2610), 12 metres, microfilm 42 reels, C-7754-C-7796.

Volume 820.

File 69.
Re Asiatic immigration, 1903-1909.

Volume 890.

File 69.3-1909.

F1d. Washington Conference on the Limitation of Armaments, 1921-1922, .6 metres, volumes 915-920.

Files of the Canadian delegation.

Volume 915.

File 1.
Chinese railways.

File 2.
China, opium traffic.

File 5.
China, telegraphic communications.

File 8.
China, new financial consortium.

File 9.
Canada, legislation and regulations respecting Asiatic immigration.

File 12.
Mandated islands.

File 13.
Land owning and other civil rights, Chinese, Japanese and other Asiatics, 1921-1922.

Volume 916.

File 16.
Anglo-Japanese alliance, and Quadruple Pacific Pact.

Volume 917.

File 20.
Chinese revenue tariff.

File 21.
China, leased territories and spheres of influence.

File 22.
China, extra territoriality.

F1g. Intergovernmental Conferences and Meetings, 1907-1958,. 30.3 metres.(volumes 2279-2393) Includes Imperial Conferences, Imperial Economic Conferences, 1932, Commonwealth Prime Ministers' meetings, United Nations General Assembly sessions, meetings of the Economic and Social Council, and of UNESCO, and Colombo Plan discussions. Finding aid 26.

F1i. Imperial Economic Conference of 1932. 4 metres(volumes 3074-3075).

Includes study of trade with Commonwealth between 1920 and 1932.
Covers trade with India.

F2b. Far Eastern Commission, 1946-1949. 6.9 metres (volumes 929-951, 2578-2585).

The Commission was established to deal with the Japanese surrender and peace terms. Mimeograph copies of the minutes of the various committees of the Commission, reports, instructions and general documents.

F2c. United Nations War Crimes Commission, 1944-1947, .3 metres (volumes 952-954), Finding aid 29.

Volume 953.
List of Japanese war criminals.

F3a. International Military Tribunal for the Far East, Tokyo, 1946-1948. 6.0 metres (volumes 973-1000, 2586-2597) Finding aid 32.

Records consist of 48,513 pages of the Tribunal Proceedings.

F3b. United States of America versus Admiral Soemu Toyoda, 1948. 1.2 metres (volumes 2598-2604), Finding aid 33.

Bound proceedings of the case against Admiral Soemu Toyoda as a war criminal.

F3c. United States of America versus Lieutenant-General Hiroshi Tamura, 1948. .6 metres (volumes 2604-2606) Finding aid 34.

Bound proceedings of the case against Lieutenant-General Tamura as a war criminal.

F4. Negotiations, and agreements regarding Commerce, Fisheries, immigration, Boundaries, 1883-1951. 1 metre.(volumes 1002-1011),

Volume 1003.
Prints 1-42, re Asiatic immigration, 1884-1925.

Volume 1004.

Bound pamphlet "Australasia" re Chinese immigration with Australian colonies, copies of "Judgment of the Supreme Court of British Columbia in re Nakane and Okakaze", 1884-1925.

Volume 1004.

Collection of reports relating to Asiatic immigration, 1907.

F6b. Canadian Delegation to the United Nations, 1945-1949, 8 metres. (volumes 1016-2067, 2612-2616), Finding aid 39.

Volume 1030.

File 246C.
Exchange of civilian internees with Japan, 1945.

Volume 1031.

File 331.
Policy re treatment of Japanese in Canada, n.d.

G1a. Central Registry Files, 1909-1955. 184.72 metres(volumes 1092-2002, 2007, 2011-2016, 2278, 2448-2451, 3205), Finding aid 47.1, 47.7.

"39" series. File numbers are consecutive within each year, not according to subject order.
Subject index exists on microfiche, and is available in the National Archives.

Volume 559.

File 1104.
Asiatic immigration into British Columbia, 1904.

Volume 1103.

File 336.
Canadian Immigration Bill No. 102, with special reference to East Indians, 1910.

Volume 1104.

File 559.
Asiatic immigration into British Columbia, 1904.

Volume 1111.

File 211.
Confidential series File 23 memorial of British Indian subjects re the immigration laws of Canada, 1911.

Volume 1112.

File 342.
Japanese emigration and colonization, 1911.

Volume 1118.

File 66.
Confidential series. File 9, facilities for British Indian subjects and general question of Hindu and Asiatic immigration, 1912.
Volume 1122.

File 412, part 2.
Attitude of some provincial governments to Japanese, re granting of licences, 1912.

Volume 1128.

File 1912-1264.
Facilities to emigrate to Canada for Armenian villagers, 1912.

Volume 1129.

File 66.
Dispatch from the Viceroy of India re the admission to Canada of two Sikh women, 1913.

Volume 1132.

File 329.
Japanese passengers, to and from Canada, 1913.

Volume 1133.

File 477.
Election of representatives of Chinese communities abroad, 1913.

Volume 1135.

File 1045.
Claims from Chinese for damages sustained during recent riots at Nanaimo, British Columbia, 1913.

Volume 1138.

File 40, part 1.
Memorandum re the immigration of families of British Indians, 1914.

Volume 1139.

File 40, part 2.
Asiatic immigration, Tara Singh, 1914.

Volume 1141.

File 188.
Monthly statistics re Japanese immigration, 1914.

Volume 1142.

File 308.
Re sale of ammunition for warlike purposes to Chinese in Canada, 1914.

File 462.
China protests employment of women in business and segregation of school children in British Columbia, 1914.

Volume 1156.

File 40.
Re forfeiture of certain seditious Indian publications, 1915.

Volume 1160.

File 469.
Despatch from British ambassador, 1915.

Volume 1162.

File 878.
Draft agreement providing for admission into Canada of Chinese labourers, 1915.

Volume 1166.

File 1939.
Complaint of Chinese Consul-general of police raids on premises of Chinese in Sault Ste-Marie, Ontario, 1915.

Volume 1185.

File 897-16.
Asiatic immigration, 1916.

Volume 1186.

File 1560-16.
Japanese immigration, 1916.

Volume 1187.

File 2336-16.
Feeling towards the Japanese in Canada, 1916.

Volume 1204.

File 43-17.
Asiatic immigration, 1917.

Volume 1221.

File 43-18.
Asiatic immigration, 1918.

Volume 1222.

File 221-18.
Complaint of Japanese consul at Vancouver against resolution of British Columbia legislature, of April 15, 1902.

Volume 1237.

File 43-19.
Asiatic immigration, 1919.

Volume 1241.

File 379-19.
Complaint against British Columbia bill prohibiting employment of white women by Chinese, 1919.

File 380.
Riots in Halifax against Chinese, 1919.

Volume 1250.

File 1919-30381.
Memorandum by Armenian mission to U.S .re recognition of the government of Armenia, 1919-1920.

Volume 1259.

File 1920-143.
Disposition of Armenia, 1920.

Volume 1274.

Files 1920-1943.
Armenian minorities treaty, 1920.

Volume 1278.

File 1920-1947.
Armenia, future status of, 1920-1921.

Volume 1285.

File 43.
League of Nations' declarations and correspondence with Asiatic Exclusion League, 1922.

File 57.
Monthly statistics re Japanese immigration, 1921-1922.

Volume 1299.

File 1921-957.
Alliances of the Caucasian states, Armenia, Georgia, etc., 1921.

Volume 1300.

File 1011.
Invitation to two officials to visit Canada re position of Asiatics in Canada, 1921-1923.

File 1011FB.
Accounts of visit of officials re Asiatic immigration.

File 1921-1047.
Armenian prisoners of war at Erzerum, League of Nations, 1921.

Volume 1301.

File 1921-178.
National home for Turkish Armenians, 1921-1923.

Volume 1321.
File 589.
Confidential prints re Asiatic immigration, 1922.

Volume 1323.

File 767 C-57.
Chinese aviation school at Esquimalt(suspected connection with Chinese Nationalist League), 1922.

Volume 1325.

File 1922-99-C.
Protection of the Armenians, Asia Minor, 1922.

Volume 1362.

File 43.
Asiatic immigration (discrimination against Indian and Japanese), 1924.

Volume 1386.

File 1413.
Amendment to Japanese Nationality Law, 1924.

Volume 1416.

File 1925-103.
League of Nations, Russian refugees, Armenian refugees, 1925.

Volume 1430.

File 789, part 1.
Japanese immigration, 1926-1929.

File 789, part 2.
Japanese immigration, 1930-1938.

File 789, part 3.
Japanese immigration, 1939-1943.

File 799FP.
Report of W.L.Mackenzie King on methods of inducement for Japanese immigrants, 1907.

Volume 1432.

File 997.
Steps taken by the government of British Columbia to restrict number of Orientals engaged in industries in the province, 1925-1927.

Volume 1484.

File 1927-44FL.
Immigration to Canada of Russian (and Armenian), refugees, 1927.

Volume 1524.

File 867.
Employment of women by Chinese in Canada, 1923-1929.

Volume 1539.

File 178.
Immigration to Canada of Chinese, proposals of Eastern Canada Chinese Mission, 1929-1932.

Volume 1541.

File 249.
Japanese in British Columbia and action of Japanese consul at Vancouver, 1929.

Volume 1549.

File 714.
Canadian interests in the Pacific(memorandum on Asiatic immigration), 1929.

Volume 1571.

File 488.
Return to Canada of Canadian citizens of Japanese origin, procedure, 1930.

File 503.
Oriental immigration to Canada, 1930.

File 758.
Naturalization regulations, Japanese, 1931.

Volume 1634.

File 737.
Passports for East Indians, 1932-1936.

Volume 1664.

File 44-AJ.
Entry into Canada of U.S. citizens of Chinese ancestry, 1933-1934.

Volume 1673.

File 744.
Immigration to Canada of Chinese, n.d.

Volume 1703.

File 490.
Franchise for East Indians in British Columbia, 1934-1935.

Volume 1749.

File 643.
Enquiry re rights of East Indians in Canada.

Volume 1771.

File 104.
Publication of documents re immigration to Canada of East Indians, 1935-1936.

Volume 1803.

File 729.
Oriental relief recipients in British Columbia, 1935-1937.

Volume 1817.

File 1937-57.
Statistics of Japanese immigration to Canada, 1937-1941.

Volume 1839.

File 589.
Property purchased by Japanese in British Columbia, 1936-1937.

Volume 1863.

File 174.
Complaint of Japanese legation re cartoons in the Canadian press, 1938.

Volume 1867.

File 263-C, parts 1-4.
Inter-departmental committee on Orientals in Canada, 1938.

Volume 1867-68.

File 1839-263, parts 1-4.
Inter-departmental committee re Orientals in Canada, 1938-1948.

Volume 1874.

File 1938-690.
Japanese boat pullers on Pacific coast, 1938-1940.

Volume 1878.

File 1939-230.
Japanese import control and export control, 1939-1941.

Volume 1891.

File 60-N.
Deportation from Canada of East Indians, 1937-1946.

Volume 1895.

File 1939-159.
Japanese fishing vessels on Pacific Ocean, 1939.

Volume 1924.

File 1939-724-U, parts 1-2.
Censorship of Japanese transit mail, 1940-1945.

Volume 1930.

File 1939-724-AU.
Interception of Japanese wireless traffic in Canada, 1941-1942.

Volume 1940.

File 1939-724-ES.
Intercepted communications re Japanese Canadians enlisted in Canadian Army, 1945.

File 1939-724-EJ.
Censorship in Canada re Japanese language instruction, 1943-1944.

Volume 1944.

File 1939-757.
Treatment of enemy aliens in wartime, 1939-1945.

Volume 1965.

File 1939-855R.
Assets of enemy aliens interned in Canada, treatment of, 1943.

Volume 1974.

File 882.
Memo re: enlistment in Canada of persons of Japanese race, 1939.

Volume 2007.

File 1939-212, parts 1-3.
Activities of Japanese in Canada, 1939-1944.

G1b. Indexes and Registers to Central Registry correspondence, 1909-1940. 5.7 metres (volumes 2017-2075), microfilm 1909-1939, reels C-6825-C-6857)(T-2392-T-2394).

This Central Registry System covers the operational files of the Department of External Affairs from its inception in 1909. Most of the files end in 1939 as a new system was put in place at the start of the Second World War. The records cover all aspects of Canada's role in foreign affairs. The records are open and the finding aid is an alphabetical index which is available on microfiche.

G2. Central Registry Files. Originals 1940-1963. 117 metres(volumes 2167-2253, 2261-2277, 2394-2412, 2439-2447, 2452, 2486-2488, 2491-1496, 2678-2958, 2962-2978, 3004-3038, 3040-3041, 3106-3127), Numerous unprocessed accessions.

Records of the main departmental registry system, commonly referred to as the "1940 series".
The central registry was begun by the Department of External Affairs in 1940 and continues until 1963.
Like series G1 it covers all aspects of the department's operations. The records are covered by the provisions of the access to information and privacy legislation. The finding aid is a list of these operational files and

includes the more recent unprocessed accessions. Finding aids 48.1, 48.2, 48.5, 48.7, 48.8.

Subject index available in the Department of External Affairs and arrangements to use it have to be made with the Historical Section, through the Under Secretary of State.

Volume 1.

File 53-FS-40.
Visit to Canada of H.S.L.Polack, some correspondence re Hindu immigration, 1941-1943.

Volume 2411.

File 102-MP-40.
Activities of Japanese diplomatic and consular officers, February-October 1941.

Volume 2412.

File 102-A2W-40.
Status of Dr. Endicott and reports re Shanghai newsletter, April 1945-May 1952.

Accession 71/690, volumes 2167-2171.

Volume 2168.

File 53-KR-40.
Visit to Canada of Premier of Burma, U Saw, 1941-1942.

Volume 2169.
Visit to Canada of Madame Chiang Kai-shek, volumes 1-2, 1942-1944.

Volume 2170.

File 53-YP-40.
Visit to Canada of Chinese goodwill mission, 1944-1945.

File 53-YQ-40.
Visit to Canada of Chinese aviation professors, 1944-1945.

Volume 2171.

File 53-QLQ-40.Visit to Canada of Generalissimo and Madame Chiang Kai-shek, 1943-1946.

Volume 2174.

File 57-12-5 Shah Volume 1. Public relations. Special events coverage. Proposal re Shah of Iran, 1965.

File 110044-AT-40 Volumes 1-4. Export of arms to India, 1949-1957.

File 110044-AT-40 Volumes 5-8. Export of arms to India, 1952-1954.

Volume 2175.

File 110044-AT-40 Volumes 9-10.
Export of arms to India, 1954.

Volume 2176.

File 110044-AT-40 Volumes 11-15.
Export of arms to India, 1954-1957.

Volume 2177.

File 110044-AT-40 Volumes 16-22.
Export of arms to India, 1957-1958.

Volume 2178.

File 110044-AT-40 Volumes 23-28.
Export of arms to India, 1958-1962.

Volume 2179.

File 110044-AT-40 Volumes 29-31.
Export of arms to India, 1958-1962.

File 110044-AT-40 Volume 32, 1962-1963.

File 37-22-1 India Volume 1.
Foreign trade. Strategy in trade controls. Export of arms and only equipment by Canada to India, 1963-1965.

Volume 2202.

File 110044-AY-40 Volumes 3-7.
Export of arms to Indonesia, 1949-1963.

Volume 2218.

File 9901-Y-40 Volume 1.
CBC/IS transcription services to India, February 1949-May 1961.

Volume 2220.

File 9901-AE-40 Volume 1.
CBC/IS transcription services-China, June 1951.

File 9901-AH-40 Volume 1.
CBC/IS transcription services to Japan, December 1951-December 1952.

File 9901-AQ-40 Volume 1.
CBC/IS transcription services to Singapore and Malaya, May 1951-August 1952.

Volume 2222.

File 9901-BJ-40 Volume 1.
CBC/IS transcription services to Turkey, October 1950-

File 9901-BK-40 Volume 1
CBC/IS transcription services to Pakistan, May 1950-

May 1963.

File 9901-BT-40 Volume 1.
CBC/IS transcription services to Iran, September 1947-November 1963.

File 9901-BW-40 Volume 1.
CBC/IS transcription services to Philippines, May 1952-September 1962.

File 9901-CA-40 Volume 1.
CBC/IS transcription services to Indo-China, November 1954-September 1963.

File 9901-CB-40 Volume 1.
CBC/IS transcription services to Ceylon, August 1951-December 1962.

File 9901-CE-40 Volume 1.
CBC/IS transcription services to Rangoon, August 1961-August 1962.

File 9901-CH-40 Volume 1.
CBC/IS transcription services to Indonesia, June 1953-January 1962.

File 9901-CR-40 Volume 1. CBC/IS transcription services to Korea, April-October 1952.

Volume 2692.

File 6-FJ-40.
Death of President Lin Sen of China, May-October 1943.

File 8-A-40.
Opium Advisory Committee of the League of Nations, June 1940-March 1946.

File 8-B-40.
Narcotics Commission, general estimates for opium supervisory body, January 1940-December 1942.

Volume 2693.

File 8-B-40.
Narcotics Commission, general estimates for opium supervisory body, January 1943-December 1949.

File 8-E-40.
Narcotics Commission, general estimates for opium supervisory body, December 1940-August 1960.

File 8-Q-40.
Control of opium in areas of the Far East reoccupied by UN, proposals, December 1942-April 1953.

Volume 2708.

File 58-KZ-40.
National status of Nisei(Japanese Canadians), February 1942-August 1944.

File 72-M-40.
Aircraft for Iran from Canada, September 1940-June 1942.

Volume 2717.

File 72-MK-40.
Passage to UK for Chinese military mission visit to Canada, February 1943-May 1946.

File 72-MZ-40.
Canadian air squadron for China, proposals, February-July 1943.

Volume 2724.

File 112-40.
Trade with China and Japan, status, January 1940-December 1946.

Volume 2738.

File 351-40.
Japanese ships for Canadian trade, March 1940-August 1945.

File 370-40.
Intercepted telegrams of Japanese officials, February-March 1940.

Volume 2748.

File 487-40.
Japan-Netherlands East Indies situation, February 1940-November 1943.

Volume 2754.

File 592-A-40.
Arrangements between Canada and Japan, release of funds of expenses of legations, July 1941-January 1950.

File 592-B-40.
Remittances between Canada and Japan, general file, November-December 1941.

File 592-C-40.
Reciprocal arrangements with Japan for release of official balances, proposals re, March 1943-March 1947.

Volume 2760.

File 621-G-3-40.
Establishment of a mixed medical commission to operate between Canada and Japan, November 1942-April 1943.

Volume 2786.

File 630-40.
Trade relations of Iran with foreign countries, March 1940-October 1959.

File 639-40.
Establishment of Far Eastern security section, May 1940-August 1942.

Volume 2798.

File 773-B-1-40, Volume 1.
Treatment of Japanese Canadians, proposals of various persons, January 1941-January 1942.

File 773-B-1-40, Volume 2.
Treatment of Japanese Canadians, proposals of various persons, January-December 1942.

File 773-B-1-40, Volume 3.
Treatment of Japanese Canadians, proposals of various persons, January 1943-June 1945.

File 773-D-40.
Treatment of Thai nationals in wartime, December 1941-May 1946.

Volume 2799.

File 773-G-40.
Movement of a school home in of Japanese girls in Oriental homes in Victoria. Proposals of United Church of Canada Board of Home Missions, March-May 1942.

File 773-H-40.
Movement from British Columbia to Toronto under the auspices of the Women's Missionary Society of the United Church of Canada of a number of Japanese young women, proposals, March 1942-July 1945.

File 791-40.
Arms for Fiji, July 1940-June 1942.

Volume 2805.

File 880-40.
Communications re interned Italians from Japanese legation, July-August 1940.

Volume 2806.

File 916-40, Volume 1.
Evacuation from Japan of British subjects, reciprocal arrangements, August 1940-May 1941.

File 916-40, Volume 2.
Evacuation from Japan of British subjects, reciprocal arrangements, June 1941-June 1942.

Volume 2807.

File 960-40.
Japan-Australia relations, January 1941-May 1959.

Volume 2809.

File 1021-40.
Japan Times and **Vancouver Sun** essay competition on Canadian-Japanese relations, August 1940.

Volume 2815.

File 1099-41.
Delhi economic conference, 1940, September 1940-April 1942.

Volume 2817.

File 1132-41.
Complaint of Japanese minister re March of Time picture "Dutch East Indies". September-October 1940.

Volume 2818.

File 1136-40.
Oriental clause in British Columbia timber sale contract, August-September 1940.

Volume 2819.

File 1166-40.
Missions in Japan, treatment of, August 1940-May 1941.

Volume 2821.

File 1227-40.
East Indians in Canada, population statistics, October 1940-March 1948.

File 1253-40.
Census of Japanese subjects in Canada by Japanese consular representatives, October 1940-December 1955.

File 1263-40.
Census of Japanese and Manchurians, October 1940-June 1941.

Volume 2824.

File 1301-40.
Proposed removal of German aviators on U.S. ships sailing to Japan, October 1940-August 1941.

File 1314-40.
Gift of wheat for China, proposals, October 1940-October 1941.

Volume 2825.

File 1339-40.
Oil for Japan and Thailand, November 1940-May 1941.

Volume 2829.

File 1408-40.
Canadian tunny fish reaching Germany via Japan, November 1940-January 1941.

Volume 2628.

File 80-M-40, Volume 1.
Premises for Canadian Minister in Tokyo, 1929-1934.

File 80-M-40, Volume 2.
Premises for Canadian Minister in Tokyo, 1934-1953.

Volume 2638.

File 1774-40. David.
Naturalization of Japanese in Canada, June 1931-January 1947.

Volume 2640.

File 2120-40.
Sale of Japanese salmon to U.K., proposals, July 1939-June 1941.

Volume 2654.

File 4606-T-40.
Census in Japan, February 1938-April 1961.

Volume 2661.

File 6045-40.
Conditions in China, report by British Embassy, March 1938-January 1948.

Volume 2687.

File 11578-B-40.
Political conditions in the Central People's Republic of China, March 1938-January 1948.

File 1439-40.
Smuggling of Japanese into U.S. from Canada by boat, December 1940.

Accession 77-78/84.

Volume 2491.

File 10463-J-40.
Annual review of political and other events in Turkey, compiled by the Canadian Ambassador, Ankara, 1948-1961.

Volume 2494.

File 10463-AD-40.
Annual review of political and other events in India, compiled by the High Commissioner, New Delhi, 1948-1960.

File 10463-AG-40.
Annual review of political and other events in Pakistan, compiled by the High Commissioner, Karachi, 1948-1959.

File 10463-AW-40.
Annual review of political and other events in Iran, compiled by the British representative, Tehran, 1951-1962.

Volume 2496.

File 10463-BD-40.
Annual review of political and other events in Indonesia, compiled by the Canadian Minister, Djakarta, 1954-1963.

File 10563-BE-40.
Annual review of political and other events in Ceylon, compiled by the High Commissioner, Colombo, 1954-1960.

G3. Central Registry Files, 1963-present(volumes 2254-2260, 2413-2437, 2473-2479, 2483-2485, 2514-2248), plus unprocessed accessions.

This Central Registry system began in 1963 and continues until the present. Like both series G1 and G2 it covers all aspects of the Department of External Affairs operations. The records are covered by the provisions of the access to information and privacy legislation. The finding aid is a list of these operational files and includes the more recent accessions. Arrangement of files is by a systematic subject approach.

Accession 80-81/22.

Political affairs, policy and background. Canadian foreign policy and relations.

Box 7.

File 20-1-2-INDIA(India).
October 1963-December 1964.

Box 8.

2. March 1965-November 1967.
3. November 1967-March 1968.
4. April-July 1968.
5. August 1968-December 1969.

File 20-1-2-INDON(Indonesia).

File 20-1-2-IRAN(Iran).
October 1963-July 1965.
2. August 1965-January 1967.
3. February 1967-August 1967.
4. September 1967-March 1968.

Box 10.

File 20-1-2-JAPAN(Japan).
September 1963-August 1966.
2. May 1966-August 1967.
3. August 1967-December 1968.

File 20-1-2-KMER(Cambodia).
August 1963-March 1968.

Box 11.

File 20-1-2-MLSIA(Malaysia).
September 1963-January 1967.
2. February 1967-June 1968

Box 13.

File 20-1-2- PAK(Pakistan).
September 1963-June 1967.

File 20-1-2- PRC(China).
September 1963-February 1964.
2. February 1964-August 1964.
3. August 1964-April 1965.
4. May 1965-May 1966.

Box 14.

5. June 1966-February 1967.
6. February 1967-March 1968.
7. April 1968-December 1968.

File 20-1-2-ROK(South Korea),
September 1963-December 1966.

Box 15.

File 20-1-2-TAIWAN(Taiwan),
September 1963-May 1966.

File 20-1-2-THAI(Thailand),
February 1964-December 1966.
2. January 1967-July 1968.

Box 16.

File 20-1-2-TURK(Turkey),
September 1963-August 1968.

Box 18.

File 20-1-2-VIET.N(North Vietnam),
September 1963-August 1968.

File 20-1-2-VIET.S(South Vietnam),
1.September 1963-October 1965,
2. August 1967-August 1968.

Box 19.

File 20-1-2-CHINA-1(China),
March-June 1968.
Review of China policy.
2. June-July 1968.
3. July-August 1968.
4. September-December 1968.

File 20-1-2-JPN-1(Japan),
1.August 1963-September 1963.
2. October 1963-August 1964.

Box 20.

3. August-December 1964,
4. January 1965-June 1966.
5. July-September 1966.
6. August 1966-December 1967.

Political affairs, policy and background. Guidance to heads of posts.

Box 22.

File 20-1-5-DKA(Jakarta),
May 1964-September 1973.

File 20-1-5-RGN(Rangoon),
October 1963-August 1975.

File 20-1-5-SGN(Saigon),
December 1963-February 1974.

File 20-1-5-TKO(Tokyo),
July 1966-August 1976.

Political affairs, reports and statistics, periodic reports.

Box 23.

File 20-PRC-2-1(China),
September 1963-November 1964.

File 20-VIET.N.-2-1(North Vietnam),
September 1963-June 1964.
2. September 1964-June 1967.
3. July-September 1967.
4. September 1967-December 1968.5. January-December 1969.

Political affairs - visits.

Box 28.

File 20-CAMB-9(Cambodia),
May 1964-November 1967.

Box 30.

File 20-INDIA-9(India),
1.October 1963-May 1965.
2. June 1965-

Box 31.

3. May 1965-March 1968.

File 20-IRAN-9(Iran),
June 1964-March 1968.
2. June 1964-May 1965.
3. May 1965-February 1967.

Box 32.

File 20-JPN-9(Japan),
September 1963-June 1967.

2. July 1967-February 1968.

File 20-MLSIA-9(Malaysia),
March 1964-June 1965.

Box 33.

File 20-ROK-9(South Korea)
February 1965-March 1968.

Box 34.

File 20-TAIWAN-9(Taiwan),
June 1964-September 1967.

Box 37.

File 20-CDA-9-FE(Far East),
August 1965-January 1967.
2. February 1967.
3. March 1967-April 1969.

Box 38.

File 20-CDA-9-FE-JPN(Far East-Japan),
June 1965-March 1968.
2. May 1968-July 1969.

File 20-CDA-9-FE-PRC(Far East-China),
February-November 1964.
2. December 1964-September 1966.
3. December 1966-July 1969.

Political affairs. Non-party groups.
Political affairs, internal security, Vietnam security situation report.

Box 50.

File 20-22-VIET.S.-1,
1. January-July 1964.
2. August 1964.
3. August-December 1964.
4. May-December 1965.

Volume 51.

File 20-22-5-VIET.S.,
Political affairs, internal security, coup d'état, South Vietnam, 1963-.

Volume 52.

File 20-24-3-INDON/MLSIA,
Political affairs, disputes, incidents, Indonesia-Malaysia, June-November 1964.

Volume 53.

Files 21-13, Military action, armistice.

File 21-13-KM-ICSC-1.
Khmer Republic, International Commission of Supervision and Control, status and immunities, September 1963-April 1964.

File 21-13-KMER-ICSC-4.
Khmer Republic, operations and investigations, February 1963-May 1965.

File 21-13-KMER-ICSC-4, part 2.
Khmer Republic, operations and investigations, part 2, May-June 1964.

File 21-13-KMER-ICSC-4, part 3.
Khmer Republic, operations and investigations, part 3, June-July 1964.

File 21-13-KMER-ICSC-4, part 4.
Khmer Republic, operations and investigations, part 4, July-September 1964.

File 21-13-KMER-ICSC-4, part 5.
Khmer Republic, operations and investigations, part 5, October 1964-August 1965.

File 21-13-KMER-ICSC-4, part 6.
Khmer Republic, operations and investigations, part 6, July 1965.

File 21-13-KMER-ICSC-5.
Indo-China, minutes of meetings, September 1963-August 1965.

Volume 54.

File 21-13-INDO-ICSC-1-FP.
Indo-China, International Commission of Supervision and Control, September 1963-December 1964.

File 21-13-LAOS-ICSC-3.
Laos, International Commission of Supervision and Control, financing, September 1960-October 1965.

File 21-13-LAOS-ICSC-4.
Laos, operations and investigations, September 1963-October 1965.

File 21-13-LAOS-ICSC-4, part 2.

File 21-13-LAOS-ICSC-4, part 3.
Laos, operations and investigations, part 3, August 1964-March 1965.

File 21-12-LAOS-ICSC-4-2 I-FP.
Laos, Makay, January-February 1964.

File 21-13-LAOS-ICSC-4-2.
Laos, Air America and Seaboard World Services, November 1963-February 1965.

File 21-13-LAOS-ICSC-4-4.
Laos.

Volume 54a.

File 21-13-LAOS-ICSC-4-6, FPS.
Laos, Dong Hene.

File 21-13-LAOS-ICSC.
Laos, September 1963-December 1967.

File 21-13-LAOS-ICSC, part 2,
Laos, January-July 1967.

File 21-13-LAOS-ICSC, part 3.
Laos, August-October 1969.

Volume 55.

File 21-13-LAOS-4-8-FP.
Laos, Thakher investigation.
Thakher investigation(Laos)

File 21-13-LAOS-5-I-FP.
Laos, minutes of meetings, April-November 1964.

File 21-13-LAOS-ICSC-6-1.
Laos, reports to co-chairmen, September-October 1963.

File 21-13-LAOS-ICSC-6-2.
Laos, reports to co-chairmen, November 1963-May 1964.

Volume 55a.

File 21-13. Military actions armistice.

File 21-13-LAOS-ICSC-6 3-FP.
Laos, reports to co-chairmen, June l964-December 1965.

File 21-13-LAOS-ICSC-7 FP only.
Laos, message from co-chairmen and Geneva Powers Commission.

File 21-13-LAOS-ICSC-7 1.
September 1963-July 1964.

Volume 56.

File 21-13-United Nations I.P.O.M.-1.
United Nations, India and Pakistan observation missions, Canadian contingent.

File 21-13-United Nations M.O.G.I.P.-1.
United Nations, military observer group in India and Pakistan, September 1963-October 1965.

File 21-13-United Nations M.O.G.I.P.-1.
United Nations, military observer group in India and Pakistan, Canadian contingent, November 1963-September 1965.

File 21-13-United Nations T.S.O.-1.
United Nations, truce supervising organization, Canadian contingent, September 1963-June 1965.

Volume 56a.

File 21-13-VIET-ICSC, part 1.
Vietnam, International Commission of Supervision and Control, part 1, September 1963-March 1965.

File 21-13-VIET-ICSC, part 2.
Vietnam, International Commission of Supervision and Control, part 2, April-June 1965.

File 21-13-VIET-ICSC, part 3.
Vietnam, International Commission of Supervision and Control, part 3, July 1965-October 1968.

File 21-13-VET-ICSC-2, part 1.
Vietnam, International Commission of Supervision and Control, administration and personnel, December 1963-October 1965.

File 21-13-VIET-ICSC-3.
Vietnam, financing, January 1964-September 1965.

File 21-13-VET-ICSC-4, part 1.
Vietnam, operations and investigation, July 1963-September 1964.

File 21-13-VIET-ICSC-4, part 2.
Vietnam, operations and investigation, part 2, October 1964-February 1965.

File 21-13-VIET-ICSC-4, part 3.
Vietnam, International Commission of Supervision and Control, operations and investigations, part 3, March-May 1965.

File 21-13-VIET-ICSC-4, part 4.
Vietnam, International Commission of Supervision and Control, operations and investigations, part 4, June-December 1965.

Volume 57.

File 21-13-VIET-ICSC-4 FPS.
Vietnam, International Commission of Supervision and Control, operations and investigations.

File 21-13-VIET-ICSC-5, part 1.
Vietnam, International Commission of Supervision and Control, minutes of meetings, July 1963-November 1964.

File 21-13-VIET-ICSC-6, part 1.
Vietnam, International Commission of Supervision and Control, interim reports and messages to co-chairmen, October 1963-January 1965.

File 21-13-VIET-ICSC-6, part 1.
Vietnam, International Commission of Supervision and Control, interim reports and messages to co-chairmen, February-March 1965.

Volume 57a.

File 21-13-VIET-ICSC-7, part 1.
Vietnam, International Commission of Supervision and Control, legal committee, September 1963-April 1965.

File 21-13-VIET-ICSC-8, part 1.
Vietnam, International Commission of Supervision and Control, monthly reports, August 1963-March 1964.

File 21-13-VIET-ICSC-8, part 2.
Vietnam, International Commission of Supervision and Control, monthly reports, February 1964-October 1965.

Volume 58.

File 21-13-VIET-ICSC-8, FPS.
Vietnam, International Commission of Supervision and Control, monthly reports.

Volume 58a.

File 21-13-VIET-ICSC-8 FPS.
Vietnam, International Commission of Supervision and Control, monthly reports.

Volume 59.

File 21-13-VIET-ICSC-8 FPS.
Vietnam, International Commission of Supervision and Control, monthly reports.

File 21-13-VIET-ICSC-8 FP.
Vietnam, International Commission of Supervision and Control.

File 21-13-VIET-ICSC-10, part 1.
Vietnam, International Commission of Supervision and Control, agenda and decisions, March 1964-March 1965.

File 21-13-VIET-ICSC-10, part 2.
Vietnam, International Commission of Supervision and Control, agenda and decisions, April-December 1965.

File 21-13-VIET-ICSC-11, part 1.
Vietnam, International Commission of Supervision and Control, future of commission and reductions, October 1963-June 1965.

Volume 60.

File 21-12-VIET-ICSC-12 FP.
Vietnam, International Commission of Supervision and Control, studies of future peace-keeping role.

File 21-13-VIET-ICSC-12-73-10 sitrep FP.
Vietnam, International Commission of Supervision and Control, Canadian delegation.

File 21-14-1. Military action-peacekeeping-policy and aims.

File 21-14-1-CYP-1.
Cyprus, February 1964.

File 21-14-1-CYP-2.
Cyprus, February 1964.

File 21-14-1-CYP-3.
Cyprus, February 1964.

File 21-14-1-CYP-4,
Cyprus, March 1964.

Volume 64.

File 21-14-Military action-housekeeping.

File 21-14-1-CYP.
Cyprus, March 1964.

File 21-14-Military action-peacekeeping.

File 21-14-4-CYP-1, part 1.
Political measures, mediations, political settlement, Cyprus, March-April 1964.

File 21-14-4-CYP-1, part 2.
Political measures, mediation, political settlement, Cyprus, May-August 1964.

File 21-14-4-CYP-1, part 3.
Political measures, mediation, political settlement, Cyprus, August 1964-January 1965.

File 21-14-4-CYP-1, part 4.
Political measures, mediation, political settlement, Cyprus, February-September 1965.

Volume 65.

File 21-14-6-U.N.F.I.C.Y.P.-1, part 1.
Special forces, U.N.F.I.C.Y.P., Mission and status, February 1964-April l965.

File 21-14-6-U.N.F.I.C.Y.P.-1, part 2.
Special forces, U.N.F.I.C.Y.P., Mission and status, April-June 1964.

File 21-14-6-U.N.F.I.C.Y.P.-1, part 3.
Special forces, U.N.F.I.C.Y.P., Mission and status, June-September 1964.

File 21-14-6-U.N.F.I.C.Y.P.-1, part 4.
Special forces, U.N.F.I.C.Y.P., Mission and status, October 1963-May 1965.

File 21-14-6-U.N.F.I.C.Y.P.-1, part 5.
Special forces, U.N.F.I.C.Y.P., Mission and status, March-August 1965.

File 21-14-6-U.N.F.I.C.Y.P.-1, part 6-FP.
Special forces, U.N.F.I.C.Y.P., Mission and status, August 1965-May 1966.

Volume 66.

File 21-14-6-U.N.F.I.C.Y.P.-2, part 1.
Special forces, U.N.F.I.C.Y.P., operations, February-May 1964.

File 21-14-6-U.N.F.I.C.Y.P.-2, part 2.
Special forces, U.N.F.I.C.Y.P., operations, June-September 1964.

File 21-14-6-U.N.F.I.C.Y.P.-2, part 3.

Special forces, U.N.F.I.C.Y.P., operations, October 1964-July 1965.

File 21-14-6-U.N.F.I.C.Y.P.-4, part 1.
Special forces, U.N.F.I.C.Y.P., Canadian contingent, December 1963-May 1964.

File 21-14-6-U.N.F.I.C.Y.P.-4, part 2.
Special forces, U.N.F.I.C.Y.P., Canadian contingent, June-December 1964.

File 21-14-6-U.N.F.I.C.Y.P.-4, part 3.
Special forces, U.N.F.I.C.Y.P., Canadian contingent, October 1964-July 1965.

File 21-14-6-U.N.F.I.C.Y.P.-7, part 1.
Special forces, U.N.F.I.C.Y.P., public relations, February-August 1964.

File 21-14-6-U.N.F.I.C.Y.P.-8, part 1.
Special forces, U.N.F.I.C.Y.P., airlift, February 1964-March 1965.

File 21-14-6-U.N.F.I.C.Y.P.-9, part 1.

Accession 80-81/060
1953-1963, 3 metres

Records of the control of Exports of Strategic materials to China Secretariat, including Secretariat papers, 1958-1960. Restricted.

Accession 83-84/233.

Box 71.

File 773-B-1-40, part 1.
Treatment of Japanese in Canada - proposals of various persons, 1941-1942.

File 773-B-1-40, part 2.
Treatment of Japanese in Canada - proposals of various persons, 1942.

File 773-B-1-40, part 3.
Treatment of Japanese in Canada - proposals of various persons, 1943-1945.

File 773-HG-40.
Movement of a school home in Assiniboia of Japanese girls in Oriental homes in Victoria -proposals of United Church of Canada Board of Home Missions, 1942.

File 773-H-40.
Movement from British Columbia to Toronto under the auspices of the Women's Missionary Society of the United Church of Canada of a number of young Japanese women - proposals, 1942-1945.

Box 91.

File 1348-40.
Exclusion of Japanese from practice of optometry in British Columbia - protest re, 1940.

Box 100.

File 1439-40.
Smuggling of Japanese in the U.S. from Canada by boat, 1940.

Accession 83-84/259.

Volume 2843.

File 1493-40.
German propaganda in Japan, November 1940-October 1941.

Volume 2854.

File 1581-40.
Detention of Japanese consular official in Vancouver, January-February 1941.

File 1592-40.
Protection of Japanese ships, legislation and reports, November 1940-May 1941.

Volume 2856.

File 1617-C-40.
Postal censorship in India, general file, June 1944-March 1950.

File 1618-40.
Interception of Japanese ships in Pacific Ocean, January-April 1941.

File 1624-40.
Activities of German raiders in Southern Pacific and Indian Ocean, December 1940-March 1946.

File 1625-40.
Allied war strategy in the Pacific Ocean, general file. Pacific War Council, November 1940-May 1948.

Volume 2857.

File 1655-B-40.
Channel of communications between Canada and Japan re protection by Argentine government of Canadian interests in Japan, December 1941-February 1942.

Volume 2858.

File 1668-40.
Termination of Treaty of Arbitration and Conciliation between Japan and the Netherlands, February 1940.

File 1698-A-40.
Precautionary measures vs. Japan and action to be taken in event of war, July-November 1941.

Volume 2859.

File 1698-B-40.
Precautionary measures vs. Japan and action to be taken in event of war, treatment of Japanese diplomats and consuls and other nationals, March-December 1941.

File 1698-C-40.
Precautionary measures vs. Japan and action to be taken in event of war, treatment of Japanese fishing vessels and miscellaneous, February-November 1941.

File 1698-D-40.
Precautionary measures in event of war by Japan vs. Netherlands East Indies, arrangements for consultation.

File 1709-40.
Remittances to Canada by Canadians in Straits Settlements, January-July 1941.

Volume 2866.

File 1836-40.
Loan of M.V. **Orange** to Australia by Netherlands East Indies, March 1941.

Volume 2870.

File 1843-X-40.
Postwar economic reconstruction plans in China, reports re, May 1943-June 1955.

Volume 2871.

File 1846-40.
Political situation in Thailand, March 1941-April 1951.

File 1848-40.
Japan National Defence Security Act, February-May 1941.

File 1851-41.
Repatriation to India of K.Zaman, February-August 1941.

Volume 2872.

File 1877-40.
Appointment of a Japanese speaking person to broadcast from the British Ministry of Information, April 1941-October 1943.

Volume 2873.

File 1892-40.
Status of passengers on Japanese ships calling at Canadian ports, April 1941.

File 1896-40.
Secret agreement between U.K. and French Indo-China, January-November 1941.

Volume 2874.

File 1954-E-40.
Canadian interests protected by Swiss government in Far East, April 1941-February 1947.

Volume 2876.

File 1966-40.
Oil storage facilities at Suva, Fiji, May 1941.

Volume 2877.

File 1969-40.
Commercial relations between Canada and Fiji, March 1941-June 1959.

Volume 2878.

File 2006-N-40.
Travel and Far East regulations and policy, April 1941-December 1946.

Volume 2883.

File 2168-40.
Application of income tax act to persons of Chinese race residents in Canada, July 1941-March 1948.

File 2172-40.
Diplomatic relations with China, proposals, June-September 1941.

Volume 2884.

File 2202-40.
Voluntary liquidation of Nickel and Lyons Ltd., of Kobe and Yokohama under Japanese government pressure, May 1941.

File 2211-40.
Rumoured suspension of Japanese shipping service to North America, July 1941.

Volume 2885.

File 2223-40.
Circular telegrams from Ministry of Economic Warfare relating to economic warfare problems in the Far East, July-October 1941.
Volume 2888.

File 2271-40.
Registration of securities in Netherlands East Indies, regulations, July 1941-April 1943.

File 2278-40.
Japanese censorship regulations, July-October 1941.

Box 141.

File 2295-AJ-2-40.
U.N.R.R.A. sub committee on agriculture for the Far East, minutes and reports, November 1944-May 1945.

File 2295-AJ-3-40.
U.N.R.R.A. Sub Committee on Health for the Far East, December 1944-July 1946.

File 2295-AJ-4-40.
U.N.R.R.A. Sub Committee on Welfare for the Far East, minutes and agenda, December 1941-October 1945.

File 2295-AJ-5-40.
U.N.R.R.A. Sub Committee on Industrial Rehabilitation for the Far East, December 1944-July 1945.

Volume 2902.

File 2336-40.
Canadian nationals evacuated from Balkans-India, July 1941.

Volume 2905.

File 2356-40.
Shipment for Norda Ltd., affected by freezing order against Japan and activities of Norda Essential Oil and Chemical Co., and subsidiaries, July-October 1941.

File 2356-A-40.
Shipment from Japan for T.S.Simins and Co., affected by freezing order versus Japan, July-October 1941.

File 2356-C-40.
Shipment of tea for Kelly Douglas Co., affected by Japan freezing order, August-October 1941.

File 2356-D-40.
Shipment of peppermint oil from Japan for E.J.Bush and Co., affected by freezing order, September-October 1941.

File 2336-E-40.
Shipment of tuna fish and peanuts from Japan for W.J.Bush and Co., affected by freezing order, October 1941.

File 2360-40.
Parcel post service between Canada and Japan, suspension of, July-August 1941.

Volume 2909.

File 2411-40.
Registration of Japanese in Canada outside of British Columbia, 1941-1942.

Volume 2911.

File 2440-40.
Payment of account due Aluminium Union Ltd., by Chinese government, August 1941-May 1942.

File 2441-40.
Return of equipment belonging to French Medical Mission at Chengtu, China, stored with Canadian Medical Mission, September-October 1941.

Volume 2914.

File 2518-40.
Precautionary measures taken by Cunard White Star re anti-Japanese feeling in Canada, July-August 1941.

Volume 2915.

File 2539-40.
Use of United Church of Canada funds in Japan by Canadian government, proposals, August-December 1941.

Volume 2920.

File 2654-40.
Establishment of a manning pool in Canada for Chinese seamen, proposals, July 1941-June 1942.

File 2668-40.
Pilot balloons from Canada for Thailand, September-October 1941.

File 2670-40.
Legal position of Canadian forces in Hong Kong, October 1941.

File 2670-A-40, volume 1.
Canadian armed forces at Hong Kong, general file, September 1941-February 1942.

File 2670-A-40, volume 2.
Canadian armed forces at Hong Kong, general file, March-August 1943.

File 2670-A-40, volume 3.
Canadian armed forces at Hong Kong, general file, September 1943-October 1946.

File 2670-B-40.
Inquiries by various persons re welfare of members of Canadian forces at Hong Kong, January 1942-December 1944.

File 2760-C-40.
Despatch of Canadian forces to Hong Kong, investigation re February-July 1942.

File 2670-D-40, volume 1.
Treatment by Japanese of prisoners of war and civilians at Hong Kong, January-December 1942.

File 2670-D-40, volume 2.
Treatment by Japanese of prisoners of war and civilians at Hong Kong, January 1943-June 1946.

Volume 2921.

File 2700-40.
India-Burma commercial relations, October 1941-April 1958.

File 2700-A-40.
India-Burma relations, July 1941-July 1961.

Volume 2925.

File 2727-Y-40.
Canadian publicity in India, July 1944-January 1948.

File 2727-AE-40, volume 1.
Canadian publicity in China, January 1943-March 1944.

Volume 2926.

File 2766-40.
Reports by various persons returning from Japan on general situation in Japan, November 1941-February 1948.

Volume 2927.

File 2795-S-40.
Paper on "Canadian air transport in the Pacific Area" submitted by Canadian Institute of International Affairs to External Affairs for comments, October 1944.

File 2795-T-40.
Article "Canada's trade with trans-Pacific countries" by A.L.Neal, submitted to External Affairs for comment, September-November 1944.

File 2837-40, volume 1.
Institute for Pacific Relations conferences, December 1941-November 1942.

Volume 2928.

File 2837-40, volume 2.
Institute for Pacific Relations conferences, December 1942-December 1947.

Volume 2930.

File 2860-40.
Commencement of war with Japan, October 1941-December 1949.

Volume 2931.

File 2863-40, volume 1.
Departures from Canada of Japanese diplomatic and consular officers re war, December 1941-January 1942.

File 2863-40, volume 2.
Departures from Canada of Japanese diplomatic and consular officers re war, January-April 1942.

File 2863-40, volume 3.
Departures from Canada of Japanese diplomatic and consular officers re war, April-July 1942.

File 2863-40, volume 4.
Departures from Canada of Japanese diplomatic and consular officers re war, August 1942-September 1945.

File 2863-A-40.
Expense re departure from Canada of Japanese diplomatic and consular officers, June 1942-July 1952.

File 2864-40, volume 1.
Departure from Japan of Canadian diplomatic officials re war, December 1941-May 1942.

File 2864-40, volume 2.
Departure from Japan of Canadian diplomatic officials re war, June-July 1942.

File 2864-40, volume 3.
Departure from Japan of Canadian diplomatic officials re war, August 1942.

File 2864-40, volume 4.
Departure from Japan of Canadian diplomatic officials re war, September 1942-July 1946.

File 2864-A-40, volume 1.
Expenses re repatriation of Canadian officials and others from the Far East on S.S.**Gripsholm,** 1942, August 1942-July 1944.

File 2864-A-40, volume 2.
Expenses re repatriation of Canadian officials and others from the Far East on S.S.**Gripsholm,** 1942, October 1944-April 1945.

Volume 2932.

File 2864-B-40, volume 1.
Department of External Affairs questionnaires for Canadians repatriated from Japan on S.S.**Gripsholm** (names only Dappen-Fairbairn), August 1942-1944.

File 2864-C-40.
Analysis of "**Gripsholm**" questionnaires prepared by US Department of State, March 1944.

Volume 2935.

File 2916-40.
Military, naval and air situation in Pacific Ocean and Far East, December 1941-August 1945.

File 2917-A-40.
Defensive measures taken on Western coast and Northern coast proposals by various persons, December 1941-November 1947.

Volume 2936.

File 2920-40.
Control of Japanese ships, November 1941-July 1942.

Volume 2937.

File 2940-40.
Closing of the Consulate-general of Thailand at Vancouver, January 1942-September 1948.

File 2948-40.

Japan-Greece relations, December 1941-October 1958.

File 2966-A-40.
Establishment of a committee to assist Spanish Consul at Vancouver in looking after Japanese interests, proposals, April-June 1942.

File 2966-B-40.
Visits of Spanish Consul General in charge of Japanese interests to External Affairs department, reports, April 1942-July 1945.

File 2966-C-40.
Channel of communications between British Columbia Security Commission and Spanish representatives in charge of Japanese interests in Canada, February 1943-December 1945.

File 2966-D-40, volume 1.
Visits by representatives of Spanish government to Japanese internment camps and settlements in Canada, arrangements and reports, 1942-1943.

File 2966-D-40, volume 2.
Visits by representatives of Spanish government to Japanese internment camps and settlements in Canada, arrangements and reports, 1943-1946.

File 2979-40.
Entry of allied troops into Portuguese Timor, December 1941.

File 2980-40.
French neutrality in Pacific War, December 1941.

Volume 2939.

File 2997-40, volume 1.
Japanese in Canada, statistics, 1941-1943.

File 2997-40, volume 2.
Japanese in Canada, statistics, 1943-1946.

Volume 2940.

File 2998-40, volume 1.
Arrangements with the Japanese re treatment of prisoners of war, general file, December 1941-April 1944.

File 2998-40, volume 2-FB.
Arrangements with the Japanese re treatment of prisoners of war, general file, May 1944-February 1946.

File 2998-A-40.
Financial arrangements between United Kingdom and Canada and Japan re treatment of prisoners of war, February 1942-July 1944.

File 2998-B-40.
Internment of Canadian women in Japan, protests, March 1942-February 1943.

File 2998-C-40, volume 1.
Exchange of information re prisoners of war and interned civilians between Canada and Japan(including nominal rolls) arrangements, 1942-1943.

File 2998-C-40, volume 2.
Exchange of information re prisoners of war and interned civilians between Canada and Japan(including nominal rolls) arrangements, 1943-1945.

Volume 2941.

File 2998-D-40, volume 1.
Visits by representatives in protecting power and International Red Cross Committee to Canadian prisoners of war and internees in Japan and Japanese occupied territory, arrangements and reports, April 1942-June 1943.

File 2998-D-40, volume 2.
Visits by representatives in protecting power and International Red Cross committee to Canadian prisoners of war and internees in Japan and Japanese occupied territory, arrangements and reports, June 1943-January 1944.

File 2998-D-40, volume 3.
Visits by representatives in protecting power and International Red Cross Committee to Canadian prisoners of war and internees in Japan and Japanese occupied territory, arrangements and reports, February 1944-April 1944.

File 2998-D-40, volume 4.
Visits by representatives in protecting power and International Red Cross Committee to Canadian prisoners of war and internees in Japan and Japanese occupied territory, arrangements and reports, April-September 1944.

File 2998-D-40, volume 5.
Visits by representatives in protecting power and International Red Cross Committee to Canadian prisoners of war and internees in Japan and Japanese occupied territory, arrangements and reports, September 1944-January 1945.

File 2998-E-40.
Transmission of cigarettes by various persons to Canadian prisoners of war and internees in the Far East, March 1942-April 1943.

File 2998-F-40.
Exchange of sick and wounded prisoners of war between allied governments and Japan, proposals, September 1942-August 1945.

File 2998-ZH-40.
Return of ashes of deceased prisoners of war on exchange ships and burials of deceased prisoners of war in Far East, policy, July 1942-November 1946.

File 2998-J-40.

Rations for Canadian prisoners of war in Japanese hands, March 1943-February 1945.

File 2998-K-40.
Employment of Canadian prisoners of war in the Far East, March 1943-August 1944.

File 2998-L-40, volume 1.
Publicity re prisoners of war in Japanese hands, June 1943-January 1944.

File 2998-L-40, volume 2.
Publicity re prisoners of war in Japanese hands, February 1944-September 1945.

Volume 2942.

File 2998-M-40.
Cruelties inflicted on prisoners of war and civilians by Japanese, protests re, April 1943-August 1944.

File 2998-N-40.
Death of Canadian prisoners of war following typhoon at Niigata, Japan, December 1943-August 1945.

File 2998-Q-40.
Broadcasting messages to and from prisoners of war in the Far East, December 1943-August 1945.

File 3010-40.
Resolutions from various Japanese organizations expressing loyalty to Canada, 1941-1942.

Volume 2945.

File 3038-40.
Evacuation of office of Canadian Trade Commissioner, Shanghai, following war with Japan, December 1941-April 1946.

File 3046-40.
Situation re mines and resources staff in Hong Kong, January-September 1942.

File 3050-A-40, volume 1.
Safety and welfare in the Far East of missionaries of the Franciscan Order following the outbreak of war with Japan, November 1942-September 1943.

File 3050-A-40, volume 2.
Safety and welfare in the Far East of missionaries of the Franciscan Order following the outbreak of war with Japan, October 1943-June 1947.

File 3050-B-40.
Safety and welfare in the Far East of missionaries of the Sulpician Order following the outbreak of war with Japan, January 1942-October 1946.

File 3050-C-40.
Safety and welfare in the Far East of missionaries of the Dominican Order following the outbreak of war with Japan, January 1942-March 1946.

File 3050-D-40.
Safety and welfare in the Far East of missionaries of the Les Sœurs de Ste. Anne following the outbreak of war with Japan, January 1942-February 1944.

File 3050-E-40.
Safety and welfare in the Far East of missionaries of the Les Sœurs Notre Dame de l'Assomption following the outbreak of war with Japan, January 1942-November 1947.

Volume 2946.

File 3050-F-40.
Safety and welfare in the Far East of missionaries of the Sœurs de la Congregation de Notre Dame following the outbreak of war with Japan, January 1942-December 1946.

File 3050-G-40.
Safety and welfare in the Far East of missionaries of the Ursuline Order following the outbreak of war with Japan, October 1941-March 1948.

File 3050-H-40.
Safety and welfare in the Far East of missionaries of the Les Sœurs Antoniennes de Marie following the outbreak of war with Japan, January 1942-October 1945.

File 3050-J-40.
Safety and welfare in the Far East of Les Frères des Écoles Chretiennes, following the outbreak of war with Japan, January 1942-February 1948.

File 3050-K-40, part 1.
Safety and welfare in the Far East of Les Sœurs de l'Immaculée Conception, following the outbreak of the war with Japan, January 1942-September 1943.

File 3050-K-40, part 2.
Safety and welfare in the Far East of Les Sœurs de l'Immaculée Conception, following the outbreak of the war with Japan, March 1943-August 1948.

File 3050-L-40.
Safety and welfare in the Far East of Les Clercs de St. Viateur, following the outbreak of the war with Japan, January 1942-December 1953.

File 3050-M-40.
Safety and welfare in the Far East of Les Missions Étrangères de Pont-Viau, following the outbreak of the war with Japan, December 1941-May 1945.

File 3050-N-40.
Safety and welfare in the Far East of Les Sœurs Missionaires de Notre Dame des Anges, following the outbreak of the war with Japan, July 1942-September 1946.

Volume 2947.
File 3050-P-40, part 1.
Safety and welfare in the Far East of missionaries of

the Jesuit Order, following the outbreak of the war with Japan, June 1942-April 1944.

File 3050-P-40, part 2.
Safety and welfare in the Far East of missionaries of the Jesuit Order, following the outbreak of the war with Japan, July 1944-December 1952.

File 3050-Q-40.
Safety and welfare in the Far East of missionaries of the Scarboro Missionary Society, following the outbreak of the war with Japan, January 1942-December 1947.

File 3050-R-40.
Safety and welfare in the Far East of Bon Pasteur Order, following the outbreak of the war with Japan, March 1942-February 1947.

File 3050-T-40.
Safety and welfare in the Far East of females of the Dominican Order, following the outbreak of the war with Japan, February 1943-November 1947.

File 3050-U-40.
Safety and welfare in the Far East of Holy Cross Order (sisters), following the outbreak of the war with Japan, April 1942-December 1945.

File 3050-V-40.
Safety and welfare in the Far East of Redemptionist Order, following the outbreak of the war with Japan, June 1944-September 1948.

File 3050-W-40.
Safety and welfare in the Far East of members of Maryknoll Order, following the outbreak of the war with Japan, April 1942-October 1945.

File 3050-Y-40.
Safety and welfare in the Far East of missionaries of Sacred Heart Order, following the outbreak of the war with Japan, March 1942-May 1946.

Volume 2948.

File 3050-Z-40.
Safety and welfare in the Far East of Couvent des Religieuses de l'Enfant Jésus, reports, following the outbreak of the war with Japan, April 1942-September 1946.

File 3050-AC-40.
Safety and welfare in the Far East of Order of Precious Blood, following the outbreak of the war with Japan, April 1942-September 1950.

File 3050-AD-40.
Safety and welfare in the Far East of Les Réligieuses Carmelites, following the outbreak of the war with Japan, May 1943-March 1947.

File 3050-AE-40.
Safety and welfare in the Far East of Order of Christian Brothers, following the outbreak of the war with Japan, June 1943-April 1948.

File 3050-AF-40.
Safety and welfare in the Far East of Les Dames de St. Maur, following the outbreak of the war with Japan, December 1943-June 1944.

File 3050-AH-40.
Safety and welfare in the Far East of Grey Sisters of Immaculate Conception, following the outbreak of the war with Japan, February 1943-February 1945.

File 3050-AJ-40.
Safety and welfare in the Far East of Christ-Roi, following the outbreak of the war with Japan, February 1943-October 1946.

File 3051-40, part 1.
Safety and welfare in the Far East of United Church of Canada, following the outbreak of the war with Japan, March-November 1942.

File 3051-40, part 2.
Safety and welfare in the Far East of United Church of Canada, following the outbreak of the war with Japan, February 1943-January 1951.

File 3051-A-40.
Safety and welfare in the Far East of Missionary Society of Church of England in Canada, following the outbreak of the war with Japan, December 1941-February 1951.

File 3051-C-40.
Safety and welfare in the Far East of the Salvation Army, following the outbreak of the war with Japan, January 1942-September 1953.

File 3051-D-40, part 1.
Safety and welfare in the Far East of China Inland Mission, following the outbreak of the war with Japan, December 1941-November 1943.

Volume 2949.

File 3051-D-40, part 2.
Safety and welfare in the Far East of China Inland Mission, following the outbreak of the war with Japan, December 1943-May 1948.

File 3051-E-40.
Safety and welfare in the Far East of Canadian Baptist Foreign Mission Board, following the outbreak of the war with Japan, January-October 1942.

File 3051-F-40.
Safety and welfare in the Far East of Free Methodist Church, following the outbreak of the war with Japan, February 1942-July 1952.

File 3051-G-40.
Safety and welfare in the Far East of Christian

Missionary Alliance Tabernacle, following the outbreak of the war with Japan, February 1942-August 1945.

File 3051-H-40.
Safety and welfare in the Far East of missionaries of Pentecostal Assemblies, following the outbreak of the war with Japan, April 1942-November 1943.

File 3051-K-40.
Safety and welfare in the Far East of missionaries of Regular Baptists of British Columbia, following the outbreak of the war with Japan, June-August 1942.

File 3051-L-40.
Safety and welfare in the Far East of Protestant Episcopal Church of US, following the outbreak of the war with Japan, April 1943-April 1945.

File 3059-40.
Japan-Argentine relations, December 1941-January 1962.

Volume 2955.

File 3135-40.
Measures taken by Argentine in war, declaration of war versus Japan and Germany, December 1941-April 1945.

File 3150-40.
US investigation of Japanese attack on Pearl Harbour, January 1942-May 1949.

Volume 2956.

File 3155-40.
Welfare in the Far East of employees of the Confederation Life Association following the outbreak of the war with Japan, January 1942-June 1946.

File 3155-A-40.
Welfare in the Far East of employees of Sun Life Assurance Company, following the outbreak of the war with Japan, February 1942-April 1948.

File 3155-B-40.
Welfare in the Far East of employees of Crown Life Insurance Company, following the outbreak of the war with Japan, January 1942-October 1945.

File 3155-C-40.
Welfare in the Far East of employees of Manufacturers Life Insurance Company, following the outbreak of the war with Japan, April 1941-October 1951.

File 3160-41, part 1.
Shipment of food and supplies to Japan for relief of allied prisoners of war and internees in the Far East, December 1941-April 1942.

File 3160-41, part 2.
Shipment of food and supplies to Japan for relief of allied prisoners of war and internees in the Far East, May-September 1942.

File 3160-41, part 3.
Shipment of food and supplies to Japan for relief of allied prisoners of war and internees in the Far East, October 1942-November 1945.

Volume 2957.

File 3191-40.
Commencement of war with Siam, December 1941-December 1945.

Volume 2958.

File 3223-40.
Thai internees in Canada, looked after by Swiss government, arrangements, February 1942-February 1947.

File 3227-40.
Assistance for distressed Canadians at Macao, February 1942-December 1945.

Volume 2962.

File 3232-F-40.
Ownership and taxation of real property in Canada bought by China, July 1942-July 1956.

Volume 2969.

File 3266-40.
Refusal by Japan to recognize protecting power for Canadian interests in the Far East, January-February 1942.

File 3267-40.
Person to person telegraphic communications between Canada and Japan and enemy occupied territories in wartime, December 1941-July 1943.

File 3274-40.
Payment to distressed Canadian nationals not interned in Far Eastern enemy occupied territories, December 1941-July 1943.

Volume 2970.

File 3274-A-40.
Payments to Chinese Canadians in Free China, April 1942-April 1950.

File 3274-A-40.
Relief payments to interned and non-interned Canadian civilians in enemy and enemy occupied territory in Far East, December 1943-November 1946.

File 3274-B-40.
Relief for Canadians in Far East, who declared repatriation, June 1942-July 1955.

File 3282-40, part 1.

446 • Ontario – Ottawa

Transmission of mail and parcels and the Far East, August 1943-November 1945.

File 3282-40, part 2.
Transmission of mail and parcels and the Far East, April 1943-January 1944.

File 3282-40, part 3.
Transmission of mail and parcels and the Far East, February 1944-January 1946.

File 3282-A-40.
Transmission of mail and parcels and the Far East, August 1943-November 1945.

File 3284-C-40.
Newsprint for India from Canada, August 1941-December 1953.

Volume 2971.

File 3284-E-40.
Motor vehicles for India from Canada, January 1940-September 1942.

File 3284-F-40.
Fish for India from Canada, August-November 1940.

File 3284-H-40.
Exchange of commodities between Canada and India, April 1942-May 1949.

File 3284-J-40.
Jute, burlap and tanned skins from India for Canada, July 1944-October 1952.

File 3290-40.
Payment of relief to Canadian prisoners of war and interned civilians in enemy occupied territory in Far East, March 1942-December 1943.

File 3290-A-40.
Relief to Canadian prisoners of war in enemy and enemy occupied territories in the Far East, December 1943-December 1945.

File 3295-40.
Relief for and repatriation of distressed Canadians evacuated to Australia and New Zealand from war areas in the Far East, general file, January 1942-September 1943.

File 3295-A-40, part 1.
Canadian nationals in China, reports, re lists of, October 1941-September 1943.

File 3295-A-40, part 2 FP.
Canadian nationals in China, reports, re lists of, October 1943-October 1948.

Volume 2972.

File 3295-B-40, part 1 FP.
Canadian nationals in Hong Kong and the Philippines, January 1942-June 1943.

File 3295-B-40, part 2.
Canadian nationals in Hong Kong and the Philippines, August 1942-December 1946.

File 3295-C-40.
Canadian nationals in India and Ceylon, March 1943-April 1947.

File 3295-D-40.
Canadian nationals in Indo-China, March 1942-August 1945.

File 3295-E-40.
Canadian nationals in Japan, January 1942-August 1946.

File 3295-F-40.
Canadian nationals in Singapore, February 1942-August 1946.

File 3295-G-40.
Canadian nationals on Wake Island, April-May 1942.

File 3295-H-40.
Canadian nationals in Malaya, May 1942.

File 3295-J-40.
Canadian nationals in Thailand, July 1942-July 1945.

File 3295-K-40.
Canadian nationals in Manchuria, July 1942-March 1946.

File 3295-M-40.
Canadian nationals in Burma, August 1942-March 1944.

File 3295-N-40.
Enquiries re welfare of various persons in the Far East, July-August 1942.

File 3295-P-40.
Enquiries re welfare of various persons in British East Indies, August 1943.

Volume 2973.

File 3327-40.
Transfer of Royal Canadian Air Force Squadron from United Kingdom to Ceylon, February-April 1942.

File 3336-40.
Japanese infiltration tactics in Dutch East Indies, report by Netherlands Information Bureau, February 1942-April 1944.

File 3353-40.
Treatment of Chinese seamen in Canadian ports, March 1942-December 1943.

Volume 2974.

File 3363-40, part 1.
Exchange of nationals other than diplomatic or official personnel between Canada and Japan, February-September 1942.

File 3363-40, part 2.
Exchange of nationals other than diplomatic or official personnel between Canada and Japan, January 1942-June 1943.

File 3363-40, part 3.
Exchange of nationals other than diplomatic or official personnel between Canada and Japan, July 1943.

Volume 2975.

File 3363-40, part 4.
Exchange of nationals other than diplomatic or official personnel between Canada and Japan, August 1943.

File 3363-40, part 5.
Exchange of nationals other than diplomatic or official personnel between Canada and Japan, August 1943-November 1953.

File 3363-A-40.
Forms of consent to repatriation and refusal to be repatriated by Japanese in Canada, also requests for repatriation, September 1942-September 1945.

File 3363-B-40.
Repatriation of Japanese nationals from Canada, expenses, 1942-1946.

File 3363-C-540.
National status of Japanese in Canada requesting repatriation to Japan, 1942-1945.

Volume 2977.

File 3445-40.
Reciprocal exchange of nationals between Canada and Thailand following outbreak of war, arrangements, February-June 1942.

Volume 2978.

File 3464-40, part 1.
Messages to and from Japanese interned in Canada, 1942-1943.

File 3464-40, part 2, FP.
Messages to and from Japanese interned in Canada, September 1943-February 1946.

Volume 3004.

File 3464-B-40, part 1.
Status and treatment of Japanese in Canada in wartime, general file, 1942-1943.

File 3464-B-40, part 2.
Status and treatment of Japanese in Canada in wartime, general file, 1942-1943.

File 3464-B-40, part 3.
Status and treatment of Japanese in Canada in wartime, general file, 1944-1945.

File 3464-C-40.
Internment of Japanese in Canada in wartime, 1942-1945.

File 3464-D-40.
Refusal of air and rail transportation and air express facilities to Japanese nationals, 1941-1948.

File 3464-E-40.
Control of Japanese newspapers, in Canada following outbreak of war with Japan, 1941-1943.

File 3464-F-40.
Registration of Japanese in Canada following outbreak of war with Japan, 1941-1942.

File 3464-G-40.
Employment of Japanese in Canada in wartime, 1941-1945.

File 3464-H-40.
Fishing licences for Japanese in Canada in wartime, 1941-1947.

File 3464-J-40.
Evacuation of Japanese from the British Columbia coastal areas, 1942-1943.

File 3464-J-40, part 2.
Evacuation of Japanese from the British Columbia coastal areas, 1943-1944.

File 3464-K-40.
P/W Information Bureau forms re Japanese interned in Canada, 1942.

Volume 3005.

File 3464-K-40, part 2.
P/W Information Bureau forms re Japanese interned in Canada, 1942-1943.

File 3464-M-40.
Religious and recreational and educational facilities for Japanese in Canada, 1942-1945.

File 3464-N-40.
Relief for families of Japanese interned in Canada, 1942-1946.

File 3464-P-40.
Rations for Japanese internees in Canada, 1942-1944.

File 3464-Q-40.
British Columbia Security Commission, 1942

File 3464-S-40.

Use of Japanese in Canada on radio transmitting and receiving apparatus in wartime, 1942-1943.

File 3464-T-40.
Formation of a Canadian Japanese construction corps in Canada, 1942-1944.

File 3464-U-40.
Trial by military court of Japanese interned in Canada, 1942.

File 3464-V-40.
Postwar treatment of Japanese in Canada.

File 3464-W-40.
Attendance at Canadian universities of persons of Japanese race, 1942.

File 3464-X-40.
Positions of Japanese in Canada under national selective service in Canada, 1942-1944.

File 3464-Z-40.
Treatment of Japanese in Canada, 1942-1947.

File 3464-AB-40.
Showing of motion pictures to Japanese at work camps in Canada, 1942.

File 3464-AC-40.
Petition from 10 Japanese women and others re release from internment of Japanese in Canada, 1945.

File 3464-AD-40.
Publicity re treatment of Japanese in Canada in wartime, 1942-1944.

File 3464-AF-40.
Payments through protecting power for Christmas presents and comforts for Japanese interned in Canada, 1942-1946.

File 3464-AG-40.
Old age pensions for Japanese in Canada, 1942.

File 3464-AH-40.
Christmas entertainment for Japanese in Canada, 1942-1943.

File 3464-AJ-40.
Advisory board on evacuation and maintenance of Japanese in Canada, establishment of, 1942-1943.

File 3464-AK-40.
New Year messages for Japanese prisoners of war and internees, 1943-1944.

File 3464-AL-40.
Postal facilities at Japanese settlements in British Columbia, 1943.

Volume 3006.

File 3464-AM-40.
Visit by S. Morley Scott to Japanese settlements, reports, 1943.

File 3464-AN-40.
Visits by various persons to Japanese internment camps and settlements in Canada, arrangements and reports, 1942-1943.

File 3464-AN-40, part 2.
Visits by various persons to Japanese internment camps and settlements in Canada, arrangements and reports, 1943-1946.

File 3464-AQ-40.
Employment of Japanese internees in Canada, 1943.

File 3464-AR-40.
Message from Japanese Red Cross to Japanese in Canada, 1943-1945.

File 3464-AS-40.
Reports of representatives of Spanish government and International Red Cross committee re Japanese in Canada made available to the Swiss authorities.

File 3464-AT-40.
Movement of Japanese from US to Canada in wartime, 1943-1945.

File 3464-AU-40.
Distribution of comforts and banks by International Red Cross committee and others among Japanese in Canada, 1942-1945.

File 3464-AV-40.
Acquisition of Japanese nationality by Japanese children born in Canada in wartime, 1943.

File 3464-AW-40.
Statement of expenditures on behalf of Japanese in Canada, 1943-1944.

File 3464-AX-40.
Remuneration of Japanese doctors, 1943.

File 3464-AY-40.
Report on Royal Jackson Commission on Japanese in British Columbia, 1943-1945.

Volume 3007.

File 3464-AZ-40.
Granting of maintenance to Buddhist priests in Canada, 1944-1945.

File 3464-BA-40.
Legal proceedings against Terue Nazuminya in Canada, 1944.

File 3464-BC-40.
Return to British Columbia of Sadame Watanabe, 1944.

File 3464-BD-40.

Uniting of Japanese families, 1944.

File 3464-BE-40.
Health of Japanese interned in Canada, reports and inquiries, re, 1944-1945.

File 3464-BF-40.
Death of Japanese interned in Canada, information re, 1942-1945.

File 3464-BG-40.
Motion pictures of Japanese settlement in Canada, 1945.

File 3464-BH-40.
Assistance for George Watanabe, 1945.

Volume 3008.

File 3521-40.
American military aid to Empire and Allied forces in the Pacific and Eastern Asia, February 1942.

File 3534-40.
Australia-Malaya Singapore relations, September 1941-July 1963.

Volume 3012.

File 3621-40.
Transmission of funds to China, procedures re, February 1942-February 1943.

Volume 3014.

File 3630-40, part 1.
Extra-territorial jurisdiction over British subjects in India, February 1942-October 1943.

File 3630-40, part 2.
Extra-territorial jurisdiction over British subjects in India, February 1942-October 1943.

File 3630-A-40.
Trial of Fr. C.M.Hoffman in Chinese courts, reports, July 1943.

File 3652-40.
Propaganda leaflets dropped by the Japanese at Hong Kong, March 1942.

Volume 3034.

File 4110-40.
US-Iran trade relations, April 1942-August 1960.

Volume 3037.

File 4166-40.
Reports and suggestions of Capt. V.C.Best re: Japanese in Canada, 1941-1943.

Volume 3110.

File 4430-40.
Japanese periodicals and publications brought back to Canada by officers of the Canadian legation in Tokyo, arrangements for perusal by British officials in Canada and US, October 1942.

Volume 3111.

File 4432-40.
Dependent allowances for wives and children of Chinese in the Canadian army, enquiry re Chinese marriage laws and customs, September 1942-May 1950.

File 4452-40.
Report on conditions in the Far East by Dr. W.S.Parsons, March 1942-May 1950.

File 4457-40.
US-China relations, October 1942-December 1946.

File 4461-40.
Gasoline for Honorary Vice-Consul of Spain at Vancouver for protection of Japanese interests, October-November 1942.

File 4462-40.
Christmas presents for Canadian prisoners of war in the Far East, October 1942-February 1946.

Volume 3112.

File 4464-40.
Repatriation from Japan of Canadian nationals, other than diplomatic, arrangements, January 1942-April 1943.

File 4464-40, part 2.
Repatriation from Japan of Canadian nationals, other than diplomatic, arrangements, May-September 1942.

File 4464-40, part 3.
Repatriation from Japan of Canadian nationals, other than diplomatic, arrangements, October 1942-October 1943.

File 4464-40, part 4.
Repatriation from Japan of Canadian nationals, other than diplomatic, arrangements, November 1943.

File 4464-40, part 5.
Repatriation from Japan of Canadian nationals, other than diplomatic, arrangements, December 1943-January 1944.

File 4464-A-40.
Repatriation from China of Canadian nationals other than diplomatic personnel, September 1942-December 1946.

File 4464-B-40.
Repatriation from the Far East of J.C.Riley, November 1943.

450 • Ontario – Ottawa

Volume 3113.

File 4464-C-40.
Expenses re repatriation of Canadian nationals in the S.S.Gripsholm, 1943, payments of, November 1943-November 1952.

File 4464-D-40.
Reports re conditions in the Far East by Canadian repatriates, September 1942-January 1944.

File 4464-D-40, part 2 FP.
Reports re conditions in the Far East by Canadian repatriates, September 1942-January 1944.

File 4464-F-40.
Repatriation of protected personnel from the Far East, December 1943-April 1944.

File 4465-H-40.
Request by Dubian I.Mario for names of Canadians repatriated from the Far East.

Volume 3116.

File 4532-40.
Turkey-Canada relations, October 1942-August 1963.

File 4558-E-40.
Premises for Canadian embassy in China, Chungking, November 1942-December 1943.

Volume 3117.

File 4558-E-40, part 2.
Premises for Canadian embassy in China, Chungking, December 1943-April 1946.

File 4558-G-40.
Establishment of Canadian embassy at Chungking, November 1941-September 1944.

File 4558-H-40.
Appointment of Patterson as counselor of the Canadian embassy at Chungking, December 1942-June 1947.
Appointment of Wing Commander J.H.Norton as air attaché to the Canadian embassy at Chungking, January-July 1943.

Volume 3118.

File 4558-P-40.
Reports on conditions by Canadian embassy, Chungking, May 1943-June 1944.

File 4558-P-40, part 2.
Reports on conditions by Canadian embassy, Chungking, July 1944-June 1948.

File 4558-V-40.
Monthly summaries from Canadian embassy in Nanking, May 1944-December 1947.

File 4558-W-40.
Evacuation of the Canadian embassy in Chungking, November 1944-April 1946.

Volume 3120.

File 4606-A-1-40.
Communism in Japan, March 1944-November 1951.

Volume 3121

File 4606-C-9-40.
Soviet Union-Japan relations, February 1941-January 1954.

File 4606-C-11-40.
Japan-Thailand relations, June 1940-February 1962.

File 4606-C-12-40.
Japan-Korea relations, June 1941-December 1955.

File 4606-C-13-40.
Treatment of assets and property of Japanese nationals in Canada, February 1942-December 1954.

File 4606-H-40.
Electrical power system in Japan, August 1942-December 1950.

File 4622-40.
Appointment of Dr. W.A.Riddle as Canadian minister to China, proposal re, October 1942.

Volume 3122.

File 4678-40.
Communist China-Cuba relations, November 1942-February 1963.

File 4683-40.
US Economic Mission to South Pacific Islands, November 1942-January 1943.

Volume 3124.

File 4697-R-40.
Renewal of prewar treaties with Japan, December 1941-July 1962.

Volume 3125.

File 4723-K-40.
US-Turkey commercial relations and lend-lease arrangements, April 1944-September 1961.

Volume 3126.

File 4725-A-40.
Sinking of the Australian hospital ship **Centaur** by the Japanese, protests re, May 1943.

Accession 83-84/268

Box 241.

File 4775-40.
Introductory speech by Madame Chiang Kai-shek at N.F.B. Canadian war production, December 1942-January 1943.

File 4791-405.
Powers of Japanese consular courts in states at war with Japan, reports, December 1942.

Box 242.

File 4830-40.
Conscription in Japan, January 1943.

File 4833-40.
United Nations nationals in the Far East(other than U.S. or Canada), reports and lists, August 1942-February 1943.

Box 243.

File 4851-B-1-40.
Chinese students to study Canadian fishery and forestry industry, arrangements, May 1944-September 1946.

File 4858-B-40.
Joint Far Eastern psychological warfare, proposals re, January-August 1944.

Box 244.

File 4881-40.
Lumber for Fiji from Canada, January 1943-October 1945.

File 4887-40.
Establishment of direct radio communication between Canada and China, proposals, February

Box 246.

File 4925-40.
Canadian nationals in the Far East, statistics and lists, February 1943-April 1947.

Box 247.

File 4929-F-40, part 2.
Support for the China and Canada Mutual Aid Pact, February-May 1944.

File 4929-F-40, part 3.
Support for the China and Canada Mutual Aid Pact, May 1944-August 1945.

File 4929-J-40.
Assistance for India under the Canadian Mutual Aid Pact, July 1943-November 1944.

File 4929-J-40, part 2.
Assistance for India under the Canadian Mutual Aid Pact, November 1944-February 1946.
File 5000-40 1 FP.

Shooting of Japanese prisoners of war in New Zealand, February 1943-February 1944.

File 5000-A-40.
Treatment of Japanese prisoners of war in New Zealand, November 1943-October 1945.

Box 251.

File 5068-A-40.
Immigration treaty between Canada and China.

File 5068-A-40, part 2.
Immigration treaty between Canada and China.

File 5068-B-40.
Immigration into, and status of Chinese in Canada.

Box 261.

File 5353-A-3-40.
Japanese sub-committee of Canadian political warfare committee, minutes and agenda, September 1943-February 1945.

File 5353-G-40.
Canadian political intelligence directed versus Japan, general file, January 1943-March 1944.

File 5353-G-2-40.
Japanese recordings from Canada for Allied Political War Committee in Australia, July-December 1944.

Box 263.

File 5356-40.
Trip to Soviet Union and China by Napier Moore, June-July 1943.

Box 264.

File 5386-40.
Religion and Christianity in China, June 1943-June 1960.

Box 267.

File 5404-X-40.
United Kingdom political warfare executive Far Eastern directives, general file, Japan, February 1944-August 1946.

File 5404-X-2-40.
Plan of political warfare versus Japan, issued by Political Warfare(Japan) Committee, London, April 1942-February 1946.

File 5404-X-3-40.
Plan of political warfare versus Burma, March-April 1944.

File 5404-X-4-40.
Plan of political warfare versus Indo-China, 1944.

File 5404-X-5-40.
Plan of political warfare versus Malaya, November 1942-June 1945.

File 5404-X-6-40.
Plan of political warfare versus Thailand, November 1942-July 1945.

File 5404-X-7-40.
Plan of political warfare versus occupied China, June-July 1944.

File 5404-4-40.
Far Eastern intelligence and propaganda reports of British Ministry of Information, September 1943-January 1946.

File 5404-AD-40.
Plan of propaganda to Free China, issued by British Ministry of Information(Overseas Planning Committee), February 1943-August 1944.

File 5414-40.
Japanese political intelligence, November 1942-December 1944.

File 5414-A-40.
Japanese broadcasts, monitoring of, December 1940-December 1945.

File 5414-B-40.
Japanese broadcasts, transcripts from India, January-August 1943.

File 5414-B-40, part 2.
Japanese broadcasts, transcripts from India, January 1943-February 1944.

File 5414-C-40.
Monitoring of Japanese broadcasts at Point Grey. Correspondence and Australian short-wave division, January 1942-December 1943.

File 5414-C-40, part 2.
Monitoring of Japanese broadcasts at Point Grey. Correspondence and Australian short-wave division, September 1943-September 1944.

File 5414-C-40, part 3.
Monitoring of Japanese broadcasts at Point Grey. Correspondence and Australian short-wave division, October 1944-May 1950.

File 5414-C-2-40.
Japanese broadcasts. Point Grey, reports, June-October 1943.

File 5414-C-2-40, part 2.
Japanese broadcasts. Point Grey, reports, November 1943-January 1944.

File 5414-C-2-40, part 3.
Japanese broadcasts. Point Grey, reports, January-February 1944.

File 5414-C-2-40, part 4.
Japanese broadcasts. Point Grey, reports, February-March 1944.

File 5414-C-2-40, part 5.
Japanese broadcasts. Point Grey, reports, April 1944.

File 5414-C-2-40, part 6.
Japanese broadcasts. Point Grey, reports, May 1944.

File 5414-C-2-40, part 7.
Japanese broadcasts. Point Grey, reports, June 1944.

File 5414-C-2-40, part 8.
Japanese broadcasts. Point Grey, reports, July-August 1944.

File 5414-C-2-40, part 9.
Japanese broadcasts. Point Grey, reports, August-September 1944.

File 5414-C-2-40, part 10.
Japanese broadcasts. Point Grey, reports, October-November 1944.

Box 269.

File 5414-C-2-40, part 11.
Japanese broadcasts. Point Grey, reports, November-December 1944.

File 5414-D-40.
Japanese broadcasts - Federal Communications Commissions reports, March 1943-August 1945.

File 5422-D-40.
Directive for political war versus Japan issued by Allied Political Warfare Committee in Australia - Japan plan, November 1942-March 1945.

File 5422-D-2-40.
Directive for political war versus Japan issued by Allied Political Warfare Committee in Australia - Indo-China plan, June 1943-July 1945.

File 5422-D-3-40.
Directive for political war versus Japan issued by Allied Political Warfare Committee in Australia - Dutch East Indies plan, June 1943.

File 5422-D-4-40.
Directive for political war versus Japan issued by Allied Political Warfare Committee in Australia - Thailand plan, November 1942-July 1945.

File 5422-D-5-40.
Directive for political war versus Japan issued by Allied Political Warfare Committee in Australia - New Guinea plan, March-June 1943.

Box 274.

File 5495-40.
Netherlands East Indies administration, political

situation - general file, July 1943-December 1946.

File 5495-A-1-40.
Appointment of Canadian liaison officer to Netherlands East Indies government establishment in Australia, proposals re, September-November 1944.

File 5495-Q-40.
Indonesia-Australia relations, November 1940-June 1963.

Box 275.

File 5538-40.
Travel to China, reports re conditions of, July 1943-February 1948.

File 5539-40.
Cost of living in China, prices, wages and controls, June 1943-September 1946.

Box 276.

File 5548-40.
Military operations in China, August 1942-June 1946.

Box 277.

File 5600-40.
Treatment of persons of East Indian origin in the Union of South Africa, May 1944-August 1947.

File 5602-40.
Transmission of mail to Netherlands nationals in Japanese hands, August-September 1943.

Box 278.

File 5650-40.
Japanese interpreters from Canada for US, requests re, August-October 1943.

File 5650-41.
Agriculture in China, legislation and reports, re August 1943-March 1958.

File 5654-40.
French Canadian units for service in Indo-China, proposals re, July-December 1943.

File 5666-40.
China-UK relations, general file, August 1943-April 1951.

File 5667-40.
China's war efforts, comments and criticism re, July 1943-August 1945.

Box 279.

File 5710-40.
Reports re organization of, and personalities of diplomatic representation in China, August 1943-February 1951.

Box 280.

File 5729-40.
Press in China, editorial opinion in the China press, reports re, August-October 1943.

File 5730-40.
Visit of Dr. Liu Shih-shun, Chinese Minister to Canada to the Maritime Provinces, August-October 1943.

File 5737-40.
Development of oil resources in China, reports re, August 1943-February 1958.

File 5741-40.
Economic and financial conditions in China, reports re, July 1942-July 1944.

File 5748-40.
Economic developments in the Far East, reports by cryptographic unit, September 1943.

Box 281.

File 5768-40.
Restraint exercised by Japanese government on cargoes prior to 28 July 1941, investigations, September-October 1943.

File 5810-40, I-FPS.
Immigration of Chinese to and from the U.S.,

regulations re, April 1943-March 1956.

File 5825-40.
Sale of property by foreigners in China, regulations re, August 1943-July 1946.

Box 284.

File 5880-40.
Participation of Canadian Friends Service Committee in work of Friends' Ambulance Unit in China, enquiry re, July 1943-April 1960.

File 5882-40.
Funds of H.F.Feaver in Japan, August-December 1943.

File 5886-40.
Soviet Union-Afghanistan relations, September 1943-June 1963.

Box 285.

File 5887-40.
Relief for India and Pakistan, proposals by various persons re(unofficial), October 1943-July 1954.

File 5901-40.
Visit to China, India and Russia of E.C.Carter, November 1943.

File 5914-40.
Cultural reconstruction movement in China, reports re, September-November 1943.

Box 286.

File 5930-B-40.
Exchange of ambassadors between China and Canada, November 1943-March 1947.

File 5937-40.
Chinese nationality law, reports re, July 1947-March 1950.

Box 291.

File 6029-40.
German Jews interned in reports re, October 1943-March 1946.

File 6053-40.
Szechwan sericulture corporation of China, export of silk etc., to Canada and imports of machinery from Canada, October 1943-October 1946.

File 6059-40.
Treatment in British ports of merchant seamen of Japanese extraction, December 1945-May 1954.

Box 292.

File 6083-40.
India-China relations, November 1943-August 1955.

File 6094-40.
Chinese Ministry of Information, reports re, November 1943-February 1947.

File 6103-40.
Industrial and mining development in China, December 1943-June 1957.

Box 293.

File 6161-40.
Trade between occupied and non-occupied China, reports re, October 1943-January 1946.

Box 294.

File 6172-40.
Enemy activities in Afghanistan, August 1941-February 1944.

File 6217-40.
Turko-Syrian boundary problems, March 1942-August 1957.

Box 295.

File 6264-40.
Registration of foreign owned firms in China, January 1944-March 1954.

File 6286-40.
Insurance business legislation in China, February 1944-May 1950.

Box 296.

File 6309-40.
Japanese translators from Canada for Australia, March 1944-October 1946.

File 6314-40.
Communication in China, February 1944-January 1962.

File 6342-40 1FP.
Economic conditions in Manchuria, January-February 1944.

Box 298.

File 6403-40.
Radio broadcasting in China, March 1944-July 1947.

File 6405-40.
Railway construction in China, March 1944-January 1945.

File 6467-40.
Publication of the laws of China, April 1944-January 1945.

Box 299.

File 6466-40
Communism in China, January 1944-October 1945.

Box 300.

File 6130-40.
India, reports re conditions in India by individuals, April 1944-August 1956.

File 6552-40.
Visit to China by Vice-President Wallace, May-July 1944.

File 6567-40.
Reports re conditions in Mongolian People's Republic (Soviet Union-Mongolian relations), June 1944-August 1960.

Box 302.

File 6669-40.
Conditions and developments in Szechwan province of China, reports re Szechwan salt administration, Chungking bridges, January 1944-January 1950.

File 6669-A-40.
Conditions and developments in Honan province in China, August 1944-January 1948.

File 6669-B-40.
Conditions and developments in Hupeh province in

China, August 1944-October 1951.
File 6669-C-40.
Conditions and developments in Shensi province in China, August 1944.

File 6669-D-40.
Conditions and developments in Kansu province in China, March-August 1944.

File 6669-E-40.
Conditions and developments in Fukien province in China, October 1944-July 1947.

File 6669-F-40.
Conditions and developments in Kwangsi province in China, May 1944.

File 6669-G-40.
Conditions and developments in Shantung province in China, December 1944-June 1948.

File 6671-40.
Conditions and developments in Shansi province in China, February 1944-November 1947.

File 6672-40.
Conditions and developments in Yunnan province in China, May 1944-September 1949.

File 6674-40.
China-Iran relations, May 1944-October 1959.

File 6676-40 1 FP.
China-Burma relations, March 1944-June 1953.

File 6681-40.
China, patent legislation, June 1944-September 1950.

File 6697-40.
Establishment of China National Resources Commission in the U.S., June 1944-July 1947.

Box 303.

File 6734-40.
Conditions and development in Kiangsi province, China, reports re, May-December 1944.

File 6742-40.
Escape of Japanese prisoners of war in Australia, August-September 1944.

File 6745-40.
Situation re Greeks in Turkey, February 1944-April 1957.

File 6794-40.
Conditions in Japanese occupied China, reports re, December 1943-April 1946.

File 6795-40.
Exchange between Australia and Canada of despatches on conditions in China, proposals re, April-September 1944.

Box 304.

File 6809-40.
Canada-Philippine relations, August 1944-October 1962.

File 6812-40.
Return of Hong Kong-China, proposals re, April 1944-January 1958.

File 6816-40.
School of Chinese Studies of the University of Toronto, information re, August 1944-November 1950.

File 6818-40.
Canadian domestic publicity on the war against Japan, proposals re, August 1944.

File 6822-40.
Reopening of the Burma road, reports re, August 1944-May 1945.

File 6832-40.
Postwar situation of Manchuria re construction plans for Manchuria, August 1944-September 1952.

Box 305.

File 6836-40.
Infringement of property rights of Baptist College in Chengtu by cattle of Dr. F.Dickinson.

File 6848-40.
China-Canada Incorporated, establishment of, October 1944-December 1945.

File 6878-40.
Escape from internment in the Far East of prisoners of war, notification re, July 1944-June 1946.

Box 306.

File 6900-40.
Franchise for Chinese Canadians, resolutions, August 1944.

File 6907-40.
Conditions of admission to Turkish ports, October 1944-April 1961.

Box 309.

File 7042-40.
Censorship in China, August 1944-November 1946.

File 7043-40.
China relations with Latin-American countries, September 1944-August 1963.

Box 310.

File 7077-40.
Position of the Moslems in China, August-November 1944.

Box 311.

File 7116-AE-40.
Information and cultural services of the Government of China, reports re, October 1943-October 1956.

File 7131-40.
Political situation and conditions in Macao, October 1943-June 1966.

File 7141-40.
Communication with former prisoners of war and internees in liberated area of the Far East, April 1941-May 1946.

Box 313.

File 7182-40.
Imperial Order of the Daughters of the British Empire donation to St. Helena's school, Poona, India, enquiry re, December 1944-July1946.

File 7182-40.
China's destiny by Chiang Kai-shek, comments and reports on, July 1943-March 1944.

Box 314.

File 7275-40.
Use of Japanese-Americans in the intelligence branch of the U.S. Army, reports re, September-December 1944.

File 7300-40.
Treatment of Chinese who have collaborated with the Japanese during the occupation of China, policy of the Chinese government re, December 1944-October 1945.

Box 315.

File 7338-40.
Status of the Bonin islands, September 1944-April 1955.

Box 316.

File 7444-40.
British intelligence agencies in China, reports re, October 1943.

Box 318.

File 7611-40.
Sino-French Committee for Scientific and Academic cooperation, activities and reports re, February-December 1944.

Box 319.

File 7921-40.
Australia-Chinese relations, general files, July 1941-December 1952.

Box 321.
File 8250-40 FP.
Postwar position of Malayan States.

File 8254-40.
Status of Korean Free Korea Movement. Activities and reports, internal conditions in Korea, December 1941-

File 8260-Y-40.
Exchanges of students between Canada and India(temporary file, original missing), May 1956-October 1958.

File 8260-AE-40.
Exchanges of students between Canada and China(including Taiwan and Formosa), July 1953-May 1963.

Box 322.

File 8295-40.
Industrial cooperation in China, reports re, October 1943-December 1948.

File 8704-40.
Future status of Sarawak and British North Borneo, June 1944-July 1962.

Box 323.

File 9030-40.
Commercial relations between China and Canada, general file, December 1940-December 1945.

File 9030-A-40.
Commercial agreement(modus vivendi) between China and Canada, November 1942-August 1954.

File 9030-D-40.
Railway equipment for China from Canada, general file, July 1942-January 1948.

File 9040-E-40.
Wheat and flour for China from Canada, September 1944-September 1946.

File 9030-F-40.
Electric power development in China, participation by Canada in, January 1942-May 1963.

File 9076-40.
Scientific liaison officer for Canadian Embassy at Nanking, proposal re, June 1944.

Box 325.

File 9161-40.
Compensation for loss of property interests in Japan and Japanese occupied territories in the Far East, procedure re placing claims, October 1941-September 1947.

File 9161-C-40.
Claims of the Sun Life Assurance Company to property in Japan, July 1942-May 1953.

File 9161-T-40.
Claims of A.R.Evans to property in Japan, January 1943-January 1958.

File 9161-AG-40.
Claims of Mrs. H.P.Trousell to property in Japan, December 1942-July 1951.

File 9161-AX-40.
Claims of Arthur A.Zimmerman to property in Japan and China, February 1942-January 1950.

File 9161-CV-40.
Claims of International Delavand Manufacturing Corporation Ltd., to property in Japan, France and Germany, June 1943-September 1947.

File 9161-DB-40.
Claims of Consolidated Mining and Smelting to property in Japan, July 1942-June 1958.

File 9161-FA-40.
Claims of H.A.Stewart to property in Japan, June 1944-September 1947.

Box 326.

File 9193-40.
Political situation in India, constitutional position in India, April 1942-May 1947.

File 9193-U-40.
India, agricultural, food situation, January 1944-December 1957.

Box 327.

File 9445-L-40.
Claim of William Buchanan to property in Hong Kong, February 1944-June 1952.

File 9445-R-40.
Claim of E.S.Widdrup to property in Hong Kong, January 1944-July 1956.

File 9445-AX-40.
Claim of Lever Brothers against Japan and U.S. government arising out of loss of certain shipments of coconut oil at Hong Kong, December 1942-February 1948.

File 9445-BD-40.
Claim for cases sustained through enemy action in Hong Kong, Empire Stevedoring Company, Ltd., February 1944-January 1948.

Box 330.

File 9820-40.
Overseas Chinese activities organisation, November 1943-March 1948.

File 9899-AE-40.
Education in China, August 1943-July 1960.

Box 335.

File 10699-J-40.
Shanghai, trade and commerce offices, appointments to, December 1942-July 1951.

File 10849-40.
Iran-U.S. relations, December 1943-June 1963.

File 11004-40.
Canadian diplomatic relations with India, November 1940-March 1963.

Box 337.

File 11318-40.
Position of the Anglo-Iranian Oil Company, August 1940-January 1951.

Box 338.

File 11494-40 1FP.
India government expenditure and revenue, May 1944-June 1963.

File 11494-C-40.
India, banking reports, September 1944-May 1957.

File 11578-C-40.
The Chinese Nationalist government foreign policy, March 1943-August 1963.

Box 341.

File 12381-40.
Japanese fisheries, general file, April 1941-October 1963.

Box 342.

File 14405-J-12-40.
Mineral products - petroleum and natural gas, Iran, October 1944-March 1952.

Accession 84-85/019.

Box 1.

File 8-U-40.
Alleged smuggling re opium into Canada by Inspector J.Mills of Shaukiwan police station in Hong Kong, January-June 1947.

File 8-AE-40, part 5.
Control traffic in opium and dangerous drugs, October 1947-January 1958.

Box 3.

File l0-DW-40.

Passport and visa regulations for entry from and to India, October 1947-August 1948.

Box 4.

File 10-ED-40.
Issuance of passports or certificates of nationality to Japanese, August 1948-October 1950.

File 10-EM-40.
Visa agreement between Canada and Turkey, October 1948-August 1963.

Box 5.

File 10-EX-40.
China, passports and visas, December 1948-April 1960.

Box 8.

File 19-CR-1-40.
Chinese awards to Canadian armed forces, May 1946-June 1948.

File 19-CR-2-40.
Chinese awards to Canadian civilians, October 1946-March 1951.

Box 12.

File 72-BP-2-40.
Air relations between China and Canada, August 1948-June 1958.

File 72-BP-3-40.
Air relations between Japan and Canada, August 1948-July 1953.

Box 14.

File 72-ABQ-40.
Postwar civilian aviation plans in Canada, March 1945-January 1955.

Box 23.

File 72-AKG-40.
Civil aviation agreement between U.S. and India, November 1946-February 1954.

File 72-AKH-40.
Civil aviation agreement between U.K. and China, January-October 1947.

File 72-AKL-40.
Civil aviation in Ceylon, general file. Agreement with U.S., February 1947-February 1962.

File 72-AKN-40.
Exchange of fifth freedom rights between Canada and U.K. re Canton Islands and Fiji, November 1946-February 1952.

Box 24.

File 72-ALS-40.
Burma, air regulations, November 1948-September 1949.

File 72-ALQ-40.
South Pacific Air Transport Council- 3rd meeting, Wellington, 1948, April 1948-March 1950.

File 72-AMJ-40.
Iran-Canada air relations, November 1949-December 1953.

File 72-AOJ-40.
Air relations between Canada and Turkey, December 1946-November 1961.

Box 25.

File 72-AOQ-40.
Civil aviation in Pakistan, February 1948-November 1963.

Box 27.

File 74-AV-1-40.
ILO 1st regional conference, Asiatic states, Ceylon, January 1950, May 1946-December 1950.

Box 32.

File 232-AH-40.
Immigration into Canada, Asiatic, March 1947-September 1963.

Box 36.

File 614-1-40.
Safeguarding and release of assets held in Canada for persons and companies of foreign countries, China, policy, September 1946-September 1963.

File 614-Q-2-40.
Safeguarding and release of Canadian assets of German nationals resident in Japan, policy, November 1948-September 1950.

File 614-R-2-40.
Release of. Japanese assets in Canada, particular cases, October 19

Box 40.

File 622-NR-40.
Release of Australian prisoners of war in the Far East, August 1945.

File 621-NU-40.
Directorate of Prisoners of War(War Office Weekly Summary re British and Allied prisoners of war in the Far East), September-November 1945.

File 656-40.
U.K.-Thailand relations, October 1946-January 1963.

Box 44.

File 773-B-1-40, part 4.
Treatment of Japanese in Canada, proposals of various persons, June-November 1945.

File 773-B-1-40, part 5.
Treatment of Japanese in Canada, proposals of various persons, January 1946-February 1949.

Box 50.

File 1426-B-40, part 13.
Reports on prisoner of war camps in Germany and Far East(East Asia consolidated reports), January-March 1945.

File 1426-B-40, part 14.
Reports on prisoner of war camps in Germany and Far East(East Asia consolidated reports), February-April 1945.

File 1426-B-40, part 15.
Reports on prisoner of war camps in Germany and Far East(East Asia consolidated reports), April-July 1945.

Box 52

File 1617-40.
India-Canada relations, including exchange of High Commissioners, November 1947-December 1956.

Box 57.

File 2006-N-40.
Travel to Far East, regulations and policy, January 1947-December 1955.

File 2006-N-1-A-40.
Clearance of persons entering Japan, procedures re, September 1946-December 1947.

File 2006-N-1-A-40, part 2.
Clearance of persons entering Japan, procedures re, January 1948-March 1952.

File 2006-N-2-40.
Clearance for entry of business representatives into Japan, special File, February 1948-October 1952.

File 2006-N-3-40.
Clearance for entry of missionaries into Japan, general file, November 1947-August 1948.

File 2006-CA-40.
Permission to travel to the Far East for members of the Order of Dominicans, January 1946-September 1947.

File 2016-40.
War measures in Burma, June 1945.

Box 62.

File 2295-AJ-40, part 2.
Committee of the Council for the Far East of U.N.R.R.A, January 1946-February 1947.

File 2295-AJ-40, part 3.
Committee of the Council for the Far East of U.N.R.R.A., March 1947.

File 2295-AJ-6-40.
U.N.R.R.A. subcommittee on displaced persons for the Far East, June-August 1945.

Box 65,

File 2295-CB-40.
U.N.R.R.A. activities in Thailand, June-August 1945.

File 2295-CD-40.
U.N.R.R.A. activities in the Netherlands East Indies, July 1945.

File 2295-CN-40.
U.N.R.R.A. supplies for Indo-China, May 1947-May 1949.

Box 75.

File 2727-AE-40, part 3.
Canadian publicity in China, December 1946-September 1962.

File 2727-AH-40.
Canadian publicity in Japan, February 1947-May 1957.

Box 76.

File 2727-AK-40.
Canadian publicity in Hong Kong, April 1947-May 1957.

File 2727-BT-40.
Cultural relations between Canada and Iran, October 1949-July 1963.

File 2727-CB-40.
Canadian publicity in Ceylon, July 1949-October 1963.

Box 78.

File 2837-40, part 3.
Institute for Pacific Relations conferences, November 1948-December 1960.

File 2997-40, part 3-FPS.
Japanese in Canada, statistics, December 1946-August 1948.

Box 79.

File 2998-D-40, part 6.
Visits by representatives of protecting power and international Red Cross committee to Canadian

prisoners of war in Japan and Japanese occupied territory, arrangements and reports, February-June 1945.

File 2998-R-40.
Food situation in civilian internment camps in Far East, June 1945-.

File 2998-S-40.
Activities of Portuguese Red Cross re prisoners of war in Far East, May-August 1945.

Box 80.

File 3050-L-40, part 2.
Safety and welfare in the Far East of the Dominican Order following the outbreak of war with Japan, October 1946-February 1957.

File 3050-M-40, part 2.
Safety and welfare in the Far East of the Order of Les Missions Étrangères de Pont-Viau, January 1945-March 1949.

File 3050-T-40, part 2.
Safety and welfare in the Far East of the Order of Sœurs Franciscains Missionaires de Marie, following the outbreak of war with Japan, December 1945-July 1954.

File 3051-G-40, part 2.
Safety and welfare in the Far East of the Christian Missionary Alliance Tabernacle, following the outbreak of war with Japan, September 1945-July 1955.

File 3227-40.
Assistance for distressed Canadians at Macao, January 1946-October 1951.

Box 81.

File 3232-AG-40.
Ownership and taxation of real properties in Canada bought by Pakistan, July 1949-July 1960.

File 3232-AT-40.
Ownership and taxation of real properties in Canada bought by Ceylon, June 1947-June 1957.

File 3284-40.
India commercial relations with Canada, October 1940-April 1956.

File 3284-D-40.
Ships for India from Canada, October 1945-October 1951.

File 3284-K-40.
Newsprint out of Indian timber research in Canada re possibility, proposed contracts for paper mills in India, April 1947-December 1952.

Box 85.

File 3363-A-40, part 2-FPS.
Forms of consent to repatriation and refusal to be repatriated by Japanese in Canada, also requests for repatriation, October 1945-March 1946.

File 3263-D-40.
Repatriation movement of Japanese from Canada to Japan, arrangements, November 1945-July 1946.

File 3263-D-40, part 2.
Repatriation movement of Japanese from Canada to Japan, arrangements, August 1946-September 1949.

File 3464-BK-40.
Payment of workmen's compensation to Japanese repatriated to Japan, January 1946-June 1955.

Box 88.

File 3857-A-40.
Beginning of Office of Canadian Trade in Hong Kong and Shanghai, February 1946-March 1946.

Box 89.

File 3978-40-part 3.
Relief for China during war, general file, June 1945-December 1949.

File 3991-B-40.
U.S.-Philippine relations, March 1947-June 1958.

Box 91.

File 4060-C-40.
Japanese war crimes, general file, International Military Tribunal for the Far East in Tokyo, September 1945-February 1946.

File 4060-C-40, part 2.
Japanese war crimes, general file, International Military Tribunal for the Far East in Tokyo, March 1946-December 1946.

File 4060-C-40, part 3.
Japanese war crimes, general file, International Military Tribunal for the Far East in Tokyo, January 1947-December 1948.

File 4060-C-40, part 4.
Japanese war crimes, general file, International Military Tribunal for the Far East in Tokyo, December 1948-June 1951.

Box 92.

File 4079-H-40.
German atrocities in the Philippines, April-November 1945.

Box 96.

File 4464-40.
Repatriation from Japan of Canadian nationals other

diplomatic personnel, arrangements, March 1945-March 1958.

File 4464-A-40.
Repatriation from China of Canadian nationals other diplomatic personnel, arrangements, March 1947-July 1961.

Box 97.

File 4558-AE-40.
Appointment of T.C.Davis as Canadian ambassador at Nanking, October 1946-May 1950.

File 4558-AK-40.
Appointment of C.S.Ronning as Canadian ambassador at Nanking, January -June 1949.

File 4606-40, part 2.
Japan political situation subsequently to entry of Japan into the war, October 1946-May 1951.

File 4606-40, part 3.
Japan political situation subsequently to entry of Japan into the war, June 1949-January 1952.

File 4606-A-40.
Japanese constitution, April 1946-September 1958.

File 4606-A-40, part 2.
Japanese constitution, February-October 1949.

File 4606-A-2-40.
Japanese foreign service, May 1947-May 1962.

File 4606-A-4-40.
Japanese personalities, May-December 1954.

File 4606-B-40, part 2.
Monitored reports re Japan, July 1947-December 1949.

File 4606-B-3-40.
Control over Japanese exports and imports, May 1949-February 1963.

File 4606-B-6-40.
Release of gold in Japan earmarked for various countries, September-October 1949.

File 4606-C-1-40.
International convention on telecommunications, accession from Japan, February 1949-August 1950.

File 4606-C-2-40.
Communication between the Japanese government and persons abroad re personal status, June 1949-May 1955.

Box 101.

File 4606-R-1-40.
Principles for Japanese farmers organization, January-December 1948.

File 4606-U-40, part 1 FP.
Far Eastern Commission, documents, July 1947-December 1951.

File 4606-U-1-40.
Far Eastern Commission, admission of new members, J January 1945-December 1950.

Box 103.

File 4723-S-40.
Treaty of Peace and Friendship between U.S. and Kingdom of Nepal, April 1947-February 1964.

Box 105.

File 4900-B-10-40.
Letters of instruction to heads of Canadian diplomatic missions abroad, Tokyo, July 1946-December 1952.

File 4900-C-1-40.
Letters of instruction to heads of Canadian diplomatic missions abroad, Ankara, December 1947-April 1961.

Box 106.

File 4900-E-40.
Letters of instruction to heads of Canadian diplomatic missions abroad, India, April 1947-November 1952.

File 4900-H-1-FP.
Letters of instruction to heads of Canadian diplomatic missions abroad, Pakistan, November 1949-January 1961.

Box 107.

File 4900-R-40.
Letters of instruction to Consul General, Manila, December 1948-September 1963.

File 4901-A-40.
U.S. Economic aid to Greece and Turkey, March 1947-January 1948.

File 4901-A-40, part 2 FP.
U.S. Economic aid to Greece and Turkey, March 1947, February 1948-December 1953.

Box 110.

File 4901-C-40.
U.S.-Ceylon relations, April 1948-July 1963.

Box 112.

File 4929-F-40.
Supplies for China under Canadian Mutual Aid Act, September 1945-March 1954.

Box 121.

File 5404-P-40.
Information re Japan for political intelligence work,

July-December 1945.

File 5414-Q-40.
Far Eastern Weekly Intelligence Summaries of British Ministry of Economic Warfare, March-May 1945.

File 5404-X-40, part 2.
UK-PWE Far Eastern Directives, general file, Japan, September 1946-January 1947.

File 5404-X-40, part 3.
UK-PWE Far Eastern Directives, general file, Japan, January-November 1947.

File 5404-Z-40.
Fortnightly Intelligence Reports(Ministry of Information, New Delhi) re Borneo, October 1945-July 1946.

File 5414-C-2-40, part 12.
Japanese broadcasts, Point Grey reports, January-February 1945.

File 5414-C-2-40, part 13.
Japanese broadcasts, Point Grey reports, March-April 1945.

File 5414-C-2-40, part 14.
Japanese broadcasts, Point Grey reports, May-August 1945.

Box 129.

File 5475-N-2-40.
Postwar disposal of Japanese islands, April 1945-July 1953.

Box 130.

File 5475-T-4-40.
International refugee organization, problem of refugees in Shanghai, December 1948-December 1949.

Box 132.

File 5475-W-4-40.
United Nations Economic and Social Council, Committee on Human Rights, complaints, treatment of Japanese in Canada, November 1948-August 1949.

Box 142.

File 5475-CR-1-40.
United Nations application for membership in United Nations and in specialized agencies, Outer Mongolia, October 1948-June 1963.

File 5475-CR-3-40.
United Nations application for membership in United Nations and in specialized agencies, Ceylon, January 1948-October 1955.

Box 143.

File 5475-CR-4-40.
United Nations application for membership in United Nations and in specialized agencies, Korea, December 1948-May 1963.

File 5475-CR-5-40.
United Nations application for membership in United Nations and in specialized agencies, Nepal, February 1949-November 1950.

File 5475-CX-2-40.
Appointment and administrative arrangements for Canadian military observers on United Nations Commission for India and Pakistan, December 1948-March 1950.

File 5475-CY-2-40, part 1 FP.
United Nations Economic Commission for Asia and the Far East, September 1946-November 1948.

File 5475-CY-2-40, part 2.
United Nations Economic Commission for Asia and the Far East, February 1949-December 1952

Box 147.

File 5475-DU-11-40.
United Nations technical assistance for Pakistan, September 1949-May 1954.

Box 149.

File 5495-40, part 2.
Netherlands East Indies administration and political situation, general file, January-August 1947.

File 5495-40, part 3.
Netherlands East Indies administration and political situation, general file, August 1947-February 1948.

File 5495-40, part 4.
Netherlands East Indies administration and political situation, general file, February-June 1948.

File 5495-40, part 5-FP.
Netherlands East Indies administration and political situation, general file, May 1948-August 1962.

Box 150.

File 5495-A-40.
Documents pertaining to the Indonesian question, January 1948-October 1959.

File 5495-B-40.
Indonesia-Netherlands relations, December 1949-August 1954.

File 5495-C-40, part 1 FP.
Political situation of Indonesia, November 1949-August 1950.

File 5495-C-1-40.
Indonesia, foreign service, August 1949-July 1962.

File 5495-E-40.
Indonesia-Philippine relations, September 1949-July 1963.

File 5495-F-40.
Indonesia-U.S. relations, December 1949-April 1961.

File 5495-G-40.
Indonesia-Canada relations, September 1949-December

File 5495-H-40.
Indonesia-India relations, December 1949-February 1963.

File 5495-J-40.
Indonesia-China relations, October 1946-December 1959.

Box 151.

File 5548-A-40.
Reorganization of the Chinese armed forces, January 1946-August 1961.

File 5550-40, part 2 FP.
Status of East Indians in Canada, general file, January 1946-July 1956.

Box 163.

File 5582-BH-4-40.
China-Canada, U.N.E.S.C.O. fellowships, CCRU project, candidates from China, October 1951-.

File 5582-BH-13-40.
Philippines-Canada, U.N.E.S.C.O. fellowships, CCRU project, candidates from Philippines, February 1949-January 1951.

Box 165.

File 5600-40.
Treatment of persons of East Indian origin in the Union of South Africa, September 1947-November 1949.

File 5710-V-40.
Reports on organizations and personalities of diplomatic representation in Japan, February 1947-August 1958.

Box 166.

File 5710-AC-40.
Reports on organizations and personalities of diplomatic representation in Pakistan, July 1947-December 1961.

File 5729-A-40.
Chinese Canadian press, December 1949-February 1951.

File 5471-40, part 3.
Economic and financial conditions in China, reports re, September 1945-October 1946.

File 5471-40, part 4.
Economic and financial conditions in China, reports re, November 1947-June 1950.

File 5761-A-40.
Chinese Maritime Customs Service, pension claims, December 1947-July 1949.

Box 168.

File 585 9-40.
Re equipment of libraries destroyed by enemy action in Europe and China, February-September 1950.

File 5860-40.
Australia-India relations, April 1946-May 1963.

Box 169.

File 5872-AH-40.
Press in Japan, reports re, January 1947-November 1963.

File 5872-BJ-40.
Press in Turkey, reports re, September 1949-March 1961.

Box 173.

File 6045-40.
Conditions in China, reports by British Embassy, February 1948-September 1957.

Box 179.

File 6624-40, part 2.
Communism in China, November 1945-January 1946.

Box 180.

File 6624-40, part 3.
Communism in China, January to November 1946.

File 6624-40, part 4.
Communism in China, October 1946-October 1949.

File 6624-40, part 5.
Communism in China, December 1949-December 1950.

File 6466-A-40.
Reports re conditions in Shanghai by the Canadian Consul General, May 1949-December 1950.

Box 181.

File 6661-A-40.
Police force in China, January 1948.

File 6609-E-40.
Conditions and developments in Chekiang province in China, July-November 1946.

File 6609-K-40.
Conditions and developments in Shantung province in China, June 1946-.

File 6609-M-40.
Conditions and developments in Sikang province in China, December 1946.

File 6609-N-40.
Conditions and developments in Kwantung province in China, October 1947-March 1948.

File 6609-P-40.
Conditions and developments in Hopei province in China, February-March 1949.

File 6686-40.
Conditions and development by Kwangchowwan leased territory, reports re, January-July 1945.

File 6687-40.
Labour conditions and organization in China, reports re, March 1946-May 1961.

File 6689-40.
Postwar situation of Shanghai municipality, July 1946-April 1950.

Box 182.

File 6804-40, part 2.
Fortnightly reports on the intelligence section of the Government of Burma and reports, December 1945-July 1946.

File 6804-40, part 3.
Fortnightly reports on the intelligence section of the Government of Burma and reports, November-December 1947.

Box 185.

File 6993-C-40, part 2.
Export credit arrangements for purchase of civilian supplies from Canada by China, April 1946-December 1948.

File 6993-C-40, part 3.
Export credit arrangements for purchase of civilian supplies from Canada by China, January 1948-January 1951.

File 6993-C-2-40.
Loan to the Ming Sung Industrial Company, April 1945-June 1947.

File 6993-C-2-40, part 2.
Loan to the Ming Sung Industrial Company, July 1947-May 1950.

File 6993-L-40.
Loan to Turkey under the terms of the Export Credits Insurance Act, proposals re, May 1946-February 1953.

Box 186.

File 7116-Y-40.
Information and cultural services of the Government of India, reports re, April 1949-March 1957.

Box 187.

File 7116-BJ-40.
Information and cultural services of the Government of Turkey, reports re, December 1949-November 1954.

File 7118-A-40.
Principles for the guidance of civil affairs officers in the Far East, April 1945-.

File 7150-40, part 2.
Welfare of Canadian nationals in the liberated Philippines, April-June 1945.

File 7150-40, part 3.
Welfare of Canadian nationals in the liberated Philippines, May 1945-July 1948.

Box 188.

File 7265-40.
Free Thai movements, reports re, August 1945.

Box 189.

File 7307-40.
Turkish foreign policy, January 1945-December 1959.

File 7307-40.
Greece-Turkey relations.

Box 190.

File 7338-A-4.
Status of the Loochoo(Ryukyu) Islands, April 1945-September 1952.

Box 191.

File 7350-P-40.
Relaxation of trading with the enemy regulations with respect to the Philippines, May-December 1945.

File 7350-S-40.
Relaxation of trading with the enemy regulations with respect to the Netherlands East Indies, August 1946-September 1948.

File 7372-40.
Reports re economic conditions in and trade of French Indo-China, June 1954-September 1954.

Box 193.

File 7477-40.
Rubber rehabilitation program for Netherlands East Indies, May-June 1945.

File 7493-40.
Research facilities in Canada for the purpose of study by Chinese professors, February-May 1945.

File 7498-A-40.
Resolutions and opinions re Netherlands East Indies nationalist movement, November 1945-April 1961.

File 7503-40.
Establishment of Chinese war transport board, January-February 1945.

Box 198.

File 7596-40.
Difficulties re production of banknotes for China, February-March 1945.

File 7607-40.
Japanese activities in Formosa, January-May 1945.

Box 199.

File 7648-40.
Post hostilities assistance to and repatriation of Canadian civilians in the Far East, March-September 1945.

File 7648-40, part 2.
Post hostilities assistance to and repatriation of Canadian civilians in the Far East, September 1945.

File 7648-40, part 3 FP.
Post hostilities assistance to and repatriation of Canadian civilians in the Far East, October-November 1945.

File 7648-40, part 4.
Post hostilities assistance to and repatriation of Canadian civilians in the Far East, November 1945-August 1952.

Box 200.

File 7648-B-40.
Lists of Canadian civilians interested in the Far East, August-September 1945.

File 7648-B-40, part 2.
Lists of Canadian civilians interested in the Far East, October 1945.

File 7648-B-40, part 3 FP.
Lists of Canadian civilians interested in the Far East, November 1945-January 1946.

File 7648-B-40, part 4.
Lists of Canadian civilians interested in the Far East, January 1946-January 1950.

File 7648-C-40.
Movement through Canada to the U.K. of British prisoners of war and civilians repatriated from the Far East, general file, July 1945-April 1946.

File 7648-D-40.
Repatriation of Canadian civilians and prisoners of war from the Far East, financial arrangements, July 1945-January 1947.

File 7648-G-40.
Press and radio publicity for Canadian repatriates from the Far East, arrangements re, September-December 1945.

File 7648-H-40.
Relief and repatriation of Canadian civilians in China, October 1945-August 1951.

File 7648-J-40.
Resumption of payments of war pensions in Japan, general file, April 1946-June 1950.

File 7648-K-40.
Relief and repatriation of persons in Japan by the Canadian mission, general file, April 1946-November 1946.

Box 203.

File 7733-40.
Sinking of ship carrying internees from Philippines to Japan, enquiry re, May - July 1945.

File 7748-40.
Ships for China, general file, May 1945-March 1947.

Box 205.

File 7799-40.
Treaty between Netherlands and the China, re relinquishment by Holland of extraterritorial privileges in China, May 1945.

File 7800-40.
Japanese casualties, reports re, June 1945.

File 7802-A-40.
Soviet Union, relations with Iran, January 1947-January 1959.

Box 207.

File 7830-40.
Argentine-China relations, general file, June 1945-.

File 7833-40.
Sino-Swedish treaty re extraterritorial jurisdiction over Swedish nationals in China, May 1945.

Box 208.

File 7889-40.
China-Philippine relations, general file, June 1945-March 1959.

Box 209.

File 7907-40.
Protection and status of Indians resident in British Commonwealth and British Empire countries, especially Indians in Ceylon, June 1945-January 1963.

File 7938-40.
Conditions in the Hong Kong area, reports re, June 1945.

File 7940-40.
China tax and tariff legislation and reports, October 1945.

Box 212.

File 8001-40.
Travel in China, regulations re, June 1945-February 1958.

Box 213,

File 8061-40.
Supplies from Canada for French Forces in the Far East, September 1945.

Box 215.

File 8097-40.
Information re Canadian personnel for use of U.S. occupation forces in Japan, July-December 1945.

Box 217.

File 8129-40.
Messages from the Emperor of Japan to Japanese nationals in Canada, September-October 1945.

File 8183-40.
Repatriation of Chinese nationals from Canada to China on board H.M.S. Implacable, November 1945.

File 8183-40.
China land policy, registration requirements, June 1945-February 1952.

Box 218.

File 8197-40.
Relief of British subjects and protection of British interests in China, September-December 1945.

Box 220.

File 8204-J-40.
Indian nationality legislation, general file, October 1947-September 1959.

File 8204-L-40.
Ceylon nationality legislation, general file, September 1948-December 1960.

Box 222.

File 8220-40.
British Foreign Office six-monthly survey of economic developments in the Far East, July 1945-.

File 8221-40.
Economic and financial conditions in Japan, enquiries from Trade and Commerce Department, October 1945-.

File 8223-40.
Repatriation of Japanese nationals from China, September 1945.

File 8225-40.
Treatment of collaborators with enemy forces in Far East, policy re, October 1945.

File 8254-A-1-40.
Claim of Korea mission to properties in Korea, March 1947-.

Box 223.

File 8254-K-40.
Korea-Korean problems at the United Nations, November 1947-November 1956.

File 8255-40.
Conditions in Korea, general, March 1947-.

Box 225.

File 8260-BJ-40.
Exchange of students between Canada and Turkey, April 1945.

File 8260-CB-40.
Exchange of students between Canada and Ceylon, July 1947.

File 8273-40.
Control over Japanese exports and imports, policy re committee No.2, economic and financial, November 1945-September 1947.

File 8273-40, part 2.
Control over Japanese exports and imports, policy re Committee No.2, economic and financial, November 1946-June 1947.

File 8273-40, part 3.
Control over Japanese exports and imports, policy re Far Eastern Commission Committee No.2, economic and financial, July-October 1947.

File 8273-40, part 4
Control over Japanese exports and imports, policy re Far Eastern Commission Committee No.2, economic and financial, November 1947-May 1948.

File 8273-40, part 5 FP.
Control over Japanese exports and imports, policy re

Far Eastern Commission Committee No.2, economic and financial, May 1948-September 1949.

Box 226.

File 8289-40.
Far Eastern Advisory Commission, publicity re, November 1945-January 1947.

Box 227.

File 8335-40.
Collection of clothing for needy children in Japan, relief for Japan, proposals re, October 1945-July 1949.

Box 228.

File 8351-40.
Reparation claims against Japan by China for losses sustained in Sino-Japanese war, October 1945.

File 8351-A-40.
Reparation claims against Japan by Australia, December 1945.

File 8351-C-40.
New Zealand claims for reparation against Japan, November 1945-.

File 8364-40, part 1 FP.
Far Eastern Commission, minutes and agenda of meetings, "basic post-surrender policy", March 1946.

File 8364-40, part 2.
Far Eastern Commission, minutes and agenda of meetings, "basic post-surrender policy", March 1948.

Box 229.

File 8364-A-40.
Far Eastern Commission, orders from the Supreme Commander Allied Powers to the Japanese government, January 1946-.

File 8364-C-40.
Far Eastern Commission, Working Committee No.1, Reparations, November 1945-June 1946.

File 8364-C-40, part 2.
Far Eastern Commission, Working Committee No.1, Reparations, July 1946-January 1947.

File 8364-C-40, part 3.
Far Eastern Committee No.1, Reparations, January-August 1947.

File 8364-C-40, part 4.
Far Eastern Commission, Working Committee No.1., Reparations, August-September 1947.

File 8364-C-40, part 5.
Far Eastern Commission, Working Committee No.1., Reparations, September 1947-February 1948.

File 8364-C-40, part 6.
Far Eastern Commission, Working Committee No.1., Reparations, February 1948-December 1949.

Box 230.

File 8364-G-40.
Far Eastern Commission, Working Committee No. 6. Aliens in Japan, September 1945-April 1949.

File 8364-J-40.
Far Eastern Commission, organization terminated, April 1952, September 1945-April 1952.

File 8364-K-40.
Far Eastern Commission, Steering Committee, minutes and reports re March 1946-May 1948.

File 8364-N-40, part 3.
Far Eastern Commission, transmitted notes, August 1947.

File 8364-N-40, part 4.
Far Eastern Commission, transmitted notes, March 1948.

File 8364-N-40, part 5.
Far Eastern Commission, transmitted notes, January 1949-.

Box 231.

File 8364-N-40, part 6.
Far Eastern Commission, transmitted notes, July 1949-.

File 8364-P-40.
Far Eastern Commission, visit to Japan by British House of Commons delegation, September 1946.

File 8364-R-40.
Restitution teams and/or reparation missions to Japan, proposals and arrangements, July 1946-.

File 8364-R-40, part 2.
Restitution teams and/or reparation missions to Japan, proposals and arrangements, July 1947-.

File 8364-R-40, part 3.
Restitution teams and/or reparation missions to Japan, proposals and arrangements, July 1948-.

File 8364-V-40.
Far Eastern commission. Inter-Allied Trade Board for Japan, April 1946-October 1947.

File 8364-Y-40.
Japanese patents, copyrights and trademarks, policy and procedure re. January 1945-March 1950. Japanese assets in neutral countries.

Box 235.

File 8376-Y-40.
Post-U.N.R.R.A. operations in China, October 1947-November 1947.

Box 240.

File 8521-40.
U.S. loan to China, policy re, December 1945-March 1957.

Box 242.

File 8547-40.
Malayan military campaign, public enquiry re, January 1946.

File 8555-40.
Claim of Esca Brook-Daykin to interest re Protectorate State of Sarawak, February-June 1946.

Box 243.

File 8562-40.
Visit of Indian food delegation to Canada, February-May 1946.

File 8350-40.
Commercial relations between U.S. and the Philippine islands, February 1946-July 1951.

File 8581-40.
Entry in Japan of Canadian insurance companies' representatives, proposals, July-October 1946.

Box 244.

File 8606-40.
Entry into New Guinea, regulations re, February 1946.

File 8620-40.
Canadian civilian liaison mission to Tokyo, expenses, June 1946-June 1948.

File 8620-I-40.
Financial transactions, Tokyo, non-departmental expenses, February 1948-July 1956.

File 8620-L-40.
Request to the Canadian government for newsprint by the British Commonwealth Occupation Forces in Japan, July 1947-September 1947.

File 8620-L-1-40.
Canadian liaison mission, Tokyo, payment of Japanese servants, policy, July 1948-November 1949.

File 8620-M-40.
Appointment of Mr. Herbert Norman as Canadian Minister to Tokyo, Japan, proposal, September 1946-December 1950.

Box 245.

File 8634-40.
Repossession of plant in Malaya by Ford Motor Company of Canada, January-October 1946.

Box 246.

File 8696-40.
Reports on U.S.-Soviet Joint Commission for Korea, January 1946-August 1951.

File 8698-40.
Conditions in Japan, general reports, Allied Council for Japan, July 1946-June 1947.

File 8698-40, part 2.
Conditions in Japan, general reports, Allied Council for Japan, July 1947-April 1948.

File 8698-40, part 3.
Conditions in Japan, general reports, Allied Council for Japan, May 1948-December 1949.

Box 247.

File 8747-40.
Japanese judicial system, report re laws and administration, April 1946-March 1961.

File 8750-40.
Japanese trade unions, March 1946-.
Box 248.

File 8767-40.
War crimes trial of Inouye Kanoe(the Kamloops Kid) general file, September 1945-June 1949.

Box 250.

File 8802-40.
Visit to Canada of Turkish purchasing commission(1946), April-August 1946.

Box 251.

File 8850-40.
Relations between China and Outer Mongolia, January 1946-March 1963.

File 8861-40.
Financial rehabilitation of the Philippines, April-August 1946.

Box 252.

File 8879-40.
Conditions in the Kurile Islands, reports re, May 1946.

Box 257.

File 8819-40.
Commercial relations between Iran and Canada, June

1946-.

File 8920-40.
Entry of Chinese ships into Canadian ports, regulations, July 1946-.

Box 258.

File 8972-40.
Participation of women in Japanese and German elections, May-June 1946.

Box 261.

File 9009-40.
Census in China, reports, June 1946-June 1956.

File 9014-40.
Hainan Island, political and economic situation, May 1947.

File 9030-T-40.
Commercial relations between Canada and China, general file, January 1946-December 1952.

Box 262.

File 9030-B-40.
Exchange of fertilizers for Formosan sugar, negotiations with China, November 1945-May 1946.

File 9030-C-40.
Newsprint paper supplies and printing machinery for China from Canada, January 1945-October 1948.

File 9082-40.
Relations between Mexico and the Philippines Republic, July 1946-October 1962.

File 9085-40.
Repatriation of Germans from China, May 1946-September 1947.

Box 270.

File 9126-40.
India - foreign policy, September 1946-December 1950.

File 9126-A-40.
United Kingdom representation in India, August-September 1946.

File 9126-B-40.
Commercial and financial relations between India and the United Kingdom, general file, August 1947-November 1962.

Box 271.

File 9138-40.
China, Yellow River flood control projects, reports re, June 1946-January 1947.

File 9145-40.
Mongols in China, political activities among, September 1946-February 1947.

Files 9161-40 to 9162-EY-40.
Individual claims against Japan.

Box 288.

File 9187-40.
Commercial relations between the Philippines and Canada, general file, August 1946-.

File 9193-40, part 2.
Political situation in India, constitutional position on India, May 1947-.

File 9193-L-40.
India, public administration, September 1946-.

File 9193-A-40.
India, control of foreigners, December 1947-.

File 9193-B-40.
Intelligence services in India, February 1948-.

File 9193-C-40.
India-Brazil relations, April 1948-.

File 9193-C-40, part 1 FP.
Indian states, general file.

Box 289.

File 9193-F-40.
India-social services, legislation reports, October 1948-.

File 9193-G-40.
India-Denmark relations, September 1949-.

File 9193-H-40.
India-Finland relations, September 1949-.

File 9193-K-40.
India, communism in, reports re, November 1949-.

File 9193-R-40.
India, economic situation, reports, October 1947-.

File 9220-40.
Economic and financial reports, activities in Formosa, October 1945-July 1963.

File 9223-40.
Supplies from Canada for British Commonwealth Occupation Force in Japan, proposals, September-October 1946.

File 9224-40.
Fishing industry in communist China, Peking Conference on Fisheries Research, October 1946-March 1961.

Box 294.

File 9260-40.
Commercial negotiations through the Canadian Commercial Corporation and the Canadian Liaison Mission, Tokyo, October 1946-May 1948.

Box 295.

File 9281-40
Appointment of Herbert Norman as tutor for Prince Mikasa in Japan, September-October 1946.

Box 296.

File 9302-40.
Middle Eastern studies in Canada and the U.S. (Institute of Islamic Studies, McGill and Middle East Institute, Washington), November 1946-May 1963.

File 9310-40, part 1 FP.
Economic situation in Siam, general file, November 1946-December 1958.

Box 299.

File 9323-AG-7-40.
Canadian Trade Commissioner, Hong Kong, September 1946-May 1956.

File 9323-AG-8-40.
Canadian Trade Commissioner, Singapore, December 1948-June 1963.

Box 301.

File 9340-40.
Soviet Union-India, relations, general, November 1946-.

File 9346-40.
Japan-India relations, general file, November 1946-.

Box 302.

File 9350-40.
New Zealand-China relations, November 1946-June 1963.

File 9364-40.
Deaf mutes in China, October 1946-January 1947.

Box 303.

File 9371-40.
Commercial relations between Canada and Turkey, June 1948-May 1954.

File 9371-A-40.
Commercial agreement between Canada and Turkey(most favoured nation treatment), August 1945-April 1948.

File 9371-B-40.
Canadian Car and Foundry Company, Ltd., commercial negotiations with Turkey, December 1946-April 1948.

Box 304.

File 9402-40.
Iran, labor situation in, January 1947-May 1960.

File 9402-A-40.
Iran, economic and financial conditions in, February 1949-December 1957.

File 9402-B-40.
Iran-Canada, diplomatic relations, April 1948-December 1957.

Box 305.

File 9408-B-40.
German refugees, entry into Canada from Shanghai, cases, September 1949-.

File 9423-C-40.
General D.MacArthur, Supreme Commander Allied Powers, statements and interviews, March 1946-.

File 9425-40.
Siam-Soviet Union relations, January 1947-.

Box 316.

File 9458-AE-40, part 1 FP.
Chinese publicity in Canada, January 1947-.

Box 318.

File 9484-F-40.
Legislation re registration of aliens in China, January 1947.

File 9487-40.
France-China relations, June 1946-May 1960.

Box 319.

File 9497-40.
Asiatic Society of Japan, activities of, January 1947-August 1949.

Box 322.

File 9543-30.
India, foreign service, organization of, February 1947-June 1960.

File 9610-40.
Turkey, labor legislation and reports, December 1946-May 1962.

Box 327.

File 9677-40.
Relations between the Netherlands East Indies and Egypt, June 1947-.

File 9706-Y-40.
Requests to Canada for professional and technical personnel by India, January 1949-July 1956.

Box 329.

File 9706-BJ-40.
Requests to Canada for professional and technical personnel by Turkey, April 1948-.

Box 329.

File 9706-BK-40.
Requests to Canada for professional and technical personnel by Pakistan, April 1948-.

Box 331.

File 9743-40.
Turkey, transportation in, March 1948-July 1951.

Box 332.

File 9776-40.
U.S. and Pakistan relations, August 1947-August 1963.

File 9803-12-40.
Canada-Philippines double taxation agreement, April 1948-June 1962.

Box 333.

File 9808-40.
India-Pakistan import and export control, regulations and reports, December 1947-May 1963.

File 9809-40.
India merchant shipping, regulations and reports, December 1947-September 1958.

File 9813-40.
Ceylon-Burma relations, April 1949-August 1963.

Box 334.

File 9820-40
Overseas Chinese activities, organization, April 1948-December 1953.

Box 335.

File 9848-40.
Relations between Afghanistan and Pakistan. The Pushtoonistan dispute, July 1947-December 1950.

File 9855-40.
Relations between Czechoslovakia and India, November 1947-January 1962.

File 9857-40.
Evacuation of Canadians in China, October 1947-July 1949.

File 9857-40, part 2.
Evacuation of Canadians in China, August 1949-September 1960.

Box 336.

File 9861-40.
Missionary work in India, October 1947-October 1959.

File 9877-40, part 1 FP.
Political situation in Hyderabad, September 1947-April 1950.

Box 337.

File 9890-40.
Policy on entry of Japanese nationals into Canada, general file, April 1947-November 1955.

File 9891-41.
Conditions in Afghanistan, June 1947-July 1957.

File 9894-40.
Canadian Club of Shanghai, activities of, April 1948.

Box 338.

File 9899-Y-40.
Education in India, June 1946-November 1960.

File 9809-AH-40.
Education in Japan, February 1946-January 1963.

Box 339

File 9899-BK-40.
Education in Karachi, December 1949-January 1962.

Box 340.

File 9908-Y-1-40.
Visit of Indian defence minister to Canada, April-June 1949.

File 9905-Y-2-40, part 1 FP.
Visit to Canada of Pandit Nehru, Prime Minister of India, April 1948-October 1949.

File 9905-Y-2-40, Part 2.
Visit to Canada of Pandit Nehru, Prime Minister of India, October 1949-September 1950.

Box 342.

File 9935-40.
Commercial relations between Canada and Pakistan, February 1948-May 1963.

File 9940-40.
Relations between China and the Netherlands, February 1948-March 1959.

Box 343.

File 9956-40.
Relations between the U.S. and Afghanistan, March 1948-September 1963.

File 9957-40.
Academia Sinica, organization and work, April 1948-.

File 9963-40.
Economic situation in Korea, January 1949-February 1959.

Box 344.

File 9968-40.
Philippines insurance legislation, January 1948-April 1959.

File 9968-A-40.
Canadian insurance interests in the Netherlands East Indies, June 1948-August 1955.

File 9983-40.
Turkey, military reports, March 1948-November 1958.
Box 345.

File 9997-40.
South Pacific Commission, organization, activities, conferences, under the auspices of, February 1948-July 1963.

File 10019-A-10.
Conditions in India, September 1948-February 1950.

Box 350.

File 10117-Y-40.
Information activities of the Canadian Mission at New Delhi, 1952.

File 10117-B-5-40.
Information activities of the Canadian Mission at Ankara, June 1949-March 1961.

Box 354.

File 10154-40.
Portugal-Pakistan relations, July 1948-February 1960.

Box 355.

File 10166-40.
Turkey, trade relations with various countries, July 1948-May 1962.

Box 356.
File 10211-40.
Japanese textile industry, January 1949-March 1961.

File 10218-40.
Economic conditions and development in the Philippines, January 1949-October 1950.

File 10267-40.
Relations between India and Roumania, December 1948-September 1960.

File 10270-40.
Relations between the Netherlands and India, December 1948-December 1962.

File 10271-40.
Relations between Yugoslavia and India, December 1948-December 1962.

File 10273-40.
Relations between Hungary and India, November 1948-June 1960.

Box 359.

File 10279-40.
India, health services in, legislation and reports, November 1947-July 1962.

File 10280-40.
India, vital census, population problem, August 1948-April 1962.

File 10281-40.
India, scientific and industrial research, legislation and reports, September 1948-August 1957.

File 10282-40, part 1 FP.
Political situation in Pakistan, September 1948-November 1954.

File 10282-A-40, part 1 FP.
Pakistan, economic situation, January 1948-September 1956.

Box 360.

File 10282-H-40.
Pakistan, government revenue and expenditure, June 1949-July 1963.

File 10282-J-40.
Pakistan, foreign exchange position, September 1949-January 1960.

File 10286-40.
Indian constitution, general file, September 1947-August 1960.

Box 361.

File 10288-40.
India, French possessions in, May 1948-August 1954.

File 10288-A-40.
The Kingdom of Nepal, U.S. relations, September 1948-July 1962.

File 10309-40.
Relations between the Soviet Union and Pakistan, June 949-August 1963.

Box 363.

File 10384-40.
Malaya, economic and financial situation, December 1948-December 1959.

File 10394-40.
Turkey, economic and financial situation, December 1948-December 1951.
Box 364.

File 10403-40.
U.K. and Ceylon, trade and financial relations, February 1949-February 1951.

Box 368.

File 10463-A-40.
Annual review of events in China, December 1948-February 1962.

Box 369.

File 10482-40.
U.K.-Pakistan relations, December 1947-August 1963.

Box 370.

File 10485-40.
Ceylon-Burma relations, October 1949-November 1956.

File 10486-40.
South Africa relations with India and Pakistan, September 1949-July 1961.

Box 371.

File 10518-40.
India-Iraq relations, December 1948-April 1960.

Box 376.

File 10627-B-40.
Visits of Indian defence authorities to Canada, May 1949-July 1963.

File 10627-C-40.
Visits of Pakistan defence authorities to Canada, June 1949-August 196

File 10640-40.
India law concerning marriage and divorce and personal status, August 1948-May 1949.

Box 377.

File 10641-40.
Japanese Agrarian Reform Law, March 1946-March 1963.

File 10648-40.
Korea-Canada commercial relations, June 1949-August 1962.

Box 380.

File 10758-40, part 1 FP.
Canadian exports to Eastern Europe and the Far East, statistics only, December 1949-April 1953.

File 10765-40.
Economic and financial conditions in Ceylon, November 1949-November 1954.

File 10780-40.
Reports on conditions in Turkey, August 1949-January 1954.

Box 381.

File 10823-40.
India-Austria relations, July 1949-February 1960.

File 10832-40.
Indonesia economic situation, June 1949-July 1953.

Box 382.

File 10857-40.
France-Philippine relations, December 1949-October 1951.

Box 383.

File 10898-40.
Claims by Canadians of Japanese ancestry for bank deposits held in the U.S., November 1949-June 1950.

Box 384.

File 10924-40.
Canadian Goodwill Trade Commission to India, Pakistan, Ceylon and Middle Eastern countries, November 1949-October 1957.

File 10932-40.
Sweden-Pakistan relations, July 1949-January 1960.

Box 386.

File 10985-40.
Science in China, September 1946-September 1959.

Box 387.

File 11011-40.
Turkey-United Kingdom relations, December 1949-May 1963.

Box 388.

File 11044-E-40.
Export of arms to Iran, August 1948-April 1963.

File 11044-G-40.
Export of arms to Thailand, February 1949-November 1953.

File 11044-T-40.
Export of arms to Turkey, January 1949-May 1963.

File 11044-AN-40.
Export of arms to Malaya, June 1949-March 1952.

File 11044-AV-40.
Export of arms to Philippines, July 1949-December 1961.

File 11044-AW-40.
Export of arms to Korea, July 1949-October 1963.

File 11044-AZ-40.
Export of arms to Indo-China, January 1949-October 1954.

File 11044-BL-40.
Export of arms to Japan, December 1949-September 1956.

File 11044-CU-40.
Export of arms to Hong Kong, April 1949-January 1954.

Box 392.

File 11045-C-40.
Export control of strategic materials from Canada to China, April 1949-October 1954.

Box 393.

File 11128-40.
Status and activity of Chinese in Canada, June 1949-August 1959.

File 11129-40.
Status of Dutch in New Guinea, July 1949-January 1950.

File 11130-40, part 1 FP.
Institute of Pacific Relations conference held in Lucknow, India, October 1950, December 1949-December 1960.

Box 401.

File 11492-40.
Diplomatic representation in India, September 1946-September 1962.

File 11493-40.
Canadian diplomatic relations with Pakistan, July 1947-August 1963.

File 11493-B-40.
Pakistan foreign service, organization of and representation abroad, November 1948-June 1963.

File 11494-A-40.
India foreign exchange position, August 1947-August 1962.

File 11494-B-40.
India, price and wage control, August 1948-July 1960.

File 11494-D-40.
India, foreign investment in, March 1949-June 1959.

File 11494-G-40.
India, trade statistics, May 1949-February 1961.

Box 404.

File 11565-40.
Treatment of East Indians in Ceylon, August 1948-August 1963.

File 11569-40, part 1 FP.
Power projects in India, April 1948-December 1958.

File 11578-A-40.
Foreign policy of the Central People's Republic of China, March 1949-May 1958.

File 11578-B-40, part 4.
Political situation in the Central People's Republic of China, March 1949-May 1958.

File 11578-B-40, part 5.
Political situation in the Central People's Republic of China, February-April 1946.

File 11578-B-40, part 6.
Political situation in the Central People's Republic of China, April-June 1946.

Box 405.

File 11578-B-40, part 7.
Political situation in the Central People's Republic of China, July 1946-February 1947.

File 11578-B-40, part 8.
Political situation in the Central People's Republic of China, March 1947-May 1948.

File 11578-B-40, part 9.
Political situation in the Central People's Republic of China, June 1948-July 1952.

File 11578-D-40.
Chinese internal development in Formosa, political and military reports, October 1946-December 1952.

Box 406.

File 11966-40.
Easter Island, December 1948-March 1954.

Box 407.

File 12201-40.
Maldive Islands, April 1948-March 1963.

Box 409.

File 12400.
Paracel-Spratly and Nansha Islands, disputes re, and conditions in, February 1947-July 1960.

Box 410.

File 12646-40.
Afghanistan-India relations, December 1947-September 1961.

Box 414.

File 14003-J-2-1-40.
Atomic energy, other countries, peaceful uses of, India, September 1947-October 1963.
File 14003-J-2-3-40.
Atomic energy, other countries, India and cooperation with Canada, September 1947-September 1959.

File 14003-J-11-1-40.
Atomic energy, other countries, Japan, August 1946-November 1962.

Box 416.

File 14400-J-6-40.
Mineral products, India, December 1947-June 1959.

Accession 84-85/150.

Box 2.

File 8-AL-40.
Control of narcotics in Japan, January 1950-January 1955.

Box 11.

File 72-AMV-40.
United States air services to the Far East, October 1950-December 1961.

Box 12.

File 720-ANJ-40.
Civil aviation in Japan, April 1952-October 1959.

File 72-ANL-40.
Japanese air agreements with other countries, March 1955-October 1963.

Box 22.

File 515-40.
Philippine immigration legislation and regulations, October 1952-January 1961.

File 621-PR-40.
Prisoners of war in Korea, August 1951-April 1954.

File 621-PR-1-40.
Postal communications with prisoners of war in Korea, March 1951-November 1952.

File 5621-PT-450.
American prisoners of war in Korea, November 1954-January 1955.

Box 29.

File 1846-40-2
Political situation in Thailand, March 1951-March 1953.

File 1846-40-3.
Political situation in Thailand, June 1953-February 1956.

File 1846-B-40.
Thailand-Australian relations, January 1952-February 1956.

Box 31.

File 2289-40.
Relations between India and United States. January 1954-

Box 33.

File 22727-Y-40.
Canadian publicity in India, February 1954-August 1957.

Box 41.

File 3978-40, part 4.
Relief for China during war, general file, February 1950-March 1951.

File 3991-40, part 2.
Constitutional and political situation in the Philippine Islands, April 1950-May 1951.

File 3991-40, part 3.
Constitutional and political situation in the Philippine islands, May 1951-June 1953.

File 3991-40, part 4.
Constitutional and political situation in the Philippine Islands, May-October 1953.

Box 42.

File 3991-40, part 6
Constitutional and political situation in the Philippine Islands, December 1953-March 1955.

File 3991-C-40.
India-Philippine relations, March 1950-July 1956.

File 3991-E-40.
Philippine legislation regarding professionals, April 1950.

File 3991-F-40.
Health in the Philippines, July 1950-August 1953.

File 3991-G-40.
Labour in the Philippines, August 1950-September 1956.

File 3991-H-40.
Public works and communities in the Philippines, August 1950-July 1955.

File 3991-J-40.
Philippine-Greece relations, September 1950-December 1955.

File 3991-M-40.
Police and armed forces in the Philippines, August 1950-September 1960.

File 3991-N-40.
Philippine-Pakistan relations, October 1950-August 1962.

File 3991-P-40.
Patents, trade marks in the Philippines, October 1950-September 1953.

File 3991-Q-40.
Philippine-Thailand relations, October 1950-July 1962.

File 3991-R-40.
Philippine-Turkey relations, November 1950.

File 3991-S-40.
Philippines tourist trade, October 1950-.

File 3991-T-40.
Argentine-Philippine relations, December 1950-.

File 3991-U-40.
Spanish-Philippine relations, January 1951-July 1962.

File 3991-V-40.
Administration of the Philippines, February 1957-.

File 3991-W-40.
Philippine foreign policy, May 1951-July 1963.

File 3991-X-40.
Sweden-Philippine relations, April 1951-.

File 3991-Y-40.
Philippines-German relations, August 1951-December 1956.

File 3991-Z-40.
Religions in the Philippines, December 1950-July 1959.

Box 44.

File 4457-40.
U.S.-China relations, May-December 1951.

File 4457-C-40.
U.K. policy in the Far East, May 1951-February 1961.

File 4558-V-40.
Monthly summaries from Canadian Embassy in Nanking, February 1950-October 1951.

File 4606-40, part 4.
Japan's political situation subsequent to entry of Japan into the war, January-February 1952.

Box 45.

File 4606-40, part 5.
Japan's political situation subsequent to entry of Japan into the war, December 1952-August 1953.

File 4606-40, part 6.
Japan's political situation subsequent to entry of Japan into the war, September 1953-August 1954.

File 4606-40, part 7.
Japan's political situation subsequent to entry of Japan into the war, April-December 1954.

File 4606-A-1-40, part 2.
Communism in Japan, January 1952-November 1957.

File 4606-A-3-40.
Japan foreign policy, March 1951-March 1957.

File 4606-A-4-40.
Japan personalities, January 1954-November 1959.

File 4606-B-40, part 3.
Monitored reports re Japan, January 1950-December 1951.

File 4606-B-40, part 4.
Monitored reports re Japan, January-December 1952.

File 4606-B-40, part 5.
Monitored reports re Japan, January 1953-December 1954.

File 4606-B-5-40.
Japanese Philippines commercial relations, April 1950-February 1957.

File 4606-B-7-40.
Japanese government overseas agencies in Canada, March 1950-November 1951.

Box 46.

File 4606-C-4-40.
Aliens in Japan, March 1952-November 1955.

File 4606-C-8-40.
Visit of Japanese officers to Canada, Japanese Minister of Finance, May 1950-September 1953.

File 4606-C-9-40, part 2.
Soviet Union-Japanese relations, March 1954-August 1956.

File 4606-C-16-40.
Japan-U.K. relations, July 1951-April 1963.

File 4606-C-17-40.
Japan-Portugal relations, September 1951-December 1960.

File 4606-C-18-40.
Japan-Philippine relations, June 1951-June 1963.

File 4606-C-19-40.
Japan-U.S. relations, October 1951-November 1955.

File 4606-C-20-40.
Japan-Italy relations, October 1951-November 1962.

File 4606-C-22-40.
Japan-Indonesia relations, November 1951-March 1963.

File 4606-C-23-40.
Channels of communication between diplomatic missions in Japan and Japanese government, February 1951-May 1952.

File 4606-C-24-40.
Japan-Burma relations, December 1954-February 1963.

File 4606-C-25-40.
Japan-Ceylon relations, December 1954-January 1963.

File 4606-D-40.
Japanese Antarctic whaling fishing, February-October 1951.

File 4606-H-2-40, part 2.
Japanese shipping and shipbuilding, September 1950-February 1961.

Box 47.

File 4606-M-40.
Japanese patents, copyrights and trademarks, May 1950-1953.

File 4606-N-1-50.
Labour in Japan, January 1954-December 1962.

File 4606-Y-40.
Japan-Pakistan relations, November 1952-February 1962.

Box 50.

File 4900-E-40.
Letters of instruction to the Head of Diplomatic Mission at India, July 1951-October 1958.

File 4900-K-40.
Letters of instruction to the Head of Diplomatic Mission at Ceylon, March 1953-October 1958.

File 4900-L-40.
Letters of instruction to the Head of Diplomatic Mission at Djakarta, March-August 1953.

File 4900-L-40, part 2.
Letters of instruction to the Head of Diplomatic Mission at Djakarta, April 1954-April 1961.

Box 56.

File 5004-R-40, part 1 FP.
Legal aspects of the Iranian Oil Company case, June 1951-December 1954.

Box 64.

File 5475-CY-2-40, part 3 FP.
United Nations Economic Commission for Asia and the Far East, January 1953-December 1954.

Box 66b.

File 5475-DU-13-40.
United Nations technical assistance for Ceylon,

September 1950-December 1952.

File 5475-DU-14-40.
United Nations technical assistance for Korea, April 1951-October 1953.

File 5475-DU-15-40.
United Nations technical assistance for Afghanistan, September 1951-April 1955.

File 5475-DU-20-40.
United Nations technical assistance for Turkey, February 1952-Novem

File 5475-DU-32-40.
United Nations technical assistance for Cambodia, December 1952-June 1959.

Box 75.

File 5475-FA-6-40.
Statements and assessments towards the United Nations policy for Burma, February 1953-September 1962.

File 5475-FA-7-40.
Statements and assessments towards the United Nations policy for Ceylon, November 1953-September 1962.

File 5475-FA-9-40.
Statements and assessments towards the United Nations policy for China(Nationalist), February 1953-February 1963.

478 • Ontario – Ottawa

Box 76.

File 5475-FA-45-40.
Statements and assessments of Canadian policy towards United Nations for Afghanistan, February 1953-September 1963.

File 5495-C-40.
Political situation of Indonesia, September 1950-May 1954.

File 5495-C-40, part 3.
Political situation of Indonesia, January-September 1952.

File 5495-C-40, part 4.
Political situation of Indonesia, October 1952-September 1953.

File 5495-C-2-40.
Indonesian foreign policy, April 1951-November 1959.

File 5495-D-40.
Indonesia-Turkey relations, December 1949-May 1959.

Box 77.

File 5495-K-40.
Indonesia-U.K. relations, January 1950-August 1963.

File 5495-L-40.
Indonesia-Ireland relations, January 1950.

File 5495-M-40.
Indonesia-Soviet Union relations, January 1950-February 1959.

File 5495-N-40.
Indonesia-New Zealand relations, January 1950-May 1963.

File 5495-P-40.
Indonesia-Sweden relations, February 1950-May 1959.

File 5495-R-40.
Indonesia-Burma relations, April-September 1951.

File 5495-T-40.
Indonesia-Portugal relations, June 1951-August 1963.

File 5495-U-40.
Indonesia-Armed forces relations, September 1951-February 1963.

File 5495-V-40.
Indonesia, digest of events in, June 1952-July 1962.

File 5495-Z-40.
Indonesia-Ceylon relations, March 1952-May 1962.

File 5507-C-40.
China-Italy relations, March 1950-January 1961.

File 5507-D-40.
China-Pakistan relations, February 1950-September 1963.

File 5507-E-40.
China-Denmark relations, March 1950.

File 5507-G-40.
China-Egypt relations, September 1950-April 1957.

Box 78.

File 5567-A-40.
Status of Burma, foreign policy, February 1951-August 1963.

File 5567-B-40.
Status of Burma-U.K. relations, March 1951-February 1963.

Box 80.

File 5582-BE-3-40.
Canadian National Committee for U.N.E.S.C.O., Japan, Osaka Cooperating Association for U.N.E.S.C.O., November 1951-November 1963.

File 5582-BH-4-40.
China-Canada U.N.E.S.C.O. fellowship, C.C.R.U. project, candidates from China, October 1951-.

Box 82.

File 5666-40.
China-U.K. relations, general file, May 1951-September 1954.

Box 83.

File 5729-40, part 2.
Press in China, editorial opinion in the Chinese press, reports re, January 1950-May 1951.

File 5729-40, part 3.
Press in China, editorial opinion in the Chinese press, reports re, June 1951-December 1957.

Box 86.

File 5870-C-40.
Australia-Korea relations, February 1953-February 1962.

File 5872-Y-40.
Press in India, reports re, May 1952-October 1963.

File 5872-AQ-40.
Press in Singapore and Malaysia, February 1954.

File 5872-BK-40.
Press in Pakistan, July 1951-October 1963.

File 5872-BW-40.
Press in the Philippines, August 1950-June 1962.

Box 88.

File 6000-Q-40.
I.B.R.D. "Pakistan Consortium", development assistance, October 1950-March 1963.

Box 89.

File 6083-40, part 2.
India-China relations, August 1954-December 1955.

Box 90.

File 6143-B-40.
Netherlands-Japan relations, May 1952-February 1962.

File 6298-A-40.
Tibetan-U.S. relations, November 1950-October 1962.

Box 91.

File 6466-40, part 6.
Communism in China, January 1951-January 1953.

File 6466-40, part 7-FP.
Communism in China, February 1953-October 1957.

Box 92.

File 6676-40, part 2.
China-Burma relations, July-November 1953.

File 6676-40, part 3.
China-Burma relations, November 1953.

File 6676-40, part 4.
China-Burma relations, December 1953-August 1954.

File 6676-40, part 5.
China-Burma relations, September 1954-.

Box 95.

File 7112-40.
U.S.-Turkey relations, November 1954-June 1963.

Box 96.

File 7116-AH-40.
Information and cultural services of the Government of Japan, reports, February 1953-February 1962.

File 7116-BW-40.
Information and cultural services of the Philippines, reports, October 1950.

Box 97.

File 7266-F-1-40.
France-Vietnam relations, September 1954-August 1963.

File 7266-H-40.
Cambodian diplomatic relations with various countries, January 1950-April 1963.

File 7266-P-40.
U.S.-Cambodian relations including Prince Sihanouk's visit to North America, June 1952-November 1960.

File 7266-P-1-40.
U.S.-Vietnamese relations, June 1952-November 1961.

File 7266-AB-40.
Australia-Vietnam relations, January 1952-September 1963.

File 7307-A-40, part 2.
Greece-Turkey relations(no data given).

Box 106.

File 8264-A-40.
Australia-Ceylon relations, October 1950-May 1963.

File 8264-C-40.
Ceylon-Italy relations, April 1951-October 1962.

File 8250-A-40, part 1 FP.
Malayan news summaries, October 1951-January 1956.

File 8250-H-40.
Malaya-U.K. relations(no data given).

File 8254-40, part 2.
Status of Korea, free Korea movement, activities and reports, political conditions in Korea, January 1952-February 1953.

File 8254-40, part 3.
Status of Korea, free Korea movement, activities and reports, political conditions in Korea, January 1953-March 1955.

File 8254-C-40.
Civil war in Korea, resolutions and correspondence with non-governmental sources, January-October 1950.

File 8254-C-40, part 2.
Civil war in Korea, resolutions and correspondence with non-governmental sources, October 1950-January 1951.

File 8254-C-40, part 3.
Civil war in Korea, resolutions and correspondence with non-governmental sources, January-April 1951.

File 8254-C-40, part 4.
Civil war in Korea, resolutions and correspondence with non-governmental sources, April 1951-May 1952.

File 8254-C-40, part 5.
Civil war in Korea, resolutions and correspondence with non-governmental sources, May-December 1952.

File 8254-C-40, part 6.
Civil war in Korea, resolutions and correspondence with non-governmental sources, November 1952-May 1953.

File 8254-C-40, part 7.
Civil war in Korea, resolutions and correspondence with non-governmental sources, April-July 1953.

File 8254-C-40, part 8.
Civil war in Korea, resolutions and correspondence with non-governmental sources, July 1953-January 1962.

Box 109.

File 8260-BT-40.
Exchange of students between Canada and Iran, May 1951-November 1963.

File 8269-CR-40.
Exchange of students between Canada and Iran, December 1951-January 1963.

Box 113.

File 8914-A-40.
Turkey, communism in, December 1951-June 1963.

Box 115.

File 8973-A-40.
All-India medical conferences, general file, October 1950-November 1966.

File 8973-B-40.
All Pakistan medical conference, general file, November 1950-October 1962.

File 9030-40, part 3.
Commercial relations between China and Canada, general file, January 1953-November 1957.

Box 125.

File 9193-40, part 4.
Political situation in India, constitutional position in India, December 1950-March 1952.

File 9193-40, part 5 FP.
Political situation in India, constitutional position in India, January 1952-March 1953.

File 9193-40, part 6.
Political situation in India, constitutional position in India, May 1953-September 1954.

Box 126.

File 9193-40, part 7.
Political situation in India, constitutional position in India, October 1954-September 1955.

File 9193-K-40.
India-Communism, reports, February 1954-December 1959.

File 9193-L-40.
India-Argentine relations, January 1950-October 1952.

File 9193-M-40.
India-Ireland relations, February 1950-November 1962.

File 9193-N-40.
India-Belgium relations, February 1950-April 1953.

File 9193-Q-40.
India-Mexico relations, June 1950-January 1962.

File 9193-U-1-40.
Unitarian service committee, proposed aid to India, September 1952-March 1959.

File 9193-V-40.
India-communications and transportation, September 1951-January 1960.

File 9193-W-40.
India-Norway, September 1951-January 1959.

File 9193-X-40.
India, small industries reports, February 1952-August 1959.

File 9200-A-40.
Iraq-Turkey relations, February 1952-August 1962.

File 9200-B-40.
Iraq-Turkey relations, March 1952-August 1963.

Box 132.

File 9423-A-40.
Political summaries in South East Asia, May 1950-March 1952.

File 9423-A-40, part 2.
Political summaries in South East Asia, March 1952-December 1958.

File 9423-B-40.
Neutral bloc in South East Asia, December 1950-April 1951.

File 9423-D-40.
Economic conditions in Asian Prime Ministers' Conference, Colombo, April 1954. January 1954-March 1959.

Box 138.

File 9456-PL-40.
Pakistan science conferences, January 1954-May 1963.

File 9456-PU-40.
Pan-Pacific Women's Association, conferences, congresses, etc. Canadian participants in, April 1952-December 1960.

Box 143.

File 9608-BW-40.
Visitors to the Philippines from Canada, September 1951.

File 9608-CK-40.
Visitors to Korea from Canada, November 1951-January 1952.

Box 147.

File 9848-40, part 2.
Relations between Afghanistan and Pakistan(the Pushtoonistan dispute), January 1951-October 1955.

File 9877-40, part 2.
Political situation in Hyderabad, August 1950-September 1953.

Box 148.

File 9899-BJ-40.
Education in Turkey, April 1951-June 1962.

File 9899-BW-40.
Education in the Philippines, July 1950-October 1955.

Box 149.

File 9909-BK-1-40, part 2.
Visit to Canada of Mr. Liaquat Ali Khan, Prime Minister of Pakistan, May-June 1950.

File 9909-BK-1-40, part 3.
Visit to Canada of Mr. Liaquat Ali Khan, Prime Minister of Pakistan, May 1950-August 1952.

Box 157.

File 10150-F-40.
Nationality law of Japan, December 1950.

File 10150-G-40.
Nationality law of China, July 1953.

Box 161.

File 10282-40, part 2.
Political situation in Pakistan, March 1952-April 1953.
Box 162.

File 10282-40, part 3.
Political situation in Pakistan, May 1953-May 1954.

File 10282-40, part 4.
Political situation in Pakistan, June 1954-November 1954.

File 10282-40, part 5.
Political situation in Pakistan, October 1954-Adjust 1955.

File 10282-1-40.
Pakistan press review, April 1952-July 1954.

File 10282-E-40.
Pakistan, Jute industry, March 1950-August 1959.

File 10282-F-40.
Pakistan census, January 1954-June 1967.

File 10282-G-40.
Pakistan and Ceylon relations, June 1951-July 1963.

File 10282-L-40.
Pakistan, foreign investment in, June 1950-January 1960.

File 10282-M-40.
Pakistan, banking reports, October 1950-May 1962.

File 10282-N-40.
Pakistan, steel industry in, March-July 1951.

File 10282-R-40.
Pakistan, labour conditions in, October 1951-July 1963.

File 10282-S-40.
Baluchistan, reports on, November 1952-July 1963.

Box 163.

File 10288-40, part 2.
India, French possessions in, general file, September 1954-April 1960.

File 10304-40, part 2.
The Kingdom of Nepal, reports, re general file, March 1953-March 1960.

Box 164.

File 10304-B-40.
The Kingdom of Nepal-China relations, June 1950-May 1963.

File 10309-A-40.
Communism in Pakistan, August 1950-May 1960.

Box 169 .

File 10483-40.
India-Pakistan relations, general file, January-December 1950.

File 10483-40, part 2.
India-Pakistan relations, general file, February 1951-March 1958.

File 10483-A-40.
India-Pakistan trade relations, February 1950-September 1960.

File 10483-B-40.
Communalism in India, February 1950-March 1963.

Box 173.

File 10600-D-40.
Law of the sea, territorial waters and fishery zones, Japan, January 1953-June 1963.

File 10600-G-40.
Law of the sea, territorial waters and fishery zones, Turkey, October 1953-August 1963.

Box 174.

File 10600-X-40.
Law of the sea, territorial waters and fishery zones, Pakistan, February 1953-June 1963.

Box 175.

File 10615-40.
Welfare of Canadian citizens in China, general file, March-December 1951.

File 10615-40, part 2.
Welfare of Canadian citizens in China, general file, December 1951-May 1954.

File 10615-40, part 3.
Welfare of Canadian citizens in China, general file, June 1952-April 1954.

File 10615-40, part 4.
Welfare of Canadian citizens in China, general file, May 1954-August 1959.

Box 177.

File 10627-M-40.
Visits of Thailand defence authorities to Canada, July 1950-October 1959.

File 10627-R-40.
Visits of Turkish defence authorities to Canada, April 1954-March 1959.

File 10627-U-40.
Visits of Japanese defence authorities to Canada, July 1954-July 1963.

Box 180.

File 10758-40, part 2 FP.
Canadian exports to Eastern Europe and the Far East, statistics only, June 1953-January 1961.

File 10765-40, part 2 FP.
Economic and financial conditions in Ceylon, December 1954-April 1956.

File 10765-A-40.
Ceylon, labour situation in, August 1953-February 1963.

Box 181.

File 10816-40.
Civil defence in the Philippines, August 1950.

Box 182.

File 10828-B-40.
Movement toward Muslim cooperation, under Pakistan, April 1952-April 1963.

File 10829-40, part 1 FP.
Ceylon, reports and general correspondence, July 1950-December 1953.

File 10829-40, part 2.
Ceylon, reports and general correspondence, January 1954.

File 10832-40, part 2.
Indonesia, economic situation in, August 1953-June 1956.

File 10832-a-40.
Indonesia, status of Canadian life assurance companies in, April 1950-December 1953.

Box 188.

File 10969-40.
Pakistan and Iran, relations, February 1950-July 1963.

File 10970-40.
Pakistan and Iraq, relations, February 1950-March 1963.

File 10973-40.
Pakistan and Australia, relations, January 1950-June 1963.

File 10977-40.
Labour in India, legislation and reports, June 1950-December 1960.

File 10978-40, part 1 FP.
Constitution of Pakistan, general file, July 1950-October 1953.

Box 189.

File 10978-40, part 2.
Constitution of Pakistan, general file, November 1953-April 1956.

File 10982-40.
Pakistan and Burma, relations, November 1950-July 1963.

File 11003-40.
Postwar situation of Singapore, December 1950-August 1955.

Box 190.

File 11015-40.
Relations between Turkey and Italy, general file, April 1950-May 1963.

File 11029-40.
Relations between Turkey and Bulgaria, general file, August 1950-October 1962.

Box 191.

File 11035-40.
Relations between Czechoslovakia and China, October 1950-August 1963.

File 11037-40.
Relations between Czechoslovakia and Pakistan, general file, October 1950-June 1959.

File 11038-40, part 14.
Commonwealth programs for economic assistance to South East Asia, October-November 1953.

Box 192.

File 11038-40, part 15.
Commonwealth programs for economic assistance to South East Asia, December 1953-June 1954.

File 11038-40, part 16 FP.
Commonwealth programs for economic assistance to South East Asia, July-September 1954.

File 11038-40, part 17.
Commonwealth programs for economic assistance to South East Asia, September-November 1954.

File 11038-40, part 18.
Commonwealth programs for economic assistance to South East Asia, December 1954-April 1955.

File 11038-2-2A-40.
Colombo plan, Pakistan capital assistance, Ganges Kabadak, March 1954-May 1955.

Boxes 192-194.

Files 11038-A-1-B-40 to 11038-A-1-AG-40.
Colombo plan, capital assistance, Ceylon 1951-1955, technical assistance.

Files 11038-A-2-G-40 to 11038i-A-2-K-40.
Colombia plan, capital assistance, India and Pakistan, 1951-1953, technical assistance.

Files 11038-A-2-l-40 to 11038-A-AR-40.
Colombo plan, capital assistance, India, 1951-1955, technical assistance.

Files 11038-A-3-A-40 to 11038-A-3-BW-40.
Colombo plan, capital assistance, Pakistan, 1951-1962, technical assistance.

Box 194.

File 11038-B-40.
Colombo plan, summary of report for cooperative economic development in South and South East Asia, distribution of, November 1950-July 1954.

File 11038-B-40, part 2 FP.
Colombo plan, summary of report for cooperative economic development in South and South East Asia, distribution of, September 1954-July 1960.

Boxes 195-197.

Files 11038-F-1-A-40 to 11038-F-1-N-40.
Colombo plan, scholarships and fellowships, Ceylon, 1951-1

Files 11038-F-2-A-40 to 11038-F-2-BT-40.
Colombo plan, scholarships and fellowships, India, 1951-1954.

Files 11038-F-3-A-40 to 11038-F-3-DN-40.
Colombo plan, scholarships and fellowships, Pakistan, 1951-1954.

Box 197.

File 11038-G-1-40.
Colombo plan, technical cooperation assistance in South East Asia, reports, May 1951-December 1952.

Box 197.

File 11038-G-1-40, part 3.
Colombo plan, technical cooperation assistance in South East Asia, reports, July 1953-February 1954.

File 11038-G-1-40, part 4-FP.
Colombo plan, technical cooperation assistance in South East Asia, reports, March 1954-December 1955.

File 11038-K-40, part 1 FP.
Colombo plan, technical assistance service reports, September 1951-October 1952.

Box 198.

File 11038-K-40, part 2 FP.
Colombo plan, technical assistance service exports, November 1952-August 1953.

File 11038-K-40, part 3.
Colombo plan, technical assistance service reports, September 1953-June 1954.

File 11038-K-40, part 4.
Colombo plan, technical assistance service reports, July 1954-September 1955.

File 11038-P-2-40.
Colombo plan, technical assistance from India, September 1951-December 1953.

Box 199.

File 11038-P-3-40.
Colombo plan, technical assistance from Pakistan, September 1951-December 1953.

File 11038-P-4-40.
Colombo plan, technical assistance from public health, January 1952-April 1953.

File 11038-Q-40.
Colombo plan, work of Canadian church missions, general file, June 1951-January 1952.

File 11038-S-40.
Colombo plan, publicity, January 1951-March 1954.

File 11038-S-40, part 2 FP.
Colombo plan, publicity, April-June 1954.

File 11038-S-40, part 2 A.
Colombo plan, publicity, July 1954-December 1955.

Box 200.

File 11038-AB-3-40.
Colombo plan, technical assistance programme, Pakistan requests for books, December 1951-May 1954.

File 11038-AB-14-A-40.
Colombo plan, technical assistance programme, Burma, December 1952-September 1954.

File 11038-AB-15-A-40 to 11038-AB-15-K-40.
Colombo plan, technical assistance programme, Thailand, 1953.

File 11038-AB-16-40.
Colombo plan, technical assistance programme, Nepal, 1951-.

File 11038-AB-17-1-40.
Colombo plan, technical assistance programme, Singapore, 1953-1955.

File 11038-AB-17-A-1-40 to 11038-AB-17-A-8-40.
Colombo plan, technical assistance programme, Malaya, 1952-1955.

File 11038-AB-17-B-1-40.
Colombo plan, technical assistance programme, North Borneo, 1951-1954.

Box 201.

File 11044-G-40.
Export of arms to Thailand, January 1953-February 1955.

Box 202.

File 11044-AN-40, part 2.
Export of arms to Malaya, April 1952-June 1953.

File 11044-AN-40, part 3.
Export of arms to Malaya, February 1954-October 1963.

Box 203.

File 11044-AZ-40, part 2.
Export of arms to Indo-China, June 1952-April 1953.

File 11044-AZ-40, part 3.
Export of arms to Indo-China, April 1953-August 1954.

File 11044-BP-40.
Export of arms to British (North)Borneo, January 1950-March 1960.

Box 204.

File 11044-CH-40.
Export of arms to New Guinea, August 1951-October 1956.

File 11044-CK-40.
Export of arms to Fiji, June 1951-May 1954.

File 11044-CM-40.
Export of arms to Canton Islands, December 1951-May 1954.

File 11044-CV-40, part 2.
Export of arms to Hong Kong, January-September 1954.

File 11044-CV-40, part 3.
Export of arms to Hong Kong, September 1954-April 1960.

File 11044-CX-40.
Export of arms to Singapore, September 1952-October 1954.

File 11044-CY-40.
Export of arms to Afghanistan, April-September 1954.

File 11045-H-40.
Export of arms to countries of the Soviet bloc, also lifting of export controls, control of the export of strategic goods to China, and U.S. foreign assets control regulations, February-December 1952.

File 11045-H-40, part 2.
Export of arms to countries of the Soviet bloc, also lifting of export controls, control of the export of

strategic goods to China, and U.S. foreign assets control regulations, January-August 1953.

File 11045-H-40, part 3.
Export of arms to countries of the Soviet bloc, also lifting of export controls, control of the export of strategic goods to China, and U.S. foreign assets control regulations, September 1953-December 1954.

Box 205.

File 11076-40.
Claims by Canadian citizens for damages resulting from police action by United Nations forces in Korea, August-September 1950.

File 11077-40.
Agrarian land reforms laws of China, texts, August 1950.

Box 209.

File 11210-40.
Canadian aircraft for Malaya, September 1950-January 1951.

File 11222-40.
Recruitment in Canada of police for Malaya, October 1950-November 1951.

File 11226-40.
Royal Canadian Air Force and Royal Canadian Navy air arm operational training in Korea, January 1951-October 1953.

Box 212.

File 11295-40.
Commercial relations between Japan and China, August 1951-May 1963.

File 11302-40.
Wheat for India from the U.S.A. and other countries, February 1951-February 1953.

File 11302-40, part 2.
Wheat for India from the U.S.A. and other countries, March 1953-August 1962.

File 11302-A-40.
Wheat for India, proposals by various persons, January-June 1951.

Box 213.

File 11305-40, par, FP.
U.K. trade and financial arrangements with Japan, March 1951-September 1963.

File 11318-40, part 4.
Position of the Iranian Oil Company(parts 2-FP and 3 missing).

Accession 84-85/215.

Box 217.

File 11344-40.
Turkey and Ireland relations, April 1951.

Box 219.

File 11414-40.
Commercial relations between Portuguese Macao and Communist China, August 1951.

Box 227.

File 11494-E-40.
India, loans from the International Bank, February 1950-July 1956.

File 11494-F-40, part 1 FP.
India, the Five-Year Plan for economic development, April 1950-December 1953.

File 11494-F-40, part 2.
India, the Five-Year Plan for economic development, February 1954-April 1956.

Box 229.

File 11549-40.
Arrest of Canadians in Japan by U.S. military police, May-July 1952.

Box 230.

File 11551-40.
Protection of Canadian interests in Iran, October 1952-October 1958.

Box 232.

File 11567.
Statistical information in Pakistan, February 1952-November 1958.

File 11568.
Political situation in Ceylon, April 1951-November 1954.

File 11568, Part 2, FP.
Political situation in Ceylon, December 1954-October 1955.

File 11568-A-40.
Ceylon, foreign policy, March 1954-January 1959.

File 11568-B-40.
Ceylon's defence and external affairs, agreements with the U.K., August 1954-August 1959.

File 11572-40.
Pakistan's defence policy, June1952-April 1963.

Box 237.

File 11578-B-40.
Political situation in the Central People's Republic of China, May1954-July 1955.

File 11592-40.
South Africa-Indonesia relations, August 1952.

File 11655-40.
Arrangements between Canada and India for inspection by Canadian inspection services of military supplies purchased in Canada by India, August 1952-1954.

Box 238.

File 11677-40.
Japanese industrial property rights in Canada, December 1952-August 1954.

Box 239.

File 11706-40.
Japan, commercial relations with various countries, March 1953-June 1962.

Box 241.

File 11756-40.
Turkey-France relations, March 1953-July 1963.

File 11757-40.
Visit to Canada of Vice President of India, Dr. Radhakrishnan, 1953, 1954, 1958, December 1952-March 1958.

File 11771-A-40.
U.S. economic assistance to South and South East Asia, November 1954-April 1955.

Box 243.

File 11811-40.
Indonesia, shipping matters, July 1953-October 1962.

File 11838-40.
Belgium-China commercial relations, August 1953-August 1962.

Box 244.

File 11872-40.
Ceylon-China relations, March 1953-October 1962.

Box 246.

File 11914-40.
Ceylon weekly press cuttings, August 1953-July 1956.

File 11927-40.
Japan-Iran diplomatic relations, November 1953-August 1960.

File 11929-40.
Pakistan-Thailand relations, November 1953-May 1962.

Box 247.

File 11955-40.
Japan-German relations, November 1953-April 1960.

File 11958-40.
Communist China-North Korea relations, political and economic relations, December 1953-July 1963.

File 11976-40.
Philippine-Korea relations, October 1953-December 1953.

File 11985-40.
Turkey-Pakistan relations, December 1953-May 1963.

File 11992-40.
Turkey-Egypt relations, January 1954-May 1958.

Box 248.

File 12015-H-40.
Claims to the subsoil of the continental shelf by the Government of Korea, February 1952-September 1953.

File 12015-N-40.
Claims to the subsoil of the continental shelf by the Government of Japan, October-November 1953.

Box 249-250.

Colombo Plan, consultative meeting, 1954, Ottawa, Burma, Cambodia, Ceylon, India, Indonesia, Laos, Nepal, New Zealand, Pakistan, U.K., U.S., Vietnam, represented, with observers from U.S., Thailand, Philippines, Japan and economic Commission for Asia and the Far East.

Box 250.

File 12026-40.
Records of Canadian prisoners of war held in Japan, October 1953-December 1954.

Box 251.

File 12038-40.
Germany-Turkey relations, March 1954-August 1963.

Box 252.

File 12056-40.
Soviet Union-Burma relations, April 1954-May 1963.

File 12069-40.
Relations between Poland and India, March 1954-November 1962.

Box 253.

File 12103-40.
German-Indonesia relations, June 1954-November 1962.

File 12104-40.
Norway-China relations, June 1954-June 1963.

File 12128-40.
Indo-China International Supervisory Truce Commission (visas, passports, etc.), July 1954-September 1963.

Box 257.

File 12397-40.
The Kurds, November 1953-April 1962.

Box 258.

File 12490-Y-40.
Exhibitions and fairs in India, July 1954-October 1962.

File 12490-Y-2-40.
Indian Industries Fair-New Delhi, November 1954-July 1960.

File 12490-AH-1-40.
Japan International Trade Fair in Osaka and Tokyo, October 1953-November 1963.

Box 259.

File 12490-CE-40.
Exhibitions and fairs in Burma, October 1954-January 1955.

File 12500-40.
Turkey-Israel relations, October 1950-July 1963.

Box 261.

File 14003-C-6-1-40.
Atomic energy, other countries, China, peaceful uses of, February 1952-July 1958.

File 14003-P-2-1-40.
Atomic energy, other countries, Pakistan, peaceful uses of, November 1953-September 1963.

Accession 84-85/225

Box 1.

File 4606-U-40 FP.
Far Eastern Commission documents, July 1947-December 1951.

File 5582-BH-4-40.
China-Canada U.N.E.S.C.O. fellowships, CCRU project, candidates from China, October 1948-January 1951.

File 7493-40.
Research facilities in Canada for purpose of study by Chinese professors, February-May 1945.

File 8004-40.
Medical personnel from Canada for China, January-September 1945.

File 8651-40.
Dental program for China, proposal, January 1946-April 1947.

Box 3.

File 11038-40 FP.
Commonwealth program for economic assistance to South East Asia, December 1953-June 1954.

File 11038-A-1-AB-40.
Colombo Plan, capital assistance, Ceylon, irrigation program, June 1951.

File 11038-A-1-AC-40.
Colombo Plan, capital assistance, Ceylon, census and statistics training, June 1951.

File 11038-A-1-AD-40.
Colombo Plan, capital assistance, Ceylon, immigration control, training facilities, January 1952-May 1953.

File 11038-A-1-AE-40.
Colombo Plan, capital assistance, Ceylon, DDT plant(coordination officers), March 1951-January 1953.

File 11038-A-1-AF-40.
Colombo Plan, capital assistance, Ceylon, iron and steel project expert, August 1951-June 1953.

File 11038-A-1-AG-40.
Colombo Plan, capital assistance, cost accountants experts, May 1952-July 1953.

Accession 84-85/226.

Box 1.

File 72.
Trans-Pacific air services, March 1941-September 1948.

File 80-4-40.
Canadian legation, Tokyo, premises taken over by the Swiss authorities, August 1942-July 1946.

Box 2.

File 443-40.
Wheat for Japan from Canada, April 1940-December 1949.

Box 3.

File 815-A-40.
Alleged attacks on Japanese hospital ships, May 1943-March 1945.

Box 4.

File 1348-40.
Exclusion of Japanese from practice of optometry in British Columbia, protest re, October-November 1940.

Box 5.

File 2289-40.
Relations between India and U.S., July 1941-December 1953.

Box 6.

File 2386-40.
Control of exports from Philippine Islands, August 1941-August 1950.

File 2727-AE-40.
Canadian publicity in China, April 1944-November 1946.

File 2864-B-40, part 2.
Department of External Affairs questionnaire for Canadians repatriated from Japan of S.S.**Gripsholm**(names only Dappen to Fairbairn), August 1942-1944.

File 2864-B-40, part 3.
Department of External Affairs questionnaire for Canadians repatriated from Japan of S.S.**Gripsholm**(names only Dappen to Fairbaum), August 1942-1944.

File 2864-B-40, part 4.
Department of External Affairs questionnaire for Canadians repatriated from Japan of S.S.**Gripsholm**(names only Dappen to Fairbaum), 1944-1945.

Box 7.

File 2966-40.
Protecting power for Japanese interests in Canada, December 1941-February 1946.

Box 8.

File 4464-40, part 6.
Repatriation from Japan of Canadian nationals other than diplomatic personnel, arrangements, January 1944-June 1948.

File 4606-40.
Japan's political situation subsequent to entry of Japan into war, September 1942-December 1947.

File 4606-B-40.
Monitored reports re Japan, February 1941-July 1947.

Box 9.

File 4929-F-40.
Supplies for China under Canadian Mutual Aid Plan(no date stated).

File 4929-F-40, part 2.
Supplies for China under Canadian Mutual Aid Plan, February-May 1944.

File 4929-F-40, part 3.
Supplies for China under Canadian Mutual Aid Plan, May 1944-August 1945.

Box 10.

File 6697-40.
Establishment of China National Resources Commission in U.S., June 1944-July 1947.

File 6812-40.
Return of Hong Kong to China, proposals, April 1944-January 1958.

Accession 85-86/551.

Volume 3411.

File 1-1918/9, part 1.
Imperial War Cabinet: Memoranda on events in India 1917-1918 by the Secretary of State for India, 1918.

Volume 3415.

File 1-1923/7, part 1.
Imperial Conference: Committee report on female French condominium in the New Hebrides.

Volume 3416.

File 1-1923/11, part 1.
Imperial Conference: Minutes on committee and report on India's contribution to the League of Nations, 1923.

File 21-1923/15, part 1.
Imperial Conference: Ministers and representatives of the United Kingdom, the Dominions and India, 1923.

Volume 3431.

File 1-1930/62D, part 1.
Imperial Conference: Statistical abstract for the several British overseas dominions and protectorates for each of the years 1913 and 1922 and 1929, 1930.

File 1-1930/62G, part 1.
Imperial Conference: Tables relating to the external trade of the United Kingdom and the Dominions and India with British and foreign countries - distinguishing principal classes of goods, 1930.

Volume 3438.

File 1-1939/1, part 1.
Joint Meetings, visits of ministers from the dominions and of a representative from India - trade in war, 1939.

File 1-1939/3, part 1.
Joint Meetings, visits of ministers from the dominions and of a representative from India -Foreign policy, strategical policy, economic warfare, shipping, civil defence, 1939.

File 1-1939/2, part 1.
Joint Meetings, visits of ministers from dominions and of a representative from India - review of the strategical situation, 1939.

File 1-1939/4, part 1.
Joint Meetings, visits of ministers from the dominions and of a representative from India - shipment of Canadian wheat to the United Kingdom, 1939.

File 1-1939/5, part 1.
Joint Meetings, visits of ministers from dominions - appreciations of probable Japanese policy in the Far East, 1939.
Volume 3451.

File 1-1965/3A, part 1.
Meeting of Commonwealth Prime Ministers, June 1965, including Cyprus. 1965.

File 1-1-1965/1, part 1.
SSEA talks with British Ministers, London December 1965, including Vietnam and Laos. 1965.

File 1-1-1965/1A, part 1.
SSEA talks with British Ministers, London December 1965, including Vietnam and Laos. 1965.

Volume 3452.

File 1-3-1965/3, part 1.
Commonwealth Economic Consultative Council, Kingston, Jamaica, September 1965, including Japan. 1965.

Volume 3468.

File 1-1964/1, part 1.
Commentary for the use of Canadian elevation to the 19th Regular Session of the United Nations General Assembly - the Korean question. 1964.

Volume 3470.

File 7-1-1948/1, part 1.
Report of the Canadian delegation to the Seventh Session of the Economic and Social Council, Geneva July to August 1948, including Regional Economic Commission for Europe, Asia and Far East, 1947.

Volume 3480.

File 29/1950-1, part 1.
Collection of papers dealing with Korea, 1950-1960.

File 29-1954/1, part 1.
Indo-China armistice agreements, 1954.

Volume 3481.

File 29-1954/2, part 1.
Indo-China notes - 1954, general situation, topography, military background. 1954.

File 29-1954/2, part 2.
Indo-China notes - notes on the History of the war and the armed forces involved. The military situation at the time of the cease fire. 1954.

File 29-1954/2, part 3.
Indo-China notes - comparative notes on armistice supervision in Korea, Cashmere and Palestine, 1954.

File 29-1954/3, part 1.
Laos Commission - basic documents, 1954.

File 29-1956/1 part 1.
Country studies - papers on South East Asia, 1956.

File 29-1958/1, part 1.
International Commission of Supervision and Control in Indo-China, interim reports, 1958.

File 29-1959/1, part 1.
International Commission of Supervision and Control in Indo-China, from the beginning of the French occupation until the appointment of the International Commission, 1954.

Volume 3482.

File 29-1961/1, part 1.
Geneva Conference for the Canadian delegation, 1961.

File 29-1961/2, part 1.
South Korea and Canada - a synopsis of various Korean developments of special interest to the Canadian Department of External Affairs, 1961.

File 29-1962/1, part 1.
Laos Conference - concluding session, July 1962.

File 29-1962/2, part 1.
Commentary on the Protocol to the Declaration on the Neutrality of Laos. Geneva, July 1962.

File 29-1964/1, part 1.
International Commission of Supervision and Control in Indo-China in Cambodia. Interim reports 8 and 9, special message, November 1963, special report, June 1964. 1962-1964.

File 29-1964/2, part 1.
Vietnam background, September 1964.

File 29/1964/3, part 1.
Report of the Liaison Team on its visit to the Canadian Delegations to the Commission for International Supervision and Control in Indo-China, 1964.

File 29/1965/1, part 1.
I.C.S.C. in Vietnam Interim reports 1-11, Special reports June 1962, Special reports February 1965. 1962-1965.

File 29-Laos, part 1.
Government, politics, and social, structure in Laos, a study of tradition and innovation, by Joel M.Halpern, Department of Anthropology, University of California, 1965.

Volume 3483.

File 36-1951-53, part 1.
Department of External Affairs Policy Papers, 1951-1953.

10. Canada and Far East, 1951-1953.

Volume 3486.

File 40-B-1930, part 1. 4.
London Naval Conference. Charts showing distribution of tonnage on ocean routes - Conference powers, 1930.

File 40-B-1930, part 1. 5.
London Naval Conference. Sea communications. Conference powers. 1930.

File 40-B-1930, part 1. 6.
London Naval Conference. Naval construction since the armistice and comparison of fleet strengths, 1930.

File 40-B-1930, part 1. 7.
London Naval Conference. Approximate capital costs and annual maintenance charges of certain types of British warships, 1930.

File 40-B-1930, part 1. 8.
London Naval Conference. Memorandum respecting proposals to be submitted by His Majesty's Government in the United Kingdom, 1930.

File 40-B-1930, part 1. 9.
London Naval Conference. British Empire. Cruiser peace distribution. January, 1930.

File 40-B-1930, part 1.10.
London Naval Conference. British Empire, U.S.A. and Japanese territorial responsibilities, 1930.

File 40-B-1930, part 1.11.
London Naval Conference. The French proposals for the Naval Conference and their compromise proposals, 1930.

File 40-B-1930, part 1.12.
London Naval Conference, Memorandum, 1930.

File 40-B-1930, part 1.13.
London Naval Conference. Delegations of the British Commonwealth. Washington Conference treaty 1921-1922. Articles affecting the actions of submarines in war, 1930.

File 40-B-1930, part 1. 14.
London Naval Conference. Delegation of the British Commonwealth. Report of the Experts Committee on the action to the taken at the Conference regarding the legal aspect of submarines, 1930.

File 40-C-1937, part 1.1.
The Brussels Conference. Reports of the Conference re Japanese intervention in China, 1937.

File 40-C-1930, part 1.2.
Conférence de Bruxelles. Rapport de la conférence Novembre re l'intervention japonaise en Chine, 1937.

Volume 3488.

File 40-C-1947 part 1.4.
Japanese Peace Conference. British Commonwealth Conference, Canberra, 1947.

File 40-C-1950 part 1.1.
Documentation for use by the Canadian delegation to the Commonwealth working party on the Japanese Treaty, London, 1950.

File 40-C-1951 part 1.1.
Japanese Peace Treaty. Telegrams and background papers, 1951.

File 8-C-Jap 1966/1 Part 1
Canada-Japan Ministerial committee, October, 1966.

Volume 3489.

File 8-C-JAP l-1963-1 part 1.
Canada-Japan Ministerial committee, commentary - September, 1963.

Volume 3494.

File 18-1-F Iran-1965/1 part 1.
Briefs and talking points for visit of Shah of Iran, May, 1965.

File 18-1-Hind-1956/1 part 1.
Visit of Mr. Nehru to Ottawa. Heads of discussion. December, 1956.

File 18-1-Hind-965/1 part 1.
Visit of Prime Minister Shastri of India - June, 1965.

File 18-1-H SKI-1959/1 part 1.
The visit of Sir John Kootelawala. Memorandum for the use of the Prime Minister, 1959.

Volume 3495.

File 19-1-B 1954/1 part 1.
Prime Minister St.Laurent's 1954 tour of Europe and Far East, 1954.

File 19-1-B 1954/1 part 2.
Prime Minister St.Laurent's 1954 tour of Europe and Far East, 1954.

File 19-1-D 1956/1 part 1. The Hon. Paul Martin brief, Asian tour, 1956.

Volume 3497.

File 19-1-BA CYP-1965/1 part 1.
Minister's visit to Cyprus, May 1965, Background briefs, 1965.

Volume 3498.

File 19-1-DB Viet-1965/1 Part 1.
The Canadian Delegation to the International Commission of Supervision and Control. Vietnam. Visit of Paul Martin to Vietnam, Briefing book, 1956.

File 20-5-4-D 1958/1 part 1.
Inspection Service, Liaison tour of posts in South East Asia, Australia and New Zealand, 1958.

File 20-5-5 DA-IND 1958/1 part 1.
Post book for India, 1958.

Accession 85-86/555.

1907 Imperial Conference.
Files I-1907-1 to 6.
Papers, minutes, agenda.

1909 Imperial Conference on defence.
Files I-1909-1 to 8a.
Proceedings, minutes, papers, correspondence.

1911 Imperial Conference.
Files I-1911-1 to 4.
Correspondence, papers, minutes.

1917 Imperial War Cabinet.

Files I-1917-1 to 9.
Minutes, papers, reports.
1917 Imperial War Conference.

Files I-I-1917-1 to 7.
Proceedings, papers, correspondence, minutes.

1918 Imperial War Cabinet.
Files I-1918-1 to 11.
Minutes, papers.

1918 Imperial War Conference.
Files I-I-1918-1 to 29.
Minutes, proceedings, papers.

1921 Imperial Conference.

Files I-1921-1 to 24.
Minutes, papers.

1923 Imperial Conference.
Files I-1923-1 to 15.
Minutes, papers, proceedings.

1923 Imperial Economic Conference.
Files I-I-1923-1 to 7.
Papers, reports, minutes.

1924 London Conference.
Files I-1924-1.
Minutes.

1926 Imperial Conference.
Files I-1926-1 to 103.
Agenda, minutes, proceedings, papers.

1927 Colonial Office Conference.
Files I-1927-1 to 2a.
Minutes, papers.

1929 Conference on Operation of Dominion Legislation.
Files I-1929-1 to 37.
Minutes and papers.

1930 Imperial Conference.
Files I-1930-1 to 65.
Minutes, papers.

1933 Imperial Conference on Economic Consultation.
Files I-1933-1 to 14.
Papers.

1937 Imperial Conference.
Files I-1937-1 to 42.
Proceedings, minutes, papers.

1939 Meetings of Dominion Ministers.
Files I-1939-1 to 8.
Minutes, correspondence.

1944 Prime Ministers' Meeting.
Files I-1944-1 to 5.
Minutes and papers.

1946 Prime Ministers' Meeting.
Files I-1946-1 to 3.

Accession 86-87/093.

Historical Division, 1930-1978. 15.6 metres. Boxes 1-52.

Includes material on the International Commission of Supervision and Control in Vietnamese.

Accession 86-87/159.

Box 1.

File 72-BP-2-40.
Air relations between China and Canada, August 1948-June 1958.

File 72-BP-3-40.
Air relations between Japan and Canada, August 1948-July 1953.

Box 2.

File 72-ABQ-40.
Postwar civil aviation plans in China, March 1945-January 1953.

Box 4.

File 72-AMJ-40.
Iran-Canada air relations, November 1949-December 1953.

File 72-AOJ-40.
Air relations between Canada and Turkey, December 1946-November 1961.

Box 13.

File 2727-BT-40.
Cultural relations between Canada and Iran, October 1949-July 1963.

Box 14.

File 4060-C-40.
Japanese war crimes, general file, International Military Tribunal for the Far East in Tokyo and nomination to the tribunal, December 1948-June 1951.

Box 15.

File 4558-AR-40.
Appointment of T.C.Davies as Canadian ambassador at Nanking, October 1946-May 1950.

File 4558-AF-40.
Appointment of Ronning as Canadian ambassador at Nanking, January-June 1949.

File 4606-E-40.
Occupation of Japan, October 1946-May 1958.

File 4606-E-2-40.
Japanese war reparations, March 1948-December 1957.

File 4606-E-6-40.
Commonwealth relations on Japan, March 1947-July 1957.

File 4606-E-8-40.
Japan's surrender, July 1947-January 1952.

Box 16.

File 4606-U-1-40.
Far Eastern Commission, admission of new members, January 1948-December 1950.

Box 17.

File 5068-B-40.
Immigration and status of Chinese in Canada, August 1949-October 1963.

Box 19.

File 5475-N-2-40.
Postwar disposal of Japanese islands, April 1945-July 1953.

Box 25.

File 5475-CR-3-40.
United Nations applications for membership in United Nations, Ceylon, January 1948-October 1955.

File 5475-CR-4-40.
United Nations applications for membership in United Nations, Korea, December 1948-May 1961.

File 5475-CR-5-40.
United Nations applications for membership in United Nations, Nepal, February 1949-November 1950.

File 5475-CX-2-40.
Appointment and administrative instructions for Canadian military observers on United Nations Commission on India and Pakistan.

Box 27.

File 5475-J-40.
Question of Chinese representation in the United Nations, general file, February 1949-September 1950.

File 5495-G-40.
Indonesian-China relations, September 1949-December 1953.

Box 32.

File 6993-C-40, part 3.
Export credit arrangements for purchase of civilian supplies from Canada by China(ship, etc.), January 1948-January 1951.

File 6993-C-2-40.
Loan to the Ming Sung Industrial Co., July 1947-May 1950.

File 6993-l-40.
Loan to Turkey under terms of the Export Credits Insurance Act, proposal, May 1946-February 1953.

File 7648-40.
Post hostilities assistance to and repatriation of Canadian civilians in the Far East.

Box 36.

File 8254-J-40.
Korea, Korean problems at the United Nations, November 1947-November 1956.

Box 37.

File 8364-J-40.
Far Eastern Commission organization, terminated, April 1950, September 1945-April 1952.

File 8364-Y-40.
Japanese patents, copyrights and trademarks, policy and procedures, February 1945-March 1950.

Box 38.

File 8620-M-40.
Application of Mr. Herbert Norman as Canadian Minister to Japan proposal, May 1946-December 1950.

Box 39.

File 8919-40.
Commercial relations between Iran and Canada, June 1946-December 1956.

Box 41.

File 9030-40.
Commercial relations between China and Canada, general file, January 1946-December 1952.

Box 44.

File 9323-AG-7-40.
Trade Commissioner Canadian at Hong Kong, September 1946-May 1956.

File 9323-AG-8-40.
Trade Commissioner Canadian at Singapore, December 1948-June 1963.

File 9323-AG-10-40.
Extension of Canadian consular services to Manila, June 1948-April 1954.

Box 45.

File 9371-40.
Commercial relations between Canada and Turkey, general file, June 1948-April 1954.

Box 46.

File 9402-B-40.
Iran-Canada diplomatic relations, April 1948-December 1957.

Box 47.

File 9515-J-40.
Appointment Major-General V.W.Odlum as Canadian ambassador to Ankara, May 1947-September 1952.

Box 49.

File 9678-40.
Canada-Pakistan relations, September 1947-December 1954.

Box 50.

File 9821-40.
Commercial relations between Canada and Burma, general file, November 1947-May 1962.

File 9935-40.
Commercial relations between Canada and Pakistan, general file, February 1948-May 1963.

File 9935-A-40.
Commercial agreement(most favoured nation treatment) between Canada and Pakistan, February-December 1948.

File 9935-B-40.
Pakistan financial relations with Canada, September 1947-January 1963.

File 9965-40.
Relations between Canada and Ceylon, February 1948-December 1960.

Box 52.

File 10354-B-40.
Exchange of military equipment between Canada and Pakistan, July 1949.

Box 54.

File 10389-40.
Japan-Canada, proposals re most favoured nation treatment for Japan, August 1948-April 1952.

File 10393-40.
Canada-Ceylon commercial relations, January 1949-March 1961.

Box 57.

File 10648-40.
Korea and Canada, commercial relations, June 1949-August 1962.

Box 60.

File 11129-40.
Status of Dutch New Guinea, July 1949-January 1950.

File 11380-40.
Canadian military observers to United Nations commission Kashmir, July 1949-August 1952.

File 11493-A-40.
Canadian diplomatic relations with Pakistan, July 1947-August 1963.
Box 61.

File 12201-40.
Maldive Islands, April 1948-March 1963.

Box 62.

File 12216-Y-40.
Extradition between Canada and India, January 1948-October 1962.

Accession 86-87/160.

Box 3.

File 72-BP-3-40.
Air relations between Japan and Canada, August 1953-February 1955.

Box 8.

File 72-ALQ-40, part 2.
South Pacific Air Transport Council, 3rd meeting, Wellington, 1948. April 1950-April 1951.

File 72-ALQ-40, part 3.
South Pacific Air Transport Council, 3rd meeting, Wellington, 1948. May 1951-January 1952.

File 72-ALQ-40, part 4.
South Pacific Air Transport Council, 3rd meeting, Wellington, 1948. February-June 1952.

File 72-ALQ-40, part 5.
South Pacific Air Transport Council, 3rd meeting, Wellington, 1948. July 1952-April 1953.

File 72-ALQ-40, part 6.
South Pacific Air Transport Council, 3rd meeting, Wellington, 1948. April-June 1953.

Box 9.

File 72-ALQ-40, part 8.
South Pacific Air Transport Council, 3rd meeting, Wellington, 1948. May-December 1954.

File 82-AMK-40.
Canada-India Air Agreement, January 1950-November 1961.

Box 15.

File 232-BL-40.
Immigration to Canada from Indo-China, October 1954-November 1959.

Box 18.

File 619-G-40.
Trials of prisoners of war in Korea by United Nations Command, February 1953-May 1956.

File 619-H-40.
Repatriation of sick and wounded prisoners of war in Korea according to Geneva Convention, March 1953-January 1954.

File 619-J-40.
Repatriation of prisoners of war in Korea after truce, according to Geneva Convention.

File 619-K-40.
Armistice in Korea, legal problems arising out of, April 1952-March 1953.

File 619-K-40, part 2.
Armistice in Korea, legal problems arising out of, February 1954.

File 619-K-40, part 3.
Armistice in Korea, legal problems arising out of, July 1954-June 1958.

File 619-L-40.
Legal questions arising out of Indo-China International Supervisory Commission, July-August 1954.

File 619-L-40, part 2.
Legal questions arising out of Indo-China International Supervisory Commission, July-August 1954.

File 619-L-40, part 3.
Legal questions arising out of Indo-China International Supervisory Commission, December 1954-January 1955.

Box 25.

File 1427-40.
Commercial relations between Canada and Japan, March 1954-September 1955.

File 1617-D-40.
Appointment of Escott Reid as Canadian High Commissioner to India, June 1952-August 1958.
Box 28.

File 2172-40, part 2.
Diplomatic relations with China, proposals, March 1952-June 1963.

Box 34.

File 3050-40, part 2.
Safety and welfare in the Far East of Roman Catholic missionaries, July 1951-March 1953.

File 3050-40, part 3.
Safety and welfare in the Far East of Roman Catholic missionaries, April 1953-July 1957.

File 3051-40.
Welfare in the Far East of United Church of Canada following outbreak of war with Japan, February 1951-April 1957.

Box 36.

File 4060-C-40, part 5.
Japan's war crimes, general file. International Military Tribunal in Tokyo and nomination to the tribunal, January 1952-March 1953.

File 4060-C-40, part 6.
Japan's war crimes, general file. International Military Tribunal in Tokyo and nomination to the tribunal, January 1952-March 1953.

Box 37.

File 4060-C-40, part 7.
Japan's war crimes, general file. International Military Tribunal in Tokyo and nomination to the tribunal, August 1953-April 1954.

File 4060-C-40, part 8.
Japan's war crimes, general file. International Military Tribunal in Tokyo and nomination to the tribunal, May 1954-June 1955.

File 4457-B-40, part 1 FP.
Canadian policy in the Far East, February--December 1951.

Box 38.

File 4606-U-40, part 2.
Far Eastern Commission's documents, January 1952-June 1954.

File 4606-U-2-40.
Far Eastern Commission minutes, February 1950-October 1951.

Box 65.
File 5475-CX-2-40, part 2.
Appointment and administrative arrangements for Canadian military observers on United Nations Commission on India and Pakistan, April 1950-April 1951.

File 5475-CX-2-40, part 3.
Appointment and administrative arrangements for Canadian military observers on United Nations Commission on India and Pakistan, May 1951-April 1953.

File 5475-CX-2-40, part 4.
Appointment and administrative arrangements for Canadian military observers on United Nations Commission on India and Pakistan, May 1953-April 1954.

File 5475-CX-2-40, part 5.
Appointment and administrative arrangements for Canadian military observers on United Nations Commission on India and Pakistan, April 1954-December 1955.

File 5475-CX-3-40.
United Nations Commission on Korea, appointment and activities of Canadian military observers of, April 1950-December 1954.

Box 75.

File 5475-EJ-40.
The question of Chinese representation in the United Nations, general file, October 1950-March 1951.

File 5475-EJ-40, part 3.
The question of Chinese representation in the United Nations, general file, April 1951-February 1953.

File 5475-EJ-40, part 4.
The question of Chinese representation in the United Nations, general file, January-November 1953.

File 5475-EJ-40, part 5.
The question of Chinese representation in the United Nations, general file, December 1953-July 1954.

File 5475-EJ-40, part 6.
The question of Chinese representation in the United Nations, general file, July 1954-August 1955.

Box 78.

File 5475-FA-21-40.
Statements and assessments of Canada's policy towards United Nations for India, February 1953-June 1962.

File 5475-FA-22-40.
Statements and assessments of Canada's policy towards United Nations for Indonesia, February 1953-October 1962.

File 5475-FA-25-40.
Statements and assessments of Canada's policy towards United Nations for Japan, July 1953-September 1962.

File 5475-FA-30-40.
Statements and assessments of Canada's policy towards United Nations for Pakistan, February 1953-October 1962.

File 5475-FA-38-40.
Statements and assessments of Canada's policy towards United Nations for Turkey, (no date given).

Box 79.

File 5475-FA-66-40.
Statements and assessments of Canada's policy towards United Nations for Thailand, February 1953-September 1962.

Box 88.

File 6466-B-40, part 2.
Resolutions re recognition of China, November 1950-March 1954.

File 6466-B-40, part 3.
Resolutions re recognition of China, April-May 1954.

File 6466-B-40, part 4.
Resolutions re recognition of China, May 1954-October 1955.

Box 89.

File 6993-C-40, part 4.
Export credit arrangements for purchase of civilian supplies. United Nations from Canada by China, February 1951-September 1962.

Box 94.

File 8254-D-40, part 3.
United Nations documents on the war in Korea, October 1950-

File 8254-D-40, part 4.
United Nations documents on the war in Korea, January 1951-

File 8254-D-40, part 5.
United Nations documents on the war in Korea, March 1951-

File 8254-D-40, part 6.
United Nations documents on the war in Korea, May 1951-

File 8254-D-40, part 7.
United Nations documents on the war in Korea, September 1951-

File 8254-G-40.
Relief arrangements for Korea, general file, July 1950-

File 8254-G-40, part 2.
Relief arrangements for Korea, general file, November 1950-

File 8254-G-40, part 3.
Relief arrangements for Korea, general file, February 1951-

File 8254-G-40, part 5.
Relief arrangements for Korea, general file, July 1951-

File 8254-G-40, part 6 FP.
Relief arrangements for Korea, general file, November 1951-

Box 96.

File 8254-G-40, part 7.
Relief arrangements for Korea, general file, December 1951-

File 8254-G-40, part 8.
Relief arrangements for Korea, general file, February 1952-

File 8254-G-40, part 9.
Relief arrangements for Korea, general file, June 1952-

File 8254-G-40, part 10.
Relief arrangements for Korea, general file, August 1952-

File 8254-G-40, part 11.
Relief arrangements for Korea, general file, December 1952-

File 8254-G-40, part 12.
Relief arrangements for Korea, general file, March 1953-

File 8254-G-40, part 13.
Relief arrangements for Korea, general file, June 1953-

File 8254-G-40, part 14.
Relief arrangements for Korea, general file, September 1953-

File 8254-G-40, part 15.
Relief arrangements for Korea, general file, December 1953-

File 8254-G-40, part 16.
Relief arrangements for Korea, general file, February 1954-

Box 97.

File 8254-G-40, part 17.
Relief arrangements for Korea, general file, May 1954-

Relief arrangements for Korea, general file, October 1954-

File 8254-G-1-40.
Red Cross social welfare team for relief work in Korea, general file, November 1950-

File 8254-G-1-40, part 2.
Red Cross social welfare team for relief work in Korea, general file, March 1951-

File 8254-G-1-40, part 3.
Red Cross social welfare team for relief work in Korea, general file, April 1954-

File 8254-G-3-40.
Donations by Canadian relief organizations to Korean relief, January 1951-

File 8254-G-3-40, part 2.
Donations by Canadian relief organizations to Korean relief, April 1953-

File 8254-G-3-40, part 3.
Donations by Canadian relief organizations to Korean relief, December 1953-

Box 98.

File 8254-G-4-40.
Visit to Korea of representatives of volunteer agencies under the auspices of United Nations K.R.A., June 1952-

File 8254-G-5-40.
Governmental contributions in kind for Korea relief, September 1952-

File 8254-G-7-40.
U.N.K.R.A. shipping policy, August 1954-

File 8254-H-40.
Preparation of background studies on Korea, September 1950-

File 8254-N-40.
Korea, Canadian representatives on the United Nations Command, Military Armistice Commission Advisory Group, reports, January 1954-

Box 99.

File 8364-N-40, part 7.
Far Eastern Commission, transmitted notes(documents to External Affairs library), January 1950-

File 8364-N-40, part 8.
Far Eastern Commission, transmitted notes(documents to External Affairs library), July 1950-

Box 109.

File 9706-BT-40.
Provision of technical assistance for the underdeveloped countries, Iran, September 1950-June 1957.

File 9706-BW-40.
Requests to Canada for professional and technical personnel by foreign governments and/or bureau in the Philippines, May 1950-June 1951.

File 9706-CE-40.
Requests to Canada for professional and technical personnel by Burma, June 1950-September 1954.

File 9706-CH-40.
Provision of technical assistance to underdeveloped areas, Indonesia, September 1950-December 1957.

File 9706-CX-40.
Direct requests training in Canada of medical officers of Pakistan's army forces, September 1952-

Box 117.
File 10389-40, part 3.
Japan-Canada proposals re most favoured nation treatment for Japan, September 1952-January 1953.

File 10389-40, part 4.
Japan-Canada proposals re most favoured nation treatment for Japan, February-August 1953.

File 10389-40, part 5.
Japan-Canada proposals re most favoured nation treatment for Japan, September 1953-January 1954.

File 10389-40, part 6.
Japan-Canada proposals re most favoured nation treatment for Japan, February-May 1954.

File 10389-40, part 7.
Japan-Canada proposals re most favoured nation treatment for Japan, June 1954-December 1956.

Box 127.

File 10818-B-40.
Korea, prisoner of war camps, provision of Canadian army officers for staffs of, June-July 1953.

File 10818-C-40.
Korea, Military Armistice Commission and participating nations' advisory group, appointment of Commonwealth officers to, June 1953-May 1959.

Box 131.

File 11038-40, part 2.
Commonwealth programme for economic assistance to South East Asia, June-August 1950.

Box 132.

File 11038-40, part 3.
Commonwealth programme for economic assistance to South East Asia, September-October 1950.

File 11038-40, part 4.
Commonwealth programme for economic assistance to South East Asia, November-December 1950.

File 11038-40, part 5.
Commonwealth programme for economic assistance to South East Asia, January-February 1951.

File 11038-40, part 6.
Commonwealth programme for economic assistance to South East Asia, February-April 1951.

File 11038-40, part 7.
Commonwealth programme for economic assistance to South East Asia, February 1950-October 1951.

File 11038-40, part 8.
Commonwealth programme for economic assistance to South East Asia, October 1951-January 1952.

File 11038-40, part 9.
Commonwealth programme for economic assistance to South East Asia, February-April 1952.

File 11038-40, part 10.
Commonwealth programme for economic assistance to South East Asia, May-December 1952.

Box 133.

File 11038-40, part 11.
Commonwealth programme for economic assistance to South East Asia, January-May 1953.

File 11038-40, part 12.
Commonwealth programme for economic assistance to South East Asia, June-August 1953.

File 11038-40, part 13.
Commonwealth programme for economic assistance to South East Asia, June-August 1953.

File 11038-1-40, part 2.
Colombo Plan, India, capital assistance, general file, January-July 1952.

File 11038-1-40, part 3.
Colombo Plan, India, capital assistance, general file, August-December 1952.

File 11038-1-40, part 4.
Colombo Plan, India, capital assistance, general file, January-June 1953.

File 11038-1-40, part 5.
Colombo Plan, India, capital assistance, general file, May 1953-February 1954.

File 11038-1-40, part 6.
Colombo Plan, India, capital assistance, general file, March-December 1954.

File 11038-1-1-40.
Colombo Plan, India, commodities(except wheat), May 1953-December 1959.

Box 134.

File 11038-1-1A-40.
Colombo Plan, India, commodities and wheat, January 1953-December 1957.

File 11038-1-2A-40.
Colombo Plan, India, capital assistance, Mayurakshi, January 1953-November 1954.

File 11038-1-2A-40, part 2 FP.
Colombo Plan, India, capital assistance, Mayurakshi, 1954-August 1959.

File 11038-1-2B-40.
Colombo Plan, India, capital assistance, Umtay, January 1953-October 1954.

File 11038-1-2B-40, part 2.
Colombo Plan, India, capital assistance, Umtay, November 1954-October 1959.

File 11038-1-6-40.
Colombo Plan, India, capital assistance, Locust Control Programme, March 1954-April 1958.

File 11038-1-10-40.
Colombo Plan, India, capital assistance, Bombay State, transport, January 1953-August 1959.

File 11038-1-11-40.
Colombo Plan, India, capital assistance, Bombay State, locomotive boilers, January 1953-September 1959.

File 11038-1-12-40.
Colombo Plan, India, capital assistance, Bombay State, All-India Medical Institute, February 1953-November 1960.

File 11038-2-40.
Colombo Plan, Pakistan, capital assistance, May-December 1951.

File 11038-2-40, part 2.
Colombo Plan, Pakistan, capital assistance, December 1951-June 1952.

File 11038-2-40, part 3.
Colombo Plan, Pakistan, capital assistance, July-December 1952.

Box 135.

File 11038-2-40, part 4.
Colombo Plan, Pakistan, capital assistance, January-June 1953.

File 11038-2-40, part 5.
Colombo Plan, Pakistan, capital assistance, July-November 1953.

File 11038-2-40, part 6.
Colombo Plan, Pakistan, capital assistance, December 1953-March 1954.

File 11038-2-40, part 7.
Colombo Plan, Pakistan, capital assistance, March-November 1954.

File 11038-2-40, part 8.
Colombo Plan, Pakistan, capital assistance, December 1954-April 1955.

File 11038-2-1-40.
Colombo Plan, Pakistan, capital assistance, provision of industrial raw materials, June 1954-December 1957.

File 11038-2-1A-40.
Colombo Plan, Pakistan, capital assistance, wheat.

Box 136.

File 11038-2-2A-40.
Colombo Plan, Pakistan, capital assistance, Ganges Kabadak, February 1953-February 1954.

File 11038-2-2B-40.
Colombo Plan, Pakistan, capital assistance, Warsak project, September 1951-June 1954.

File 11038-2-2B-40.
Colombo Plan, Pakistan, capital assistance, Warsak project, September 1951-June 1954.

File 11038-2-2B-40, part 2.
Colombo Plan, Pakistan, capital assistance, Warsak project, June 1954-May 1955.

File 11038-2-2C-40.
Colombo Plan, Pakistan, capital assistance, Mianwali project, February 1953-March 1954.

File 11038-2-2D-40, part 1 FP.
Colombo Plan, Pakistan, capital assistance, Karnfuti project, January 1953-September 1960.

File 11038-2-2E-40.
Colombo Plan, Pakistan, capital assistance, Punjab tubewell(canal Hydel)(Shadiwell), January 1953-October 1954.

File 11038-2-2E-40, part 2.
Colombo Plan, Pakistan, capital assistance, Punjab tubewell(canal Hydel)(Shadiwell), November 1954-December 1956.

File 11038-2-4-40.
Colombo Plan, Pakistan, capital assistance, Thal cement plant, January 1953-March 1954.

File 11038-2-4-40, part 2.
Colombo Plan, Pakistan, capital assistance, Thal cement plant, March-September 1954.

Box 137.

File 11038-2-4-40, part 3.
Colombo Plan, Pakistan, capital assistance, Thal cement plant, March-September 1954.

File 11038-2-5-40.
Colombo Plan, Pakistan, capital assistance, Thal livestock farm, September-December 1953.

File 11038-2-5-40, part 2.
Colombo Plan, Pakistan, capital assistance, Thal livestock farm, January 1954-December 1955.

File 11038-2-6-40.
Colombo Plan, Pakistan, capital assistance, Beaver aircraft for pest control, February 1953-October 1960.

File 11038-2-6A-40.
Colombo Plan equipment to Pakistan for F.A.O. livestock control project in Saudi Arabia, April 1953-

File 11038-2-8-40.
Colombo Plan, Pakistan, capital assistance, aerial resources survey, January 1952-October 1954.

File 11038-2-8-40, part 2.
Colombo Plan, Pakistan, capital assistance, aerial resources survey, November 1954-July 1956.

File 11038-2-11-40.
Colombo Plan, Pakistan, capital assistance, railway ties, January 1953-December 1956.

File 11038-2-14-40.
Colombo Plan, Pakistan, capital assistance, counterpart funds, December 1954-November 1960.

File 11038-3-40, part 2.
Colombo Plan, Ceylon, capital assistance, September 1952-

Box 138.

File 11038-3-40, part 3.
Colombo Plan, Ceylon, capital assistance, May-September 1954.

File 11038-3-40, part 4.
Colombo Plan, Ceylon, capital assistance, October 1954-May 1955.

File 11038-3-1-40.
Colombo Plan, Ceylon, capital assistance, commodities(flour), May 1953-December 1957.

File 11038-3-3-40.
Colombo Plan, Ceylon, capital assistance, Gal Oya project, December 1952-June 1957.

File 11038-3-5-40.
Colombo Plan, Ceylon, capital assistance, agricultural maintenance stations, July 1953-May 1959.

File 11038-3-5a-40.
Colombo Plan, Ceylon, capital assistance, drainage and irrigation equipment, July 1953-May 1959.

File 11038-3-6-40.
Colombo Plan, Ceylon, capital assistance, pest control, June 1953-May 1959.

File 11038-3-7-40.
Colombo Plan, Ceylon, capital assistance, fisheries project, December 1952-January 1956.

File 11038-3-7-40, part 2.
Colombo Plan, Ceylon, capital assistance, fisheries project, September 1953-February 1954.

File 11038-3-7-40.
Colombo Plan, Ceylon, capital assistance, fisheries project, December 1952-January 1956.

File 11038-3-7-40, part 2.
Colombo Plan, Ceylon, capital assistance, fisheries project, September 1953-February 1954.

File 11038-3-7-40, part 3.
Colombo Plan, Ceylon, capital assistance, fisheries

project, March-July 1954.

File 11038-3-7-40, part 4.
Colombo Plan, Ceylon, capital assistance, fisheries project, July-September 1954.

File 11038-3-7-40, part 5.
Colombo Plan, Ceylon, capital assistance, fisheries project, October-December 1954.

Box 139.

File 11038-3-8-40.
Colombo Plan, Ceylon, capital assistance, photographic survey, October 1954-December 1955.

File 11038-3-9-40.
Colombo Plan, Ceylon, capital assistance, Polytechnic Institute, July 1953-August 1959.

File 11038-3-11-40.
Colombo Plan, Ceylon, capital assistance, diesel locomotives, August 1953-May 1959.

File 11038-3-11C-40.
Colombo Plan, Ceylon, capital assistance, railway ties(sleepers) diesel locomotives, June 1954-May 1959.

File 11038-3-13-40.
Colombo Plan, Ceylon, capital assistance, rural road development, February 1953-January 1960.

File 11038-3-14-40.
Colombo Plan, Ceylon, capital assistance, provision of telecommunication equipment to Colombo Airport, Ratamalana, April 1954-June 1960.

File 11038-4-40.
Colombo Plan, Indonesia, capital assistance, July 1953-December 1957.

File 11038-5-40.
Colombo Plan, meeting of the Consultative Committee, 1954, Ottawa, September 1953-September 1954.

File 11038-5A-40.
Colombo Plan, meeting of the Consultative Committee, 1955, Singapore, December 1954-August 1955.

Box 141.

File 11038-A-1-40, part 1 FP.
Colombo Plan, capital assistance, Ceylon, technical cooperation in South and South East Asia, September 1951-June 1952.

File 11038-A-1-40, part 2.
Colombo Plan, capital assistance, Ceylon, technical cooperation in South and South East Asia, September 1951-June 1952.

File 11038-A-1-40, part 3.
Colombo Plan, capital assistance, Ceylon, technical cooperation in South and South East Asia, July-December 1952.

File 11038-A-1-40, part 4.
Colombo Plan, capital assistance, Ceylon, technical cooperation in South and South East Asia, January-April 1953.

File 11038-A-1-40, part 5.
Colombo Plan, capital assistance, Ceylon, technical cooperation in South and South East Asia, May-September 1953.

File 11038-A-1-40, part 6.
Colombo Plan, capital assistance, Ceylon, technical cooperation in South and South East Asia, October 1953-February 1954.

File 11038-A-1-40, part 7.
Colombo Plan, capital assistance, Ceylon, technical cooperation in South and South East Asia, March-May 1954.

File 11038-A-1-40, part 8.
Colombo Plan, capital assistance, Ceylon, technical cooperation in South and South East Asia, June-August 1954.

Box 142.

File 11038-A-1-40, part 9.
Colombo Plan, capital assistance, Ceylon, technical cooperation in South and South East Asia, August-October 1954.

File 11038-A-1-40, part 10.
Colombo Plan, capital assistance, Ceylon, technical cooperation in South and South East Asia, November 1954-May 1955.

File 11038-A-1-BA-40.
Colombo Plan, capital assistance, Ceylon, fisheries development expert, January 1954-January 1955.

File 11038-A-2-40.
Colombo Plan, Council for Technical Cooperation in South and South East Asia, India, December 1950-June 1952.

File 11038-A-2-40, part 2.
Colombo Plan, Council for Technical Cooperation in South and South East Asia, India, July 1952-April 1953.

File 11038-A-2-40, part 3.
Colombo Plan, Council for Technical Cooperation in South and South East Asia, India, May-December 1953.

File 11038-A-2-40, part 4.
Colombo Plan, Council for Technical Cooperation in South and South East Asia, India, January-September 1954.

File 11038-A-2-40, part 5.
Colombo Plan, Council for Technical Cooperation in South and South East Asia, India, October 1954-April 1955.

File 11038-A-2-40, part 6.
Colombo Plan, Council for Technical Cooperation in South and South East Asia, India, July 1954-December 1955.

File 11038-A-3-40.
Colombo Plan, capital assistance, Pakistan, technical cooperation in South and South East Asia, December 1950-September 1952.

File 11038-A-3-40, part 2.
Colombo Plan, capital assistance, Pakistan, technical cooperation in South and South East Asia, February 1952-December 1953.

Box 143.

File 11038-A-3-40, part 3.
Colombo Plan, capital assistance, Pakistan, technical cooperation in South and South East Asia, January-August 1954.

File 11038-F-1-40.
Colombo Plan, offers by Canada of fellowships and scholarships to Ceylon, March 1951-December 1954.

File 11038-F-2-40.
Colombo Plan, offers by Canada of fellowships and scholarships to India, April-October 1954.

File 11038-F-2-40, part 2.
Colombo Plan, offers by Canada of fellowships and scholarships to India, November 1954-January 1955.

Box 144.

File 11038-F-3-40.
Colombo Plan, technical assistance, Pakistan, general correspondence concerning fellowships and scholarships, April 1951-January 1955.

Box 145.

File 11038-AD-10-40.
Colombo Plan, cooperative missions from Canada, August 1952-June 1953.

Box 146.

File 11038-AB-10-40, part 2.
Colombo Plan, cooperative missions from Canada, July 1953-June 1954.

File 11038-AB-14-40.
Colombo Plan, technical assistance programme, Burma, experts, training, equipment, September 1952-November 1954.

File 11038-AB-14-40, part 2.
Colombo Plan, technical assistance programme, Burma, experts, training, equipment, December 1954-August 1955.

File 11038-AB-15-40.
Colombo Plan, technical assistance programme, Thailand, general file, January 1953-December 1958.

File 11038-AB-17-A-40.
Colombo Plan, technical assistance programme, Malaya, general file, December 1953-February 1955.

File 11038-AC-40.
Canadian government loan to India, proposals, June-September 1952.

File 11038-AF-40.
Colombo Plan, technical assistance programme, Laos, August 1954-September 1956.

File 11038-AF-40.
Colombo Plan, technical assistance programme, Cambodia, November 1950-December 1954.

File 11038-AH-40.
Colombo Plan, technical assistance programme, Vietnam, July 1951-February 1956.

Box 149.

File 11073-40.
War in Korea, legal questions, June 1950-March 1957.

File 11129-40, part 2.
Status of Dutch New Guinea, October 1950-October 1952.

File 11129-40, part 3.
Status of Dutch New Guinea, February 1953-September 1954.

File 11129-40, part 4.
Status of Dutch New Guinea, September-November 1954.

File 11129-40, part 5.
Status of Dutch New Guinea, November 1954-December 1955.

Box 152.

File 11302-B-40.
Canadian wheat for India, April 1950-May 1951.

File 11302-B-40, part 2.
Canadian wheat for India, May 1951-August 1962.

Box 163.

File 11562-26-40.
Visit to Canada of Shigeru Yoshida, Prime Minister of Japan, October 1953-November 1954.

Box 166.

File 11563-5-5-40.
Visit of Prime Minister abroad, Pakistan, January 1953-February 1954.

File 11563-5-5-40, part 2 FP.
Visit of Prime Minister abroad, Pakistan, February-October 1954.

File 11563-6-6-40, part 1 FP.
Visit of Prime Minister abroad, India, July 1952-January 1954

File 11563-6-6-40, part 2.
Visit of Prime Minister abroad, India, February 1954.

File 11563-6-6-40, part 3.
Visit of Prime Minister abroad, India, March 1954--January 1955.

Box 167.

File 11563-5-7-40.
Visits of the Prime Minister abroad, Ceylon, September 1953-June 1954.

File 11563-5-8-40.
Visits of the Prime Minister abroad, Indonesia, September 1953-May 1954.

File 11563-5-9-40.
Visits of the Prime Minister abroad, Philippines, September 1953-July 1954.

File 11563-5-10-40.
Visits of the Prime Minister abroad, South Korea, September 1953-April 1954.

File 11563-5-11-40.
Visits of the Prime Minister abroad, Japan, September 1953-December 1954.

File 11583-40.
Wheat for Pakistan from Canada, June 1952-August 1957.

Box 169.

File 11679-A-40.
Food relief for Pakistan(East Bengal, India and Nepal), 1954, August 1954-September 1955.

Box 170.

File 11744-40.
Peking International Economic Conference, March-July 1953.

File 11766-40.
Closing of office of the Canadian Consulate at Shanghai, June 1951-January 1952.

Box 171.

File 11871-40.
Relations between Canada and Thailand, July 1953-June 1963.

File 11975-40.
International North Pacific Fisheries Commission(U.S., Canada, Japan), June-December 1953.

File 11975-40, part 2.
International North Pacific Fisheries Commission(U.S., Canada, Japan), March 1952-October 1955.

Box 172.

File 12017-40.
Termination of war with Japan, March 1951-December 1956.

File 12022-40.
Article 16 of Japanese peace terms, distribution by International Red Cross of indemnities to Allied prisoners of war of Japan, August 1951-May 1954.

File 12022-40, part 2.
Article 16 of Japanese peace terms, distribution by International Red Cross of indemnities-Allied prisoners of war of Japan, June 1954-December 1955.

File 12022-40, part 3.
Article 16 of Japanese peace terms, distribution by International Red Cross of indemnities to Allied prisoners of war of Japan, December 1955-October 1961.

Box 173.

File 12113-40.
International transportation arrangements in Indo-China for the International Supervisory Commission in Indo-China, February 1954-February 1961.

File 12113-A-40.
Landing clearances for the Royal Canadian Air Force aircraft en route to Indo-China carrying members of the International Supervisory Commission, August 1954-August 1955.

File 12130-40.
Indo-China Truce Commission, administrative arrangements, July 1954-February 1958.

File 12130-40, part 2.
Indo-China Truce Commission, administrative arrangements, September-November 1954.

File 12130-40, part 3.
Indo-China Truce Commission, administrative arrangements, December 1954-February 1955.

File 12130-B-40.
International Supervisory Commission, Hanoi, Vietnam, personnel arrangements, August 1954-May 1955.

File 12130-C-40.
International Supervisory Commission, Vientiane, Laos, August 1954-August 1956.

File 12130-D-40.
International Supervisory Commission, Phnom Penh, Cambodia, personnel arrangements, August 1954-December 1955.

File 12130-E-40.
International Supervisory Commission, Saigon, Vietnam, personnel arrangements, July 1954-December 1955.

Box 174.

File 12173-40.
Afro-Asian(Bandung) conferences, June 1954-March 1955.

Box 175.

File 12386-3-40.
International Convention for the High Seas of the North Pacific Ocean(International North Pacific Fisheries Commission), April 1954-December 1955.

Accession 86-87/336.

Box 20.

File 72-ALQ-40, volume 9.
South Pacific Air Transport Council, 3rd meeting, Wellington, 1948, January-November 1955.

File 72-ALQ-40, volume 10.
South Pacific Air Transport Council, 3rd meeting, Wellington, 1948, December 1955-October 1956.

File 72-ALQ-40, volume 11.
South Pacific Air Transport Council, 3rd meeting, Wellington, 1948, October 1956-October 1957.

File 72-ALQ-40, volume 12.
South Pacific Air Transport Council, 3rd meeting, Wellington, 1948, November 1957-May 1959.

File 72-ALQ-40, volume 13.
South Pacific Air Transport Council, 3rd meeting, Wellington, 1948, September 1958-August 1959.

File 72-ALQ-40, volume 14.
South Pacific Air Transport Council, 3rd meeting, Wellington, 1948, September-December 1959.

Box 22.

File 72-AOH-40.
Air relations between Canada and Pakistan, October 1956-October 1961.

Box 29.

File 114-B-40, volume 3.
19th International Red Cross Conference, New Delhi, 1957, general file, September-October 1957.

File 114-B-40, volume 4.
19th International Red Cross Conference, New Delhi, 1957, general file, September-October 1957.

Box 30.

File 114-B-40, volume 5 & FP.
19th International Red Cross Conference, New Delhi, 1957, general file, November 1957-August 1961.

File 114-B-1-40.
19th International Red Cross Conference, New Delhi, 1957, draft rules for the limit action of the danger incurred by the civilian population in time of war, January 1956-September 1957.

File 114-B-1-40, volume 2.
19th International Red Cross Conference, New Delhi, 1957, draft rules for the limit action of the danger incurred by the civilian population in time of war, September 1957-June 1959.

Box 44.

File 619-l-40.
Legal questions arising out of Indo-China International Supervisory Commission, January-May 1956.

File 619-l-40, volume 2.
Legal questions arising out of Indo-China International Supervisory Commission, June-September 1956.

File 619-l-40, volume 3.
Legal questions arising out of Indo-China International Supervisory Commission, September 1956-April 1958.

File 619-l-40, volume 4.
Legal questions arising out of Indo-China International Supervisory Commission, May 1958-November 1960.

File 619-l-1-40.
Otter airplane crash, Laos. Indo-China International Supervisory Commission, March 1958-January 1959.

File 621-pt-40.
American prisoners of war in Korea, January 1955-November 1962.

File 654-A-40.
Visit to Canada of Japanese training ship **Nippon maru,** May 1958.

Box 47.

File 960-40.
Japan-Australia relations, July 1959-July 1963.

Box 56.

File 1617-40.
India-Canada relations(including exchange of High Commissioner), January 1957-December 1958.

File 1617-40, volume 2.
India-Canada relations(including exchange of High Commissioner), January 1959-May 1961.

File 1617-E-40.
Appointment of Chester Ronning as Canadian High Commissioner to India, January-August 1957.

Box 78.

File 2963-B-40.
Registration of Japanese in Canada(census of overseas Japanese), October-November 1955.

Box 80.

File 3284-40, volume 3.
India commercial relations with Canada, May 1956-December 1958.

File 3284-40, volume 4.
India commercial relations with Canada, January 1959-July 1963.

Box 92.

File 4457-D-40.
Visit of Paul Martin to Asia, general file, 29 August 1956-25 November 1957.

File 4457-D-1-40.
Visit of Paul Martin to Philippines, 22 October 1956-17 January 1957.

File 4457-D-2-40.
Visit of Paul Martin to South Vietnam, 7 October 1956-5 March 1957.

File 4457-D-3-40.
Visit of Paul Martin to Cambodia, 9 October 1956-17 January 1957.

File 4457-D-4-40.
Visit of Paul Martin to Laos, 12 October 1956-17 January 1957.

File 4457-D-5-40.
Visit of Paul Martin to Thailand, 16 October 1956-13 December 1956.

File 4457-D-6-40.
Visit of Paul Martin to Indonesia, 12 October 1956 to 29 November 1956.

File 4457-D-9-40.
Visit of Paul Martin to Singapore, Burma, Malaya, 16 October 1956-17 January 1957.

File 4457-D-10-40.
Visit of Paul Martin to Ceylon, 12 October 1956-17 January 1957.

File 4457-D-11-40.
Visit of Paul Martin to India, 1 October 1956-22 January 1957.

File 4457-D-12-40.
Visit of Paul Martin to Pakistan, 12 October 1956-17 January 1957.

File 4457-D-13-40.
Visit of Paul Martin to Hawaii, San Francisco, Wake, and Guam, 16 October 1956-7 February 1957.

File 4558-E-40.
Premises for Canadian embassy in China, Chungking address; No. 97, Shen Hsien Tung Chieh(Fairy Grotto Street), 2 March 1959-29 November 1962.

File 4606-40, volume 8.
Japanese political situation subsequent to entry of Japan into the war, 3 January 1955-24 April 1956.

File 4606-40, volume 9.
Japanese political situation subsequent to entry of Japan into the war, 15 April 1956-28 February 1957.

Box 93.

File 4606-40, volume 10.
Japanese political situation subsequent to entry of Japan into the war, 27 February 1957-27 November 1957.

Box 94.

File 4606-40, volume 11.
Japanese political situation subsequent to entry of Japan into the war, 9 December 1957-31 May 1958.

File 4606-40, volume 12.
Japanese political situation subsequent to entry of Japan into the war, 6 June 1958-31 December 1958.

File 4606-40, volume 13.
Japanese political situation subsequent to entry of Japan into the war, 5 January 1959-30 December 1959.

File 4606-A-1-40, volume 3.
Communism in Japan, 10 December 1957 to 28 December 1962.

File 4606-A-3-40, volume 3.
Japan, foreign policy, 15 April 1958-5 December 1958.

File 4606-A-3-40, volume 4.
Japan, foreign policy, 6 January 1959-29 January 1962.

File 4606-B-40, volume 6.
Monitored reports re Japan, 10 January 1955-21 November 1956.

Box 95.

File 4606-B-40, volume 7.
Monitored reports re Japan, 13 December 1956-18 February 1958.

File 4606-B-40, volume 8.
Monitored reports re Japan, 16 May-19 December 1958.

File 4606-B-40, volume 9.
Monitored reports re Japan, 5 January 1959-26 April 1960.

File 4606-C-9-40, volume 3.
Soviet Union-Japan relations, 5 September 1956-19 January 1958.

File 4606-C-9-40, volume 4.
Soviet Union-Japan relations, 7 January 1958-2 December 1959.

File 4606-C-12-40, volume 2.
Japan-Korea relations, 24 December 1955-15 May 1959.

File 4606-C-12-40, volume 3.
Japan-Korea relations, 4 June 1959-26 May 1960.

File 4606-C-13-40, volume 2.
Treatment of assets and property of Japanese nationals in Canada, 4 January 1955-3 October 1962.

Box 96.

File 4606-C-14-40, volume 2.
Japan-China relations, 6 May 1955-9 December 1959.

File 4606-C-14-40, volume 3.
Japan-China relations, 27 November 1959-3 July 1962.

File 4606-C-19-40, volume 2.
Japan-U.S. relations, 13 February 1956-22 January 1960.

File 4606-C-21-40, volume 2.
Japan-Canada relations, 2 February 1955-29 March 1957.

File 4606-C-21-40, volume 3.
Japan-Canada relations, 1 April 1957-31 July 1958.

File 4606-C-21-40, volume 4.
Japan-Canada relations, 5 August 1958-31 December 1959.

File 4606-C-26-40.
Japan-Colombia relations, 12 January 1955-4 February 1958.

File 4606-C-27-40.
Japan-Paraguay relations, 20 December 1956-15 April 1958.

File 4606-C-28-40.
Japan-Ecuador relations, 15 January-12 February 1957.

File 4606-C-29-40.
Japan-Denmark relations, 5 February 1957-7 August 1958.

File 4606-C-30-40.
Japan-Brazil relations, 6 February 1957-10 April 1962.

File 4606-C-31-40.
Japan-Cuba relations, 13 February 1957-11 October 1962.

File 4606-C-32-40.
Japan-Dominican Republic relations, 13 February 1957-16 September 1961.

File 4606-C-33-40.
Japan-Haiti relations, 13 February-4 April 1957.

File 4606-C-34-40.
Japan-Mexico relations, 13 February 1957-26 October 1962.

File 4606-C-35-40.
Japan-Peru relations, 13 February 1957-11 August 1961.

File 4606-C-36-40.
Japan-Uruguay relations, 13 February 1957-16 September 1957.

File 4606-C-37-40.
Japan-Venezuela relations, 13 February 1957-26 February 1958.

File 4606-C-38-40.
Japan-Sweden relations, 18 March 1952-22 September 1960.

File 4606-C-41-40.
Japan-Turkey relations, 16 May 1957-24 April 1963.

File 4606-C-42-40.
Japan-Libya relations, 21 August 1957.

Box 97.

File 4606-E-2-40, volume 2.
Japanese war reparations, 2 January 1958-8 February 1963.

File 4506-K-40, volume 2.
Disasters in Japan, 1 October 1959-16 December 1960.

File 4606-W-40.
Japan-New Zealand relations, 12 March 1956-4 September 1963.

File 4606-X-40.
Japan-Ethiopia relations, 22 November 1956-13

November 1957.

File 4606-Z-40.
Japan-Austria relations, 6 December 1956-4 May 1962.

File 4606-AB-40.
Japan-France relations, 14 December 1956-13 June 1963.

Box 104.

File 4901-M-6-40, volume 2.
Commonwealth Liaison Committee, general file, 13 September 1955-21 May 1958.

File 4901-M-6-40, volume 3.
Commonwealth Liaison Committee, general file, 13 June 1958-13 August 1959.

File 4901-M-6-40, volume 4.
Commonwealth Liaison Committee, general file, 17 August 1959-7 September 1960.

File 4901-M-6-A-40, volume 9.
Commonwealth Liaison Committee, documents and minutes of meetings, 6 June 1956-18 December 1957.

File 4901-M-6-A-40, volume 10.
Commonwealth Liaison Committee, documents and minutes of meetings, 8 September 1958-18 February 1959.

File 4901-M-6-A-40, volume 11.
Commonwealth Liaison Committee, documents and minutes of meetings, 10 February 1958-15 March 1961.

File 4901-M-6-B-40, volume 2-FP.
Commonwealth Liaison Committee, trade with the Sino-Soviet bloc, 14 January 1959-7 December 1962.

Box 138.

File 5475-CX-2-40, volume 6.
Appointment and administrative arrangements for Canadian military observers on United Nations Commission on India and Pakistan, 6 January 1956-19 June 1957.

File 5475-CX-2-40, volume 7.
Appointment and administrative arrangements for Canadian military observers on United Nations Commission on India and Pakistan, 8 July 1957-29 September 1960.

File 5475-CX-5-40.
Permanent seat for India in the Security Council, 16 November 1955-10 March 1959.

File 5475-CY-2-40, volume 5.
United Nations Economic Commission for Asia and the Far East, 2 July 1956-22 December 1958.

File 5475-CY-2-40, volume 6.
United Nations Economic Commission for Asia and the Far East, 8 January 1959-29 February 1960.

Box 160.

File 5475-EA-5-40, volume 1-FP.
United Nations Refugees Emergency Fund, Chinese refugees in the Far East, 10 March 1955-15 May 1962.

Box 165.

File 5475-FA-35-40.
Statements and assessments of Canada's policy towards United Nations for Philippines, 20 July 1956-9 October 1962.

File 5475-FA-35-40, volume 2.
Statements and assessments of Canada's policy towards United Nations for Philippines, 14 January 1958-31 August 1962.

File 5475-FA-75-40.
Statements and assessments of Canada's policy towards United Nations for Laos, 7 November 1956-1 October 1962.

File 5475-FA-77-40.
Statements and assessments of Canada's policy towards United Nations for Vietnam, 18 January 1957-12 January 1959.

File 5475-FA-80-40.
Statements and assessments of Canada's policy towards United Nations for Malaya, 19 November 1957-5 October 1962.

File 5475-FA-83-40.
Statements and assessments of Canada's policy towards United Nations for Nepal, 15 September 1958-9 October 1962.

Box 166.

File 5475-FA-84-40.
Statements and assessments of Canada's policy towards United Nations for Cambodia, 1 October 1959-3 October 1962.

Box 169.

File 5495-B-40, volume 3.
Indonesia-Netherlands relations, 5 December 1957-24 August 1960.

File 5495-B-1-40.
Imprisoned Dutch citizens in Indonesia, 13 June 1955-30 April 1959.

File 5495-C-40, volume 5.
Political situation in Indonesia, 24 September 1959-15 October 1962.

File 5495-C-2-40, volume 1.
Indonesia, foreign policy, 6 May 1959-30 August 1963.

File 5495-G-40, volume 3.
Indonesia-Canada relations, 2 January 1958-19 October 1960.

File 5495-G-1-40, volume 1-FP.
Asamara Oil Corporation(formerly called New British Dominion Oil Co.), 26 July 1958-31 December 1958.

Box 170.

File 5495-M-40.
Indonesia-Soviet Union relations, 2 April 1959-1 June 1963.

File 5495-W-40.
Indonesia-Czechoslovakia relations, 28 March 1956-21 January 1963.

File 5495-Y-40.
Indonesia-Poland relations, 7 June 1957-26 June 1962.

File 5507-B-40, volume 2.
Military action by Nationalists against Communist China, 6 May 1955-23 May 1963.

File 5567-C-40.
Status of Burma-Czech relations, 8 February 1957-3 April 1962.

File 5567-D-40.
Status of Burma-Yugoslav relations, 21 December 1956-15 July 1959.

Box 179.

File 5600-40, volume 9.
Treatment of persons of East Indian origin in the Union of South Africa, 9 September 1957-29 August 1960.

File 5651-40, volume 2.
Agriculture in China, legislation and reports re, 16 April 1958-17 October 1963.

File 5710-AR-40.
Reports re organizations of and personalities of diplomatic representation in Manila, 16 February 1959-19 June 1962.

Box 185.

File 5729-40, volume 4.
Press in China, editorial opinion in the Chinese press, reports re, 20 January 1958-7 March 1960.

Box 186.

Press in Iran, reports re, 12 November 1959-8 August 1963.

File 5872-CA-40.
Press in Indo-China, reports re, 27 September 1956.

File 5872-CH-40.
Press in Indonesia, reports re, 3 February 1955-13 June 1963.

Box 190.

File 6000-R-40.
I.B.R.D.-Indian consortium(discussions on India's financial position), 11 June 1958-17 August 1959.

File 6045-A-40.
Developments in China, reports, 10 February 1959-23 August 1963.

Box 197.

File 6676-40, volume 6.
China-Burma relations, 5 September 1956-15 November 1957.

File 6676-40, volume 7.
China-Burma relations, 21 January 1958-17 June 1963.

Accession 86-87/360.

Box 203.

File 7116-CH-40.
Informational and cultural services of the government of Indonesia, reports, March 1955.

File 7266, part 1.
Laos-Vietnam relations, September 1956-April 1959.

File 7266, part 2.
Laos-Vietnam relations, April 1959-September 1962.

File 7266-A-40.
Bulgaria-Vietnam relations, January 1956-October 1962.

File 7266-B-40, part 1.
Cambodia-Vietnam relations, January 1956-March 1957.

File 7266-B-40, part 2.
Cambodia-Vietnam relations, April 1957-May 1958.

File 7266-B-40, part 3.
Cambodia-Vietnam relations, June-July 1958.

File 7266-B-40, part 4.
Cambodia-Vietnam relations, January 1958-March

1960.

File 7266-C-40.
Canada-Laos relations, January 1956-January 1958.

File 7266-C-40, part 2.
Canada-Laos relations, October 1958-December 1962.

File 7266-C-1-40.
Canada-Vietnam relations, June 1956-March 1963.

Box 205.

File 7266-C-2-40.
Canada-Cambodia relations, 17 November 1955-15 August 1963.

File 7266-D-40.
Canada-Cambodia relations(including visit of Prince Sihanouk of Cambodia to Peking), 24 January 1956-27 December 1960.

File 7266-D-2-40.
China-Laos relations, 5 April 1955-19 June 1963.

File 7266-E-40.
Czechoslovakia-Vietnam relations, 6 January 1955-14 January 1960.

File 7266-E-1-40.
Czechoslovakia-Cambodian relations, 20 September 1956-27 December 1960.

File 7266-F-40.
France-Cambodian relations, 11 January 1956-3 January 1963.

File 7266-F-2-40.
France-Laos relations, 12 August 1955-9 July 1963.

File 7266-G-40.
Hong Kong-Vietnam relations, 23 January 1956.

File 7266-J-40.
India-Cambodia relations, 23 November 1955-13 August 1963.

File 7266-J-1-40.
India-Laos relations, 12 January 1956-13 August 1963.

File 7266-J-2-40.
India-Vietnam relations, 4 April 1955-31 August 1963.

File 7266-K-40.
Poland-Vietnam relations, 14 February 1956-19 April 1963.

File 7266-K-1-40.
Poland-Cambodia relations, 24 April 1956-15 February 1963.

File 7266-K-40.
Poland-Vietnam relations, 14 February 1956-19 April 1963.

File 7266-K-1-40.
Poland-Cambodia relations, 24 April 1956-15 February 1963.

File 7266-L-40.
Soviet Union-Cambodia relations, 24 January 1956-14 May 1963.

File 7266-L-1-40.
Soviet Union-Vietnam relations, 8 February 1956-23 May 1963.

File 7266-L-2-40.
Soviet Union-Laos relations, 3 July 1956-12 August 1963.

File 7266-M-40.
Sudan-Vietnam relations, 26 January 1956.

File 7266-N-40.
U.K.-Vietnam relations, 29 September 1956-25 September 1962.

File 7266-N-1-40.
U.K.-Laos relations, 21 March 1956-18 April 1963.

File 7266-N-2-40.
U.K.-Cambodia relations, 12 September 1956-30 November 1962.

File 7266-P-2-40.
U.S.-Laos relations, 13 April 1956-30 August 1960.

File 7266-Q-40.
Thailand-Cambodia relations, 22 March 1956-31 December 1959.

Box 206.

File 7266-Q-1-40.
Thailand-Laos relations, 14 March 1956-4 July 1963.

File 7266-R-40.
Indonesia-Laos relations, 26 March 1956-3 June 1963.

File 7266-R-1-40.
Indonesia-Vietnam relations, 11 January 1957-24 September 1962.

File 7266-S-1-40.
Japan-Vietnam relations, 30 May 1956-28 August 1963.

File 7266-S-2-40.
Japan-Cambodia relations, 24 February 1955-23 February 1962.

Philippine-Laos relations, 1 February 1956-11 June 1962.

File 7266-U-40.
Korea-Vietnam relations, 9 December 1955-6 August 1962.

File 7266-V-40.
Roumania-Vietnam relations, 2 May 1956-20 September 1960.

File 7266-W-40.
Egypt-Laos relations(volume 2 transferred to 50405-B-40, volume 3 transferred to 12653-B-40), 20 June 1956-15 January 1958.

File 7266-W-1-40.
Egypt-Cambodia relations(volume 2 transferred to 50405-B-40, volume 3 transferred to 12653-B-40), 4 April 1957.

File 7266-X-40.
Israel- Indo-China relations(Cambodia, Vietnam), 9 July 1956-19 February 1957.

File 7266-Y-40.
Spain-Cambodia relations, 29 June-7 August 1956.

File 7266-Z-40.
Denmark-Laos relations, 13 November 1956-9 January 1957.

File 7266-AB-1-40.
Australia-Laos relations, 26 February 1957-24 April 1963.

File 7266-AB-2-40.
Australia-Cambodia relations, 2 April 1957-14 December 1962.

File 7266-AC-40.
Pakistan-Cambodia relations, 17 January 1957.

File 7266-AC-1-40.
Pakistan-Laos relations, 19 June 1957.

File 7266-AD-40.
Yugoslavia-Cambodia relations, 29 January 1957-10 December 1959.

File 7266-AH-1-40.
Yugoslavia-Vietnam relations, 15 March 1957-25 March 1958.

File 7266-AE-40.
Ceylon-Cambodia relations, 20 February 1957.

File 7266-AF-40.
Portugal-Laos relations, 2 April 1957.

File 7266-AG-40.
New Zealand-Vietnam relations, 2 August 1957- 20August 1963.

File 7266-AH-40.
Burma-Vietnam relations, 6 August 1957-22 May 1958.

File 7266-AH-1-40.
Burma-Laos relations, 21 March 1958-9 March 1962.

Box 213.

File 7802-A-40, volume 2.
Soviet Union, relations with Iran, 2 February-8 June 1959.

File 7802-A-40, volume 3.
Soviet Union, relations with Iran, 9 June 1959-30 August 1960.

Box 215.

File 7938-40, volume 2.
Conditions in the Hong Kong area, reports re, 6 January 1956-28 March 1963.

Box 221.

File 8246-E-40.
Ceylon-Spain relations, 23 April 1955-16 January 1956.

File 8250-B-40.
Malay Independent Constitutional Commission for Malaya, proposals re nominations of Canadian member, 19 August 1955-12 October 1961.

Box 222.

File 8250-D-40.
Malayan Independence celebrations.
General file(Mr. McDonnell's visit), 29 December 1956-31 July 1957.

File 8250-D-40, volume 2.
Malayan Independence celebrations.
General file(Mr. McDonnell's visit), 2 August-31 August 1957.

File 8250-D-40, volume 3.
Malayan Independence celebrations.
General file(Mr. McDonnell's visit), 15 August-21 July 1960.

File 8250-D-1-40.
Malayan Independence celebrations.
Mr. McDonnell's visit-San Francisco, Hawaii, Wake, Guam and Singapore, 2 August-29 October 1957.

File 8250-D-2-40.
Malayan Independence celebrations.
Mr. McDonnell's visit to New Delhi, Karachi, Beirut and London, 30 July 1957 to 6 March 1958.

File 8250-K-40.
Federation of Malaya newsletter(from Malayan High Commissioner in London), 21 October 1957 to 26 June 1959.

File 8254-40, volume 4.
Status of Korea, free Korea movement, activities and reports, political conditions in Korea, 1 April 1955-18 December 1957.

File 8254-40, volume 5.
Status of Korea, free Korea movement, activities and reports, political conditions in Korea, 8 January 1958-24 March 1959.

File 8254-40, volume 6.
Status of Korea, free Korea movement, activities and reports, political conditions in Korea, 1 April 1959-30 April 1960.

File 8254-40, volume 8.
Status of Korea, free Korea movement, activities and reports, political conditions in Korea, 5 August 1959-30 June 1961.

Box 223.

File 8254-F-1-40.
Fortnightly report of events in Korea(by British Embassy in Peking) (duplicate copy to go to File 8254-40), 6 September 1957-26 June 1959.

File 8254-F-1-40, volume.
Fortnightly report of events in Korea(by British Embassy in Peking) (duplicate copy to go to File 8254-40), 9 July 1959-30 August 1960.

File 8254-G-40, volume 19.
Relief arrangements for Korea, general file, 3 February 1955-29 April 1955.

File 8254-G-40, volume 20-FP.
Relief arrangements for Korea, general file, 3 May-31 August 1955.

Box 224.

File 8254-G-40, volume 21.
Relief arrangements for Korea, general file, 13 July-31 December 1955.

File 8254-G-40, volume 22.
Relief arrangements for Korea, general file, 4 January-29 June 1956.

File 8254-G-40, volume 23.
Relief arrangements for Korea, general file, 3 July 1956-15 April 1957.

File 8254-G-40, volume 24-FP.
Relief arrangements for Korea, general file, 20 April 1957-25 November 1958.

File 8254-G-40, volume 25.
Relief arrangements for Korea, general file, 8 December 1958-21 November 1960.

File 8254-G-6-40.
Korea rehabilitation of proposals for the employment of Canadian troops in reconstruction projects in Korea, 28 May 1958-9 September 1964.

File 8254-J-40, volume 2.
United Nations cemetery in Korea, 1 April 1955-1 March 1956.

File 8254-J-40, volume 3.
United Nations cemetery in Korea, 13 June 1956-28 October 1958.

File 8254-J-40, volume 4-FP.
United Nations cemetery in Korea, 23 January 1959-15 November 1962.

Box 225.

File 8254-K-40, volume 3.
Korea, Korean problems at the United Nations, 6 November 1958.

File 8254-K-40, volume 4-FP.
Korea, Korean problems at the United Nations, 4 January 1959-15 November 1960.

File 8254-L-40.
Korea, Neutral Nations Supervisory Commission, 31 January 1955-29 February 1956.

File 8254-L-40, volume 2 FP.
Korea, Neutral Nations Supervisory Commission, 2 March 1956-30 April 1956.

File 8254-L-40, volume 3.
Korea, Neutral Nations Supervisory Commission, 1 May-3 July 1956.

File 8254-L-40, volume 4.
Korea, Neutral Nations Supervisory Commission, 3 July-30 October 1956.

Box 226.

File 8254-L-40, volume 5.
Korea, Neutral Nations Supervisory Commission, 8 November 1956-30 December 1957.

File 8254-L-40, volume 6.
Korea, Neutral Nations Supervisory Commission, 10 January 1959-4 December 1962.

File 8254-N-40, volume 2.
Korea, Canadian representative on the United Nations Command, Military Armistice Commission Advisory Group, reports, 17 December 1957-23 May 1963.

File 8254-P-40.
Korea-Soviet Union relations, 20 June 1956-7 March 1963.

File 8254-Q-40.
Korea, situation in North Korea, 31 January 1956-27 March 1958.

File 8254-Q-40, volume 2.
Korea, situation in North Korea, 31 January 1956-27 March 1958.

File 8254-R-40.
Korea-U.K. relations, 6 December 1956-18 September 1962.

File 8254-S-40.
Korea-Indonesia relations, 27 May 1957-20 November 1962.

File 8260-11-40.
Chair of Commonwealth Studies, New Delhi University, proposals re granting fellowship-an Indian student, 21 December 1956.

Box 227.

File 8260-CH-40.
Exchange of students between Canada and Indonesia, 29 May 1957-29 May 1961.

File 8260-CV-40.
Exchange of students between Canada and Fiji Islands, 17 December 1956-31 August 1961.

Box 239.

File 9030-40, volume 4.
Commercial relations between China and Canada, general file, 2 December 1957-30 September 1958.

File 9030-40, volume 5.
Commercial relations between China and Canada, general file, 3 October 1958-8 March 1960.

File 9030-G-40.
Patent and trade mark agreement between Canada and the Republic of China(Formosa).

Box 246.

File 9126-40, volume 7.
India, foreign policy, 4 March-20 June 1955.

File 9126-40, volume 8.
India, foreign policy, 23 June-20 December 1955.

File 9126-40, volume 9.
India, foreign policy, 8 November 1955-29 November 1956.

File 9126-40, volume 10.
India, foreign policy, 4 December 1956-8 September 1958.

File 9126-40, volume 11.
India, foreign policy, 3 October 1958-21 September 1962.

Box 247.

File 9126-C-40.
India-Syria relations, 26 February 1957.

File 9126-D-40.
India-Saudi Arabia relations, 19 December 1955-26 February 1957.

Box 249.

File 9161-40, volume 4 FP.
Compensation for loss of property interests in Japan and Japanese occupied territories in the Far East, procedures re placing claims, 5 January 1956-19 December 1957.

File 9161-40, volume 5.
Compensation for loss of property interests in Japan and Japanese occupied territories in the Far East, procedures re placing claims, 6 January 1958-30 October 1962.

File 9161-B-1-40.
Claim of Des Révérends Sœurs du Précieux Sang concerning Sino-Japanese conflict, 8 March 1956-14 February 1961.

File 9161-GM-40.
Claim of R.M.Andrews to property in Japan, 15 September 1958-30 November 1959.

Box 251.

File 9193-40, volume 8-FP.
Political situation in India, constitutional position in India, 3 October 1955-19 December 1956.

File 9193-40, volume 9.
Political situation in India, constitutional position in India, 31 December 1956-13 December 1959.

File 9193-40, volume 10.
Political situation in India, constitutional position in India, 9 January 1958-23 December 1958.

File 9193-40, volume 11.
Political situation in India, constitutional position in India, 28 November 1959-27 March 1962.

Box 252.

File 9193-R-40, volume 3.
India -economic situation, reports, 3 October 1955-29 November 1957.

File 9193-R-40, volume 4.
India -economic situation, reports, 22 January 1958-31 August 1960.

File 9193-U-40, volume 2.
India -agriculture, food situation, 17 January 1958-26 July 1963.

File 9193-Z-40.
India -North Eastern and Eastern Frontiers, including protectorate states, 8 August 1955-2 December 1962.

File 9193-AB-40.
India -proposed acquisition by Simcoe, North Ontario, of Queen Victoria statue from Lucknow, India, 11 September 1957-12 November 1957.

Box 258.

File 9310-40, volume 2.
Economic situation in Siam, general file, 2 January 1959-18 September 1963.

File 9323-B-14-40.
Canadian consular matters in Burma, 14 August 1958-25 May 1959.

File 9323-B-16-40.
Canadian consular matters in Iran, 13 February 1959-6 December 1960.

Box 261.

File 9340-40, volume 2.
Soviet Union-India relations, general, 5 May 1955-19 February 1960.

File 9340-A-40.
Soviet Union-India relations, Bulganin-Khrushev visit to India, 18 November 1955-8 December 1962.

File 9371-40, volume 4.
Commercial relations between Canada and Turkey, general file, 8 January-30 September 1958.

File 9371-40, volume 5.
Commercial relations between Canada and Turkey, general file, 1 October 1958-7 October 1963.

Box 263.

File 9402-A-40, volume 2.
Iran -economic and financial conditions in, 11 February 1958-30 November 1960.

File 9402-B-40, volume 2.
Iran-Canada, diplomatic relations, 21 January 1958-28 October 1959.

File 9402-B-40, volume 3.
Iran-Canada, diplomatic relations, 13 November 1959-20 February 1962.

File 9423-F-40.
Inter-regional trade and coordinated economic planning, Bandung or Asian powers, 27 March 1958-30 July 1962.

File 9423-G-40.
Coordination of information, activities in South East Asia, 28 August 1958-20 June 1962.

File 9544-40, volume 2.
India -protection of interests of Canadian life insurance companies operating in India, appointment of representatives re, 14 January 1955-8 June 1960.

Box 279.

File 9557-B-40, volume 2.
Establishment of courier service to Indo-China and other posts en route, 1 November 1955-23 May 1963.

Box 283.

File 9678-40, volume 2.
Canada-Pakistan relations, 13 January 1959-28 April 1961.

Box 286.

File 9803-22-40.
Canada-Pakistan Double Taxation agreement, 16 September 1959-25 June 1963.

Box 287.

File 9820-40, volume 4.
Overseas Chinese, activities, organization, 9 September 1958-15 January 1963.

File 9821-A-40.
Canada-Burma relations, 19 May 1955-23 December 1959.

Box 288.

File 9848-40, volume 3.
Relations between Afghanistan and Pakistan(the Pushtoonistan dispute) Afghanistan relations with Pakistan, 16 November 1955-9 June 1960.

File 9890-40, volume 2.
Policy on entry of Japanese nationals into Canada, general file, 9 December 1955-30 May 1961.

File 9891-40, volume 2.
Conditions in Afghanistan, 26 September 1957-21 December 1959.

File 9891-40, volume 3.
Conditions in Afghanistan, 29 December 1959-24 May 1963.

File 9899-AQ-40.
Education in Malaya, 23 March 1959-15 October 1962.

File 9899-CA-40.
Education in Indo-China, 13 November 1957-2 April 1958.

File 9899-CB-40.
Education in Ceylon, 2 June 1955-24 October 1961.

File 9899-CH-40.
Education in Indonesia, 31 July 1956-23 August 1962.

Box 291.

File 9963-40, FPS.
Economic situation in Korea.

File 9965-B-40.
Visit to Canada of Prime Minister of Ceylon, S.W.R.D. Bandaranaike, 6 July 1956-6 February 1957.

Box 300.

File 10168-40, volume 2 FP.
Financial and economic situation in Burma, 10 November 1955-18 January 1960.

Accession 86-87/414.

Box 305.

File 10218-40, volume 4.
Economic conditions and development in the Philippines, 28 July 1956-27 May 1963.

File 10218-40, volume 5-FP.
Economic conditions and development in the Philippines, 5 July 1959-23 October 1962.

Box 309.

File 10301-K-40.
Canadian High Commissioner at Kuala Lumpur, 30 December 1958-18 June 1963.

File 10304-C-40.
The Kingdom of Nepal-Canada relations, 2 June 1956-9 August 1963.

File 10304-D-40.
The Kingdom of Nepal-Japan relations, 12 September 1956-20 March 1962.

Box 310.

File 10348-C-40.
Reporting from Djakarta, 31 March 1958-17 July 1963.

File 10348-D-40.
Reporting from Manila, 11 April 1958-3 December 1962.

File 10348-E-40.
Reporting from Singapore, 11 April 1958-3 December 1962.

Box 312.

File 10389-40, volume 8.
Japan-Canada, proposals re most favoured national treatment for Japan, 7 January-12 December 1957.

File 10389-40, volume 9.
Japan-Canada, proposals re most favoured national treatment for Japan, 13 January-29 August 1958.

File 10389-40, volume 10.
Japan-Canada, proposals re most favoured national treatment for Japan, 2 September 1958-11 March 1959.

File 10389-40, volume 11.
Japan-Canada, proposals re most favoured national treatment for Japan, 6 May-20 July 1959.

File 10389-40, volume 12-FP.
Japan-Canada, proposals re most favoured national treatment for Japan, 21 July-31 December 1959.

Box 313.

File 10394-40, volume 2.
Turkey, economic and financial situation, 15 January 1955-17 April 1956.

File 10394-40, volume 3.
Turkey, economic and financial situation, 10 July 1956-29 August 1958.

File 10394-40, volume 4.
Turkey, economic and financial situation, 21 July 1958-13 December 1959.

Box 321.

File 10463-BL-40.
Political review, annual review of political and other events in Korea by Canadian mission in Austria, 10 January 1955-8 January 1960.

File 10463-BU-40.
Political review, annual review of political and other events in Malaya by Canadian mission in Austria, 19 February-5 March 1959.

Box 322.

File 10483-40, volume 3.
India-Pakistan relations, general file, 1 April 1958-28 February 1959.

File 10483-40, volume 4.
India-Pakistan relations, general file, 4 March-28 December 1959.

Box 334.

File 10600-N-40.
Law of the sea, territorial waters and fishing zones, position on and/or claims relating thereto, consultations for international conferences, Cambodia, Burma, Thailand, Vietnam, 16 May 1958-6 July 1961.

File 10600-AK-40.
Law of the sea, territorial waters and fishing zones, position on and/or claims relating thereto, consultations for international conferences, Indonesia, Philippines, 17 December 1957-18 March 1963.

Box 335.

File 10600-AJ-40.
Law of the sea, territorial waters and fishing zones, position on and/or claims relating thereto, consultations for international conferences, Afghanistan, 4 May 1959-8 November 1960.

File 10600-AO-40.
Law of the sea, territorial waters and fishing zones, position on and/or claims relating thereto, consultations for international conferences, China(communist), 4 September 1958-2 February 1961.

File 10600-AM-40.
Law of the sea, territorial waters and fishing zones, position on and/or claims relating thereto, consultations for international conferences, Iran, 7 July 1958-29 June 1962.

File 10600-B-40.
Law of the sea, territorial waters and fishing zones, position on and/or claims relating thereto, consultations for international conferences, Ceylon, 14 April 1958-26 October 1961.

File 10600-BE-40.
Law of the sea, territorial waters and fishing zones, position on and/or claims relating thereto, consultations for international conferences, Malaya, 24 March 1958-20 June 1963.

Box 336.

File 10600-BR-40.
Law of the sea, territorial waters and fishing zones, position on and/or claims relating thereto, consultations for international conferences, Korea, 20 February 1958-3 February 1961.

File 10615-B-40, volume 2.
China -Canadians visiting Communist China, demands by Chinese Communists authorities for ransom payments, 21 January 1958-29 April 1959.

File 10615-B-40, volume 3.
China -Canadians visiting Communist China, demands by February, Communists authorities for ransom payments, 22 May 1959-21 December 1961.

Box 344.

File 10828-C-40.
Pakistan-Saudi Arabia relations, 8 August 1956-26 January 1960.

File 10828-D-40.
Pakistan-Sudan relations, 26 October 1956-26 January 1960.

File 10828-E-40.
Pakistan-Hungary relations, 31 July 1956.

File 10828-F-40.
Pakistan-Syria relations, 21 January-15 October 1957.

File 10829-40, volume 4.
Ceylon, reports and general correspondence re, 12 October 1955-13 July 1956.

File 10829-40, volume 5.
Ceylon, reports and general correspondence re, 19 July 1956-17 April 1963.

File 10829-A-40.
Ceylon, armed forces, reports re, 21 February 1955-30 April 1962.

File 10832-40, volume 3.
Indonesia, economic situation in, 4 July 1956-20 December 1957.

File 10832-40, volume 4-FP.
Indonesia, economic situation in, 16 December 1957-31 December 1959.

Box 349.

File 11003-40, volume 2.
Postwar position of Singapore, 2 September 1955-28 August 1956.

File 11003-40, volume 3.
Postwar position of Singapore, 4 September 1956-28 September 1956.

File 11003-40, volume 4.
Postwar position of Singapore, 8 October-18 December 1957.

File 11003-A-40, volume 1-FP.
Economic situation in Singapore, 12 November 1959-

22 September 1962.

Box 350.

File 11038-40, volume 19-FP.
Commonwealth programme for economic assistance to South East Asia, 2 May-8 December 1955.

File 11038-40, volume 20.
Commonwealth programme for economic assistance to South East Asia, 28 December 1955-28 September 1956.

Box 351.

File 11038-40, volume 21-FP.
Colombo Plan, capital assistance, 27 September 1956-27 May 1957.

File 11038-40, volume 22.
Colombo Plan, capital assistance, 10 June 1957-25 March 1958.

File 11038-40, volume 23.
Colombo Plan, capital assistance, 25 March-25 September 1958.

File 11038-40, volume 24.
Colombo Plan, capital assistance, 3 October 1958-15 March 1959.

File 11038-40, volume 25.
Colombo Plan, capital assistance, 16 March-30 June 1959.

File 11038-40, volume 26-FP.
Colombo Plan, capital assistance, 2 July-30 December 1959.

File 11038-1-40, volume 7.
Colombo Plan, India, capital assistance, general file, 4 January-31 May 1955.

File 11038-1-40, volume 8.
Colombo Plan, India, capital assistance, general file, 2 May 1955-31 July 1956.

Box 352.

File 11038-1-40, volume 9.
Colombo Plan, India, capital assistance, general file, 16 August 1956-25 July 1957.

File 11038-1-40, volume 10.
Colombo Plan, India, capital assistance, general file, 27 August 1957-23 December 1958.

File 11038-1-40, volume 11.
Colombo Plan, India, capital assistance, general file, 4 September 1958-31 July 1959.

File 11038-1-40, volume 12.
Colombo Plan, India, capital assistance, general file, 1 August 1959-30 June 1960.

File 11038-1-1A-40, volume 2.
Colombo Plan, India, commodities, wheat, 3 January 1958-23 April 1960.

File 11038-1-2C-40.
Colombo Plan, India, capital assistance, rural and small town electrification, 31 January 1955-30 December 1959.

File 11038-1-2D-40.
Colombo Plan, India, capital assistance, Kunday hydro-electric project, 12 October 1955-30 November 1956.

File 11038-1-2D-40, volume 2-FP.
Colombo Plan, India, capital assistance, Kunday hydro-electric project, 17 December 1956-6 December 1960.

Box 353.

File 11038-1-8-40.
Colombo Plan, India, capital assistance, aid, India aerial magnetic survey, 16 September 1955-31 July 1956.

File 11038-1-8-40, volume 2.
Colombo Plan, India, capital assistance, aid, India aerial magnetic survey, 2 August 1956-2 January 1960.

File 11038-1-9-40.
Possible Canadian aid under Colombo Plan for Indian oil exploration, 18 July 1956-2 January 1960.

File 11038-1-13-40.
Colombo Plan, India, capital assistance, provision of an atomic reactor by Canada, 15 March-14 October 1955.

File 11038-1-13-40.
Colombo Plan, India, capital assistance, provision of an atomic reactor by Canada, 15 October 1955-31 January 1956.

File 11038-1-13-40.
Colombo Plan, India, capital assistance, provision of an atomic reactor by Canada, 30 January-30 April 1956.

File 11038-1-13-40.
Colombo Plan, India, capital assistance, provision of an atomic reactor by Canada, 2 May 1956-31 January 1958.

File 11038-1-13-40, volume 5.
Colombo Plan, India, capital assistance, provision of an atomic reactor by Canada, 2 February 1958-28 November 1959.

File 11038-1-13-40, volume 6.
Colombo Plan, India, capital assistance, provision of an atomic reactor by Canada, 2 December 1959-2 December 1960.

Box 354.

File 11038-1-14-40.
India, Calcutta milk scheme, 29 March 1956-3 August 1960.

File 11038-1-16-40.
Colombo Plan, India, capital assistance, Upper Sileru project, 16 June 1959-19 July 1960.

File 11038-1-17-40.
Colombo Plan, India, capital assistance, Chambel Valley development scheme(Rana Pratap sugar and Kotah dam sites), 23 May 1959-9 December 1960.

File 11038-1-18-40.
Colombo Plan, India, capital assistance, Bhimkund project, 22 May 1959-27 June 1960.

File 11038-2-40, volume 9-FP.
Colombo Plan, Pakistan, capital assistance, 28 April 1955-30 November 1956.

File 11038-2-40, volume 10-FP.
Colombo Plan, Pakistan, capital assistance, 3 December-28 April 1958.

File 11038-2-40, volume 11.
Colombo Plan, Pakistan, capital assistance, 6 June-22 December 1958.

File 11038-2-40, volume 12.
Colombo Plan, Pakistan, capital assistance, 2 January-29 December 1959.

File 11038-2-1-40, volume 2.
Colombo Plan, Pakistan, capital assistance, provision of industrial raw materials, 22 September 1958-4 November 1960.

Box 355.

File 11038-2-1A-40, volume 2.
Colombo Plan, Pakistan, capital assistance, wheat, 1 September 1956-31 December 1958.

File 11038-2-1A-40, volume 3.
Colombo Plan, Pakistan, capital assistance, wheat, 2 January 1959-24 November 1960.

File 11038-2-1A-40, volume 3.
Colombo Plan, Pakistan, capital assistance, wheat, 2 January 1959-24 November 1960.

File 11038-2-2A-40, volume 3.
Colombo Plan, Pakistan, capital assistance, wheat, 1 June 1955-25 June 1958.

File 11038-2-2A-40, volume 4-FP.
Colombo Plan, Pakistan, capital assistance, wheat, 7 July 1958-3 February 1960.

File 11038-2-2B-40, volume 3.
Colombo Plan, Pakistan, capital assistance, Warsak project, 8 June-24 November 1955.

File 11038-2-2B-40, volume 4.
Colombo Plan, Pakistan, capital assistance, Warsak project, 28 November 1955-31 May 1956.

File 11038-2-2B-40, volume 5.
Colombo Plan, Pakistan, capital assistance, Warsak project, 1 June-26 July 1956.

File 11038-2-2B-40, volume 6.
Colombo Plan, Pakistan, capital assistance, Warsak project, 9 August-21 December 1956.

Box 356.

File 11038-2-2B-40, volume 7.
Colombo Plan, Pakistan, capital assistance, Warsak project, 2 January-28 June 1957.

File 11038-2-2B-40, volume 8-FP.
Colombo Plan, Pakistan, capital assistance, Warsak project, 3 July 1957-26 February 1958.

File 11038-2-2B-40, volume 9.
Colombo Plan, Pakistan, capital assistance, Warsak project, 4 March-12 December 1958.

File 11038-2-2B-40, volume 10.
Colombo Plan, Pakistan, capital assistance, Warsak project, 2 February 1959-23 March 1960.

Box 357.

File 11038-2-2E-40, volume 3.
Colombo Plan, Pakistan, capital assistance, Punjab Tubewell(Canal Hydel) (Shadiwell), 7 January 1957-18 September 1959.

File 11038-2-2E-40, volume 4-FP.
Colombo Plan, Pakistan, capital assistance, Punjab Tubewell(Canal Hydel) (Shadiwell), 5 October 1959-7 November 1960.

Box 358.

File 11038-2-2F-40.
Colombo Plan, Pakistan, capital assistance, Khulna Steam Thermal project, 29 April 1955-25 October 1960.

File 11038-2-3-40, volume 2.
Colombo Plan, Pakistan, capital assistance, Dacca-Chittagong link and electrical distribution scheme in East Bengal, 22 March 1957-25 October 1960.

File 11038-2-4-40, volume 4.
Colombo Plan, Pakistan, capital assistance, Thal cement plant, 2 October 1956-7 October 1960.

File 11038-2-5-40, volume 3.
Colombo Plan, Pakistan, capital assistance, Thal livestock farm, 3 January 1956-22 December 1958.

File 11038-2-8-40, volume 3.
Colombo Plan, Pakistan capital assistance, aerial resources survey, 7 August 1956-10 November 1960.

File 11038-2-12-40.
Pakistan milk survey, 24 September 1956-21 July 1959.

File 11038-2-13-40.
Colombo Plan, Pakistan, capital assistance, Atomic Energy programme, 3 July 1956-2 May 1960.

File 11038-2-15-40.
Colombo Plan, Pakistan, capital assistance, Warsak transmission line, 25 April 1958- 28 July 1960.

File 11038-2-16-40.
Colombo Plan, Pakistan, capital assistance, Chittagong transmission line, Kharmaphuli, 5 April 1958-14 July 1960.

File 11038-2-17-40.
Colombo Plan, Pakistan, capital assistance, Sukkur Thermal Power project, 30 October 1958-7 December 1960.

Box 359.

File 11038-2-18-40, volume 1-FP.
Colombo Plan, Pakistan, capital assistance, pre-stressed concrete products factory, 19 December 1958-24 November 1960.

File 11038-3-40, volume 5.
Colombo Plan, Ceylon, capital assistance, general file, 26 June 1955-30 November 1956.

File 11038-3-40, volume 6.
Colombo Plan, Ceylon, capital assistance, general file, 3 December 1956-30 September 1957.

File 11038-3-40, volume 7.
Colombo Plan, Ceylon, capital assistance, general file, 1 October 1957-25 November 1958.

File 11038-3-40, volume 8.
Colombo Plan, Ceylon, capital assistance, general file, 3 December 1958- 28 April 1960.

File 11038-3-1-40, volume 2.
Colombo Plan, Ceylon, capital assistance, commodities(flour), 8 January 1958-23 November 1960.

File 11038-3-3-40, volume 2.
Colombo Plan, Ceylon, capital assistance, Gal Oya project, 18 July 1957-24 November 1959.

Box 360.

File 11038-3-7-40, volume 6.
Colombo Plan, Ceylon, capital assistance, fisheries project, 4 January-31 March 1955.

File 11038-3-7-40, volume 7.
Colombo Plan, Ceylon, capital assistance, fisheries project, 1 April-30 June 1955.

File 11038-3-7-40, volume 8.
Colombo Plan, Ceylon, capital assistance, fisheries project, 5 July-30 November 1955.

File 11038-3-7-40, volume 9.
Colombo Plan, Ceylon, capital assistance, fisheries project, 1 December 1955-15 February 1956.

File 11038-3-7-40, volume 10.
Colombo Plan, Ceylon, capital assistance, fisheries project, 16 February-31 July 1956.

File 11038-3-7-40, volume 11.
Colombo Plan, Ceylon, capital assistance, fisheries project, 2 August 1956-1 May 1957.

File 11038-3-7-40, volume 12-FP-1.
Colombo Plan, Ceylon, capital assistance, fisheries project, 7 January-25 November 1958.

File 11038-3-7-40, volume 13.
Colombo Plan, Ceylon, capital assistance, fisheries project, 7 January-25 November 1958.

File 11038-3-7-40, volume 14-FP.
Colombo Plan, Ceylon, capital assistance, fisheries project, 3 December 1958-6 December 1960.

Box 361.

File 11038-3-8-40, volume 2.
Colombo Plan, Ceylon, capital assistance, photographic survey, 27 December 1955-28 May 1958.

File 11038-3-8-40, volume 3.
Colombo Plan, Ceylon, capital assistance, photographic survey, 5 June 1958-11 December 1959.

File 11038-3-15-40.
Colombo Plan, Ceylon, capital assistance, cranes for Colombo Harbour, 20 January 1956-4 May 1959.

File 11038-3-16-40.
Colombo Plan, Ceylon, capital assistance, counterpart funds, 2 February 1956-10 May 1960.

File 11038-3-17-40, volume 1-FP.
Colombo Plan, Ceylon, capital assistance, request for financial and economic aid, 20 May 1958-10 February 1960.

File 11038-4-40, volume 2.
Colombo Plan, Indonesia, capital assistance, 23 January 1958-27 February 1959.

File 11038-4-40, volume 3.
Colombo Plan, Indonesia, capital assistance, 2 March 1959-2 December 1960.

Box 362.

File 11038-5-A-40, volume 2.
Colombo Plan, meeting of the consultative committee, 1955, Singapore, 1 September-16 November 1955.

File 11038-5-A-40, volume 3-FP.
Colombo Plan, meeting of the consultative committee, 1955, Singapore, 23 September 1955-4 January 1956.

File 11038-5-B-40.
Colombo Plan, meeting of the consultative committee, 1956, Wellington, 21 March-30 November 1956.

File 11038-5-B-40, volume 2-FP.
Colombo Plan, meeting of the consultative committee, 1956, Wellington, 8 December 1956-5 September 1957.

Box 363.

File 11038-5-D-40.
Colombo Plan, meeting of the consultative committee, 1957, Saigon, 30 November 1956-30 August 1957.

File 11038-5-C-40, volume 2-FP.
Colombo Plan, meeting of the consultative committee, 1957, Saigon, 2 September 1957-15 April 1959.

File 11038-5-C-1-40.
Colombo Plan, meeting of the consultative committee, 1957, Saigon, accommodation and travel arrangements, 4 September 1957-13 May 1958.

File 11038-5-C-2-40.
Colombo Plan, meeting of the consultative committee, 1957, Saigon, trip of the Hon. W.J.Brown, 12 September-21 November 1957.

File 11038-5-C-2-40, volume 2.
Colombo Plan, meeting of the consultative committee, 1957, Saigon, trip of the Hon. W.J.Brown, 22 November-20 December 1957.

Box 364.

File 11038-5-F-40, volume 2-FP.
Colombo Plan, meeting of the consultative committee, 1958, Seattle, 1 November 1958-28 October 1959.

Box 365.

File 11038-8-40.
Colombo Plan, capital assistance, Singapore, 22 October 1955-19 September 1960.

File 11038-9-40.
Colombo Plan, capital assistance, Philippines, 24 May 1957-24 April 1959.

File 11038-9-40, volume 2.
Colombo Plan, capital assistance, Philippines, 21 May 1958-28 August 1959.

File 11038-9-40, volume 3.
Colombo Plan, capital assistance, Philippines, 2 September 1959-23 November 1960.

File 11038-10-40.
Colombo Plan, capital assistance, Burma, 3 January-29 December 1956.

File 11038-10-40, volume 2.
Colombo Plan, capital assistance, Burma, 2 January-30 December 1957.

Box 366.

File 11038-10-40, volume 3.
Colombo Plan, capital assistance, Burma, 2 January-30 June 1958.

File 11038-10-40, volume 4.
Colombo Plan, capital assistance, Burma, 3 July 1958-26 March 1959.

File 11038-10-40, volume 5.
Colombo Plan, capital assistance, Burma, 7 April-24 December 1959.

File 11038-11-40.
Colombo Plan, capital assistance, Mekong River Project, 23 July 1957-18 June 1958.

File 11038-11-40, volume 2.
Colombo Plan, capital assistance, Mekong River Project, 5 July 1958-13 March 1959.

File 11038-11-40, volume 3.
Colombo Plan, capital assistance, Mekong River Project, 17 March-30 June 1959.

File 11038-11-40, volume 4.
Colombo Plan, capital assistance, Mekong River Project, 2 July-30 September 1959.

File 11038-11-40, volume 5.
Colombo Plan, capital assistance, Mekong River Project, 6 October-30 December 1959.

File 11038-12-40.
Colombo Plan, capital assistance, Cambodia, 1 April 1955-30 December 1959.

Box 367.

File 11038-12-A-40.
Colombo Plan, capital assistance, Laos, 27 January

1956-1 December 1960.

File 11038-12-B-40.
Colombo Plan, capital assistance, Vietnam, 22 October 1956-31 July 1958.

File 11038-12-B-40, volume 2.
Colombo Plan, capital assistance, Vietnam, 21 May-28 November 1958.

File 11038-12-B-40, volume 3.
Colombo Plan, capital assistance, Vietnam, 12 November 1958-24 October 1960.

File 11038-13-B-40.
Colombo Plan, capital assistance, North Borneo, Sarawak, Brunei, 14 November 1956-26 May 1960.

File 11038-14-B-40.
Colombo Plan, capital assistance, Malaya, 23 April 1957-19 March 1959.

File 11038-14-B-40, volume 2.
Colombo Plan, capital assistance, Malaya, 3 April-28 August 1959.

File 11038-14-B-40, volume 3-FP.
Colombo Plan, capital assistance, Malaya, 1 September 1959-25 January 1960.

File 11038-14-1-40.
Colombo Plan, capital assistance, Malaya, aerial survey, 15 November 1956-1 December 1959.

Box 368.

File 11038-14-2-40.
Colombo Plan, capital assistance, Malaya, fisheries project, 2 August 1957-4 November 1960.

File 11038-14-3-40.
Colombo Plan, capital assistance, Malaya, Wheat and Foodstuff programme, 5 March 1959-30 November 1960.

File 11038-14-4-40.
Colombo Plan, capital assistance, Malaya, hydro-electric survey, 19 December 1956-23 November 1960.

File 11038-15-40.
Proposed establishment of a Canada Colombo Plan office in Saigon, 18 September 1957-26 May 1960.

File 11038-16-40.
Colombo Plan, presentation of books to medical libraries in South and South East Asia, 10 July 1958-26 May 1959.

File 11038-16-40, volume 2.
Colombo Plan, presentation of books to medical libraries in South and South East Asia, 9 June 1959-27 July 1960.

File 11038-A-40, volume 6.
Colombo Plan, council for cooperation Commonwealth technical assistance scheme for technical cooperation in South and South East Asia, general file, 8 January-28 July 1955.

File 11038-A-40, volume 7-FP.
Colombo Plan, council for cooperation Commonwealth technical assistance scheme for technical cooperation in South and South East Asia, general file, 17 May 1955-27 September 1956.

File 11038-A-40, volume 8-FP.
Colombo Plan, council for cooperation Commonwealth technical assistance scheme for technical cooperation in South and South East Asia, general file, 1 October 1956-6 December 1960.

Box 369.

File 11038-A-1-40, volume 11.
Colombo Plan, capital assistance, Ceylon, technical cooperation in South and South East Asia, 5 March-15 June 1955.

File 11038-A-1-40, volume 12.
Colombo Plan, capital assistance, Ceylon, technical cooperation in South and South East Asia, 16 June-14 October 1955.

File 11038-A-1-40, volume 13.
Colombo Plan, capital assistance, Ceylon, technical cooperation in South and South East Asia, 17 October 1955-23 January 1956.

File 11038-A-1-40, volume 14.
Colombo Plan, capital assistance, Ceylon, technical cooperation in South and South East Asia, 24 January-30 April 1956.

File 11038-A-1-40, volume 15.
Colombo Plan, capital assistance, Ceylon, technical cooperation in South and South East Asia, 2 May-28 September 1956.

File 11038-A-1-40, volume 16.
Colombo Plan, capital assistance, Ceylon, technical cooperation in South and South East Asia, 1 October 1956-27 February 1957.

File 11038-A-1-40, volume 17.
Colombo Plan, capital assistance, Ceylon, technical cooperation in South and South East Asia, experts and equipment, 1 March-29 August 1957.

File 11038-A-1-40, volume 18-FP.
Colombo Plan, capital assistance, Ceylon, technical cooperation in South and South East Asia, experts and equipment, 3 September 1957-28 May 1958.

Box 370.

File 11038-A-1-40, volume 19.
Colombo Plan, capital assistance, Ceylon, technical cooperation in South and South East Asia, experts and equipment, 4 June 1958-28 January 1960.

File 11038-A-2-40, volume 7.
Colombo Plan, Council for Technical Cooperation in South and South East Asia, India, 3 January 1956-27 June 1957.

File 11038-A-2-40, volume 8.
Colombo Plan, Council for Technical Cooperation in South and South East Asia, India, 12 July 1957-30 June 1958.

File 11038-A-2-40, volume 9.
Colombo Plan, Council for Technical Cooperation in South and South East Asia, India, 3 July 1958-30 June 1959.

File 11038-A-2-40, volume 10.
Colombo Plan, Council for Technical Cooperation in South and South East Asia, India, 6 July 1959-5 December 1960.

File 11038-A-2-G-40, volume 3.
Colombo Plan, capital assistance, India and Pakistan, biological control laboratory, 12 April 1958-19 October 1960.

File 11038-A-2-AS-40.
Colombo Plan, capital assistance, India, Canadian Medical mission, 7 July 1955-8 October 1957.

File 11038-A-2-AS-40, volume 2-FP.
Colombo Plan, capital assistance, India, Canadian Medical mission, 1 March 1957-20 November 1958.

Box 371.

File 11038-A-3-40, volume 4.
Colombo Plan, capital assistance, Malaya, hydro-electric survey, 19 December 1956-23 November 1960.

File 11038-15-40.
Proposed establishment of a Canada Colombo Plan office in Saigon, 18 September 1957-26 May 1960.

File 11038-16-40.
Colombo Plan, capital assistance, Pakistan, technical cooperation in South and South East Asia, 1 June 1955-14 December 1956.

File 11038-A-3-40, volume 6.
Colombo Plan, capital assistance, Pakistan, technical cooperation in South and South East Asia, 1 January 1957-27 October 1959.

File 11038-A-3-40, volume 7.
Colombo Plan, capital assistance, Pakistan, technical cooperation in South and South East Asia, 2 November 1959-7 December 1960.

File 11038-A-4-40.
Colombo Plan, capital assistance, Burma, experts in general, 2 January-30 April 1956.

File 11038-A-4-40, volume 2.
Colombo Plan, capital assistance, Burma, experts in general, 2 May-31 October 1956.

File 11038-A-4-40, volume 3.
Colombo Plan, capital assistance, Burma, experts in general, 3 November 1956-26 September 1957.

File 11038-A-4-40, volume 4.
Colombo Plan, capital assistance, Burma, experts in general, 9 October 1957-28 August 1958.

File 11038-A-4-40, volume 5.
Colombo Plan, capital assistance, Burma, experts in general, 1 September 1958-30 May 1959.

File 11038-A-4-40, volume 6.
Colombo Plan, capital assistance, Burma, experts in general, 1 June 1959-25 November 1960.

Box 372.

File 11038-C-40, volume 3.
Colombo Plan, appointments to Technical Cooperation Bureau, general file, 9 September 1955-30 April 1956.

File 11038-C-40, volume 4.
Colombo Plan, appointments to Technical Cooperation Bureau, general file, 1 May 1956-28 September 1960.

File 11038-F-40, volume 3.
Colombo Plan, offer by Canada of fellowships and scholarships to countries in South and South East Asia, 1 February-26 April 1956.

File 11038-F-40, volume 4-FP.
Colombo Plan, offer by Canada of fellowships and scholarships to countries in South and South East Asia, 1 May 1956-26 February 1957.

File 11038-F-40, volume 5-FP.
Colombo Plan, offer by Canada of fellowships and scholarships to countries in South and South East Asia, 5 March-31 December 1957.

File 11038-F-40, volume 6.
Colombo Plan, offer by Canada of fellowships and scholarships to countries in South and South East Asia, 7 January 1958- 30 June 1959.

File 11038-F-40, volume 7.
Colombo Plan, offer by Canada of fellowships and scholarships to countries in South and South East Asia, 2 July 1959-22 November 1960.

Box 373.

File 11038-F-1-40, volume 2.
Colombo Plan, offers by Canada of fellowships and scholarships to Ceylon, 5 January-30 June 1955.

File 11038-F-1-40, volume 3.
Colombo Plan, offers by Canada of fellowships and scholarships to Ceylon, 1 July-31 October 1955.

File 11038-F-1-40, volume 4.
Colombo Plan, offers by Canada of fellowships and scholarships to Ceylon, 1 November 1955-30 September 1956.

File 11038-F-1-40, volume 5.
Colombo Plan, offers by Canada of fellowships and scholarships to Ceylon, 1 October 1956-30 August 1957.

File 11038-F-1-40, volume 6.
Colombo Plan, offers by Canada of fellowships and scholarships to Ceylon, 1 September 1957-23 July 1958.

File 11038-F-1-40, volume 7.
Colombo Plan, offers by Canada of fellowships and scholarships to Ceylon, 6 August 1958-26 May 1960.

File 11038-F-2-40, volume 3.
Colombo Plan, offers by Canada of fellowships and scholarships to Ceylon, 1 February-30 April 1955.

File 11038-F-2-40, volume 4.
Colombo Plan, offers by Canada of fellowships and scholarships to Ceylon, 1 May-13 September 1955.

File 11038-F-2-40, volume 5.
Colombo Plan, scholarships and fellowships, India, 1 May-30 June 1958.

File 11038-F-2-40, volume 13.
Colombo Plan, scholarships and fellowships, India, 2 September-27 November 1958.

File 11038-F-2-40, volume 14.
Colombo Plan, scholarships and fellowships, India, 1 December-15 December 1958.

File 11038-F-2-40, volume 15.
Colombo Plan, scholarships and fellowships, India, 16 December-17 December 1958.

File 11038-F-2-40, volume 16.
Colombo Plan, scholarships and fellowships, India, 18 December 1958-30 January 1959.

File 11038-F-2-40, volume 17.
Colombo Plan, scholarships and fellowships, India, 2 February-31 March 1959.

File 11038-F-2-40, volume 18.
Colombo Plan, scholarships and fellowships, India, 1 April -30 April 1959.

File 11038-F-2-40, volume 19.
Colombo Plan, scholarships and fellowships, India, 1 May-31 May 1959.

File 11038-F-2-40, volume 20.
Colombo Plan, scholarships and fellowships, India, 1 June-15 July 1959.

File 11038-F-2-40, volume 21.
Colombo Plan, scholarships and fellowships, India, 16 July-30 October 1959.

Box 376.

File 11038-F-3-40, volume 2.
Colombo Plan, technical assistance - Pakistan - general correspondence concerning fellowships and scholarships to Pakistan under the Colombo Plan for Economic Development, February-October 1955.

File 11038-F-3-40, volume 3.
Colombo Plan, technical assistance - Pakistan - general correspondence concerning fellowships and scholarships to Pakistan under the Colombo Plan for Economic Development, November 1955-August 1956.

File 11038-F-3-40, volume 4.
Colombo Plan, technical assistance - Pakistan - general correspondence concerning fellowships and scholarships to Pakistan under the Colombo Plan for Economic Development, September 1956-May 1957.

File 11038-F-3-40, volume 5.
Colombo Plan, technical assistance - Pakistan - general correspondence concerning fellowships and scholarships to Pakistan under the Colombo Plan for Economic Development, June-December 1957.

File 11038-F-3-40, volume 6.
Colombo Plan, technical assistance - Pakistan - general correspondence concerning fellowships and scholarships to Pakistan under the Colombo Plan for Economic Development, December 1957-June 1958.

File 11038-F-3-40, volume 7.
Colombo Plan, technical assistance - Pakistan - general correspondence concerning fellowships and scholarships to Pakistan under the Colombo Plan for Economic Development, July-September 1958.

File 11038-F-3-40, volume 8.
Colombo Plan, technical assistance - Pakistan - general correspondence concerning fellowships and scholarships to Pakistan under the Colombo Plan for Economic Development, October-December 1958.

File 11038-F-3-40, volume 9.
Colombo Plan, technical assistance - Pakistan - general correspondence concerning fellowships and scholarships to Pakistan under the Colombo Plan for Economic Development, January-April 1959.

File 11038-F-3-40, volume 10.
Colombo Plan, technical assistance - Pakistan - general correspondence concerning fellowships and scholarships to Pakistan under the Colombo Plan for Economic Development, April-September 1959.

File 11038-F-3-40, volume 11.
Colombo Plan, technical assistance - Pakistan - general correspondence concerning fellowships and scholarships to Pakistan under the Colombo Plan for Economic Development, October-December 1959.

Box 377.

File 11038-F-6-40.
Colombo Plan, offers of technical assistance from Asian countries, 24 December 1957-20 November 1959.

File 11038-F-7-40.
Colombo Plan, technical assistance, AF, trainees, 5 October 1955-31 July 1956.

File 11038-F-7-40, volume 2.
Colombo Plan, technical assistance, Burma, trainees, 2 August-28 December 1956.

File 11038-F-7-40, volume 3.
Colombo Plan, technical assistance, Burma, trainees, 3 March-30 July 1957.

File 11038-F-7-40, volume 4.
Colombo Plan, technical assistance, Burma, trainees, 1 August-30 December 1957.

File 11038-F-7-40, volume 5.
Colombo Plan, technical assistance, Burma, trainees, 2 January-30 June 1958.

File 11038-F-7-40, volume 6.
Colombo Plan, technical assistance, Burma, trainees, 2 July-31 December 1958.

File 11038-F-7-40, volume 7.
Colombo Plan, technical assistance, Burma, trainees, 6 January-31 July 1959.

File 11038-F-7-40, volume 8.
Colombo Plan, technical assistance, Burma, trainees, 4 August 1959-31 August 1960.

File 11038-G-40, volume 5.
Colombo Plan, technical cooperation assistance in South East Asia, agenda and minutes, 5 July 1955-27 June 1956.

File 11038-G-40, volume 6.
Colombo Plan, technical cooperation assistance in South East Asia, agenda and minutes, 7 July 1956-15 July 1957.

Box 378.

File 11038-G-40, volume 7-FP.
Colombo Plan, technical cooperation assistance in South East Asia, agenda and minutes, 16 July 1957-30 June 1958.

File 11038-G-40, volume 8.
Colombo Plan, technical cooperation assistance in South East Asia, agenda and minutes, 2 July-29 August 1958.

File 11038-G-40, volume 9-FP.
Colombo Plan, technical cooperation assistance in South East Asia, agenda and minutes, 5 September-31 December 1958.

File 11038-G-40, volume 10.
Colombo Plan, technical cooperation assistance in South East Asia, agenda and minutes, 5 January-28 April 1959.

File 11038-G-40, volume 11.
Colombo Plan, technical cooperation assistance in South East Asia , agenda and minutes, 8 May-7 August 1959.

File 11038-G-40, volume 12.
Colombo Plan, technical cooperation assistance in, agenda and minutes, 1 September-30 December 1959.

Box 379.

File 11038-G-1-40, volume 5-FP.
Colombo Plan, technical cooperation assistance in South East Asia, reports, 17 January-22 November 1956.

File 11038-G-1-40, volume 6.
Colombo Plan, technical cooperation assistance in South East Asia, reports, 3 December 1956-6 December 1957.

File 11038-G-1-40, volume 7.
Colombo Plan, technical cooperation assistance in South East Asia, reports, 6 February 1958-3 August 1960.

File 11038-H-40, volume 3.
Colombo Plan, Council for Technical Cooperation in South and South East Asia, contribution and cost, 24 January-22 December 1955.

File 11038-H-40, volume 4.
Colombo Plan, Council for Technical Cooperation in South and South East Asia, contribution and cost, 21 December 1955-30 November 1956.

Box 380.

File 11038-H-40, volume 5-FP.
Colombo Plan, Council for Technical Cooperation in South and South East Asia, contribution and cost, 11 December 1956-27 May 1958.

File 11038-H-40, volume 6.
Colombo Plan, Council for Technical Cooperation in South and South East Asia, contribution and cost, 3 June 1958-15 November 1960.

File 11038-H-1-40.
Colombo Plan, financial and administration of bureau, 4 February 1955-31 August 1960.

Box 381.

File 11038-J-40, volume 3.
Colombo Plan exhibition, 1952, 4 January 1956-24 April 1959.

File 11038-K-40, volume 5-FP.
Colombo Plan, technical assistance, service reports, 1 February 1956-16 June 1960.

File 11038-S-40, volume 3.
Colombo Plan publicity, 21 December 1955-31 March 1956.

File 11038-S-40, volume 4.
Colombo Plan publicity, 4 April-27 July 1956.

File 11038-S-40, volume 5.
Colombo Plan publicity, 1 August-31 October 1956.

File 11038-S-40, volume 6-FP.
Colombo Plan publicity, 1 November 1956-31 January 1957.

Box 382.

File 11038-S-40, volume 7-FP.
Colombo Plan publicity, 1 February-17 March 1957.

File 11038-S-40, volume 8.
Colombo Plan publicity, 21 May-30 October 1957.

File 11038-S-40, volume 9.
Colombo Plan publicity, 6 December 1955-31 July 1958.

File 11038-S-40, volume 10.
Colombo Plan publicity, 29 August 1958-28 August 1959.

File 11038-S-40, volume 11-FP.
Colombo Plan publicity, 16 September 1959-21 December 1960.

File 11038-S-1-40.
Colombo Plan, trainees, publicity re, 23 December 1957-28 September 1958.

File 11038-S-1-40, volume 3.
Colombo Plan, trainees, publicity re, 5 October 1959-25 April 1960.

Box 383.

File 11038-S-2-40.
Colombo Plan, requests for information in, 23 October 1957-30 December 1960.

File 11038-S-3-40.
Colombo Plan, distribution of publications on(other than annual reports), 30 January 1957-28 October 1960.

File 11038-S-4-40.
Colombo Plan, publicity, articles and speeches, 15 January 1957-28 July 1961.

File 11038-S-6-40.
Colombo Plan, information officers' conference, 18 November 1957-22 June 1959.

File 11038-S-6-40, volume 2-FP.
Colombo Plan, information officers' conference, 20 October 1959-29 September 1960.

File 11038-S-7-40.
Colombo Plan, films, 31 December 1957-20 December 1960.

File 11038-S-8-40.
Colombo Plan, photos, 21 November 1956-14 August 1963.

Box 384.

File 11038-S-9-40.
Colombo Plan, Interdepartmental Committee on External Aid, Committee on Information, 22 May 1959-7 November 1960.

File 11038-S-10-40.
Colombo Plan, anniversary celebrations, 28 May 1959-24 February 1961.

File 11038-V-40, volume 3.
Colombo Plan, enquiries by various persons, 4 January 1955-26 December 1957.

File 11038-V-40, volume 4.
Colombo Plan, enquiries by various persons, 3 January 1958-21 November 1960.

File 11038-Z-40, volume 2.
Colombo Plan, capital and technical assistance, publicity, general file, 8 September 1955-23 October 1959.

File 11038-Z-40, volume 3-FP.
Colombo Plan, capital and technical assistance, publicity, general file, 6 November 1959-24 July 1960.

File 11038-AB-2-40, volume 4.
Colombo Plan, technical assistance, requirements from Indonesia, experts and training facilities, 24 January-31 August 1955.

File 11038-AB-2-40, volume 5.
Colombo Plan, technical assistance, requirements from Indonesia, experts and training facilities, 1 September-29 November 1955.

File 11038-AB-2-40, volume 6.
Colombo Plan, technical assistance, requirements from Indonesia, experts and training facilities, 1 December-31 July 1956.

Box 385.

File 11038-AB-2-40, volume 7.
Colombo Plan, technical assistance, requirements from Indonesia, experts and training facilities, 1 August-31 December 1956.

File 11038-AB-2-40, volume 8.
Colombo Plan, technical assistance, requirements from Indonesia, experts and training facilities, 2 January-31 July 1957.

File 11038-AB-2-40, volume 9.
Colombo Plan, technical assistance, requirements from Indonesia, experts and training facilities, 31 July 1957-28 February 1958.

File 11038-AB-2-40, volume 10.
Colombo Plan, technical assistance, requirements from Indonesia, experts and training facilities, 13 February-31 March 1958.

File 11038-AB-2-40, volume 11.
Colombo Plan, technical assistance, requirements from Indonesia, experts and training facilities, 2 April-31 July 1958.

File 11038-AB-2-40, volume 12.
Colombo Plan, technical assistance, requirements from Indonesia, experts and training facilities, 5 August 1958-27 February 1959.

File 11038-AB-2-40, volume 13.
Colombo Plan, technical assistance, requirements from Indonesia, experts and training facilities, 2 March-15 April 1959.

File 11038-AB-2-40, volume 15.
Colombo Plan, technical assistance, requirements from Indonesia, experts and training facilities, 2 June-31 July 1959.

File 11038-AB-2-40, volume 16.
Colombo Plan, technical assistance, requirements from Indonesia, experts and training facilities, 4 August 1959-18 February 1960.

Box 386.

File 11038-AB-14-40, volume 3.
Colombo Plan, technical assistance programme, Burma, experts, trainees, equipment, 2 September-29 December 1955.

File 11038-AB-15-40, volume 2.
Colombo Plan, technical assistance programme, Thailand, general file, 12 January 1959-2 December 1960.

File 11038-AB-15-40, volume 10.
Colombo Plan, technical assistance programme, Malaya, 4 August-27 November 1959.

File 11038-AE-15-40, volume 11.
Colombo Plan, technical assistance programme, Malaya, 1 December 1959-31 May 1960.

File 110380-AB-17-B-40, volume 2.
Colombo Plan, technical assistance programme, United Kingdom colonies, North Borneo, 29 January 1957-29 January 1960.

File 11038-AD-40.
Colombo Plan, exhibits(photographs and displays), 31 January 1955-28 August 1959.

File 11038-AD-40, volume 2.
Colombo Plan, exhibits(photographs and displays), 3 September 1959-27 September 1961.

File 11038-AE-40.
U.S. Atomic Energy Research and Training Centre, 29 September 1955-29 June 1957.

Box 387.

File 11038-AE-40, volume 2-FP.
U.S. Asian Atomic Energy Research and Training Centre, 3 July 1957-4 May 1959.

File 11038-AF-40, volume 2.
Colombo Plan, technical assistance programme, Laos, 2 October 1956-13 February 1959.

File 11038-AG-40, volume 3.
Colombo Plan, technical assistance programme, 12 March 1959-11 October 1960.

File 11038-AG-40, volume 2.
Colombo Plan, technical assistance programme, Cambodia, 6 January-20 December 1955.

File 11038-AG-40, volume 3.
Colombo Plan, technical assistance programme, Cambodia, 28 December 1955-27 September 1956.

File 11038-AG-40, volume 4.
Colombo Plan, technical assistance programme, Cambodia, 2 October 1956-31 December 1957.

File 11038-AH-40, volume 5.
Colombo Plan, technical assistance programme, Cambodia, 7 January 1958-27 May 1960.

Box 388.

File 11038-AH-40, volume 2 FP.
Colombo Plan, technical assistance programme, Vietnam, 1 March 1956-24 June 1957.

File 11038-AH-40.
Colombo Plan, technical assistance programme, Vietnam, 2 July 1957-23 December 1958.

File 11038-AH-40, volume 4.
Colombo Plan, technical assistance programme, Vietnam, 7 January-29 May 1959.

File 11038-AH-40, volume 5.
Colombo Plan, technical assistance programme, Vietnam, 1 June-30 September 1959.

File 11038-BL-40, volume 6.
Colombo Plan, technical assistance programme, Vietnam, 1 October 1959-1 December 1960.

File 11038-AK-40.
Colombo Plan, technical assistance programme, Japan, 1 June 1959-12 August 1960.

Box 390.

File 11044-BL-40, volume 2.
Export of arms from Canada to Japan, 3 October 1956-22 July 1957.

File 11044-BL-40, volume 3.
Export of arms from Canada to Japan, 1 October-25 November 1957.

File 11044-BL-40, volume 4.
Export of arms from Canada to Japan, 8 June 1958-17 December 1959.

File 11044-Far Eastern-40, Volume 5.
Export of arms from Canada to Japan, 8 June 1958-17 December 1959.

Box 391.

File 11045-H-40, volume 4.
Japanese and Far Eastern control of exports to countries of the Soviet bloc, also titled export controls, control of the export of strategic goods to China and U.S. foreign assets control regulations, 6 January 1955-27 January 1956.

File 11045-H-40, volume 5.
Japanese and Far Eastern control of exports to countries of the Soviet bloc, also titled export controls, control of the export of strategic goods to China and U.S. foreign assets control regulations, 27 January-26 September 1956.

File 11045-H-40, volume 6.
Japanese and Far Eastern control of exports to countries of the Soviet bloc, also titled export controls, control of the export of strategic goods to China and U.S. foreign assets control regulations, 1 October 1956-14 May 1957.

File 11045-H-40, volume 7.
Japanese and Far Eastern control of exports to countries of the Soviet bloc, also titled export controls, control of the export of strategic goods to China and U.S. foreign assets control regulations, 15 May-30 June 1957.

File 11045-H-40, volume 8.
Japanese and Far Eastern control of exports to countries of the Soviet bloc, also titled export controls, control of the export of strategic goods to China and U.S. foreign assets control regulations, 2 July 1957-29 April 1958.

File 11045-H-40, volume 9.
Japanese and Far Eastern control of exports to countries of the Soviet bloc, also titled export controls, control of the export of strategic goods to China and U.S. foreign assets control regulations, 6 May 1958-24 April 1963.

Box 418.

File 11477-40.
Request by the Canadian Liaison Mission in Tokyo by Canadians for assistance in obtaining visas for entry to Formosa, procedure re, 20 February-10 March 1955.

File 11494-F-40, volume 3.
India, the Five Year Plan for Economic Development, 1 May 1956-24 October 1962.

File 11500-B-40, volume 2.
Non-official visitors from Canada to Asia, the Far East, Africa and Australia(excluding journalists, defence authorities and cultural personages), 5 January 1956-19 August 1960.

Box 430.

File 11568-40, volume 5.
Political situation in Ceylon, 2 January 1957-28 May 1959.

File 11568-40, volume 6.
Political situation in Ceylon, 10 June 1959-19 May 1960.

File 11568-C-40.
Ceylon, use of official languages, 29 March 1956-2 May 1963.

File 11568-D-40.
Ceylon-Netherlands relations, 9 October 1956-17 February 1961.

File 11568-E-40.
Ceylon-Sweden relations, 17 August 1955-20 December 1956.

File 11568-F-40.
Ceylon-Denmark relations, 6 February 1957.

File 11578 to 40.
Organization of the Central People's Government of China, 17 September 1959-14 December 1962.

File 11578-A-40, volume 2.
Foreign policy of the Central People's Republic of China, 3 June 1958-31 December 1959.

File 11578-A-1-40.
China-Roumania relations, 24 January 1957-9 August 1963.

File 11578-A-2-40.
China-Hungary relations, 24 January 1957-30 March 1962.

File 11578-A-3-40.
China-Israel relations, 1 February 1957-16 June 1959.

File 11578-A-4-40.
China-Sudan relations, 28 June 1956-7 August 1962.

File 11578-A-5-40.
China-Syria relations(for prior correspondence to 1956 see File 50055-B-40), 30 November 1955-8 November 1957.

File 11578-A-6-40.
China-Ghana relations, 4 March 1957-24 May 1962.

(no file cited in finding aid)
China-Iraq relations, 12 March 1957-4 August 1961.

File 11578-A-8-40.
China-Lebanon relations, 9 June 1956-18 November 1960.

File 11578-A-9-40.
China-Jordan relations, 28 November 1956-28 May 1959.

File 11578-A-11-40.
China-Singapore relations, 13 March 1959-20 May 1960.

File 11578-B-40, volume 12.
Political situation in the Central People's Republic of China, 16 August 1955-24 July 1956.

File 11578-B-40, volume 13.
Political situation in the Central People's Republic of China, 3 August 1956-28 June 1957.

File 11578-B-40, volume 14.
Political situation in the Central People's Republic of China, 2 July 1957-28 May 1958.

Box 431.

File 11578-B-40, volume 15.
Political situation in the Central People's Republic of China, 1 June 1958-31 March 1959.

File 11578-B-40, volume 16.
Political situation in the Central People's Republic of China, 1 April-28 May 1959.

File 11578-B-40, volume 16.
Political situation in the Central People's Republic of China, 1 April-28 May 1959.

File 11578-B-40, volume 17.
Political situation in the Central People's Republic of China, 4 June 1959-11 January 1960.

File 11578-B-40, volume 18-FP.
Political situation in the Central People's Republic of China, 1 December 1959-30 June 1960.

File 11578-D-40, volume 4-FP.
The Chinese internal development in Formosa, political and military reports, 18 May 1959-16 August 1963.

File 11578-E-40.
Resolutions and correspondence from individuals re Formosa and the coastal islands, 20 January 1955-25 October 1960.

File 11578-F-40.
China, language reform in, 11 December 1957-17 March 1958.

Box 434.

File 11655-A-40.
Arrangements between Canada and Pakistan for inspection by Canadian inspection services of military supplies purchased in Canada by India, 14 June-4 July 1956.

Box 435.

File 11679-A-40, volume 2.
Flood relief for Pakistan(East Bengal, India and Nepal), 5 October 1955-25 September 1956.

File 11679-A-40, volume 3.
Flood relief for Pakistan(East Bengal, India and Nepal), 1 October 1956-30 December 1957.

File 11679-A-40, volume 4.
Flood relief for Pakistan(East Bengal, India and Nepal), 2 January-30 June 1958.

File 11679-A-40, volume 5.
Flood relief for Pakistan(East Bengal, India and

Nepal), 7 July 1958-30 March 1960.

File 12113-A-40, volume 2.
Landing clearances for Royal Canadian Air Force aircraft en route to Indo-China carrying members of the International Supervisory Commission, 2 September 1955-23 September 1957.

File 12113-A-40, volume 3.
Landing clearances for Royal Canadian Air Force aircraft en route to Indo-China carrying members of the International Supervisory Commission, 16 October 1957-26 October 1960.

File 12130-A-40, volume 4.
Indo-China truce commission, personnel arrangements, 1 March-18 May 1955.

File 12130-A-40, volume 5.
Indo-China truce commission, personnel arrangements, 2 June-23 November 1955.

File 12130-A-40, volume 6.
Indo-China truce commission, personnel arrangements, 1 December 1955-11 June 1956.

Box 452.

File 12130-A-40, volume 7-FP.
Indo-China truce commission, personnel arrangements, 1 July 1956-19 June 1957.

File 12130-B-40, volume 2.
International Supervisory Commission, Hanoi, Vietnam, personnel arrangements, 3 June 1955-28 December 1956.

File 12130-B-40, volume 3.
International Supervisory Commission, Hanoi, Vietnam, personnel arrangements, 3 January 1957-8 March 1963.

File 12130-C-40, volume 2.
International Supervisory Commission, Vientiane, Laos, personnel arrangements, 5 March 1956-31 May 1962.

File 12130-D-40, volume 2.
International Supervisory Commission, Phnom Penh, Cambodia, personnel arrangements, 25 January 1956-1 April 1963.

File 12130-E-40, volume 2.
International Supervisory Commission, Saigon, Vietnam, personnel arrangements, 11 January 1956-26 December 1957.

File 12130-E-40, volume 3.
International Supervisory Commission, Saigon, Vietnam, personnel arrangements, 2 January 1958-1 April 1963.

File 12130-K-40, volume 2.
Indo-China truce commission, welfare, recreation and leave facilities for Canadian personnel, 7 June 1956-8 August 1959.

File 12130-L-40.
Vietnam electoral commission, personnel for, 28 January 1955-1 April 1956.

File 12130-M-40, volume 5.
Common pool of funds provided for the International Supervisory Commission in Indo-China and correspondence relating to expenses of the international secretariat and national delegations, 30 June 1959-20 December 1961.

File 12130-N-40.
Indo-China Truce Commission, insurance scheme, 5 June 1956-8 May 1963.

File 12135-E-40.
International Truce Commission, Canadian offices, premises, general, 14 February 1955-14 May 1963.

File 12135-F-1-40.
Indo-China truce commission, Canadian offices, furnishings, inventory of, 23 January 1956-24 April 1963.

Box 453.

File 12135-H-40, volume 2.
Diplomatic bag arrangements between External Affairs and Canadian offices in Indo-China, 1 June 1956-11 April 1963.

File 12135-J-40.
Royal Canadian Air Force airlift to Indo-China, 1955, 15 August 1955-30 October 1958.

File 12148-40.
Czech-Bandung relations, 26 October 1955-14 January 1960.

File 12173-40, volume 2.
Afro-Asian (Bandung) conferences, 1 April-28 October 1955.

File 12173-40, volume 3.
Afro-Asian (Bandung) conferences, 1 May-28 December 1955.

File 12173-40, volume 4.
Afro-Asian(Bandung) conferences, 9 January 1956-32 January 1958.

File 12173-40, volume 5.
Afro-Asian(Bandung) conferences, 1 February-27 November 1958.

File 12173-40, volume 6-FP.
Afro-Asian(Bandung) conferences, 1 December 1958-30 May 1959.

File 12173-40, volume 7.
Afro-Asian(Bandung) conferences, 1 June 1959-31 December 1960.

File 12173-C-40.
Asian-International Supervisory Commission legal consultative committee, 12 December 1956-13 April 1962.

Box 456.

File 12193-40.
Yugoslavia-China relations, 14 January 1955-14 June 1963.

File 12199-40.
Egypt-India relations, 19 February 1955-7 February 1958.

Box 459.

File 12242-40.
German Democratic Republic-Chinese People's Republic relations, 8 June 1955-5 February 1963.

File 12256-A-40.
Arts council of Ceylon, 8 November 1955.

File 12259-50, volume 3.
Disputes arising under article 15a of the Japanese peace treaty, 16 September 1958-30 June 1959.

File 12259-50, volume 4.
Disputes arising under article 15a of the Japanese peace treaty, 2 July 1959-15 September 1960.

File 12264-40.
Commercial claim by H.F.Pollock and Co., against the Government of Pakistan, 3 July 1956-28 November 1957.

File 12266-40.
Claim by the Redemptorist Fathers to property in Indo-China, 18 July 1957.

File 12273-40.
China-Iceland relations, 15 July-29 August 1955.

Box 461.

File 12294-40.
Poland-Burma relations, 15 November 1955-22 March 1957.

File 12295-40.
Scandinavia-Burma relations, 16 November 1955-18 April 1958.

Box 462.

File 12311-40.
Training of young Japanese farmers in Canada, 15 November 1955-30 November 1958.

File 12311-40, volume 2.
Training of young Japanese farmers in Canada, 9 December 1958-29 October 1963.

File 12321-40.
Canadian delegation to Indo-China, publicity re distribution of material for, 6 August 1955-27 February 1957.

File 12334-40.
Indonesia-Latin America relations, 30 September 1955-3 September 1959.

Box 466.

File 12335-40.
Italy-India relations, 19 January 1956-7 December 1962.

File 12360-40.
Ceylon-Poland relations, 22 February 1956-9 May 1963.

File 12361-40.
Ceylon-Roumanian relations, 29 February 1956-17 August 1962.

File 12364-40.
India-Albania relations, 9 March 1956.

Box 467.

File 12366-40.
Korea-Turkey relations, 16 March 1956-10 June 1960.

File 12368-40.
India-Iran relations, 16 December 1955-22 May 1963.

File 12369-40.
India-France relations, 15 March 1956-19 November 1962.

File 12371-40.
Visit to the U.S. and Canada of President Sukarno of Indonesia, 12 May-31 May 1956.

File 12371-40, volume 2.
Visit to the U.S. and Canada of President Sukarno of Indonesia, 1 June 1956-19 September 1957.

File 12376-40.
Navigation aids in Korean waters, 20 January-14 April 1956.

File 12379-40.
Relations between German Democratic Republic and India, 17 April 1956-9 March 1960.

File 12382-40.
India, questions in the Lok Sabha(House of People) or Rajya Sabha(Council of States), 2 March-14 December 1956.

Box 470.

File 12390-40.
Religion in Ceylon, 21 October 1955-21 July 1963.

File 12391-40.
Ceylon-Greece Union relations, 11 May 1956-14 August 1963.

File 12395-40.
India-Sudan relations, 10 May 1956.

File 12496-40.
India-Spain relations, 27 July 1955-3 November 1958.

File 12398-40.
The Five Principles - Panch Shila, 11 January 1956-29 June 1961.

File 12399-40.
India-Greece relations, 23 May 1956.

File 12401-40.
Buddhist Jayanti celebrations in Commonwealth countries, 30 December 1955-6 August 1958.

File 12402-40.
Indonesia-France relations, 6 June 1956-9 May 1962.

File 12405-40.
Request from the Indian government for the loan of four service tank repair technicians, 18 June 1956-8 August 1956.

File 12419-40.
Lebanon-Indian relations, 25 July 1956-9 January 1963.

Box 471.

File 12420-40.
New Zealand-Thailand relations, 27 February 1956-17 January 1963.

File 12422-40.
United Kingdom-Ceylon relations, 30 May 1956-31 July 1963.

File 12423-40.
Turkey, social conditions in, 19 April 1957-29 July 1963.

File 12434-40.
Turkey-Libya relations, 10 August 1956-15 November 1957.

File 12439-40.
Czechoslovakia-Ceylon relations, 1 April 1955-7 December 1962.

File 12440-40.
Reporting from Hong Kong, 6 September 1956-30 August 1963.

File 12444-40.
Switzerland-Burma relations, 25 September-13 November 1956.

File 12445-40.
Ceylon-Germany relations, 20 January 1955-25 October 1962.

File 12446-40.
Singapore, labour situation in, 6 September 1956-15 October 1962.

Box 484.

File 12532-40.
Saudi Arabia-Turkey relations, 25 March 1957-2 April 1958.

Box 484.

File 12536-40.
Switzerland-Philippine relations, 6 November 1956-16 April 1957.

File 12540-40.
Pakistan-Germany relations, 13 March 1957-3 August 1963.

File 12549-40.
Turkey-Afghanistan relations, 27 June 1956-17 March 1960.

File 12557-40.
Switzerland-Pakistan relations, 8 May 1957-23 June 1959.

Box 485.

File 12560-40.
Czechoslovakia-Afghanistan relations, 25 April 1957-12 December 1960.

File 12562-40.
Ceylon-Egypt relations, 16 May-12 November 1957.

File 12588-40.
India-Sweden relations, 25 June 1957-27 November 1962.

Box 486.

File 12593-40.
Spain-Pakistan relations, 11 July 1957-21 April 1959.

Box 487.

File 12501-40.
Pakistan-Jordan relations, 15 August 1957-7 October 1960.

File 12614-40.
Malaya-Egypt relations, 13 September 1957-15 January 1958.

File 12620-40.
Malaya, foreign policy, 2 October 1957-27 December 1962.

File 12624-40.
Ceylon, Malaya service, 22 May 1957-7 July 1961.

Box 488.

File 12628-40.
Ceylon, 10th anniversary of independence, 1958, 29 November 1957-28 February 1958.

File 12631-A-40.
Office of Canadian High Commissioner, Kuala Lumpur, expenses and accounts, 9 September 1957-24 June 1963.

File 12631-A-1-40.
Office of Canadian High Commissioner, Kuala Lumpur, premises, chancery, 31 December 1957-24 June 1963.

File 12631-A-2-40.
Office of Canadian High Commissioner, Kuala Lumpur, premises, official residence, 18 April 1958-5 October 1960.

File 12631-A-3-40.
Office of Canadian High Commissioner, Kuala Lumpur, premises, staff accommodation, 3 April 1958-23 May 1963.

File 12631-G-40.
Appointment of Arthur Redpath Menzies as High Commissioner for Canada in Federation of Malaya, 7 December 1957-20 December 1961.

Box 490.

File 12653-D-40.
United Arab Republic-Cambodia relations, 21 November 1958.

File 12653-E-40.
United Arab Republic-Ceylon relations, 9 January 1959-7 December 1962.

Box 491.

File 12653-P- 40.
United Arab Republic-India relations, 22 May 1958-29 April 1963.

File 12653-Q-40.
United Arab Republic-Japan relations, 5 April 1957-22 May 1962.

File 12653-S-40.
United Arab Republic-Malaya relations, 21 May 1958-27 May 1960.

File 12653-U-40.
Afghanistan-Malaya relations, 14 April 1958-6 February 1962.

File 12653-X-40.
United Arab Republic-Turkey relations, 14 April 1958-29 July 1963.

Box 492.

File 12653-E-40.
United Arab Republic-Indonesia relations, 22 May 1956-18 January 1962.

File 12655-40.
Scholarships for Canadians in the humanities and social sciences in India, Pakistan and Ceylon, 14 October 1957-12 November 1958.

Box 495.

File 12677-40.
Malaya, labour situation, 11 November 1957-22 January 1963.

Box 497.

File 12687-E-40, volume 1-FP.
Prime Minister's Commonwealth tour, 1958, Pakistan, 18 August-15 December 1958.

File 12687-F-40.
Prime Minister's Commonwealth tour, 1958, India, 18 August-14 September 1959.

File 12687-G-40.
Prime Minister's Commonwealth tour, 1958, Ceylon, 18 August 1958-17 July 1959.

File 12687-H-40.
Prime Minister's Commonwealth tour, 1958, Malaya, 18 August 1958-16 October 1959.

File 12687-J-40.
Prime Minister's Commonwealth tour, 1958, Indonesia, 8 September-12 December 1958.

Box 502.

File 12766-40.

New Zealand-India relations, 17 October 1958-14 May 1963.

File 12767-40.
New Zealand-Malaya relations, 11 October-3 November 1958.

File 12771-40, volume 1-FP.
Commercial relations between Canada, Malaya and Singapore, 24 September 1957-31 October 1963.

File 12772-40.
Vietnam-Thailand relations, 9 June 1958-1 August 1963.

File 12779-40.
Diplomatic representation in Indonesia, 31 December 1958-26 September 1962.

File 12787-40.
Singapore, political situation, 6 January 1958-25 June 1959.

Box 503.

File 12787-40, volume 2.
Singapore, political situation, 3 July 1959-29 December 1961.

File 12796-40.
Laos-Iran relations, 26 February 1958-27 February 1959.

File 12802-40.
China, relations with various countries, 21 May 1959-16 May 1963.

File 12803-40.
Ceylon's relationship to the Commonwealth, 23 January 1959-13 July 1962.

File 12810-40.
Iran, relations with various countries, 20 May 1959-7 August 1963.

File 12810-A-1-40.
Iran-Afghanistan relations, 26 May 1959-14 June 1963.

File 12811-40.
Indonesia, relations with various countries, 5 June 1959-26 August 1963.

File 12812-40.
Japan, relations with various countries, 9 June 1959-25 September 1962.

File 12816-40.
Afghanistan to Canada relations, 15 October 1957-12 August 1963.

Box 505.

File 12826-40.
Southeast Asian Friendship and Economic Treaty-SEAFET, 16 January 1959-29 April 1963.

File 12829-40.
Pakistan, transfer of the capital city, 22 January 1959-16 June 1962.

File 12830-40.
Iran, defence, 19 August 1959-6 May 1962.

File 12832-B-1-40.
Death of the honorable S.W.R.D. Bandaranaike, Prime Minister of Ceylon, 24 September 1959-18 July 1962

File 12832-V-1-40.
Health of his Majesty Sisanag Vong, King of Lao, 1959, 30 October-18 December 1959.

File 12833-40.
Cyprus-Commonwealth relations, 19 September 1959-14 January 1960.

Box 508.

File 12919-40.
Turkey-Yugoslavia relations, 17 October 1957-11 July 1962.

File 12992-6-5-40.
Passport office, travel to China, Formosa and mainland, 12 August 1958-21 November 1963.

File 12992-7-7-5-5-40.
Passport office, passports for persons of Chinese origin, 23 April 1958-10 January 1963.

Box 521.

File 14003-B-12-1-40.
Atomic energy, Burma, peaceful uses of, 2 January 1956.

File 14003-J-2-3-40.
Burma energy, India, cooperation with Canada, 1 October 1959-10 May 1960.

File 14003-J-3-1-40.
Atomic energy, Indo-China, peaceful uses of, 10 September 1958.

File 14003-J-4-1-40.
Atomic energy, Indonesia, peaceful uses of, 17 April-16 June 1958.

File 14003-J-4-3-40.
Atomic energy, Japan, cooperation with Canada, 24 September 1957-15 November 1961.

Box 522.

File 14003-J-11-3-40.

File 14003-J-11-3-40, volume 1.
Atomic energy, Japan, cooperation with Canada, 19 January 1957-30 October 1958.

File 14003-J-11-3-40, volume 2.
Atomic energy, Japan, cooperation with Canada, 5 November 1958-15 April 1959.

File 14003-J-11-3-40, volume 3.
Atomic energy, Japan, cooperation with Canada, 16 April-30 June 1959.

File 14003-J-11-3-40, volume 4.
Atomic energy, Japan, cooperation with Canada, 1 July 1959-27 October 1961.

File 14003-P-2-3-40.
Atomic energy, Pakistan, cooperation with Canada, 24 August 1956-31 October 1963.

File 14003-T-7-1-40.
Atomic energy, Turkey, peaceful uses of, 12 January 1959-28 February 1962.

File 14003-T-7-3-40.
Atomic energy, Turkey, cooperation with Canada, 18 December 1959-17 July 1963.

Box 523.

File 14030-B-12-1-40.
Foreign aid received by other countries, Burma, general file, 7 August 1958-18 January 1960.

Box 530.

File 14030-J-2-1-40.
Foreign aid received by other countries, India, general file, 8 July 1958-18 January 1960.

File 14030-J-3-1-40.
Foreign aid received by other countries, Indo-China, general file, 27 November 1958-28 July 1960.

File 14030-M-2-1-40.
Foreign aid received by other countries, Malaya, general file, 30 July-6 November 1958.

File 14030-P-2-1-40.
Foreign aid received by other countries, Pakistan, general file, 24 September 1958-11 July 1960.

Box 534.

File 14053-C-4-40.
G.A.T.T.(General Agreement on Tariffs and Trade) accession or association, waivers, re negotiations of schedules, article XXVIII; 4, Ceylon, 31 July 1959-6 April 1962.

File 14053-C-15-40.
G.A.T.T.(General Agreement on Tariffs and Trade) accession or association, waivers, re negotiations of schedules, article XXVIII; 4, Cambodia, 15 February 1959-16 April 1963.

File 14053-J- 11-40.
G.A.T.T.(General Agreement on Tariffs and Trade) accession or association, waivers, re negotiations of schedules, article XXVIII; 4, Japan, 1958-17 July 1963.

File 14053-P- 2-40.
G.A.T.T.(General Agreement on Tariffs and Trade)accession or association, waivers, re negotiations of schedules, article XXVIII; 4, Pakistan, 7 July 1958-6 July 1961.

Box 535.

File 14053-T- 7-40.
G.A.T.T.(General Agreement on Tariffs and Trade) or association, waivers, re negotiations of schedules, article XXVIII; 4, Turkey, 21 October 1958-27 June 1963.

Accession 89-90/029.

Finding aid FA 25-7, part 1.

Box 1.

File 1(s), volume 1.
French relations with China:1940-1943

Box 3.

File 2-R(s), volume 1.
Japanese offer of mediation between Soviet Union and Germany, September 1943-September 1944.

File 2-T(s), volume 1.
Soviet-Japanese Relations, November 1940-March 1946.

Box 5.

File 4-AA(s), volume 1.
Attacks of H.F.Angus re Japanese Policy, February 1942-December 1945.

File 5(s).
Visit-Canada of Jam Sahib of Nawanagar, October-November 1942.

File 5-A(s), volume 7-8.
Disputes between India and Pakistan - general file. Transferred to 50015-40.

File 5-B(s), volume 1.
India-Pakistan Defence Arrangement, Transferred to 50016-40.

File 5-C(s), volumes 1-2.
Arrangements for Possible Evacuation of Canadians from India and Pakistan, October 1946-November 1948.

File 5-D(s), volume 1.
Collection of Funds for Establishment of a Sikh State in Northern India, October 1947-June 1948.

File 5-E(s), volume l.-2.
India's Relationship to the Commonwealth. Transferred to 9193-D-40.

File 5-F(s),volume 1.
Relations between India and the United States. Transferred to 2239-40.

File 5-G(s), volume 1.
Visit to Canada of Pandit Jawaharlal Nehru, October 1949. Transferred to 9908-Y-2-40.

Box 8.

File 7-Q(s)
Post War Settlement in the Far East, July 1943-July 1945.

Box 11.

File 7-AL(s), volume 1.
Post War Position in Indo-China and other French colonies. Transferred to 50052-40.

Box 13.

File 7-BP(s), volume 1.
Security in South East Asia and the South West Pacific, February 1944.

Box 19.

File 7-CK(s), volume 1.
Post-Hostilities administration of Malaya and British territories in Borneo. Transferred to 8704-40.

File 7-CQ(s), volume 1.
British Strategic Requirements in India and the Indian Ocean, September 1944.

Box 20.

File 7-CZ(s), volume 1.
Council of Foreign Ministers of United States, United Kingdom, Soviet Union, France and China-establishment of, July 1945-January 1946.

Box 24.

File 8-J(s), volume 1.
Spanish Relations with Puppet Government of Philippines, November 1943.

File 11-A(s), volume 1.
Turkish Commercial and Cultural Relations with Germany, September 1940-June 1944.

File 11-C(s), volume 1.
Taxation in Turkey, December 1942-March 1944.

File 11-C(s), volume 1.
Turkey - Supplies of Military Equipment, May 1943-August 1948.

File 11-D(s), volume 1.
Turkish participation in the War and Relations with Belligerents. Transferred to 50137-40 and 50138-40, November 1940-December 1945.

File 11-E(s), volume 1.
Turkish Political Situation. Transferred to 50138-40.

File 11-G(s), volume 1.
Turkish-Italian Diplomatic Relations. August 1943.

File 11-H(s), volume 1.
Reports re Diplomatic Representatives in Turkey. Transferred to 50151-40.

Box 25.

File 12-12(s), volume 1.
Control of Communications to and between Persia and Iraq, September 1941-October 1943.

File 12-E(s), volume 1.
Persia-Japan Relations, August 1941-April 1942.

File 12-F(s), volume 1.
Agreement between U.K., Iraq and Iran re Navigation and Conservation of the Shatt-Al-Arab Waterway, April 1945.

Box 27.

File 19(s), volume 1.
Royal Canadian Air Force Squadrons for Middle and Far East, October 1941-January 1943.

Box 28.

File 22-T(s), volume 1.
Japanese Balloon-Bomb, December 1944-May 1945.

Box 29.

File 25(s), volume 1.
Supply routes to China, May 1942-September 1943.

File 25-A(s), volume 1.
Financial arrangements with China - general, December 1941-February 1944.

File 25-B(s), volume 1.
Visit to America of Mme Chiang Kai-shek, June 1943-December 1944.

File 25-C(s), volume 1.
Chinese-Tibetan relations. Transferred-6209-40

File 25-D(s), volumes 1-10.
Political situation and economic conditions in China. Transferred to 50055-50.

File 25-F(s), volume 1.
Chinese request for air reinforcement in Pacific, July-September 1941.

File 25-G(s).
Chinese foreign policy and relations with Allies - general, May 1941-January 1946.

File 25-H(s), volume 1.
Chinese Goodwill Mission to United Kingdom, July-September 1943.

File 25-J(s), volume 1.
Disclosure of military information to the Chinese, January-March 1944.

File 25-K(s), volume 1.
Visit of Lord Louis Mountbatten to China, December 1943.

File 25-L(s), volume 1.
Chinese intelligence organizations, December 1943-October 1944.

File 25-N(s), volume 1.
Protection of Allied property in liberated areas of China, September-November 1945.

File 25-P(s), volume 1.
Status and activities of Chinese in Canada. Transferred to 11128-40.

File 25-Q(s), volume 1.
Financial relations between China-Canada. Transferred to 50059-40.

File 28-A(s), volume 1.
Japan war plans and policy, January 1942-April 1943.

Box 30.

File 32-C(s)
Portugal-Japan relations, December 1941-February 1945.

File 32-D(s), volume 1.
Defence of Portuguese possessions, June 1941-February 1943.

File 38(s), volume 1.
Japanese shipping situation, January-February 1943.

Box 31.

File 41-E-5(s), volume 1.
War-operational reports from National Defence Department - Far East, April-September 1945.

File 41-E-5(s), volume 2.
War-operational reports from National Defence Department - Far East, October-December 1945.

Box 39.

File 68-E(s), volume 1.
Participation of New Zealand in war against Japan, July-September 1944.

File 68-F(s), volume 1.
Plans for combined Royal Canadian Air Force Bomber Force for the war against Japan, March-August 1945.

File 69(s), volume 1.
Neutrality of Sweden and relations with belligerents, March 1940-May 1948.

Box 40.

File 75(s), volume 1.
Government supervision of foreign language groups in Canada, June 1943.

File 77(s), volume 1.
Arrangement for rubber production in liberated areas of the Far East, October 1943.

File 89-A(s), volume 1.
Argentina -supply of arms from Japan, July-August 1943.

File 94-A(s), volume 1.
Mission of General Hurley to Middle and Far East - Resignation of General Hurley and appointment of General Marshall as United States Ambassador to China, September 1944-December 1945.

Box 41.

File 101-B(s), volume 1.
Netherlands Armed Forces, reports re, July 1949-February 1950.

File 104(s), volume 1 and FP.
Postwar treatment of Japanese in Canada and United States, August 1943-October 1944.

File 104(s), volume 2 and FP.
Postwar Treatment of Japanese in Canada and United States, November 1944-December 1945.

File 104-A(s), volume 1.
Postwar disposal of Japanese Islands. Transferred to 5475-N-2-40.

File 104-B(s), volume 1.
Negotiation re the surrender of Japan, August-September 1945.

File 104-C(s), volumes 1-4.
Occupation and control of Japan. Transferred to 500651-40.

File 104-D(s), volume 1.
Inter-Allied action re Japanese and other enemy assets and United Nations assets seized by Japanese, September 1945-April 1946.

File 104-E(s), volume 1.
Disposition of the Japanese fleet, October 1945-October 1946.

File 104-F(s), volume 1.
Conditions in the Far East, report re. Transferred to 50062-40.

File 104-G(s), volume 1.
Reparation from Japan. Transferred to 8364-C-40.

File 104-H(s), volume 1.
Canadian participation in the investigation of Japanese science and technology. Transferred to 8690-40.

File 104-J(s), volume 1.
International Military Tribunal for the Far East, investigation of, March 1947-December 1948.

File 104-J-1(s), volume 1.
Termination of participation by Canada in the Japanese war crimes trials, February-October 1947.

File 104-K(s), volumes 1-5.
Peace treaty with Japan, negotiations re. Transferred to 50051-40.

Box 43.

File 123-B(s), volumes 1-4.
Activities of D.DeKobbe - correspondence re Japanese interest, January-December 1943.

File 123-C(s), volumes 1-2.
Activities of D.DeKobbe - Marichu Alba correspondence, February 1943-January 1944.

File 123-D(s), volumes 1-3.
Activities of D.DeKobbe - Schwartz intercepts, October 1942-September 1945.

File 123-E(s), volume 1.
Activities of D.DeKobbe - Schwartz -Kobbe correspondence, January-November 1943.

File 123-F(s), volumes 1-2.
Activities of D.DeKobbe -correspondence re Spanish interest, May 1943-December 1944.

File 123-G(s), volume 1.
Activities of D.DeKobbe -Vancouver-Madrid correspondence, January 1943-January 1944.

File 123-H(s), volume 1.
Activities of D.DeKobbe -register sheets of intercepted correspondence, July-October 1943.

Box 47.

File 152(s), volume 1.
Welfare of Canadian prisoners of war at Hong Kong. Transferred to 2670-A-40.

File 152-A(s), volume 1.
Publication of reports on the fighting at Hong Kong in 1941, August 1946-May 1948.

File 152-B(s), volume 1.
Security of Hong Kong. Transferred to 50063-40.

Box 48.

File 162(s), volume 1.
Peace overtures by Japan, November 1944-August 1945.

Box 49.

File 193(s), volume 1.
Japanese diplomats captured in Northern Italy and Germany- treatment of, May-June 1945.

Box 53.

File 204(s), volumes 1-2.
Status of Korea. Transferred to 50067-40.

File 204A(s), volumes 1-4.
United Nations Temporary Commission on Korea, April 1947-January 1948(volume 1). Transferred to 50058-40.

File 204-A-1(s), volume 1.
Communication arrangement and security arrangements for Canadian representative on United Nations Temporary Commission on Korea, January-October 1948.

File 204-A-2(s), volume 1-2.
United Nations Temporary Commission on Korea- documents, February-June 1948.

Box 54.

File 204-A-2(s), volume 1-2.
United Nations Temporary Commission on Korea- documents, June-November 1948.

File 204-A-3(s), volume 1.
Appointment of Canadian representative on the United

Nations Temporary Commission on Korea, December 1947-January 1948.

File 204-B(s), volume 1.
Military Reports re Korea. Transferred to 50069-40.

File 207(s), volume 1.
Release of secret documents in connection with the Pearl Harbour inquiry in the United States, November 1945-March 1946.

Box 55.

File 223(s), volume 1.
Evacuation of European women and children from the Netherlands East Indies, proposals re, December 1945-April 1946.

Box 58.

File 234-B(s), volume 1.
Censorship planning for the war with Japan 1944, September 1944.

Box 69.

File 305-A(s), volume 1.
Burma- Evacuation Arrangements for British subjects(Europeans) and American citizens, August 1948-March 1949.

Box 70.

File 323-C(s), volume 1.
Production and Export of Military Equipment by India, April 1949.

Accession 89-90/292.

Finding aid 25-5. Part 21.

Box 2.

File 10-P-40, FP only.
Pass Visa Feeds- specimen of special passport issued by Japanese Minister of Foreign Affairs.

Box 3.

File 19-EA-40, volume 1.
Honours and awards for service in Korea under angle of United Nations - general, May 1951-September 1962.

File 19-EA-3-40, FP only.
Special United Kingdom awards for service in Korea.

File 26-BD-40, FP only.
Appointment of S.Yoshizawa as Japanese Minister at Ottawa.

Box 5.

File 72-BP-40, FP only, for Volume 1.
Trans-Pacific Air Services.

File 72-BP-40 FP only, for Volume 3.
Trans-Pacific Air Services.

Box 10.

File 325-40, FP only.
United States trade with China and Japan - Statistics.

Box 12.

File 515-40, FP only.
Philippine Immigration Legislation and Regulations.

Box 13.

File 592-40, volume 1.
Economic policy toward Japan, April 1940-June 1941.

File 592-40, volume 2 and FP.
Economic policy toward Japan, July-August 1941.

File 592-40, volume 3.
Economic policy toward Japan, September 1941-March 1949.

Box 14.

File 614-R-1-40, volume 1.
Release of German assets in Japan, Cases, August 1943-September 1956.

Box 15.

File 621-W-40, volume 1.
Release from internment of refugees doctors for service with the Red Cross in China, September-December 1941.

Box 18.

File 861-A-40, volume 1.
Arrest of Canadian nationals by Japanese Authorities, July 1940-June 1944.

Box 23.

File 1493-40, FP only.
German propaganda in Japan.

Box 24.

File 16555-40, volume 1.
Canadian interests in Japan to be taken care of by Argentine government in event of war with Japan - arrangements, December 1940-May 1943.

File 1846-4, FP only.
Political situation in Thailand.

Box 25.

File 1955-W-40, volume 1.
Procedures and instruction in Far Eastern Division. August 1953-June 1963.

File 2006-N-1-40, volume 2.
Travel to Communist China - enquiries re, June 1961-November 1963.

File 2006-CA-40, FP only.
Permission to travel to Far East for members of Order of Dominicans.

Box 32.

File 2727-AX-40, FP only.
Canadian publicity in Hong Kong.

File 2864-B-40, FP only.
Department of External Affairs. Questionnaires for Canadians repatriated from Japan on S.S. **Gripsholm** (names only - Dappen to Fairbairn).

Box 33.

File 2998-D-40, FP only.
Visits by representative of protecting power and International Red Cross Committee to Canadian prisoners of war and internees in Japan and Japanese occupied territory - arrangements and reports.

File 3051-G-40, FP only.
Welfare and safety in the Far East of missionaries of the Christian Missionary Alliance Tabernacle following the outbreak of war with Japan.

File 3160-40, FP only.
Shipment of food and supplies to Japan for relief of prisoners of war and internees in the Far East.

Box 34.

File 3363-D-40, FP only.
Repatriation movement of Japanese from Canada to Japan arrangements.

File 3630-40, FP only.
Extra-territorial jurisdiction over British subjects in India.

Box 36.

File 3991-40, FP only.
Constitution and political situation in Philippine Islands.

File 3991-B-1-40, volume 1.
United States War Damage Commission in Philippines, December 1950-May 1951.

File 4079-H-40, FP only.
German atrocities in the Philippines.
Box 37.

File 4457-40, volume 2.
United States-China - relations, June 1946-March 1951.

File 4457-40, volume 3.
United States-China - relations May 1951-December 1957.

File 4464-40, FP only.
Repatriation from Japan of Canadian nationals, other than diplomatic personnel - arrangements.

File 4558-Q-40, volume 2.
Movements of Canadian Ambassador at Chungking and Nanking and staff, February 1948-March 1951.

File 4558-V-40, volume 2.
Monthly summaries from Canadian Embassy in Nanking, December 1947-December 1949.

File 4558-AK-40, FP only.
Appointment of Mr. C.A.Ronning as Canadian Ambassador at Nanking.

File 4558-AL-40, FP only.
Appointment of J.R.Maybee as Canadian Vice-consul at Nanking.

File 43606-B-7-40, FP only.
Japanese government overseas agencies in Canada.

File 4606-C-21-40, volume 1.
Japan-Canada relations, December 1951-December 1954.

Box 38.

File 46065-D-40, FP only.
Japanese Antarctic whaling - fishing(aquatic industries).

File 4606-E-4-40, FP only.
Allied Council for Japan.

File 4606-F-40, volume 1.
Annual review of events in Japan by Head of Canadian Liaison Mission in Tokyo, December 1948-December 1959.

File 4606-F-1-40, volume 1.
Monitored report re Japan, January-April 1951.

File 4606-N-40, FP only.
Japanese aluminium industry.

File 4606-N-1-40, FP only.
Labour in Japan.

Box 39.

File 4851-40, volume 1.
Canada-China relations - general, September 1942-June 1958.

File 4851-40, volume 2 and FP.
Canada-China relations - general, November 1961-August 1963.

Box 40.

File 4900-E-40, FP only.
Letters of instruction to the head of Canadian Mission at India.

File 4900-K-40, FP only.
Letters of instruction to the head of Canadian Mission at India.

Box 41.

File 4949-F-40, FP only.
Supplies for China under Canadian Mutual Aid Act.

Box 43.

File 5000-40, FP only.
Shooting of Japanese prisoners of war in New Zealand.

Box 50.

File 5475-CY-2-40, FP only.
United Nations Economic Commission for Asia and the Far East.

File 5475-DU-11-40, FP only.
United Nations technical assistance for Pakistan.

File 5475-EA-3-40, FP only.
United Nations and ICEM refugee emergency fund to assist European refugees in China.

File 5475-EJ-40, volume 7.
The question of Chinese representation in the United Nations - general file, June 1955-October 1956.

File 5475-EJ-40, volume 8.
The question of Chinese representation in the United Nations, general file, November 1956-September 1958.

Box 51.

File 5475-EJ-40, volume 9.
The question of Chinese representation in the United Nations, general file, September 1958-September 1959.

File 5475-EJ-40, volume 10.
The question of Chinese representation in the United Nations, general file, October 1959-January 1961.

File 5475-EJ-1-40, volume 1.
The question of Chinese representation in the United Nations - resolutions re, general correspondence with non-government sources, October-December 1950.

File 5475-EJ-1-40, volume and FP.
The question of Chinese representation in the United Nations - resolutions re, general correspondence with non-government sources, December 1950-January 1951.

File 5475-EJ-1-40, volume 3.
The question of Chinese representation in the United Nations - resolutions re, general correspondence with non-government sources, February 1951-September 1958.

File 5475-EJ-1-40, volume 4.
The question of Chinese representation in the United Nations - resolutions re, general correspondence with non-government sources, September 1958-May 1959.

File 5495-A-40, FP only.
Documents pertaining to the Indonesian questions.

Box 52.

File 5507-B-40, volume 1.
Military action by Nationalists against Communist China, June 1949-December 1954.

File 5507-C-40, volume 1.
China-Italy relations, March 1950-June 1961.

Box 54.

File 5741-40, volume 5.
Economic and financial conditions in China - reports re, December 1950-November 1952.

File 5741-40, volume 7.
Economic and financial conditions in China - reports re, September 1953-November 1954.

File 5741-40, volume 8.
Economic and financial conditions in China - reports re, December 1954-February 1958.

File 5741-40, volume 9.
Economic and financial conditions in China - reports re, March 1958-April 1959.

File 5741-40, volume 10.
Economic and financial conditions in China - reports re, May-December 1959.

File 5741-40, volume 11.
Economic and financial conditions in China - reports re, December 1959-June 1960.

File 5741-40, volume 12.
Economic and financial conditions in China - reports re, June 1960-January 1961.

File 5741-40, volume 13.
Economic and financial conditions in China - reports re, February 1961-May 1962.

File 5741-40, volume 14.
Economic and financial conditions in China - reports re, June 1962-October 1963.

Box 55.

File 5872-AER-40, volume 1.
Press in China - reports re, September 1960-May 1963.

File 5872-BK-40, FP only.
Press in Pakistan - reports re.

Box 58.

File 6045-40, volume 3.
Conditions in China - report by British Embassy, December 1957-October 1960.

File 6083-40, volume 2.
India-China relations, August 1954-December 1955.

File 6083-40, volume 3.
India-China relations, January 1956-April 1959.

Box 59.

File 6083-40, volume 4.
India-China relations, May-October 1959.

File 6466-A-40, volume 1.
Reports re conditions in Shanghai by the Canadian Consul-general, May 1949-December 1950.

File 6466-A-40, volume 2.
Reports re conditions in Shanghai by the Canadian Consul-general, January 1951-January 1956.

File 6466-B-40, volume 5.
Resolutions re recognition of China, November 1955-February 1956.

File 6466-B-40, volume 7.
Resolutions re recognition of China, March 1956-February 1960.

Box 61.

File 7266-D-1-40, volume 1.
China-Vietnam relations, January 1951-June 1963.

Box 66.

File 8250-F-40, volume 1.
Malaya-India relations, April 1957-December 1958.

File 8250-G-40, volume 1.
Malaya-Indonesia relations, April 1956-December 1963.

File 8250-J-40, volume 1.
Malaya-Thailand relations, October 1957-July 1963.

File 8250-L-40, volume 1.
Malaya-Japan relations, November 1957-October 1958.

File 8254-F-40, volume 1 and FP.
White Paper on Korea and Indo-China - production and distribution of, August 1950-October 1958.

File 8254-J-40, FP only.
United Nations cemetery in Korea.

File 8254-K-40, FP only.
Korea- Korean problems at the United Nations.

File 8254-N-40, FP only.
Korea- Canadian representative on the United Nations Command - Military Armistice Commission Advisory Group - reports.

File 8260-A H-40, volume 1.
Exchange of students between Canada and Japan, July 1951-November 1963.

File 8364-40, FP only.
Far Eastern Commission - minutes and agenda of meetings "Basic Post-Surrender Policy" (volume 3 transferred to File 4606-W-2-40).

Box 67.

File 8392-A-40, volume 1 and FP.
Yugoslavia - relations with Greece and Turkey, July 1946-January 1954.

Box 73.

File 9161-40, FP only.
Compensation for loss of property interests in Japan and Japanese occupied territories in the Far East - procedures re placing claims.

File 9161-D-40, FP only.
Claim of Aluminium Secretariat Ltd. to property in Japan.

File 9161-G-40, volume 1.
Holiness Movement Church in Canada against China and Japan re death of Mr. and Mrs. A.Caswell and destruction of Church property in China, June 1939-May 1961.

File 9161-Q-40, FP only.
Claim of Canadian Pacific Railway Co. Ltd. to property in Japan.

Box 74.

File 9161-T-40, FP only.
Claim of A.R.Evans to property in Japan.

File 9161-GT-40, FP only.
Claim of W.A.Dickson to property in China 1939 and also for injury.

File 9190-40, volume 1.
Naturalization of Chinese in Canada - regulations re, May 1942-July 1954.

File 9193-R-40, volume 2.
India- economic situation - reports, March 1953-

September 1955.

Box 75.

File 9402-D-40, volume 1.
Iran- foreign policy, March 1951-July 1963.

Box 76.

File 9445-L-40, FP only.
Claim of William Buchanan to property in Hong Kong.

File 94465-40, FP only.
Siamese Claims Commission - establishment and activities of.

Box 78.

File 9458-Y-40, FP only.
Indian publicity in Canada- general and policy. File including all sorts of publicity from India.

File 9474-N-40, FP only.
Claim of property in Philippines Islands and Singapore of Mrs. Knollys.

Box 80.

File 9780-Q-40, volume 1.
Claim against China for death of George Hamilton Cattanach, August-September 1954.

File 9780-R-40, volume 1.
Claim against China to property by Harry Hussey, August 1954-June 1966.

Box 81.

File 9891-40, FP only.
Conditions in Afghanistan.

Box 83.

File 10282-D0-40, volume 1.
Pakistan- agriculture and food situation, April 1950-March 1959.

File 10282-D0-40 volume 2.
Pakistan- agriculture and food situation, May 1959-September 1972.

Box 84.

File 10301-G-40, volume 1.
Canadian High Commissioner at Karachi - reports of tours, ceremonies and functions attended, entertainments given etc., February 1950-May 1963.

File 10304-E-40, volume 1.
The Kingdom of Nepal - India relations, January 1957-July 1963.

Box 89.

File 10615-B-40, volume 1.
China- Canadians visiting Communist China - demands by Chinese Communist authorities for ransom payments, December 1954-December 1957.

Box 94.

File 10951-40, FP only.
Inquiries re compensation for Japanese internment - Article 14 of the Treaty.

File 11038-40, volume 1 and FP.
Commonwealth programme for economic assistance to South East Asia, December 1949-June 1950.

File 11038-1-15-40, FP only.
Colombo Plan: India - capital assistance - counterpart funds.

File 11038-2-3-40, volume 1 and FP.
Colombo Plan - Pakistan - capital assistance - Dacca Chittagong link and electrical distribution scheme in East Bengal, July 1953-December 1956.

File 11038-3-3-40 FP only.
Colombo Plan: Ceylon - capital assistance - Gal Oya project.

File 11038-5-E-40, volume 1 and FP.
Colombo Plan: Meeting of the Consultative Committee, 1959, Djakarta, Indonesia, September 1958-October 1959.

File 11038-5-E-40, volume 2.
Colombo Plan: Meeting of the Consultative Committee, 1959, Djakarta, Indonesia, October 1959-August 1960.

File 11038-5-F-40, volume 1 and FP.
Colombo Plan: Meeting of the Consultative Committee, 1960, Tokyo, October 1959-September 1960.

Box 95.

File 11038-6-40, volume 2.
Colombo Plan - Meeting of the Group - minutes and documents, October 1956-October 1957.

File 11038-6-40, volume 3.
Colombo Plan - Meeting of the Group - minutes and documents, January-December 1958.

File 11038-6-40, volume 1.
Colombo Plan - Interdepartmental Committee on External Aid Policy, December 1958-August 1959.

File 11038-6-C-40, volume 2.
Colombo Plan - Interdepartmental Committee on External Aid Policy, September 1959-June 1960.

File 11038-6-D-40, FP only.
Colombo Plan - Scholarships Advisory Panel Committee.

File 11038-A-2-40, FP only.
Colombo Plan - Council for Technical Cooperation in South and South East Asia - India.

File 11038-G-40, FP only.
Colombo Plan - Technical Cooperation assistance in South East Asia, agenda and minutes.

File 11038-K-40, FP only.
Colombo Plan - Technical assistance.

Box 96.

File 11038-AB-2-40, volume 1.
Colombo Plan -Indonesia - training of in land and land development transmigration from Mr. Siswadi, November 1953-July 1954.

File 11038-AB-2-B-40, volume 1.
Canadian assistance to technical education in Indonesia, November 1955-August 1960.

File 11038-AB-14-40, FP only.
Colombo Plan - technical assistance program - Burma - experts, trainees, equipment.

File 11038-AB-17-40, volume 2.
Colombo Plan - technical assistance programme - United Kingdom colonies, general files, September 1955-December 1959.

File 11038-AB-17-A-40, volume 2.
Colombo Plan - Technical assistance, Malaya, January - December 1955.

File 11038-AB-17-A-40, volume 3.
Colombo Plan - Technical assistance, Malaya, January-October 1956.

File 11038-AB-17-A-40, volume 4.
Colombo Plan - Technical assistance, Malaya, November 1956-July 1957.

File 11038-AB-17-A-40, volume 5.
Colombo Plan - Technical assistance, Malaya, August 1957-April 1958.

File 11038-AB-17-A-40, volume 6.
Colombo Plan - Technical assistance, Malaya, May-August 1958.

File 11038-AB-17-A-40, volume 7.
Colombo Plan - Technical assistance, Malaya, April-December 1958.

File 11038-AB-17-A-40, volume 8.
Colombo Plan - Technical assistance, Malaya, January-April 1959.

Box 97.

File 11038-AB-17-A-40, volume 9.
Colombo Plan - Technical assistance, Malaya, May-July 1959.

File 11038-AB-17-B-40, FP only.
Colombo Plan - Technical assistance, United Kingdom colonies, North Borneo.

File 11044-BM-40, volume 1.
Export of arms from Canada to Cyprus, January 1950-November 1961.

File 11044-BS-40, volume 1.
Export of arms from Canada to China, June 1946-December 1947.

File 11044-BS-40, volume 2.
Export of arms from Canada to China, October 1948-November 1950.

File 11044-BS-40, volume 3.
Export of arms from Canada to China, January 1951-October 1963.

Box 98.

File 11152-E-40, volume 1.
Peking premises, October 1949-January 1951.

File 11279-40, volume 1.
United Kingdom trade and economic relations with China, October 1950-September 1963.

File 11318-40, volume 2 and FP.
Position of the Anglo-Iranian Oil Company, June-October 1951.

Box 103.

File 11561-GB-40, volume 1.
Privileges and immunities for Canadian representatives in Iran, June 1959-September 1960.

Box 104.

File 11568-40, FP only.
Political situation in Ceylon.

File 11568-A-40, volume 2.
Ceylon foreign policy, February 1959-August 1963.

File 11578-A-10-40, volume 1.
China-Asia commercial relations, January 1958-June 1961.

File 11578-B-40, volume 10 and FP.
Political situation in the Central People's Republic of China, August 1952-April 1954.

File 11578-D-40, volume 1.
The Chinese internal development in Formosa- political and military reports, October 1946-December 1952.

Box 105.

The Chinese internal development in Formosa- political and military reports, January 1950-January 1951.

File 11578-D-40, volume 3.
The Chinese internal development in Formosa-political and military reports, February 1955-May 1959.

File 11619-40, FP only.
Appointment of Mr. G.R.Heasman as Canadian Ambassador to Djakarta, Indonesia.

Box 107.

File 11741-40, volume 1.
Control of Canadian shipping engaged in trade with Communist China and North Korea, March 1953-August 1961.

Box 108.

File 11973-40, volume 2.
Eastern Economist - India - annual review, January 1956-December 1958.

Box 109.

File 12130-40, FP only.
Indo-China Truce Commission - personnel arrangements.

File 12130-40, volume 8
Indo-China Truce Commission - personnel arrangements, July 1954-June 1962.

File 121320-M-40, volume 2.
Common pool of funds provided for the International Supervisory Commission in Indo-China and correspondence relating to expenses of the International Secretariat and national delegations, October 1955-December 1956.

File 121320-M-40, volume 3.
Common pool of funds provided for the International Supervisory Commission in Indo-China and correspondence relating to expenses of the International Secretariat and national delegations, January-May 1957.

File 121320-M-40, volume 4 and FP.
Common pool of funds provided for the International Supervisory Commission in Indo-China and correspondence relating to expenses of the International Secretariat and national delegations, June 1957-May 1959.

File 12135-J-40, volume 2.
Royal Canadian Air Force Christmas airlift to Indo-China, 1955, July 1959-November 1962.

File 12145-40, volume 1.
British Commonwealth forces in Korea, disposal of warlike stores by, Canadian policy re, November 1954-October 1956.

Box 111.

File 12343-A-40, FP only.
Intelligence on Sino-Soviet bloc, economic activities in under-developed areas - biweekly reports by working group of the Economic Intelligence Committee.

Box 112.

File 12412-40, volume 1.
China-Formosa relations, June 1956-September 1962.

File 12440-40, FP only.
Reporting from Hong Kong.

Box 114.

File 12653-P-40, FP only.
United Arab Republic-India relations.

File 12671-BK-40, volume.
Sports and recreation in Pakistan, December 1958-January 1959.

File 12850-N-2-1-40, FP only.
Visit to Canada of the King of Nepal, 1960.

Box 116.

File 14030-C-4-1-40, volume 1.
Foreign aid received by other countries, Ceylon, general file, July-September 1958.

File 14053-J-4-40, volume 1.
G.A.T.T. - or Association, Waivers, re negotiations of schedules, Article XXVIII: 4, Indonesia, July 1959-November 1961.

File 14405-J-12-A-40, volume 1.
Mineral product, petroleum and natural gas, Anglo-Iranian Co., January 1953-May 1960.

Accession 1990-91/001.

Finding aid 25-5-20, part 1.

Box 2.

File 10-H-40-AJIR.
Cyprus, volume 1. Policy re Canadian passport - impounding of by foreign government -AHIR, Cyprus, May-November 1962.

Box 7.

File 19-EP-40, volume 1.
Thailand - honours and awards to Canadian civilians, cases, April 1960.

File 58-AE-2-40, volume 1.
National status of Wing Jongeng(Wing Chung) Wu, March-June 1961.

File 58-AE-3-40, volume 1.
National status of Wong, Katherine, February-June 1962.

File 58-FEB-5-40, volume 1.
National status in Far East, January 1962-September 1963.

Box 22.

File 72-AOS-40, volume 1.
Air relations between Canada and Thailand, March 1960-September 1962.

File 72-AOV-40, volume 1.
Civil aviation in Iran, May-November 1960.

File 72-AOX-450, volume 1.
Air relations between Canada and Philippines, June 1960-August 1963.

File 72-APA-40, volume 1.
Civil aviation in Burma, April 1961-December 1962.

Box 36.

File 500-93-40, volume 1.
Visit of H.M.C.S. **Assiniboine**, **Ottawa**, **Saguenay**, **St. Laurent** to Yokosuka and Kobe, Japan, March-April 1962. January-February 1960.

File 500-103-40, volume 1-FP.
Visit of R.C.N. to Far East, 1962, July 1961-June 1962.

File 1529-40, volume 3.
Commercial relations between Canada and Indonesia, April 1963-January 1964.

File 1617-40, volume 4.
India-Canada relations, including exchange of High Commissioners), June 1961-September 1962.

Box 45.

File 1617-40, volume 5.
India-Canada relations, including the exchange of High Commissioners, October 1962-August 1963.

Box 46.

File 846-40, volume 6.
Political situation in Thailand, January 1960-May 1963.

Box 66.

File 4457-B-40, volume 3.
Canadian policy in the Far East, January 1961-August 1963.

Box 69.

File 4606-40, volume 14.
Japanese political situation, subsequent to entry of Japan into the war, January-June 1960.

File 4606-40, volume 15.
Japanese political situation, subsequent to entry of Japan into the war, June-October 1960.

File 4606-40, volume 16.
Japanese political situation, subsequent to entry of Japan into the war, November 1960-December 1961.

File 4606-40, volume 17.
Japanese political situation, subsequent to entry of Japan into the war, January 1962-September 1963.

Box 70.

File 4606-A-4-40, volume 3-FP.
Japan- personalities, January 1960-July 1963.

File 4606-B-40, volume 10-FP.
Monitored reports re Japan, April 1960-February 1962.

File 4606-B-40, volume 11.
Monitored reports re Japan, April 1962-September 1963.

File 4606-C-9-40, volume 5.
Soviet Union-Japan relations, January 1960-December 1961.

File 4606-C-9-40, volume 6.
Soviet Union-Japan relations, December 1961-August 1962.

File 4606-C-12-40, volume 4.
Japan-Korea relations, August 1960-August 1963.

File 4606-C-12-1-40, volume 1.
Japan-North Korea relations, August 1961-August 1963.

File 4606-C-14-40, volume 4.
Japan-China relations, June 1961-August 1963.

File 4606-C-14-40, volume 1.
Japan-Nationalist China relations, January-September 1962.

File 4606-C-19-40, volume 3.
Japan-United States relations, May 1960-February 1962.

File 4606-C-19-40, volume 4.
Japan-United States relations, February 1962-August 1963.

File 4606-C-21-40, volume 5.
Japan-Canada relations, January-February 1960.

File 4606-C-21-40, volume 6.
Japan-Canada relations, March 1960-May 1961.

File 4606-C-21-40, volume 7.
Japan-Canada relations, June 1961-September 1962.

File 4606-C-21-40, volume 8.
Japan-Canada relations, October 1962-July 1963.

File 4606-C-21-1-40, volume 2-FP.
Visit of Canadian Prime Minister to Japan, 1961, April 1960-October 1961.

File 4606-C-21-1-40, volume 1.
Visit of Canadian Prime Minister to Japan, 1961, October-November 1961.

File 4606-C-43-40, volume 1.
Japan-Outer Mongolia relations, July-December 1961.

File 4606-F-40, volume 2-FP.
Annual review of events in Japan by Head of Canadian Liaison Mission in Tokyo January 1960-January 1963.

Box 72.

File 4723-V0-40, volume 1.
U.S.A.-Japan trade relations, January 1961-October 1963.

Box 73.

File 4900-C-25-40, volume 1.
Letters and instructions to the Head of Diplomatic Mission as - Cyprus. April 1961-July 1962.

File 4900-H-40, volume 2.
Letters and instructions to the Head of Diplomatic Mission as - Pakistan. July-August 1963.

File 4900-K-40, volume 2.
Letters and instructions to the Head of Diplomatic Mission as - Ceylon, May-September 1960.

Box 88.

File 5475-K-29-40, volume 1.
World Health Organization - 14th World Health Assembly - New Delhi, 1961, January 1960-July 1961.

Box 101.

File 475-CX-2-40, volume 8.
Appointment and administrative arrangements for Canadian military observers on United Nations Commission on India and Pakistan, October 1960-September 1963.

File 5475-CY-2-40, volume 7.
United Nations Economic Commission for Asia and Far East, March 1960-February 1962.

File 5475-CY-2-40, volume 8.
United Nations Economic Commission for Asia and Far East, March 1962-April 1963.

File 5475-CY-2-40, volume.9.
United Nations Economic Commission for Asia and Far East, May-October 1963.

Box 112.

File 5475-EJ-40, volume 11.
The question of Chinese representation in the United Nations, general file, February 1961-June 1963.

File 5475-EJ-40, volume 12.
The question of Chinese representation in the United Nations, general file, July-November 1961.

File 5475-EJ-40, volume 13.
The question of Chinese representation in the United Nations, general file, November 1961-January 1962.

File 5475-EJ-40, volume 14.
The question of Chinese representation in the United Nations, general file, February 1961-August 1963.

File 5475-EJ-1-40, volume 5.
The question of Chinese representation in the United Nations, resolutions re, general correspondence with non-government sources, August 1960-November 1962.

Box 114.

File 5475-FA-28-40, volume 2-FP.
Statements and assessments of Canada's policy towards United Nations for Cyprus, September 1960.

File 5475-FA-108-40, volume 1.
Statements and assessments of Canada's policy towards United Nations for Outer Mongolia, October 1962.

Box 115.

File 5475-GX-40, volume 1.
International cooperation year(World Peace Year proposals made by India at the 16th United Nations General Assembly session), September 1961-October 1962.

Box 116.

File 5475-GX-40, volume 2.
International cooperation year(World Peace Year proposals made by India at the 16th United Nations General Assembly session),November 1962-March 1963.

File 5475-GX-40, volume 3.
International cooperation year(World Peace Year proposals made by India at the 16th United Nations General Assembly session), April-July 1963.

File 5495-B-40, volume 4.
Indonesia-Netherlands relations, November 1960-August 1963.

File 5495-B-40, volume 2.
Indonesia-United States relations, May 1961-July 1963.

File 5495-B-40, volume 4.
Indonesia-Canada relations, March 1960-August 1963.

Box 127.

File 5729-40, volume 5.
Press in China - editorial opinion in the Chinese press, reports re, April 1960-September 1963.

Box 128.

File 5741-40, volume 14.
Economic and financial conditions in China, reports re, June 1962-October 1963.

Box 130.

File 5872-CQ-40, volume 1.
Press in Cyprus, reports re, June 1963.

Box 135.

File 6000-Q-40, volume 2.
International Bank for Reconstruction and Development - Pakistan Consortium development assistance to Pakistan, April-October 1963, FP.

File 6000-R-40, volume 2.
International Bank for Reconstruction and Development - Indian Consortium(discussions on India's financial position), February 1960-May 1961.

Box 136.

File 6000-R-40, volume 3.
International Bank for Reconstruction and Development - Indian Consortium(discussions on India's financial position), June 1961-May 1962.

File 6000-R-40, volume 4 & FP.
International Bank for Reconstruction and Development - Indian Consortium(discussions on India's financial position), June 1960-May 1961.

Box 137.

File 6083-40, volume 6.
India-China relations, February-December 1960.

File 6083-40, volume 7.
India-China relations, January 1961-August 1962.

File 6083-40, volume 8.
India-China relations, September-November 1962.

File 6083-40, volume 9.
India-China relations, November 1962.

File 6083-40, volume 10.
India-China relations, December 1962-January 1963.

Box 138.

File 6083-40, volume 1.
India-China relations, February-August 1963.

Box 152.

File 6466-B-40, volume 8.
Resolution re recognition of China, March 1960-August 1963.

File 6576-40, volume 2.
Reports re conditions in Mongolian People's Republic(Soviet Union-Mongolia relations), January 1961-November 1962.

File 6576-40, volume 3 & FP.
Reports re conditions in Mongolian People's Republic(Soviet Union-Mongolia relations), March 1962-August 1963.

Box 156.

File 6993-C-2-40, volume 9.
Loan to the Ming Sung Industrial Co., October 1960-September 1962.

Box 158.

File 7116-AQ-40, volume 1.
Information and cultural services of the Government of Malaya, reports re, June 1961.

File 7131-A-40, volume 1.
Timor, general file, political situation, conditions in etc., May 1960-April 1963.

Box 159.

File 7266-B-40, volume 5.
Cambodia-Vietnam relations, April 1960-December 1961.

File 7266-B-40, volume 6.
Cambodia-Vietnam relations, January-September 1962.

File 7266-B-40, volume 7.
Cambodia-Vietnam relations, October-November 1962.

File 7266-B-40, volume 8.
Cambodia-Vietnam relations, December 1962-August 1963.

File 7266-B-1-40, volume 3.
Laos-Vietnam relations, October 1962-July 1963.

File 7266-C-40, volume 3.
Canada-Laos relations(including visits of Crown Prince of Laos to North America (January-August 1963).

File 7266-D-40, volume 2.
China-Cambodia relations(including visit of Prince Sihanouk of Cambodia to Peking), January 1961-May 1963.

File 7266-L-3-40, volume 1.
Laos- relations with Communist countries(other than Soviet Union and China), January-August 1963.

File 7266-P-40, volume 2.
United States-Cambodia relations(Including Prince Sihanouk's visit to North America), January 1961-August 1963.

File 7266-P-1-40, volume 2.
United States-Vietnam relations, December 1961-August 1963.

File 7266-P-2-40, volume 2.
United States-Vietnam relations, December 1961-August 1963.

Box 160.

File 7266-Q-40, volume 2.
Thailand-Cambodia relations, January 1960-September 1962.

File 7266-Q-40, volume 3 & FP.
Thailand-Cambodia relations, October 1962-August 1963.

Box 161.

File 7307-40, volume 2.
Turkish foreign policy, January 1960-July 1963.

Box 167.

File 8250-C-40, volume 1 & SF.
Canada-Malaya relations P.S. special file kept in file pocket. Visit of Tun Razak, Deputy Prime Minister, visit to Canada, April 1963(special file), March-May 1963.

File 8250-C-40, volume 3 & FP.
Canada-Malaya relations, January-August 1963.

File 8250-E-40, volume 2.
Malaya-Singapore relations(including greater Malaysia), October 1961-February 1962.

File 8250-E-40, volume 3.
Malaya-Singapore relations(including greater Malaysia), October 1961-February 1962.

File 8250-E-40, volume 4.
Malaya-Singapore relations(including greater Malaysia), January-April 1963.

File 8250-E-40, volume 5 & FP.
Malaya-Singapore relations(including greater Malaysia), May-July 1963.

Box 168.

File 8250-E-40, volume 6 & FP.
Malaya-Singapore relations(including greater Malaysia), August-September 1963.

File 8250-E-1-40, volume 1.
Malaysia Day celebrations, July-August 1963.

File 8250-G-40, volume 2.
Malaya-Indonesia relations, March-August 1963.

File 8250-M-40, volume 1.
Malaya- relations with various countries (correspondence prior to January 1960 see File 12620-40), February 1960-June 1963

File 8254-540, volume 7 & FP.
Status of Korea- free Korea movement -Activities and reports, political conditions in Korea, May 1960-February 1961.

File 8254-540, volume 9.
Status of Korea- free Korea movement -Activities and reports, political conditions in Korea, May 1961-May 1962.

File 8254-40, volume 10.
Status of Korea- free Korea movement -Activities and reports, political conditions in Korea, June 1962-June 1963.

File 8254-540, volume 11.
Status of Korea- free Korea movement -Activities and reports, political conditions in Korea, July-August 1963.

File 8254-A-40, volume 1.
Korea- diplomatic relations with various countries, July 1961-April 1963.

File 8254-F-1-40, volume 3.
Fortnightly report of events in Korea(by British Embassy in Peking) (Duplicate copy to go on 8354-40.), September 1960-September 1961.

File 8254-F-1-40, volume 3.
Fortnightly report of events in Korea(by British Embassy in Peking) (Duplicate copy to go on 8354-40, September 1961-September 1962.

File 8254-F-1-40, volume 4.
Fortnightly report of events in Korea(by British Embassy in Peking) (Duplicate copy to go on 8354-40), September 1962-August 1963.

File 8254-K-40, volume 5.
Korea- Korean problems at the United Nations, November 1960-March 1961.

File 8254-K-40, volume 6.
Korea- Korean problems at the United Nations, March-December 1961.

File 8254-K-40, volume 7.
Korea- Korean problems at the United Nations, January 1962-August 1963.

File 8254-P-1-40, volume 1.
North Korea-USSR relations, July 1961-November 1962.

File 8254-T-40, volume 1 & FP.
North Korea relations with various countries, June 1961-July 1963.

8254-U-40, volume 1.
Korea-New Zealand relations, June 1961-July 1963.

Box 172.

File 8260-Y-40, volume 2.
Exchanges of students between Canada and India, January 1960-June 1963.

File 8260-BW-40, volume 1.
Exchanges of students between Canada and the Philippines, including scholarships and fellowships, September 1960-January 1963.

File 8260-CA-1-40, volume 1.
Exchanges of students between Canada and Cambodia, including scholarships and fellowships, August 1961-September 1963.

File 8260-CY-40, volume 1.
Exchanges of students between Canada and British Guyana. January 1963-.

File 8260 DC-40, volume 1.
Exchanges of students between Canada and Laos, September 1961.

Box 176.

File 8600-BM-40, volume 1.
Opening of foreign consulates in Canada - Turkey, June 1962-March 1963.

File 8620-Y-1-40, volume 3.
Canadian Embassy, Tokyo, residence and chancellery, February 1960-May 1963.

File 8620-Y-3-C-40, volume 2.
Canadian Embassy, Tokyo, premises, staff accommodation - Qu' Appelle House, July 1961-March 1963.

File 8620-Y-3-E-40.
Canadian Embassy, Tokyo. Construction of staff accommodation within compound, February 1960-May 1963.

Box 179.

File 8919-4, volume 3.
Commercial relations between Iran and Canada, July 1960-October 1963.

Box 182.

File 9030-40, volume 6.
Commercial relations between China and Canada, general file, April 1960-May 1961.

Box 183.

File 9030-40, volume 7.
Commercial relations between China and Canada, general file, May-December 1961.

File 9030-40, volume 8.
Commercial relations between China and Canada, general file, January-September 1962.

File 9030-40, volume 9.
Commercial relations between China and Canada, general file, October 1962-February 1963.

File 9030-40, volume 10.
Commercial relations between China and Canada, general file, March-July 1963.

File 9030-40, volume 11.
Commercial relations between China and Canada, general file, July-October 1963.

Box 184.

File 9118-S-40, volume 1.
Programme of inspection by departmental security officer Far East and Middle East, February 1961-February 1962.

Box 186.

File 9187-40, volume 2.
Commercial relations between the Republic of the Philippines and Canada, general file, November 1962-September 1963.

File 9193-40, volume 12.
Political situation in India, constitutional position in India, April 1962-August 1963.

File 9193-K-40, volume 3.
India- Communism in, reports re, January 1960-May 1963.

Box 187.

File 9193-R-40, volume 5.
India- economic situation, reports September 1960-February 1963.

File 9193-AC-40, volume 1.
India- relations with various countries, February 1960-May 1963.

File 9200-A-40, volume 2.
Iraq-Turkey relations, August 1962-August 1963.

File 9235-E-1-40, volume 3.
Purchase of property for office of Canadian High Commissioner, New Delhi, in the diplomatic enclave, January 1960-May 1961.

File 9235-E-1-40, volume 4.
Purchase of property for office of Canadian High Commissioner, New Delhi, in the diplomatic enclave, April 1961-August 1962.

File 9235-E-1-40, volume 3.
Purchase of property for office of Canadian High Commissioner, New Delhi, in the diplomatic enclave, September 1962-May 1963.

Box 189.

File 9258-A-4-1-40, volume 2.
Universal Postal Union Congress, admission of the Federation of Malaya and other states, January 1962-September 1963.

Box 192.

File 9323-B-19-40, volume 1.
Canadian consular matters in Cyprus, August 1961-June 1962.

Box 194.

File 9340-40, volume 3.
Soviet Union-India relations, general, January 1960-August 1963.

Box 196.

File 9402-A-40, volume 3.
Iran- economic and financial conditions in, December 1960-December 1961.

File 9402-A-40, volume 4-FP.
Iran- economic and financial conditions in, January 1962-September 1963.

File 9402-B-40, volume 1.
2500th anniversary of Iranian monarchy, July 1960-February 1963.

Box 203.

File 9515-H-1-40, volume 2.
Furnishings for the Canadian Ambassador at Ankara, January 1961-May 1963.

File 9515-X-2-40, volume 4.
Canadian Embassy, Ankara - premises, residence, January 1960-April 1963.

File 9515-X-2-A-40, volume 2.
Canadian Embassy, Ankara - premises, new residence, September 1962-May 1963.

File 9515-X-3-40, volume 3.
Canadian Embassy, Ankara - premises, staff accommodations, May 1962-April 1963.

Box 206.

File 9543-40, volume 2.
India- Foreign Service- organization of, July 1960-October 1962.

Box 208.

File 9678-40, volume 3.
Canada-Pakistan relations, May 1961-May 1963.

File 9678-40, volume 4.
Canada-Pakistan relations, June-September 1963.

Box 211.

File 9821-A-40, volume 2.
Canada-Burma relations, January 1960-September 1963.

File 9848-40.
Relations between Afghanistan and Pakistan(The Pushtoonistan dispute), Afghanistan-relations with Pakistan, July 1960-August 1963.

File 9861-40, volume 2.
Missionary work in India, January-April 1960.

File 9890-40, volume 3.
Policy on entry of Japanese nationals into Canada, general file, June 1961-November 1963.

File 9899-Y-40, volume 2.
Education in India, January 1961-November 1963.

Box 212.

File 9899-BT-40, volume 1.
Education in Tehran, Iran, August 1960-November 1963.

File 9899-CE-40, volume 1.
Education in Burma, January-October 1960.

Box 213.

File 9918-E-5-40, volume 1.
National Defence College - Tour - India(New Delhi), November 1961-April 1963.

File 9918-E-9-40, volume 1.
National Defence College - Tour - Malaya(Kuala Lumpur), November 1961-August 1963.

File 9918-E-11-40, volume 1.
National Defence College - Tour - Pakistan-Rawalpindi(Karachi), August 1961-April 1963.

File 9918-E-14-40, volume 1.
National Defence College - Tour - Thailand(Bangkok), December 1961-May 1963.

File 9918-E-15-40, volume 1.
National Defence College - Tour - Turkey-Istanbul(Ankara), November 1961-August 1963.

File 9918-E-18-40, volume 1.
National Defence College - Tour - Iran(Teheran), November 1961-April 1963.

Box 214.

File 9965-40, volume 2.
Relations between Canada and Ceylon, January 1961-August 1963.

File 9983-40, volume 2.
Turkey - Military reports, June 1960-December 1962.

File 9983-40, volume 3.
Turkey - Military reports, January-July 1963.

Box 217.

File-Y-40, volume 4.
Information activities of the Canadian Office at New Delhi, reports re, January 1960-November 1963.

File 10117-BX-40, volume 1.
Information activities of the Canadian Office at Thailand, reports re, January 1962- .

File 10117-CA-40, volume 1.
Information activities of the Canadian Office at Laos, reports re, November 1962-September 1963.

File 10117-CA-3-40, volume 1.
Information activities of the Canadian Office at Vietnam, reports re, February-April 1960.

File 10117-CB-40, volume 2-FP.
Information activities of the Canadian Office at Colombo, Ceylon, reports re, March 1961-October 1963.

File 10117-CE-40, volume 1.
Information activities of the Canadian Office at Burma, reports re, January 1962-.

File 10117-CQ-40, volume 1.
Information activities of the Canadian Office at Cyprus, reports re, April 1961-September 1963.

Box 219.

File 10166-40, volume 2.
Turkey- trade relations with various countries, May 1962-October 1963.

File 10168-40, volume 3-FP.
Financial and economic situation in Burma, February 1960-October 1963.

Box 222.

File 10190-E-1-40, volume 1.
Canadian Consul-general at Manila- premises, chancery, October 1960- .

File 10190-E-2-40, volume 2.
Canadian Consul-general at Manila- premises -official residence, January 1962-May 1963.

Box 230.

File 10304-40, volume 3.
The Kingdom of Nepal- reports re general file, April 1960-August 1963.

File 10304-F-40, volume 1.
The Kingdom of Nepal- relations with various countries, January 1960-August 1963.

Box 232.

File 10484-40, volume 2.
Malaya- economic and financial situation, January 1960-October 1963.

File 10389-40, volume 13.
Japan-Canada: proposals re extending most-favoured nation treatment for Japan, January-July 1960.

File 10389-40, volume 14.
Japan-Canada: proposals re extending most-favoured nation treatment for Japan, August-October 1960.

File 10389-40, volume 15.
Japan-Canada: proposals re extending most-favoured nation treatment for Japan, November 1960-January 1961.

File 10389-40, volume 16.
Japan-Canada: proposals re extending most-favoured nation treatment for Japan, February-March 1961.

File 10389-40, volume 17.
Japan-Canada: proposals re extending most-favoured nation treatment for Japan, March-April 1961.

File 10389-40, volume 18.
Japan-Canada: proposals re extending most-favoured nation treatment for Japan, April-July 1961.

File 10389-40, volume 19.
Japan-Canada: proposals re extending most-favoured nation treatment for Japan, July 1961-November 1961.

File 10389-40, volume 20-FP.
Japan-Canada: proposals re extending most-favoured nation treatment for Japan, December 1961-November 1962.

File 10389-40, volume 21.

Japan-Canada: proposals re extending most-favoured nation treatment for Japan, December 1962-June 1963.

File 10389-40, volume 22.
Japan-Canada: proposals re extending most-favoured nation treatment for Japan, July-October 1963.

Box 234.

File 10389-1-40, volume 1.
Commercial relations with Ryukyu Islands, September 1961-March 1963.

File 10393-40, volume 2.
Canada-Ceylon: commercial relations, April 1961-October 1963.

File 10394-40, volume 5.
Turkey- economic and financial situation, January 1960-April 1962.

File 10394-40 volume 6.
Turkey - economic and financial situation, April 1962-October 1963.

Accession 1990-91/001.

Finding aid 25-5, part 2.

Box 238.

File 10438-AE-40, volume 2.
Visits between Communist China and Canada, general file, January 1960-June 1963.

Box 239.

File 10464-K-40, volume 1.
Recognition of Cyprus, April 1960-April 1961.

File 10483-40, volume 5.
India-Pakistan relations, general file, January 1960-December 1961.

File 10483-40, volume 6.
India-Pakistan relations, general file, January-November 1962.

Box 240.

File 10483-40, volume 7.
India-Pakistan relations, general file, December 1962-February 1963.

File 10483-40, volume 8.
India-Pakistan relations, general file, March-July 1963.

File 10523-A-40, volume 1.
Canadian trade and commercial relations with British Guyana, April 1961-October 1963.

Box 245.

File 10615-B-40, volume 4.
China- Canadians visiting Communist China - demands by Chinese Communist authorities for ransom payments, January 1962-September 1963.

Box 246.

File 10648-40, volume 2.
Korea and Canada - commercial relations, October 1962-October 1963.

File 10660-J-3-40, volume 3.
Officer of High Commissioner for Karachi - staff accommodation, December 1961-September 1962.

File 10660-J-3-40, volume 4.
Officer of High Commissioner for Karachi - staff accommodation, October 1962-May 1963.

File 10660-J-6-40, volume 1.
Officer of High Commissioner for Karachi - premises Islamabad, February 1962-May 1963.

Box 248.

File 10699-T-40, volume 2.
Hong Kong - Trade and Commerce Offices - appointments to, May 1962-January 1963.

File 10765-40, volume 5-FP.
Economic and financial conditions in Ceylon, October 1961-August 1963.

Box 252.

File 10824-R-40, volume 1.
Trinidad and Tobago - political and economic development, September 1961-May 1963.

File 10824-R-1-40, volume 1.
Trinidad and Tobago - independence ceremonies, June 1962-September 1963.

File 10824-R-2-40, volume 1.
Trinidad and Tobago - Foreign Service(including Canadian assistance to), December 1961-June 1963.

File 10824-R-3-40, volume 1.
Trinidad and Tobago economic situation, July 1961-August 1963.

File 10824-R-4-40, volume 1.
Trinidad and Tobago - foreign policy, April 1962-May 1963.

File 10824-R-5-40, volume 1.
Trinidad and Tobago -relations with Canada, January 1962-January 1963.

File 10824-R--C-40, volume 1.
Trinidad and Tobago - relations with various countries, October 1961-August 1963.

Box 253.

File 10828-G-40, volume 1.
Pakistan-relations with various countries., April 1960-July 1963.

File 10832-40, volume 5.
Indonesia - economic situation in, January-December 1960.

File 10832-40, volume 6.
Indonesia - economic situation in. January 1961-October 1963

File 10832-B-40, volume 1.
Indonesian file 8-years Plan(including Canadian participation in), May-September 1961.

Box 257.

File 11004-40, volume 2.
Canadian diplomatic relations with India, May-June 1963.

File 11038-40, volume 27.
Colombo Plan - capital assistance, January-April 1960.

File 11038-40, volume 28.
Colombo Plan - capital assistance, May-August 1960.

Box 258.

File 11038-40, volume 29.
Colombo Plan - capital assistance, September-November 1960.

File 11038-1-40, volume 13.
Colombo Plan - India, capital assistance, general file, July-December 1960.

File 11038-1-1-40, volume 2.
Colombo Plan - India- commodities(except wheat), January-December 1960.

File 11038-1-1A-40, volume 3.
Colombo Plan - India- commodities - wheat, April-November 1960.

File 11038-2-40, volume 13.
Colombo Plan - Pakistan- capital assistance, January-July 1960.

File 11038-2-40, volume 14-FP.
Colombo Plan - Pakistan- capital assistance, August-December 1960.

Box 259.

File 11038-2-2B-40, volume 11.
Colombo Plan - Pakistan- capital assistance, Warsak project, March-November 1960.

File 11038-2-2B-40, volume -FP.
Colombo Plan - Pakistan- capital assistance, Warsak project, March-November 1960.

File 11038-2-19-40, volume 1.
Colombo Plan - Pakistan- capital assistance. Geramara-Goalpara transmission line, May-October 1960.

File 11038-2-20-40, volume 1.
Colombo Plan - Pakistan- capital assistance. Comilla-Sylhet transmission line, May-November 1960.

File 11038-2-21-40, volume 1.
Colombo Plan -Pakistan- capital assistance. Sangu Hydro-Electric and Irrigation project, May-November 1960.

File 11038-2-22-40, volume 1.
Colombo Plan - Pakistan- capital assistance. Transmission line and power plant for Karnafuli Paper Mill, May-August 1960.

File 11038-3-40, volume 9.
Colombo Plan - Ceylon- capital, general file, May-December 1960.

File 11038-3-8-40, volume 4.
Colombo Plan - Ceylon- capital assistance, Photographic survey, January-July 1960.

File 11038-5-F-40, volume 2.
Colombo Plan - meeting of the Consultative Committee - 1960- Tokyo, October 1960-May 1962.

File 11038-6-C-40, volume 3.
Colombo Plan - Interdepartmental Committee on external aid policy, July-December 1960.

Box 260.

File 11038-10-40, volume 6.
Colombo Plan - capital assistance-Burma, January-October 1960.

File 11038-10-40, volume 7.
Colombo Plan - capital assistance-Burma, November-December 1960.

File 11038-11-40, volume 6-FP.
Colombo Plan - capital assistance- Mekong River project, January-March 1960.

File 11038-11-40, volume 7.
Colombo Plan - capital assistance- Mekong River project, April-November 1960.

File 11038-12-40, volume 2.
Colombo Plan - capital assistance- Cambodia, January-December 1960.

File 11038-14-40, volume 4.
Colombo Plan - capital assistance- Malaya, February-May 1960.

File 11038-14-40, volume 5.
Colombo Plan - capital assistance- Malaya, June-November 1960.

File 11038-16-40, volume 3.
Colombo Plan -Presentation of books-medical libraries in South and South East Asia, August-November 1960.

Box 261.

File 11038-180-40, volume 2.
Proposed visit of Minister-India and Pakistan - inaugural celebration for Warsak, Kundah and Circa, March-December 1960.

File 11038-A-1-40, volume 20.
Colombo Plan -capital assistance - Ceylon, technical Cooperation in South and South East Asia - experts and equipment., February-November 1960.

File 11038-A-5-40, volume 1.
Colombo Plan - Appointment of attachés abroad, August-November 1960.

File 11038-B-40, volume 3-FP.
Colombo Plan - summary of report for cooperative economic development in South and South East Asia, distribution of, September 1960-May 1962.

File 11038-F-1-40, volume 8.
Colombo Plan - offers by Canada of fellowships and scholarships-Ceylon, June-December 1960.

File 11038-F-2-40, volume 23-FP.
Colombo Plan - scholarships and fellowships- India, February-July 1960.

File 11038-F-2-40, volume 24.
Colombo Plan - scholarships and fellowships- India, August-December 1960.

File 11038-F-7-40, volume 9.
Colombo Plan - technical assistance - Burma trainees, September-December 1960.

Box 262.

File 11038-G-40, volume 13.
Colombo Plan- technical cooperation assistance in South East Asia, agenda and minutes, January-March 1960.

File 11038-G-40, volume 14.
Colombo Plan - technical cooperation assistance in South East Asia, agenda and minutes, April-August 1960.

File 11038-G-40, volume 15.
Colombo Plan - technical cooperation assistance in South East Asia, agenda and minutes, September-November 1960.

File 11038 -S-40, volume 12-FP.
Colombo Plan - publicity, January 1961-July 1963.

File 11038-S-1-40, volume 4.
Colombo Plan - trainees - publicity re, May-December 1960.

File 11038-S-1-40, volume 5.
Colombo Plan - trainees, publicity re, January-September 1961.

File 11038-S-1-40, volume 6.
Colombo Plan - trainees, publicity re, October 1961-January 1962.

Box 263.

File 11038-S-1-40, volume 7.
Colombo Plan - trainees, publicity re, February-September 1962.

File 11038-S-1-40, volume 8.
Colombo Plan - trainees, publicity re, October 1962-September 1963.

File 11038-5-2-40, volume 2.
Colombo Plan - requests for information in, January 1961-September 1963.

File 11038-S-3-40, volume 2.
Colombo Plan - distribution of publications on(other than annual reports), November 1960-June 1963.

File 110398-S-4-40, volume 2.
Colombo Plan - publicity, articles and speeches, November-December 1961.

File 11038-S-6-40, volume 3-FP.
Colombo Plan - Information Officers conference, October 1960-October 1961.

File 11038-S-7-40, volume 2.
Colombo Plan - films, January 1961-September 1962.

File 11038-S-9-40, volume 2.
Colombo Plan - Interdepartmental Committee on External Aid Committee on Information, January-July 1961.

File 11038-S-10-40, volume 2-FP.
Colombo Plan - anniversary celebrations, February 1962-

File 11038-S-10-40, volume 3.
Colombo Plan - anniversary celebrations, February-June 1962.

File 11038-Z-40, volume 4.
Colombo Plan - capital and technical assistance, publicity, general file, August 1960-January 1961.

File 11038-Z-40, volume 5.
Colombo Plan - capital and technical assistance, publicity, general file, January 1961-September 1963.

Box 264.

File 11038-AB-2-40, volume 17.
Colombo Plan - technical assistance, requirements for Indonesia, experts and training facilities, February-August 1960.

File 11038-AB-2-40, volume 18.
Colombo Plan - technical assistance, requirements for Indonesia, experts and training facilities, September-December 1960.

File 11038-AB-17-40, volume 3.
Colombo Plan - Technical Assistance Programme. United Kingdom colonies, general file, January-December 1960.

File 11038-AB-17-A-40, volume 12.
Colombo Plan - Technical Assistance Programme - Malaya, June-December 1960.

File 11038-AB-17-B-40, volume 3.
Colombo Plan - Technical Assistance Programme, United Kingdom colonies. North Borneo, February-November 1960.

File 11038-AD-40, volume 3.
Colombo Plan - Exhibits(photographs and displays), October 1961-October 1963.

File 11038-AG-40, volume 6.
Colombo Plan - Technical Assistance Programme, Cambodia, June-November 1960.

Box 265.

File 11044-BL-40, volume 6.
Export of arms from Canada-Japan, January 1960-September 1961.

File 11044-BL-40, volume 7.
Export of arms from Canada-Japan, October 1961-March 1963.

File 11044-BL-40, volume 8.
Export of arms from Canada-Japan, April-October 1963.

Box 270.

File 11124-6-Y-40, volume 1.
Canada Council non-resident fellowships programme, India, February 1960-November 1963.

File 11124-6-AH-40, volume 1.
Canada Council non-resident fellowships programme, Japan, October 1960-July 1963.

File 11124-6-AQ-40, volume 1.
Canada Council non-resident fellowships programme, Malaya, November 1960-December 1962.

Box 271.

File 11124-6-BK-40, volume 1.
Canada Council non-resident fellowships programme, Pakistan, September 1960-April 1962.

File 11124-6-BT-40, volume 1.
Canada Council non-resident fellowships programme, Iran, October 1960.

File 11124-6-BW-40, volume 1.
Canada Council non-resident fellowships programme, Philippines, April-May 1961.

File 11124-6-CA-40, volume 1.
Canada Council non-resident fellowships programme, Indo-China, April 1962.

File 11124-6-CA-1-40, volume 1.
Canada Council non-resident fellowships programme, Cambodia, October 1960-May 1961.

File 11124-6-CB-40, volume 1.
Canada Council non-resident fellowships programme, Ceylon, March 1961.

File 11124-6-CH-40, volume 1.
Canada Council non-resident fellowships programme, Indonesia, September 1960-May 1961.

File 11124-6-CR-40, volume 1.
Canada Council non-resident fellowships programme, Korea, February-March 1961.

File 11156-K-3-40, volume 3.
Office of the High Commissioner, Colombo, premises, staff accommodation, January 1962-April 1963.

File 11156-N-40, volume 1.
Appointment of James George as High Commissioner at Colombo, Ceylon, April-September 1960.

Box 274.

File 11336-24-40, volume 5.
Establishment and organization for offices of the High Commissioner, New Delhi, June 1961-May 1963.

Box 275.

File 11336-44-40, volume 3.
Establishment and organization for the Canadian Embassy, Tokyo, July 1960-April 1963.

File 11336-48-40, volume 5.
Establishment and organization for offices of the High Commissioner, Karachi, November 1962-May 1963.

Box 278.

File 11384-C-40, volume 1.
Defence research assistance to India, July 1962-May 1963.

File 11384-E-40, volume 1.
Military assistance to Trinidad and Tobago, September 1962-August 1963.

File 11384-G-0, volume 1.
Military assistance to India, Air Defence Mission, December 1962-April 1963.

File 11384-G-40, volume 2-FP.
Military assistance to India - Air Defence Mission, May-September 1963.

File 11384-H-40, volume 1.
Defence Research assistance to Pakistan, January 1962-August 1963.

File 11394-K-40, volume 1.
Military assistance to Malaya, May-August 1963.

Box 286.

File 11561-BL-40, volume 1.
Privileges and immunities for Canadian representatives in Turkey, November 1962-April 1963.

File 11562-128-40, volume 1.
Visit to Canada of King of Laos, 1963, December 1962-March 1963.

Box 287.

File 11568-40, volume 7.
Political situation in Ceylon, June 1960-May 1961.

File 11568-40, volume 8.
Political situation in Ceylon, June 1961-March 1962.

File 11568-40, volume 9.
Political situation in Ceylon, April 1962-August 1963.

Box 288.

File 11568-G-40, volume 1.
Ceylon- relations with various countries, March 1960-August 1963.

File 11568-H-40, volume 1.
Ceylon- immigration and emigration policy, October 1961-November 1962.

File 11572-1-40.
Pakistan- military attaché reports, January-July 1963.

File 11578-A-40, volume 3.
Foreign policy of the Central People's Republic of China, January-April 1960.

File 11578-A-40, volume 4.
Foreign policy of the Central People's Republic of China, May-September 1960.

File 11578-A-40, volume 5.
Foreign policy of the Central People's Republic of China, October 1960-August 1963.

File 11578-B-40, volume 19.
Political situation in the Central People's Republic of China, July-November 1960.

File 11578-B-40, volume 20.
Political situation in the Central People's Republic of China, December 1960-May 1962.

Box 289.

File 11578-B-40, volume 21.
Political situation in the Central People's Republic of China, June 1962-July 1963.

File 11596-J-1-40, volume 2.
Canadian Embassy, Djakarta, chancery, January 1961-May 1963.

Box 290.

File 11596-J-3-A-40, volume 2.
Canadian Embassy, Djakarta, staff residence Polonia, January 1960-May 1963.

File 11596-J-3-D-40, volume 2.
Canadian Embassy, Djakarta, premises, staff residence Krakatku House, October 1961-May 1963.

Box 291.

File 11619-N-40, volume 1.
Appointment of J.P.Sigvaldaon as Ambassador of Canada to Djakarta, Indonesia, October 1960-March 1961.

Box 292.

File 11679-A-40, volume 6.
Food relief for Pakistan(East Bengal, India and Nepal), - 1954. April-August 1960.

File 11679-A-40, volume 7.
Food relief for Pakistan(East Bengal, India and Nepal), - 1954. September-December 1960.

File 11679-A-40, volume 8.
Food relief for Pakistan(East Bengal, India and Nepal), - 1954. January-November 1961.

File 11679-A-40, volume 9.
Food relief for Pakistan(East Bengal, India and Nepal), - 1954. November 1961-October 1963.

Box 293.

File 11706-40, volume 2.
Japan- commercial relations with various countries, July 1962-October 1963.

Box 297.

File 11913-40, volume 3.
British Guyana - political situation - Communism, September-October 1961.

File 11913-40, volume 4-FP.
British Guyana- political situation - Communism, November 1961-February 1962.

Box 298.

File 11913-40, volume 4-FP.
British Guyana- political situation - Communism, November 1961-February 1962.

File 11913-40, volume 5.
British Guyana- political situation - Communism, February-July 1962.

File 11913-40, volume 6.
British Guyana- political situation - Communism., August-December 1962.

File 11913-40, volume 7.
British Guyana- political situation - Communism, January-May 1963.

File 11913-40, volume 8.
British Guyana- political situation - Communism, May-June 1963.

File 11913-40, volume 9.
British Guyana - political situation - Communism, July-August 1963.

Box 299.

File 11958-A-40, volume 1.
South Korea -Communist China relations, May-December 1962.

File 12022-40, volume 4-FP.
Article 16 of Japanese Peace Treaty - distribution by International Red Cross of indemnities to Allied prisoners of war of Japan, February 1962-June 1963.

Box 300.

File 12087-40, volume 2.
Canada-Korea relations - including proposals for exchange of diplomatic representatives, January 1962-August 1963.

Box 301.

File 12113-A-40, volume 4.
Landing clearance for Royal Canadian Air Force aircraft en route to Indo-China carrying members of the International Supervisory Commission, November 1960-December 1962.

File 12130-A-40, volume 9.
Indo-China Truce Commission - personnel arrangements, July 1962-February 1963.

File 12130-C-40, volume 3.
International Supervisory Commission - Vientiane, Association of South East Asian Nations- personnel arrangements, June 1962-April 1963.

File 12130-M-040, volume 6.
Common pool of funds provided for the International Supervisory Commission in Indo-China and correspondence relating to expenses of the International Secretariat and national delegations, January 1962-May 1963.

Box 303.

File 12173-40, volume 8.
Afro-Asian(Bandung) conference, January 1961-August 1963.

Box 305.

File 12214-DG-40, volume 1.
Procedure re service of documents, taking of evidence, letters of request and rogatory commissions in Canada and Vietnam, November 1960-June 1962.

Box 306.

File 12216-AE-40, volume 1.
Extradition between Canada and Iran, August 1960-May 1961.

Box 332.

File 12490-BT-40, volume 1.
Exhibitions and fairs in Iran-Canadian participation, March 1961-March 1962.

File 12490-CA-3-40, volume 1.
Exhibitions and fairs in Saigon, Vietnam - Canadian participation, May 1960-June 1962.

Box 336.

File 12631-A-2-40, volume 2.
Office of Canadian High Commissioner, Kuala

Lumpur, premises-accommodation, January 1961-May 1963.

File 12631-D-1-40, volume 1.
Office of Canadian High Commissioner, Kuala Lumpur Inventory of furnishings, November 1960-April 1963.
Box 337.

File 12653-R-40, volume 1.
United Arab Republic-Laos relations, February-April 1961.

Box 339.

File 12670-AH-40, volume 1.
Cultural competitions, exhibitions, fairs and festivals in Japan, invitation to Canada to attend, April 1960-June 1964.

File 12670-BK-40, volume 1.
Cultural competitions, exhibitions, fairs and festivals in Pakistan, invitation to Canada to attend, August 1961-October 1962.

File 12670-BT-40, volume 1.
Cultural competitions, exhibitions, fairs and festivals in Iran - invitation to Canada to attend, April 1960-April 1963.

File 12670-AH-40, volume 1.
Cultural competitions, exhibitions, fairs and festivals in the Philippines, invitation to Canada to attend, October 1961-August 1963.

File 12670-CR-40, volume 1.
Cultural competitions, exhibitions, fairs and festivals in Japan, invitation to Canada to attend, March 1961-June 1963.

Box 340.

File 12671-AH-40, volume 1.
Sports and recreational activities in Japan, February-July 1961.

File 12671-CH-40, volume 1.
Sports and recreational activities in Indonesia, August 1962-November 1963.

File 12680-A-40, volume 1.
Appointment of Mr. McGaughey as Ambassador to Burma and Thailand and also High Commissioner to Malaya, October 1961-May 1963.

File 12706-A-1-40, volume 2.
Canadian Minister at Tehran, premises, chancery, January 1962-April 1963.

Box 337.

File 12706-A-2-40 volume 2.
Canadian Minister at Tehran, premises, residence, January 1960-November 1961.

File 12706-A-2-40, volume 3.
Canadian Minister at Tehran, premises, residence, January 1962-May 1963.

Box 341.

File 12706-A-3-40, volume 2.
Canadian Minister at Tehran, premises -staff accommodations, August 1961-May 1963.

File 12706-D-1-40, volume 1.
Canadian Minister at Tehran, inventory, June 1960-June 1963.

Box 347.

File 12816-A-40, volume 1.
Afghanistan- relations with other countries, March 1960-August 1963.

Box 349.

File 12832-R-1-40, volume 1.
Death of Tunku Abdul Rahman, Paramount Ruler of Malaya, 1960. April 1960-.

File 12832-S-1-40, volume 1.
Death of H.M.King Norodom Suramarit of Cambodia, 1960. April-August 1960.

File 12833-40, volume 2.
Cyprus-Commonwealth relations, January-March 1960.

File 12833-40, volume 3-FP.
Cyprus-Commonwealth relations, April 1960-January 1961.

File 12833-40, volume 4.
Cyprus-Commonwealth relations, February 1961-May 1963.

File 12833-1-40, volume 1.
Cyprus-Canada - commercial relations, January 1960-August 1963.

Box 355.

File 12850-J-5-1-40, volume 1.
Visit to Canada of the Shah of Iran and Queen Farah - 1961. May-August 1960.

File 12850-J-11-1-40, volume 1.
Visit to Canada of Crown Prince and Princess of

Japan - Fall 1960. May 1960-April 1961.

File 12850-J-12-2-40, volume 1-FP.
Visit to Canada of Mr. Ikeda, Japanese Prime Minister, January 1960-June 1961.

File 12850-J-12-2-40, volume 2.
Visit to Canada of Mr. Ikeda, Japanese Prime Minister, June-July 1961.

File 12850-M-2-1-40, volume 1.
Visit to Canada of Tunku Abdul Rahman, Prime Minister of the Federation of Malaya, July-October 1960.

File 12850-M-2-1-40, volume 2-FP.
Visit to Canada of Tunku Abdul Rahman, Prime Minister of the Federation of Malaya, October 1960-January 1961.

File 12850-M-2-1-40, volume 3.
Visit to Canada of Tunku Abdul Rahman, Prime Minister of the Federation of Malaya, September 1960-April 1961.

Box 356.

File 12850-P-2-2-40, volume 1.
Visit to Canada of Mr. Ayub, President of Pakistan, March 1961-October 1962.

Box 360.

File 12878-40, volume 1.
Albania-China relations, September 1960 - August 1963.

File 12881-40, volume 1.
Colombo Plan general, capital and technical assistance. December 1960-July 1961.

File 12881-40, volume 2.
Colombo Plan, general, capital and technical assistance, August-October 1961.

File 12881-40, volume 3.
Colombo Plan, general, capital and technical assistance, November 1961-August 1962.

File 12881-40, volume 4.
Colombo Plan, general, capital and technical assistance, September 1962-April 1963.

File 12881-40, volume 5.
Colombo Plan, general, capital and technical assistance, May-October 1963.

Box 361.

File 12881-6-40, volume 1.
Mekong River projects, December 1960-March 1962.

File 12881-B-12-40, volume 1.
Colombo Plan , capital and technical assistance-Burma, November 1963.

File 12881-J-2-40, volume 1-FP.
Colombo Plan, capital and technical assistance to India, November 1960-February 1962. October 1963.

File 12881-C-4-40, volume 1.
Colombo Plan, capital and technical assistance to Ceylon, December 1960-October 1963.

File 12881-J-2-40, volume 1-FP.
Colombo Plan, capital and technical assistance to India, November 1960-February 1962.

Box 362.

File 12881-J-2-40, volume 2.
Colombo Plan, capital and technical assistance to India, February 1962-October 1963.

File 12881-J-3-40, volume 1-FP.
Colombo Plan, capital and technical assistance to Indo-China, Afghanistan and Nepal, December 1960-October 1963.

File 12881-J-4-40, volume 1.
Colombo Plan, capital and technical assistance to Indonesia, December 1960-October 1963.

File 12881-M-2-40, volume 1.
Colombo Plan, capital and technical assistance to Malaya, October 1961-August 1963

File 12881-P-2-40, volume 1-FP.
Colombo Plan, capital and technical assistance to Pakistan, November 1960-October 1963.

File 12881-S-9-40, volume 1-FP.
Colombo Plan, capital and technical assistance to Singapore, Brunei, Borneo and Sarawak, December 1960-May 1961.

File 12881-T-3-40, volume 1-FP.
Colombo Plan, capital and technical assistance to Thailand, December 1960-February 1962.

Box 363.

File 12882-B-44-40, volume 1.
Canadian aid to British Guyana and British Honduras, December 1960-March 1962.

File 12882-B-44-40, volume 2.
Canadian aid to British Guyana and British Honduras, April-November 1962.

File 12883-40, volume 1-FP.
Canadian commercial relations with Hong Kong, December 1960-August 1963.

Box 364.

File 12883-40, volume 2.
Canadian commercial relations with Hong Kong, September-October 1963.

File 12884-40, volume 1.
Organization of the Japanese Government, December 1960-September 1961.

File 12891-40, volume 1.
Administrative arrangements for Canadian delegation to the Conference on Laos in Geneva, April 1961-June 1962.

Box 366.

File 12898-C-4-40, volume 1.
Export financing to Ceylon, August 1961-May 1963.

File 12898-J-2-40, volume 1.
Export financing to India, June 1961-October 1963.

File 12898-P-2-40, volume 1.
Export financing to Pakistan, July 1961-August 1963.

File 12898-P-6-40, volume 1.
Export financing to Philippines, August 1961-.

Box 369.

File 12937-40, volume 1.
Canada-Japan - Ministerial Committee, June 1961-February 1963.

Box 370.

File 12937-40, volume 2.
Canada-Japan Ministerial Committee, February-August 1963.

File 12942-F-40, volume 1.
Syria-Turkey relations, October 1961-June 1963.

File 12944-40, volume 1-FP.
Cyprus- defence, January 1961-April 1962.

File 12945-40, volume 1.
Cyprus- economic situation, general, December 1962.

Box 371.

File 12946-40 volume 1.
Cyprus- relations with other countries, August 1960-May 1963.

File 12946-A-40, volume 1.
Cyprus- relations with Greece and Turkey, December 1960-August 1963.

File 12949-40, volume 1.
Hong Kong- Premises, general, September 1962-May 1963.

File 12964-40, volume 1.
Western Samoa, general, February-December 1961.
Box 372.

File 12964-40, volume 2.
Western Samoa, general, January 1962-August 1963.

File 12984-40, volume 1.
Sino-Afro-Asian relations, May 1962-August 1963.

Box 373.

File 12991-40, volume 1.
Formosa(Nationalist China), Canada relations, May 1962-June 1963.

File 12992-7-5-2-1-40, volume 1.
Passport Office - passport facilities for East Indians, March 1961-December 1963.

Box 382.

File 14003-C-6-3-40, volume 1.
Atomic energy - other countries - China - cooperation with Canada, February - November 1962.

File 14003-J-2-3-40, volume 3.
Atomic energy, other countries, India, cooperation with Canada, June 1960-March 1961.

Box 383.

File 14003-J-2-3-40, volume 4.
Atomic energy, other countries, India, cooperation with Canada, April 1961-March 1962.

File 14003-J-2-3-40, volume 5.
Atomic energy, other countries, India, cooperation with Canada. April 1962-January 1963.

File 14003-J-2-3-40, volume 6.
Atomic energy, other countries, India, cooperation with Canada, January-May 1963.

File 14003-J-2-3-40, volume 7.
Atomic energy, other countries, India, cooperation with Canada, May-August 1963.

File 14003-J-2-3-40, volume 8.
Atomic energy, other countries, India, cooperation with Canada, August-October 1963.

File 14003-J-6-1-40, volume 1.
Atomic energy, other countries, Iran, peaceful uses of, July 1960-January 1963.

File 14003-J-11-1-40, volume 2.
Atomic energy, other countries, Japan, peaceful uses of, January-July 1963.

File 14003-J-11-3-40, volume 5.
Atomic energy, other countries, Japan, cooperation with Canada, November 1961-December 1962.

File 14003-J-11-3-40, volume 6.
Atomic energy, other countries, Japan, cooperation with Canada, January-November 1963.

Box 391.

File 14020-C-14-9-40, volume 1.
Commonwealth Educational Plan, visit to Canada of Mr. V.S.Jha, July 1960-April 1961.

File 14020-C-14-9-40, volume 2.
Commonwealth Educational Plan, visit to Canada of Mr. V.S.Jha, May 1961-July 1963.

File 14020-C-14-12-40, volume 1.
Commonwealth Conference on the Teaching of Science

in the Schools, Ceylon 1963, July 1962-October 1963.

Box 392.

File 14020-J-4-1-40, volume 1.
Other countries foreign aid programmes, Indonesia, general file, January-March 1960.

Box 397.

File 14053-J-2-40, volume 1.
G.A.T.T. - Accession or Association, waivers re negotiations of schedules, Article XXVIII: 4-India, February 1960-April 1962.

Box 403.

File 14500-3-4-40, volume 1.
O.E.E.C./O.E.C.D. - Turkish Consortium, December 1962-October 1963.

Box 407.

File 14500T--24-40, volume 1.
O.E.E.C./O.E.C.D., general, financial and economic policy in trade, agriculture and fisheries, Turkey, July-August 1961.

File 15000-B-12-40, volume 1-FP.
Representatives of other countries in Canada, Burma, Heads of post, May 1962-March 1963.

File 15000-C-26-40, volume 1-FP.
Representatives of other countries in Canada, China, Heads of post, October 1962-March 1963.

File 15000-C-26-1-40, volume 1.
Representatives of other countries in Canada, China, political advisers, May-June 1963.

File 15000-C-26-11-4, volume 1.
Representatives of other countries in Canada, China, in Vancouver, May 1962-March 1963.

Box 408.

File 15000-J-6-40, volume 1.
Representatives of other countries in Canada, India, Heads of post, May 1962-June 1963.

File 15000-J-10-1-40, volume 1.
Representatives of other countries in Canada, Indonesia, in Ottawa, March 1962-July 1963.

File 15000-J-12-40, volume 1.
Representatives of other countries in Canada-Iran. Heads of post, August-December 1962.

File 15000-J-12-1-40, volume 1.
Representatives of other countries in Canada, Iran, political advisers, March-July 1963.

Box 409.
File 15000-J-36-40, volume 1.
Representatives of other countries in Canada, Japan, political advisers, February 1962-July 1963.

File 15000-J-36-40, volume 1.
Representatives of other countries in Canada, Japan, political advisers, July -December 1963.

File 15000-J-36-40, volume 1.
Representatives of other countries in Canada, Japan. Heads of post, January-May 1963.

File 15000-J-36-11-40, volume 1.
Representatives of other countries in Canada, Japan, in Montréal, April-July 1962.

File 15000-J-36-12-40, volume 1.
Representatives of other countries in Canada, Japan, in Toronto, October 1962.

File 15000-J-36-13-40, volume 1.
Representatives of other countries in Canada, Japan, in Vancouver, January-July 1963.

File 15000-J-36-14-40, volume 1.
Representatives of other countries in Canada, Japan, in Winnipeg, September 1962-April 1963.

File 15000-K-2-40, volume 1.
Representatives of other countries in Canada, Korea. Heads of post, December 1962-May 1963.

File 15000-P-8-40, volume 1.
Representatives of other countries in Canada, Pakistan. Heads of post, October 1962-May 1963.

File 15000-P-8-2-40, volume 1.
Representatives of other countries in Canada, Pakistan, military advisers, February-June 1962.

File 15000-P-24-40, volume 1.
Representatives of other countries in Canada-Philippines, in Vancouver, August 1962-February 1963.

Box 410.

File 15000-T-8-40, volume 1.
Representatives of other countries in Canada, Thailand, in Ottawa, March 1962-May 1963.

File 15000-T-19-40, volume 1.
Representatives of other countries in Canada, Trinidad, Heads of posts, August-December 1962.

File 15000-T-19-1-40, volume 1.
Representatives of other countries in Canada, Trinidad, political advisers, September-November 1962.

File 15000-T-19-2-40, volume 1.
Representatives of other countries in Canada, Trinidad, in Montréal, September-December 1962.

File 15000-T-24-1-40, volume 1.
Representatives of other countries in Canada, Turkey, political advisers, May-October 1962. File 15000-T-24-1-40, volume 1.
Representatives of other countries in Canada, Turkey, military advisers, August-October 1962.

Box 411.

File 15001-J-10-1-40, volume 1.
Canadian representatives abroad, Indonesia, political advisers, March-June 1963.

File 15001-J-12-40, volume 1.
Canadian representatives abroad, Iran, heads of post, November 1962-February 1963.

File 15001-J-12-1-40, volume 1.
Canadian representatives abroad, Iran, consular advisers, September-December 1961.

File 15001-J-36-40, volume 1.
Canadian representatives abroad, Japan, Heads of post, October-December 1962.

File 15001-J-36-1-40, volume 1.
Canadian representatives abroad, Japan- political advisers, November 1962-March 1963.

File 15001-M-6-2-40, volume 1.
Canadian representatives abroad, Kuala Lumpur, trade and commerce advisers, May-September 1962.

Box 412.

File 15001-P-8-40, volume 1.
Canadian representatives abroad, Pakistan, heads of post, October 1962-July 1963.

File 15001-P-8-3-40, volume 1.
Canadian representatives abroad, Pakistan, military advisers, July-September 1962.

File 15001-P-24-40, volume 1.
Canadian representatives abroad, Philippines, heads of post, August 1962-March 1963.

File 15001-P-24-1-40, volume 1.
Canadian representatives abroad, Philippines, political, administrative and consular, June 1962-March 1963.

File 15001-T-24--1-40, volume 1.
Canadian representatives abroad, Trinidad, Heads of post, May 1962-March 1963.

File 15001-T-24-40, volume 1H
Canadian representatives abroad, Turkey, heads of post, September 1962-January 1963.

Box 415.

File 15500-10-15-40, volume 1.
NATO Ministerial Meeting, Ottawa, May 1963.

Administrative arrangements, Turkey delegations, February-April 1963.

Record Group 26. Citizenship and Immigration, 1949-1966.

In 1966 became Department of Manpower and Immigration.

A. Deputy Minister's Records, 1923-1972.

Contains statistical information, 1880-1964, on immigration policy, including East Indians.

Volume 71.
Bulletins on Canadian Citizenship Act, memoranda re Chinese applicants for citizenship, etc., 1947-1951.

A1c. Deputy Minister's Registry Files(Block) 1939-1972.

Volumes 90-147, 151, 161-170, 172-173, 13.62 metres

Volume 121.

File 3-30-5.
Canada-Japan ministerial meetings(correspondence re immigration matters), 1964-1966.

Volume 123.

File 3-32-21.
Orientals, re immigration to Canada, 1960-1963.

Volumes 125, 126.

File 3-33-7, parts 1-4.
Chinese immigration, 1936-1964.

Volume 127.

File 3-33-15.
East Indian immigration, 1946-.

Volume 128.

File 3-33-19, part 1.
Admission to Canada from Japan(with a copy of briefs from National Japanese Canadian Citizens Associations, 1951, 1953 and report on re-establishment of Japanese in Canada, 1944-1946), 1947-1957.

Volume 130

File 3-33-33.
Admission from Turkey, 1951-1957.
A2a. Miscellaneous Records, 1923-1971. Legal files, 1923-1964, .8 metres Volumes 70-74.

C. Statistical Records, 1880-1964.

Statistical tabulation.(Immigration) 1880-1964. 11.65 metres volume 16-64, and 61A-61G.
Monthly tabulation, volumes 25-64, and 61A-61G.

Monthly statistics of immigration.

Miscellaneous tabulation, volume 16-24.

Statistics for special groups, include Japanese, 1928-1933.

Record Group 27. Labour.

A. Ministers' Office, 1921-1947, 1973-1983.

Records of the Honourable Humphrey Mitchell 1921-1947, 3 ft.(volumes 618-622).

Volume 618.

File 8.
Binder 2(includes references to Japanese Canadians, 1943-1945).

Volume 619.

File 1.
Reference volume 1943.

B. Deputy Minister's Office 1921-1947, 1973-1983,1900-1978.

B1. Lacelle Files, volumes 65-274, 1902-1945.

Volume 130, File 601-3-4.
Conscription of East Indians for the Canadian army, 1943.

Volume 169.

File 614.02:11, parts 1-2.
Japanese placement, policy and plans, 1942-1944.

Volume 169.

File 614.02:11, part 3.
Proposed Japanese settlement, pictures, n.d.

Volume 169.

File 614.02:11, parts 1-2.
Japanese placement in Québec and the Maritimes, 1943-1945.

Volume 170.

File 614.02:11, parts 1-2.
Japanese placement in Alberta, 1942-1943.

File 614.02:11, parts 1-2.
Transfer of Japanese from British Columbia to Manitoba, 1942-1944.

Volume 171.

File 614.02:11, parts 1-2.
Relief and medical attention to indigent Japanese, 1942-1944.

File 614.02:11, parts 1-18.
British Columbia Security Commission- summary of expenditures - financial statements re evacuation of Japanese, 1942-1944.
Volume 174.

File 614.02:11.
Expenditure reports 1946, of Japanese division of Department of Labour, n.d.

File 614.02:11.
Expenditure reports, Japanese division of Department of Labour, 1946-1947.

Volume 174-79.

File 614.02:11-1, parts 1-19.
Japanese situation in Canada, general, 1942-1944.

Volume 174-81.

File 614.02:11-7, parts 1-11.
Japanese situation in Canada, Ontario - plans for Japanese workers, 1942-1944.

Volume 182.

File 614.02, no. 3009.
Report of the Royal Commission to enquire into the welfare and maintenance of Japanese in the interior settlements of British Columbia, 1943-1944.

Volume 182.

File 614.02, no. 3009.
Report of his Honour Judge Cameron re Japanese inquiry at Vancouver, 1942.

B6. Committees. Conferences, Meetings. 1920-1966, volumes 837-931. 19.9 metres

Volume 914.

File 8-9-109, parts 1-2.
Interdepartmental Committee on Orientals in British Columbia, and interim report, 1938-1939.

C. Public Relations and Information Services Branch.

Accession 87-88/108.

C1. Press Clipping Division, 1900-1971, 113.9 m, volume 1000-1477.

Volume 1337.

File S 2-7.
Japanese(clippings), 1938-1944.

Volume 1338.

File S 1-7.
Japanese(clippings), 1944-1946.

Volume 1339,.

File S-1-7.
Japanese(clippings), 1946-1947.

Volume 1340.
Japanese(clippings), 1947.

L. Councils, Commissions, Bureau.

Inquiries, Task forces, 1919-1981.

L1. National Labour Supply Council, 1919-1951, 1.95 metres(volumes 630-639).

Volume 632.

File 77.
Farm labour problems - Oriental menace, 1941.

N. National Selective Service, National Selective War Services, 1939-1947, 17.7 metres (volumes 967-999, 1478-1526).

Volume 998.

File 2-114-15.
Aliens, Chinese, 1943-1945.

Volume 999.

File 2-114-16.
National war services - aliens, Japanese, 1943-1945.

File 2-114-27.
Aliens, Indians, 1943-1944.

File 2-115-22.
Aliens, Turks(national war services), 1943-1945.

Volume 1486.

File 2-153, parts 1-4.
East Indians, 1940-1946.

File 2-153-1.
East Indians in British Columbia, franchise, 1942-1943.

Volume 1489.

File 2-184.
Orientals, national war service, 1941.

Volume 1496.

File 2-B-184.
National war services - military service of, division B, 1941.
Volume 1500.

File 2-12-184.
National war services - Orientals, British Columbia, division K, 1941.

Volume 1508.

File 10-1-14.
Postponement of military training of East Indians, 1942-1943.

Volume 1527 to 1529.

Japanese division, 1942-1965.

N2. Office Files of Raymond Ranger, and other National Selective Service officials, 1940-1951. 7.6 metres (volumes 3000-3054).

Volume 3004.
National selective service, mobilization section, Chinese enlistment, 1944.

Volume 3022.
Imp. document no. 21, re Chinese admission, 1942.

Volume 3026.
Cabinet committee on Japanese questions - agendas and minutes of meetings, 1945-1948.

Volume 3518.

File 3-26-1, part 3DB.
Memorandum presented by the East Indian Canadian Citizens Welfare Association, Vancouver, British Columbia and the Khalsa Diwan society, 1963.

O. Japanese Division, 1940-1965. Volumes 640-662, 1527-1529.

Volumes 640-662, 1527-1529.
These records contain extensive files of correspondence, memoranda, and statistics on the administration of Japanese Canadian affairs, 1942-1965. File titles include administrative orders, property permits, placement, settlements, repatriation, education, training, refugees, and intercepted letters. See finding list for list of files.

P. Employment Service Branch.

P1. Employment Service Branch, 1942-1968, 3 metres, volumes 600-612.

Volume 608.

File 6-34-4.
Use of Japanese labour in Canadian industry, 1964-1965.

Q. Immigration Farm Placement Bureau, 1943-1965.

General Registry Files, 1943-1965, 4.1 metres, volumes 275-293.

Volume 288.

File 1-26-42.
Immigrants from China, 1948.

Record Group 29. National Health and Welfare.

Contains records on quarantine and Immigration Medical Service.

Central Registry File S.

Volume 169.

File 236-1-4.
Old age assistance, blind persons and disabled assistance - Japanese evacuated from West Coast, 1948-1949.

Volume 182.

File 302-1-13.
Public health services, transportation of Chinese coolies through Canada, 1919.

Volume 290.

File 403-1-12.
Quarantine, general, Japanese disaster, 1923(refugees), 1923.

Volume 299.

File 414-1-1, part 2.
Leprosy, repatriation of Chinese lepers detained on Bentinck Island, 1923-1931.

Volume 552.

File 321-3-11, parts 1-3.
Narcotics, Chinese medicines, anti-opium pills, etc., 1929-1934.

E. Special and International Organisations.

Colombo Plan, 1951-1969, volumes 1007-1009. 1.5 feet.

Includes Public Health Mission from South East Asia. Observation tour to study T.B. in Canada by experts from India.

Accession 81-82/184.

World Health Organization, 1931-1979. Volumes 993-1066, 1555, 1679.

Record Group 30. Canadian National Railways(Devlin papers).

Volume 604B.

File J5275.
Chinese, 1960.

Record Group 33. Royal Commissions.

Series 7. Royal Commission on Japanese Claims.

Volume C41.

Files 219-222.
Royal Commission on Japanese claims to investigate into losses sustained by Japanese of Vancouver on occasion of riots in Vancouver, in September 1907(correspondence, claims for damages, expense accounts, hearings, copy of report and miscellaneous papers).

Series 8. Royal Commission on Oriental Immigration.

Volume C37.

File 203.
Correspondence written in Chinese, table of Asiatic immigration in British Columbia, re U.S. head tax regulations, census count of 1901, copy of resolutions passed by city of Vancouver, 28 October 1907, for exclusion of Asiatics from Canada, correspondence from companies desiring Asiatic labourers to Canadian Nippon Supply Co., Ltd., 1907.

File 204.
Newspaper editorials criticizing King's failure to investigate violations of Immigration Act, correspondence, etc. of Canadian Nippon Supply Co., British Columbia General Contract Co. Ltd., Wellington Colliery Co. Ltd., etc.

File 205.
Minutes of evidence of Royal Commission to inquire into methods by which Oriental labourers have been induced to come to Canada, 1907.

Volume C38.

File 207.
Re Oriental labour desired by companies, arrivals of steamships with immigrants, formation of Bocho Immigration Company, etc., 1907.

File 208.
Draft reports, summary of evidence of Royal Commission, 1907.

Volume C39.

File 208.
Report of Royal Commission, 1907.

File 210
Report of W.L.MacKenzie King, resumé of report of Royal Commission on Chinese immigration, 1885, report on Chinese and Japanese immigration, 1902, etc., 1907.

Series 9. Royal Commission on Chinese Claims.

Volume C39.

File 211.
Memoranda, reports, and appointments to investigate losses sustained by Chinese during riots in Vancouver, September 1907, list of claimants for damages, 1908.

File 212.
Record books, cheque stubs of payments, etc., 1908.

File 213.
Evidence presented, accounts, statements, copy of declaration of Chuin Quay, etc., 1908.

Volume C40.

File 215-118.
Notarized copies of declarations of actual damages as result of riots, 1908.

Series 60. Royal Commission to Investigate Charges that Japanese Black Dragon Society was Operating in British Columbia. J.C.A.Cameron, Chief Commissioner.

Volume 1.
Report of proceedings, exhibits, copy of notice outlining regulations governing persons of Japanese race, map showing area to be evacuated by Japanese, etc., 1942.

Volume 2.
Volumes 2 and 3 of report of proceedings, 1942.

Series 69. Royal Commission on Japanese Property Losses. H.I.Bird, Chief Commissioner.

Volumes 1-79.
These records include transcripts, exhibits, reports and correspondence. The first 74 volumes contain individual case files regarding claims for loss of property. See finding aid for list of files.

Series 80. Bilingualism and Biculturalism Commission.

Volume 56.

File 750-534.
National Japanese Canadian Citizens Association in Ontario, brief, December 1965.
Volume 129.

File 585E.
Background papers, annual meeting of the Japanese Canadian Citizens Association, Toronto, March 1965.

Volume 120.

File 631E.
Report, private meeting with Japanese Canadians, Vancouver, 12 May l965, June 1965.

Volume 130,.

File 634E.
Report, private meeting with Chinese Canadian group, Vancouver, 13 May 1965.

Volume 131,

File 679E.
Letter from Reverend Andrew Lam, St. John the Baptist Anglican church, Fort Garry, re hopes of citizens of Chinese ethnic origin, 19 July 1965.

Series 120. Royal Commission on Organization, Authorization and Despatch of the Canadian Expeditionary Force to the Crown Colony of Hong Kong, 1942. Sir Lyman P. Duff, Chief Commissioner. .6 metres volumes 1-3.

Record Group 35. Interdepartmental Committees.

Series 7. Public Records Committee.

Volume 22.

File 22, parts 1-2.
Department of Labour - report on the administration of Japanese affairs during World War II.

Volume 24.
Account of war activities of Department of Justice - internment operations, etc. World War II, 1948.

Record Group 36. Boards, Offices and Commissions.

Series 27, British Columbia Security Commission, 1942-1948, 4.92 metres, volumes 1-44.

These records contain extensive files of correspondence, memoranda, reports and clippings for the period 1942-43. Subjects include evacuation and resettlement, accommodation, welfare, education, property purchases, progress reports, arrangements with provincial governments, Royal Canadian Mounted Police reports, and British Columbia settlements(Tashme, Slocan, Sandon, New Denver, Lemon Creek, Kaslo, Greenwood).

Volume 1.

Files 1, 11, 17, 17a, 17b, 18, 20.
Includes distribution of Japanese, 1942-1949.

Volume 2.

Files 31, 34, 35, 37, 40, 45, 50, 53.
Include Citizens' Defence Committee, 1942, detention and internment, 1942, 1944, 1942-1945.

Volume 3.

Files 53a, 57, 59, 66, 71, 76, 77, 79.
Includes internees, agitators, detention building, Japanese Canadian Citizens' League, evacuation, 1942-1946.

Volume 4.

Files 90, 100, 120, 127-129.
British Columbia police and Royal Canadian Mounted Police, self-supporting Japanese, 1942-1948.

Volume 5.

Files 130-132.
Self-supporting Japanese communities, 1942-1947.

Volume 6.

Files 132A, 133, 133A.
Self-supporting Japanese communities, 1942-1947.

Volume 7.

Files 134, 136, 137, 144, 163, 171, 172, 178.
Communities, interior housing projects, contracts, agreement, parliamentary enquiries, 1942-1945.

Volume 8.

Files 18-182, 199, 201, 202.
Includes property purchases, damage to immigration sheds, progress reports, evacuation from New Westminster, 1942-1947.

Volume 9.

Files 203-208, 213, 214.
General policy, evacuation, Royal Canadian Mounted Police, and police reports, 1942-1948.

Volume 10.

Files 163, 305, 306, 313, 320, 323, 327.
Press coverings, releases, welfare, hospitalization, general "cities" protests.

Volume 11.

Files 400, 403, 434, 436, 506.
Includes trust accounts, education, 1942-1950.

Volume 12.

Files 500-501.
General, 1942-1948.

Volume 13.

Files 503, 513, 514.
Policy, repatriations, reports to Ottawa, 1942-1945.

Volume 14.

File 516.
Summer school, 1943-1948.

Volume 15.

Files 607, 610, 612-615, 622.
American repatriation Japanese nationals, committees, 1942-1946.

Volume 16.

Japanese Canadian Citizenship League, 1942-1946.

Volume 17.

File S 622, 625, 626, 628, 629.
Repatriation, community analyses, evacuation surveys, 1944-1945.

Volume 19.

File 630.
Inspection trips, Japanese interior projects, Ottawa officials, Red Cross and Department of External Affairs, also reports, there on, 1945.

Volume 20.

File 639.
Naturalized Canadians, where husbands signed and wives did not, 1946.

Volume 34.

Files 2201, 2202.
Committee on Japanese, 1943-1948. Cabinet Committee on Japanese problems, notice of meetings, etc.

Volume 35.

File 2203.
Special cabinet committee on claims by Japanese evacuees, 1947.

Volume 35.

File 2562.
A Journal of Opinion Published by Japanese Canadian Committee for Democracy, miscellaneous issues for 1946, 1947, 1946-1947.

Volumes 36-37.

File 2501.

Heart Mountain Sentinel published weekly at an American Japanese Evacuation Centre, 2 volumes, 1942-1945, 1942-1945.

Volume 38-40.

File 2503.
The New Canadian, "An independent weekly for Canadians of Japanese origin", 3 volumes, 1944-1949.

Volume 41.

File 2505.
Miscellaneous articles and pamphlets re Japanese in Canada and the United States, n.d.

Volume 41-42.

File 2505.
Japanese high schools, calendars, yearbooks, etc., n.d.

Volume 43.

File 3009.
Report of his Honour Judge J.C.A.Cameron re Japanese inquiry at Vancouver, British Columbia, 1942.

Record Group 38. Veterans's Affairs. 3

D2. Subject File S.

Volume 177.
Several files on Japanese camps operated by the Department of Mines and Resources.

D3. Veterans' Land Administration.

Volume 368A.

File BC-1906-B.
McLaren, Robert Craig, 1946-1959.

Volume 368A.

File BC-1880-A.
Neale, Kenneth, 1944-1960.

File BC-1871-B.
Foulkes, David John, 1944-1962.

File BC-1870-B.
Staples, Jack Harold, 1944-1957.

File BC-1869-B.
Armstrong, Harry, 1946-1952.
Veterans' Land Administration. Central Registry, 1942-1982, volumes 403-404.

Relate to various aspects of acquisition of former Japanese properties in British Columbia from the Custodian of Enemy Property by the Director, Veterans' Administration.

Record Group 42. Marine Branch.

IIB1. Central Registry Files, 1887-1973.

Volume 152.

File 27713.
Desertion of Chinese crews in British Columbia, 1906.

Volume 224.

File 34366.
Granting of marine engineer's certificate to Orientals, 1913-1917.

Volume 255.

File 37467.
Canadian Pacific Railway steamers carrying Chinese, 1916-1919.

Volume 283.

File 45431.
Canadian Pacific Railway steamers, carriage of returning Chinese to Canada, 1918-1919.

IIC1. Central Registry Files, 1923-1936.

Volume 392.

File 58-0-20.
Shipping of seamen, general employment of Asiatics and Orientals.

Record Group 43. Railways and Canals.

Volume 922.

File 961, part 4.
Canadian Pacific Railway, including some letters to Chinese workers, 1890-1892.

Record Group 44. National War Service.

Volume 37.

Chinese War Relief Fund national campaign in

January 1947, January 1947.

Record Group 55. Treasury Board.

Volume 557, File 2-12.
Correspondence with Immigration and Colonization(volume 1) includes letters re refunds of head tax on Chinese, appointment of controllers of Chinese immigration, etc., 1923-1933.

Record Group 58. Auditor General.

C. Office of the Auditor General, 1936-1974.

Audit Subject Files, 1890, 1936-1953. 8.2 metres(Volumes 11-511)

Volumes 12-13, 47.
There are numerous files on the audit of the Custodian of Enemy Property's activities including the Vancouver Branch, 1947-1953. See finding aid for list of files.

Accession 74-75/83.

Boxes 61-64.393-394.

Files on the audit of the Custodian of Enemy Property, 1947-1958. There is one file on the awards recommended by the Bird Commission(Box 62). See finding aid for list of files.

Record Group 64. Wartime Prices and Trade Board.

Volume 732.

File 32-17, part 3.
Red Cross requirements [includes correspondence on Chinese War Relief Fund providing relief to China,etc.], 1945-1950.

Volume 738.

File 32-30.
Aid to China, Canadian aid to China fund, 1944-1948.

Record Group 68. Registrar General.

1908-1918 general index.

p.750. Charter to "the Canadian Japanese Social and Athletic Club, Ltd." (1917).

Record Group 74. External Aid Office, 1955-1976.
318.9 metres

Canadian International Development Agency since 1968.

Warsak Files volume 1-11.

Warsak hydroelectric project on North West Frontier. Bilateral assistance program between Pakistan and Canada.

Applications for 1955 and 1958.

Accession 80-81/063

Planned program Country Files, 1965-1976. Boxes 80-150.

Equipment and supplies for.

Colombo Plan, general file, 1958-1970.

Asian Development Bank, 1968-1969.

Burma, 1968-1969.

Cambodia, 1955-1969.

Ceylon, 1954-1966.

India, 1952-1968.

Indonesia, 1959-1970.

Laos, 1967-1970.

Malaysia, 1956-1969.

Pakistan, 1962-1969.

Thailand, 1964-1969.

Vietnam, 1958-1970.

Singapore, 1957-1967.

Canadian International Development Agency.

Trainee files, 1955-1968, .67 metres

Commonwealth Scholarship Fellowship Program, 1961-1969.

Accession 75-76/59.

Volumes 8-11.

Sample of application dated 1961-1968.
Includes students from Ceylon, India and Pakistan.

Accession 80-81/100.

List of trainees.
Sample of application.
Includes students from Ceylon, India and Pakistan.

Accession 80-81/104.

List of trainees.
Sample of application.
Includes students from Ceylon, India and Pakistan.

International Projects, 1959-1970.

Accession 80-81/103.

Technical and development assistance. 173 boxes.

Ceylon, 1959-1970.

India, 1964-1970.

Malaysia, 1962-1970.

Pakistan, 1964-1970.

Vietnam, 1964-1968.

Singapore, 1956-1966.

Thailand, 1956-1966.

Accession 80-81/103.

Boxes 384-438.

Administration and operational records, 1950-1963.

Burma,

Cambodia, 1963-1966.

Ceylon, 1961-1966.

India, 1959-1968.

Indonesia, 1964-1967.

Laos, 1966-1967.

Malaysia, 1965-1968.

Pakistan, 1959-1968.

Sarawak, 1960-1965.

Singapore, 1964.

Thailand, 1964-1966.

Vietnam, 1960-1967.

Korea, 1963-1967.

Philippines, 1962-1966.

Colombo Plan.

Record Group 76. Immigration, 1865-1977.

I. Central Registry File Series.

A. First Central Registry Series, 1873-1968.
Volumes 1-692 on microfilm.

Volumes 1-676.
Files on all subjects.

Finding aids. There is a complete file list.

Index to First Central Registry Files, 1892-1024. 21 reels, T5571-T5592.

Index to First Central Registry Files, 1924-ca. 1946. 5 microfilm reels, M-1986-M-1990.

Volume 83.

File 9309, part 1, reel C-4750.
Japanese emigration, 1891-1908.

File 9309, part 2, reel C-4750.
Japanese emigration, 1908.

Volume 84.

File 9309, part 3, reel C-4750.
Clippings Japanese immigration (report of inquiry), 1908-1909.

File 9309, part 4, reel C-4750.
Japanese immigration, 1909-1910.

File 9309, part 6, reel C-4750.
Japanese immigration, 1912-1914.

File 9309, part 7, reel C-4750.
Japanese immigration, 1914-1917.

File 9309, part 8, reel C-4751.
Japanese immigration, 1917-1918.

Volume 85.

File 9309, part 9, reel C-4751.
Japanese immigration, 1918-1919.

File 9309, part 10, reel C-4751.
Japanese immigration, 1919-1920.

File 9309, part 11, reel C-4751.
Japanese immigration, 1921-1923.

File 9309, part 12, reel C-4751.
Japanese immigration, 1923-1925.

File 9309, part 13, reel C-4751.
Japanese immigration(lists), 1925-1930.

Volume 86.

File 9309, part 14, reel C-4751-C-4752.
Japanese immigration, 1930-1936.

File 9309, part 15, reel C-4752.
Japanese immigration, 1936-1938.

File 9309, part 16, reel C-4752.
Japanese immigration, 1938.

File 9309, part 17, reel C-4752.
Japanese immigration(report), 1938-1941.

File 9309, part 18, reel C-4752.
Japanese immigration(report), 1941-1947.

Volume 87.

File 9309, part 19, reel C-4752.
Japanese immigration(report), 1947-1949.

File 9309, part 19, reel C-4753.
Japanese immigration, 1947-1949.

File 9309, part 20, reel C-4753.
Japanese immigration, 1947-1949.

File 9309, reel C-4753.
Reports of board of review on illegal immigration(Japanese), 1938.

File 9309, part 1, reel C-4753.
Japanese immigration, form file(lists), 1908-1909.

File 9309, part 2, reel C-4753-C-4754.
Japanese immigration, form file(lists), 1909-1910.

File 9309, part 3, reel C-4753.
Japanese immigration, newspaper clippings, 1942-1945.

Volume 88.

File 9309, part 3, reel C-4754.
Japanese immigration, form file(lists), 1910-1911.

File 9309, part 4, reel C-4754.
Japanese immigration, form file(lists), 1911.

File 9309, part 5, reel C-4754.
Japanese immigration, form file(lists), 1911.

File 9309, part 6, reel C-4754.
Japanese immigration, form file(lists), 1911-1912.

File 9309, part 7, reel C-4754.
Japanese immigration, form file(lists), 1912.

File 9309, part 8, reel C-4754.
Japanese immigration, form file(lists), 1912.

Volume 89.

File 9309, part 9, reel C-4755.
Japanese immigration, form file(lists), 1912.

File 9309, part 10, reel C-4755.
Japanese immigration, form file(lists), 1912-1913.

File 9309, part 11, reel C-4755.
Japanese immigration, form file(lists), 1913.

File 9309, part 12, reel C-4755.
Japanese immigration, form file(lists), 1913.

File 9309, part 13, reel C-4755.
Japanese immigration, form file(lists), 1913.

Volume 90.

File 9309, part 14, reel C-4755.
Japanese immigration, form file(lists), 1913.

File 9309, part 15, reel C-4755.
Japanese immigration, form file(lists), 1913-1914.

File 9309, part 16, reel C-4756.
Japanese immigration, form file(lists), 1914.

File 9309, part 17, reel C-4756.
Japanese immigration, form file(lists), 1914.

File 9309, part 18, reel C-4756.
Japanese immigration, form file(lists), 1914.

Volume 91.

File 9309, part 19, reel C-4756.
Japanese immigration, form file(lists), 1914.

File 9309, part 20, reel C-4756.
Japanese immigration, form file(lists), 1914-1915.

File 9309, part 21, reel C-4756.
Japanese immigration, form file(lists), 1915-1916.

File 9309, part 22, reel C-4757.
Japanese immigration, form file(lists), 1916.

File 9309, part 23, reel C-4757.

Japanese immigration, form file(lists), 1916.
Volume 92.

File 9309, part 24, reel C-4757.
Japanese immigration, form file(lists), 1916-1917.

File 9309, part 25, reel C-4757.
Japanese immigration, form file(lists), 1917.

File 9309, part 26, reel C-4757.
Japanese immigration, form file(lists), 1917.

File 9309, part 27, reel C-4757.
Japanese immigration, form file(lists), 1917-1918.

File 9309, part 28, reel C-4757 to C-4758.
Japanese immigration, form file(lists), 1918.

File 9309, part 29, reel C-4758.
Japanese immigration, form file(lists), 1918.

Volume 93.

File 9309, part 31, reel C-4758.
Japanese immigration, form file(lists), 1918-1919.

File 9309, part 32, reel C-4758.
Japanese immigration, form file(lists), 1919-1920.

Volume 121.

File 23635, part 1, reel C-4784.
Chinese immigration, 1895-1909.

File 23635, part 2, reel C-4784.
Chinese immigration, report by W.L.MacKenzie King, 1908-1911.

File 23635, part 3, reel C-4784.
Chinese immigration, 1911-1918.

File 23635, part 4, reel C-4784.
Chinese immigration, 1918-1919.

File 23635, part 5, reel C-4784.
Chinese immigration, 1919-1924.

File 23635, part 6, reel C-4785.
Chinese immigration, 1924-1943.

Volume 122.

File 23635, part 7, reel C-4785.
Chinese immigration, 1943-1948.

File 23635, part 8, reel C-4785.
Chinese immigration, 1948-1949.

File 23635, part 9, reel C-4785.
Chinese immigration, 1949-1950.

File 23635, part 10, reel C-4785.

Chinese immigration.151-1952.

Volume 125.

File 27114, reel C-4736,
Immigration of Armenians to Western Canada.
D.M.Quin, manager. 1895-1905.

Volume 215.

File 89616, part 1, reel C-7366.
Armenian relief fund. Admissions of orphans to Canada(photographs) 1922-1926.

File 89616, part 2, reel C-7366.
Armenian relief fund. Admission of orphans, 1926-1928.

File 89616, part 3, reel C-7366.
Armenian relief fund. Bringing orphans to Canada, 1928-1934, 1944.

Volume 223.

File 111414, reel C-7372.
Registration of Chinese in Canada under section 18 of the Chinese Immigration Act of 1923, 1942-1943, 1958.

Volume 226.

File 116193, part 1, reel C-7375.
Hong Kong(photographs and plans), 1923-1942.

File 116193, part 2, reel C-7375.
Administration and inspection at Hong Kong, 1945-1949.

Volume 280.

File 536999, part 1, reel C-10279-C-10280.
Emigration of Hindoos, 1904,1906-1907.

File 536999, part 2, reel C-10280.
Emigration of Hindoos(including British Honduras, labour(East Indian) ordinances, 1908), 1907-1908.

File 536999, part 3, reel C-10,280.
Emigration of Hindoos, 1908-1911.

File 536999, part 4, reel C-10,280.
Emigration of Hindoos, 1911-1912.

Volume 300.

File 279907, part 1, reel C-7849,
Immigration from Turkey and Armenia, 1903-1915, 1919-1923.

File 279907, part 2, reels C-7849-C-7850.
Immigration from Turkey and Armenia, 1923-1928.

File 279907, part 3, reel C-7850.

Immigration from Turkey and Armenia, 1929-1934, 1936-1938, 1940, 1946-1949.

Volume 342.

File 361435, reel C-10250.
Fred Yoshi, alias Kiyoshi Suhinto, Vancouver, smuggling Japanese into Canada, 1920-1921, 1928-1932.

Volume 363.

File 462223, reel C-10264.
White Canada Association, Vancouver, British Columbia, information on statistics on Japanese in Canada, 1934-1938.

File 467977, part 1, reel C-10264 to C-10265.
Consul-general for Japan, Ottawa, 1906-1911, 1912-1925.

File 467977, part 2, reel C-10265.
Consul-general for Japan, Ottawa, Ontario, 1928, 1930-1931, 1933-1944, 1948.

Volume 368.

File 488557, reel C-10268.
Privy Council reference from Colonial Office relating to Armenians in Brantford, Ontario, who wish to obtain permission for their families to rejoin them from Armenia, 1906-1907.

Volume 382.

File 532462, reel C-10278.
Investigation by Royal Canadian Mounted Police of illegal entry of Japanese, 1931-1934.

Volume 385.

File 536999, part 5, reel C-10280.
Emigration of Hindoos, 1912-1913.

File 536999, part 6, reel C-10280.
Emigration of Hindoos, 1913.

File 536999, part 7, reel C-10280.
Emigration of Hindoos(appeals against deportation), 1913.

File 536999, part 8, reel C-10280.
Emigration of Hindoos, 1913-1914.

File 536999, part 9, reel C-10280.
Emigration of Hindoos, 1914-1916.

File 536999, part 10, reel C-10280.
Emigration of Hindoos(including **Extracts from Minutes of Proceedings and Papers laid before the Imperial War Conference)**, 1917, 1916-1918.

Volume 386.

File 536999, part 11, reel C-10280 to C-10281.
Emigration of Hindoos(including **Extracts from Minutes of Proceedings and Papers laid before the Imperial War Conference,** 1917, 1917-1919.

File 536999, part 12, reel C-10281.
Emigration of Hindoos(including **Summary of proceedings and documents on Conference of Prime Ministers**), 1921, 1919-1921.

File 536999, part 13, reel C-10281.
Emigration of Hindoos(copies of acts), 1921-1923.

File 536999, part 14, reel C-10281.
Emigration of Hindoos(copies of acts)(lists),1922-1935.

File 536999, part 15, reel C-10281.
Emigration of Hindoos, 1934-1939.

Volume 387.

File 536999, part 16, reel C-10281.
Emigration of Hindoos(lists), 1939-1943.

File 536999, part 17, reel C-10281.
Emigration of Hindoos(lists), 1943-1947.

File 536999, part 18, reel C-10281 to C-10282.
Emigration of Hindoos(lists), 1947-1948.

File 536999, part 19, reel C-10282.
Emigration of Hindoos(lists), 1948-1949.

File 536999 R.O., part 1.
Registering certificates of identification to Hindoos leaving on a visit, 1913-1919.

Volume 388.

File 536999 R.O., part 2, reel C-10282.
Registering certificates of identification to Hindoos leaving on a visit(pamphlet), 1919-1922.

File 536999 R.O., part 3, reel C-10282.
Registering certificates of identification to Hindoos leaving on a visit, 1923-1954.

File 536999 British, part 1, reel C-10282.
Reports from W.C.Hopkinson on Hindoo matters(copies), 1914-1919.

File 536999 British, part 2, reel C-10282.
Reports from W.C.Hopkinson on Hindoo matters, 1919-1921.

File 536999 clippings, part 1, reel C-10282.
Newspaper clippings on Hindoos, 1913-1914.

File 536999 clippings, part 2, reels C-10282 to C-10283.
Newspaper clippings on Hindoos, 1914-1915, 1918.

File 536999 clippings, part 3, reel C-10283.
Newspaper clippings on Hindoos, 1918, 1920, 1922.

Volume 393.

File 561280, reel C-10286.
Ocean Steamship Company, Liverpool, England. Bonds covering escape of two Japanese, T.Obano and M.Ohishi(in Vancouver, British Columbia), 1906.

Volume 397.

File 565225, reel C-10289.
Chick Sexing Association of America, admission of chick sexing experts from Japan, 1933-1937.

Volume 401.

File 574351, reel C-10292.
G.L.Milne(medical inspector and immigration agent) Vancouver, British Columbia, escape of Japanese from schooner **Swan maru**, 1906.

Volume 470.

File 716275, reel C-10407.
G.L.Milne sends fine of $350.00 for allowing seven Japanese to land at Union Bay, British Columbia, without properly entering customs at that place, German ship S.S. **Wanguard**, 1907.

Volume 474.

File 729921, part 1, reel C-10410.
Asiatics, Orientals(Japanese, Chinese, East Indians), (list), 1907-1922.

File 729921, part 1, reel C-10410.
Asiatics, Orientals(Japanese, Chinese and East Indians), (pamphlets), 1922-1925.

File 729921, part 3, reel C-10410 to C-10411.
Asiatics, Orientals(Japanese, Chinese and East Indians), 1925-1932, 1934-1939.

File 729921 clippings, reel C-10411.
Newspaper clippings on Asiatic immigration(Japanese, Chinese and East Indians) 1907, 1909-1922.

Volume 491.

File 761402, reel C-10425.
A.Lavergne, member of Parliament, Montmagny, Québec. Japanese syndicate acquiring land in Alberta in order to settle colonists there, 1906, 1908, 1913.

Volume 503.

File 781181, reel C-10606.
Richard L.Drury, Victoria, British Columbia, appointed as a special officer of the Immigration branch for immigration work in Japan, 1908-1909.

Volume 512.

File 817172, reel C-10653.
J.B.Harkin wants employment in the fishing industry retained for Canadians(Japanese):1910-1948.

Volume 546.

File 304845, reel C-10632
Inquiries from the Fiji islands, 1908-1911.

Volume 550.

File 805806, reel C-10634.
Khoren Andonian, destitute at Batoum, Russia, makes application for repatriation to Canada(Armenian), 1908-1909.

Volume 551.

File 806018, reel C-10635.
Francis W. Giddens, Department of Labour, Ottawa, Ontario, statement re Chinese, Japanese, and Hindu immigration, 1908-1909.

Volume 556.

File 806652, reel C-10638.
Business manager, **Free Press**, Ottawa, Ontario. Printing pamphlet, **East Indians in British Columbia**(copies), 1909.

Volume 561.

File 808722, part 1, reel C-10641.
W.C.Hopkinson, Vancouver, British Columbia, appointed to the immigration staff at Vancouver, British Columbia(Hindu immigration), 1909-1914.

File 808722, part 2, reel C-10,641.
W.C.Hopkinson, Vancouver, British Columbia, appointed to the immigration staff at Vancouver, British Columbia(Hindu immigration), 1914-1916, 1918.

Volume 563.

File 808904, reel C-10644.
General enquiries from Persia, 1909, 1912-1913.

Volume 566.

File 806977, reel C-10638.
United States Commissioner of Immigration, Montréal, Québec. Report on number of Japanese and Hindoos entering United States, 1907 and 1909.

Volume 568.

File 812274, reel C-10647.
A.B.Barnard, Deputy Director of Intelligence, India, photographs and fingerprints of reports(Hindus), 1909, 1911-1912, 1920-1926.

Volume 576.

File 815661, reel C-10652.
Chinese conditions: 1912, 1921-1932, 1935-1938.

Volume 578.

File 817172, reel C-10653.
J.B.Harkin wants employment in the fishing industry on the Fraser River to be retained for Canadians(Japanese), 1910, 1912-1916, 1918-1919, 1933 and 1948.

Volume 584.

File 820636, reel C-10658.
Honourable Frank Oliver, Minister of the Interior, Ottawa, Canada. prevalence of hookworm among Hindus, among Hindus applying for admission to U.S. and among the negroes(blacks) of the U.S., 1910-1914, 1918, 1922-1923, 1943.

Volume 601.

File 879545, part 1, reel C-10,669.
Hindoo immigration, sailing of 400 Hindoos by chartered vessel **Komagata maru**, 1914.

File 879545, part 2, reel C-10,669.
Hindoos sailing from Shanghai to Vancouver, British Columbia on S.S. **Komagata maru**, 1914.

File 879545, part 3, reel C-10,669.
Hindoos sailing from Shanghai to Vancouver, British Columbia on S.S. **Komagata maru**(photo), 1914.

File 879545, part 4, reel C-10,669.
Hindoos sailing from Shanghai to Vancouver, British Columbia on S.S. **Komagata maru**, 1914.

Volume 602.

File 879545, part 5, reel C-10,669 to C-10,670.
Hindoos sailing from Shanghai to Vancouver, British Columbia on S.S. **Komagata maru** (publication), 1914.

File 879545, part 6, reel C-10,670.
Hindoos sailing from Shanghai to Vancouver, British Columbia on S.S. **Komagata maru**, 1914-1915.

File 879545, part 7, reel C-10,670.
Hindoos sailing from Shanghai to Vancouver, British Columbia on S.S. **Komagata maru**, 1915-1922.

File 879545, part 8, reel C-10,670.
Hindoos sailing from Shanghai to Vancouver, British Columbia on S.S. **Komagata maru**, 1936, 1938, 1942, 1952.

Volume 647.

File A66589, part 1, reel C-10586.
Repatriation of Japanese(lists), 1941-1943, 1945.

File A66589, part 2, reel C-10587.
Repatriation of Japanese(lists), 1946-1947.

Volume 669.

File C57382, reel C-10603.
Transit of German refugees from Shanghai, China through Canada(Jewish), 1949.

Volume 674.

File C92656, reel C-10677.
Admission of Jewish refugees from Shanghai(lists), 1950.

File C92656, reel C-10677.
Admission of Jewish refugees from Shanghai, China(lists), 1950.

Volume 675.

File D46144, reel C-10677.
Greek Embassy, Ottawa, Ontario, admission of 200 Greeks from China(lists), 1951-1952.

Volume 712.

Reel C-13421.
Control certificates, Chinese immigration(c.1, 5, 28, 30, 36), 1899-1953.

B. Central Registry Files. Second Central Registry series("500" block) 1911-1970 (volumes 676, 677, 689 to 692, and 743 to 930), 7 microfilm reels(C-10678, C-10687 to C-10688, C-13487, and M-1983 to M-1985).

l. Central Registry files, "500" block, 1911-1971. 40.2 metres (volumes 689-692, 718-725, 743-930), and 2 microfilm reels(C-10687 to C-10688).

This series consists of the Immigration Service's core policy and subject files active in the period from World War II to 1966.

Volumes 743 to 930 are the main run of files in this series. Volumes 689 to 692, reels C-10,687 and C-10,688, document questions and answers in the House of Commons, including individual cases, immigration and employment policy and statistics, U.S. draft dodgers and deserters, and refugees issues from 1957 to 1970.

Volumes 718-725 relate to the Immigration Inspection Service on irregularities in immigration.

Finding aids.

Subject index to "500" block and related files, ca. 1925-1962. 3 microfilm reels M-1983 to M-1985.

Complete list of files in this series available.

The file classification manual indicates some of the files created in this series.

Volume 713.

Reel C-13421.
Register of Chinese Immigration, Central District(Toronto), 1923-1953.

Volume 796.

File 546-1-526, part 1.
Medical examinations of immigrants from China and Hong Kong, 1950-1957.

File 546-1-526, part 2.
Medical examinations of immigrants from China, Hong Kong and Formosa, 1958-1966.

Volume 802.

File 547-5-567.
Security examination of immigrants in India, 1962-1966.

File 547-5-580.
Security examination of persons from Korea, 1963-1966.

File 547-5-611.
Security examination of immigrants in the Philippines, 1961-1966.

Volume 803.

File 547-5-629.
Security examination of immigrants in Thailand, 1966.

File 548-8, part 1.
Processing of Chinese applications (including form 55b procedures), 1951-1956.

File 548-8, part 2.
Processing of Chinese applications (including form 55b procedures), 1956-1961.

Volume 804.

File 548-8, part 3.
Processing of Chinese applications (including form 55b procedures), 1961-1963.

File 548-8, part 4.
Processing of Chinese applications (including form 55b procedures), 1964-1966.

Volume 808.

File 548-12-578.
Processing of applications, Japan, 1965-1966.

Volume 819.

File 552-1-5-522.
Immigration from Burma, 1963-1966.

File 552-1-524.
Immigration from Ceylon, 1960-1065.

File 552-1-526, part 1.
Immigration from China, general files, 1952-1955.

File 552-1-526, part 2.
Immigration from China, policy and instructions, 1955-1958.

File 552-1-526, part 3.
Immigration from China, policy and instructions, 1958-1962.

File 552-1-526, part 4.
Immigration from China, policy and instructions, 1962-1963.

Volume 820.

File 552-1-526, part 5.
Immigration from China, policy and instructions, 1964-1966.

Volume 821.

File 552-1-548.
Immigration from the Fiji Islands, general file , 1953-1966.

Volume 822.

File 522-1-567, part 1.
Immigration from India, 1950-1961.

File 522-1-567, part 2.
Immigration from India, 1961-1966.

Volume 823.

File 552-1-537.
Immigration from Iran, general file, 1951-1956.

File 552-1-569.
Immigration from Indonesia, 1950-1964.

File 552-1-570.
Immigration from Iran, general file, 1951-1966.

Volume 824.

File 552-1-578, part 1.
Immigration from Japan, general file, 1950-1957.

File 552-1-578, part 2.
Immigration from Japan, general file, 1957-1964.

File 552-1-578, part 3.
Immigration from Japan, general file (reading list enclosed), 1964-1966.

File 552-1-580.
Immigration from Korea, general file, 1896-1966.

Volume 826.

File 552-1-606.
Immigration from Pakistan, general file, 1953-1966.

File 552-1-611, part 1.
Immigration from the Philippines, 1929-1963.

File 552-1-611, part 2.
Immigration from the Philippine Islands, 1929-1963.

Volume 829.

File 552-1-632.
Immigration from Turkey, general file, 1951-1966.

Volume 831.

File 5521-10-567, part 1.
Canada-India Immigration agreement, policy and instructions, 1951-1952.

File 5521-10-567, part 2.
Canada-India Immigration agreement, policy and instructions, 1953-1954.

File 5521-10-567, part 3.
Canada-India immigration agreement, policy and instructions, 1955-1956.

File 5521-10-567, part 4.
Canada-India immigration agreement, policy and instructions, 1957-1959.

Volume 832.

File 5521-10-567, part 5.
Canada-India immigration agreement, policy and instructions, 1959-1962.

File 5521-10-567, part 6.
Canada-India immigration agreement, policy and instructions, 1963-1966.

File 552-10-606, part 1.
Canada-Pakistan immigration agreement, policy and instructions, 1951-1956.

Volume 850.

File 553-148-567.
Admission to Canada of students from India, 1920-1966.

File 553-148-578.
Movement of students from Japan, 1960-1965.

File 533-148-592.
Movement of students from Malaysia (formerly Malaya, Singapore, etc.) policy and instructions, 1960-1964.

File 553-10-606.
Movement of students from Pakistan, 1962-1964.

Volume 854.

File 554-3, part 1.
Immigration to Canada of Armenians, general file, 1950-1961.

File 554-3, part 2.
Immigration to Canada of Armenians, general file, 1961-1966.

File 554-5.
Asiatics, general policy, 1953-1963.

File 554-6.
Asiatic immigration, 1923-1950.

Volume 861.

File 555-54-526, part 1.
Chinese refugees in Hong Kong(and refugees in China) general file, 1946-1961.

File 555-54-526, part 2.
Chinese refugees in Hong Kong(and refugees in China) general file, 1962-1963.

File 555-54-526, part 3.
Special movement of Chinese refugees from Hong Kong, operational control, 1962-1963.

Volume 862.

File 554-54-526-5.
Tibetan refugees, general file, 1959-1966.

Volume 866.

File 555-54-632.
Refugees in Turkey, general file, 1951-1963.

Volume 867.

File 556-1-524.
Immigration laws and regulations, Ceylon, 1942-1961.

Volume 868.

File 556-1-567.
Immigration laws and regulations, India, 1945-1950.

File 556-1-570.
Immigration laws and regulations, Iran, 1960.

File 556-1-606.
Immigration laws and regulations, Pakistan, 1948-1950.

File 556-1-611.
Immigration laws and regulations, Philippines, 1930-1963.

Volume 870.

File 556-3-570.
Alien labor laws and regulations, Iran, 1959.

Volume 871.

File 557-3-578, part 2.
Establishment of Japanese enterprises and entry of personnel, 1961-1966.

Volume 873.

File 557-40-12, part 1.
Canadian church organizations proposals for entry of Chinese immigrants from Hong Kong, 1960-1963.

File 557-40-12, part 2.
Canadian church organizations proposals for entry of Chinese immigrants from Hong Kong, 1964-1966.

Volume 876.

File 560-2-578.
Citizenship regulations, Japan, 1916-1950.

File 560-2-606.
Citizenship regulations, Pakistan, 1951.

File 560-6-526, part 1.
Status adjustment of Chinese illegally in Canada, 1960-1961.

File 560-6-526, part 2.
Status adjustment of Chinese illegally in Canada, policy and procedure, 1961-1962.

File 560-6-526, part 3.
Status adjustment of Chinese illegally in Canada, policy and procedure, 1962-1963.

Volume 877.

File 560-6-526, part 4.
Status adjustment of Chinese illegally in Canada, policy and procedure, 1962-1963.

File 560-6-526, part 5.
Status adjustment of Chinese illegally in Canada, policy and procedure, 1965-1966.

File 560-6-567.
Status adjustments of East Indians who have entered Canada illegally, 1961-1965.

Volume 895.

File 569-2.
Passport and visa regulations for Chinese nationals, 1938-1964.

Volume 896.

File 569-9-510.

Passport regulations, Cambodia, 1954.

File 569-9-524.
Passport regulations, Ceylon, 1950-1965.

Volume 898.

File 569-9-561.
Passport regulations, Maldive Islands, 1966.

File 569-9-567.
Passport regulations, India, 1953-1966.

File 569-9-569.
Passport regulations, Indonesia, 1950-1964.

File 569-9-570.
Passport regulations, Iran, 1954-1966.

Volume 899.

File 596-9-
Passport regulations, Japan, 1918-1965.

Volume 900.

File 596-9-606.
Passport regulations, Pakistan, 1953-1963.

File 569-9-611.
Passport regulations, Philippines, 1953-1964.

File 569-9-621.
Passport regulations, Singapore, 1960-1965.

Volume 901.

File 555-54-632.
Refugees in Turkey, general file, 1951-1963.

File 569-9-641.
Passport regulations, Vietnam, 1953-1966.

Volume 903.

File 569-30-522.
Issuance of Canadian visas to persons from Burma, 1953-1966.

File 569-30-524.
Issuance of Canadian visas to persons from India, 1950-1963.

File 569-30-526.
Issuance of Canadian visas to persons from China, 1949-1960.

Volume 904.

File 569-30-567.
Issuance of Canadian visas to persons from India, 1950-1965.

File 569-30-569.
Issuance of Canadian visas to persons from Indonesia, 1960-1961.

File 569-30-570.
Issuance of Canadian passports to persons from Iran, 1958-1966.

File 569-30-578.
Issuance of visas to persons from Laos, 1959.

Volume 905.

File 569-30-578.
Issuance of Canadian visas to persons from Japan, 1959-1966.

File 569-30-592.
Issuance of Canadian visas to persons from Malaysia(formerly Malaya, Singapore, etc.), 1950-1958.

File 569-30-611.
Issuance of Canadian visas to persons from the Philippines, 1953-1963.

File 569-30-621.
Issuance of Canadian visas to nationals from Singapore, 1965.

File 569-30-632.
Issuance of Canadian visas to persons from Turkey, 1953-1966.

File 569-30-580.
Issuance of Canadian visas to persons from Korea, 1960.

File 569-30-589.
Issuance of Canadian visas to persons from North Korea, 1963-1964.

File 569-30-606.
Issuance of Canadian visas to persons from Pakistan, 1955-1962.

Volume 906.

File 569-36-524.
Passport and visas agreements, Ceylon, 1949-1950.

Volume 907.

File 569-36-570.
Passport and visa agreements, Canada-Iran, 1959-1961.

File 569-36-578.
Passport and visas agreements, Canada-Japan, 1954-1965.

File 569-36-632.
Passport and visa agreements, Canada-Turkey, 1949-1963.

Volume 914.

File 581-3-2, part 1.
Japanese agricultural students, general file, 1955-1959.

File 581-3-2, part 2.
Japanese agricultural students, general file, 1960.

Volume 917.

File 584-2-641.
Entry of nationals of Vietnam for medical treatment, 1965-1966.

Volume 920.

File 585-12-578.
Repatriation of Japanese from Canada, 1945-1966.

C. Central Registry Files. Third Central Registry series(5000 block), 1948-1979.
The Third Central Registry series of immigration records contains the core policy and subject files of Immigration headquarters in Ottawa between 1966 and 1977.
This was replaced by a fourth series, 8000 block in about 1977.

1. Central Registry Files, 5000 block(unclassified files), 1967-1973, 67.5 metres

VI. **Chinese immigration records, 1885-1953**, .9 metres(volumes 693-703, 712, 713), 5 microfilm reels, C-9510 to C-9513, C-13421.

The Department of Customs was made responsible for the administration of the Chinese Immigration Act of 1885, and a general register was to be maintained for Chinese immigrants who entered Canada. In 1893, the Department of Trade and Commerce was established, and customs officers, as controllers of Chinese immigration were to report to the Deputy Minister of Trade and Commerce. In 1911, the administration of the Act was transferred to the Immigration branch of the Department of the Interior, and the Immigration branch was responsible for the administration of the Act until 1947.

A CI.6 certificate was issued to all Chinese who had entered Canada before 1885, and a CI.5 certification to Chinese immigrants who arrived after 1885, and paid the head tax. CI.9 and CI.9A certificates were issued to persons wishing to leave Canada temporarily.

A. General registers of Chinese immigration, 1885-1903, .9 metres(volumes 694-703), 4 microfilm reels, C-9510 to C-9513.
Gives information on Chinese immigrants, some as early as 1860, including village and province of birth in China. General registers numbers 11-to 18, 1903-1949, are found in Record Group 76, accession 84-85/062, with a microfilm version in 84-85/238.

B. New Westminster Agency, register of Chinese immigration, 1887-1898, 1907 and 1908, .075 metres(Volume 693), one microfilm reel(C-9510).

In 1885, the Collectors of Customs at Victoria, Nanaimo, New Westminster, and the sub-Collectors of Customs at Osoyoos and Kootenay and all collectors and acting collectors of customs, as controllers of Chinese immigration, having to register Chinese immigrants, collect head tax, and issue C.I. certificates of identification.

1. Register of Chinese immigrants, Port of New Westminster, 1887--1898, 1907 and 1908, .075 metres(Volume 693), one microfilm reel, C-9510.

List of Chinese immigrants who registered and paid the head tax at New Westminster, British Columbia.

C. Central district, registers and certificates of Chinese immigration, 1899-1953, .05 metres,(volumes 712,713), one microfilm reel, C-13421.

Immigration activities for Toronto were controlled by Central District Headquarters. Chinese moving in or out of Canada were required to register their movement with the controllers of Chinese immigration at Toronto.

1. Register of Chinese immigration (Toronto), 1923-1953(Volume 713), one microfilm reel, C-13421.

Chinese register number 2, created in the Office of Immigration's central district(Toronto), and used to control Chinese immigration to and temporary emigration from Canada, particularly outward CI.9 registrations. Register number 1 for registrations before 1923 has apparently not survived.

2. Sample C.I. certificates, C.I.5, CI.28, C.I.30, and C.I.36, 1899-1953(Volume 712), one microfilm reel, C-13421.

The certificate system was used to control the movement of Chinese in and out of Canada, and of seamen sailing out of the Great Lakes system These certificates seem to have never been used.

VII. Asiatic immigration records, 1949-1973,(volumes 714, 716-718).

These files document the admission to Canada of individual immigrants classified as "Asiatic" under restrictive regulations and quota agreements. The files were opened between l949 and 1967. They are numbered sequentially and prefixed by the letter "AN". The files in Volume 716-718 were chosen for transfer to the National Archives Canada in 1979 as relating to cases of special historical or legal interest. These involve persons of specially desirable or questionable status(such as specialist scientists and successful entrepreneurs on the one hand, or criminal, deportees and other irregular entrants on the other).

Between 1907 and 1967, prospective and accepted immigrants to Canada, classified as "Asiatics" or "Asians" were subject to special restrictions, separate from those placed on Chinese immigrants.
"Asians" included Japanese, ethnic East Indians(from the Indian subcontinent, West Indies, Africa and elsewhere), Pakistanis, Ceylonese, Filipinos, and other inhabitants of East Asia and the Middle East.

The restrictive Orders in Council aimed at "Asiatics" between 1908 and 1960 are listed on pages 125-191 of R.Sampat-Mehta's **International barriers** (Ottawa, Harpell Press, 1973), these restrictive orders were definitively rescinded by the new immigration regulations in 1967.

1. "Asiatic" case files, 1949-1973.
At least five series of case files have been opened at various dates since the 1920s to document the arrival of individuals classed as "Asiatics" under the exclusionary Orders in Council. The oldest appear to be the "Hindu" (H prefix) files, a few examples of which survive in the Record Group 76 accessions V84-85/279 and V85-86/472. These may have been superseded by the Record Group 76 "AN" (Asian or Asiatic) files described in Series VII 1a below. A few examples survive in accessions at the Vancouver Federal Records Centre of files prefixed M(Malaysian or Malayan), T(Thai) and J(Japanese).

a. **AN(Asiatic or Asian) case files, 1949-1973**, .6 metres,(volumes 716-718).

2. Register of immigrants under India, Pakistan and Ceylon quota agreements, 1951-1967, 4 cm. (Volume 714).

Asian immigration(as opposed to Chinese immigration) had been almost entirely prohibited since 1930, by Order in Council 2115. This excepted only spouses and minor children of Canadian citizens. The 1951 agreements expanded the admissible Asians to include aged parents, and a limited number of persons from each country.

VIII. Employment and Immigration Commission(Immigration branch) inspection services, 1950-1976, 1.9 metres(volumes 727-735).

A. Chinese case files compiled by the inspection service of the department during the investigation by the Royal Canadian Mounted Police of illegal and fraudulent immigration practices among Chinese immigrants and agents during the early 1960s. These are coded in the DIC and CH files series, 1950-1963(85 metres, volumes 727-732).

C. Printed, near print material and reports on various departmental activities in the 1960's and 1970's. Of particular note is a report entitled **Chinese immigration: Hong Kong immigration office**, by H.K. Abbott, Director of Inspection Services, 1959, (Volume 735).

Accession 83-84/345.

Records of legal counsel, Robert Philip Brooks case, 1918-1972, 1.8 metres. Boxes 1-6.

Brooks was an American businessman who was deported from the Philippines in 1962, as a result of wide variety of charges against himself and associates including tax evasion, tobacco smuggling, currency violations, theft of stock and bribery. He came to Canada and acquired landed immigrant status in 1963, but was ordered deported in 1968. The case was tried in the Supreme Court in 1972-1974, and Brooks was finally ordered deported.
File list available.

Accession 83-84/346.

In the 1970s a series of secret subject files, the security or "SF" series were amalgamated with unclassified "5000" subject files on similar topics, and segregated by the department, before they were transferred to this accession.

File lists and indexes available.

Box 4.

File 5003-1-6058.
Ports and posts, Seoul, South Korea, 1970-1973.

Box 6.

File 5175-1-526, part 1.
Illegal entry, China, 1963-1970.

File 5175-1-526, part 2.
Illegal entry, China, 1971-1975.

File 5175-1-611, Volume 1.
Illegal entry, Philippines, -1969.

File 5175-1-611, Volume 2.
Illegal entry, Philippines, 1969-1970.

File 5180-2-1/611.
Crimes and irregularities, passports and visas, passports lost and invalidated, Philippines, 1968-1975.

File 5185-6-1-526.
Crimes and irregularities, illegal entry, misrepresentation, Chinese, 1971-1976.

Box 9.

File 5260-1-546.
Diplomatic relations, Taiwan, 1947-1976.

File 5260-1-641, Volume 1.
Diplomatic relations, South Vietnam, 1973-1975.

File 5260-1-713, volume 1.
Diplomatic relations, North Vietnam, 1973-1976.

Box 10.

File 5420-1-526.
Examination, stage "B", China, 1949-1973.

File 5420-1-569.
Examination, stage "B", Indonesia, 1964-1969.

Box 11.

File 5420-1-578.
Examination, stage "B", Japan, 1953-1973.

File 5420-1-629.
Examination, stage "B", Thailand, 1966-1967.

File 5420-1-710.
Examination stage "B", Bangladesh, 1972-1974.

Box 12.

File 5450-1-511, part 1.

Asia, 1967-1969.

File 5450-1-564.
Hong Kong, 1966-1969.

File 5450-1-567.
India, 1967-1969.

Accession 83-84/347.

Box 1.

File SF-C-25, part 1.
Chinese fraudulent visa practices in Hong Kong (U.S. report), 1955-1965.

File SF-H-5.
Immigration irregularities.

File SF-I-10, part 1.
Return to Canada of repatriates to Sino-Soviet bloc countries, 1955-1961.

File SF-I-26, volumes 1, 2.
Investigation, Chinese immigration, general(adjustment program), 1959-1964.

Box 2.

File SF-N-32.
Irregularities in Canadian immigration office in New Delhi, 1967.

Accession 83-84/348.

Chinese case files, ca. 1900-1966, 29.4 metres, boxes 1-92.

Records consist of individual Chinese immigration case files in the "CH" series, created by federal officials to screen prospective immigrants to which the Chinese Immigration Act(1885-1947) applied. Many files also contain documentation on immigration of relatives arriving after the repeal of the Act in 1947. Some contain extremely detailed genealogical reviews, family trees, interviews describing family life in home villages in China, and formal documentation for immigration inquiries or immigration appeal board cases. Arrival records for many of these individuals are found in the registers of Chinese immigration in Record Group 76, series VI.

This accession is continued in Accession 84-85/041 and 84-85/527.
The finding aid is a nominal file list. Nominal indexes to these files are Accession 85-86/002 and 85-86/051. Files originally created in the first Central Registry series are indexed in 85-86/005, but there is no conversion list to indicate where these files are found in the "CH" series.

Accession 83-84/349.

Immigration division, Central Registry Files, 5000 block(unclassified volumes), 1938-1979, 67.1 metres, boxes 1-215, 13a, 31a, 46a, 46b, 66a, 98a, 144a, 192a, 197a, 198a, 199a, 200a. Boxes 1-32, 13A and 31A now processed with permanent status, Record Group 76, volumes 1002-1060.

Includes most of the remaining files of the third Central Registry filing system of the Immigration branch, called the "5000" block, because of its base-numbering system(in the range 5000-5999 with subnumbers). It follows the "500" block registry system (see Record Group 76, volumes 717-725, and 743-930) on, 1 April 1966. Active files in "5000" series were brought forward into the "8000" block. Files include immigration law, policy, history and statistics, and many relate to foreign countries, and foreign immigration posts. No individual case files in this series.

Box 15.

File 5000-25-606.
Pakistan, 1972.

Box 18.

File 5003-1-410.
Ports and posts, Hong Kong, China, 1965-1974.

File 5003-1-411.
Ports and posts, New Delhi, India, 1967-1973.

Box 19.

File 5003-1-487.
Ports and posts, Islamabad, Pakistan, 1967-1973.

File 5003-1-489.
Ports and posts, Tokyo, Japan, 1970-1973.

File 5003-1-491.
Ports and posts, Manila, Philippines, 1968-1973.

Box 20.

File 5003-1-6045.
Ports and posts, Peking, China, 1972-1973.

Box 21.

File 5020-1-510.
Adoption, Khmer Republic, 1975-1976.

File 5020-1-564.
Adoption, Hong Kong, 1963-1973.

File 5020-1-567.
Adoption, India, 1963-1976.

File 5020-1-580.
Adoption, Korea, 1968-1976.

File 5020-1-606.
Adoption, Pakistan, 1962-1963.

File 5020-1-629.
Adoption, Thailand, 1976.

File 5020-1-710, volume 1.
Adoption, Bangladesh, 1972.

File 5020-1-710, volume 2.
Adoption, Bangladesh, 1972.

File 5020-1-710, volume 3.
Adoption, Bangladesh, 1973-1974.

File 5020-3.
Adoption, Hong Kong teenage project, 1967-1972.

Box 28.

File 5110-2-410.
Assisted passage scheme, warrant reports, Hong Kong, 1970-1973.

File 5110-2-441.
Assisted passage scheme, warrant reports, New Delhi, India, 1968-1973.

Box 29.

File 5110-2-487.
Assisted passage scheme, warrant reports, Islamabad, Pakistan, 1970-1972.

File 5110-2-489.
Assisted passage scheme, warrant reports, Tokyo, Japan, 1970-1972.

File 5110-2-491.
Assisted passage scheme, warrant reports, Manila, Philippines, 1968-1973.

Box 30.

File 5110-2-6057.
Assisted passage scheme, warrant reports, Singapore, 1976.

Box 32.

File 5175-1-548.
Illegal entry, Fijians, 1963-1974.

File 5175-1-567.
Illegal entry, Indians, 1974-1975.

Box 33.

File 5175-1-567, part 1.
Illegal entry, Indians, 1967-1970.

File 5175-1-567, part 2.
Illegal entry, Indians, 1971.

File 5175-1-567, part 3.
Illegal entry, Indians, 1971.

File 5175-1-567, part 4.
Illegal entry, Indians, 1971.

File 5175-1-567, part 5.
Illegal entry, Indians, 1972.

File 5175-1-567, part 6.
Illegal entry, Indians, 1972-1973.

File 5175-1-567, part 7.
Illegal entry, Indians, 1974.

File 5175-1-567-2, part 1.
Illegal entry, Indians, N.I.A.L., 1971-1972.

File 5175-1-567-2, part 2.
Illegal entry, Indians, N.I.A.L., 1972-1973.

File 5175-1-570.
Illegal entry, Iranians, 1970-1974.

Box 34.

File 5175-1-580.
Illegal entry, Koreans, 1969-1975.

File 5175-2-606.
Illegal entry, Pakistan, 1970-1977.

File 5175-1-611, volume 3.
Illegal entry, Philippines, 1970.
File 5175-1-611, volume 4.
Illegal entry, Philippines, 1970-1971.

File 5175-1-611, volume 5.
Illegal entry, Philippines, 1971.

File 5175-1-611, volume 6.
Illegal entry, Philippines, 1972.

File 5175-1-611, volume 7.
Illegal entry, Philippines, 1973-1976.

Box 35.

File 5175-1-632.

Illegal entry, Turkey, 1969-1974.

Box 36.

File 5175-41-526.
Smuggling of persons to U.S., Chinese, 1971-1973.

Box 37.

File 5180-2-1-510.
Lost and invalidated passports, Khmer(formerly Cambodia), 1970-1971.

File 5180-2-1-522.
Lost and invalidated passports, Burma, 1966-1976.

File 5180-2-1-524.
Lost and invalidated passports, Sri Lanka(Ceylon), 1969-1972.

File 5180-2-1-548.
Lost and invalidated passports, Fiji Islands, 1977.

Box 38.

File 5180-2-1-564.
Lost and invalidated passports, China, 1966-1969.

File 5180-2-1-567, part 1.
Lost and invalidated passports, India, 1966-1967.

File 5180-2-1-569.
Lost and invalidated passports, Indonesia, 1966-1973.

File 5180-2-1-570.
Lost and invalidated passports, Iran, 1970-1974.

File 5180-2-1-578, part 1.
Lost and invalidated passports, Japan, 1975-1976.

File 5180-2-1-580.
Lost and invalidated passports, Korea, 1977.

File 5180-2-1-592.
Lost and invalidated passports, Malaysia, 1969-1970.

File 5180-2-1-605.
Lost and invalidated passports, Bhutan and Nepal, 1974.

File 5180-2-1-606, volume 1.
Lost and invalidated passports, Pakistan, 1971.

File 5180-2-1-611.
Lost and invalidated passports, Philippines, 1974-1976.

File 5180-2-1-629.
Lost and invalidated passports, Thailand, 1967-1975.

File 5180-2-1-632.
Lost and invalidated passports, Turkey, 1973-1976.

File 5180-2-1-710.
Lost and invalidated passports, Bangladesh, 1977.

Box 39.

File 5195-1-564.
Travel agencies, Hong Kong, 1968-1976.

Box 40.

File 5195-1-611.
Travel agencies, the Philippines, 1966-1976.

File 5230-1-510.
Deportation, Cambodia, 1975-1978.

File 5195-1-567.
Travel agencies, India, 1967-1975.

Box 41.

File 5230-1-526.
Deportation, China, 1958-1978.

File 5230-1-564.
Deportation, Hong Kong, 1968-1978.

File 5230-1-569.
Deportation, Indonesia, 1977-1978.

Box 52.

File 5260-1-526.
Diplomatic relations, People's Republic of China, 1970-1976.

File 5260-1-567.
Diplomatic relations, India, 1970-1973.

File 5260-1-568.
Diplomatic relations, Laos, 1974.

File 5260-1-578.
Diplomatic relations, Japan, 1972-1973.

File 5260-1-580.
Diplomatic relations, Republic of Korea, 1971-1974.

File 5260-1-606.
Diplomatic relations, Pakistan, 1972-1976.

Box 73.

File 5420-1-567.
Stage "B", India, 1966-1974.

File 5420-1-578.
Criminal records, Japan, 1969.

File 5420-1-580.
Stage "B", Korea, 1966-1973.

File 5420-1-606.
Stage "B", Pakistan, 1967-1970.

File 5420-1-611.
Stage "B", Philippines, 1966-1970.

Box 74.

File 5425-4-1-570.
Non-immigrants, Iran, 1974-1975.

Box 80.

File 5425-13-578.
Exchange agreements with foreign countries, Japan, 1971-1975.

Box 81.

File 5450-1-502.
Foreign countries, Afghanistan, 1973.

File 5450-1-522.
Foreign countries, Burma, 1968.

Box 82.

File 5450-1-548.
Immigration from foreign countries, Fiji, 1976.

File 5450-1-567, volume 2.
Foreign countries, India, 1969-1978.

File 5450-1-578.
Foreign countries, Japan, 1967-1975.

File 5450-1-580.
Foreign countries, Korea, 1966-1973.

File 5450-1-606.
Foreign countries, Pakistan, 1968-1974.

File 5450-1-611.
Foreign countries, Philippines, 1968-1972.

Box 83.

File 5450-1-621.
Foreign countries, Singapore, 1968-1974.

File 5850-1-708.
Foreign countries, Western Samoa, 1970.

File 5450-1-710.
Foreign countries, Bangladesh, 1971-1972.

Box 85.

File 5420-2-524.
Immigration to foreign countries, Sri Lanka, 1976.

File 5450-2-567.
Immigration to foreign countries, India, 1968-1970.

File 5450-2-578.

Box 86.

File 5450-1-629.
Immigration from foreign countries, Thailand, 1974-1975.

Box 87.

File 5450-3-567.
India, 1972.

Box 94.

File 5500-11-2-6020, volume 1.
Monthly operational reports, Islamabad, 1969-1978.

File 5500-11-2-6029, volume 1.
Monthly operational reports, New Delhi, 1969-1978.

Box 96.

File 5500-11-2-6041, part 1.
Monthly operational reports, Tokyo, 1969-1976.

Box 97.

File 5500-11-2-6057, part 1.
Monthly operational reports, Singapore, 1973-1974.

File 5500-11-2-6057, part 2.
Monthly operational reports, Singapore, 1975-1978.

File 5500-11-2-6058, part 1.
Monthly operational reports, Seoul, 1973-1978.

Box 98.

File 5500-11-2-6065, part 1.
Monthly operational reports, Tehran, 1975-1978.

File 5500-11-2-6076.
Monthly operations reports, Bangkok, Thailand, 1978.

Box 102.

File 5630-1-567.
Medical examination, India, 1966-1975.

File 5630-1-570.
Medical examination, Iran, 1967-1971.

File 5630-1-578.
Medical examination, Japan, 1967-1968.

File 5630-1-580.
Medical examination, Korea, 1968-1973.

File 5360-1-592.
Medical examination, Malaysia, 1969-1973.
File 5360-1-605.

Medical examination, Nepal, 1971.

File 5630-1-606.
Medical examination, Pakistan, 1966-1973.

File 630-1-611.
Medical examination, Philippines, 1967-1973.

Box 103.

File 5630-1-710.
Medical examination, Bangladesh, 1972.

Box 107.

File 5750-3, volume 1.
Armenians, 1966-1969.

File 5750-3, volume 2.
Armenians, 1969-1976.

Box 109.

File 5750-2, volume 1.
Race, sect, or religious groups, Kurds, 1975-1976.

Box 110.

File 5780-1-567.
Refugees, India, 1971.

File 5780-1-629, volume 1.
Refugees, Thailand, 1975-1977.

Box 111.

File 5780-1-632.
Refugees, Turkey, 1968-1969.

Box 121.

File 5786-1, volume 13.
Refugees, Tibetan, movement, general, 1972-1973.

File 5786-1, volume 14.
Refugees, Tibetan, movement, general, 1973-1974.

File 5786-1, volume 15.
Refugees, Tibetan, movement, general, 1974-1975.

File 5786-1, volume 16.
Refugees, Tibetan, movement, general, 1975-1976.

Box 122.

File 5786-1, volume 3.
Refugees, Tibetan, movement, general, 1967-1968.

File 5786-1, volume 4.
Refugees, Tibetan, movement, general, 1968-1969.

File 5786-1, volume 5.
Refugees, Tibetan, movement, general, 1969.

File 5786-1, volume 6.
Refugees, Tibetan, movement, general, 1969.

File 5786-1, volume 7.
Refugees, Tibetan, movement, general, 1969.

File 5786-1, volume 8.
Refugees, Tibetan, movement, general, 1970.

File 5786-1, volume 9.
Refugees, Tibetan, movement, general, 1970.

File 5786-1, volume 10.
Refugees, Tibetan, movement, general, 1971.

File 5786-1, volume 11.
Refugees, Tibetan, movement, general, 1971.

File 5786-1, volume 12.
Refugees, Tibetan, movement, general, 1971-1972.

Box 123.

File 5786-1, volume 1.
Refugees, Tibetan, movement, general, 1966-1967.

File 5786-1, volume 2.
Refugees, Tibetan, movement, general, 1966-1967.

File 5786-1 ONT, volume 1.
Refugees, Tibetan, movement, general, Ontario region, 1971.

File 5786-1 ONT, volume 2.
Refugees, Tibetan, movement, general, Ontario region, 1971-1972.

File 5786-1 ONT, volume 3.
Refugees, Tibetan, movement, general, Ontario region, 1972-1974.

File 5786-1 PR, volume 1.
Refugees, Tibetan, movement, general, Ontario region, 1971.

File 5786-1 PR, volume 2.
Refugees, Tibetan, movement, general, Ontario region, 1971.

File 5786-1 PR, volume 3.
Refugees, Tibetan, movement, general, Prairie region, 1972.

File 5786-1 PR, volume 4.
Refugees, Tibetan, movement, general, Prairie region, 1972-1974

Box 124.

File 5786-1 QUE, volume 1.

Refugees, Tibetan movement, general, Québec region, 1971.

File 5786-1 QUE, volume 2.
Refugees, Tibetan movement, general, Québec region, 1971.

File 5786-1 QUE, volume 3.
Refugees, Tibetan movement, general, Québec region, 1971-1972.

File 5786-1 QUE, volume 4.
Refugees, Tibetan movement, general, Québec region, 1972-1976.

File 5800-2-710.
Repatriation to Bangladesh, 1972.

Box 132.

File 5850-2-510.
Selection and processing, Khmer(Cambodia), 1971-1972.

Box 133.

File 5850-2-567.
Selection and processing, India, 1966-1974.

File 5850-2-569.
Selection and processing, Indonesia, 1976-1978.

File 5850-2-578.
Selection and processing, Japan, 1966-1978.

File 5820-2-580.
Selection and processing, Korea, 1966-1972.

File 5850-2-606, volume 1.
Selection and processing, Pakistan, 1967-1972.

File 5850-2-606, volume 2.
Selection and processing, Pakistan, 1973-1974.

File 5850-2-621.
Selection and processing, Singapore, 1967-1972.

File 5850-2-632.
Selection and processing, Turkey, 1969.

File 5850-2-641, volume 1.
Selection and processing, Vietnam, 1964-1969.

File 5850-2-641, volume 2.
Selection and processing, Vietnam, 1970-1975.

File 5850-2-710.
Selection and processing, Bangladesh, 1972-1973.

File 5850-3-502.
Immigration from Afghanistan, 1967-1973.

Box 134.

File 5850-3-510.
Immigration from Khmer(formerly Cambodia), 1969-1975.

File 5850-3-5-11.
Immigration from Asia, 1971-1973.

Box 136.

File 5850-3-548.
Immigration from Fiji Islands, 1966-1974.

Box 137.

File 5850-3-567, volume 1.
Immigration from India, 1966-1970.

File 5850-3-567, volume 2.
Immigration from India, 1970-1973.

File 5850-3-567, volume 3.
Immigration from India, 1974-1976.

File 5850-3-568.
Immigration from Laos, 1969-1975.

File 5850-3-569.
Immigration from Indonesia, 1966-1974.

File 5850-3-570.
Immigration from Iran, 1966-1975.

Box 138.

File 5850-3-578, part 1.
Immigration from Japan, 1966-1973.

File 5850-3-578, part 2.
Immigration from Japan, 1973-1974.

File 5850-3-580.
Immigration from Korea, 1966-1974.

Box 139.

File 5850-3-589.
Immigration from North Korea, 1974.

Box 140.

File 5850-3-606, volume 1.
Immigration from Pakistan, 1966-1971.

File 5850-3-611, volume 1.
Immigration from Philippines, 1966-1971.

File 5850-3-611, volume 2.
Immigration from Philippines, 1972-1973.

Box 141.

File 5850-3-629.
Immigration from Thailand, 1966-1973.

File 5850-3-621.
Immigration from Singapore, 1966-1974.

File 5850-3-632.
Immigration from Turkey, 1966-1976.

Box 142.

File 5850-3-641, volume 10.
Immigration from South Vietnam, 1976.

File 5850-3-641, volume 11.
Immigration from South Vietnam, 1976.

File 5850-3-641, volume 12.
Immigration from South Vietnam, 1976.

Box 143.

File 5850-3-641, volume 1.
Immigration from South Vietnam, 1972-1974.

File 5850-3-641, volume 2.
Immigration from South Vietnam, 1974-1975.

File 5850-3-641, volume 3.
Immigration from South Vietnam, 1975.

File 5850-3-641, volume 4.
Immigration from South Vietnam, 1975.

File 5850-3-641, volume 5.
Immigration from South Vietnam, 1975.

File 5850-3-641, volume 6.
Immigration from South Vietnam, 1975.

File 5850-3-641, volume 7.
Immigration from South Vietnam, 1975.

File 5850-3-641, volume 8.
Immigration from South Vietnam, 1975.

File 5850-3-641, volume 9.
Immigration from South Vietnam, 1975.

File 5850-3-2-641, volume 1.
Immigration from South Vietnam, Vietnam emergency operations, statistics, 1975.

File 5850-3-2-641, volume 2.
Immigration from South Vietnam, Vietnam emergency operations, statistics, 1975.

Box 144.

File 5850-3-3-641.
Immigration from South Vietnam, transportation, 1975-1976.

File 5850-3-4-641, volume 1.
Immigration from South Vietnam, financial arrangements, 1975-1976.

File 5850-3-5-641, volume 2.
Immigration from South Vietnam, Khmer emergency operations, Project 29, 1975.

File 5850-3-5-641, volume 2a.
Immigration from South Vietnam, Khmer emergency operations, Project 29, 1975.

File 5850-3-5-641, volume 3. 1975.
Immigration from South Vietnam, Khmer emergency operations, Project 29, 1975.

File 5850-3-5-641, volume 4.
Immigration from South Vietnam, Khmer emergency operations, Project 29, 1975.

File 5850-3-5-641, volume 6.
Immigration from South Vietnam, Khmer emergency operations, Project 29, 1975.

File 5850-3-5-641, volume 7.
Immigration from South Vietnam, Khmer emergency operations, Project 29, 1975-1976.

File 5850-3-5-641, volume 8.
Immigration from South Vietnam, Khmer emergency operations, Project 29, 1976.

File 5850-3-5-641, volume 9.
Immigration from South Vietnam, Khmer emergency operations, Project 29, 1976.

File 5850-3-5-641, volume 10.
Immigration from South Vietnam, Khmer emergency operations, Project 29, 1977.

File 5850-3-5-641, volume 11.
Immigration from South Vietnam, Khmer emergency operations, Project 29, 1977.

File 5850-3-5-641, volume 12.
Immigration from South Vietnam, Khmer emergency operations, Project 29, 1977.

File 5850-3-5-641, volume 13.
Immigration from South Vietnam, Khmer emergency operations, Project 29, 1977.

File 5850-3-5-641, volume 14.
Immigration from South Vietnam, Khmer emergency operations, Project 29, 1978.

File 5850-3-5-641, volume 15.
Immigration from South Vietnam, Khmer emergency operations, Project 29, 1978.

File 5850-3-5-641, volume 16.
Immigration from South Vietnam, Khmer emergency operations, Project 29, 1978.

File 5850-3-5-641, volume 17.
Immigration from South Vietnam, Khmer emergency operations, Project 29, 1978.

File 5850-3-5-641, volume 18.
Immigration from South Vietnam, Khmer emergency operations, Project 29, 1978.

File 5850-3-5-641, volume 19.
Immigration from South Vietnam, Khmer emergency operations, Project 29, 1978.

File 5850-3-7-641.
Immigration from South Vietnam, publicity, 1975-1976.

File 5850-3-8-641.
Immigration from South Vietnam, family allowance, 1975.

Box 147.

File 5850-3-675.
Immigration from Gilbert and Ellice Islands, 1966-1968.

File 5850-3-710, volume 1.
Immigration from Bangladesh, 1971-1972.

File 5850-3-710, volume 2.
Immigration from Bangladesh, 1972.

File 5850-3-710, volume 3.
Immigration from Bangladesh, 1972-1974.

File 5850-3-710, volume 4.
Immigration from Bangladesh, 1974-1976.

Box 150.

File 5850-6-4-611.
Occupational selections, domestics, Philippines, 1965-1974.

Box 153.

File 5850-6-24-611.
Occupational selection, nurses, Philippines, 1965-1975.

Box 159.

File 5855-1-567, volume 1.
Processing of applications, India, 1970-1976.

File 5855-1-578.
Processing of applications, Japan, 1967-1976.

Box 160.

File 5855-1-7-13.
Processing of applications, North Vietnam(Democratic Republic of Vietnam), 1973-1975.

Box 163.

File 5855-4-34.
Philcan Personnel Consultants, Ltd., 1974.

File 5855-4-34.
Philcan Personnel Consultants, Ltd., 1975.

File 5855-4-46.
Philippine Manpower Centre, 1978.

Box 166.

File 5855-9-1/411.
Overseas Area Offices, New Delhi, India, 1966-1976.

Box 167.

File 5855-9-1-487.
Overseas area offices, Islamabad, Pakistan.

File 5855-7-1-489.
Overseas area offices, Tokyo, Japan, 1966-1973.

Box 178.

File 5865-3-2-12, volume 1.
Indian Immigrant Aid Service, 1973-1976.

Box 179.

File 5865-3-2-16, volume 1.
Korean Canadian Association, 1973-1976.

File 5865-3-2-22, 1.
Silayon Filipino Community Centre, 1973-1976.

File 5865-3-2-26.
Centre d'Orientation & Adaptation(Armenians), 1974-1976.

Box 181.

File 5865-3-2-49.
La société des armeniens d'Istanbul, 1973-1975.

File 5865-3-2-56.
Comité d'aide aux réfugits vietnamiens(Montréal), 1975-1976.

Box 184.

File 5865-7-3.
East Indians, 1974-1976.

Box 187.

File 5870-3-3.
Asian Studies, Inc., 1975.

Box 192.

File 3-33-25.
Admission to Canada from Philippines, 1952-1956.

Box 203.

File 5905-4-567.
Agreements, Canada-India, 1973.

Box 206.

File 5965-1-510.
Passports and visas, Khmer Republic, 1973.

File 5965-1-511.
Passports and visas, Asia, 1973.

File 5965-1-522.
Passports and visas, Burma, 1973-1976.

File 5965-1-524.
Passports and visas, Sri Lanka, 1972-1977.

File 5965-1-548.
Passports and visas, Fiji Islands, 1973-1974.

File 5965-1-561.
Passports and visas, Maldive Islands, 1973.

File 5965-1-567.
Passports and visas, India, 1969-1976.

File 5965-1-568.
Passports and visas, Laos, 1975-1976.

File 5965-1-569.
Passports and visas, Indonesia, 1973-1976.

File 5965-1-570.
Passports and visas, Iran, 1966-1973.

Box 207.

File 5865-1-578.
Passports and visas, Japan, 1970-1976.

File 5965-1-606.
Passports and visas, Pakistan, 1972-1973.

File 5965-1-611.
Passports and visas, Philippines, 1972-1977.

File 5965-1-629.
Passports and visas, Thailand, 1973.

File 5965-1-5-580.
Passports and visas, Korea, 1974-1977.

File 5965-1-632.
Passports and visas, Turkey, 1973.

File 5965-1-641.
Passports and visas, Vietnam, 1968-1975.

Box 208.

File 5161-1-721.
Passports and visas, Brunei, 1973-1974.

File 5965-1-675.
Passports and visas, Gilbert and Ellice Islands, 1973.

File 5965-1-701.
Passports and visas, Bangladesh, 1972-1973.

File 5965-1-701.
Passports and visas, New Hebrides, 1969.

File 5965-1-708.
Passports and visas, Western Samoa, 1973.

Box 209.

File 5965-5-1-522.
Canadian visas, general, Burma, 1966-1973.

File 5965-5-1-560.
Canadian visas, general, Laos, 1967-1976.

File 5965-5-1-580.
Canadian visas, South Korea, 1967-1976.

File 5965-5-1-589.
Canadian visas, North Korea, 1968-1976.

File 5965-5-1-606.
Canadian visas, Pakistan, 1972-1976.

File 5965-5-1-611.
Canadian visas, Philippines, 1967-1973.

File 5965-7-629.
Canadian visas, Thailand, 1967.

File 5865-5-1-641.
Canadian visas, South Vietnam, 1969-1976.

File 5965-5-1-713.
Canadian visas, North Vietnam, 1967-1974.

File 5965-5-1-721.
Canadian visas, general, Singapore, 1967-1974.

Box 211.

File 5965-7-570.
Iran, 1968-1973.

File 5965-7-578.
Japan, 1967-1974.

File 5965-7-580.
Korea, 1972-1973.

File 5965-7-629.
Thailand, 1971.

Accession 83-84/350.

Index cards for Central Registry("5000" block) File series, ca. 1960-1980, .9 metres, boxes 1-3.

"Case" nominal index.
Most of the names are for persons making representations to the department, or criminals. Few are for individual immigrants.

Subject index
Detailed subject index to the "5000" block, mainly for the 1960s to the 1977, but with a few to 1980.

Index to comments from the public on bill C-24. Bill C-24 subsequently became the Immigration Act of 1976.

Accession 84-85/003.

Immigration branch, Toronto, Chinese case files, c.1900-1966, 36 metres, PARC boxes 1643-1762.

As part of its numerous duties, the Immigration Branch received and screened applications from Chinese currently residing in Canada for the admission of friends and relatives wishing to enter Canada. These records consist of individual Chinese case files created by Immigration Branch officials for the purposes of screening those individuals wishing to enter Canada. As such, they contain documents such as application forms, Immigration Appeal Board testimony, history of employment and previous residence letters, and statutory declarations of proposed immigrants.
The finding list is a PARC list.

Accession 84-85/041.

Chinese case files, c.1900-1966, 42.6 metres, boxes 99-240.

This accession continues the "CH" file series described in accession 83-84/348. The series is completed in 84-85/527.
The finding aid is a nominal file list.

Accession 84-85/062.

Chinese division, Chinese Immigration ledgers, 1903-1949, 2.4 metres.
The Chinese Immigration Act of July 1885, allowed for the control of Chinese immigration and the registration of Chinese in Canada. This accession contains three types of ledgers used for these purposes.

1) Eight general registers of Chinese immigration(1903-1949), which are arranged numerically by serial number and declaration number in rough chronological order. Two indexes arranged by the CI 28 or CI 36 number of each immigrant.

2) One Chinese register number 2(1912-1913) from the Central District(Toronto) used to control Chinese immigration to and temporary emigration from Canada.

3) Two reports of exempt admissions at Victoria(1913-1930) and Vancouver (1914-1924). These ledgers document Chinese immigrants who applied for exemptions from the restrictions of the Immigration Act.

Register of Chinese immigrants(1910-1949) admitted into the colony of Newfoundland.
Finding aid is a file list.

Accession 84-85/238.

Chinese division, Chinese immigration registers and miscellaneous records, 1903-1950, 4 reels(microfilm reel numbers T-3484 to T-3487).
This accession consists of microfilm copies of four groups of registers and indexes relating to Chinese immigration and one ship's passenger list, as follows:

1. Eight general registers of Chinese immigration, nos. 11 to 18(1903-1949).

2. Index to holders of C.I. 28 certificates, by number of certificate, 24 January 1912-19 July 1947 (reel T-3486).

3. Index to holders of C.I. 36 certificates, by number of certificate, 28 January 1913-16 February 1949. appears to cover arrivals up to ca. 1912 only (reels T-3486 and T-3487).

4. Register of Chinese immigrants to Newfoundland, 1910-1950. Organized by date of arrival(reel T-3487).

5. Passenger list, **Empress of Russia,** lists names of immigrants from Hong Kong, destined for Victoria, Vancouver and Seattle, landing at Victoria on 8 March 1935, and at Vancouver on 25 March 1935.
Finding aid available.

Accession 84-85/239.
Index covers years 1908-1918, but omits Victoria and Vancouver.

Accession 84-85/240.

Records of entry: ships' manifests, manifest indexes and index retakes, ship notifications of arrival, entry lists, Chinese immigration records,

and juvenile immigration indexes, 1865-1953, 330 reels, microfilm reels T-5733 to T-6062. These are working duplicates only, except for item 6 and part of item 3.

Items 1 to 5 were copies from the master negatives in accessions 85-86/585 and 85-86/586. Further information on these records can be found in Record Group 76 inventory entries for Series V(records of entry, 1865-1908, and juvenile indexes); Series VI(Chinese division); and Accession 85-86/004.

1. Ships' passenger lists, 1906-1919(reels T-5733 to T-5918, T-6056 and T-6058).
Copies of ships' manifests listing names of persons docking at the six official immigration seaports in Canada and the six in the United States.
The most important for Asian immigrants are the records for: Vancouver, British Columbia. 18 January 1907-11 June 1919(reels T-5849 to T-5858).

Victoria, British Columbia, 7 July 1907-4 February 1919(reels T-5859 to T-5873).

Positive records, similar to those in Accession 84-85/581. Master negatives are in Accession 85-86/585.

2. Manifest indexes and manifest index retakes, 1907-1920(reels T-5819 to T-5980 and T-6059 to T-6062).

3. Ship notifications of arrival, 1865-1922(reels T-5981 to T-5985).

(c) Draft versions: lists of ships arriving at including Vancouver and Victoria(1905-1922).

4. Border entry lists, 1908-1918(reels T-5986 to T-6033).

Monthly lists of immigrants passing into Canada are various border ports of entry, with some for Pacific seaports.

5. Juvenile immigration indexes.

Two indexes relate to British emigrant children coming to Canada.

6. Chinese immigration records, C.I.9a series(reels T-6038 to T-6055).

Working positive copies and master negatives of filmed C.I.9 certificates and related lists, documenting the departure and return of Chinese persons in Canada who left the country temporarily through the major West Coast ports, 1910-1953. The C.I.9 certificates were issued to ordinary travellers, and the C.I.9a certificates to crews of ocean-going vessels in four groups as follows:

(a) C.I.9 certificates, Vancouver and Victoria, 1910-1952.
Microfilm copies of C.I.9. certificates issued to Chinese immigrants who left Canada temporarily through the Ports of Vancouver and Victoria between 1910 and 1952. The certificates contain travel information, identification data, and photograph in four series, as follows:

1. Victoria (first series: persons born abroad) C.I.9 numbers 15701 to 37100, 7 September 1910-9 April 1920(reels T-6038 to T-6045).

2. Victoria (second series: native-born persons).C.I.9 numbers 1 to 2375, 7 May 1913-24 July 1952(reel t-6046).

3. Vancouver (first series: persons born abroad).C.I.(numbers 17175 to 31399), 28 September 1910-23 July 1919(reels T-6047 to T-6051).

4. Vancouver (second series: native born persons) C.I.9 numbers 1 to 3240. 29 June 1915-8 September 1939(reel T-6052).

The finding aid is a microfilm shelf list indicating the first and last certificate on each reel. There is no nominal index.

(b) C.I.9 and C.I.9a out-registration: lists of certificate holders, Vancouver and Victoria, 1913-1951.
Monthly lists of holdings of C.I.9 and C.I.9a certificates(for ordinary travellers and ships' crewmen respectively), and of "native-born" Chinese issued at the Ports of Vancouver and Victoria from 1913-1953. Lists were compiled monthly by the local controllers of Chinese immigration and forwarded to Ottawa in letter form They were originally part of first Central Registry files 830533-Victoria and 830533-Vancouver, but now arranged in chronological order in annual files.
Unique positive records, in two series as follows:

1. Victoria. April 1913-March 1953, file parts 2-31(reel T-6053).

2. Vancouver. January 1913-February 1953, file parts 1-32(reel T-6054).

(c) C.I.9 and C.I.9a out-registrations (Victoria): lists of persons readmitted and certificates cancelled, 1912-1953, and certificates cancelled, 1912-1953.
Monthly lists of Chinese-Canadians who left Canada temporarily through the port of Victoria(under C.I.9 and C.I.9a certificates or without certificates, as "native-born" persons) between about 1910 and 1953, and who have been readmitted to Canada; and lists of persons whose failure to return within the prescribed time period.

Parts 1 to 31 of the file contain monthly lists of persons leaving Canada through Victoria, who have been legally admitted between 1911 and 1953 at Victoria, various other British Columbia land, sea and air ports, and occasionally ports elsewhere in Canada. Part 32 consists of monthly lists of persons who failed to return to Canada within the time limit prescribed by the Chinese Immigration Act, or regulations, 1922-1953. The microfilm is a unique master negative. No nominal index.

Victoria readmission lists, October 1911-December 1953, file parts 1-31(reel T-6055), cancellation lists, May 1922-December 1
953, file part 32(reel T-6055).

Accession 84-85/527.

Chinese case files, ca. 1900-1966, 16.8 metres, boxes 241-296.

Continues and completes the "CH" file series described in Accession 83-84/348 and 84-85/041.

Finding aid is a nominal file list.

Accession 84-85/581.

Records of entry, ships' passenger manifests and ship notifications of arrival, 1865-1921, 189 reels(microfilm reels T-4689 to T-4697, T-4699 to Y-4732, T-4734 to T-4757, T-4759 to T-4818, T-4820 to T-4834, T-4836 to T-4859, T-4851 to T-4859, T-4861 to T-4877, T-493, T-503, T-508, T-512, T-514, T-516, T-519, and T-520).

Ships' passenger lists(manifests) for vessels arriving at Canadian and American ports, between 1908 and the end of 1919, also two indexes to annual ship arrivals between 1865 and the end of 1922. Names of persons on ships arriving at six official ports of entry in Canada, and six in the United States. Those listed for American ports, show only the names of persons intending to proceed to Canada. Of the twelve ports, the two most significant ports for Asian immigrants are Vancouver(1909-1919) and Victoria(1908-1919). Finding aids available.

Accession 84-85/761.

Draft indexes to ship arrivals at Québec, Halifax, St. Johns, Vancouver, Victoria and New York, and ther American ports, 1865-1922.

Accession 85-86/001.

Box 2.

File SF-C-88, volume 1.
Conference for Solidarity on Vietnam(Hemispheric Conference to end the War in Vietnam), October 1968, November 1968.

File SF-C-88, volume 2.
Conference for Solidarity on Vietnam(Hemispheric Conference to end the War in Vietnam), October 1968, 1968-1969.
File SF-C-92, volume 1.
Committee of Solidarity with Vietnam, 1968-1969.

File SF-C-92, volume 2.
Committee of Solidarity with Vietnam, 1969-1971.

File SF-C-92, volume 3.
Committee of Solidarity with Vietnam, 1971-1973.

File SF-C-98, part 1.
Chinese journalists, general, 1964-1971.

File SF-C-98, part 2.
Chinese journalists, general, 1972-1978.

File SF-C-101.
Conference on International Law and the Vietnam War(York University, Toronto), May-June 1970.

File SF-C-149.
Canadian Society for Asian Studies(Fredericton conference, 1977, entry of North Koreans), May-June 1977.

Box 3.

File SF-E-34.
East Indian Defence Committee, Toronto, 1976-1977.

File SF-G-65.
Gomeg Yarns, Ltd.,(joint venture with Jari Industries, Ltd., of India), 1971-1976.

File SF-H-35, part 1.
Hong Kong police serving with the Royal Canadian Mounted Police, 1961-1980.

File SF-I-52.
International Assembly of Christians in Solidarity with the Indo-Chinese People, Québec, 1972, entry of Vietnamese delegates, 1972, 1975.

File SF-l-59.
Official of Global Finance Company, Hong Kong, proposals for student and agricultural immigration, 1973-1974.

Box 4.

File SF-N-43.
National Chinese Opera Theatre(Taiwanese opera company), September 1973.

File SF-T-28.
Teach-ins, international, on China(University of Toronto, 1965-1966), 1965-1966.

File SN-P-32.
Pugwash Conference(on Science and Technology, 1960, and on Vietnam, 1970, admission of Chinese and Vietnamese representatives), 1960, 1980.

Accession 85-86/002.

Chinese Immigration division, Chinese telegraphic code, nominal index and partial(romanized) alphabetical index to case files, 1960-1984, 77,647 cards, cabinet nos. 1-4.

One of two nominal indexes to the Chinese and Hong Kong immigration case files of the "CH" and "HK" series of which the National Archives of Canada holds examples in Record Group 76, volumes 727-732, and Accession 83-84/348, 84-85/003, 84-85/041, 84-85/527, 85-86/054, 85-86/265, 85-86/266 and v-84-85/279. Part of the other index(alphabetical by romanized surname) is found in Accession 85-86/051. The code index was created in the Chinese records unit of the Immigration records office in the early 1970s and abandoned at an unknown later date.
The accession is in two parts. The Chinese Telegraphic Code card index covers the Chinese-character form of the names of individuals whose case files were active between about 1970 and 1984, which contain documents dated as early as the 1890s. As well as the main subject of each case file, names of principal family members are indexed including dependents and sponsored relatives.
Parallel to this index is the romanized-name index(accession 85-86/051) which must be used where the exact Chinese-character name is unknown or has Western first and middle names.

Accession 85-86/004.

Records of entry, border entry lists, manifest indexes, and ships notification of arrival, 1865-1922. 999 reels. Includes Chinese.

Accession 85-86/005.

Central Registry files(first series), nominal and subject index, 1893-1924, 21 reels(reels T-5571 to T-5591).

A microfilm copy of the master subject and nominal index to operational and case files in the Immigration branch's first Central Registry system, active from 1893 to ca. 1949. Files from this system that have survived in their original form are now found in Record Group 76 1a(volumes 1-676, 679-689, and 712), series VII(Box 715), series X(volumes 737-742) and parts of accession 81-82/198.
The index consists of (a) nominal entries for immigrant case files, names of correspondents, name of immigration officers, (b) personnel and administration files; and (c) subject entries.
For subject indexes to records from 1924 onwards, see Record Group 76, series I A 2, reels M-1983 to M-1990.

Accession 85-86/006.

Index to records for years 1893-1924.

Accession 85-86/040.

Canada Immigration Centre, Yarmouth, Nova Scotia, immigration case files, 1971-1982, .20 metres, box 1.

Sixteen immigration case files, relating to individual persons' immigration to Canada. One file concerns local sponsorship of Vietnamese refugees("boat people").

Accession 85-86/050.

Immigration case file, Canada Immigration center, Vancouver, 1918-1984, .3 metres, box 1.

An "F" sampling of regular and Chinese files(individuals with surnames beginning with "F") and files involving the office of the Minister of Employment and Immigration and other senior level("minister's interest") files. Included with the case files is one file on the status adjustment program(amnesty for Chinese people illegally in Canada) for the Pacific region, 1965-1970.
No finding aids for this material.

Accession 85-86/051.

Chinese Immigration division, romanized alphabetical index to case files, 1900-1970, 74,655 cards, tray nos. 1-38.

Part of the Immigration Branch's master index to romanized versions of names of Chinese immigrants documents in the headquarters Chinese case file series. The index covers files now found in Record Group 76,

Accessions 83-84/348, 84-85/041, and 84-85/527, with related references to files in other Accessions. Cards for files still in the possession of employment and Immigration Canada, and those for Accession 85-86/265, have been retained by the department. Cards for files held at regional or local offices(e.g. Accessions 84-85/003, V85-86/674, and V85-86/475) are not included.
Each card gives a file number either in the "CH" or the first Central Registry series. Most of the references are dated after 1945, but some refer to 1900-1910, for families where immigration has spanned several generations.
Chinese-character version in accession 85-86/002.

Accession 85-86/052.

Canada Immigration centres, Québec and Ontario regions, historical case files and "F" sample case files, HQ 2 to HQ 4 series, 1975-1980,

6 metres, boxes 1-2.

Box 1 contains a case file on the self-styled acting president of the South Molucca Islands.

Accession 85-86/054.

Chinese case files, "F" sample, 1900-1970, 1.8 metres, boxes 1-6.

Sample from a group of files dated before and after 1967, for persons whose surnames begins with the letter "F". For the "CH"-series Chinese case files.

Accession 85-86/265.

Chinese case files, 1900-1967, 21 metres, boxes 1-70.

Individual Chinese case files created by Immigration Branch officials for the purpose of screening individuals who wish to enter Canada, and containing family trees, application forms, Immigration Appeal Board testimony, histories of employment and previous residence, and statutory declarations of proposed immigrants. Contains files used in investigations under the 1973 status adjustment programs

Accession 85-86/266.

Chinese case files, "F" sample, 1912-1973, .3 metres, box 1.

"CH"-series Chinese case files, consisting of a sample of closed files containing material dated before and after 1967, for persons whose surnames begin with the letter "F".

Accession 85-86/589.

Subject index to Central Registry Files of Secret series 500 block. Security(SF) block, and records of 1945-1970, 98640 cards in trays 1-16.

Accession 86-87/332.

Immigration intelligence subject files, 1950-1984, 10.8 metres, boxes 1-36.

The Intelligence Division of Employment and Immigration Canada collects information and provides advice and support on security matters to immigration agents. The Intelligence Division relies heavily on information gathered by the Royal Canadian Mounted Police, as well as by other Canadian provincial and municipal police forces, Interpol, and police forces and intelligence sources in other countries. The files are from the 200, 300, 400, and 700 blocks of a special file series prefixed by "IH"; they are not part of Employment and Immigration's Central Registry system. All Royal Canadian Mounted Police "secret" correspondence, specific Royal Canadian Mounted Police reports, and all "top secret" documentation have been removed from files by the Intelligence Division before transfer to the National Archives of Canada and destroyed.

Includes numerous files on illegal Chinese and other Asian immigrants, Chinese gangs in Canadian cities, etc.

File list, from which personal names have been deleted.

Accession 86-87/353.

Chinese immigrant records, romanized alphabetical index to case files, ca. 1900-1983, 42,412 cards.

This is a further portion of the nominal(romanized) card index to names found in the Chinese case files of the CH series. The index contains annotations, some as late as 1983. In alphabetical order by surname, middle name and given name.

Accession 86-87/354.

Chinese immigration records - Chinese family trees(form IMM 692), 1949-1972, .3 metres, Hong Kong 1.

These are specialized genealogical cross-reference charts or "Chinese family trees"(form IMM 692) completed by Immigration staff between 1964 and 1972, during investigations of illegal Chinese immigration under the Chinese Adjustment Statement Programs. Almost all the persons documented arrived in Canada between 1949 and 1972.

The Chinese Adjustment Statement Program was a continuing amnesty for persons of Chinese ancestry who had made false statements to secure landed immigrant status before 1960, in particular false claims of close family relationship to their sponsors in Canada(creating "paper" as opposed to "true" families). Royal Canadian Mounted Police investigations into their immigrations frauds resulted in a massive series of raids on Chinese-Canadian individuals, organizations, and businesses in May 1960. Reaction to these events led to the announcement by the Minister on 9 June 1960, of the Chinese Adjustment Statement Program(modelled on a similar American initiative) by which individuals were allowed to come forward voluntarily, "adjust" their status and remain in Canada. The program's procedures were simplified in late 1962(see minister's statement dated 16 November 1962) and continued in force, despite periodical re-evaluations, until October 1973. At that date the small number remaining eligible claims were merged with several other non-Chinese amnesty programs as the general "Status Adjustment Program". By that time, the status of between 10,300 and 13,000 persons of

Chinese ancestry had been adjusted under the program. The Chinese family trees appear to have been created primarily as aids to nominal indexing of the complex "paper" and "true" family names involved in the adjustments, and to cross-reference related case files. They may have been filled out by special Chinese records indexing officers. Each sheet is headed with person's name and his/her case file number in the CH series.

Accession 87-88/095.

Immigration, overseas posts, Hong Kong, London, Seattle, Cash Records 1982-1986. .60 metres, boxes 1 and 2.

Record Group 82. Immigration Appeal Board.

Responsibilities for deportation orders prior to 1967.

Record Group 84. Parks Canada.

Volume 64.

File ENG-20-3.
Japanese internment camps and projects - engineering and construction service, 1942-1945.

Volume 132.

File ENG-20-3.
Japanese internment camps and projects, engineering and construction service, 1942-1945.

Volume 148.

File J-165, part 1.
Jasper Park - war activities, alternate service work of Japanese.

Volume 210.

File EC-7-27, part 1.
Engineering and construction - Jasper work camps, Jasper, Yellowhead, Blue River, general, 1942-1943.
File U2003, Parts 3-5.

Japanese nationals - Ontario - general, 1942-1946.

Engineering and construction, Blue River, general, 1944-1947.

File EC-7-27-1.
Engineering and construction - movement and control of Japanese workcamps, 1942-1946.

File-7-28.
Engineering and construction - Japanese work camps, Revelstoke(plans, photos), 1942-1946.

File EC-7-28-1.
Engineering and construction - Japanese work camps, movement and control, 1942-1944.

Volume 212.

File EC-7-27, Part 2.
Engineering and construction - movement and control, Japanese work camps, 1942-1946.

Volume 281.

File J-165.
Jasper park, war activities, alternate service work of Japanese, 1939-1951.

Record Group 85. Northern Affairs Program.

C. Northwest Territories and Yukon Branch, 1894-1954.

1. Central registry Files, 1897-1954, 72.6 metres, (volumes 567-613, 653-669, 746-1043, 1929).

Volume 1014, File 17775.
A.Iriye(Japanese) - Indian act, 1947.

Volume 1023, File 18679.
Estate of M. Yuasa(Japanese) - Dawson, Yukon Territory.

Record Group 88. Surveys and mapping.

The following records are in the process of being reorganized and possibly transferred to another record group.

Volume 21.

File EC1-1-10. Parts 1-2.
Japanese work camps - financial, 1942-1947.

File EC5-1-18, Parts 1-4.
Japanese work camps, equipment, 1942-1949.

Volume 211.

File EC7-27, Part 2.

File EC7-24. Parts 1-3.
Japanese work camps - projects, general, 1941-1946.

Volume 36.

File EC7-24-1, Parts 1-2.
Japanese work camps - control and regulations, 1942-1947.

File EC7-24-2.
Japanese work camps - welfare, 1942-1946.

Volume 37.

File EC7-24-3.
Japanese work camps - reports, 1942-1946.

File EC7-24-4.
Japanese work camps - censored letters, 1942-1944.

Volume 38.

File EC7-26.
Ontario Japanese work camps - general, 1942-1946.

File EC7-26-1.
Movement and control - Japanese camps - Ontario, 1942-1944.

File EC7-29.
Clinton, Princeton, Japanese work camps, 1942.

Volume 39.

File EC7-30.
Hope, Princeton, Japanese work camps, general, 1942-1949.

Volume 47-48.

File U2000.
Japanese nationals, general, 1942-1945.

Volume 48.

File U2003, Parts 1-2.
Japanese nationals - regulations, 1942-1945.

Volume 48.

File U2004, Part 1.
Japanese nationals - staff, 1942.

Volume 49.

File U2003, Parts 1-2.
Japanese nationals - Ontario - general, 1942.

Volume 50.

Volume 51, File U2003, Parts 1-2.
Japanese nationals - British Columbia, 1942.

Volume 52.

File U2003, Parts 3-4.
Japanese nationals - British Columbia, 1942.

Volume 53.

File U2003, Parts 5-6.
Japanese nationals - British Columbia, 1942.

Volume 54.

File U2003, Parts 7-8.
Japanese nationals - British Columbia, 1942.

Volume 55,

File U2003, Parts 9-10.
Japanese nationals - British Columbia, 1942-1943.

Volume 56.

File U2003, Parts 11-12.
Japanese nationals - British Columbia, 1943-1944.

Volume 57.

File U2003, Parts 13-14.
Japanese nationals - British Columbia, 1944.

Record Group 117. Office of the Custodian of Enemy Property

Volume 20.

File 229-31.
Armenian claims, accounts, vouchers and receipts, 1931-1975.

C. Vancouver office.

1. Office Files. 1891, 1904-1911, 1913-1914, 1941-1958, 1.5 metres (volume 1-2, 267-272), microfilm reels C-9434 to C-9480.

In 1942 the Vancouver office was organized into the Enemy Section which administered the property of individuals interned as "enemy aliens" including those of German, Italian and Japanese extraction and into the Evacuation Section which administered the property of the Japanese Canadians who were removed from the coastal areas and relocated to the interior of British Columbia, the prairies, Ontario or Quebec. Both sections reported to a Director who, in turn, reported to the Deputy Custodian in Ottawa.

The subject files include the minutes of the two advisory committees on the disposal of property, correspondence with the Royal Canadian Mounted Police, Custodian policy, the Pacific Co-op Union and other cooperatives whose shares were held by Japanese Canadians, reports from outside accounting firms and agents, motor vehicles, sales, evaluation of properties, including those sold to D.V.A., legal opinions, internal office procedure, Custodian staff, cheques issued, the Bird Commission and the Far Eastern Commission, primarily for the period 1941 to 1952. Records predating 1941 deal with past land transactions. A few files exist as paper files; most of the Vancouver office files exist only on microfilm, a process which was carried out during 1951 prior to the closing of the branch office one year later. The files were not part of the numbered registry system, therefore they are in no particular order, although an attempt to group series of like files together is evident from the file list.
The finding aid is a file list for the paper files, a subject

index to the records on microfilm and a microfilm conversion list.

Reels C-9299 to C-9480.
These reels contain records created by Vancouver office, 1942-1951, and include case files on individual Japanese Canadians(over 15,000) plus records relating to property claims, repatriation. Bird Commission, accounting and other financial matters as well as Custodian policy. See finding aid for file list and index of names.

2. Ledgers. 1942-1952, 1.51 metres(volumes 69-95).

Following the recommendation of an accounting firm, the Custodian's office in Vancouver instituted two ledger systems: one for "enemies" and one for "evacuees." The ledgers contain many numbered entries on the money held in trust and real estate. The agricultural lands register, for example, indicates various expenses paid by the Custodian on behalf of Japanese Canadians, property taxes with the lot number and address given, water bills, mortgages, liens on cars, life insurance, plumbing and house repairs, sales commissions, etc. The evacuees' ledgers record such information as name, registration and file numbers, expenses for repairs, taxes, valuation fee, commissions, liabilities, real estate operation disbursement, cash or income from bank accounts, cash, real estate operation disbursement, cash or income from bank accounts, cash, real estate, miscellaneous assets and securities. Most entries are accounts for real estate. Most ledgers concern the administration of the evacuees' property for 1942-1949.

3. Case Files and index. 1942-1951, 135 microfilm reels C-9299 to C-9434.

The Vancouver office file system included an extensive series of cases, one for each Japanese Canadian over the age of sixteen who was removed from the coastal area of British Columbia. Over 15,600 case files were opened. The basis for each file is the "JP" form which record such information as name, address, age, marital status, occupation, employer, spouse's name, children's names, citizenship, information on a "J" form records brief information on individuals who had no property in the protected area. The files vary in length and may include a personal property summary, liability summary, real property summary, list of chattels, their value and date sold at public auction, Royal Canadian Mounted Police exhibit forms, inventories, legal documents, correspondence on the disposition of property, Bird Commission claims and awards and the occasional personal memo on family members for the period 1942 to 1951.

The case files are arranged numerically and exist only on microfilms. An alphabetical index is available. This index gives the name and address of the individuals, the case file number, family members and their file numbers and sometimes the relocation address. The microfilm conversion lists individuals on what reel a particular case file is located.

4. Business records. 1909-1950, 15.71 metres(volumes 96-267).

About one hundred firms owned or controlled by individuals of Japanese extraction were confiscated by the Canadian government and turned over to the Custodian's office. The latter acquired the essential business records of these companies in order to administer them during the World War II. Most companies were later acquired by the Custodian. This series includes corporation minutes and by-laws, accounting ledgers indicating inventories, sales, wages, expenditures and disbursements, share certificate books, bank deposit slips and the occasional income tax forms. Some ledger entries date back to 1909, some are written partly in Japanese and partly in English. The businesses were engaged in fishing, fish processing, lumbering, dry goods, food services, banking and publishing. The records are arranged in rough alphabetical order.
The finding aid is a list of companies and the types of records as well as the inclusive dates.

Record Group 118. Manpower and Immigration. Formerly Department of Citizenship and Immigration, Record Group 26 until 1966. In 1976 becomes Employment and Immigration Canada.

Policy, organizational, finance and administrative records on the immigration program from the 1940s onwards, especially in volumes 51-64 and accessions 77-78/103, 81-82/117, 84-85/120, and 84-85/566. Employment programs tied directly into immigration policy are documented in Record Group 118, especially 85-86/071.

Accession 84-85/R.

"Life in Canada" questionnaires completed by recent Ugandan immigrants and by recent visitors, tourists and farmer immigrants, 1971-1979.

Documentary Art and Photography Division.

Aitken, Kate, 1891-1971.
Radio broadcaster.
Photographs, 1880-1966.
Includes visits to Korea, Pakistan, Singapore and Japan in the 1950s.
SEIFRIED

Anderson, Patrick.
Poet and teacher.
Black and white. 703 photographs.
Includes photographs of the Far East used in his writings.
SEIFRIED

Baldwin, Charles O.
Black and white. 48 photographs, 1895-1896.
Includes photographs of Japan.
SEIFRIED

Bando, T.
Black and white photograph.
Road gang of Japanese internees, Yellowhead, British Columbia, March 1942.
SEIFRIED

Bergevin, A.F.
Noir et blanc, 206 photographies, couleur, 31. 1892.
Voyage autour du monde; photos prises aux Indes, et au Japon.SEIFRIED

Birks, Gerald W., 1872-1950.
Black and white, 31 photographs, 1910-1931.
Include views in India, China and Japan.SEIFRIED

British Columbia Security Commission.
Black and white. 160 photographs, 1942-1946.
Activities of Canadians of Japanese origin interned in camps in British Columbia, 1942-1946.
SEIFRIED

Buck, Tim, 1891-1973.
Black and white, 344 photographs, ca. 1930-ca. 1970.
Trips by Tim Buck, leader of the Communist Party of Canada, including China and Vietnam.
SEIFRIED

Canada. Department of External Affairs.
Black and white. 646 photographs, 1940-1960.
Include album on Japanese internment camps in British Columbia, and visit of Dr. Sukarno of Indonesia to Canada.
SEIFRIED

Canada. Department of External Affairs.
Black and white. 214 photographs, 1949-ca. 1959.
Include visit of Indian Prime Minister Jawaharlal Nehru, Mrs. L. and Mrs. Indira Gandhi to Ottawa, Toronto and Vancouver, 1949.
SEIFRIED

Canada. Department of Industry, Trade and Commerce.
Black and white. 165 photographs, 1921-ca. 1970.
Include Trade Commissioner's office in Tientsin.
SEIFRIED

Canada. Department of Labour.
42 photographs.
Relocation of Japanese Canadians in Manitoba.

Canada. Department of Manpower and Immigration.
Black and white. 5,337 photographs, 1958-1960.
Urban and rural areas across Canada, showing activities and occupations of immigrants, including Japanese, and Chinese.
SEIFRIED

Canada. Department of National Defence.
Black and white. Approximately 500,000 photographs, 1919-1953.
Include series P(South Pacific), S.F.(Special Forces, Korean War), H.U.(H.M.C.S. **Huron,** Korean War), I.R.(H.M.C.S. **Iroquois,** Korean War), S.O.(H.M.C.S. **Sioux,** Korean War).
SEIFRIED

Canada. Gouverneur general.
Noir et blanc. 12 photographies, 1914.
Différents aspects de l'incident du **Komagata maru** à Vancouver.
SEIFRIED

Canada. Information Canada. Expositions Branch.
Black and white. 200 photographs, 1915-1970.
Include Canadian participation at Osaka World's Fair, 1970.
SEIFRIED

Canada. Ministère des Affaires Extérieures.
Noir et blanc. 87 photographies, 1930.
Délégation canadienne à Japon.
SEIFRIED

Canada. Ministère du Secrétariat d'État.
Noir et blanc. 128 photographies, couleur 3.
Son Altesse Impériale le Shah d'Iran, Muhammed Rizah Pahlavi.
SEIFRIED

Canada. National Parks Branch.
18 boxes of photographs, ca. 1915-1950.
Includes Japanese internment farms.

SEIFRIED
Canada. Supreme Court.
Black and white. 14 photographs, 1887-1904.
Includes a portrait of Quai Shing.
SEIFRIED

Canadian Girls in Training.
Black and white. 702 photographs, 14 coloured.
Activities including Hong Kong, Indonesia, and Korea.
SEIFRIED

Canadian Government Exposition Centre.
Black and white, 246 photographs, colour 69.
Photographic coverage of Canadian participation in Expo '70, Osaka, Japan.
SEIFRIED

Canadian International Development Agency.
Black and white 14 photographs, colour 42, 1965-1970.
Activities of students and staff of the Coady International Institute, St. Francis Xavier University, Antigonish, cooperative projects by their graduates in India, Malaysia and the Philippines.
SEIFRIED

Carter, Thelma Nelson, 1902-1980.
Politician, feminist, editor.
Black and white 28 photographs, colour 10.
Views of Dorise Nielsen including photographs of her and others in China, where she worked from 1957 until her death in 1980.
SEIFRIED

Cavouk.
Toronto portrait photographer.
23 photographs.
Includes portrait of Dr. Hsieh-yen Shih.
SEIFRIED

Chinese Benevolent Association.
Black and white l photograph, ca. 1920.
Group photograph of members of the Association at a Chinese school in Victoria.
SEIFRIED

Clark, Andrew, 1952-
Ottawa, Ontario photographer.
Black and white, 21 photographs, 1976.
Photos of people taken in Asia and Africa.
SEIFRIED

Drew, George Alexander, 1894-1973.
Toronto, Ontario politician.
Activities of the Drew family in Canada, Western Europe, North Africa and Asia.
SEIFRIED

Ebdon, Frank W., 1905-
Black and white 19 photographs, colour 1, 1940-1966.
Ebdon at ceremony marking battle for Hong Kong, December 8. 1966.
SEIFRIED

Ellefsen, Marc.
Photographe.
Noir et blanc, 13,503, couleur 38,212, ca. 1960- ca. 1978.
Photographies commerçiales, incluant Japon,
SEIFRIED

Ellefsen, Marc, 1932-1978.
Noir et blanc 54,000 photographies, ca. 1970-ca. 1978.
Photographies des voyages, incluant Osaka.
SEIFRIED

Ells, Sidney Clarke, 1878-1971.
Mining engineer, public servant.
Black and white 360 photographs, colour 235.
Include views of China, l914-1948.
SEIFRIED

Endicott, James G., 1898-
Black and white 1,000 photographs, (1895-ca. 1955)
Scenes of the life of James Endicott, and James G. Endicott, with Mary Austin, wife of the latter, include coverage of their periods as missionaries in China.
SEIFRIED

Foster, Margaret C.
Missionary.
Black and white 108 photographs, 1939-1954.
Include views of evacuation of Japanese Canadians to the interior of British Columbia, and settlements in British Columbia and Ontario, 1942-1954.
SEIFRIED

Herridge, Herbert Wilfred, 1895-1973.
Politician.
Black and white 58 photographs, colour 15, 1930-1970.
Include activities of Chinese Canadian students, Trail, British Columbia.
SEIFRIED

Hoe, Wanda Joy.
Black and white 3 photographs, 1900-1939.
Chinese immigrants to Canada.
SEIFRIED

Hundle, T.S.
Black and white, 2 photographs.
Sikh funeral procession and pyre in Vancouver, including view of Sikh temple.
SEIFRIED

Hunter, George.
Black and white 46 photographs, 1965.
Canadian Trade Show, Tokyo, Japan.
SEIFRIED

Jenkins, F.M.D., 1859-1930.
Public servant and musician.
Black and white 36 photographs, ca. 1890-1927.
Include aspects of Ruth Jenkins' life in China as a missionary, 1920-1927.
SEIFRIED

Kitagawa, E.
Black and white l photograph, 1919-1920.
Hockey team, Asahi Athletic Club, Vancouver.
SEIFRIED

Kitagawa, E.
Black and white 2 photographs.
Minister of Citizenship and Immigration Ellen Fairclough with representatives of the immigration committees of the National Japanese Canadian Citizenship Association and the Chinese Canadian Association, 20 June, 1958.
SEIFRIED

Kohashigawa, K.
Black and white 1 photograph, 1910.
Messrs. Kohashigawa and Takayesu, immigrants from Okinawa, Lethbridge.
SEIFRIED

Kohashigawa, K.
Black and white 7 photographs, colour 1, 1910-1975.
Activities of the Kohashigawa family in Vauxhall, Coaldale, and Lethbridge, the Japanese warship **Kirishima kan.** 1919, New Year's party of Okinawan

Issei in Southern Alberta, at Lethbridge.
SEIFRIED

Lewis, Allan C.T., 1885-
Lawyer.
Black and white 154 photographs, 1904-1907.
Include views of Madras, Ceylon, Hong Kong and China.
SEIFRIED

Matsubara, Keitaro.
Black and white 13 photographs, 1944-1947.
Activities and members of the family of Rev. Keitaro Matsubara on the sugarbeet farm of D.P.Froebe, near Holmwood, Manitoba, ca. 1944-1947; sugarbeet fields and machinery.
SEIFRIED

Matsumoto, Isamu.
Black and white 1 photograph, 1946.
Embarkation of Japanese-Canadian internees, Slocan City, British Columbia.
SEIFRIED

Measures, W. Howard, 1894-
Government official.
Black and white 202 photographs, 1920-1964.
Include views and portraits of events and personalities involved in the international life of Canada during the period 1920-1964, including Prime Minister Jawaharlal Nehru of India and Mrs. Indira Gandhi at Queenston power house, 23 October, 1949.
SEIFRIED

Meredith, Brian.
Journalist.
Black and white 14 photographs, 1951.
Presentation of the United Nations' flag to the 25th Canadian Infantry Brigade, Korea, May 16, 1951.
SEIFRIED

Miyagawa, George Sutekichi, 1899-
Black and white 16 photographs, 1916-1947.
July First celebration by the Japanese community, Vancouver, in the Miyagawa home, family, and activities. Mr. S.Miyagawa's World War II internment card.
SEIFRIED

Miyazaki, Masajiro, 1899-
Osteopath.
Black and white 13 photographs, 1924-1943.
Portrait of the Vancouver chapter of the Japanese Students Christian Association of North America, 1924, view of a Japanese evacuation settlement, 1943, group portraits of the Japanese Student Club of the University of British Columbia annual graduation banquet, 1934-1939.
SEIFRIED

Murray, L.F.
Black and white 10 photographs, ca. 1900-1945.

Includes views of Onagawa bay, Honshu, Japan, 9 August, 1945.
SEIFRIED

Nakayama, C. Gordon.
Minister.
Black and white 44 photographs, 1909-1960.
Activities of Rev. Gordon G. Nakagawa, Anglican minister in Vancouver, Prince Rupert, and Slocan, and Coaldale and Lethbridge, during the period 1930-1960. Some photographs relate to Japanese Canadian citizens displaced by measures taken during World War II.
SEIFRIED

National Film Board of Canada.
Black and white 368 photographs, ca. 1914-1918.
Include photographs for a documentary on Norman Bethune, 1966.
SEIFRIED

National Film Board of Canada.
Black and white 740 photographs, colour 200. 1960-1965.
Include visits of the Shah of Iran and the Prime Minister of India, Mr. Lal Bahadur Sastri, 1965.
SEIFRIED

Nielsen, Dorise Winnifred, 1902-1980.
Politician and preacher.
Black and white 2 photographs, ca. 1940-1966.
One photograph shows Dorise Nielsen with Chinese people in front of the temple at the Summer Palace of former Emperors, China, 1966.
SEIFRIED

Nishima, C.
Black and white photograph, 1929.
Group portrait of officers of the Japanese vegetable farmers cooperative, Lethbridge.
SEIFRIED

Odlum, Victor Wentworth, 1880-1971.
Soldier, journalist, diplomat.
Black and white 53 photographs, ca. 1914-1965.
Include photographs as Canadian ambassador to China and Turkey.
SEIFRIED

Packard, Frank Lucius.
Black and white photograph, 1920-1930.
Canadian author Frank L. Packard and J.P.Marquand(possibly the American author) in the Forbidden City, Peking, China.
SEIFRIED

Panter, Richard.
Engineer.
Black and white 9 photographs, 1949-1950.
Includes two views of Harry Shigeta.
SEIFRIED

Raymond(Alberta) Young Peoples Society.
Black and white photograph, 1948.
Eugene Hattori, first child born in Lethbridge of Japanese evacuee parents and his sister Susan.
SEIFRIED

Reford, Robert.
Businessman and amateur photographer.
Black and white 841 photographs, 1885-1890.
Include views of Japanese immigrants on the west coast.
SEIFRIED

Ridsdale, George F.
Collector.
Black and white 176 photographs, 1890-1920.
Include views of Chinese immigration to Canada.
SEIFRIED

Ross, Graham.
Black and white photograph, 1919.
Portrait of Dr. Norman Bethune, with associates at the Hospital for Sick Children, London, England.
SEIFRIED

Sakamoto, Mas.
Black and white photograph, 1958.
Original members of the Cho Jo Kai(Old age pensioners club) Lethbridge.
SEIFRIED

Sasaki, Steve.
Black and white photograph. ca. 1943.
Tashme, British Columbia, overflow camp, a non-denominational internment camp for Japanese Canadians.
SEIFRIED

Sato. S.S.
Black and white 4 photographs,1923.
Rev. and Mrs. S.S.Sato and family at Steveston, British Columbia.
SEIFRIED

Shing Wah Daily News.
Color 4 photographs, 1977.
Interior of the print shop of the **Shing Wah Daily News.**
SEIFRIED

Silverthorne, F.G.
Black and white photograph, 1945.
Nisei soldiers who volunteered for Pacific training, Brantford, Ontario.
SEIFRIED

Stevens, Henry Herbert, 1878-1973.
Politician.
Black and white 89 photographs, ca. 1911-1919.
Includes the **Komagata maru** incident.
SEIFRIED

Stevenson, William.
Black and white 383 photographs, colour 76, 1960-1969.
Include touristic photographs taken by Mr. Stevenson in Formosa and China.

Stursberg, Peter.
Journalist and author.
Black and white 28 photographs, 1907-1923.
Includes race tiffin, Foochow, 1907.
SEIFRIED

Stursberg, Peter.
Black and white l8 photographs, 1,418, 1938-1971.
Includes slides of trip to China in l971 with Chester Ronning.
SEIFRIED

Tamayose, Art.
Black and white 23 photographs, 1915-1973.
Includes Okinawan community in Southern Alberta.
SEIFRIED

Tashiro, Eiji.
Black and white 5 photographs. 1934-1940.
Includes Japanese community in Mission, British Columbia, including members of one of the earliest judo clubs in Canada.
SEIFRIED

Tata, Sam.
Montreal photographer.
Black and white 52 photographs, 1948-1974.
Includes aspects of daily life in Tokyo, Hong Kong, Shanghai.

Black and white 3 photographs, 1941-1943.
Portraits taken in Shanghai of Michel Harriz, M. White-Steven's, and Diana Chang.

Noir et blanc photographie, 1973.
Sam Tata photographie par son neveu Karli Brown, age de 9 ans, à Hong Kong.

Noir et blanc 54 photographies, 1956-1981.
Les montréalais vus par Sam Tata entre l956 et 1976, portraits de photographes canadiens ou étrangers de réputation internationale.

Noir et blanc 2 photographies, 1948, 1973.
Portraits des photographes Henri Cartier-Bresson à Bombay, en 1948, et de Brian Bake à Hong Kong en 1973.
SEIFRIED

Trudeau, Pierre, 1919-
Politician.
Black and white 991 photographs, colour 845, 1968-1976.
Visits by the Prime Minister to foreign countries, including Japan, Iran, Pakistan, Indonesia, India, Sri Lanka, and China.
SEIFRIED

Tucker, M.Grace, 1902-
Missionary.
Black and white 10 photographs, colour 1, 1942-1944.
Activities of Japanese families evacuated to Slocan City, British Columbia.
SEIFRIED

Uchida, Matasaburo, 1900-
Black and white 14 photographs, 1942-1945.
Activities and staff of the Slocan Community Hospital, New Denver, British Columbia.
SEIFRIED

Watts, Ruth Jenkins.
Missionary.
Black and white 64 photographs, 1921.
Photos by R.J.Watts in China, missionaries, missions and mission activities, famine struck China.
SEIFRIED

Whitton, Charlotte, 1896-1975.
Social worker, writer, politician.
Black and white 778 photographs, ca. 1914 - ca. 1972.
Includes Indira Gandhi.
SEIFRIED

Wong, Christine P.
Black and white 29 photographs, colour 7, 1958-1960.
Career of Dorise Winnifred Nielsen, former United Progressive Party member, and feminist, who joined Peking's Foreign Languages Publishing House in 1957, and worked there until her death in 1980.
SEIFRIED

National Film, Television and Sound Archives.

Les actualités, number 24.
35 mm, b&w, 43.9 mètres.
Canada 1943.
Deposited April 1979.

Flight lieutenant Cheng lands at St. Hubert in an Avro Anson and is greeted by the commanding officer, Group Commander Scott. She inspects an honour guard of Royal Canadian Air Force WDS, and is honoured by Montreal Chinese Womens' Society, at a banquet, Miss Cheng, still in uniform, addresses the gathering.

Bamboo, Lions, and Dragons.
3/4 inch videocassette, 26 minutes.
Canada 1979.

"Two families, the Changs and the Lims, tell the story of the Chinese community in Vancouver from widely different perspectives. Chang Yun arrived in Canada in 1908. His generation never integrated into the Canadian mainstream, partly because of the passage of the Asiatic Exclusion Act that fostered racism. By contrast Liz and Herbert Lim were born in Canada and grew up in Chinatown. They now live in the suburbs, totally acculturated to Canadian ways...

Belles of the South Seas.
16 mm, b&w positive, 106.7 metres
Castle Films, U.S., 1920's?
Deposited March 1982.

Documentary on natives of the South Sea islands.

British Canadian Pathe News.
Videotape.
Canada, 1920.

Includes visit of Japanese sailors in Mexico City. Mexican girls pose with officers and men of the cruiser **Yakumo**, in return the Japanese give an exhibition of kendo and jiujitsu.

C.B.C. Newsmagazine, 20 March 1954.
16 mm and b&w print, 850 feet.
Canada.
Deposited 20 April 1976.

Includes pictorial essay on property expropriation of Chinese community on Elizabeth Street in Toronto, shot of community's commercial buildings, entertainment, sequence on Chinese moving business to Brampton, sequence on operation of Chinese newspaper press and on Chinese opera.

C.B.C. Newsmagazine, 30 October 1955.
16 mm, b&w print, 850 feet.
Canada.
Deposited 20 April 1976.

Includes sequence of TV cameraman filming a Chinese festival.

C.B.C. Newsmagazine, 11 March 1956.
16 mm, b&w, 850 feet.
Canada.
Deposited 20 April 1976.

Includes Indo-China War, security measures taken by the Southeast Asian collective defence treaty and its members, Pakistan, Thailand, Philippines, Australia and U.S. against Communist aggressions, shot of the King of Laos.

C.B.C. Newsmagazine, 16 September 1956.
16 mm, b&w, 850 feet.
Canada.

Includes Indo-China.

C.B.C. Newsmagazine, 7 October 1956.
16 mm, b&w, 850 feet.
Canada.
Deposited 20 April 1976.

Includes Indo-China.

C.B.C. Newsmagazine, 20 October 1957.
16 mm, b&w, 128 feet.
Canada.
Deposited 20 April 1976.

Includes brief shots of fighting in Korea, Indo-China, and stills of Nehru.

C.B.C. Newsmagazine, 5 January 1958 - The Week's Highlights.
3/4 inch, b&w videocassette, 3 minutes.
Canada, Canadian Broadcasting Corporation.

Television magazine story about events in India, Indonesia.
1. India. India gives its support to the government of Indonesia in its conflict with the Netherlands.
2. Indonesia. 50,000 Dutch are expelled from Indonesia by the government. Dutch refugees shown in transit on their way to Malaya.

C.B.C. Newsmagazine, 12 January 1958.
Videotape.
Canada 1958.

Television public affairs program includes report from Djakarta by William Stephenson on the political instability in Indonesia. Includes views of Java and Sumatra and discussion of the severe economic crisis affecting Indonesia, weakness of the Sukarno government and the legacy of Dutch colonial rule.

C.B.C. Newsmagazine, 8 February 1958.
Canada, 1958.

Television public affairs program includes report by Douglas Lachance on the unstable political situation in Cyprus. Footage depicting Cypriot Greeks and Turks demonstrating and rioting and public address by Dr. Fazil Kuchuk, leader of the Cypriot Turks, also interview with the Governor of Cyprus, Sir Hugh Foote and editor of Turkish-language newspaper. William Stephenson reports on the economic and political chaos in Indonesia following its independence from the Dutch, includes footage of the poor in Jakarta, empty businesses and idle ship in the harbour, noteworthy interview with Prime Minister Djuanda, former Prime Minister and government officials, exiled Iran Queen Sunassa, and Dutch nationals departing the country.

C.B.C. Newsmagazine, 18 February 1958.
16 mm, b&w, 850 feet.
Deposited 20 April 1976.

Includes coverage of Indo-China and Cyprus.

C.B.C. Newsmagazine, 23 February 1958.
16 mm and b&w print, 34 feet.

Canada.
Deposited 20 April 1976.

Residents of Vancouver's Chinese community celebrate the start of the Chinese lunar calendar year, parade, beauty queen, Chinese lion dance, etc. are part of this celebration.

C.B.C. Newsmagazine, 1 November 1959.
Videotape.
Canada, 1959.

Television public affairs programs profile of Prime Minister Jawaharlal Nehru of India, including footage of Nehru visiting remote areas of India and meeting with world leaders such as President Kwame Nkrumah of Ghana, Premier Chou En-lai of the People's Republic of China, and President Ayub Khan of Pakistan. In an interview Nehru discusses the strained relations between China and India over recent border skirmishes. Additional topics discussed by Nehru are India's food production, Russian aid to India, individual freedoms, decentralization of government and Nehru's future political plans.

C.B.C. Newsmagazine(network), 6 December 1959. The War of Ideas.
Videotape.

Special documentary program on India entitled **The War of Ideas** written and directed by Michael MacLean. Film captures the widely varied Indian landscape and its diverse peoples, shows how ancient customs and beliefs flourish side by side with the latest advances in science and technology. We see street scenes of Delhi with its beautiful temples and its "untouchables", many of who live and die in the streets. In rural areas the villages are seen conducting most activities with primitive tools. Aerial shots of the Bhakra Dam high in the Himalayas shows teams of labourers toiling with pick and shovel to complete a vast irrigation project. Evidence of India's dependence on foreign aid is recorded in footage of the Canadian-financed nuclear reactor near Bombay and the Soviet-financed steel mills at Bhilai and Bokaro. Additional sequences on the southern state of Kerala where a communist government organized agricultural cooperatives. In an interview, Prime Minister Jawaharlal Nehru discusses his government's policy of cooperation and persuasion rather than compulsion as India strives to solve its social and economic problems.

C.B.C. Newsmagazine, 21 September 1965.
Videotape.
Canada 1965.

Television newspecial from the United Nations building in New York. Discussion of the conflict in Jammu and Kashmir, territory of Northwestern Indian subcontinent, parts of which are claimed by India and Pakistan, and whose northern border is disputed by the People's Republic of China, and the political turmoil that reigns in Sikkim, Indian state which is threatened by a Chinese invasion. Includes sequences on military manoeuvres of both Indian and Tibetan troops in the mountains of Sikkim, speech segments by Pakistani Minister of law, S.M.Zafer and Indian representative, Muhammad Ali Shagla at the U.N. Security Council meeting, interview with Canadian External Affairs Minister Paul Martin, and filmed interview with a Pakistani representative, Muhammad Ayoub and a Minister of the Indian controlled area of Kashmir, Sayeed Murkazeen, who declare their respective claims over the disputed territory and comment on the U.N.'s ceasefire resolution.

C.B.C. Radio News Summary.
Canada, 1962.

Items include failure of second attempt of American scientists to explode nuclear device over the Pacific, picketers in Montréal protest presence of Communist China trade delegation to Canada to negotiate purchase of more Canadian wheat.

C.B.C. TV News. First edition, 16 June 1962.
Studio recording of a television news recording.

Includes resignation of South Korean premier.

C.B.C. TV News Library, number 004(anti-Kutch demonstrations).
Videotape.
United Kingdom, in Hindi.

Sound footage of demonstrations in India against border negotiations with Pakistan. Demonstrators yell slogans, raise fists, and carry placards reading "no talks with Pakistan" and "do not give away Kutch", a territory of India which Pakistan also claims. A cutaway shows negotiators from India and Pakistan entering a meeting room and seating themselves.

C.B.C. TV News Library, number 374.
Videotape.
Canada, 1956.

Item on Federal Minister of Trade and Commerce, Clarence Decatur Howe's visit to Japan where he is shown inspecting a Tokyo food factory. Footage includes a shot of Canadian departmental officials, including Mitchell Sharp.

Canada at War, part 6, Turn of the Tide.
16 mm, b&w positive, 950 feet.
Deposited May 1977.

Period between October 1942 and July 1943. Includes U.S. marines landing on Guadalcanal and the Solomons.
This is an American version of Canada at War, called Men in Combat.
Description based on Canadian version.

Canada harvests record wheat crop for war.
35 mm, b&w positive, 375 feet.
U.S., 1940's.

Includes grain being loaded onto wagons by Japanese-Canadian farm labourers(deported from the West Coast).

Chinese Funeral Parade, 1918.
35 mm, b&w positive, 100 feet.
Deposited 3 November 1972.

Location: Victoria, British Columbia, Yates Street. Delegation of Chinese Canadians follows horse-drawn hearse to cemetery.

Daily Life in the Solomons.
16 mm and b&w positive, 250 feet.
New Zealand, 1940's.
Deposited September 1976.

New Zealand fighter wing stationed in the Solomons goes through a typical day. A transport plane brings mail. Aerials of air raids on Japanese installation by U.S. bombers. Various shorts of wrecked Japanese freighters. Sequence on native life and fraternizing between natives and airmen.

Elizabeth is Queen.
35 mm, colour positive, parts 1-6, 4491 feet.
Great Britain, 1953.
Deposited July 1977.

Includes the Queen of Tonga at coronation ceremony.

The Fifth Estate, 6 February 1979.
Videotape.
Canada, 1979.

Includes report on the "ethnic" Chinese refugees from Vietnam, includes footage of the "boat people" escaping Vietnam and eventually arriving in Canada, views of Hanoi, Ho Chi Minh City(formerly Saigon) and Cholon, the former Chinese quarter of Saigon. Translation of an interview with Viet Cong army captain who recounts how the Viet Cong defeated the Americans and comments by a Chinese refugee in Canada.

Fishing camp at Campbell River, Cannery at Steveston and tugboats in Vancouver.
1/2 inch colour videocassette, 8 minutes.
Canada, 1938-1939.

Includes sequences on Japanese fisherman and his family working on nets on a wharf.

5000 Miles.
16 mm colour print, 693 feet.
Canada, 1965.
Deposited August 1977.

Includes sequence of Montréal Chinatown.

French-speaking World - the Hour of Independence.
16 mm, b&w, 1014 feet.
Canada, 1963.

Effect of independence on France's ties with her former colonies, a look at independence movements in French colonies and France's reaction to them, including Indo-China, shots of drawings illustrating colonial wars, Ho Chi Minh arriving in France for talks with leaders.

A Friend at the Door.
16 mm b&w positive, 1000 feet.
Canada, 1950.
Deposited August 1977.

Includes sequences of Nanaimo Chinatown and inhabitants.

Gateway to Asia.
35 mm, b&w positive, 950 feet.
Canada, 1945.
Deposited April 1977.

The role of British Columbia in the postwar world, with flashbacks to the province's contribution to the war effort, wartime sequence on idle Japanese Canadian fishing fleet, vacant houses and a relocation camp, sequence on Chinatown, on Sikhs at work, sequence on violent Japanese kamikaze attacks on U.S. warships.

The Grand Design.
b&w positive, 352 feet.
U.N. 1951.

Includes footage of war in Indonesia, Kashmir and Korea.

[Hon. Allen Joseph MacEachen Far East trip]
1/2 inch colour videocassette, 21 minutes.
Canada 1976.

Television news report on the Secretary of State for External Affairs, Hon. Allen MacEachen's visit to the Far East in September 1976. Global TV reporter Peter Trueman is on location with Canadian delegation in Indonesia, Malaysia, New Zealand and Australia. Report includes footage on: official welcome by Indonesia's Foreign Minister Adam Malik, shots of President Soeharto of Indonesia, Jakarta market place, slums, and train overflowing with passengers hanging on body of locomotive, official Malaysia reception and shows of hospital supported by Canadian funds, island of Bali where MacEachen and staff spend rest stop, Bali market and rice paddies. Interview with MacEachen included, with comments on the tour and Canadian involvement in the Far East.

Inquiry, 20 July 1964, the Japanese Canadians.
1/2 inch b&w videocassette, 30 minutes.
C.B.C. Canada.

Television documentary film looks at the tragedy of Japanese Canadians during World War II when they were evacuated from their homes in British Columbia to inland prison camps, because of government suspicion of enemy invasion by Japanese at the occurrence of Pearl Harbour attack. The film also probes in the uncertainty of Japanese rights in Canada today, and includes actual footage of the evacuation, sequences on life in row camps, personal narratives of evacuees who lost their land and personal belongings and who were sometimes separated from their families; interviews with Minister H.A.Stevens of the Bennet government in British Columbia, explaining government's suspicions of Japanese agents among these citizens, reports on racial discrimination in Canada in reference to Japanese and interview with a Japanese lawyer.

Jalan, Jalan: a Journey in Sundanese Java.
3/4 inch videocassette. colour, 20 minutes.
Canada, 1973.

An abridged and revision version of **Wet Earth and Warm People** made for the younger audience, this is a film without commentary about, with all the sights and sounds, color and tempo of life of the exotic Indonesian islands in the Java sea. Here "Jalan, Jalan" can mean either going on a journey or simply taking a stroll. It is a film of surprises - the bustling, half modern, half-ancient city of Jakarta, capital of the island republic, and in the lovely countryside where rice fields reach distant mountains.

Japanese Canadians at Play.
16 mm, colour positive, 1056 feet.
Canada 1952.

Amateur documentary. Various events held by the Toronto Japanese Canadian Citizens Association, including the visit to the top of the Canadian Bank of Commerce building in Toronto, family outing to Center Island(Toronto), the Japanese Canadian Golf Club tournament in Toronto at the Rouge Hills Golf Club, a visit to the C.N.E.; an international Nisei tournament of tennis held between Toronto and Cleveland; view of the Ami club, a baseball organization of the Toronto Nisei Girls' Softball League, the Toronto International Nisei Softball Tournament at Trinity Park(between Toronto, Montréal, Cleveland and New York with the finals shown played on Labour Day between Montréal and Cleveland. The winning Montréal team receives the J.C.C.A. cup. The Toronto baseball club, the Oldtimers play an exhibition game at St.Clair stadium. The Toronto J.C.C.A. executives take to the beach. Map of Canada indicating the Japanese Canadian population in each province.

MacArthur back in Philippines.
16 mm, b&w positive, 11 feet.
U.S., 1944.
Deposited July 1977.

MacArthur is shown wading through surf being true to his promise "I shall return".

Marketplace, 16 February 1974, [Performance of the Barrett government in British Columbia].
1/2 inch vtr cassette, 28 minutes.
Canada.

Includes sequence on Chinese labour working on a Fraser Valley farm.

Nakagawa, G.F.
15 items, colour, b&w film, 2 hours, 37 minutes.

Contains filmed records of the travels of G.F.Nakagawa throughout Canada and abroad, and of his experiences in the Canadian internment camps for Japanese during the war years, 1936-1940's.

National Press Theatre, 3 May 1984.
Canada, 1984.

Part of press conference held by representatives of Japanese auto dealers in Canada about import restrictions on Japanese cars.

National Press Theatre, 12 June 1984.
Canada, 1984.

Press conference held by Gerald Regan, Minister of International Trade to announce agreement with Japanese officials concerning import restrictions of Japanese automobiles into Canada.

National Press Theatre, 20 June 1984.
VHS audiorecording.
Canada, 1984.

Press conference held by officials of the Ministry of State for Multiculturalism, David M. Collenette(Minister of State), Kerry Johnston(Director-general for Multiculturalism Canada) and Dhiru Patel(Chief, Race Relations Division). Among the issues raised were government provisions in the new act regarding individual compensation to Japanese-Canadians who suffered deprivation and injustice during World War II.

National Press Theatre, 28 January 1985.
Canada 1985.

Press conference held by the National Association of Japanese Canadians represented by Art Miki to report on the breakoff of the negotiations between the N.A.J.C. and the government. In an opening statement and in a question period that follows, Mr. Miki addresses the following topics and issues: misunderstandings and area of conflict between the N.A.J.C. and the federal government; type of negotiation required by the N.A.J.C. and its agenda of issues including monetary compensation for economic losses suffered by Japanese Canadians detained in internment camps during World War II, possible N.A.J.C. scenarios if the federal government decides to act unilaterally.

National Press Theatre, 12 April 1985.
Canada, 1985.

Press conference held by the Japanese ambassador to Canada, Kiyoaki Kikuchi, to announce his government's decision to apply new external economic measures intended to encourage foreign exports to Japan. In an opening statement and subsequent question period, the following topics were discussed: Japanese non-tariff barriers reduction, the productivity of western nations, foreign understanding of Japanese trading patterns, unique characteristics of the policy's trade barrier reductions, and comments on the power of the Japanese bureaucracy.

National Press Theatre, 8 July 1985.
Canada, 1985.

Press conference held by the Department of External Affairs officials, John G.Hayden, Director General, East-Asia Bureau, Richard V. Gorham, Canadian ambassador to China, Russell H.Davidson, Director of East-Asia Relations Division, to provide background information on the visit of the President of China, Li Xiann Tan. In an opening statement and subsequent question period, the following topics were discussed; Chinese-Canadian political, trade and investment relations, prospects for sale of Canada reactors to China, Pierre Elliot Trudeau's peace mission visit to China, President Li's background and itinerary in Canada

National Press Theatre, 16 July 1985.
VHS audio recording.
Canada, 1985.

Press conference held by a delegation from China representing the Ministry of Foreign Affairs, including Ji Peng Fei, state counsellor and Zhu Qizhen, Director of Information, to report on their visit to Canada. In opening statements and subsequent question period the following items were discussed: Sino-Canadian capacity for reaching understanding and developing relations, need for cooperation in economic matters and an outline of current trade relations, establishment of a Chinese trade show in Canada, omission in signing communication and technology agreements, Canadian participation in the development of hydroelectric power in China, meeting with Prime

Minister Brian Mulroney, and American disapproval of Chinese family planning practices.

National Press Theatre, 31 July 1985.
VHS audio recording.
Canada, 1985.

Press conference held by S.J.S.Chhatwal, Indian High Commissioner, to announce a settlement between the Prime Minister of India and the Akali Party in the Panjab, and to talk about the Air India disaster and the support given by the High Commissioner of India to grieving families in Canada. In an opening statement and subsequent question period the following items were discussed: the position of the Indian government relating to extremists, suspension of flights to Canada by Air India and the inquest being conducted on the crash.

National Press Theatre, 31 July 1985.
Audio recording.
Canada, 1985.

Press conference held by the Japanese Embassy in Canada, represented by Tadashi Ikeda, Minister and Charge d'affaires, to release Japan's new economic and commercial policy relating to foreign goods and foreign markets. In an opening statement and subsequent question period the following items were discussed: objectives of the new Japanese economic policy, impact of import quotas and the U.S./Canada free trade discussions on Japanese trade policy, the nature and motives of Japanese tariff reductions on foreign goods including references to G.A.T.T. talks, and the current potential for a trade war between Japan and the United States.

National Press Theatre, 9 January 1986.
Canada, 1986.

Press briefing conducted by Senior Policy Advisor to the Prime Minister, Dr. Charles Macmillan and Japan C. McCloskey, Director General of the Pacific Bureau of External Affairs, on the up-coming visit of Japan's Prime Minister, Yasuhiro Nakasone. The agenda and objectives of the visit are discussed, with special mention of the current global issues to be raised, including arms control. Concerns raised by members of the press include: automobile import quotas, voluntary trade restraints, U.S. protectionism, Japan-U.S. trade policy, Canada-U.S. trade policy, and the importance of security of supply for Japan.

National Press Theatre, 13 January 1986.
Canada, 1986.

Press conference held by Dr. Charles Macmillan, Senior Policy Advisor to the Prime Minister, Derek Burney, Associate Under-Secretary of State for External Affairs, and Barry Steers, Canada's
Ambassador to Japan, concerning the current visit of Japanese Prime Minister Yasuhiro Nakasone. In opening statements and responses to questions from the press, Macmillan reports on Nakasone's visit to Northern Telecom's manufacturing facilities in Brampton, Ontario, his speech in Parliament, and topics discussed with Prime Minister Mulroney and other officials, including agreements on a student exchange program, the provisions of an accord with the U.S. to eliminate tariff barriers on computer parts. Topics still to be discussed include free trade, arms control, terrorism, and Canadian assistance to Asia.

National Press Theatre, 13 January 1986.
Canada, 1985.

Press conference held by Seiichiro Otsuka, official spokesman for Japanese Prime Minister Yasuhiro Nakasone, currently visiting Canada. He is accompanied by Takashi Kagami, Director of International Press Division of the Ministry of Foreign Affairs. Otsuka reports on agreements reached by Nakasone and Mulroney in their talks together relating to: the need to further economic development; investment and trade expansion between Canada and Japan, an early conclusion to the Science and Technical Cooperation Agreement, revision of taxes on imports, the student exchange program, the promotion of grass-roots understanding between the two countries, and the issue of free trade between Canada and the United States.

National Press Theatre, 24 April 1986.
Canada, 1986.

Press briefing conducted by Dr. Fred Doucet, Senior Adviser to the Prime Minister, and Sylvia Ostrey, personal representative of the Prime Minister for the economic summit in Tokyo. In opening statements Doucet describes international events in which Prime Minister Mulroney recently took part, including meetings with the Prime Ministers of Japan and the United States and with leaders of third world countries as valuable preparation for the Tokyo summit meeting of May 4-6, 1986. Issues relevant to the summit agenda raised during questions from the press include: the blurring of economic and political issues, interdependency in today's world, exchange rates, hegemony within developing countries, Canada's role as a spokesman for developing countries, the General Agreement on Tariffs and Trade talks, Libya's role in terrorism, the role of the United Nations, and the possible addition of Canada to the Group of Five(finance ministers from Britain, France, Japan, West Germany and the United States).

[The Netherlands and India]
1/2 inch, b&w videocassette tape, 40 minutes.
U.S., 1900's.

Travelogue on Indonesia in early 1900's under Dutch rule. Aboard a Dutch liner, a group of Europeans visit some of its territories, namely Malaysia, Java and Bali. The film depicts Indonesian life in cities and villages, and shows sequences on luxurious hotels and palaces, ruins of Hindu and Buddhist temples, street merchants, coconut carvings and batik hand-printing, rice harvest, Indonesian dances, public bathing, native funeral processions and musical instrumentalists.

90 Minutes Live, 11 February 1977.
1/2 inch colour VTR cassette, 75 minutes.
Canada.

Television public affairs program with host Peter Gzowski and his guests, includes novelist and filmmaker James Clavell, talks about his book **Shogun**, his experience as a prisoner of war in Japan during World War II, Japanese culture and their attitude towards war, and the unjust treatment Japanese Canadians received from the Canadian government during this.

90 Minutes Live, 19 May 1977, [Japanese drummers]
1/2 inch color, 5 minutes.
Canada.

Peter talks to Mona Kanadapa(?), representative for the Japanese Canadian centennial celebrations, who introduces performance by group of Japanese drummers, "ondakoza".

People - the Chinese in Canada.
16 mm b&w, 1048 feet.
Canada, 1955.

Docudrama on the difficult adaptation of a newly landed Chinese youth to life in Toronto. Sequences: a session in a Department of Citizenship and Immigration office, the city of Toronto in daytime and at night, language classes, Chinatown shops and people, demolition and slums, the despair of the young man and his eventual realization that he can be happy in his new land.

Southern Hemisphere cruise on the Good ship Carinthia.
b&w videocassette tape, 100 minutes.

Travel film on Mrs. Frank A.Wright's long extended voyage of the South Seas aboard the ship **Carinthia**. Includes map illustration of her itinerary, film sequences including Tahiti, Raratonga island, Port Moresby, New Guinea, Indonesian ports and cities, Singapore, Penang Island, Colombo, Sri Lanka.

Stevenson, William, 1924-
Tapes. 3 hours(approx.)

William Stevenson was educated in London, England. He worked as a reporter after World War II on various London newspapers. He immigrated to Canada in 1947, worked as a journalist for the
Toronto Star and **Star Weekly**, and later became a producer for the C.B.C.
This collection contains reports by William Stevenson about Communist China, the lives of its citizens and the changes that accompanied the arrival of Communist propaganda. Included is a collection of historical sound recordings, radio programs and messages, and recorded television programs, 1950s-1973 silent and sound films, videotapes(32 hrs, 30 mins).
The collection contains outtakes, printing elements and source material from the production of the telecast **A Man Called Intrepid**. Political leaders John F. Kennedy, Mao Tse-tung, Winston Churchill, Marshal Tito, Adolf Hitler, F.D.Roosevelt, Benito Mussolini, Leonid Brezhev and many others appear frequently. There are also sequences on major international events during the 1940s and in the years following the two world wars, 1940s-1973.
GUENETTE

Thunder in the East.
16 mm b&w positive, 375 feet.
Canada, 1950.

A presentation of the issues which precipitated the Korean conflict, a survey of Asia's struggle for nationhood and its resolve to identify and solve its problems.
Includes North Koreans cheering a Soviet Army detachment as it marches through their streets, a statue of Mahatma Gandhi is unrobed at its first showing, Sukarno is being cheered as his motorcade weaves through swarming crowds, Sukarno and Nehru greet each other at a meeting, their wives being present. A Siamese king is paraded in traditional style and is then shown being whisked away in a limousine, Mao Tse-tung reviews troops of the Chinese People's Republic Army. Jawaharlal Nehru is greeted by his daughter Indira aboard a vessel.

Tuesday Night, 8 January 1972.
Canada, 1972.

Television presentation on the events of including "ping-pong diplomacy" in China, Nixon's visit to China, and Canada's Trade Minister Jean-Luc Pepin's visit to Peking, United Nation's acceptance of China and rejection of Taiwan, Japanese emperor Hirohito's visit to Alaska, and royal tour of the West Coast.

Tuesday night - Khmer! Khmer!, Cambodia in conflict.
1/2 inch colour, VTR cassette, 60 minutes.
Canada, 17 August 1972.

Television documentary examining the current upheaval in Cambodia including extensive sequences on Cambodia's way of life, its art, music, and culture prior to its wars and political crisis, a profile on the deposed Cambodia Chief of State Prince Norodom Sihanouk, whose nationalistic outlook and policies of economic austerity led to his dismissal and subsequent replacement by Prince Sirik Matak, comments from Sihanouk and Alan Dawson, former UPI chief, speaking in Phnom Penh, voice-over commentary traces Cambodia's history from French colonization, Japanese domination during World War II, Cambodia's independence in 1953, and the current fragmentation and destruction of Cambodian society by the invasion forces of the United States, North and South Vietnam and Thailand.

U.S. Marines Crush Japs in Marianas.
16 mm, b&w positive, 30 feet.
U.S. 1944.
Deposited July 1977.

Violent action, much smoke, marines using flame throwers, Japanese surrendering, burning, falling off a cliff.

The Way it is, 15 October 1967.
Videotape.
Canada, 1967.

Includes land dispute over Saltspring Island, British Columbia, originally owned by the Japanese Canadian Teratsu Yuwosoki who lost it during the Japanese evacuation in Canada during World War II. Now, at the age of 87 years, Yuwosoki discusses the case. He is attempting to get his land back by laying charges. Report includes interviews with the Yuwosoki family and some of their former neighbours on Saltspring Island.

The Way it is, 18 February 1968.
Videotape.
Canada, 1968.

Includes report on the severe unemployment and starvation crisis in Calcutta, India. Includes riot scenes of people protesting in the streets against the newly-elected leaders of the Central Parliament, sequences on poor and crowded living conditions, people dying of starvation, shots of left-wing leaders who have undergone many prison sentences, and comments by Mihir Sen(lawyer) and S. Bannerji(Communist ex-minister) who describe the desperate situation. Also includes an interview with father Robert Drinan, Jesuit priest of Boston College Law School and co-author of a report which documents 1,100 cases of war crimes committed by Americans and their allies in Vietnam. Father Drinan accuses the American government of violating international law and expresses his concern over the impact this state of "lawlessness" will have on youth in America. Includes footage showing the torture of Viet-Cong prisoners, and the indiscriminate killing of civilians.

The Way it is, 9 March 1969.
Videotape.
Canada 1969.
Includes Bill Saywell(Professor of Chinese Studies at Toronto University) talk with Norman Endicott(Chinese-born Canadian and Professor of History at Toronto university) about Canada's impending diplomatic recognition of Red China.

Weekend, 7 March 1971.
2-inch videotapes.
Canada, 1971.

Television news program includes report on war crimes and atrocities committed by U.S. troops in the Philippine islands(1895-1901) and in the Vietnam war(1961-1975). Shown are still photographs and archival film of American soldiers, including Senator George Hoar, Senator John L.Beveridge, Brigadier General Jacob Smith, Secretary of War Elihu Root, Major General Leonard Wood, and President "Teddy" Roosevelt. Noteworthy sequences include corpses of slain Filipinos, an emaciated Filipino in an American concentration camp. Excerpt of a speech by Senator Howard Taft. Philippine regular and guerrilla armies, and sequence of the aftermath of the bombing of Dresden and Nagasaki. Comments are made by Telford Taylor, former U.S. prosecutor at Nuremberg and former American soldiers in Vietnam regarding their contact or involvement with the commission of atrocities.

Wet Earth and Warm People.
3/4 inch colour videocassette, 58 minutes.
Canada, 1971.

"Candid glimpses of Indonesia and its people, in and around the capital, Jakarta, capturing the flavor of like in this fertile crescent of tropical islands, as it focuses on the Indonesian people caught between the past and the conflicting options of the future - to change or not to change from long established patterns of life to ones more influenced by Western technology.

Historical Sound Recording Section.

Shimpo, Mitsuru.
Collection of interviews with Japanese Canadians, 1971, by Dr. M. Shimpo.
REP/1972-73.

**National Library of Canada,
395 Wellington Street,
Ottawa, Ontario, K1A 0N4.
Tel:(613)996-1318**

Shastri Institute.

Archival materials on microfilm from the Shastri Institute.

Government of India. General administrative reports, 1869-1927, reels 1-6.
Government of India. Proscribed publications, pre-1947, reels 1-63(including 32a)

B.D.Chaturvedi collection, reels 1-42(including 23a)
B.D.Chaturvedi, 1892- Journalist and author.

Jehangir Cowasjee collection, reels 1-7.
Papers of Jehangir Cowasjee, 1873-1934, Industrialist.

Jayakar papers, reels 1-243.
Private Papers of Mukund Ramarao Jayakar, 1873-

Saint Catharines.

Brock University Library,
Brock University,
500 Glenridge Street,
St. Catharines, Ontario. L2S 3A1.
Tel: (905)688-5550.

Theses and dissertations

Jawaid, Sohail.
The Naxalite movement in India, origin and failure of the Maoist revolutionary strategy in West Bengal, 1967-1971. M.A. thesis 1979.
CT

Ma, Pow How.
Manpower development and nation building, Singapore's experience. M.A. thesis 1978.
CT

Ng, Wang-chun.
The People's Republic of China and her relations with the countries of the Association of South-East Asian Nations. M.A. thesis 1977.
CT

Poong, Moi-eng.
Relations between Malaysia and the PRC, 1963-1975, evolution of adjustment to a multipolar international system M.A. thesis 1979.
CT

Quddus, Muhammed A.
The problem of National integration in plural societies, a case study of Pakistan, 1947-1971. M.A. thesis 1976.
CT

Sokolow, Alexander.
The nature of Avidya in Buddhism and Vedanta. M.A. thesis 1975.
CT

Toronto

Anglican Church of Canada,
General Synod Archives,
600 Jarvis Street,
Toronto, Ontario, M4Y 2J6.
Tel:(416)924-9192, ext. 278.

Personal manuscript collections, Church archives and photographs are indexed in a four-drawer card index.

GS75-103. Missionary Society of the Church in Canada(M.S.C.C.).

Series 1. Board of Management and Executive Committee. 1884-1968.

Boxes 1-8.

Minutes and indexes to minutes.

Series 2. Committees 1903-1968.

Box 9.

Series 2.02. Includes minutes of the Foreign Missions Committee, 1903-1904.

Box 12.

Series 2:06. Committee on Overseas Missions, Minutes, 1904-1955.

Series 3. General Secretary's materials, 1897-1976.

Series 3.1. Lewis NormanTucker, 1903-1912

Box 46.

File 1. Foreign Letter book. Letters White and missionaries in China. Indexed. 1910.

Box 48.

File 2. Bishop of Honan appointment, 1909.

Series 3.2. Sydney Gould, 1910-1938.

Box 58.

File 2. Orientals in British Columbia, 1914-1936.

Box 60.

File 1. China - Ruth E. Jenkins, 1925-1926.

File 2. China - B. K. Jones, 1914.

File 3. China - S. Kelsey, 1917.

File 4. China - Kerswell, 1914.

File 5. China - Elizabeth W. McIntosh, 1915-1927.

File 6. China - Mabel E. Naisbitt, 1924.

File 7. China - Mary G. Peters, 1925-1927.

File 8. China - Dr. E.Margaret Phillips, 1912-1915.

File 9. China - Florence Rapson, 1927.

File 10. China - Katherine H. Robbins, 1915-1925.

File 11. China - Violet Shaw, 1915-1923.

File 12. China - Canon G.E. Simmons, 1920-1935.

File 13. China - Dr. Catherine H. Travis, 1918-1928.

File 14. China - Gladys Trivett, 1920-1923.

File 15. China - A.J. Wade, 1918.

File 16. China - May Watts, 1935-1938.

File 17. China - William C. White, 1911-1935.

File 18. China - Annual Reports, 1913-1931.

File 19. China - Honan Mission Conference Minutes, 1913-1937.

File 20. China - Miscellaneous, 1908-1938.

File 21. China - Visits to China and Japan, 1923-1924.

Box 61.

File 1. India - Kangra Local Governing Board - Minutes, 1912-1922.

File 2. India- Kangra Local Governing Board - Correspondence 1905-1925.

File 3. India - Educational Sub-Committee, 1927-1933.

File 4. India - Evangelistic Sub-Committee, 1930-1933.

File 5. India - Medical Sub-Committee, 1925-1930.

File 6. India - Kangra Missionary Conference, 1918-1934.

File 7. India - Kangra staff meetings, 1916-1918.

File 8. India - Dr. G.B. Archer, 1911-1920.

File 9. India - W.A. Earp, 1913-1921.

File 10. India - F.S. Ford, 1912-1936.

Box 62.
File 1. India - Canon E. Guilford (8 files) 1916-1930.

Series 3.2. Sydney Gould, 1910-1938.
File 1. India - Florence Martyn, 1920.

File 2. India - D.M. Rose (5 files), 1916-1931.

File 3. India - C.R.H. Wilkinson (4 files), 1926-1938.

File 4. India - Map of the District of Kangra.

Box 63A.

File 1.Japan - Conference Minutes, 1911-1940.

File 2.Japan - Advisory Committee Minutes, 1915-1940.

File 3 Japan - Mid-Japan Workers (Japanese), 1915-1940.

File 4.Japan - Diocesan Synod Minutes, 1913-1918.

File 5. Japan - Proposal re: Diocese in, 1910-1921.
Box 64.

File 1. Japan - South Tokyo Quarterly Magazine, 1898-1906.

File 2. Japan - Pastoral letter - Wm. Awdry, 1905.

File 3. Japan - Bishop H.J. Hamilton, 1913-1940.

File 4. Japan - F . M. Kennedy, 1911-1914.

File 5. Japan - Hilda Robinson, 1912-1922.

Box 65.

File 1. Japan - J. Cooper Robinson, 1913-1923.

File 2. Japan - Egerton Ryerson, 1910-1912.

File 3. Japan - Paul Shinji Saski, 1935-1938.

File 4. Japan - Rev. Charles Harper Shortt, 1911-1918.

File 5. Japan - Victor Spencer, 1912-1937.

File 6. Japan - Richard K. Start, 1928-1938.

File 7. Japan - Dr. Jon.G. Waller, 1911-1937.

File 8. Japan - Horace G. Watts, 1916-1937.

File 9. Japan - Miscellaneous, 1934-1939.

File 10.Jerusalem and East, 1909-1929.

Box 66.

File 1. Armenian Work, 1928-1934.
Box 67.

File 7. Church Missionary Society - India, 1911-1936.

Box 72.

File 1. Provincial Board of Missions to Orientals in British Columbia. Japanese Evacuees - Correspondence, 1938-1943.

File 2. Japanese East of the Rockies, 1944-1957.

Box 76.

File 8. China - Honan, Correspondence, 1935-1951.

File 9. China -Honan, Budgets, 1941-1949.

File 11. China Loan, American Church Mission,

Shanghai to Canadian Church Mission, 1942-1943. Box 77.

File 1. China - Andrew, Ven. G. Andrew, 1916-1954.

File 2. China - Brown, Dr. Richard, 1918-1944.

File 3. China - Cheng, Rev. C.Y., 1948-1949.

File 4. China - Clark, Miss Greta, 1939-1948.

File 5. China - Coates, Mae, 1947.

Box 78.

File 1. China - Gibberd, Grace, 1919-1946.

File 2. China -Gilbert, H.H., 1938-1952.

File 3. China - Howard, Miss Frances D - Missionary Society of the Church in Canada, 1947-1948.

File 4. China - Howard, Miss Frances D. - Other missionaries , 1947-1948.

File 5. China - Howard, Miss Frances D. - WA, 1947-1948.

File 6. China - Kelsey, Miss S.D.S. 1919-1948.

File 7. China - Lewis, Rundall, 1946-1949.

File 8. China - Peters, Miss Mary G., 1945-1946.

File 9. China - Scovil, Rev. G. Coster, 1942-1948.

File 10. China - Scovil, Mrs. Mary, 1941-1946.

Box 79.

File 1. China - Simmons, Mrs. G.E., 1932-1946.

File 2. China - Simpson, Rev. William, 1940-1949.

File 3. China - Simpson, Mrs. Mary (Searle), 1934-1946.

File 4. China -Tamblyn, William Gordon, 1945-1947.

File 5. China -Tsen, Lindel, 1930-1945.

Box 80.

File 1. China -Tsen, Lindel, 1946-1951.

File 2. China -Tseng, Rev. Francis, 1939-1951.

File 3. China -Wang, Rev. Stephen. 1941-1954.

File 4. China -Watts, Miss May, 1938-1946.

File 5. China -White, William C., 1934-1954.

File 6. China-Williston, Constance, 1947.

Box 81.

File 1. China-News from China, 1938-1954.

File 2. China- Lessons to be learned from Experience of Christian Missionaries in China, 1951-1952.

File 3. China-Conference re: Honan funds, 1947-1952.

File 4. China-Conference re: Post War Work, 1942.

File 5. China- Bishop White's report of Honan Situation, 1946.

File 6. China - College of Chinese Studies, 1946-1955.

File 7. China - Correspondence with External Affairs Department. re: Property held and missionaries , 1938-1947.

File 8. China - Bishop Y.Y. Tsu, 1943.

File 9. China - Chung Hua Sheng Kung Hui - Constitution and Canons, General Synod reports, 1918-1937.

Box 82.

File 1. China - Bishop Frank Norris, 1933.

File 2. China - Hong Kong, 1951-1958.

File 3. China - Central Theological School, Shanghai, 1947-1951.

File 4. China - Account Books, 1946-1948.(7)

Box 83.

File 1. India - Amritsar Diocese, 1950-1959.

File 2. India - Baring Christian College, 1948.

File 3. India - Barrackpore Diocese, 1956-1959.

File 4. India - C.I.P.B.C., 1952-1955.

File 5. India - Colombo Plan, Ottawa, 1951.

File 6. India - Blackaller, D.W., 1956.

File 7. India - Balderston, Olive, 1946-1954.

File 8. India - Carson, Jessie, 1939-1943.

File 9. India - Davis, Eldon, 1946-1948.

File10. India - DeBlois, Audrey E., 1933-1939.

File11. India - Dustan, Rev.T.M., 1945-1948.

File12. India - Edgar, Annie, 1939-1943.

File13. India - Elliott, Edna, 1943.

File14. India - Guiton, Geoffrey, 1939-1947.

File15. India - Hanson, Helen, 1938-1954.

File16. India - Haslam, Florence J., 1941-1954.

File17. India - Holtby, Mary, 1939-1946.

File18. India - Jackson, Constance V., 1938-1954.

File19. India - Lang, S.R., 1958-1959.

File 20. India - McRae, Rev. John, 1958-1959.

File 21. India - Miller, Jessie, 1941-1944.

File 22. India - Nattress, Marion, 1941-1947.

File 23. India - Nichols, Dr. Florence L., 1946-1950.

File 24. India - Peel, Donald H, 1952-1954.

File 25. India - Peter, Rev. F.A., 1945-1948.

Box 84.

File 1. India - Peter, Rev. F.A., 1949-1952.

File 2. India - Smith, Wilfred C., 1943-1944.

File 3. India - Wilkinson, C.R.H., 1935-1954.

File 4. India - Wylie, J.F., 1946.

File 5. India - Correspondence. re: Missionary entry into India, 1949-1956.

File 6. India - Flood Relief Appeal, 1955-1957.

File 7. India - Maple Leaf Hospital, Kangra, 1941.

File 8. India - Lady Willingdon Hospital, Manali, Kulu, 1941-1951.

File 9. India - Dr. H.G. Watts report, 1951.

File10. India - Annual Reports, 1939-1958.

File 11. India - Technical Services Association, Pakistan, Annual Reports, 1956-1958.

File 12. Japan - Archer, Miss A.L., 1937-1941.

Box 85.

File 1. Japan - Bailey, Miss Helen, 1937-1940.

File 2. Japan - Bowman, Miss N.F., 1936-1940.

File 3. Japan - Clench, Miss M., 1937-1941.

File 5. Japan - Elliott, Miss Edna, 1937-1940.

File 6. Japan - Fletcher, Shirley, 1954.

File 7. Japan - Foerstel, Miss Marie, 1937-1959.

File 8. Japan - Harrison, Mary, 1955.

File 9. Japan - Hamilton, F., 1936-1941.

File 10. Japan - Hawkins, Miss F., 1937-1959.

File 11. Japan - Heaslett, S., 1936-1940.

File 12. Japan - Horobin, Miss H., 1937-1957.

File 13. Japan - Isaac, Irene, 1936-1940.

File 14. Japan - "K", 1938-1940.

File 15. Japan - Lane, Miss E.A., 1938-1941.

File 16. Japan - McAlpine, Rev. J.A., 1939-1940.

File 17. Japan - McSherry, H.J., 1948-1953.

File 18. Japan - Miller, Miss Jessie, 1937-1950.

File 19. Japan - Miller, Miss Jessie, 1969-1970.

File 20. Japan - Moss, Adelaide F., 1937-1940.

File 21. Japan - Powell, Miss L., 1938-1959.

File 22. Japan - Powles, Cyril, 1949-1953.

File 23. Japan - McDonald, John, 1955-1959.

Box 86.

File 1. Japan - Powles, P.S.C., 1937-1959.

File 2. Japan - Reid, Mrs. F.B., 1935-1940.

File 3. Japan - Robinson, Miss Hilda, 1937-1954.

File 4. Japan - Sasaki, Bishop, 1939-1940.

File 5. Japan - Savary, Reg, 1937-1954.

Box 87.

File 6. Japan - Shadan, 1936-1940.

File 7. Japan - Shaw, Miss L.L., 1937-1941.

File 8. Japan - Sheppard, Alison, 1954.

File 9. Japan - Shore, Miss G., 1937-1941.

File 10. Japan - Smith, Norman, 1948-1955.

File 11. Japan - Spencer, Victor, 1934-1939.

Box 88.

File 1. Japan - Spencer, Victor, 1940-1942.

File 2. Japan - Start, Dr. R.K., 1936-1957.

File 3. Japan - Waller, Rev. J.G., 1935-1947.

File 4. Japan - Watts, Rev. H.G., 1937-1941.

File 5. Japan - Wilkinson, Miss Rhoda, 1937-1941.

File 6. Japan - Young, Miss N.M., 1939-1940.

Box 89.

File 1. Japan - Annual reports, 1952-1958.

File 2 Japan - Minutes of Japan Mission, 1932-1940.

File 3 Japan - Correspondence in Japanese, 1940-1941.

File 4 Japan - Financial Statements, 1939-1941.

File 5 Japan - A.A.A. Funds, 1945-1948.

File 6. Japan - Fire Insurance, 1937-1940.

File 7. Japan - Japan International Christian University, 1949-1955.

File 8. Japan - "Planes of Living", 1949-1950.

File 9. Japan - Committee on East Asia - New York Bulletins re:Japan, 1940.

File 10. Japan - Committee on East Asia - re Japan, 1942-1945.

File 11 Japan - Nippon Sei Ko Kai - Bishop Michael Yashiro, 1946-1959.

File 12 Japan - Nippon Sei Ko Kai- Magazines, etc., 1893-1940.

File 13 Japan - Miscellaneous papers, 1938-1963.

File 14 Japan - Prayer Book Revision, 1953-1958.

File 15. Japan - Canadian Academy, 1952-1955.

Box 90.

File 1. Other Overseas - Jerusalem and East, 1941-1944.

File 4. Other Overseas - Singapore, 1957-1958.

File 3. Special - Interchurch Committee on Japanese in Canada, 1943.

Box 91.

File 4. Special - South India Proposed Union Booklets, 1943-1952.

Box 93.

File 3. W.H.Gale - Provincial Board of Missions to Orientals in British Columbia, 1946-1952.

File 4. Ken Imai - Japanese East of the Rockies, 1952-1959.

File 5. Grace Tucker - Japanese Canadian Work., 1947-1948

File 6. H.G.Watts - trip to Japan report, 1946.

Series 3-4. Alfred Henry Davis, 1959-1976

File 10. Work among Japanese - Toronto, 1960-1961.

File 11. Provincial Board of Missions to Orientals in British Columbia, 1960 -1961.

Box 97.

File 9. India- Bishop Anand, 1960-1966.

File 10. India - Barrackpore - Bishop Bryan, 1959-1961.

File 11. India - Kashmir, 1959.

File 12. India - Dr. S.R. Lang, 1960-1961.

File 13. India - Dr. Florence Farmer, 1961.

File 14. India - Dr. James Wilkes, 1958-1960.

File 15. India - Mrs. B.S. Chandar, 1960.

File 16. India - Baring Union College, 1960-1961.

File 17. India - Miss Margaret Burns, 1960.

File 18. India - Dr. F.A. Philbrook, 1962.

File 19. India - Rainawari Hospital, Kashmir, 1959-1960.

File 20.India - Women's Christian College, Chandigarh, 1961.

File 21. India - Ajnala Christian Rural Training Centre, 1960.

File 22. India - Newsletters, 1956-1968.

Box 98.

File 1. Japan - General, 1960-1965.

File 2. Japan - Bishop Ueda - Hokkaido, 1960-1961.

File 3. Japan - Bishop Kurose, 1959-1960.

File 4. Japan - Miss H. Horobin, 1956-1960.

File 5. Japan - Miss F. Hawkins, 1958-1961.

File 6. Japan - Rev. J. MacDonald, 1960-1962.

File 7. Japan - Rev. R.N. Savary, 1952-1960.

File 8. Japan - Marie Foerstel, 1962.

File 9. Japan - Kobe Diocese, 1960-1961.

File 10. Japan - Osaka Diocese, 1960.

File 11. Japan - Nagano Clinic, 1959-1960.

File 12. Japan - Nikkapu Grant, 1961.

File 13. Japan - Miss Cecelia Benns, 1961.

File 14. Japan - Newsletters, 1963-1965.

File 15. Japan - Hong Kong and Bishop Hall, 1961.

File 16. East Asia - Chung Chi College, 1961.

File 17. East Asia - Bishop White Memorial Scholarship Fund (Hong Kong), 1960-1961.

File 18. Pakistan - General, 1960.

File 19. Pakistan - Rev. F. Peter, 1956-1961.

File 20. Pakistan - Mr. Moti Lal Malakar, 1961.

File 22. Other Overseas - Korea, 1956-1962.

File 24. Other Overseas - Ceylon, 1956.

Series 4. Field Secretary's Files, 1941-1959.

Series 4.1. Horace Godfrey Watts, 1941-1952.

Box 99.

File 1. China, 1948-1952.

File 2. Japan, 1940-1954.

Box 100.

File 1. India Trip, 1950-1952.

File 2. Simla, 1952.

Series 4.2. Alfred Henry Davis, 1952-1959.

File 3. Deputations, Bishop Daly, Korea, 1955.

File 9. Annual Summaries of Misssionary Society of the Church in Canada. Activities, 1956-1959.

File 10. Japan, 1956-1959.

File 11. Indian Act Study, 1959.

File 12. India, General, 1955-1959.

File 13. Parkash Samuels, 1956 -1959.

Box 101.

File 1. China, 1956-1958

File 4. Pakistan, 1959.

Series 5. Financial Records, 1877-1963.

File 10. Kangra Mission - Cash Summary sheet, 1913.

Box 103.

File 6. Honan missions, 1909-1912.

Box 108.

File 11. Honan, China Property, 1911-1948.

File 12. Kangra Property, 1911-1934.

File 13. Japan Mission.

File 21. Japanese Mission Property, Vancouver.

Series 6. Overseas Personnel, 1907-1940.

Box 116.

File 1. Foreign missionaries of the Mission Society of the Church of England in Canada. 1907.

File 2. Index of Mission Society of the Church of England in Canada, as at 1st January, 1936 and later, 1936-1940.

File 3. China, 1936-1940.

File 4. India, 1936-1940.

File 5. Japan, 1936-1941.

Series 7. Publications Department, 1943-1957.

Box 117.

File 9. F. MacNaghten - Missionary in India, 1943-1947.

Series 8. Publications-Official Records, 1901-1957.

Series 8.4. Printed Committee Reports, 1908-1934.

Box 124.

File 14. Report of the Commision re: Mid-Japan and

Honan, 1934.

Series 9. Publications - 1904-1975.

Series 9.05. Leaflets, 1904-1935.

Box 130.

File 3. The Kangra Mission, by George B.Archer, 1914.

Kangra Medical Work, by Miss I. Abdulla.

Coversations on India, China and Japan, by ARGUS(after 1913).

Our Mission Station in Japan, by Miss Loretta L.Show(after1925).

Series 9.06. Popular Information Series, 1917-1948.

Includes materials on China, India and Japan and on Orientals in Canada.

Series 9.07. Missionary Information, 1940-1963.

Box 131.

Missionary Intelligence Series and Missionary Capsule Series.

Series 9.09. Mission Study books, 1921-1965.

Boxes 132-134.

Include materials on China, India and Japan.

Series 9:14.Publications by subject, [1903?]-1963.

Box 137.

Includes materials on China, India and Japan and on Canadian Japanese.

Series 10. Photograph and Audio Visual Collections.

Series 10.4. Lantern Slides and Lectures.

Box 138-139.

File 3. The Island Empire of the East.

File 4. Canadian Diocese of Honan, China.

File 5. India, No.l, by R.H.A. Haslam.

File10. Japan, No.4, R.M. Millman, 1917.

File11. Honan Lecture, III.

File12. Life of a Missionary in India, No.3.

File 16. The Women of Japan.

File 17. Japan, No.1.

File 18. China, Honan.

File 19. India, No.4 - Medical & India.

File 26. Lecture on Japan, by R.M. Millman.

File 27. India, Lecture 6A, by R.H.A. Haslam.

File 28. India, Lecture 6B, by R.H.A. Haslam.

File 31. Diocese of Mid-Japan, Nagoya and Out-Stations.

Box 140.

File 11. Diocese of Mid-Japan [5000, 4000, 4001].

File 12. Section Set on Japan III.

File 13. Japan Lantern Slides, Hamilton.

File 14. Japan, Tokyo to Nagasaki - J.C. Robinson.

File 20. China.

File 21. A Visit to Kangra.

File 22. India, Missionary Society of the Church in Canada #2.

File 23. India - Lecture A.

File 24. [India] - Lantern Address II.

File 25. [India] - Lecture III - C.

File 26. India #4 - Medical and India [2019].

File 27. India #5 - Five Minute Talks #1.

File 28. India #5 - Five Minute Talks #2.

File 29. India #5 - Five Minute Talks #3.

File 30. India #5 - Five Minute Talks #4.

File 31. India.

GS75-106. Council for Social Service.

Box 9.

File 1. Gambling, 1945-1992.

File 6. Immigration - Anglican Ministrations to Non Anglo-Saxons. 1956-1959.

File 7. Immigration - Canadian Port Chaplains, 1956-1970.

File 8. Immigration - Chinese, 1965-1968.

File10. Immigration - Hong Kong Teenagers, 1961-1968.

File 11. Immigration - Hong Kong Teenagers - Ancaster -John Heather - Fung Kam Lung, 1966-1970.

Box 10.

File 1. Immigration - Hong Kong Teenagers - Baie D'Urfe(Beaurepaire) - Christ Church - A.D. Thornton- Tam Po Yin (girl), 1965-1972.

File 2. Immigration - Hong Kong Teenagers - Ottawa - Desmond Bowen - St. John's - Lai Che Sun(brother) and Lai Kam Sheung (sister), 1968-1975.

File 3. Immigration - Hong Kong - Canadian Government.-Correspondence, 1965-1972.

File 4. Immigration - Hong Kong - Ontario Government-Correspondence, 1966-1970.

File 5. Immigration - Hong Kong - Quebec Government-Correspondence, 1967-1969.

File 6. Immigration - Hong Kong - International Social Service - Ottawa - Correspondence, 1966-1970.

File 7. Immigration - Hong Kong - International Social Service and Social Welfare Department, Hong Kong - Correspondence, 1965-1968.

File 8. Immigration - Have arrived in Canada - A - L, 1966-1972.

File 9. Immigration - Have arrived in Canada - M - Z.

File 10. Immigration - Ministries to Newcomers, 1966-1972.

GS76-9. National and World Project.

Box 7.

India, 1966-1972.

National Christian Council of India, 1971-1972.

Church of North India, 1971-1972.

- other dioceses, 1971.

Church of South India, 1971-1972.

Christian Institutions, 1972.

Christian Medical College and Hospital - Ludhiana/Vellore, 1971-1972.

Baring Union Christian College, 1970-1972.

Amritsar, 1971-1972.

- Bishop Anand, 1962-1964.

- Mrs. Chandar, 1971-1980.

Barrackpore, 1971-1972.

Sunderbans Project, 1970-1973.

Dacca, 1972.

Pakistan, 1970-1971.

Nippon Sei Ko Kai, 1966-1972.

- Hokkaido, 1971-1972.

- Kyoto 1971.

- Mid-Japan, 1971-1972.

- Okinawa, 1971-1972.

- Osaka, 1971.

- Tokyo, 1970-1972.

Box 8.

South Pacific Council, 1971-1972.

- Melanesia, 1970-1972.

- Papua New Guinea, 1971-1972.

- Polynesia, 1972.

South East Asia Council, 1971-1972.

Diocese of Hong Kong, 1968-1972.

Kei Oi Welfare Centre, 1971-1972.

St. Christopher's Home, 1971.

Kuching Diocesan Office, 1971-1972.

Sabah Diocesan Office, 1970-1972.

Singapore and Malaya,1971-1972.

Seoul, 1971-1972.

West Malaysia, 1972.

Taejon, 1971.

Philippine Independent Church, 1971-1972.

Burma, 1971-1972.

Inter-Church Committee on World Development Education, 1972-1975.

Mission Interpretation Reports, 1973-1975.

Phyllis L. Cowan - Newsletters, 1957-1969.

Missionaries -Baldwin, William, 1957-1980.

Box 9.

Bolton, Venerable K.C., 1971-1975.

Coffin, Peter R., 1973-1978.

Coleman, Kenneth Armstrong, 1953-1972.

Crabb, Alison, 1974-1984.

Draper, Rev. James, 1973-1974.

Fife, Prof. J.R., 1973-1980.

Fisher. Penelope, 1970-1971.

House, Rev. E.E., 1969-1975.

Major, Rev. Carl, 1966-1977.

Powles, Rev. C.H., 1968-1971.

Box 10.

Task Force on Overseas Work, 1969-1977.
Theological Education Fund, 1972-1974.

United Church/Anglican Church meetings, 1972-1974.

United Church/Anglican Church/Christian Church, Senior Staff Consultation, 1973.

GS 76-15. Women's Auxilary Founded to Promote Missionary Effort.

Box 20.

10.2 Overseas.

India, 1935-1958.

Church of England Zenana Society, 1898-1906.

Japan, 1891-1901.

Box 21.

13.11 Pakistan Embroidery Committee. Correspondence and reports, 1966-1973.

GS80-5. Primate's World Relief and Development Fuid.

Box 1.

File 2. 71.HKG.001 Kowloon Workers' Mutual Benevolent Corporation, 1968-1979.

File 3. 74.HKG.003F Fisherman Village, 1974-1976.

File 4. 74.IND.009F Calcutta Cathedral Relief Services, 1974-1977.

File 5. 75.IND.014 Bombay - BUILD, 1975.

File 6. 76.IND.017 Calcutta Development Education, 1976-1977.

File 7. 76.IND.018 St. Thomas Vocational School, 1976-1978.
File 8. 76.INC.001F Assistance to Refugees, 1975-1978.

File 9. 76.INN.003F Second Leadership Training, 1976-1978.

File 10. 74.KOR.002 Agape Coffee House, 1972-1977.

File 11. 76.KOR.005F Communications and Publication Project, 1977.

File 12. 76.KOR.007F Community Organization - Siheung, Seoul, 1977-1978.

File 13. 75.KOR.008F Chunju Urban Industrial Mission, 1977-1979.

File 14. 75.NEP.001 Pokahara Boys' Boarding School, 1975-1976.
File 15. 73.PHI.003 Rehabilitation Program-Southern Diocese, 1973-1978.

File 16. 75.PHI.006 Process Education Development and Research, 1975-1976.

File 17. 76.SRL.004F Kandy Industrial Institute, 1976.

File 18. 77.SRL.007 Electricity for Navajeefanam - 77.6, 1977-1979.

File 19. 77.TUR.001 Development Foundation of Turkey, 1976-1977.

File 20. 77.VTN.003 "New Economic Area"-Food Production.

File 21. 77.VTN.004F Vietnam Water Supply, 1977.
Box 2.

File 24. 77.30 St. Barnabas Hospital, Papua, New Guinea, - 74.4, 1976-1978.

File 25. 77.PAR.003 Scholarships - Bossey, 1977.

File 26. 76.PNG.009 Rural Development Service, 1977-

1978.

File 27. 76.PNG.010 Wantok, 1975-1977.

File 28. 77.GLO.019 G.A.T.T.-Fly: International Sugar Workers Conference, 1974-1977.

File 29. 71.GLO.003F WCC - Program to Combat Racism, Correspondence, 1971-1976.

File 30. 77.GLO.021 International Seminar on Training for Non-violent Action, 1977.

File 31. 76.PAC.002F Pacifique '77, 1976-1977.

GS80-8. National World Program.

Amritsar Diocese, Church of North India, 1976-1977.

Amritsar Diocese, Financial, 1973-1977.
Barrackpore Diocese, 1976-1977.

Church of North India, 1975-1977.

Council of the Church of East Asia, 1975-1977.

Hong Kong, Kei Oi Welfare Centre, 1975-1977.

Japan, 1976-1977.

Mid-Japan Diocese, Nagoya Student Centre, 1976-1977.

Seoul Diocese - Korea, 1976-1977.

United Society for the Propagation of the Gospel, 1976-1977.
West Malaysia Diocese, 1973-1977.

Retired Missionaries.

GS81-19. World Mission.

Box 5. 1973-1978.

Asia and the South Pacific Area secretary, 1974.

Council of the Church of East Asia past correspondence, 1978.

Philippines project, 1973-1975.

Philippines - Saint Andrews, 1973-1974.

Philippines - political - past correspondence, 1978.

Joint Council (P.I.C.-P.E.C.) 1973-1974.

South East Asia, 1975.

South East Asia Council, 1974.

Philippines trip - T.M.S., 1970-1971.

Sabah diocese - 1974.

West Malaysia diocese - 1973-1974.

Kuching diocese, 1973 -1975.

China - general, 1974.

Korea - Seoul diocese - 1973.
Korea - Seoul diocese - past correspondence, 1976.

Korea - political - past correspondence, 1978.

Hong Kong diocese - past correspondence, 1978.

Hong Kong diocese, 1973-1975.

Kei Oi welfare centre, Hong Kong, 1973.

Singapore diocese, 1973.

Dr. Peter Leung, 1975-1976.

Thailand- human rights, political, etc., 1978.

Burma, 1973-1974.

Box 6. 1973-1978.

Nagoya Y.M.C.A. - N.S.K.K. 1973-1975.

N.S.K.K.(Nippon Sei Ko Kai) - college work, 1973-1974.

N.S.K.K.(Nippon Sei Ko Kai) - External Relations Committee, 1973-1974.
N.S.K.K.(Nippon Sei Ko Kai) - financial, 1976-1978.

N.S.K.K.(Nippon Sei Ko Kai) -Internal Relations Committee, 1975.

N.S.K.K.(Nippon Sei Ko Kai)- P.I.M. 1975.

Japan - general, 1974.

Mid-Japan diocese - Nagoya Student Centre, 1973-1975.

Sri Lanka - Rt. Rev. Wikremesinghe, 1975-1976.

Bangla Desh, 1976-1977.

Sri Lanka - correspondence, 1976-1978.

Polynesia diocese, 1973-1974.

Church of North India, 1973-1976.

Church of North India Related Missions Committee, 1978.

Sunderbans project - India C.I.D.A. 338-90/a6-11, 1970-1982.

Diocese of Amritsar, 1973-1977.

Amritsar Diocese - financial, 1978.

Barrackpore Diocese - financial, 1977-1978.

Calcutta Diocese - Rt. Rev. R.W.Bryan, 1974-1978. Baring Union Christian College, 1973-1976.

Church of South India - correspondence, 1978.

Church of South India - correspondence - Mrs. G. Ratnam, 1977.

Church of South India, 1973.

Church of Pakistan, 1975.

Karen Moore, 1976-1977.

Christian Conference of Asia, 1975-1978.

Episcopal Church of the U.S.A.(E.C.U.S.A.) - Asiaamerica Ministry, 1974-1975.

New Guinea Diocese, 1973-1974.

Melanesia Diocese, 1973-1974.

South Pacific, 1974.

Box 10. 1975-1978.

Canada-China program, 1977-1978.

Canada-China program, financial, 1975-1978.

GS82-9. Pakistan M.R.I. Mutual responsibility and interdependence).

Pakistan Embroideries Project founded 1947. Correspondence and reports, 1955-1965, 1967-1983.

GS84-4. World missions .

North India, 1980-1981.

Correspondence, 1979-1981.

Diocese - Amritsar, 1979-1981.

- Barrackpore, 1980-1982.

- Vellore/Ludhiana committee, 1974-1981.Financial, 1981.

Bishop Memorial Hospital plans, 1982.

R.M.C. - C.N.I.- correspondence, 1981.

R.M.C.- financial, 1980-1981.

Synod meetings - minutes - 1981.

Synod materials, 1980-1981.

Wilkinson appeal, 1980-1982.

GS85-11. World Mission.

Box 4.

Canada-Asia working group, 1977-1979.

Canada-China program, 1978-1979.

N.C.C. - East Asia office, 1977.

Division of Overseas Ministry, 1978-1979.

Committee for East Asia/Pacific, 1977-1979.

Southern Asia committee, 1979.

South Pacific joint action group, 1977-1979.

Pacific Theological College, 1975-1979.

South Pacific Anglican Council, 1977-1979.

Pacific Conference of Churches, 1976-1989.

Diocese of Polynesia - financial, correspondence, 1975-1979.

Diocese of Papua New Guinea, 1977-1979; Church of Melanesia, 1977-1978.

Box 5.

Philippines - correspondence, 1980.

Indochina - refugees, 1979.

Christian Conference of Asia, 1979.

Council of the Church of East Asia, 1974-1979.

Diocese of West Malaysia, 1978-1979.

Korea, 1979-1980.

St. Christopher's Home, 1977-1978.

Kei Oi Welfare Centre(Hong Kong), 1978-1979.

Church of North India - financial, 1979-1980.

Church of North India - Related Mission Committee, 1979-1980.

N.S.K.K.(Nippon Sei Ko Kai) - External Relations Committee, 1976.

N.S.K.K.(Nippon Sei Ko Kai) - P.I.M., 1980.

South Pacific Anglican Council, 1975-1979.

Asia - Forum on Human Rights, 1979-1980.

GS86-5. World Mission.

Box 1.

Asia - general -other reflections and reports, 1980-1982.

Asia - political - regional, 1982.

Trudeau's South East Asia trip, 1983, 1982-1983.

Visiting clergy from overseas, 1981, 1981.

World Student Christian Federation(W.C.S.F.), 1982.

Asian Christian Art Association, 1982.
Canada - China program - minutes, 1978-1982.

- conference Montréal, 1981, 1981-1982.

Canada Foundation for Asia and the Pacific, 1981-1982.

China delegation, 1981.

Box 2.

Church of North India - Bhandare visit, 1981-1983.

- Santram's visit, 1981.

Council of the Church of East Asia - correspondence financial, 1979-1981.

P.I.M. consultation, Philippines, 1983, 1982-1983.
Japan/Papua New Guinea exchange, 1982.

Japan - Nippon Sei Ko Kai correspondence, 1978-1979.

GS87-15. World Mission.

Box 1.

Christian Conference of Asia, 1981-1983.

Council of the Church of East Asia, 1980-1981.

Box 2.

Hong Kong , 1983-1984.

Japan - general, 1984.

Korea - Bad Boll meeting, 1982.

Korea - financial, 1980-1982.

North Korea, 1980-1984.

Korea - regional P.I. M., 1979.

South Korea, 1980-1983.

GS89-6. World Mission:Asia/South Pacific.

Box 1

File 1. Anglican Mission Event, 1980.

File 2. ACC - Mission Issues and Strategies, 1982-1983.

File 3. Appeal/apportionment, 1981-1988.

File 4. Church Missionary Society - correspondence, 1977-1982.

File 5. Rhea Whitehead, 1983.

File 6. China - General, 1979-1984.

File 7. China - Rev. Li Tim Oi, 1981-1984.

File 8. China - World Council of Churches, 1985-1986.

File 9. Japan - Kyoto and Mid-Japan Diocese, 1976-1981.

File l0. Japan - NSKK, 1980-1985.

File 11. Japan - Overseas Missionaries in Canada - John Kominami, 1979-1982.

File 12. Christian Broadcasting System, 1981-1982.

File 13. Chun Doo Hwan - Visit to Ottawa, 1982

File 14. External Affairs Correspondence, 1982.

File 15. Koreans in Canada, 1979.

File 16. North American Coalition for Human Rights in Korea, 1981-1984.

File 17. National Council of Churches in Korea, 1980-1984.

File 18. Oo-Chung Lee, 1980.

File 19. Mark Suk - Mark Jung, 1976-1982.

File 20. Political Arrests/Detentions, 1977-1984.

File 22. Diocese of West Malaysia - Correspondence, 1981-1984.

File 23. Malaysia - Diocese of Sabah, 1975-1980.

File 24. Gordon Finney, 1981-1988.

File 25. South Pacific Anglican Council - PIM, 1983.

File 26. Pacific Theological College, 1984-1986.

Box 2.

File 1. Philippines - Jerry Aquino, 1980-1981.

File 2. Philippines - Abdias dela Cruz, 1982-1984.

File 3. Philippines - Bishop P. Dela Cruz, 1979-1984.

File 4. Philippines - Ecumenical Staff Conference, 1982-1983.

File 5. Philippines - Human Rights, 1984.

File 6. Filipinos in Canada/Immigration requests, 1978.

File 7. National Commissions on Social Justice and Human Rights, 1984-1985.

File 8. Philippines - National Priests Organization,

1982-1984.

File 9. Philippines - NORLUCEDEC, 1985.

File 10. Philippines - Projects, 1976-1977.

File 11. Philippines - Visayas - Mindanao (P.I.C.-P.E.C.), 1981-1984

File 12. P.I.C. - Campus Ministry, 1985.

File 13. Philippines - P.I.C. - General, 1980-1985.

File 14. Canada China Program, 1979-1984.

File 15. N.C.C.-USA - East Asia & Pacific Joint Action Group, 1985.

File 16. N.C.C.-USA - Commissions on Education for Mission, 1979.

File 17. N.C.C.C (USA) - North American Ecumenical Conference on the Unification of Korea, 1985.

File 18. N.C.C.C DOM, 1981-1983.

File 19. NNCUSA Philippine Joint Action Group, 1983-1985.

File 20. N.C.C.-USA - United Church Board for World Ministries, 1979-1983.

File 21. WCC - correspondence, 1980-1981.

File 22. WCC - Commissions on World Mission and Evangelism,1980-1985.

File 23. WCC - Program to Combat Racism,1978-1980.

GS90-23. Primate's World Relief and Development Fund.

Box 1.

File 1. 87.IND.056 India Socio-Legal Education-Extension Training Program, 1986-1987.

File 2. 82.JAP.002F Center for Christian Response to Asian Issues,1982-1987.

File 3. 85.KOR.022F St. Michael's Young Women's Hostel, Masan, Korea,1985-1986.

File 4. 85.KOR.024 Labour Management Counselling Centre Seoul, Korea, 1985-1988.

File 5. 83.PHI.154B PHIL-ICFID Project - MPDC Program, Budget, 1985-1988.

Box 2.

File 1. 84.PHI.028F Philippine Episcopal Church Human Rights Program, 1984-1988.

File 2. 86.PHI.038F Kaigorotan Assistance, 1985-1987.

File 3. 87.PHI.047.6 CREATE - Visayas Blacksmith Shops - Samar, Bohol, Cebu, 1987-1990.

File 4. 87.PHI.048.6 Santa Maria Community Waterworks Project, 1987-1990.

File 5. 87.PHI.054 Coconut Livelihood, 1987-1990.

Box 3.

File 1. 87.PHI.055 Grassroots, 1987-1990.

File 2. 87.PNG.020 Nambaiyufa Water Project, 1987-1989.

File 3. 83.SOI.006F Water Supply Project, Marapona Village, Malaita Province, 1983-1989.

File 4. WES.001F Agricultural Equipment Project, 1975-1990.

File 5. 82.ELS.007F Psychological Orientation & Social Promotion (CREDHO), 1981-1985.

File 6. 83.ELS.009F Family Settlement & Collective Poultry Farm (CREDHO), 1982-1986.

File 7. 85.ELS.012 CREDHO - Sewing and Dressmaking Project, 1985-1988.

File 8. 85.ELS.014 CREDHO - La Virtud Cooperative, 1985.

File 9. 87.ELS.017 Coop for Graduates of CREDHO Sewing Program, 1987.

GS90-31. World Mission: Asia/Pacific.

Box 1.

File1. Burma Council of Churches - Program, 1984.

File 2. Burmese Anglican Students at Trinity College, Singapore, 1985.

File 3. The Burma Council of Churches Integrated Budget, 1986.

File 4. Burma - Portable Generator, Diocese of Sitwe, 1986.

File 5. Burmese Office Typewriter, Diocese of Mandalay, 1987.

File 6. Burma Council of Churches Integrated Budget, 1987.

File 7. Office furniture, Missionary Diocese of Myitkyina, 1988.

File 8. Burmese Hymnal with Music, 1988.

File 9. BCC Integrated Budget, 1988.

File 10. China & Philippines - Leadership Development, 1984.

File 11. World Anglican Chinese Clergy Conference, 1984.

File 12. China Leadership Development - Scholarships, 1985.

File 13. China Leadership Development - Scholarships, 1986.

File 14. Amity Foundation - English Teachers, 1986-1987.

File 15. Publications Nanjing Theological Seminary, 1988-1989.

File 16. K.H. Ting/G.S. May visit for Emmanuel College, Toronto, Honorary Doctorate, 1989.

File 17. Christian Conference of Asia Programme Support, 1985-1986.

File 18. CAWG FIM - Intern, 1985-1986.

File 19. Christian Conference of Asia Programme Support, 1987.

File 20. Christian Conference of Asia Programme Support, 1988.

File 21. Asia Youth Assembly & Related Travel, 1984.

File 22. Sri Lanka - Christian Experimental Liturgy Organization, 1984-1985.

File 23. Peter and Ann McCalman Sabbatical CIRS Consultation, 1984.

File 24. CIRS Consultation, 1984.

File 25. Sri Lanka - N.C.C.C Commissions for Justice and Peace, 1984.

File 26 CSI Priorities, 1984.

File 27. CNI Priorities, 1984.

File 28. CNI film, 1984-1985.

File 29. Sri Lanka - Film in SCM and Church Related Work, 1984.

File 30. CNI-Bishop's College Building Appeal, Calcutta, 1985.

File 31. CSI Priorities, 1985.

File 32. CNI - Diocese of Amritsar ~Jeep Fund" Appeal, 1985.

File 33. CNI-Serampore College Solidarity Fund, 1986.

File 34. Asian Workshop on Music and Liturgy, 1986.

File 35. CNI - Construction of Bishop's Residence and Diocesan Office Complex, 1985.

File 36. CSI Priorities, 1987.

File 37. CNI Vocational Training and Rehabilitation Centre, 1987.

File 38. CNI Serampore College Solidarity Fund, 1987.

File 39. CNI - Purchase of Amritsar Diocesan Centre, 1987.

File 40. Sri Lanka - Diocese of Kurunagala Continuing Education, 1987.

File 41. CSI Priorities, 1988.

File 42. Sri Lanka - Repair of Church Buildings, Vicarages, etc. Diocese of Colombo, 1989.

File 43. Japan - Peace and Justice in N.E. Asia, 1984.

File 44. Japan - M.Powles Study of Women in Japanese Church, 1985.

File 45. Japan Centre for Christian Response to Asian Issue CCRAI, 1987-1989.

File 46. Korea - St. Michael's Theological College Class Room, 1984.

File 47. CCA Assembly June, 1985.

File 48. N.C.C. - Integrated Budget, 1984.

File 49. Korea Christian Broadcasting System, 1984.

File 50. John Lee doctoral studies in Toronto, 1984-1985.

File 51. West Daegu Evergreen School, Educational Material, 1985-1986.

File 52. N.C.C. - Integrated Budget, 1985.

File 53. Korea - St. Michael's Seminary Building, 1985-1989.

File 54. Korea - Christian Broadcasting System, 1984-1985.

File 55. Korea - St. Peter's Education Center Training Material, 1976-1985.

File 56. Korea Church Women United, 1985-1987.

File 57. The Rev. John Lee - Graduate study, 1986.

File 58. Bishop of Pusan's Travel to Anglican Centre Seminar, Rome, 1985-1986.

File 59. Korea - Integrated Budget, 1986.

File 60. Korea - Anglican Priests' Corps for the Realization of Justice (APCRJ), 1986-1988.

Box 2. .

File 1. Korea - Integrated Budget, 1987.

File 2. Mask Dance Missionary Committee (Korea 8311), 1987.

File 3. Anglican Church in Korea Human Rights Program, 1987.

File 4. Emergency Appeal for Bishop of Taejon Housing, 1987.

File 5. Sang-ju - Renovation of St. Nicholas' Church, Korea , 1987-1988.

File 6. Integrated Budget, 1988.

File 7.International Consultation on Peace and Justice in Korea, 1988.

File 8. Mask Dance Missionary Committee (Korea 8311) 1988.

File 9. Equipment for Pyongyang Church, 1988-1989.

File 10. Malaysia - Community Education Programmes Expansion: Kindergarten/Hostel, 1986.

File 11. Malaysia - Support for Doctoral Thesis Publication, 1986-1988.

File 12. Malaysia- Exchange Program for Youths, 1984-1986.

File 13. Seminari Malaysia Grant, 1986-1987.

File 14. Clergy Refresher Course - Diocese of West Malaysia, 1987-1988.

File 15. Sabah Language Studies, 1987-1988.

File 16. Pacific Theological College, 1984.

File 17. Fiji - Extension to St. John's Training Centre, 1984-1987.

File 18. Kilikali Youth Centre, 1984-1987.

File 19. Pacific Conference of Churches, 1984-1985.

File 20. Bishop Patteson Theological Centre, 1985.

File 21. New Caledonia - Kanak Scholarships, 1986.

File 22. Pacific Theological College, 1985.

File 23. Pijin Project Coordinator, 1985.

File 24. Bishop Patteson Theological Centre Repairs, 1985-1986.

File 25. Burma Youth Group Furniture Project, 1986-1987.

File 26. Pacific Theological College - Women's Studies, 1986-1987.

File 27. Kindergarten House - BPTC, 1986.

File 28. PNG - St. Francis Library, 1985-1987.

File 29. SPAC - Theological college survey, 1987.

File 30. Pacific Conference of Churches Budget, 1987.

File 31. Martyrs' Memorial School Renovations PNG, 1986-1987.

File 32. Publication of Melanesian Institute Catalyst, 1987.

File 33. Pacific Theological College, 1987.

File 34. Solomon Islands Christian Association Centre, 1987-1988.

File 35. P.N.G. Ecumenical Christian Youth Centre, 1987.

File 36.Lotus Pasifika Publications Computer, 1987-1988.

File 37. Fiji Emergency Grants, 1987-1988.

File 38. Pacific Conference of Churches, 1988.

File 39. Fiji - Pacific Theological College, 1988-1989.

File 40. B.P.T.C. Water Tank and Auxiliary Pump, 1988.

File 41. Vanuatu Cyclone Relief, 1985.

File 42. Pijin Dictionary Translation, 1986.

File 43. Pijin Project Building, 1986-1987.

Box 3.

File 1. P.I.C.-N.P.O.(National Priests Organization) Continuing Education Program, 1984-1985.

File 2. P.I.C.-P.E.C. Visayas-Mindanao Regional Council, 1984-1985.

File 3. Philippines - Land Rights Consultation, 1984-1985.

File 4. I.R.C. - Formation Program, 1984-1986.

File 6. Aglipay Central Theological Seminary Building, 1985-1986.

File 7. P. Coffin travel to Philippine Solidarity Conference, 1985.

File 8. Kalibo Student Centre/Multipurpose Building (P.I.C.), 1985.

File 9. Water supply, Tabuk Diocesan Headquarters (P.E.C.), 1985-1986.

File 10. N.C.C.- Philippine Integrated Budget, 1987.

File 11. Books for Aglipay Central Theological Seminary, 1986-1989.

File 12. Books for St. Paul's Theological Seminary - Philippines, 1986-1989.

File 13. Grassroots Renewal and Evangelism through Biblical Approach (G.R.E.B.A.), 1986.

File 14. Association of Women in Theology (A.W.I.T.) Programme Support, 1986.

File 15. I.R.C.P Evaluation Study, 1985-1986.

File 16. Grassroots Evangelism and Conscientization (G.R.E.A.C.), 1986-1987.

File 17. National Priests Organization (N.P.O.) Philippines, 1985-1987.

File 18. Reconstruction of Church Buildings destroyed by Typhoons, 1985-1986.

File 19. Support for Asian Delegates attending the Nanjing '86 Conference, 1985-1986.

File 20. Transportation for National Program Coordinator Filipino Exposure Trip for Youth, 1986.

Box 4.

File 1. Clergy-Laity Formation Program (CLFP-NL), 1987.

File 2. St. Andrew's Theological Seminary - Program and Faculty Development, 1986-1988.

File 3. Repair of National Program Coordinator's car, 1986-1987.

File 4. Ecumenical Council for Theological Education, 1986-1987.

File 5. Aglipayan Resource Centre - N.P.O.(National Priests Organization), 1986-1987.

File 6. N.C.C.P. - Integrated Budget (Philippines 8300), 1987.

File 7. I.R.C.P. - Programme Support, 1987-1988.

File 8. Clergy-Laity Formation Program -NL, 1987.

File 9. P.I.C. - Repair and Repainting of Diocesan Centre, 1987-1989.

File 10. Philippines - A.C.T.S. Water Tank Proposal, 1987-1988.

File 11. Philippines - National Council of Churches of the Philippines(N.C.C.P.) Integrated Budget, 1988.

File 12. P.E.C. - Zabala Sabbatical, 1987-1988.

File 13. P.E.C. - National Office Building, 1988-1990.

File 14. P.I.C. - Central Office transport, 1988-1990.

File 15. SATS - Lagunzad Sabbatical, 1988-1989.

File 16. Overseas Personnel - McShane, 1984-1991.

GS92-18. World Mission Asia/Pacific.

Box 1.

File 1. Goal IIO Evaluation - O/S Personnel, 1990.

File 2. Trip reports (3 files), 1985-1989.

File 3. Overseas Personnel Procedures, 1985-1989.

File 4. Job description - Regional Mission coordinator, 1978-1988.

File 5. Budget, 1980-1987.

File 6. World Mission - New design, 1985-1986.

File 7. Overseas Income Tax Regulations, 1975-1985.

File 8. Canadian Asia Working Group, 1985-1989.

File 9. Canada China Program, 1984-1990.

File 10. Canada China Programme - Remandating, 1987-1989.

File 11. China Partnership Visit - Ecumenical Theological Students, 1987.

File 12. Association for Theological Education in South East Asia Funding, 1984-1990.

File 13. Christian Conference of Asia Assembly(Korea), 1985.

File 14. Christian Conference of Asia - Finances, 1983-1990.

Box 2.

File 1. Council of the Church of East Asia PIM Consultation, Sabah, November, 1987.

File 2. Council of the Church of East Asia - Review and Evaluation Committee meeting, Taiwan, 1988-1989.

File 3. Council of the Church of East Asia Youth Consultation, 1990.

File 4. Council of the Church of East Asia - Finances, 1984-1989.

File 5. World Student Christian Federation - Asia/Pacific Region, 1984-1990.

File 6. World Student Christian Federation, Asia/Pacific Region Women's bi-regional meeting, 1989.

File 7. Burma - Burma Council of Churches, Scholarship Programme AIM A/P #202, 1986-1990.

File 8. Burma - Burma Council of Churches integrated budget, 1989-1990.

File 9. Myanmar - Archbishop Andrew's Visit to Hong Kong, etc. A/P AIM #248, 1990.

File 10. China - Chinese Theological Students in Canada #131, 1987-1990.

File 11. China - Support of Hong Kong Amity Foundation Office AIM #260, 1990-1991.

File 12. China - Theological Student Doctoral Studies in Canada - Ms. Jin Yan #170, 1988-1990.

File 13.Canada China Program "Living the Gospel in Society", Edinburgh, 1988-1989.

File 14. India - Church of South India Cyclone Relief AIM A/P #258, 1990.

File 15. India - Bishop's College - Leadership Training Program AIM A/P #254, 1990.

File 16. India - Satyaniketan ("Abode of Truth"), Theological College - Library Book Grant #209, 1989.

File 17. India - Church of North India - Human Resources Sharing Program A/P #222, 1990.

File 18. India - Request to cover travel expenses for Dr. T. Das A/P #223, 1988-1990.

File 19. India - Serampore College Solidarity Fund, 1988-1992.

File 20. India - Christian Institute for Sikh Studies Program Support #149, 1987-1990.

File 21. India - Support of Church of North India, Scholarship student - Rev. Hemata Dutta A/P #168, 1988-1990.

File 22. Indochina - World Council of Churches Round Table People to People Programs AIM A/P #266, 1990.

File 23. Korea - St. Michael's Lecture Series - Anglican Centennial A/P #245, 1990.

File 24. Korea - Pokkeri Rectory (Taejon Diocese) AIM #262, 1990.

File 25. Korea - OCK-PO, Kuo-Jae Island, Korea #203, 1989.

File 26. Korea - N.C.C. Korea Integrated Budget #205, 1989-1990.

File 27. Korea - Rev. John (Jaejoung) Lee, 1981-1988.

File 28. Papua New Guinea - Diocese of Aipo Rongo, New Parish Development #189, 1988-1989.

File 29. Papua New Guinea - Divine Word Institute #188, 1988-1989.

File 30. Papua New Guinea - Umben Magazine, translation into Hiri Motu Language #185, 1988-1989.

File 31. Papua New Guinea - Theological Student Support at Bishop Patteson Centre #144, 1987-1990.

File 32. Papua New Guinea - The Rev. Peter Moi - Degree Level Studies at Holy Spirit #136, 1987-1990.

File 33. Papua New Guinea - Development Program for Youths 87 #132, 1986-1989.

Box 3.

File 1. Philippines - St. Andrew's Theological Seminary Local Faculty Development #123, 1987-1990.

File 2. Philippines - Filipino Book of Common Prayer Project #96, 1986-1991.

File 3. Philippines - Institute for Religion and Culture (ICRP) grant #150, 1987-1989.

File 4. Philippines - Institute for Religion and Culture (ICRP) Budget A/P #226, 1989-1990.
File 5. Philippines - student - Danilo M. Ocampo #193, 1989.

File 6. Philippines - SATS TEE Program #171, 1988-1989.

File 7. Philippines - P.E.C. Consolidated Motorcycles for Ministry Project #160, 1988-1989.

File 8. Philippines - P.E.C. Liturgical Conference AIM A/P #263, 1990

File 9. Philippines - P.E.C. - Bible Inculturation Course #164, 1988-1990.

File 10. Philippines - - Rebuilding of St. Joseph's, Galatoc A/P #255, 1990.

File 11. Philippines - National Priests Organization(N.P.O.) Integrated Program #152, 1987-1991

File 12. Philippines - Institute for Studies in Asian Church and Culture (ISACC) #186, 1988-1990.

File 13. Philippines - ECTEEP -Support for 1988 Budget AIM #211, 1987-1990.

File 14. Philippines - Asian Unity for Beginners #128, 1987-1991.

File 15. Philippines - Earthquake Emergency Relief AIM #257, 1990-1991.

File 16. Philippines - P.I.C. Delegates to World Council of Churches Assembly, Canberra A/P 1991/6, 1990-1991.

File 17. Philippines - National Council of Churches of the Philippines(N.C.C.P.) Integrated Budget, 1989 #206, 1988-1990.

File 18. Philippines - Brian Allan, 1984-1992.

File 19. Thailand - Long Tail Canoe & Motor #201, 1987-1989.

File 20. Sri Lanka - National Council of Churches-Sri Lanka)N.C.C.-SL Secretariat Building AIM #261, 1990.

File 21. Sri Lanka Church Reconstruction Emergency Appeal #181, 1988.

File 22, Sri Lanka - Diocese of Colombo Leadership Development A/P #232, 1989-1990.

File 23. Sri Lanka - Support for Overseas Scholarship for Jeffrey Abayasekra #177, 1987-1990.

File 24. Sri Lanka - N.C.C. Commissions for Justice and Peace # 61, 1986-1988.

File 25. Sri Lanka - Emergency Financial Support # 140 and Continuing Education for Clergy, 1987-1988.

File 26. South Pacific Association of Theological Schools A/P #264, 1990.

File 27. Solomon Islands - Holo Prayer Book (Ysabel) A/P #251, 1990.

File 28. Samoa - Cyclone Ofa Emergency Relief A/P #249, 1990.

File 29. Halapua - Winston Diocese of Polynesia Fiji Islands #159, 1987-1990.

File 30. Pacific Theological College - Women's Program 1990 A/P #228, 1989-1990.

File 31. Vanuatu - Cyclone Anne (Torres) Disaster - Rebuilding request #175, 1988-1991.

File 32. Diocese of Solomons - West Kwara'ae Prayer Book #187, 1988-1990.

File 33. Solomon Islands - Airahu Training Centre Development #138, 1987-1990.

File 34. Solomon Islands - Luesalo Training Center #58, 1985-1987.

File 35. Solomon Islands - Melanesian Brotherhood building project A/P #213, 1987-1990.

File 36. Solomon Islands - Pauline Bradbrook, 1987-1990.

File 37. Solomon Islands - Student - John Falea #192, 1988-1991.

File 38. Japan - CCRAI 1990 Budget A/P 239, 1990.

File 39. Japan - Nomura Visit to Canada April 1990 A/P #242, 1989-1990.

File 40. Japan - Korea Christian Social Center Program Budget #52, 1985-1986.

GS92-29. Primate's World Relief and Development Fund: Asia/Pacific
Textual records - 1980-1992. 15 in.

Box 1.

File 1. 86.ASR, 008F. Asia-Pacific Mission for Migrant Filipinos, 1985-1988.

File 2. 89.ASR.01A APMMF, 1989-1992.

File 3. 90.ASR.07A DAGA, 1990-1991.

File 4. 89.BAN, 02A Multisectoral Rural Development, 1989-1990.

File 5. 86.BAN.03A Women's Group Formation, 1990.

File 6. 86.BRM.003F Urban Rural Mission, 1987-1988.

File 7. 89.BRM.01A Burma Urban Rural Mission, 1989.

File 8. 90.BRM.02A Burma Urban Rural Mission, 1990.

File 9. 90.IND.05A PUDAR, 1990-1991.

File 10. 90.IND.08A Organizing Thru Action Lokonnoyana, 1989-1991.

File 11. 87.KOR.028 Anglican Priests Corps, 1986-1988.

File 12. 87.KOR.031.6 Emergency Legal Aid Fund for Prisoners in Korea, 1987-1988.

File 13. 89.KOE.01A Yongdongpo Urban Industrial Mission, 1980-1990.

File 14. 89.KOE.05A Korea Church Women Prostitution Program, 1987-1991.

File 15. 89.KOE.06A Korea Human Rights Committee N.C.C.K, 1988-1991.

File 16. 89.KOE.08A (7902) Korea Christian Farmers, 1986-1991.

File 1A. Christian Commissions for Development in Bangladesh (CCDB), 1987-1989.

Box 2.

File 1. 86.PHI.042F Cooperative Education Seminar, 1986-1988.

File 2. 87.PHI.049.6 Concerns Rising Over Prostitution, 1984-1990.

File 3. 87.PHI.052 Amakan Rice, 1986-1991.

File 4. 88.PHI.057 Asia Consultation of Prostitutes and Concerned Women Activists, 1988-1990.

File 5. 88.PHI.058 Clear-Education Campaign, 1987-1989.

File 6. 88.PHI.059 KMP - Peasant Movement of the Philippines, 1988-1989.

File 7. 89.PHI.01A Teatro Obrero, 1989-1990.

File 8. 89.PHI.03A Protestant Lawyers League of the Philippines, 1989.

File 9. 89.PHI.04A Council of Peoples Development, 1989.

File 10. 89.PHI.05A Minority Peoples National Secretariat, 1989-1990.

File 11. 89.PHI.07A Farmers Development Centre (FARDEC), 1989-1990.

File 12. 89.PHI.08A Development Agency for Tribes in the Cordillera (DATC), 1989-1990.

File 13. 89.PHI.12A Agrarian Reform Organizers, 1989-1990.

File 14. 89.PHI.13A Grassroots Evangeliztion and Conscientization, 1989-1991.

File 15. 89.PHI.15A Alaminos Small Fisherman Association (ASFA), 1989-1991.

File 16. 89.PHI.16A Documentary on Philippine Workers, 1989.

File 17. 89.PHI.18A Kaibigan, 1989-1991.

File 18. 90.PHI.38A Farmer's Development Centre(FARDEC), 1990.

Box 3.

File 1. 89.PHI.22A Community Education Through Peoples Theatre, 1989-1991.

File 2. 90.PHI.31A Teatro Obrero, 1990-1991.

File 3. 90.PHI.35A CPA - Core Funding, 1990-1992.

File 4. 90.PHI.37A Development Agency for the Tribes in the Cordillera (DATC), 1990-1991.

File 5. 90.PHI.44A VEMJP - Education Campaign, 1989-1991.

File 6. 90.PHI.46A Promotion of Church People's, Rights, 1990-1991.

File 7. 80.SRL.O11F Christian Workers' Fellowship, 1980-1991.

File 8. 82.SRL.013F URM - Rural Initiatives, 1982-1990.

File 9. 87.SRL.017 Squatter Settlement & Human Upliftment Project, 1987.

File 10. 87.SRL.018F N.C.C. Sri Lanka Women's Desk, 1987.

File 11. 89.SRL.02A Women's Development Centre, 1989-1992.

File 12. 89.SRL.04A New World Publications, 1989-1991.

File 13. 89.SRL.06A Samagi Block Brick Makers, 1989-1990.

File 14. 89.KOE.02A Labour Management Counselling Centre Kyung Gi, 1988-1991.

GS93-01. Primate's World Relief and Development Fund:Asia/Pacific Region.
Textual records. 1986-1993. 10 in.

Box 1.

File 1. CCC - Committee on International Affairs, 1987-1990.

File 2. N.C.C.I - NDAC [National Development Advisory Council], 1988-1989.

File 3. 2216.05 Ecumenical Center for Development /IDEA, 1990.

File 4. 2219.13 P.E.C. [Philippine Episcopal Church] Philippines, 1989.

File 5. John Whitehall, 1989-1990.

File 6. 2231.8 CUFID, 1987-1988.

File 7. 86.KOR.027 Korea Christian Action Organization, 1986-1990.

File 8. Selwyn College Solomon Islands [Reconstruction], 1986-1987.

File 9. 88.SOI.05A Selwyn College Reconstruction [Solomon Islands], 1988-1990.

File 10. 89.IND. IDEA [Institute for Development Education and Action, India], 1988-1990.

File 11. 89.KOE.04A Nanumae Zib (House of Sharing) [Korea], 1988-1989.

File 12. 89.PHI.02A Northern Antique Development Program (NORADEP) [Philippines], 1989-1990.

File 13. 89.PHI.11A CEBU Relief and Rehabilitation Centre [Philippines], 1989-1991.

Box 2.

File 1. 90.IND.10A Calcutta the Other City PUDAR [India], 1990-1991.

File 2. 89-KOE.03A Christian Institute for Justice and Development (CIJD) [Korea]1988-1992.

File 3. 89-KOE.07A Christian Action Organization Korea, 1989-1990.

File 4. 89.PHI.19A Visayas Human Rights Conference and Education Campaign [Philippines], 1989-1900.

File 5. 90.KOE.14A Nanumae Zib [House of Sharing] 1989-1992.

File 6. 90.PHI.34A Resource Centre for Philippine Concerns, 1990-1992.

File 7. 90.PHI.36A CPA - Education Campaign on the Environment [Philippines]1990-1991.

File 8. 90.PHI.39A Minority People's National. Secretariat (KANP) [Philippines], 1990.

File 9. 90.PHI.40A National Lawyer's Conference on Agrarian Reform (CARLS) [Philippines], 1990-1993.

File 10. 90.PHI.45A Protestant Lawyers League of the Philippines, 1990-1992.

File 11. 90.PHI.49A GREAC (Grassroots Evangelization and Conscientization) [Philippines], 1989-1990.

File 12. 90.PHI.51A Community Theatre EDCADS [Philippines], 1990-1991.

File 13. 91.PHI.03A Teatro Obrero - Core Support [Philippines], 1991.

File 14. 91.PHI.05A GREAC (Grassroots Evangelization and Conscientization) [Philippines], 1991-1992.

GS93-05. World Mission: Asia/Pacific.
Textual records. 1985-1992. 5 in.

Box 1.

File 1. Grant for Asia/Pacific participants in Anglican Encounter, Brazil AP 1992/1, 1992.

File 2. Andrew Mya Han - Burma, 1981-1983.

File 3. Burma - Myanmar - Holy Cross Theological College Vehicle A/Pl991/18, 1991.

File 4. Canadian Forces Chapel Offerings Committee, 1985-1990.

File 5. Canadian Forces Chapel Offerings Committee, 1991-1992.

File 6. India/Sri Lanka - General Inquiries, 1987-1988.

File 7. Church of North India correspondence, 1985-1989.

File 8. Church of North India - Related Missions Committee - North American Section, 1985-1987.

File 9. Church of North India - Partners in Mission Committee - North American Section, 1987-1992.

File 10. Church of North India - Visit report of Peter and Ann McCalman, 1985.

File 11. Church of the Province of India, Pakistan.

File 12. India - Christian Institute for Sikh Studies A/Pl99 1/2, 1991.

File 13. India - Ditt Memorial Centre - A/Pl991/19, 1990.

File 14. India - South Asia Theological Research Institute (SATHRI) A/P #224, 1989-1990.

File 15. Japan - NSKK(Nippon Sei Ko Kai) Centennial, 1986-1987.

File 16. Japan - NSKK(Nippon Sei Ko Kai) Consultation Costs AIM A/P 208, 1989.

File 17. Japan - NSKK(Nippon Sei Ko Kai) - PIM, 1979-1985.

File 18. Sri Lanka - Diocese of Kurunagala - Motorcycles A/Pl99 1/3 2, 1991.

File 19. Sri Lanka - National Christian Council of Ceylon - Justice and Peace Commissions A/Pl991/3, 1991.

File 20. Sri Lanka - Rev. Sydney Knight at Anglican Church of Canada Liturgy Conference A/Pl991/25, 1991.

GS93-20. Primate's World Relief and Development Fund: Asia/Pacific Region.
Textual records. 1980-1993.

Box 1.

File 1. 83.SOI.005F Housing Project, 1983-1985.

File 2. 87.PNG.06A Development Project for Youth, 1987-1990.

File 3. 87.PNG.018 Youth Project truck - Madang, 1987-1991.

File 4. 87.PNG.021 Aradep Air Strip, 1987-1991.

File 5. 88.PNG.05A Training Course in Social Counselling, 1988-1989.

File 6. 88.PNG.022 Community Based Rehabilitation Program, 1988-1992.

File 7. 89.BAN.02A Multisectoral Rural Development Program, 1989-1992.

File 8. 89.KOE.09A Chung Ju Urban Industrial Mission, 1986-1990.

File 9. 89.K0E.l0A Mission to Labour & Industry, Inchon, 1980-1990.

File 10. 89.KOE.llA Ulson Labour Counselling Centre, 1987-1990.

File 11. 89.PNG.02A Tadup Village Rice Cultivation Project, 1989.

File 12. 89.PNG.03A St. Andrews youth Training, 1988-1991.

File 13. 89.PNG.04A Training Course in Social Counselling, 1989-1992.

File 14. 89.SOI.02A NORII Association on Wakabout Sawmill, 1989-1990.

File 15. 89-SOI.03A Popular Development Education Program:, 1989-1992.

File 16. 89.SRL.05A Women's Commissions of the National Council of Churches of Sri Lanka, 1989-1991.

File 17. 89.VTN.01A Tudu Irrigation, 1989-1991.

Box 2.

File 1. 90.ASR.09A Ecumenical Coalition on Third World Tourism, 1990-1993.

File 2. 90.BAN.05A Ubinig - Core Support, 1990-1991.

File 3. 90.BAN.06A Ubinig - Publication & Information Campaign, 1990-1991.

File 4. 90.PHI.33A Northern Luzon Human Rights Organization, 1990-1991.

File 5. 90.PHI.38A Farmer's Development Centre, Fardec, 1990-1991.

File 6. 90.PHI.48A Clear - BCEPZ Factory Workers, 1990-1993.

File 7. 90.SRL.09A World Solidarity Forum on Sri Lanka for Justice and Peace, 1989-1991.

File 8. 90.SRL.llA CWF - Plantation Service Committee, 1988-1991.

File 9. 90.SRL.12A Samagi Block Brickmakers Vehicle, 1990-1992.

File 10. 90.SRL.13A Samuha Youth Farm, CWF, 1990-1991.

File 11. 91.BRM.0lA WCC-URM, 1991.

File 12. 91.IND.01A PUDAR - Calcutta the Other City, 1991-1992.

File 13. 91.IND.02A Lokonnoyana- Organizing Through Action, 1991.

File 14. 91.PHI.07A KAMP - 3rd Organizational Congress, 1990-1992.

File 15. Development Agency for Tribes in the Cordillera (DATC) - Core Support, 1991-1993.

Box 3.

File 1. 91.PHI.11A CPD - UN Educational Campaign, 1991-1992.

File 2. 91.PHI.18A Promotion of Church People's Rights, 1991-1992.

File 3. 91.PHI.19A VEMJP - Provincial Assemblies, 1991-1992.

File 4. 91.PHI.20A Cebu Relief and Rehab Centre (CRRC), 1991-1992.

File 5. 91-PHI.23A CODE NGO - National NGO Congress, 1991-1992.

File 6. 91.SRL.01A CWF - Gami Seva Sevana, 1991.

File 7. 91.SRL.03A Christian Workers Fellowship Core, 1991-1993.

File 8. 91.SRL.09A CWF - Samuha Youth Farm, 1991-1992.

File 9. 91.SRL.10A Commissions of Justice & Peace), 1991.

File 10. 92.PHI.04A GREAC(Grassroots Evangelization and Conscientization), 1991-1992.

File 11. 92.PHI.05A CPA Core, 1991-1993.

File 12. 92.PHI.06A P.E.C.(Philippine Episcopal Church) Literacy Campaign, 1992.

File 13. 92.PHI.08A Council for People's Development, 1992.

File 14. 92.PHI.21 CPAR - Second Congress, 1992-1993.

File 15. 92.PNG.01A Christian Institute for Counselling Training Courses, 1992-1993

File 16. 2.SRL.02A Women's Development Centre, 1992-1993

GS93-22. World Mission: Asia/Pacific Region.
Textual records. 1975-1993. 25 in.

Box 1.

File 1. A/P - AIM Projects, 1986-1989

File 2. McLaughlin Research on AIM/Apportionment Split, 1987-1988

File 3. AIM-917-143-1987 WSCF - A/P Region Program Budget, 1986-1988

File 4. AIM-917-220-1990 Pacific Conference of Churches Integrated Budget, 1989-1991.

File 5. AIM-917-227-1990 PNG - St. Paul's Mission District, Sogeri Lowland (Port Moresby Diocese), 1989-1991.

File 6. AIM-917-231-1990 Philippines - CLFP(Cergy Laity Formation Program) - NL 1990-1993 Program, 1989-1990.

File 7. AIM-917-234-1990 Malaysia - Sabah Language Studies, 1990.

File 8. AIM-917-236-1990 Malaysia - Support of Anglican Lecturer at S.T.M, 1990.

File 9. AIM-917-237-1990 Malaysia - Rebuilding of Anglican Community Centre, Ipoh, Diocese of West Malaysia, 1989-1990.

File 10. AIM-917-238-1990 Malaysia - Rebuilding of Christ Church, Jinjang, Diocese of West Malaysia, 1990.

File 11. AIM-917-238-1990 Philippines - P.I.C. - Cagayan Valley POEMS Program, 1989-1992.

File 12. AIM-917-253-1990 Solomon Islands - Diocese of Temotu Training Centre Development, 1989-1992.

File 13. AIM-917-265-1990 Solomon Islands - Mothers' Union Provincial Projects, 1989-1991.

File 14. AIM-917-01-1991 Polynesia - Bishop Bryce Sabbatical, 1991.

File 15. AIM-917-08-1991 Philippines - Institute for Studies in Asian Church and Culture (ISACC), 1990-1991.

File 16. AIM-917-11-1991 SPAC Women's Conference, 1990-1991.

File 17. AIM-917-12-1991 Fiji - Lotu Pasifik Productions - Photocopying Machine, 1990-1991.

File 18. AIM-917-16-1991 Clergy/Laity Formation Program-Northern Luzon, Inc. (Partnership Grant), 1990-1991.

File 19. AIM-917-21-1991 Philippines - P.I.C. Diocesan CNP Projects, 1991;

File 20. AIM-917-22-1991 Korea - Saenuri Shinmun, 1991.

File 21. AIM-917-24-1991 Polynesia - Savusavu Parish Van, Fiji, 1991-1992.

File 22. AIM-917-27-1991 Pacific - Support of Pacific Desk (CICARWS), 1989-1992.

File 23. AIM-917-29-1991 PNG - St. Francis, Koki, Priests's House, 1990-1991.

File 24. AIM-917-30-1991 Philippines - Rev. J. Laus - A.C.C. Clergy Conference, 1991.

File 25. AIM-917-34-1991 PNG - Diocese of Popondota Capital Development, 1991.

File 26. AIM-917-35-1991 Solomon Islands - Pamua Training Centre, 1991-1992.

File 27. AIM-917-39-1991 Philippines - P.E.C. Youth Assembly, 1990-1992

File 28. AIM-917-43-1991 PNG - Ecumenical Theological Studies - UPNG, 1990-1991.

File 29. AIM-917-44-1991 [and 28] Solomon Islands - B.P.T.C. Up-Grading, 1990-1992.

File 30. AIM-917-46-1991 Solomon Islands - Tikopia Disaster Appeal, 1991-1992.

File 31. AIM-917-05-1992 Solomon Islands - Jejevo Parish Hall (Ysabel Dio), 1991-1993.

File 32. AIM-917-12-1992 Solomon Islands - Training of Librarian at B.P.T.C , 1992.

File 33. AIM-917-18-1992 PNG - Diocese of Aipo Rongo -Wewak Parish Vehicle, 1992-1993.

Box 2.

File 1.1211.07 ORC - Correspondence Financial - Publications, 1986-1987.

File 2.1212.01 Brian Allan - Correspondence, 1981-1992.

File 3. 1212.02 Brian Allen - Finance, 1983-1989.

File 4. 1214.02 John Lee - Financial, 1983-1988.

File 5. 1217.00 Peter, Rev. Friedrich A. and Miss. Elsa G. Peter, 1980-1989.

File 6. 1232.06 Japan - National Christian Council of Japan (N.C.C.J), 1982-1985.

File 7. 1232.07 Japan - NSKK - National - Correspondence, 1985-1989.

File 8. 1232.07 Japan - NSKK - National, Financial, Irene Isaac Estate, 1982-1987.

File 9. 1232.09 Japan - NSSK - National - Powles/Hamilton Bursary, 1978-1989.

File 10.1232.11 Japan - Japanese Women and the Church- Report by Marjorie A. Powles, 1985-1987.

File 11.1232.13 Japan - Fingerprinting of Aliens, 1985-1986.

File 12. 1233.00 Korea - Anglican Church "Council ofAdvice", 1987-1991.
Box 3.

File 1. 1233.02 Korea - Anglican Church in Korea - Diocese of Busan, 1979-199.

File 2. 1233.04 Korea - Christian Institute for the Study of Justice and Development, 1981-1987.

File 3.1233.10 Korea -Human Rights, 1985-1988.

File 4. 1233.12 Korea - Kim Dae Jung, 1980-1986.

File 5. 1233.18 Korea -Anglican Church in Korea, National Office, 1985-1988 .

File 6. 1233.21 Korea - Projects, 1985-l986.

File 7. 1233.22 Korea -Anglican Church in Korea - St. Michael's Theological Seminary, 1984-1989.

File 8. 1233.23 Korea - Anglican Church in Korea- Diocese of Seoul, 1979-1989.

File 9. 1233.27 Korea - Anglican Church in Korea- Diocese of Taejon, 1979-1990.

File 10. 1231.03 Irian Jaya- Refugees, 1985-1986.

File 11. 1234.01 Malaysia - Diocese of West Malaysia - Correspondence, 1985-1989.

File 12. 1234.01 Malaysia - Diocese of West Malaysia - Financial, 1983-1986.

File13. 1234.06 Malaysia - Diocese of West Malaysia - Seminari Theoloji Malaysia (STM), 1979-1988.

File 14. 1234.07 Malaysia - Richard Toase -West Malaysia, 1981-1988.

File 15. 1234.08 Malaysia-Diocese of Kuching, 1976-1989.

File 16. 1234.09 Malaysia-Diocese of Sabah, 1984-1986.

File 17. 1234.14 Malaysia-Women's Program of Daya Rakyat. (Grassroots Research Centre), 1986-1987.

File 18. 1235.04 Pacific Conference of Churches, 1981-

1987.

File 19. 1235.05 Pacific Theological College, Suva, Fiji Islands, 1984-1989.

File 20. 1235.06 South Pacific Anglican Council - General Correspondence, 1988-1989.
File 21. 1235.06 South Pacific Anglican Council - Financial, 1983-1989.

Box 4.

File 1. 1235.08 Church of Melanesia - General Correspondence, 1985-1989.

File 2. 1235.08 Church of Melanesia - Diocese of Malaita, 1989.

File 3. 1235.08 Church of Melanesia - Diocese of Vanuatu, 1983-1990.

File 4. 1235.08 Church of Melanesia - Diocese of Ysabel, 1984-1989.

File 5. 1235.08 Church of Melanesia - Projects, 1986-1988.

File 6. 1235.12 Papua New Guinea, 1986-1989.

File 7. 1235.15 Diocese of Polynesia, 1983-1989.

File 8. 1236.07 Philippines - Ecumenical Center for Development, 1985-1988

File 9. 1236.08 Philippines - Ecumenical Movement for Justice and Peace, 1980-1984.

File 10. 1236.11 Philippines - Guimaras Unified Action for Rural Development (GUARD), 1985.

File 11. 1236.12 Philippines - Human Rights from 1985, 1988-1990.

File 12. 1236.13 Philippine Human Rights Congress, 1985-1988.

File 13. 1236.15 Philippines - Institute for Religion and Culture, 1984.

File 14. 1236.24 Philippines - Massey Fergusson Project, 1986-1987.

File 15. 1236.26 Philippines - National Council of Churches, 1980-1989.

File 16. 1236.33 Philippines - Peasant Education and Organizing Program Towards Liberational Enlightment (PEOPLE), 1989.

File 17. 1236.36 Philippines - Projects, 1986-1989.

File 18. 1236.38 Philippines - United Church of Christ in the Philippines, 1984-1988.

Box 5.

File 1. 1237.02 Philippine Episcopal Church - Correspondence, 1978-1989.

File 2. 1237.07 Philippine Episcopal Church - Diocese of Central Philippines, 1981-1989.
File 3. 1237.08, Philippine Episcopal Church - Diocese of Northern Luzon (Bontoc), 1981-1986.

File 4. 1237.09. Philippine Episcopal Church - Diocese of Northern Luzon(Tabuk), 1986.

File 5. 1237.10 Philippine Episcopal Church - Diocese of Southern Philippines, 1979-1989.

File 6. 1237.11 Philippines - P.E.C. - Nishga-Cordillera Exchange, 1986-1987.

File 7. 1238.01 Philippine Independent Church - Financial, 1979-1988.

File 8. 1238.02 Philippine Independent Church - Correspondence, 1985-1989.

File 9. 1238.04 Philippine Independent Church - Diocese of Antique and Paluwan, 1984-1989.

File 10. 1238.06 Philippine Independent Church - Diocese of Cebu, Bohol, and Masbat, 1986-1989.

File 11. 1238.12 Philippine Independent Church - Abdias Dela Cruz, 1984-1986.

File 12. 1238.13 Philippine Independent Church - Porfirio Dela Cruz, 1985-1989.

Box 5.

File l. 1238.14 Philippine Independent Church - National Priests Organization, 1980-1983.

File 2. 1238.14 Philippine Independent Church - St. Andrew's Seminary, 1984-1988.

File 3. 1238.15 Philippines - P.I.C. GREAC (Grassroots Evangelization and Conscientization)Program Support, 1988.

File 16. 1238.16 Philippine Independent Church - Exchange, Fr. Robespierre Noreno, 1987-1989.

File 17. 1240.01 Taiwan, 1975-1989.

File 18. 1259.00 Canada China Program, 1988-1990.

File 19. 1266.06 WSCF - Canadian SCN Asia Visit, 1987.

File 20. Dr. Thakur Das research on Amritsar, 1991.

File 21. India. Church of Northern India. Bursar. Rv. P.K.Tandy visit, 1991-1992.

Anglican Church of Canada - Archives • 633

GS93-28. Missionary Society of the Church in Canada/NWP.

Box 1.

File 1. IAA-l Diocese of Amritsar, 1962-1970.

File 2. Amritsar-Financial Statements, 1959-1967.

File 3. IA-l CIPBC - Metropolitan, Rt. Rev. H.L.J. DeMel, 1964-1968.

File 4. IA-3 Amritsar Budget, 1967-1970.

File 5. IA.A-3 Amritsar Budget, 1964-1966.

File 6. Peel, Donald - paper on A Suggested Training in the Faith Program for the Diocese of Amritsar, 1965.

File 7. I-39 The Rev.John B. Wade, Amritsar, 1962-1965.

File 8. IAG.I-5 Baring Union Christian College, Batala, 1963-1970.

File 9. A.A.1-6 Christian Rural Training Centre, Ajnala, 1964-1966.

Box 2.

File 1. I.22 Amritsar Diocesan Board of Women's Work Mrs. B.S. Chandar, 1963-1966.

File 2. IA.A.I-3 Lady Willingdon Hospital, Manali - Dr. Peter Snell, 1964-1966.

File 3. I-1 India - General, 1970.

File 4. I.14 Landour Community Hospital, Mussoorie, Uttar Pradesh, 1964-1965.

File 5. IAAI-2 Maple Leaf Hospital, Kangra, 1967-1968.

File 6. I.50 Nan Niahl Chang Paul Trust, 1963-1965.

File 7. I.5 Overseas Scholarship Assistance, Diocese of Amritsar, 1960-1966.

File 8. IAAI-4 St. Thomas Higher Secondary School, Simla, 1961-1968.

File 9. IA.A.1-7 Spring View Property, Landour, 1962-1966.

File 10. I-2 Diocese of Amritsar Standing Committee, 1962-1966.

File 11. IAB-1 Diocese of Barrackpore - Rt. Rev. R.W. Bryan, 1963-1970.

File 12. IAB-3 Barrackpore Diocese, 1969-1970.

File 13. IB-4 Barrackpore Lay Training, John McRae, 1969-1970.

File 14. M-1 Burma - General, 1970.

File 15. IA.C-2 Durgapur Building Project, 1962-1967.

File 16. I.63 Kalyani Project Diocese of Barrackpore, 1965.

File 17. MA/D-l Karachi, 1965-1968.

Box 3.

File 1. MA/E-I-2 Kinnaird College, Lahore, 1968.
File 2. MAE-1 Lahore, 1968-1970.

File 3. IA.E-1 Diocese of Lucknow Rt. Rev. J. Amritanand, 1965-1966.

File 4. MA/D-I-l Quetta Mission, Karachi, 1968.

File 5. MA/E-I-l Technical Services Association, Lahore, 1965-1968.

File 6.IB.G.I-l Vellore Christian Medical College and Hospital, 1989.

File 7. J-2 NSKK General, 1970.

File 8. I-7 New Life Sanitorium, Nagano. The Rev.J.R. Toyooka, 1964-1966.

File 9. J-7 Dioceses - General, 1970.

File 10. The Nagoya Student Centre, the Rev. R.B.Mutch, 1964-1967.

File 11. J-39 Wakkanai Grant re Rev. K. Hayashi, 1965.

File 12. J-57 Bishop Hamilton and Bishop Powles Memorial Scholarship, 1963-1966.

File 13. JA-l Hokkaido - General, 1970.

File 14. JA-2 Hokkaido - Fukujuen, 1970.

File 15. JA-2 NSKK External Affairs Committee - Rt. Rev. D.M. Goto, 1964-1967.

File 16. JA-3 NSKK Loan Fund Mr. G.S. Lehman, 1963-1969.

File 17. JA-6 College Work Project - NSKK, 1968-1970.

File 18. JAA-l Diocese of Hokkaido, 1966-1969.

File 19. JAD-l Diocese of Mid-Japan(2), 1964-1970.

Box 4.

File 1. JA.D.I-2 Love the Blind Centre, Gifu, 1964-1966.

File 2. JADI-3 Nagoya Student Centre, 1967.

File 3. JAD-3 Toyoda, 1964-1967.

File 4. JAE.1 Diocese of Osaka, 1963-1970.

File 5. JAGI-l Fukujuen Children's Home, 1969.

File 6. KA-1 Polynesia - General, 1965-1970.

File 7. KA-l South Pacific Council - General, 1965-1970.

File 8. KB-1 Melanesia - General, 1968-1970.

File 9. L-1 South East Asia Council, 1964-1970.

File 10. N-4 The Bishop in Korea - The Rt. Rev. J.C.S.Daly, 1959-1965.

File 11. L.18 Diocese of Jesselton, North Borneo, 1964-1965.

File 12. LAA-1 Diocese of Hong Kong, 1963-1970.

File 13. LAC-1 Diocese of Kuching, 1989.

File 14. LC-1 Papua New Guinea - Diocesan Office, 1964-1970.

File 15. LD-1 Sabah - Diocesan Office, 1970.

File 16. LAF-1 Diocese of Seoul, 1989.

File 17. LAE-1 Diocese of Singapore and Malaya, 1964-1970.

File 18. LAH-1 Diocese of Taejon, 1969-1970.

File 19. LH-1 Philippine Independent Church, 1970.

GS93-30. Primate's World Relief and Development Fund: Asia/Pacific Region.

Box 1.

File 1. 88.SOI.014 Kolomola Sawmill Project Solomon Islands(A13), 1988-1993.

File 2. 91.BAN.03A Ekota Women's Program, 1991-1993.

File 3. 91.PHI.09A DATC(Development Agency for Tribes in the Cordillera), R&R Northern Benguet [Philippines], 1991-1993.

File 4. 91.PHI.16A Kaibigan R & R, Returnees from M.E. [Philippines], 1991-1993.

File 5. 91.PHI.26A Northern Luzon Human Rights Organization, 1991-1992.

File 6. 91.SRL.07A Development Education N.C.C.-SL [Sri Lanka], 1991-1993.

File 7. 92.ASR.06A Asian Migrant Centre [Hong Kong], 1991-1993.

File 8. 92.PHI.16A VEMJP [Philippines], 1992-1993.

Box 2.

File 1. 89.PHI.08A Human Rights Program of the P.E.C., 1989-1993.

File 2. 90.KOE.13A CSPID 1988-1991, 1990-1993.

File 3. 90.PHI.43A Village Blacksmithing and Tool Dispersal Ints, 1990-1993.

File 4. 91.BRM.02A Burma Water Supply, 1991.

File 5. 91.KOE.06A Saenuri Shinmun Ecumenical Paper, 1991-1993.

File 6. 91.SRL.06A N.C.C.-SL Transportation, 1991-1993.

File 7. 92.BRM.02A Nobel Peace Laureates Mission to Burma, Feb/93, 1993.

File 8. 92.CHN.01A Amity Foundation - Water Wells 1990-1993.

File 9. 92.PHI.03A Protestant Lawyers League of the Philippines (PLLP), 1992-199.

File 10. 92.SRL.09A Conference: Promotion of Peace in Sri Lanka, 1992-1993.

File 11. 90.PAC.03A 6th Nuclear Free Independent Pacific Conference, 1990.

GS94-04. Primate's World Relief and Development Fund

Development Coordinator Asia/Pacific Region. Textual records. --1985-1994-- 5 in.

Box 1.

File 1. 92.ASR.08A - Org: Forum Asia Project: Human Rights, Development, 1992-1993.

File 2. 92.BAN.03A Org: CCDB PRJ: People's Participatory Development Program, 1992-1993.

File 3. 92.IND.0lA ORG: PUDAR PRJ: Women's Program, 1992-1993.

File 4. 92.PHI.02 ORG: Solidaridad Foundation PRJ: Resource Centre for Philippine Concerns, 1992-1994.

File 5. 92.SRL.07A ORG: CWF PRJ: Plantation Service Committee - Core Program, 1982-1993.

File 6. 86.SOI.010 Maloa Copra Processing Centre, 1986-1994.

File 7. 87.SOI.011 Aulupeine Water, 1988-1994.

File 8. 88.SOI.012 Lede Uunimenu Water Supply, 1988-1994.

File 9. 92.IND.03A PUDAR - Phase III, Calcutta, Other City, 1992-1994.

File 10. 89.PNG.024 Dogura Water Supply, 1989-1994.

File 11. 91.SOI.02A Olumburi Water Supply Diocese of Malaita, 1990-1994.

File 12. 91.SOI.05A Namusifue Water Supply, Diocese of Malaita, 1988-1994.
File 13. 92.PHI.19A KAMP - Core Funding, 1991-1993.

File 14. 93.KOE.03A Human Rights Committee, N.C.C.K, 1991-1994.

File 15. 93.PHI.O1A GREAC(Grassroots Evangelization and Conscientization), 1993-1994.

File 16. 93.PHI.09A D.A.T.C. - 1993, Core Program, 1993-1994.

GS94-13. Primate's World Relief and Development Fund:
Asia/Pacific.

Box 1.

File 1. 93-ASR.021 Asian Migrant Centre - Core Program Funding, 1993-1994.

File 2. 92.IND.02A Lokonnoyana - Organizing thru Action, 1992-1993.

File 3. 93.KOE.06A CSPID - MSLI-K Program, 1993-1994.

File 4. 92.PHI.15A CRRC - Funding for skills training and rehabilitation work, 1992-1994.

File 5. 92.KOE.O1A CISJD WCC, 1992-1993.

Personal papers.

M63-1. White, William C.
Papers relate to Bishop White's interest in archaeology, including the tombs at Loyang.
Papers relating to his life and work as a missionary are also on microfilm and are in the University of Toronto Library and include much information on the period 1897-1934.

Box 1. Honan activities, 1909-1923.

Box 2. Correspondence 1896-1941, 1945-1958, and biographical file.
Box 3. Sermons and articles.
Class e. Missionary reports from Honan, 1910-1929, typed.

M75-14. Gibberd, Grace W.
Papers. 1935-1945. 2 inches.
The papers of Grace Gibberd, Church of England missionary in China, who returned to Canada in 1945. Manuscript describing the activities of missionaries in China during the Sino-Japanese war 1937-1945. Diary of 20 days travel in Honan during the war, 30 October to 18 November 1940. Photographs.

M80-2. Hamilton, James Heber, 1862-1952. Bishop of Mid-Japan.
Went to Japan in January 1892, and resigned See of Mid-Japan in 1934.i.?Japan:
Includes biographical sketch, clippings, 1892-1899, 1912, notebooks containing journals 1892-1894, and four photographs.

M81-26. Chung hua sheng kung hui, Diocese of Honan.
Originals, 1911-43. 61 pages.
Typescript and ms. register of marriages from 3 January 1911 to 3 May 1934, including marriages on extemporized forms from 1 December 1938 to 2 October 1943 in the Diocese of Honan. Also register of baptisms in the same diocese from 1912-1936. miscellaneous copies of banns, applications for marriage and certificates of marriage. In a portfolio. none of the persons registered bear Chinese names.
ULM

M93-04. Harriet Mitchell Horobin, 1897-1990.
Missionary in Japan, 1923-1940, 1949-1962.
Letters, 1984-1990

Photograph collection.

Large collections of mounted photographs, arranged by name of person photographed, or by subject of scene. Sizable representation of Asian scenes. 11 drawers.

P7506. C.R.H.Wilkinson Collection.
92 photographs of scenes in Amritsar diocese and other locations. Some are medical and Church activities, dated 1941-1954. One is dated 1914.

P7526. Diocese of Mid-Japan.
488 photographs illustrating Japanese situations and Church activities, mostly 1921-1936, with a few for the 1980's.

P7809. Gibberd, Grace W.
17 photographs, illustrating travel in China, October - November 1940, hampered by the flooding of the Yellow river.
P8006. Bishop White.
Photographs and rubbings. includes five sets of rubbings of Jewish memorial stones at Kaifeng, 1903, Bishop White's junk, photographs of Church activities in Honan in the 1940's.

P8209. Pakistan M.T.I. Embroidery project.
14 photographs of the project, one dated 1963.

Malaysia.
27 photographs, mostly of Sarawak, illustrating local customs and situations in 1970.

P8456. Missionary Society for the Church in Canada.
64 glass negatives and prints of China and Japan. Three are dated 1921, 1931, and 1944. Showing local scenes and some church activities.

P8494.
265 Photographs illustrating Church activities including Amritsar diocese, Hong Kong, Barrackpore, Japan, Pakistan, Polynesia, Melanesia, Papua New Guinea. Dated photographs from 1961 to 1968.

P75-103. Missionary Society.
Approximately 1035 photographs dealing with China and Japan.

P93-12. Harriet Mitchell Horobin, 1897-1990.
91 photographs, same taken in Japan, 1902-1987.

The John Holmes Library,
Canadian Institute for International Affairs,
14 King's College Circle,
Toronto, Ontario M5S 2V9
Tel: (416)979-1851.

Papers presented to the National Archives of Canada in 1976 and 1978. Microfilmed by the National Archives on five reels, M-4618 to M-4622.

Minute Books, 1928-1961.
Minute books of the Institute.

Edgar J.Tarr, 1932-1961. 66 cm.(volumes 1-4)
Papers relating to various conferences, miscellaneous correspondence relating to World Affairs and general information on both the Canadian Institute for International Affairs and the Institute of Pacific Relations. There is also included some personal material concerning Edgar J.Tarr.

Volume 1.

Correspondence, 1932-1950.

Volume 2.

Conferences.
Atlantic Conference, 1941;42
British Commonwealth Conference: Agenda Committee, 1937.
British Commonwealth Relations Conference - London, 1945. 1943/45 British Commonwealth Relations Conference:1943-1949.
Commonwealth Nations Conference 1948/49/
International Studies Conference 1937, 1940.
Montebello Conference 1943.

Sydney Conference, 1937/38.

General.
Reid, Escott - special memorandum - "The Future of the Institute" 1938.

Rockefeller Foundation, 1936/1944.

World Affairs.
Correspondence 1936-1943.
Volume 3.

World Affairs.

Conferences:
Atlantic City Conference, 1943/1946
Hot Springs Conference 1944/1945
Mont Tremblant Conference 1942.
Mont Tremblant Conference: Canadian Group
Ottawa Conference: Sir Frederick Whyte 1943.
Yosemite Conference 1935.

General.
India 1935/1949
International Research - D.P.E.Corbett 1932/1947

Personal.
Correspondence China, 1937/1950

MacKenzie, Norman A.M. 1911, 1927-1966. 66 cm.(volumes 4-7).
The majority of the MacKenzie papers deals with the Canadian Institute for International Affairs, while a small portion consists of general information and material relating to the Institute for Pacific Relations.
Canadian Institute for International Affairs, 1927-1928.

Volume 4.

Canadian Institute for International Affairs, 1927-1928.

Volume 5.

Canadian Institute for International Affairs, 1929-1930.

Volume 6.

Canadian Institute for International Affairs, 1931-1933.

Volume 7.

Canadian Institute for International Affairs, January-July 1934.

Volume 8.

15th Annual Study Conference - "Canada in a Two Power World", "Canada's Economic Future", "Canada and the Far East" 1948.

Volume 9

32nd Annual Study Conference - "Canada and the

Asian World" 1963/1965

Volume 11.

Institute for Pacific Relations - 4th General Session - Held in China 1931.Institute for Pacific Relations - Documentation , 1952. 1952.
Institute for Pacific Relations, 1953. 1951/1954

Institute for Pacific Relations - General 1951/1960.

Volume 12.

Conferences.

Institute for Pacific Relations - Proposal and Admissions of Councils 1932/1934

Institute for Pacific Relations - Review 1933/1934

Institute for Pacific Relations - Finances 1933/1934

Institute for Pacific Relations - Canadian Data Paper/Manuscript 1954.

Institute for Pacific Relations -1957, 1956/1957.

Institute for Pacific Relations - 1958, 1954/1958.

Institute for Pacific Relations - 1960, 1959/1961.

Volume 14.

General Conferences.

British Commonwealth/ U.S. Relations - Round Table 1945/1946.

Volume 18.

University of Guelph 1968. "Conference on China" 1966/1968

Volume 20.

General.

Pacific Affairs - University of British Columbia 1960/1962

Volume 21.

Institute for Current World Affairs, 1961-1974. 30 cm. (volumes 21-22)
There are ten file folders of newsletters concerning topical news items and information from countries around the world.

File 3 and File 4, Newsletters.

Hong Kong, 1962/1966.

Japan, 1966/1968.

File 5, File 6 and File 7, Newsletters.

Papua and New Guinea, 1967/1971.

File 8, File 9 and File 10, Newsletters.
Japan, 1973.
Thailand, 1973/1974.

China Inland Mission/Overseas Missionary Fellowship,
1058 Avenue Road,
Toronto, Ontario, M5N 2C56
Tel:(416)489-4660.

Background note.
Founded in 1865 by Dr. J.Hudson Taylor, the China Inland Mission(CIM) accepted Canadians as early as 1886, two years before expanding from England into North America. The largest mission in China, it eventually operated in 16 of the 18 provinces as well as Tibetan and Mongolian borderlands. It was particularly famous for its unrelenting conservatism in evangelistic methods and its insistance on missionaries adapting to Chinese living conditions. Due to its international character, Canadians were scattered throughout its China missions, although distinguishable concentrations appeared in Kwangsi, Kweichow, Szechuan andHunan as well as theChefoo School for missionaries ' children and the Shanghai business offices. Unfortunately for historians' purposes, many of their records were lost when the Mission evacuated from Shanghai in 1951. Further Canadian records were destroyed when theMission moved to its present Canadian premises in 1955.

Holdings
The main holdings of the China Inland Missions/Overseas Missionary Fellowship are located in England at the School of Oriental and African Studies, University of London. In North America the main holdings are at the Billy Graham Center Archives, Wheaton College, Wheaton, Illinois, with small collections at the United States

Headquarters office and the Canadian Headquarters in Missisauga, Ontario or Regional Office, Toronto, Ontario:

A. Minutes, financial records, correspondence and personnel files:

Personnel card list. Sketchy information on some 400 missionaries who registered as Canadians on initial departure.

B. Separate Collections of Papers:

The Chefoo School Archives. A small collection relating to Chefoo School for Missionaries' Children, orginally at Chefoo, later at Kuling and now in Japan, Malaysia and the Philippines. Includes class photographs since 1890s, and the bi-annual **The Chefusian** and also photographs of various school buildings. The Archives are on deposit.

C. Unpublished Manuscripts, Key Monographs and Memorabilia:
The library has about 800 books, including most of the China Inland Missions and Overseas Missionary Fellowship publications, as well as other older China-related books and books on other Asian countries.
In addition to the library volumes, the depository has a collection of Chinese Bibles, hymn books, devotional literature, language study texts and dictionaries compiled by missionary personnel.

4 volumes as follows: -
Taylor, J.Hudson, China's Spiritual Need and Claims.
Broomhall, B. A Missionary Band(The Cambridge Seven).
Broomhall, B., The Evangelization of the World(2 copies).

Handwritten record of all applicants to the China Inland Mission from 1887 to the early twentieth century.

D. Pamphlets and Periodicals.

A. **Occasional Papers,** 1866-1875.

B. **China's Spiritual Need and Claims,** 1887(Seventh edition).

C. **China's Millions**(Australian edition), 1932-1950.

D. **China's Million**s:(United Kindom), 1875-1952 (1901 issue missing).

The Millions, 1953-1952.
East Asia Millions, 1965-1976.

E. **China's Millions**(North America), 1891-1952

The Millions, 1953-1960.
East Asia Millions, 1961-1976.

F. **Young China**(United Kingdom), 1924-1950(1933-1936 and1946-1948 issues are missing).

G. **Young China**(North America), 1927-1948
Annual reports of the missions from 1910 to present.

H. **C.I.M. Monthly Notes,** 1896-1938
(September-December 1890 issues missing).

I. **C.I.M. Field Bulletin,** 1939-1952.
(December 1941, January-August 1942, January-July 1943, November-December 1944, March -December 1951, January-December 1952 issues missing).

J. **C.I.M.List of Missionaries,** 1895-1930.

K. **C.I.M. Directories,** 1931-1977 to present(list of members of the Mission)(July 1935, 1938, 1945, 1951, 1971, 1974 issues missing).

L. **C.I.M. Annual Report,** 1906-1959(1908-1909, 1922, 1926, 1939, 1946 issues missing).

M. **C.I.M. Code,** 1907 and 12929. (1922 Supplement).

N. **C.I.M. and O.M.F. Review,** 1951-1964.

O. **Principles and Practice. C.I.M. and O.M.F.** 1925, 1968, 1976.

P-S. Publications on Chinese language, dictionaries, atlases, Chinese customs.

T. Index for Story of the C.I.M. by Dr. Henry Frost.

U. First 40 chapters of the Story of the Beginning of the Work of the C.I.M. in North America, by Dr.Henry Frost.

V. List and Simple Details of North American C.I.M. Missionaries, 1887-1932.

W. Minutes of North America C.I.M. Council Meetings, 1897-1979.

Y. Photographs.

E. Audiovisual materials.

Three excellently captioned albums for 1890-1910, 1910-1915, and 1915-1920.
Sundry photographs, albums and curios from China particularly.

Chefoo School Archives.

A. **Chefoo Magazine,** 1908-1979.

B. Children of C.I.M. and O.M.F. Lists.

C.I.M.December 1892, January 1898, February 1900, August 1903, March 1906, September 1906, February 1908, December 1908, March 1910, March 1912, March 1914, July 1915, January 1918, January 1920, March 1922, August 1923, October 1925, November 1927, October 1929, June 1931, February 1933, February 1935, February1937, March 1939, March 1941, Decemeber 1945, December 1949.

O.M.F. January 1956, January 1958, January 1960, January 1962, January 1964, January 1966, January 1969, August 1973, September 1978.

C. Photographs of School groups, buildings etc. 1895-1978.

Frost, Henry.
Article:Henry Frost's Influence on Rowland V.Bingham(SIM)

Circular letters:The first four.
Correspondence from James Hudson Taylor.
Index to Frosts's **Story of the CIM.**
Report: Farewell to first North American Party.
Forming of First Council.

Michel, David.
William S. Clark of Sapporo, Pioneer educator and Church planter in Japan(Hokkaido), an account of an American educator(1826-1886) of Massachusetts. Thesis.

Shanghai Newsletters to Home Directors, Secretaries and Council Members, 1920s-1950s.
Hongkong Newsletters, 1950s.

Taylor, James Hudson.
Newspaper account of James Hudson Taylor's last day.
Circular on Special Support.
Correspondence:1888-1892.
Correspondence regarding his resignation as General Director and some points concerning the **Principles and Practice**.
Diary showing engagements and other matters.
Financial policy.

Metropolitan Toronto Reference Library,
789 Yonge Street,
Toronto, Ontario, M4V 2G8
Tel:(416)393-7000.

Mission clippings.
2 microfiches.
Clippings on missions in China, 1909--1925.i.3China:
MITCHELL

Mitchell, Dorothy Elizabeth, 1890-1966.
Papers. 1931-1945. 132 pieces and 169 photographs.
Dorothy Mitchell was a missionary with the Church of England in Peiping, and in Ta tung fu, Shensi, from 1931
to 1941. In 1941, when she was forced to leave because of the war, she moved to Victoria, British Columbia.
Photographs of China, chiefly of missionaries .

O'Brien, Henry, 1836-1931.
Papers. 1853-1931. 11 volumes, and 489 pieces, 28 cm.
Practiced law in Toronto for 60 years, and from 1865 to 1922 was editor of the **Canada law journal.** A member of St. Paul's Anglican Church, and especially interested in home and foreign missions . Member of the board of the China Inland Mission.
Includes correspondence from family and friends.
Correspondents include Rosalind Goforth, Violet S. Gillies and Marion Neale, all missionaries to China.

Archives of Ontario,
77 Grenville Street,
Toronto, Ontario, M7A 2R9.

Tel:(416)965-5317.

Immigrant communities in Toronto.

The archives collects materials related to immigrant communities in Ontario, including the Korean, Japanese,

Chinese and Vietnamese. These include some manuscript records on Japanese and Korean Churches in Canada, and several oral histories with related personal documentation.
MITCHELL

The records of the Attorney General and the Ontario Provincial Police contain immigrant records. Other records, as court records and business registrations could provide additional information.

Record group 9. Ministry of Industry, Trade and Industry.

Series 23: Ministry of Industry, Trade and Technology. Industry and Trade division, Executive director's general correspondence, 1972-1979, 27 cubic feet.

Should contain a few individual files relating to Ministry of Trade and Industry missions to Asian cities as well a few files relating to proposed Industry and technology joint ventures between Ontario and Asian companies.

Series 30: Ministry of Industry and Tourism, Industry and Trade division, program files, 1957-1978, 119 cubic feet.
Japan Trade Council, Asian Trade delegations, Ontario engineering projects in Asian countries, "product of prospecting missions " to Asia and the Ministry in Tokyo.

Series 33: Ministry of Industry and Tourism, Industry and Trade division, missions files, 1959-1979, 34 cubic feet.
May contain files relating to Ministry of Industry and Trade missions to Asian countries.

Series 34: Ministry of Trade and Tourism, Industry and Trade division, Marketing Branch, Marketing company files, 1961-1968, 6 cubic feet.
May contain files on Asian companies seeking to import and sell Ontario products.

Series 35: Ministry of Industry and Tourism, Industry and Trade division. Shows and Trade fair files, 1963-1978. 5 cubic feet.
May contain files on Asian Trade or industrial exhibitions.

Series 43: Ministry of Industry and Tourism, Industry division, Trade development branch, Trade missions files, 1974-1978, 3 cubic feet.
May contain files relating to Ministry Trade missions to Japan, Hong Kong, etc.

Series 92: Ministry of Industry and Trade, Industry division, entrepreneur case files, 1973-1983, 8 cubic feet. Includes files relating to Asia businessmen seeking to emigrate to Ontario and establish businesses.

Series 93: Ministry of Industry and Tourism, Industry division, Trade development branch, country information files, 1974-1978, 2 cubic feet.
Includes files relating to economic conditions in specific countries(including Asia countries), Trade fairs, proposed and existing company Trade ventures.
Series 96: Ministry of Industry and Trade, Industry and Trade division, Industry and Trade development branch- special areas, directors administrative files, 1977-1978, 7 cubic feet.
May include correspondence with Asian field offices of the Ministry of Industry and Trade and correspondence relating to Trade and Industry ventures.

Kuursela, Oliver.
Papers. MU 687. 2 in. 1937-1948.
Business papers, include list of Japanese internees working in World War II period.
ONTARIO

Wallace, Nathaniel Clarke.
Minister and Controller of Customs, December 1892 - March 1893. Customs were directly responsible for Chinese immigration, 1885-1893.

**Archives of the Presbyterian Church of Canada,
Knox College,
59 St. George Street,
Toronto, Ontario, M5S 1P6.
Tel:(416)595-1297.**

Presbyterian Church in Canada. General Board of Missions/ Board of World Mission. Foreign Missions Collection, 1880-1980.

Presbyterian Church in Taiwan.

Box 1.

File l01-A-1. 1957-1980.
Presbyterian Church in Taiwan General Assembly. Annual Reports, Correspondence, Lectures concerning the Presbyterian Church in Taiwan (Photographs removed to Graphics Collection).

File 101-A-2 .1972.
Presbyterian Church in Taiwan.
General Assembly Agenda, Worship, Order of Business for General Assembly 1972 (Illustrated).

File 101-A-3. 1972-1980.
Presbyterian Church in Taiwan.
General Secretary Correspondence.

File 101-A-4. 1960-1971.
Presbyterian Church in Taiwan.
General Secretary Correspondence.

Box 2.

File 101-A-5. 1969-1980.
Presbyterian Church in Taiwan.
Assistant General Secretary Correspondence.

File 101-A-6. 1964-1968.
Presbyterian Church in Taiwan.
Assistant General Secretary Correspondence (Photograph removed to Graphics Collection).

File 101-A-7. 1963.
Presbyterian Church in Taiwan.
Assistant General Secretary Correspondence.

File 101-A-8. 1967-1970.
Presbyterian Church in Taiwan.
Treasurer Correspondence.

File 101-A-9. 1967.
Presbyterian Church in Taiwan.
Membership in World Council of Churches.
"Statement Concerning the Nature of the Church and Membership of the Presbyterian Church of Formosa in the World Council of Churches".

File 101-A-10. 1964.
Presbyterian Church in Taiwan.
Delegation of August 1964 Correspondence re: Visitors from Taiwan.

File 101-A-11. 1961-1965.
Presbyterian Church in Taiwan.
General Assembly Centenary Plans, Special gifts, History of the Presbyterian Church in Taiwan.

File 101-A-12. 1955-1958.
Presbyterian Church in Taiwan.
General Assembly: Planning Committee Correspondence, Proposals of the Planning Committee.

Box 3.

File 101-B-1. 1956-1976.
Presbyterian Church in Taiwan North Synod Correspondence, Reports, General Assembly material for 1956-1958.

File 101-C-1. 1933-1937.
Presbyterian Church in Taiwan.
Presbytery of North Formosa Correspondence, Minutes.

File 101-C-2.1962-1965.
Presbyterian Church in Taiwan.
Christian Mobile Clinics Three booklets re the Christian Mobile Clinics operated by the Presbyteries (Illustrated).

File 101-D-1. 1927-1932.

Presbyterian Church in Taiwan.
North Formosa Mission Council Minutes.

File 101-D-2. 1933-1937.
Presbyterian Church in Taiwan
North Formosa Mission Council Minutes.

File 101-D-3. 1938-1951.
Presbyterian Church in Taiwan.
North Formosa Mission Council Minutes.

File 101-D-4. 1952-1957.
Presbyterian Church in Taiwan.
North Formosa Mission Council Minutes.
Box 4.

File 101-D-5. 1960-1966.
Presbyterian Church in Taiwan.
Canadian Committee of Mission Council Minutes.

File 101-D-6. 1973-1980.
Presbyterian Church in Taiwan.
Canadian Committee of Mission Council: Secretary Correspondence, Scattered copies of minutes from Canadian Committee.

File 101-D-7. 1965-1972.
Presbyterian Church in Taiwan.
Canadian Committee of Mission Council: Secretary. Correspondence. Scattered copies of minutes from Canadian Committee (Architectural drawings of new construction of MacKay Memorial Hospital removed)

File 101-D-8. 1958-1964.
Presbyterian Church in Taiwan.
Canadian Committee of Mission Council: Secretary. Correspondence. Scattered copies of minutes from Canadian Committee (Photographs removed to Photo Collection).

Box 5.

File 101-D-9. 1955-1957.
Presbyterian Church in Taiwan.

Canadian Committee of Mission Council: Secretary Correspondence.

File 101-D-10. 1950-1954.
Presbyterian Church in Taiwan.
Canadian Committee of Mission Council: Secretary Correspondence.

File 101-D-11. 1950-1965.
Presbyterian Church in Taiwan.
Canadian Committee of Mission Council: Treasurer Correspondence.

Box 6.

File 101-D-12. 1955-1970.
Presbyterian Church in Taiwan.
Canadian Committee of Mission Council: Chairman Correspondence.

File 101-D-13. 1957-1960.
Presbyterian Church in Taiwan.
"Aims and Functions of the Orientation Committee" Report of Mission Council outlining direction and policy.

File 101-D-14. 1954-1955.
Presbyterian Church in Taiwan.
Mission Council: Theological Education Committee. Correspondence, Report, Material utilized to generate this report Architectural drawings removed).

File 101-D-15. 1963-1965.
Presbyterian Church in Taiwan.
English Committee of Mission Council Minutes.
File 101-D-16. 1954-1960.
Presbyterian Church in Taiwan.
Joint Meetings of Missionaries Minutes, Constitution of the North Formosa Mission Council.

File 101-D-17. 1958-1978.
Presbyterian Church in Taiwan.
Mission Council Correspondence, Minutes.

File 101-D-18. 1954-1962.
Presbyterian Church in Taiwan.
Taiwan Missionary Fellowship Pamphlets, Surveys.

File 101-D-19. 1944.
Presbyterian Church in Taiwan.
Committee on Church and Industrial Society. Pamphlet "Report of the Student in Industrial Society".

File 101-D-20. 1959-1970.
Presbyterian Church in Taiwan.
Mountain Work. Correspondence, Reports, Minutes. (Consultative Group for Translation into Tribal Languages), Three pamphlets (Illustrated).

File 101-D-21. 1930-1935;1960-1968.
Presbyterian Church in Taiwan.
Property Committee. Correspondence, Reports, Minutes.

Box 7.

File 101-D-22. 1977-1980.
Presbyterian Church in Taiwan.
Personnel Committee. Correspondence, Minutes, Reports.

File 101-D-23. 1973-1976.
Presbyterian Church in Taiwan.
Personnel Committee Correspondence, Minutes, Reports.

File 101-D-24. 1959-1972.
Presbyterian Church in Taiwan.
Personnel Committee. Correspondence, Minutes, Reports.

File 101-D-25. 1973-1980.
Presbyterian Church in Taiwan.
Consultative Committee. Correspondence, Minutes, Reports.

File 101-D-26. 1968-1972.
Presbyterian Church in Taiwan.
Consultative Committee. Correspondence, Minutes, Reports (Photograph removed to Graphics Collection).

File 101-D27. 1962-1968.
Presbyterian Church in Taiwan. Consultative Committee. Correspondence, Minutes, Reports.

File 101-D-28. 1962-1969.
Presbyterian Church in Taiwan.
Ecumenical Consultative Committee. Minutes, Correspondence.

File 101-D-29. 1956-1965.
Presbyterian Church in Taiwan.
Joint Policy Committee (Relations between Churches and Missionaries) Reports.

File 101-D-30. 1961-1963.
Presbyterian Church in Taiwan.
Consultation of Secretaries (Secretaries of Boards working with the Presbyterian Church in Taiwan) Minutes, Correspondence.

File 101-D-31. 1933-1934.
Presbyterian Church in Taiwan.
Canadian General Assembly Committee re Formosa Correspondence.

File 101-D-32. 1968-1978.
Presbyterian Church in Taiwan.
Scholarship Committee. Correspondence, Applications (Photographs removed to Graphics Collection).

Box 9.(no box 8 noted in finding aid)

File 101-E-1. 1961-1981.
Presbyterian Church in Taiwan.
Changhua Christian Hospital. Correspondence, Newsletters, Constitution, Financial statements, Histories, Pamphlet: "Changhua Christian Hospital 1896-1981"(Illustrated).

File 101-E-2. 1966-1973.
Presbyterian Church in Taiwan. MacKay Memorial Hospital:General Correspondence, Reports (Photographs removed to Graphics Collection) (Architectural drawings removed).

File 101-E-4. 1958-1960.
Presbyterian Church in Taiwan. MacKay Memorial Hospital. C.H.Holleman, M.D. Correspondence.

File 101-E-5. 1956-1960.
Presbyterian Church in Taiwan. MacKay Memorial Hospital. New Staff Correspondence.

Box 10.

File 101-E-6. 1969.
Presbyterian Church in Taiwan. MacKay Memorial Hospital. Expansion Plans Reports, Program outline (Photograph removed to Graphics Collection) (All Architectural drawings removed).

File 101-E-7. 1967.
Memorial Hospital: re: Cobalt Teletherapy Unit. Correspondence.

File 101-E-8.
Presbyterian Church in Taiwan. MacKay Memorial Hospital. Publications and Reports, Booklets outlining the history and work of MacKay Memorial Hospital, various years, many illustrated, includes reports from 1884-1885 and 1888.

File 101-E-9. 1953-1974.
Presbyterian Church in Taiwan. Happy Mount Leprosy Colony Correspondence, Reports, Article re: burial of Dr. Gushue-Taylor (1954), Pamphlet "Stretch Forth thine Hand", Booklet commemorating the 40th anniversary of Happy Mount Leprosy Colony (includes an Order of Service).

File 101-E-10. 1962-1967.
Presbyterian Church in Taiwan. Taiwan Christian Service Correspondence, Reports.

File 101-E-11. 1967-1968.
Presbyterian Church in Taiwan. University Christian Service Centre, Tainan Correspondence, Report, Outline of intent.

File 101-E-12.
Presbyterian Church in Taiwan Taipei Theological College Correspondence (Architectural drawings removed).

File 101-E-13. 1955.
Presbyterian Church in Taiwan. Taipei Bible School. Correspondence, Reports. (Photographs of Architectural drawings removed to Graphics Collection).

File 101-E-14. 1961-1963.
Presbyterian Church in Taiwan. Taipei Language Institute Correspondence.

File 101-E-15. 1955-1974.
Presbyterian Church in Taiwan. Hsin Chu Bible School Correspondence, Minutes, Reports.

Box 11.

File 101-E-16. 1928-1956.
Presbyterian Church in Taiwan. Tamsui School Property Correspondence, Legal Documents (Photographs removed to Graphics Collection).

File 101-E-17. 1957.
Presbyterian Church in Taiwan. Tam Kang Middle School Correspondence, Pamphlets (Illustrated) (Photographs removed to Graphics Collection) (Map of school grounds removed).

File 101-E-18. 1958-1979.
Presbyterian Church in Taiwan Tainan Theological College. Correspondence, Reports, Newsletters, Illustrated Pamphlets, Booklets, Postcard (Architectu

File 101-E-19. 1963-1980.
Presbyterian Church in Taiwan. Yu-Shan Theological Institute (also known as Mount Morrison) Correspondence, Reports, Illustrated Newsletters,

Booklet "Preparing Workers for Mountain Churches in Taiwan", Postcard, Illustrated Pamphlets, 20th Anniversary booklet, Information re: Eileen Black (Artist's rendition removed) (Architectural drawing removed).

Box 12.

File 101-E-20. 1958-1980.
Presbyterian Church in Taiwan. Taiwan Theological College. Correspondence, Minutes, Reports Newsletter, Illustrated Booklets, (Photographs removed to Graphics Collection) (Architectural drawings removed).

File 101-E-21. 1958-1979.
Presbyterian Church in Taiwan. Tunghai University. Correspondence, Reports, Illustrated Pamphlets and Booklets.

File 101-E-22. 1967-1972.
Presbyterian Church in Taiwan. Tamsui Institute for Business Administration Correspondence, Illustrated Pamphlet (Photo removed to Photo Collection) (Architectural drawings removed).

File 101-F-1. 1971-1980.
Presbyterian Church in Taiwan. Interboard Finance Correspondence.

File 101-F-2. 1967-1980.
Presbyterian Church in Taiwan. Canadian Committee: Finance Correspondence, Financial statements.

File 101-F-3. 1970-1980.
Presbyterian Church in Taiwan. Church Finance: General Correspondence.

Box 13.

File 101-F-4. 1967-1970.
Presbyterian Church in Taiwan. Financial Statements Reports.

File 101-F-5. 1967-1966.
Presbyterian Church in Taiwan. Financial Statements Reports, Correspondence.

File 101-F-6. 1960-1961.
Presbyterian Church in Taiwan. Church of Christ in China Funds Correspondence, Financial reports.

File 101-F-7. 1957-1960
Presbyterian Church in Taiwan. Canadian Aid to China Trust Fund Correspondence.

File 101-F-8. 1966-1967.
Presbyterian Church in Taiwan. Field and Mission Finance Correspondence.

File 101-F-9. 1956-1960.
Presbyterian Church in Taiwan. Purchase of Vehicles Correspondence.

File 101-F-10. 1956-1962.
Presbyterian Church in Taiwan. Budgets Correspondence, Financial Statements.
File 101-F-11. 1946-1950.
Presbyterian Church in Taiwan. Finance: Li Thian Su: Correspondence.

Box 14.

File 101-F-12. 1968-1980.
Presbyterian Church in Taiwan. Special Gifts Correspondence, Reports.

File 101-F-13. 1959-1968.
Presbyterian Church in Taiwan. Special Gifts Correspondence, Reports (includes centennial gifts).

File 101-F-14. 1963-1966.
Presbyterian Church in Taiwan. Special Gifts: Youth Centre Correspondence.

File 101-F-15. 1965.
Presbyterian Church in Taiwan. Special Gifts: Stone Churches Correspondence.

File 101-F-16. 1961-1965.
Presbyterian Church in Taiwan. Special Gifts: Library Fund Correspondence.

File 101-G-1. 1964-1972.
Presbyterian Church in Taiwan. Caldwell, Georgine. Correspondence, Personal Reports.

*** NOTE: All personnel material i.e. medical reports have been removed to the Head Offices of the Presbyterian Church in Canada.

File 101-G-3. 1956-1960.
Presbyterian Church in Taiwan. Copland, E. Bruce. Correspondence, Reports, Newsletters, Informational Material collected by Bruce Copland (Photo removed to Graphics Collection).

Box 15.

File 101-G-4. 1956-1972. Presbyterian Church in Taiwan. Costerus, Chris correspondence, Reports.

File 101-G-5. 1949.
Presbyterian Church in Taiwan. deGroot, L.L. correspondence.

File 101-G-6. 1927-1967.
Presbyterian Church in Taiwan. Dickson, James. (Material in this file was collected by Dr. W.H.Fuller and donated to the Board of World Missions on August 23, 1968) Correspondence, Newsletters, Reports, Copy of Memorial Service - June 25, 1968, Copy of booklet "Stranger than Fiction" (Illustrated) (Photographs removed to Graphics Collection).

File 101-G-7. 1952-1965.
Presbyterian Church in Taiwan. Dickson, James. Correspondence, Newsletters, Pamphlets, Applications from Taiwanese Students (Photos removed to Photo Collection) (File includes correspondence from Dr. Gushue-Taylor).

File 101-G-8. 1938-1951.
Presbyterian Church in Taiwan. Dickson, James Correspondence, Newsletters (File includes correspondence from G.W. MacKay)

File 101-G-9. 1965-1972.
Presbyterian Church in Taiwan Ellis, H. Ted. Correspondence, Newsletters.

Box 16.

File 101-G-10. 1962-1972.
Presbyterian Church in Taiwan. Embree, Bernard L. M. Correspondence, Newsletters.

File 101-G-11. 1962-1972.
Presbyterian Church in Taiwan. Gamble, Louise. Correspondence, Reports.

File 101-G-12. 1963-1973.
Presbyterian Church in Taiwan. Garvin, M.L. Correspondence, Reports, Tribute to Mary E. Garvin.

File 101-G-13. 1959-1972.
Presbyterian Church in Taiwan. Geddes, Jack. Correspondence, Christmas Card(Illustrated).

File 101-G-14. 1957-1969.
Presbyterian Church in Taiwan. Gordon, S. Moore. Correspondence, Newsletters, Newsclippings (Illustrated).

File 101-G-15. 1941-1955.
Presbyterian Church in Taiwan. Gushue-Taylor, G. Correspondence (Including correspondence re Gushue-Taylor Memorial Building).

File 101-G-16. 1941-1951.
Presbyterian Church in Taiwan. MacKay, G.W. Correspondence, Reports.

File 101-G-17. 1950-1962.
Presbyterian Church in Taiwan. MacMillan, Hugh. Correspondence, Newsletters, Reports, Newsclippings (Illustrated).

File 101-G-18. 1945-1949.
Presbyterian Church in Taiwan. MacMillan, Hugh. Correspondence, Reports (Photographs removed to Graphics Collection).

Box 17.

File 101-G-19. 1953-1961.
Presbyterian Church in Taiwan. MacMillan, Hugh booklets authored by H. MacMillan: "The Church of the Iona Stone" (Illustrated), "Youth in a Younger Church" (Illustrated), "Builder Abroad"(Illustrated), "Then Till Now in Formosa"(Illustrated).

File 101-G-20. 1960-1963.
Presbyterian Church in Taiwan. Malcolm, George. Correspondence, Newsletter (Illustrated).
File 101-G-21. 1958-1977.
Presbyterian Church in Taiwan. McGill, Clare. Correspondence, Booklets (Written in Tayal).

File 101-G-22. 1965-1972.
Presbyterian Church in Taiwan. Petrie, Diane. Correspondence, Reports, - Newsclippings (Illustrated) (Photograph removed to Graphics Collection).

File 101-G-23. 1970-1972.
Presbyterian Church in Taiwan. Randall, Joy M.R. Correspondence, Newsletters.

File 101-G-24. 1960-1965.
Presbyterian Church in Taiwan. Roberts, Thomas. Correspondence, Newsletters.

File 101-G-25. 1969-1972.
Presbyterian Church in Taiwan. Sutherland, James. Correspondence, Reports.

File 101-G-26. 1969-1971.
Presbyterian Church in Taiwan. Taylor, Isabel. Correspondence.

File 101-G-27. 1968-1969.
Presbyterian Church in Taiwan. Welsh, Wilma. Correspondence, Newsletters, Designation Service (Illustrated).

Box 18.

File 101-G-28. 1968-1969.
Presbyterian Church in Taiwan. Williams, Gordon. Correspondence.

File 101-G-29. 1959-1967.
Presbyterian Church in Taiwan. Wilson, Donald J. Correspondence, Newsletters.

File 101-H-1. 1970-1980.
Presbyterian Church in Taiwan. General Correspondence, Reports (Photographs removed to Graphics Collection).

File 101-H-2. 1954-1968.
Presbyterian Church in Taiwan. General Correspondence, Reports, Obituary for Rev. T.W. Wu. (Illustrated).

File 101-H-3. 1954-1968.
Presbyterian Church in Taiwan. General Correspondence(Photograph removed to Graphics Collection) .

Box 19.

File 101-H-4. 1927-1974.
Presbyterian Church in Taiwan. General Reports. Miscellaneous reports on various topics, Histories of Mission work in Taiwan.

File 101-H-5. 1955-1975.
Presbyterian Church in Taiwan. Formosa Confidential. Reports, Correspondence, Informational Pamphlets re Taiwanese Self Determination.

File 101-H-6. 1961-1969
Presbyterian Church in Taiwan. Political Data. Reports, Correspondence, Informational Material re Taiwanese Self Determination.

File 101-H-7. 1980.
Presbyterian Church in Taiwan. Our National Fate. Correspondence, Reports, Informational Material particularly concerning the arrest of Rev. Kau of the Presbyterian Church in Taiwan.

File 101-H-8. 1971-1979.
Presbyterian Church in Taiwan. Our National Fate. Correspondence, Reports, Informational Material.

Box 20.

File 101-H-9. 1954-1959.
Presbyterian Church in Taiwan. Dr. Vicedom: Aboriginal Study Correspondence.

File 101-H-10. 1957.
Presbyterian Church in Taiwan. Dr. Vicedom: Preliminary Report Correspondence, Report.

File 101-H-11. 1958-1960.
Presbyterian Church in Taiwan. Dr. Vicedom: Manuscript Revisions Correspondence, Reports.

File 101-H-12.
Presbyterian Church in Taiwan.
Dr. Vicedom: Untitled Manuscript.

File 101-H-13. 1957-1961.
Presbyterian Church in Taiwan.
Dr. Vicedom: "Faith that Moves Mountains" Correspondence, Report, Manuscript.

File 101-H-14. 1967.
Presbyterian Church in Taiwan. Dr. Vicedom: Correspondence re: Manuscript Correspondence, Reports.

File 101-H-15.
Presbyterian Church in Taiwan. Dr. Vicedom: Original Copy Manuscript .

File 101-H-16. 1953-1975.
Presbyterian Church in Taiwan. Reports.

File 101-H-17. 1964-1965.
Presbyterian Church in Taiwan. Centenary Information on events, Histories, Booklets.

ile 101-H-18. 1953-1955.
Presbyterian Church in Taiwan. North Formosa Mission. Reports, Histories.

File 101-H-19. 1977-1980.

Presbyterian Church in Taiwan. Taiwan Property Correspondence.
Box 21.

File 101-H-20. 1965-1972.
Presbyterian Church in Taiwan. New Century Mission Movement. Correspondence, Reports, Untitled Manuscript (Photographs removed to Graphics Collection).

File 101-H-21. 1972.
Presbyterian Church in Taiwan. Taiwan Centennial: Chairman's Visit Correspondence, Report.

File 101-H-22. 1972.
Presbyterian Church in Taiwan. G.L. MacKay Centennial Service. Correspondence, Copies of Commemorative Articles.

File 101-H-23. 1975.
Presbyterian Church in Taiwan. The Spirit Movement among Tayal Churches in Taiwan Report paper prepared by Rev. Clare McGill.

File 2101-H-24. 1967.
Presbyterian Church in Taiwan. Relationship to World Council of Churches Correspondence, Statement.

File 101-H-25. 1958.
Presbyterian Church in Taiwan. Furniture Inventory Correspondence.

File 101-H-26. 1952-1965.
Presbyterian Church in Taiwan. Visitations to Taiwan Correspondence, Itineraries, Reports (Photographs from E.H. Johnson's Trip in 1961 removed to Photo Collection).

File 101-H-27. 1954-1975.
Presbyterian Church in Taiwan. General Material on Education Correspondence, Reports, Curriculum, Conference Materials.

File 101-H-28. 1940-1959.
Presbyterian Church in Taiwan. Leprosy Work. Correspondence, Reports, Histories: (Happy Mount Leprosy Colony) (Taiwan Leprosy Relief Association) (Photographs removed to Graphics Collection).

File 101-H-29. 1960-1970.
Presbyterian Church in Taiwan. Material on Medical Work Correspondence, Reports, Survey.

File 101-H-30. 1960.
Presbyterian Church in Taiwan. Women's Work in North Formosa. Reports on Women's position in the Church.

File 101-H-31.
Presbyterian Church in Taiwan. Social Work Information on Social Work in Taiwan (Canada House, Christian Centre, Kaoshiung Life Line).

Box 22.

File 101-H-32. 1964.
Presbyterian Church in Taiwan. Pilgrim's Progress Report on Theatre Play: "Pilgrim's Progress" (Photographs removed to Graphics Collection).

File 101-H-33.
Presbyterian Church in Taiwan. Formosan Christian Youth Fellowship Newsletter.

File 101-H-34. 1956-1966.
Presbyterian Church in Taiwan. Jackson, Harold M. Correspondence.

File 101-H-35. 1941-1942.
Presbyterian Church in Taiwan. Hermanson, Hildur K. Correspondence and Reports on her work.

File 101-H-36. 1941-1942.
Presbyterian Church in Taiwan. Stevens' Trust. Correspondence re: Dr. E. Steven's Trust Fund.

File 101-I-1. 1947-1962.
Presbyterian Church in Taiwan. Newsletters. Newsletters (Note: Newsletters may also be located in the author's personnel file.).

File 101-I-2. 1970-1986.
Presbyterian Church in Taiwan. **Rice Bowl.** Newsletter published by the Canadian Missionaries in Taiwan.

File 101-I-3. 1963-1972.
Presbyterian Church in Taiwan. China: News and Views Newsletter.

File 101-I-4. 1963.
Presbyterian Church in Taiwan. Bulletin of Taiwan Evangelical Fellowship. Newsletter. One Issue.

File 101-I-5. 1967.
Presbyterian Church in Taiwan. Formosa:Newsletter - One Issue.

File 101-I-6. 1973-1978.
Presbyterian Church in Taiwan. Taiwan Church Growth Bulletin Newsletter published by the Taiwan Church Growth Society.

File 101-I-7. 1956-1960.
Presbyterian Church in Taiwan. Taiwan Christian Year Book Survey of Christian Movement in Taiwan - Two Issues.

File 101-I-8.
Presbyterian Church in Taiwan. General Information re: The Presbyterian Mission in Taiwan Pamphlets, Booklets.

File 101-I-9.
Presbyterian Church in Taiwan. General Information re: Christianity in Taiwan.

GUYANA

Presbyterian Mission in British Guyana is part of the Assembly of Reformed Churches, commonly referred as the C.A.R.C.

Box 23.

File 102-A-1. 1957-1973.
C.A.R.C. Clerk Correspondence, Reports from Caribbean Assembly of Reformed Churches (C.A.R.C.).

File 102-A-2. 1964-1973.
C.A.R.C. General Assembly Minutes, Reports, Correspondence, Copies of the Constitution.

File 102-A-3. 1964-1968.
C.A.R.C. General Assembly Minutes, Reports, Correspondence, Constitution (Photographs removed to Graphics Collection).

File 102-A-4. 1965.
C.A.R.C. E.H. Johnson Visit Correspondence, Report (Photographs removed to Graphics Collection).

File 102-A-5. 1965-1970.
C.A.R.C. Grant material. Correspondence.

Box 24.

File 102-B-1. 1966-1980.
C.A.R.C. Synod of Trinidad and Grenada. Correspondence.

File 102-B-2. 1967-1968.

C.A.R.C. Trinidad Centenary 1968. Correspondence, Newspaper clippings.

File 102-B-3.
C.A.R.C. Trinidad: Publications and Reports. Report from 1887, "The Presbyterian Mission" (1911), "The Trinidad Presbyterian" (1912), 100th Anniversary of Susamacher Presbyterian Church (1974).
File 102-B-4. 1964-1978.
C.A.R.C. Synod of Jamaica and Grand Cayman. Correspondence, Reports, Minutes.
File 102-C-1. 1962-1967.
C.A.R.C. Joint Council of Presbyterian Churches in British Guyana .Correspondence, Draft of Constitution, Minutes.
File 102-C-2. 1967.
C.A.R.C. British Guyana: Joint Presbytery and Mission Council Meetings. Minutes.

File 102-C-3. 1946-1962.
C.A.R.C. Canadian Presbytery in British Guyana. Correspondence, Minutes.

File 102-C-4. 1961-1966.
C.A.R.C. Presbytery of Guyana. Minutes of Presbytery and related Committees.

File 102-C-5. 1969-1980.
C.A.R.C. Presbytery of Guyana. General Correspondence.

File 102-C-6.
C.A.R.C. Presbytery of Guyana. Information Copy of Constitution, Church Dedication Service.

File 102-C-7. 1961-1967.
C.A.R.C. Guyana Presbyterian Church. Minutes of Presbytery and related Committees (See also File 102-C-11).

Box 26.

File 102-C-8. 1972-1980.
C.A.R.C. Guyana Presbyterian Church: Clerk. Correspondence, Reports, Minutes.

File 102-C-9. 1962-1971.
C.A.R.C. Guyana Presbyterian Church: Clerk. Correspondence, Reports, Minutes.

File 102-C-10. 1969-1970.
C.A.R.C. Guyana Presbyterian Church: Treasurer. Correspondence, Reports.

File 102-C-11. 1964-1980.
C .A.R.C . Guyana Presbyterian Church: General. Correspondence Correspondence, Reports, Minutes.

File 102-C-12. 1970.
C.A.R.C. Guyana Presbyterian Church: re Administrative Handover Minutes.

File 102-C-13. 1954-1967.
C.A.R.C. Statement of Relations between Presbyterian Church in Canada and the Guyana Presbyterian Church. Drafts and Copies of Statement, Copy of Statement re Canadian Missionary Goals in Guyana.

File 102-C-14.
C.A.R.C. Presbyterian Church in Guyana: General Information. Copies of "News and Views", History, Formal handing over Ceremony (1974).
Draft Manual for the Guyana Presbyterian Church.

Box 26.

File 102-D-1. 1958-1963.
C.A.R.C. Consultative Assembly. Reports, Statements, Correspondence, Minutes.

File 102-D-2. 1968-1977.
C.A.R.C. Guyana: Scholarship Committee.

Correspondence (See also 102-D-3).

File 102-D-3.1956-1973.
C.A.R.C. Guyana: Personnel Committee. Correspondence (Includes scholarship materials i.e. forms, guidelines).

File 102-D-4. 1957-1958.
C.A.R.C. Guyana: Property Committee. Correspondence, Report.

File 102-D-5. 1962-1970.
C.A.R.C. Guyana Mission Council: Secretary. Correspondence.

File 102-D-6. 1955-1961.
C.A.R.C. Guyana Mission Council: Secretary. Correspondence.

File 102-D-7. 1950-1954.
C.A.R.C. Guyana Mission Council: Secretary. Correspondence (Photographs removed to Graphics Collection) (Architectural drawings removed).

Box 27.

File 102-D-8. 1941-1949.
C.A.R.C. Guyana Mission Council: Secretary. Correspondence.

File 102-D-9. 1955-1965.
C.A.R.C. Guyana Mission Council: Chairman. Correspondence, Reports (Architectural drawings removed).

File 102-D-10. 1950-1970.
C.A.R.C. Guyana Mission Council: Treasurer. Correspondence, Reports.

File 102-D-11. 1886-1961.
C.A.R.C. Guyana Mission Council. Reports from the

Mission Council and the Canadian Presbyterian Mission.

File 102-D-12. 1915-1920.
C.A.R.C. Guyana Mission Council: Minutes.

Box 28.

File 102-D-13. 1921-1925.
C.A.R.C. Guyana Mission Council. Minutes (fragile).

File 102-D-14. 1926-1929.
C.A.R.C. Guyana Mission Council. Minutes(fragile).

File 102-D-15. 1930-1939.
C.A.R.C. Guyana Mission Council. Minutes (fragile).

File 102-D-16. 1940-1949.
C.A.R.C. Guyana Mission Council: Minutes.(fragile).

Box 29.

File 102-D-17. 1950-1956.
C.A.R.C. Guyana Mission Council. Minutes.

File 102-D-18. 1957-1959.
C.A.R.C. Guyana Mission Council. Minutes.
File 102-D-19. 1960-1967.
C.A.R.C. Guyana Mission Council. Minutes.

Box 30.

File 102-E-1. 1974-1980.
C.A.R.C. U.T.C.W.I.: (Union Theological College of the West Indies) Correspondence, Reports, Booklets, Newsletters.

File 102-E-2. 1967-1973.
C.A.R.C. U.T.C.W.I.: Correspondence, Reports, Dedication Service.

File 102-E-3. 1964-1966.
C.A.R.C. U.T.C.W.I. Correspondence, Reports.

File 102-E-4. 1967-1975.
C.A.R.C. U.T.C.W.I. Minutes, Reports (From Board of Governors, various Committees and Conferences).

File 102-E-5. 1959-1966.
C.A.R.C. U.T.C.W.I. Minutes, Reports (From Board of Governors, various Committees and Conferences) (Includes material from the Union Theological Seminary) (Architectural drawings removed).

Box 31.

File 102-E-6. 1978-1980.
C.A.R.C. U.T.C.W.I.: Pitamber Project. Correspondence re: Dr. Dayanand Pitamber.

File 102-E-7. 1955-1964.
C.A.R.C. Union Theological Seminary: Dr. W. Farris. Correspondence, Reports.

File 102-E-8. 1954-1958.
C.A.R.C. Guyana: Bethel College. Correspondence, Reports (Prepared primarily by Dr. W. Farris).

File 102-E-9. 1944-1967.
C.A.R.C. Guyana: Berbice High School. Correspondence, Reports, Financial statements, Histories (Architectural drawings removed).

File 102-E-10. 1957-1958.
C.A.R.C. Guyana: Berbice High School. Correspondence, Reports re: Special discussions in June 1958.

Box 32.

File 102-E-11. 1976-1980.
C.A.R.C. Guyana Extension Seminary. Correspondence, Reports.

File 102-E-12. 1965-1974.
C.A.R.C. Guyana: St. Columba House. Correspondence.

File 102-E-13. 1973-1976.
C.A.R.C. Trinidad: St. Andrew's Theological College. Correspondence.

File 102-E-14. 1966-1976.
C.A.R.C. University of Guyana. Reports.

File 102-E-15. 1962-1964.
C.A.R.C. Better Hope Training Centre Correspondence, Reports (Architectural drawings removed).

File 102-E-16. 1960-1963.
C.A.R.C. Primary School Material. Correspondence, Reports, Statements.

File 102-E-17. 1943-1949.
C.A.R.C. Guyana: Corentyne High School. Correspondence.

File 102-F-1. 1973-1977.
C.A.R.C. Guyana: Finance. Correspondence.

File 102-F-2. 1938-1970.
C.A.R.C. Guyana: Financial Statements. Correspondence, Statements.

Box 33.

File 102-F-3. 1960-1980.
C.A.R.C. Guyana: Treasurer. Correspondence, Reports.

File 102-F-4. 1972-1980.
C.A.R.C. Guyana: Special Gifts Correspondence.

File 102-F-5. 1966.
C.A.R.C. Missionary Finance. Correspondence.

File 102-F-6. 1967-1968.
C.A.R.C. Guyana: Requisition Sheets Financial Statements.

File 102-F-7. 1956.
C.A.R.C. Guyana: Pension Plan Correspondence.

File 102-F-8. 1950-1951.
C.A.R.C. Furniture Inventory.

File 102-F-9. 1958-1964.
C.A.R.C Guyana: Statistics and Estimates Reports.

File 102-F-10. 1962-1965.
C.A.R.C. Guyana: Income Tax Data. Correspondence.

File 102-G-1. 1971-1972.
C.A.R.C. Buckhurst, Joan. Correspondence, Report.

File 102-G-2. 1953-1964.
C.A.R.C. Cropper, Grace. Correspondence, Obituary for J.B. Cropper (n.d.).

File 102-G-3. 1959-1960.
C.A.R.C. Crozier, Murray. Correspondence.

File 102-G-4. 1948-1961.
C.A.R.C. DeCastro, Clement. Correspondence.

File 102-G-5. 1941-1945.
C.A.R.C. Dickson, James. Correspondence.

Box 34.

File 102-G-6. 1956-1961.
C.A.R.C. Duncanson, Robert G. Correspondence, Newsclippings.

File 102-G-7. 1968-1971.
C.A.R.C. Dunn, Zander. Correspondence, Newsletters, **A Short History of St. Paul's Presbyterian Church.**

File 102-G-8. 1941-1947.
C.A.R.C. Elder, John. Correspondence, Reports.

File 102-G-9. 1948-1962.
C.A.R.C. Elder, John. Correspondence, Reports, Service of Appreciation (Photographs removed to Photo Collection).

File 102-G-10. 1956-1966.
C.A.R.C. Farris, W.J.S. Correspondence, Reports.

File 102-G-11. 1928-1930.
C.A.R.C. Fisher, R. Gibson. Reports from Essequebo Field (Illustrated with Photos of various Mission Buildings, Schools, Missionaries, Catechists, Natives and sights of the field. Areas include: Hamburg, Golden Fleece and Suddie - *Note: All photographs remain in the reports.) (See also File 102-I-18).

Box 35.

File 102-G.12. 1959-1961.
C.A.R.C. Glazier, Kenneth M. Correspondence.

File 102-G-13. 1956-1957.
C.A.R.C. Hamilton-Pollard, D.W. Correspondence, Reports.

File 102-G-14. 1968--1973.
C.A.R.C. , Johnston, Geoffrey. Correspondence, Reports.

File 102-G-15. 1956-1966.
C.A.R.C. MacDonald, Alexander S. Correspondence, Reports, Newsletters.

File 102-G-16. 1960.
C.A.R.C. MacDonald, Alexander S. Thesis by Alexander MacDonald "A Divided Church in a Divided Nation: British Guyana" (*Loose Pages - Handle with Care*).

Box 36.

File 101-G-17. 1965-1970.
C.A.R.C. McDonald, Anna. Correspondence.

File 101-G-18. 1942-1945.
C.A.R.C. MacKay, George William. Correspondence.

File 102-G-19. 1960-1967.
C.A.R.C. Muchan, Joseph. Correspondence, Reports Biographical Sketch (Photograph removed to Graphics Collection).

File 102-G-20. 1960-1971.
C.A.R.C. Murphy, David. Correspondence, Reports, Newsletters (Photographs removed to Graphics Collection).

File 102-G-21. 1967-1970.
C.A.R.C. Murphy, David. Finance. Correspondence.

File 102-G-22. 1954-1960.
C.A.R.C. Reoch, Allan. Correspondence.

File 102-G-23. 1945-1948.
C.A.R.C. Rumball, W.E.P. Correspondence.

File 102-G-24. 1969.
C.A.R.C. Seunarine, James. Correspondence.

File 102-G-25. 1961-1963.
C.A.R.C. Shields, Robert M. Correspondence, Reports.

File 102-H-1. 1971.
C.A.R.C. Guyana Council of Churches. Constitution.

File 102-H-2. 1976-1980.
C.A.R.C. Caribbean Conference of Churches. Correspondence, Reports, Newsletter: **Christian Action.**

File 102-H-3. 1970-1975.
C.A.R.C. Caribbean Conference of Churches. Correspondence, Reports, Newsletter: **Christian Action.**

Box 37.

File 102-I-1. 1966-1980.
C.A.R.C Caribbean: General Correspondence. Correspondence, Reports.

File 102-I-2. 1970-1971.
C.A.R.C. Ecumenical Consultation for Development. Correspondence, Reports.

File 102-I-3. 1963-1977.
C.A.R.C. Ecumenical Committee on Missions in the Caribbean (Southern) (E.C.O.M.I.C.S.) Correspondence, Reports.

File 102-I-4. 1973-1980.
C.A.R.C. Guyana: General Correspondence.

File 102-I-5. 1953-1972.
C.A.R.C. Guyana: General Correspondence.

Box 38.

File 102-I-6. 1951-1952.
C A.R.C. Guyana: General Correspondence. Correspondence, Reports.

File 102-I-7. 1950-1951.
C.A.R.C. Guyana: General Correspondence, Reports.

File 102-I-8 1948-1949.
C.A.R.C. Guyana: General Correspondence, Reports.

File 102-I-9. 1944-1947.
C.A.R.C. Guyana: General Correspondence, Reports.

Box 39.

File 102-I-10. 1943-1960.
C.A.R.C. Guyana: Reports, Report Summaries.

File 102-I-11. 1963-1966.
C.A.R.C. Guyana: Political Situation. Correspondence, Reports, Newsletters.

File 102-I-12. 1967.
C.A.R.C. Guyana: Ministers' Retreat - 1967. Correspondence.

File 102-I-13. 1971-1972.
C.A.R.C. West Indian Immigrants. Correspondence re: West Indians in Canada.

File 102-I-14. 1964-1967.
C.A.R.C. Guyana: Government Leaders. Correspondence with Government Officials - including the High Commissioner for Canada.

File 102-I-15. 1972.
C.A.R.C. Guyana: D. Pitamber. Trip Correspondence, Report.

File 102-I-16. 1939-1976.
C.A.R.C. Visitations to Guyana. Correspondence, Reports from visits to Guyana and Caribbean by prominent Church Leaders: E.H. Johnson, C.A. Dunn, E. Roberts, H. Tetley, R. Reith, W.A. Cameron.

File 102-I-17. 1955-1974.
C.A.R.C. General Information on Education. Correspondence, Reports, Materials from the Undercroft Centre and the Guyana Institute for Social Research and Action (G.I.S.R.A.).

File 102-I-18. 1927-1962.
C.A.R.C. Guyana: W.M.S. material. - Three reports from Rev. R.G. Fisher 1927-30 (Illustrated) (See also file 102-G-ll), One report from L.A. Reith 1961-62 (See also file 102-I-16).

File 102-J-1. 1946-1966.
C.A.R.C. Guyana: Newsletters (Note: Newsletters may also be located in the author's personnel file).

Box 40.

File 102-J-2. 1937-1945.
C.A.R.C. Guyana: Periodical: Issues from April 1937 December 1945 (With gaps).

File 102-J-3.
C.A.R.C. Guyana: General Information re: Canadian Mission in Guyana. Booklets, Pamphlets, Orders of Service, Histories.

File 102-J-4.
C.A.R.C. General Information re: Christianity in the Caribbean. Pamphlets, Histories.

JAPAN

Box 55.

File 104-A-1. 1974-1978.
Korean Christian Church in Japan. General Assembly. Correspondence, Reports.

File 104-A-2. 1975-1980.
Korean Christian Church in Japan. General Secretary. Correspondence, Reports.

File 104-A-3. 1971-1974.
Korean Christian Church in Japan. General Secretary. Correspondence, Reports.(Architectural drawings removed)

File 104-A-4. 1966-1970.
Korean Christian Church in Japan. General Secretary. Correspondence, Reports.

Box 56.

File 104-A-5. 1961-1965.
Korean Christian Church in Japan. General Secretary. Correspondence, Reports (Photographs removed to Graphics Collection).

File 104-A-6. 1963-1967.
Korean Christian Church in Japan. Moderator .Correspondence, Report..

File 104-A-7. 1963-1970.
Korean Christian Church in Japan. General Assembly. Annual Reports.

File 104-A-8. 1962-1965.
Korean Christian Church in Japan. Joint Reports of the Korean Christian Church, Japan in Japan and the Presbyterian Church in Canada Reports (from various Committees -many Illustrated).

File 104-A-9. 1968.
Korean Christian Church in Japan. Rev. In Ha Lee: Trip to Canada Correspondence.

File 104-A-10. 1957-1964.
Korean Christian Church in Japan. Rev. Yoon Tai Oh Correspondence (One time moderator of K.C.C.J. and Executive Committee Chairman).

File 104-B-1. 1966-1980.
Korean Christian Church in Japan. Canadian Committee. Correspondence (Photographs removed to Graphics Collection).
Box 57.

File 104-B-2. 1973-1976.
Korean Christian Church in Japan. Personnel Committee. Correspondence. China.

File 104-B-3. 1972-1979.
Korean Christian Church in Japan. Scholarship Committee Correspondence. Applications (Photographs removed to Graphics Collection).

File 104-B-4. 1977-1980.
Korean Christian Church in Japan. J.N.A.C. (Japan-North American Commissions on Cooperative Mission). Correspondence, Minutes, Reports.

File 104-B-5. 1972-1976.
Korean Christian Church in Japan. J.N.A.C. Correspondence, Reports.

File 104-B-6. 1975-1979.
Korean Christian Church in Japan. J.N.A.C.: Minutes, Correspondence, Reports.

File 104-B-7. 1972-1974.
Korean Christian Church in Japan. J.N.A.C.: Minutes, Correspondence, Reports.

Box 58.

File 104-B-8. 1961-1966.
Korean Christian Church in Japan. Missionary Committee. Correspondence, Minutes, Reports.

File 104-B-9. 1963-1969.
Korean Christian Church in Japan. Missionary Committee. Senriyama Property. Correspondence, Reports (Architectural drawings removed).

File 104-B-10. 1939-1955.
Korean Christian Church in Japan. Mission Council: Secretary. Correspondence, Reports.

File 104-B-11. 1950-1966.
Korean Christian Church in Japan. Mission Council: Treasurer. Correspondence, Statements.

File 104-B-12. 1937-1940.
Korean Christian Church in Japan. Mission Council. Minutes.

File 104-B-13. 1938.
Korean Christian Church in Japan. Mission Council. Property. Correspondence

Box 59.

File 104-C-1. 1970-1979.
Korean Christian Church in Japan. Korean Christian Centre. Correspondence, Reports.

File 104-C-2. 1974-1980.
Korean Christian Church in Japan. Research Action Institute (R.A.I.K.) Correspondence, Reports, Newsletters.

File 104-C-3. 1959-1967.
Korean Christian Church in Japan. International Christian Institute. Correspondence, Pamphlets.

File 104-C-4. 1961.
Korean Christian Church in Japan. Tokyo Union Theological Seminary. Report, Pamphlet.

File 104-C-5. 1960.
Korean Christian Church in Japan. Tokyo Church Youth Centre. Correspondence (Architectural drawings removed).

File 104-C-6. 1955.
Korean Christian Church in Japan. Yodogawa Christian Hospital. Booklet.

File 104-D-1.
Korean Christian Church in Japan. Finance: Canadian Committee. Correspondence, Statements.

File 104-D-2. 1972-1980.
Korean Christian Church in Japan. Special Gifts. Correspondence

File 104-D-3. 1972-1980.
Korean Christian Church in Japan. Church Finance.

Correspondence, Statements.

File 104-D-4. 1966-1970.
Korean Christian Church in Japan. Japan: Treasurer. Correspondence, Statements.

Box 60.

File 104-D-5. 1967-1968
Korean Christian Church in Japan. Requisition Sheets Statements.

File 104-D-6. 1966-1970.
Korean Christian Church in Japan. Finance: R. Anderson Correspondence.

File 104-D-7. 1961-1964.
Korean Christian Church in Japan. Finance: R. Talbot Correspondence.

File 104-D-8.1963-1964.
Korean Christian Church in Japan. Income Tax Data Statements.

File 104-D-9. 1962.
Korean Christian Church in Japan. Estimates. Statements, Correspondence.

File 104-D-10, . 1967-1968.
Korean Christian Church in Japan. Special Projects. Correspondence.

File 104-D-11.1966-1967.
Korean Christian Church in Japan. Overseas Student - Finance. Correspondence.

File 104-E-1. 1961-1970.
Korean Christian Church in Japan. Anderson, Robert K. Correspondence, Biographical Material.

File 104-E-2. 1963-1971.
Korean Christian Church in Japan. Davis, H. Glen. Correspondence, Newsletters.

File 104-E-3. 1971.
Korean Christian Church in Japan. Hyndman, Mavis. Correspondence, Biographical material.

File 104-E-4. 1962-1970.
Korean Christian Church in Japan. McIntosh, John H. Correspondence, Newsletters (Photograph removed to Graphics Collection).

File 104-E-5. 1969.
Korean Christian Church in Japan. Nakamura, Tamiko. Correspondence.

File 104-E-6. 1955-1961.
Korean Christian Church in Japan. Powell, Donald H. Correspondence, Newsletters.

Box 61.

File 104-E-7. 1958-1965.
Korean Christian Church in Japan. Talbot, Rodger. Correspondence, Newsletters (Photographs removed to Graphics Collection).

File 104-E-8. 1940-1949.
Korean Christian Church in Japan. Young, L.L. and Chapman, Gordon. Correspondence, Reports.

File 104-F-1. 1962-1978.
Korean Christian Church in Japan. National Christian Council of Japan. Correspondence, Reports.

File 104-G-1. 1965-1980.
Korean Christian Church in Japan. General Correspondence, Reports, Newsletters (Photographs removed to Graphics Collection) (Architectural drawings removed).

File 104-G-2. 1952-1964.
Korean Christian Church in Japan. General Correspondence, Reports.(Photographs removed to Graphics Collection).

File 104-G-3. 1946-1951.
Korean Christian Church in Japan. General Correspondence, Reports (Photographs removed to Graphics Collection).

Box 62.

File 104-G-4. 1949-1970.
Korean Christian Church in Japan. General Reports (Including Reports on visits to Japan).

File 104-G-5. 1974-1980.
Korean Christian Church in Japan. Korean Minority Issue. Correspondence, Statements, Reports (Photographs removed to Graphics Collection).

File 104-G-6. 1969-1973.
Korean Christian Church in Japan. Korean Minority Issue Correspondence, Reports.

File 104-G-7. 1969-1973.
Korean Christian Church in Japan Policy Papers, Correspondence, Reports, Statements.

File 104-G-8. 1962-1972.
Korean Christian Church in Japan. Relationship with Presbyterian Church in Canada. Correspondence, Statements.

File 104-G-9. 1962.
Korean Christian Church in Japan. Missionary Language Orientation Statements.

File 104-H-1. 1945-1968.
Korean Christian Church in Japan. Newsletters (Note: Newsletters may also be located in the author's personnel file).

File 104-H-2. 1964-1967.

Korean Christian Church in Japan. Newsletters: **Japan Mission Newsletter** - A compilation of reports on and from a variety of missionaries.

File 204-H-3. 1966-1967.
Korean Christian Church in Japan. **Koinonia** newsletter of the K.C.C.J.

File 104-H-4.
Korean Christian Church in Japan. Canadian Mission in Japan. Correspondence, Reports, Histories, Newsclippings, Booklets, Pamphlets, (Includes Material re: Wm. Kerr and Caroline MacDonald) (Photographs removed to Graphics Collection).

File 104-H-5.
Korean Christian Church in Japan. Christianity in Japan. Reports, Pamphlets, Histories.

INDIA

Box 63.

File 105-A-1. 1962-1980.
Church of North India. General Assembly. Correspondence, Minutes, Reports, Statement of priorities, History (Map removed).

File 105-A-2. 1973-1980.
Church of North India. Moderator and General Secretary. Correspondence, Reports, Minutes.

File 105-A-3. 1959-1972.
Church of North India. Moderator and General Secretary. Correspondence, Reports.

File 105-A-4. 1967.
Church of North India. Dr. Gerbachan Singh: Visit to Canada Correspondence.

File 105-A-5. 1959-1965.
Church of North India. Reports of General Assembly. Reports from United Church of Northern India, copy of Constitution, Reports of Committees to General Assembly.
Box 64.

File 105-A-6. 1973-1975.
Church of North India. Policies and Priorities. Statements, Reports, Minutes, Copy of Constitution.

File 105-A-7. 1957-1970.
Church of North India. Church Union. Correspondence, Reports, Statements, Minutes, Booklets: all concerning the creation of the Church of North India (Map removed).

File 105-A-8. 1960-1970.
Church of North India. Church Union: Inauguration. Copies of Inauguration and proposed services.

File 105-A-9. 1958-1970.
Church of North India. Church Union: Publications. Periodicals concerning Church Union.

File 105-B-1. 1970-1980.
Church of North India. Diocese of Bhopal. Correspondence (primarily with Bishop), Reports.

File 105-B-2. 1970-1979.
Church of North India. Diocese of Lucknow. Correspondence (primarily with Bishop).

File 105-B-3. 1973-1976.
Church of North India. Diocese of Lucknow. Reports.

File 105-B-4. 1976.
Church of North India. Diocese. Other Reports, Newsclippings.

Box 65.

File 105-C-1. 1937-1976.
Church of North India. Vindhya/Satpura Church Council. Correspondence, Reports, Minutes.

File 105-D-1. 1967-1980.
Church of North India. Bhil Mission Council. Secretary. Correspondence, Minutes.

File 105-D-2. 1965-1966.
Church of North India. Bhil Mission Council. Secretary. Correspondence, Minutes.

File 105-D-3. 1962-1964.
Church of North India. Bhil Mission Council. Secretary. Correspondence, Reports, Financial Statements.

Box 66.

File 105-D-4. 1952-1961.
Church of North India. Bhil Mission Council. Secretary. Correspondence, Reports.

File 105-D-5. 1946-1951.
Church of North India. Bhil Mission Council. Secretary. Correspondence, Reports.

File 105-D-6. 1888-1947.
Church of North India. Bhil Mission Council. Secretary. Correspondence, Reports.

Box 67.

File 105-D-7. 1941-1947.
Church of North India. Bhil Mission Council. Miscellaneous Correspondence.

File 105-D-8. 1948-1952.
Church of North India. Bhil Mission Council. Miscellaneous Correspondence.

File 105-D-9. 1927-1949.
Church of North India. Bhil Mission Council. Minutes.

File 105-D-10. 1950-1958.
Church of North India. Bhil Mission Council. Minutes.

Box 68.

File 105-D-11. 1959-1966.
Church of North India. Bhil Mission Council. Minutes.

File 105-D-12. 1967-1968.
Church of North India.Bhil Mission Council. Minutes.

File 105-D-13. 1949-1968.
Church of North India.Bhil Committee. Minutes - includes: Executive Minutes (1950-1968) Joint Policy Minutes (1966), Work Council Minutes (1949).

File 105-D-14. 1925-1964.
Church of North India. Bhil Reports - includes: Annual Reports, Committee Reports.

File 105-D-15. 1966-1967.
Church of North India. Bhil Economic Life Committee. Correspondence, Minutes.

File 105-D-16. 1965.
Church of North India. Bhil Affairs Committee. Minutes.

File 105-D-17. 1963-1965.
Church of North India. Bhil Consultative Committee. Correspondence, Minutes.

File 105-D-18. 1950-1951.
Church of North India. Bhil Medical Committee. Minutes.

File 105-D-19. 1961-1969.
Church of North India. Bhil Newsletters (Note: Newsletters may also be located in the author's personnel file).
Box 69.

File 105-D-20.
Church of North India. Bhil General Information. Booklets - "50 Golden Years", "Among the Bhils", "Bhil Field Stories 1944", Information for Canadian Missionaries (includes a copy of the Handbook of Rules), Statements on Mission work Policy (Map removed)

File 105-D-21. 1950-1979.
Church of North India. Jhansi Mission Council. Secretary. Correspondence, Minutes.

File 105-D-22. 1941-1949.
Church of North India. Jhansi Mission Council. Secretary. Correspondence.

File 105-D-23. 1917-1940.
Church of North India. Jhansi Mission (Gwalior). Correspondence, Reports, Minutes.

Box 70.

File 105-D-24. 1893-1915.
Church of North India. Jhansi Mission (Gwalior). Correspondence, Reports, Minutes.

File 105-D-25. 1941-1949.
Church of North India. Jhansi Mission Council. Treasurer. Correspondence, Reports.

File 105-D26. 1950-1953.
Church of North India. Jhansi Mission Council. Miscellaneous Correspondence.

File 105-D-27. 1937-1950.
Church of North India. Jhansi Mission Council. Minutes.

Box 71.

File 105-D-28. 1951-1966.
Church of North India. Jhansi Mission Council. Minutes.

File 105-D-29. 1909-1918.
Church of North India. Jhansi Gwalior Mission. Minutes

File 105-D-30. 1939-1940.
Church of North India. Jhansi Negotiations with American Presbyterians. Correspondence.

File 105-D-31. 1961-1964.
Church of North India. Jhansi American Bible Society. Correspondence re: Rev. Russell Self.

File 105-D-32. 1956-1957.
Church of North India. Jhansi Evangelical Fellowship of India.

File 105-D-33. 1900-1964.
Church of North India. Jhansi Reports - with gaps, One bound volume includes histories as well as early reports.

Box 72.

File 105-D-34.
Church of North India. Jhansi Histories.Various histories of missions work in Jhansi area.

File 105-D-35.
Church of North India. Jhansi Mission Policy.

Policies and rules for Mission and missionaries.

File 105-D-36. 1961-1970.
Church of North India. Jhansi Bundelkhand Church Council. Correspondence, Statements of Policy.

File 105-D-37. 1959.

Church of North India. Joint Mission Council of Jhansi and Bhil. Minutes.

File 105-D-38. 1978-1980.
Church of North India. C.N.I. Related Churches. Correspondence, Reports, Minutes.

File 105-D-39. 1965-1977.
Church of North India. C.N.I. Related Churches. Correspondence, Reports, Minutes.

File 105-D-40. 1961-1977.
Church of North India. Episcopal and Missionary Personnel Committee .Correspondence

File 105-D-41. 1966-1969.
Church of North India. Scholarship Committee. Daniel Sunderlal Correspondence, Biographical material (Photographs removed to Graphics Collection)

Box 73.

File 105-D-42. 1967-1972.
Church of North India. Trust Association. Correspondence, Legal Papers.

File 105-D-43. 1944-1946.
Church of North India. India Committee. Minutes, Correspondence

File 105-E-1.1974-1980
Church of North India. A.C.C.I. Secretary. Correspondence, Reports, Minutes.

File 105-E-2. 1968-1973.
Church of North India. A.C.C.I. Secretary. Correspondence, Reports, Minutes (Photographs removed to Graphics Collection)

File 105-E-3. 1972-1976.
Church of North India. A.C.C.I. Economic Development. Correspondence

File 105-E-4. 1972-1980.
Church of North India. A.C.C.I. Medical Board. Correspondence, Reports

Box 74.

File 105-E-5. 1958-1980.
Church of North India. Jobat Hospital. Correspondence, Reports, Charts, Copy of Constitution, (Architectural drawings removed)

File 105-E-6. 1967-1969.
Church of North India. Jobat Hospital. Administrator. Correspondence, Biographical material on Bruce Nigel (Photographs removed to Graphics Collection)

File 105-E-7. 1956-1966.
Church of North India. Jobat Hospital. Nursing School Correspondence, Reports, Minutes, copy of Constitution (Architectural drawings removed)

(Photographs removed to Graphics Collection).

File 105-E-8. 1964.
Church of North India. Jobat Hospital. X-Ray Machine. Correspondence.

File 105-E-9. 1965.
Church of North India. Jobat Hospital. T.B. Ward. Correspondence (Includes material on X-Ray Machine) (Architectural drawings removed)

File 105-E-10. 1962-1963.
Church of North India. Jobat Hospital. Improvement Plans Report.

File 105-E-11. 1962-1964.
Church of North India. Jobat Hospital. Ambulance Correspondence

File 105-E-12 1960-1978.
Church of North India. Serampore College. Correspondence, Booklets

File 105-E-13. 1957-1980.
Church of North India. Helen MacDonald Secondary School Correspondence, Reports, Minutes, Copy of Constitution

Box 75.

File 105-E-14. 1972-1979.
Church of North India. Bangalore - United Theological College Correspondence

File 105-E-15. 1971.
Church of North India. Christian Association for Radio and Audio Visual Service (C.A.R.V.A.S.) Correspondence.

File 105-E-16. 1972.
Church of North India. Christian Training Centre Reports.

File 105-E-17. 1963-1965,
Allahabad Agricultural Institute. Correspondence, Booklets, Newletters
File 105-E-18. 1950-1966.
Church of North India. Landour Language School. Correspondence, Minutes, Booklets

File 105-E-19. 1965
Church of North India. Jhansi Youth Centre. Correspondence

File 105-E-20. 1964-1980.
Church of North India. North India Theological College. Correspondence, Minutes, Reports

File 105-E-21. 1959-1966.
Church of North India. Christian Institute. Correspondence, Reports.

File 105-E-22. 1962-1975.

Church of North India. Ecumenical Christian Centre. Correspondence, Booklets, Reports.

File 105-E-23. 1954-1977.
Church of North India. Ludhiana Christian Medical College. Correspondence, Reports, Histories, Newletters.

File 105-E-24.
Church of North India. Ludhiana Christian Medical College. General Information. Pamphlets, Histories, Newletters (Including "Here in Ludhiana")

Box 76.

File 105-E-25. 1956-1980.
Church of North India. Vellore Christian Medical Centre. Correspondence, Reports, Minutes, Histories.

File 105-E-26.
Church of North India. Vellore Christian Medical Centre. General Information Pamphlets, Histories, Newsletters, Reports.

File 105-E-27. 1972-1980.
Church of North India. Baring Union Christian College. Correspondence, Reports, Newsletters

File 105-E-28. 1978-1980.
Church of North India. Woodstock School. Correspondence, Reports, Minutes, Pamphlets, Newsletters.

Box 77.

File 105-E-29. 1976-1977.
Church of North India. Woodstock School for Missionaries' Children.
Correspondence, Reports, Minutes, Pamphlets

File 105-E-30. 1974-1975.
Church of North India. Woodstock School. Correspondence, Reports, Minutes.

File 105-E-31. 1971-1973.
Church of North India. Woodstock School. Correspondence, Reports, Minutes, Newletters.

Box 78.

File 105-E-32. 1966-1971.
Church of North India. Woodstock School. Correspondence, Reports, Minutes.
File 105-E-33. 1953-1965.
Church of North India. Woodstock School.

Correspondence, Reports, Minutes.

File 105-E-34. 1964-1970.
Church of North India. Woodstock School. Advisory Board. Minutes.

File 105-E-35.

Church of North India. Woodstock School. Pamphlets, Reports.

File 105--F-1. 1976-1980.
Church of North India. Church of North India. Treasurer. Correspondence, Reports.

Box 79.

File 105-F-2. 1970-1975.
Church of North India. Church of North India. Treasurer. Correspondence, Reports. (Architectural drawings removed)

File 105-F-3. 1970-1980.
Church of North India. A.C.C.I.: Treasurer. Correspondence, Reports.

File 105-F-4. 1971-1976.
Church of North India. Bhil Finance - Mission Committee. Correspondence, Reports.

File 105-F-5. 1950-1970.
Church of North India. Bhil Treasurer. Correspondence, Reports.

File 105-F-6. 1941-1949.
Church of North India. Bhil Treasurer. Correspondence, Reports.

Box 80.

File 105-F-7. 1967-1968.
Church of North India. Bhil Requisition Sheets. Statements.

File 105-F-8. 1952-1968.
Church of North India. Bhil Finance - Missionary & Field. Correspondence, Reports.

File 105-F-9. 1940-1963.
Church of North India. Bhil Financial Statements.
File 105-F-10. 1964-1968.
Church of North India. Bhil Financial Statements.

File 105-F-11. 1959-1964.
Church of North India. Bhil Business Manager. Correspondence, Reports.

File 105-F-12. 1962-1968.
Church of North India. Bhil Income Tax. Correspondence, Reports.

File 105-F-13. 1958-1965.
Church of North India. Bhil Statements and Estimates. Financial Statements.
Box 81.

File 105-F-14. 1967-1968.
Church of North India. Bhil Special Projects. Correspondence.

File 105-F-15. 1951-1977.

Church of North India. Jhansi Canadian Treasurer. Correspondence, Reports.

File 105-F-16. 1940-1950.
Church of North India. Jhansi Canadian Treasurer. Correspondence, Reports.

File 105-F-17. 1967-1968.
Church of North India. Jhansi Requisition Sheets. Statements.

File 105-F-18. 1966-1967.
Church of North India. Jhansi Finance - Missionary & Field. Correspondence.

File 105-F-19. 1937-1966.
Church of North India. Jhansi Financial Statements.

Box 82.

File 105-F-20. 1906-1930.
Church of North India. Jhansi (Gwalior) Property. Contracts, Deeds.

File 105-F-21. 1958-1962.
Church of North India. Jhansi Statements and Estimates. Correspondence, Financial Statements.

File 105-F-22. 1960-1965.
Church of North India. Jhansi Income Tax. Correspondence, Reports.

File 105-F-23. 1976-1980.
Church of North India. Special Gifts. Correspondence.

File 105-F-24. 1972-1975.
Church of North India. Special Gifts. Correspondence.

File 105-F-25. 1970-1980.
Church of North India. Finance: Bhopal Diocese. Correspondence, Reports.

File 105-F-26. 1973-1979.
Church of North India. Finance: Lucknow Diocese. Correspondence.

File 105-F-27. 1974-1976.
Church of North India. Finance: Baring College. Correspondence, Reports, Statements (Photographs removed to Graphics Collection) (Architectural drawings removed).

File 105-F-28. 1978-1980.
Church of North India. Finance; Indore Graduate School. Correspondence.

File 105-F-29. 1968-1980.
Church of North India. Inter Mission Business Office. Correspondence.

File 105-G-1. 1964-1965.
Church of North India. Carter, Arnold K. Correspondence, Reports, Newsclippings (Photographs removed to Graphics Collection).

Box 83.

File 105-G-2. 1962-1963.
Church of North India. Carter Arnold K. Correspondence, Reports Newsclippings (Photograph removed to Graphics Collection).

File 105-G-3. 1953-1954.
Church of North India. Cheshire, John. Correspondence, Reports.

File 105-G-4. 1954-1960.
Church of North India. Cunningham, Ian. Correspondence, Reports.
File 105-G-5. 1968.
Church of North India. Douglas, Donald E. Correspondence, Report.

File 105-G-6. 1963-1968.
Church of North India. Horrell, W. Roger. Correspondence, Reports, Newsletter.

File 105-G-7. 1966-1970.
Church of North India. Howard, Desmond. Correspondence, Reports, Newsletters.
File 105-G-8. 1956-1968.
Church of North India. Knox, Fred. Correspondence.

File 105-G-9. 1936-1939.
Church of North India. Lowther, A.A. Reports.

File 105-G-10. 1958-1968.
Church of North India. McIntosh, Alvin. Correspondence, Reports.
File 105-G-11. 1966-1971.
Church of North India. MacKay, Angus. Correspondence.

Box 84.

File 105-G-12. 1954-1965.
Church of North India. MacKay, Angus. Correspondence, Reports.

File 105-G-13. 1956-1970.
Church of North India. Milne, James, W. Correspondence, Reports

File 105-G-14. 1945-1953.
Church of North India. Muchan, Joseph. Newsletters.

File 105-G-15. 1956-1966.
Church of North India. Murray, John. Correspondence, Reports.
File 105-G-16. 1958-1968.
Church of North India. Nichol, Mary. Correspondence, Reports (Photographs removed to Graphics Collection)

File 105-G-17. 1943-1949.
Church of North India. Quinn, William R. Correspondence, Reports.

File 105-G.-18. 1955-1969.
Church of North India. Self, Russell T. Correspondence. Reports, Newsletters.

File 105-G-19. 1967-1970.
Church of North India. Sherrick, Mary. Correspondence, Report.

Box 85.

File 105-G-20. 1940-1949.
Church of North India. Smith, Wilfred C. Correspondence, Reports (Photograph removed to Graphics Collection).

File 105-G-21. 1966-1967.
Church of North India. Tanzer, Herbert. Correspondence.

File 105-G-22. 1911.
Church of North India. Wilkie, John Correspondence.

File 105-G-23. 1957-1964.
Church of North India. Williams, Jack A. Reports.

File 105-G-24. 1965-1967.
Church of North India. W.M.S. Personnel. Correspondence, Newsletters.

File 105-G-25. 1955-1965.
Church of North India. Wood, Clarence L. Correspondence, Reports, Obituary

File 105-H-1. 1964-1976.
Church of North India. National Christian Council of India. Correspondence, Reports, Minutes, Publications.

File 105-H-2. 1955-1963.
Church of North India. National Christian Council of India. Reports, Minutes.

Box 86.

File 105-I-1. 1970-1980.
Church of North India. General Correspondence, Reports.

File 105-I-2. 1950-1969.
Church of North India. General Correspondence, Reports (Map removed).

File 105-I-3. 1972-1973.
Church of North India. Jubilee Celebrations. Correspondence

File 105-I-4. 1949-1969.
Church of North India. Medical Information. Correspondence, Report

File 205-I-5. 1972-1980.
Church of North India. Property. Correspondence, Reports, Legal Documents

Box 87.

File 105-I-6. 1965-1968.
Church of North India. India Consultation. Correspondence, Reports, Minutes

File 105-I-7. 1978.
Church of North India. Visit of J.M. Das. Correspondence

File 105-I-8. 1951-1961.
Church of North India. Overseas Candidate Information. Correspondence, Reports

File 105-I-9. 1879-1970.
Church of North India. General Reports, Annual Reports: 1879, 1883, 1887, 1906, 1915 (Photographs removed to Graphics Collection)

File 105-I-10.
Church of North India. India: Sunday School Materials. Correspondence, Booklets [ca. 1915]

File 105-I-11. 1961-1975.
Church of North India. Relationship with Presbyterian Church in Canada. Statements

File 105-IJ-1. 1946-1970.
Church of North India. Newsletters (Note: Newsletters may also be located in the author's personnel file)

File 105-J-2. 1883-1884.
Church of North India. Opposition to work at Indore. Volume of Letters, editorials and extracts from Indian newspapers relating opposition to Church Mission work at Indore

Box 88.

File 105-J-3. 1904-1908.
Church of North India. **The Journal of the Gwalior Mission** Periodical: Bound Volumes I, III, IV. *(Experienced a series of name changes during its history - i.e. **The Journal of the Gwalior Presbyterian Mission, Journal of the Canadian Presbyterian Mission, Gwalior India**)

File 105-J-4. 1909-1911.
Church of North India. **The Journal of the Gwalior Mission,** Periodical: Bound Volumes V, VI, VII *(See 105-J-3)

File 105-J-5. 1911-1914.
Church of North India. **The Journal of the Gwalior Mission,** Periodical: Bound Volumes VIII, IX, X *(See 105-J-3)

Box 89.

File 105-J-6. 1914-1917.
Church of North India. **The Journal of the Gwalior Mission,** Periodical: Bound Volumes XI, XII, XIII. *(See 105-J-3).

File 105-J-7. 1917-1923.
Church of North India. **The Journal of the Gwalior Mission, Periodical**: Bound Volumes - Numbers stop at XVII *(See 105-J-3)

File 105-J-8. 1925.
Church of North India. **The Journal of the Gwalior Mission,** Periodical: Bound Volumes *(See 105-J-30)

File 105-J-9. 1919-1928.
Church of North India. **The Journal of the Gwalior Mission**, Periodical: Loose copies - single issues *(See 105-J-3)

Box 90.

File 105-J-10. 1939-1940.
Church of North India. Newsletter: **The Central India Torch,** Two issues

File 105-J-11. 1962-1963.
Church of North India. Newsletter: **Church Union: News and Views** , Two issues
File 105-J-12. 1960-1967.
Church of North India. Newsletter: **The United Church Review** Publication - series containing gaps.

File 105-J-13.
Church of North India. General Information re: Christianity in India Booklets, Histories, Pamphlets.

CHINA

File 106-A-1. 1942-1946.
China. Church of Christ in China. Correspondence, Minutes, Reports.

File 106-A.-2. 1947-1949.
China. Church of Christ in China. Correspondence, Minutes, Reports.

File 106-A-3. 1950-1952.
China. Church of Christ in China. Correspondence, Minutes, Reports

File 106-A-4.
China. Church of Christ in China. Church Union Booklets, Report

File 106-B-1. 1919-1940.
China. Mission Council Minutes, Correspondence, Reports, Booklets, Histories.
Box 92.

File 106-B-2. 1939-1951.
China. Christian Literature Society. Correspondence, Reports.

File 106-C-1. 1946-1955.
China. College of Chinese Studies. Correspondence, Reports, Minutes.

File 106-C-2. 1946-1948.
China. Moukden Medical College. Correspondence.

File 106-C-3. 1920.
China. Shantung Christian University: School of Medicine. One Booklet.

File 106-C-4. 1919.
China. Canton Christian College. One Booklet.

File 106-C-5. 1975.
China. China Graduate School of Theology. Pamphlet, Newsletter.

File 106-D-1. 1937-1940
China . Finance. Statements.

File 106-E-1. 1944-1956.
China. Andrews, J. Eldon .Correspondence, Reports.

File 106-E-2. 1939-1947.
China. Davis, William G. Correspondence, Reports.

Box 93.

File 106-E-3. 1974-1975.
China. Johnson, Edward H. Correspondence, Reports.

File 106-E-4. 1942-1949.
China. Ransom, Malcolm. Correspondence, Reports.

File 106-E-5. 1949-1951.
China. Ransom, Malcolm. Correspondence, Reports.

File 106-E-6. 1938-1945.
China. Reoch, Allan & Johnson, E.H. Correspondence, Reports.

File 106-E-7. 1952-1954.
China. Zia, Z.K. Correspondence.

File 106-F-1. 1973-1974.
China. General. Correspondence.

File 106-F-2. 1976-1977.
China. Ting, K.H. Correspondence.

File 106-F-3. 1972.
China. Canadian China Society Pamphlets.

File 106-F-4. 1936-1938.
China. Manchuria Property. Correspondence, Legal Documents.

File 106-F-5. 1946-1949.
China. War Relief.

AFGHANISTAN

Box 97.

File 108-A-1. 1969-1980.
Afghanistan International Mission. Correspondence, Report, Copy of Constitution (Photograph removed to Graphics Collection).

File 108-A-2. 1977-1980.
Afghanistan. International Mission. Minutes, Reports.

File 108-A-3. 1973-1976.
Afghanistan. International Mission. Minutes, Reports.

Box 98.

File 108-A-4. 1969-1972.
Afghanistan. International Mission. Minutes, Reports.

File 108-B-1. 1972-1982.
Afghanistan. International Mission. Finance Correspondence, Reports.

File 108-C-1. 1969-1971.
Afghanistan. International Mission. Reoch, John A. Correspondence, Newsletters.

NEPAL

Box 109-A-1. 1974-1976.
Nepal - United Mission. Correspondence, Reports.
Box 109-A-2. 1976-1980.
Nepal - United Mission. Minutes, Reports, Newsletters.

Box 109-A-3. 1972-1975.
Nepal - United Mission. Minutes, Reports, Newsletters.

Box 99.

File 109-B-1. 1975-1979.
Nepal - United Mission. Finance. Correspondence.
File 109-C-1. 1973-1976.
Nepal - United Mission. Personnel Secretary. Correspondence, Reports.

KOREA

File 110-A-1. 1919-1980.
Presbyterian Church of Korea. Mission Correspondence, Reports, Book commemorating Class of 1919 of Chosen Christian College in Seoul, Korea (Illustrated),

ASIA

Box 103.

File 203-D-1. 1970-1979.
Inter Church Organizations. Christian Conference of Asia. Correspondence, Reports, Booklets.

File 203-D-2. 1972-1976.
Inter Church Organizations. Christian Conference of Asia. Urban Industrial Mission Committee. Correspondence.

File 203-D-3. 1974-1976.
Inter Church Organizations. Christian Conference of Asia. Finance. Correspondence.

SOUTH EAST ASIA

File 203-E-1. 1973-1980.
Inter Church Organizations. Fund for Theological Education in South East Asia. Correspondence, Reports, Minutes.

Box 104.

File 203-E-2. 1969-1972.
Inter Church Organizations. Fund for Theological Education in South East Asia. Correspondence, Reports, Minutes.

File 203-H-2. 1967-1969.
Inter Church Organizations. N.C.C.C. East Asia Department. Correspondence, Minutes, Report.

File 203-H-3. 1964-1965.
Inter Church Organizations. N.C.C.C. East Asia Department. Committee on Theological Education. Correspondence, Report.

File 203-H-4. 1956-1969.
Inter Church Organizations. N.C.C.C. East Asia Department. Taiwan. Correspondence, Reports, Minutes.

File 203-H-5. 1972.
Inter Church Organizations. N.C.C.C. East Asia Department. Japan. Correspondence.i.?Japan:

File 203-H-6. 1957-1975.
Inter Church Organizations. N.C.C.C. East Asia Department. China. Correspondence, Reports, Minutes.

File 203-H-7. 1966-1973.
Inter Church Organizations. N.C.C.C. Southern Asia Department. India. Correspondence, Report.

Box 105.

File 203-H-13. 1971.
Inter Church Organizations. N.C.C.C. Committee on U.S. Asian Policy. Correspondence, Reports.

GOVERNMENTS

Box 109.

File 205-B-1. 1972-1976.
Governments. Foreign. Bangladesh. Correspondence.
File 205-B-2. 1972-1974.
Governments. Foreign. China. Correspondence.

TOURS

Box 111.

File 207-A-1. 1977-1978.
Tours. Orient: Spring 1978. Correspondence.

File 207-B-1. 1948.
Tours.Taiwan. 1948. Letter from J.A.Munro and Miss L.K.Pelton.

File 207-B-2. 1952.
Tours. Taiwan. 1952. Report from W.A.Cameron and G.D.Johnston.

File 207-B-3. 1954-1955.
Tours. Taiwan. 1954-1955. Reports re: State of Church in Taiwan, Mission Council, Church supported Institutions.

File 207-B-4. 1954.
Tours. Taiwan. 1954. Reports, Correspondence re: Schools.

Box 112.

File 207-B-5. 1955.
Tours. Taiwan. 1955. Reports from E.H.Johnson and J.L.W.McLean.

File 207-B-6. 1956.
Tours. Taiwan. 1956. Correspondence, Reports from E.H.Johnson.

File 207-B-7. 1957-1961.
Tours. Taiwan. 1961. Correspondence, Reports from E.H.Johnson re: Property Holdings.

File 207-B-8. 1960-1961.
Tours. Taiwan. 1961. Correspondence, Reports from E.H.Johnson re: Property Holdings (Architectural drawings removed).

File 207-B-9. 1961.
Tours. Taiwan. 1961. Correspondence with E.H.Johnson.

File 207-B-10. 1957-1961.
Tours. Taiwan. 1961. Correspondence with E.H.Johnson, Reports, Newsclippings(Photographs removed to Graphics Collection).

File 207-B-11. 1961.
Tours. Taiwan. 1961. Correspondence re: Tam Kang School Property Problem(Photographs removed to Graphics Collection).

File 207-B-12. 1961.
Tours. Taiwan. 1961. Correspondence re: Tainan College Property Problem.

File 207-B-13. 1962-1963.
Tours. Taiwan. 1963. Correspondence, Reports from R.M.Ransom (Photogaph removed to Graphics Collection).

File 207-C-1. 1956.
Tours. Japan. 1956. Correspondence, Report from E.H.Johnson.

File 207-C-2. 1961.
Tours. Japan. 1961. Reports from E.H.Johnson.

File 207-C-3. 1963.
Tours. Japan. 1963. Reports, Correspondence with R.M.Ransom (Photographs removed to Graphics Collection).

File 207-C-4. 1975-1976.
Tours. Japan. 1976. Correspondence.

Box 113.

File 207-D-1. 1961.
Tours. Caribbean. 1961. Correspondence with R.M.Ransom.

File 207-D-2. 1962-1963.
Tours. Caribbean. 1963. Reports.

File 207-D-3. 1970.
Tours. Caribbean. 1970. Reports.

File 207-E-1. 1950.
Tours. British Guyana. 1950. Report from W.A.Cameron.

File 207-E-2. 1954.
Tours. British Guyana. 1954 .Report from E.H.Johnson.

File 207-E-3. 1957.
Tours British Guyana: 1957. Correspondence, Reports, Minutes.

File 207-E-4. 1958.
Tours. British Guyana. 1958. Report from E.H.Johnson.

File 207-E-5. 1960.
Tours. British Guyana. 1960. Report from E.H.Johnson (Includes short note on Jamaica).

File 207-E-6. 1962.
Tours. British Guyana. 1962. Correspondence with E.H.Johnson.

File 207-G-1. 1952.
Tours. India. 1952. Reports from Miss Helen E.Bricker

(Includes information on Taiwan).

File 207-G-2. 1955-1956
Tours. India. 1956. Correspondence with E.H.Johnson.

File 207-G-3. 1955-1956.
Tours. India. Bhil Visit 1956. Correspondence, Reports with E.H.Johnson.

File 207-G-4. 1959.
Tours. India. 1959. Correspondence with E.H.Johnson.

File 207-G-5. 1962-1963.
Tours. India. 1963. Correspondence with R.M.Ransom.

File 207-G-6. 1963.
Tours. India. Madras Conference 1963. Correspondence, Reports.

Box 114.

File 207-G-7. 1971.
Tours. India. South Asia - Crisis Conference. Correspondence, Report.

File 207-G-8. 1971-1972.
Tours. India-Pakistan: 1971. Correspondence, Report.

File 207-G-9. 1971.
Tours. India. 1971. Correspondence re: Miss M.E.Whale.

File 207-G-10. 1972.
Tours. India and Bangladesh 1972. Correspondence, Reports from E.H.Johnson.

File 207-G-11. 1976.
Tours. India. 1976. Correspondence, Reports.

File 207-G-12. 1977-1978.
Tours. India. 1977. Correspondence, Reports.

File 207-H-1. 1955-1965.
Tours. Johnson, E.H. Trips. Correspondence, Reports from various Missions including India, Taiwan.

File 207-I-1. 1948-1949
Tours. Overseas Delegation: 1948-1949. Report on Missions in China, Japan, Taiwan and India - Prepared by Miss L.K.Pelton and J.A.Munro.

SPECIAL GIFTS

Box 115.

File 208-B-1. 1967-1970.
Special Gifts. Missions: Caribbean Correspondence.

File 208-B-2. 1965-1970.
Special Gifts. Missions: India Correspondence, Newsletters.

File 208-B-3. 1965-1971.
Special Gifts. Missions: Japan. Correspondence.

File 208-B-4. 1965-1971.
Special Gifts.Missions: Taiwan. Information.

OVERSEAS VISITORS

Box 116.

File 210-A-1. 1971-1972.
Overseas Visitors. India: Bishop Patro Correspondence.

File 210-E-1. 1974.
Overseas Visitors. Japan: Dr. In Ha Lee Correspondence.

File 210-F-1. 1972.
Overseas Visitors. Taiwan: Tsi Tan Correspondence.

Administrative Records of the General Board of Missions/Board of World Mission. Correspondence 1964-1987. General Correspondence 1964-1987.

File 1989-1009-2-1. 1978-1984.
Association for Theological Education in South East Asia.

File 1989-1009-2-7. 1981-1987.
Canadian Council of Churches. Canada/China

Programme.

File 1989-1009-2-10. 1980-1986.
Canadian Council of Churches - Vellore/Ludhiana Committee.

File 1989-1009-2-12. 1977-1987.
Christian Conference of Asia.

File 1989-1009-3-2. 1983-1987.
Ecumenical Forum - Canada-Asia Working Group.

File 1989-1009-3-8. 1974-1987.
Korean Ministries.
File 1989-1009-3-11 1983-1987.
N.C.C.C./D.O.M./East Asia.

File 1989-1009-3-14. 1980-1982.
Overseas Visitors - India.

File 1989-1009-4-1. 1978.
Overseas Visitors - D.S. Kim and K.S. Choi.

File 1989-1009-4-2. 1980-1981.
Overseas Visitors - Korean Christian Church in Japan.

File 1989-1009-4-5. 1980
Overseas Visitors - Presbyterian Church in Taiwan.

File 1989-1009-5-7. 1977-1985.

United Board for Christian Higher Education in South East Asia.

Administrative Records of the General Board of Missions/Board of World Mission. Home Missions, 1911-1982. Administrative Correspondence, 1927-1976.
File 1988-1003-67-7. 1961-1972.
Chinese .

File 1988-1003-67-8. 1963.
Chinese Advisory Committee(Photograph removed to Graphics Collection).

File 1988-1003-67-9. 1968-1970.
Chinese Conference.

Administrative Records of the General Board of Missions/Board of World Mission. Mission Education 1946-1983. Director's Correspondence, 1946-1983.

File 1988-1003-78-15. 1966-1968.
China Book - Study Materials.

File 1988-1003-78-16. 1973-1974.
China Consultation.

File 1988-1003-78-17. 1969.
China Seminar - Associated Church Press.

File 1988-1003-78-18. 1967.
Chiu, Rev. Teng Kiat - Visitor.
File 1988-1003-78-19. 1973.
Churchmen's Seminar on Exploring Canada's new relationship with China.

File 1988-1003-81-8. 1968-1969.
Correspondence. Also includes newsletter of General Board of Missions and Map of British Guiana mission stations.

File 1988-1003-81-10.1971.
Includes report by Rev. E.F. Roberts on Guyana visit.

File 1988-1003-81-25. 1970.
Hunter, Mr. and Mrs. Neale - Visit - Roman Catholics from Australia who taught in China.
File 1988-1003-84-10. 1962-1966.
Newsletters - Japan . Includes newsletters by Talbot. Davis and Nakamura.

File 1988-1003-84-12. 1962.
Newsletters - Rev. R.M.Shields - British Guiana.

File 1988-1003-84-13. 1958-1963.
Newsletters - Rev. and Mrs. Talbot - Japan. Includes illustration of the Talbot family.

File 1988-1003-84-25. 1968-1969.
Overseas Missions Includes "Report on My Investigation of Hospitals in India" by G. Nigel Bruce 1968.
Administrative Records of the General Board of Missions/Board of World Mission. Overseas Missions 1925-1982. Administrative Correspondence 1925-1976.

File 1988-1003-43-15. 1965.
Field Visits - Rev. D.T. Evans - Formosa, Japan, India.

File 1988-10032-44-2. 1966-1968.
Formosa - Overseas Students.

File 1988-1003-46-2. 1965-1967.
St. Andrew's, Victoria Gift to St. Andrew's of Taiwan Theological.

File 1988-1003-46-11. 1968-1971.
Taiwan - Special Projects.

File 1988-1003-49-1. 1971-1976.
Scholarship - Rev. Jalal Masih Daniel. Includes photograph of Rev. Daniel.

File 1988-1003-49-4. 1970-1979.
Scholarship - Rev. Took Sam Kim.

File 1988-1003-49-6. 1971-1978.
Scholarship - Kyung Hee Lynn (nee Park).

File 1988-1003-49-7. 1971.
Scholarship - Rev. Wen-Yen Peng.

File 1988-1003-49-8.
Scholarship - I-Shin Wu.

File 1988-1003-49-10. 1974-1979.
Scholarship - James Chia-Shih Chen.

File 1988-1003-50-1. 1975-1976.
Scholarship - Dr. C.M. Kao.

File 1988-1003-50-2. 1975-1976.
Scholarship - Dr. Ram Singh.

File 1988-1003-50-3. 1977-1978.
Scholarship - Dr. Ram Singh. Includes report "New Canadians in Multicultural Canada" by Dr. Singh.

File 1988-1003-50-4. 1975-1980.
Scholarship - C.J. Su. Includes photograph of C.J. Su.

File 1988-1003-50-8. 1977-1982.
Scholarship - Shin -Wan Kim.

File 1988-1003-51-3. 1974-1975,
Research and Planning- China Task Force.

File 1988-1003-52-9. 1973-1975.
Centennial Projects. Korean Christian Church in Japan.

File 1988-1003-52-10. 1973-1976.
Centennial Committee - Visitors - New Hebrides.

File 1988-1003-52-12. 1974-1975.
Centennial Committee - Visitors - Taiwan.

File 1988-1003-52-13. 1974-1975.

Centennial Committee - Visitors - Japan.

File 1988-1003-52-15. 1974-1975.
Centennial Committee -Visitors-India.
Administrative Records of the General Board of Missions/Board of World Mission. Overseas Missions, 1925-1982. General Subject Correspondence 1848-1976.

File 1988-1003-55-4. 1966-1968.
Mrs. Lillian Dickson(Taiwan). Includes correspondence with James Dickson.

Administrative Records of the General Board of Missions / Board of World Mission. Overseas Missions 1925-1982. Overseas Joint Policy Committee [1934]-1972.
Series Description This was a joint committee of the General Board of Missions and the Women's Missionary Society(Western Division) to deal with policy matters overseas. The record series consists of the subject files of the committee. Included is material on church union in India and Nigeria. Minutes of the committee will be found under Committee Minutes Joint Committees 1988-1003-35-11 to 1988-1003-36-2. Patrons may also wish to see Home Missions Policy
Committee Minutes, General Policy Committee Minutes, Overseas Policy Committee Minutes, and Board of World Mission Policy Committee Minutes. One other subgroup related to these records is the Policy Document which details the guidelines for missionaries at home and overseas.

File 1988-1003-62-19. 1962
British Guiana - Study Day. Notes only.

File 1988-1003-62-23. 1958.
Church Union in Nigeria and Northern India.

File 1988-1003-62-24. 1965.
Church Union in Nigeria and Northern India.

File 1988-1003-62-27. 1955-1964.
Formosa - Church/Mission Relations.

File 1988-1003-62-29 [1967].
India - Guidelines.

File 1988-1003-63-1. 1952-1966.
India - Bhil Field Policy. Includes Report of M.E.Whale's visit to Bhil, 1956.

File 1988-1003-63-2. [196?].
India - Bhil Field Policy - Education.

File 1988-1003-63-3. 1960-1963.
India - Bhil Field Policy - Findings Committee Reports.

File 1988-1003-63-4. 1960-1961.
India - Bhil Field Policy - Guiding Principles.

File 1988-1003-63-5. 1956-1958.
India - Bhil Field Policy - Medical Work.

File 1988-1003-63-6. 1956-1957.
India - Bhil Field Policy - School of Nursing.

File 1988-1003-63-7. 1966-1967.
India - Bhil - Reorganization of New Congregations.

File 1988-1003-63-8. 1960.
India - Jhansi - Helen MacDonald Memorial School.

File 1988-1003--63-9. 1938-1961.
India - Jhansi - Policy Statement.

File 1988-1003-63-10. 1959-1964.
Japan.

File 1988-1003-63-24. 1935-1937.
"Shrine Question."

Administrative Records of the General Board of Mission/Board of World Mission. Overseas Missions, 1925-1982. Overseas students, 1954-1978.

File 1988-1003-64-6. 1958-1961.
Bun-ti, Rev. O (Rev. Wen Ch'ih Hu).

File 1988-1003-64-9. 1962-1966.
Chang, Mr. Chin-un.

File 1988-1003-64-10. 1960-1963
Chang, H.C. and T.S.

File 1988-1003-64-11. 1964-1966.
Cheh, Rev. Kyong Shik Choi. Includes photographs of Rev. Cheh.

File 1988-1003-64-12. 1966-1969
Chen, Mr. Su Ti Tan.

File 1988-1003-64-13. 1959-1960.
Cheng, Rev. John S.

File 1988-1003-64-14. 1960-1962
Cheng, Rev. L/K and Rev. L/M.

File 1988-1003-64-15. 1957-1960.
Chou, Mr. Frank.

File 1988-1003-64-19. 1962-1964.
Hwang, Rev. Chia Sheng.

File 1988-1003-64-20. 1968-1970.
Hwang, Rev. Ee-Seng.

File 1988-1003-64-21. 1969-1971.
Japan.

File 1988-1003-65-2. 1959-1960.
Kang, Mr. Pau I.

File 1988-1003-65-4. 1956-1960.
Kiel, Ik Hyun.

File 1988-1003-65-5. 1963.
Kim, Elder C.T.

File 1988-1003-65-6. 1956-1963.
Kim, Rev. Duk Sing.

File 1988-1003-65-7. 1963-1964.
Kim, Rev. K.C. Includes photographs of Rev. Kim.

File 1988-1003-65-12. 1954-1957.
Lee, In Ha.

File 1988-1003-65-13. 1960-1962.
Lin, Mr. Cheng-Mo (Yoshi).

File 1988-1003-65-14. 1960.
Li u, H.Y.

File 1988-1003-65-15. 1965-1968.
Loh, Rev. I-jin.

File 1988-1003-66-1. 1956-1958.
Ramsaroop, Rev. Neil - Study Plans.

File 1988-1003-66-2. 1966-1969.
Shieh, Mr. S.

File 1988-1003-66-6. 1959-1961.
Wu, Rev. T.T.

File 1988-1003-66-7. 1954-1958.
Yang, Ching-an.

File 1988-1003-66-8. 1969-1970.
Yun, Rev. C.U.

Administrative Records of the General Board of Missions/Board of World Mission. Research and Planning, 1973-1980.

File 1988-1003-87-7. 1974-1975
China Correspondence.

File 1988-1003-87-8. 1975-1976.
China Correspondence.

File 1988-1003-87-9. 1977-1978
China Mission Documents - North American Directory.

File 1988-1003-87-10. 1975
China Reports - April.

File 1988-1003-87-11. 1974-1977
China Reports - E.H. Johnson.

File 1988-1003-87-12. 1975-1976.
China Statement.

File 1988-1003-87-13. 1973.
Johnson, E.H. - China Correspondence.

File 1988-1003-87-14. 1973-1974.
Johnson, E.H. - China Correspondence (Photographs removed to (Graphics Collection).

File 1988-1003-87-15. 1975-1978.
Johnson, E.H. - China Correspondence.

File 1988-1003-87-16. 1975-1976.
Johnson, E.H.- Personal and Miscellaneous. Correspondence.

File 1988-1003-88-1. 1977.
Race Relations in Toronto. Ram Singh Studies. See also 1988-1003-50-2 and 1988-1003-50-3.

Records of the Women's Missionary Society(Western Division), 1914-1986.

File 1988-7004-9-14.1927-1945.
Chinese in Canada. Reports and correspondence of W.M.S. missionaries .

File 1988-7004-9-15. 1946-1948.
Chinese in Canada. Reports and correspondence.

File1988-7004-22-1. 1950-1954.
Chinese in Canada - Correspondence relating to staff salaries, conditions of service and general administration and management, .

File 1988-7004-22-2.
Chinese in Canada.

File 1988-7004-22-4. 1963.
Chinese in Canada-Conference Notes, circulars, reports and correspondence concerning assessment spiritual state and effectiveness of work among Chinese in Canada.

File 1988-7004-22-5.
Chinese in Canada-Montréal. Reports of and correspondence with deaconesses in Montréal concerning work with Chinese Church.

File 1988-7004-22-6. 1951-1953.
Chinese in Canada-Montréal.

File 1988-7004-22-7. 1954-1955.

Chinese in Canada-Montréal.

File 1988-7004-22-8. 1956-1958.
Chinese in Canada-Montréal .

File 1988-7004-23-1. 1959-1960.
Chinese in Canada-Montréal .

File 1988-7004-23-2. 1961-1963.
Chinese in Canada.

File 1988-7004-23-3. 1947-1955.
Chinese in Canada-Toronto. Reports of and

correspondence with deaconesses in Toronto concerning work in Chinese Kindergarten and with Chinese Church.

File 1988-7004-23-4. 1950-1952.
Chinese in Canada-Toronto.

File 1988-7004-23-5. 1956-1958.
Chinese in Canada-Toronto.

File 1988-7004-23-6. 1959-1960.
Chinese in Canada-Toronto.

File 1988-7004-23-7. 1947-1951.
Chinese in Canada-Vancouver. Reports of and correspondence with deaconesses in Vancouver concerning work in Chinese Kindergarten and with Chinese Church.

File 1988-7004-24-1. 1952-1953.
Chinese in Canada-Vancouver.

File 1988-7004-24-2. 1954-1955.
Chinese in Canada-Vancouver.

File 1988-7004-24-3. 1956-1958.
Chinese in Canada-Vancouver.

File 1988-7004-24-4. 1958-1960.
Chinese in Canada-Vancouver.

File 1988-7004-24-5. 1947-1951.
Chinese in Canada-Victoria. Reports of and correspondence with deaconesses in Victoria concerning Chinese Kindergarten and Chinese Church.

File 1988-7004-24-6. 1952-1955.
Chinese in Canada-Victoria.

File 1988-7004-24-7. 1956-1957.
Chinese in Canada-Victoria.

File 1988-7004-25-1. 1958-1960.
Chinese in Canada-Victoria.

File 1988-7004-25-2. 1956-1960.
Chinese in Canada-Windsor. Reports of and correspondence with deaconesses in Windsor concerning establishment of Chinese school and work with Chinese women through the Chinese congregation.

Records of the Women's Missionary Society(Western Division) 1914-1986. Records of the Overseas Mission Department. Secretary for British Guiana.

File 1988-7004-47-1. 1938-1944.
Annual Reports, Canadian Presbyterian Mission.

File 1988-7004-47-2. 1927.
Report of the General Board of Missions on visit to British Guiana and survey of missions field.

File 1988-7004-47-3. 1927-1939.
Correspondence. Publications.

File 1988-7004-47-4 1935-1947.
Church Record of the Canadian Presbyterian Mission in British Guiana.

Secretary for India.

File 1988-7004-47-5. 1924.
Reports of missionaries .
Typescript and published annual reports and letters from missionaries .

File 1988-7004-2-7. 1930.
Reports of missionaries .

File 1988-7004-47-6. 1938.
Reports of missionaries .

File 1988-7004-47-7. 1939.
Reports of missionaries .

File 1988-7004-47-8. 1940.
Reports of missionaries .

File 1988-7004-47-9. 1941.
Reports of missionaries .

File 1988-7004-47-10. 1942.
Reports of missionaries .

File 1988-7004-47-11. 1944.
Reports of missionaries .

File 1988-7004-47-12. 1945.
Reports of missionaries .

File 1988-7004-47-13. 1921.
Letter from missionary, Margaret McKellar, published letter.

File 1988-7004-47-14. 1935-1940.
Jhansi Mission Council. Historical Sketch, minutes and address to Council Executive

File 1988-7004-47-15. 1944.
Report on Jhansi Mission of Rev. A.A. Lowther
A Study of Mass Movements and of the bearing upon the Jhansi Mission.

File 1988-7004-47-16. 1923-1925.
The Central India Torch. Journal of the Canadian Presbyterian Mission in Central India.

File 1988-7004-47-17. 1925-1928.
Journal of the Canadian Presbyterian Mission in Central India.

File 1988-7004-47-18. 1918-1942.
Ludhiana - Women's Christian Medical

College. Various publications relating to publicity and fund-raising.

File 1988-7004-47-19. 1921.
Madras - Women's Christian College. Publications concerning publicity.

File 1988-7004-47-20. 1925-1946.
Madras - St. Christopher's Training College Publications.

File 1988-7004-47-21. 1930-1942.
Vellore. Missionary Medical College for Women. Publications concerning publicity.

File 1988-7004-47-22. 1928-1947.
General Reports of visits by delegations to the Bhil Field; notes on missionaries and missions work; and booklet **What the Simon Report Means**: S.K.Ratcliffe.
Japan Secretary/Secretary for Koreans in Japan.

File 1988-7004-48-1. 1927.
Report on Koreans in Japan "Report of delegates on the matter of establishing missions work among the Koreans in Japan"

File 1988-7004-48-2. 1937-1941.
Annual Reports of missionaries.

File 1988-7004-48-3. 1935.
Correspondence with missionaries.

File 1988-7004-49-4. [ca. 1930s].
Publications. Various publications concerning missions of Canadian Presbyterians to Koreans in Japan.
Formosa Secretary.

File 1988-7004-48-5. 1927.
Annual Report. Report to the General Board of Missions on missions in North Formosa.

File 1988-7004-48-6. 1934, 1935.
Annual Reports of North Formosa Mission.

File 1988-7004-48-7. 1927.
Diary of Anne Senior. Typescript diary of missionary at MacKay Memorial Hospital containing information on W.M.S in Formosa, women's work, hospital work and personal activities (Photographs removed to Graphics Collection: B-530-FC; B- 531-FC; B-532-FC; B-533-FC; B-534-FC. 535-FC; B-536-FC; B-537-FC; B-538-FC).

File 1988-7004-48-8.1925-1934.
Historical Notes. Reports, articles and letters compiled for the sixtieth anniversary of the Canadian Mission in Formosa and the tenth anniversary of the W.M.S.

File 1988-7004-48-9. 1935.
The Shrine Question. Reports and articles by missionaries relating to the Japanese law compelling schools to bow towards Shinto Shrines.

File 1988-7004-48-10. 1948.
Report on Post-War Missions.

Manchuria, China and South China. Secretary for China.

File 1988-7004-48-11. 1933-1939.
Annual Reports of Missions. Printed and published reports of Canadian Presbyterian Mission.

File 1988-7004-48-12. 1924.
Correspondence with missionaries . Circular letters from missionaries (Photographs removed to Photograph-539-FC; also unidentified).

File 1988-7004-48-13. 1927-1929.
Correspondence with missionaries.

File 1988-7004-48-14. 1936-1946.
Correspondence with missionaries .

File 1988-7004-48-15. 1927.
Report on visit to Manchuria.
Report of delegation to General Board of Missions concerning establishment of missions .

File 1988-7004-48-16. 1930-1939.
Church of Christ in China - periodicals.
Information bulletins issued by partner church of Canadian Presbyterian Mission.

File 1988-7004-48-17. 1946-1947.
Church of Christ in China - periodicals.

File 1988-7004-48-18. 1933-1937.
Publications. Various publications concerning co-operation in missions in China.

Overseas Executive Secretary/Executive Director of Overseas Missions.

British Guiana. Guyana.

File 1988-7004-49-5. 1955-1962.
Annual Reports of missionaries .

File 1988-7004-49-6. 1967-1969.
Annual Reports of missionaries .

File 1988-7004-49-7. 1947, 1967-1969.
Correspondence with missionaries
Correspondence and reports of W.M.S. (W.D.)

missionaries in Guyana (Photograph removed to Graphics Collection: I-1066-FC).

File 1988-7004-49-8. 1953-1959.
Mission Council. Correspondence and minutes of

Mission Council concerning mainly W.M.S.(W.D.) missionaries and support(Photographs removed to Graphics Collection: unidentified).

File 1988-7004-49-9. 1966-1967
Missions Council. .

File 1988-7004-49-10. 1954-1957.
Canadian Presbyterian Mission. Reports, newscuttings and leaflets relating to history and future planning for Canadian Presbyterian missions in British Guiana (Photographs removed to Graphics Collection: I-183-FC; B-529- FC).

File 1988-7004-49-11. 1961-1964.
Canadian Presbyterian Mission. Correspondence, Mission reports and reports and minutes of the Guiana Presbytery of the Presbyterian Church in Canada relating to independence struggles and internal civil disturbances.

File 1988-7004-49-12. 1965-1968.
Guyana Presbyterian Church. Reports, publications and minutes of Church relating to youth work, organization and structure and local congregations.

File 1988-7004-49-13. 1965-1969.
Christian Education and Women's Organizations. Reports, newsletters, leaflets, correspondence, minutes and addresses relating to visits of W.M.S. (W.D) officers to Guyana and the development of women's organizations and their work in Christian Education.

India

File 1988-7004-50-1. 1955.
Annual Reports of missionaries .

File 1988-7004-50-2. 1957.
Annual Reports of missionaries .

File 1988-7004-50-3. 1959.
Annual Reports of missionaries .

File 1988-7004-50-4. 1960.
Annual Reports of missionaries .

File 1988-7004-50-5. 1961.
Annual Reports of missionaries .

File 1988-7004-50-6. 1962.
Annual Reports of missionaries .

File 1988-7004-50-7. 1965.
Annual Reports of missionaries .

File 1988-7004-50-8. 1966.
Annual Reports of missionaries .

File 1988-7004-50-9. 1967.
Annual Reports of missionaries .

File 1988-7004-50-10. 1968.
Annual Reports of missionaries .

File 1988-7004-50-11. 1969.
Annual Reports of missionaries .

File 1988-7004-50-12. 1954-1955.
Correspondence with delegates.
Correspondence with Mary Whale on delegation to survey W.M.S. (W.D.) work at Jhansi.

File 1988-7004-50-13. 1962-1964.
Correspondence with missionaries . Circular letters, personal correspondence and reports of W.M.S. (W.D.) missionaries in Jhansi and Bhil Field (Photographs removed to Graphics Collection: G-143- FC).

File 1988-7004-50-14. 1965-1966.
Correspondence with missionaries
File 1988-7004-50-15. 1967-1968.
Correspondence with missionaries

File 1988-7004-50-16. 1969-1970.
Correspondence with missionaries . (Photographs removed to Graphics Collection: I-174-FC; I-1097-FC).

File 1988-7004-50-17. 1952-1966.
Mission Policy. Reports and correspondence relating to policy; includes Committee on Southern Asia of National Christian Council(U.S.).

File 1988-7004-50-18. 1965-1968.
Mission Administration. Minutes and policy papers, relating to proposals for a missionary council/administrative council.

File 1988-7004-50-19. 1964-1967.
Bhil Field Mission Council Correspondence, minutes and reports (Photographs removed to Graphics Collection: unidentified).

File 1988-7004-50-20. 1958-1964.
Establishment of Vindhya Satpura Administrative Council Reports, evangelistic surveys and policy papers relating to recommendations for replacement of Mission Council with an administrative council.

File 1988-7004-50-21. 1969-1972.
Vindhya Satpura Administrative Council for Christian Institutions Minutes and notes.

File 1988-7004-51-1. 1952-1969.
Vellore Christian Medical College. Correspondence relating to work of missionaries and nurses (Photographs removed to Graphics Collection: 1-210-FC; B-524-FC; G-129-FC; G-130-FC).

File 1988-7004-51-2. 1960-1964.
Jobat Christian Hospital. Articles and reports; constitution of hospital (Photographs removed to

Graphics Collection: 1-1098-FC; B-521 FC;).

File 1988-7004-51-3. 1969.
Ludhiana Medical College and Hospital. Newsletter(Photographs removed to Graphics Collection: I-198-FC; G-140-FC; G-141-FC; G-142-FC; unidentified).

File 1988-7004-51-4. 1967.
Vellore and Ludhiana Committee Constitution.

File 1988-7004-51-5. 1952-1964.
Helen MacDonald Higher Secondary School, Jhansi. Reports on school relating to proposed changes in administration; minutes of Advisory Council and of discussions on future planning.

File 1988-7004-51-6.1967-1968.
Helen MacDonald Higher Secondary School Jhansi.

File 1988-7004-51-7. 1961.
Education Reports. Reports on Education in India and Christian Education among the Balahis of India.
File 1988-7004-51-8. 1945, 1949.
National Christian Council (U.S.) Committee on India and Pakistan Conference material relating to changes in missions policies following independence and separation of India and Pakistan.

File 1988-7004-51-9. 1966-1968.
United Church of North India Draft statements of faith, constitution and statistical reports relating to union of churches in North India.

File 1988-7004-51-10. n.d.
Maps of Mission Fields in India. Various maps showing Canadian Presbyterian missions fields.

File 1988-7004-51-11. (ca.1962-1969).
General Correspondence, reports and notes: includes letter to Indira Gandhi; report on missions work in India and other missions fields; copies of compiled historical notes on Dr. John Buchanan, missionary in Amkhut (1898 - 1913).

Koreans in Japan.

File 1988-7004-52-1. 1955-1968.
Annual Reports of missionaries .

File 1988-7004-52-2. 1962-1968.
Annual Reports of Co-operative Work of Presbyterian Church in Canada and the Korean Christian Church, Reports produced by missionaries: includes photographs glued to reports.

File 1988-7004-52-3. 1962-1963.
Correspondence with missionaries and Korean Christian Church in Japan Correspondence, reports relating mainly to work of the W.M.S. (W.D) missionary and work with women and children supported by W.M.S.(W.D.).

File 1988-7004-52-4. 1964-1967.
Correspondence with missionaries and Korean Christian Church in Japan (Photographs removed to Graphics Collection: G-146-FC).

File 1988-7004-52-5. 1968-1969.
Correspondence with missionaries and Korean Christian Church, Japan (Photographs removed to Graphics Collection: I-186-FC; 1-1107-FC; G-144- FC).

File 1988-7004-52-6. 1956-1964.
Missionary Policy. Reports, minutes and policy papers concerning the relationship of Canadian Presbyterian Missionaries to the Korean Christian Church in Japan and proposal for their membership of the Korean Christian Church in Japan (Photographs removed to Graphics Collection: I-1100-FC; I-1101-FC; I-1102-FC; B-528-FC; G- 135-FC; G-136-FC; G-137-FC; G-138-FC).

Formosa/Taiwan.

File 1988-7004-53-1. n.d.
Annual Reports of missionaries .

File 1988-7004-53-2. 1952
Annual Reports of missionaries .

File 1988-7004-53-3. 1955.
Annual Reports of missionaries .

File 1988-7004-53-4. 1957.
Annual Reports of missionaries .

File 1988-7004-53-5. 1958.
Annual Reports of missionaries .

File 1988-7004-53-6. 1959.
Annual Reports of missionaries .

File 1988-7004-53-7. 1962.
Annual Reports of missionaries .

File 1988-7004-53-8. 1963.
Annual Reports of missionaries .

File 1988-7004-53-9. 1964.
Annual Reports of missionaries .

File 1988-7004-53-10. 1967.
Annual Reports of missionaries .

File 1988-7004-53-11. 1968.
Annual Reports of missionaries .

File 1988-7004-53-12. 1969.
Annual Reports of missionaries .

File 1988-7004-53-13. 1960.
Correspondence with missionaries . Circular letters, reports and personal correspondence of W.M.S.(W.D.) missionaries concerning activities and support.

File 1988-7004-53-14. 1965-1966.
Correspondence with missionaries .

File 1988-7004-53-15. 1968-1970.
Correspondence with missionaries . (Photographs

removed to Graphics Collection: I-658-FC).

File 1988-7004-53-16. 1951-1959.
Mission Policy. Reports, articles, circulars, minutes and correspondence relating to the work of the Presbyterian Church in Canada and the Presbyterian Church of Formosa: includes policy discussions on relationship of missions to the Presbyterian Church of Formosa (Photographs removed to Graphics Collection: B-525-FC; B-527-FC; G-126- FC; G-127-FC; G-128-FC; G-132-FC; G- 133-FC; G-134-FC; unidentified).

File 1988-7004-53-17. 1960-1964.
Mission Administration. Reports, correspondence, minutes and newscuttings relating to the work of W.M.S.(W.D.) in supporting projects of the Presbyterian Church of Formosa and women missionaries (Photographs removed to Graphics Collection: G-145-FC).

File 1988-7004-53-18. 1965--1966.
Mission Administration. (Photographs removed to Graphics Collection: I-317-FC).

File 1988-7004-53-19. 1961-1969.
Mission Administration.

File 1988-7004-53-20.1961-1969.
Women's Work. Correspondence with Secretary of the Women's Work Committee of the Presbyterian Church of Formosa concerning W.M.S.(W.D.) support for programmes, and for training of and scholarships for women(Photographs removed to Graphics Collection: I-1105-FC, G-139-FC; unidentified).

File 1988-7004-53-21. 1965.
Centenary of Presbyterian Church.
Publications and typescript copies of booklets concerning history and work of the Presbyterian Church of Formosa/Taiwan and centenary publications. Also includes centenary booklet for MacKay Memorial Hospital.

Administration.

File 1988-7004-55-5. 1960-1965.
Scholarships - Correspondence, minutes and reports concerning W.M.S. (W.D.) sponsorship of students and church workers at universities in Canada and Japan.

File 1988-7004-55-8. 1957-1962.
Overseas Joint Policy Committee. Includes material on the relationship between the Presbyterian Church in Canada and partner churches in Formosa and India, along with general policy on missions.

File 1988-7004-56-2. 1949.

Report of Overseas Delegation to Japan, Taiwan, and India, 1948-1949.

File 1988-7004-56-3. 1952-1953.
Reports of E.H.Johnson's visit to Formosa Reports and correspondence of General Secretary of Student Volunteer Movement,

File 1988-7004-56-4. 1959-1961.
Reports of visits to missions fields. Reports on visits by various personnel of W.M.S. (W.D.) and General Board of Missions to India, Nigeria, Jamaica, British Guiana, Taiwan and Japan.

File 1988-7004-56-5. 1968.
Reports on visits to Formosa, Japan and India.

File 1988-7004-56-6. 1968.
Report on visit to Guyana. Reports on visits by Executive Director of Overseas Missions.

File 1988-7004-
Report on visit to Guyana. Report on visit by Executive Director of Overseas Missions

File 1988-7004-56-10. 1953, 1957-1958.
Interdenominational Mission Information.
Circulars and leaflets relating to World Council of Churches and to various missions in India, Hong Kong, Philippines, South Africa, British Guiana and Southern Asia.

Records of the Women's Missionary Society(Western Division), 1914-1986.
Records of the Publications Department.

Records of the Editor, the **Glad Tidings.** File.

Subject Reference Files.

File 1988-7004-58-1.
China. Circular Letters of missionaries and reports concerning to Honan.

File 1988-7004-58-2. 1921-1947.
China. Letters and articles concerning missions in

Manchuria. (Photograph removed to Graphics Collection: I-1103-FC3).

File 1988-7004-58-3. 1926-1941.
Formosa. Typescript and manuscript articles, letters and publications relating mainly to Happy Mount Leprosy Colony and other missions work in Formosa.

File 1988-7004-58-4. 1928.
India. Typescript and manuscript articles and reports concerning missions in Gwalior.

File 1988-7004-58-7. 1936-1947.
Home Missions. Reports and correspondence concerning Italian, French, Hungarian and Chinese work in Canada and St. Margaret's Girl's Centre, Toronto.(Photograph removed to Graphics Collection: I-1108-C).

File 1988-7004-58-8. 1949-1950

Articles and Letters concerning history of Canadian Presbyterian Mission in New Hebrides at centenary of founding of missions.

File 1988-7004-58-10. n.d.
Dr. Marion Oliver, missionary in India. Manuscript biography with editorial notes.

File 1988-7004-58-11.
Dr. & Mrs. John Wilkie, missionaries in India. Biographical articles.

File 1988-7004-58-12. 1921-1932.
Dr. Caroline MacDonald, missionary in Japan. Biographical articles, correspondence, publications and newscuttings: includes material compiled for memorial articles and services on death of Dr. MacDonald.

File 1988-7004-58-13.
Miss Bertha M. Robson, missionary in India. Articles on educational missions work.

File 1988-7004-58-14. (ca. 1930-1932)
Tui Chang Mai (Mrs. George Leslie MacKay) missionary in Formosa. Biographical articles, transcript of radio talk.

File 1988-7004-58-15. 1930-1940.
Dr. Margaret O'Hara, missionary in India. Letters and articles, mainly compiled for memorial articles after Dr. O'Hara's death; also includes manuscript notebook with descriptions of life in India.

File 1988-7004-58-16. 1933-1934, 1948-1950.
Miss Bessie M.MacMurchy, missionary in India. Personal correspondence, circular letters and newscuttings concerning experiences of Miss MacMurchy in Vellore and other parts of India: includes newscuttings on politics and religion in India sent by Miss MacMurchy to the Editor, **The Glad Tidings** and newspaper articles written by Miss MacMurchy.

File 1988-7004-59-1. 1939.
Dr. Elizabeth Beatty, missionary in India. Biographical articles..

File 1988-7004-62-20.
Missionary Education - Formosa. Map of Formosa showing Canadian Presbyterian missions field, map of S.E.Asian countries, circulars concerning Canadians in Taiwan and annual reports of missionaries.

File 1988-7010-2, 3. 1926.
Joint G.B.M./W.M.S. (W.D.) Delegation to British Guiana. Report and correspondence of Mrs. Mary McKerroll on visit to missions field.

File 1988-7010-1-20. ca. 1967-1980.
Reference Papers - Barwani, India. Material collected for history of missions work at Barwani (Photographs removed to Graphics Collection)

File 1988-7010-1-21. n.d.
Plans. Unidentified plans, possibly of Christian Education building or Nursery School in Japan

(Koreans in Japan)

Kirkwood, Kenneth P. **Canadian missionary activities in the Japanese Empire**, 1933. Manuscript in Korean.

Dr. Vicedom. Untitled manuscript re missions to mountain people of Taiwan, 1961.

Records of the Women's Missionary Society (Western Division) 1914-1986 Scrapbooks.

File 1988-7010-1-19. ca. 1936.
Scrapbook. Contains newspaper photographs of missionaries in India, Formosa, Japan and British Guiana.

McNeely, M.Verne.
Papers, 1909-1962, 45 cm.
Correspondence, articles and photographs about her life in China with various missions, mostly Chinese